D0998403

1 PETER

VOLUME 37B

THE ANCHOR BIBLE is a fresh approach to the world's greatest classic. Its object is to make the Bible accessible to the modern reader; its method is to arrive at the meaning of biblical literature through exact translation and extended exposition, and to reconstruct the ancient setting of the biblical story, as well as the circumstances of its transcription and the characteristics of its transcribers.

THE ANCHOR BIBLE is a project of international and interfaith scope: Protestant, Catholic, and Jewish scholars from many countries contribute individual volumes. The project is not sponsored by any ecclesiastical organization and is not intended to reflect any particular theological doctrine. Prepared under our joint supervision, THE ANCHOR BIBLE is an effort to make available all the significant historical and linguistic knowledge which bears on the interpretation of the biblical record.

THE ANCHOR BIBLE is aimed at the general reader with no special formal training in biblical studies; yet it is written with the most exacting standards of scholarship, reflecting the highest technical accomplishment.

This project marks the beginning of a new era of cooperation among scholars in biblical research, thus forming a common body of knowledge to be shared by all.

William Foxwell Albright
David Noel Freedman
GENERAL EDITORS

THE ANCHOR BIBLE

1 PETER

◆

A New Translation
with Introduction and Commentary

JOHN H. ELLIOTT

THE ANCHOR BIBLE
Doubleday
New York London Toronto Sydney Auckland

THE ANCHOR BIBLE
PUBLISHED BY DOUBLEDAY
a division of Random House, Inc.
1540 Broadway, New York, New York 10036

Library of Congress Cataloging-in-Publication Data

Bible. N.T. Peter, 1st. English. Elliott. 2000.
1 Peter : a new translation with introduction and commentary / by John H. Elliott.— 1st ed.
p. cm. — (The Anchor Bible ; v. 37B)
Includes bibliographical references (p.) and indexes.
ISBN 0-385-41363-7 (alk. paper)
1. Bible. N.T. Peter, 1st—Commentaries. I. Elliott, John Hall. II. Title. III. Bible. English. Anchor Bible. 1964 ; v. 37B.

BS192.2.A1 1964 .G3 vol. 37B
[BS2795.3]
220.7'7 s—dc21
[227'.92077] 00–021940
CIP

Printed in the United States of America
December 2000

First Edition

10 9 8 7 6 5 4 3 2 1

In loving memory of my dear parents
Charles E. Elliott (died 8-23-86)
and
Nietta H. Elliott (died 8-6-91)
whose constant love and Christian example
modeled for me the joy of following
in the footsteps of Christ

CONTENTS

◆

LIST OF MAPS

◆

PREFACE

◆

This commentary, like most of our undertakings, is part of a larger personal story. Actual writing on this commentary began in 1990, but my research on 1 Peter has a far longer history. A class on 1 Peter at Concordia Seminary in 1957, with Martin Scharlemann as instructor, first aroused my curiosity concerning this letter and especially its relevance to Martin Luther's teaching concerning the priesthood of all believers. At the Wilhelms-Universität in Münster, Westphalia, Germany, with Professor Karl Heinrich Rengstorf as my "Doktorvater," I pursued this issue in my doctoral dissertation, *The Elect and the Holy*, which was published by E. J. Brill in 1966 as volume 12 in the Supplement Series to *Novum Testamentum*. Further publications on 1 Peter followed over the years. All of these studies were produced with the help of many student research assistants, to whom I now wish to extend my heartfelt thanks: Arthur Geiger, Gary Simpson, Mark Jesenko, Burton Procter, S.J., Joseph Romeo, Claire Marie Heesacker Kahn, Rosendo Urrabazo, C.M.F., Mary Romo, Rev. Joanna Percival, Shoshana Chaim, Alan Martinez Ramirez, Rev. Steven Black, Chris Seeman, Seth Solomonow, Garrett Phipps, Daniel Peterson, and Kourtney Hallum.

During a sabbatical leave in 1977–78, while I was Scholar in Residence at the Institut zur Erforschung des Urchristentums in Tübingen, Germany (fall 1977) and a representative of the Catholic Biblical Association of America, teaching a course on 1 Peter at the Pontifical Biblical Institute in Rome (spring 1978), I completed two further monographs on 1 Peter. The one, *1 Peter: Estrangment and Community*, published by the Franciscan Herald Press in 1979, I dedicated to the Jesuit community of the Bellarmino, where I lived as a Lutheran *paroikos* and *fratello*, and to Concordia Seminary-in-Exile, the remnant of the seminary in which I had previously taught. The other volume, *A Home for the Homeless*, was published by Fortress Press in 1981. A commentary on *James, I–II Peter and Jude*, coauthored with R. A. Martin, appeared in 1982. Other articles and essays followed, including the entry on 1 Peter in the *Anchor Bible Dictionary* (1992), and material on 1 Peter that served as an illustration of exegetical and social-scientific analysis in my 1993 study, *What Is Social-Scientific Criticism?* (Fortress Press). In the course of delivering a lecture at the University of Basel in 1986, I and my wife, Linde, enjoyed the gracious hospitality of Bo Reicke and his wife. It was a delightful occasion when Professor Reicke and I, over Schweizer Delikatessen, could personally exchange our respective views on this New Testament writing that had occupied our common attention for so long. Conversations over the years with other good friends and "primo-petrophiles," including Frederick Danker, William Dalton, Raymond Brown,

Kazuhito Shimada, Ernest Best, Thomas Herron, and Barth Campbell have helped me hone my thinking on 1 Peter probably more than I am even aware.

My colleagues of the Context Group and several of my students have patiently read and generously critiqued several portions of earlier drafts of this commentary. To them and to K. C. Hanson, in particular, I owe a huge debt of thanks. My old friend Robert Wilken has faithfully reminded me of the attention of the Church Fathers to this pastoral letter and, while our appreciation of historical criticism may differ somewhat, my attention to these rich sources of spiritual wisdom reflects the influence of his gentle persuasion.

I am also grateful to the University of San Francisco for two past sabbatical leaves (1990–1991, 1998–1999), which provided time for the commencement and completion of the manuscript, and to the able staff of Gleeson Library, especially Hille Novak and Eric Ewen, for aid in obtaining many of the volumes and articles necessary for this research. To Dr. Gabriele Schroeder for her expert assistance in the electronic formatting of this manuscript I owe a special *herzlichen Dank.*

Professor David Noel Friedman was a writer's delight to have as an editor, especially for the humor and grace in which he couched his trenchant suggestions for improvement and clarity. How much all of us Anchor Bible authors owe to Noel for his eagle eye, immense erudition, and wise counsel! To Noel and Prof. Astrid Beck, my resolute *paraklētoi*, who saved this tome from bureaucratic limbo, meinen unaussprechlichen Dank! I am also most grateful to editors Andrew Corbin of Doubleday and Beverly Fields of Eisenbrauns for their peerless editing as well as their gracious style of collaboration.

Last, and decidely not least, I thank my geliebte Frau Linde for reading this manuscript with such an able and accurate eye, but most of all for being patient with my preoccupation with this *wissenschaftliches Kind* over the past ten years.

Shortly before I commenced this volume, my father died, and during the first year of writing my mother also passed away. While the minutiae of this commentary were beyond their ken, the spirit of the letter that it examines filled their hearts and souls. I dedicate this commentary to their loving memory.

The Feast of St. Michael and All Angels,
September 29, 1998
John H. Elliot

ABBREVIATIONS

◆

PRINCIPAL ABBREVIATIONS

AB	Anchor Bible
ABD	D. N. Freedman et al. (eds.). *The Anchor Bible Dictionary*. 6 vols. New York: Doubleday, 1992
ABR	*Australian Biblical Review*
AGJU	Arbeiten zur Geschichte des antiken Judentums und des Urchristentums
AJBI	*Annual of the Japanese Biblical Institute*
AnBib	Analecta biblica
AnBoll	Analecta Bollandiana
ANF	The Ante-Nicene Fathers
ANRW	H. Temporini and W. Haase (eds.). *Aufstieg und Niedergang der römischen Welt: Geschichte und Kultur Roms im Spiegel der neueren Forschung*. Berlin: de Gruyter, 1972–
AOSTS	American Oriental Society Translation Series
AR	*Archiv für Religionswissenschaft*
ASNU	Acta seminarii neotestamentici upsaliensis
AsSeign	*Assemblées du Seigneur*
ATANT	Abhandlungen zur Theologie des Alten und Neuen Testaments
AThR	*Anglican Theological Review*
AUSS	*Andrews University Seminary Studies*
BA	*Biblical Archaeologist*
BAGD	Walter Bauer. A *Greek-English Lexicon of the New Testament and Other Early Christian Literature*, translated and adapted by W. F. Arndt and F. W. Gingrich. 2d ed. F. W. Gingrich and F. W. Danker. Chicago: University of Chicago Press, 1979
BARev	*Biblical Archeology Review*
BBB	Bonner biblische Beiträge
BBET	Beiträge zur biblischen Exegese und Theologie
BDF	F. Blass and A. Debrunner. A *Greek Grammar of the New Testament and Other Early Christian Literature*, translated and revised by R. W. Funk. Chicago: University of Chicago Press, 1961
BeO	*Bibbia e oriente*
BETL	Bibliotheca ephemeridum theologicarum lovaniensium

Author's note: For abbreviations of ancient texts, series, and corpora of inscriptions and papyri, see Index of Scriptural and Other Ancient References.

BFCT	Beiträge zur Förderung christlicher Theologie
BHH	B. Reicke and L. Rost (eds.). *Biblisch-historisches Handwörterbuch: Landeskunde, Geschichte, Religion, Kultur. 4 vols.* Göttingen: Vandenhoeck & Ruprecht, 1962–1966
BHT	Beiträge zur historischen Theologie
Bib	*Biblica*
BibLeb	*Bibel und Leben*
BibS(F)	Biblische Studien (Freiburg, 1895–)
Billerbeck	[H. L. Strack and] P. Billerbeck. *Kommentar zum Neuen Testament aus Talmud und Midrasch*. 6 vols. Munich: Beck, 1922–1956
BK	*Bibel und Kirche*
BL	*Bibel und Liturgie*
BSac	*Bibliotheca sacra*
BT	*The Bible Translator*
BTB	*Biblical Theology Bulletin*
BWANT	Beiträge zur Wissenschaft vom Alten und Neuen Testament
BZ	*Biblische Zeitschrift*
BZAW	Beihefte zur Zeitschrift für die alttestamentliche Wissenschaft
BZNW	Beihefte zur Zeitschrift für die neutestamentliche Wissenschaft
CBC	Cambridge Bible Commentary
CBQ	*Catholic Biblical Quarterly*
CBQMS	Catholic Biblical Quarterly Monograph Series
CChr	Corpus Christianorum
CGTC	Cambridge Greek Testament Commentary
CIG	A. Boeckh (ed.) *Corpus inscriptionum graecarum*. 4 vols. Berlin, 1828–1877 [Also see Inscriptions and Papyri in the Index]
CNT	Commentaire du Nouveau Testament
ConBOT	Coniectanea biblica: Old Testament Series
ConNT	Coniectanea neotestamentica
CQR	*Church Quarterly Review*
CRINT	S. Safrai and M. Stern (eds.). Compendia rerum iudaicarum ad Novum Testamentum. 2 vols. Assen: Van Gorcum, 1974–1976
CSEL	Corpus scriptorum ecclesiasticorum latinorum
CTM	*Concordia Theological Monthly*
CurTM	*Currents in Theology and Mission*
DB	F. Vigouroux (ed.). *Dictionnaire de la Bible*. 5 vols. Paris: Letouzey et Anè, 1895–1912
DBSup	L. Pirot and A. Robert (eds.). *Dictionnaire de la Bible: Supplement*. Paris, 1928–
EB	Echter Bibel
Ebib	Etudes bibliques
EDNT	H. Balz and G. Schneider (eds.). *Exegetical Dictionary of the New Testament*. 3 vols. Grand Rapids: Eerdmans, 1990–1993

EHAT Exegetisches Handbuch zum Alten Testament
EJ *Encyclopedia Judaica*. 14 vols. Jerusalem: Magnes, 1972
EKKNT Evangelisch-katholischer Kommentar zum Neuen Testament
EKL E. Fahlbusch et al. (eds.). *Evangelisches Kirchenlexikon*. 4 vols. 3d ed. Göttingen, 1985–1996
EncBib *Encyclopaedia Biblica*
EncBrit *Encyclopaedia Britannica*. 15th ed. Chicago: Encyclopaedia Britannica, 1974
ErFor Erträge der Forschung
ErJb *Eranos Jahrbuch*
EstBib *Estudios bíblicos*
ETL *Ephemerides theologicae lovanienses*
ETR *Etudes théologiques et religieuses*
EvQ *Evangelical Quarterly*
EvT *Evangelische Theologie*
EWNT H. Balz and G. Schneider (eds.). *Exegetisches Wörterbuch zum Neuen Testament*. 3 vols. Grand Rapids: Eerdmans, 1990–1993
Exp *Expositor*
ExpTim *Expository Times*
FB Forschung zur Bibel
FRLANT Forschungen zur Religion und Literatur des Alten und Neuen Testaments
FTS Freiburger theologische Studien
GCS Die Griechischen christlichen Schriftsteller. Leipzig, 1897–
GNT[4] K. Aland et al. (eds.). *Greek New Testament*. 4th ed. New York: United Bible Societies, 1994
GNT Grundrisse zum Neuen Testament
Greg *Gregorianum*
GThT *Gereformeerd theologisch tijdschrift*
HBC J. L. Mays et al. (eds.). *Harper's Bible Commentary*. San Francisco: Harper & Row, 1988
HBD P. J. Achtemeier et al. (eds.). *Harper's Bible Dictionary*. San Francisco: Harper & Row, 1985
HBT *Horizons in Biblical Theology*
HDAC J. Hastings (ed.). *A Dictionary of the Apostolic Church*. New York: Scribner's, 1916–1918
HDB J. Hastings (ed.). *A Dictionary of the Bible*. 5 vols. 2d ed. New York: Scribner's, 1901–1904
HDCG J. Hastings (ed.). *A Dictionary of Christ and the Gospels*. 2 vols. Edinburgh: T. & T. Clark, 1906–1908
HERE J. Hastings (ed.). *Encyclopedia of Religion and Ethics*. New York: Scribner's, 1908–1927
HeyJ *Heythrop Journal*
HNT Handbuch zum Neuen Testament
HNTC Harper's New Testament Commentaries
HTKNT Herders theologischer Kommentar zum Neuen Testament

HTR	*Harvard Theological Review*
HTS	Harvard Theological Studies
HUCA	*Hebrew Union College Annual*
HUT	Hermeneutische Untersuchungen zur Theologie
IB	G. A. Buttrick et al. (eds.). *Interpreter's Bible.* 12 vols. New York, 1951–1957
IBS	*Irish Biblical Studies*
ICC	International Critical Commentary
IDB	G. A. Buttrick (ed.). *Interpreter's Dictionary of the Bible.* 4 vols. Nashville: Abingdon, 1962
IDBSup	K. Crim (ed.). *Interpreter's Dictionary of the Bible: Supplementary Volume.* Nashville: Abingdon, 1976
IG	*Inscriptiones graecae.* Editio minor. Berlin, 1924– [Also see inscriptions and Papyri in the Index]
Int	*Interpretation*
ISBE	G. W. Bromily (ed.). *International Standard Bible Encyclopedia.* Rev. ed. 4 vols. Grand Rapids: Eerdmans, 1979–1988
ITQ	*Irish Theological Quarterly*
JAC	*Jahrbuch für Antike und Christentum*
JB	Jerusalem Bible
JBC	R. E. Brown et al. (eds.). *The Jerome Biblical Commentary.* 2 vols in one. Englewood Cliffs: Prentice-Hall, 1968 [cf. *NJBC*]
JBL	*Journal of Biblical Literature*
JBR	*Journal of Bible and Religion*
JECS	*Journal of Early Christian Studies*
JEH	*Journal of Ecclesiastical History*
JETS	*Journal of the Evangelical Theological Society*
JQR	*Jewish Quarterly Review*
JRelS	*Journal of Religious Studies*
JRS	*Journal of Roman Studies*
JSJ	*Journal for the Study of Judaism in the Persian, Hellenistic, and Roman Periods*
JSNT	*Journal for the Study of the New Testament*
JSNTSup	Journal for the Study of the New Testament: Supplement Series
JSOT	*Journal for the Study of the Old Testament*
JSOTSup	Journal for the Study of the Old Testament: Supplement Series
JSPSup	Journal for the Study of the Pseudepigrapha: Supplement Series
JSS	*Journal of Semitic Studies*
JTS	*Journal of Theological Studies*
KD	*Kerygma und Dogma*
KJV	King James Version
LB	Living Bible
LCL	Loeb Classical Library
LD	Lectio divina

Louw-Nida	J. P. Louw and E. A. Nida (eds.). *Greek-English Lexicon of the New Testament Based on Semantic Domains*. 2 vols. New York: United Bible Societies, 1988
LSJ	H. G. Liddell and R. Scott, *A Greek-English Lexicon*, rev. H. S. Jones and R. McKenzie. Oxford: Clarendon, 1968
LTK	*Lexikon für Theologie und Kirche*
LW	*Luther's Works*. J. Pelikan and H. T. Lehmann (eds.). 55 vols. St. Louis: Concordia/ Philadelphia: Muhlenberg and Fortress, 1955–1986
LXX	Septuagint (Greek Old Testament)
MBPF	Münchener Beiträge zur Papyrusforschung und antiken Rechtsgeschichte
MeyerK	H. A. W. Meyer. *Kritisch-exegetischer Kommentar über das Neue Testament*
MM	J. H. Moulton and G. Milligan. *The Vocabulary of the Greek Testament Illustrated from the Papyri and Other Non-literary Sources*. London: Hodder & Stoughton, 1930
MNTC	Moffatt New Testment Commentary
MTZ	*Münchener theologische Zeitschrift*
NAB	New American Bible
NABPR	National Association of Baptist Professors of Religion
NASB	New American Standard Bible
NCCHS	R. D. Fuller et al. (eds.). *A New Catholic Commentary on Holy Scripture*. London: Nelson, 1969
NCB	New Century Bible
NCE	W. J. McDonald et al. (eds.). *New Catholic Encyclopedia*. 15 vols. New York: McGraw-Hill, 1967
NEB	New English Bible
NedTT	*Nederlands theologisch tijdschrift*
Neot	*Neotestamentica*
NHC	Nag Hammadi Codex
NICNT	New International Commentary on the New Testament
NIGTC	New International Greek Testament Commentary
NIV	New International Version
NJB	New Jerusalem Bible
NJBC	R. E. Brown et al. (eds.). *The New Jerome Biblical Commentary*. Englewood Cliffs: Prentice-Hall, 1990
NKJV	New King James Version
NovT	*Novum Testamentum*
NovTSup	Novum Testamentum, Supplements
NRSV	New Revised Standard Version
NRTh	*La nouvelle revue théologique*
NTAbh	Neutestamentliche Abhandlungen
NTD	Das Neue Testament Deutsch

NTG[26], *NTG*[27]	K. Aland et al. (eds.). *Novum Testamentum Graece*. Stuttgart: Deutsche Bibelgesellschaft. 26th ed., 1979. 27th ed., 1993
NTS	*New Testament Studies*
NTT	*Norsk Teologisk Tidsskrift*
NTTS	New Testament Tools and Studies
OBO	Orbis biblicus et orientalis
OCD	N. G. L. Hammond and H. H. Scullard (eds.). *Oxford Classical Dictionary*. 2d ed. Oxford: Clarendon, 1970
OGIS	W. Dittenberger (ed.). *Orientis graeci inscriptiones selectae*. 2 vols. Leipzig, 1903–1905 [Also see Inscriptions and Papyri in the Index]
OTP	J. H. Charlesworth (ed.). *The Old Testament Pseudepigrapha*. 2 vols. New York: Doubleday, 1983
OtSt	*Oudtestamentische Studiën*
PCB	*Peake's Commentary on the Bible*. New York: Thomas Nelson, 1962
PG	J.-P. Migne (ed.). Patrologia graeca. 162 vols. Paris, 1857–1886
PGL	G. W. H. Lampe (ed.). *Patristic Greek Lexicon*. Oxford: Clarendon, 1968
PGM	K. Preisendanz (ed.). *Papyri graecae magicae: Die griechischen Zauberpapyri*. Berlin, 1928
PL	J.-P. Migne (ed.). Patrologia latina. 217 vols. Paris, 1844–1864
PLSup	Patrologia latina Supplements
PVTG	A. M. Denis and M. de Jonge (eds.). Pseudepigrapha Veteris Testamenti Graece. Leiden: Brill
PW, PWSup	A. Pauly and G. Wissowa (eds.). *Realencyclopädie der classischen Altertumswissenschaft*, and supplementary volumes. Stuttgart: Metzlersche, 1894–
QD	Quaestiones disputatae
RAC	T. Klauser et al. (eds.). *Reallexikon für Antike und Christentum*. 17 vols. Stuttgart: Hiersemann, 1950–
RB	*Revue biblique*
RE	*Realencyklopädie für protestantische Theologie und Kirche*
ResQ	*Restoration Quarterly*
RevExp	*Review and Expositor*
RevistB	*Revista bíblica*
RevQ	*Revue de Qumran*
RevScRel	*Revue des sciences religieuses*
RGG[2]	H. Gunkel et al. (eds.). *Die Religion in Geschichte und Gegenwart*. 2d ed. 5 vols. Tübingen: Mohr (Siebeck), 1927–1932
RGG[3]	K. Galling. (ed.). *Die Religion in Geschichte und Gegenwart*. 3d ed. 7 vols. Tübingen: Mohr (Siebeck), 1957–1965
RHE	*Revue d'histoire ecclésiastique*

RHPR	*Revue d'histoire et de philosophie religieuses*
RivB	*Rivista biblica*
RNT	Regensburger Neues Testament
RocTKan	*Roczniki Teologiczno-Kanoniczne*. Lublin
RQ	*Römische Quartalschrift für christliche Altertumskunde und Kirchengeschichte*
RSPT	*Revue de sciences philosophiques et théologiques*
RSR	*Recherches de science religieuse*
RSV	Revised Standard Version
RTL	*Revue théologique de Louvain*
RTP	*Revue de théologie et de philosophie*
RVV	Religionsgeschichtliche Versuche und Vorarbeiten
SacBib	La Sacra Bibbia
SANT	Studien zum Alten und Neuen Testament
SBB	Stuttgarter biblische Beiträge
SBLDS	Society of Biblical Literature Dissertation Series
SBLMS	Society of Biblical Literature Monograph Series
SBLSP	Society of Biblical Literature Seminar Papers
SBS	Stuttgarter Bibelstudien
SBT	Studies in Biblical Theology
SC	Sources chrétiennes
ScEccl	*Sciences ecclésiastiques*
ScrHier	Scripta hierosolymitana
SE	*Studia evangelica I, II, III* (= TU 73 [1959], 87 [1964], 88 [1964])
SEÅ	*Svensk exegetisk årsbok*
SEG	Supplementum Epigraphicum Graecum
SIG^{3}	W. Dittenberger (ed.). *Sylloge inscriptionum graecarum*. 4 vols. 3d ed. Leipzig, 1915–1924 [Also see Inscriptions and Papyri in the Index]
SJT	*Scottish Journal of Theology*
SKKNT	Stuttgarter kleiner Kommentar, Neues Testament
SNT	Studien zum Neuen Testament und seiner Umwelt
SNTSMS	Society for New Testament Studies Monograph Series
SR	*Studies in Religion/Sciences religieuses*
ST	*Studia theologica*
StudBib	Studia Biblica
SUNT	Studien zur Umwelt des Neuen Testaments
SVF	H. von Arnim (ed.). *Stoicorum Veterum Fragmenta*. 4 vols. Leipzig: Teubner, 1903–1924
SwJT	*Southwestern Journal of Theology*
TAik	*Teologinen aikakauskirja*
TBNT	L. Coenen et al. (eds.). *Theologisches Begriffslexikon zum Neuen Testament*. Wuppertal: Brockhaus, 1967–1972
TBü	Theologische Bücherei: Neudrucke und Berichte aus dem 20. Jahrhundert
TBT	*The Bible Today*

TCatArg	*Revista de la Facultad de Teología de la Pontifica Universidad Católica Argentina*
TD	*Theology Digest*
TDNT	G. Kittel and G. Friedrich (eds.). *Theological Dictionary of the New Testament*, translated by G. W. Bromiley. 10 vols. Grand Rapids: Eerdmans, 1964–1976
TEV	Today's English Version
TGl	*Theologie und Glaube*
THAT	E. Jenni and C. Westermann (eds.). *Theologisches Handwörterbuch zum Alten Testament*. 2 vols. Munich: Kaiser / Zurich: Theologischer Verlag, 1971–1976
TLZ	*Theologische Literaturzeitung*
TNTC	Tyndale New Testament Commentaries
TQ	*Theologische Quartalschrift*
TRE	G. Krause and G. Müller (eds.). *Theologische Realenzyklopädie*. Berlin, 1977
TRu	*Theologische Rundschau*
TS	*Theological Studies*
TSK	*Theologische Studien und Kritiken*
TT	*Teologisk Tidsskrift*
TTKi	*Tidsskrift for Teologi og Kirke*
TToday	*Theology Today*
TTZ	*Trierer theologische Zeitschrift*
TU	Texte und Untersuchungen
TynBul	*Tyndale Bulletin*
TZ	*Theologische Zeitschrift*
UNT	Untersuchungen zum Neuen Testament
USQR	*Union Seminary Quarterly Review*
VC	*Vigiliae christianae*
VCaro	*Verbum Caro*
VD	*Verbum domini*
VF	*Verkündigung und Forschung*
Vulg.	Latin Vulgate translation of Jerome
VL	Vetus Latina, Old Latin
VT	*Vetus Testamentum*
VTSup	Vetus Testamentum Supplements
WA	*D. Martin Luthers Werke*. Kritische Gesamtausgabe. Weimar: Hermann Böhlau, 1883–
WBC	Word Biblical Commentary
WMANT	Wissenschaftliche Monographien zum Alten und Neuen Testament
WTJ	*Westminster Theological Journal*
WUNT	Wissenschaftliche Untersuchungen zum Neuen Testament
ZAW	*Zeitschrift für die alttestamentliche Wissenschaft*
ZKG	*Zeitschrift für Kirchengeschichte*
ZKT	*Zeitschrift für katholische Theologie*
ZMR	*Zeitschrift für Missionskunde und Religionswissenschaft*
ZNW	*Zeitschrift für die neutestamentliche Wissenschaft*
ZST	*Zeitschrift für systematische Theologie*
ZWT	*Zeitschrift für wissenschaftliche Theologie*

OTHER ABBREVIATIONS

AD	Anno Domini (year of our Lord)
act.	active
adj.	adjective
adv.	adverb
aor.	aorist
art.	article
b.	indicates a tractate of the Babylonian Talmud
Bar.	Baraita
BC	Before Christ
BCE	Before the Common Era (= BC)
CE	Common Era (= AD)
ca.	*circa* (about, approximately)
cf.	confer, compare
ch(s).	chapter(s)
col(s).	column(s)
conj.	conjunction
dat.	dative
def.	definite
ed(s).	editor(s), edited by
ep(s).	epistle(s)
ET	English translation
et al.	et alii (and others)
fem.	feminine
frg(s).	fragment(s)
Gem.	Gemara
Gk.	Greek
HB	Hebrew Bible
Heb.	Hebrew
imperf.	imperfect
indic.	indicative
infin.	infinitive
Lat.	Latin
lit.	literally
LXX	Septuagint (Greek Version of OT)
m.	indicates a rabbinic tractate of the Mishnah
𝔐	Majority Text (NT textual witnesses)
masc.	masculine
MS(S)	manuscript(s)
MT	Masoretic (Hebrew) Text
neut.	neuter
n(n).	note(s)
nom.	nominative
n.s.	new series
NT	New Testament
obj.	objective
opt.	optative
OT	Old Testament
p	pesher (commentary)
pap.	papyrus
par.	parallel(s)
part.	participle
pass.	passive
perf.	perfect
pl.	plural
p(p).	page(s)
pl(s).	plate(s)
prep.	preposition(al)
pres.	present
pron.	pronoun
Ps.-	Pseudo-
1Q, 2Q, etc.	numbered caves of Qumran, followed by abbreviation of MS cited
R.	Rabbi (as title for any rabbi)
rev.	revised
ser.	series
sing.	singular
subj.	subject
s.v.	*sub voce* (under the word)
Sync.	Georgius Syncellus's Greek text of *1 Enoch*
T.	*Testament* (of)
Tg.	Targum
Theod.	Greek translation of the Hebrew Bible by Theodotion
trans.	translator, translated by
v(v)	verse(s)
v.l.	*varia lectio* (variant reading)
Vulg.	Vulgate
y.	indicates a tractate of the Jerusalem (Yerushalmi) Talmud

INTRODUCTION

INTRODUCTION

◆

INTRODUCTORY OVERVIEW

The commentary of Bo Reicke on 1 and 2 Peter and Jude inaugurated the Anchor Bible series in 1964. The portion devoted to 1 Peter comprised a mere seventy-one pages. From this time to the present, the once lamentable status of 1 Peter as one of the benignly neglected writings of the NT has improved considerably. Numerous commentaries on 1 Peter in various languages have appeared, new exegetical methods have been applied to this writing, and a host of important monographs have brought much new light to bear on what Martin Luther at a pivotal period of Church history considered to be one of the key writings of the entire NT.

In 1976 I described the treatment of 1 Peter in the exegetical guild as that of an "exegetical step-child" (Elliott 1976/1986). This comment was made in connection with my review of the third edition of Francis W. Beare's influential commentary on 1 Peter published in 1970 (1st ed. 1947; 2d ed. 1958). The first edition of this work appeared in the same year as did the second edition of the groundbreaking and brilliant commentary of Edward Gordon Selwyn (1st ed. 1946). These English-language commentaries represent two strikingly different conceptions of 1 Peter, its genre, authorship and theology, its time and place of composition, and its relation to other Christian and secular writings and cultural currents. Beare's work echoed critical German research of the first half of the twentieth century, especially in locating 1 Peter within the orbit of the Mystery Religions, in regarding it as originally a homily later put into letter form, and in assuming its direct reliance on the writings of Paul. Selwyn's study, on the other hand, in its introductory material, commentary, and rich "Additional Notes," expanded on positions taken toward 1 Peter in the English-speaking world. An important exception where Selwyn appropriated the work of German Form Critics was his extensive Essay II on "The Inter-relation of I Peter and other N.T. Epistles" (Selwyn 1947, 363–466). Here he argued that the numerous affinities between 1 Peter and other NT writings were due not to literary dependency but to a common use of preexistent Christian tradition. Among subsequent major commentaries, those of L. Goppelt (1978; ET 1993) and N. Brox (1976; 2d ed. 1986) are significant for disengaging 1 Peter from prevailing theories of official Roman persecution and attributing the suffering described in the letter to the local harassment of the addressees as a vulnerable and disparaged minority, a view also advanced independently by the present author (Elliott 1979, 1981/1990, 1982, 1992a). An earlier commentary of this century predating Reicke's, the outstanding volume of U. Holzmeister (1937), provided a wealth of linguistic observations, useful summaries of earlier research, and rich documentation of patristic sources relevant to 1 Peter.

Since the commentaries of Selwyn and Beare at midcentury, numerous monographs have also been devoted to this writing, focusing on a variety of passages and issues: 2:4–10 (Elliott 1966b); 2:18–25 and 5:1–4 (Bosetti 1990); 3:18–22/3:18–4:6 (Reicke 1946; Dalton 1965, 2d ed. 1989; Vogels 1976; Reichert 1989); suffering (Millauer 1976; Cervantes Gabarrón 1991); strangerhood (Elliott 1979, 1981/1990; Feldmeier 1992; Martin 1992a); household management (Balch 1981; Elliott 1981/1990; Lamau 1988; Bosetti 1990; Gielen 1990; Prostmeier 1990); ecclesiology (Spörri 1925; Goldstein 1975; Elliott 1979, 1981/1990; Schröger 1981b; Lamau 1988); and the alleged reception of the Gospel of Matthew in 1 Peter (Metzner 1995); see also the more general studies of Munro 1983; J. Rousseau 1986; Schutter 1989; Thurén 1990, 1995; and the collection of essays in Perrot 1980 and Talbert 1986. For overviews of research and developing areas of consensus, see Wand 1955; Martin 1962; Elliott 1966, 10–13; 1976; Schierse 1976; Sylva 1980, 1986; Cothenet 1980, 13–42, 269–74; 1988; Hoops 1983; Neyrey 1984; Senior 1984; Childs 1985, 446–62; Achtemeier 1988, 1–3; Prostmeier 1990, 15–37, 477–55; T. W. Martin 1992a: 3–39. Extensive bibliographies of literature on 1 Peter have been published by Sylva (1982/1986) and, more recently, by Casurella (1996; 1,573 books and articles). On critical research prior to the twentieth century, see especially Huther 1851/1881, 35–36; Weiss 1906; Moffatt 1918, 318–44; and Holzmeister 1937, 148–510.

In view of this sizable body of research on 1 Peter over the past thirty years, a fresh accounting of this NT letter in the Anchor Bible series appears in order.

The regard for 1 Peter in the history of the Church has varied signficantly over the course of time. Since the end of the first century, Christian authors such as Clement of Rome (*1 Clement*, ca. 95 CE) and Bishop Polycarp of Smyrna in Asia Minor (*Letter to the Philippians*, before 140 CE) were inspired by its words of consolation, exhortation, and hope. In the following centuries it was quickly and universally embraced in both the East and the West as an indisputable statement of the church's faith, teaching, and practice. Although it gained an early inclusion in the church's scriptural canon, citations of it by the Church Fathers were relatively few in number, as were the commentaries devoted to it in the Middle Ages. According to Holzmeister (1937, 404–5), 1 Pet 5:8 was the most frequently cited of all the words of 1 Peter; eventually 1 Pet 5:8–9 was given an honored place as the scriptural reading in the daily office of Compline, part of the Divine Office dating back to the fifth century. Mention could also be made of a study (Galloway 1988) proposing an extensive influence of 1 Peter on the well-known Anglo-Saxon Medieval poem, *The Seafarer*, and the spirituality of Medieval missionaries (St. Boniface) and pilgrims. 1 Peter 5:6–9 was also interpolated into the Eighth Step of Humility of the Rule of St. Benedict in two tenth-century English manuscripts.

In the sixteenth century, however, the letter of 1 Peter as a whole suddenly rose to special prominence among the NT writings under the powerful influence of Martin Luther. In his "Preface to the New Testament" (1522), Luther ranked 1 Peter among "the true and noblest books of the New Testament" containing "the true kernel and marrow of all the books." For this reformer, 1 Peter, along with the Gospel of John, Romans, Galatians, and Ephesians constituted

> the books that show you Christ and teach you all that is necessary and salvatory for you to know, even if you were never to see or hear any other book or doctrine. . . . For in them you do not find many works or miracles of Christ described, but you do find depicted in masterly fashion how faith in Christ overcomes sin, death, and hell, and gives life, righteousness, and salvation. This is the real nature of the gospel, as you have heard. (*Luther's Works*, 35.361–62)

In addition to the eloquent evangelical message of the letter as a whole, upon which he preached on numerous occasions, Luther saw in 1 Pet 2:5, 9 in particular a fundamental biblical basis for his revolutionary doctrine of the "priesthood of all believers," assuring for these verses a paramount place in all subsequent discussions of the ministry and order of the church down to the present time; see the DETAILED COMMENT on 2:4–10. In the piety of the post-Reformation period, the letter's call for resolute faith in Christ, the Church's cornerstone, and for constancy in opposition to the devilish foe inspired the poetry of countless hymns as well.

In more recent time, 1 Peter has also been assigned a more prominent role in the church's liturgy. The current *Revised Common Lectionary* now includes eight readings from 1 Peter: one on every Holy Saturday, one in Lent of Year B, and six during the Easter season of Year A.

In academic scholarship since the advent of modern biblical criticism, however, 1 Peter has met with a more mixed reaction. For some commentators, 1 Peter presents "a gallant and high-hearted exhortation which breathes a spirit of undaunted courage and exhibits as noble a type of piety as can be found in any of the New Testament writings outside the gospels" (Wand 1934, 1) and represents "a microcosm of Christian faith and duty, the model of a pastoral charge" (Selwyn 1947, 1) or "one of the most pastorally attractive and vigorously confident documents of the New Testament" (J. N. D. Kelly 1969, 1). Others, by contrast, have viewed it as an unimaginative echo of Pauline thought and an inferior product of later "Paulinism," devoid of originality and evangelical spirit.

Considering the many historical, literary, and theological questions that this composition poses, it was no exaggeration when S. Neill in his 1964 survey of NT interpretation referred to 1 Peter as "a storm-centre of New Testament studies" (Neill 1964, 343). While Neill's verdict may still hold true, prevailing opinion on this writing has shifted noticeably since Reicke's commentary (1964) and much earlier and more negative assessment of 1 Peter. The last third of this century has been marked by a raft of studies that, reassessing the premises of earlier conclusions, have led to clearer insight into the letter's situation and strategy and, as a result, to a greater appreciation of 1 Peter as a creative synthesis of multiple strands of early Christian thought, an eloquent voice of Roman Christianity, and a moving call to steadfastness and hope in the face of hostility.

One aim of the present second edition of the commentary on 1 Peter is to take this shift into account, to trace the vacillating course of scholarship, and to reflect the results of more recent research that have led to a more positive assessment of the letter and its distinctive contribution to early Christian life and thought.

A COMMENT ON THE TRANSLATION

In a certain sense, the translation that emerges from a comprehensive analysis of a biblical text is the jewel of the commentary's crown. The challenge for any translator is to convey in an equivalent modern idiom the rhetorical and literary properties of the original biblical text, the character and consistency of its vocabulary, its line of thought, its literary coherence, rhetorical power, and religious spirit. This translation aims at providing an idiomatic, dynamic equivalent in English to the original Greek. At the same time, it also seeks to reflect in its English vocabulary the consistency of the vocabulary of the original Greek so that the reader might gain an impression of the linguistic and thematic consistency of the composition. This results in a translation that is more literal than idiomatic in most instances, but one that, for study purposes, reveals the linguistic coherence of the original text. The translation is also structured to convey the syntactic consistencies and inconsistencies of the original Greek and to display the literary devices such as parallelism, chiasm, and inclusion that provide structure to the subunits in particular. Throughout the commentary use is made of the terms "Israel," "Israelite," and, where appropriate, "Judean," in place of the conventional but less accurate terms "Judaism, "Jew," and "Jewish."

A COMMENT ON THE FORMAT OF THE COMMENTARY

The structure or outline of the Greek text is discussed below as part of the General Introduction. The Commentary proceeds in accord with this outline. Commentary on each unit of the text includes an *Introduction* that situates it within the letter as a whole. This is followed by *Notes* designed to clarify text-critical questions, questions of syntax, semantics, literary patterns, social and cultural matters, and the pragmatic thrust of specific verses or units. A concluding *Commentary* summarizes the chief features and emphases of the unit. Subsequent *detailed comments* are designed for readers who wish to consider in greater detail features of the text, its sources, its theological ramifications, and the scholarly discussions. The works listed at the conclusion of each unit of the Commentary indicate the chief studies on specific aspects of that particular unit. Other studies cited throughout the Commentary are listed in *Bibliographies* located after the *General Introduction*. The first is a list of all commentaries on 1 Peter from antiquity to the present. Through the end of the nineteenth century the commentaries are listed in *chronological* order. Commentaries published in the twentieth century are listed in *alphabetical* order. The insightful commentary of P. J. Achtemeier on 1 Peter in the Hermeneia series (1996) appeared too late to be considered in the present work. A second bibliography lists all monographs and articles directly on 1 Peter and the Apostle Peter with an aim toward completeness. A third bibliography lists other literature cited in the Commentary.

1. Genre and Integrity

The genre and integrity of this writing have been a focus of ongoing scholarly debate. Until the advent of modern biblical criticism, 1 Peter was regarded as a genuine letter. This earlier view, however, was called into question by a series of modern scholars.

On the one hand, 1 Peter bears all the typical features of a genuine letter. In terms of its structure, it has the three formal requisites of a genuine letter: (a) a personal epistolary prescript identifying the chief sender and intended recipients (1:1–2), (b) a letter body (1:3–5:11), and (3) a personal epistolary conclusion (5:12–14). The latter contains a personal commendation of the letter's courier, Silvanus (v 12ab), a reference to the act and aim of writing (v 12c), greetings from the co-senders (v 13), an urging of a gesture of familial affection (v 14a), and a concluding wish for peace (v 14b). Indications are that the author did not know the recipients personally; no addressees are mentioned by name, and it is clear from 1:12 and 1:25b that they were evangelized by persons other than the senders. Nevetheless, pragmatically 1 Peter manifests the three typical *functions* of a letter as a mode of personal correspondence (Koskenniemi 1956, 35–47), namely, (1) establishing or maintaining personal contact between senders and recipients (*philophronēsis*); (2) serving as a means for making the author(s) present to the addressees (*parousia*); and (3) initiating a conversation or communicative interaction between sender and addressee (*homilia*), the aim of which is indicated in 5:12.

Although the final and present form of 1 Peter is a letter, the form of its *original* components has been the subject of sustained debate (surveyed by R. P. Martin 1962; Beasley-Murray 1963, 251–58; Elliott 1966, 11–13; J. N. D. Kelly 1969, 15–20; Dalton 1989, 62–71). Adolf von Harnack (1897, 451–65) was the first to claim that 1 Peter consisted of an original homily (1:3–5:11), to which a later teacher or confessor (ca. 90 CE) added an epistolary framework (1:1–2; 5:12–14), dispatching the ensemble as a letter. Soltau (1905) soon concurred, adding instances of supposed "interpolations" to the writing. In support of this homily theory, R. Perdelwitz (1911) claimed to have found indications of the letter's composite character, including a supposed break in thought between 4:11 (doxology) and 4:12 (new address) and a shift in situation from potential (1:3–4:11) to actual (4:12–5:11) suffering. Section 1:3–4:11, he suggested, contained a discourse directed to Christian neophytes at the occasion of their baptism. When the persecution of which the discourse spoke had become a reality, the speaker composed a letter of encouragement (4:12–5:14), joined it to the homily, and, adding 1:1–2, gave it its current shape. The author was not the Apostle Peter but some anonymous figure of the second century under the influence of the cult of Cybele.

W. Bornemann (1919–1920) expanded further on this theory. The absence of personal information concerning the author and the audience gives the writing, he claimed, the appearance of an address rather than a personal letter. He cites the mention of baptism (3:21) and numerous references to Ps 33[34] in 1 Peter in support of a hypothesis that 1:3–5:11 constituted a baptismal homily based on Ps 33[34] originally given by Silvanus (ca. 90 CE) somewhere in Asia Minor. At the request of guests from the provinces mentioned in 1:1 who were present, Silvanus transcribed the homily and dedicated it to them (1:1b–2d), adding "by Silvanus" at the end (cf. 5:12). A generation later, as the NT canon was being assembled, an unknown redactor attributed the letter to Peter (1:1a) and also added the remainder of 5:12–14 to imply Petrine authorship (in Rome).

Subsequently this baptismal homily theory, popular among German scholars (e.g., Windisch 1930/1951; Jülicher and Fascher 1931, 199–200; Hauck 1936/1957, 35–36), found favor with others as well (e.g., Streeter 1929, 129–34; Danielou 1950, 141; Fransen 1960; Beasley-Murray 1963, 256–58; Reicke 1964, 74–75; Beare 1947/1970, 25–28, 180; Leaney 1967, 8; Fitzmyer 1968, 363; and Marxsen 1968, 234–35; 1979, 389 [claiming "no material connection" between 1:3–5:11 and its epistolary framework, 1:1–2; 5:12–14]).

Elaborations of the composite theory and the assumed cultic setting of 1 Peter proposed that the document does not merely incorporate baptismal material or a baptismal homily but constitutes the transcript of an actual baptismal liturgy. H. Preisker argued this case in his supplement to the third edition of Windisch's commentary (Windisch-Preisker 1951, 156–60). In 1:3–4:11, he saw a "worship service of a baptismal community" and in 4:12–5:11, a "concluding service of the entire congregation," "the oldest document of an early Christian worship service" (1951, 157). F. L. Cross (1954) concurred in the main with Preisker but took the theory a step further. Stressing parallels between the Greek terms for "suffer" (*paschō*) and "Passover" (*Pascha*) as well as affinities between 1 Peter and the Paschal rites of the *Apostolic Tradition of Hippolytus* (baptism and confirmation followed by a eucharist), he suggested that 1:3–4:11 records "the Celebrant's part" of a baptismal eucharist occurring in the Paschal Vigil (Cross 1954, 31). A. R. C. Leaney (1964) agreed with Cross, noting similarities to the Passover Haggadah. M.-E. Boismard (1956b,

1957, 1961, 1966), while not concurring entirely with Preisker, attempted, on the basis of affinities between 1 Peter and James, 1 John, Titus, Romans, and Colossians, to identify fragments of a baptismal liturgy in 1:3–5, 1:13–2:10 and 3:18–22, with an allusion to the eucharist in 2:5 (cf. also Gryglewicz 1958).

On the whole, theories such as these, based on the alleged composite character of 1 Peter, must be judged more imaginative than cogent. They find no support in the manuscript evidence, which attests no form of 1 Peter other than its present complete form. Nor is their suspicion about the literary coherence of the letter justified.

The verses of the "epistolary framework" (1:1–2; 5:12–14) are not unrelated to or isolable from the remainder of the letter but are thoroughly consistent lexically and thematically with the content of 1:3–5:11. In regard to 1:1–2, for instance, see "Jesus Christ" (cf. 1:3 [2×], 7, 13; 2:5; 3:21; 4:11); "elect" (2:4–10; "co-elect," 5:13); "strangers" (cf. 2:11 and 1:17; also 1:14–17; 4:2–4); "diaspora" (cf. "alien residence," 1:17 and "Babylon," 5:13); "according to" (cf. 1:3, 15, 17; 2:11; 3:7; 4:6 [2×]; 4:19; 5:2); "foreknowledge of God" (cf. 1:20); "God the Father" (cf. 1:3, 17); "through the sanctifying action" (cf. the pervasive theme of holiness and purity in 1:14–16, 19, 22; 2:5, 9; 3:5); "of the Spirit" (cf. 1: 12; 4:14; also 2:5); "obedience" (cf. 1:14, 22; 3:6 and "disobey," 2:7, 8; 3:1, 20; 4:17); "blood" (cf. 1:19) and references to the suffering and death of Jesus Christ (1:11; 2:21–24; 3:18; 4:1, 13; 5:1); "grace" (cf. 1:10, 13; 2:19, 20; 3:7; 4:10; 5:5, 10, 12); "peace" (cf. 3:11; 5:14).

With respect to 5:12–14, see "trustworthy" (*pistos*; cf. 1:21; 4:19; *pisteuō*, *pistis* as "trust," 1:8; 2:6, 7; 1:15, 7, 9, 21; 5:9); "brother" (cf. "brotherhood," 2:17; 5:8; "brotherly love," 1:22; 3:8; and "children" for believers, 1:14; 3:6); "briefly" (cf. 1:6; 5:10); "exhorting" (cf. 2:11; 5:1); "witnessing fully" (cf. "I . . . a witness," 5:1); "dependable" [*alēthē*] (cf. "truth" [*alētheia*], 1:22); "grace of God" (cf. 1:2, 10, 13; 3:7; 4:10; 5:5, 10); "Babylon" (cf. "diaspora," 1:1); "co-elect" (cf. "elect," 1:1; 2:4–10); "my son" (cf. familial terminology for believers, 1:14; 3:6); "one another" (cf. 1:22; 4:9; 5:5); "kiss" [*philēma*] (cf. *phil-* terms in 1:22; 3:8; 4:9); "love" (cf. 1:8, 22; 2:17; 4:8 [2×]); "beloved" (2:11; 4:12); "peace" (cf. 1:2; 4:11); "in Christ" (cf. 3:16; 5:10); amen (cf. 4:11).

The doxology of 4:11 is prompted by the preceding reference to glorifying God (4:11c; cf. also 2:12 and 4:16) and, as most NT doxologies, marks not the end of a document but only the conclusion of one unit of thought. The section beginning with 4:12 does not introduce a "new" situation of actual suffering, since the actual suffering and abuse of the readers is presumed earlier in the letter (2:12, 15, 18–20; 3:9; 3:13–17; 4:1–6; cf. also 5:1, 7–10). What is distinctive in 4:12–19 is rather the constellation of ideas giving a positive valuation to innocent suffering. The frequent use of the verb *paschein* ("suffer," 12×) is prompted not by liturgical recollection during the paschal (*pascha*) vigil but by the actual suffering of the addressees, which is the chief focus of this letter of comfort and exhortation. Mention of baptism (3:21), and its related imagery (rebirth, 1:3, 23; 2:2; sanctification, 1:2, 15–16, 22; 2:5, 9; 3:5, 15; Exodus and redemption, 1:13, 18–19) and exhortation (1:14–16, 22–23; 2:1–3; 4:1), reveals the use of common Christian liturgical, catechetical, Christological, and hortatory material associated with baptism. But this constitutes no clear evidence that the document itself or any segment thereof was a baptismal homily or liturgy. The readers' baptism is a presumption rather than a central focus of the letter. With regard to the liturgy theory, its proponents could not even agree on its components or agents. Preisker imagined a baptism's taking place between vv 21 and 22 of ch. 1 (as did Cross) but attributed an array of liturgical acts to diverse speakers: a "prayer-psalm" (1:3–12), an "instructional discourse" (1:13–21), a "baptismal dedication" (1:22–25), a "festal song" (2:1–10) ascribed to a speaker imbued with the Spirit, an "exhortation" issued by a new speaker (2:11–3:12), an apocalypse contributed by "ein Apokalyptiker" (3:13–4:7a), an "epistolary replacement" for a closing prayer (4:7b–11), a further apocalypse introducing the concluding service involving all members (4:12–19), a hortatory discourse (5:1–9) by the same speaker of 2:11–3:12, a blessing by a presbyter (5:10), and a doxology spoken by the whole congregation (5:11).

Cross, on the other hand, envisioned a different liturgical structure and speaker: an opening prayer (1:3–12), a formal charge to the baptismal candidates concluding with the administration of baptism (1:13–21), a welcome of the baptized into the community (1:22–25), an address on the fundamentals of the sacramental life concluding with a eucharist (2:1–10), an address on the duties of Christian discipleship (2:11–4:6), final admonitions and doxology (4:7–11), and an address to the entire congregation gathered with the newly baptized (4:12–5:11). The entirety of 1:3–4:11 he attributed to a single speaker, with no clear explanation of 4:12–5:11. Neither author made clear how and why such a liturgy was put into an epistolary form and dispatched as a letter.

These liturgy proposals were indeed "impressive in their breath-taking ingenuity" (so J. N. D. Kelly 1969, 18) but were mutually inconsistent and excessively conjectural. Consequently they have come under intense criticism and have failed to win scholarly support (see Moule 1956/1957; Stibbs and Walls 1959, 58–63; Cranfield 1960, 11–13; Thornton 1961; R. P. Martin 1962; Beasley-Murray 1963, 251–58; Dalton 1965, 62–71 / 1989, 69–75; J. N. D. Kelly 1969, 15–20; Beare 1970, 220–26; Hill 1976; Achtemeier 1988, 208–10; Goppelt 1993, 16–18). Their speculative reconstruction of what is not stated in the text and their arbitrary reading of what is there (including the exaggeration of literary breaks, differences in style, and temporal discontinuities) simply fail to convince.

Several of these objections apply equally to the baptismal homily theory. The letter contains only one explicit mention of baptism (3:21) and, though echoing much baptismal catechetical tradition, the writing is concerned not with clarifying the nature of baptism as such but with addressing the issue of suffering and with stressing the participation that baptism effects into the suffering of the crucified and resurrected Lord. Reliance on baptismal and other forms of tradition accounts for the language and formulas in 1 Peter without requiring a theory that seeks to explain the obscure through the more obscure. The relative absence of personal detail may be expected in a letter that is addressed so broadly to Christians of several provinces and that focuses on what they all share in common—namely, suffering from outsiders' hostility. In addition to the absence of any analogue for a homily incorporated into a letter and a compelling reason for incorporating a homily, the main weakness of the homily theory is its failure to demonstrate the letter's lack of literary integrity (including the alleged unconnectedness of 1:1–2 and 5:12–14 to the vocabulary and themes of the body of the letter) and hence any cogent reason why 1 Peter cannot be regarded as a coherent letter thematically, stylistically, and rhetorically. Finally, comparable contemporary examples of Christian homilies or liturgies embodied in letters are completely lacking.

These facts also militate against the earlier interpolation theories of Soltau (1905) and Völter (1906) as well as Moule's (1956–1957, 7–11) two-letter hypothesis. The proposal that numerous secondary insertions were made into an earlier composition by a later redactor has been convincingly rejected by Clemen (1905) and Moffatt (1918, 343–44). Moule's notion that 1 Peter incorporates two letters, one of which (2:11–4:11) was originally addressed "to those not yet under actual persecution" and the other (4:12–5:11) written "to those in the refining fire," with 1:1–2, 1:3–2:10, and 5:12–14 common to both, misconstrues, as do other partition theories, the actuality of suffering throughout the letter and finds no support in any external manuscript evidence. To all of these theories the sober axiom of Occam applies: *entia non sunt multiplicanda extra necessitatem*, "no increase of entities beyond their necessity."

Accordingly, the theory that 1 Peter, as we now have it, is the product of the combination of independently composed parts is both undemonstrated and unnecessary. "To say that the letter, or most of it, is a baptismal homily or liturgy is to treat as explicit, direct, and prominent what is only implicit, presupposed, and subsidiary" (Hill 1976, 189). The consistency and coherence of its language, style, themes, arrangement, and line of argumentation indicate that 1 Peter from the outset was conceived, composed, and dispatched as an integral, genuine letter. This conclusion represents the position of the vast majority of recent research on 1 Peter.[1]

The hortatory aim (5:12) and mood of 1 Peter, along with its inclusion of much hortatory and parenetic material clearly qualify it as a "parenetic/hortatory letter" (Stowers 1986, 96–97; T. W. Martin 1992a, 81–134), where "parenetic" refers to its aim and mood (hortatory) and does not imply a simple juxtaposition of disparate, general injunctions lacking any thematic unity.

---

[1]See Wrede 1900 (against Harnack); Selwyn 1947–1948; van Unnik 1956–1957, 79–80; 1980, 62–63; T. C. G. Thornton 1961 (against Cross); R. P. Martin 1962; van Unnik 1962a or b; Dalton 1965/1989; Elliott 1966a; 1981/1990, 1982, 1992; Spicq 1966a; J. N. D. Kelly 1969; Best 1971; Hill 1976; Schelkle 1976; Cothenet 1980; Senior 1980; Balch 1981; Berger 1984a, 133; Shimada 1985; Brox 1986; Lohse 1986; J. Rousseau 1986; Frankemölle 1987; Grudem 1988; Lamau 1988; Michaels 1988; Achtemeier 1988; Reichert 1989; Schutter 1989; Bosetti 1990; Davids 1990; Prostmeier 1990; Thurén 1990; Cervantes Gabarrón 1991a; Feldmeier 1992; Hillyer 1992; T. W. Martin 1992a; Goppelt 1993; R. A. Campbell 1994; J. W. Thompson 1994; Krodel 1995; P. Perkins 1994.

Addressed to a wider audience than the letters of Paul and specifically to communities of the Diaspora (1:1), 1 Peter is similar to the letter of James, which is also addressed generally to Christians "in the Diaspora" (Jas 1:1); cf. also the wider audience addressed by the letter of the Jerusalem Council (Acts 15:23–29) and the NOTE on 1 Pet 1:2 (below). As a *Diaspora letter* urging the maintenance of a distinctive and holy way of life in union with God in an alien environment, 1 Peter is perhaps closest to the Diaspora letter of the Epistle of Jeremiah (ca. 100 BCE), which was addressed to the exiles in Babylon and which urged its audience to "take care not to become at all like the foreigners or to let reverence for these gods [of theirs] possess you when you see the multitude before and behind them worshipping them, but say in your heart, 'It is you, O Lord, whom we must worship'" (Ep Jer 1:5–6). For letters addressed by Israelites to others of the Diaspora, see also Jer 29:4–23; 2 Macc 1:1–9; 1:10–2:18; and 2 *Bar.* 78–87 (2d century CE), a similar letter of consolation and exhortation.

The sequence of the provinces mentioned in 1 Pet 1:1 (with Pontus and Bithynia separated and mentioned first and last, though they formed a single province), moreover, may even suggest the circular route to be taken by the bearer of the letter (see 5.1 below and the NOTE on 1:2) and qualify it as an *encyclical* or *circular letter* as well.

In view of 1 Peter's broad audience and its concern with the situation of the Christian brotherhood in Asia Minor, Babylon-Rome, and throughout the world (5:9), it eventually was associated with other writings of the NT (James, 2 Peter, 1–3 John, Jude) as one of the seven "catholic" or "general" epistles (Eusebius, *Hist. eccl.* 2.23–25).

2. Sources and Affinities

2.1. The Citation and Use of Sacred Scripture

The Old Testament reckons prominently among the sources of 1 Peter and is by far the source to which explicit reference is most frequently made. Cited consistently according to the Greek version (LXX), the OT supplied the author with a rich source of direct quotations, allusions, and motifs. References involve not simply single texts or passages but occasionally blocks of material, as Dodd (1953) has shown was typical for NT writers in general. On the whole, 1 Peter appears to contain at least eight citations of the OT (LXX) and from ten to twelve allusions. Three types of usage are evident (following, with modifications, the classification and criteria of Schutter [1989, 35–36]: quantity and degree of correspondence of terminology; length of terminological correspondence; nature and degree of modifications).

1. Citations
   1.1. Citations with introductory formula or term
   - 1:16 *dioti gegraptai* [*hoti*], Lev 19:2
   - 1:24–25 *dioti*, Isa 40:6–8
   - 2:6–8 *dioti periechei en graphēi*, Isa 28:16
   - 2:25 *gar*, Isa 53:6; cf. Ezek 34:5, 16
   - 3:10–12 *gar*, Ps 33[34]:13–17

   1.2. Citations involving sufficient quantity of text and degree of correspondence, with preceding term:
   - 4:8 *hoti*, Prov 10:12 (closer to MT than LXX)
   - 4:14c *hoti*, Isa 11:2
   - 4:18 *kai*, Prov 11:3 LXX
   - 5:5c *hoti*, Prov 3:34 LXX
   - 5:7b *hoti*, Wis 12:13

   In these cases, the simple *hoti* functions like *dioti* in announcing substantiations drawn from the OT; in 3:5 *gar* likewise precedes a reference to OT matriarchs and Sarah (Gen 18:12).

   1.3. Citations involving sufficient quantity of text and degree of correspondence, lacking a preceding term
   - 2:3 Ps 33:8[34:7]
   - 2:7b Ps 117[118]:22
   - 2:8a Isa 8:14
   - 2:9 Exod 19:5–6; cf. 23:22 LXX; Isa 43:20–21
   - 2:10 Hos 1:6, 9; 2:1, 3, 25 LXX
   - 2:11 Gen 23:4; cf. Ps 38:13 LXX
   - 3:14c Isa 8:12
   - 3:15a Isa 8:13

2. Allusions
   2.1. Allusions reproducing sufficient quantity of text to indicate reference to a specific OT text segment, often in modified form
   - 2:12 Isa 10:3
   - 2:17 Prov 24:21
   - 2:22 Isa 53:9
   - 2:23 Isa 53:6, 12
   - 2:24a Isa 53:4, 5, 12
   - 2:24d Isa 53:5

2:25a Isa 53:6
2:25b Ezek 34:4–5, 16
3:6ab Gen 18:12
3:6c Prov 3:25
3:20 Gen 6–8
3:22 Pss 109[110]:1; 8:6–7
5:7 Ps 54[55]:23

2.2. Possible allusions (insufficient quantity to indicate with certainty one of several possible OT sources; allusion to further material of larger blocks of OT texts that are cited [Dodd 1953])

1:18 Isa 52:3
1:19 Isa 53:7; cf. Exod 12:5, 29:38
1:21 Isa 52:13
1:25b Isa 40:9
2:4a Ps 33[34]:6
2:9 Isa 42:12; Mal 3:17 or Hag 2:9
3:13 Isa 50:9
3:18b Isa 53:11 LXX
4:17 Ezek 9:6
4:18 Ps 31[32]:5
5:8 Ps 21[22]:14

2.3. Incipient allusions (OT reference dependent on an exegetical tradition for its recognition)

1:19 Isa 52–53 (pre-Petrine Christological interpretation; cf. Isa 52–53 in 2:21–25)
2:24 Deut 21:23 (*epi to xylon*; for NT interpretation, see Wilcox 1977; Hengel 1977)
3:19–20 Gen 6:1–4 (for interpretive tradition, see A.T. Hanson 1980; Dalton 1984)

2.4. Iterative allusions (anticipating or resuming part of an OT text cited elsewhere by author; use suggested by literary context)

1:15 paraphrases Lev 19:2 cited in 1:16
1:23 paraphrases Isa 40:6–8 cited in 1:24–25a
1:25b resumes Isa 40:8 cited in 1:25a
2:4a paraphrases Ps 33:6; Ps 33 cited in 3:10–12
2:4c paraphrase of Ps 117[118]:22 cited in 2:7a
2:4d paraphrase of Isa 28:16 cited in 2:6
2:5 paraphrase of Exod 19:6 cited in 2:9

Further iterative allusions may be involved in the following cases as well:

1:1 *eklektoi* anticipating Isa 43:20 alluded to in 2:9

1:3, 13, 21; 3:5 *elpis*; cf. Ps 33[34]:9, 23

1:14 *tekna*; cf. Ps 33[34]:12

1:17; 2:17, 18; 3:2, 16 *phobos*; cf. Ps 33[34]:8, 10, 12

1:18 *elytrōthēte*; cf. Ps 33[34]:23

2:1 paraphrase of Ps 33[34]:14 cited in 3:10

2:11 *paroikoi*; cf. Ps 33[34]:5

2:12 anticipating Ps 33[34]:15 cited in 3:11

2:12, 14; 3:17; 4:15 *kakopoieō* etc.; cf. Ps 33[34]:15, 17 cited in 3:10–12

2:14, 15; 3:6, 17; 4:19 *agathopoieō* etc. cf; Ps 33[34]:15

2:16 *douloi* (*theou*); cf. Ps 33[34]:22

3:7e anticipates Ps 33[34]:13 cited in 3:10

3:8 *tapeinophrones*; 5:5b *tapeinophronsynē*; cf. Ps 33[34]:19 (*tapeinous*)

3:9 anticipating Ps 33[34]:13 cited in 3:10

3:13–14 paraphrasing Ps 33[34]:10–12 cited in 3:10–12; cf. also *makarios* and Ps 33[34]:9

3:16 *prautētos*; cf. Ps 33[34]:3

4:14, 16 *onomati*; cf. Ps 33[34]:4

5:5b anticipating Prov 3:34 LXX cited in 5:5c

5:6a resuming same proverb cited in 5:5c

3. Biblicisms (informal idiom characteristic of Greek-speaking Israelite piety, informed by the language of the LXX). Examples include:

1:2 Dan 4:1 or 6:26 Theod.

1:3 Sir 16:12

1:7 Prov 17:3; 27:21; Zech 13:9; Mal 3:2b–3; Sir 2:5

1:10 1 Macc 9:26

1:12 Ps 84:12; Lam 3:50; *1 En.* 9:1; 16:3

1:13 Exod 12:11; Jer 1:17; Prov 31:17

1:17 Jer 3:19; Ps 88[89]:27; Ps 61[62]:12; Prov 24:12

1:23 Dan 6:27; Theod. 2:5, 9; 2 Macc 2:17

2:9 Isa 9:2

2:11 Gen 23:4; Ps 38[39]:13

2:23 Jer 11:20

2:25 Ezek 34:5, 6; Job 10:12; Wis 1:6

3:3–4 Isa 3:18–24

3:19 Ps 87[88]:4, 6

4:12 Prov 17:3; cf. above, 1 Pet 1:7
4:14 Pss 71[72]:19; 78[79]:9
4:19 2 Macc 1:24
5:4 Isa 28:5
5:6 Gen 16:9; Exod 3:19; 6:1; Deut 9:26; Job 30:20
5:7 Wis 12:13

For discussion of the above biblicisms, see Schutter 1989, 41–43. Mention might also be made of the numerous lexical and thematic similarities between 1 Peter and the Wisdom of Solomon (1 Pet 1:3–2:10/Wis 2–5, 17–20; 3:19–20/Wis 14:6–7; 4:2–4/Wis 14:23–26; and 2:9/Wis 17:2).

In some instances where the LXX is cited, the text of 1 Peter is closer to the readings of Codex Alexandrinus than to Codex Vaticanus (2:6 [Vaticanus omits *ep' autōi*]; 2:10; 2:22; 3:10). In a few cases, the citation is closer to the Hebrew text than the LXX (1:24; 2:6b), and in yet other instances minor variations from both LXX and MT are evident (1:25; 2:6a; 2:8, 22, 24; 5:5).

From the above list of approximately 46 OT citations and allusions (excluding iterative allusions and biblicisms), it is immediately apparent that 1 Peter makes abundant use of the OT in its Greek version and employs a speech rooted in the language and metaphors of Sacred Scripture. Four books of the Pentateuch (Genesis, Exodus, Leviticus, Deuteronomy), four of the latter prophets (Isaiah, Hosea, Ezekiel, Malachi) and three of the Writings (Psalms, Proverbs, Job) are represented, with a concentration on three writings in particular, Isaiah (21×), Psalms (11×), and Proverbs (6×). From the Greek OT (LXX), use was made of no fewer than 24 text segments or combinations of texts.

The citation of Ps 33[34] in 3:10–12 and the number of further terminological affinities with this psalm (see iterative allusions above) led Bornemann (1919–1920) to hypothesize that 1 Peter was a baptismal homily based on this OT text in particular, a proposal amply discussed and cogently refuted by Schutter (1989, 44–49).

As Schutter also has noted (1989, 43), in addition to simple citations and allusions, six more complex modes of usage are evident: (1) the abbreviation or "telescoping" of texts (2:10 [Hos 1–2]; 2:22–25 [Isa 53]); (2) catenas of texts assembled around specific motifs (2:6–8 [stone passages]; 2:9–10 [people of God passages] cf. Elliott 1966b, 16–49); (3) the conflation of multiple texts (1:19 [Isa 53:7; Exod 12:5]; 2:9 [Exod 19:5–6; Isa 43:20–21; 42:12; Mal 3:17]; 2:24 [Isa 53:4, 1; Deut 21:23]; 5:8 [Ps 22:14; Job 1:7]); (4) presupposition of the wider text-plot (1:18–19 [Isa 52:3]; 1:24–25 [Isa 40:6–8]; 2:3–4 [Ps 33:5–8(34:4–7)]; 2:22–25 [Isa 53]); (5) association of the text with a familiar exegetical tradition (1:18–19 [Isa 52:3 and the Exodus motif]; 2:24 [Deut 21:23 and the Cross]; 3:19–20 [Gen 6:1–4 and the Fall of the Heavenly Watchers]); and (6) a combination of text catenas (2:6–8, 9–10) used for expounding the theme of the election and holiness of God's covenant people (2:4–10).

Linking the eschatological community with the history of God's covenant people, this material served to stress the social estrangement and oppression of God's people as resident aliens in diaspora (1:1, 17–18; 2:11; 3:6 [Gen 23:4; cf. Gen 12:1–20, 20:1–18; Isa 52:3, 5]; 3:10–12 [Ps 33[34]]; 5:8–9, 13 [Jer 50–51]); their election and holiness (1:15–16 [Lev 19:2]; 2:5, 9 [Exod 19:6; Isa 43:20; Hos 1:6, 9; 2:1, 3, 25]); the rejection, suffering, and exaltation of the Messiah-Servant (2:4–8 [Isa 8:14; 28:16; Ps 117[118]:22]; 2:22–24 [Isa 53:4, 6, 9]); divine redemption of the righteous and oppressed (1:13 [Exod 12:11]; 1:17–19; cf. 1:2 [Exod 12–15; Isa 52:3, 5]); the examples of Sarah (3:5–6 [Gen 18:12]) and Noah (3:20 [Gen 6–8]); fear of God rather than man (2:17 [Prov 24:21]; 3:6 [Prov 3:25]; 3:14–15 [Isa 8:12–13]); moral conduct (3:10–12 [Ps 33:13–17(34:12–16)]; 4:8 [Prov 10:12]); the imminence of divine judgment (2:12 [Isa 10:3]; 4:17 [Ezek 9:6]; 4:18 [Prov 11:31 LXX]); and God's nurture (2:3 [Ps 33[34]:9]) and exaltation of the humble (5:5 [Prov 3:34 LXX]; 5:7 [Ps 54[55]:23]). Motifs and themes of the Exodus and Passover tradition also figure prominently (sprinkling of the blood of the Passover lamb, 1:2, 19; inheritance, 1:4; 3:7, 9; girding of loins, 1:13; redemption, 1:18; Exodus covenant and election, 2:4–10; cf. 1:1 and 5:13; alien residence, 1:17; 2:11; mighty hand of God, 5:6).

The Petrine author makes abundant use of the OT, but the letter as a whole is no discernible "midrash" or "homily" on any particular OT text or combination of texts. If we understand "midrash" as interpretation whose focus is a *text* and whose aim is expounding the meaning of that text, then none of the sections of 1 Peter can be regarded as "homiletic midrash" (against Schutter 1989). Nor has Bornemann (1919–1920) made a convincing case for regarding it a homiletic exposition of Ps 33[34]. Its primary focus and aim is not an OT text to be interpreted but a suffering community to be consoled and strengthened (as Schutter himself [1989, 172–76] acknowledges). The letter employs a diversity of OT texts, motifs, and themes in order to illustrate the ancient heritage to which the Christian brotherhood is heir and to provide scriptural and hence authoritative substantiation for its message of affirmation and exhortation.[2]

2.2. AFFINITIES WITH OTHER LITERATURE AND TRADITIONS OF ISRAEL

1 Peter contains no explicit citation of the OT Pseudepigrapha, the writings of Qumran, or the works of Philo and Josephus. On the whole, however, the

---

[2] On the use of the OT in 1 Peter see also Smits 1955, 351–69; Leaney 1964; Cipriani 1966b; Elliott 1966; Lea 1968, 1980; Hillyer 1970; Davey 1973; Snodgrass 1977; Cothenet 1980, 28–29; Sandevoir 1980; Schlosser 1980; Detering 1981; Osborne 1981b; Goppelt 1982, 152–58; Pryor 1986a, 1986b; Glenny 1987; Voorwinde 1987; Green 1990; McCartney 1989; Oss 1989; Cervantes Gabarrón 1991a, 97–102 and the NOTES on 2:4–10, 21–25; 3:10–12, and 18–22.

author is clearly familiar with concepts, terminology, traditions, and perspectives evident in this diverse body of literature.

1 Enoch

Although not quoted explicitly in 1 Peter, *1 Enoch* (especially chs. 6–36, 65–67, 106–8) is one important representative of a broad Israelite tradition concerning the Noachic Flood and its surrounding events. This tradition contains several concepts, motifs, and themes upon which the Petrine author drew in 3:19–20 and illustrates as well the cosmology presumed in these verses, as first recognized by F. Spitta (1890) and then examined by subsequent scholars (see the full survey by W. Dalton [1965/1989] and on *1 Enoch* in particular, 1989, 163–76). See the NOTES and DETAILED COMMENT 1 on 3:18–22; compare also 1 Pet 1:12 and *1 En.* 1:2; 16:3. On the use of Israelite-Christian tradition in 1 Peter, see also Cothenet 1980, 32–33.

The Qumran Literature

The Qumran writings and 1 Peter are similar in their eschatological perspective, use of the OT, their conception of the community as an elect and holy people of the covenant in conflict with outsiders, and their ethical rigor concerning admission to and behavior within the community. However, substantial differences are also evident, particularly regarding the conceptualization and identification of the Messiah and the strategy of the community vis-à-vis society. Whereas the Qumran community embraced an ascetic ethic and geographical withdrawal from society, 1 Peter promoted a stance of active yet critical engagement with outsiders in anticipation of their conversion (2:12; 3:2). H. Braun (1966, 282–89) discussed analogous views and perspectives (in relation to 1 Pet 1:2, 5, 11; 2:1–3, 4–9, 22, 23, 25; 4:10, 11; 5:2, 3, 5, 13) but concluded that 1 Peter is in no way "qumranic" (Braun 1966, 288). Goppelt (1993, 69–70 and passim) notes, in somewhat exaggerated fashion, various ideational similarities (see his comments on 1:1, 2, 3–5, 11–12, 14–15, 22–2:3; 2:4–10; 3:21; 4:1, 12–13, 17; 5:2, 8) but claims no actual instances of direct quotation or allusion. Indeed, in no instance can any direct influence be demonstrated (Elliott 1966b, 26–27, 209–13; Snodgrass 1977, 101–2). He agrees with Lohse's assessment (1986, 49–50) that the similarities instead are traceable to the use made in 1 Peter of "traditional material that is appropriated in already christianized form." This material, such as the notion of the expiatory power of suffering and death (4:1), judgment beginning with the house of God (4:17–18), the oriental form of the epistolary greeting in 1:2, and reminiscences of the Jesus tradition of the Synoptics point to the familiarity of the Petrine author with tradition originating in an earlier Palestinian provenance (Lohse 1986, 51; Goppelt 1993, 33–35). For discussions of the similarities and differences between Qumran and Christianity in general see, e.g., Cross 1961, 195–243; Mansoor 1964, 153–63; Gaster 1976, 1–31, 547–67; and the literature cited by Fitzmyer 1975, 119–30.

Philo of Alexandria

On the whole, the similarities between 1 Peter and Philo are of a general nature and entail no instance of literary dependency. The writings of Philo illustrate the perspectives of a Diaspora Israelite on the social and cultural conventions of the age and the tense relation of Israel to secular society, a situation that offered an analogy for the dilemma of the Jesus movement. One remarkable affinity between 1 Peter and Philo, however, involves their common appeal to and similar exposition of the covenant formula of Exod 19:3–6 (1 Pet 2:5, 9; cf. Philo, *Sobr.* 66; *Abr.* 56; see Elliott 1966a, 96–101; 1981, 170–74 and the NOTES on 2:4–10). Like Philo, the Petrine author also knew and adapted the Hellenistic household management (*oikonomia*) tradition in 2:13–3:7; compare 5:1–5a (Elliott 1981/1990, 208–20; Prostmeier 1990, 278–99). Both authors also shared social perspectives typical of Diaspora Judaism and its familiarity with Greco-Roman social, cultural, and ethical traditions. However, the report transmitted by Eusebius (*Hist. eccl.* 2.17.1) that Philo "conversed at Rome in the days of Claudius with Peter, who at that time was preaching to the people there" lacks any further corroboration.

Flavius Josephus

Like Philo, Josephus illustrates an Israelite perspective on Israel and its relation to its social environment. But Josephus' more positive, if not fawning, assessment of Rome distinguishes his position from that of both Philo and 1 Peter. It has been suggested (Balch 1981, 81–116) that the Petrine author used Hellenistic tradition concerning household management (2:13–3:7) to mount a defense of Christianity similar to the apologia of Israel presented by Josephus in *Against Apion* 2.147. But clear differences between the audiences and overall strategies of 1 Peter and Josephus make this hypothesis quite unlikely (Elliott 1981/1990, 110–12, 213–33; compare also Balch 1986 and Elliott 1986a).

2.3. AFFINITIES WITH GRECO-ROMAN THOUGHT, DICTION, AND CULTURE

At no point does the Petrine author cite an ancient secular text, though he appears acquainted with the language, rhetoric, diction, moral exhortation (virtues, vices, household management tradition), and literary conventions of the Greco-Roman world. The similarities of thought and expression are attributable, as in the case of the contemporary Israelite Diaspora literature, to a familiarity with the cultural heritage and contemporary parlance of Hellenistic culture in general.[3] Rather than Greek or Roman literature, it is primarily the

[3] For affinities with various classical writings see Wettstein 1751–1752, 2:681–97; Selwyn 1947–1948, 25–27, 499–501; Mussies 1972, 236–38; Balch 1977, 1981, 1988; Bovon 1978, 34–38; Elliott 1981/1990, 208–20; Adinolfi 1988, 1991a, 1991b, 1991c, 1991d; and the Index of the present commentary.

Greek version of the OT and Israelite and Christian oral tradition shaped in a Hellenistic context that supplied and influenced the content and formulations of the letter. On key values and behavioral scripts of the Circum-Mediterranean cultures in general that also are reflected in 1 Peter (e.g., honor-shame, gender constructs, views of social order and domestic roles, etc.), many instructive studies are now at hand.[4]

2.4. NEW TESTAMENT AFFINITIES AND COMMON CHRISTIAN TRADITION

2.4.1. From Literary Dependency to Common Use of Preexistent Tradition: A Shift in Theories

Scholars have long noted numerous correspondences (including terms, formulations, and themes) between 1 Peter and many other NT writings. The assessment of these "parallels" however, has undergone a significant shift in the twentieth century. Earlier literary-critical studies regarded them as the product of direct literary dependency, usually on the part of the Petrine author. See the extensive list of scholars from F. C. Baur (1856) to Schutter (1989) in Shimada 1991, 78–80 and his earlier 1966 study as well. The influential German scholar, H. J. Holtzmann (1885, 313–15), in fact opined on the basis of these affinities that the Petrine author must have known and used most of the NT writings, an amazing claim repeated in more recent time by Beare (1970, 219). Such literary dependence, it was assumed, could then serve as a basis for reaching conclusions about the letter's date, geographical provenance, authorship, aim, and its relation to Paul, Pauline theology, and the Pauline circle in particular. One such conclusion was that the Petrine author was an unoriginal spirit and dependent for his chief ideas and formulations on other early Christian writers, especially Paul.

The most comprehensive, yet rarely cited, example of this treatment of NT similarities is the 1913 study of O. D. Foster. In a 145-page analysis, Foster discussed and tabulated similarities between 1 Peter, the Apostolic Fathers (1913, 381–411) and the canonical writings of the NT (1913, 411–533). In regard to the latter, he noted a total of 408 affinities in terminology and/or thought with varying degrees of proximity (Foster 1913, 534). From this comparative analysis he concluded that the author of 1 Peter "was not an original writer" (1913, 376) but made extensive use of the Pauline epistles (219 references, including the Deutero-Paulines), with particular dependence upon Romans (63 references, summary list, 1913, 44) and Ephesians (45 references, summary list on p. 454). According to Foster, the author of 1 Peter also knew Galatians, Colossians,

---

[4] See Malina 1986a, 1986b, 1686c, 1988a, 1988b, 1989, 1992, 1993d, 1994; Malina-Neyrey 1988, 1996; Malina-Rohrbaugh 1992; Malina-Pilch 1993; Neyrey 1986, 1988, 1990, 1991, 1993, 1994; Pilch 1991a, 1991b, 1991c, 1993, 1995; Elliott 1686c, 1987, 1993c, 1995a; Esler 1995.

Hebrews, and possibly 1 Corinthians but shows no knowledge of the Q source or literary dependence upon the Gospels. Similarities between 1 Peter and James and the Johannine literature he took as evidence of their literary dependence on 1 Peter (Foster 1913, 377–78).

Foster's analysis tempered the extravagant claim of Holtzmann, but his premise was the same: that literary similarity must indicate literary dependency. Studies proceeding on this premise, however, regularly disagreed regarding specific instances and degrees of similarity and their exegetical or historical implications. Moreover, the lack of agreement concerning the criteria for determining "similarities," the direction of dependence, and the exegetical and historical implications of these affinities resulted in a welter of divergent and inconclusive theories regarding virtually all aspects of the letter and its place within the history of early Christianity.[5]

The emergence of Form and Tradition Criticism in the 1920s brought a new perspective to bear on this issue. With these analyses, the specific *forms* of the similar material, the association of forms of communication (oral as well as written) with specific social settings and activities of the community (*Sitze im Leben*), the history of the transmission and modification of these formal units, and the ideological interests of the tradents became a focus of attention. These exegetical operations have shown that underlying all of the NT writings was a body of oral tradition upon which all NT authors drew in various ways. Form critics have identified and categorized various "forms" of this tradition (kerygmatic, hortatory, catechetical, liturgical, etc.), explained their origin, tradents, combination over time, and the various uses of these traditional forms of communication for purposes of instruction, exhortation, polemic, apologetic, and worship. This material constituted a large reservoir of teaching upon which all of the writers of the NT, including the Petrine author, drew in the composition of their writings. It is reliance on this fluid stream of tradition, influenced by both Israelite and Hellenistic cultural currents and conventions, that accounts for most of the lexical, thematic, and formal features that the NT writings have in common. While literary dependency still remains a likely explanation of the relation, for instance, between Jude and 2 Peter, the Synoptics, Colossians and Ephesians, and perhaps the Pastorals, this is not the case with 1 Peter. The correspondences between this letter and other NT writings is, rather, due to their authors' common, while varied, use of a wide stream of Christian oral tradition. The affinities listed below, then, are to be regarded from this perspective.

With respect to the *Pauline and Deutero-Pauline writings*, Romans and Ephesians are the letters with which 1 Peter shares the greatest number of lexical and thematic affinities.

---

[5] For further representative listings and examinations of parallels see Nestle-Aland *NTG* marginalia; Usteri 1886, 279–335; Bigg 1902, 15–24; Holzmeister 1937, 105–24; Barnett 1941, 51–69; Stibbs-Walls 1959, 45–48; Selwyn 1947, 461–66; Shimada 1966, 1985, 1991; D. H. Schmidt 1972; Brox 1978a; Goppelt 1993, 28–35; Elliott 1992a, 271–72.

For 1 Peter and *Romans*, see 1 Pet 1:14–16 (Rom 12:2); 1:21 (Rom 4:24); 1:22; 3:8–9 (Rom 12:9–19); 2:4–10 (Rom 9:25, 32–33); 2:5 (Rom 12:l; 15:16, 31); 2:6–8 ([= Isa 28:1ab; Ps 117[118]:22; Isa 8:14] Rom 9:33 [= Isa 28:16a; Isa 8:14; cf. Isa 28:16b]; cf. Rom 14:13); 2:10 ([= Hos 1:6, 9; 2:1, 25] Rom 5:25–26 [= Hos 2:25; 2:1]); 2:13–17 (Rom 13:1, 3, 7); 3:8–9 (Rom 1:9–21); 3:22 (Rom 8:34); 4:1 (Rom 6:7, 10); 4:8–11 (Rom 12:3–13); 4:12–13, 5:1 (Rom 8:17, 18); 5:12 (Rom 5:2); cf. also Boismard 1966, 1423–27.

For 1 Peter and *Ephesians*, see 1 Pet 1:2, 20 (Eph 1:4–5); 1:3[–12] (Eph 1:3 [–14]; cf. 2 Cor 1:3[–11]; 1:3–5 (Eph 1:18–19); 1:13 (Eph 6:14); 1:14–18, 4:2–3 (Eph 4:17–18; 5:8); 1:20 (Eph 1:4); 2:1 (Eph 4:25, 31); 2:4–6 (Eph 2:19–22); 2:18–20 (Eph 6:5–9); 3:1 (Eph 5:22); 3:7 (Eph 5:25–33); 3:18, 22 (Eph 1:20–21; 4:8–10); 5:8–9 (Eph 6:11–13).

The lexical and thematic similarities of Romans and 1 Peter and their use of similar OT texts once had led many scholars to postulate the direct dependency of the latter upon the former (see, e.g., Seufert 1874, 386; Hort 1898, 116; Knopf 1912, 14; Foster 1913, 424–42; Beare 1970, 217, 219; and the studies listed in Shimada 1993). However, Shimada's extensive and meticulous analysis of the pertinent passages and his clarification of the valid critieria for comparative analysis have now definitively shown that "a direct literary dependence of I Peter on Romans cannot be demonstrated" (Shimada 1993, 135).

The literary dependency of 1 Peter on Ephesians, as claimed by various authors,[6] also has been cogently refuted by Shimada (1991). The attribution of 1 Peter and Ephesians to a common author (Seufert 1881) has justly gained no followers; on the differences, see also Elliott 1981/1990, 255.

In regard to 1 Peter's relation to both Romans and Ephesians, it is now recognized that several factors argue against literary dependency and rather for independent use of common tradition. These include the different senses and uses of identical or similar terms (e.g., *dikaios, dikaiosynē*), the different mode of employment and combination of similar formulas or OT texts (e.g., 1 Pet 2:4–10; Rom 9:19–33), and the different mode of exhortation (indicative followed by imperatives in Romans and Ephesians; the opposite in 1 Peter).[7] This attention to the sometimes subtle and other times obvious differences among textual "parallels" is essential, of course, for assessing 1 Peter's relation to *all* the NT writings.

Affinities between 1 Peter and *Galatians, 1–2 Thessalonians,* and *1–2 Corinthians* listed by Foster (1913, 411–23) involve nothing more than common terminology and ideas; on the affinities of 1 Peter and *Colossians,* see Boismard 1966, 1428–29, and on the affinities of 1 Peter and *1 John,* Boismard 1966, 1420–21. These are Christian commonplaces that are not peculiar to these

[6] For example, Moffatt 1918, 337–38; Coutts 1957; Beare 1970, 219; D. H. Schmidt 1972, 33–35, 57–58 and especially Mitton 1950; 1951, 176–97, 279–315.

[7] See Percy 1946, 433–40; Selwyn 1947, 384; Lohse 1957/1986; Brox 1978a, 183–85; 1986, 47–51; Goppelt 1993, 28–30; Shimada 1966, 1991, 1993.

documents but common to early Christianity, as Selwyn (1947–1948, 369–84) emphasized. This fact, however, undermines Selwyn's claim that affinities between 1–2 Thessalonians and 1 Peter betray the mind and hand of a common author, namely the Silvanus mentioned in 1 Thess 1:1; 2 Thess 1:2; and 1 Pet 5:13; see the telling critique of Rigaux 1956, 105–11.

For similarities between 1 Peter and the *Pastorals*, compare 1 Pet 1:3–5 (Titus 3:4–7); 2:1 (Titus 3:3); 2:9 (Titus 2:14); 2:13–3:7, 5:1–5 (1 Tim 2:1–2, 8–15; 6:1–2; Titus 2:1–10; 3:1–2; cf. Eph 5:22–6:9; Col 3:18–4:1); 3:18, 22 (1 Tim 3:16); cf. also Boismard 1966, 1422–23. On the dependency of the Pastorals upon 1 Peter, see Hofrichter 1987. These similarities, however, generally involve kerygmatic and parenetic formulations typical of early Christian tradition. Boismard's theory (1956a, 1956b, 1961, 1966) that baptismal hymns and a baptismal liturgy underlie the affinities of 1 Peter and Titus, however, claims more than can be demonstrated. The rather idiosyncratic notion of Munro (1983), that similarities between 1 Peter and Romans, Ephesians, Colossians, as well as the Pastorals are evidence of a "pastoral stratum" secondarily added to these documents to inculcate submission to the imperial authorities and to dissociate Christianity from Israel, has been cogently criticized by Dijkman (1984, 10–19; 1987).

On the whole, an earlier preoccupation with lexical similarities generally overlooked the notable differences in the way terms and formulas were used and interpreted. A closer scrutiny of the latter has demonstrated peculiarities of 1 Peter that make dependency on the Pauline and Deutero-Pauline writings highly unlikely. Varied use of a common reservoir of tradition more adequately accounts for these affinities in the case of 1 Peter, Ephesians, and the Pastorals. A further factor accounting for the contacts of 1 Peter with Romans, in particular, is the likely association of both writings with Rome. Romans was part of the broad stream of Christian tradition known to the Christian community of Rome, tradition upon which the Petrine author so extensively drew.

Similarities between 1 Peter and *James* include 1 Pet 1:1 (Jas 1:1); 1:6–7; 4:12 (Jas 1:2–3, 12; cf. Wis 3:5–6); 1:23–2:2 (Jas 1:18–22); 5:8–9 (Jas 4:7); and the common OT citations of Isa 40:6–8 (1 Pet 1:24–25; Jas 1:10–11), Prov 10:12 (1 Pet 4:8; Jas 5:20), and Prov 3:34 (1 Pet 5:5; Jas 4:6); cf. also Boismard 1966, 1419–20. Literary critics differed in their assessment of these similarities. Some postulated a Petrine dependency on James (Vowinkel 1899; Meyer 1930, 81); others, the reverse (Knopf 1912, 6–7; Moffatt 1918, 338; Ferris 1939). Similar situations of social stress, however, similar sectarian insider-outsider perspectives, and use of similar sources (OT, especially Isaiah and Proverbs; persecution tradition) best account for these affinities (Brox 1978a, 186; Lohse 1986, 49; Goppelt 1993, 31). L. T. Johnson (1995, 54–55), however, is correct in stressing that such similarities are far outweighed by more important Christological and ecclesiological differences. On the whole, while James and 1 Peter are both addressed to communities in the Diaspora, are both hortatory in tone with common appeal to Wisdom tradition, and are both intent on reinforcing the distinctions of insiders and outsiders, they also differ significantly in their general perspectives. James focuses predominantly on the internal life of the community and the issue of integrity (personal, social, and cosmic; cf. Elliott 1993), whereas 1 Peter addresses the problematic nature of insider-outsider relations and the factor of innocent suffering analyzed from a Christological perspective.

Affinities of 1 Peter with *Hebrews* include 1 Pet 1:1, 2:11 (Heb 11:13); 1:2 (Heb 12:24); 1:23 (Heb 4:12); 2:24 (Heb 10:10); 2:25, 5:4 (Heb 13:20); 3:9 (Heb 12:17); 3:18 (Heb 9:28); 4:14 (Heb 13:13) and the themes of social alienation and solidarity with the suffering of Jesus Christ. Similarities between these two writings (see Foster 1913, 480–92) led Ferris (1930) to postulate the literary dependence of Hebrews on 1 Peter. While these documents reflect a similar situation of social alienation and suffering and employ similar motifs and themes, including solidarity with the suffering of Jesus Christ, the differences in theological and cosmological perspectives far outweigh the similarities (see Elliott 1981/1990, 156–57, 251 and Brox 1978a, 185). For a more extended list and discussion of parallels, see Attridge (1989, 30–31), who also regards both writings as drawing on a "large body of common traditions" (so also Brox 1978a, 185). There is merit to Michaels' (1988, xliv) conjecture that affinities of 1 Peter (written in Rome) with Hebrews (possibly written in Rome) and Romans (addressed to Rome) may reflect theological tradition and perspectives of the Roman Christian community.

Links with the *Gospel of Mark* and the *Synoptic tradition* include 1 Pet 1:18 (Mark 10:45); 2:4–8 ([= Ps 117[118]:22] Mark 12:1–12 par. [= Ps 117[118]:22]); 2:5, 4:17 (Mark 3:31–35 par.); 2:18–3:7, 5:2–5a (Mark 10:2–45 par., domestic instruction for the household of God); 1 Pet 1:19–21, 2:21–25, 3:18 (Mark 14–16 par.); 4:13 (Mark 13:9–13 par.); and 1 Pet 5:2–5 (Mark 10:35–45 par.); 5:8 (Mark 13:33, 37). On the similarities of the Gospel of Mark and 1 Peter in general, see Scharfe 1893; van Dodewaard 1949; Schattenmann 1954–1955 (claiming, unconvincingly, that 1 Peter is a commentary on and criterion for the authenticity of Mark 13); and Elliott 1983 (noting similarities in eschatological perspective, a common accent on Jesus' suffering, death, and resurrection, and this as the bond joining believers and Christ, a similar distinction between insiders and outsiders, and a common Roman provenance). These similarities likewise are due not to literary dependence but to reliance on preexisting tradition known to the community at Rome (Best 1971, 54; Elliott 1983, 190–93).

Affinities with specific *Dominical sayings* preserved in the Synoptic Gospels include 1 Pet 1:10–12 (Matt 13:17; Luke 24:26); 1:13 (Luke 12:35); 1:17 (Matt 6:9; Luke 11:2); 2:12 (Matt 5:16); 2:19–20 (Luke 6:27–36); 3:9 (Matt 5:38–42/Luke 6:29–30); 3:14 (Matt 5:10); 4:5 (Matt 12:36); 4:13–14 (Matt 5:10–11/Luke 6:22–23, 28); 5:6 (Luke 14:11); 5:7 (Matt 6:25–34). For a more extensive list, see Chase 1900b, 787–88. For the most part, these affinities are restricted to two blocks of sayings tradition in Matthew and Luke, both of which are traceable in their totality to the parenetic tradition of the early Church (Best 1969–1970). Except for 1 Pet 2:18–20, 1 Peter is generally closer to Matthean than Lukan formulations (cf. Metzner 1995). In their transmission, these sayings and other thematic teaching underwent considerable reformulation (Nauck 1955; J. P. Brown 1963; Elliott 1970).

The correspondences between 1 Peter and the Synoptics in general are the result of a similar but varied use of the Jesus sayings, hortatory tradition, and tradition pertaining to Jesus' passion.[8] The recent claim that 1 Peter was directly dependent on Matthew (Metzner 1995) underestimates the differences among the affinities, fails to adequately consider the mutual use of common tradition, and begs the question as to the relative dating of these writings.

R. Gundry (1966–1967; 1974) pointed to numerous affinities between 1 Peter and the words of Jesus in the *Gospel of John* that he alleged were mediated by Peter and that thus supported the apostolic authorship of 1 Peter (see also Maier 1984, following Gundry). The similarities, however, involve traditional motifs and themes (e.g., rebirth [1 Pet 1:3, 23/John 3:3, 7], reciprocal love [1 Pet 1:22; 3:8; 4:8/John 13:34; 15:12], Jesus as shepherd and the commission to tend the flock [1 Pet 2:25; 5:4/John 10:11, 14; 1 Pet 5:2/John 21:15–17]) that are too general to prove exclusive association with the Apostle Peter or anything more than similar reliance on common Christian tradition (so Best 1969/1970; Brox 1978a, 182–92; and Goppelt 1993, 33–35).

The tradition used in 1 Peter and the Jesus tradition incorporated in the Synoptic Gospels, as Goppelt (1993, 33–35) aptly noted, "travelled the same road of development": emergence in the Palestinian church and embellishment in the Hellenistic church, with Rome as one important locale of their convergence.

1 Peter also displays some remarkable affinities with the *Petrine Speeches of Acts* that also suggest the use of common tradition.There is general agreement concerning the difficulty but not impossibility of distinguishing preexistent tradition from Lukan redaction in the speeches of Acts (1:16–23; 2:14–37; 3:12–26; 4:8–12; 5:29–32; 10:34–44; 11:5–17; 15:7–11; cf. Wilcox 1975). Selwyn's claim (1947, 33–36) that similarities of these speeches with the content of 1 Peter indicate Peter's authorship of the letter is hardly demonstrable. However, several affinities (terms, motifs, themes) do point to certain consistent features of early Christian tradition associated with Peter and to possible elements of Petrine tradition existing prior to both writings. For affinities between 1 Peter and the Petrine speeches, compare 1 Pet 1:2, 20 (Acts 2:23; 3:18); 1:3, 21; 3:18 (Acts 2:31–36; 3:13, 15, 26); 1:5, 9, 10 (Acts 4:12; cf. 13:26, 47); 1:5, 20 (Acts 2:17); 1:6, 8; 4:13 (Acts 2:26); 1:10 (Acts 2:17, 18); 1:14 (Acts 3:17); 1:17 (Acts 10:34; 15:9); 1:18 (Acts 3:6); 1:21; 3:21–22 (Acts 2:32–36; 3:15; 4:10; 10:40); 2:4, 7 ([= Ps 117:22] Acts 4:11 [= Ps 117:22]); 2:21–25 ([= Isa 53] Acts 3:13, 26; 4:27, 30 [= Isa 53; cf. 8:32–33]); 2:24 (Acts 5:30; 10:39); 3:18 (Acts 2:31; 3:14); 3:22 (Acts 2:33–36; 5:31); 4:5 (Acts 10:42); 5:1 (Acts 1:8, 22; 2:32; 3:15; 5:32; 10:39, 41).

---

[8]So Selwyn 1947, 23–24 and passim; J. P. Brown 1963; Spicq 1966; Best 1971; Elliott 1970; Brox 1976, 187–90; Millauer 1976; Maier 1985.

These affinities reveal not only lexical but also thematic similarities:

1. Use of *Christos* in Acts as both a title (13×) and a proper name (13×), several of which, respectively, are associated with Peter (Acts 2:31, 36; 3:18, 20; 2:38; 3:6; 4:10; 9:34; 10:36; 11:17); 1 Peter (22×);
2. Depiction of Christ as "servant (*pais*) of God" modeled after Isa 53 (Acts 3:13, 26; cf. 4:27, 30; 1 Pet 2:21–25);
3. Portrayal of Christ as the "holy and just one" (Acts 3:14; 1 Pet 3:18 and 2:22–23);
4. Focus on the suffering, rejection, death, and resurrection of the Christ (Acts 2:23–24, 31–36; 3:13–18, 26; 4:10–12; 10:39–40; 1 Pet 1:3, 21; 2:21–24; 3:18, 22; 4:1–2, 13);
5. Reference to the "tree" of crucifixion (Acts 5:30; 10:39; 1 Pet 2:24);
6. Christ as the rejected "stone" with identical use of Ps 117[118]:22 (Acts 4:11; 1 Pet 2:4, 7);
7. Christ not abandoned in Hades (Acts 2:24–32; 1 Pet 3:19–22);
8. Reference to the "name" of Christ (Acts 2:21, 38; 3:6, 16; 4:10–12, 17; 1 Pet 4:14); suffering for the name (Acts 4:17, 18, 28, 40–41; 10:16; 1 Pet 4:14); cf. the sole NT appearances of *Christianos* in Acts 11:26; 26:28 and 1 Pet 4:16;
9. Reference to the "foreknowledge" of God (Acts 2:23; 10:42; cf. 4:28; 1 Pet 1:2);
10. Stress on obedience to God (Acts 5:29, 32; 1 Pet 1:2, 14, 22; 2:15; 3:17; 4:12, 19);
11. "Judge of the living and the dead" (Acts 10:42; 1 Pet 4:5);
12. "Impartiality" of divine judgment (Acts 10:34; 15:9; 1 Pet 1:17);
13. OT prophets' foretelling the suffering and glorification of the Christ (Acts 2:23, 29–35; 3:18, 21, 24; 10:43; 1 Pet 1:10–11);
14. Reception of the Holy Spirit (Acts 2:17, 38; 15:8; 1 Pet 1:2; 4:13);
15. Baptism (Acts 2:38; 1 Pet 3:21);
16. Election (Acts 15:7; 1 Pet 1:1; 2:4–10; 5:13);
17. Salvation available to all righteous believers (Acts 10:43; 11:2–27; 15:7–11; 1 Pet 1:5, 9, 10, 18–19; 2:2, 10, 12; 3:2, 21; 4:6);
18. Peter the Apostle as "witness" (Acts 2:32; 3:15; 10:39–41; 1 Pet 5:1, 12).

Maier's proposal (1984) that "brief catechisms" underlay the affinities of the Petrine speeches, 1 Peter, and the Gospels, like Selwyn's catechism hypothesis, claimed a more organized schema than could be demonstrated. Whether these similarities reflected smaller elements of tradition, however, is another matter. On the basis of the association between the term *Christos* and "suffering," Smalley (1973) concluded that "an apostolic christological tradition lies behind both Acts and I Peter, and 'Peter', actually or indirectly, is its spokesman" (Smalley 1973, 92). The totality of the affinities listed above constitutes further support for this conclusion and indicates important themes associated with the Apostle Peter in the memory of the early Church. Cullmann (1958, 33–69) considered Acts and its Petrine speeches as a reliable source of information concerning Peter and features of his activity and teaching (stress on the inclusive scope of the Gospel, on Jesus Christ as suffering servant [the earliest of the Church's Christologies], and on the atoning character of Jesus' death [Cullmann 1958, 66–68]). These features are prominent in 1 Peter as well, and this letter, like the material underlying the redacted speeches of Acts, could well be testimony to the Church's early memory of Peter.[9]

Affinities between 1 Peter and 2 *Peter* and *Jude* include the following, of which their common reference to the Flood tradition is most significant, as the NOTES on 3:19–21 indicate. Compare 1 Pet 1:1, 2 (2 Pet 1:1, 2; Jude 2); 1:5, 7, 13; 5:1, 4 (2 Pet 1:16; 3:3, 10, 12); 1:10–11 (2 Pet 1:19–20); 1:15, 2:4–10 (2 Pet 1:10; 3:11); 1:17, 4:5, 17 (2 Pet 3:7); 1:19 (2 Pet 3:14); 3:19–20 (2 Pet 2:4–5; 3:5–6; Jude 6). Beyond the similar initial greetings of the salutations, the similarities involve mainly traditional themes (election, holiness, coming of the Lord, and prophecy), among which the common reference to Noah and Flood as a sign of condemnation and salvation is the most noteworthy. The letters differ significantly, however, in vocabulary, style, sources, situations addressed, and theology.[10] Virtually all scholars today assume the priority of 1 Peter (perhaps alluded to in 2 Pet 3:1), but few see any direct dependence of 2 Peter or Jude on 1 Peter, although Mayor (1907, cxiv) thinks that 2 Peter "shows signs of careful study of 1P," and Boobyer 1957 argues for direct use of 1 Peter in 2 Peter. On the whole, the dissimilarities in language, style, and themes far outweigh the lexical similarities and indicate different authors and little influence of 1 Peter upon 2 Peter. On the relation of the two writings and the possible allusion to 1 Peter in 2 Pet 3:1, see below under 10. EXTERNAL ATTESTATION.

Correspondences between 1 Peter and *Revelation* are equally sparse. Both documents address Asia Minor communities and both treat situations of suffering, though Revelation, in contrast to 1 Peter, speaks of the deaths of some of the faithful (Rev 2:13; 7:14; 18:24). They both refer to the city of Rome as "Babylon" (1 Pet 5:13; Rev 14:8; 16:19; 17:5; 18:10, 21), as occurs in writings after 70 CE, but display contrary views of Roman rule. Textual affinities are mainly restricted to the common but different use of Exod 19:6 (1 Pet 2:4–10; Rev 1:5–6; 5:9–10; 20:6; cf. Elliott 1966b, 107–20; Schüssler Fiorenza 1972).

In summary, correspondences between 1 Peter and other NT writings can no longer be regarded as evidence of literary dependency. Form-critical and

---

[9] On 1 Peter and the Petrine speeches, see Seyler 1832; Cullmann 1958, 66–68; Wand 1934, 28; Selwyn 1947, 33–36; Hunter 1957, 78; Spicq 1966c, 53–61; Brox 1978a, 187–88; Dijkman 1984, 148–53; Maier 1984. On Peter in Acts, see Brown et al. 1973, 39–56.

[10] On lexical and other similarities and noteworthy differences between 1 Peter and 2 Peter, see Mayor 1907/1965, lxviii–cv; Holzmeister 1949; Boobyer 1957; Davey 1970; and Bauckham 1988, 3716–18.

Tradition-critical analysis of the NT writings including 1 Peter has shown that the numerous affinities among virtually all of the NT writings are the result not of literary dependency but of a common, varied use of a wide stream of oral and written tradition (Selwyn 1947, 363–466; Lohse 1954/1986; J. N. D. Kelly 1969; 11–15; Best 1971; Elliott 1976; Millauer 1976; Brox 1978a, 1986; Cothenet 1980; Vanhoye 1980; Michaels 1988, xl–xlv; Goppelt 1993, 33–35).

E. G. Selwyn was the first to systematically analyze the material of 1 Peter along form-critical lines, and his commentary with its appended essay "On the Inter-relation of I Peter and other N.T. Epistles" (Selwyn 1947, 365–466) marks a milestone of research on 1 Peter and its intertextuality. Through a detailed comparison of the material of 1 Peter with other NT writings, Selwyn demonstrated that the lexical and thematic correspondences were due not to the literary dependency of 1 Peter on other NT literature but to common yet varied use of a broad reservoir of early Christian tradition. Subsequent studies on 1 Peter and related NT texts have confirmed and expanded upon this fundamental conclusion of Selwyn.

Selwyn's work was not totally original but expanded on the publications of two earlier authors, A. Seeberg (1903/1960) and P. Carrington (1940). Seeberg in his novel study, *Der Katechismus der Urchristenheit*, "The Catechism of Primitive Christianity" (1903; reprinted 1960), in anticipation of later form-critical analysis, had proposed that certain verses of 1 Peter (1:11, 18–21; 3:18–22; 4:5) derived from an early Christian creed (reconstructed on p. 80) which, together with traditional ethical instruction, formed part of an early Christian catechism circulating in oral form between 30–50 CE. G. Klein (1909) took Seeberg's theory a step further by suggesting a connection between Christian catechetical instruction (exemplified by the *Didache*) and "Jewish diaspora propaganda literature" (with use of Ps 33[34] as in Pseudo-Phocylides, "the oldest catechism for Gentiles" [Klein 1909, 137–43]).

In his 1940 study, *The Primitive Christian Catechism*, Philip Carrington, apparently independently of Seeberg and Klein, similarly concluded that passages common to 1 Peter, Colossians, Ephesians, and James were the result of common use of a "primitive Christian catechism" designed for the instruction of proselytes. This catechism, linked with baptism and based on Lev 17–19, according to Carrington, constituted a "neo-levitical holiness code." Its four main themes were "put off" (evil), "be subject," "be watchful," "resist" (the devil). It also included an introductory prayer for wisdom and knowledge and a statement concerning the reception of the word of truth in baptism "as reenactment of creation, new birth or the sowing of a seed" (Carrington 1940, 31). The catechism comprised a common "pattern" of oral tradition indebted to Israelite tradition and was employed about the year 50 CE in the Gentile mission.

Selwyn (1947, 17–24) identified four types of sources used in 1 Peter: (1) liturgical hymnic material; (2) a "persecution fragment"; (3) catechetical schemas; and (4) sayings of Jesus (*Verba Christi*). Essay II of his commentary (Selwyn

1947, 365–466) contains an extensive discussion of these sources, which builds on the work of Seeberg and especially Carrington. Here Selwyn hypothesized two "baptismal forms" used in 1 Peter and other NT writings. A "very early baptismal Form" (B1) reflected in the material common to 1 Peter and 1–2 Thessalonians was "compiled under the influence of the Apostolic Decree of Acts xv, involved the idea of the Church as a 'neo-Levitical community,'" and contained "teaching on abstinence from sensual sins, on Love as the fulfillment of Holiness, on Worship, and on the conduct expected of catechumens" (Selwyn 1947, 19). The association of Silvanus with this material suggested to Selwyn that he was the author who adopted this catechetical tradition in 1 Peter and the Thessalonian letters (1947, 383–84).

This early baptismal form, Selwyn postulated (1947, 19; 384–439), was subsequently incorporated in a later baptismal form (B2) reflected in material common to 1 Peter, Romans, Colossians, Ephesians, James, and Philippians. This form also included a fragment on catechumen virtues based largely on Prov 3 and Ps 33[34], as well as teaching on creation or new birth, renunciation of Gentile vices, social subordination, watchfulness and prayer, steadfastness, and Church order (Selwyn 1947, 19, 384–439). This catechetical form circulated in the Church about 50–55 (1947, 19, 460).

Furthermore, in material common to 1–2 Thessalonians, 1 Peter, Acts, Romans, 1 Corinthians, Philippians, James, and in certain sayings of Jesus (Matthew, Mark, and Luke), Selwyn also detected evidence of a "persecution form" calling for joy in suffering, which was developed with persecution in view, eschatological in character, and rooted in the teaching of Jesus (1947, 18, 439–58, 461).

For Selwyn (1947, 17–24), these catechetical patterns and persecution form, along with liturgical material (2:6–10; Ps 33[34] as "hymn for catechumens," and 3:18–22), and sayings of Jesus (*Verba Christi*) belonging to a "hortatory type of tradition" (1947, 24), comprised the four chief sources utilized in 1 Peter in addition to the OT. Common use of this common tradition, he convincingly has shown, explains the numerous lexical and thematic similarities among the NT writings and decisively discredits theories of direct literary dependency (Selwyn 1947, 19–20, 384). Beare (1970, 220–26) is one of the sole recent voices still holding out for 1 Peter's literary dependency on much of the NT. Form-critical studies subsequent to Selwyn's groundbreaking work, however, have confirmed the existence and diverse use of a common reservoir of tradition of which 1 Peter and other NT writings made use.

This employment of tradition, however, is too varied in subject matter, wording, and sequence of material to sustain Selwyn's theory of one or more schematized baptismal catechisms. This applies as well to more recent attempts to link the tradition to other forms of schematic "catechisms" (i.e., an earlier "Jerusalem Catechism" [Dijkman 1984] or "brief catechisms" with OT roots [Maier 1984]). The evidence, rather, indicates independent and varied use of a flexible oral tradition involving not large catechetical patterns but smaller units of material: stable kerygmatic and creedal formulas, and baptismal-catechetical, liturgical, and parenetic formulations with specific semantic fields that have been employed in similar social situations.[11]

1 Peter, it is now generally agreed, is an "épître de la Tradition" (Spicq 1966, 37) and an epistolary "carrefour" (Vanhoye 1980) in which various streams of tradition intersect (Brox 1978a, Cothenet 1980, 26–36; Vanhoye 1980, 97–128; Goppelt 1993, 26–35). Traces of these diverse traditions in 1 Peter will be noted throughout this commentary. The various modes of employment of this tradition, illuminated in turn by subsequent redaction-critical studies, have clarified the specific literary and theological characteristics of 1 Peter, as of all the NT writings.

2.4.2. Forms of Christian Tradition Employed in 1 Peter

2.4.2.1. Christological and Kerygmatic Formulas: Creedal and Hymnic Forms?

There is as yet no consensus as to whether the Christological tradition employed in 1 Peter (1) already was in the form of integrated hymns or creeds or (2) consisted primarily of independent Christological or kerygmatic formulas not yet integrated into fixed hymns or creeds.

The Christological and kerygmatic formulas have a typical content, form, structure, and function:

(1) The content concerns Jesus Christ, his being the one

- who was "foreknown (by God) before the foundation of the world and was made manifest at the end of the ages" (1:20)
- who, in his lifetime, "did no wrong nor was guile found in his mouth" (2:22)
- who was "rejected by humans but (was) elect, honored in God's sight" (2:4)
- who suffered for you (2:21b)
- who "when insulted did not insult in return" (2:23a)
- (who) "when suffering did not threaten" (2:23b) but rather committed his cause to the One (God) who judges justly (2:23c)
- who "himself bore our sins in his body on the tree" (2:24a)
- "by whose/his bruise you have been healed" (2:24d)
- who "suffered for sins once for all" (3:18a)
- (who was) "a righteous one (who suffered) for unrighteous ones" (3:18b)
- (who) was "put to death in the flesh" but who was "made alive in the spirit" (3:18d,e; 4:1a)

[11] General studies on the indebtedness of 1 Peter to this common tradition include Lohse 1954/1986; Nauck 1955; Shimada 1966; Best 1969–1970, 1971; Brox 1978a, 1986; Cothenet 1980, 26–36; Vanhoye 1980, 97–128; Goppelt 1993, 26–36 and passim; as well as investigations of the Petrine creedal or hymnic material by Bultmann (1947) and others (see the NOTES and DETAILED COMMENTS on 2:21–25 and 3:18–22).

- whom God raised from the dead and gave glory (1:21b; cf. resurrection of Jesus Christ, 1:3a; 3:22c)
- who "went into heaven" (3:22b; cf. 3:19)
- "who is at the right (hand) of God" (3:22a)
- to whom "angels and authorities and powers are subordinated" (3:22c)
- who will be revealed/manifested (1:7, 13; 5:4)
- see also the "sufferings" and "glories" of (the) Christ (1:11; 4:13; 5:1bc)

(2) Their form is that of brief formulas (1:11; 4:13; 5:1bc), declarative clauses (2:21b, 22, 23c; 3:18ab), relative pronominal clauses (2:22, 23, 24a,d; 3:22a), and participial phrases (1:20, 21b; 2:4; 3:22b,c; 5:4; cf. 1:7, 13), occasionally entailing paralleled contrasts (1:20a/b; 2:4c/d; 3:18d/e) and sometimes presented in sequence (2:21–24; 3:18, 22).

(3) Their structure occasionally involves statements arranged as parallelisms with rhythmic cadence (1:20; 2:4, 22–24; 3:18, 22).

(4) The function of these kerygmatic formulas regarding Jesus Christ, his appearance, life, suffering, death, and resurrection is to establish both the basis and model for Christian belief, behavior, hope, and trust in God. Frequently this kerygmatic material simultaneously is employed to support and explain preceding imperatives often derived from hortatory tradition (Lohse 1986). This sequence varies from Pauline style, where imperatives follow preceding indicatives.

Several scholars have suspected that some of these kerygmatic formulas may have been parts of fixed creeds or hymns.[12] Texts of 1 Peter thought to contain traditional creedal formulas or hymnic patterns include the following:

- 1:2, triadic structure (cf. also 1:3–12); reference to God the Father (1:2; 3–5), Holy Spirit (1:2b; 10–12), and Jesus Christ (1:2c; 6–9); cf. Matt 28:19
- 1:3–12, "entrance hymn" (Windisch); "prayer-psalm" (Preisker); "prayer" (Coutts; Cross); cf. 2 Cor 1:3–12; Eph 1:3–14; Col 1:3–5
- 1:3–5, fragment of baptismal hymn (Boismard); cf. Titus 3:3–5
- 1:20, fragment of creed/hymn cited further in 3:18–19, 22 (Bultmann and others)
- 2:1–10, "hymn" (Windisch), "festal song" of three strophes (Preisker)
- 2:6–10, "hymn" of two strophes (Selwyn 1947, 268–81)
- 2:21–24 (25), "Christ hymn" (Windisch-Preisker; Bultmann; Deichgräber; and others)

[12] Windisch 1930, 65, 70; R. Bultmann 1947, Selwyn 1947, 17–18, 268–81; Cullmann 1943, 14–15; Windisch-Preisker 1951; Boismard 1956b, 1957, 1961, 1966; Schille 1962, 45–46; Deichgräber 1967, 140–43, 169–73; Goldstein 1974; Wengst 1974, 83–86; Millauer 1976, 15–84; 90–103; Schlosser 1980, 83–93; Brox 1986, 134; Lohse 1986, 56–59; Richard 1986; Dalton 1989, 109–19; Reichert 1989, 355–74; Goppelt 1993, 207–10.

- 3:18–19a, 22, fragments of a "Christ hymn" (Windisch; Bultmann; Jeremias; Boismard; Dalton; Deichgräber; Hunzinger; and others)
- 5:5–9, "baptismal hymn" (Boismard)

There are several problems with this hypothesis, however, (see also the NOTES and DETAILED COMMENTS on 1:20, 2:18–25 and 3:18–22):

(1) Much of this form-critical work still remains highly conjectural and controverted. Reconstruction of the original forms of these hymns in particular often involves hypothetical and arbitrary alterations of the present NT texts in order to create coherent and symmetrical forms. This is illustrated by the analyses of Preisker and R. Bultmann (1947/1964) in particular; see the critiques of Lohse (1954/1986), Jeremias (1949), R. P. Martin (1962), and Deichgräber (1967).

(2) None of the NT hymns or creeds on which there is a consensus presents a complete parallel to the various and separated material of 1 Peter. Bultmann and followers therefore have to speculate about *membra disiecta*, parts of hymns/creeds that have been separated and cited independently of one another in 1 Peter (e.g., elements of a coherent hymn that were separated and cited independently in 1:19–21; 2:21–24; 3:18–22), with inadequate explanation of the motivation for this procedure.

(3) There is no consensus among proponents of this theory concerning the identification of the original genre, content, context, and theme of this hymnic or creedal material on the one hand and Petrine redactional elements and procedure on the other.

Consequently, the most that can be stated with certainty is that 1 Peter incorporates isolated phrases and formulas of Christological and kerygmatic tradition but not that this material was embodied in demonstrable hymnic or creedal sources.

2.4.2.2. Tradition and Forms Associated with Baptism and Baptismal Catechesis

It was Selwyn in particular, who directed attention to several affinities between 1 Peter and tradition and catechesis associated with baptism.[13] See, for example:

(1) Use of the technical term for baptism (*baptisma*) and explanation of its nature: 3:21.

(2) Metaphorical baptismal terminology: "born again," 1:3, 22; "newborn babies," 2:2; cf. Titus 3:5–7; John 3:3–8; 1 John 3:9–10; 5:1–5; Jas 1:18; see also the related motifs of "newness of life" (Rom 6:4; Gal 6:15; 2 Cor 5:17; Col 3:10; Eph 2:15; 4:22–24; Titus 3:4) and "adoption" as children of God (Rom 8:15; Gal 4:4–7; Eph 1:5); motifs derived from Israelite Passover tradition (oppression and redemption of house of Jacob as resident aliens in Egypt; liberation from

[13] On baptismal motifs and themes in 1 Peter, see Seeberg 1903/1960; Carrington 1940; Selwyn 1947, 369–461; Cross 1954, 28–35; Boismard 1956a (listing paschal lamb, new people, holiness, obedience to the word, new worship, living stone); Kosala 1985; Lohse 1954/1986. See also Beasley-Murray 1963, 251–62 on baptism in 1 Peter and his overview of baptismal treatise theories.

darkness, death, and external political control through sacrificed lamb's blood; abandonment of Egypt and past condition of enslavement; wilderness wanderings; divine covenant at Sinai with elect and holy people of God); cf. Danielou 1950, 141; Adinolfi 1967b.

(3) Baptism into the "name" of Christ and bearing this name: 4:14; cf. Acts 2:38; 8:16; 10:48; 19:5; 1 Cor 1:13; 6:11.

(4) Baptism as sharing in Christ's suffering, death, and resurrection: 1:3, 21; 2:21–24; 3:18–22; 4:1, 13; cf. Rom 6:1–11; 1 Cor 15:29; Col 2:12–13; 3:1–7; Eph 5:14; Mark 10:38; Luke 12:50.

(5) Baptism as the "call" of God: 1:15; 2:9, 21; 3:9; 5:10; cf. Rom 8:30; Eph 4:4; 2 Thess 2:13–14; 1 Tim 6:12; 2 Tim 1:9.

(6) Baptism as experience of divine mercy: 1:3; 2:10; cf. Rom 11:30–31; Titus 3:5–7.

(7) Baptism as conferral of the Holy Spirit, sanctification, and purification: 1:2, 14–16, 21, 22; 2:5, 9; cf. Acts 2:38; 8:14–17; 10:44–48; Rom 8:15–23; 1 Cor 6:11; Eph 4:26–27; 1 Thess 4:1–8; 2 Thess 2:13; Titus 3:5–7; 1 John 3:3.

(8) Baptism linked with trinitarian formula: 1:2; cf. Matt 28:19 and *Did.* 7:1–3; 2 Thess 2:13–14.

(9) Baptism as means for becoming the "children" of God: 1:14; cf. Rom 8:14–17; Gal 3:26–27; 4:5–7; 1 John 3:1–2, 7, 10; "heirs" of God: 1:4; 3:7; cf. Rom 8:14–17; Gal 3:25–29; 4:7; Titus 3:5–7; and calling God "Father": 1:17; cf. Rom 8:15–16; Gal 4:6; 1 John 3:1–2; 5:1–5.

(10) Baptism as linked with hearing the word of truth, the gospel: 1:12, 22–25; 4:17; cf. Rom 6:17; Col 1:5–6; 3:16; Eph 1:13; 1 Thess 1:5–6.

(11) Baptism as transition and transformation expressed in antitheses: "formerly-now": 1:14–17; 2:9, 25; 4:2–4; "from darkness to light": 2:9; cf. Rom 13:12; Col 1:13; Eph 5:8–14; 1 Thess 5:4–5; Heb 6:4; 10:32; "death-life": 2:24; cf. Rom 6:3–11; "flesh-spirit": 2:11/2:5; 3:18; 4:1, 6; cf. Rom 7:5; 8:1–5; Gal 3:3.

(12) Baptism's moral responsibilities: renunciation of, and abstinence from evil on the one hand: 2:1, 11; 3:9; 4:2–4, 15; cf. Acts 15:29; Rom 12:2, 17; 13:12; Col 3:5–9; Eph 4:25–31; Heb 12:1; Jas 1:21; 1 John 2:15; holy, God-pleasing behavior on the other: 1:14–16, 22; 2:12; 3:16; cf. Rom 6:1–23; Eph 4:23; Col 3:12–17; 1 Thess 4:1–12, 15; Jas 1:22–27; 1 John 3:4–10.

Israelite antecedents of this tradition concerning baptismal conversion included regulations regarding entrance into the Qumran community (1QS), Diaspora missionary instruction (e.g., *Joseph and Asenath*), and probably instruction associated with proselyte baptism (Selwyn 1947, 369–72; van Unnik 1980, 3–82; cf. George 1964, 1–32).

The specific themes, terms, and motifs that can be assigned to a common Christian baptismal tradition remain a matter of debate. Selwyn's maximalist proposal concerning the common material and its use in 1 Peter also includes material on "worship" (1 Pet 1:17; 2:4, 9), "catechumen virtues" (2:3–4; 2:16; 3:8–12; 4:8–11), "church unity and order" (1:12; 4:8–11; 5:1–2, 5–6), and a "social code" of subordination and humility (2:13–3:8; 5:5–6). The scope and schema of this proposal, however, cannot be established with certainty on form-critical grounds. K. Berger (1984a, 130–35), on the other hand, has proposed that numerous elements of a "post-conversion admonitory discourse" with the theme of "return to baptism" (1:13–3:12; 4:7–11; 5:6–9) and "martyrium parenesis" (3:13–4:6; 4:12–19) constitute the major components of the letter. What is clear, nonetheless, regarding 1 Peter is that, although baptism is mentioned explicitly only once, the fact of the readers' baptism constitutes a fundamental presupposition and reference point of its exhortation. The Petrine author draws heavily from a wide stream of Christian teaching concerning baptism, its blessings and responsibilities, to console and instruct the beleaguered converts of Asia Minor.

2.4.2.3. *Further Liturgical Tradition*

Apart from the question of 1 Peter's originally constituting a baptismal liturgy, there is nonetheless evidence of the influence of Israelite and early Christian liturgical tradition:

- 1:2, trinitarian formula related to baptism; cf. Matt 28:19; *Did.* 7:1–4; 2 Thess 2:13–14
- 1:3–5, eulogy/blessing with hymnic predicate for God (1:3a); *agalliaō* (1:6, 8; 4:13), occurring frequently in cultic contexts
- 2:9, a variation on Exod 19:5–6 (*basileion, hierateuma*), cited in association with liturgical formulations in Rev 1:5–6; 5:9–10; 20:6
- 4:11; 5:11, doxologies and "amen" (cf. Rev 1:6; 5:13; also 1 Tim 6:16; Jude 25; etc.)
- 5:14, kiss of love/peace, extended in liturgical settings

The theory that this material reflects elements of a baptismal-eucharist liturgy of which 1 Peter is a transcription has been discussed above. In regard to 1 Pet 2:1–10 in particular, Lohmeyer (1937, 296) and Selwyn (1947, 294–98) considered these verses "eucharistic" as well as baptismal, with 2:3 ("you have tasted that the Lord is good"), 2:4 ("draw near"), "priestly community" and "spiritual sacrifices" in v 5 pointing to the "worshipping community gathered for the celebration of the Eucharist" (Selwyn 1947, 297). This proposal, however, seriously exaggerates the supposed "cultic" coloration of this text and ignores the function of these particular verses: 1 Pet 2:3 derives from Ps 33:9 (not a cultic psalm) and describes metaphorically the reception of the "milk of the word" in the preceding verse, not the reception of the eucharistic bread and wine (though in later centuries these words were sung during the Eucharistic liturgy [*Apos. Con.* 8.13.16; Cyril of Jerusalem, *Myst. Cath.* 5.20; Jerome, *Epist.* 71.6]). 1 Peter 2:4 ("continuing to come to him"), possibly an adaptation of v 6 in the same psalm, is not an invitation to the eucharist but an acknowledgment of the believers' continued loyalty to the Lord, which establishes the basis for their comparison with Jesus in vv 4b–5. Nowhere in 1 Peter, moreover, is "holy priestly community" (2:5) developed as an appellation for a community offering a eucharistic sacrifice. Rather, this expression derives from Exod 19:6 (cf. 2:9) and is used to affirm the elect and holy character of the Christian community as God's eschatological covenant people rather than the cultic function of individual members as priests. The parallels in Rev (1:5–6; 5:9–10; 20:6) bear a certain formulaic, liturgical flavor (cf. "new song," Rev 5:9) but nothing patently eucharistic. 1 Peter 2:6–10 consists of combined OT passages and terms joined with instructive application to the readers and nonbelievers in a sequence hardly liturgical or hymnic in character.

Thus, only "to offer spiritual sacrifices" (2:5f) has cultic overtones. But this phrase anticipates and interprets 2:9 ("that you might declare the praises of him who called you out of darkness into his marvelous light"). It is used in conjunction with its subject, "holy priestly community," not to refer to eucharistic sacrifice (nowhere intimated in 1 Peter) but to describe the entire holy mode of conduct, obedience, and witness requisite of God's covenant people (cf. Elliott 1966b, 174–88). The eucharistic liturgy surely would have been an appropriate occasion for celebrating the fact of Christian communal identity affirmed in these verses, as it is today. However there is simply insufficient evidence to indicate that such a liturgy was the context that the author of 1 Peter presumed.

The remaining liturgical formulations in 1 Peter were influenced by the liturgical formulas and practice of the early Church. On the doxologies of 4:11d and 5:11 in particular, see Shimada 1966, 396–421 and the NOTES on 4:11 and 5:11. This liturgical tradition, like the Christological and kerygmatic traditions and OT citations and allusions, was cited to affirm the concepts, traditions, and practices that the senders and recipients had *in common* and thus to demonstrate and affirm the *bonds of belief and worship* that united the Christians in Rome with those in Asia Minor. The manner in which other traditional material was employed will be discussed below in connection with a description of the letter's strategy.

2.4.2.4. *Hortatory Tradition*

Antecedents of this material are found in Israelite Palestinian writings (Qumran) concerning moral instruction and community regulations and Diaspora Israelite ethical instruction (OT Pseudepigrapha; Philo; Pseudo-Phocylides) and missionary propaganda (*Joseph and Asenath*) as well as in Greco-Roman ethical catalogues of vices and virtues and moral instruction associated with household management (*oikonomia*) that were also adopted and adapted by Israelite Diaspora teachers and mediated to their Christian successors (linked with observation of Mosaic Law and obedience to the will of God).

The forms and content of the hortatory material in 1 Peter include:

(1) Stock terms, phrases, formulas used for the purpose of instruction, admonition, encouragement (e.g., *parakaleō*, *anastrephō*, etc., *agathopoieō* etc., *hypotassō*, etc.).

(2) Imperative finite verbs (generally present and aorist tenses, approximately 51 in 1 Peter), adjectives used imperativally ("be X not Y," 3:8–9), or participles used imperativally when not accompanied by finite verbs and when expressing communal rules and regulations (7 in 1 Peter).

(3) Short, succinct imperatival injunctions, often listed in succession: 1 Pet 2:1; 3:8–9; 4:7–11; 5:2–3 (cf. Rom 12: 9–21; 1 Thess 5:14–22; Matt 5–7/Luke 6).

(4) Gnomic material from OT Wisdom tradition: 1 Pet 3:10–12 (Ps 33[34]: 13–17); 4:8 (Prov 10:12 MT; cf. Jas 5:20); 4:18 (Prov 11:31 LXX); 5:5c (Prov 3:34 LXX; cf. Jas 4:6); 5:6, alluding to Ps 54[55]:23 LXX (cf. Jas 4:10; Matt 6:25).

(5) Stock lists of vices to be avoided and virtues to be manifested (vices: 2:1; 4:3, 15; 5:2–3; virtues: 3:8; 4:8–11; 5:2–3; cf. Rom 1:29–31; 13:13; 1 Cor 5:10–13; 6:9–10; 2 Cor 12:20–21; Gal 5:19–23; Eph 4:2–3, 31; 5:3–13; Phil 4:8; Col 3:5–9, 12–13; 1 Tim 1:9–10; 6:11; 2 Tim 3:2–9, 10–12; 2:22; Titus 1:8; 2:2–9; 3:1–3; Rev 21:7–8; 22:14–15). On codes of virtues and vices in the NT, Hellenism, and Israel, see Vögtle 1936; Wibbing 1959; K. Berger 1984a, 148–54.

(6) Standard instruction concerning "household management" (*oikonomia*) and associated domestic relations (husband/wife; parents/children; older/younger persons; owners/slaves); the relations of gods/humans and city-state/citizens can also be included. See 1 Pet 2:18–3:7; 5:1–5a; cf. Eph 5:22–6:9; Col 3:18–4:1; 1 Tim 2:8–15; 5:3–8; 6:1–2; 1 John 2:12–14; *1 Clem.* 21:6–9, 38:2; Pol. *Phil* 4:1–6; *Barn.* 19:5–7; *Did.* 4:9–11; Ign. *Pol.* 5:1–2; 4:1–6:2. On civic duties, see 1 Pet 2:13–17; cf. Rom 13:1–7; 1 Tim 2:1–3; Titus 3:1–3. On the *oikonomia* tradition or "household codes" in 1 Peter, see the DETAILED COMMENTs and BIBLIOGRAPHIES on 2:13–17 and 2:18–25.

(7) *Verba Christi* used in exhortation; see 1 Pet 2:12 (Matt 5:16); 2:19–20 (Luke 6:32–34); 3:14 (Matt 5:10); 5:1–5 (Matt 20:20–28/Mark 10:35–45/Luke 22:24–27); see Selwyn 1947, 25–27; J. P. Brown 1963; Spicq 1966c; Gundry 1966–1967, 1974; Elliott 1970; Best 1971; Maier 1984.

(8) Finally, Selwyn (1947, 439–58) conjectured that the Petrine author relied on a "persecution form" giving a positive valuation of suffering. Nauck (1955) critically assessed Selwyn's theory and identified at least six certain texts illustrating an ancient oral tradition with the theme of "joy in suffering" and a structure of acclamation-condition-summons-substantiation: Jas 1:2, 12; 1 Pet 1:6; 4:13–14; Matt 5:11–12; and Luke 6:22–23 (cf. also *2 Bar.* 48:48–50; 52:5–7; 54:16–18). Traces of this tradition are also found in Heb 10:32–36; Rom 5:3–5; 2 Cor 8:20; 1 Thess 1:6; Acts 5:41; 2 Cor 4:17–18; 2 Thess 1:4–6. The origin of this tradition was not the "Lord's teaching," as Selwyn had proposed, but earlier Israelite apocalyptic teaching providing a positive rationale for innocent suffering in the midst of the Maccabean crisis (Jdt 8:25–27; Wis 3:4–6; 2 Macc 6:28, 30; 4 Macc 7:22; 9:29; 11:12; cf. Kuhn 1952); on suffering as testing and refinement in Qumran see also 1QS IV 20; VIII 4. In the messianic community's similar encounter with social hostility, this tradition of calling for joy in the midst of suffering served as a means of reassurance that divine protection was unfailing and that steadfast loyalty in the face of innocent suffering, as in the case of the Christ, was certain of divine vindication. No other writing of the NT was as dependent on this tradition as was 1 Peter (Nauck 1957, 80); the related themes of joy amidst suffering, solidarity with the suffering and vindicated Christ, and meeting the test of faith pervade the letter from opening to close (1:6–8; 2:18–25; 3:13–4:1; 4:12–16; 5:8–9, 10–11; see also Lohse 1954/1986; J. Thomas 1968; Villiers 1975).

This hortatory material could be described as "parenesis," as long as the term "parenesis" is understood to constitute not just imperatival formulations of a general nature but exhortation that was variously adapted and applied to *specific occasions*. (On parenesis in general, see Kamlah 1964; MacDonald 1990; and Perdue and Gammie 1990.)

In conclusion, various forms of diverse traditions have been employed and combined by the Petrine author. Their liberal use and combination in the letter suggest that our author was attempting to appeal to an audience of diverse and mixed backgrounds, Israelite and Hellenistic, in citing traditions with which they were familiar and to which they could resonate. As will be discussed below, the amount and diversity of the tradition incorporated into 1 Peter is one of the several factors pointing to its origin among the Christians of Rome, a converging point of diverse traditions shared by many writings of a Roman provenance (Mark, Hebrews, Luke–Acts? *1 Clement*, Hermas; cf. also Paul's letter to the Romans). Features of the Petrine redaction and merging of this traditional material are discussed throughout the present commentary; see, in particular, the NOTES, COMMENTARY, and DETAILED COMMENTS on 2:4–10; 2:18–25; and 3:18–22.

2.4.3. The Relation of 1 Peter to Paul and the Pauline Writings: A Reappraisal

The foregoing conclusion has particular bearing upon the often-discussed issue of 1 Peter's relation to Paul, the Pauline and Deutero-Pauline writings, the Pauline mission field, and the supposed "Paulinism" of 1 Peter.

It is possible, if not probable, that the Petrine author was familiar with one or more of Paul's letters (esp. Romans). Yet 1 Peter contains not a single explicit reference to Paul or to any of his letters, in contrast to 2 Peter (cf. 3:15). Earlier literary critics, however, assumed that several lexical and thematic similarities between 1 Peter and the Paulines was self-evident proof of 1 Peter's literary dependency on Paul.[14] 1 Peter, it was said, was simply an "Abklatsch paulinischer Rede," a mere aping of Pauline speech. This theory that 1 Peter was dependent on Paul and a product of later Paulinism, especially popular among German scholars but repeated more recently by Beare (1970, 219), still has its advocates.[15] The recent dissertation by Reichert (1989; reviewed by Elliott 1992a) is but the latest illustration of the lengths to which some go to preserve the presumption of a contact with Pauline thought or a conflict with distorters of Pauline teaching.

---

[14] See, e.g., Holtzmann 1885; Foster 1913; Jülicher-Fascher 1931, 189–200; Barnett 1941, 51–68; and several scholars listed in Shimada 1966, 18–53, 428–34; 1991, 78–80 (from 1856 to 1989).

[15] For example, Làconi 1967; Marxsen 1968, 233–38; 1979, 379; Beare 1970; Fischer 1973, 15; 1976; Goldstein 1975, Vielhauer 1975, 580–89; H. Koester 1982, 292–95; Migliasso 1986; cf. Munro 1983.

To be sure, there are discernible similarities between 1 Peter and the Pauline letters (cf. Brox 1978a; 1986, 50; Schröger 1981b, 223–25). In both cases we are dealing with letters as the preferred medium of communication, letters manifesting a similar structure, and letters with a similar use of epistolary conventions. There is some but not total overlap in the Asia Minor communities addressed (Galatia and Asia but not Bithynia-Pontus or Cappadocia). The letters have in common a significant amount of vocabulary, ideas, themes, and even formulas. Only Paul and 1 Peter, moreover, employ the expression *en Christōi* (1 Pet 3:16; 5:10, 14; approximately 164× in Paul) or refer to the "charisms" with which all believers are endowed (1 Pet 4:10–11; Rom 12:3–8; 1 Cor 12:4–13, 27–30). Certain OT texts, too, are cited in combination only by these two authors (the connnection of passages from Isa 8 and 28 with Hosea 2, cited in Rom 9:25–33 and 1 Pet 2:4–10).

Most of the theological features that they share in common (e.g., a theocentric focus on God's action through Christ; appeal to Scripture; accent on grace, call, election, holiness, availability of salvation to all who believe; Christ's suffering, death, and resurrection; solidarity with Christ in suffering; imminence of the end and divine judgment; the household as metaphor for Christian community and believers as brothers and sisters in the faith) constitute elements of general Christian teaching and proclamation. With the possible exception of the "in Christ" formula, few, if any, of these basic Christian themes were developed exclusively by Paul. He contributed to this tradition, "but it was not determined by him" (Goppelt 1993, 30). These features reflect, not ideas unique to Paul that were then borrowed by the Petrine author, but features typical of the early Christian proclamation and teaching in general, upon which both authors drew. 1 Peter is especially close at points to passages in Romans, but *none* of these affinities can be shown to be the result of *direct literary borrowing*. By the time 1 Peter was written, Paul's letter to the Romans belonged to the body of teaching and traditional exhortation collected at Rome. The author of 1 Peter drew freely from this material, as did subsequent Christians writing from Rome.[16]

Many of the themes common to Paul and 1 Peter, moreover, were interpreted differently by each author. For example, while Paul also stresses the divine election of believers (Rom 11:26–29), this theme nowhere receives the elaboration in Paul that it does in 1 Pet 2:4–10, and never does Paul cite Exod 19:6, a key text for 1 Peter. The Petrine expression "co-elect" (5:13) likewise appears nowhere in Paul. Both require upright conduct, but Paul's concern for distinguishing faith from "works" or obedience to the Law is no concern for the Petrine author. The term *dikaiosynē*, used by Paul for "God's righteousness," in 1 Peter denotes human upright behavior, as in Matthew and in Israel generally. Paul viewed the *charismata*, of which he mentioned many, as products of the

[16] See Best 1971, 32–34; Vanhoye 1980; Elliott 1979; 1981/1990, 267–95; R. E. Brown 1983, 87–216; Lohse 1986, 52–55; Mullins 1991, 139–48 and passim; Goppelt 1993, 32.

Holy Spirit (Rom 12:3–8; 1 Cor 12:4–13, 27–30). The Petrine author, on the other hand, mentions only two charisms and associates them not with the Holy Spirit and the image of the Body of Christ but with household management (4:10–11). Both authors depict the community metaphorically as a household (Gal 6:10; 1 Pet 2:5; 4:17), but only in 1 Peter is this image used as an organizing symbol throughout the letter. Both refer to the Holy Spirit, but the Petrine author far less frequently than Paul. Both mention sin, which for the Petrine author, however, is not a menacing force outside a person, as for Paul, but a personal act. For the Petrine author the term "soul" has the Semitic sense of "self" or "life," whereas for Paul it identifies a lower, sinful nature. Paul, in contrast to 1 Peter (2:19, 20) never uses the term *charis* in the sense of "credit." Even where similarities involve citations of Scripture (Hos 2:23 [Rom 9:19–26; 1 Pet 2:10]; Isa 8:14 and 28:16 [Rom 9:30–32; 1 Pet 2:4–8]), Paul and 1 Peter employ different formulations and present different interpretations.

Features characteristic of Paul are absent in 1 Peter and vice versa. Nowhere in 1 Peter is use made of the characteristic Pauline term *ekklēsia*, while Paul never identifies the Christians as "strangers and resident aliens" (1 Pet 1:1; 2:11; cf. 1:17). "Body of Christ," a key image for Paul, makes no appearence in 1 Peter, whereas "brotherhood" (1 Pet 2:17; 5:9) and "flock of God" (1 Pet 5:2), significant concepts in 1 Peter, occur nowhere in Paul. Paul never employs the terms *agathopoiia* and *agathopoieō*, so basic to the exhortation of 1 Peter. Paul never addressses elders (*presbyteroi*), as does 1 Peter (5:1); nor does he ever refer to himself as an elder (contrast 1 Pet 5:1, *sympresbyteros*). 1 Peter displays a preference for aorist imperatives (22×), whereas Paul generally uses the present verb in commands. The sequence of indicative followed by imperative, so typical of Paul, is reversed in 1 Peter. Many OT texts cited in 1 Peter receive no mention whatsoever in Paul (Gen 18:12; 23:4; Exod 19:6; Lev 19:2; Ps 33[34]; Isa 11:2; 53; Prov 3:34; 10:12; 11:31). Other features characteristic of 1 Peter likewise have no counterpart in Paul (rebirth as a metaphor for conversion; the distinctive definition of baptism in 3:21; the linking of the elect community with Christ, the elect stone of God [2:4–10]; the use of Isa 53 to present Jesus as the suffering servant of God and model for believers; the reference to the cross as the "tree" [2:21–25]; the mention of the term *Christianos* [4:16]; and the depiction of Christ as "chief shepherd" [5:4]). In contrast to Paul, 1 Peter manifests no interest in the tension between the Messiah and the Mosaic Law or believers and the House of Israel. The fundamental social contrast in 1 Peter is, rather, between believers and "Gentiles" (a term in 1 Peter for all, including Israelites, who reject the gospel, but not so employed by Paul). 1 Peter also differs from the Pauline letters in terms of its destination, with two provinces addressed (Bithynia-Pontus, Cappadocia) that were not sites of Pauline missions and were not the target of Pauline letters. Whereas Paul wrote to urban churches, 1 Peter is a general letter addressed not to cities but to communities of provinces encompassing much rural territory. 1 Peter and the Pauline letters were addressed to different localities and focus on different issues with different theological constructs, sets of vocabulary, and social aims.

Finally, 1 Peter and the letters of Paul differ in tone and spirit. As one author has noted, Jean Guitton of the Académie française, introducing the work of Carlo Martini on the Greek text of 1 Peter (Martini 1968, x), 1 Peter differs from Paul in being "less ingenious, less systematic, less flashy, less personal, less obscure, but more tender, more human, more pastoral."

The differences between 1 Peter and the Pauline writings are numerous and striking. They constitute incontestable evidence that, while one or more of the Pauline letters may have been known to the author of 1 Peter, the Petrine author constructed, on the basis of the same tradition known to Paul, a distinctive pastoral message and spoke with a distinctive voice. Proponents of this more nuanced assessment of the relationship of 1 Peter to Paul and the Pauline letters, stressing a mutual reliance on preexistent tradition, have increased in number and now represent the majority view.[17]

Consequently, it can no longer be claimed that the Petrine author was dependent on Paul for his thoughts and formulations, that he was a representative of exclusively Pauline theology, that he was a member of a Pauline or post-Pauline circle, or that he was in dialogue or dispute with Pauline theology or its distortions. Rather he, like Paul, relied for his inspiration and message on a broad stream of early Christian tradition. It is this that accounts for their similarities. On the other hand, each author, in the manner in which he employs and merges these traditions, also reveals his distinctive theological concerns and social agenda. The notion of a supposed "Paulinism" of 1 Peter has no solid basis in the textual evidence and ought finally be abandoned. It is high time for 1 Peter to be liberated from its "Pauline captivity" and read as a distinctive voice of the early Church. Cullmann's comment (1958, 69), uttered forty years ago, still remains valid and bears repeating: "Later times have often been unjust to Paul by putting him in the shadow of Peter. Theologically, however, scholars seem to me to be unjust to Peter when they put him entirely in the shadow of Paul, or regard him as Paul's antagonist devoid of understanding for the great Pauline insights." Careful comparison of 1 Peter and the writings of Paul continues to bear out this sage observation.

2.5. PETRINE TRADITION IN THE NEW TESTAMENT

Efforts occasionally have been made to identify a stream of tradition in the NT (as attested by 1 Peter, 2 Peter, the Gospel of Mark, Petrine speeches in Acts,

[17] See, *inter alios*, Selwyn 1947, 20–21, 363–466; Stibbs-Walls 1959, 31–48; Dalton 1965/1989; Elliott 1966b; 1976, 246–48; 1980; 1981/1990, 267–95; 1992, 271–72; Shimada 1966, 1991, 1993; J. N. D. Kelly 1969, 11–15; Best 1971, 28–36; Lindemann 1979, 252–61; Brox 1977, 1978a, 1978b; 1986, 47–51; Neugebauer 1979, 71–74; Cothenet 1980, 33–36; 1988, 3692–94; Vanhoye 1980; Schröger 1981b, 223–28; K. Berger 1984a; Dijkman 1984; Lohse 1986; Richard 1986; Frankemölle 1987, 24–26; Michaels 1988, xl–xlv; Lamau 1988; Davids 1990, 5–6; Prostmeier 1990, 24–37; T. W. Martin 1992a; Goppelt 1993, 28–30; Krodel 1995, 70–80.

and more recently John) linked specifically with the Apostle Peter as an eyewitness of Jesus and guarantor of the antiquity and veracity of Christianity's proclamation.[18] Scharfe, for instance, spoke of a "Petrine current" within the NT, and Testa, of "Petrine schools" of thought. Form-critical and redaction-critical analysis, however, has demonstrated that the great majority of NT texts cited as evidence of "Petrine tradition" involves forms of tradition only *secondarily* associated with Peter for a variety of ideological reasons. Such is clearly the case with 1 Peter and the Gospels in regard to the sayings of Jesus. In the Gospels generally, Peter is the *typical* rather than unique disciple: a flawed, failed, and forgiven follower enlisted as witness to God's saving action in Jesus the Messiah. A comparison of 1 Peter and the epistolary literature of the NT reveals no instance of tradition associated *only* with Peter. At the same time, certain images and concepts do recur in association with Peter (Peter as first among and spokesman for the disciples, apostle, confessor, failed-but-forgiven witness to the risen Christ, missionary, fisher of humans, and shepherd) that serve as stones in the later construction of an integrated Petrine mosaic (cf. R. E. Brown, Donfried, and Reumann, eds. 1973, 157–68). The final word also has not yet been spoken concerning the correspondences between the Petrine speeches of Acts and 1 Peter. The extent to which these correspondences may reflect authentic words of Peter is still an agenda item for future research. What is obvious in 1 Peter, the NT, and in later Christian literature is the gradual emergence of a body of theological themes and images associated with the Apostle Peter that are employed in literature attributed to Peter and that are appropriated in the shaping of the contours of ecclesisatical orthodoxy. Equally obvious is the association of this tradition with Rome, the place of Peter's final ministry and death. On this latter issue, see below concerning the letter's place of composition.

3. VOCABULARY, STYLE, AND COMPOSITIONAL DEVICES AND PATTERNS

3.1. VOCABULARY

The Greek text of 1 Peter contains a total of 1,675 words and a vocabulary of 547 terms, 61 of which occur nowhere else in the NT. The following vocabulary list is based primarily on the work of Dr. K. Shimada (Fukura, Japan) and Prof. S. Pisano (Pontifical Biblical Institute, Rome) and is correlated with the vocabulary published by Prof. M. Adinolfi (1988, 199–215).

Terms that are <u>underlined</u> are unique to 1 Peter in the NT (*hapax legomena*). New Testament *hapax legomena* in 1 Peter also occurring in the LXX are

[18] For example, B. Weiss 1855; Scharfe 1893; Elert 1911; van Dodewaard 1949; Selwyn 1947, 27–36; Schattenmann 1954–1955; Walls in Stibbs and Walls 1959, 31–36; Spicq 1966a; Gundry 1966–1967, 1974; Testa 1967; Maier 1984.

indicated by an asterisk (*). Italicized verses involve OT quotations. Terms in 1 Peter associated with the main entry (terms with the same root or synonyms or antonyms) give some indication of the letter's semantic fields. The numbers immediately following each entry compare occurrences in 1 Peter with total NT occurrences.

Terms

Abraam	(1/73) 3:6. Cf. *Sarra*, *Noē*
agathopoieō	(4/8) 2:15, 20; 3:6, 17. Cf. *poieō agathon*, 3:11. Contrast *kakopoieō*, *kakoō*
agathopoiia	(1/1) 4:19. Cf. *agathopoieō*, *agathopoios*
*agathopoios**	(1/1) 2:14. Cf. *dikaios*. Contrast *kakopoios*
agathos	(7/104) 2:18; 3:*10*, *11*, 13, 16 (2×), 21. Contrast *kakia*, *kakos*
agalliaō	(3/11) 1:6, 8; 4:13. Cf. *chairō*
agapaō	(4/141) 1:8, 22; 2:17; 3:*10*
agapē	(3/116) 4:8 (2×); 5:14. Cf. *philadelphia*
agapētos	(2/61) 2:11; 4:12
aggelos	(2/175) 1:12; 3:22. Cf. *anaggellō*, *euaggelizō*, *euaggelion*
hagiazō	(1/27) 3:15. Cf. *hagiasmos*, *hagios*, *hagnizō*
hagiasmos	(1/10) 1:2. Cf. *hagiazō*, *hagios*
hagios	(7/233) 1:12, 15 (2×), 16 (2×); 2:5, 9; 3:5. Cf. *hagnos*, *amōmos*, *aspilos*, *katharos*. Contrast *hamartōlos*, *asebēs*, *rhypos*
hagnizō	(1/7) 1:22. Cf. *hagnos*, *hagiazō*, *hagiasmos*, *hagios*
agnoia	(1/4) 1:14. Cf. *agnōsia*. Contrast *dianoia*, *ennoia*
hagnos	(1/8) 3:2. Cf. *hagnizō*, *hagios*, *hagiazō*, *hagiasmos*, *amōmos*, *aspilos*, *katharos*
agnōsia	(1/2) 2:15. Cf. *agnoia*. Contrast *gnōsis*
adelphos	(1/343) 5:12. Cf. *adelphotēs*, *philadelphos*, *philadelphia*, *hyios*, *brephos*, *teknon*, *patēr*, *oikos*
*adelphotēs**	(2/2) 2:17; 5:9. Cf. *adelphos*, etc.
adikos	(1/12) 3:18. Contrast *dikaios*, *dikaiosynē*
*adikōs**	(1/1) 2:19. Contrast *dikaiōs*
adolos	(1/1) 2:2. Contrast *dolos*
aei	(1/7) 3:15
athemitos	(1/2) 4:3. Cf. *adikos*
haima	(2/97) 1:2, 19. Cf. *paschein* (of Christ), 2:21, 23; 3:18; 4:1; *pathēmata* (of Christ), 1:11; 4:13; 5:1
aischrokerdōs	(1/1) 5:2. Cf. *aischynomai*, etc. Contrast *timē*, etc.

aischynomai (1/5) 4:16. Cf. *kataischynō*. Contrast *timaō*

aiteō (1/70) 3:15

aiōn (4/123) 1:25; 4:11 (2×); 5:11

aiōnios (1/70) 5:10. Contrast *oligon*

akrogōniaios (1/2) 2:6. Cf. *gōnia*

alētheia (1/109) 1:22. Cf. *alēthēs*

alēthēs (1/26) 5:12. Cf. *alētheia*

alla (16/635) 1:15, 19, 23; 2:16, 18, 20, 25; 3:4, 14, 16, 21; 4:2, 13; 5:2 (2×), 3

allēlōn (4/100) 1:22; 4:9; 5:4, 14

allotriepiskopos (1/1) 4:15. Cf. *episkopeō, episkopē, episkopos*

amarantinos (1/1) 5:4. Cf. *amarantos, aphthartos*. Contrast *phthartos*

*amarantos** (1/1) 1:4. Cf. *amarantinos*

hamartanō (1/42) 2:20. Contrast *agathopoieō*

hamartia (6/173) 2:22, 24 (2×); 3:18; 4:1, 8. Cf. *kakia, rhypos*. Contrast *dikaiosynē*

hamartōlos (1/47) 4:18. Cf. *asebēs, kakopoios*. Contrast *agathopoios, dikaios*

amēn (2/126) 4:11; 5:11

amianton (1/4) 1:4. Cf. *hagios, amōmos, aspilos, katharos*

amnos (1/4) 1:19. Cf. *probaton, poimēn, poimnion, poimainō, archipoimēn*. Contrast *leōn*

amōmos (1/8) 1:19. Cf. *hagios, hagiazō, hagiasmos, hagnizō, amianton, aspilos, katharos*

anaggellō (1/13) 1:12. Cf. *euaggelizō, euaggelion*

anagennaō (2/2) 1:3, 23. Cf. *artigennētos, brephos, teknon*, etc.

*anagkastōs** (1/1) 5:2

*anazōnnymi** (1/1) 1:13. Cf. *perithesis, egkomboomai*. Contrast *apothesis, apotithēmi*

anapauō (1/12) 4:14

anastasis (2/42) 1:3; 3:21. Cf. *egeirō, zōopoieō*, etc. Contrast *thanatoō, nekros*

anastrephō (1/9) 1:17. Cf. *epistrephō*, 2:25; *poreuō*, 4:3

anastrophē (6/13) 1:15, 18; 2:12; 3:1, 2, 16. Cf. *anastrephō, epistrephō; agathopoieō, agathopoiia, agathopoios, kalē erga*

agathos (7/104) 2:18; 3:10, 11, 13, 16 (2×), 21. Cf. *kalos*. Contrast *kakos, kakia, kakoō, kakopoieō, kakopoios*

anapherō (2/9) 2:5, 24

anachysis (1/1) 4:4
aneklalētos (1/1) 1:8. Cf. *laleō*, etc.
aneu (2/3) 3:1; 4:9
anēr (3/216) 3:1, 5, 7. Cf. *gynē*
anthos (2/4) 1:24 (2×)
anthrōpinos (1/7) 2:13
anti (2/22) 3:9 (2×)
antidikos (1/5) 5:8. Contrast *dikaios*, *dikaiosynē*
antiloidoreō (1/1) 2:23. Cf. *loidoreō*, *blasphēmeō*, *epēreazō*, *katalaleō*, *katalalia*, *oneidizō*
antistēmi (1/14) 5:9. Cf. *apechō*
antitassō (1/5) 5:5. Contrast *hypotassō*
antitypos (1/2) 3:21. Cf. *typos*
anypokritos (1/6) 1:22. Cf. *hypokrisis*
hapax (1/14) 3:18
apeitheō (4/14) 2:8; 3:1, 20; 4:17. Cf. *apisteuō*
apeileō (1/2) 2:23
apekdechomai (1/8) 3:20
apechō (1/19) 2:11. Cf. *apoginomai hamartiais*, 2:24; *pauō hamartiais*, 4:1; *apotithēmi*. Contrast *echō*
apisteuō (1/8) 2:7. Cf. *apeitheō*. Contrast *pisteuō*, *pistis*, *pistos*
apo (5/45) 1:12; 3:10, 11; 4:17 (2×)
apoginomai (1/1) 2:24. Cf. *pauō hamartiais*, 4:1; *apechō*, *apotithēmi*, *apothesis*
apodidōmi (2/47) 3:9; 4:5
apodokimazō (2/9) 2:4, 7. Cf. *dokimazō*, 1:7
apothesis (1/2) 3:21. Cf. *apotithēmi*, *apechō*. Contrast *perithesis*, 3:3
apokalyptō (3/26) 1:5, 12; 5:1. Cf. *apokalypsis*, *dēloō*, *phaneroō*. Contrast *kalyptō*
apokalypsis (3/18) 1:7, 13; 4:13. Cf. *apokalyptō*, etc.
apollymi (1/90) 1:7
apologia (1/8) 3:15
*aponemō** (1/1) 3:7
apostellō (1/131) 1:12. Cf. *apostolos*, *pempō*
apostolos (1/79) 1:1. Cf. *apostellō*
apotithēmi (1/9) 2:1. Cf. *apothesis*; *apechō*, *apoginomai hamartiais*, 2:24; *pauō hamartiais*, 4:1. Contrast *paratithēmi*, *tithēmi*

aprosopolēmptōs (1/1) 1:17. Cf. *prosōpon*

argyrion (1/21) 1:18. Cf. *chrysion*

aretē (1/5) 2:9 (plural usage is a NT *hapax legomenon*). Cf. *doxa, epainos, timē*

arketos (1/2) 4:3

arti (2/36) 1:6, 8. Cf. *nyn*

artigennētos (1/1) 2:2. Cf. *anagennaō, brephos, tekna, zaō*, etc.

*archipoimēn** (1/1) 5:4. Cf. *poimēn, poimainō, poimnion, amnos, probaton*

archō (1/85) 4:17

asebēs (1/9) *4:18*. Cf. *athemitos, hamartōlos, kakopoios*. Contrast *dikaios*

aselgeia (1/10) 4:3

Asia (1/18) 1:1

asthenē (1/25) 3:7

aspazomai (2/59) 5:13, 14

aspilos (1/4) 1:19. Cf. *hagiazō, hagiasmos, hagios, hagnizō, amōmos, katharos*

asōtia (1/3) 4:4

auxanō (1/22) 2:2

auta (2/46) 1:12; 5:9

autēn (3/127) 3:*11*; 4:1, 4

autēs (1/166) *1:24*

auto (1/3) 4:10

autoi (2/87) 1:15; 2:5

autois (1/550) 1:11

auton (3/944) 1:21; 3:6; 5:7

autos (3/152) 2:24; 3:6; 5:10

autou (10/1396) 1:3, 21; 2:9, 14, 21, 22, 24; 3:*12*; 4:13; 5:10

autōi (6/843) 1:21; 2:2, 6; 3:22; 5:7, 11

autōn (3/555) 3:*12*, 14; 4:19

aphthartos (3/7) 1:4, 23; 3:4. Cf. *amarantinos, amarantos*. Contrast *phthartos*

aphrōn (1/11) 2:15. Contrast *homophrōn*, 3:8; *sōphroneō*, 4:7; *tapeinophrōn*, 3:8

Babylōn (1/12) 5:13. Cf. *diaspora*, 1:1. Contrast *Siōn*, 2:6

baptisma (1/20) 3:21

basileion (1/2) 2:9. Cf. *basileus; genos, ethnos, laos, oikos basileus* (2/115) 3:13, 17. Cf. *basileion*

Bithynia (1/2) 1:1

bioō (1/1) 4:2. Cf. *zaō, zōē, zōopoieō*

blasphēmeō (1/34) 4:4. Cf. *loidoreō, antiloidoreō, loidoria, katalaleō, katalalia, epēreazō, oneidizō*

boulēma (1/3) 4:3

brephos (1/8) 2:2. Cf. *anagennaō, artigennētos; teknon*, etc., *oikos*, etc.

gala (1/5) 2:2

gar (10/1036) 2:19, 20, 21, 25; 3:5, *10*, 17; 4:3, 6; 4:15

genos (1/20) 2:9. Cf. *ethnos, laos, basileion, hierateuma, oikos*

geuomai (1/15) 2:3

ginomai (6/667) 1:15; 2:7; 3:6, 13; 4:12; 5:3

glōssa (1/50) 3:*10*

gnōsis (1/29) 3:7. Cf. *prognōsis*. Contrast *agnoia*, 1:14; *agnōsia*, 2:15

goggysmos (1/4) 4:9

graphē (1/50) 2:16

graphō (2/190) 1:16

grēgoreō (1/22) 5:8

*gynaikeios** (1/1) 3:7. Cf. *gynē*

gynē (3/209) 3:1 (2×), 5. Cf. *gynaikeios; anēr*

gōnia (1/9) 2:7. Cf. *akrogōniaios*

de (29/2771) 1:7, 8, 12, 20, 25; 2:4, 7, 9, 10 (2×), 14, 23; 3:8, 9, *11*, *12*, 14, 15, 18; 4:6, 7, 16 (2×), 17, 18; 5:5b, 5, 10. Cf. *men*

deēsis (1/18) 3:*12*. Cf. *proseuchē*, 3:7; 4:7

dexios (1/54) 3:22

deon (1/102) 1:6. Cf. *thelēma tou theou*, 2:15; 3:17; 4:2, 19

despotēs (1/10) 2:18

dēloō (1/7) 1:11. Cf. *apokalyptō, apokalypsis, phaneroō*

dia (18/666) 1:3, 5, 7, 12, 20, 21, 23; 2:5, 13, 14, 19; 3:1, 14, 20, 21; 4:11; 5:12 (2×)

diabolos (1/37) 5:8

diakoneō (3/36) 1:12; 4:10, 11

dianoia (1/12) 1:13. Cf. *ennoia*. Contrast *agnoia*

diaspora (1/3) 1:1. Cf. *spora; Babylōn*

diasōzō (1/8) 3:20. Cf. *sōzō, sōtēria*

didōmi (2/416) 1:21; 5:5c

dikaios (3/79) 3:12, 18; 4:18. Cf. *dikaiosynē, dikaiōs, ekdikēsis*. Contrast *adikos, asebēs, hamartōlos*

dikaiōs (1/5) 2:23. Cf. *dikaios, dikaiosynē*. Contrast *adikōs*

dio (1/53) 1:13

dioti (3/24) 1:16, 24; 2:6

diōkō (1/44) 3:11

dokimazō (1/22) 1:7. Cf. *dokimion*. Contrast *apodokimazō*

dokimion (1/2) 1:7. Cf. *dokimazō*, etc.

dolos (3/11) 2:1, 22; 3:10. Contrast *adolon*, 2:2

doxa (10/165) 1:7, 11, 21, 24; 4:11, 13, 14; 5:1, 4, 10. Cf. *doxazō; aretē, epainos, stephanos, timē*, etc.

doxazō (4/61) 1:8; 2:12; 4:11, 16. Cf. *doxa*

doulos (1/124) 2:16. Cf. *oiketēs*. Contrast *despotēs, eleutheria, eleutheros*

dynamis (2/118) 1:5; 3:22. Cf. *ischys, kratos, krataios*

ean (1/343) 3:13. Cf. *ei*

heautou (4/320) 1:12; 3:5; 4:8, 10

eggizō (1/42) 4:7

egeirō (1/143) 1:21. Cf. *anastasis, zōopoieō, zōe*, etc. Contrast *thanatoō, nekros*

<u>*egkomboomai*</u> (1/1) 5:5. Cf. *perithesis, anazōnnymi*. Contrast *apothesis, apotithēmi*

egkoptō (1/5) 3:7

egō (2/1713) 1:16; 5:13

ethnos (3/162) 2:9, 12; 4:3. Cf. *genos, basileion, hierateuma, laos, oikos*

ei (15/513) 1:6, 17; 2:3, 19, 20 (2×); 3:1, 14, 17; 4:11 (2×), 14, 16, 17, 18. Cf. *ean*

eidōlolatria (1/4) 4:3

eimi (11/2450) 1:16, [16], 21, 25; 2:15, 25; 3:3, 4, 20, 22; 4:11; 5:12

eirēnē (3/91) 1:2; 3:11; 5:14

eis (42/1753) 1:2, 3, 4 (2×), 5, 7, 8, 10, 11 (2×), 12, 21 (2×), 22, 25, 25; 2:2, 5, 7, 8, 9, 9, 14, 21; 3:5, 7, 9, 12, 20, 21, 22; 4:2, 4, 6, 7, 8, 9, 10, 11; 5:10, 11, 12

eite (2/65) 2:13, 14

ek (8/915) 1:3, 18, 21, 22, 23; 2:9, 12; 4:11

hekastos (2/81) 1:17; 4:10

ekdikēsis (1/9) 2:14. Cf. *dikaiosynē, dikaios*. Contrast *epainos exzēteō* (1/7) 1:10

ekklinō (1/3) *3:11*

eklektos (4/22) 1:1; 2:4, 6, 9. Cf. *syneklektē*; *entimos*, etc.

hekousiōs (1/2) 5:2

ekpiptō (1/10) *1:24*

ektenēs (1/1) 4:8

ektenōs (1/3) 1:22

eleeō (2/32) 2:10 (2×). Cf. *eleos*

eleos (1/27) 1:3. Cf. *eleeō*

eleutheria (1/11) 2:16. Cf. *eleutheros*

eleutheros (1/23) 2:16. Cf. *eleutheria*. Contrast *doulos*

elpizō (2/31) 1:13; 3:5. Cf. *elpis*

elpis (3/57) 1:3, 21; 3:15. Cf. *elpizō*

emplokē (1/1) 3:3

en (49/2713) 1:2, 4, 5 (2×), 6 (2×), 7, 11, [12], 13, 14, 15, 17, 22; 2:2, 6, 6, 12 (2×), *12*, 18, 22, 24; 3:2, 4, 15 (2×), 16 (2×), 19 (2×), 20, 22; 4:2, 3, 4, 11, 12, 13, 14, 16, 19; 5:1, 2, 6, 9, 10, 13, 14 (2×)

*endysis** (1/1) 3:3

ennoia (1/2) 4:1. Cf. *dianoia*, 1:13; *agnoia*, 1:14

entimos (2/5) 2:4, 6. Cf. *timios*, *polytimos*, *timē*, *timaō*; *eklektos*, *makarios*, *doxa*, *epainos*. Contrast *aischrokerdōs*, *aischynomai*, *kataischynō*

enōpion (1/93) 3:4

exaggellō (1/1) 2:9. Cf. *euaggelizō*, *euaggelion*, *aggelos*

*exeraunaō** (1/1) 1:10. Cf. *eraunaō*

exousia (1/102) 3:22

exōthen (1/13) 3:3. Contrast *kryptos*

epainos (2/11) 1:7; 2:14. Cf. *aretē*, *doxa*, *timē*. Contrast *ekdikēsis*

epakoloutheō (1/4) 2:21

*eperōtēma** (1/1) 3:21

epēreazō (1/2) 3:16. Cf. *blasphēmeō*, *katalaleō*, *katalalia*, *loidoreō*, *loidoria*, *oneidizō*

epi (9/878) 1:13, 20; 2:6, 24, 25; 3:*12* (2×); 4:14; 5:7

epieikēs (1/5) 2:18. Contrast *skolios*

epithymeō (1/16) 1:12. Cf. *epithymia*

epithymia (4/38) 1:14; 2:11; 4:2, 3. Cf. *epithymeō*

epikaleō (1/30) 1:17. Cf. *kaleō, parakaleō*
*epikalymma** (1/1) 2:16
*epimartyreō** (1/1) 5:12. Cf. *promartyreō, martys*
epipotheō (1/9) 2:2
epiriptō (1/2) 5:7
episkopeō (1/2) 5:2. Cf. *episkopē, episkopos*
episkopē (1/4) 2:12. Cf. *episkopeō, episkopos*
episkopos (1/5) 2:25. Cf. *episkopē, episkopeō*
epistrephō (1/36) 2:25. Cf. *anastrephō, anastrophē*. Contrast *planoō*
epiteleō (1/10) 5:9. Cf. *telos*
epopteuō (2/2) 2:12; 3:2. Cf. *horaō*
eraunaō (1/6) 1:11. Cf. *exeraunaō*
ergon (2/169) 1:17; 2:12. Cf. *katergazomai*
eschatos (2/52) 1:5, 20. Cf. *telos, kairos, hetoimōs*
hetoimos (2/17) 1:5; 3:15. Cf. *hetoimōs; eschatos*, etc.
hetoimōs (1/3) 4:5. Cf. *hetoimos*
euaggelizō (3/54) 1:12, 25; 4:6. Cf. *euaggelion, anaggellō, exaggellō*
euaggelion (1/76) 4:17. Cf. *euaggelizō*, etc.
eulogeō (1/42) 3:9. Cf. *eulogētos, eulogia, logia*
eulogētos (1/8) 1:3. Cf. *eulogeō, eulogia, logia*
eulogia (1/16) 3:9. Cf. *eulogētos, eulogeō, logia*
euprosdektos (1/5) 2:5
heuriskō (2/176) 1:7; 2:22
eusplagchnos (1/2) 3:8
echō (5/705) 2:12, 16; 3:16; 4:5, 8. Contrast *apechō*
zaō (7/140) 1:3, 23; 2:4, 5, 24; 4:5, 6. Cf. *zōē, zoopoieō; bioō*. Contrast *thanatoō, nekros*
zēlōtēs (1/8) 3:13
zēteō (2/117) 3:*11*; 5:8.
zōē (2/135) 3:7, *10*. Cf. *zaō, zōopoieō; anagennaō, artigennētos, brephos, tekna*. Contrast *thanatoō, nekros*
zōopoieō (1/11) 3:18. Cf. *zaō, zōē; egeirō, anastasis*. Contrast *thanatoō, nekros*
ē (6/342) 1:11, 18; 3:3, 9, 17; 4:15
hēgemōn (1/20) 2:14
hēmera (3/338) 2:*12*; 3:*10*, 20
hēmas (1/166) 1:3. Cf. 3:18 *v.l.*

hēmōn (3/395) 1:3; 2:24 (cf. *hymōn, v.l.*); 4:17 (cf. *hymōn, v.l.*)

hēsychios (1/2) 3:4

thanatoō (1/11) 3:18. Cf. *nekros*, 1:3, 21; 4:5, 6. Contrast *zaō, zoopoieō, zōē, bioō*

thaumastos (1/6) 2:9

thelēma (4/62) 2:15; 3:17; 4:2, 19. Cf. *thelō*

thelō (2/207) 3:*10*, 17. Cf. *thelēma*

themelioō (1/5) 5:10. Cf. *oikodomeō, oikos*

theos (39/1314) 1:2, 3, 5, 21 (2×), 23; 2:4, 5, 10, 12, 15, 16, 17, 19, 20; 3:4, 5, 17, 18, 20, 21, 22; 4:2, 6, 10 11 (3×); 4:14, 16, 17 (2×), 19; 5:2 (2×), 5, 6, 10, 12. Cf. *kyrios*, 2:13; 3:*12* (2×)

thrix (1/15) 3:3

thysia (1/28) 2:5

iaomai (1/26) 2:24

idios 3:1, 5

*hierateuma** (2/2) 2:5, 9. Cf. *genos, basileion, ethnos, laos*

himation (1/60) 3:3

hina (13/673) 1:7; 2:2, 12, 21, 24; 3:1, 9, 16, 18; 4:6, 11, 13; 5:6

histēmi (1/152) 5:12

ischys (1/10) 4:11. Cf. *dynamis, kratos, krataios*

ichnos (1/3) 2:21

katharos (1/26) [1:22]. Cf. *hagios, hagiazō, hagiasmos, hagnizō, amōmos, aspilos*

katho (2/4) 4:13. Cf. *kathōs*

kathōs (1/178) 4:10. Cf. *katho*

kai (71/8947) 1:1, 2 (2×), 3, 4 (2×), 7 (2×), 8, 10, 11, 15, 17, 19, 21 (2×), 23, 24 (2×); 2:1 (4×), 5, 6, 8, 8, 8, 11, 16, 20 (2×), 21, 25; 3:1, 3, 4, 5, 6, 7, *10* (2×), *11* (2×), *12*, 13, 14, 16, 18, 19, 21, 22 (2×); 4:1, 3, 5, 6, 7, 11, 13, 14, 18, *18*, 19; 5:1 (2×), 4, 12, 13

kairos (4/85) 1:5, 11; 4:17; 5:6. Cf. *chronos, eschatos, telos*

kakia (2/11) 2:1, 16. Cf. *kakos, kakopoieō, kakopoios, kakoō; hamartia, rhypos*. Contrast *agathos*, etc.

kakopoieō (1/4) 3:17. Cf. *poiountas kaka*, 3:12. Contrast *agathopoieō, agathopoiia*

*kakopoios** (3/3) 2:12, 14; 4:15. Contrast *agathopoios*, etc.

kakos (5/50) 3:9 (2×), *10, 11, 12*. Contrast *agathos, kalos*

kakoō (1/6) 3:13. Cf. *kakopoieō*, etc. Contrast *agathopoieō*, etc.

kaleō	(6/148) 1:15; 2:9, 21; 3:6, 9; 5:10. Cf. *epikaleō*, *parakaleō*
kalos	(3/99) 2:12 (2×); 4:10. Cf. *agathos*, 2:18; 3:10, 11, 13, 16, 21. Contrast *kakos*, *kakia*, etc.
kalyptō	(1/8) 4:8. Contrast *apokalyptō*, *deloō*, *phaneroō*
kardia	(3/156) 1:22; 3:4, 15
kata	(10/471) 1:2, 3, 15, 17; 2:11; 3:7; 4:6 (2×), 19; 5:2
katabolē	(1/11) 1:20
kataischynō	(2/13) 2:6; 3:16. Cf. *aischynomai*, *aischerdōs*. Contrast *timaō*, *timē*, etc.
katakyrieuō	(1/4) 5:3. Cf. *kyrios*
katalaleō	(2/5) 2:12; 3:16. Cf. *katalalia*; *loidoreō*, *antiloidoreō*, *epēreazō*, *blasphēmeō*, *oneidizō*
katalalia	(1/2) 2:1 Cf. *katalaleō*, etc.; *loidoria*, 3:9
katapinō	(1/7) 5:8
katartizō	(1/13) 5:10
kataskeuazō	(1/11) 3:20
katergazomai	(1/22) 4:3. Cf. *ergon*
kerdainō	(1/17) 3:1
kephalē	(1/75) 2:7
kēryssō	(1/61) 3:19
kibōtos	(1/6) 3:20
*kleos**	(1/1) 2:20
kleptēs	(1/16) 4:15
klēronomeō	(1/18) 3:9. Cf. *klēronomia*, *synklēronomos*, *klēroi*
klēronomia	(1/14) 1:4. Cf. *klēronomeō*, etc.
klēros	(1/11) 5:3 (plural *klēroi* is NT *hapax legomenon*). Cf. *klēronomeō*, etc.
koinōneō	(1/8) 4:13. Cf. *koinōnos*
koinōnos	(1/10) 5:1. Cf. *koinōneō*
komizō	(2/11) 1:9; 5:4. Cf. *lambanō*, 4:10
kosmeō	(1/10) 3:5. Cf. *kosmos*
kosmos	(3/185) 1:20; 3:3; 5:9. Cf. *kosmeō*
*krataios**	(1/1) 5:6. Cf. *kratos*, etc.
kratos	(2/12) 4:11; 5:11. Cf. *krataios*, *dynamis*, *ischys*
kreitton	(1/19) 3:17
krima	(1/27) 4:17. Cf. *krinō*
krinō	(4/114) 1:17; 2:23; 4:5, 6. Cf. *krima*

kryptos (1/17) 3:4. Contrast *exothen*

ktisis (1/19) 2:13. Cf. *ktistēs*

*ktistēs** (1/1) 4:19. Cf. *ktisis*; *patēr*

kyrios (8/718) of God, 2:13; 3:*12* (2×); of Jesus Christ, 1:3, 25; 2:3; 3:15; of Abraham, 3:6

kōmos (1/3) 4:3. Cf. *oinophlygia*, *potos*

laleō (2/298) 3:*10*; 4:11. Cf. *aneklalētos*. Contrast *katalaleō*, *katalalia*

lambanō (1/238) 4:10. Cf. *komizō*

laos (3/141) 2:9, *10*, 10. Cf. *genos*, *ethnos*, *basileion*, *hierateuma*, *oikos*

leōn (1/9) 5:8. Contrast *amnos*, *poimnion*, *probaton*

lithos (5/58) 2:4, 5, 6, 7, 8. Cf. *petra*, 2:8

logia (1/4) 4:11. Cf. *logizomai*, *logikos*, *logos*; *rhēma*,

logizomai (1/40) 5:12. Cf. *logia*, *logikos*, *logos*

logikos (1/2) 2:2. Cf. *logia*, *logizomai*, *logikos*, *logos*

logos (6/331) 1:23; 2:8; 3:1 (2×), 15; 4:5. Cf. *rhēma*

loidoreō (1/4) 2:23. Cf. *loidoria*, *antiloidoreō*, *epēreazō*, *katalaleō*, *blasphēmeō*, *oneidizō*

loidoria (2/3) 3:9 (2×). Cf. *loidoreō*, etc., *katalalia*, 2:1

lypeō (1/26) 1:6. Cf. *lypē*, *paschō*, *pathēma*

lypē (1/15) 2:19. Cf. *lypeō*, *paschō*, *pathēma*

lytroō (1/3) 1:18

makarios (2/50) 3:14; 4:14. Cf. *entimos*, etc., *epainos*. Contrast *aischrokerdōs*, *aischynomai*, *kataischynō*

makrothymia (1/14) 3:20. Cf. *prothymōs*. Contrast *epithymia*

Markos (1/8) 5:13. Cf. *Petros*, *Silouanos*

martys (1/35) 5:1. Cf. *epimartyreō*, *promartyromai*

mataios (1/6) 1:18

mellō (1/110) 5:1

melō (1/10) 5:7

men (4/181) 1:20; 2:14; 3:18; 4:6. Cf. *de*

menō (2/118) 1:23, 25

merimna (1/6) 5:7

meta (2/467) 1:11; 3:16

mē (14/1055) 1:8, 14; 2:6, 16; 3:6, 7, 9, *10*, 14; 4:4, 12, 15, 16; 5:2. Cf. *mēde*, *mēdeis*, *mēketi*, *ou*, *oude*

mēde (3/57) 3:14; 5:2, 3. Cf. *mē*, etc.

mēdeis (1/85) 3:6. Cf. *mē*, etc.

mēketi (1/21) 4:2. Cf. *mē*, etc.

molis (1/7) 4:18

monon (1/66) 2:18

mou (1/559) 5:13

*mōlōps** (1/1) 2:24. Cf. *haima*, *lypeō*, *lypē paschō*, *pathēma*

nekros (4/128) 1:3, 21; 4:5, 6. Cf. *thanatoō*. Contrast *zaō*, *zōē*, *zōopoieō*, *bioō*

neōteros (1/11) 5:5. Contrast *presbyteros*

nēphō (3/6) 1:13; 4:7; 5:8

nyn (5/148) 1:12; 2:10 (2×), 25; 3:21. Contrast *pote*, *proteron*

Nōe (1/8) 3:20. Cf. *Sarra*, *Abraam*

xenizō (2/10) 4:4, 12

xenos (1/14) 4:12. Cf. *philoxenos*; *parepidēmos*, *paroikos*, *paroikia*

xērainō (1/15) 1:24

xylon (1/20) 2:14

oida (2/321) 1:18; 5:9. Cf. *gnōsis*, *syneidēsis*. Contrast *agnoia*, *agnōsia*

oiketēs (1/4) 2:18. Cf. *doulos*, *oikos*, etc. Contrast *despotēs*

oikokodomeō (2/40) 2:5, 7. Cf. *oikos*, etc., *themelioō*

oikonomos (1/10) 4:10. Cf. *oikos*, etc.

oikos (2/112) 2:5; 4:17. Cf. *oiketēs*, *oikodomeō*, *oikonomos*, *paroikia*, *paroikos*, *synoikeō*; *teknon*, *hyios*, *patēr*, *adelphos*, *adelphotēs*, *philadelphia*, *philadelphos*, *philēma*, *anēr*, *gynē*, *hypotassō*

oinophlygia (1/1) 4:3. Cf. *kōmos*, *potos*

oktō (1/8) 3:20

oligon (4/40) 1:6; 3:20; 5:10, 12

homoiōs (3/31) 3:1, 7; 5:5

homophrōn (1/1) 3:8. Cf. *tapeinophrōn*, *sōphroneō*. Contrast *aphrōn*

oneidizō (1/9) 4:14. Cf. *katalaleō*, *katalalia*, *loidoreō*, *antiloidoreō*, *loidoria*, *epērazō*, *blasphēmeō*

onoma (2/228) 4:14, 16. Cf. *Christianos*

hoplizō (1/1) 4:1. Cf. *strateuō*

hopōs (1/53) 2:9

horaō (1/114) 1:8 (2×); 2:6; 3:10. Cf. *epopteuō*

osphys (1/8) 1:13

hostis (1/154) 2:11

hote (1/102) 3:20

hoti (16/1285) 1:12 [16], 16, 18; 2:3, 15, 21; 3:9, 12, 18; 4:1, 8, 14, 17; 5:5, 7

ou (13/1619) 1:8, 12, 18, 23; 2:6, 10 (2×), 18, 22, 23 (2×); 3:3, 21. Cf. *oude, mē, mēde, mēdeis, mēketi*

oude (1/139) 2:22. Cf. *ou*, etc.

oun (6/493) 2:1, 7; 4:1, 7; 5:1, 6

ouranos (3/372) 1:4, 12; 3:22

ous (1/36) 3:12

houtos (1/1388) 2:7

houtōs (2/208) 2:15; 3:5

ophthalmos (1/100) 3:12

pathēma (4/16) 1:11; 4:13; 5:1, 9. Cf. *paschō, sympatheis; lypeō, lypē, haima, mōlōps*

para (2/191) 2:4, 20

paradidōmi (1/120) 2:23. Cf. *patroparadotos*

parakaleō (3/109) 2:11; 5:1, 12. Cf. *kaleō, epikaleō*

parakyptō (1/4) 1:12

paratithēmi (1/19) 4:19. Cf. *tithēmi*. Contrast *apotithēmi, apothesis*

parepidēmos (2/3) 1:1; 2:11. Cf. *paroikos, paroikia, xenos, diaspora, Babylon*

parerchomai (1/29) 4:3. Cf. *proserchomai*, 2:4

paroikia (1/2) 1:17. Cf. *paroikos, oikos; parepidēmos, xenos, philoxenos, diaspora, Babylon*

paroikos (1/4) 2:11; cf. *paroikia*, etc., *parepidēmos*

pas (18/1226) 1:15, 24 (2×); 2:1 (3×), 13, 17, 18; 3:8, 15; 4:7, 8, 11; 5:5, 7, 8, 11

paschō (12/40) 2:19, 20, 21, 23; 3:14, 17, 18; 4:1 (2×), 15, 19; 5:10. Cf. *pathēma; lypeō, haima, mōlōps; sympatheis*

patēr (3/415) 1:2, 3, 17. Cf. *ktistēs, anagennaō*, etc.; *oikos*, etc.; *patroparadotos*

<u>*patroparadotos*</u> (1/1) 1:18. Cf. *paradidōmi; patēr*

pauō (2/15) 3:10; 4:1

peirasmos (2/21) 1:6; 4:12

pempō (1/79) 2:14. Cf. *apostellō*

peri (5/331) 1:10 (2×); 2:15, 18; 5:7

periechō (1/2) 2:6

<u>*perithesis*</u>* (1/1) 3:3. Cf. *anazōnnymi, egkomboomai*. Contrast *apothesis, apotithēmi*

peripateō (1/95) 5:8. Cf. *poreuō*

peripoiēsis (1/5) 2:9

petra (1/15) 2:8. Cf. *lithos*

Petros (1/154) 1:1. Cf. *Silouanos, Markos*

pisteuō (3/241) 1:8; 2:6, 7. Cf. *pistis, pistos*. Contrast *apisteuō, apeitheō*

pistis (5/243) 1:5, 7, 9, 21; 5:9. Cf. *pisteuō*, etc., *pistos*

pistos (3/67) 1:21; 4:19; 5:12. Cf. *pisteuō*, etc., *pistis*

planaō (1/39) 2:25. Contrast *epistrephō*

plēthos (1/31) 4:8. Cf. *plēthynō*

plēthynō (1/12) 1:2. Cf. *plēthos*

pneuma (8/379) 1:12, 11, 12; 3:4, 18, 19; 4:6, 14. Contrast *sarx*

pneumatikos (2/26) 2:5 (2×). Cf. *pneuma*

poieō (3/565) 2:22; 3:11, 12. Cf. *agathopoieō, agathopoiia, agathopoios; kakopoieō, kakopoios*

poikilos (2/10) 1:6; 4:10

poimainō (1/11) 5:2. Cf. *poimēn, archipoimēn, poimnion*

poimēn (1/18) 2:25. Cf. *poimainō, archipoimēn, poimnion*, etc.

poimnion (2/5) 5:2, 3. Cf. *probaton, amnos, archipoimēn*. Contrast *leōn*

poios (2/32) 1:11; 2:20

polys (1/353) 1:3. Cf. *polytimos*

polytimos (1/3) 1:7. Cf. *timios, entimos, timaō, timē; aretē, doxa, epainos, polytelēs, makarios*. Contrast *aischrokerdōs, aischynomai*, etc.

Pontos (1/2) 1:1

poreuomai (3/150) 3:19, 22; 4:3. Cf. *anastrephō*

pote (3/29) 2:10; 3:5, 20. Cf. *proteron*, 1:14. Contrast *nyn*

*potos** (1/1) 4:3. Cf. *oinophlygia, kōmos*

pou (1/47) 4:8

praüs (1/4) 3:4. Cf. *praütēs; tapeinos, tapeinophrōn*

praütēs (1/11) 3:16. Cf. *praüs; tapeinophrosynē, tapeinos*. Contrast *hyperēphanos*

presbyteros (2/65) 5:1, 5. Cf. *sympresbyteros*. Contrast *neōteros*

pro (2/47) 1:20; 4:8

probaton (1/37) 2:25. Cf. *amnos, poimainō, poimēn, poimnion, archipoimēn*. Contrast *leōn*, 5:8

proginōskō (1/5) 1:20. Cf. *prognōsis, gnōsis*

prognōsis (1/2) 1:2. Cf. *proginōskō, gnōsis*. Contrast *agnōsia, agnoia*

_prothymōs_*	(1/1) 5:2. Cf. _makrothymia_. Contrast _epithymia_
promartyromai	(1/1) 1:11. Cf. _epimartyromai_, 5:12; _martys_, 5:1
pros	(3/696) 2:4; 3:15; 4:12
prosagō	(1/5) 3:18. Cf. _proserchomai_
proserchomai	(1/87) 2:4. Cf. _prosagō_
proseuchē	(2/36) 3:7; 4:7. Cf. _deēsis_
proskomma	(1/6) 2:8
proskoptō	(1/8) 2:8
prosōpon	(1/74) 1:14
proteron	(1/11) 1:14. Cf. _pote_
prophēteuō	(1/28) 1:10. Cf. _prophētēs_
prophētēs	(1/114) 1:10. Cf. _prophēteuō_
prōton	(1/60) 4:17
_ptoēsis_*	(1/1) 3:6. Cf. _tarassō_, _phobeō_, 3:6, 14
pyr	(1/71) 1:7. Cf. _pyrōsis_
pyrōsis	(1/3) 4:12. Cf. _pyr_
rhantismos	(1/2) 1:2
rhēma	(2/68) 1:25, 25. Cf. _logos_, _logia_
_rhypos_*	(1/1) 3:21. Cf. _hamartia_, _kakia_, etc.
sarkikos	(1/7) 2:11. Cf. _sarx_
sarx	(7/147) 1:14; 3:18, 21; 4:1 (2×), 2, 6. Cf. _sarkikos_. Contrast _pneuma_
Sarra	(1/4) 3:6. Cf. _Abraam_, _Nōe_
sthenoō	(1/1) 5:10
Silouanos	(1/4) 5:12. Cf. _Petros_, _Markos_
Siōn	(1/7) 2:6. Contrast _Babylon_, 5:13
skandalon	(1/15) 2:8
skeuē	(1/23) 3:7
skolios	(1/4) 2:18. Contrast _epieikēs_
skotos	(1/30) 2:9. Contrast _phōs_
_spora_*	(1/1) 1:23. Cf. _diaspora_
stereos	(1/4) 5:9. Cf. _stērizō_
stephanos	(1/18) 5:4. Cf. _doxa_, etc.
stērizō	(1/14) 5:10. Cf. _stereos_
stoma	(1/78) 2:22
strateuomai	(1/7) 2:11. Cf. _hoplizō_
sygklēronomos	(1/4) 3:7. Cf. _klēros_, _klēronomeō_, _klēronomia_

symbainō	(1/8) 4:12. Cf. *syntrechō*
*sympathēs**	(1/1) 3:8
*sympresbyteros**	(1/1) 5:1. Cf. *presbyteros*
syneidēsis	(3/30) 2:19; 3:16, 21. Cf. *oida*, etc.
*syneklektos**	(1/1) 5:13. Cf. *eklektos*
*synoikeō**	(1/1) 3:7. Cf. *oiketēs, oikonomos, oikodomeō, oikos*, etc.
syntrechō	(1/3) 4:4. Cf. *syschēmatizō, symbainō*
syschēmatizō	(1/2) 1:14. Cf. *symbainō, syntrechō*
sōzō	(2/106) 3:21; 4:18. Cf. *diasōzo, sōtēria*
sōma	(1/142) 2:24
sōtēria	(4/45) 1:5, 9,10; 2:2. Cf. *sōzō, diasōzō*
sōphroneō	(1/6) 4:7. Cf. *tapeinophrōn, homophrōn*. Contrast *aphrōn*
tapeinos	(1/8) 5:5. Cf. *tapeinophrōn, praüs, hypotassō*. Contrast *hyperēphanos*, 5:5
tapeinophrosynē	(1/7) 5:5. Cf. *tapeinos*, etc.
*tapeinophrōn**	(1/1) 3:8. Cf. *tapeinos*, etc.
tapeinoō	(1/14) 5:6. Cf. *tapeinos*, etc., *hypotassō*. Contrast *hypsoō*
tarassō	(1/17) 3:14. Cf. *phobeō, ptoēsis*
tauta	(1/238) 1:11
tautēn	(1/52) 5:12
teknon	(2/99) 1:14; 3:6. Cf. *brephos, hyios, patēr, adelphos, adelphotēs, philadelphia, philadelphos, oikos*, etc.
*teleiōs**	(1/1) *1:13*
telos	(4/41) 1:9; 3:8; 4:7. Cf. *epiteleō, eschatos, kairos*
tēreō	(1/70) 1:4. Cf. *phroureō*
ti	(1/549) 4:17
tithēmi	(2/101) 2:6, 8. Cf. *paratithēmi*. Contrast *apotithēmi, apothesis*
timaō	(2/21) 2:17 (2×). Cf. *timē*, etc. Contrast *aischynomai, kataischynō*
timē	(3/41) 1:7; 2:7; 3:7. Cf. *timaō, timios*, etc.; *aretē, doxa, epainos*
timios	(1/13) 1:19. Cf. *entimos, polytimos, polytelēs, makarios*. Contrast *aischrokerdōs*
tís, tí	(3/552) 1:11; 3:13; 4:17
tis, ti	(6[7]/518) 2:19; 3:1, 13; 4:11 (2×), 15; [5:8]
tou'nantion	(1/3) 3:9
touto	(7/316) 1:25; 2:19, 20, 21; 3:9, 20; 4:6
toutōi	(1/91) 4:16

typos (1/14) 5:3. Cf. *antitypos*

hydōr (1/76) 3:20

hyios (1/375) 5:13. Cf. *brephos, teknon, patēr, adelphos, adelphotēs, philadelphia, philadelphos, oikos*, etc.

hymas (15/433) 1:4, 10, 12, 15, 20, 25; 2:9; 3:13, 15, 18 (cf. *hēmas, v.l.*), 21; 4:14; 5:6, 10, 13

hymeis (2/235) 2:9; 4:1

hymin (14/608) 1:2, 12 (2×), 13; 2:7, 21; 3:15; 4:12 (3×); 5:1, 2, 12, 14

hymōn (21[22]/555) 1:7, [9], 13, 14, 17, 18, 21, 22; 2:12 (2×), 21, 25; 3:2, 7, 15, 16; 4:4, 15; 5:7 (2×), 8, 9. Cf. *hymōn* as *v.l.* in 2:24; 4:17

hypakoē (3/15) 1:2, 14, 22. Cf. *hypakouō*

hypakouō (1/21) 3:6. Cf. *thelēma tou theou* (2:15; 3:17; 4:2, 19), *hypotassō*. Contrast *apeitheō*

hyper (2/149) 2:21; 3:18

hyperēphanos (1/5) 5:5. Cf. *hypsoō*. Contrast *tapeinos*, etc.

hyperechō (1/5) 2:13

hypo (2/217) 2:4; 5:6

*hypogrammos** (1/1) 2:21

hypokrisis (1/6) 2:1. Contrast *anypokritos*

hypolimpanō (1/1) 2:21

hypomenō (2/17) 2:20 (2×). Cf. *hypopherō*

hypotassō (6/38) 2:13, 18; 3:1, 5, 22; 5:5. Cf. *hypakouō, hypomenō*. Contrast *antitassō*

hypopherō (1/3) 2:19. Cf. *hypomenō*

hypsoō (1/20) 5:6. Cf. *hyperēphanos*. Contrast *tapeinoō*, etc.

phainō (1/34) 4:18

phaneroō (2/49) 1:20; 5:4. Cf. *apokalyptō, apokalypsis, dēloō*

pherō (1/68) 1:13

phthartos (2/6) 1:18, 23. Contrast *aphthartos, amarantos, amarantinos*

phthonos (1/9) 2:1

philadelphia (1/6) 1:22. Cf. *philadelphos, philēma, philoxenos, adelphos, adelphotēs; agapaō, agapē*

*philadelphos** (1/1) 3:8. Cf. *philadelphia*, etc.

philēma (1/7) 5:14. Cf. *philadelphia*, etc.

philoxenos (1/3) 4:9. Cf. *philadelphia*, etc.; *xenos*

[*philophrōn**] (1/1) [*v.l.* in 3:8; cf. NTG, *homophrōn*]

phimoō (1/7) 2:15

phobeō (3/95) 2:17; 3:6, 14. Cf. *phobos; tarassō*

phobos (5/47) 1:17; 2:18; 3:2, 14, 16. Cf. *ptoēsis*
phoneus (1/7) 4:15
phroureō (1/4) 1:5. Cf. *tēreō*
phylakē (1/46) 3:19
phōs (1/73) 2:9. Contrast *skotos*
chairō (2/74) 4:13 (2×). Cf. *chara, aggaliaō*
chara (1/59) 1:8. Cf. *chairō*
charis (10/155) 1:2, 10, 13; 2:19, 20; 3:7; 4:10; 5:5, 10, 12. Cf. *charisma*
charisma (1/17) 4:10. Cf. *charis*
cheilos (1/7) 3:10
cheir (1/176) 5:6
chorēgeō (1/2) 4:11
chortos (3/15) 1:24 (3×)
chrēstos (1/7) 2:3
chronos (4/54) 1:17, 20; 4:2, 3. Cf. *kairos, eschatos, telos*
chrysion (3/13) 1:7, 18; 3:3. Cf. *argyrion*
psychē (6/101) 1:9, 22; 2:11, 25; 3:20; 4:19
*ōryomai** (1/1) 5:8
hōs (27/505) 1:14, 19, 24 (2×); 2:2, 5, 11, 12, 13, 14, 16 (3×), 25; 3:6, 7 (2×); 4:10, 11 (2×), 12, 15 (2×), 16; 5:3, 8, 12
hōste (2/84) 1:21; 4:19

Proper Names

Abraam (1/73) 3:6
Asia (1/18) 1:1
Babylōn (1/12) 5:13. Cf. *diaspora*, 1:1
Bithynia (1/2) 1:1
Galatia (1/4)1:1
Iēsous Christos (9[10]/905) 1:1, 2, 3 (2×), 7, 13; 2:5; 3:21; 4:11 (*Christos* [*Iēsous*, 5:10]). No absolute occurrences of *Iēsous* only. Cf. *Christos*, abs.
Kappadokia (1/2) 1:1
Markos (1/8) 5:13
Nōe (1/8) 3:20
Petros (1/154) 1:1
Pontos (1/2) 1:1

Sarra (1/4) 3:6
Silouanos (1/4) 5:12
Siōn (2/7) 2:6
Christianos (1/3) 4:16. Cf. *onoma*, 4:16
Christos (22/529) abs. (13×) 1:11 (2×), 19; 2:21; 3:15, 16, 18; 4:1, 13, 14; 5:1, 10 (*Christos* [*Iēsous*]), 14. *Iēsous Christos* (9×)1:1, 2, 3 (2×), 7, 13; 2:5; 3:21; 4:11; cf. *kyrios*, 1:3, 25; 2:3; 3:15

Definite Articles

hai 3:[1], 5 (2×)
hē 2:7; 3:20; 4:11; 5:13
ho 1:3 (2×), 24; 2:3, 6; 3:3, 4, *10*, 13; 4:1, 3, 11 (2×), [17], *18* (2×); 5:1 (2×), 5, 8, 10 (2×), 13
hoi 1:10; 2:7, 10, 18; 3:7, 16; 4:19
ta 1:11; 5:9
tais 1:14; 2:24; 3:15
tas 1:11, 13, 22; 2:9, 24; 3:7; 4:19
tēi 1:14, 22; 2:24; 4:12, 13; 5:9 (2×)
tēn 1:13, 21; 2:11, 15, 16, 17; 3:2, *10*, 16; 4:1, 4, 8; 5:5, 6, 7, 10
tēs 1:7, 9, 10, 13, 17, 18, 22; 2:11, 16; 3:1, 4, 15; 4:4, 13, 14; 5:1, 4
to 1:3, 7, 9, 11, 17, 24, 25, 25 (2×); 2:2, 9, 15, 24; 3:7, 8, 17; 4:2, 3, 7, 11; 4:14 (2×), 17 (2×), 19; 5:2, 11
tois 2:7, 12, 18 (3×), 21; 3:1, 5, 19; 4:13; 5:14
ton 1:3, 7; 2:9, 15; 3:4 (2×), *10*, 13, 17 (2×), 25; 3:14, 15; 4:2, 16; 5:4
tou 1:3, 7; 2:9, 15; 3:4 (2×), *10*, 13, 17, 20 [22]; 4:13, 14, 17 (4×), 19; 5:1, 2, 3, 4, 6, 12 (2×)
tous 1:5, 21; 4:11; 5:11
tōi 2:[5], 8, 22, 23, 24 (2×); 3:1, 4, 6, 7, 15, 18; 4:5, 16, 17; [5:9]
tōn 1:12, 20; 2:11, 12, 15, 25; 3:1; 4:3, 11; 4:17; 5:1, 3, 9

Relative Pronouns

ha 1:12 (2×)
hēn 3:20; 5:12
hēs 1:10; 3:6; 4:11
ho 2:8; 3:4, 21
hoi 2:8, 10; 4:5
hois 1:12
hon 1:8 (2×); 2:4, 7

hos	2:22, 23, 24; 3:22
hou	2:24
hōi	1:6; 2:12; 3:16, 19; 4:4, 11; 5:9
hōn	3:3

Peculiarities of the terminology include:

- 61 terms occurring nowhere else in the NT. Several of these *hapax legomena* (34/35 of which appear in the LXX) are employed to express fundamental emphases in the letter: the Christian community as "brotherhood" (*adelphotēs*—in consonance with the letter's traditional familial terminology ["brother," "brotherly love," "children," God as "Father," community as "house(hold) of God"]), and as covenantal "priestly community" (*hierateuma*, 2:5, 9); "doing what is right" (*agathopoios*, 2:14; *agathopoiia*, 4:19) and "doing what is wrong" (*kakopoios*, 2:12, 14; 4:15)—key terms of its moral instruction
- numerous terms among these *hapax legomena* of classical origin (*anagkastōs, anachysis, apechesthai epithymiōn, apogenesthai* [metaphorical], *apothesis, bioun, emplokē, oinophlygia, homophrōn, hoplizein, patroparadotos, prothymōs*) or terms for which there is no earlier or contemporary parallel (*allotriepiskopos, amarantos, amarantinos, aneklalētos, aprosōpolēmptōs* [Hebraism], *artigennētos, perithesis*)
- seventy-four terms occurring only twice in the NT
- seventy terms (including proper names) occur less than five times in the NT, including *agnoia, agnōsia, athemitos, akrogōniaios, amianton, amnos, antitypos, apothesis, aspilos, asōtia, aphthartos, amarantos, basileion, Bithynia, Galatia, diaspora, dokimion, doxai* (pl.) *epakoloutheō, episkopē, epopteuō, ichnos, kakopoieō, Kappadokia, katalalia, logikos, loidoreō, lytroō, paroikia, paroikos, parepidēmos, Pontos, prognōsis, pyrōsis, rhantismos, Sarra, Silouanos, stereos, synklēronomos, syntrechō, syschēmatizō, hypopherō, philoxenos, chorēgeō, Christianos*—all terms figuring prominently in the consolation and exhortation of the letter
- relative to its length, the most frequent use of *paschō* (12×), "suffer," in a single NT writing; cf. also *pathēma* (4×)
- relative to its length, the most frequent use of *hypotassō* (6×), "be subordinate to," in a single NT writing
- relative to its length, the most frequent use of the comparitive particle *hōs* ("as," "like") in the NT (27×). The use is varied, and sense is determined by the context. On some occasions, *hōs* clearly indicates a comparison or simile: "A is like B" (1:19, 24; 3:6); on other occasions, it marks something thought to be the case, that is not the case: "As though A were B but is not or should not be so" (2:12, 16b; 4:12, 15 [2×]; 5:3); third, it can identify an actual quality of someone that is affirmed as true or a case that is literally true: "A is B" (2:13, 14, 16a; 4:16; 5:12). The remaining instances are closest to this third sense: *hōs* introduces something (B) which is real or true of A

in either a literal or metaphorical sense: "As the X that you are" (1:14; 2:2, 5, 11, 16c, 25; 3:7; 4:10, 11 [2×])

- in addition to the unique NT occurrences of *agathopoiia* (4:19) and *agathopoios* (2:14), four of the eight NT occurrences of *agathopoieō* and all of the NT occurrences of *kakopoios* (3×); cf. also *kakopoieō* (1/4)
- the rare identification of the believer as *christianos* ("Christian," 4:14), occurring elsewhere in the NT only in Acts 11:26 and 26:28
- Some terms unique to 1 Peter in the NT occur also in certain LXX writings (marked by *) or related literature. Particular note might be made of: *sympathēs* (1 Pet 3:8/4 Macc 5:25; 13:23; 15:4) and *sympathēs* combined with *philadelphoi* or *philadelphia* (only in 1 Pet 3:8 and 4 Macc 13:23); *adelphotēs* (1 Pet 2:17, 5:9/1 Macc 12:10, 17; 4 Macc 9:23; 10:3, 15; 13:19, 27); *philadelphos* (1 Pet 3:9/2 Macc 15:14; 4 Macc 13:21; 15:10; cf. *philadelphia* [1 Pet 1:22/4 Macc 13:23, 26; 14:1—only LXX occurrences); see also *agathopoieō* (1 Pet 2:15, 20; 3:6, 17/1 Macc 1:2; 2 Macc 1:2; cf. *T. Benj.* 5). For *agathopoiia* (singular in NT, 1 Pet 4:19), see *T. Jos.* 18:2. See also: *kata to poly autou eleos* (1 Pet 1:3/*T. Naph.* 4:3); *amnos amōmos* (1 Pet 1:19/*T. Jos.* 19:8). Compare also similar phrases in 1 Pet 1:22 and *T. Gad* 6:3; and 1 Pet 2:9 and *T. Jos.* 19:3; and 1 Pet 2:25b and *T. Gad* 5:3. Such lexical and phraseological resemblances amply illustrate the familiarity of our author with the language of both Diaspora and Palestinian Hellenistic Israel and formative Christianity

Further distinctive features of its vocabulary include:

- preference for *syn*-composites of which all are unique (*sympathēs*, 3:8; *sympresbyteros*, 5:1; *syneklektos*, 5:13; *synoikeō*, 3:7) or rare in the NT (*sygklēronomos*, 3:7; *symbainō*, 4:12; *syntrechō*, 4:4, *syschēmatizō*, 1:14; cf. *syneidēsis*, 2:19; 3:16, 21)
- occurrences of *hypo*-composites, (*hypomenō*, *hypotassō*, *hypopherō*) and *phil*-composites (*philadelphia*, *philadelphos*; *philēma*; *philoxenos*)
- *repetition* of identical or related terms, including several not occurring elsewhere in the NT: *agathopoieō*, *agathopoiia*, *agathopoios*; *agathos*; *agalliaō*; *agapaō*, *agapē*; *aggelos*; *hagios*; *adelphotēs*; *haima*; *amēn*; *apokalyptō*, *apokalypsis*; *anagennaō*, *artigennētos*; *anastasis*, *egeirō*; *anastrephō*, *anastrophē*; *apeitheō*; *dolos*, *adolon*; *doxa*, *doxazō*; *eklektos*, *syneklektē*; *euaggelizō*, *euaggelion*; *zaō*, *zōopoieō*, *zōē*; *theos*; *Iēsous Christos*; *hierateuma*; *kakopoios*; *kairos*; *krinō*, *krima*; *nyn*; *menō*; *xenizō*; *oikos*, *oiketēs*, *oikonomos*, *oikodomeō* *synoikeō*; *phthartos*; *paschō*, *pathēma*; *patēr*; *pisteuō*, *pistis*, *pistos*, *apisteuō*; *poimnion*, *poimainō*, *poimēn*, *archipoimēn*; *poreouomai*; *sarx*, *sarkikos*; *sōtēria*, *sōzō*; *syneidēsis*; *tapeinos*, *tapeinophrosynē*, *tapeinophrōn*, *tapeinoō*; *telos*; *timaō*, *timē*, *entimos*, *polytimos*, *timios*; *hypakoē*, *hypomenō*, *hypotassomai*; *philadelphia*, *philadelphos*, *philēma*, *philoxenos*; *charis*; *Christos*; *chrysion*; *psychē*; *hōs*. These repetitions often serve either as link-words joining subsections of the letter or as means for maintaining thematic consistency throughout the composition.

Much of the distinctive vocabulary of 1 Peter involves extensive *semantic fields* signaling major concepts and themes of the letter:

- depiction of the Christian community as "strangers" and "resident aliens" (*parepidēmoi, paroikoi, paroikia*; cf. *diaspora, Babylon*)
- a variety of related terms pertaining to hostility and shaming treatment of believers by their neighbors (*blasphēmeō; epēreazō; kakoō; katalaleō, katalalia; loidoreō, antiloidoreō, loidoria; oneidizō*; cf. *laleō*)
- a variety of related terms indicating the honorable and distinctive status of Christians before God (*eklektos, syneklektos; hagios, hagiasmos, hagnos, katharos, amōmos, aspilos*, etc; *timē, timaō, timios, entimos, polytimoteros* [contrast terms of shame: *aischynomai, aischrokerdōs, kataischynō*]; *makarios; doxa, doxazō*)
- several related terms for holiness, purity etc. (*hagiazō, hagios, hagiasmos; hagnizō, hagnos; amiantos; amōmos; aspilos; katharos; hierateuma*)
- an extensive semantic field depicting the community as the *household* or *family* of God (*oikos tou theou*; God as *patēr* who rebirths [*anagennaō*, cf. *artigennētos*]; believers as brotherhood [*adelphotēs*] and family members [*tekna, adelphos, hyios*] who practice brotherly love [*philadelphia, philadelphos, philēma, philoxenos, agapē*]) and numerous terms of the *oik*-root (*oikos, oiketēs, oikodomeō, oikonomos, synoikeō*) referring to the affairs of the household or to those separated from home (*paroikos, paroikia; parepidemos; diaspora*)
- an extensive semantic field pertaining to conduct (*anastrephō, anastrophē; agathopoieō, agathopoiia, agathopoios; agapaō, agapē, agapētos; apeitheō; apotithēmi; antistēmi; dikaios, dikaiosynē, dikaiō, adikos, adikōs; hamartanō, hamartia, hamartōlos; kalē erga; kakopoieō, kakopoios, kakia; pisteuō, apisteō; poreuō; syntrechō; philadelphia, philadelphos; philoxenos*); norms of conduct (*thelēma tou theou, phobos* [*tou theou*], *syneidēsis* [*tou theou*]; *athemitos*); quality of conduct and character (*agathos, anypokritos, hagios, kalos* etc.); the attitude of humility (*tapeinoō, tapeinos, tapeinophrosynē, tapeinophrōn; hēsychios; prautēs*) and respect for authority and order (*hypotassō, timaō*); cf. also the vice lists in 2:1, 4:3; and 4:15
- a field of terms indicating the letter's eschatological perspective (*eschatos, kairos, telos; apokalyptō, apokalypsis, phaneroō, dēloō*) and contrast of transience vs. permanence (*apollymi; phthartos, aphthartos; amiantos, amarantos, amarantinos; menei eis ton aiōna; eis tous ainōnas tōn aiōnōn*) or of "once" (*pote*)/"now" (*nyn*), distinguishing former from present existence.

The vocabulary, moreover, displays noteworthy differences from that employed by Paul. There is no use of *ekklēsia* ("church") and no mention of such Pauline concerns as "law," "circumcison," "cross" (cf. *xylon*, 2:24, rather than *stauros*), "body of Christ," or *diōkō* for "persecute" (except in the psalm quotation in 3:11 and with a different, positive sense), though usage of this latter term certainly would have been appropriate. The terms *dikaios* (3:12, 18; 4:18) and *dikaiosynē* (2:24; 3:14) bear a conventional Israelite sense ("righteous, upright behavior"), as in Matthew, but in contrast to Paul. These lexical differences are an important indication of the distance between 1 Peter and Paul, both conceptually and temporally.

How much can be made of the few connecting particles used and the absence of such particles as *ara*, *ge*, *epei*, *epeidē*, *te*, *dē*, *pou*, *pōs*, and particularly *an*, however, is another matter. The conclusion of Bigg (1902, 4–5) that "this fact alone [the absence of *an*] is sufficient to show that the writer was not a Greek" seems to rest too much on too little.

For a discussion of the vocabulary and *hapax legomena* of 1 Peter, see Holzmeister 1937, 84–93, with an inclusion of tabular comparisons of 1 Peter's lexical affinities with 2 Peter, Mark, the Petrine speeches of Acts, and the rest of the NT; see also Mussies 1972, 236–38 for affinities between 1 Peter and Dio Chrysostom, and Adinolfi 1988 for lexical and conceptual affinities between 1 Peter and the Greco-Roman world. On the metaphors and images employed in 1 Peter, see Elliott 1981/1990, 165–266; Puig Tarrech 1980, 331–402; Achtemeier 1988; Feldmeier 1992; R. P. Martin 1992.

3.2. STYLE

In 1 Peter an abundance of diverse traditions is integrated in a composition that nevertheless is consistent in style and coherent in theme.[19] Its relatively polished Greek contains few vulgar elements and reveals an author of some education (Radermacher 1926; Wifstrand 1948, 180). It manifests a semitic appreciation of parallelism (1:2, 20, 24; 2:4, 4–5, 6, 8, 10, 13–14, 16, 17, 18, 19–20, 20, 22, 23, 25; 3:3–4, 9, 10–12, 17, 18d, 18e, 19/22b, 21b–c; 4:6, 11, 14–16, 17b–18; 5:1, 2–3, 5:5c, 6–7) allied with a Hellenistic preference for substantival expressions resulting in an abundance of abstract nouns. Like the epistle of James, it resembles the "edifying language of the hellenized synagogue" (Wifstrand 1948, 180) and displays abundant affinities in vocabulary and style to Classical writings (listed in Selwyn 1947, 499–501, and the Index of the present volume). On the whole, it most closely resembles the middle style of Greek rhetoric, "neither heavily ornamented nor without artifice" (J. W. Thompson 1994, 250). On the rhetoric of 1 Peter, see Ellul 1990; Thurén 1990; I. H. Marshall 1991; Campbell 1995; and Slaughter 1995.

Several features indicate the rhetorical competence and literary refinement of the author:

- the near-Classical employment of the definite article and exact use of tenses

[19] Relevant studies on the letter's style and rhetoric include Bigg 1902, 2–7; Mayor 1907, lxxxix–cv; Radermacher 1926; Holzmeister 1937, 82–104; Selwyn 1947, 25–28; Daube in Selwyn 1947, 467–88; Wifstrand 1948; Quacquarelli 1967, 425–42; Best 1971, 49; van Rensburg 1990; Thurén 1990, 1995; Campbell 1995; Snyder 1995.

- the dramatic accumulation of synonyms for effect: 1:3–5 (*eis elpida, eis klēronomian, eis sōterian*); 1:7 (*eis epainon kai doxan kai timēn*); 1:18 (*amōmou kai aspilou*); 2:6 (*akrogōniaion eklekton entimon*); 2:9 (*genos eklekton, basileion, hierateuma, ethnos hagion, laos eis peripoiēsin*); see also 3:3b–d; 3:8; 4:3b; 4:15; 5:2c–3a; and 5:10d (*katartisei, stērixei, sthenōsei, themeliōsei*)
- alliteration and assonance: 1:4 (*aphtharton kai amianton kai amaranton*); 1:6 (*poikilois peirasmois*); 1:10–11a (*exezētēsan kai exēraunēsan . . . eraunōntes*); 1:19 (*amnou amōmou kai aspilou*); 2:12 (*kalēn . . . katalalousin . . . kakopoiōn . . . kalōn*); 2:15 (*tōn aphronōn anthrōpōn agnōsian*); 2:16 (*eleutheroi . . . epikalymma echontes . . . eleutherian*); 2:18–20 (*hypotassomenoi . . . hypopherei . . . hypomeneite . . . hypomeneite; hōs . . . hōs . . . hōs*); 2:21 (*hyper hymōn hymin hypolimpanōn hypogrammon*); 2:25 (*probata planōmenoi*); 3:2 (*hagnēn anastrophēn*); 3:14 (*phobon . . . phobēthēte*); 3:16 (*katalaleisthe kataischynthōsin*); 3:17 (*theloi to thelēma tou theou*); 3:18b (*dikaios hyper adikōn*); 4:4 (*autēn tēs asōtias anachysin*); 4:11 (*aiōnos tōn aiōnōn*); 4:12 (*pyrōsei pros peirasmon*); 5:2a (*poimanate to . . . pomnion*); 5:2c–3 (*mē, mēde, mēde; anagkastōs, hekousiōs, aischerdōs, prothymōs*); 5:3 (*katakyrieuontes tōn klērōn*); 5:10 (*katartisei, stērixei, sthenōsei, themeliōsei*); 5:12 (*parakalōn kai epimartyrōn*)
- paranomasia: 2:23 (*loidoroumenos, anteloidorei*); 3:9 (*kakon anti kakou, loidorian anti loidorias*); 3:17 (*ei theloi to thelēma tou theou*; cf. 2:15; 4:2, 19); 4:10 (*charisma, charitos*); 5:2 (*poimanate . . . poimnion*)
- hendiadys (the expression of one idea by two or more nouns linked by "and"): 2:25; 3:15; 4:14
- the anaphoric sequential repetition of terms: 1:3–5 (*eis, eis, eis*); 2:16 (*hōs, hōs, hōs*); 2:22–24 (*hos, hos, hos, hou*); 3:1, 7 (*homoiōs*; cf. 5:5); 4:14–18 (*ei, ei, ei, ei*); 5:2–3 (*mē, mēde, mēde*)
- the repetition of terms and themes for rhetorical effect and for maintaining continuity of thought (see under 3.1. VOCABULARY)
- rhetorical questions: 2:20; 3:13; 4:17b–18 (2×)
- the sensitive use of optative verbs: 1:2; 3:14, 17
- the proper distinction of tenses (4:3; cf. 4:1) and of prepositions (1:2)
- the adept use of prepositions: 1:2 (*kata/en/eis*), 3–5 (*eis* 3× for purpose), 22 (*en/eis/ek*); 2:2 (*en/eis*)
- an appropriate use of infinitives (4:17; 5:8)
- a refined and variegated use of the comparative particle *hōs* (27×)
- the abundance of participial constructions (116×), many of which are appended as extensions of the main verb (a special aspect of Petrine style [Radermacher 1926, 289]): 1:3b, 4b, 5a, 6b, 8a,b, 9a,10, 11a, 13a, 15a, 18a, 20a,b, 23a; 2:13b, 14a, 15b (2×), 16b, 19c, 20b (2×), 20d (2×), 21c, 23a,b, 24b, 25a; 3:2a, 5d, 7d, 9a,c, 16b, 17a,c, 18d,e, 19a, 20c, 22b,c; 4:3b, 4d, 10b, 12b, 13b; 5:2b, 3a, 7a, 8c, 9b, 10b,c, 12d). Participles also serve to introduce sentences: 1:13, 14, 18, 22; 2:1, 4, 12, 18; 3:1, 7, 9, 13, 17; 4:1, 8, 9; 5:4, 7). For constructions with the participle *echontes*, see 2:12, 16; 3:16; 4:5, 8

- a predilection for relative clauses (31×): 1:3b, 5a, 6a, 8b, 10a, 12a,b,c; 2:22–24; 3:3a, 5a, 6c, 19a, 20d, 21a, 22a; 4:4a, 5a, 11d; 5:7b, 9a, 11
- a frequent use of relative pronouns as clausal connectives: 1:5a, 8 (2×), 10, 12 (3×), 21; 2:4a, 8 (2×), 10 (2×), 11, 22, 23, 24a (2×); 3:3a, 4c, 6c, 20d, 21a, 22a,c; 4:4a, 5a, 11d; 5:9b, 11, 12; see also the use of *en hōi*, in particular, as a circumstantial connective (1:6; 2:12; 3:16, 19; 4:4)
- a predilection for comparisons and comparative particles (*hōs* [27×], *katho*, [4:13], *kathōs* [4:10]; cf. *homoiōs* [3:1, 7; 5:5]) and a related fondness for metaphor: e.g., rebirth (1:3, 23) and numerous interrelated familial and household metaphors (God as Father, believers as children, newborn babies, brothers [and sisters], household stewards, son, inheritance, brotherly love, etc.); faith-gold (1:7); girding loins of mind (1:13); Christ as lamb (1:19); word as seed, milk, stone (1:23–25; 2:2–3, 8); flesh as grass (1:24); Christ, believers as living stone(s) (2:4, 5, 6–8); darkness, light (2:9); military metaphors (2:11; 4:1; cf. 1:5); believers as slaves of God (2:16); sheep (2:25; 5:2, 3) and God or Christ as shepherd (2:25; 5:4); female as vessel (3:7); baptism, its prototype, and effect (3:21); fire, fiery trial (1:6; 4:12); elders as shepherds (5:2); crown of glory (5:4); hand of God (5:6); Devil as lion (5:8); God's calling, protecting, strengthening, etc. (1:15; 2:9; 5:10); Babylon (5:13)
- a preference for aorist imperatives (26×: 1:13, 15, 17, 22; 2:2, 13, 17a; 3:10, 11 [4×], 14 [2×], 15; 4:1, 7 [2×]; 5:2, 5 [2×], 6, 8 [2×], 9, 12) over present imperatives (8×: 2:17b,c,d; 3:3; 4:12, 13b, 16, 19)
- a preference for the sequence of a negative followed by a positive: 1:8, 10–11/12; 14/15, 18/19, 23, 24/25; 2:1/2; 2:4c/d; 2:10a/b, c/d; 2:11/12; 2:16b/c; 2:20; 2:23a,b, 25a/b; 3:3/4, 9ab/c, 11, 13, 14/15, 16, 18d/e, 21b/c: 4:2b/c, 6b/c, 12/13, 15/16, 16b/c; 5:2c/d, 5:2e/f, 5:3a/b; 5:5c
- twenty-three instances of the construction in which various attributes are inserted between an initial article and a final substantive: 1:10, 11a, 11b, 14, 17, 21; 2:9, 15; 3:1, 2, 3 (9 intervening terms!), 15, 16; 4:2, 4, 8, 12, 13, 14; 5:1, 4, 9, 10
- "step" constructions in which subordinate clauses are themselves qualified by subordinate clauses: 1:17–21; 3:19–22
- the circumstantial use of *ei* in a de facto sense ("since," "because X is the case"): 1:17; 2:3; 4:14, 17, 18
- numerous ellipses

(1) Ellipses of the verb *eimi*: 1:3 (*eulogētos* [*estin*] *o theos*); 1:24a (*pasa sarx* [*estin*] *hōs chortos*); 2:5d; ([*hymeis este*] *oikos pneumatikos*); 2:9a (*hymeis de genos eklekton* [*este*]); 2:10 (*hoi pote* [*ēte*] *ou laos, nyn de* [*este*] *laos theou; hoi* [*ēte*] *ouk ēleēmenoi, nyn de* [*este*] *eleēthentes*); 2:20a (*poion kleos* [*estin*]); 3:12 (*ophthalmoi kyriou epi dikaiou* [*estin*]); 3:13 (*tis ho kakōsōn hymas* [*estin*]); 3:14 and 4:14 (*makarioi* [*este*]); cf. also 2:19a, 20f; 3:8; 4:3a, 9, 17a,c.

(2) Ellipses of other verbs: 4:11 (*ei tis lalei, hōs logia* [*laleitō*]; *ei tis diakonei, hōs ex ischyos hēs chorēgei o theos* [*diakoneitō*]); 4:16 (*ei de hōs christianos* [*paschei*]); 4:17b (*ei de prōton aph' hēmōn* [*archetai*]; see also 2:16a; 3:10c, 15b; 5:13b.

(3) Ellipses of nouns, pronouns, etc: 1:9 ([*hymōn*] *psychōn*); 2:11 (*parakalō* [*hymas*] *apechesthe*); 2:23 (*paredidou* [*heauton*] *tōi krinonti*); 3:7 (*hōs asthenesterōi skeuei tōi gynaikeiōi* [*skeuei*]); cf. also 1:18b (*phthartois* [*hōs*] *argyriōi ē chrysiōi*) and 1:8a, 8b, 12b, 12c, 15b, 18b, 21c, 22c; 2:11a, 12c, 18a; 3:3b, 4b, 7d, 22a; 4:19b; 5:3a, 9a, 13a.

- interjections/conditional qualifications: 1:6 (*ei deon*); 3:17 (*ei theloi to thelēma tou theou*); 5:12 (*hōs logizomai*); cf. 3:20d (*tout' estin oktō psychai*)
- use of *en* instrumentally: 1:2, 5a, 6b, 12, 17, 22; 2:2, 18; 3:2, 4; 4:16, 19; 5:14
- accusative-with-infinitive constructions: 5:9, 12
- asyndeton: 2:6, 9, 10; 3:8, 18b, 18d, 18e; 4:3; 5:8, 10
- relative or conditional clauses immediately following a conjunction: 3:1c; 3:14a; 3:16c; 4:13a
- refererence to vices in the plural: 2:1; 4:3; contrast Rom 1:29; Gal 5:19–20
- triads (a) textual: 1:4, 7, 19; 2:6b; 3:3, 22; 5:1; (b) structural 1:2a–c; 1:3–12 (3–5/6–9/10–12); 1:3–5 ([*eis/eis/eis*], 3c/4:a–5a/5b); 5:2–3 (2c, 2d, 3)
- quartads: 4:15; 5:10
- pentads: 2:1; 3:8; 4:3 (5+1)

Several features illustrate the *predominantly hortatory tone* of the letter:

- the broad semantic field of terms for conduct (see above)
- fifty-four imperatival constructions (1:13, 14, 15, 17, 22b; 2:1, 2, 11, 12, 13, 16, 17 [4×], 18; 3:1, 3–4, 7, 8, 9 [2×], 10–11 [5×], 14 [2×], 15, 16a, 16b; 4:1, 7b [2×], 8, 9, 10b, 11a, 11b, 12, 13, 15, 16 [2×], 19; 5:2–3, 5a, 5b, 6, 7, 8 [2×], 9, 14a) including the imperatival use of adjectives (3:8) and participles (1:14b; 2:1, 12a, 18a; 3:1, 7b, 9, [2×]; 16b; 4:8, 10b; 5:7a). On participles with imperatival force in 1 Peter, see Daube in Selwyn 1947, 467–88; Meecham 1947; Salmon 1963; Kanjuparambil 1983; Gielen 1990, 478–83; Snyder 1995)
- the predominant use of 2d-person plural pronouns (51/52×) and verbs; contrast 1st-person plural pronouns only in 1:3 (2×) and 4:17 (unlikely variants in 2:24 and 3:18), the 1st-person plural verb *zēsōmen* in 2:24c; and the 1st-person singular verbs in 2:11, 5:1 and 5:12 (2×)
- the parenetic use of *oun* ("therefore," 2:1, 7; 4:1, 7; 5:1, 6; cf. 1:13)
- numerous antitheses, frequently contrasting believers-nonbelievers or former-present types of behavior: 1:10–11/12 14/15, 18/19, 23b, 24/25a; 2:4c/d; 7a/7b–8/9–10, 10a/b, c/d, 12b/d, 16b/c, 17, 18c, 20bc/d–f; 23 (2×), 24b/c, 25a/b; 3:3/4, 9ab/c, 11, 12ab/c, 13/14ab, 14c/15a, 17a/c, 18d/e, 20/21, 21b/c; 4:2, 6b/c, 12/13, 15/16, 17b/c, 18a/b; 5:2c, 2d, 3a, 5:5c; 5:6–7/8–9/10–11, occasionally with homoioteleuton in antitheses (2:14; 3:18; 4:6); cf. also 1:8a, 8b
- the sequence of initial imperatives followed by supporting indicatives: 1:14–15/16; 1:17/18–21; 2:1/2–3; 2:13–14/15–16; 2:18–20/21–25; 3:3–4/5; 3:8–9c/9d; 3:13–17/18–22; 4:1ab/c–6; 4:12–13a/13b; 4:15–16/17–19; 5:2–3/4; 5:5ab/c; 5:6–7a/7b; 5:8a/b; 5:9a/b. This sequence differs markedly from

Paul, who normally employs an indicative/imperative arrangement. Our author's preference for aorist imperatives over present imperatives (see above) likewise contrasts with Pauline style
- the persistent stress on conduct consistent with the "will of God" (2:15; 3:17; 4:2, 19) or "mindfulness" of God and God's will (2:19; 3:16, 21); cf. also 3:4 ("in God's sight"); 4:6 ("according to God's standard"); 5:4 ("in accord with God")
- exhortation supported by many OT citations or allusions that also conclude preceding imperatives (1:16, 24–25; 2:3, 22–25; 3:10–12; 4:8b, 18; 5:5c, 7b, 8b). Kerygmatic material similarly is employed to support preceding imperatives (1:18–21; 2:21–24; 3:18–22; 4:6).

Certain less refined stylistic features are also evident:

- the use of *eis* rather than *en* in 3:20d and 5:12 and omission of the definite article where expected (1:5 [*kairos eschatos*), 10 [*prophētai*], 12 [*aggeloi*]; 2:6 [*graphē*]; 3:1 [*gynaikes*], 7 [*charis zōēs*]; 4:5 [*nekroi kai zōntes*]; 5:1 [*presbyterous en hymin*]). With *pneuma* designating the divine spirit the article occurs in 4:14 but not in 1:2, 12. Determinative genitive constructions explain the absence of the article elsewhere (1:2, 3, 5, 7, 9, 19; 2:12; 3:12, 20; 4:18)
- occasional omission of a *men* in a contrast including *de*: 2:14; 4:15–16
- occasional Semitisms: 1:13 (*tas osphyas tēs dianoias hymōn*); 1:14 (*tekna hypakoēs*); 2:8 (*lithos proskommatos, petra skandalou*, OT citation); 2:12 (*en hēmerai episkopēs*); see also numerous divine passives (referring to action of God): 1:2d, 5b, 7c, 12a,b, 13b, 18a, 20a,b, 23a; 2:5c, 6c, 7d, 8c, 10c, 21a, 22b, 24d, 25b; 3:9d, 16d, 18e, 20d, 22c; 4:18a; 5:1c, 4a
- omission of the article in determinative genitive constructions (1:2, 3, 5, 7, 9, 19; 2:12; 3:12, 20; 4:18); cf. also 1:13 (*elpizein epi ti* [locative dative] and 4:3 (*poreuesthai en*).

Some instances of unusual or problematic grammar and syntax include 1:2 (*eis* with sense of "because"); 1:11 (*eis tina ē poion kairon*); 2:5 (relation of verb *oikodomeisthe* to nominative *oikos*); 3:7 (singular *skeuos* with implied plural *gynaixi*); 3:21 (antecedent of *ho*, relation of nouns); 3:19 (sense and function of *en hōi*, relation of vv 19 and 20); 4:2 (relation of 4:2 *eis to . . . biōsai* to 4:1); nature of relation of *blasphēmountes* (4:4) to foregoing; 5:9 (*ta auta tōn pathēmatōn* and syntax); 5:12 (relation of 5:12e to 5:12d). See the respective NOTES.

3.3. COMPOSITIONAL DEVICES AND PATTERNS

Various proposals have been made concerning the structure of the letter. These have often been dependent upon judgments made concerning the integrity of the document and the nature of its genre. The foregoing discussion of the issues of genre and integrity has shown that a preponderance of evidence indicates that the present text of 1 Peter reflects its original shape and content and that 1 Peter therefore is best regarded as an integral letter.

Among those regarding 1 Peter as a letter, opinion concerning its structure still varies widely. Some scholars (e.g., Bigg [1902, 6]; Brox [1986, 16]) find little evidence of a definite structure with clearly defined units. Most other commentators, however, find an array of means for discerning the letter's structural contours. The pioneering work of W. Dalton (1965, 72–86; 1989, 93–108) marks a significant advance beyond earlier studies in this regard. Building on A. Vanhoye's structural analysis of Hebrews, Dalton called attention to various compositional devices that provide clues to the letter's structure (inclusions, link-words, prior announcement of theme, repetition of key words, shift from indicative to imperative voice, symmetrical organization of the material). Subsequent studies either following the lead of Vanhoye and Dalton (e.g., Volpi 1984; Bosetti 1990; Cervantes Gabarrón 1991) or employing other but similar modes of detailed literary analysis (Chevallier 1971; du Toit 1974; Combrink 1975; Elliott 1979, 14–15; 1992a, 272; Antoniotti 1985; Ellul 1990) have led to partial but not complete consensus. The problem here has less to do with the criteria agreed upon than with the mode of their application and differing sensitivities to the letter's general line of thought. One of several areas of concurrence, however, involves a rejection of the opinion (e.g., Brox 1986) that the letter lacks sufficient indications of structure with clearly discernible units.

The clearest indicators of structure include the composition's epistolary framework, its means of announcing themes, its inclusions, its chiasms, its transitions from declarative statement (indicative mood) to exhortation (imperative mood) and vice versa, its link-words, and other compositional patterns (patterns of subunits, commencements and conclusions of subunits).

3.3.1. *The Epistolary Framework*

At the outset it is clear that 1:1–2 and 5:12–14 together form the epistolary framework of the entire letter and envelop the composition in one grand inclusion. Such an inclusion (use of identical or similar terms or images at the beginning and end of a unit, section, or composition to mark their commencement and close) is indicated by the following parallels:

1:1–2	*5:12–14*
Peter, an apostle of Jesus Christ	I have written; cf. Silvanus, Mark
to the elect strangers	co-elect [brotherhood]
of the Diaspora	at Babylon
Jesus Christ	in Christ
grace	grace
peace	peace
salutation (1:2)	greetings (5:14)

Both the prescript (1:1–2) and the postscript (5:12–14), moreover, sound themes (divine foreknowledge, sanctification, obedience, passion of Christ, grace, familial terminology) that reverberate throughout the letter, as has been discussed above.

In regard to the body of the letter (1:3–5:11), the following indications of structure are evident.

3.3.2. *Announcement of Themes*

1:1–2d	election (2:4–10); strangerhood (1:17; 2:11); divine foreknowledge (1:20); God the Father (1:3, 17); sanctification (1:14–16; 2:5, 9; cf. 1:22; 3:5, 15); Spirit (1:11–12; 4:14; cf. 2:5); obedience (1:14, 22); blood of Jesus Christ (1:19 and references to Christ's suffering); grace (10×); peace (3:11)
1:3–12	an introductory section announcing the themes to be developed in 1:13–5:11 more fully (mercy, rebirth, living hope, resurrection of Jesus Christ, permanent inheritance, divine protection, salvation, joy in suffering, suffering as test, revelation of Jesus Christ, salvation as grace, bearing witness, sufferings and glories of Christ, good news for you)
2:11–12	exhortation introducing themes and semantic fields of 2:11–5:11: avoiding deadly cravings that war against life (4:1, 2–4); maintaining honorable conduct among the Gentiles (2:13–5:11); slander and verbal abuse (2:15; 3:9, 16; 4:4, 14–16); Gentiles' observing good deeds of believers (3:2); distinction from Gentiles (4:1–6); glorifying God (4:11, 16; 5:11).

3.3.3. *Inclusions*

1 Peter contains a diversity of inclusions that bracket larger and smaller units of the letter.

Some inclusions embrace *larger units* of the letter:

1:1–2/5:12–14	the frame of the entire letter
1:3–5:11	suffering a little while (1:6/5:10); glory (1:7/5:10); unfading (*amaranton*, 1:4 / *amarantinon*, 5:4); grace (1:10/5:10)
1:3–2:10	mercy of God (*eleos*, 1:3 / *ouk eleēmenoi*, *eleēthentes*, 2:10); praise of God (*eulogētos*, 1:3; *aretai*, 2:9)
2:11–4:11	*paroikoi*, 2:11 / *oikonomoi*, 4:10 (*oik*-root terms); wage war (*strateuontai*, 2:11) / arm yourselves (*hoplisasthe*, 4:1); good behavior (*kalēn anastrophēn*, 2:11) / good household stewards (*kaloi oikonomoi*, 4:10); Gentiles (*ethnē*, 2:11/4:3); speaking slander (*katalalousin*, 2:12) / speaking as oracles of God (*lalei*, 4:11); glorify God (*doxasōsin*, 2:12) / His is the glory (*hōi estin hē doxa*, 4:11)

4:12–5:11	suffering (*pathēmata*, 4:13 / *pathontas*, 5:10; cf. also *hoi paschontes*, 4:19; *pathēmata*, 5:1/9); glory (*doxēs*, 4:13/5:10; cf. also 4:16, 5:1).

Other inclusions embrace and mark *smaller units*:

1:1–2	Jesus Christ (1:1/2)
1:3–12	(Jesus) Christ (1:3/11); heavens (*ouranois*, 1:4 / *ouranou*, 1:12)
1:13–21	hope (1:13/21); cf. also chiastic structure, as noted below under Chiasms
2:4–10	elect (2:4/9; cf. 2:6)
2:13–17	emperor (2:13/17); cf. be subordinate to every creature (*pasēi ktisei*, 2:13) / honor everyone (*pantas*, 2:17)
2:21–25	"for" (*gar*) clauses (2:21a/2:25) bracket vv 21b–24
3:1–6	(be) subordinate to own *husbands* (3:1, *hypotassomenai tois idiois andrasin*, 3:1 /5–6); cf. also chiastic structure under Chiasms
3:13–17	*kakōsōn* (harm, 3:13) / *kakopoiountas* (doing what is wrong, 3:17); zealots for what is right (*tou agathou*, 3:13) / doing what is right (*agathopoiountas*, 3:17); suffer (3:13/17)
3:18–4:6	put to death in the flesh, made alive in the spirit (3:18) / judged in the flesh but made alive in the spirit (4:6)
3:18–22	Christ (3:18/21–22); God (*tōi theōi*, 3:18) / *theou*, 3:22); having gone (*poreutheis*, 3:19/22); cf. angelic spirits (*pneumasin*, 3:19) / angels, authorities, powers (*aggelōn kai exousiōn kai dynameōn*, 3:22)
4:1–6	flesh (*sarki*, 4:1/6); will of God (*thelēmati theou*, 4:2 / *kata theon*, 4:6; contrast of God vs. humans, 4:2/6)
4:7–11	all (*pantōn*, 4:7 / *pasin*, 4:11); cf. also 4:8
5:1–4	glory (*doxēs*, 5:1/4); (glory) about to be revealed (*mellousēs apokalyptesthai*, 5:1) / when the chief shepherd is manifested (*phanerōthentos tou archipoimenos*, 5:4); shepherd (*poimainate*, 5:2 / *archipoimenos*, 5:4)
5:5b(6)–11	God (*theou*, 5:5b, 6/10–11); grace (5:5c/10); powerful (*krataian*, 5:6 / *kratos*, 5:11).

Still other inclusions occur *within subunits or verses:*

2:1	"all" (*pas*) frames five vices listed
2:4–8	stone (*lithos*, 2:4/8)
2:6–8	"I am setting (*tithēmi*, 2:6) / "as they were set (*etethēsan*) to do," 2:8c
2:16	"as (*hōs*) (free persons)" / "as (*hōs*) (slaves of God")
2:17	"honor (all persons)" / "honor (the emperor)," with chiastic structure
2:19–20	"this is creditable" (2:19a/20f), with chiastic structure.

3.3.4. *Chiasms*

Chiasms (inverted parallelisms with an A B B′ A′ structure) involving either units or verses include:

1:13–21 A. hope (v 13)
B. holiness (of believers, vv 14–16)
B′. holiness (of Christ, vv 17–20)
A′. hope (1:21)

1:24 A. "was withered
B. the grass (v 24c)
B′. the flower (v 24d)
A′. falls"

2:12 A. when they (the Gentiles) slander you (v 12bα)
B. as those who do what is wrong (v 12bβ)
B′. from observing your honorable deeds (v 12c)
A′. they may glorify God on the day of visitation (v 12d)

2:17 A. Honor everyone (v 17a)
B. love the brotherhood (v 17b)
B′. revere God (v 17c)
A′. honor the emperor (v 17d)

2:20 A. for what credit (*kleos*) is it (v 20a)
B. if, when you do what is wrong and are beaten, you patiently endure? (v 20bc)
B′. if, however, when you do what is right and suffer, you patiently endure, (v 20de)
A′. this is creditable in God's sight (*touto charis para theōi*) (v 20f)

2:21–25 A. For (*gar*) to this you have been called (v 21a)
B. Christ also suffered (vv 21b–24c)
B′. by his bruise you have been healed (v 24d)
A′. For (*gar*) you were straying as sheep, but now have been returned (v 25ab)

2:21 A. For to this you have been called (v 21a)
B. because Christ also suffered for you (v 21b)
B′. leaving you an example (v 21c)
A′. that you should follow in his footsteps (v 21d)

3:13 A. Who then shall harm you (v 13a)
B. if you are zealots for what is right? (v 13b)
B′. If, however, you should suffer for doing what is right (v 14a),
A′. how honored you are! (v 14b)

4:16 A. If, however, [any of you suffers] as a Christian (v 16a)
B. you should not feel shamed (v 16b)
B′. but should rather glorify God (v 16cα)
A′. with this name (v 16cβ)

5:6 A. Allow yourselves, therefore, to be humbled (v 6aα)
B. under the powerful hand of God (v 6aβ)
B′. so that he may exalt (v 6bα)
A. you (v 6bβ)
5:7 A′. (you) cast all your anxiety
B. upon him
B′. for he
A′. cares about you

For other proposed but questionable chiasms, see Combrink 1975. Parallelisms other than chiasms generally occur *within* units or verses and are less indicative of structural units: 1:2a/b/c, 14/15, 18/19, 20a/b, 24–25a; 2:4c/d, 4–5, 6b/c, 7a/7b–8, 10a/b, c/d, 13b–14, 16a/b/c, 18c/d, 19–20, 22, 23, 24b/c, 25a/b; 3:3/4, 9a,b/c, 10–12, 13/14, 17a/c, 18a,b, d/e, 21b/c; 4:1a,b, 2, 6b/c, 11a/b, 12/13, 14/15/16, 17bc/18ab; 5:1a,b,c, 2c–3, 5:5c, 6–7, 13, 14). See, however, the parallelism of 2:4 (Jesus Christ, living stone) / 2:5 (believers, living stones) and of 2:4 (related to vv. 6–8) / 2:5 (related to vv. 9–10).

3.3.5. Transitions

Transitions from declarative statement (predominant indicative mood) to exhortation (predominant imperatival mood) and vice versa include the following:

Declarative	*Imperatival*
1:3–12	1:13–17
1:8–21	1:22
1:23–25	2:1–2
2:3; 2:4–10	2:11–12; 2:13–14
2:15–16	2:17; 2:18
2:19–20; 2:21–25	3:1–4
3:5–6	3:7; 3:8–9c
3:9d; 3:10–12; 3:13	3:14–16
3:17; 13:8–22	4:1–2
4:3–6; 4:7a	4:7b; 4:8a
4:8b	4:9–11c
4:11d	4:12–14a
4:14b	4:15–16
4:17–18	4:19; 5:1–3
5:4	5:5 5:6–9
5:10–11; 5:12a–d	5:12e
5:13	5:14a
5:14b	

3.3.6. *Commencement Indicators*

Terms occurring at and signaling the beginning of sections include:

- "strangers" (*parepidēmoi*, 1:2; 2:11)
- "hope" (*elpis, elpisate*, 1:3 [1:3–12], 13 [1:13–21]) at the outset of units
- "therefore" (parenetic *oun* initiating exhortation: 2:1 [2:1–3]; 4:1 [4:1–6], 7 [4:7–11]; 5:1 [5:1–5], 6 [5:6–11])
- "beloved" (*agapētoi*, vocative address of readers introducing exhortation, 2:11; 4:12)
- "exhort (*parakaleō*, introducing imperatives [2:11/2:13ff.; 4:12/13ff])
- "be subordinate" (*hypotassō*, an imperative verb initiating exhortation: 2:13 [2:13–17], 18 [2:18–20 (25)]; 3:1 [3:1–6]; 5:5a [5:5a])
- "Christ" initiating traditional Christological material (2:21b [2:21b, 22–24]); 3:18 [3:18–22]; at outset see also 4:1 [4:1–6]; 4:13 [4:12–19]; 5:1 [5:1–5]; cf. also 2:4 ("to him" = "Lord" [2:3] as antecedent [2:4–10])
- "likewise," "in turn," (*homoiōs*, introducing further groups addressed in exhortation: 3:1a [3:1–6], 7a; 5:5a

3.3.7. *Conclusion Indicators*

Items indicating the conclusions of sections include:

- OT citations concluding major or minor sections

  (1) Major: catena of OT passages (2:4–10) concluding 1:3–2:10; Ps 33 [34]:13–17 (1 Pet 3:10–12) concluding 2:11 (13)–3:12.

  (2) Minor: 1:16 (Lev 19:2) concluding 1:14–16; 1:24–25a (Isa 40:6–8) concluding 1:22–25; 2:17 (allusion to Prov 24:21 LXX) concluding 2:13–17; 2:22–25 (Isa 53) concluding 2:18–25; 5:5c (Prov 3:34 LXX) concluding 5:1–5.

- Terms occurring at and signaling the conclusion of sections: "proclaim good news" (*euaggelizō*, 1:12, 25; 4:6); "good news" (*euaggelion*, 4:17); "finally" (*to de telos*, 3:8 [2:13–3:9 (12)]).
- Doxologies with "amen" (4:11 [4:7–11]; 5:11 [5:5b–11]).

3.3.8. *Compositional Patterns*

1 Peter also manifests certain repeated patterns of argumentation. These include the following:

1. A. Initial main statement
   B. Negative qualification
   C. Positive qualification
   D. Conclusion

Examples:

1:13–16
A. 1:13
B. 1:14 *mē* . . .
C. 1:15 *alla* . . .
D. 1:16 *dioti* + OT citation

1:17–21
A. 1:17
B. 1:18 *ou* . . .
C. 1:19–20 *alla* . . .
D. 1:21 with final *hōste* clause

1:22–25
A. 1:22
B. 1:23a *ouk* . . .
C. 1:23b *alla* . . .
D. 1:24 *dioti* + OT citation (and application, 1:25)

2:13–17
A. 2:13–14 + *hoti* explanatory statement (2:15–16a)
B. 2:16b *mē* . . .
C. 2:16c *alla* . . .
D. 2:17

2:18–20 (25)
A. 2:18 + *gar* explanatory statement (2:19)
B. 2:20a–c *poion* . . .
C. 2:20de *alla* . . .
D1. 2:20e
D2. 2:21–25 *eis touto gar* introducing traditional material

3:8–9 (12)
A. 3:8
B. 3:9a,b *mē* . . .
C. 3:9c *tounantion de* . . .
D1. 3:9d *hoti* clause
D2. 3:10–12 *gar* + OT citation

3:1–6
A. 3:1–2
B. 3:3 *ouch* . . .
C. 3:4 *alla* . . .
D. 3:5–6 *gar* explanatory clause

3:13–17
A. 3:13–14b
B. 3:14c *mē* . . .
C. 3:15–16 *de* . . .
D1. 3:17 *gar* explanatory clause
D2. 3:18–22 *hoti* introducing traditional material

4:1–6
A. 4:1
B. 4:2–4 *mēketi* . . . *mē* . . .
C. 4:5
D. 4:6 *eis touto gar* introducing explanatory clause

4:12–19
A. 4:12–14 (involving negative [4:12], positive [4:13a + *hina* (purpose), 4:13b]; makarism [4:14a]; plus explanation [*hoti*, 4:14b])
B. 4:15 *mē* . . .
C. 4:16 *de* . . .
D. 4:17–19 (involving explanatory *hoti* clause [4:17a], two *ei* clauses [4:17bc,18] and final *hōste* clause [4:19])

5:1–4
A. 5:1–2b
B. + C. 5:2c–3 (three antithetical phrases)
5:2c *mē . . . / alla . . .*
5:2d *mēde . . . / alla . . .*
5:3 *mēde . . . / alla . . .*
D. 5:4

2. A. Initial negative imperative
B. Positive
C. Conclusion

Examples:

2:1–3
A. 2:1
B. 2:2
C. 2:3 *hoti* + OT citation

2:11–12
A. 2:11
B. 2:12a
C. 2:12b–d *hina* purpose clause

3. In 3:1–12 and 5:1–5, units of domestic and internal communal exhortation, a similar pattern is also apparent, with the primary difference being the sequence of those addressed (subordinates—superordinates or vice versa).

3:1–6	wives, be subordinate to your own husbands	5:1–4	elders
3:7	husbands in turn	5:5a	younger persons in turn, be subordinate to the elders
3:8–9	injunctions to all	5:5b	injunctions to all
3:10–12	concluding OT citation	5:5c	concluding OT citation

3.3.9. Link-Words

Words (terms, motifs, themes) can function, as do relative clauses in 1 Peter, to join verses and thereby integrate and extend the line of thought. Occasionally they are only apparent in the original Greek.

(1) Link-words (*Stichworte, mots crochets*) that *join units* include the following:

1:1–2/1:3–12	God, father (1:2/3); Jesus Christ (1:1, 2 / 1:3, 7,11); Spirit (1:2/12); grace (1:2/10); you (1:2/4, 7, 10, 12)
1:3–12/13–21	God (1:3/21); father (1:3/17); hope (1:3/13, 21); grace (1:10/13); reveal/revelation (1:5, 7, 12/13); *timē/timios* (1:7/19; cf. 20b); last (1:5/20); *pistis/pistos* (1:9/21). Cf. 1:1–2/13–21 foreknowledge (1:2/19); obedience (1:2/14); blood (of Christ) (1:2/19)
1:13–21/22–25	your (1:21/22); *hagios/hagnizō* (1:15–16/22; cf. *amōmos, aspilos*, 1:19a); God (1:21/23). Cf. born again (1:3/23); love (1:8/23); *psychai* (1:9/22); proclaim good news (1:12/25)
1:22–25/2:1–3	unhypocritical/hypocrisy (1:22/2:1); born anew/newborn (2:2/1:22; cf. 1:3); word/of the word/word (1:22/2:1; cf. 1:25); Lord (1:25/2:3). Cf. salvation (1:5, 9/2:2)
2:1–3/4:10	*as* newborn babies / *as* living stones (1:22/2:5; cf. 1:14 as obedient chidren); purify/holy (1:22/2:5, 9d); of the word/word (2:2/8). Cf. brotherly love / household of God (1:22/2:5)
2:4–10/11–12	as living stones / as resident aliens and strangers (2:5/11; cf. 1:1, 17); household of the Spirit (*oikos penumatikos*) / resident aliens (*paroikoi*) (2:5/11); God (2:4, 5, 10/12)
2:11–12/13–17	*as* resident aliens and strangers / *as* free, not *as* . . . , *as* slaves of God (2:12/16; cf. 2:13–14); do what is wrong

	(2:12/13; cf. 2:16); good conduct, good deeds / do what is right (2:12/14, 15); God (2:12/15, 16, 17). Cf. household/brotherhood (2:5/17)
2:13–17/18–20	slaves of God (*douloi*, 2:16) / household slaves (*oiketai*, 2:18); be subordinate (2:13/18); *phobeō/phobos* (2:17/18); God (2:15, 17/19, 20)
2:18–20/21–25	*touto* (2:19, 20/21); *gar* (2:20/21); suffer (2:19, 20/21, 23); sin (2:20/22, 24a,b); unjustly/justly (2:19/23)
2:18 (21)–25/3:1–6	be subordinate (2:18/3:1, 5); *phobos* (reverence, respect) (2:18/3:2); *para theōi/enōpion tou theou* (2:20/3:4); do good (2:20/3:6)
3:1–6/7	husbands (3:1, 5/7); likewise, in turn (3:1/7); *as* Sarah / *as* weaker vessel, *as* coheirs (3:6/7c,e); *gynaikes/gynaikeios* (3:1, 5/7c)
3:8–9/2:13–3:7	all of you (3:8) referring to all persons and groups addressed in 2:13–3:7; *sygklēronomois/sympatheis* (syncomposites) (3:7/8); coheirs/inherit (3:7/9d). Cf. because to this you have been called (2:21a/3:9b)
3:8–9/10–12	(do) evil, what is wrong (3:9/10c, 11, 12); cf. life (3:7/10); do what is right (3:6; 2:14, 15, 20/3:11); *dikaioi/dikaiosynē* (2:24c/3:12); prayers (3:7/12)
3:10–12/13–17	*poiountas kaka/kakōsōn* (3:12/13); *dikaious/dikaiosynē* (3:12/14); do what is right (3:11/17; cf. 2:14, 15, 20; 3:6). Cf. also the continuation of earlier themes: suffer (2:19–20, 21, 23; 1:6/3:14, 17); not fear (3:6/14); *hagiazō* (cf. 1:15–16; 2:5, 9; 3:5/3:15); hope (1:3, 13, 21; 3:5/3:15); gentle (3:4/16); *phobos* (reverence) (1:17; 3:2/3:14, 16); good conscience (*syneidēsis*) (2:19/3:16); slander (2:12/3:16); good conduct (2:12; 3:1, 2; 1:15, 17, 18 / 3:16); will of God (2:15/3:17; cf. 2:20)
3:13–17/18–22	Christ (3:15, 16/18, 21); suffer (3:14, 17 / 3:18); doing what is right/righteous (3:14/18; cf. unrighteous, 3:18); God (3:17/18, 21, 22); *syneidēsis* (3:16/21)
3:18–22/4:1–6	Christ (3:21; cf. 3:15, 16/4:1); suffer (3:18; cf. 3:17/4:1, 2); flesh (3:18, 21 / 4:1a,c, 2, 6); sin (3:18/4:1); God (3:18, 21, 22 / 4:2, 6); *poreuō* (3:19, 22 / 4:3); *en hōi* (3:19/4:4); made alive (*zōopoiētheis*) / living (*zōntas*), live (*zōsi*) (3:18/4:5, 6); put to death in the flesh, made alive in the spirit/judged in the flesh . . . , might live in the spirit . . . (3:18/4:6)
4:1–6/7–11	God (4:2, 6/10, 11a,b); Christ (4:1/11). Cf. stay alert (*nēphō*) (1:13/4:7); love (one another) (1:22; 2:17; cf. 3:8); *oikonomoi* (4:10; cf. *oikos*, 2:5; *oiketai*, 2:18; *synoikeō*, 3:7); *charisma* (4:10; cf. *charis* 1:10, 13; 3:7); glory to God (4:11; cf. 2:12)

4:7–11/12–19	beloved/love (4:8/12); Christ (4:11/13, 14); glory, glorify (4:11/13, 14, 16); God (4:11/14, 16, 17, 19); end (*telos*) (4:7/17); sin, sinner (4:8/18; cf. 2:20, 22, 24; 3:18; 4:1). Cf. surprise (4:4/12); *symbainō* (4:4/12)
4:12–19/5:1–4	Christ (4:13, 14 / 5:1); sufferings (of Christ) (4:13/5:1); reveal (4:13/5:1); glory (4:13/5:1, 4); share(r) (*koinōneite/koinōnos*, 4:13/5:1); God (4:14, 16, 17, 18 / 5:2). Cf. also *poimanate, episkopountes* (5:2; cf. *poimena kai episkopon*, 2:25 and *archipoimenos*, 5:4); *poimnion* (5:2, 3; cf. *probata*, 2:25); *klēroi*, 5:3; cf. *klēronomia*, (1:4; *klēronomeō*, 3:9; *sygklēronomos*, 3:7); *typoi* (5:3; cf. *typos*, 3:21); *phaneroō* (5:4 cf. 1:20); *amarantinon* (5:4; cf. *amarantos*, 1:4)
5:1–4/5a	elders (5:1/5a)
5:1–5a/5b–11	God (5:2/5c, 6, 10–11); *hōs* phrases (5:5:3/8); Christ (5:1/10); suffering(s) (5:1/9, 10); all (*pas*) (5:5b/7, 10; cf. *pantes* + *de* marking conclusion, 5:5b/3:8); glory (5:1, 4/10).
5:5b–11/12–14	brotherhood/brother (5:9/12; cf. 2:17; brotherly love, 1:22; 3:8); briefly (*oligon*, 5:10/12); grace (5:12/5:5b, 10; cf. 1:2, 10. 13; 3:7, 10; 4:10), God (5:5b, 6, 10/12); *allēloi* (5:5b/14; cf. 1:22; 4:9); all (5:5b/5:14); in Christ (5:10/14; cf. 3:16).

(2) Link-words also are used to join verses *within* units and occasionally occur within inclusions:

1:1–2	Jesus Christ (1:1, 2)
1:3–12	you (1:4, 5/6–9/10–12); salvation (1:5/6–9/10–12); reveal (1:5, 6/12); exult (1:6, 8); glory (1:7/11); Christ (1:7/11, 12)
1:13–21	*dianoia/agnoia* (1:13, 14); *hōs* (1:14, 19); holy (15, 16); cf. *amōmos, aspilos*, 1:19); 1:13; God (1:21a,b)
2:1–3	*dolos/adolon* (2:1, 2)
2:4–10	stone(s) (2:4/5/6–8); God (2:4/10); rejected (2:4/7c); elect (2:4/6/9); *entimos/timē* (2:4, 6/7); you (2:5/7a/9–10); priestly community (2:5, 9); holy (2:5, 9); set (2:6, 8); people (2:9, 10)
2:11–12	*hōs* (2:11, 12)
2:13–17	*eite* (2:13b, 14a); emperor (2:13/17); *hōs* (2:13, 14, 16 [3×]); God (2:15, 16, 17)
2:18–20	*hypo*-terms (*hypotassomenoi*, 2:18; *hypopherei*, 2:19; *hypomeneite*, 2:20c,d); *touto* (2:19a/20f); God (2:19, 20); suffer (2:19, 20); creditable (2:19, 20f; cf. *kleos*, 2:20a)
2:21–25	who, whose (Christ) (2:22, 23, 24a,d); sin (2:22, 24a,b); *dikaiōs, dikaiosynē* (2:23, 24); you (verb) (2:24d, 25; cf. 2:21)

3:1–6	wives (3:1/5); subordinate (*hypotassomenai*) to own husbands (3:1/5); cf. Sarah obeyed (*hypēkousen*) Abraham (3:6a)
3:7	*hōs* (3:7c,e)
3:8–9	bless, blessing (3:8c,d)
3:10–12	good (3:10b, 11a); evil (3:10c, 11, 12)
3:13–17	*kakōsōn/kakopoiountas* (3:13/17); right-good (3:13/16 [2×]) / do what is right (3:17); suffer (3:14/17); *phobos* (of humans, 3:14c / of God, 3:16)
3:18–22	Christ (3:18, 21); *peri, hyper* (3:18a,b); God (3:18c, 20, 20, 21, 22); *poreutheis* (3:19/22b); *diesōthēsan, sōizei* (3:20/21)
4:1–6	suffer in the flesh (4:1a,c); flesh (4:1a,c, 2, 6); humans vs. God (4:2, 6); *chronos* (4:2, 3); *krinai, krithōsi* (4:5, 6); *zōntas, zōsi* (4:5/6); dead (4:5/6)
4:7–11	*pas* (4:7, 8); *eis heautous, eis allēlous, eis heautous* (4:8, 9, 10); *diakonountes, diakonei* (4:10, 11); *charisma, charis* (4:10a,c); *eis tis lalei hōs, ei tis diakonei hōs* (4:11a,b); God (4:11a,b,c)
4:12–19	you (4:12, 13, 14, 15); Christ, Christian (4:13, 14, 16); sufferings, suffer (4:13, 15, 19); glory, glorify (4:13, 14, 16); if (4:14, 16, 17, 18); name (4:14, 16); God (4:14, 16, 17, 19); *apo* (4:17a,b)
5:1–4	Christ (5:2; cf. *archipoimenos*, 5:4); glory (5:2/4); God (5:2a,c); three antitheses (with *mē[de]/alla*, 5:2c,d; 5:3)
5:5–11	all (5:5b, 7, 10); you (5:5b, 6, 7, 8, 9,10,11); humility, humble (5:5b,c, 6); *hoti* (5:5c, 7b); God (5:5c, 6–7, 10); grace (5:5c, 10); powerful, power (5:6, 11); sufferings, suffer (5:9, 11)
5:12–14	you (5:12, 13, 14); I (5:12 b,c); greet (5:13, 14); Silvanus, a faithful *brother*; co-elect (*brotherhood*); Mark my *son* (5:12, 13).

4. Literary Structure and Outline

The various compositional devices listed above, taken together, indicate the following subunits of the letter: 1:1–2; 1:3–12; 1:13–21; 1:22–2:3; 2:4–10; 2:11–12; 2:13–17; 2:18–25; 3:1–7; 3:8–12; 3:13–17; 3:18–22; 4:1–6; 4:7–11; 4:12–19; 5:1–5:5a; 5:5b–11; 5:12–14. These passages, however, are not independent units of thought lacking literary connection or logical coherence (against Bigg 1902, 6; Brox 1986, 35–36). A smoothly flowing continuity of thought is effected especially through link-words joining subunits and through repetitions of key themes.

1 Peter 1:1–2 and 5:12–14 form the epistolary framework of the composition, employing vocabulary and announcing key themes developed in the body of the letter (against Von Harnack 1898; Marxsen 1979; and others who claim that 1:1–2 and 5:12–14 were later additions to the composition with no thematic connections to the body of the letter).

The body of the letter (1:3–5:11) opens with an affirmation of the collective identity and divinely conferred dignity of the believing community as the elect and holy household of God (1:3–2:10) brought into being by God's mercy (1:3; 2:10).

In 2:11–5:11 the conduct of this community and its several groups of members in society is addressed, with a consistent focus on the need for honorable, upright behavior and doing what is right in the face of hostility, abuse, and undeserved suffering.

In this second major section of the letter, 2:11–12 serves as a major transitional unit or hinge. These two verses reiterate key ideas of 1:3–2:10 (cf. 1:1, 9, 14–16, 17, 22; 2:1, 9) while at the same time shifting to an hortatory tone and stating a general principle and chief goal of Christian conduct (avoidance of evil, maintaining honorable conduct among nonbelievers to the glory of God) that is then developed in the specific exhortations that follow (2:13–5:11). They are thus "at once resumptive and prefatory" (Selwyn 1947, 169), providing a logical transition from what has previously been stated concerning the identity of the holy people of God to exhortation concerning the holy and honorable conduct (*anastrophē kalē, kala erga*, 2:12) of God's household in a hostile (*katalalousin hymōn hōs kakopoiōn*, 2:12) society, details of which are contained in virtually all the subunits of 2:13–5:11.

Although 2:13–17 introduces a specific subunit on responsibility in the civic realm and the theme of "subordination" not mentioned in 2:11–12, some scholars would see 2:12 and 5:11 ("glorify God," "glory of God") forming a major inclusion framing 2:11–5:11. Others detect a major section in 2:11–4:11 marked and framed by this same theme of glorification as well as other alleged correspondences (*paroikous/oikonomoi*; *kalēn . . . kalōn/kaloi*; *katalalousin/lalei*). Still others see 2:11–4:19 as forming a major section, with 5:1 (*parakalō*) and its direct address mirroring 2:11 and marking a new and final section (5:1–11). 1 Peter 2:13–17, however, clearly forms a new and distinct subunit of thought distinguished from 2:11–12 and introduces a theme of subordination, which extends from 2:13 through 3:7 and is resumed again in 5:5a. (For surveys of the various proposals concerning the major divisions of the letter, see Bosetti 1990, 21–29; Cervantes Gabarrón 1991a, 23–53; and T. W. Martin 1992a, 3–39, 277–84.)

The lack of consensus on the major divisions of the latter half of the letter ultimately is of minor importance, however, since its general line of thought in any event is patently clear.

After 1 Pet 2:11–12, which sets the hortatory mood and focus for what follows, 2:13–3:12 urges the doing of what is right and respect for order in the civil

(2:13–17) and domestic (2:18–25; 3:1–7) realms, with the entire community then addressed in 3:8–12.

1 Peter 3:13–17 continues the focus on upright behavior and doing what is right, with hostile opposition and innocent suffering now moving to the foreground of attention. This exhortation is supported by a Christological statement (3:18–22), repeating the pattern employed earlier in 2:18–20 supported by 2:21–25. In 4:1–6 our author draws out the implications of 3:18–22 for the moral behavior of the believers vis-à-vis Gentile outsiders and in 4:7–11 then urges conduct supportive of the internal cohesion of the community.

1 Peter 4:12–19, which introduces the final part of the body of the letter (4:12–5:11), presents a constellation of reasons for regarding suffering not as something alien to Christians but as a reason for joy and an opportunity to glorify God. 1 Peter 5:1–5a treats the specific responsibilities of elders/shepherds-overseers and subordinate younger persons in the faith for maintaining the unity of the community. 1 Pet 5:5b–11 directs attention once again to the entire community (cf. 3:8–12), all of whose members are urged to humble themselves before the God of grace, resist the Devil, and trust in God's power and care. 1 Peter 5:12–14 constitutes the epistolary conclusion of the letter, matching the prescript of 1:1–2, and reiterates earlier themes affirming the familial solidarity of the letter's senders and addressees.

AN OUTLINE OF 1 PETER

The following is an outline taking into consideration the several subunits, thematic clusters, and likely major divisions of the letter:[20]

1:1–2	Epistolary Prescript
1:3–2:10	By God's Mercy Believers are Reborn an Elect and Holy People
1:3–12	Praise to God for the Saving Benefits of His Mercy
1:13–21	The Hope and Holy Conduct of the Children of God
1:21–25	Familial Love and Rebirth through the Word of the Gospel
2:1–3	Renunciation of Evil; Nourishment and Growth through the Word
2:4–10	Election and Rejection: Christ, Believers, Nonbelievers; Consolidation and Honor of the Household of God

[20] For varying proposals regarding the structure of 1 Peter see Holzmeister 1937, 165–72; Selwyn 1947, 4–6; Reicke 1964, 75; Dalton 1965, 72–86 / 1989, 93–108; Chevallier 1971; Frederick 1975, 17–18; Manke 1975; Combrink 1975; Elliott 1979, 17–22; 1981/1990, 234–36; 1982, 67–70; Balch 1981, 123–31; Volpi 1984; Antoniotti 1985; Talbert 1986; Frankemölle 1987, 20–23; Michaels 1988, xxxiv–vii; Reichert 1989, 103–43; Schutter 1989, 19–84; Bosetti 1990, 30–45; Thurén 1990, 126–63, 1995, 88–183; van Rensburg 1990; Cervantes Gabarrón 1991a, 53–112, 417–34; Feldmeier 1992, 133–51; T. W. Martin 1992a, 41–267; Goppelt 1993, vi–viii, 20–21.

2:11–12	Transition: Aliens and Strangers Are to Maintain Honorable Conduct among the Gentiles to the Glory of God
2:13–3:12	Honorable Subordinate Conduct in Civil and Domestic Realms
2:13–17	Honorable Subordinate Conduct in the Civil Realm
2:18–25	Honorable Subordinate Conduct in the Domestic Realm: Household Servants and the Servant of God
3:1–7	Honorable Subordinate Conduct in the Domestic Realm: Subordinate Wives (3:1–6) and Respectful Husbands
3:8–12	Honorable Conduct in Civil and Domestic Realms: Concluding Exhortation to All
3:13–4:6	Doing What Is Right in the Face of Hostility
3:13–17	Doing What Is Right despite Innocent Suffering
3:18–22	Christ the Suffering Righteous One: His Suffering, Death and Resurrection as the Basis for Believers' Salvation and Vindication
4:1–6	Obedience to God's Will Distinguishes Suffering Believers from Sinful Outsiders; God's Condemnation of Sinners and Vindication of the Faithful
4:7–11	Maintaining the Solidarity of the Household of God to the Glory of God
4:12–5:11	Joy and Solidarity in Suffering, Commmunal Unity, and Trust in God
4:12–19	Suffering and Doing What Is Right as Joyous Solidarity with Christ and Honor with God
5:1–5a	Maintaining the Unity of the Community: Responsible Elders and Subordinate Younger Persons
5:5b–11	The Mutual Humility of All, Resisting the Devil, and Trusting in the Power and Care of God
5:12–14	Epistolary Postscript

In conclusion, these features of the letter's vocabulary, style, and disposition of thought reveal a compositional consistency and an author who had a facile command of Koine Greek and skill at persuasive argumentation and epistolary composition. While the quality of the writing does not quite match that of Hebrews or the Gospel of Luke, its author "was quite awake to the difference between good Greek and bad, and used the language with freedom and a not inconsiderable degree of correctness" (Bigg 1902, 5). The tone of the letter is pastoral in character, involving a skillful blending of exhortation and consolation in accord with its stated purpose (5:12). While manifesting acquaintance with the conventions of rhetoric and epistolary composition, the letter is animated more by the passion of a preacher with an eye on the audience than by the artistry of a composer of a literary epistle (Moffatt 1918, 322). The extent to which these aspects of vocabulary, style, and composition have a bearing on the identity of the author is discussed below in conjunction with the issue of authorship.

5. THE ADDRESSEES AND THEIR SITUATION

5.1. THE GEOGRAPHICAL LOCATION OF THE ADDRESSEES

The initial words of the letter's prescript (1:1) indicate its address to persons residing in Asia Minor (modern-day Turkey), an early beachhead of the messianic movement in the Mediterranean Diaspora and the place of its most extensive early growth.[21] (See Map 1).

The five names of the address (Pontus, Galatia, Cappadocia, Asia, Bithynia) designate not regions but Roman provinces (Elliott 1981/1990, 60) located mainly west of the Halys River and north of the Taurus Mountains that stretch east–west across the territory formerly known as Anatolia, with Bithynia-Pontus united by the Romans as a single province. The amount of territory covered by these provinces is approx. 129,000 square miles, about the size of the state of Montana; thus, 1 Peter is addressed to a larger area than any other letter of the NT, with James (see its vaguely formulated address, "to the twelve tribes in the Diaspora," 1:1) constituting the only possible exception. For this reason, both 1 Peter and James are classified among the "general" or "catholic" letters of the NT (James, 1–2 Peter, 1–3 John, Jude), though they still constitute particular messages for particular audiences facing particular sets of cirumstances.

These lands were formerly territories and independent kingdoms of Anatolia that, in the course of Rome's eastward military expansion from 133 BCE onward, were progressively subdued, annexed, and constituted as Roman provinces. By 17 CE, this vast amount of territory, comprising a population of approximately 8,500,000 (see Broughton 1938, 812–16), had been organized into four Roman provinces with Bithynia and Pontus united as a single province in 65/63 BCE. The separate mention of Pontus and Bithynia is no indication that the names designated native regions rather than Roman provinces. In this case the omission of reference to the adjacent regions of Paphlagonia, Phrygia, Pisidia, and Lycaonia would be difficult to explain. Inscriptional evidence, moreover, attests the occasional independent mention of Bithynia and Pontus in references to groups of Asia Minor provinces (e.g., CIL 3.318, an

---

[21] On the geographical location of the addressees, see Hort 1898, 157–84; Selwyn 1947, 47–52; Beare 1970, 38–43; Puig Tarrech 1980, 116–19; Elliott 1981/1990, 59–65; cf. also Koester 1982b, 1, 20–22, 45–47. On the provinces of 1:1, their history, topography, economy, heterogeneous ethnic composition, and social life, see Ramsay 1893; J. Weiss 1901/1951; Mommsen 1909; Monumenta Asiae Minoris Antiqua 1928–1937; Broughton 1938; Calder and Keil 1939; A. H. M. Jones 1940, 27–29, 41–46, 67–72; Magie 1950; Rostovtzeff 1953, 1957; Eddy 1961; R. North 1963; Leipoldt 1966; Peters 1970; Bean 1971; Cramer 1971; Dewdney 1971; A. H. M. Jones 1971; Avi-Yonah 1978, 169–72; Sahin, Schwertheim, and Wagners, eds. 1978; Hemer 1912; Brixhe 1987; Mitchell 1993; Gill and Gempf 1994, 291–362, 377–95. For maps of Asia Minor and early Christianity, see Putzger 1961 (maps 16, 26–27, 28); Aharoni and Avi-Yonah 1968 (maps 183, 238, 263, 264); M. Grant 1971, 57–58, 60, 63, 70–71; A. H. M. Jones 1971, 28; Littell 1976, 10; Hammond 1981 (maps 26a, 28); Cornell and Matthew 1982, 107, 150–55; May 1984, 52–53, 82–83, 88–89, 90–91.

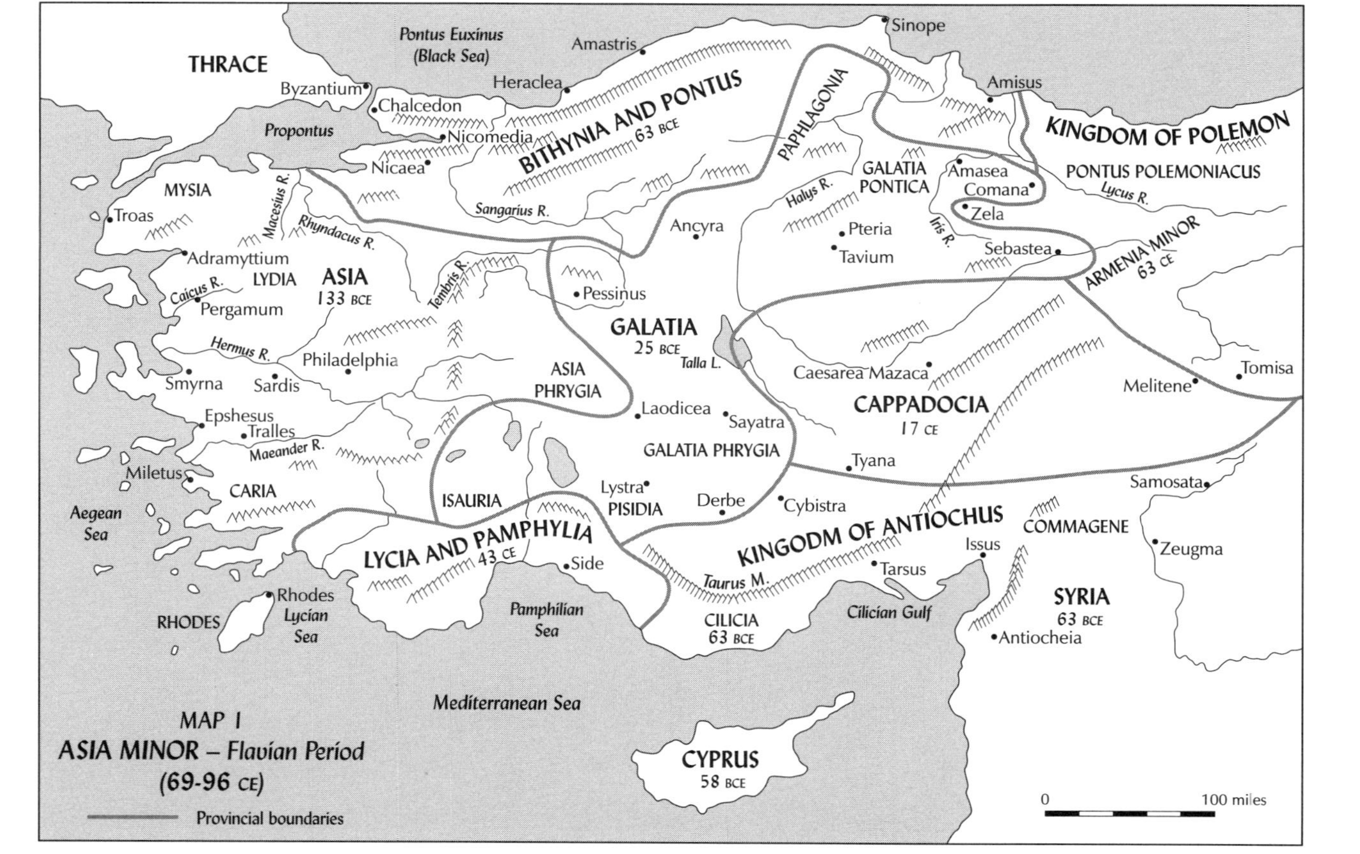

MAP I
ASIA MINOR – *Flavian Period*
(69-96 CE)

inscription on a milestone of the road from Ancyra to Doryleum, [dated July 80–June 81 CE]) referring to roads constructed by Titus and Domitian: ". . . vias provinciarum Galatiae, Cappadociae, Ponti, Pisidiae, Paphlagoniae, Lycaoniae, Armeniae Minoris staverunt"; note also CIL 3.249: ". . . ASIAM BITHYN GALAT CAPPODOC LYCIAM PAMPHL CILIC CYPRUM PONTUM PAPHLAG," referring to Asia, Bithynia, Galatia, Cappodocia, Lycia, Pamphilia, Cilicia, Cyprus, Pontus, and Paphlagonia. Strabo's description of the geography and history of Asia Minor (*Geogr.*, books 12–14) makes it clear that the Taurus Mountain range extending from east to west across the southern expanse of Asia Minor was a determining factor of geographical and political boundaries. The provinces included in 1 Peter 1:1 and the omission of the provinces of Lycia and Pamphilia south of this mountain indicate that the letter was sent to the totality of Christian communities residing in the whole of Roman Asia Minor north and west of the Taurus.

The successive subjection of these areas to Persian, then Greek, then Roman rule contributed to the cultural diversity of this region but failed to achieve any political or cultural unification of the territories. The provinces of Asia and Bithynia-Pontus had shorelines bordering on the Aegean and Black Seas, respectively, and ports that were open to sea trade and travelers from Italy and other points to the west and south. By contrast, the territories of Galatia and Cappadocia featured a central plateau and a wild mountainous interior where Hellenization and Romanization had made little headway. Cities, moreover, the primary institution through which Greek and Roman culture was established, receive no mention in this letter. The diverse topography of this area of Asia Minor and the abundance of natural boundaries (mountains, rivers, lakes, forests) helped to perpetuate its economic, political, and cultural heterogeneity down through late antiquity. The inland territory relied on an economy of farming, herding, and mining. Villages and forts dotted the landscape, along with imperial and royal domains. In contrast to the littoral areas, the interior was relatively sparsely populated. Christianity made its headway mostly in villages and household communities (on the rural conditions presupposed in 1 Peter, see Puig Tarrech, 1980, esp. 395–97; and Elliott 1981/1990, 59–65).

Bithynia, named after a Thracian tribe, was situated in the northeastern corner of Asia Minor and bordered on the Propontis and the south shore of the Black Sea. Ruled earlier by local dynasts, it initially had maintained its independence after the conquest of Asia Minor by Alexander the Great. Its chief cities of Nicomedia and Prusa were founded in the third century BCE. After decades of Roman intervention, this region was ceded to Rome by Nicomedes III in 74 BCE. Under Pompey (63 BCE) it was joined with Pontus to the east to form a single province (Bithynia-Pontus). It was rich in luxuriant forests and quarries of precious stones; in addition to timber for shipbuilding, agriculture, fishing, and trade were mainstays of its economy. 1 Peter provides the earliest attestation of Christians in Bithynia (-Pontus).

Pontus lay adjacent to the eastern border of Bithynia and likewise constituted a portion of the north coast of Asia Minor bordering on the Black Sea.

Some coastal cities had been founded by the Greeks in the sixth century BCE (Amisos, Sinope, Kotyora, Kerasus, Trapezus); its hinterland had been ruled by Iranian-Persian princes. Its population was a mixture of natives, Iranians, and Greeks, where Hellenization made only slow and partial headway. The kingdom of Pontus, founded by Mithridates I (301 BCE), was gradually expanded by his successors. Initial friendly relations between the kings of Pontus and Rome eventually degenerated into hostility and decades of war under the leadership of Mithridates VI Eupator Dionysius (120–63 BCE). Following Pompey's victory in 63 BCE, this territory was annexed and divided by Rome. A western section was combined with Bithynia to form the single Roman province of Bithynia-Pontus. Other parts of Pontus were annexed to Galatia (*Pontus Galaticus*) or Cappadocia (*Pontus Cappadociacus*). In 37 BCE, much of eastern coastal Pontus was given to Polemon as puppet king. Later reorganizations of these territories took place under Vespasian (72 CE) and Trajan (ca. 107/113 CE; cf. Magie 1950, 1:491–96, 574–75; 2:1349–56, 1435–39; and Broughton 1938, 597; Elliott 1981/1990, 91).

Israelites from Pontus who were pilgrims in Jerusalem at Pentecost in the early 30s heard Peter's proclamation of the gospel (Acts 2:9) and perhaps were among the first believers to spread the gospel in Pontus. Pontus was the birthplace of Aquila (and probably of his wife, Priscilla, Acts 18:2–3), both early believers. This famous couple traveled widely throughout the Mediterranean, with residences in Rome (Acts 18:2; Rom 16:3), Ephesus (1 Cor 16:19; 2 Tim 4:19) and Corinth (Acts 18:1–3). They were already adherents of the Jesus movement prior to Paul's arrival in Corinth, where they labored together as leather-workers (ca. 53–55 CE, Acts 18:2–3). Along with the Pentecost pilgrims, they provide evidence of the early spread of the Jesus movement in the north of Asia Minor, independent of the Pauline mission. Half a century later, Pliny the Younger, an imperial legate of Trajan charged with ordering affairs in Bithynia-Pontus, encountered persons denounced to him as "Christians" and exchanged correspondence with his emperor concerning the handling of the situation (Pliny, *Ep.* 10.96–97). By this time, Pliny noted, Christianity had spread throughout the towns and the countryside of Pontus (*Ep.* 10.96.9–10). Later in the second century, Lucian (*Alex.* 25.38) speaks of the large number of Christians in Pontus, and Dionysius, bishop of Corinth, addressed one letter to "the church at Amastris and others in Pontus" and another to the church of Nicomedia. Sinope in Pontus was also the home of the notorious Marcion (Eusebius, *Hist. eccl.* 4.23.185–86). (On Bithynia-Pontus under Roman rule, see Sherwin-White 1966, 525–29; and on the Pliny-Trajan correspondence, see the NOTES on 1 Pet 4:12–19.)

Southwest of Pontus lay the inland territory of Galatia. Galatia took its name from the Celts or "Gauls" (*Galatikai*) who, at the height of Celtic power and expansion, had migrated into this region from Europe across the Hellespont in 278 BCE. Its three main tribes were the Trocmi, Tectosages, and Tolistobogii. From 189 BCE onward, Rome increased its control over the Galatians and eventually annexed their territory in 25 BCE. Galatian tribal organization and its chief centers at Ancyra, Tavium, and Pessinus were little influenced by Hellenization and urbanization. Here even "towns were uncommon" (A. H. M. Jones 1971, 181). This was an area populated by a "rustic people" with "no taste for town life" (Jones 1971, 117). A Christian presence here in the mid-50s is clear from Paul's letter to the Galatians, in which, it is noteworthy, no mention of cities occurs, contrary to virtually all of Paul's other letters. Thus Galatians, like the later 1 Peter, suggests a rural rather than urban location of the Christians in this province.

South and east of Galatia lay Cappadocia, the easternmost region of the Anatolian highlands. Cappadocia had earlier been the site, along with Pontus, of the ancient Hittite Empire. Under later Persian rule, these regions were divided into large estates controlled by feudal lords or temple estates that served as centers of worship of Iranian deities. Still later it came under the control of Perdiccas, one of Alexander's successors, but remained the least Hellenized and urbanized of all the Anatolian territories. Eventually also conquered by Pompey, it was made a vassal kingdom of Rome and subsequently, following the death of its last king, Archelaus, a Roman province (17 CE). From 72 CE until the reign of Trajan (98–117 CE), together with Pontus, Galatia, and Paphlagonia, it was under the administration of a Roman legate. The presence there of military forts attested its strategic importance to Rome as a buffer zone against the Parthians to the east. Much of Cappadocia consisted of an inaccessible plateau and volcanic ranges. Agriculture and herding were the chief bases of its economy. Israelite pilgrims from Pontus were also among those in Jerusalem for the Pentecost festival and Peter's address (Acts 2:9). Similar to Bithynia and Pontus, there is no record of any Pauline activity in Cappadocia.

Asia was the most intensively Hellenized and urbanized of all of the provinces named in 1 Pet 1:1. In the third and second centuries BCE, Pergamum had been the most important kingdom of Anatolia. Ruled by the Attalids, this territory was eventually ceded by testament to Rome by its last king, Attalus III Philometor (138–133 BCE) and was made a Roman province in 133 BCE. Rich in cities, natural resources, trade and commerce, and industries, including textile, dye, and other factories manned by royal slaves, Asia became one of Rome's principal sources of revenue and power in Asia Minor. Huge war indemnities were imposed following the insurrections of Mithridates, as well as the decuma (1/10th of all produce) and other penalties and taxes. (On the Roman exploitation of Asia Minor, see Dickey 1928). Among the provinces mentioned in 1 Peter, Asia was the primary site of the Pauline mission in western Asia Minor, though Israelite Pentecost pilgrims (Acts 2:9) may also have played some role in the missionizing of Asia.

The population of these provinces included natives (local aristocrats, administrators, and ordinary citizens), freed persons (former slaves who had been manumitted [*liberti*]), a massive number of slaves (*douloi, oiketai, servi*), as well as a sizable number of resident aliens (*paroikoi, metoikoi, katoikoi*), strangers passing through (*parepidēmoi, xenoi*), a small number of Roman officials and military veterans, and numerous Israelite communities that had been accorded special rights and privileges (living according to their own law, grants of land for farming and viticulture, exemption from tithes on produce, and the protected right to send an annual temple tax to Jerusalem; cf. Josephus, *Ant.* Books 14, 16). Population figures for these provinces are difficult to determine. Broughton (1938, 812–16; table on p. 815) proposed a total population of 8,500,000; Reicke (1968, 302–12), on the other hand, reckoned, less convincingly, with half this total. Here in Asia Minor, as in Syria and Egypt, Diaspora Israelites were particularly numerous (ca. 1 million), and evidence of their presence in both urban and rural areas is abundant (Philo, *Legat.* 245, 280–82, 314–15; Josephus, *Ant.* 12.119, 125, 129, 147–53; 14.213–64; 16.6; 1 Macc. 15:22–23; *Sib. Or.* 3:271; cf. also Acts, the Pauline letters, and Revelation).[22]

In regard to the number of Christians in Asia Minor, Reicke (1968, 302–4) envisions a growth from approximately 40,000 before 67 CE to more than 80,000 after the year 100 CE. This is a conservative figure, however, based on a minimal total population estimate. In any case, it is clear that it was Asia Minor where the Jesus mission established an early and substantial beachhead. It is also clear that it was the extensive dispersion of Israelites in Asia Minor that provided the starting point and communication network of the Christian mission there, and enabled its rapid growth. Parallel to the campaigns of Paul initiated among the communities of Galatia and Asia, it may have been Cappadocian, Pontic, and Asian Israelites returning from their Pentecost pilgrimage (Acts 2) who first brought the messianic message to their compatriots at home. Selwyn notes that

> an excellent road ran from the Cilician Gates northwards through Cappadocia and Galatia to Amisus on the Euxine, probably the first city on that coast to receive the Gospel; and at Mazaca (Caesarea [in Cappadocia]) it crossed another fine route which the enterprise of Ephesian traders had utilized so effectively as to direct the commerce of Cappadocia from Sinope [on the Black Sea coast] to their own Levantine sea-board. Syrian Antioch occupied a key position in relation to both routes; and we can be sure that the Christian Church there would lose little time in following up with a more thorough evangelization the trail of the Gospel first blazed by the returning pilgrims. (Selwyn 1947, 46)

By the time of 1 Peter, however, recruits from among the Gentiles probably had begun to outnumber their Israelite counterparts. More is said in the letter about the past history of the former, and it is upon the difficulties that these

---

[22] For treatments of the Israelite Diaspora, including specific references to Asia Minor, see Galanté 1937–1939; von Harnack 1908/1962, 1–18; Juster 1914, 1:188–94; Applebaum 1974a, 420–63; Blanchetière 1974; Safrai 1974, 184–215; Stern 1974, 117–83; Tcherikover 1974, 287–89; Trebilco 1991a; Feldman 1993, 69–74.

former pagans were having in the termination of previous associations that the letter particularly focuses (1:14–16, 18–19; 2:9–10, 11–12; 4:1–6, 12–19).[23]

This evidence concerning the geographical location of the addressees has significant implications for the letter in general (Elliott 1981/1990, 64–65):

(1) The vast expanse of territory mentioned in 1:1, some 129,000 square miles, presupposes an *extensive expansion of the Christian mission* following the activity of Paul and prior to the composition of 1 Peter.

(2) The predominantly *rural* feature of the provinces other than Asia and the absence of any mention of cities point to the rural location of the letter's addressees, who formed pockets of households dispersed across the landscape of Asia Minor. This is consistent with the absence of the term *ekklesia*, so basic a concept in Paul's urban mission, and with the prominence given the image of the household in this letter. This marks 1 Peter as a notable exception to the generalization that early Christianity everywhere constituted an "urban phenomenon."

(3) The *situation* of the addressees, particularly of those in the interior of Asia Minor, cannot be assumed to be that confronted by Christians in the cities and Hellenized province of Asia, as reflected in the writings of Paul, the Revelation of John, and Acts. In the inland and highland areas, the social tension between Christians and natives instead would have been typical of the animosity regularly directed by natives against displaced and foreign outsiders, with Rome playing no role at all.

(4) The several aspects of the diversity characterizing these provinces historically, geographically, politically, ethnically, and culturally suggest the inevitable *heterogeneity* of the communities addressed. A movement with members of diverse regions, cultures, and religious backgrounds presents the practical challenge of establishing some sense of a singular social identity and promoting an effective measure of social cohesion. Hostility from the natives and pressure to conform to local standards of comportment would have made this challenge even more critical. The letter's stress on the common identity and solidarity of the Christian brotherhood can be seen as an attempt to address this issue.

(5) These factors decisively differentiate the addressees of 1 Peter from the mission field of Paul. Paul did not campaign at all in Bithynia-Pontus or Cappadocia; he worked in and wrote to urban, not rural, communities; and his earlier mission of the 50s reached only a partial amount of the territory circumscribed by 1 Pet 1:1.

(6) The *sequence of the names* mentioned in 1:1 is unusual in that it commences with Pontus and concludes with Bithynia, though Bithynia-Pontus actually formed a single province. The separate mention of Pontus and Bithynia

---

[23] On early Christianity in Asia Minor, see Ramsay 1904; von Harnack 1908, 2:182–229; Dickey 1928; Streeter 1929, 99–136; Foakes-Jackson and Lake, eds. 1933, vol. 5; S. E. Johnson 1958, 1972, 1975; Bauer 1971, 61–94; Littell 1976 (maps 4, 6, 7, 10); H. P. Müller 1976; Hemer 1979; Oster 1992.

could reflect popular usage; see Acts 16:7 (Bithynia) and 18:2 (Pontus). Mention of both portions of the united province here, however, together with their separation and sequence, has prompted the plausible suggestion that this reflected the *circular route* taken by the courier, Silvanus, in the delivery of the letter.

This proposal, advanced by Hort, following a suggestion of Ewald (1870), was accepted by later commentators including Moffatt (1918, 327), Selwyn (1947, 47, indicating possible roads used); Elliott (1981/1990, 60), and Hemer (1978). Commencing his journey at some point in Pontus (Sinope according to Hort, but Hemer's case for Amisus is more persuasive), Silvanus then would have proceeded south through contiguous parts of Galatia (Amisus to Amasea) and Cappadocia (Amasea to Caesarea Mazaca), then turned westward toward Asia along one of the interior trade routes (Caesarea Mazaca to Sardis), and finally northward to reach the Christians in Bithynia (Sardis to Nicomedia). Commencement of the delivery route at Pontus in northern and eastern Asia Minor, a location remote from any place of activity of the Apostle Peter, is best explained by the likelihood that the letter's courier had arrived there by ship. If, as is probable, "Babylon" in 5:13 stands for Rome, the locality of Peter's final ministry, then it would have been a sea voyage from Rome that would have brought the courier, Silvanus, to this point of disembarkation. It was a similar voyage by sea that took Pliny the Younger from Rome to Asia Minor when he undertook his responsibilities in Bithynia-Pontus (Pliny, *Ep.* 10.15–17). For Mediterranean trade routes by sea and land, see MAP 2.

Upon completing his journey in Bithynia, Silvanus would have returned to Italy and Rome via ship from one of the ports of Bithynia such as Nicomedia (cf. also Puig Tarrech 1980, 118–19). For Silvanus' journey from and to Rome and his circular route within Asia Minor, see MAP 3.

Though based only on circumstantial evidence, this theory regarding the route taken by Silvanus has considerable merit. It is compatible with the theory of the origin of the letter in the city of Rome and with the sea and land routes one would have taken when traveling from Rome to Pontus, from Pontus to provinces lying south and west, and finally from Bithynia back to Rome. Second, it explains why Pontus and Bithynia are separated and mentioned first and last in the letter's address. Third, this route through several provinces is consonant with the general, rather than personalized, content of the letter, which addresses a general condition affecting numerous segments of the messianic movement in Asia Minor north of the Taurus Mountains. Finally, this proposed route is consistent with the fact that Cilicia, Lycia, and Pamphylia are not included in the address, since they lie primarily to the south of the Taurus range. Beare's claim (1970, 42–43) that Pontus and Bithynia were mentioned first and last in the list to give them prominence as the "storm centre" of anti-Christian persecution in Trajan's time is hardly a cogent counterproposal, since it rests on the unfounded premises of the letter's composition during Trajan's reign (98–117 CE) and of a Rome-sponsored persecution of Christians at this time (see below, under 5.3. SITUATION).

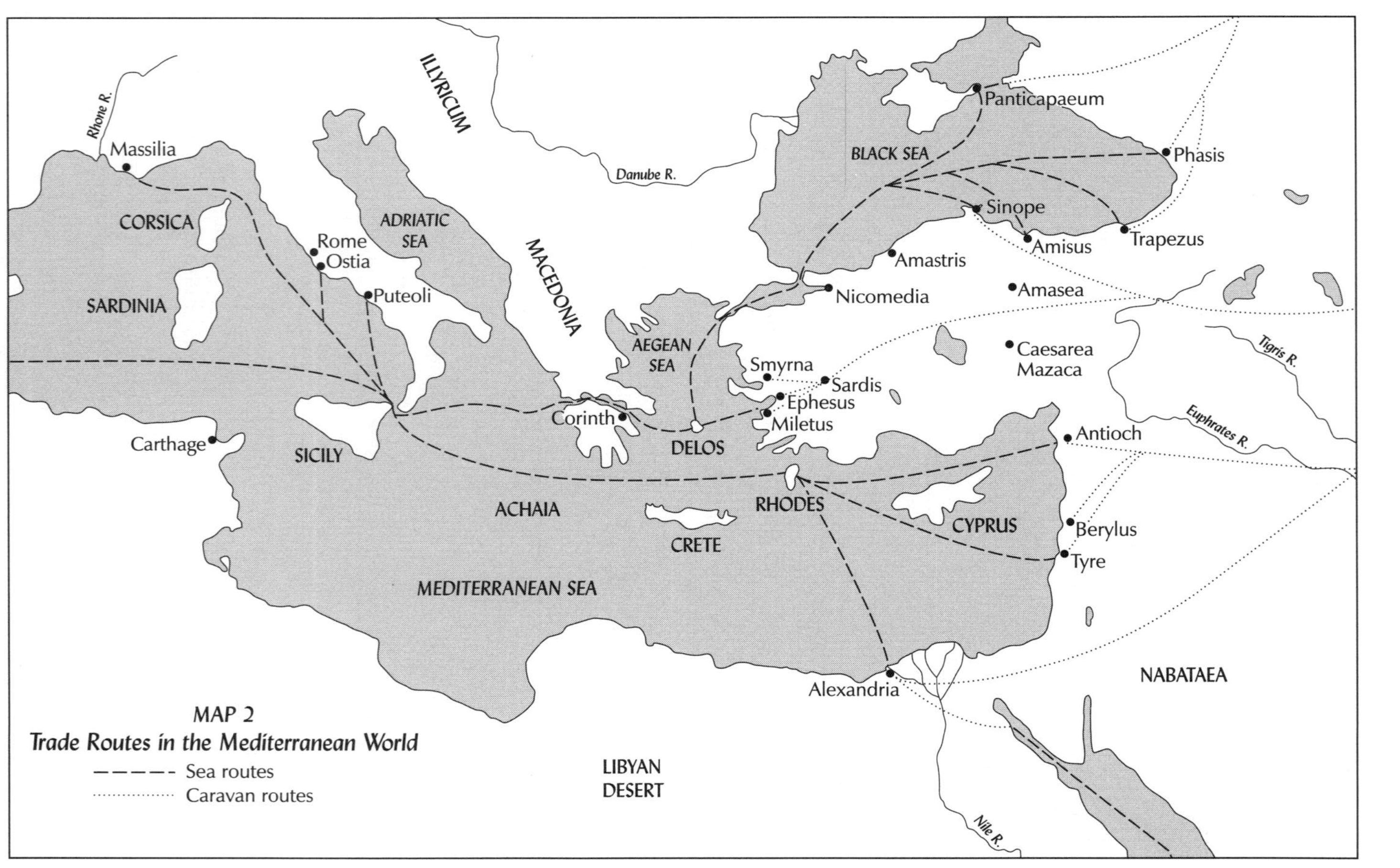

MAP 2

Trade Routes in the Mediterranean World

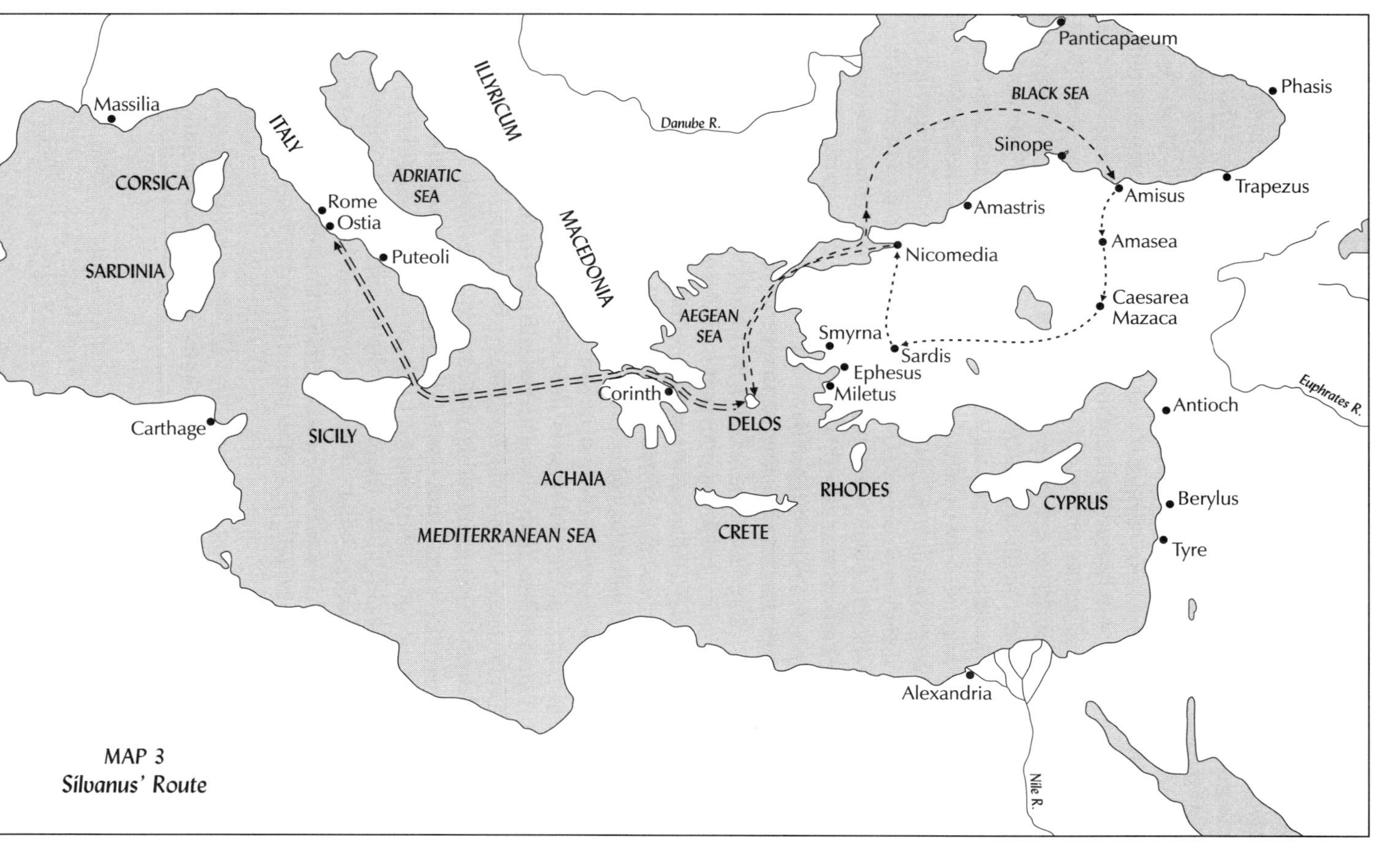

MAP 3
Silvanus' Route

5.2. THE PERSONS AND GROUPS ADDRESSED: A SOCIAL PROFILE

In comparison with the *explicit* information on the geographical location of the addressees, information on the personal and social identity of the addressees is at best *inferential* and reflective of what the author presumes to know concerning his hearers/readers and their situation.[24] Here we can speak at most of the "implied" readers—that is, the readers as presupposed and construed by the author and as indicated in the following data of the letter.

(1) The addressees are presumed to be "strangers" and "resident aliens" in the areas they inhabit (1:1, 17; 2:11; see the respective NOTES). This designation indicates that their political, legal, and social situation was a precarious one, similar to the multitude of the déclassé and homeless strangers, who lacked, or were deprived of, local citizenship and its privileges (Rostovtzeff 1957, 1:345–46; Elliott 1981/1990, 67–72). *Paroikoi*, "by-dwellers," were distinguished legally from complete strangers (*xenoi*) and belonged to an institutionalized class ranked socially below the citizen population and above freed-persons, slaves, and complete strangers (Dickey 1928, 406; Rostovtzeff 1957, 1:236–37). In addition to natives dispossessed of their lands which were annexed to expanding cities, this group included strangers from abroad (tradespersons, artisans, teachers, and traveling missionaries) who had taken up residence for more than thirty days. Excluded from voting and landholding privileges as well as from the chief civic offices and honors, they enjoyed only limited legal protection, were restricted in regard to intermarriage, commerce, transmission of property, and land tenure, could be pressed into military service, and were susceptible to severer forms of civil and criminal punishment. While allowed limited participation in local cultic rites, they were excluded from priestly offices, but still shared full responsibility with the citizenry for all financial burdens, such as tribute, taxes, and production quotas (Elliott 1981/1990, 35–37, 67–69). Their different languages, clothing, customs, religious traditions, and foreign roots set these aliens apart and exposed them to suspicion and hostility on the part of the native population and to charges of wrongdoing and conduct injurious to the well-being of the commonwealth and the favor of the gods. As resident aliens, the addressees of 1 Peter were exposed to such charges (2:11–12, 15; 3:16; 4:12–14, 15), and thus their condition of *paroikia* (1:17) accounts for much of the suffering with which this letter is concerned (see also the NOTES on 1:1, 17, and 2:11).

(2) Certain portions of the letter have all the addressees in mind (1:1–2; 1:3–2:10; 3:8–12; 3:13–4:11; 5:5b–11). On the other hand, the author reckons

[24] On the people addressed, their ethnic, social, and cultural composition and status, and their religious identity and formation as a conversionist sect, see Elliott 1981/1990, 59–118; see also Selwyn 1947, 42–47; Best 1971, 14–20; Puig Tarrech 1980, 119–29, 395–97; Lamau 1988, 81–105; Michaels 1988, xlv–lv.

also with the existence of specific groups, for whom he has specific instructions: free persons (2:13–17; cf. *hōs eleutheroi*, 2:16); domestic slaves (2:18–20) but no reciprocal group of owners/masters; wives with nonbelieving husbands (3:1–6); husbands with believing wives (3:7); community elders/leaders (5:1–5a); and recent converts (5:5b). From the minimal evidence in 1 Peter, it is impossible to determine how many of these free persons may have enjoyed local provincial or Roman citizenship. In any case, such citizenship would not have been enjoyed by any of the addressees who were strangers and resident aliens in the literal sense. It was only in the year 212 CE that the emperor Caracalla conferred Roman citizenship on all free persons of the empire. On the little that can be inferred concerning their economic status and modes of employment, see Elliott 1981/1990, 69–72.

(3) All of the addressees are presumed to be believers in Jesus Christ, called and elected by God, sanctified by the divine Spirit, redeemed by Jesus Christ (1:1, 3–5, 10–12, 14–16, 17–21, 22–25; 2:2–3, 4a, 5, 7, 9–10; etc.), who entered the community through conversion and baptism (3:21; cf. 1:3, 22–23; 2:2), were committed to obedience to God's will (1:2; 2:15; 3:17; 4:2, 19), and anticipated the final revelation of Jesus Christ (1:7, 13; 4:13; 5:1). As such they belonged to the messianic movement originating within Israel, but at present they were distinguished from other Israelite groups by the demeaning label "Christian" (4:16).

(4) They were presumed not to be eyewitnesses of Jesus (1:8) but to have been evangelized through missionaries other than the senders of the letter (1:12, 25).

(5) An *ethnically mixed audience* is also presumed, comprising persons of both Israelite and pagan origin. The Israelite origin of some is indicated by

- the preponderance of concepts, terms, and images drawn from Israel's Scripture and tradition: the concepts of election (1:1; 2:4–10; 5:13) and holiness or purity (1:2, 14–16, 22; 2:5, 9; 3:5); the numerous allusions to the Passover and the exodus ("gird loins," 1:13; *paroikia*, 1:17; cf. 2:11; redemption, 1:18–19; lamb, 1:19; Exod 19:5–6 in 2:4–10); the story of Hosea (2:10); the Israelite use of the terms "Diaspora" (1:1) and "Babylon" (5:13)
- the conception of the believers' "inheritance" as permanent and undefiled in contrast to the defiled land of Israel (1:4)
- mention of OT prophets and their inquiry concerning the Christ, with a stress on the believers as recipients of the good news of salvation in contrast to these prophets (1:10–12)
- mention of Sarah and Abraham (3:6) and allusion to Abraham in 2:12 with the phrase "resident aliens and visiting strangers" (recalling Gen 23:4, known to Israelites but lost on Gentiles)
- reference to the holy matriarchs of Israel as models of conduct (3:5) and identification of the female believers as "children of Sarah" (3:6)
- reference to the Israelite tradition concerning the Flood, the disobedient angels, and to the family of Noah as a model of salvation (3:19–21)

- use of the term "Gentiles" (*ethnē*) as designation for outsiders opposed to insiders (2:12) and their God (2:12; 4:2–4), in continuity with Israelite usage
- condemnation of behavior proscribed in the Decalogue (4:16)
- ascription of the letter to Peter (1:1) and mention of Silvanus (5:12) and Mark (5:13)—all representatives of the Jerusalem church with whom former Israelites rather than Gentiles would more likely have been familiar. On the whole, these factors point to an author and an audience steeped in the Scripture, tradition, and history of Israel.

Readers of a predominantly Israelite origin were presumed among the Fathers. Eusebius (*Hist. eccl.* 3.1.2) cites Origen who in the third volume of his *Commentary on Genesis* observed: "But Peter, it seems, preached in Pontus and Galatia and Bithynia, in Cappadocia and Asia, to those Jews who were of the Dispersion" (cf. also *Hist. eccl.* 3.4.2, "Peter . . . in his acknowledged Epistle . . . writes to those of Hebrew parentage of the Dispersion in Pontus and Galatia, Cappadocia and Asia and Bithynia"). This assumption of the Greek Fathers eventually became the "traditional" view as held by Erasmus, Calvin, B. Weiss, and numerous other scholars. (On the "Jewishness of 1 Peter" and its audience, see also Michaels 1988, xlix–lv.)

At the same time, other internal evidence indicates that persons of a *pagan origin*, perhaps the majority, were also presumed among the audience. This is indicated by references to traits more characteristic of former pagans than Israelites: the addressees' earlier "ignorance" of God (1:14), their former "Gentile" immoral conduct and associations (4:2–4; cf. 1:14–16, 17; 2:1, 11; 4:15), their ransom from the "futile conduct inherited from your ancestors" (1:18), their divine call "from darkness to light" (2:9), and their once being alienated from God (2:10, though this could describe former Israelites as well). Among these persons may have been previous Gentile sympathizers with and proselytes to Israel (cf. van Unnik 1980, 3–82).

The use of the term "Gentiles" (*ethnē*, 2:12; 4:3) does not require that the author and audience were of exclusively Israelite origin. This collective term, once used by Israel to designate all non-Israelites (as *gōyîm*) is now employed in 1 Peter to identify collectively all non-Christians as the new "outsiders" and negative reference group. Here we have one of the several sectarian strategies of the messianic movement in its sectarian phase, in which traditional terminology and social distinctions are taken over from the parent body of Israel but invested with new and different meaning. (On the sectarian features of the movement and the sectarian elements of 1 Peter's strategy, see Elliott 1981/1990, 73–84, 102–18; 1993a, 70–86; 1995b.)

On the whole, the letter's content, combination of Israelite and Hellenistic traditions, and mode of argumentation indicate that the author reckoned with a mixed audience—some of Israelite roots and some of pagan origin. This mixed ethnic composition would be consistent with the heterogeneity of the populations of Asia Minor in general and with the constituencies of the Christian communities described throughout the NT. As I. H. Marshall (1973, 283) has correctly observed: "a differentiation between Hellenistic Jewish and Hellenistic Gentile churches in the early period is entirely without foundation. . . . There is thus no specifically Hellenistic Gentile Christianity to be found in the New Testament. No single New Testament document can be labeled as basically Gentile, but for almost every document it is possible to demonstrate its mixed Jewish-Gentile character."

(6) The author further presupposed that there were tenets of faith and Christian baptismal instruction, Christian values and norms, and formulas of worship that were known to and shared by senders and recipients and that illustrated and reinforced the bonds that united them (*eidotes* [1:18; 5:9]; "we," "our," "us" [1:3; 2:24a,b,c; 4:17]; and passim for traditional formulas).

(7) Presupposed was also their respect for the authority of the Apostle Peter and his teaching (1:1; 5:1, 12) as well as a knowledge of and respect for Silvanus (5:12) and Mark (5:13), close colleagues of Peter.

(8) Mention of the distinguishing label "Christian" (4:16) indicates that the movement to which the addressees belonged was a messianic sect of Israel now distinguished from other Israelite coalitions and factions by the name "Christian" (4:16) and in the process of disengaging from its parent body socially and ideologically. Impelled by its universalist gospel to engage in a worldwide mission to all ethnic groups and classes, this missionary movement, as a conversionist sect (Elliott 1981/1990, 73–84, 102–18), was required to interact with rather than withdraw from society and to offer to all with whom it came into contact a vision and form of life and hope superior to what its converts had previously known.

(9) The predicament of the addressees, however, as presumed in the letter, was that they formed a dispersed alien minority within a larger, generally hostile, society (Elliott 1981/1990; Brox 1977, 1986; Goppelt 1993). They were presumed to have been exposed to hostility, verbal abuse, and degrading shaming from ignorant (2:15) native outsiders (2:12, 15; 3:6? 9, 13, 16; 4:4, 14; cf. 5:8–9), a harassment that had led to their innocent suffering (1:6; 2:12, 19–20; 3:14, 17, 18; 4:1, 2, 13, 16, 19; 5:8–9, 10). Presumed also in this connection was the addressees' knowledge (*eidotes*) of the worldwide suffering of the Christian brotherhood (5:9). With this final point we have arrived at the question of the precarious situation of the addressees presumed in this letter.

5.3. THE PRECARIOUS SITUATION OF THE ADDRESSEES

The concept *situation* refers to the set of circumstances, as perceived, described, and diagnosed by the Petrine author, that prompted this letter's composition and dispatch. The most prominent and repeatedly emphasized feature of the addressees' situation as portrayed in 1 Peter is the undeserved suffering that they were undergoing as a result of the disparagement and abuse to which they were subjected by hostile nonbelievers. While commentators agree on this point, only in more recent time has a consensus emerged regarding the nature, agents, and motives of this hostility. Positions on this issue are also related to positions taken on the author of the letter, its genre, integrity, and date.

Prior to the mid-1970s and occasionally thereafter, commentators sought to trace the suffering of which 1 Peter speaks to an assumed hostility toward or official proscription of Christianity on the part of Rome, beginning with Nero in the mid-60s CE (e.g., Windisch 1951, 80; Knox 1953; Beare 1970, 30–34, 188; Schrage and Balz 1973, 63; Downing 1988; Molthagen 1995). Proponents of this view attempted to link the situation and date of 1 Peter to the reign of Nero (54–68), Domitian (81–96), or Trajan (98–117). This approach to the question generally has been abandoned in more recent time for several weighty reasons (cf. Elliott 1976, 251–52; 1981/1990, 78–84; 1992a, 274).

The Petrine author describes the suffering of which he speaks as worldwide in scope (5:9). This suffering could not have been the result of an official persecution of Christians by Rome because, as historians have long noted, the first worldwide persecution of Christians officially undertaken by Rome did not occur until the persecution initiated by Decius (249–251 CE) in 250 CE (on the Decian persecution, see Eusebius, *Hist. eccl.* 6.39.1–42.6; 7.1.; *Sib. Or.* 13:81–88). Prior to this time, anti-Christian actions against individuals or groups were sporadic, generally mob-incited, locally restricted, and unsystematic in nature. Initiated on the whole by natives who perceived members of the messianic movement as threatening local peace and order, pogroms occurred only sporadically, with provincial Roman governors drawn in mainly to adjudicate the issues (see Colwell 1970; Krodel 1971).[25]

Nero's attack on the Christians of Rome in the mid-60s, according to the Roman historian Tacitus (ca. 117 CE), was prompted by his quest for scapegoats to blame for a devastating fire (July 64 CE) which had destroyed four-fifths of the city. Seeking to divert blame from himself for having set the fire to make room for a new palace, he charged those people known as *Christiani* with arson, rounded them up, and had them burned in his garden on Vatican hill (Tac., *Ann.* 15.44; cf. also Eusebius, *Hist. eccl.* 2.25.1–8). This pogrom, however, was confined to the city itself, resulted in no official proscription of Christianity, and set no official precedent for any policy of Rome toward the Christian movement in general. Suetonius, another Roman historian and contemporary of Tacitus, also records that Nero attacked Christians in Rome (Suet., *Nero* 16).

[25] On the persecutions in general, see Workman 1906/1980; Canfield 1913; T. Lewis 1918; Colwell 1939/1970; Millburn 1945; Zeiller 1949; Fuchs 1950; Guterman 1951; Sherwin-White 1952/1966a, 772–87; 1964; Last 1954; J. Vogt 1954; Frend 1958, 1967; Wlosok 1959; de Ste. Croix 1963, 1964; Barnard 1964; Grégoire 1964; Coleman-Norten 1966; Frend 1966; Barnes 1968; E. J. Bickerman 1968; Freudenberger 1969; Krodel 1971; Moreau 1971; Musurillo 1972, lvii–lxii; Keresztes 1973, 1979, 1984, 1989; Vittinghoff 1984; Benko 1980, 1985b; Potter 1992; Sordi 1994; Bowersock 1995; Molthagen 1995.

This was not, however, for any complicity in the fire of Rome, which he relates in a separate context (*Nero* 38), but for their constituting "a sect given to a novel and malicious superstition." Although writing more than 50 years after the fire of 64 CE and well aware of imperial policies in this period, neither Tacitus nor Suetonius gives any indication that Nero's action against the Christians of Rome marked the beginning of an official, empire-wide prosecution of Christianity. Within the Christian comunity, apparently a misunderstanding of a comment by Tertullian (*Apol.* 5), cited by Eusebius (*Hist. eccl.* 2.25.4), that "Nero was the first to attack this opinion [Christianity]," was responsible for the erroneous notion that the empire-wide prosecution of Christians inaugurated by Decius in 250 CE was the continuation of a policy established by Nero. On the so-called "institutum Neronianum" and the absence of any official Neronian edict proscribing Christianity generally, see Borleffs (1952). Actually, Eusebius himself noted the occasional nature of anti-Christian outbreaks: "sometimes it was the people, at others the local rulers, who laid their plots against us so that *even without there being open persecution, partial ones in particular provinces* sprang up" (*Hist. eccl.* 3.33.2, emphasis mine). As to the Flavian emperors, there is no evidence whatever of anti-Christian aggression on the part of Vespasian (69–79 CE) and Titus (79–81 CE). Domitian (81–96 CE) had his difficulties in Rome with the senatorial aristocracy and philosophers, particularly during the latter years of his reign (93–96). His suspicion of intrigue on the part of some senators (Suet., *Dom.* 10–15), his execution of his cousin Flavius Clemens, and his banishment of Clemens' wife, Flavia Domitilla, on the charge of atheism in 95 (Dio Cassius 67.13–14, possibly because they favored alien Israelite rites), had nothing to do, however, with an attack on Christianity as such. As an isolated incident it provides no basis for an assumption of anti-Christian antipathies on Domitian's part or an intent to exterminate the Christian movement. His rule of the provinces was an enlightened one, with "little evidence of cruelty or even of pretensions to grandeur," and was marked by "both vigour and intelligence" (Magie 1950, 1:577; see also B. W. Jones 1979, 1992; L. L. Thompson 1990, 95–115, 146–67, 171–72). Except for the final years of his life, Domitian and the Flavian house in general had brought to the empire a period of tranquility, stability, and prosperity.[26]

Trajan was informed of the existence of Christians in Pontus by his legate Pliny (ca. 111–112 CE). But in their exchange of correspondence (Pliny, *Ep.* 10.96–97) concerning Pliny's handling of the problem, neither makes reference to any official Roman policy proscribing Christianity, a fact that strongly suggests that none existed. Pliny met with obstinacy on the part of some of the Christians but found no crimes with which to charge them and concluded that they were guilty of nothing more than adhering to a "depraved superstition"

[26] For rejection of any Christian persecution under Domitian, see also Millburn 1945; Barnard 1964; Bell 1978; and J. C. Wilson 1993.

(*Ep*. 10.96.8). Trajan (Pliny, *Ep*. 10.97) expressly forbade the hunting down and punishment of Christians for any other reason than possible criminal behavior, urging leniency and toleration in dealing with the incident. Here, too, the problem was confined in scope, in this case to Pontus. On this correspondence, its date after 1 Peter, and its limited relevance for 1 Peter, see the NOTES on 1 Pet 4:12–19.

There is thus no evidence external to 1 Peter indicating any official anti-Christian Roman policy that could have prompted the suffering of which the letter speaks. Nothing *within* the letter, moreover, indicates such a situation. 1 Peter itself contains no reference to Roman hostility toward Christianity or to Roman trials and displays no animus against Rome. The letter contains only one direct and unambiguous reference to Roman rule (the emperor and his governors, whose tasks are to reward those doing what is right and punish those doing wrong, 2:14) and expressly urges the readers to respect their authority (2:13) and to honor the emperor (2:17), advice hardly imaginable if Christians at the time were suffering from official Roman persecution. The attempt to link 1 Peter with putative Roman persecutions of Christianity, therefore, has now been abandoned by the majority of recent commentators, who point rather to local harassment as the cause of the suffering mentioned in this letter.[27]

A comprehensive consideration of the content of 1 Peter provides a clearer picture of the nature and actual causes of the suffering experienced by the Christians of Asia Minor and elsewhere. 1 Peter contains more uses of the term *paschō* (12×) than any other NT writing (2:19, 20, 21, 23; 3:14, 17, 18; 4:1 [2×], 15, 19; 5:10); for the related noun *pathēma*, see 1:11; 4:13; 5:1, 9; for terms and images for suffering, see also *lypeō* (1:6), *lypē* (2:19), Jesus' shedding of blood (1:2, 19) and his "bruise" (2:24d), his rejection by humans (2:4c), and the verbal abuse he endured (2:23).

The believers had been upright and honorable in their behavior (3:13–14, 16); their suffering was undeserved (2:19) and comparable with the innocent suffering of Jesus Christ (2:21–25; 3:18; 4:1). The cause of this suffering is also clearly indicated: persistent slander and verbal abuse from nonbelieving outsiders aimed at demeaning, shaming, and discrediting the Christians in the court of public opinion. The nature of this abuse and insult is primarily verbal, not physical (rightly stressed by Neugebauer 1979, 62), as the terms for this harassment clearly indicate: "slander" (*katalaleō*; 2:12, 3:16), "disparage" (*epēreazō*, 3:16), "malign" (*blasphēmeō*, 4:4), "reproach" (*oneidizō*, 4:14); com-

---

[27] These include J. N. D. Kelly 1969, 5–11; McGaughey 1969; Best 1971, 36–42; Elliott 1976, 251–52; 1981/1990, 78–84; 1992a, 274; Neugebauer 1979, 62; Lepelley 1980; Brox, 1977; 1986, 24–34; Frankemölle 1987, 13–17; Plümacher 1987; Achtemeier 1988, 211; Cothenet 1988, 3701–4; Lamau 1988, 49–79; Michaels 1988, lxiii–lxvi; Davids 1990, 10; Prostmeier 1990, 51–64; Feldmeier 1992, 105–32; Hillyer 1992, 2–3, 5; Goppelt 1993, 36–45. See also the NOTES on 2:11–12; 2:13–17; 3:13–17; 4:12–19; 5:8–9. On the absence of Roman persecution in Asia Minor in the first century, see also Yarbro-Collins 1985 and L. L. Thompson 1986.

pare "insult," used in relation to Jesus Christ (*loidoreō*, *loidoria*, *antiloidoreō*, 2:23); and "harm" (*kakon* and *kakoō*, 3:9, 13). No mention is made of physical aggression, trials, torture, or execution of the believers. No use is made of the terms *diōkō* and *diōgmos* ("persecute, persecution"), words customarily employed to depict more violent forms of oppression (cf. Matt 5:11–12, 10:17–23; Mark 10:30; Luke 11:49; 21:12; John 15:20; Acts 9:4–5; 13:50; 22:4; Rom 8:35; 1 Cor 4:12, 15:9; 2 Cor 12:10; Gal 1:13, 23; 2 Thess 1:4). It was rathter ignorance regarding these strangers and aliens on the part of outsiders (2:15; 3:15) that led to suspicion and accusation of wrongdoing (2:12, 2:19–20); surprise and maligning as a result of Christians' withdrawing from previous association with outsiders (4:4); intimidation (3:6, 14); disparagement of the believers' good conduct in Christ and their reproach as "Christ lackeys" (4:16) because of their affiliation with Jesus Christ (4:14). This suffering was the same as that being experienced by the worldwide Christian brotherhood (5:9).

Their condition as "strangers" and "resident aliens" (1:1, 17; 2:11) figured prominently among the factors that made the addressees vulnerable to such harassment. There is, however, a difference of opinion on how these terms are to be taken and how they apply to the addressees. According to one view, the believers *became* resident aliens as a result of their adherence to Christianity. But this is open to serious question, if "resident aliens" (*paroikoi*) is used literally, since no legal policy existed whereby persons converting to Christianity were reduced to the legal, economic, and social status of *actual* resident aliens. Consequently, this view requires the supposition that the author only *compared* the addressees to strangers and aliens or that he used the terms only metaphorically (strangers and aliens in a supposedly "spiritual" sense). Neither of these suppositions, however, is without problems. The numerous references in the Bible to Israel, Abraham, Moses, and other individuals and groups as "strangers" and "resident aliens" in *paroikia* are all literal, not metaphorical, and occur in descriptions of the social predicament accompanying the status of such strangers and resident aliens. In 1 Peter, where the believers are expressly linked with Sarah and Abraham (3:6) and where the expression "resident aliens and strangers" (2:11) derives from the description of Abraham in Gen 23:4, these terms appear to have the same actual sense that they do in descriptions of Abraham and Israel. Assumption of a metaphorical sense is also connected with the notion that the Petrine author portrays the believers in a "spiritual" sense as exiles or pilgrims on earth yearning for a home in heaven. This notion, however, lacks any basis in this letter and appears far removed from the author's actual intent.

On the other hand, a literal sense of *parepidēmoi*, *paroikoi*, and *paroikia* fits the context of 1 Peter, its social situation and that of early Christianity in general, and the theological strategy of the letter in particular. On this reading, the letter was addressed to persons who were actual strangers and resident aliens in Asia Minor prior to their conversion and who remained so after their conversion (cf. Elliott 1981/1990, 21–58). Comprising both resident aliens living in these provinces for a greater period of time[28] and visiting strangers briefly passing through, this group of persons, as we may envision it, encountered missionaries of the messianic movement and was attracted to this new community as a way of attaining a haven of acceptance, security, and belonging in an alien and often hostile environment. It was with such persons that the messianic sect, itself a missionary religion on the move, first came into contact as it traveled along the trade routes of the Empire (Beskow 1970). Indeed, most of its missionaries themselves had the status of actual strangers and aliens as they moved from place to place in areas far removed from their homeland. After joining the movement, however, these Asia Minor strangers and aliens found that adherence to an exotic Israelite sect did not bring freedom from local suspicion and hostility but only exacerbated it. Part of our author's reponse to this dilemma, as we shall soon see, was to enlarge the concept of "resident aliens" to include all the spiritual children of Abraham and Sarah, the prototypical "resident aliens and strangers." In this process, the condition of the actual alien status of *some* of the addressees provided the experiential basis for metaphorically portraying *all* of the recipients as sharing the social condition but also the divine vocation of Israel's first and prototypical resident aliens.

The insults and disparagment encountered by the addressees was typical of the hostility regularly leveled against strangers who were seen as lacking roots in and loyalty toward the local community and therefore were perceived as threatening the common weal and favor of the gods. Israel, the parent body of this messianic sect, frequently had encountered similar treatment as a "superstition" with a singular commitment to Yahweh, and its social aloofness often was decried as *amixia* ("standoffishness"), "misanthropy," and "hatred of the human race" (cf. Josephus, Ag. *Ap*. 2.95; Tac., *Hist*. 5.5.1; Diod. Sic., *Hist*. 34.1–2). While the derogatory label "Christian" ("partisan of Christ" [Messiah]) with which the believers were stigmatized indicated their perceived connection with Israel and its messianic hope and their association with the Israelite crucified years ago in Jerusalem, this label also distinguished them from other Israelite factions and now made them also vulnerable to the charge of being a "new and depraved superstition" (*nova ac prava superstitio*; cf. Tac., *Ann*. 15.44; Suet., *Nero* 16.2).

The *verbal nature* of the aggression and the absence of any mention of official hearings, trials, and executions make it clear that no formal organized state persecution is envisioned here. The curiosity shown by the natives concerning the hope that filled the Christians (3:15) illustrates the difference and distance between believers and nonbelievers. The "reply" (*apologia*) "requested" (*aitounti*) by the nonbelievers in clarification of this hope, moreover, is far removed from official trials demanding a self-defense on the part of the persons accused of criminal offenses (see the NOTE on 3:15).

---

[28] On *paroikoi* in Asia Minor, see Dickey 1928, 398–99; Broughton 1938, 637–45; Magie 1950, 149, 225, 1037–38; and Rostevtzeff 1957 (index, under "by-dwellers").

In sum, the manner in which Christian suffering is mentioned, described, and addressed in this letter points not to organized Roman persecution as its cause but to local social tensions deriving from the social, cultural, and religious differences demarcating believers from their neighbors. It is not the punitive actions of Roman authorities but those of alienated (4:4), suspicious (2:15; 3:15), slanderous (2:12; 3:16), and hostile (3:9, 13) local populations that 1 Peter describes. Such popular opposition could conceivably lead to hearings and official trials.[29] 1 Peter, however, makes no mention of such trials. In contrast to the demoralization and despair that a state-initiated persecution might provoke, the perspective of the Petrine author is remarkably positive. Unjust slander, he notes, can be countered by good behavior, outsider ignorance can be overcome (2:15), and detractors can even be won to the Christian cause (2:12; 3:1). The letter presupposes a situation in which the addressees were not being treated as "enemies of the state" but were made victims of social discrimination because of their being strangers and aliens both socially and religiously, because of their similarity to Israel in their distinctiveness and nonconformity, and because of their adherence to an exotic Israelite sect stigmatized as "Christian." This situation differentiates 1 Peter from the writings of Paul. It reflects the tension and conflict of the messianic movement not with mainstream Israel, as was the case with Paul, but with society at large and locates this letter in a new epoch in the history of the primitive church (Moffatt 1918, 323). If this precarious situation of innocent suffering was not to lead to disillusionment, despair, defection, and the ultimate demise of the movement in Asia Minor, those who suffered had to be provided with a persuasive rationale for remaining firm in their faith and resolute in their commitment to God, Jesus Christ, and one another.

6. AIM, STRATEGY, AND THEOLOGICAL CONCEPTS

Our author's statement in 5:12 comes closest to summarizing the content and aim of his letter: to bear full witness to the grace of God in which his addressees stand and to encourage them to stand fast in this grace. Consideration of the full content of the letter reveals a constellation of key features involved in the author's strategy for effectively addressing the predicament faced by the readers. Before examining these factors, we can eliminate various theories regarding the letter's aim that must be dismissed as untenable.

Nothing in the letter supports the idiosyncratic view advanced by F. C. Baur (1856) and others (Lewis 1899; McNabb 1935; Trilling 1971), that 1 Peter was an "Unionsschrift" whose goal was to effect a synthesis or reconciliation

[29] See Mark 13:9–13 par.; Matt 5:11–12/Luke 6:22–23; Matt 10:17–22; Luke 12:11–12; 21:12–17; Acts 18:1–11; 23:23–26:32.

between Pauline and Petrine poles of the Christian mission (Baur 1856, 219–20) or whose aim was to lend Petrine authority to the universalist theology of Paul (Strathmann 1943, 275; Mussner 1976, 53, 55), as the cogent critique by Brox (1975, 79; 1977, 1–4; 1978b, 116–20; 1986, 46) makes clear. This view, prompted not by the content of 1 Peter but by a notion of conflict, mediation, and resolution within early Christianity, finds no support in the letter itself, which makes no mention of Paul whatsoever and focuses on an entirely different set of issues.

Nor do literary affinities with the Pauline writings support the view that 1 Peter was composed by a "Paulinist" intent on transmitting, in albeit diluted form, the Pauline gospel to Pauline communities. The communities addressed include areas not reached by Paul (Bithynia-Pontus, Cappadocia), and the affinities are the result not of a Paulinist aping Paul but of a common use of preexisting tradition, as noted above. Nor has a convincing case been made for the further idosyncratic view (Reichert 1989) that 1 Peter was written to reject certain erroneous Deutero-Pauline views that were cited and refuted in 3:18–22 (for a critique, see Elliott 1992b). Nor was its intention "to renew the expectation of the parousia in the face of the persecution of Christians," as Koester (1982, 295) proposes. The imminence of Christ's final coming is assumed in this letter rather than debated or defended. Along with mention of the nearness of the end (4:7) and of judgment (4:4–6, 17), this expectation serves as a motivation for the letter's exhortation rather than as a point requiring demonstration.

The focus of this letter is the innocent suffering of Christian believers and the dilemma this presented concerning the believers' relation to and behavior among hostile outsiders. This suffering, if continued and ignored, eventually would have led to discouragement, despair, and possible defection from the Christian community, for it would have undermined the confidence, cohesion, and commitment of its members. Suffering and the opprobrium of "strangeness," to be sure, could have been minimized or eliminated through the simple step of conformity and social assimilation. But this would have entailed the sacrifice of the moral distinctiveness and communal exclusiveness to which the sect owed its existence. One important goal of this conversionist sect was the attraction and conversion of outsiders (2:12; 3:2), an aim that would be decisively thwarted if it espoused a strategy of social and moral accommodation (against Balch 1981, 1986, whose restricted focus on the household "code" and inattention to the letter's overall missionary orientation and strategy resulted in a fatal misconstrual of its aim and message; see Elliott 1986a; Achtemeier 1988, 218–22, 235; and Dalton 1989, 104–5). The continued existence and growth of the community as a whole depended on maintaining those elements of their communal life, which suffering and continued hostility threatened to undermine: namely, a common sense of their unique, divinely-conferred identity and purpose, a sustaining social cohesion, and fervent commitment to mission nurtured by a unifying faith and hope involving steadfast loyalty to God, Jesus

Christ, and the brotherhood. It is precisely this constellation of factors that the letter was designed to promote.

Inquiry concerning the author's strategy entails more than considering his "theological aim or purpose." This strategy involves the manner in which the letter has been designed, in genre, content, structure, and rhetorical argument, to have a persuasive effect (both cognitional and emotional) upon its addressees and to move them toward effective social action and renewed religious commitment in response to their precarious situation.

In general, the letter itself serves as a direct group-to-group communication assuring the beleaguered addressees of the concern and support of their brothers and sisters abroad. In terms of its content, it is arranged and designed to motivate its audience to meet the challenge posed by their social alienation, abuse, and unjust suffering. More specifically, this message is designed (1) to enhance the readers' awareness of their collective dignity and privileged status with God over against their low status in society and to strengthen their resolve to dissociate from former, preconversion modes of conduct, allegiance, and alliance; (2) to encourage social cohesion and solidarity *within* the Asia Minor movement so that it will present a united front against abuse from outsiders; and (3) to provide a persuasive rationale for the courageous endurance of suffering and for continued commitment to God, Jesus Christ, and one another in the face of suffering that threatens to undermine hope, trust, and fidelity.

Our author addresses the paramount issue head-on and acknowledges the fact that believers indeed are suffering unjustly (1:6; 2:12, 15, 18–20; 3:9, 13–17; 4:1, 4, 6b, 12–14, 16, 19; 5:8–9, 10), setting this problematic fact within the context of the tension between their social estrangement and their divine vocation, their homelessness in society and their at-home-ness in the family of God. He reminds them of the grace, favor, and honor conferred by God upon the believing community (1:1–2, 3–2:10, 18–20; 3:4, 7, 9, 10–12, 14, 18c, 21; 4:5–6, 10–11, 14, 18, 19; 5:1, 4, 5b–7, 9–11, 12). He stresses their redemption through and solidarity with Jesus Christ (1:2, 8, 10–12, 13, 18–21, 23–25; 2:2–3, 4–10, 18–25; 3:15–16, 18–22; 4:1, 11, 13, 14, 16; 5:1, 4, 10). He recasts unjust suffering in a positive light (1:6–7; 2:12, 18–25; 3:9, 13–22; 4:1–2, 5–6, 12–19; 5:1, 6–11). He calls for holy, distinctive, and honorable conduct in society (1:14–16; 2:11–12, 13–17; 3:1–7, 8–9, 10–12, 13–17; 4:1–3, 15, 19) as well as for continued commitment to God (1:21; 2:9, 12, 13, 15–16, 17c, 18–20; 3:4–5, 7f, 10–12, 16, 17; 4:2–3, 5–6, 7b, 10–11, 16, 19; 5:2–4, 6–7, 12f), Jesus Christ (1:8; 2:2–3, 4a, 7a; 3:15, 16; 4:14, 16; 5:1, 2–4, 10, 14), and one another (1:22; 2:17b; 3:8; 4:8–11; 5:2–3, 5a, 5b). And he assures his readers that the divine grace already experienced "in Christ" and in the household of God is a basis for steadfastness in faith, holy conduct, persistence in doing what is right, and confident hope in the salvation soon to be realized at Christ's final appearance (1:10, 13, 3:7e; 4:10; 5:5, 10, 12).

Our author thus reassures his readers that, despite their vulnerable condition as strangers and resident aliens in society, through baptism and conversion they have been born anew as children of God and now constitute an elect and holy family of God united through faith in Jesus Christ, the elect of God (1:3–2:10). In society, however hostile, they, as the household of God, are to lead honorable and holy lives in obedience to God's will, in emulation of their suffering and exalted Lord, with loyalty and love toward one another, and with trust and hope in the One who is their creator, father, judge, and protector. Their innocent suffering is not a bane to be bemoaned but a test of faith, a paradoxical badge of honor, and an opportunity for glorifying God (2:11–5:11).

In regard to the first point, the letter opens with an affirmation of the distinctive communal identity of the believers and their privileged status with God in contrast to their demeaned status and reputation in society (1:1–2; 1:3–2:10).

(1) Believers, our author affirms, have been elected (1:1; 2:4–10; cf. 5:13), sanctified (1:2, 14–16, 22; 2:4–10), and reborn (1:3, 23; 2:2–3) by God as God's children (1:14), who as such now constitute the household or family of God (2:5).

(2) This new life has been inaugurated through the resurrection of Jesus Christ from death to life (1:3, 21; 2:4) and is made available to those who believe in Jesus as the resurrected Christ (2:4–5, 7a, 9–10) and who have undergone a baptism that unites them with the resurrected Christ (3:21).

(3) Their experience of the Christ and the good news of salvation has put them in a more favored position than the prophets and even the angels (1:10–12, 23–25; 2:4–10).

(4) Reborn by God's mercy (1:3), not from perishable but imperishable seed, namely the word of God (1:23–25), as newborn infants they are nourished by this word (2:2–3) and are being constructed by God as a household of the Spirit (2:5), the end-time elect and holy covenant people of God (2:4–10).

(5) This passage from old to new life is a passage from futility (1:18) to hope (1:13, 21; cf. 3:15). It is to be set on a course of salvation (2:2; 3:21) ready to be revealed in the last propitious time (1:5).

(6) The divine origin of their new life and their divinely conferred dignity make them one with God (1:14–16), with Christ (2:4–5, 7a, 9–10; 18–25; 3:18–22; 4:1, 13, 14; 5:1), and with one another as brothers and sisters of one family, one brotherhood bound in loyalty and love (1:22; 2:17; 3:8; 4:8; 5:9). United by faith in Christ, believers form one community "in Christ" (3:16; 5:10, 14), one "flock of God" (5:2) under Christ the shepherd (2:25; 5:4).

(7) This union with God, the Holy One (1:16), and Christ, the holy lamb (1:19), is to be manifested in a holy way of life subject ultimately to the will of God (2:15; 3:17; 4:2, 19) and marked by reverence for God (1:17; 2:17, 18; 3:2, 16) and by following in the footsteps of Jesus Christ (2:21–25).

(8) Union with God and Jesus Christ simultaneously sets the believing community apart from the nonbelievers (2:7b) or "disobedient" (2:7b, 8; 3:1; cf. the disobedient angels of 3:20) or "Gentiles" (2:12; 4:3) who oppose God (4:2–4), reject Christ and the gospel (2:4c, 7b–8; 2:23; 4:17), and reproach his followers (2:12, 15; 3:9, 16; 4:4, 14, 16). Conversion involves dissociation as well as association: association with a new source of life and dissociation from one's former

ignorant, immoral, and futile conduct (1:14, 18; 2:1, 11) as well as from former associates still immersed therein (4:1–4).

This stress on difference and dissociation is expressed through the numerous contrasts and antitheses filling the letter: "before-after," "former(ly)-now," "darkness-light," contrasting preconversion and present states (1:14–15; 2:9, 10, 25; 4:2–3); prophets, angels-you (1:10–12); perishable-imperishable (1:4, 7, 23, 24); humans-God (2:4, 17; 4:2–3, 5–6; 5:5c); honorable-dishonorable conduct, doing what is right-doing what is wrong (2:11–12, 14–15, 16, 18–20, 23, 24bc; 3:3–4, 8–9, 10–12, 17; 4:1–3, 15–16, 19; 5:2–3, 5c); believers-nonbelievers (2:7–10, 12, 15; 3:1, 13, 15–16; 4:2–6, 17–18); shame and suffering from humans (2:12, 15, 18d, 19c, 20bd; 3:9ab, 13, 14, 16, 17; 4:1c, 4, 6b, 13a, 14a, 16a, 19a; 5:8b, 9b, 10c)-honor from God (1:3–5, 8, 9, 10–12, 18–19, 23, 25b; 2:3a, 5, 7a, 9–10, 16, 19a, 19f, 24c–25; 3:9d, 13, 14, 18c, 21a; 4:6b, 10, 13bc, 14bc, 18, 19; 5:1c, 4, 5c, 6b, 7b, 10b, 10d, 12e); trust in God-resisting the Devil and his minions (5:6–10). Christians, in a word, form a "contrast society," as Lohfink (1984, 122–32, 163–70) terms it, a holy community charged with living lives of "holy non-conformity" (cf. Goppelt 1993, 109–11), and rejecting "culture's claim to [ultimate] loyalty." This is the position classically described as "Christ against Culture" in H. R. Niebuhr's seminal study, *Christ and Culture* (1956, 45–82). This advocacy of dissociation, however, is not to be confused with a recommendation of physical withdrawal as undertaken, for instance, by the Qumran community. Instead, believers are to remain engaged with their neighbors, to live in accord with general standards of honorable behavior, insofar as this is possible without compromising loyalty to God and Jesus Christ, and to practice a higher form of morality, which may eventually attract even erstwhile detractors to the faith (2:12).

To encourage solidarity and cohesion within the Christian community in Asia Minor, our author develops the social and moral implications of the believers' union with God and Jesus Christ. To be "reborn" (1:3, 23; 2:2–3) by God the Father (1:2, 3, 17) is to be God's "children" (1:14), united with one another by the bonds characteristic of family and kinship loyalties. Constituting a "household of the Spirit" (2:5), a "household of God" (4:17), a "brotherhood" of faith (2:17; 5:9; cf. 5:13), they are to maintain the unity of the community through constant "brotherly and sisterly love" (1:22; 2:17b; 3:8; 4:8; 5:14), respect for order and reciprocal responsibilities (2:18–20; 3:1–7; 5:1–5a), mutual humility (3:8; 5:5b), like-mindedness, compassion, tenderheartedness (3:8), hospitality (4:9), and mutual service (4:10–11; cf. 5:3). See also the comments on ecclesiology below.

Finally, to equip his readers for confronting undeserved abuse and suffering, our author urges that they remain steadfast in their commitment and allegiance. This calls for constant faith, trust, and hope in God (1:3, 5, 7, 9, 13, 21; 3:10–12, 15; 5:5c–7, 10), reverence for God (1:17; 2:17, 18; 3:2, 16), obedience (1:14, 22) and mindfulness (2:19; 3:16, 21) of God's will (2:15; 3:17; 4:2, 19; 5:2c, 5), love and fidelity toward Jesus Christ (1:8; 2:3, 4, 6, 7; 3:15), as well as familial loyalty toward one another. Such commitment is made possible by the divine grace, mercy, and honor already experienced (1:1–2; 1:3–2:10, 24–25;

3:14, 21; 4:11, 14; 5:5c–7, 10, 12). God's power in raising, glorifying, and vindicating Jesus Christ (1:3, 11, 21; 2:4; 3:18–22) is the power (1:5; 4:11; 5:10–11) that also sustains and empowers those united with Christ. It is this divine grace, mercy, and power that provide the basis and means for their steadfastness in faith, holy conduct, persistence in doing what is right, self-entrustment to God's care, and confident hope in the salvation soon to be realized at Christ's final appearance.

The abuse and suffering of the believers are the chief manifestations of their paradoxical situation: their estrangement in society, on the one hand, and their union with God, on the other. The revaluation our author gives to this suffering, accordingly, is one of the paramount features of his strategy and of his letter's good news:

(1) Innocent suffering, he stresses, constitutes a divine testing of the purity and constancy of faith and trust in God (1:6–7; 4:12).

(2) It unites suffering believers with their suffering Lord (2:18–25; 3:13–22; 4:1, 13; 5:1) and suffering believers everywhere (5:9). Therefore, suffering is nothing strange to those who are followers of the Christ (4:12–13).

(3) As the suffering Christ was exalted, vindicated, and glorified by God (1:11, 19, 21; 3:18–22; 5:1), so those who suffer innocently and remain faithful will likewise be exalted, vindicated, and glorified (1:6–9; 2:4–5, 18–25; 3:13–22; 5:1, 10).

(4) Since innocent suffering effects solidarity with the suffering Christ, it is a cause for rejoicing (1:6–7; 4:13) both now and in the future, when his glory will be revealed. Suffering should lead not to grief or despair but to "rejoicing with exultation."

(5) Innocent suffering is also not a cause for fear but an opportunity for "sanctifying the Christ as Lord in your hearts" (3:15).

(6) It is an occasion for liberation from sin (4:1–2).

(7) Innocent suffering is blessed by the divine Spirit of glory (4:14b) and hence a sign of being honored by God (4:14; cf. 3:14).

(8) Suffering from being stigmatized as a "Christian" is not a cause for feeling shamed but an occasion for glorifying God (4:16).

(9) The suffering of the believers is a sign of the divine judgment that has begun with God's own people, "us," the household of God (4:17). It is thus a further indication of the imminence of the end and the nearness of salvation (4:18), and with it a termination of suffering; note also 1:6 and 5:10 on the brief duration of this suffering.

(10) All who suffer innocently can confidently entrust their lives to their faithful Creator and thereby persevere in doing what is right. In this light, salvation is not redemption *from* suffering but rescue *through* suffering.

(11) Thus, even in suffering believers have cause for rejoicing (1:6–8; 4:13) and reason for hope (1:13, 21; 3:15) in God's power to protect (1:5; 5:7), strengthen (5:10), save (1:9; 2:2; 3:21), and ultimately bring his children to glory (1:7; 5:10).

In sum, suffering, despite one's innocence, is not a bane but a blessing, not an occasion for shame but an opportunity for honor. This is the most extensive theological commentary on Christian suffering found in the NT.[30]

THEOLOGICAL CONCEPTS OF THE LETTER

Since 1 Peter is not a theological treatise but a particular message of encouragement and exhortation for a particular situation, its theological concepts are not easily isolable but are interwoven into one coherent line of thought. Following one time-honored approach, however, we might summarize these concepts according to the traditional categories of concepts: God, Christ and salvation, eschatology, and ecclesiology and ethics.[31]

1. God

1 Peter is thoroughly theocentric in its theology (Beare 1970, 51–52; Frankemölle 1987, 64). God (*theos* occurring 39×; *kyrios*, 3×) is the gracious author and completer of the believers' new life in Christ. It is by God that the Messiah was foreknown before the foundation of the world, was revealed at the end of the ages (1:20), was raised to life and glory (1:21; cf. 1:3, 11; 3:21–22), and soon will be finally manifested (5:1, 4). It is likewise in accord with God's foreknowledge (1:2) and mercy (1:3; 2:10) that persons once alienated from God are elected (1:2; 2:4–10; 5:13), reborn (1:3; cf. 1:23; 2:2), united in the new household or family of God (2:4–10), guarded by God's power (1:5; 5:5, 10–11), and brought to salvation (1:5, 9, 10; 2:2; 3:21) and glory (1:7; 5:1, 4, 10). It was to God that Jesus Christ was obedient (1:2; 2:21–24), and it is to God that his followers likewise direct their faith (1:21), hope (1:21; cf. 1:3, 13; 3:15), obedience (1:14, 22; 2:15–16, 19; 3:16, 17, 21; 4:2; cf. 2:5), reverence (1:17; 2:17, 18; 3:2, 16), and trust (4:19; 5:7). God's spirit initially sanctified the addressees (1:2b), enabled the proclamation of the good news (1:12), prompts acceptable sacrifices (2:5c), and now rests upon all who suffer innocently (4:14). God is the ultimate, definitive, and impartial judge of human conduct (1:17; 2:23; 4:5, 6, 17), the one who is now bringing the age to a close (4:7, 17), and the focal figure of praise (1:3; 2:9) and glorification (1:3; 2:9; 4:11, 16; 5:10, 11). God is the originator of rebirth (1:3), the one who calls (1:15; 2:9, 21; 3:9; 5:10), and the

[30] On the theme of suffering in 1 Peter, see Filson 1955; Selwyn 1947, 78–81, 439–58; Nauck 1955; Sander 1966; Hall 1976; Hill 1976; Millauer 1976; Losada 1980; Kirk 1981; Omanson 1982; Cervantes Gabarrón 1991a; Davids 1990, 30–44; Talbert 1991, 42–57.

[31] On the letter's theology in general, see Bigg 1902, 33–52; Selwyn 1947, 64–115; Beare 1945; 1970, 50–60; Zedda 1962; L. Morris 1965, 316–33; Ashcraft 1982; W. D. Kilpatrick 1982; Brox 1986, 253–58; Frankemölle 1987, 20–24, 26–27; Michaels 1988, lxvii–lxxv; Reichert 1989; Davids 1990, 14–23.

one who elects both Jesus Christ (2:4) and the believers (1:1; 2:9–10; 5:13). God is the one whose praises are proclaimed (2:9), who receives the glory (2:12; 4:11; 5:11), and whose spirit rests upon the believers (4:14). Note also all the divine passives that have God as their subject (1:2d, 5b, 7c, 12a, 12b, 13b, 18a, 20a, 20b, 23a; 2:5c, 6c, 7d, 8c, 10c, 21a, 22b, 24d, 25b; 3:9d, 16d, 18e, 20d, 22c; 4:18a; 5:1c, 4a). This theocentricity of the letter and its abundant use of OT thought concerning God, with Jesus functioning exclusively as mediator, situate 1 Peter within the early and still Israelite perspective of the Christian movement. According to the Petrine author, Christian life begins with God's calling, is subject to God's will, is sustained by God's grace, and is aimed at God's glorification.

2. *Jesus Christ and Salvation*

Jesus Christ plays a central role in God's saving action. For the designation "Jesus Christ," see 1:1, 2, 3, 7; 2:5; and 4:11; with 2:5 and 4:11 (*dia Iēsou Christou*) expressing his mediatorial role; for "Christ," see 1:11, 19; 2:21; 3:15, 18; 4:1, 13; with 3:15 and 4:13 containing the articular "the Christ"; for Jesus Christ as "Lord" (*kyrios*) see 1:3, 25; 2:3; 3:15. Jesus, according to our author, has been revealed or manifested by God as the Christ/Messiah and inaugurator of the end of the ages (1:18–19). From the preexisting tradition, the Petrine author stresses two related poles of Jesus Christ's activity: (1) his innocent suffering in obedient submission to God (1:2, 11, 19; 2:4c, 22–23; 4:1, 13a; 5:1) and atoning death (2:21b, 24; 3:18abd); and (2) his resurrection/exaltation to glory (1:3, 11, 21; 2:4d, 7d; 3:18e, 19a, 21d–22; 4:13c; 5:1, 4, 10). His suffering and death were sacrificial, vicarious, atoning, and redemptive (1:2, 18–19; 2:21, 24; 3:18abc). His resurrection, glorification, and vindication are the ultimate demonstration of God's power to save. Sharing in his resurrection through baptism (3:21) is the basis for the believers' rebirth (1:3), new life (2:5, 24), confidence in salvation (3:21), and their trust and hope in God (1:21). This resurrection is also described as his being made alive (3:18e; cf. 2:4b, "living stone") as well as his election (2:4d), honoring (2:4d; cf. 3:22), and glorification (1:11; 4:13; 5:1) by God—all features to be shared by his believers as well. Through his resurrection, believers are reborn (1:3) and saved (3:21). By him believers are brought to God (3:18c), and "through him" believers offer spiritual sacrifices acceptable to God (2:5) and glorify God (4:11c).

Many of these Christological motifs and other images (flawless and faultless lamb, 1:19; rejected-elect, honored, living stone, 2:4; shepherd, 2:25; chief shepherd, 5:4) derive from preexisting Christological tradition and are developed in a distinctive manner throughout the letter; see esp. 2:4–10, 21–25; 3:18–22; and 5:2–4, where the creative blending of motifs and traditions is clearly evident.

Particular emphasis is given in this letter to Christ's role as both exemplar and enabler. Experiencing the same human rejection as the believers (2:4c), he nevertheless lived as God's obedient suffering servant (2:21–24; 3:18b; cf. 1:2) and serves as a model of obedience and subordination to God's will for all rejected believers, who share in his obedience and innocent suffering (2:18–25; 3:13–17; 4:1, 12–13; 5:1, 10). As he was elected by God (2:4, 6) and raised to life (2:4, "living stone"; 3:18e) and glory, so his followers are "living stones" (2:5a) and an elect and holy people (1:1; 2:5–10; 5:13), who live for doing what is right (2:24c), and who will share in his exaltation, vindication, and glory (3:18c; 4:12–13; 5:1, 4, 10). At the same time, it is he whose innocent suffering on behalf of others (2:21b, 22–24a,e; 3:18ab) leads believers to God (3:18c; cf. 4:13) and makes upright conduct possible (2:24bd; 4:1–3). Consequently his life, vicarious suffering, death, and resurrection are not only the pattern but also the empowering basis and motivation for the conduct and hope of his followers.

Jesus, the suffering, dead, and resurrected Christ, is also the central content of the good news (1:12, 25; cf. 4:17), the word by which the believers were reborn (1:23–25) and nourished (2:2), and over which nonbelievers stumble (2:8).

In their entirety these Christological motifs and themes of 1 Peter have eschatological, soteriological, ecclesiological, and ethical implications as well and in their complexity constitute the dynamo, so to speak, that gives this letter of encouragement and exhortation its evangelical and rhetorical power.

While the letter contains no developed doctrine of the Trinity, elements for this doctrine may be seen in the threefold distinctions of 1:2 (God, Spirit, Jesus Christ) and the triadic structure of 1:3–12 (God, 1:3–5; Jesus Christ, vv 6–9; and Holy Spirit, vv 10–12).

The letter's soteriological language and imagery are likewise rich and varied. God has elected a people (1:1; 2:4–10; 5:13) and sanctified its members through the Spirit (1:2, 15–16, 22; 2:5, 9); rebirthed them through the imperishable word (1:3, 23; 2:2); and made them alive (2:5, 24c; cf. 4:6). God has given them a lasting inheritance (1:4; 3:7, 9), the prospect of salvation (1:5, 9, 10; 2:2; 3:21; 4:18) and glorification (1:7; 4:13; 5:1, 4, 10), and a cause for hope (1:3, 13, 21; 3:15; cf. 3:5) and joy (1:6; 4:13). God has called them (1:15; 2:9, 21; 3:9; 5:10); redeemed them by Christ's holy blood (1:2, 18); favored them with grace (1:2, 10, 13; 3:7; 4:10; 5:5, 10, 12) and peace (1:2; 3:11; 5:14); honored them (1:7; 2:7a; 3:14; 4:14); gathered them as a flock (2:25); and consolidated them as a household (2:5; 4:17; 5:10). This action of a salvation-in-process is a manifestation of God's grace, mercy (1:3; 2:10), and power (1:5; 4:11; 5:6, 11) manifested preeminently in the resurrection of Jesus Christ (1:3, 21; 3:18, 21), in which believers now share through faith and baptism (1:21; 2:4–5; 3:21).[32]

3. *Eschatology*

With Jesus Christ's having inaugurated the last of the ages (1:20b), a vibrant *eschatological consciousness* pervades this letter and animates its ethical exhortation. Several motifs of early Christian eschatology are in evidence. The endtime

[32] On the letter's Christology and soteriology, see Kraft 1950–1951; J. M. Lewis 1952; D. G. Miller 1955; Müller 1962; Davies 1972; Delling 1973; Romo 1977; Olson 1979; van Unnik 1980c 3–82; Cothenet 1982; Richard 1986; Kennard 1987; Cervantes Gabarrón 1991a; Sywulka 1991.

(4:7) has been inaugurated by the revelation of Jesus as the crucifed and resurrected Messiah/Christ (1:20; cf. 1:2, 20; 2:4, 21–25; 3:18–22; 4:13; 5:1). The judgment of God (1:17; 2:23c; 4:5; cf. 3:12—but not "wrath" of God—contrast 1 Thess 1:10; Rom 1:18), therefore, is now at hand. It has already begun with the household of God (4:17a, 18a) but embraces all humankind (4:5, 17b, 18b) and is executed according to each one's deeds (1:17). Believers now live between the first (1:20) and imminent final (1:7; 4:13; 5:1, 4) revelation of Christ and must conduct themselves "in the remaining time in the flesh" not "in accord with human cravings but in accord with the will of God" (4:2; cf. 1:14–16). For now (1:12; 2:10; 3:21), in contrast to their former life (1:17; 2:10, 25) they have heard the good news (1:12, 25), are reborn (1:3), and constitute the eschatological people of God (2:4–10). From the author's perspective, this remaining time (cf. also 1:17) will be a relatively "brief" period (*oligon* in 1:6b and 5:10c) and calls for constant vigilance and alertness (1:13; 4:7; 5:8). The present experience of grace and glory, moreover, already offers a foretaste of the glory yet to come (see the NOTE on 3:9).

This eschatological awareness, in turn, lends an urgency to the ethical exhortation of the letter (1:17; 4:1–6, 7–11, 12–19; and 5:1–4). Though employing the terms "reveal" (*apokalyptō*, 1:15, 12; 5:1) and "revelation" (*apokalypsis*, 1:7, 13; 4:13), our author manifests no interest in apocalyptic timetables and scenarios as found, for example, in Paul, the Gospels, and 2 Peter (1 Cor 15:23–28; 1 Thess 4:16–17; 2 Thess 2:1–11; Mark 13 par.; 2 Pet 3:7). In contrast to Paul (Gal 1:12) and the author of Revelation (Rev 1:1–2), our author makes no claim to be passing on any privileged revelation. Nor does one find here a dualistic contrast as in Paul, between the present evil age and the coming age (e.g., Rom 8:18–21, 38; Gal 1:4; 2 Cor 5:17) or the duality of corrupt flesh versus Spirit. No cosmic clash is presented between the forces of good and evil, despite the references to God, the Devil (5:9), and the cosmic powers (3:22). Our author presents no pessimistic view of the present age, but manifests a positive outlook marked by confidence in God's power and hope for the future (1:13, 21; 3:15).

The contrast and conflict on which 1 Peter focuses is not cosmological but social—the contrast between a holy community united with God and a society alienated from God. The author speaks not of "new creation," however, but of personal rebirth and transformed communal life in a hostile environment. The perspective thus is eschatological but without any apocalyptic shadowing (see Michaels 1988, xlvi–xlix; Prostmeier 1990, 88–99). The end, for this author, is a time of redemption through Christ, of a testing of faith through suffering, of impartial judgment, and of a culmination of the salvation promised to the elect and holy people of God—a time calling for vigilance, fidelity, joy, trust, and hope. On the letter's eschatological perspective, see also Vitti 1931; Selwyn 1956; Parker 1994.

4. *Ecclesiology and Ethics*

1 Peter is one of the most church-oriented writings of the NT, though the word "church" (*ekklēsia*) never occurs. While the believers occasionally are depicted

as "living stones" (2:5) united by faith with Christ the "living stone" (2:4) or as "sheep" returned to their guardian and overseer (2:25) or as "children" of Sarah (3:6, regarding Christian wives), it is the plethora of *collective terms and images* employed to emphasize the community-forming dynamic of salvation and the communal identity of the redeemed that is one of the most striking features of this letter. Believers are depicted as constituting collectively a "house(hold) of the Spirit" (2:5d) or "house(hold) of God" (4:17), a "holy priestly community" (2:5e, 9b), an "elect stock" (2:9a), a "royal residence" (2:9b), a "holy people" (2:9d), a "people for (God's) possession" (2:9e), "God's people" (2:10b), a "brotherhood" (2:17; 5:9), "the flock of God" (5:2; cf. 2:25), and those who are "in Christ" (3:16; 5:10, 14).

These collective terms state explicitly what other metaphors for the act of salvation and its community-building effect imply: God's action of electing (1:1; 2:9; 5:13), sanctifying (1:2, 14–16, 22), fathering (1:3, 23; 2:2; cf. 1:17) or (pro)creating (4:17; cf. 2:13), building (2:5; 5:10), and gathering together (2:25) believers into *one communal entity*. Most of these terms were honorific predicates of ancient Israel, the imperiled and yet privileged people of God whom our author sees in the present company of believers, the children of Sarah and Abraham (3:6; 2:11), as the continuation and culmination. These collective predicates are applied to the believing community as the eschatological people of God and are designed to underscore the fact that believers scattered across Asia Minor and throughout the world neverthess form one communal entity, one collective body of believers in Jesus Christ who have been united by God and who must stand together in mutual support and familial solidarity.

While this community is implicitly distinguished from any among the House of Israel (1:4, 12) or elsewhere who reject Jesus as Messiah and mediator of salvation, the author shows no interest in a critique of contemporary Israel, as Goldstein (1976), Brox (1981; 1986, 49, 103) and others have correctly observed. Israel's early history and special status with God are treated as the initiation and model of a relationship with God that culminates in those now united with God through Christ. This blatant appropriation of the nomenclature of ancient Israel is a strategy typical of a sect seeking to legitimate itself by claiming to be the "true" representation of the body to which it once belonged. Other than this, the issue of Christianity's relation to contemporary Israel is largely ignored. The social interaction on which the letter exclusively focuses is that between the believing community and a hostile society, whose members are identified as "nonbelievers" (2:7b), "disobedient" (2:8; 3:1; 4:17) or "Gentiles" (2:12; 4:3). Israelites who reject Jesus as Messiah would be included in these designations, but nowhere is contemporary Israel a focus of attention or critique, in contrast to the Pauline letters and the Gospels.

Of the various ecclesial concepts employed in this letter, it is the symbolization of the community as the *household of God* that serves as the root metaphor and organizing ecclesial image in 1 Peter (cf. Elliott 1981/1990, 165–266; followed by Dalton 1990, 904). There is in 1 Peter a more extensive and consistent employment of *oikos*-related terminology and imagery than in any other writing of the NT. *Oikos* is used twice to designate the Christian readers as the "house(hold) of the Spirit" (2:5) or the "house(hold) of God" (4:17). The related verb *oikodomeō* is used in the passive voice to describe God's construction and integration of the house(hold) of faith (2:5). Slaves are specifically addressed as "household slaves" (*oiketai*, 2:18), whereas the more frequently occurring NT term is *douloi*. The verb *synoikeō* (sole NT occurrence) is used in reference to husbands' "living together" with their wives (3:7). "Household stewards" (*oikonomoi*) is the term employed to depict the recipients as servants of God's varied grace (4:10). Finally, *paroikos* (2:11) and *paroikia* (1:17) are linguistically related yet socially contrasting terms indicating the condition of Christians *within society*.

The household and familial character of the community is further highlighted by yet other expressions and images. The believing community is called a "brotherhood" (*adelphotēs*, 2:17; 5:9; cf. 5:13), whose members are urged to be "brother [and sister] lovers" (*philadelphoi*, 3:8), constantly engaged in maintaining the unity of the brotherhood through "brotherly [and sisterly] love" (*philadelphia*, 1:22–23), with *adelphotēs* and *philadelphoi* employed only here in the NT (cf. also Puig Tarrech 1980, 378–87). Silvanus is described as one such "faithful brother" (5:12) and Mark, as "my son" (5:13). The "kiss of love" that the author urged his addressees to share was in fact a gesture of family-like affection and solidarity. Believers, moreover, are called "children" of God (1:14), who as "Father" (1:2, 3, 17) brought them to new life (1:3, 23), provides nourishment for "newborn babies" (2:2–3), and builds them together as a house(hold) or family (2:5). Finally, use is made of "household management" (*oikonomia*) tradition to instruct the members of the household of God on proper deportment within the civil and domestic structures of society (2:13–3:7) as well as within the believing community (cf. also 5:1–5a). With this ensemble of household and familial terminology and imagery, our author has constructed a unifying concept of the community as the household or family of God called to live as God's holy and obedient children in a hostile society.

The psychological, social, and religious power of this familial metaphor derives in great part from the significance of the family as the fundamental unit of ancient social life and of kinship, kin, and kin-like relations as a basic principle of social ordering. Israel's history begins with the house of Abraham; it is the house of Jacob that covenants with God at Sinai; and it is within the House of Israel that the messianic movement centered in Jesus of Nazareth had its origin. Jesus redefined his *oikos* (family) as consisting no longer of his blood kin but of "whoever does the will of my father in heaven" (Matt 12:50; cf. Mark 3:35; Luke 8:21). He thereby established a new fictive-kin model of community that was to inspire the values, internal relations, and conduct of this movement for years to come. Historically, the *oikos* was the fundamental social locus, basis, and focus of the Christian mission as it moved "from household to household" (cf. Elliott 1981/1990, 198–200; 1984; 1991; Klauck 1981a, 1981b, 1982, 1992). And it was the symbol of the community as "house(hold) of God" (1 Tim

3:15; Heb 3:1–6; 10:21) or "household of faith" (Gal 6:10) that the movement used to express its communal identity and internal solidarity as well as its independence and distinctiveness vis-à-vis "outsiders" (1 Thess 4:10–12; Col 4:5; cf. 1 Cor 5:9–12). The household/family (*oikos*) thus provided the conceptual model, the vocabulary, and pattern of roles, relationships, and responsibilities for envisioning the collective identity of the movement, its organization, its familial values of love, loyalty, emotional commitment, hospitality and social order, its relation to God, and its demarcation from all outsiders.[33]

In 1 Peter, these aspects and functions of the household model are particularly prominent, perhaps more so than in any other writing of the NT. Beyond providing a vocabulary for affirming the distinctive collective identity of the Christian community, its union with God, and the bonds that unite brothers and sisters in love and loyalty, it also provided a means for consoling and encouraging readers confronting social alienation and its consequences as strangers and resident aliens (*paroikoi*). In this letter, *paroikia/paroikos* and *oikos tou theou* are linguistic correlates while at the same time functioning as social contrasts. The unsettling and debilitating experience of the readers was their experience of alienation and homelessness (*paroikia*), socially and religiously, in a hostile society. As reborn children of God, however, they have found a new place of belonging, divine protection, a supportive brotherhood, and a basis for hope as the *oikos tou theou*, the household and family of God. *Paroikoi* they are, and *paroikoi* in society they should remain, for in the family of God they have found a home (*oikos*) for the homeless. In this contrast of homelessness and "at-home-ness," the concept of the household of God serves as a potent symbol socially, psychologically, and religiously for addressing the predicament of social estrangement and for integrating the experiences of life and the expressions of faith.

The distinctive identity of the community, in turn, is to be manifested in a distinctive mode of conduct. A holy, set-apart community is to lead a holy, set-apart way of life. On the one hand, the believers are called to a level of morality equal or superior to that of their neighbors, such as acting honorably, respecting authority and order, maintaining harmonious domestic relations, not using freedom as a pretext for wrongdoing, doing what is right (2:13–3:12), along with the approved virtues of modesty (3:4; 4:15) and avoiding evil (2:1; 4:15). On the other hand, a holy mode of life requires that they avoid or abandon the vices

---

[33] On house, household, family, house churches, and familial metaphors in the NT and the early Church, see Filson 1939; Judge 1960; Aalen 1962; Weigandt 1963; Delling 1965; Strobel 1965; Schenke 1971; Lührmann 1975; Henning 1978; P. Schmidt 1978; Von Allmen 1981; Elliott 1981/1990, 165–266; 1984, 1991; Klauck 1981a, 1981b, 1982, 1992; Legido Lopez 1982; Vogler 1982; White 1982; Gnilka 1983; Malherbe 1983; Verner 1983; Aguirre 1984; Dassmann 1984; Gielen 1986; Laub 1986; Ohly 1986; Lorenzen 1987; Birkey 1988; Crosby 1988; Branick 1989; Schöllgen 1988; Grey 1989; Schäfer 1989; Barton 1991; Oliver and van Aarde 1991; Lampe 1992; B. F. Meyer 1992; De Vos 1993; Jacobs-Malina 1993; Love 1993; Rusam 1993; Banks 1994; Blue 1994; Carter 1994; Kraft 1994; Wagner 1994; Matson 1995; Osiek 1996.

typical of their past and characteristic of persons alienated from God (1:14–16; 4:2–4). The ultimate norm of their behavior is not cultural conformity but reverence for God (1:17; 2:17; 3:2, 16) and mindfulness of and obedience to God's will (2:15–16, 19–20; 3:16, 17, 21; 4:2, 19; 5:2; cf. 3:4), as exemplified by Jesus Christ (1:2; 2:21–24; 3:18). Humility, so despised in Greco-Roman society, is essential for all believers, superordinates and subordinates alike (3:8; 5:5b–6) and, in a reversal of traditional roles, humble household slaves are *first* addressed as examples for the entire household of faith. In their subordination to their husbands, wives are declared Sarah's children in doing what is right (3:6). Conjugal life is to be motivated not only by a desire for harmony but by the fact that both wives and husbands are "co-heirs of the grace of life" (3:7). A clear distinction is drawn between the honor due the emperor as to all persons, the love that binds only the brotherhood (2:17; cf. 1:22; 3:8; 4:8; 5:14) and the reverence reserved only for God (2:17). Just as Christ's story—his rejection and suffering at the hands of humans and his exaltation and honoring by God—establishes the plot for their story and its glorious outcome (1:6–9, 18–21; 2:4–10, 24–25; 3:18–22; 4:12–14; 5:1, 4, 10), so his obedient submission to God's will serves as the pattern for their conduct as well (2:21–23; 4:1–2; 5:3, 5–6). Such behavior (*anastrophē*, 1:15, 17; 2:12; 3:1, 2, 16) entails living in a holy fashion (1:14–16, 22; 3:2), having pure hearts (1:22), doing good deeds (1:17; 2:12), doing what is right (2:14, 15, 20; 3:6, 10–12, 17; 4:19) in contrast to doing what is wrong (2:1, 12, 14, 16; 3:9, 10–12, 17; 4:2–3, 15), righteous conduct (2:24; 3:12, 14; 4:18), being subordinate and respectful of order (2:13, 18; 3:1, 5; 5:5a), nonretaliation (3:9; cf. 2:23), pursuing peace (3:11; cf. 1:2; 5:14), love and support of fellow-believers (1:22; 2:17; 3:8; 4:8–11; 5:14), selfless leadership (5:2–4), humility (3:8; 5:5, 6), gentleness (3:4, 16), alertness (1:13; 4:7; 5:8), sound judgment (4:7), and resisting the Devil (5:8–9).

This kind of conduct is distinctive, defensive, and attractive. It distinguishes believers from nonbelievers (1:14–16; 4:2–4), it refutes suspicions and charges of wrongdoing (2:15), and it can lead detractors themselves to join believers in the glorification of God (2:12; 3:1–2). Behind the exhortation of the letter lies a clear interest in an effective mission to nonbelievers and an optimistic view of its effectiveness. This simultaneous convergence with and divergence from the norms and values of the society is consistent with the sectarian movement's twofold need to maintain its distinctive identity, exclusive loyalties, and honorable conduct as God's holy people, on the one hand, and to win adherents to the faith, on the other. Finally, the outcome of this conduct, faithfulness, and perseverance in suffering on the part of the believers themselves will be their own share in the grace, inheritance, and salvation yet to be revealed (1:4, 7, 9, 13; 2:2; 3:7, 9; 4:6c, 13c, 17–19; 5:1, 4, 10).[34]

---

[34] On the letter's ecclesiology and ethics, see Spörri 1925; Bolkestein 1942; Thils 1943; Brandt 1953; van Unnik 1954–1955; Swigchem 1955; Soucek 1960; Völkl 1961, 370–80; Kline 1963; Jonsen 1964; Schütz 1964; Lippert 1965; Elliott 1966b, 1968, 1970, 1976, 1979, 1981/1990, 1985, 1986, 1992a, 1995a; J. W. Thompson 1966; Schückler 1967; Sleeper 1968; Frattalone 1971; Phillips 1971;

Ultimately, the conflict that 1 Peter addresses might be described as a conflict about honor and shame, those pivotal values of ancient Mediterranean society (see Elliott 1995a). In the bitter struggle between the Anatolian Christians and their local neighbors, the chief weapon of attack employed by the latter was a barrage of verbal abuse designed to demean, discredit, and shame the believers as social and moral deviants endangering the common good. This procedure of public shaming was employed as a means of social control with the aim of pressuring the minority community to conform to conventional values and standards of conduct. Unrelenting abuse, in turn, resulted in undeserved suffering on the part of the believers and if unchecked could have led to their demoralization, despair, or even defection.

The response to this situation that our author recommends is not the conventional one of returning insult for insult but, rather, engagement in honorable conduct which could have three possible consequences for the abusive nonbelievers: the silencing of ignorant detractors (2:15), winning them to the Christian cause (2:12) or, if the slander continued, the exposure of the slanderers to the judgment of God, who would put the shamers to shame (3:16).

To move the beleaguered believers to this course of action, our author reminds them of the dignity and honor they already enjoy as a result of their baptismal incorporation into the household of God and their solidarity with their shamed but divinely honored Lord Jesus Christ (1:3–2:10). This honor from God is to be manifested in an honorable way of life in society (2:11–5:11). To suffer for doing what is right is honor before God (3:14; cf. 2:20). To be reproached because of allegiance to Christ is likewise a mark of honor assured by the experience of God's presence (4:14). To suffer as a Christian, a Christ-lackey, is no cause for shame (4:16ab) but, to the contrary, an opportunity for glorifying and honoring God (4:16c). The believers' honorable conduct, like that of Christ (2:21–25; 3:18), will ultimately be vindicated by God, the final arbiter of honor and shame.

In the transposition of honor and shame into a theological key, honor ultimately is ascribed not according to blood and birth, as convention would dictate; nor is it achieved by any heroic act of valor and *andreia* ("manliness," "courage"). Instead, it is conferred by an act of divine grace, by the favor of a God who gives grace to the lowly (5:5); a divine patron who raises slaves to the status of sons and daughters (2:18–25) and wives to the status of coheirs of the grace of life (3:1–7); who covenants with a lowly house of Jacob and exalts it to the status of God's very own special possession, his elect and holy people; and

---

Schlier 1972; Bruni 1973; Chevallier 1974, 1978; Bojorge 1975; Carter 1975; Frederick 1975; Furnish 1975; Goldstein 1975; Wolff 1975; Schröger 1976, 1981b, 1985; Refoulé 1979, 1990; Kohler 1982; Kendall 1985; Russell 1975; Cothenet 1979; Balch 1981, 1986; Brox 1981; Cothenet 1980–1981; Dalton 1981–1982; Winberry 1982a; R. E. Brown 1984; Warden 1986; Richardson 1987; Lamau 1988; Achtemeier 1988; Prostmeier 1990; Söding 1990; Feldmeier 1992; T. W. Martin 1992a; Schertz 1992; Zerbe 1993; Volf 1994. See also the studies on household instruction listed in the BIBLIOGRAPHY on 1 Pet 2:18–25.

who incorporates disgraced strangers and aliens into a graced family of God (2:4–10). On the one hand, 1 Peter illustrates how much the struggle between early Christianity and its social environment was a battle over social standing and social rating, honor disputed and honor paradoxically claimed. On the other hand, the letter also illustrates how honor and shame provided the idiom for conceptualizing the relationship of the social and the sacred, the experiencing of the countervailing grace or honor conferred by God in the face of social disgrace and shame. For Christians at odds with their environment and pressured to conform and assimilate, honor and shame are theologically redefined in this letter and reckoned according to a calculus of divine reversal, preeminently expressed in God's honoring of the shamed Messiah and honoring of those who share both his innocent suffering and his glorious vindication.

7. AUTHORSHIP

The issues of the authorship, place, and date of composition are inextricably related. Furthermore, decisions on these issues are also connected to positions taken on other questions, including the composition's genre; its literary integrity or nonintegrity; its literary affinities with other NT writings, especially those of Paul; its address; and its historical setting. Positions taken on any of these issues affect the position taken on authorship and vice versa. As a consequence, the question of the letter's authorship remains a highly controversial issue.

In general, three main theories concerning authorship have been advanced: (1) the letter was written by Peter himself; (2) it was composed by Silvanus, writing as Peter's secretary (*amanuensis*), either during the apostle's lifetime or soon after his death; (3) it was a pseudonymous composition written in Peter's name and apostolic authority.

7.1. PETER AS AUTHOR

7.1.1. Arguments for Direct Authorship by Peter

From antiquity until the advent of modern biblical criticism, the traditional view was that Peter himself wrote the letter (see Eusebius, *Hist. eccl.* 4.14.9 et al.). Modern scholars who continue to hold this view[35] adduce the following points in support of their position, several of which, however, are met by compelling counterarguments:

[35] These include Hort 1898; Stegmann 1917; Moffatt 1918, 334–35; and 1947; Wohlenberg 1923; Schlatter 1937; Lenski 1945; Cranfield 1950; Charue 1951; Franco 1962; Love 1954; van Unnik 1954, 1955, 1964; Hunter and Homrighausen 1957; Michaelis 1961; Gundry 1966–1967; Guthrie 1970; Thurston 1974; J. A. T. Robinson 1976; Neugebauer 1979; Grudem 1988; Michaels 1988 (as a possibility).

(1) The author explicitly identifies himself in 1:1 as the Apostle Peter.

(2) The author's further identification of himself as a "witness to the sufferings of the Christ" (5:1) is consistent with what is said of Peter as witness elsewhere in the NT (Luke 24:44–47 and especially the Petrine speeches and narratives of Acts; see the NOTE on 5:1). Further instances in which the author speaks in the first-person singular (2:11; 5:12b,c) or includes himself with the addressees ("we"/"us," 1:3; 2:24; 4:17) are compatible with Peter as author.

(3) The author's knowledge of and consistent appeal to the OT and OT figures (Sarah, Abraham, Noah and family) fit what might be expected of Peter, an Israelite.

(4) The theology of 1 Peter reflects early Christian thought. Its vibrant eschatology, theocentricity (focused on God as ultimate agent of salvation) and Servant of God Christology are typical of an early stage of Christian thought and consonant with views and teachings attributed to Peter elsewhere in the NT.

(5) Further ideas and images (e.g., impartiality of God [1:17], discipleship [2:21–24, 5:3], humility [3:8; 5:5–6], sheep-shepherd image [2:25; 5:2–4]) found here are also associated with Simon Peter in the Gospels and Acts (so especially Gundry 1966–1967; 1974; Maier 1984; for a more moderate position, see Moule 1955–1956; and Best 1971, 51–54).

(6) The rudimentary character of the church order (5:1–5a) presupposed in the letter and its concept of charisms (4:10–11) also point to an early date of composition compatible with Petrine authorship.

(7) Peter had had early contact with Israelite pilgrims from Pontus, Cappadocia, and Asia at the Pentecost festival in Jerusalem, according to Acts 2:9–11, a contact that possibly could explain his writing now to believers in these provinces (1:1).

(8) If Silvanus is not identified in 5:12 as the courier of the letter (as some supporters of authenticity hold), he may be identified as a secretary writing at Peter's behest while the apostle was still alive; on this point, see below.

(9) Post-NT tradition unanimously attests Peter's presence and death in Rome, the likely location to which "Babylon" (5:13) refers as the place of the letter's composition (see below and the NOTE on 5:13).

(10) The reference to "Mark, my son" (5:13) indicates an intimate relationship, perhaps reaching back to their early contact in Jerusalem (Acts 12:1–17). Their collaboration in Rome is attested in post-NT tradition (see the NOTE on 5:13).

(11) No connection is made in the letter between the suffering experienced by the believers and Roman anti-Christian aggression, thereby suggesting a date of composition prior to Nero's attack on the Christians of Rome (ca. 64–65 CE).

(12) 1 Peter "exhibits none of the telltale pointers to pseudonymity, such as a self-conscious straining after verisimilitude or the barely concealed assumption that the apostolic age lies in the past" (J. N. D. Kelly 1969, 30), in contrast to 2 Peter, a clearly pseudonymous writing manifesting these traits; notice the fuller name "Simon Peter" (2 Pet 1:1); Peter's "reminder" (1:12 and 3:1); allusion to Jesus' transfiguration at which Peter was present (1:16–17); and reference to "brother Paul" (3:15).

(13) The early acceptance of the letter as Petrine (from Irenaeus onward) and its early and unchallenged reception into the canon (see below under EXTERNAL ATTESTATION AND CANONICITY) testify to the assumption of its apostolic authenticity.

7.1.2. Arguments against Direct Authorship by Peter

Beginning with objections first raised by Herman Heimart Cludius (1808), an increasing number of scholars has grown convinced that the letter could not have been written by Peter himself (see the surveys by Hutter 1881, 35–36; and Prostmeier 1990, 15–37). Some objections carry greater weight than others, though cumulatively they make a cogent case:

(1) The polished Attic style, Classical vocabulary (Selwyn [1947, 499–501] lists over 200 possible Classical parallels; see also the INDEX in the present commentary), and rhetorical quality of this Greek composition make it one of the more refined writings in the NT. It is difficult to reconcile a composition of such quality with the Galilean fisherman Simon Peter whose mother tongue was Aramaic and who was described as "unschooled" (Acts 4:13). Simon Peter may also have spoken a primitive Greek, given the Hellenized condition of Galilee and the bilingual capabilties of Jesus and perhaps of his disciples as well. His ability in Greek, however, apparently was so inadequate that Mark, according to later tradition (Papias, cited in Eusebius, *Hist. eccl.* 3.39.15; Iren. *Haer.* 3.1.2), was required to serve as Peter's interpreter in Rome (see also the NOTE on 5:13).

(2) The numerous OT quotations in this letter are cited from the Greek Septuagint (LXX), not the Hebrew or Aramaic Targums with which Simon Peter would have been acquainted. The many OT allusions are even more telling, for they indicate a writer thinking in terms of the LXX, not the Hebrew (Best 1971, 49–50). The skillful interweaving of these LXX texts is likewise difficult to reconcile with an unschooled, Aramaic-speaking fisherman, whose Bible would have been Hebrew and whose language of worship would have been Palestinian Aramaic.

(3) The letter contains little mention of Jesus' teaching (apart from a few sayings never explicitly ascribed to Jesus) and virtually nothing of Jesus' life and ministry (apart from his suffering, death, and resurrection), a fact difficult to reconcile with one of Jesus' closest disciples. Although the author refers to himself as a "witness" in 5:1, the term does not mean "eyewitness" but one who bears testimony to Christ's suffering and glory. The claim that 1 Peter contains numerous "Petrine reminiscences" (Gundry, Maier) is greatly exaggerated (see Best 1969–1970; and the discussion above [2.4] concerning 1 Peter's NT affinities).

(4) There is no historical evidence that Peter himself missionized in Asia Minor, and 1 Peter contains no mention of any direct personal contact between Peter and the addressees. While pilgrims from Asia Minor may have heard Peter in Jerusalem, the author makes no reference to this, and from 1:12 it is clear

that he does not include himself among the evangelists who first preached the gospel to the readers. The ties that bind author and addressees are less personal than social and spiritual. Both belong to a worldwide brotherhood of faith and are similarly strangers and aliens in the Diaspora, undergoing similar types of animosity and suffering (1:1; 5:8–9, 11, 12–13). The weight of this as an argument against Petrine authorship, however, is uncertain. Paul wrote to communities that he did not found (Romans, Colossians; cf. the household of Philemon), and 1 Peter could be another instance of this as well. Post-NT tradition, in fact, even spoke of Peter's missionary activity in Asia Minor, a notion either inferred from 1 Pet 1:1 or perhaps known from local sources (see Origen [in Eusebius, *Hist. eccl.* 3. 1]; Epiphanius [*Pan.* 27.7], stating that Peter often visited Pontus and Bithynia; Jerome [*Vir. ill.* 1]; *Acts of Peter and Andrew* [Peter and Andrew in Cappadocia and Pontus]).

(5) The author presents himself as "the co-elder" (5:1), a unique designation never used by or attributed to Peter elsewhere in the NT, leading some commentators to suspect that at this point the actual writer of the letter is speaking (see the NOTE on 5:1).

(6) Were Peter the author of this letter from Rome, he would have been writing at a time when Paul too was there. In this case, however, as Krodel (1995, 64) points out, the absence of any mention of Paul, despite the letter's address to two provinces missionized by Paul, "becomes incomprehensible."

(7) Several factors, moreover, point to a date of composition after 70 CE and thus provide a further reason for discounting Peter as writer, since the apostle, according to the consensus of early Church tradition (Tert., *Scorp.* 15; Origen, in Eusebius, *Hist. eccl.* 3.1.3; Lact., *Mort.* 2; Macarius Magnus, *Unigenitus* 3.22, 4.4) died about 65–67 CE, in the aftermath of Nero's anti-Christian pogrom (see the NOTE on 5:13). For these factors, see below under DATE OF COMPOSITION.

(8) No Christian writer before Irenaeus (ca. 180 CE, *Haer.* 4.9.2) names Peter as the author. 1 Peter was likely known to both Clement of Rome (*1 Clement*) and Polycarp (*Letter to the Philippians*), but neither explicitly mentions Peter as author. Lack of reference to 1 Peter in the Muratorian Canon, in the Latin churches before the time of Cyprian, and in the Syriac tradition before the Peshitta of the fifth century is also curious for a writing supposedly from the pen of the Apostle Peter.

Other objections, though frequently advanced, are based on faulty premises and therefore can be dismissed as unconvincing and irrelevant:

(1) It has been judged "unlikely" that the historical Peter would refer to himself by his nickname "Peter" (and without the article) rather than by his personal name, Simon son of Jonah/John (Krodel 1995, 66). In 2 Peter, however, a composition viewed by virtually all scholars as pseudonymous, the use of "Symeon Peter" is considered one of the devices employed by the actual author to give the appearance of authorship by Peter. Little, in other words, can be concluded from the form of the name by itself.

(2) The letter, it is said, appears to be addressed to persons from a predominantly Gentile background, while Peter's mission was supposedly restricted to "Jews." This supposition rests exclusively on Paul's comment in Gal 2:7–8 that Peter missionized among the "circumcised," while Paul focused on Gentiles. This comment, however, even if accurate in general terms, cannot be taken entirely restrictively. Not only is it at variance with the portrait of Peter in Acts, where Peter is reported to have converted the Gentile Cornelius and his family and to have supported a mission to the Gentiles (Acts 15)—hardly total Lukan fabrications—it is also questionable on sociological grounds, for how could any mission be restricted to only one ethnic group in communities that were all composed of Israelites and Gentiles?

(3) Peter, it is claimed, would not have written to areas missionized by Paul. Besides involving sheer conjecture, this objection fails to recognize that only two of the provinces (Galatia and Asia) are known to have been areas of Pauline activity. The totality of the regions addressed in 1 Peter was hardly "Pauline turf."

(4) The claim occasionally has been made (Jülicher and Fascher 1931, 192–93; Marxsen 1979, 379) that if the name "Peter" were not present in 1:1, nothing in the writing would lead its readers to imagine Peter as its author. These and other scholars, assuming that the affinities of 1 Peter with the letters of Paul put 1 Peter in the Pauline camp, declared the author of 1 Peter to be a "Paulinist." On this basis they ruled out Simon Peter as author, since the apostle himself never would have merely aped Pauline thought and phraseology. This line of thinking, going back to Cludius (1808), is now recognized as mistaken, since its premise is erroneous. It is now acknowledged that 1 Peter is not a mere *Abklatsch* (inferior copy) of Paul's ideas and formulations. The Petrine-Pauline affinities are instead the result of a common use of preexisting Christian tradition.

Such acknowledgment notwithstanding, K. M. Fischer (1973, 15; 1978) in fact went so far as to imagine that originally *PAULOS* stood in 1 Pet 1:1 and was later mistakenly read as *PETROS*, a conjecture finding no support whatsoever in the manuscript tradition in which *PETROS* is always present. The related suggestion of Krodel (1995, 66–67) likewise finds no support in the manuscripts and is equally unconvincing. He proposed that if the name in 1:1 had been abbreviated, the difference between an abbreviated "Peter" and an abbreviated "Paul" would have entailed no more than a stroke of the pen or stylus. Such a change from Paul to Peter, he imagines, could have occurred "by accident" prior to 2 Peter (cf. 3:1) or perhaps was made by the author of 2 Peter himself. One can only concur with Krodel's own admission that this theory, prompted by a desire to see 1 Peter as "a pseudonymnous Pauline letter" (1995, 67), is indeed "farfetched" (Krodel 1995, 66). On the whole, the effort to force 1 Peter into a Pauline mold must be judged a tendentious failure that contributes nothing toward solving the question of the authorship of 1 Peter.

(5) Those who assume that the original genre of 1 Peter was not a letter but a homily or liturgy later put into letter form rule out Peter as author because

the stages of the gradual construction of this mixed genre, along with other factors, presuppose a length of time after the death of Peter ca. (65–67 CE).[36] The composition, however, is clearly an integral letter so that this point too has no bearing on the question of authorship.

Even when these five objections are discounted as irrelevant, the preceding points 1–8 are of such weight that they have led a majority of scholars to deem the direct Petrine authorship of 1 Peter to be an untenable position (listed below under 7.3 and 7.4). Other solutions concerning the question of authorship must be considered. One such possibility, in the mind of several scholars, is that a secretary was involved in the composition of the writing.

7.2. THE SECRETARY HYPOTHESIS AND SILVANUS AS AMANUENSIS

One attempt to salvage some degree of Peter's immediate involvement in the letter's composition involves the hypothesis that Peter dictated or conceived the substance of the message which was then put into final literary form by a secretary (*amanuensis*), either prior to Peter's death or soon thereafter. This secretary either (1) is not named or, as most who favor this hypothesis think, (2) is expressly identified in 5:12 as "Silvanus, the faithful brother."

Secretaries were indeed employed in NT times for the drafting of letters (Doty 1973, 41; cf. also Roller 1933; E. R. Richards 1991; and Pliny, *Ep*. 9.36), as is clearly the case in Paul's use of Tertius in the composition of Romans (16:22) and as perhaps also is implied by Paul's addition of a greeting "in his own hand" (1 Cor 16:21; cf. Gal 6:11; Phlm 19). The first alternative (1), however, is sheer conjecture, with no textual basis whatsoever. Virtually all scholars favoring this secretarial hypothesis, therefore, point to 5:12 and claim that the expression *dia Silouanou* indicates that Silvanus was the writer.[37]

Silvanus as secretary or drafter of the letter, it is argued, could account for factors arguing against its immediate composition by Peter. These include the refined quality of the letter's Greek and its citation of the Greek Bible, the absence of references to Jesus and his ministry, the affinities of 1 Peter with the Pauline letters, its address to Asia Minor communities, and its supposed reflection of Pauline thought—factors all explained if Silvanus, the more "cosmopolitan"

---

[36] For example, von Harnack 1897; Perdelwitz 1911; Bornemann 1919–1920; Streeter 1929; Windisch 1930; Windisch and Preisker 1951; Leaney 1967; Beare 1970; Marxsen 1979.

[37] Scholars espousing this view include Seufert 1885b; Usteri 1886; von Soden 1899; Monnier 1900; Bigg 1902; Zahn 1909; Wohlenberg 1923; Radermacher 1925; Holzmeister 1937; Selwyn 1947; McNeile and Williams 1958; van Unnik 1954–1955; 1962a, 763–64; Stibbs and Walls 1959; Schneider 1961; Reicke 1964; Spicq 1966; Klijn 1967; Fitzmyer 1968; J. N. D. Kelly 1969; Schelkle 1976; Arichea and Nida 1980; Dalton 1989; Davids 1990; and Goppelt 1993. Bigg (1902, 195) and others (Wikenhauser 1963a, 506; Dalton 1989, 91), following a proposal made by Pseudo-Hilarius, further speculate that Peter himself wrote 5:12–14 to authenticate Silvanus's words. Among the translations, compare "with the help of Silvanus" (NIV) and "I am sending this note to you through the courtesy of Silvanus" (*Living Bible*).

figure and erstwhile colleague of Paul in Asia Minor, had drafted the letter at Peter's instigation. Selwyn (1947, 14–17) in fact went so far as to propose that alleged correspondences between 1 Peter and 1–2 Thessalonians were due to Silvanus's role in the writing of all three letters.

The sole *textual ground* on which this theory is based, the words of 5:12, however, does not sustain this proposal, and other factors militate against it as well.

As shown in the NOTE on 5:12, the construction, "I/we have written through X" (*egrapsa/egrapasamen dia* + Name), was a conventional formula for identifying not the secretary of a letter but its bearer or courier, as an abundance of evidence attests. Thus in 5:12 Silvanus is identified and commended ("the faithful brother, as I regard him") as the letter's *courier*, not its drafter. Additional points also argue against this proposal. There is no textual indication whatever that 5:12–14 was added personally by Peter. On the other hand, if these lines were by the secretary Silvanus, the accompanying self-commendation would be nothing short of "massive self-praise" (Brox 1986, 242). There is no reason to believe that the three terms in 1 Pet 5:1 ("co-elder," "witness," "sharer") supposedly describing Peter would better fit Silvanus. Nothing is known of Silvanus's literary capabilties, and consequently this theory would merely be substituting one unknown for another. Selwyn's attempt to link 1 Peter with 1–2 Thessalonians was convincingly refuted by Rigaux (1956, 105–11). Michaels (1988, 307) cogently observes that "if Silvanus had even a small part in writing the letter, it is more plausible that his name would have been linked with Peter's at the outset (as it was with Paul's in 1 Thess 1:1; 2 Thess 1:1)." Affinities of 1 Peter with the Pauline letters in general are due to common use of preexisting tradition. In no Christian writings after 1 Peter, moreover, is Silvanus ever mentioned as the letter's drafter, let alone its author.

The somewhat related theory of Bornemann (1919–1920) and others that 1 Peter originally was a homily by Silvanus that eventually was put into the form of a letter by a later unknown person and ascribed to Peter only compounds the unknowns. It involves not only a misreading of the function of Silvanus in 5:12 but also an indemonstrable homily theory and a postulation of yet another unknown author.

With the textual linchpin of this hypothesis removed and other objections weighing strongly against it, the notion of Silvanus as secretary or author or drafter of 1 Peter (or homilist of 1:3–4:11) represents little more than a counsel of despair and introduces more problems than it solves, as noted by Beare (1970, 212–16), Best (1971, 55–59), Brox (1986, 242), Lohse (1986, 41–42), and others.

7.3. 1 PETER AS A PSEUDONYMOUS LETTER

The factors discussed above make it virtually certain that 1 Peter is a pseudonymous letter ascribed to the Apostle Peter and produced not by Silvanus but either by someone remaining anonymous or by some group to which reference in the letter is made.[38] Of these two alternatives, the latter is now gaining the favor of a growing number of scholars.

"The use of the pseudonym," Beare (1970, 48) rightly points out, "need not trouble us in the slightest; the feeling that it is somehow fraudulent is a purely modern prejudice." The term pseudonymity, like its kindred term, pseudepigraphy, "is itself morally neutral" (Danker 1980, 129); both terms simply denote writings ascribed to persons other than their actual writers.[39] Writing in the name of someone else was a relatively common phenomenon in Greco-Roman philosophical circles and in the biblical communities as well. The OT contains writings (or sections thereof) ascribed to persons other than their actual authors (the 5 books of "Moses," the book of "Daniel," chs. 40–66 of Isaiah, chs. 9–14 of Zechariah; psalms of "David," proverbs of "Solomon"). No less than 65 extrabiblical works are found among the OT pseudepigrapha, and several pseudonymous writings appear among the NT books as well (James, 1–2 Peter, Jude, 1–2 Timothy, Titus, Ephesians, and possibly 2 Thessalonians; see Charlesworth 1983; 1992, 537–40, 540–41). Such pseudonymous or pseudepigraphical works fall into different literary categories with various motives for ascription (see the seven listed by Charlesworth 1992, 540. In general, the biblical and related pseudepigraphal books presume divine inspiration and are ascribed to deceased authoritative figures of the past (patriarchs, sages, prophets, kings, apostles) in whose religious stream of tradition the actual authors believed themselves to stand and under whose authority they claimed to write. As Danker (1995, 84) has noted in regard to 2 Peter, "pseudepigraphy is a device whereby a writer adopts the persona of a deceased and revered authority figure for communication with contemporaries. In most cases there was no attempt to deceive the public, but to say, 'If N. N. were living, this is what N. N. would say to us.'" This is the case with 1 Peter as well. Ascription of the letter to Peter would have been intended to identify its message as reflective of and consistent with the actual witness and pastoral concerns of the Apostle Peter.

The practice in the ancient Church of attribution of documents to Peter is well attested. In addition to 1 and 2 Peter, further writings ascribed to Peter include the *Gospel of Peter, the Apocalypse of Peter,* a letter of Peter to James

---

[38] Proponents of the letter's pseudonymity include Cludius 1808; von Harnack 1897; Perdelwitz 1911; Knopf 1912; Gunkel 1906–1917; Windisch 1930; Jülicher and Fascher 1931; Hauck 1933; Wand 1934; Hunzinger 1965; Windisch and Preisker 1951; Kee, Young, and Froehlich 1965; Leaney 1967; Marxsen 1968, 1979; Beare 1970; Best 1971; D. H. Schmidt 1972, 7–18; Schrage and Balz 1973; Goldstein 1975; Kümmel 1975; Brox 1975, 1978a, 1986; Vielhauer 1975; Elliott 1976, 1979, 1981/1990, 1982, 1992a; Millauer 1976; Mussner 1976; Cothenet 1980, 1988; Danker 1980; R. Pesch 1980; Senior 1980; Schröger 1981b; Koester 1982; Spivey-Smith 1982; Frankemölle 1987; Lamau 1988; Reichert 1989; Schutter 1989; Prostmeier 1990; Feldmeier 1992; Goppelt 1993; Duling and Perrin 1994; D. L. Barr 1995; Krodel 1995; Perkins 1994.

[39] On pseudonymity and pseudepigraphy in general and with relevance for 1 Peter specifically, see also K. Aland 1965; Speyer 1969, 1971, 1977; Brox 1973, 1975a, 1975b, 1977, 1978b; K. Koch 1976; Meade 1986; Bauckham 1988c; Dalton 1989, 77–91, 82–86; E. E. Ellis 1992.

(attached to the *Clementine Homilies*), and an apologetic writing known as the *Preaching of Peter* (*Kērygma Petrou*). All are works of the second or later centuries, composed long after the apostle's death. Besides 1 and 2 Peter, some others also achieved a temporary measure of canonical standing. The *Apocalypse of Peter* appears in the Muratorian fragment; the *Gospel of Peter* was initially accepted in the Syrian church but later rejected by Serapion, bishop of Antioch (ca. 199–211 CE).

7.3.1. Various Conjectures concerning Individual Authors

Some scholars favoring the pseudonymity of 1 Peter regard Silvanus as the actual author (e.g., Seufert 1885b, 352–54). This theory, however, is vulnerable to many of the same objections applying to the theory of Silvanus as secretary. Still more problematic in this case is the notion that an author who thought that his own name lacked renown and therefore wrote under the name Peter, then "slipped" and revealed himself as author in 5:12. In addition to mistaking *dia Silouanou* as a reference to the author rather than the courier, this would be an instance without parallel in the pseudepigraphic literature (Brox 1986, 242). Most supporters of the letter's pseudonymity, however, take 5:12 to indicate Silvanus as courier, not author, but vary in regard to the possible motives prompting the ascription of the letter to Peter and the mention of Silvanus and Mark by name.

Some commentators theorize unconvincingly that Silvanus and Mark, taken as earlier associates of Paul, are named to connect 1 Peter with Paul and his Asia Minor mission. While the Silvanus and Mark mentioned here are most likely the same persons who earlier accompanied Paul on his journeys through Asia Minor (cf. Acts 15:22–18:5; 2 Cor 1:19; 1 Thess 1:1; 2 Thess 1:1; Acts 13:5, 13; 15:37, 39; Col 4:10; 2 Tim 4:11; Phlm 24) and therefore still could have been known to the communities there, the places addressed in 1 Peter include provinces *beyond* the reach of the Pauline mission (i.e., Bithynia-Pontus and Cappadocia), where the Paul-Silvanus-Mark association would not necessarily have been known. The theory that Silvanus and Mark were mentioned in 1 Peter to forge some link between this letter and Paul is further undermined by the fact that 1 Peter, in contrast to 2 Peter (which refers explicitly to "our beloved brother Paul," 3:15), makes no mention of Paul and displays no effort at effecting any connection with Paul, let alone at bringing about a "unification" of Petrine and Pauline factions of the church, as Brox (1978) points out in his critique of the *Unionsthese* of F. C. Baur (1856) and followers.

Restricting attention only to the name Peter, on the other hand, and attributing the letter to an anonymous "co-presbyter" (cf. 5:1), writing in Peter's name (e.g., Prostmeier 1990, 139–40), fails to account for the reasons that prompted the references to the names Silvanus and Mark. Brox, who treats the pseudonymity of 1 Peter most extensively (1975, 1978a, 1978b; 1986, 43–47), maintains, along with Beare (1970, 48–50), that the names Silvanus and Mark are simply part of the "device of pseudonymity," with little further significance, similar to the personal names mentioned in the pseudepigraphic Pastorals (Brox 1975, 85–86). He does allow the possibility, however, that Silvanus and Mark were mentioned because of their place in tradition concerning the Apostolic Council (Acts 15) and Peter's association with Mark in Jerusalem (Acts 12:12). This possibility was left undeveloped by Brox but is discussed below.

Brox thus represents a version of the view that 1 Peter was composed by an unknown author writing in Peter's name, an author who, however, violates the "Petrine fiction" and speaks directly as co-elder in 5:1 (see Prostmeier 1990, 139–40 for a similar view). Both Peter as author and Rome ("Babylon") as the place of the letter's origin, according to Brox (1975, 96), were part of the "fiction" of the letter. On this assumption, Brox then concludes that either (1) the letter was ascribed to Peter because it was written, actually or fictively, in Rome (the city with which Peter was linked), or (2) it was written in the name of Peter and therefore linked with Rome. This conclusion, however, is less than satisfactory. Why the author inconsistently violates the fiction of Petrine authorship and in 5:1 chooses to speak directly as co-elder is never adequately explained. Moreover, Paul too was in Rome. On Brox's reasoning, the letter could just as well have been attributed to Paul. Why then was it actually ascribed to Peter and why the accompanying references to Silvanus and Mark? A closer consideration of these questions has led to a more likely scenario, the second version of the third view (3b): the letter originated within a Petrine group in Rome, writing in the name of its leading figure, the Apostle Peter.

Conjectures, on the other hand, that the actual author was Mark (Eichhorn, Kühl), or Barnabas (McGiffert) or the author of Acts (Seufert) or Aristion of Smyrna (Streeter) can only be viewed as exegetical curiosities (see Brox 1978, 110).

7.3.2. 1 Peter as a Letter from a Petrine Group in Rome

The theory that the letter emerged from a Petrine group in Rome was first proposed in rudimentary form by Best (1971, 62–63) and Senior (1980, xiv–xv) and was developed more extensively by the present writer (Elliott 1979, 32–36; 1980; 1981/1990, 267–95; 1982, 66; 1992, 277–78). Numerous scholars now consider the theory plausible, if not probable.[40] Factors supporting this theory include the following points:

(1) Peter, like Paul and other missionaries, did not work alone, and therefore the existence of a Petrine group was inevitable from a social and practical point of view. In Peter's case, there is also NT evidence of groups of which he was a member or leading figure: besides his prominent place among "the twelve" (Mark 3:13–19 par.), eleven (Acts 1:13), and seven (John 21:2) disciples, he also worked in smaller groups; note, for instance, "Peter and those with

[40] Blevins 1982, 402–3; Bauckham 1983, 146–51, 160–61, 167; 1988b, 3739; R. E. Brown and Meier 1983, 130; J. L. Price 1987, 401; Michaels 1988, lxvi; Soards 1988; Knoch 1991; Mullins 1991, 139–48; Duling and Perrin 1994, 477; R. P. Martin 1994, 94; D. L. Barr 1995, 442.

him" (Mark 1:36; Luke 8:45 [variant reading]; 9:32; Mark 16 [*conclusio brevior*]; cf. Ign. *Smyrn.* 3:2); Peter, James, and John of Zebedee (Mark 5:37/Luke 8:51; Mark 9:2/Matt 17:1/Luke 9:28; Mark 14:33/Matt 26:37; Luke 5:10) and Andrew (Mark 1:16–20/Matt 4:18–22; Mark 1:29; 13:3; Acts 1:13); Peter and Andrew (John 1:40–42, 44; cf. 6:8); Peter and John (Luke 22:8; Acts 3:1, 3, 4, 11; 4:13, 19; 8:14); Peter "and another disciple (whom Jesus loved)" (John 18:15; 20:2, 3, 4; 21:15–23); Peter and James of Zebedee (Acts 12:1–3); Peter (Cephas), James (brother of the Lord), and John (Gal 2:9) or Cephas and James (Gal 1:18–19); Peter and the brothers of the Lord (1 Cor 9:5; Acts 1:13–14; 12:17; 15; Gal 1:18–19; 2:9, 11–12; compare Mark 16:7 with Matt 28:10 and John 20:17); Peter and the household of Mary (including John Mark, Acts 12:12–17). "These groupings may reflect not only familial (Andrew) or local (Galilee, Jerusalem, Antioch, Corinth?) associations, but also teams of ministry, groups of leaders, and circles of support" (Elliott 1981/1990, 273).

(2) That Peter, like Paul and others, worked in groups or teams is also likely from a sociological perspective, for this accords with the dynamics of a social and religious movement. The experience, thoughts, visions, and actions of one person only become socially relevant and effective when they are shared by a group or groups of sympathizers. The "big man" view of history, according to which single (male!) individuals affected the course of events has now been exposed as a figment of nineteenth-century imagination. In actuality it was, and only could have been, persuasive and powerful groups leading collective movements that altered the course of history. As the Jesus movement advanced beyond Palestine, it grew in strength through the formation of team missions and group ministries, conversion of households, and establishment of social networks. Although there is more NT evidence for the existence and collective activities of a Pauline group, there is no reason to doubt and every practical reason to assume that other missionaries and leaders such as Simon Peter, John, and James also had their groups of associates, co-workers, aides, and supporters. (For a brief but welcomed consideration of the phenomenon of groups within early Christianity, see Berger 1977, 226–34.)

(3) The explicit naming of Silvanus and Mark in 1 Pet 5:12–13 makes sense if they were actually intimate colleagues of the Apostle Peter and associated with the composition and dispatch of the letter in Peter's name.

(4) The personal association of these three persons is compatible with what is recorded of them in Acts. Peter and Silvanus/Silas were both present at the "Apostolic Council" in Jerusalem years earlier, and both played key roles in the council's promotion of the Gentile mission (Acts 15). Peter spoke in favor of this mission (Acts 15:7–11), and Silvanus and Judas Barsabbas were "leading men among the brothers" and "prophets," who delivered the letter of this council to the believers in Antioch (Acts 15:22–34). Subsequently Silvanus joined Paul in a mission to regions of Asia Minor and Greece (Acts 15:40–18:22; 2 Cor 1:19; 1 Thess 1:1; 2 Thess 1:1).

In Jerusalem, Silvanus and Peter also had contact with Mark, in all likelihood the same person identified in 1 Pet 5:13 as "my [Peter's] son" (see the

NOTE on 5:13). Mark too had visited regions of southern Asia Minor as a member of Paul's first mission to this area (Acts 12:25–14:28) and after separating from Paul (Acts 15:36–39) perhaps rejoined the apostle at a later date (cf. Col 4:10; 1 Tim 4:11; Phlm 24). If the place of imprisonment from which Colossians was written (cf. Col 4:3, 10, 18) was Rome, this would also put Mark in Rome, though this can hardly be stated with certainty. Whatever may have brought these three figures, who were associates in Jerusalem, eventually together again in Rome, the intimate relation among them indicated in 1 Pet 5:12–13 is consistent with their earlier collaboration.

(5) The absence of any further information concerning Silvanus and Mark indicates that they, like Peter, were assumed to have been known to the addressees by reputation, even though not necessarily through personal contact. The only Silvanus and Mark who could have been so well known must have been these members of the Jerusalem mother church who also had had contact with at least some of the Asia Minor communities.

(6) The role of Silvanus in 1 Peter is identical to his role earlier in Jerusalem. In each case he is a prominent person ("leading man among the brothers . . . prophet," Acts 15:22, 32; "faithful brother," 1 Pet 5:12) entrusted with the task of delivering a letter, in which Peter had a part, to distant brothers and sisters in Asia Minor.

(7) The naming of Silvanus and Mark, along with the ascription of the letter to Peter, serves several purposes related to the thrust of the letter as a whole:

First, the personal names personalize the letter and its message. In contrast to Hebrews or 1 John, 1 Peter enhances the personal bond between senders and recipients, by including the names of figures known to the letter's audience. The explicit descriptions of Silvanus and Mark as "brother" and "son" not only express their intimate relation to Peter but also are appropriate in a letter that characterizes the believing community as a "brotherhood" (2:17; 5:9) and family or household of God (2:5; 4:17). Both, along with Peter, are members of the brotherhood in Rome now in personal touch with the brotherhood in Asia Minor.

Second, the names authorize the content of the message and give it weight and a personal "seal" (Goppelt 1993, 50–52). The careers and reputations of the three persons named are linked with the earliest phase of the messianic movement in Palestine, its crucial developments and decisions, and its worldwide mission. Their ministry from east to west and points in between and now their concern for the brotherhood in Asia Minor illustrate the inclusive ethnic and geographical dimensions of the universal grace of God of which their letter speaks. Given their roots in Palestine, they also confirm the antiquity of the traditions contained in the letter; and the origin of their letter in "Babylon"/Rome (see below), a prominent gathering point of diverse Christian traditions (Vanhoye 1980), explains the rich diversity of these traditions (Hellenistic as well as Palestinian; Goppelt 1993, 30, 33–36).

Third, of this group, Peter was the chief and central figure. He was undoubtedly known to the addressees already as apostle and early follower of Jesus

Christ and proclaimer of Jesus' suffering and resurrection, perhaps via the Pentecost pilgrims from Pontus, Cappadocia, and Asia present at his Pentecost address in Jerusalem (Acts 2:1–42). "Peter was the one among the Twelve most open to the Gentiles, and so he may have been the patron of the Jerusalem mission to the Gentiles in the disapora" (R. E. Brown, in Brown and Meier 1983, 131 n. 277). The witness in this letter to God's inclusive grace and indiscriminate judgment, to Christ as "stone," to his words, to the atoning power of his death, to following in the footsteps of Christ, God's suffering servant, and to sharing in his resurrection and glory is in complete accord with what is said of Peter elsewhere in the NT (Cullmann 1958, 65–69), and it is Peter's name, ministry, and witness combined with his own suffering and death that give this letter its ultimate authority and power. Attribution of this letter to the Apostle Peter appropriately identifies the one within the Roman community to whom its content and theology most owed their origin and inspiration.

In this light, the issue of the specific person *writing* the letter assumes secondary importance to the person to whom the letter is *ascribed*. While 1 Peter is pseudepigraphic because not directly written by Peter, it was ascribed to the apostle not simply because Peter was known to have been in Rome, the place of the letter's origin (so Brox 1975, 96), or because its alleged aim was to reconcile "Pauline" communities in Asia Minor with a Petrine group at the capital. As a letter from the Petrine group in Rome of which Silvanus and Mark were members, it was ascribed to Peter the Apostle because the group responsible for its composition knew that they were expressing not primarily their own ideas but rather the perspectives and teaching of their foremost leader, the Apostle Peter. The letter is then "Petrine" in the secondary sense that it embodies and transmits the theology and pastoral concerns of the chief figure of this Petrine circle.

At the same time, the letter contains a blend of further diverse traditions representative of early Christian proclamation, teaching, and worship in general—a body of tradition gradually coalescing at Rome (Vanhoye 1980). Thus, 1 Peter is not only a testament to the Petrine legacy but also an expression of the theology of the Roman church of which Peter was a leading figure. On this tradition and its reflection in 1 Peter, see also below under Rome as the letter's place of composition.

Since it is under the name of the Apostle Peter that this letter from the Petrine community in Rome was written, and since a single author is presumed in 2:11 and 5:11, the singular term "author" or "Petrine author" will be used throughout the commentary for the one who, on behalf of the Petrine group, wrote this letter in Peter's name.

This issue of the letter's ascription to or authorship by Peter is inextricably linked with the tradition concerning Peter's ministry and death in Rome. This fact leads to the issues of the letter's place of composition and dating.

8. PLACE OF COMPOSITION

Various proposals have been made concerning the letter's place of composition, with Rome preferred by the great majority of commentators.

(1) Antioch in Syria has been proposed by some scholars, most notably Boismard (1957; cf. also Hunzinger 1965: "Syrian–Asia Minor area"). A legend known to Origen (*Hom. Luke* 6.1) and Eusebius (*Hist. eccl.* 3.36.2) identified Peter as the first bishop of Antioch and the immediate predecessor to Ignatius. If historically accurate, it would allow Antioch as a place of origin of a letter from Peter. The legend, however, apparently developed after Ignatius, who makes no mention of Peter as his predecessor, and so the legend lacks historical value. Boismard (1957, 183) claimed that, since the letter's alleged teaching on Christ's descent to the underworld (1 Pet 3:19) was first attested by the Syrian church and, since the designation "Christian" (1 Pet 4:16) originated in Antioch, 1 Peter must have originated in Antioch. 1 Peter 3:19, however, refers to a heavenly *ascent*, not "descent," of Christ and manifests no relation to the later doctrine of Christ's *descensus ad inferos* (see the NOTE and DETAILED COMMENT on 3:19). The currency of the label "Christian" in Rome in the mid-60s, on the other hand, would make Rome as likely a candidate for the letter's place of origin as Antioch. 1 Peter, moreover, differs notably in its theology, concerns, and church order from the letters of Ignatius, bishop of Antioch. It makes no reference to themes typical of Christianity in the east (e.g., conflict with Israel and gnosticism) but is far closer to writings of the western church (Hebrews, Mark, Luke–Acts, *1 Clement*, Hermas), as Goppelt (1993, 48) has noted.

(2) Asia Minor occasionally has been suggested by others,[41] but an origin here is also most unlikely. The letter was known here at an early date. Both Papias and Polycarp were acquainted with it (see below under ATTESTATION), but this is simply consistent with its *address* to this region and indicates nothing about its place of origin. The claim of Hunzinger (1965, 77) and Vielhauer (1975, 588) that apocalyptic writings were composed in areas to which they were addressed is an unsubstantiated generalization and in any case has no bearing on 1 Peter, which is hardly an "apocalyptic letter" (against Michaels 1987; 1988, xlvi–xlix; and Schutter 1987). Moreover, Hunzinger's postulation of a Syrian–Asia Minor origin is inconsistent with his recognition that in 1 Peter Rome is signified as "Babylon," which the letter clearly indicates as its place of origin (5:13).

(3) The letter's place of origin is indicated explicitly as "Babylon" in 5:13, a term used figuratively for Rome in the opinion of the vast majority of scholars.

(3.1) There is little to commend taking "Babylon" literally as a reference to either the Babylon in Mesopotomia or the Babylon located in the Nile Delta of

[41] See Knopf 1912, 25; Streeter 1929, 131–34; Hunzinger 1965, 77; Vielhauer 1975, 587–88; Marxsen 1979, 389, 391; Reichert 1989, 525–29.

Egypt. Mesopotamian Babylon was virtually desolate in the first century CE, and Babylon on the Nile, founded by refugees from Mesopotamian Babylon, was at this time a Roman military garrison. Neither of these localities was associated in tradition with Peter, Silvanus or Mark, or Christian communities in general (see the NOTE on 5:13 on these sites).

(3.2) On the other hand, the term "Babylon" often was used figuratively of Rome in Israelite and Christian literature following the Roman conquest of Judea in 70 CE (see *2 Bar.* 11:1; 67:7; 77:12, 17, 19; 79:1; 80:4; *4 Ezra* 3:1–5:20; 10:19–48; 11:1–12:51; 15:43–63; 16:1–34; *Sib. Or.* 3:63–74, 303–13; 5:137–78; Rev 14:8; 16:19; 18:2, 10, 21; and several rabbinic texts cited in the NOTE on 5:13).

(3.3) The association of Peter, 1 Peter, and Mark with Rome (but no other place bearing the name Babylon), moreover, is a consistent feature of the post-NT Christian tradition from *1 Clement* (5:1–7) and Ignatius (*Rom.* 4:3) onward (see the NOTE on 5:13 for details). It was there, tradition held (see the NOTE on 5:13), that Peter also died (ca. 65–67 CE), most likely in connection with the devastating fire of 64 CE and Nero's execution of Christians as the alleged arsonists, as described by Tacitus (*Ann.* 15.41, 44).

(3.4) The origin of 1 Peter at Rome, moreover, also has early attestation by Papias and Clement of Alexandria (*Hyp.* 6; see Eusebius, *Hist. eccl.* 2.15.2).

In comparison with this unanimous voice of the tradition, other interpretations of "Babylon" as referring to an indeterminate place, perhaps as a metaphor for "life in exile," are unpersuasive (see the NOTE on 5:13). The figurative use of "Babylon" for Rome, the literary tradition of the association of Peter with Mark in Rome, and both the literary and archaeological evidence pointing to Peter's final ministry, death, and burial in Rome make the equation of "Babylon" and Rome virtually certain in the opinion of the majority of commentators.[42]

There are no grounds in 1 Peter, however, for regarding "Babylon" as a "code name" for Rome designed to conceal the locality of the author from readers outside the Christian community, as may have been the case with Revelation (so also Goppelt 1993, 375). In contrast to Revelation, 1 Peter engages in no negative critique of Rome and nowhere associates Roman officials with harassment of the believers. Only once in the letter is reference made to Rome's authority (2:14, 17d), where respect and subordination are enjoined in regard to the emperor and his governors. The honorable conduct for which 1 Peter calls would hardly disturb outsiders or strike them as subversive, so a code name for its place of origin would be unnecessary. "Babylon" symbolizes Rome, in accord with tradition, as the seat of world power and the capital of a nation, which like the Mesopotamian Empire of old, subdued the land of Judea, displaced its inhabitants, and ushered in a new era, for better or worse, in the history of God's people. For the Petrine author this similarity between Rome and Babylon

[42] See also Smothers 1926–1927; Galling and Altaner 1950; Kuhn 1964; Hunzinger 1965; Schlier 1968; Thiede 1986.

was more a given than an issue for discussion. The city of Rome, like the provinces of Asia Minor, was part of the Diaspora (1:1) in which the members of the brotherhood were scattered. Those sending this letter lived socially as strangers and aliens in Rome just as did the addressees in the Roman provinces of Asia Minor. In parallelism with "Diaspora," "Babylon" stands for Rome and expresses the fact that addressees and senders shared a common experience of displacement and resulting vulnerability.

(3.5) Rome is a plausible point of origin for an encyclical letter addressed to Asia Minor, particularly if, as is likely, the remote Pontus is mentioned first in the address of 1:1 because it would be the point of arrival of Silvanus, the letter-bearer, traveling by ship from the west. With the conclusion of his circular route in Bithynia, he would return, again by ship, to Rome via the port of Puteoli or Ostia (see above, 5. THE ADDRESSEES AND THEIR SITUATION, and also the NOTE on 1:1).

(3.6) The largest city in the Roman Empire, with a population of about one million persons, most of whom were slaves and former slaves, Rome was a gathering place for many foreign groups (La Piana 1927). Israelites were one element of this foreign population for over two hundred years, and it is likely that their several synagogue communities provided the initial basis and network for the mission of the messianic movement there. Paul, writing to believers in Rome in the mid-50s, greeted at least five distinct household groups (Rom 16:3–16; vv 3–5, 10, 11, 14, 15; cf. Lampe 1991). This plurality of groups coincides with the plurality of Israelite synagogues (and absence of central organization) as well as with the plurality of cultural and religious views presumed by Paul among the Roman believers. What is known concerning the presence and diverse nature of Christian groups in Rome clearly allows for the existence of a distinct circle gathered around Peter, a group of which Silvanus and Mark (as later tradition attests) were members. These groups, moreover, all formed household communities none of which was identified as *ekklēsia*, two features that are also consonant with the household imagery and absence of the term *ekklēsia* in 1 Peter.[43]

(3.7) Rome as the location, destination, and meeting place of so many early Christians was the gathering site of a variety of cultural and theological traditions, many of which are merged in 1 Peter (Cothenet 1980, 27–36; Vanhoye 1980). This would also explain its similarities in terminology, formulas, thought, and diction with other writings of a Roman provenance (Romans, Hebrews, Mark, Luke–Acts [?], *1 Clement*, and Hermas), as a number of scholars have pointed out.[44] These correspondences, while generally insufficient to

[43] On early Christianity in Rome in general, see Vielliard 1959; Pietri 1976; R. E. Brown and Meier 1983, 92–216; Lampe 1989; R. E. Brown 1990; Jeffers 1991; Mullins 1991; Wiefel 1991; Snyder 1992; Fitzmyer 1993, 25–39.

[44] J. N. D. Kelly 1969, 11–12; Best 1971, 32–36; Millauer 1976, 192–93; Elliott 1982, 64; 1983, 190–94; R. E. Brown and Meier 1983, 134–39, 166–76; R. E. Brown 1984, 75–76; Brox 1986, 42; Lohse 1986, 53–55; Bosetti 1990, 287–91; Mullins 1991, 143–458 and passim; Goppelt 1993, 32, 48.

demonstrate direct literary dependency, do suggest a common reservoir of tradition in Rome upon which numerous authors drew, including the group responsible for 1 Peter. The affinities of 1 Peter and Romans in particular suggest that Romans was known to the Petrine author as part of the tradition of the Roman community (Kelly, Best, Elliott, Brown and Meier, Brox). Both documents, moreover, appear to have been known to the author of *1 Clement* as well (Elliott, Millauer, Brox, Lohse, Bosetti, Goppelt), as elements of this Roman tradition. R. E. Brown (1983a, 128–39; 1984, 75–83) also finds it plausible for a letter from Rome to be directed to communities of northern Asia Minor, given the likelihood that both regions shared the same type of Christianity that had its origins in Jerusalem. "With the fall of Jerusalem and the flight of Jewish Christians . . . from Jerusalem, Rome, where Peter had died, became a main [speaker] for a Christianity that remained strongly appreciative of the Jewish heritage" (R. E. Brown, 1983, 132).

"Behind the letter," Goppelt (1993, 48) aptly comments, "stood the church in the capital of the world." Here were displaced believers who were well acquainted with harassment and suffering and who could speak to this issue in the name of their former leader, the Apostle Peter. Soon after 1 Peter, the Roman church's reputation for the love and hospitality that 1 Peter so frequently urges (1:22; 2:17; 3:8; 4:8; 5:14) was noted by Ignatius, who describes the Roman believers as "preeminent in love" (*Rom. inscr.*).

On the one hand, then, our letter was ascribed to Peter because it was believed to embody and transmit key elements of the Petrine legacy. On the other hand, it also reflects the perspectives and interests of the Roman group associated with the apostle and its concern for the welfare of the Christian brotherhood beyond its urban borders. It affirms the bond that unites the Roman wing of the worldwide brotherhood with its beleaguered brothers and sisters in Asia Minor, a bond involving a common experience of suffering, a common confidence in the grace of God, and a common hope in the salvation yet to be realized. By reaching across the waters to the communities of Asia Minor, the letter establishes a bridge between the Church at the heart of the Roman Empire and the heaviest concentration of Christians anywhere in the Roman world. It represents the first of many efforts on the part of the Church at Rome to support and influence Christian communities abroad. In the course of the following centuries, this bridge will be traveled frequently in both directions.

9. Date of Composition

The letter contains no explicit statement regarding its date of composition so the date must be determined on the basis of circumstantial evidence. This includes (1) the earliest external attestation of its existence and (2) internal evidence relating to its date of composition and its corollaries: authorship, situation, genre, and place of origin. Divided opinion on these last issues is accompanied by disagreement concerning its date as well. Consideration of external and internal evidence indicating the upper and lower temporal limits of its composition is perhaps the most useful way to address this issue.

9.1. THE DATE BEFORE WHICH 1 PETER WAS WRITTEN

(1) External attestation of 1 Peter aids in establishing the date before which it had to have been written (*terminus ad quem*). Irenaeus (*Haer.* 4.9.2., ca. 180 CE) was the first to cite 1 Peter explicitly. Use of or allusions to 1 Peter, however, are found earlier in the first half of the second century, in the writings of Papias (Eusebius, *Hist. eccl.* 3.39.17, ca. 140 CE), Polycarp (*Phil*), and 2 Peter (3:1; see below under EXTERNAL ATTESTATION). The author of *1 Clement*, a letter from Rome to the church of Corinth in about 95 CE, also appears to have known and been influenced by 1 Peter. This is suggested by the numerous terms (many of them rare or unique to these two writings) and references to OT texts common to these two documents (see below under EXTERNAL ATTESTATION). In this case, 1 Peter was composed prior to 95 CE, the date when *1 Clement* was written in the opinion of most but not all scholars (contrast Herron 1988, 103, "ca. 70 AD").

(2) A date prior to 95 CE, in turn, is consistent with a comment by Pliny (*Ep.* 10.96), who, concerning Christians in Pontus (ca. 111–112 CE), states that some had renounced their faith "twenty years ago"—in other words, about 92 CE—a fact to which 1 Peter does not yet make reference. 1 Peter, though addressed in part to Pontic Christians (1:1) and though replete with references to harassment and suffering, contains no reference to defections; thus, they are likely to have occurred after its composition. The earliest date before which 1 Peter must have been written is then 92 CE.

(3) This upper limit is also consistent with the different situations in 1 Peter and Revelation. By the time of Revelation (ca. 95 CE), the condition of Christianity in Asia, another of the provinces addressed in 1 Peter (1:1), had worsened. In contrast to the absence of any mention of martyrs' deaths in 1 Peter and its neutral perspective on Roman rule, the later writing of Revelation indicates that many believers had died (2:13; 6:9–10; 16:6; 18:24; 19:2) and displays a thoroughly negative view of Rome, now portrayed as a violent agent of Satan (Rev 12–18).

(4) A composition before 92 CE is also consistent with factors mentioned earlier (see above on AUTHORSHIP) and features that distinguish it from late NT writings. These include the early character of the letter's theology (its vibrant eschatology and expectation of an immiment coming of Christ, theocentricity, early Servant of God Christology), its appreciation of charisms and its undeveloped church order, its lack of any appeal to apostolic authority as a motivation for its moral instruction, and the absence of any mention of internal heresies

or conflicts with gnosticism so typical of late-first-century and early-second-century writings (Pastorals, 1–3 John, Jude, 2 Peter, letters of Ignatius). The sole focus of 1 Peter is the relation of the Christians to hostile outsiders. "Here alone is the locus of conflict and confession" (Neugebauer 1979, 64–65).

A composition prior to Peter's death (ca. 65–67 CE) would be required if the letter were written by him or a secretary under his direction and so a date not later than 67 CE is favored especially by all proponents of direct Petrine authorship and most advocates of the secretary theory.[45] Given the strong likelihood of the letter's pseudonymity (see above under 7. AUTHORSHIP), however, there is nothing else requiring such an early date and certainly not a date (ca. 54 CE) prior to Romans (against Weiss and Kühl). In actuality, several factors point to its having been written at a date sometime after 70 CE. This evidence, however, does not include the harassment and suffering mentioned in 1 Peter. As indicated above (under SITUATION [5.3]), it was the abuse of hostile neighbors that caused this suffering, not worldwide anti-Christian actions initated by Rome and its emperors, the first instance of which was that of Decius (249–251 CE). Nero's pogrom against the Christians of Rome was an ad hoc attack limited to the city of Rome. Domitian and Trajan may have suspected Christians, like other foreign groups from the east, of wrongdoing, but neither undertook any official actions against the Christian movement as a whole, and Trajan specifically forbade hunting Christians down (Pliny, *Ep.* 10.97). Thus, efforts at relating 1 Peter to alleged "universal persecutions" of Christianity by Nero (54–68 CE) or Domitian (81–96 CE) or Trajan (98–117 CE) proceed from a false premise and hence are misguided and unconvincing.[46] Nor can a case for a late date of 1 Peter be made on the basis of its alleged literary "dependence" on many other NT writings. In reality, as discussed above (under 2. SOURCES AND AFFINITIES), its affinities with other NT writings are the result of a common use of preexistent tradition.

9.2. THE DATE AFTER WHICH 1 PETER WAS WRITTEN

Several factors are relevant in determining the date after which 1 Peter was written (*terminus a quo*):

(1) The correspondences between 1 Peter and Romans are close and numerous enough to suggest knowledge of Romans on the part of the Petrine author,

---

[45] For example, Hort 1898; Bigg 1902; Holzmeister 1937; Selwyn 1947; Stibbs and Walls 1959; Schneider 1961; van Unnik 1962a; Reicke 1964; Spicq 1966; Fitzmyer 1968; J. N. D. Kelly 1969; Guthrie 1970; J. A. T. Robinson 1976, 150–69; Neugebauer 1979; Dalton 1989; Davids 1990; Hillyer 1992; cf. also Michaels 1988.

[46] Against Cludius 1808; Baur 1856; Holtzmann 1885; von Soden 1899; Soltau 1905; Gunkel 1906–1917; Völter 1906; Knopf 1912; Knox 1953; MacCaughey 1969; Beare 1970; Downing 1988; Molthagen 1995; and others arguing along these lines; cf. Elliott 1976, 251–53.

thereby requiring a date for 1 Peter after the composition and arrival of Romans in Rome (ca. 56–58 CE). How much later than Romans it was written, however, must be determined by a consideration of further evidence.

(2) A clearer and more certain indication of the letter's composition after 70 CE is the author's use of "Babylon" as a reference to Rome (5:13) as the letter's place of origin (see above, under 8. PLACE OF COMPOSITION). The association of "Babylon" with Rome as a latter-day Babylon and destroyer of Jerusalem and the Temple is attested in documents only *later* than 70 CE (*2 Bar.* 11:1; 67:7; *Sib. Or.* 5:143, 159; *4 Ezra* 3:1, 28, 31); passages in Revelation (14:8; 16:19; 17:5; 18:2, 10, 21) are also relevant unless, as is sometimes suggested, this writing, though composed in the mid-90s CE, reflects the progress of the Judean Revolt in the late 60s. This use of "Babylon" for Rome in writings only postdating the destruction of Jerusalem and the Temple in 70 CE makes it highly likely that 1 Peter likewise was composed after 70 CE, as well as by someone other than the Apostle Peter who, according to tradition, died in the mid-60s. This point, made initially by Hunzinger (1965), has been considered a decisive indication of the letter's post-70 dating by most subsequent commentators. This dating, in turn, is consistent with internal evidence against direct authorship by Peter.

(3) The vast scope of the letter's address (four provinces comprising ca. 129,000 sq. mi. and two provinces not reached by Paul [Bithynia-Pontus and Cappadocia]) requires the allowance of sufficient time for the spread of Christianity into this area subsequent to the missions of Paul in the 50s.

(4) The letter's distance from the Pauline period and the early 60s is also indicated by the growth and coalescence of diverse traditions reflected in 1 Peter, a coalescence not yet found in the Pauline writings.

(5) The conflict treated in 1 Peter is no longer primarily an inner-Israel debate over Jesus as Messiah, observance of the Mosaic Law, circumcision, diet, and calendar, as with Paul. It concerns instead the struggle of an Israelite sect now identified as "Christian" (a term not used by and probably unknown to Paul) with hostile outsiders, all of whom are classified together as "Gentiles" (a usage not yet found in Paul).

(6) Other features in the letter are also consistent with a post-70 dating and temporal distance from Paul. These include its minimal references to the Holy Spirit, in contrast to Paul (and especially its lack of any association of the Holy Spirit with charisms [4:9–11]); its reference to elders (absent in Paul) and their identification as "shepherds" and "overseers," a development not yet in evidence in the Pauline writings but attested in Acts 20:17–35 (80s CE); and other traditions (discipleship and *imitatio Christi*; Noah, Flood and Enochic traditions; Petrine traditions; more developed household-management tradition) that it has in common with NT writings of the 70–100 period (Gospels, Acts, Ephesians, Jude, 2 Peter).

(7) If the sequence of the provinces (1:1) reflects the realignment of the adjacent provinces of Pontus, Galatia, and Cappadocia under Vespasian in 72 CE (see Filson 1962; Elliott 1981/1990, 60, 91), this would indicate 72 CE as an upper limit of the *terminus a quo* of 1 Peter's composition.

(8) Finally, a dating after 72 CE and before 93–96 CE, the last tumultuous years of Domitian's reign, would accord with the era of tranquility, stability, and prosperity established in the mid-Flavian period, which allowed the extensive growth of Christianity in Asia Minor presumed in 1 Peter (cf. Elliott 1981/1990, 84–87). The absence of any Roman-Christian hostility at this time would explain the neutral stance toward Roman rule manifested in the letter (2:13–17), in contrast to the demonization of Rome by the seer of Revelation, writing about 95 CE.

The combination of the relevant factors involving both external and internal evidence, in sum, favors a dating of 1 Peter sometime in the period between 73 and 92 CE.[47]

10. EXTERNAL ATTESTATION AND CANONICITY

10.1. EXTERNAL ATTESTATION

Until Irenaeus (the first Christian author to cite 1 Peter with explicit reference to Peter as author [ca. 180 CE]), all possible attestations to the existence and influence of 1 Peter are of the nature of allusions.

1 Clement

1 Clement is in all probability the first writing attesting the existence and influence of 1 Peter. This epistle from Rome (ca. 96 CE, according to most scholars, with Herron 1988, 103 [ca. 70 CE] representing a minority opinion) does not cite 1 Peter explicitly. However, the numerous lexical and thematic affinities that they share make it likely that Clemens Romanus knew and alluded to 1 Peter (along with Romans and Hebrews) as part of the local tradition of the Roman church.[48]

---

[47] Scholars favoring this or a more general time frame (dates between 70 and 100) for varieties of reasons, some more compelling than others, include von Harnack 1897; Perdelwitz 1911; Knopf 1912; Bornemann 1919–1920; Streeter 1929; Strathmann 1943; Windisch and Preisker 1951; Hunziger 1965; Marxsen 1968; Best 1971; Schrage 1973; Kümmel 1975; Millauer 1975; Vielhauer 1975; Elliott 1979, 1981/1990, 1982, 1992; Cothenet 1980; R. Pesch 1980; Balch 1981; Schröger 1981b; R. E. Brown-Meier 1983; R. E. Brown 1984; Brox 1986; Frankemölle 1987; Lamau 1988; Reichert 1989; Schutter 1989; Gielen 1990; Prostmeier 1990; Feldmeier 1992, Goppelt 1993; Duling and Perrin 1994.

[48] So J. N. D. Kelly 1969, 12; Best 1971, 32–36; Hagner 1973; Millauer 1976, 192–93; Elliott 1982, 64; Brox 1978, 186–87; Cothenet 1980, 17–18; Brown and Meier 1983, 166–76; Lohse 1986, 53–55; Bosetti 1990, 287–91; Mullins 1991, 144–45; Goppelt 1993, 31–32, 48.

Among the following affinities, an asterisk (*) marks especially striking correspondences:

1 Peter	*1 Clement*
1:1–2	1:1–2
1:1; etc. *eklektos*	1:1; etc. *eklektos*
1:8	7:2–4
1:11	8:1
1:15–16	7:1
1:17 *paroikia*	1:1 *paroikeō*
1:18–19	7:2–4*
2:9g	59:2*; cf. 36:2
2:13–17	61:1
2:13	37:3
2:21	16:17
2:22–24 (= Isa 53)	16:3–14* (= Isa 53:1–12)
2:25	61:3
3:6	4:8; 31:2; etc.
3:10–12 (= Ps 33:13–17a)	22:1–7 (= Ps 33:12–18)
3:20 Noah	7:6; 9:4 Noah
4:8 (= Prov 10:12 diverging from MT and LXX)	49:5 (= Prov 10:12 similar divergence from MT and LXX)
4:10	38:1
4:11; 5:10–11	chs. 64, 65
5:1	5:4
5:5a	57:1
5:5c (= Prov 3:34), with 30.2* (Prov 3:34, with *theos* replacing *kyrios*)	30:2* (= Prov 3:34, with *theos* replacing *kyrios*)

1 Clement has 327 words in common with 1 Peter, including the following, several of which (marked by *) occur in the NT only in 1 Peter or rarely elsewhere in the NT:

*agathopoiia**	1 Pet 4:19; *1 Clem.* 2:2, 7; 33:1; 34:2. Cf. *agathopoieō*, 1 Pet 2:15, 20; 3:6, 17; *agathopoios*, 1 Pet 2:14
*adelphotēs**	1 Pet 2:17; 5:9; *1 Clem.* 2:4
amiantos	1 Pet 1:4; *1 Clem.* 29:1
amōmos	1 Pet 1:19; *1 Clem.* 1:3; 35:5; 36:2; 37:1; 45:7; 50:2

aprosōpolēmptōs	1 Pet 1:17; *1 Clem.* 1:3
arketos	1 Pet 4:3; *1 Clem.* 49:3
charis hymin kai eirēne plēthyntheiē	1 Pet 1:2; *1 Clem. inscr.*
diasōzō (with Noah and flood)*	1 Pet 3:20; *1 Clem.* 9:4; cf. 7:6
eklektos	1 Pet 1:1; 4:2, 6, 9; cf. *syneklektos*, 5:13; 1 *Clem.* 1:1; 2:4; 6:1; 46:3, 4, 8; 49:5; 52:2; 58:2; 59:2
episkopē (for day of judgment)	1 Pet 2:12; *1 Clem.* 50:3
epopteuō	1 Pet 2:12; 3:2; *epoptēs*, *1 Clem.* 59:3
*hypogrammos**	1 Pet 2:21; *1 Clem.* 5:7; 16:17; 33:8
ktistēs (of God)*	1 Pet 4:19; *1 Clem.* 19:2; 59:3; 62:2
krateia cheir	1 Pet 5:6; *1 Clem.* 28:2
paroikia, *paroikos*	1 Pet 1:17; 2:11; *paroikeō*, *1 Clem. inscr.*
parepidēmos	1 Pet 1:1; cf. 2:11; *parepidēmeō*, *1 Clem.* 1:2
poimnion	1 Pet 5:2, 3; *1 Clem.* 16:1; 44:3; 54:2; 57:2
syneidēsis	1 Pet 2:19; 3:16, 21; *1 Clem.* 1:3; 2:4; 34:7; 41:1; 45:7
*tapeinophrōn**	1 Pet 3:8; *1 Clem.* 19:1; 38:2
timios (with blood of Christ)	1 Pet 1:19; *1 Clem.* 7:4; cf. 21:6
*timēn aponemein**	1 Pet 3:7; *1 Clem.* 1:3
philadelphia	1 Pet 1:22; *1 Clem.* 47:5; 48:1
philoxenos	1 Pet 4:9; *1 Clem.* 12:3; *philoxenia*, *1 Clem.* 1:2; 10:7; 11:1; 12:1

Important motifs or themes in 1 Peter also reappear in *1 Clement*: elect, election (*eklektos*, *eklegomai*, *eklogē*); call, calling (*kaleō*); glory (*doxa*); hope (*elpis*, *elpizō*); will of God (*thelēma tou theou*); obedience (*hypakoē*, *hypakouō*); order (*taxis*) and subordination (*hypotassō*); humility (*tapeinophrōn*, *tapeinophrosynē*); and so on. The two writings also have OT citations in common (Ps 33[34]; Prov 10:2; 3:34; and Isa 53), as well as common references to Noah (see above). These affinities, in sum, make it highly probable that 1 Peter was among the Roman writings known to and used by the author of *1 Clement*.

2 Peter

2 Peter, written sometime in the first half of the second century (see Elliott 1992a, 282–87), is the only NT writing to make an apparent reference to 1 Peter, if, as is commonly thought, 2 Pet 3:1 ("This is now the second letter that I have written to you") is taken as a reference to 1 Peter and not Jude, which 2 Peter

obviously incorporates. However, the pronounced Hellenistic vocabulary and conceptuality of 2 Peter and other dissimilarities in style, content, and theological perspective clearly indicate different authors, the different use of the same terminology, and the minimal degree of 2 Peter's "indebtedness" to 1 Peter (see Mayor 1907/1965, lxviii–cv; Holzmeister 1949; Boobyer 1957; Bauckham 1983, 143–47; 1988b, 3716–18). Dissimilarities in the two writings were already apparent to the Church Fathers, as Jerome illustrates, commenting on differences in vocabulary and style (*Cat. Script. Eccles.* 1; *Epist.* 120.11). The early observations of dissimilarities undoubtedly played a role in the different reception and canonical history of both documents, the early acknowledgment of 1 Peter as Petrine, and doubts concerning the Petrine authorship of the latter. Affinities noted by scholars include the following:

1 Peter	*2 Peter (and Jude)*
1:1 "Peter"	1:1 "Peter"; cf. 3:1
1:1 etc. "elect"	1:10, "election"; cf. Jude 2
1:2 greeting	1:2; cf Jude 2
1:3, 17 "Father"	1:17
1:7, 13; 4:13; 5:1,4	1:16, revelation, coming of
1:7 etc. "glory"	1:3 etc.
1:10–11 "prophets"	1:20–21; 3:2
1:14–16; etc. "holy"	3:11, 14; cf. Jude 20
1:15, 19	3:14
1:17; 4:5, 17 "judgment"	3:7
1:19	3:14; cf. 2:13
1:22; 2:17; 3:8; 4:8; 5:9	1:7
2:12; 3:2 *epopteuō*	1:16
2:16	2:19
3:19 "disobedient angel-spirits"	2:4; cf. Jude 6
3:20, Noah, Flood	2:5; 3:6
4:2–4	2:2, 10–22
4:7	3:10
4:11d	3:18b
4:19 "creator"	3:5

On the relation of 2 Peter to 1 Peter, see also above, 2. SOURCES AND AFFINITIES. Bauckham (1983, 146; 1988, 3738–39) and Soards (1988), following Elliott (1981/1990, 267–95 in regard to 1 Peter), allow for the possibility that both documents are products of different authors of a Petrine circle in Rome.

Epistle of Barnabas

Barnabas, whose date is not absolutely certain (ca. 70–100 or 130 CE), manifests some lexical affinities with 1 Peter but contains no certain allusions or citations:

1 Peter	*Barnabas*
1:2c, 19	5:1
1:3	16:8
1:9	1:5
1:11	5:6
1:17	4:12, 19
2:4–7 (= Isa 28:16; Ps 117[118]:22)	6:2 (= Isa 28:16; Ps 117[118]:22, 23)
2:5	16:10
2:9	14:6
4:5	7:2

Shepherd of Hermas

The *Shepherd of Hermas*, a writing from Rome within the first half of the second century CE, likewise contains several affinities with 1 Peter, but no certain allusions or citations: (cf. Massaux 1950, 321–23):

1 Peter	*Shepherd of Hermas*
1:7	*Vis.* 4.3.4
2:5	*Vis.* 3.5
4:6	*Sim.* 9.16.5
4:14	*Sim.* 9.28
5:7, 8–9	*Vis.* 3.11.3; 4.2.4–5

Didache

The *Teaching of the Twelve Apostles* or *Didache* (first half of 2d century CE) has several affinities with 1 Peter involving possible allusions but no certain citations (cf. Massaux 1950, 642–43):

1 Peter	*Didache*
1:13	16:1
2:1; 4:2–3, 15	2:1–7; 3:1–6, 9; 5:1–3
2:11	1:4
2:18	4:11
2:19–20	1:3
3:9	1:3
4:9	4:7
4:11	4:1
4:12	16:5

Polycarp, Letter to the Philippians

Polycarp, bishop of Smyrna in Asia Minor (died 155/56 CE), in his *Letter to the Philippians* (before 140 CE), included a few clear citations of, as well as allusions to material in 1 Peter, in addition to references to Paul's letters, particularly Philippians. He refers explicitly to Paul (3:2; 9:1; 11:2, 3) because he writes to the same community that years ago had received a letter from Paul (Philippians) but refers only implicitly to Peter ("Paul and the other apostles," 9:11). Eusebius (*Hist. eccl.* 4.14.9), however, noted Polycarp's knowledge and use of 1 Peter: "Now Polycarp, in the said writing of his to the Philippians, extant to this day, has employed certain testimonies taken from the former epistle of Peter."

1 Peter	Polycarp, *Philippians*
1:2 *plēthyntheiē*	*Inscriptio*, *plēthyntheiē*
1:3a	12:2*
1:8	1:3*
1:10–11	6:3
1:13, 21	2:1*
1:21	12:2
2:1	2:2; 11:1
2:11	5:3*
2:12	10:2*
2:13	10:2*
2:21–24	5:2
2:21	8:2*; cf. 10:1
2:24, 22	8:1*
3:1–6	4:2
3:8a; 5:5b	9:1
3:8b	10:1*
3:9a	2:2*
3:13	6:3*
3:14	2:3
4:5	2:1
4:7	7:2*
4:8	3:3
4:14, 16	8:2
5:1	6:1
5:2–3	6:1
5:5a	5:3*
5:5b	10:2*
5:12ab	14:1
5:12f	10:1

*An asterisk marks virtually certain citiations.

Martyrdom of Polycarp

The *Martyrdom of Polycarp* (second half of second century CE) contains several possible allusions to 1 Peter but no certain citations.

1 Peter	*Martyrdom of Polycarp*
1:2	*Inscriptio*
1:3a	*Inscriptio*
1:7	15:2
1:8; 4:13	18:3
1:9	19:2
2:5	14:2
2:13–15	10:2
2:21	1:2
2:25	19:2
3:18; 1:19	17:2
4:11	14:3
4:16	10:1
5:1	1:1; cf. 2:1
5:4	17:1; 19:2
5:10–11	20:2
5:12	20:1

Papias of Hierapolis

Papias was bishop of Hierapolis, Asia Minor, in approximately 140 CE. According to Eusebius (*Hist. eccl.* 3.39.1–17), this "companion of Polycarp" and author of five extant treatises (*Hist. eccl.* 3.39.1), including *Expositions of the Oracles of the Lord*, would "inquire as to the discourses of the elders, what Andrew or what Peter said," out of preference for the oral rather than the written word (*Hist. eccl.* 3.39.4). However, he also "used testimonies drawn from the former Epistle of John, and likewise from that of Peter" (*Hist. eccl.* 3.39.17). In this same context, Eusebius also notes that Papias recalled the witness of the elder John that the Gospel of Mark was written by Mark, a "follower of Peter" who served as "the interpreter of Peter," writing "accurately, albeit not in order, all that he [Peter] recalled of what was either said or done by the Lord" (*Hist. eccl.* 3.39.15). This is the earliest external witness to an association between Peter and Mark and is quite possibly reflective of their association in 1 Pet 5:13.

Justin Martyr

Justin Martyr (ca. 100–165 CE), a native of Palestine and later apologist in Ephesus and Rome, authored two writings containing possible echoes of 1 Peter: a *Dialogue with Trypho the Jew* (ca. 135 CE) and a *First Apology* (ca. 155 CE). In

Bigg's opinion (1902, 10), "it is probable, but not certain, that Justin knew I Peter." The common ideas, however, with the possible exception of *Dial.* 116 ("we are the true high priestly race of God"; cf. 1 Pet 2:9) may reflect no more than the influence of Christian tradition. (See also Massaux 1950, 565–68.)

1 Peter	*Justin Martyr*
1:3, 23	*1. Apol.* 61
2:5	*Dial.* 116
2:6	*Dial.* 114
2:9	*Dial.* 116*
2:10	*Dial.* 199
3:20	*Dial.* 138
4:12	*Dial.* 116
5:8–9	*Dial.* 103

Another apologist, Theophilus of Antioch, in his letter *Ad Autolycum* (2.34), possibly alludes to 1 Pet 1:18 (*mataios, patroparadotos*). (On Justin, as well as Aristides, Tatian, Athenagoras, and Theophilus, see also Holzmeister 1937, 132.)

Melito of Sardis

Melito, bishop of Sardis (flourished ca. 160–170 CE), in his *Apology* to the Emperor Antoninus, uses a phrase reminiscent of 1 Pet 1:4 ("eternal inheritance that does not perish"). It is his Paschal Homily, *Peri Pascha* (*On the Passover*), however, that reveals more striking similarities with the terminology and thought of 1 Peter. Especially noteworthy are *Pascha* 12 (*aspilon amnon kai amōmon*; cf. 1 Pet 1:19) and *Pascha* 68 (*basileian, hierateuma, laon periousion*; cf. 1 Pet 2:9). Beyond these lexical affinities, which, because of the singularity of the involved terms, allow the possibility of literary dependency, several other similarities in terminology and theme can be noted: association of Exod 12 and Isa 53 with Christ (4–10, 64; cf. 1 Pet 1:13, 19; 2:12–25); passover and suffering (46); lamb, sheep, and ransom (67, 103; cf. 1 Pet 1:18–19); contrast of perishable-imperishable (3–4, 39; cf. 1 Pet 1:18–19, 23–24); ancient *typos* as model for the future (3, 34–39, 40; cf. 1 Pet 3:20–21); *xylon* for cross (70, 71, 95, 96, 97, 104; cf. 1 Pet 2:24). These similarities point at least to an oral tradition of interpretation linking the redemptive death of Christ with the Passover and Isa 53, a tradition attested by both 1 Peter and the *Peri Pascha* of Melito.

1 Peter		Melito, *Peri Pascha*	
1:4		45	
1:5	believers "guarded"	30	Israel "guarded" (*phrouroumenos*)
1:13		13	
1:18		67	

1:19	*amnou amōmou kai aspilou*	12*	*aspilon amnon kai amōmon*; 44; 67; 71
2:9	*basileian, hierateuma, laos eis peripoiēsin*	68*	*basileian, hierateuma, laon periousion*
2:24		70; 104	

On *Peri Pascha* and its references or allusions to 1 Peter, see Bonner 1940; Perler 1966; Hall 1979.

Letter to Diognetus, 2 Clement, Apologetic, Apocryphal, and Other Writings

The *Letter to Diognetus* (late 2d century) contains possible allusions to 1 Peter in 5:16 (1 Pet 2:19); 9:2 (1 Pet 3:18); 9:3 (1 Pet 2:24). *2 Clement* (late 2d century) contains a possible allusion to 1 Pet 1:20 (*2 Clem.* 14:2; cf. Massaux 1950, 161–62). See Massaux on the use of 1 Peter by Athenagoras (1950, 588, 590), Theophilus of Antioch (1950, 602), and in *Sib. Or.* (1950, 445–46).

Among the NT *apocryphal writings* (2d–3d centuries), compare *Prot. Jas.* 15:4 and 1 Pet 5:6; *Ep. Apos.* 10 and 1 Pet 1:12.

The Christian interpolations of the *Testaments of the Twelve Patriarchs* may reflect allusions to a few passages in 1 Peter; compare 1 Pet 1:3 and *T. Naph.* 4:3; 1 Pet 1:19 and *T. Jos.* 19:8; 1 Pet 1:22 and *T. Gad* 6:1; and 1 Pet 4:14 and *T. Benj.* 4:4.

Among the *Acts of the Christian Martyrs*, possible allusions to 1 Peter are found in the *Acts of the Martyrs of Vienne and Lyons* (177 CE) (Eusebius, *Hist. eccl.* 5.1.25, 52; 5.2.6 [1 Pet 5:8]; 5.2.5 [1 Pet 5:6]), the *Acts of the Scillitan Martyrs* (9 [1 Pet 2:17]), and the *Martyrdom of Bishop Fructuosus and His Deacons* (7 [1 Pet 5:4]).

Irenaeus of Lyons

Irenaeus (ca. 180 CE, bishop of Lyons in Gaul and previously in Asia Minor and Rome) is the first writer to cite from 1 Peter with explicit reference to Peter as author: *Haer.* 4.9.2 ("Peter says in his epistle," citing 1:8); 5.7.2 ("this is what was said by Peter," citing 1:8); 4.16.5 ("Peter says," citing 2:16); 4.34.2. See also Eusebius, *Hist. eccl.* 4.9.2, 15.5; 5.7.2; and allusions to 1 Peter in the letter of the martyr churches of Lyons and Vienne (Eusebius, *Hist. eccl.* 5.1.26: 1 Pet 5:8; 5:2, 5; 5:6).

Tertullian of Carthage

Tertullian (ca. 160–ca. 220) refers to Peter as having written to "the Christians of Pontus" and then cites 2:21 and 4:12–16 (*Scorp.* 12); 1 Pet 2:17 is also cited in *Scorp.* 14. See also *Adv. Jud.* 10 (1 Pet 2:22); *Marc.* 4.13 (1 Pet 2:8); *Or.* 15 (cf. 1 Pet 3:3; 1 Tim 2:9), 20 (1 Pet 3:1–6).

Clement of Alexandria

Clement of Alexandria (ca. 150–215), as Bigg (1902, 12) has noted, "quotes very freely from every chapter of the Epistle . . . in his *Hypotyposes*" (cf. Eusebius, *Hist. eccl.* 6.14.1). See also *Paed.* 1.6 (1 Pet 2:1–3); 3.11 (1 Pet 2:18; 3:8, 12); 3.12 (1 Pet 1:17–19; 3:12–13; 4:3); *Strom.* 3.12 (1 Pet 2:11–12, 15–16); 4:18 (1 Pet 1:21–22; 1:14–16); 4.20 (1 Pet 1:6–9); *Quis div.* 23 (1 Pet 1:12), 38 (1 Pet 4:8); *Protr.* 4 (1 Pet 2:9), 9 (1 Pet 2:3 [ascribed erroneously to Paul]; 3:10–12, 13); and *Adum.* on 1 Peter (from the Latin translation of Cassiodorus; cf. ANF 2.571–73).

Origen of Alexandria

According to Eusebius (*Hist. eccl.* 6.25.8), Origen (ca. 185–ca. 254), in his *Commentary on John*, book 5, observes that "Peter, on whom the church of Christ is built, against which the gates of Hades shall not prevail, has left one acknowledged epistle, and, it may be, a second one, for it is doubted." In this same commentary (13.13.84), he alludes to terminology in 1 Pet 2:5 ("living stones," "holy priestly community," "spiritual sacrifices"). In his *Commentary on Genesis*, book 3 (cf. Eusebius, *Hist. eccl.* 3.1), he states that Peter evangelized Judeans of the Diaspora in Pontus, Galatia, Bithynia, Cappadocia, and Asia, although this may have been only an inference from 1 Pet 1:1. In his *Commentary on Matthew*, book 1 (cf. Eusebius, *Hist. eccl.* 6.25.5), he refers to 1 Peter as the "catholic epistle" in which Peter refers to Mark, the author of the Gospel, as "my son" (1 Pet 5:13).

Cyprian of Carthage

Cyprian, bishop of Carthage (died 258), cites 1 Pet 2:21 in *Pat.* 9 and 1 Pet 2:9 in *Test.* 3.11.

Eusebius of Caesarea

Eusebius (ca. 260–ca. 340), bishop of Caesarea, recounts in his *Ecclesiastical History* various bits of information preserved in early Christian tradition concerning Peter and 1 Peter:

Book 1.1. Origen is quoted as telling of the labors of those among the twelve apostles as known to tradition, and Peter is said to have labored in the districts of Asia mentioned in 1 Peter.

Book 2.3.2. The letter was accepted by all the ancient presbyters.

Book 3.3.4; 3.4.2; 3.25.2. Eusebius reckons only 1 Peter among the several writings bearing Peter's name as "genuine and acknowledged by the elders of olden time" (3.3.4) and includes this epistle among the acknowledged writings (3.25.2). The letter, he notes, was addressed to "those of Hebrew parentage of the Dispersion in Pontus and Galatia, Cappadocia and Asia and Bithynia" (3.4.2).

Book 3.39.6. Papias, bishop of Hierapolis in Asia, used testimonies from 1 Peter and 1 John.

Book 4.14.9. Polycarp used testimonies from 1 Peter in his letter to the Philippians.

Book 5.8.7. Irenaeus used the letters of 1 Peter and 1 John.

Book 6.25.8. 1 Peter is included among the *homologoumena* (commonly accepted writings) in the canon of Origen.

For references to 1 Peter in Basilides, the Valentinians, the Marcosians, and Marcion, see Bigg (1902, 12–13) and Holzmeister (1937, 133). On the Old Latin version, the Muratorian Fragment, and the reception of 1 Peter in the Post-Nicene church, see Holzmeister (1937, 125–48).

The four volumes of *Biblica Patristica* (1975, 1977, 1980, 1987) list the following number of citations of passages in 1 Peter: vol 1: 250; vol. 2: 200; vol. 3: 495; vol. 4: 194; thereby placing 1 Peter 14th, 14th, 13th, and 16th, respectively, among the NT documents cited in the works of the four volumes.

10.2. Canonicity

From the preceding survey, it is clear that the attestation and reception of 1 Peter in the post-NT church was "widespread, early, and clear" (Selwyn 1947, 38). From the second century onward it formed an undisputed part of the NT canon and eventually was grouped among the seven so-called "Catholic Epistles." No mention is made of 1 Peter in the Muratorian Canon (second or third century), though there is reference to the *Apocalypse of Peter*. The omission may have been accidental, as in the case of Hebrews. Given the mutilated condition of the Muratorian Fragment, no final judgments can be made concerning its possible contents. There is minimal trace of its use in the Latin churches, but it does not appear in Syriac until the Peshitta of the fifth century. On the other hand, the Bodmer Papyrus ($\mathfrak{P}^{72}$), a third- or early fourth-century papyrus from Egypt, contains the entire texts of 1 Peter, 2 Peter and Jude and attests their combined circulation in Egypt during this period. Moreover, Origen (died 253 CE) and Eusebius (died ca. 340) list it among the *homologoumena* or acknowledged writings (Origen, *Comm. Matt.*, book 1; Eusebius, *Hist. eccl.* 3.3.1, 4; 3.2; 3.25.2; 6.25.5). It was included in the canon of the Greek church (Athanasius, *Easter Letter* of 367) as one of the seven Catholic Epistles (Council of Laodicea, canon 59 [363 CE]) and eventually within the Syrian canon (Peshitta, fifth century) as well. With the single exception of 1 John, 1 Peter is the only one of the Catholic Epistles whose authority was never questioned. "Aside from the four Gospels and the letters of Paul, the external attestation for 1 Peter is as strong, or stronger, than that for any NT book" (Michaels 1988, xxxiv). "In the earliest Christian literature outside the NT (i.e., AD 90–190)," Chase (1900b, 781) has observed, "it is second only to the Gospels and the

Pauline Epistles in the extent of the influence which it exercised on the language and thoughts of writers widely separated from each other in place and in circumstances."[49]

11. THE TEXT OF 1 PETER AND ITS TRANSMISSION

The Greek text of 1 Peter is relatively well preserved. It is contained in three papyri, sixteen uncials from the fourth to tenth centuries, more than 550 minuscules of the ninth to sixteenth centuries, and a number of passages in the lectionaries.[50]

The three papyri witnesses to 1 Peter comprise:

𝔓[72], Bodmer Papyri VII and VIII (3d–4th century), the earliest manuscript of 1 Peter, which contains the texts of 1 Peter, 2 Peter, and Jude. Several other writings are also contained in this codex: apocryphal correspondence between Paul and the Corinthians, eleven of the *Odes of Solomon*, the *Paschal Homily* of Melito of Sardis, the *Apologia* of Phileas (Egyptian bishop martyred 307 CE), the *Protevangelium of James*, and the Septuagintal text of Ps 33 and 34 (quoted in 1 Peter). 𝔓[72] displays close affinities to the uncials A (Alexandrinus) and B (Vaticanus), the minuscules 104, 424, 326, 81, and the Sahidic version, though the reliability of the latter ought not to be overestimated.

𝔓[74], Bodmer Papyrus XVII, which contains parts of Acts, James, 2 Peter, 1 John, 2 John, 3 John, and Jude, as well as 1 Peter (1:1–2, 7–8, 13, 19–20, 25; 2:6–7, 11–12, 18, 24; 3:4–5). Its relatively late dating (6th–7th century) tends to minimize its importance.

𝔓[81] (4th century), which contains only two fragments of 1 Peter; namely, 2:20–3:1 and 3:4–12.[51]

Uncial codices that, in addition to 𝔓[72], contain the complete Greek text of 1 Peter include Sinaiticus (א, 4th century); Vaticanus (B, 4th century), Alexandrinus (A, 5th century), Ephraemi Syri Rescriptus (C, 5th century, omitting only 1:1–2; 4:5–5:14); P (6th century); Ψ (044, 8th–9th century); 048 (5th century).

Portions of 1 Peter are also included in 093 (6th century, containing 2:22–24; 3:1, 3–7); 0206 (4th century, containing 5:5–13); 0247 (5th/6th century, containing 5:13–14). These nine codices constitute the "constant witnesses" to 1 Peter and are normally subsumed under the "Majority Text," as described and cited in the standard critical Greek edition of the New Testament edited by K. Aland et al., *Novum Testamentum Graece* (27th ed.; Stuttgart: Deutsche

[49] On the attestation and place of 1 Peter in the canon, see Chase 1900b, 779–81; Schelkle 1976, 15–17; Brox 1986, 39–40; Michaels 1988, xxxi–xxxiv; Roloff, in Goppelt 1993, 53–55.

[50] See Beare 1970, 1–24; Duplacy and Amphoux 1980; and Roloff, in Goppelt 1993, 55–57.

[51] On papyrus witnesses to 1 Peter, see also Junack and Grunewald 1986, 67–100.

Bibelstiftung, 1993). Specifically, the designation "Majority Text" (cited in the present commentary as "𝔐") includes: (1) all witnesses to the "Koine" or "Byzantine Text" ("Koine text," the nomenclature used in *NTG*[25] but replaced in *NTG*[26] and *NTG*[27]) for the Catholic Epistles including 1 Peter: H (014), L (020), S (029), and many minuscules; and (2) the "constant witnesses," which, for 1 Peter, include: 𝔓[72], 𝔓[74], 𝔓[81], ℵ (01), A (02), B (03), C (04), P (025), Ψ (044), 048, 093, 0206, 0247, 0285, and those witnesses that are cited only when they differ from the Majority Text: K (108), L (020), 33, 81, 323, 614, 630, 1241, 1739, 2495; and the minuscules: 69, 322, 623, 945, 1243, 1505, 1846, 1852, 1881, 2298, 2464 (see Aland and Aland 1989, Index, p. 344).

Further witnesses to the text of 1 Peter include, besides the cursives and lectionary readings: ancient translations of the Greek into other languages, including Latin (Old Latin, Vulgate), Syriac (Peshitta, Philoxenian, Harclean, Palestinian), Egyptian dialects (Sahidic, Akhmimic, Middle Egyptian, Coptic), Armenian, Georgian, and others, and the citations by the Church Fathers. By the third century, 1 Peter and 2 Peter were combined and circulated together, as attested by the Bodmer Papyrus VIII (𝔓[72]).[52]

The translation and interpretation in the present commentary are based on the 27th edition of *Novum Testamentum Graece* (1993), equivalent to the 4th edition of the *Greek New Testament* (New York: United Bible Society, 1994).

The state of the text and the history of its transmission present no major problems or variant readings that significantly affect the wording or meaning of the text in general. Of the 105 total verses in 1 Peter, 70 verses are free of variants. Readings that vary from the text adopted in *NTG*[27] will be discussed and evaluated in the present commentary, as appropriate. Thirty-eight instances of noteworthy variants are discussed by Metzger (1971, 687–98). The commentary by Michaels (1988) offers the fullest treatment to date of the textual variants as they occur throughout the letter.[53]

12. THE HISTORICAL, SOCIAL, AND THEOLOGICAL SIGNIFICANCE OF 1 PETER

1 Peter illustrates the situation of the Jesus movement at an early sectarian stage of its development: its predicament of social alienation and its strategy for survival and growth. In the face of public slander, insult, unjust accusation of

---

[52] On a fragment of 1 Pet 3:2–21 (*recto*) and 3:22–4:1 (*verso*), in a 5th-century Coptic (Sahidic) codex, see Willis 1964.

[53] On the textual attestation of 1 Peter and text-critical questions, see also Tischendorf 1872, 273–300; Harris 1902a, 1902b, 1909, 1929–1930; Holzmeister 1937, 83–84; J. P. Wilson 1942–1943; Salmon 1951; Thiele 1958, 1965; Testuz 1959; Beare 1961, 1964; Garcia del Moral 1961; Massaux 1963; King 1964; Willis 1964; Quinn 1965; Thiele 1965; Daris 1967; Martini 1968; Metzger 1968; Carder 1970; Duplacy 1969–1970; Davey 1970; W. L. Richards 1974, 1975, 1976; Schelkle 1976, 16–17; Duplacy and Amphoux 1980; Rodgers 1981; Junack and Grunewald 1986; K. Aland and B. Aland 1989; Bethge 1993; Wachtel 1995; Amphoux and Outtier 1996.

wrongdoing, and the suffering resulting from such treatment by nonbelieving outsiders, the Jesus movement was called upon to demonstrate its honor, distinctive holiness, and moral integrity and faithfully to maintain its commitment to God, Jesus Christ, and one another, with the hope of gaining even erstwhile detractors to its cause. In this letter of encouragement and exhortation, the predicament of innocent suffering and its positive value receives more sustained attention than anywhere else in the NT. The paradox of Christianity's forming an honored household of God despite its status as a community of strangers and aliens is matched by the paradox of its joy in suffering and its fervent hope despite oppression. Publicly shamed by outsiders, believers are honored by God and, in solidarity with their suffering Lord, will also be vindicated on the day of judgment. Thus, the letter assures its readers, they can persevere in faith and doing what is right because of their union with Jesus Christ and their confidence and trust in God's power and fatherly support.

One of the several noteworthy features of 1 Peter is the diverse range of Israelite, Hellenistic, Palestinian Christian, and Diaspora Christian traditions used in the letter. This diversity is directly related to the persons associated with its composition, their catholic experiences and sensibilities, and also to the letter's place of origin. At the same time, the skillful combination and interweaving of these traditions witness to the creative ability of its author to fashion an integrated message that speaks powerfully of the "ties that bind" one suffering branch of the Christian brotherhood with another.

The letter also offers one of the most sustained reflections on innocent suffering in the entire NT. Its extensive focus upon and positive valuation of innocent Christian suffering make 1 Peter one of the most pastoral of the New Testament writings.

Without once identifying Jesus Christ as "servant," its Servant of God Christology, elaborated through use of the servant song in Isa 53, is one of the most developed and moving expressions of this Christology in the early Church.

1 Peter also represents one of the the most extensive discourses in the NT on the engagement of the Christian community with non-Christian society, involving both respect for social order and witness of holy nonconformity. Its contrast between Christians as strangers and resident aliens in society and being "at home" in the family of God, along with its elaboration on the divine election that binds believers with their elect Lord, are among the most creative ecclesial formulations in the NT.

The response advocated by 1 Peter to the predicament of Christian social and religious estrangement within a hostile environment became in many ways a harbinger of the course that the Church subsequently followed. In 1 Peter we meet the aspects of Christian community that, it is said, accounted for the Church's eventual ascendancy and consolidation within the Roman Empire: maintenance of a distinctive communal identity in the Christian movement, solidarity in suffering, radical promotion of internal cohesion and fraternal love, and an offering of a place of belonging to society's aliens and strangers. 1 Peter proclaimed the Christian gospel in such an effective and compelling fashion that it was soon received into the Church's canon as a treasured witness of Christian faith, constancy in affliction, and hope in God's sustaining care. In subsequent centuries, its teaching on God's grace, on Jesus as Suffering Servant, on the Church as the body of God's elect and holy people in a hostile world, on the reciprocal service of all the faithful, and on vigilance against evil have inspired two millennia of Christian theology, preaching, hymnody, liturgical practice, and personal spirituality.

From the Reformation period onward, a prevailing view of 1 Peter held that this writing was an appeal to beleaguered Christians to remain steadfast and beyond reproach and to consider themselves as pilgrims on earth looking forward to their eventual homecoming in heaven. Representative of this view are the comments of John Calvin, writing in 1551: "Peter's purpose in this Epistle is to exhort the faithful to a denial and contempt of the world, so that they may be free from carnal affections and all earthly hindrances, and aspire with their whole soul after the celestial kingdom of Christ" (ET of Calvin's commentary on *The Epistle of Paul the Apostle to the Hebrews and The First and Second Epistles of St. Peter* [1963, 227]). In contrast to this perspective on reading and interpreting 1 Peter, which presumes an unwarranted contrast between a pilgrimage on earth and a home in heaven, the present commentary seeks to show how the essential perspective of this letter concerns, not a cosmological contrast between life on earth and home in heaven, but a social tension between maintaining the identity and integrity of the Christian people of God and experiencing the abuse and pressures of a hostile society.

Read in this light, this passionate call to holy behavior and steadfast commitment in the face of societal hostility takes on an eloquence and a power often overlooked in conventional treatments of this letter. It accounts for the regard in which this letter has been held, especially at moments in Christian history when the evangelical witness of the Church was sorely tested and when the clash between Church and culture was particularly severe. It is thus not surprising that the letter has held a particular significance for "Diaspora Christian communities" of all ages. For these communities on the margin of mainstream Christianity or communities undergoing oppression either within the larger Church or within a hostile macrosociety, the letter's positive revaluation of *paroikia* existence and innocent suffering, its good news concerning God's neverfailing grace and power manifested in Jesus Christ, its bold call for persistence in holiness and exemplary conduct, and its assurance of hope and salvation for all who follow faithfully in the footsteps of their rejected and vindicated Lord have constituted a pastoral message of good news beyond measure. The extent to which this oft-neglected writing of the NT assumes a more central place in the teaching and preaching of the Church depends on the extent to which these powerful elements of its message receive their deserved due.

BIBLIOGRAPHY

◆

1. COMMENTARIES ON 1 PETER

◆

Commentaries through the nineteenth century are listed in chronological order and commentaries of the twentieth century in alphabetical order. These commentaries are not included among the studies listed at the conclusion of each unit of 1 Peter in the present commentary.

ANTIQUITY

Clement of Alexandria. "Adumbrationes in epistolam Petri primam catholicam." In *Adumbrationes Clementis Alexandrini in epistolas canonicas*. Pages 203–6 in vol. 3 of GCS 17. Berlin: Akademie, 1970.

Cyril of Alexandria. "In epistolam I B. Petri." In *Fragmenta in epistolas catholicas*. Columns 1011–16 in PG 74.

Didymus of Alexandria. "In epistolam S. Petri primam enarratio." In *In epistolas catholicas enarratio*. Columns 1755–72 in PG 39.

———. *Didymi Alexandrini in epistolas canonicas brevis enarratio*, ed. F. Zoepl. NTAbh 4/1. Münster: Aschendorff, 1914.

John Chrysostom. "In primam S. Petri epistolam." In *Fragmenta in epistolas catholicas*. Columns 1053–58 in PG 64.

Jerome. "B. Petri apostoli epistola prima." In *Divina Bibliotheca, pars tertia*. Columns 877–82 in PL 29.

Ammonius of Alexandria. "Fragmentum in primam S. Petri epistolam." Columns 1607–10 in PG 85.

Hesychius. "Fragmentum in primam epistolam S. Petri." Columns 1389–90 in PG 93.

Cassiodorus. "Epistola Petri apostoli ad gentes." In *Complexiones canonicarum epistularum septem*. Columns 1361–68 in PL 70.

Paterius. "In epistolam S. Petri primam." In *Liber de expositione Veteris ac Novi Testamenti: Sextus, de testimoniis in epistolas catholicas*. Columns 1097–1100 in PL 79.

Luculentius. "Lectio epistolae I beati Petri apostoli." In *In aliquot Novi Testamenti partes commentarii*. Columns 857–60 in PL 72.

Pseudo-Euthalius. "Prioris catholicae Petri epistolae." In *Elenchus capitum septem epistolarum catholicarum*. Columns 679–82 in PG 85.

Pseudo-Oecumenius. "Petri Apostoli prior epistola catholica." In *Commentarii in epistolas catholicas*. Columns 509–78 in PG 119.

Pseudo-Hilary of Arles. "Epistola Beati Petri Apostoli Prima." In *Expositio in epistolas catholicas*. Columns 83–106 in PLSup 3.

MIDDLE AGES

Bede, the Venerable. *Super epistolas catholicas expositio: In primum epistolam Petri.* Columns 41–68 in PL 93. ET: "Commentary on 1 Peter." Pages 69–122 in *Commentary on the Seven Catholic Epistles,* trans. D. Hurst. Cistercian Studies Series 82. Kalamazoo: Cistercian, 1985.

Isho'dad of Merv. Pages 38–39, 51–53 in *Acts of the Apostles and Three Catholic Epistles.* Volume 4 of *The Commentaries of Isho'dad of Merv, Bishop of Hadatha (c. 850 A.D.) in Syriac and English.* Horae Semiticae 10. Edited and translated by M. D. Gibson. Cambridge: Cambridge University Press, 1913.

Walafridus Strabo. "Epistola I B. Petri." In *Glossa ordinaria.* Columns 679–88 in PL 114.

Pseudo-Theophylact. "Expositio in epistolam primam S. Petri." Columns 1189–1252 in PG 125.

Alulfus. "Expositio super I epistolam B. Petri apostoli." In *De expositione Novi Testamenti.* Columns 1385–88 in PL 79.

Euthymius Zigabenus. Pages 519–66 in vol. 2 of *Commentarius in XIV epistolas S. Pauli et VII catholicas,* ed. N. Kalogeras. Athens: Perrê, 1887.

Dionysius Bar Salibi. Pages 134–37 in vol. 53 (text), and pp. 103–5 in vol. 60 (translation) of *In Apocalypsin, Actus et Epistulas catholicas,* ed. and trans. I. Sedlaček. Corpus scriptorum christianorum orientalium, Scriptores Syri 2/101. Paris, 1909–1910.

Martinus Legionensis. "Expositio in epistolam I B. Petri apostoli." Columns 217–52 in PL 209.

Gregorius Barhebraeus. Pages 27–29 in *In Actus apostolorum et Epistulas catholicas adnotationes Syriace e recognitione M. Klamroth.* Göttingen: Dieterich, 1878.

Pseudo-Thomas. Pages 368–98 in vol. 31 of *In septem epistolas canonicas.* Paris, 1873–1882.

16TH CENTURY

Erasmus, D. *Annotationes in Novum Testamentum.* 1516. 2d ed., 1519. 3d–5th eds.: Basel: Rauracorum, 1522–1535. *Paraphrases in Novum Testamentum.* Columns 1081–1100 in vol. 7 of *Opera omnia.* Leiden: Petrus van der Aa, 1706.

Luther, M. *Epistel Sanct Petri gepredigt und ausgelegt.* Wittenberg: Nickel Schyrtenz, 1523. Pages 259–399 in vol. 12 of *D. Martin Luthers Werke: Kritische Gesamtausgabe.* Weimar, 1966. ET: "Sermons on the First Epistle of St. Peter." Pages 1–145 in *The Catholic Epistles,* trans. M. H. Bertram. Volume 30 of *Luther's Works,* ed. J. Pelikan. St. Louis: Concordia, 1967. A combination of Luther's 1523 sermons and his 1539 commentary is contained in M. Luther, *The Epistles of St. Peter and St. Jude,* ed. and trans. J. N. Lenker. Minneapolis, 1904. Reprinted, Grand Rapids: Kregel, 1982 and updated 1990.

____. *Enarrationes Martini Lutheri in epistolas D. Petri duas et Judae unam in quibus quidquid omnino ad Christianismum pertinet consumatissime digestum leges,* trans. M. Butzer. Strassburg, 1524.

Bullinger, H. *In D. Petri apostoli epistolam utranque.* Heinrychi Bullingeri commentarius. Zurich: Christoph Mense, 1534.

de Leuwis, D. *In omnes catholicas epistolas, necnon Acta apostolorum & apocalypsin, ac nonnullos hymnos ecclesiasticos, commentarii doctissimi*. Paris: le Preux, 1542.

Calvin, J. "Epistola Petri apostoli prior." *Commentarius in epistolas catholicas Joannis Calvini opera quae supersunt omnia* (1551). Reprinted, cols. 205–92 in vol. 55. Corpus Reformatorum 83. Braunschweig: Schwetschke, 1896. ET: Pages 227–323 in *The Epistle of Paul the Apostle to the Hebrews and the First and Second Epistles of St. Peter*, trans. W. B. Johnston; ed. D. W. and T. F. Torrance. Calvin's Commentaries 12. Edinburgh: Oliver & Boyd / Grand Rapids: Eerdmans, 1963.

Coglerus, J. *In Epistolas Petri Commentarius*. Wittenberg, 1564.

Alley, W. *Ptochomuseion . . . Bishop of Exeter upon the First Epistle of Saint Peter*. London: John Day, 1565.

Hessels, J. *In priorem B. Pauli apostoli ad Timotheum epistolam commentarius: Alter item eiusdem authoris commentarius in priorem B. Petri apostoli canonicam epistolam*. 2 vols. Louvain: Bogardum, 1568.

Hemmingius, N. Pages 667–708 in *Commentaria in omnes epistolas apostolorum Pauli, Petri, Iudae, Iohannis, Iacobi, et in eam quae ad Hebraeos inscribitur, scripta, recognita, emendata et alicubi aucta*. Frankfurt am Main, 1579.

17TH CENTURY

Aretius, B. Pages 487–507 in *Commentarii in Domini nostri Jesu Christi Novum Testamentum*. Bern: le Preux, 1607.

Winckelmann, J. *Commentarii in utramque Epistolam Petri*. Wittenberg, 1608.

Serarius, N. *Prolegomena bibliaca et commentaria in omnes epistolas canonicas*. Paris: Lippius, 1612.

Estius, W. *In omnes beati Pauli et septem catholicas apostolorum epistolas commentarii*. Douai, 1614–1616. Pages 1149–1201 in vol. 2 of *Absolutissima in omnes beati Pauli septem catholicas apostolorum epistolas commentaria*. Cologne: Henning, 1631 / Paris: Leonarrd, 1658.

Byfield, N. *Sermons upon the First Chapter of the First Epistle General of Peter*. London: Butler & Griffen, 1617.

———. *A Commentary, or "Sermons upon the Second Chapter of the First Epistle of Saint Peter."* London: Lownes, 1623.

Cornelius à Lapide. *Epistolarum canonicarum*. Commentaria in scripturam sacram 19. Antwerp: Nuntium, 1627. 2d ed., 1628. Edited by A. Crampon: Paris: Vivès, 1857–1863.

Laurentius, J. *S. apostoli Petri epistola catholica prior, perpetuo commentario explicata*. Campis: Laurentius, 1640. Reprinted with *Epistola catholica posterior*. Amsterdam, 1647.

Gerhard, J. *Commentarius super priorem D. Petri epistolam*, ed. J. E. Gerhard. Jena: Reiffenberger, 1641.

Pareus, D. Pages 180–237 in *Commentarii in epistolas canonicas Jacobi, Petri et Judae*, ed. P. Pareus. Geneva, 1641.

Schotanus, M. *Conciones in I. Epistolam Petri*. Franeker, 1644.

Amyraut, M. *Paraphrase sur les épîtres catholiques de S. Jacques, S. Pierre, S. Jean et S. Jude*. Saumur: Lesnier, 1646.

Trapp, J. "The First Epistle General of St. Peter." *A Commentary or Exposition upon All the Books of the New Testament.* London: R. W., 1647. 2d ed., 1656. Reprinted, pp. 705–17 in *A Commentary on the New Testament.* London: Dickinson, 1865. Reprinted, Grand Rapids: Zondervan, 1958.

Grotius, H. Pages 1–37 in *Annotationum in Novum Testamentum, pars tertia ac ultima.* Paris: Pepingué, 1650.

Rodgers J. *A Godly and Fruitful Exposition upon All the First Epistle of Peter.* London: Field, 1650.

Horneius, C. *In epistolam catholicam Sancti Apostoli Petri priorem: Expositio litteralis,* ed. J. Horneius. Braunschweig: Duncker, 1654.

Crell, F. J. Pages 269–84 in *Commentarius in primam Petri apostoli epistolam.* Volume 2 of *Johannis Crellii Franci opera omnia, exegetica, didactica et polemica.* Freiburg: Philaleth, 1656.

Estius, W. Pages 1149–1201 in vol. 2 of *In omnes beati Pauli et aliorum apostolorum epistolas commentaria.* Paris, 1658.

Gomarus, F. *In priorem S. Petri epistolam explicatio.* Pages 679–705 in *Opera theologica omnia,* ed. F. Gomarus. Amsterdam: Jansson, 1664.

Calov, A. Pages 1463–1531 in vol. 2 of *Biblia Novi Testamenti illustrata.* Frankfurt: Wust, 1676. 2d ed., Dresden: Zimmermann, 1719.

Goltzius, D. *Schriftmatige verklaringe en toepassinge tot geestelijck gebruyck, van de eerste (en tweede) algemeyne Sendbrief des apostels Petri.* Amsterdam: Boeckholt, 1689–1691.

Leighton, R. *A Practical Commentary upon the First Espistle of St. Peter.* Vol. 1: York: White, 1693. Vol. 2: London: Keble, 1694. Edited by W. West: London: Bohn, 1853 / Longmans, 1870. Reprinted, Grand Rapids: Kregel, 1972.

Antonides, T. *Schriftmatige verklaringe over den eersten algemeinen sendbrief van den H. Apostel Simeon Petrus.* Leeuwarden: Hoogslagh, 1698.

18TH CENTURY

Bibliander, T. *Richtige Harmonie der heiligen Schrift Alten und Neuen Testamentes in 4 Theilen.* Görlitz, 1705.

Alexandre, N. *Commentarius litteralis et moralis in omnes epistolas Sancti Pauli apostoli et in VII epistolas catholicas.* Rouen, 1710. 2d ed., Paris: Bettinelli, 1768.

Laurentius, G. M. *Kurtze Erklärung des ersten (und andern) Briefs St. Petri: In Tabellen verfasset . . . Sammt angehängter kurtzen Paraphrasi.* Halle: Waÿsenhaus, 1716.

Streson, C. *Meditationes in I et II Epistolas Petri.* Amsterdam, 1717.

Calmeth, A. Pages 794–831 in vol. 8 of *Commentaire littéral sur tous les livres de l'Ancien et du Nouveau Testament.* Paris, 1707–1726.

van Alphen, H. S. *De eerste algemeene sendbrief van den apostel Petrus, ontleedender wyse verklaard, en tot syn oogmerk toegepast.* Utrecht: van Paddenburg and Kroon, 1734.

Lange, J. *Urim ac Thummim (Licht und Recht) seu exegesis epistolarum Petri ac Joannis.* Halle: Orphanotrophe, 1712. 2d ed., 1734.

Wolf, J. C. Pages 681–97 in *Curae philologicae et criticae in sanctorum apostolorum Jacobi, Petri, Judae et Joannis epistolas, hujusque Apocalypsin.* Hamburg: Kisner, 1735.

Bengel, J. A. *Gnomon Novi Testamenti*. Tübingen: Schramm, 1742. 2d ed., 1759. 3d ed., 1773. ET: "Annotations on the First Epistle of Peter." In *Gnomon of the New Testament*, trans. C. T. Lewis and M. R. Vincent. Edinburgh: T. & T. Clark, 1857–1858.

Benson, G. *A Paraphrase and Notes on the Seven (Commonly Called) Catholic Epistles, viz. St. James, I St. Peter, II St. Peter, St. Jude, I, II, III of St. John*. London: Waugh, 1749 / London: Waugh & Fenner, 1756.

Wettstein, J. J. Pages 681–97 in *Continens Epistolas Pauli, Acta Apostolorum, Epistolas Canonicas et Apocalypsin*. Volume 2 of *Novum Testamentum Graecum editionis receptae cum lectionibus variantibus codicum mss., editionum aliarum versionum, et patrum nec non commentario pleniore ex scriptoribus veteribus hebrais, graecis et latinis historiam et vim verborum illustrante*. Amsterdam: Dommeriana, 1751–1752. Reprinted, Graz: Akademische Druck- und Verlagsanstalt, 1962.

Wesley, J. *Romans to Revelation*. Volume 2 of *Explanatory Notes upon the New Testament*. 1754. Reprinted, Grand Rapids: Baker, 1983.

von Matthaei, C. F. *SS. apostolorum septem epistolae catholicae*. Riga: Hartknoch, 1782.

Semler, J. S. *Paraphrasis in epistolam I. Petri, cum latinae translationis varietate et multis notis*. Opera varia 7. Halle: Hemmerdian, 1783.

Pott, D. J. *Epistolae catholicae graecae perpetua annotatione illustratae*. Göttingen: Dieterich, 1786.

Morus, S. F. N. Pages 98–186 in *Praelectiones in Jacobi et Petri epistolas*, ed. C. A. Donat. Leipzig: Sommer, 1794.

19TH CENTURY

Meyer, F. B. *Trial by Fire: Expositions of the First Epistle of Peter*. New York: Revell, 1800.

Augusti, J. C. W. *Die katholischen Briefe, neu übersetzt und erklärt mit Excursen und einleitenden Abhandlungen herausgegeben*. Lemgo: Meyer, 1801–1808.

de Clorivière, P., and Pierre, J. *Explication des Épîtres de S. Pierre*. Paris, 1809. 2d ed., 1864.

Hensler, C. G. *Der erste Brief des Apostels Petrus übersetzt und mit einem Kommentar versehen*. Sulzbach: Seidel, 1813.

Hottinger, J. J. *Epistolae Jacobi atque Petri cum versione germanica et commentario latino*. Leipzig: Dyckiana, 1815.

de Kanter, H. P. *Commentatio in locum I. Petri v. 1–4*. Leiden: Luchtmans, 1823.

Eisenschmid, G. B. *Die Briefe des Apostels Petrus übersetzt, erläutert und mit erbaulicher Betrachtung begleitet*. Ronnenberg, 1824.

Hahn, J. M. *Betrachtungen auf all Tage des Jahrs über den ersten Brief Petri*. Tübingen: Fues, 1824.

Clark, A. "The First General Epistle of Peter." Pages 1875–1908 in vol. 2 of *The Holy Bible Containing the Old and New Testaments*. London: Butterworth, 1825. New edition: London: Tegg, 1838, New Testament.

Steiger, W. *Der erste Brief Petri mit Berücksichtigung des ganzen biblischen Lehrbegriffes ausgelegt*. Berlin: Oehmigke, 1832. ET: *Exposition of the First Epistle of Peter*. Edinburgh: T. Clark, 1836.

Mayerhoff, E. T. *Historisch-critische Einleitung in die petrinischen Schriften nebst einer Abhandlung über den Verfasser der Apostelgeschichte*. Hamburg: Perthes, 1835.

Schichthorst, J. D. *Entwicklung des ersten Petrusbriefs*. Stuttgart, 1836.

Jenks, W., ed. *I & II Peter*. The Comprehensive Commentary on the Holy Bible. Brattleboro: Fessending, 1834–1838.

Bloomfield, S. T. *I & II Peter*. In The Greek Testament with English Notes. Boston: Perkins-Marvin, 1837.

Jachmann, K. R. *Commentar über die katholischen Briefe mit genauer Berücksichtigung der neuesten Auslegungen*. Leipzig: Barth, 1838.

Liebich, E., and Burg, E. J. *I und II Petrus*. Hirschberger Bibel. 3d ed. Hirschberg: Krahn, 1846.

de Wette, W. M. L. *Kurze Erklärung der Briefe des Petrus, Judas und Jakobus*. Kurzgefasstes exegetisches Handbuch zum Neuen Testament 3/1. Leipzig: Weidmann, 1847. 2d ed., Leipzig: Hirzel, 1865. 3d ed., 1885.

Brown, J. *Expository Discourses on the First Epistle of the Apostle Peter*. Edinburgh: Oliphant, 1848. 2d ed., 1849. 3d ed., 1886. Reprinted as *First Peter*. Edinburgh and Carlisle, Pennsylvania: Banner of Truth, 1975.

Alford, H. Pages 331–88 in *PETROU* A. The Greek Testament . . . A Critical and Exegetical Commentary 4. London: Rivington's, 1849. Boston: Lee and Shepard / New York: Lee, Shepard, and Dillingham, 1872. Reprinted most recently, Grand Rapids: Baker, 1980.

Mason, A. J. *The First Epistle General of Peter*. A Bible Commentary for English Readers. London: Cassell, 1850.

Demarest, J. T. A *Translation and Exposition of the First Epistle of the Apostle Peter*. New York: Moffet, 1851.

Huther, J. E. *Kritisch-exegetisches Handbuch über den 1. Brief des Petrus, den Brief des Judas und den 2. Brief des Petrus*. MeyerK 12. Göttingen: Vandenhoeck & Ruprecht, 1851. 2d ed., 1860. 3d. ed, 1867. 4th ed., 1877. ET: *Critical and Exegetical Handbook to the General Epistles of James, Peter, John and Jude*, trans. D. B. Croom. Edinburgh: T. & T. Clark, 1881. [Cited as 1851/1881]

Besser, W. F. *Die Briefe St. Petri in Bibelstudien für die Gemeinde ausgelegt*. Bibelstunden 8. Halle: Mühlmann, 1854.

Steinmeyer, F. L. *Disquisitio in epistolae Petrinae prioris*. Berlin: Wiegandt & Grieben, 1854.

Barnes, A. *Notes, Explanatory and Practical, on the General Epistles of James, Peter, John, and Jude*. New York: Harper, 1855. Reprinted, Grand Rapids: Baker, 1949.

Wiesinger, A. *Der erste Brief des Apostels Petrus*. Olshausens Commentar über sämtliche Schriften des Neuen Testaments 6/2. Königsberg: Unzer, 1856.

Wordsworth, C. *The General Epistles, Book of Revelation, and Indices: The New Testament of our Lord and Saviour Jesus Christ in the Original Greek, with Introduction and Notes*. London: Rivingtons, 1856–1860. 2d ed., 1861. 4th ed., 1864.

Reiche, J. G. Pages 245–83 in *Epistolam ad Hebraeos et epistolas catholicas continens*. Commentarius criticus in Novum Testamentum: Quo loca graviora et difficiliora lectionis dubiae accurate recensentur et explicantur 3. Göttingen: Dieterich, 1857.

Fronmüller, G. F. C. *Die Briefe Petri und der Brief Judä*. J. P. Lange's Theologisch-homiletisches Bibelwerk 14. Bielefeld: Velhagen & Klasing, 1859. 2d ed., 1862. 3d ed., 1871. 4th ed., 1890. ET: *The Epistles General of Peter*, trans. J. I. Mombert. A Commentary on the Holy Scriptures: New Testament 9. New York:

Scribner's, 1867. Reprinted as "The First Epistle General of Peter" in vol. 9 of *Lange's Commentary on the Holy Scriptures*. Grand Rapids: Zondervan, n.d.

Schott, T. F. *Der erste Brief Petri erklärt*. Erlangen: Deichert, 1861.

Harms, L. *Auslegung der ersten Epistel S. Petri*. Hermannsburg: Missionshausbuchdruckerei, 1869.

Lillie, J. *Lectures on the First and Second Epistles of Peter*. New York: Scribner's, 1869. Reprinted, Minneapolis: Klock & Klock, 1978.

Ewald, J. "Petrus' Sendschreiben." Pages 1–73 in *Sieben Sendschreiben des Neuen Bundes übersetzt und erklärt*. Göttingen: Dieterich, 1870.

Bisping, A. *Erklärung der sieben katholischen Briefe*. Exegetisches Handbuch zum Neuen Testament 8. Münster: Aschendorff, 1871.

Cook, F. C. "The First Epistle General of Peter." Pages 155–220 in *The Holy Bible according to the Authorized Version (A.D. 1611) with an Explanatory and Critical Commentary and a Revision of the Translation, by Bishops and Other Clergy of the Anglican Church: The New Testament*. The Speaker's Commentary 4, ed. F. C. Cook. London: Murray, 1871–1876 / New York: Scribner, Armstrong, 1871.

Drach, P. "Première épître catholique de l'apôtre Saint Pierre." Pages 76–110 in *Épîtres catholiques*. La Sainte Bible 25. Paris: Lethielleux, 1873. 2d ed., 1889. 3d ed., 1912.

Hundhausen, L. J. *Das erste Pontifikalschreiben des Apostelfürsten Petrus*. Mainz: Kirchheim, 1873.

von Hofmann, J. C. K. *Der erste Brief Petri*. Volume 7/1 in *Die heilige Schrift Neuen Testaments zusammenhängend untersucht*, ed. J. C. K. von Hofmann. Nördlingen: Beck, 1875.

Camerlynck, A. *Commentarius in epistolas catholicas*. Bruges: Beyaert, 1876. 5th ed., 1909.

Reuss, E. *Les épîtres catholiques*. Le NT 5. Paris, 1878.

Caton, N. T. A *Commentary and an Exposition of the Epistles of James, Peter, John and Jude*. 1879.

Plumptre, E. H. *The General Epistles of St. Peter and St. Jude*. Cambridge Bible for Schools and Colleges. Cambridge: Cambridge University Press, 1879. 14th ed., 1903.

Witz, C. A. *Der Erste Brief Petri*. Vienna: Braumüller, 1881.

Keil, C. F. *Kommentar über die Briefe des Petrus und Judas*. Leipzig: Dörffling & Franke, 1883.

Mason, A. J. "The First Epistle of St. Peter." Pages 383–436 in vol. 3 of A *New Commentary on Holy Scripture*, ed. C. J. Ellicott. London: Cassell, 1884. Reprinted, pp. 385–436 in Ellicott's Commentary on the Whole Bible 4. Grand Rapids: Zondervan, 1959.

Kühl, R. *Die Briefe Petri und Judä*. MeyerK 12. 5th ed. Göttingen: Vandenhoeck & Ruprecht, 1887. 6th ed., 1897.

Usteri, J. M. *Wissenschaftlicher und praktischer Commentar über den ersten Petrusbrief*. Zurich: Höhr, 1887.

de Wette, W. M. L. *Die katholischen Briefe*. Halle: Anton, 1887.

Burger, K. *Der erste Brief Petri*. Strack-Zöcklers kurzgefasster Kommentar über das Neue Testament 4. Nördlingen: Beck, 1888.

Johnstone, R. *The First Epistle of Peter*. Edinburgh: T. & T. Clark, 1888.

Williams, N. M. *Commentary on the Epistles of Peter*. An American Commentary on the New Testament 6. Philadelphia: American Baptist Publication Society, 1888.

Caffin, B. C. *The First Epistle General of Peter.* The Pulpit Commentary 22. London: Kegan Paul, Trench, 1889. Reprinted, Peabody, Massachusetts: Hendrickson, 1980.

Kögel, R. *Der erste Brief Petri in zwanzig Predigten ausgelegt.* 3d ed. Bremen, 1890.

Schaff, P., ed. *I & II Peter.* International Illustrated Commentary. New York: Scribner's, 1890.

von Soden, H. *Hebräerbrief, Briefe des Petrus, Jakobus, Judas.* Hand-Commentar zum Neuen Testament 3/2. Freiburg im Breisgau: Mohr, 1890. 3d ed., 1899.

Weiss, B. *Die katholischen Briefe: Textkritische Untersuchungen und Textherstellung.* Lepizig. 1892. ET: *Thessalonians to Revelation,* trans. G. H. Schodde and E. Wilson. A Commentary on the New Testament 4. New York: Funk & Wagnalls, 1906.

Goebel, S. *Die Briefe des Petrus: Griechisch, mit kurzer Erklärung.* Gotha: Perthes, 1893.

Lumby, J. R. Pages v–xiv, 671–754 in *The Epistles of St. Peter.* Expositor's Bible 6. New York: Armstrong, 1893.

Couard, H. *Die Briefe des Petrus, Judas und Johannes.* Potsdam: Stein, 1895.

de Hartog, A. H. *Uitlegkundige werken: Korte aanteekeningen op den eersten brief van den apostel Petrus.* Amsterdam: Fernhout, 1895.

Sadler, M. F. *The General Epistles of SS. James, Peter, John and Jude.* London: Bell, 1885.

Beck, J. T. *Erklärung der Briefe Petri,* ed. J. Lindenmeyer. Gütersloh: Bertelsmann, 1896.

Donner, J. H. *De eerste algemeene zendbrief van den apostel Petrus.* Leiden: Donner, 1896.

Tuck, R. "The First Epistle General of Peter." Pages 1–167 in *A Homiletical Commentary on the General Epistles of I. and II. Peter, I. II. and III. John, Jude, and the Revelation of St. John the Divine.* The Preacher's Complete Homiletical Commentary. New York: Funk & Wagnalls, 1896.

Weidner, R. F. *Annotations on the General Epistles of James, Peter, John, and Jude.* New York: Christian Literature, 1897 / New York: Scribner's, 1905.

Hort, F. J. A. *The First Epistle of St. Peter I.1–II.17: The Greek Text with Introductory Lecture, Commentary, and Additional Notes.* London: Macmillan, 1898.

20TH CENTURY
(ALPHABETICALLY)

Achtemeier, P. J.
1988 1 Peter. Pages 1279–85 in *HBC.*
1996 *1 Peter.* Hermeneia. Minneapolis: Fortress.

Adams, J. E.
1979 *Trust and Obey: A Practical Commentary on First Peter.* Grand Rapids: Baker.

Ambroggi, P. de
1957 La prima epistola di Pietro. Pages 87–157 in *Le Epistole cattoliche di Giacomo, Pietro, Giovanni e Giuda.* SacBib 14/1. 3d ed. Turin: Marietti. [1st ed., 1947]

Arichea, D. C. Jr., and E. A. Nida
1980 *A Translator's Handbook on the First Letter from Peter.* Helps for Translators. New York: United Bible Societies.
Baljon, J. M. S.
1904 *Commentaar op de Katholieke Brieven.* Utrecht: van Boekhoven.
Ball, C. S.
1966 First Peter. Pages 239–78 in vol. 6 of *The Wesleyan Bible Commentary.* Grand Rapids: Eerdmans.
Barbieri, L. A.
1978 *First and Second Peter.* 2d ed. Chicago: Moody. [1st ed., 1975]
Barclay, W.
1976 *The Letters of James and Peter.* 2d ed. Daily Study Bible. Philadelphia: Westminster.
Barth, G.
1967 *Commentario à Primera Épístola de Pedro.* São Leopoldo: Sinodal.
Bauer, J. B.
1971 *Der erste Petrusbrief.* Die Welt der Bibel, Kleiner Kommentar 14. Düsseldorf: Patmos.
Beare, F. W.
1970 *The First Epistle of Peter: The Greek Text with Introduction and Notes.* 3d ed. Oxford: Blackwell. [1st pub., 1947; 2d ed., 1958]
Beasley-Murray, G. R.
1965 *The General Epistles: James, 1 Pt., Jude, 2 Pt.* Bible Guides 21. Nashville: Abingdon / London: Lutterworth.
Beelen, J. T., and A. van der Heeren
1932 *De Katholieke Brieven.* Bruges: Beyaert-Storie.
Bénétreau, S.
1984 *La première épître de Pierre.* Commentaires évangéliques de la Bible. Vaux-sur-Seine: EDIFAC.
Bennett, W. H.
1901 *The General Epistles: James, Peter, John, Jude.* Century Bible 17. New York: Frowde.
Best, E.
1971 *I Peter.* NCB. London: Oliphants / Grand Rapids: Eerdmans.
Bigg, C. A.
1902 *A Critical and Exegetical Commentary on the Epistles of St. Peter and St. Jude.* ICC. 2d ed. Edinburgh: T. & T. Clark. [1st ed., 1901]
Billerbeck, P. (and H. L. Strack)
1926 Der erste Brief Petri. Pages 762–68 in *Die Briefe des Neuen Testaments und die Offenbarung Johannis.* Volume 3 of *Kommentar zum Neuen Testament aus Talmud und Midrasch.* Munich: Beck. [2d ed., 1954]
Blaiklock, E. M.
1977 *First Peter: A Translation and Devotional Commentary.* Waco, Texas: Word.
Blenkin, G. W.
1914 *The First Epistle General of Peter.* Cambridge Greek Testament for Schools and Colleges. Cambridge: Cambridge University Press.
Blum, E. A.
1981 1 Peter. Pages 207–54 in *Hebrews–Revelation.* Expositor's Bible Commentary 12. Grand Rapids: Zondervan.

Boatti, A.
1932 *Le Lettere cattoliche tradotte dal testo greco e annotate*. S. Scrittura 15. Sale Tortonese: Ermite. [2d ed., Milan, 1933]
Bolkestein, M. H.
1952 *De Kerk in de Wereld: De eerste Brief van Petrus*. Amsterdam: Holland Uitgeversmaatschappij.
1972 *De Brieven van Petrus en Judas: De Predeking van het Nieuwe Testament*. 2d ed. Nijkerk: Callenbach. [1st ed., 1963]
Bosio, E.
1990 *Epistola agli Ebrei–Epistole cattoliche: Giacomo, Ia e IIa Pietro, Giuda, Ia, IIa, IIIa Giovanni–Apocalisse*. Turin: Claudiana.
Bowman, J. W.
1962 The First Epistle of Peter. Pages 116–55 in *Hebrews, James, I and II Peter*. The Layman's Bible Commentary 24. London: SCM.
Briscoe, D. S.
1993 *1 Peter: Holy Living in a Hostile World*. Wheaton, Illinois: Shaw.
Brown, D.
1934 *I and II Peter*. Critical Commentary 6. Grand Rapids: Zondervan.
Brownson, W.
1975 *Tried by Fire: The Message of I Peter*. Grand Rapids: Baker.
Brox, N.
1986 *Der erste Petrusbrief*. EKKNT 21. 2d ed. Zurich: Benzinger / Neukirchen-Vluyn: Neukirchner Verlag. [1st ed., 1976]
Brun, L.
1949 *Forste Petersbrev tolket*. Oslo: Aschehoug.
Calloud, J., and F. Genuyt
1982 *La première épître de Pierre: Analyse sémiotique*. LD 109. Paris: Cerf.
Calmes, T.
1907 *Les épîtres catholiques*. 3d ed. Paris: Bloud. [1st ed., 1905]
Camerlynck, A.
1909 *Commentarius in Epistolas Catholicas*. 5th ed. Commentarii Brugenses in S. Scripturam. Bruges: Beyaert.
Cash, W. W.
1947 *The First Epistle of St. Peter*. London: Church Book Room.
Cedrar, P. A.
1984 Pages 105–200 in *James, First and Second Peter, Jude*. The Communicator's Commentary 11. Waco, Texas: Word.
Chaine, J.
1939 *Les épîtres catholiques*. Paris: Gabalda.
Charue, A.
1951 Première Épître de S. Pierre. Pages 443–74 in *Les épîtres catholiques*. Sainte Bible 12. 3d ed. Paris: Gabalda. [1st ed., 1938]
Clowney, E. P.
1988 *The Message of 1 Peter: The Way of the Cross*. The Bible Speaks Today. Downers Grove, Illinois: InterVarsity.
Cochrane, E. E.
1965 *The Epistles of Peter: A Study Manual*. Grand Rapids: Baker.
Coffman, J. B.
1979 *Commentary on James, 1 and 2 Peter, 1, 2 and 3 John*. Abilene: ACU.

Corley, K. E.
1994 1 Peter. Pages 349–60 in *A Feminist Commentary*. Volume 2 of *Searching the Scriptures*. Edited by E. Schüssler Fiorenza. New York: Crossroad.

Cothenet, E.
1984 Pages 7–48 in *Les Épîtres de Pierre*. Cahiers Évangile 47. Paris: Cerf.

Craddock, F. B.
1995 *First and Second Peter and Jude*. Westminster Bible Companion. Louisville: Westminster John Knox.

Cramer, G. H.
1967 *First and Second Peter*. Everyman's Bible Commentary. Chicago: Moody.

Cranfield, C. E. B.
1950 *The First Epistle of Peter*. London: SCM.
1960 *I and II Peter and Jude*. Torch Bible Commentaries. London: SCM / New York: Harper & Row.
1962 I Peter. Pages 1026–30 in *PCB*. New York: Thomas Nelson.

Dalton, W. J.
1969 I Peter. Pages 1246–51 in *NCCHS*.

Danker, F. W.
1980 *A Commentary on Hebrews, 1 and 2 Peter, 1, 2 and 3 John and Jude*. In *Invitation to the New Testament: Epistles IV*. Garden City, New York: Doubleday-Image.

Davids, P. H.
1990 *The First Epistle of Peter*. NICNT. Grand Rapids: Eerdmans.

Díaz, R. M., and G. M. Camps
1958 1, 2 Sant Pere. Pages 67–140 in *Epistoles Catòliques-Apocalipsi*. La Bíblia de Montserrat 22. Montserrat.

Dowd, S.
1992 1 Peter. Pages 370–72 in *The Women's Bible Commentary*. Edited by C. A. Newson and S. H. Ringe. London: SPCK.

Elliott, J. H.
1966a *Doxology: God's People Called to Celebrate His Glory—A Biblical Study of I Peter in 10 Parts*. St. Louis: Lutheran Laymen's League.

Elliott, J. H., and R. A. Martin
1982 *James, I–II Peter/Jude*. Augsburg Commentary on the New Testament. Minneapolis: Augsburg. [Chinese translation by B. Luk (*James*) and A. Chow (*I–II Peter/Jude*). Hong Kong: Taosheng, 1988]

English, E. S.
1941 *The Life and Letters of St. Peter*. New York: Gaeblein.

Erdman, C. R.
1919 *The General Epistles*. Philadelphia: Westminster.

Fabris, R.
1980 *Lettera di Giacomo e Prima Lettera di Pietro*. Collana Lettura pastorale della Bibbia. Bologna: Dehoniane.

Felten, J.
1929 *Die zwei Briefe des heiligen Petrus und der Judasbrief*. Regensburg: Manz.

Fermin de la Cot
1921 *Epístolas católicas*. Barcelona: Labrana.

Ferrin, H. W.
1942 *"Strengthen Thy Brethren": Pointers from Peter for Power in Christian Living—A Devotional Exposition of the First Epistle of Peter.* Grand Rapids: Zondervan.

Fitzmyer, J. A.
1968 The First Epistle of Peter. Pages 362–68 in vol. 2 of *JBC*.

Franco, R.
1962 Primera Carta de San Pedro. Pages 219–97 in *Cartas de San Pedro*. La Sacrada Escritura, Nuevo Testamento 3. Biblioteca de Autores Cristianos 214. Madrid.

Frankemölle, H.
1987 *1. Petrusbrief, 2. Petrusbrief, Judasbrief.* Die Neue Echter Bibel: Kommentar zum Neuen Testament mit der Einheitsübersetzung 18/20. Würzburg: Echter.

Gaebelein, A. C.
1916 *The First and Second Epistles of Peter.* Annotated Bible. New York: Our Hope.

Goppelt, L.
1993 *A Commentary on I Peter.* Edited by F. Hahn. Translated and augmented by J. E. Alsup. Grand Rapids: Eerdmans. [Translation of *Der erste Petrusbrief.* 8th ed. MeyerK 12/1. Göttingen: Vandenhoeck & Ruprecht, 1978]

Gourbillon, J. G., and F. M. du Buit
1963 *La première épître de Saint Pierre.* Évangile. Cahiers Bibliques 50. Paris.

Greijdanus, S.
1929 *De Brieven van de Apostelen Petrus en Johannes, en de Brief van Judas.* Kommentaar op het Nieuwe Testament 13. Amsterdam: van Bottenburg.

Grudem, W. A.
1988 *The First Epistle of Peter.* TNTC. Grand Rapids: Eerdmans.

Gryglewicz, F.
1959 *Listy katolickie: Pierwszy list św. Piotra—Drugi list św. Piotra.* Pismo święte Nowego Testamentu 11. Poznań: Pallotinum.

Gunkel, H.
1906–17 *Der erste Brief des Petrus.* Volumes 2–3 of *Die Schriften des Neuen Testaments.* Göttingen: Vandenhoeck & Ruprecht.

Harrison, P. V.
1992 *James, 1, 2 Peter, and Jude.* Randall House Bible Commentary. Nashville: Randall House.

Hart, J. H. A.
1897–1910 The First Epistle General of Peter. Pages 3–80 in vol. 5 of *The Expositor's Greek Testament.* London: Hodder & Stoughton.

Hastings, J.
1924 *The First and Second Epistle of St. Peter and the Epistle of St. Jude.* The Speaker's Bible. London: Speaker's Bible Office.

Hauck, F.
1936 *Die Briefe des Jakobus, Petrus, Judas und Johannes.* NTD 10. Göttingen: Vandenhoeck & Ruprecht. [8th ed., 1957]

Heeren, A. van der
1932 *De Katholieke Brieven vertaald en uitgelegd.* Beelen NT. Bruges: Beyaert.

Heijkoop, H. L.
1970 *De eerste brief van Petrus*. Winschoten: Woord der Waarheid.

Henry, M.
1953 *Acts to Revelation*. Volume 6 of *Matthew Henry's Commentary on the Whole Bible*. New York: Revell.

Hiebert, D. E.
1984 *First Peter: An Expositional Commentary*. Chicago: Moody.

Hillyer, N.
1992 *1 and 2 Peter, Jude*. New International Biblical Commentary. Peabody, Massachusetts: Hendrickson.

Holmer, U., and W. de Boor
1976 Pages 13–183 in *Die Briefe des Petrus und der Brief des Judas*. Wuppertaler Studienbibel. Wuppertal: Brockhaus.

Holtzmann, O.
1926 *Die Petrusbriefe und der Judasbrief*. Das Neue Testament nach dem Stuttgarter griechischen Text übersetzt und erklärt 2. Giessen: Alfred Töpelmann.

Holzmeister, U.
1937 *Epistula Prima S. Petri Apostoli*. Volume 1 of *Commentarius in Epistulas SS. Petri et Judae, Apostolorum*. Cursus Scripturae Sacrae 3/13. Paris: Lethielleux.

Houwelingen, P. H. R.
1991 *I Petrus: Rondzendbrief uit Babylon*. Kampen: Kok.

Hunter, A. M., and E. G. Homrighausen
1957 The First Epistle of Peter: Introduction, Exegesis and Exposition. Pages 76–159 in vol. 12 of *IB*.

Janzen, H. H.
1951 *Glaube und Heilung: Eine schlichte Auslegung von 1. Petrus, Kapitel 1,1–4,7*. Karlsruhe.

Jones, J. C.
1900 *Studies in the First Epistle of Peter*. London: Bible Christian Book Room.

Jowett, J. H.
1970 *The Epistles of St. Peter: A Practical and Devotional Commentary*. London: Hodder & Stoughton, 1905. Reprinted Grand Rapids: Kregel.

Kasteren, J. P. van
1911 *De eerste brief van den apostel Petrus*. Utrecht: van Rossum.

Kelcy, R. C.
1972 *The Letters of Peter and Jude*. Austin, Texas: Sweet.

Kelly, J. N. D.
1969 *The Epistles of Peter and of Jude*. HNTC. New York: Harper & Row.

Kelly, W.
1923 *The First Epistle of Peter*. 2d ed. London: Weston. [1st ed., 1904]

Ketter, P.
1950 *Hebräerbrief, Jakobusbrief, Petrusbriefe, Judasbrief*. Die Heilige Schrift für das Leben erklärt 16/1. Freiburg: Herder.

Keulers, J.
1946 *De Katholieke Brieven en het Boek der Openbaring*. De boeken van het NT 7. Roermond.

Kistemaker, S. J.
1987 *Exposition of the Epistles of Peter and of the Epistle of Jude*. New Testament Commentary. Grand Rapids: Baker.
Knoch, O. B.
1990 *Der Erste und Zweite Petrusbrief, Der Judasbrief*. RNT. Regensburg: Pustet.
Knopf, R.
1912 *Die Briefe Petri und Judae*. 7th ed. MeyerK 12. Göttingen: Vandenhoeck & Ruprecht.
Köder, S.
1977 *Ein Hirtenbrief der Hoffnung*. 2d ed. Stuttgart: Katholisches Bibelwerk.
Kretzmann, P. E.
1922–24 *I and II Peter*. Popular Commentary on the New Testament 2. St. Louis: Concordia.
Krodel, G.
1977 The First Letter of Peter. Pages 51–80 in *Hebrews, James, 1 and 2 Peter, Jude, Revelation*. Proclamation Commentaries. Philadelphia: Fortress.
1995 1 Peter. Pages 42–83, 146–47 in *The General Letters: Hebrews, James, 1–2 Peter, Jude, 1–3 John*. Rev. ed. Proclamation Commentaries. Minneapolis: Fortress.
Kupferschmid, A.
1964 *Lebendige Hoffnung: Der erste Petrusbrief ausgelegt*. Meines Fusses Leuchte. Zurich: Gotthelf.
Lange, J. P.
1949–51 *I and II Peter*. Column 23 of *Commentary on the Holy Scriptures*. Translated and edited by P. Schaff. Grand Rapids: Zondervan.
Leaney, A. R. C.
1967 *The Letters of Peter and Jude: A Commentary on the First Letter of Peter, a Letter of Jude and the Second Letter of Peter*. CBC. Cambridge: Cambridge University Press.
Leconte, R.
1961 *Les épîtres catholiques*. Sainte Bible de Jérusalem. 2d ed. Paris: Cerf. [1st ed., 1953]
Leighton, R.
1972 *Commentary on First Peter*. Grand Rapids: Kregel. [Reprint of London 1853 ed.]
Lenski, R. C. H.
1966 *The Interpretation of the Epistles of St. Peter, St. John, and St. Jude*. Columbus: Lutheran Book Concern, 1938; reprinted, Minneapolis: Augsburg.
Lilje, H.
1954 *Die Petrusbriefe und der Judasbrief*. Bibelhilfe für die Gemeinde 14. Kassel: Oncken.
McFayden, J. R.
1924 *Through Eternal Spirit: A Study of Hebrews, James, and 1 Peter*. London: Clarke.
Macknight, J.
1949 *Apostolical Epistles*. Grand Rapids: Baker.

McKnight, S.
1996 *1 Peter.* NIV Application Commentary. Grand Rapids: Zondervan.
Maclaren, A.
1910 *First and Second Peter.* Expositions of Holy Scripture. New York: Armstrong.
Macleod, A. N.
1951 *The First Epistle of Peter: A Commentary.* Hong Kong: Christian Witness Press. [Chinese]
Madsen, P.
1912 *Peters forste Brev.* Copenhagen.
Maly, E. H.
1960 *The Epistles of Saints James, Jude, Peter.* New Testament Reading Guide 12. Collegeville, Minnesota: Liturgical.
Margot, J. C.
1960 *Les Épîtres de Pierre: Commentaire.* Geneva: Labor et Fides.
Marshall, I. H.
1991 *1 Peter.* InterVarsity Press New Testament Commentary. Downers Grove, Illinois: InterVarsity.
Masterman, J. H. B.
1900 *The First Epistle of St. Peter.* London: Macmillan.
Maycock, E. A.
1957 *A Letter of Wise Counsel.* New York: World Christian Books.
Meyer, F. B.
1950 *Tried by Fire: Expositions of the First Epistle of Peter.* Grand Rapids: Zondervan.
Michaels, J. R.
1988 *1 Peter.* WBC 49. Waco, Texas: Word.
Michl, J.
1968 *Die katholischen Briefe.* RNT 8/2. 2d ed. Regensburg: Pustet. [1st ed., 1953]
Miller, D. C.
1993 *On This Rock: A Commentary on I Peter.* Princeton Theological Monograph Series 34. Allison Park, Pennsylvania: Pickwick.
Moffatt, J.
1928 *The General Epistles of James, Peter, and Jude.* Moffatt New Testament Commentary. London: Hodder & Stoughton / Garden City, New York: Doubleday, Doran. [2d ed., 1947]
Monnier, J.
1900 *La première Épître de l'Apôtre Pierre.* Macon: Protat.
Moorhead, W. G.
1910 *Outline Studies in the New Testament: Catholic Epistles—James, 1 and 2 Peter, 1, 2, 3 John, and Jude.* New York: Revell.
Mounce, R. H.
1982 *A Living Hope: A Commentary on 1 and 2 Peter.* Grand Rapids: Eerdmans.
Nes, M. van
1931 *De Brief an de Hebreen, de Brief van Jakobus, de eerste Brief van Petrus: Tekst en Uitleg.* Groningen: Wolters.

Neyrey, J. H.
1983 *First Timothy, Second Timothy, Titus, James, First Peter, Second Peter, Jude.* Collegeville Bible Commentary 9. Collegeville, Minnesota: Liturgical.

Nisbert, A.
1982 *An Exposition of 1 and 2 Peter.* Edinburgh.

Olsson, B.
1982 *Första Petrusbrevet.* Kommentar till Nya Testamentet 17. Stockholm: EFS.

Patterson, P.
1982 A *Pilgrim Priesthood: An Exposition of the Epistle of First Peter.* Nashville: Nelson.

Perkins, D.
1995 *First and Second Peter, James, and Jude.* Interpretation. Louisville: John Knox.

Pesch, R.
1980 *1. Petrusbrief.* Volume 1 of *Die Echtheit eures Glaubens.* Biblische Orientierung. Freiburg: Herder.

Pfendsack, W.
1952 *Dennoch getrost: Eine Auslegung des 1. Petrus-Briefes.* Basel: Reinhardt.

Phillips, J. B.
1976 *Peter's Portrait of Jesus: A Commentary on the Gospel of Mark and the Letters of Peter.* London: Collins and World.

Purkiser, W. T.
1974 *Hebrews, James, Peter.* Beacon Bible Expositions 11. Kansas City: Beacon Hill.

Pury, R. de
1948 *Pierres vivantes: Commentaire de la première Épître de Pierre.* 2d ed. Neuchâtel: Delachaux & Niestlé. [1st ed., 1944]

Rees, P. S.
1962 *Triumphant in Trouble: Studies in I Peter.* Westwood, New Jersey: Revell.

Reicke, B.
1964 Pages 67–139 in *The Epistles of James, Peter and Jude: Introduction, Translation, and Notes.* AB 37. Garden City, New York: Doubleday.

Rendtorff, H.
1951 *Getrostes Wandern: Eine Einführung in den ersten Brief des Petrus.* Die Urchristliche Botschaft 20. 7th ed. Hamburg: Furche. [6th ed., Berlin: Furche, 1929]

Reuss, J.
1959 *Die katholischen Briefe.* Echter Bibel 3. Würzburg: Herder.

Ross, J. M. E.
1918 *The First Epistle of Peter.* London: Religious Tract Society.

Salguero, J., and M. Garcia Cordero
1965 *Epístolas Católicas, Apocalypsis.* Biblia Commentada 7. Madrid.

Schelkle, K. H.
1976 *Die Petrusbriefe, Der Judasbrief.* HTKNT 13/2. 3d ed. Freiburg: Herder. [1st ed., 1961]

Schiwy, G.
1970 *Weg ins Neue Testament—Kommentar und Material, IV: Nach-Paulinen.* Würzburg: Echter.

1973 *Die katholischen Briefe*. Der Christ in der Welt 6. Das Buch der Bücher 12. Aschaffenburg: Pattloch / Stein am Rhein: Christiana.

Schlatter, A.
1928 Pages 5–80 in *Die Briefe des Petrus, Judas, Jakobus; der Brief an die Hebräer; die Briefe und die Offenbarung des Johannes*. Erläuterungen zum Neuen Testament 3. 4th ed. Stuttgart: Calwer. [1st ed., 1910]

Schneider, J.
1961 *Die Briefe des Jakobus, Petrus, und Johannes*. NTD 10. 9th ed. Göttingen: Vandenhoeck & Ruprecht

Schrage, W., and H. Balz
1973 Der erste Petrusbrief. Pages 59–117 in *Die "Katholischen" Briefe: Die Briefe des Jakobus, Petrus, Judas und Johannes*. 11th ed. NTD 10. Göttingen: Vandenhoeck & Ruprecht.

Schroder, D.
1985 *First Peter: Faith Refined by Fire*. Newton, Kansas: Faith and Life.

Schwank, B.
1969 *The First Epistle of Peter*. Translated by W. Kruppa. New York: Herder & Herder. [Translation of *Der erste Brief des Apostels Petrus*. Düsseldorf: Patmos, 1963]

Schwank, B., and A. Stöger
1981 *The First Epistle of St. Peter; The Second Epistle of St. Peter*. New Testament for Spiritual Reading. New York: Crossroad.

Schweizer, E.
1972 *Der erste Petrusbrief*. Zürcher Bibelkommentare. 3d ed. Zurich: Theologischer Verlag. [1st ed., Zurich: Zwingli, 1942; 2d rev. ed., 1949]

Scott, T.
1930–32 *I and II Peter*. In *The Holy Bible, with Explanatory Notes*. Boston: Armstrong.

Seethaler, P. A.
1985 *1. und 2. Petrusbrief, Judasbrief*. SKKNT 16. Stuttgart.

Selwyn, E. G.
1947 *The First Epistle of St. Peter: The Greek Text with Introduction, Notes, and Essays*. 2d ed. London: Macmillan / New York: St. Martin's. [1st ed., 1946]

Senior, D.
1980 *1 and 2 Peter*. New Testament Message 20. Wilmington, Delaware: Glazier.

Setzer, S. M.
1989 *We Are a Chosen People of God*. ELCA Lutheran Youth Organization 1989–90 Bible Studies. Minneapolis: Augsburg Fortress.

Södergren, C. J.
1925 *The First Epistle of Peter*. Rock Island, Illinois: Augustana.

Speyr, A. von
1961 *Der Jakobusbrief, Die Petrusbriefe*. Volume 1 of *Die katholischen Briefe*. Einsiedeln: Johannes.

Spicq, C.
1966a *Les Épîtres de Saint Pierre*. Sources Bibliques 4. Paris: Gabalda.

Staffelbach, G.
1941 *Die Briefe der Apostel Jakobus, Judas, Petrus und Johannes*. Lucerne: Räber.

Stibbs, A. M., and A. F. Walls

1959 *The First Epistle General of Peter.* TNTC. London: Tyndale / Grand Rapids: Eerdmans.

Stöckhardt, G.

1984 *Lectures on the First Epistle of St. Peter.* Translated by E. W. Koehlinger. Fort Wayne, Indiana: Concordia Theological Seminary Press. [Translation of *Kommentar über den ersten Brief Petri*. St. Louis: Concordia, 1912]

Stöger, A.

1954 *Bauleute Gottes: Der erste Petrusbrief als Grundlegung des Laienapostolats.* Lebendiges Wort 3. Munich.

Stoginannos, V. P.

1980 *Prôte Epistole Petrou.* Hermêneia Kainês Diathêkês 15. Thessalonica: Pournara.

Stronstad, R.

1983 *Models for Christian Living: The First Epistle of Peter.* Companion Bible Commentary. Vancouver: CLM.

Thompson, C. H.

1971 The First Epistle of Peter. Pages 921–30 in *The Interpreter's One-Volume Commentary on the Bible*. Nashville: Abingdon.

Trempela, P. N.

1956 *Hê pros Hebraious kai hai hepta katholikai.* Volume 3 of *Hypomnêma eis tas epistolas tês kainês diathêkês.* Athens: Adelphotês theologôn hê Zôê.

Unnik, W. C. van

1973 Peter, Epistles of Saint. Pages 743–45 in volume 17 of *EncBrit.* 14th ed.

Vaganay, L.

1930 *L'Evangile de Pierre.* Paris: Gabalda.

Valentine, F.

1981 *Hebrews, James, 1 and 2 Peter.* Layman's Bible Book Commentary 23. Nashville: Broadman.

Vanni, U.

1975 *Lettere di Pietro, Giacomo, Giuda.* Rome: Paoline.

Vaughan, C., and T. D. Lea

1988 *1–2 Peter, Jude.* Bible Study Commentary. Grand Rapids: Zondervan.

Vrede, W.

1932 Der erste Petrusbrief. Pages 79–117 in *Die katholischen Briefe: Judas-, Petrus-, und Johannesbriefe.* 4th ed. Die Heilige Schrift des Neuen Testaments. Bonner NT 9. Bonn: Hanstein.

Waltemyer, W. C.

1936 *The First Epistle of Peter.* New Testament Commentary. Philadelphia: United Lutheran Church in America.

Wand, J. W. C.

1934 *The General Epistles of St. Peter and St. Jude.* Westminster Commentaries. London: Methuen.

Weisiger, C. N.

1961 *The Epistles of Peter.* Grand Rapids: Baker.

Willmering, H.

1953 The First Epistle of St. Peter. Pages 1177–80 in *A Catholic Commentary on Holy Scripture*. Edited by B. Orchard et al. New York: Nelson.

Windisch, H.
1930 *Die katholischen Briefe*. 2d ed. HNT 15. Tübingen: Mohr. [1st ed., 1911]
Windisch, H. (and H. Preisker)
1951 *Die katholischen Briefe*. HNT 4/2. 3d revised and augmented ed., with appendix by H. Preisker, pp. 152–62. Tübingen: Mohr.
Wohlenberg, G.
1915 *Der erste und zweite Petrusbrief und der Judasbrief*. Kommentar zum Neuen Testament 15. Leipzig: Deichert. [3d ed., 1923]
Woods, G. N.
1976 *A Commentary on the New Testament Epistles of Peter, John and Jude*. Nashville: Abingdon.
Wouters, S., P. N. Kruyswijk, and J. A. Schep
1940 *De Brieven van Jakobus, Petrus, Johannes, en Judas*. Kampen: Kok.
Wuest, K. S.
1947 *First Peter in the Greek New Testament for the English Reader*. Grand Rapids: Eerdmans.
Yeager, R. O.
1984 *Petrou A*. Pages 53–189 in vol. 17 of *The Renaissance New Testament*. Gretna, Louisiana: Pelican.
Zampini, S.
1922 *Pietro e le sue Epistole*. Milan: Hoepli.
Zedda, S.
1962 *Il messaggio spirituale di S. Pietro*. Rome: Paoline.
Zilz, W.
1958 *Lebendige Hoffnung: Eine Auslegung des I. Petrusbriefes*. Lahr-Dinglingen: St. Johannis.
Zoellner, F.
1935 *Der erste Petrusbrief, für die Gemeinde ausgelegt*. Potsdam: Stiftungsverlag.

2. STUDIES ON 1 PETER AND PETER THE APOSTLE

◆

Aalen, S.
1972 Oversettelsen av ordet *eperôtêma* i dåpsstedet 1 Petr. 3,21. *TTKi* 43:161–75.

Achtemeier, P. J.
1988 Newborn Babes and Living Stones: Literal and Figurative in 1 Peter. Pages 207–36 in *To Touch the Text: Biblical and Related Studies*. J. A. Fitzmyer Festschrift. Edited by M. P. Horgan and P. J. Kobelski. New York: Crossroad.
1993 Suffering Servant and Suffering Christ in 1 Peter. Pages 176–88 in *The Future of Christology*. L. E. Keck Festschrift. Edited by A. J. Malherbe and W. A. Meeks. Minneapolis: Fortress.

Adinolfi, M.
1965–66 Temi dell' Esodo nella 1 Pt. *Studi Biblici Franciscani Liber Annuus* 16:299–317.
1967a Stato civile dei Cristiani "forestieri e pellegrini" (1 Pt 2:11). *Antonianum* 42:420–34.
1967b Temi dell' Esodo nella 1 Petr. Pages 319–36 in *San Pietro: Atti della XIX settimana Biblica Italiana*. Edited by A. Bea et al. Brescia: Paideia.
1988 *La prima lettera di Pietro nel mondo greco-romano*. Bibliotheca Pontificii Athenaei Antoniani 26. Rome: Antonianum.
1991a Appunti erodotei su Dio e l'uomo: Un confronto con 1 Pt. *RivB* 39: 223–29.
1991b L'Autorità civile nelle diatribe di Epitteto alla luce della 1 Pt. Pages 93–103 in *Ellenismo e Bibbia: Saggi storici ed esegetici*. Rome: Dehoniane.
1991c La deontologia stoica di Ierocle e il codice domestico della 1 Pt. Pages 105–22 in *Ellenismo e Bibbia: Saggi storici ed esegetici*. Rome: Dehoniane.
1991d La metanoia della tavola di Cebete alla luce della 1 Pt. *Antonianum* 60 (1985):579–601. Reprinted pp. 123–43 in *Ellenismo e Bibbia: Saggi storici ed esegetici*. Rome: Dehoniane.

Adrianopoli, L.
1935 *Il mistero di Gesù nelle Lettere di San Pietro*. Turin: Società editrice internazionale.

Agnew, F. H.
1983 1 Peter 1:2: An Alternative Translation. *CBQ* 45:68–73.

Aland, K.
1960 Der Tod des Petrus in Rom. Pages 35–104 in *Kirchengeschichtliche Entwürfe*. Gütersloh: Gütersloher / Mohn.

Allison, D. C., Jr.
1992 Peter and Cephas: One and the Same. *JBL* 111:489–95.
Ambroggi, P. de
1933a Il concetto di salute nei discorsi e nelle lettere di Pietro. *Scuola Cattolica* 61:319–36.
1933b La salvezza nelle lettere di S. Pietro. *Scuola Cattolica* 61:431–46.
1947 Il sacerdozio dei fedeli secondo la prima di Pietro. *Scuola Cattolica* 75:52–57.
Antoniotti, L.-M.
1985 Structure littéraire et sens de la Première Épître de Pierre. *Revue Thomiste* 85:533–60.
Applegate, J. K.
1992 The Coelect Woman of 1 Peter. *NTS* 32:587–604.
Appolonj-Ghetti, B. M., A. Ferrua, E. Josi, and E. Kirschbaum
1951 *Esplorazioni sotto la confessione di San Pietro in Vaticano*. Vatican City.
Arichea, D. C. Jr.
1977 God or Christ? A Study of Implicit Information. *BT* 28:412–18.
Arichea, D. C., Jr., and E. A. Nida
1980 *A Translator's Handbook on the First Letter from Peter*. Helps for Translators. New York: United Bible Societies.
Arndt, W.
1929 Studies in First Peter. *CTM* 9:38–46, 354–62.
1934 Die Lehre von der Inspiration nach 1 Petr. 1, 10–12. *CTM* 5:192–98.
1948 A Royal Priesthood. *CTM* 19:241–49.
Arvedson, T.
1950 *Syneidêseôs agathês eperôtêma*: En studie till 1 Ptr. 3,21. *SEÅ* 15:55–61.
Ashcraft, M.
1982 Theological Themes in I Peter. *Theological Educator* 13:55–62.
Asseldonk, O. van
1978 Le Lettere di San Pietro negli scritti di San Francesco. *Collectanea Franciscana* 48:67–76.
Augusti, J. C. W.
1808 *Nova, qua primae epistolae Petri authentiam oppugnatur, hypothesis sub examen vocata*. Jena.
Bagshawe, W.
1674 *The Riches of Grace Displayed in . . . 2 Ephes. 7th Verse, to Which Is Added the Privilege of Passive Obedience from I Peter 4,14*. London: Parkhurst.
Baird, J. A., and J. D. Thompson
1989 *A Critical Concordance to I, II Peter*. Rev. ed. Computer Bible 32. Wooster, Ohio: Biblical Research.
Balch, D. L.
1981 *Let Wives be Submissive: The Domestic Code in I Peter*. SBLMS 26. Chico, California: Scholars Press.
1984 Early Christian Criticism of Patriarchal Authority: 1 Peter 2:11–3:12. *USQR* 39:161–73.

1986 Hellenization/Acculturation in 1 Peter. Pages 79–101 in *Perspectives on First Peter*. Edited by C. H. Talbert. National Association of Baptist Professors of Religion Special Studies Series 9. Macon, Georgia: Mercer University Press.

Balocco, A. A.

1966 Avviando alla lettura di S. Pietro. *Rivista Lasall* 33:180–213.

Bammel, E.

1964–65 The Commands in 1 Peter ii.17. *NTS* 11:279–81.

Banks, W. L.

1966 Who Are the Spirits in Prison? *Eternity Magazine* 17:23, 26.

Barnes, W. W.

1913 *The Place of Peter in the Early Church (up to* A.D. *451)*. Th.D. Dissertation, Southern Baptist Theological Seminary.

Barr, A.

1961 Submission Ethic in the First Epistle of Peter. *Hartford Quarterly* 20:27–33.

Barr, D. L.

1995 Peter as the Exhorting Elder: First Peter. Pages 438–43, 450–51 in *New Testament Story: An Introduction*. 2d ed. Belmont: Wadsworth.

Barr, G. K.

1997 The Structure of Hebrews and of 1st and 2nd Peter. *IBS* 19:17–31.

Barr, J.

1975 *Bʾrṣ—molis*: Prov. xi.31, 1 Pet iv.18. *JSS* 20:149–64.

Barth, G.

1966 1 Petrus 1, 3–9: Exegese, Meditation und Predigt. *Estudios teológicos* 6:148–60.

1981 Taufe als Bitte um ein gutes Gewissen in 1 Petrus 3,21. Pages 111–16 in *Die Taufe in frühchristlicher Zeit*. Biblisch-theologische Studien 4. Neukirchen-Vluyn: Neukirchener Verlag.

Bartina, S.

1964 Pedro manifesta su poder primacial (1 P 2,25). *Cultura Biblica* 21: 333–36.

Bartling, V.

1939 Pilgrims of Hope: An Exposition of the Argument of First Peter. *CTM* 10:10–24.

Barton, J. M. T.

1950 The Spirits in Prison (1 Pt 3:19). *Scripture* 4:181–82.

Bauckham, R.

1988a James, 1 and 2 Peter, Jude. Pages 303–17 in *It Is Written: Scripture Citing Scripture*. Edited by D. A. Carson and H. G. M. Williamson. Cambridge: Cambridge University Press.

1992a The Martyrdom of Peter in Early Christian Literature. *ANRW* 2.26.1:539–95.

1992b Spirits in Prison. Pages 177–78 in vol. 6 of *ABD*.

Bauer, J. B.

1978a Aut maleficus aut alieni speculator (1 Petr. 4.15). *BZ* n.s. 22:109–15.

1978b Der erste Petrusbrief und die Verfolgung unter Domitian. Pages 513–27 in *Die Kirche des Anfangs*. H. Schürmann Festschrift. Ed. R. Schnackenburg, J. Ernst, and J. Wanke. Erfurter theologische Studien 38. Leipzig: St. Benno.

Baur, F. C.
1856 Der erste petrinische Brief, mit besonderer Beziehung auf das Werk: *Der petrinische Lehrbegriff* von Bernhard Weiss. *Theologisches Jahrbuch* 15:193–240.

Bea, A., et al., eds.
1967 *San Pietro: Atti della XIX Settimana Biblica*. Brescia: Paideia.

Beare, F. W.
1943 Sequence of Events in Acts 9–15 and the Career of Peter. *JBL* 62:295–306.
1945 The Teaching of First Peter. *AThR* 27:284–96.
1961 The Text of 1 Peter in the Bodmer Papyrus ($\mathfrak{P}^{72}$). *JBL* 80:253–60.
1964 Some Remarks on the Text of 1 Peter in the Bodmer Papyrus ($\mathfrak{P}^{72}$). Pages 263–65 in *SE III*. TU 88. Berlin: Akademie.

Bennetch, J. H.
1944 Exegetical Studies in 1 Peter. *BSac* 101:193–98.

Benoit, P.
1961 La Primauté de S. Pierre selon le Noveau Testament. *Istina* 2 (1955): 305–34. Reprinted pp. 250–84 in vol. 2 of *Exégèse et Théologie*. Paris: Cerf.

Bergh, H.
1784 *De drangredenen tot een levendig . . . eene leerde over I Petr. V. vs.* 7. Te Deventer: Brower.

Bernard, J. A.
1916 The Descent into Hades and Christian Baptism (A Study of 1 Peter III, 19ff). *Exp* 8/64:241–74.

Best, E.
1960 Spiritual Sacrifice: General Priesthood in the New Testament. *Int* 14:273–99.
1969 1 Peter II 4–10: A Reconsideration. *NovT* 11:270–93.
1969–70 1 Peter and the Gospel Tradition. *NTS* 16:95–113.
1986 A First Century Sect. *Irish Biblical Studies* 8:115–21.

Bethge, H.-G.
1993 Der Text des ersten Petrusbriefes im Crosby-Schøyen-Codex (Ms. 193 Schøyen Collection). ZNW 84:255–67.

Bieder, W.
1950 *Grund und Kraft der Mission nach dem ersten Petrusbrief*. Theologische Studien 29. Zurich: Zwingli.
1963 Der Descensus Jesu Christi und die Mission der Christen. *Kirchenblatt für die reformierte Schweiz* 119:306–9.

Bindley, T. H.
1929 1 Peter 3,18f. *ExpTim* 41:43.

Bischoff, A.
1906 "*Allotri(o)episkopos* [Part 1]." ZNW 7:271–74.
1908 "*Allotri(o)episkopos*[Part 2]." ZNW 9:171.

Biser, E.
1959 Abgestiegen zu der Hölle. *MTZ* 9:205–12, 283–93.

Bishop, E. F. F.
1951 *Oligoi* in 1 Pet. 3:20. *CBQ* 13:44–45.

1953 The Word of a Living and Unchanging God: 1 Peter 1,23. *The Muslim World* 43:15–17.

Blazen, I. T.

1983 Suffering and Cessation from Sin according to 1 Peter 4:1. *AUSS* 21: 27–50.

Blendinger, C.

1967 Kirche als Fremdlingschaft (1 Petrus 1:22–25). *Communio Viatorum* 10:123–34.

Blevins, J. L.

1982 Introduction to 1 Peter. *RevExp* 79:401–13.

Blinzler, J.

1949 *Ierateyma*: Zur Exegese von 1 Petr. 2:5 u. 9. Pages 49–65 in *Episcopus: Studien über das Bischofsamt*. Michael von Faulhaber Festschrift. Edited by the Theologische Fakultät der Universität München. Regensburg: Gregorius.

1953 Simon der Apostel, Simon der Herrenbruder und Bischof Symeon von Jerusalem. Pages 25–55 in *Passauer Studien*. Simon Konrad Landersdorfer Festschrift. Passau: Theologische Hochschule.

Boismard, M.-É.

1956a La typologie baptismale dans la première épître de Saint Pierre. *La Vie Spirituelle* 94:339–52.

1956b Une liturgie baptismale dans la Prima Petri, I: Son influence sur Tit, 1 Jo. et Col. *RB* 63:182–208.

1957 Une liturgie baptismale dans la Prima Petri, II: Son influence sur l'épître de Jacques. *RB* 64:161–83.

1961 *Quatre hymnes baptismales dans la première épître de Pierre*. LD 30. Paris: Cerf.

1966 Pierre (Première Épître de). Columns 1415–56 in vol. 7 of *DBSup*.

Bojorge, H.

1975 Fundamentación y normas de la conducta cristiana según la 1ª carta de Pedro. *RevistB* 37:269–77.

Bolkestein, M. H.

1942 De Kerk in haar vreemdelingschap volgens de eerste brief van Petrus. *Nieuwe Theologische Studiën* 25:181–94.

1961 Het tijbegrip in de eerste brief van Petrus. Pages 140–49 in *Woord en Wereld*. K. H. Miskotte Festschrift. Edited by H. C. Touw. Amsterdam: de Arbeiderspers.

Bonnardière, A.-M. de la

1980 La prédication du Christ aux esprits en prison d'après l'interprétation de Saint Augustin. Pages 247–67 in *Études sur la première lettre de Pierre*. LD 102. Paris: Cerf.

Boobyer, G. H.

1957 The Indebtedness of 2 Peter to 1 Peter. Pages 34–53 in *New Testament Essays*. T. W. Manson Festschrift. Edited by A. J. B. Higgins. Manchester: Manchester University Press.

Borchert, G. L.

1982 The Conduct of Christians in the Face of the "Fiery Ordeal" (1 Peter 4:12–5:11). *RevExp* 79:451–62.

Boring, M. E.
1993 Interpreting 1 Peter as a Letter (Not) Written to Us. *Quarterly Review* 1:89–111.

Bornemann, W.
1919–20 Der erste Petrusbrief: Eine Taufrede des Silvanus? *ZNW* 19:143–65.

Bornhauser, K.
1921 Jesu Predigt für die Geister. *Allgemeine Evangelisch-Lutherische Kirchenzeitung* 54:322–24.

Bosetti, E.
1990 *Il Pastore: Cristo e la chiesa nella Prima lettera di Pietro*. Associazione Biblica Italiana. Supplementi alla Rivista Biblica 21. Bologna: Dehoniane.
1996 I cristiani come stranieri nella Prima lettera di Pietro. *Ricerche Storico-Bibliche* 8:317–34.

Botha, J.
1988 Christian and Society in 1 Peter: Critical Solidarity. *Scriptura: Journal of Bible and Theology in Southern Africa* 24:27–37.

Botte, B.
1934 L'idée du sacerdoce des Fidèles dans la tradition, I: L'Antiquité chrétienne. Pages 21–28 in *La Participation active des fidèles au culte*. Cours Conférence des Semaines Liturgiques 11. Louvain.

Bovon, F.
1978 Foi chrétienne et religion populaire dans la première épître de Pierre. *ETR* 53:25–41.

Brandt, W.
1953 Wandel als Zeugnis nach dem 1. Petrusbrief. Pages 10–25 in *Verbum Dei manet in aeternum*. O. Schmitz Festschrift. Edited by W. Foerster. Witten: Luther.

Bratcher, R. G.
1984 *A Translator's Guide to the Letters of James, Peter, and Jude*. New York: United Bible Societies.

Brauer, N.
1951 *The Meaning and Significance of the Suffering and Death of Christ as Found in I Peter*. STM Thesis. St. Louis: Concordia Theological Seminary.

Braun, H.
1940 *Das Leiden Christi: Eine Bibelarbeit über den 1. Petrusbrief*. Theologische Existenz heute 69. Munich: Kaiser.

Braunfels, W.
1976 Petrus, Apostel, Bischof von Rom. Columns 158–74 in vol. 8 of *Lexikon der christlichen Ikonographie*. Edited by E. Kirschbaum. Rome: Herder.

Brinley, J. B.
1987 The Type and Antitype 1 Petr 3, 21. *Christian Quarterly* April:244.

Brooke, G. J.
1990 Laos: A Biblical Perspective for a Theology of "The People of God." *Modern Churchman* 32:32–40.

Brooks, O. S.
1974 1 Peter 3:21: The Clue to the Literary Structure of the Epistle. *NovT* 16:290–305.

Brown, E. F.
1907 1 Peter v 9. *JTS* 8:450–52.

Brown, R. E.
1976 Peter. Pages 654–57 in *IDBSup*.
1983a The First Epistle of Peter. Pages 128–39 in *Antioch and Rome: New Testament Cradles of Catholic Christianity*. Edited by R. E. Brown and J. P. Meier. New York: Paulist.
1983b The Roman Church in the Second Christian Generation (A.D. 65–95): I Peter and Hebrews. Pages 128–58 in *Antioch and Rome: New Testament Cradles of Catholic Christianity*. Edited by R. E. Brown and J. P. Meier. New York: Paulist.
1984 The Petrine Heritage in I Peter: The Church as the People of God. Pages 75–83 in *The Churches the Apostles Left Behind*. New York: Paulist.

Brown, R. E., K. P. Donfried, and J. Reumann, eds.
1973 *Peter in the New Testament: A Collaborative Assessment by Protestant and Roman Catholic Scholars*. Minneapolis: Augsburg / New York: Paulist.

Brownrigg, R.
1974 Andrew and Peter: Brothers from Bethsaida. Pages 41–83 in *The Twelve Apostles*. London: Weidenfeld & Nicholson / New York: Macmillan.

Brox, N.
1975a Zur pseudepigraphischen Rahmung des ersten Petrusbriefes. *BZ* 19:78–96.
1977a Situation und Sprache der Minderheit im ersten Petrusbrief. *Kairos* 11:1–13.
1978a Der erste Petrusbrief in der literarischen Tradition des Urchristentums. *Kairos* 20:182–92.
1978b Tendenz und Pseudepigraphie im ersten Petrusbrief. *Kairos* 20:110–20.
1981 "Sara zum Beispiel": Israel im 1. Petrusbrief. Pages 484–93 in *Kontinuität und Einheit*. F. Mussner Festschrift. Edited by P.-G. Müller and W. Stenger. Freiburg: Herder.

Bruce, F. F.
1979 *Peter, Stephen, James, and John: Studies in Early Non-Pauline Christianity*. Grand Rapids: Eerdmans.

Bruni, G.
1973 La communità cristiana nella prima lettera di Pietro. *Servitium* 7/30: 278–86.

Brunk, G. R., III
1978 The Missionary Stance of the Church in 1 Peter. *Mission-Focus* 6:1–4.

Brusten, C.
1905 La descente aux enfers selon les apôtres Paul et Pierre. *Revue de Théologie et des questions religieuses* 1905:346–54.

Bullinger, E. W.
1895 *"The Spirits in Prison": An Exposition of 1 Pet iii 17–iv* 6. London: Eyre & Spottiswoode. Reprinted pp. 141–63 in *Selected Writings*. London: Lamp, 1960.

Bultmann, R.
1947 Bekenntnis- und Liedfragmente im ersten Petrusbrief. Pages 1–14 in *Coniectanea Neotestamentica in Honorem Antonii Fridrichsen*. ConNT 11. Lund: C.W.K. Gleerup.

Burtness, J. H.
1969 Sharing the Suffering of God in the Life of the World: From Text to Sermon on I Peter 2:21. *Int* 23:277–88.

Busto, J. R.
1993 Alegraos según compartís las padecimientos de Cristo. *Manresa* 65: 139–52.

Butler, J.
1996 Grace and Suffering: A Study in 1 Peter. *Notes on Translation* 10:58–60.

Calloud, J.
1980 Ce que parle veut dire (1 P 1, 10–12). Pages 175–206 in *Études sur la première lettre de Pierre*. LD 102. Paris: Cerf.

Campbell, B.
1995 *Honor, Shame, and the Rhetoric of 1 Peter.* Th.D. Dissertation, Fuller Theological Seminary.

Cantinat, J.
1959 La Première Épître de Saint Pierre. Pages 577–89 in *Introduction à la Bible*. 2 vols. Edited by A. Robert and A. Feuillet. *II: Nouveau Testament.* Tournai: Desclée.

Caragounis, C. C.
1990 *Peter and the Rock*. BZAW 58. Berlin: de Gruyter.

Carcopino, J.
1966 Pierre (Fouilles de Saint). Pages 1375–1415 in vol. 7 of *DBSup*.

Carrez, M.
1980 L'esclavage dans la première épître de Pierre. Pages 207–17 in *Études sur la première lettre de Pierre*. LD 102. Paris: Cerf.

Carrington, P.
1951 Saint Peter's Epistle. Pages 57–63 in *The Joy of Study: Papers on New Testament and Related Subjects to Honor F. C. Grant*. Edited by S. E. Johnson. New York: Macmillan.

Carter, F. S.
1975 *The Theme of Obedience in the First Epistle of Peter.* Ph.D. Dissertation, Duke University.

Case, S. J.
1918a Peter. Pages 191–201 in vol. 2 of *HDAC*.
1918b Peter, Epistles of, A: First Peter. Pages 201–7, 209 in vol. 2 of *HDAC*.

Castellini, G. M.
1958 Vestigi di una liturgia baptismale nella prima lettera di S. Pietro. *Ephemerides Liturgicae* 72:220–23.

Castelot, J. J.
1967 Peter, Apostle, St. Pages 200–205 in vol. 11 of *NCE*.

Casurella, A.
1996 *Bibliography of Literature on First Peter.* NT Tools and Studies 16. Leiden: Brill.

Caviglia, G.
1981 *Le ragioni della speranza cristiana (1 Pt 3,15): Ma piuttosto l'intera teologia fondamentale*. Turin: Leumann.

Cerfaux, L.
1939 *Regale Sacerdotium*. *RSPT* 28:5–39. [Reprinted pp. 283–315 in vol. 2 of *Recueil Lucien Cerfaux: Études d'exégèse et d'histoire religieuse*. BETL 6–7. Gembloux: Duculot, 1954]

Cervantes Gabarrón, J.
1991a *La pasión de Jesucristo en la Primera Carta de Pedro: Centro literario y teológico de la carta*. Institución San Jerónimo 22. Estella (Navarra): Verbo Divino.
1991b El pastor en la teología de 1 Pe. *Estbib* 49:331–51.

Charue, A.
1951 Première Épître de S. Pierre. Pages 435–74 in vol. 12 of *Sainte Bible*. 3d ed. Edited by L. Pirot. Revised by A. Clamer. Paris: Letouzey et Ané.

Chase, F. H.
1900a Peter (Simon). Pages 756–79, 817 in vol. 3 of *HDB*.
1900b Peter, First Epistle of. Pages 779–96, 817–18 in vol. 3 of *HDB*.

Cherian, C. M.
1960 The Christian Way (1 Peter). *Clergy Monthly* 23:81–90.

Chester, A., and R. P. Martin
1994 *The Theology of the Letters of James, Peter, and Jude*. New York: Cambridge University Press.

Chevallier, M.-A.
1971 1 Pierre 1/1 à 2/10: Structure littéraire et conséquences exégétiques. *RHPR* 51:129–42.
1974 Condition et vocation des chrétiens en diaspora: Remarques exégétiques sur la 1re épître de Pierre. *RSR* 48: 387–400.
1978 Israël et l'Église selon la Première Épître de Pierre. Pages 117–30 in *Paganisme, Judaïsme, Christianisme: Influences et affrontements dans le monde antique*. Mélanges offerts á Marcel Simon. Paris: de Boccard.
1980 Comment lire aujord'hui la première épître. Pages 129–54 in *Études sur la première lettre de Pierre*. LD 102. Paris: Cerf.

Chevrot, G.
1959 *Simon Peter*. Chicago: Scepter.

Childs, B. S.
1985 I Peter. Pages 446–62 in *The New Testament as Canon: An Introduction*. Philadelphia: Fortress.

Chin, M.
1991 A Heavenly Home for the Homeless: Aliens and Strangers in 1 Peter. *TynBul* 42:96–112.

Cipriani, S.
1966 L'unitarietà del disegno della storia della salvezza nella 1[a] lettera di Pietro. *RivB* 14:385–406.
1981 Sacerdozio "commune" e "ministeriale" nella 1[a] lettera di Pietro. *Lateranum* 47:31–43.
1986 Lo "Spirito di Cristo" come "spirito di profezia" in 1 Pt. 1,10–12. Pages 157–67 in *Ecclesiae Sacramentum*. Edited by G. Lorizio and V. Scippa. A. Marranzini Festschrift. Pontificia facoltà teologica dell'Italia meridionale 2. Naples: D'Auria.
1990 "Evangelizzazione" e "missione" nella prima lettera di Pietro. *Richerche storico-bibliche* 2:125–38.

Clark, S. D.
1982 Persecution and the Christian Faith. *Theological Educator* 13:72–82.

Clarke, W. K. L.
1914 The First Epistle of St. Peter and the Odes of Solomon. *JTS* 15:47–52.

Clavier, H.
1954 *Petros-petra*. Pages 101–7 in *Neutestamentliche Studien für Rudolf Bultmann*. BZNW 21. Berlin: Alfred Töpelmann.

Clemen, C.
1902 The First Epistle of St. Peter and the Book of Enoch. *Exp* 6/4:316–20.
1905 Die Einheitlichkeit des 1. Petrusbriefes verteidigt. *TSK* 78:619–28.

Clowney, E. P.
1989 *The Message of 1 Peter: The Way of the Cross—The Bible Speaks Today*. Downers Grove, Illinois: InterVarsity.

Cocagnac, A. M.
1968 *Pierre, pécheur du Christ*. Paris: Cerf.

Colecchia, L. F.
1977 Rilievi su 1 Piet. 2,4–10. *RivB* 25:179–94.

Combrink, H. J. B.
1975 The Structure of 1 Peter. *Neotestamentica* 9:34–63.

Cone, O.
1902 The Epistles of Peter: First Peter. Columns 3677–83 in vol. 3 of *EncBib*. London: Black.

Connick, C. M.
1972 Pages 338–43 in *The New Testament: An Introduction to Its History, Literature, and Thought*. Encino, California: Dickenson.

Conzelmann, H., and A. Lindemann
1977 Der erste Petrusbrief. Pages 308–11 in *Arbeitsbuch zum Neuen Testament*. Uni-Taschenbücher 52. Tübingen: Mohr (Siebeck).

Cook, D.
1980 I Peter iii.20: An Unnecessary Problem. *JTS* 31:72–78.

Coppens, J.
1969 Le Sacerdoce royal des fidèles: Un Commentaire de I Petr. II, 4–10. Pages 61–75 in *Au service de la parole de Dieu: Mélanges offerts á Monseigneur André-Marie Charue*. Gembloux: Duculot.

Cordero, M. G.
1959 El sacerdocio real en 1 P. 2:9. *Cultura Bíblica* 16:321–23.

Corley, K. E.
1994 1 Peter. Pages 349–80 in *A Feminist Commentary*. Edited by E. Schüssler Fiorenza. Volume 2 of *Searching the Scriptures*. New York: Crossroad.

Cothenet, E.
1969 Le Sacerdoce des fidèles d'après la 1[a] Pierre. *Esprit et Vie* 11:169–73.
1971 Béni soit Dieu (1 P 1,3–9). *AsSeign* 23:26–33.
1974 La Première épître de Pierre, L'épître de Jacques. Pages 138–54 in *Le ministère et les ministères selon le Nouveau Testament*. Edited by J. Delorme. Parole de Dieu 10. Paris: Seuil.
1979 Liturgie et vie chrétienne d'après I Pierre. Pages 97–113 in *La liturgie—expression de la foi: Conférences Saint-Serge, 1978*. Rome.

1980 Les Orientations actuelles de l'exégèse de la première lettre de Pierre. Pages 13–42, 269–74 in *Études sur la première lettre de Pierre*. LD 102. Paris: Cerf.

1980–81 Le Réalisme de l'espérance chrétienne selon 1 Pierre. *NTS* 27:564–72.

1982 La Portée salvifique de la résurrection du Christ d'aprés I Pierre. Pages 249–62 in *La Pâque du Christ, mystère de Salut*. F. X. Durrwell Festschrift. Edited by M. Benzerath et al. Paris: Cerf.

1984 Pages 7–48 in *Les Épîtres de Pierre*. Cahiers Évangiles 47. Paris: Cerf.

1985 Pierre (saint) apôtre. Columns 1452–86 in vol. 12 of *Dictionnaire de spiritualité ascétique et mystique, doctrine et histoire*. Edited by Marcel Viller et al. Paris: Beauchesne.

1988 La Première [Épître] de Pierre: Bilan de 35 ans de recherches. *ANRW* 2.22.5:3685–3712.

Coutts, J.

1957 Ephesians I.3–14 and I Peter I.3–12. *NTS* 3:115–27.

Covolo, E. dal

1995 L'Interpretazione origeniana di 1 Petri 2,9. Pages 567–75 in *Origeniana Sexta: Origene et la Bible / Origen and the Bible*. BETL 118. Louvain: Peeters.

Cramer, J.

1891 Exegetica et critica, II: Het glossematisch karacter van 1. Petr. 3:19–21 en 4:6. Pages 73–149 in vol. 7 of *Nieuwe Bijdragen op het gebied van godgeleerdheid en wijsbegeerte*. Utrecht.

Cranfield, C. E. B.

1958 The Interpretation of 1 Peter 3:19 and 4:6. *ExpTim* 62:269–72.

Cross, F. L.

1954 *I Peter: A Paschal Liturgy*. London: Mowbray.

Cullmann, O.

1958 *Peter: Disciple–Apostle–Martyr: A Historical and Theological Essay*. Translated by F. V. Filson. New York: Meridian.

Dacquino, P.

1967 Il sacerdozio del nuovo populo di Dio e la prima lettera di Pietro. Pages 291–317 in *San Pietro: Atti della XIX settimana Biblica Italiana*. Edited by A. Bea et al. Brescia: Paideia.

Dale, R. W.

1896a Christians and Social Institutions (1 Peter ii.11–iii.7). *Exp* 1896:287–95.

1896b Like Minded (1 Peter iii.8–12). *Exp* 1896:349–57.

1896c A Spiritual House (1 Peter ii.5). *Exp* 1896:127–36.

Dallman, W.

1930 *Peter: Life and Letters*. St. Louis: Concordia.

Dalmer, J.

1898–99 Zu 1. Petri 1,18–19. Pages 75–87 in BFCT 2/6. Gütersloh: Bertelsmann.

Dalton, W. J.

1964a Christ's Proclamation to the Spirits (1 Peter 3:19). *Australian Catholic Record* 41:322–27.

1964b Proclamatio Christi spiritibus facta: Inquisitio in textum ex prima Epistola S. Petri 3:18–4:6. *VD* 42:225–40.

1965 Christ's Victory over the Devil and the Evil Spirits. *TBT* 2:1195–1200.

1968 Interpretation and Tradition: An Example from 1 Peter. *Greg* 49:11–37.
1970 Le Christ, espérance des chrétiens dans un monde hostile (1 P 3,15–18). *AsSeign* 27:18–23.
1974 "So That Your Faith May Also Be Your Hope in God" (I Peter 1:21). Pages 262–74 in *Reconciliation and Hope: New Testament Essays on Atonement and Eschatology.* L. L. Morris Festschrift. Edited by R. Banks. Exeter: Paternoster / Grand Rapids: Eerdmans.
1977 Review of H.-J. Vogels, *Christi Abstieg ins Totenreich und das Läuterungsgericht an den Toten* (Freiburg: Herder, 1976). *Bib* 58/4:585–88.
1979 The Interpretation of 1 Peter 3,19 and 4,6: Light from 2 Peter. *Bib* 60:547–55.
1982a The Church in 1 Peter. Pages 79–91 in *Jerusalem: Seat of Theology.* Edited by D. Burrell, P. Du Brul, and W. Dalton. Jerusalem: Ecumenical Institute for Theological Research.
1982b La rigenerazione alla vita cristiana (1 Pt 1,3). *Parola, Spirito e Vita* (Bologna) 5:234–46.
1984 1 Peter 3:19 Reconsidered. Pages 96–106 in vol. 1 of *The New Testament Age.* B. Reicke Festschrift. Edited by W. C. Weinrich. Macon, Georgia: Mercer University Press.
1989 *Christ's Proclamation to the Spirits: A Study of 1 Peter 3:18–4:6.* AnBib 23. 2d rev. ed. Rome: Pontifical Biblical Institute. [1st ed., 1965]
1990 The First Epistle of Peter. Pages 903–8 in *NJBC.*

Danielou, J.
1967 Pierre dans le judéo-christianisme hétérodox. Pages 443–58 in *San Pietro: Atti della XIX Settimana Biblica.* Edited by A. Bea et al. Brescia: Paideia.

Danker, F. W.
1967a Brief Review of J. H. Elliott,*The Elect and the Holy. CTM* 38:329–32.
1967b 1 Peter 1:24–2:17: A Consolatory Pericope. *ZNW* 58:93–102.

Daris, S.
1967 *Un nuovo frammento della Prima Lettera di Pietro (1 Petr 2,20–3,12).* Papyrologica Castroctaviana 2. Barcelona: Papyrologica Castroctaviana.

Daube, D.
1947 Participle and Imperative in I Peter. Appended note on pp. 467–88 in E. G. Selwyn, *The First Epistle of St. Peter.* 2d ed. London: Macmillan.

Dautzenberg, G.
1964 *Sôtêria psychôn* (1 Petr. 1, 9). *BZ* n.s. 8:262–76.

Davey, G. R.
1970 *Philological Notes in the Two Epistles of St. Peter: An Examination of the Greek and Syriac Texts of the Two Petrine Epistles, and their Interrelation and their Theology.* Ph.D. Dissertation, Melbourne.
1973 Old Testament Quotations in the Syriac Version of I and II Peter. *Parole de l'Orient* 3:353–64.

Davids, P. H.
1986 Suffering: Endurance and Relief. *First Fruits* (1986):7–11.

Davidson, J. A.
1940 *The Petrine Conception of the Christian Life.* Ph.D. dissertation, Temple University, Philadelphia.

Davies, P. E.

1972 Primitive Christology in I Peter. Pages 115–22 in *Festschrift to Honor F. Wilbur Gingrich*. Edited by E. H. Barth and R. E. Cocroft. Leiden: Brill.

Déault, R. le

1961 Le Targum de Gen 22,8 et 1 Pt 1,20. *RSR* 49:103–6.

Deering, R. F.

1961 *The Humiliation-Exaltation Motif in I Peter.* Th.D. Dissertation, Southern Baptist Theological Seminary.

De Haan, M. R.

1954 *Simon Peter: Sinner and Saint*. Grand Rapids: Zondervan.

Deist, F. E.

1970 Van die duisternis tot sy merkwaardige lig (1 Petr. 2,9) in die lig van Elephantine. *Nederduitse Gereformeerde Teologiese Tydskrif* 11:44–48.

Delling, G.

1963 Taufe und Taufmotive im I. Petrusbrief, im Johannes-Evangelium und im I. Johannesbrief. Pages 82–96 in *Die Taufe im Neuen Testament*. Berlin: Evangelische.

1973 Der Bezug der christlichen Existenz auf das Heilshandeln Gottes nach dem ersten Petrusbrief. Pages 95–113 in *Neues Testament und christliche Existenz*. H. Braun Festschrift. Edited by H. D. Betz and L. Schottroff. Tübingen: Mohr (Siebeck).

Detering, P. E.

1981 Exodus Motifs in First Peter. *Concordia Journal* 7:58–65.

Díaz Carbonell, R.

1965 Pedro, Epístolas de San. Pages 966–79 in vol. 5 of *EncBib*.

Dibelius, M.

1930 Petrusbriefe. Pages 1113–15 in vol. 4 of *RGG*^{2}.

Diderichsen, B.

1975 *Allotrioepiskopos* (1 Pet 4,15) og *eperôtêma* (1 Pet 3,21) belyst ved Plinius dys brev til Trajan (ep x, 96). Pages 35–41 in *Hilsen til Noack*. B. Noack Festschrift. Edited by N. Hyldahl and E. Nielsen. Copenhagen: Gad.

Dierkens, L. H. B. E.

1919 "Nauwelijks zalig" (vix salvabitur 1 Pet. 4,18). *Nieuwe theologische Stuidiën* 2:188.

Dijkman, J. H. L.

1984 *The Socio-religious Condition of the Recipients of I Peter.* Ph.D. Dissertation, University of the Witwatersrand, Johannesburg.

1986 *Hoti* as an Introductory Formula to the Catechetical References in I Peter. Pages 260–70 in *A South African Perspective on the New Testament*. B. M. Metzger Festschrift. Edited by J. H. Petzer and P. J. Hartin. Leiden: Brill.

1987 I Peter: A Later Pastoral Stratum? *NTS* 33:265–71.

Dinkler, E.

1939 Die ersten Petrusdarstellungen. Ein archäologischer Beitrag zur Geschichte des Petrusprimates. *Marburger Jahrbuch für Wissenschaft* 11:1–80.

1959 Die Petrus-Rom Frage: Ein Forschungsbericht [Part 1]. *TRu* n.s. 25:189–230, 289–335.

1961 Die Petrus-Rom Frage: Ein Forschungsbericht [Part 2]. *TRu* n.s. 27: 33–64.
1966 Die Petrus-Rom-Frage: Ein Nachtrag. *TRu* n.s. 31:232–53.

Dixon, M. C.
1989 *Discipleship in I Peter as a Model for Contextual Mission*. Th.D. Dissertation, Southern Baptist Theological Seminary.

Dockx, S.
1984 Chronologie de la vie de saint Pierre. Pages 161–78 in *Chronologies néotestamentaires et Vie de l'Église primitive: Recherches exégétiques*. Leuven: Peeters.

Dodewaard, J. van
1949 Die sprachliche Übereinstimmung zwischen Markus-Paulus und Markus-Petrus, II: Markus-Petrus. *Bib* 30:218–38.

Donfried, K. P.
1992 Peter. Pages 251–63 in vol. 5 of *ABD*.

Downing, F. G.
1988 Pliny's Prosecution of Christians: Revelation and 1 Peter. *JSNT* 34:105–23.

Dschulnigg, P.
1994 Aspekte und Hintergrund der Theologie des 1. Petrusbriefes. *TGl* 84:318–29.
1996 *Petrus im Neuen Testament*. Stuttgart: Katholisches Bibelwerk.

Duling D. C., and N. Perrin
1993 The First Letter of Peter and the Petrine School. Pages 473–79, 504 in *The New Testament: Proclamation and Parenesis, Myth and History*. 3d rev. ed. Fort Worth: Harcourt Brace College Publishers.

Duplacy, J.
1969–70 Le texte occidentale des épîtres catholiques. *NTS* 16:397–99.

Duplacy, J., and C.-B. Amphoux
1980 A propos de l'histoire du texte de la première épître de Pierre. Pages 155–73 in *Études sur la première lettre de Pierre*. LD 102. Paris: Cerf.

Dupont-Roc, R.
1995 Le jeu des prépositions en 1 Pierre 1,1–12: De l'espérance finale à la joie dans les épreuves présentes. *EstBib* 53:201–12.

Durken, D.
1955 First Peter. *Worship* 29:382–84.

du Toit, A. B.
1974 The Significance of Discourse Analysis for New Testament Interpretation and Translation: Introductory Remarks with Special Reference to 1 Peter 1:3–13. *Neot* 8:54–80.

Duvall, T. J.
1919 The First Epistle of Peter. *RevExp* 16:194–205.

Ebright, H. K.
1917 *The Petrine Epistles: A Critical Study of Authorship*. Cincinnati: Methodist Book Concern.

Edelkoort, A. H.
1934 *De rijkdom in Christus: Bijbellezingen over I Petrus I*. Rotterdam: Dorteweg.

Ehrman, B. D.
1990 Cephas and Peter. *JBL* 109:463–74.

Elert, W.

1911 *Die Religiosität des Petrus: Ein religionspsychologischer Versuch*. Leipzig: Deichert.

Elliott, J. H.

1966b *The Elect and the Holy: An Exegetical Examination of I Peter 2:4–10 and the Phrase* basileion hierateuma. NovTSup 12. Leiden: Brill.

1968 Death of a Slogan: From Royal Priests to Celebrating Community. *Una Sancta* [USA] 25:18–31.

1970 Ministry and Church Order in the New Testament: A Traditio-historical Analysis (1 Pt 5,1–5 & plls.). *CBQ* 32:367–91.

1976 The Rehabilitation of an Exegetical Step-Child: 1 Peter in Recent Research. *JBL* 95:243–54. Reprinted pp. 3–16 in *Perspectives on First Peter*. Edited by C. H. Talbert. NABPR Special Study Series 9. Macon, Georgia: Mercer University Press, 1986.

1979 *1 Peter: Estrangement and Community*. Herald Biblical Booklets. Chicago: Franciscan Herald.

1980 Peter, Silvanus and Mark in I Peter and Acts: Sociological-Exegetical Perspectives on a Petrine Group in Rome. Pages 250–67 in *Wort in der Zeit: Neutestamentliche Studien*. K. H. Rengstorf Festschrift. Edited by W. Haubeck and M. Bachmann. Leiden: Brill.

1981/1990 *A Home for the Homeless: A Sociological Exegesis of I Peter, Its Situation and Strategy*. Philadelphia: Fortress / London: SCM, 1981. 2d expanded ed.: *A Home for the Homeless: A Social-Scientific Criticism of I Peter, Its Situation and Strategy, With a New Introduction*. Minneapolis: Fortress, 1990.

[Portuguese translation of 1st ed. of *A Home for the Homeless*, by J. Rezende Costa: *Um lar para quem não tem casa: Interpretação sociológica da primeira carta de Pedro*. Coleção Biblia e Sociologia 3. São Paulo: Paulinas, 1985]

[Spanish translation of 2d ed. of *A Home for the Homeless*, by C. Ruiz-Garrido: *Un hogar para los que no tienen patria ni hogar: Estudio crítico social de la Carta primera de Pedro y de su situación y estrategia*. Estella (Navarra): Verbo Divino, 1995]

1982 Salutation and Exhortation to Christian Behavior on the Basis of God's Blessings (1 Pet 1:1–2:10). *RevExp* 79:415–25.

1983 The Roman Provenance of 1 Peter and the Gospel of Mark: A Response to David Dungan. Pages 182–94 in *Colloquy on New Testament Studies. A Time for Reappraisal and Fresh Approaches*. Edited by B. Corley. Macon, Georgia: Mercer University Press.

1985 Backward and Forward "In His Steps"—Following Jesus from Rome to Raymond and Beyond: The Tradition, Redaction, and Reception of 1 Peter 2:18–25. Pages 184–209 in *Discipleship in the New Testament*. Edited by F. Segovia. Philadelphia: Fortress.

1986a 1 Peter, Its Situation and Strategy: A Discussion with David Balch. Pages 61–78 in *Perspectives on First Peter*. Edited by Charles H. Talbert. NABPR Special Study Series 9. Macon, Georgia: Mercer University Press.

1992a Peter, First Epistle of. Pages 269–78 in vol. 5 of *ABD*.

1992b Review of A. Reichert, *Eine urchristliche praeparatio ad martyrium. Studien zur Komposition, Traditionsgeschichte und Theologie des 1. Petrusbriefes*. (BBET 22; Frankfurt am Main: Peter Lang, 1989). In *CBQ* 54:369–71.

1993a Social-Scientfic Criticism of a Biblical Text: 1 Peter as an Example. Pages 70–86 in *What Is Social-Scientific Criticism?* Guides to Biblical Scholarship, New Testament Series. Minneapolis: Fortress.
1995a Disgraced yet Graced: The Gospel according to 1 Peter in the Key of Honor and Shame. *BTB* 25:166–78.
1997 Review of R. Metzner, *Die Rezeption des Matthäusevangeliums im 1. Petrusbrief: Studien zum traditionsgeschichtlichen und theologischen Einfluss des 1. Evangeliums auf den 1. Petrusbrief* (WUNT 2/74; Tübingen: Mohr (Siebeck), 1995). In *JBL* 116:379–82.

Elliott, J. H., and W. Thompson
1974 Peter in the New Testament: Old Theme, New Views. *America* 130:53–54.

Elliott, J. K.
1972 *Kêphas: Simôn Petros: Ho Petros*: An Examination of New Testament Usage. *NovT* 14:241–56. [Reprinted pp. 125–38 in *Essays and Studies in New Testament Criticism*. Estudios de Filologia Neotestamentaria 3. Cordoba: el Alemandro, 1992]

Ellul, D.
1990 Un exemple de cheminement rhétorique: I Pierre. *RHPR* 70:17–34.

Elton, G. E.
1966 *Simon Peter: A Study of Discipleship*. Garden City, New York: Doubleday.

English, E. S.
1941 *The Life and Letters of St. Peter*. New York: Our Hope/Gabelein.

Erbes, C.
1901 Petrus nicht in Rom, sondern in Jersualem Gestorben. *Zeitschrift für Kirchengeschichte* 22:1–47, 161–224.

Erbes, K.
1919 Was bedeutet *allotrioepiskopos* 1 Ptr. 4,15? ZNW 19:39–44.
1921 Noch etwas zum *allotrioepiskopos*? ZNW 20:249.

Erickson, M. J.
1995 Is There Opportunity for Salvation after Death? *BSac* 152:131–44.

Ericson, N. R.
1981 Interpreting the Petrine Literature. Pages 243–66 in *The Literature and Meaning of Scripture*. Edited by M. A. Inch and C. Hassell. Grand Rapids: Baker.

Ermoni, V.
1909 La cristologia dell' epistole di Pietro. *Rivista storico-critica* 5:85–93.

Evang, M.
1989 *Ek kardias allêlous agapêsate ektenôs*: Zum Verständnis der Aufforderung und ihrer Begründungen in 1 Petr 1,22f. ZNW 80:111–23.

Fabris, R.
1995 Elementi apocalittici nelle lettere di Pietro e di Giuda. *Ricerche storico-bibliche* 7:85–102.

Falconer, R. A.
1903–4 A Prophet of the New Israel: A Study in the First Epistle of Peter. *ExpTim* 15:259–63.

Farrer, F. W.
1883 St. Peter; The First Epistle of St. Peter. Pages 60–97 in *The Early Days of Christianity*. New York: Funk & Wagnalls.

Fascher, E.
1938 Petrus. Columns 1335–61 in vol. 38 of *PW*. [Reprinted pp. 175–223 in *Sokrates und Christus: Beiträge zur Religionsgeschichte*. Leipzig, 1959]
1961 Petrusbriefe. Pages 257–60 in vol. 5 of *RGG*[3].

Fedalto, G.
1983 Il toponimo di 1 Petr. 5,13 nella esegesi di Eusebio di Cesarea. *Vetera Christianorum* 20:461–66.

Feinberg, J. S.
1986 1 Peter 3:18–20: Ancient Mythology and the Intermediate State. *WTJ* 48:303–36.

Feldmeier, R.
1992 *Die Christen als Fremde: Die Metapher der Fremde in der antiken Welt, im Urchristentum und im 1. Petrusbrief*. WUNT 64. Tübingen: Mohr (Siebeck).

Ferris, T. E. S.
1930 A Comparison of 1 Peter and Hebrews. *CQR* 119:123–27.
1939 The Epistle of James in Relation to I Peter. *CQR* 128:303–8.

Ferrua, A.
1952 La storia del sepolcro di San Pietro. *La Civiltà Cattolica* 103:15–29.

Feuillet, A.
1974 Les "sacrifices spirituels" du sacerdoce royal des baptisés (1 P 2,5) et leur préparation dans l'Ancien Testament. *NRTh* 96:704–28.

Fillion, L.
1912a Pierre (Première Épître de Saint). Pages 380–98 in vol. 5 of *DB*.
1912b Pierre (Saint). Pages 356–79 in vol. 5 of *DB*.

Filson, F. V.
1940 Peter. Pages 19–51 in *Pioneers of the Primitive Church*. New York: Abingdon.
1955 Partakers with Christ: Suffering in First Peter. *Int* 9:400–412.
1962 Peter. Pages 749–57 in vol. 3 of *IDB*.

Findlay, J. A.
1935 *A Portrait of Peter*. New York: Abingdon.

Finegan, J.
1964 The Life of Peter. Pages 302–15 in *Handbook of Biblical Chronology*. Princeton: Princeton University Press.
1976 The Death and Burial of St. Peter. *BARev* 2:3–8.

Fink, J.
1978 Das Petrusgrab: Glaube und Grabung. *VC* 32:255–75.

Fink, P. R.
1967 The Use and Significance of *en hôi* in 1 Peter. *Grace Journal* 8:33–39.
1969 *The Literary Style of Peter and Its Relationship to the Exegesis of the Petrine Epistles*. Th.D. Dissertation, Dallas Theological Seminary.

Finkbiner, F. L.
1960 *Church and State from Paul to 1 Peter*. Th.D. Dissertation: Southern California School of Theology.

Fischer, K. M.
1978 Der erste Petrusbrief. Pages 199–216 in *Einleitung in die Schriften des Neuen Testaments, I: Die Briefe des Paulus und Schriften des Paulinismus*. Edited by H.-M. Schenke and K. M. Fischer. Gütersloh: Gütersloher/Mohn.

Fitzmyer, J. A.
1981 Aramaic *Kephâʾ* and Peter's Name in the New Testament. Pages 112–24 in *To Advance the Gospel*. New York: Crossroad.

Foakes-Jackson, F. J.
1927a Evidence for the Martyrdom of Peter and Paul in Rome. *JBL* 46:74–78.
1927b *Peter, Prince of Apostles: A Study in the History and Tradition of Christianity*. London: Hodder & Stoughton / New York: Doran.

Foster, O. D.
1913 Pages 363–538 in *The Literary Relations of "The First Epistle of Peter" with Their Bearing on Date and Place of Authorship*. Transactions of the Connecticut Academy of Arts and Sciences 17. New Haven: Yale University Press.

Fouard, C. H.
1982 *Saint Peter and the First Years of Christianity*. Translated by G. F. X. Griffith. New York and London: Longmans, Green. [ET of *Saint Pierre et les premières années du christiansme*. Paris: Lecoffre, 1886. 3d ed., 1893]

France, R. T.
1977 Exegesis in Practice: Two Samples. Pages 252–81 in *New Testament Interpretation: Essays on Principles and Methods*. Edited by I. H. Marshall. Grand Rapids: Eerdmans.

Francis, J.
1980 "Like Newborn Babes": The Image of the Child in 1 Peter 2:2–3. Pages 111–17 in *Papers on Paul and Other New Testament Authors*. Sixth International Congress on Biblical Studies, Oxford 1978. StudBib 3. Edited by E. A. Livingstone. JSNTSup 3. Sheffield: JSOT Press.

Fransen, I.
1960 Une homélie chrétienne. *Bible et Vie Chrétienne* 31:28–38.

Frattalone, R.
1967 Antropologia naturale e soprannaturale nella prima lettera di San Pietro. *Studia Moralia* 5:41–111.
1971 *Fondamenti dell' agire morale secondo la 1ª Pt. Il battezzato sulle orme di Cristo*. Collana studi e ricerche 11. Bologna: Dehoniane.

Frederick, S. C.
1975 *The Theme of Obedience in the First Epistle of Peter*. Ph.D. Dissertation, Duke University.

Fridrichsen, A.
1947 Till 1 Petr. 3,7. *SEÅ* 12:143–47.

Frings, J.
1925 Zu 1 Petr 3,19 und 4,6. *BZ* 17:75–88.

Fritsch, C. T.
1966 *To Antitypon* (1 Pt 3:21; Heb 9:24). Pages 100–107 in *Studia Biblica et Semitica*. T. C. Vriezen Festschrift. Wageningen: Veenman.

Fry, E.
1990 Commentaries on James, 1 and 2 Peter, and Jude. *Bible Translator* 41: 326–36.

Fuller, R. H.
1966 1 Peter. Pages 155–60 in *A Critical Introduction to the New Testament*. London: Duckworth.

Furnish, V. P.
1975 Elect Sojourners in Christ: An Approach to the Theology of I Peter. *Perkins Journal* 28:1–11.

Gaddy, W.
1982 Preaching from 1 Peter. *RevExp* 79:473–85.

Gaechter, P.
1958 *Petrus und seine Zeit*. Innsbruck: Tyrolia.

Galbiati, E.
1979 L'escatologia delle lettere di S. Pietro. Pages 413–23 in *San Pietro: Atti della XIX Settimana Biblica*. Edited by A. Bea et al. Brescia: Paideia, 1967. Reprinted pp. 259–69 in *Scritti minori* 1. Brescia: Paideia.

Gale, H. M.
1939 *The Validity of the Petrine Tradition in the Light of Modern Research.* Ph.D. Dissertation, Boston University.

Galloway, A.
1988 1 Peter and *The Seafarer. English Language Notes* 25:1–10.

Galot, J.
1961 La descente du Christ aux enfers (1 P 3:18–20). *NRTh* 83:471–91. [Abridged ET: Christ's Descent into Hell. *TD* 13 (1965):89–94]

Gamba, G. G.
1982 L'evangelista Marco segretario-"interprete" della prima lettera di Pietro? *Salesianum* 44:61–70.

Gangel, K. O.
1969 Pictures of the Church in I Peter. *Grace Journal* 10:29–35.

García del Moral, A.
1961a Crítica textual de 1 Pt 4:14. *EstBib* 20:45–77.
1961b Sentido trinitario de la expresión "Espíritu de Yavé" de Is 11:2 en 1 Ptr 4:14. *EstBib* 20:169–206.
1961c El sujeto secondario de los Dones del Espiritu Santo, a la luz de 1 Pt 4,14. *Teología Espiritual* 5:443–58.

García del Moral, A., and O. P. Garrido
1962 *Interpretacion apostolica de Is. XI,2 en I Pdr IV,14*. Granada.

Gardner-Smith, P.
1954 Peter, First Epistle of. Pages 635–37 in vol. 17 of *EncBrit*.

Garofalo, S.
1959 Verità, unità, e pace nelle Lettere di S. Pietro. *Tabor* 27:128–41.

Garofalo, S., et al., eds.
1968 *Studi Petriani*. Rome: Istituto dei studi romani.

Gatzweiler, K.
1970 Prix et exigencies de la condition chrétienne (1 P 1,17–21). *AsSeign* 24:16–20.

Gerkan, A. von
1952–53 Die Forschung nach dem Grab Petri. *ZNW* 44:196–205.

Gewalt, D.
1966 *Petrus: Studien zur Geschichte und Tradition des frühen Christentums.* Doctoral Dissertation, Heidelberg University.

Geyser, A. S.
1959 Die name van Petrus en 1 Petrus. *Hervormde Teologiese Studies* 15:92–100.

Ghiberti, G.
1988 Le "sante donne" di una volta (1 Pt 3,5). *RivB* 36:287–97.
1992 L'Apostolo Pietro nel Nuovo Testamento: La discussione e i testi. *ANRW* 2.26.1:462–538.

Giaquinta, C.
1980 "Vuestra hermandad que está en el mundo" (1 Pe 5,9): Apuntos bíblicos para una eclesiología. *Teología* (Buenos Aires) 17:14–27.

Gielen, M.
1990 *Tradition und Theologie neutestamentlicher Haustafelethik: Ein Beitrag zur Frage einer christlichen Auseinandersetzung mit gesellschaftlichen Normen*. BBB 75. Frankfurt am Main: Hain.

Giesen, H.
1986 Kirche als Gottes erwähltes Volk: Zum Gemeindeverständnis von 1 Petr 2,4–10. *Theologie der Gegenwart* 29:140–49.
1989 Hoffnung auf Heil für alle: Heilsgegenwart für die Glaubenden (1 Petr 3,18–22). *SNT* 14:93–150.

Gillman, J.
1992 Silas. Pages 22–23 in vol. 6 of *ABD*.

Glaze, R. E.
1982 Introduction to 1 Peter. *Theological Educator* 13:23–34.

Glenny, W. E.
1987 *The Hermeneutics of the Use of the Old Testament in 1 Peter*. Th.D. Dissertation, Dallas Theological Seminary.

Goetz, K. G.
1927 *Petrus als Gründer und Oberhaupt der Kirche und Schauer von Gesichten nach den altkirchlichen Berichten und Legenden: Eine geschichtlich-exegetische Untersuchung*. UNT 13. Leipzig: Hinrichs.

Goldstein, H.
1973 Die politischen Paränesen in 1 Petr 2 und Röm 13. *BibLeb* 14:88–104.
1974 Die Kirche als Schar derer, die ihrem leidenden Herrn mit dem Ziel der Gottesgemeinschaft nachfolgen: Zum Gemeindeverständnis von 1 Petr 2,21–25 und 3,18–22. *BibLeb* 15:38–54.
1975 *Paulinische Gemeinde im ersten Petrusbrief*. SBS 80. Stuttgart: Katholisches.
1979 Das heilige Volk das zuvor kein Volk war: Christengemeinde ohne Judenpolemik—1 Petr 2,4–10. Pages 279–302 in *Gottesverächter und Menschenfeinde? Juden zwischen Jesus und frühchristicher Kirche*. Edited by H. Goldstein. Düsseldorf: Patmos.

Golebiewski, E.
1965 Dieu nous console dans l'épreuve (1 P 5,6–11). *AsSeign* 57:17–23.

Gontard, L.
1905 *Essai critique et historique sur la première épître de Saint Pierre*. Lyons.

Gonzalez, G. G., and J. L. Gonzalez
1989 *A Faith More Precious Than Gold: A Study of I Peter*. n.p.: John Milton Society for the Blind. [Braille]

Goodspeed, E. J.
1954 Some Greek Notes, IV: Enoch in 1 Peter 3:19. *JBL* 73:84–92.

Goppelt, L.

1969 Mission ou révolution? La responsabilité du Chrétien dans la societé d'aprés la Première Épître de Pierre. *Positions Luthériennes* 194:202–16.

1972 Prinzipien neutestamentlicher Sozialethik nach dem 1. Petrusbrief. Pages 285–96 in *Neues Testament und Geschichte: Historisches Geschehen und Deutung im Neuen Testament.* O. Cullmann Festschrift. Edited by H. Baltensweiler and B. Reicke. Zurich: Theologischer Verlag / Tübingen: Mohr.

1982 The Responsibility of Christians in Society according to the First Epistle of Peter. Pages 161–78 in vol. 2 of L. Goppelt, *Theology of the New Testament.* Edited by Jürgen Roloff. Grand Rapids: Eerdmans. [ET of Die Verantwortung der Christen in der Gesellschaft nach dem 1. Petrusbrief. Pages 490–508 in vol. 2 of *Theologie des Neuen Testaments.* Vielfalt und Einheit des apostolischen Christuszeugnisses. Edited by J. Roloff. Göttingen: Vandenhoeck & Ruprecht, 1976]

Gourges, M.

1978 La première épître de Pierre. Pages 75–87 in A *la droite de Dieu: Résurrection de Jésus et actualisation de Psaume 110:1 dans le Nouveau Testament.* Ebib. Paris: Gabalda.

Grandbery, J. C.

1910 Christological Peculiarities in the First Epistle of Peter. *American Journal of Theology* (1910):62–81.

Grant, M.

1994 *Saint Peter.* London: Weidenfeld & Nicholson.

Grappe, C.

1992 *D'un temple à l'autre: Pierre et l'Église primitive de Jérusalem.* Études d'historie et de philosophie religieuses 71. Paris: Presses universitaires de France.

Gray, J. C.

1903 The First Epistle General of St. Peter. Pages 541–68 in vol. 5 of *The Biblical Encyclopedia.* Cleveland: Barton.

Green, G. L.

1980 *Theology and Ethics in 1 Peter.* Ph.D. Dissertation, Aberdeen University.

1990 The Use of the Old Testament for Christian Ethics in 1 Peter. *TynBul* 41:276–89.

Griffith-Thomas, W. H.

1916 A Study of 1 Peter 3:19ff. *Exp* 8/69:237–41.

Grosheide, F. W.

1954 Kol 3, 1–4; 1 Petr 1, 3–5; I Jo 3,1–2. *GThT* 54:139–47.

1960 I Petrus 1, 1–12. *GThT* 60:6–7.

Gross, C. D.

1989 Are the Wives of 1 Peter 3.7 Christians? *JSNT* 35:89–96.

Grudem, W. A.

1986 Christ Preaching through Noah: 1 Peter 3:19–20 in the Light of Dominant Themes in Jewish Literature. *Trinity Journal* 7:3–31.

Gryglewicz, F.

1957 Tio upomnien św. Piotra do "starszych" (1 Pe 5,2s). *RocTKan* 4:114–21.

1958a Pierwotna Liturgia chrzto św. Jako zrodlo pierwszego listu św. Pietra (An original Baptismal Liturgy as Source of the First Epistle of St. Peter). *Ruch Biblijny i Liturgiczny* 11:206–10.
1958b Rola cytatów W pierwszym líscie św. Piotra (The Role of the Citations in 1 Peter). *RocTKan* 5:67–72.
1959 Opis Końca swiata u św. Piotra i w Qumran. *Ruch Biblijny i Liturgiczny* 12:278–82.

Gschwind, K.
1911 *Die Niederfahrt Christi in die Unterwelt. Ein Beitrag zur Exegese des Neuen Testaments und zur Geschichte des Taufsymbols.* NTAbh 2/3–5. Münster: Aschendorff.

Guarducci, M.
1953 *Cristo e San Pietro in un Documento precostantiniano della necropoli Vaticana.* Rome: Bretschneider.
1958 *I graffiti sotto la confessione di San Pietro.* Vatican City: Libreria Editrice Vaticana.
1960 *The Tomb of St. Peter, the New Discoveries in the Sacred Grottoes of the Vatican.* New York: Hawthorn.
1965 *Le Reliquie di Pietro sotto la Confessione della Basilica Vaticana.* Vatican City: Libreria Editrice Vaticana.
1982 Die Ausgrabungen unter St. Peter. Pages 364–414 in *Das frühe Christentum im römischen Staat.* Edited by R. Klein. 2d ed. Wege der Forschung 267. Darmstadt: Wissenschaftliche.

Gülzow, H.
1969 Die Haustafeln: Der erste Petrusbrief. Pages 67–76 in *Christentum und Sklaverei in den ersten drei Jahrhunderten.* Bonn: Habelt.

Gundry, R. H.
1966–67 Verba Christi in I Peter: Their Implications concerning the Authorship of I Peter and the Authenticity of the Gospel Tradition. *NTS* 13:336–50.
1974 Further Verba on Verba Christi in First Peter. *Bib* 55:211–32.

Guthrie, D.
1970 The First Epistle of Peter. Pages 771–813 in *New Testament Introduction.* 3d rev. ed. Downers Grove, Illinois: InterVarsity.

Haenchen, E.
1960–61 Petrus-Probleme. *NTS* 7:187–97.

Halas, S.
1984 Sens dynamique de l'expression laos eis peripoiêsin en 1 P 2,9. *Bib* 65: 254–58.

Hall, R.
1976 For to This You Have Been Called: The Cross and Suffering in 1 Peter. *ResQ* 19:137–47.

Hall, S. G.
1973 Paschal Baptism. Pages 239–51 in *SE* 6. Edited by E. A. Livingstone. TU 112. Berlin: Akademie.

Hallencreutz, C. F.
1978 Ett Folk pa Väg. *Svensk Missionstidskrift* 66:13–29.

Hamblin, R. L.
1960 *An Analysis of First Peter with Special Reference to the Greek Participle.* Th.D. Dissertation, Southwestern Baptist Theological Seminary.

1982 *Triumphant Strangers: A Contemporary Look at First Peter.* Nashville: Broadman.

Hanson, A. T.
1981–82 Salvation Proclaimed, I: 1 Peter 3:18–22. *ExpTim* 93:100–112.

Harmon, G. M.
1898 Peter: The Man and the Epistle. *JBL* 17:31–39.

Harris, J. R.
1901 A Further Note on the Use of Enoch in 1 Peter. *Exp* 6/4:346–49.
1902a On a Recent Emendation in the Text of St. Peter. *Exp* 6/5:317–20.
1902b The History of a Conjectural Emendation. *Exp* 6/6:378–90.
1909 An Emendation to 1 Peter II.8. *Exp* (1909-A):155–63.
1919 The Religious Meaning of 1 Peter V.5. *Exp* 8/18:131–39.
1911 Two Flood Hymns of the Early Church. *Exp* 8/10:405–17.
1929–30 An Emendation to 1 Peter i.13. *ExpTim* 41:43.

Harrison, E. F.
1940 Exegetical Studies in I Peter [Part 1]. *BSac* 97:200–210, 325–34, 448–55.
1941 Exegetical Studies in I Peter [Part 2]. *BSac* 98:69–77, 183–93, 307–19, 459–68.

Haselhurst, R. S. T.
1926 Mark, My Son. *Theology* 13:34–36.

Heeren, A. van der
1911 Epistles of St. Peter. Pages 752–55 in vol. 11 of *The Catholic Encyclopedia.* Edited by C. G. Herbermann et al. New York: Appleton.

Heiene, G.
1992 En analyse av 1 Pet 2, 13–17 med henblikk på tekstens aktualitet for politisk etikk. *Tidsskrift for Teologi og Kirke* 63:17–31.

Heimann, P.
1991 *Der griechische Weg zu Christus. Elemente zum Verständnis des Ersten Petrusbriefes.* Stuttgart: Urachhaus.

Hemer, C. J.
1978 The Address of 1 Peter. *ExpTim* 89:239–43.

Heussi, K.
1936 *War Petrus in Rom?* Gotha: Klotz.
1937 War Petrus wirklich römischer Märtyrer? *Die Christliche Welt* 51 (February):162–71.
1949 Die Entstehung der römischen Petrustradition. *Deutsches Pfarrerblatt* (1949):82–83, 301–2, 501–4.
1955 *Die römische Petrustradition in kritischer Sicht.* Tübingen: Mohr (Siebeck).

Hiebert, D. E.
1980a Designation of the Readers in 1 Peter 1:1–2. *BSac* 137:64–75.
1980b Peter's Thanksgiving for Our Salvation. *Studia Missionalia* 29:85–103.
1982a Selected Studies from 1 Peter, Part 1: Following Christ's Example—An Exposition of 1 Peter 2:21–25. *BSac* 139:32–45.
1982b Selected Studies from 1 Peter, Part 2: The Suffering and Triumphant Christ—An Exposition of 1 Peter 3:18–22. *BSac* 139:146–58.
1982c Selected Studies from 1 Peter, Part 3: Living in the Light of Christ's Return—An Exposition of 1 Peter 4:7–11. *BSac* 139:243–54.
1982d Selected Studies from 1 Peter, Part 4: Counsel for Christ's Under-Shepherds—An Exposition of 1 Peter 5:1–4. *BSac* 139:330–41.

Hilgenfeld, A.
1873 Der erste Petrus-Brief [Part 1]. *ZWT* 16:465–98.
1876 Der erste Petrus-Brief [Part 2]. *ZWT* 19:149–54.

Hill, D.
1976 On Suffering and Baptism in I Peter. *NovT* 18:181–89.
1982 "To Offer Spiritual Sacrifices . . ." (1 Peter 2:5): Liturgical Formulations and Christian Paraenesis in 1 Peter. *JSNT* 16:45–63.

Hillyer, N.
1969a The Servant of God. *EvQ* 41:143–60.
1969b Spiritual Milk . . . Spiritual House. *TynBul* 20:126.
1970 First Peter and the Feast of Tabernacles. *TynBul* 21:39–70.
1971 "Rock-Stone" Imagery in I Peter. *TynBul* 22:58–81.

Hobbie, P. H.
1993 From Text to Sermon: I Peter 2:2–10. *Int* 47:170–73.

Hofius, O.
1975 Seid bereit zur Verantwortung: Christ sein heisst auskunftsfähig sein (1 Petrus 3,15b–16a). *RefK* 116:45–57.

Hofrichter, P.
1987 Strukturdebatte im Namen des Apostles: Zur Abhängigkeit der Pastoralbriefe untereinander und vom ersten Petrusbrief. Pages 101–16 in *Anfänge der Theologie: CHARISTEION*. J. B. Bauer Festschrift. Edited by N. Brox et al. Graz: Styria.

Holdsworth, J.
1980 The Sufferings in 1 Peter and "Missionary Apocalyptic." Pages 225–32 in *Studia Biblica 1978*. Edited by E. A. Livingstone. JSNTSup 3. Sheffield: JSOT Press.

Holzmeister, U.
1922 "Exordium prioris S. Petri" (1 Petr. 1,1–2). *VD* 2:209–12.
1929 "Dei . . . Spiritus super vos requiescit" (1 Petr. 4,14). *VD* 9:129–31.

Hoops, M. H.
1983 First Peter: A Renewed Appreciation? (A Review of selected issues in Petrine Studies). *Trinity Seminary Review* 5:3–14.
1985 First Peter: A Community at Witness. *Trinity Seminary Review* 7:30–39.

Ho-Sang, D.
1989 *The New Age and the Interpretation of 1 Peter*. Ph.D. Dissertation, Oxford University.

Hugelé, P.
1983 L'obéissance du croyant à Jésus-Christ dans la première Épître de Pierre. *Carmel* 32:252–57.

Hughes, H. D.
1971 *A Developmental Approach to the Christology of the Petrine Canonical Tradition*. Ph.D. Dissertation, Baylor University.

Huidekopper, F.
1890 *The Belief of the First Three Centuries concerning Christ's Mission to the Underworld*. 8th ed. New York: Francis.

Hunzinger, C.-H.
1965 Babylon als Deckname für Rom und die Datierung des I. Petrusbriefes. Pages 67–77 in *Gottes Wort und Gottes Land*. H.-W. Hertzberg Festschrift. Edited by H. Graf Reventlow. Göttingen: Vandenhoeck & Ruprecht.

1970 Zur Struktur der Christus-Hymnen in Phil. 2 und 1. Petr. 3. Pages 142–56 in *Der Ruf Jesu und die Antwort der Gemeinde*. J. Jeremias Festschrift. Edited by E. Lohse, C. Buchard, and B. Schaller. Göttingen: Vandenhoeck & Ruprecht.

Hutton, J. A.
1922 A Ruling from First Peter. *Exp* 8/23:420–27.

Iersel, B. van
1956 Ihr seid ein königliches Priestertum: Bildsprache oder Wirklichkeit? *T'H. Land* 9:23–26.

James, S. A.
1985 Divine Justice and the Retributive Duty of Civil Government. *Trinity Journal* 6:199–210.

Janse, W.
1982 De verhouding tussen "vlees" en "geest" in 1 Petrus [Part 1]. *Theologia Reformata* 25:244ff.
1983 De verhouding tussen "vlees" en "geest" in 1 Petrus [Part 2]. *Theologia Reformata* 26:13ff.

Jensen, J. P.
1891 *Om Kristi praediken for aanderne 1 Petr 3, 18–22*. Copenhagen.
1903 *Laeren om Kristi Nedfahrt til de Döde*. Copenhagen.

Jeremias, J.
1949 Zwischen Karfreitag und Ostern: Descensus und Ascensus in der Karfreitagstheologie des Neuen Testaments. *ZNW* 42:194–201.

Ji, W. Y.
1983 4th Sunday of Easter. *Concordia Journal* 9:65–66.

Johnson, D. E.
1986 Fire in God's House: Imagery from Malachi 3 in Peter's Theology of Suffering (1 Pet. 4:12–19). *JETS* 29:285–94.

Johnson, L. T.
1986 1 Peter. Pages 430–41 in *The Writings of the New Testament. An Interpretation*. Philadelphia: Fortress.

Johnson, S. E.
1960 The Preaching to the Dead. *JBL* 79:48–51.

Johnston, G.
1961 The Will of God, V: In 1 Peter and 1 John. *ExpTim* 72:237–40.

Jones, J. C.
1887 *Studies in the First Epistle of Peter*. London.

Jones, P. R.
1982 Teaching First Peter. *RevExp* 79:463–72.

Jones, R. B.
1949 Christian Behavior under Fire (The First Epistle of Peter). *RevExp* 46:56–66.

Jones-Haldeman, M.
1988 *The Function of Christ's Suffering in I Peter 2:21*. Th.D. Dissertation, Andrews University.

Jonge, M. de
1956–57 Vreemdelingen en bijwoners: Enige opmerkingen naar aanleding van 1 Pt. 2, 11 en verwante teksten. *NedTT* 11:18–36.

Jonsen, A. R.
1964 The Moral Teaching of the First Epistle of St. Peter. *ScEccl* 16:93–105.

Jossa, G.
1996 La sottomissione alle autorità politiche in 1Pt 2,13–17. *RivB* 44:205–11.

Jülicher, A., and E. Fascher
1931 Der erste Petrusbrief. Pages 189–200 in *Einleitung in das Neue Testament*. 7th ed. Tübingen: Mohr (Siebeck).

Karrer, M.
1989 Petrus im paulinischen Gemeindekreis. ZNW 80:210–31.

Karrer, O.
1963 *Peter and the Church: An Examination of Cullmann's Thesis*. Translated by R. Walls. QD 8. Freiburg: Herder.

Kayalaparampil, T.
1977 Christian Suffering in I Peter. *Biblehashyam* (Kottayam, Kerala, India) 3:7–19.
1989 Christian People: A Royal Priesthood (A Study on 1 Peter 2:9). *Biblehashyam* 15:154–69.

Kee, H. C., F. W. Young, and K. Froehlich
1965 Ethics for Exiles: I Peter and James. Pages 355–89 in *Understanding the New Testament*. 2d ed. Englewood Cliffs, New Jersey: Prentice-Hall.

Kelly, W.
1872 *The Preaching to the Spirits in Prison: I Peter III.18–20*. London: Morrish. London: Weston, 1900. Reprinted Denver: Wilson Foundation, 1970.

Kendall, D. W.
1984 *The Introductory Character of 1 Peter 1:3–12*. Th.D. Dissertation, Union Theological Seminary, Richmond, Virginia.
1985 The Christian's Vocation: The Call to Holiness according to the First Epistle of Peter. *Asbury Seminary Review* 40:3–12.
1986 The Literary and Theological Function of 1 Peter 1:3–12. Pages 103–20 in *Perspectives on First Peter*. Edited by C. H. Talbert. Macon, Georgia: Mercer University Press.
1987 On Christian Hope: 1 Peter 1:3–9. *Int* 41:66–71.

Kennard, D. W.
1986 *The Doctrine of God in Petrine Theology*. Th.D. Dissertation, Dallas Theological Seminary.
1987 Petrine Redemption: Its Meaning and Extent. *JETS* 30:399–405.

Kesich, V.
1981 1 Peter and the Doctrines of Primitive Christianity. Pages 129–48 in *Orthodox Synthesis*. Edited by J. J. Allen. Crestwood, N.Y.: St. Vladimir's Seminary.

Ketter, P.
1947 Das allgemeine Priestertum der Gläubigen nach dem 1 Petrusbrief. *TTZ* 56:43–51.

Kiley, M.
1987 Like Sara: The Tale of Terror behind 1 Peter 3:6. *JBL* 106:689–92.

Kilpatrick, G. D.
1986 1 Peter 1:11: *Tina ê poion kairon*. *NovT* 28:91–92.

King, M. A.
1964 Notes on the Bodmer Manuscript of Jude and 1 and 2 Peter. *BSac* 121:54–57.

Kira, K.
1960 1 Pe. 3:18–4:6 et la descente aux enfers du Christ. *JRelS* 34:62–76.

Kirk, G. E.
1981 Endurance in Suffering in 1 Peter. *BSac* 138:46–56.

Kirkpatrick, W. D.
1982 The Theology of First Peter. *Southwestern Journal of Theology* 25:58–81.

Kirschbaum, E.
1959 *The Tombs of St. Peter and St. Paul.* New York: St. Martin's.

Klauser, T.
1956 *Die römische Petrustradition im Lichte der neuen Ausgrabungen unter der Petruskirche.* Arbeitsgemeinschaft für Forschung des Landes Nordrhein-Westfalen, Geisteswissenschaft 24. Cologne: Westdeutscher.

Kline, L.
1963 Ethics for the Endtime: An Exegesis of 1 Pt. 4: 7–11. *ResQ* 7:113–23.

Knapp, P.
1887 1 Petr 3, 17ff und die Höllenfahrt Jesu Christi. *Jahrbücher für Deutsche Theologie* 23:177–228.

Knoch, O. B.
1973 *Die "Testamente" des Petrus und Paulus: Die Sicherung der apostolischen Überlieferung in der spätneutestamentlichen Zeit.* SBS 62. Stuttgart: Katholische.
1976 "Wir haben durch die Auferstehung Jesu Christi von den Toten eine lebendige Hoffnung" (1 Pet 1,3): Die Hoffnung der Christen zwischen "Schon" und "Noch Nicht." *Dienst und Glaube* 52:92–99.
1981 Petrus und Paulus in den Schriften der Apostolischen Väter. Pages 241–60 in *Kontinuität und Einheit.* F. Mussner Festschrift. Edited by P. Müller. Regensburg: Pustet.
1990 Die Petrusschule in Rom: Die Stellung des Petrus in der Kirche. Pages 143–46 in *Der Erste und Zweite Petrusbrief, Der Judasbrief.* RNT. Regensburg: Pustet.
1991 Gab es eine Petrusschule in Rom? Überlegungen zu einer bedeutsamen Frage. *SNT* 16:105–26.

Knox, J.
1953 Pliny and 1 Peter: A Note on 1 Peter 4:14–16 and 3:15. *JBL* 72:187–89.

Koch, H.
1938 Petrus. Columns 1335–61 in vol. 19/2 of *PW.*

Kögel, J.
1902 *Die Gedankeneinheit des ersten Briefes Petri: Ein Beitrag zur neutestamentlichen Theologie.* BFCT 6,5–7. Gütersloh: Bertelsmann.

Körtner, U.
1980 Markus der Mitarbeiter des Petrus. *ZNW* 71:160–73.
1983 *Papias von Hierapolis. Ein Beitrag zur Geschichte des frühen Christentums.* FRLANT 133. Göttingen: Vandenhoeck & Ruprecht.

Köster, F.
1831 Über die Leser, an welche der Brief des Jakobus und der erste Brief des Petrus gerichtet ist. *TSK* 4:581–88.

Koester, H.

1982a The Letters of Peter and the Legacy of Paul. Pages 292–97 in vol. 2 of *Introduction to the New Testament*. Philadelphia: Fortress.

Koger, A. D., Jr.

1988 *The Question of a Distinctive Petrine Theology in the New Testament*. Ph.D. Dissertation, Baylor University.

Kohler, M.-E.

1982 La Communauté des Chrétiens selon la première Épître de Pierre. *RTP* 114:1–21.

Kokot, M.

1974 Znaczenie "nasienia niezniszczalnego" w 1 P 1,23 (The Significance of "Incorruptible Seed" in 1 P 1,23). *Collectanea Theologica* 44:35–44.

Kosala, K. C. P.

1985 *Taufverständnis und Theologie im Ersten Petrusbrief*. Doctoral Dissertation, Kiel University.

Kowalski, S.

1938 *La descente de Jésus-Christ aux enfers selon la doctrine de saint Pierre*. Roznan.

1949 De descensu Christi ad inferos in prima S. Petri epistola. *Collectanea Theologica* 21:42–76.

Krafft, E.

1950–51 Christologie und Anthropologie im ersten Petrusbrief. *EvT* 10:120–26.

Küchler, M.

1986 Sara und "Herr" Abraham: Die Unterordnung als Schmuck der Frau (1 Petr 3,1–6). Pages 64–70 in *Schweigen, Schmuck und Schleier: Drei neutestamentliche Vorschriften zur Verdrängung der Frauen auf dem Hintergrund einer frauenfeindlichen Exegese des Alten Testaments im antiken Judentum*. Göttingen: Vandenhoeck & Ruprecht.

Kügler, U.-R.

1976 *Die Paränese an die Sklaven als Modell urchristlicher Sozialethik*. Th.D. Dissertation. Erlangen-Nürnberg.

Kümmel, W. G.

1975 The First Epistle of Peter. Pages 416–24 in *Introduction to the New Testament*. Rev. ed. Nashville: Abingdon.

Küschelm, R.

1983 "Lebendige Hoffnung" (1 Petr 1,3–12). *BL* 56:202–6.

Kvanvig, H. S.

1985 Bruken av Noahtradisjonene i 1 Pet 3:20f. *TTKi* 56:81–98.

Làconi, M.

1967 Tracce dello stile e del pensiero di Paolo nella prima lettera di Pietro. Pages 367–94 in *San Pietro: Atti della XIX Settimana Biblica*. Edited by A. Bea et al. Brescia: Paideia.

Lake, K.

1911a Peter, Epistles of. Pages 295–97 in vol. 21 of *EncBrit*.

1911b Peter, St. Pages 285–88 in vol. 21 of *EncBrit*.

Lamau, M.-L.

1986 Exhortation aux esclaves et hymne au Christ souffrant dans la Première Épître de Pierre. *Mélanges de Science Religieuse* 43:121–43.

1988 *Des Chrétiens dans le monde: Communautés pétriniennes au Ier siècle.* LD 134. Paris: Cerf.

Lamparter, H.
1960 *Lebensbewältigung oder Wiedergeburt. Eine biblische Besinnung über 1 Petrus 1, 3–9.* Metzingen: Brunnquell.

Lampe, P.
1979 Das Spiel mit dem Petrus-Namen: Matt. XVI.18. *NTS* 25:227–45.

Land, D. T.
1981 *The Concept of Christian Hope In 1 Peter.* Th.D. Dissertation, Southwestern Baptist Seminary.

Landeira, J.
1966 *Descensus Christi ad Inferos in 1 Pet 3:18–20.* Doctoral Dissertation, Pontifical Lateran University, Rome.

Langkammer, H.
1987 Jes 53 und 1 Petr 2,21–25: Zur christologischen Interpretation der Leidenstheologie von Jes 53. *BL* 60:90–98.

Lash, J. A.
1982 Fashionable Sports: Hymn-Hunting in I Peter. Pages 293–97 in *SE* 7. Edited by E. A. Livingstone. TU 126. Berlin: Akademie.

LaVerdiere, E. A.
1969 Covenant Theology in 1 Peter 1:1–2:10. *TBT* 42:2909–16.
1974 A Grammatical Ambiguity in 1 Pet 1:23. *CBQ* 36:89–94.

Lea, T. D.
1968 *Peter's Use of the Old Testament.* Th.D. Dissertation, Southwestern Baptist Theological Seminary.
1980 How Peter Learned the Old Testament. *SwJT* 22:96–102.
1982 1 Peter: Outline and Exposition. *SwJT* 24:17–45.

Leaney, A. R. C.
1964 I Peter and the Passover: An Interpretation. *NTS* 10:238–51.

Leclerq, H.
1939 Pierre (Saint). Columns 822–981 in vol. 14/1 of *Dictionnaire d'archéologie chrétienne et de la liturgie.* Paris: Letouzey et Ané.

Lecomte, P.
1981 Aimer la vie: 1 Pierre 3/10 (Psaume 34/13). *ETR* 56:288–93.

Leconte, R.
1961 Pages 79–117 in *Les Épîtres catholiques.* La Sainte Bible de Jerusalem. 2d ed. Paris.

Le Déaut, R.
1961 Le Targum de Gen 22,8 et 1 Pet 1,20. *RSR* 49:103–6.

Légasse, S.
1988 La soumission aux authorités d'après 1 Pierre 2. 13–17: Version spécifique d'une parénèse traditionelle. *NTS* 34:378–96.

Lepelley, C.
1980 Le contexte historique de la Première Lettre de Pierre. Pages 43–64 in *Études sur la première lettre de Pierre.* LD 102. Paris: Cerf.

Lewis, F. W.
1899 Note on the Date of the First Epistle of Peter. *Exp* 5/10:319–20.

Lewis, J. M.
1952 *The Christology of the First Epistle of Peter.* Th.D. Dissertation, Southwestern Baptist Theological Seminary.

Lietzmann, H.
1927 *Petrus und Paulus in Rom.* 2d ed. Berlin: de Gruyter.
1936 Petrus, römischer Märtyrer. *Sitzungsberichte der preussischen Akademie der Wissenschaften, philosophisch-historische Klasse* (December 3, 1936): 391–410.

Lillie, J.
1978 *Lectures on the First and Second Epistles of Peter.* Scribner's, 1898. Reprinted, Minneapolis: Klock & Klock.

Lippert, P.
1965 Leben als Zeugnis: Ein Beitrag des ersten Petrusbriefes zur pastoraltheologischen Problematik der Gegenwart. *Studia Moralia* 3:226–68.
1968 Der erste Petrusbrief. Pages 61–87 in *Leben als Zeugnis: Die werbende Kraft christlicher Lebensführung nach dem Kirchenverständnis neutestamentlicher Briefe.* Stuttgarter biblische Monographien 4. Stuttgart: Katholisches Bibelwerk.

Lips, H. von
1994 Die Haustafel als "Topos" im Rahmen der urchristlichen Paränese: Beobachtungen anhand des 1. Petrusbriefes und des Titusbriefes. *NTS* 40:261–80.

Lohse, E.
1986 Parenesis and Kerygma in 1 Peter. Pages 37–58 in *Perspectives on First Peter.* Translated by J. Steely. NABPR Special Study Series 9. Macon, Georgia: Mercer University Press. ET of Paränese und Kerygma im 1. Petrusbrief. *ZNW* 45 (1954) 68–89. [Cited as 1954/1986]

Losada, D.
1980 Suffir por el nombre de Cristiano en la Primera Carta di Pedro. *RevistB* 42:85–101.

Love, J. P.
1954 The First Epistle of Peter. *Int* 8:63–87.

Lowe, J.
1956 *Saint Peter.* Oxford: Clarendon.

Ludwig, J.
1952 *Die Primatworte Mt 16,18 in der altkirchlichen Exegese.* NTAbh 19/4. Münster: Aschendorff.

Lugo Rodríguez, R.
1991 El verbo *hypotassein* y la parénesis social de 1 Pe 2, 11–17. *Efemerides Mexicana* 9:57–70.
1992 La primera carta de San Pedro en los estudios actuales. *Efemerides Mexicana* 10:269–73.

Lumby, J. R.
1876 Style and Character of St. Peter. *Exp* 3/1:264–82.
1890 1 Peter III.17. *Exp* 5/1:142–47.

Lyonnet, S.
1955 De ministerio romano S. Petri ante adventum S. Pauli. *VD* 33:143–54.

MacCaughey, J. D.
1969 Three "Persecution Documents" of the New Testament. *ABR* 17:27–40.

1983 On Re-reading 1 Peter. *ABR* 31:33–44.

MacDonald, M. Y.

1990 Early Christian Women Married to Unbelievers. *SR* 19:221–34.

Maiburg, U.

1984 Christus der Eckstein: Ps 118,22 und Jes 28,16 im Neuen Testament und bei den lateinischen Vätern. Pages 247–56 in *Vivarium*. T. Klauser Festschrift. Edited by J. Engemann. JAC Ergänzungsband 11. Münster: Aschendorff.

Maier, G.

1984 Jesustradition im 1 Petrusbrief? Pages 85–128 in *The Jesus Tradition Outside the Gospels*. Edited by D. Wenham. Volume 5 of *Gospel Perspectives*. Sheffield: JSOT Press.

Malte, E. C.

1949 The Message of the First Epistle of Peter for our Day. *CTM* 20:728–74.

Manke, H.

1975 *Leiden und Herrlichkeit: Eine Studie zur Christologie des 1 Petrusbriefes*. Doctoral Dissertation, Westfälische Wilhelms-Universität, Münster.

Manley, G. T.

1944 Babylon on the Nile. *EvQ* 16:138–46.

Manns, F.

1984a La maison où réside l'Esprit, 1 P 2,5 et son arrière-plan juif. *Studii Biblici Franciscani Liber Annuus* 34:207–24.

1984b Sara, modèle de la femme obéissante: Étude de l'arrière-plan juif de 1 Pierre 3,5–6. *BeO* 26:65–73.

Marco, A. de

1964 *The Tomb of St. Peter: A Representative and Annotated Bibliography of the Excavations*. NovTSup 8. Leiden: Brill.

Margot, J.-C.

1979 1 Pierre 1.3–9. Pages 231–42 in *Traduire sans trahir. La théorie de la traduction et son application aux textes bibliques*. Lausanne: L'Age d'Homme.

Marshall, I. H.

1991 Rhetoric in 1 Peter. *ExpTim* 102:317.

Marshall, J. S.

1946 "A Spiritual House, an Holy Priesthood" (1 Petr ii, 5). *AThR* 28:227–28.

Martelet, G.

1980 Das Lamm, erwählt vor Gründung der Welt. *Internationale katholische Zeitschrift "Communio"* 9:36–44.

Martimort, G. A.

1972 Vingt-cinq ans de travaux et recherches sur la mort de saint Pierre et sa sépulture (1946–1968). *Bulletin de littérature ecclésiastique* 73:73–101.

Martin, R. P.

1962 The Composition of I Peter in Recent Study. Pages 29–42 in *Vox Evangelica: Biblical and Historical Essays by Members of the Faculty of the London Bible College*. Edited by R. P. Martin. London: Epworth.

1986a Peter. Pages 802–7 in vol. 3 of *ISBE*.

1986b Peter, First Epistle of. Pages 807–15 in vol. 3 of *ISBE*.

1994 I Peter. Pages 87–133 in *The Theology of the Letters of James, Peter, and Jude*. Edited by A. Chester and R. P. Martin. Cambridge: Cambridge University Press.

Martin, T. W.

1992a *Metaphor and Composition in 1 Peter*. SBLDS 131 Atlanta: Scholars Press.

1992b The Present Indicative in the Eschatological Statements of 1 Pet 1:6, 8. *JBL* 111:307–12.

Martini, C., ed.

1968 *Beati Petri Epistulae ex Papyro Bodmeriana VIII transcriptae*. 2 vols. Milan: Pizzi.

Marrucchi, O.

1934 *Pietro e Paolo a Roma*. 4th ed. Turin: Marietti.

Marxsen, W.

1968 The First Epistle of Peter. Pages 233–38 in *Introduction to the New Testament: An Approach to Its Problems*. Philadelphia: Fortress.

1979 Der Mitälteste und Zeuge der Leiden Christi: Eine martyrologische Begründung des "Romprimats" im 1. Petrusbrief? Pages 377–93 in *Theologia crucis—Signum crucis*. E. Dinkler Festschrift. Edited by C. Andresen and G. Klein. Tübingen: Mohr (Siebeck).

Massaux, E.

1963 Le texte de la Ia Petri du Papyrus Bodmer VIII ($\mathfrak{P}^{72}$). *ETL* 39:616–71.

May, G.

1967 Die Zeit ist da, dass das Gericht anfange am Hause Gottes. Pages 41–49 in *Geschichtswirklichkeit und Glaubensbewährung*. F. Miller Festschrift. Edited by F. C. Fry. Stuttgart: Evangelisches.

Mayerhoff, E. T.

1835 *Historisch-kritische Einleitung in die petrinischen Schriften*. Hamburg: Perthes.

McCartney, D.

1989 *The Use of the Old Testament in the First Epistle of Peter*. Th.D. Dissertation, Westminster Theological Seminary.

1991 *Logikos* in 1 Peter 2,2. ZNW 82:128–32.

McKelvey, R. J.

1961–62 Christ the Cornerstone. *NTS* 8:352–59.

McNabb, V.

1935 Date and Influence of the First Epistle of St. Peter. *Irish Ecclesiastical Record* 45:596–613.

McNeile, A. H., and C. S. C. Williams

1953 I Peter. Pages 213–24 in *Introduction to the New Testament*. 2d ed. Oxford: Clarendon.

Meecham, H. G.

1936–37 The First Epistle of St. Peter. *ExpTim* 48:22–24.

1953–54 A Note on I Peter ii.12. *ExpTim* 65:93.

Mees, M.

1973 Petrustraditionen im Zeugnis kanonischen und ausserkanonischen Schrifttums. *Augustinianum* 13:185–203.

Metzner, R.

1995 *Die Rezeption des Matthäusevangeliums im 1. Petrusbrief: Studien zum traditionsgeschichtlichen Einfluss des 1. Evangeliums auf den 1. Petrusbrief*. WUNT 2/74. Tübingen: Mohr (Siebeck).

Michaelis, W.
1961 Erster Petrusbrief. Pages 282–88 in *Einleitung in das Neue Testament* (and pp. 36–37 in supplementary volume). 3d ed. Bern: Berchtold Haller.

Michaels, J. R.
1966–67 Eschatology in I Peter III.17. *NTS* 13:394–401.
1987 Jewish and Christian Apocalyptic Letters: 1 Peter, Revelation, and 2 Baruch 78–87. Pages 268–75 in *SBL 1987: Seminar Papers*. SBLSP 26. Atlanta: Scholars Press.

Michl, J.
1948 Petrus als Seelsorger. *BK* 3:15–24.
1973 Die Presbyter des ersten Petrusbriefes. Pages 48–62 in *Ortskirche—Weltkirche*. J. Döpfner Festschrift. Edited by H. Fleckenstein et al. Würzburg: Echter.

Migliasso, S.
1986 Il paolinismo di prima Pietro. *RivB* 34:519–41.

Miguéns, M.
1969 La "passion" du Christ total (1 P 2,20b–25). *AsSeign* 25:26–31.

Mildenberger, M.
1979 "Seid allezeit zur Verantwortung bereit vor jedem" (1 Pt 3,15) . . . : Ist das Christentum aggressiv? Pages 321–50 in *Christentum im Spiegel der Weltreligionen*. Edited by H. J. Loth and A. L. Loth. Stuttgart.

Millauer, H.
1976 *Leiden als Gnade: Eine traditionsgeschichtliche Untersuchung zur Leidenstheologie des ersten Petrusbriefes*. Europäische Hochschulsschriften 23, Theologie 56. Bern: H. Lang / Frankfurt am Main: P. Lang.

Miller, D. G.
1955 Deliverance and Destiny: Salvation in First Peter. *Int* 9:413–25.
1995 The Resurrection as the Source of Living Hope: An Exposition of I Peter 1:3. *HBT* 17:132–40.

Miller, L.
1995 *Christianisme et Société dans la première lettre de Pierre: Histoire de l'interprétation, interprétation de l'histoire*. Ph.D. Dissertation, Strassburg.

Minear, P. S.
1982 The House of Living Stones: A Study of 1 Peter 2:4–12. *Ecumenical Review* 34:238–48.

Mitton, C. L.
1950 The Relationship between I Peter and Ephesians. *JTS* n.s. 1:67–73.

Moffatt, J.
1918 The (First) Epistle of Peter. Pages 318–44 in *An Introduction to the Literature of the New Testament*. 3d rev. ed. Edinburgh: T. & T. Clark.

Mole, J.
1961 Laymanship (I P 2:9). *SJT* 14:380–89.

Molthagen, J.
1995 Die Lage der Christen im römischen Reich nach dem 1. Petrusbrief. *Historia* 44:422–80.

Moorehead, W. G.
1915 The First Epistle of Peter. Pages 2351–55 in vol. 4 of *The International Standard Bible Encyclopedia*. Edited by J. Orr et al. Chicago: Howard-Severance.

Moret, J.
1967 *Simon Bar Jona, un homme de foi*. Paris: Apostolat des Éditions.
Morris, L.
1965 The First Epistle General of Peter. Pages 316–33 in *The Cross in the New Testament*. Exeter: Paternoster / Grand Rapids: Eerdmans.
Morris, W. D.
1926–27 1 Peter iii.19. *ExpTim* 38:470.
Moule, C. F. D.
1950 Sanctuary and Sacrifice in the Church of the New Testament. *JTS* n.s. 1:29–41.
1955–56 Some Reflections on the "Stone" Testimonia in Relation to the Name Peter. *NTS* 2:56–58.
1956–57 The Nature and Purpose of I Peter. *NTS* 3:1–11.
Müller, H.
1962 La obra salvifica de la conversion ségún la primera epístola de S. Pedro. *RevistB* 24:1–10, 76–83.
Mullins, M.
1991 The First Letter of Peter. Pages 139–48, 267–73 in *Called to Be Saints: Christian Living in First-Century Rome*. Dublin: Veritas.
Muñoz León, D.
1978 Un reino de sacerdotes y una nación santa (Ex 19,6): La interpretación neotestamentaria de nuestro texto a la luz setenta y de las traducciones targúmicas. *EstBib* 37:149–212. [Pages 170–82 on 1 Peter]
Munro, W.
1983 *Authority in Paul and Peter: The Identification of a Pastoral Stratum in the Pauline Corpus and I Peter*. SNTSMS 45. Cambridge: Cambridge University Press.
Mussner, F.
1976 *Petrus und Paulus: Pole der Einheit—Eine Hilfe für die Kirchen*. QD 76. Freiburg: Herder.
Myrant, R.W.
1956 *Petrine Theology*. Th.D. Dissertation, Dallas Theological Seminary.
Nardelli, M.
1967 *Pietro e Paolo apostoli a Roma*. Brescia: Franciscanum.
Nauck, W.
1955 Freude im Leiden: Zum Problem einer urchristlichen Verfolgungstradition. *ZNW* 46:68–80.
1957 Probleme des frühchristlichen Amtsverständnisses (1 Ptr 5,2f.). *ZNW* 48:200–220.
Nestle, E.
1898–99 1 Pet 1.2. *ExpTim* 10:188–89.
Neugebauer, F.
1979 Zur Deutung und Bedeutung des 1. Petrusbriefes. *NTS* 26:61–86.
Neumaier, R.
1978 *Das neue Menschsein nach dem Zeugnis des Neuen Testaments enfaltet am 1. Petrusbrief, Kap. 1,1–2,10*. Metzingen: Franz.
Newman, M. L.
1963 *The People of the Covenant*. Nashville: Abingdon.

Neyrey, J. H.
1984 First Peter and Converts. *TBT* 22:13–18.
1985 Peter, the First Letter of. Pages 778–80 in *HBD*.
Nickelsburg, G. W. E.
1981 Enoch, Levi, and Peter: Recipients of Revelation in Upper Galilee. *JBL* 100:575–600.
Niemann, R., ed.
1994 *Petrus, der Fels des Anstosses*. Stuttgart: Kreuz.
Nixon, R. E.
1968 The Meaning of "Baptism" in 1 Pt 3:21. Pages 437–41 in *SE* 4. TU 102. Berlin: Akademie.
North, J. L.
1993 Qui cum percuteretur non repercussit (1 Pet 2:23): The Christian Trajectory of a Non-Christian Motif. Pages 316–37 in vol. 1 of *Philologia Sacra: Biblische und patristische Studien*. 2 vols. H. H. Frede and W. Thiele Festschrift. Edited by R. Gryson. Vetus Latina: Aus der Geschichte der lateinischen Bibel 24/1–2. Freiburg: Herder.
Nouel, P. C.
1957 Le Christ notre rançon: Le témoignage de Pierre. *Cahiers Évangiles* 25:45–50.
O'Connor, D.
1991 Holiness of Life as a Way of Christian Witness. *International Review of Missions* 80:17–26.
O'Connor, D. W.
1969 *Peter in Rome: The Literary, Liturgical and Archeological Evidence*. New York: Columbia University Press.
1975 Peter in Rome: A Review and Position. Pages 146–60 in *Early Christianity*. M. Smith Festschrift. Edited by J. Neusner. Part 2 of *Christianity, Judaism and other Greco-Roman Cults*. Leiden: Brill.
1992 Peter the Apostle, Saint. Pages 330–33 in vol. 9 of *The New Encyclopaedia Britannica: Micropaedia*. 15th ed. Chicago: Encyclopaedia Britannica.
Odeland, S.
1901 Kristi praediken for "aanderne i forvaring" (1 Petr. 3, 19). *NTT* 2:116–44, 185–229.
Ogara, F.
1936a Adversarius . . . diabolus tamquam leo rugiens. *VD* 16:166–73.
1936b Caritas operit multitudinem peccatorum (1 Pet.4,7b-11). *VD* 16:129–35.
1936c In hoc enim vocati estis: Quia et Christus passus est pro nobis . . . (1 Pt 2:11–19, 21–25). *VD* 16:97–106.
1937 Quis est qui vobis noceat, si boni aemulatores fueritis? (1 Pt 3:8–15). *VD* 17:161–65.
Olson, V. S.
1979 *The Atonement in 1 Peter*. Th.D. Dissertation, Union Theological Seminary, Richmond, Virginia.
Olsson, B.
1984 Ett hem för hemlösa: Om sociologisk exeges av NT. *SEÅ* 49:89–108.
1995 A Social-Scientific Criticism of 1 Peter. Pages 827–46 in *Texts and Contexts: Biblical Texts in Their Textual and Situational Contexts*. Lars

Hartman Festschrift. Edited by T. Fornberg and D. Hellholm. Oslo: Scandinavian Press.

Omanson, R.
1982 Suffering for Righteousness' Sake (1 Pet. 3:13–4:11). *RevExp* 79:439–50.

Ordonez, V.
1956 El Sacerdocio de los Fideles (Sentido escrituristico textual). *Revista Española de Teología* 64:359–79.

Osborne, T. P.
1981a *Christian Suffering in the First Epistle of Peter.* S.T.D. Dissertation, University of Louvain.
1981b L'utilisation des citations de l'Ancien Testament dans la première épître de Pierre. *RTL* 12:64–77.
1983 Guide Lines for Christian Suffering: A Source-Critical and Theological Study of 1 Peter 2, 21–25. *Bib* 64:381–408.

Oss, D. A.
1989 The Interpretation of the "Stone" Passages by Peter and Paul: A Comparative Study. *JETS* 32:181–200.

Otranto, G.
1970 Il sacerdozio commune dei fedeli nei riflessi della 1 Petr. 2,9 (I e II secolo). *Vetera Christianorum* 7:225–46.

Otto, W.
1883 Die Auslegung von 1 Petr 3, 17–22 in besonderer Beziehung auf 1 Petr 3, 21. *Zeitschrift für kirchliche Wissenschaft und kirchliches Leben* (1883): 83–96.

Paciorek, A.
1976 Obraz Piotra w pierwotnej gminie (The Petrine Image in the Primitive Community). *Studia Theologica Varsaviensia* 14:85–98.

Page, S. H. T.
1974 *The Suffering of Christ in 1 Peter, with Special Attention to the Background of the Concepts Employed.* Doctoral Dissertation, Manchester University.

Palmer, C. L.
1985 *The Use of Traditional Materials in Hebrews, James and 1 Peter.* Th.D. Dissertation, Southwestern Baptist Theological Seminary.

Papa, B.
1980 Spirito Santo e battesimo nella prima lettera di Pietro. *Nicolaus* 8: 295–300.

Parker, D. C.
1994 The Eschatology of 1 Peter. *BTB* 24:27–32.

Parsons, S. P.
1978 *We Have Been Born Anew: The New Birth of the Christian in the First Epistle of St. Peter (I Petr. 1:3,23).* Doctoral Dissertation, Pontificia Studiorum Universitas a S. Thomas Aquino in Urbe. Rome.

Patsch, H.
1969 Zum alttestamentlichen Hintergrund von Röm 4, 25 und I. Petrus 2, 24. *ZNW* 60:273–79.

Patterson, D. K.
1982 Roles in Marriage: A Study in Submission—1 Peter 3:1–7. *Theological Educator* 13:70–79.

Patton, W. W.

1882 Exegesis of 1 Petr 3, 18–20. *The New Englander* (1882):83–96.

Pearson, B. A.

1989 James, 1–2 Peter, Jude. Pages 371–406 in *The New Testament and Its Modern Interpreters*. Edited by E. J. Epp and G. W. MacRae. Atlanta: Scholars Press.

Pearson, S. C.

1993 *The Christological Hymnic Pattern of 1 Peter*. Th.D. Dissertation. Fuller Theological Seminary.

Peeters, R. J.

1986 Imitatio Christi: Samenhang en theologie in Petr 3,13–4,6. Pages 130–54 in *Bij de put van Jakob: Exegetische opstellen*. Theologische Faculteit Tilburg 5. Tilburg.

Pellend, L.

1949 Le sacerdoce des fidèles. *ScEccl* 2:5–26.

Penna, A.

1954 *San Pietro*. Brescia: Morcelliana.

1967 Il "senatoconsulto" del 35 D.C. e la prima lettera di S. Pietro. Pages 337–66 in *San Pietro: Atti della XIX Settimana Biblica Italiana*. Edited by A. Bea et al. Brescia: Paideia.

Pennington, M. B.

1987 *Daily We Follow Him: Learning Discipleship from Peter*. Garden City, New York: Doubleday-Image.

Perdelwitz, R.

1911 *Die Mysterienreligion und das Problem des I. Petrusbriefes: Ein literarischer und religionsgeschichtlicher Versuch*. RVV 11/3. Giessen: Alfred Töpelmann.

Perkins, D. W.

1982 Simon-Rock: An Appraisal of Peter in the New Testament Witness. *Theological Educator* 13:42–54.

Perkins, P.

1994 *Peter: Apostle for the Whole Church*. Columbia: University of South Carolina Press.

Perrot, C.

1980 La descente aux enfers et la prédication aux morts. Pages 231–46 in *Études sur la première lettre de Pierre*. LD 102. Paris: Cerf.

Perrot, C., ed.

1980 *Études sur la première lettre de Pierre*. LD 102. Paris: Cerf.

Pesch, R.

1971 The Position and Significance of Peter in the Church of the New Testament: A Survey of Current Research. Pages 21–35 in *Papal Ministry in the Church*. Edited by H. Küng. Concilium 64. New York: Herder & Herder.

1979 Peter in the Mirror of Paul's Letters. Pages 291–309 in *Paul de Tarse: Apôtre de notre temps*. Edited by L. De Lorenzi. Rome: Abbaye de S. Paul.

1980 *Simon Petrus: Geschichte und geschichtliche Bedeutung des ersten Jüngers Jesu Christi*. Päpste und Papsttum 15. Stuttgart: Hiersemann.

1993 "*Petros, Simōn*." Pages 81–85 in vol. 3 of *EDNT*.

Pesch, W.
1970 Zu Texten des Neuen Testaments über das Priestertum der Getauften. Pages 303–15 in *Verborum Veritas*. G. Stählin Festschrift. Edited by O. Böcher and K. Haacker. Wuppertal: Brockhaus.

Philipps, K.
1971 *Kirche in der Gesellschaft nach dem 1. Petrusbrief*. Gütersloh: Gütersloher/Mohn.

Pietrantonio, R.
1980 Sacerdocio corporativo y ministerios eclesiales en la 1ª Carta de Pedro. *RevistB* 42:195–208.

Pilch, J. J.
1991a "Visiting Strangers" and "Resident Aliens." *TBT* 29:357–61.

Pinto da Silva, A.
1984 A proposito del significato di 1 Pt 3, 18–4,6. *Salesianum* 46:473–86.

Piper, J.
1980 Hope as the Motivation of Love: 1 Peter 3:9–12. *NTS* 26:212–31.

Plooij, D.
1913 De Descensus in 1 Petrus 3:19 en 4:6. *TT* 47:145–62.

Plumpe, J. C.
1943 Vivum saxum, Vivi lapides: The Concepts of "Living Stones" in Classical and Christian Antiquity. *Traditio* 1:1–14.

Poelman, R.
1966 St. Peter and Tradition. *Human Virtue* 21:50–65. [ET of Saint Pierre et la Tradition. *Lumen Vitae* 20 (1965): 632–48]

Pompei, A., ed.
1975 *Pietro nella Sacra Scrittura*. Florence: Città di Vita.

Prete, B.
1984 L'espressione *hê en Babylôni syneklektê* di 1 Pt. 5,13. *Vetera Christianorum* 21:335–52.

Price, J. J. H.
1977 *Submission-Humility in 1 Peter: An Exegetical Study*. Ph.D. Dissertation, Vanderbilt University.

Price, J. L.
1987 The First Letter of Peter. Pages 398–403, 416–17 in *The New Testament: Its History and Theology*. New York: Macmillan.

Prigent, P.
1992 I Pierre 2, 4–10. *RHPR* 72:53–60.

Prostmeier, F.-R.
1990 *Handlungsmodelle im ersten Petrusbrief*. FB 63. Würzburg: Echter.

Pryor, J. W.
1986a First Peter and the New Covenant (1). *Reformed Theological Review* 45:1–4.
1986b First Peter and the New Covenant (2). *Reformed Theological Review* 45:44–51.

Puig Tarrech, A.
1980 Le milieu de la Première épître de Pierre. *Revista Catalana de Teología* (Barcelona) 5:95–129, 331–402.

Quacquarelli, A.

1967 Similitudini, sentenze e proverbi in S. Pietro. Pages 425–42 in *San Pietro: Atti della XIX Settimana Biblica Italiana*. Edited by A. Bea et al. Brescia: Paideia.

Quinn, J. D.

1965 Notes on the Text of the P[72]: 1 Pt 2,3; 5,14; and 5,9. *CBQ* 27:241–49.

Radermacher, L.

1926 Der erste Petrusbrief und Silvanus. *ZNW* 25:287–99.

Rainey, K. T.

1967 *The Death of Christ in Petrine Thought*. Th.D. Dissertation, New Orleans Baptist Theological Seminary.

Ramos, F. F.

1970 El sacerdocio de los creyentes (1 Pet. 2:4–10). Pages 11–47 in *Sacerdocio ministerial y laical*. Teologica del Sacerdocio 2. Burgos: Aldecoa.

Ramsay, W. M.

1893 The Church and the Empire in the First Century, III: The First Epistle Attributed to S. Peter. *Exp* 4/8:282–96.

Rasco, E.

1981 Il "sangue prezioso" di Cristo nella prima lettera di Pietro. Pages 851–64 in *Sangue e Antropologia biblica*. Edited by F. Vattioni. Rome: Pia Unione Preziosissimo Sangue.

Rebeiro, C. A.

1981 The Primary Focus of Catechesis in 1 Peter. *Word and Worship* 14: 145–52.

Redigonda, L. A.

1977 Simon Pietro a Roma (nota storico-archeologica). *Sacra Doctrina* 22: 183–215.

Rees, P. S.

1962 *Triumphant in Trouble: Studies in 1 Peter*. Westwood, New Jersey: Revell.

Refoulé, F.

1979 Bible et éthique sociale: Lire aujourd'hui 1 Pierre. *Le Supplément* 131: 457–82.

1990 Soumission et liberté. *Vie Spirituelle* 690:331–42.

Reichert, A.

1989 *Eine urchristliche* praeparatio ad martyrium: *Studien zur Komposition, Traditionsgeschichte und Theologie des 1. Petrusbriefes*. BBET 22. Frankfurt am Main: Peter Lang.

Reicke, B.

1946 *The Disobedient Spirits and Christian Baptism: A Study of I Pet. III.19 and Its Context*. ASNU 13. Copenhagen: Munksgaard.

1954 Die Gnosis der Männer nach I. Ptr. 3,7. Pages 296–304 in *Neutestamentliche Studien für Rudolf Bultmann*. BZNW 21. Berlin: Alfred Töpelmann.

Renner, F.

1970 Exkurs 7: Einheit und Struktur des ersten Petrusbriefes. Pages 156–60 in *An die Hebräer: Ein pseudographischer Brief*. Münsterschwarzacher Studien 14. Münsterschwarzach: Vier Türme.

Rensburg, J. J. J. van
1990 The Use of Intersentence Relational Particles and Asyndeton in First Peter. *Neotestamentica* 24:283–300.

Rhijn, C. H. van
1875 *De jongste bezwaren tegen de echtheid van den eersten Brief van Petrus getoest*. Utrecht.

Riber, M.
1966 Un modelo de catequeis bautismal: Sugerencias, en torno a la carta primera de Pedro, para una catequeis de adultos. *Cultura Biblica* 23: 323–31.

Richard, E.
1986 The Functional Christology of First Peter. Pages 121–40 in *Perspectives on First Peter*. Edited by C. H. Talbert. Macon, Georgia: Mercer University Press.

Richards, G. C.
1931 1 Peter iii.21. *JTS* 32:77.

Richardson, R. L., Jr.
1987 From "Subjection to Authority" to "Mutual Submission": The Ethic of Subordination in 1 Peter. *Faith and Mission* 4:70–80.

Rigato, M. L.
1990 Quali i profeti di cui nella 1 Pt 1,10? *RivB* 38:73–90.

Rigaux, B.
1967 Saint Peter in Contemporary Exegesis. Pages 147–79 in *Progress and Decline in the History of Church Renewal*. Edited by R. Aubert. Concilium 27. New York: Paulist.
1973 1 Tm 3,16; 1 P 3,18–22; He 1,3–4. Pages 160–69 in *Dieu l'a ressuscité: Exégèse et théologie biblique*. Studii biblici franciscani analecta 4. Gembloux: Duculot.

Rigg, W. H.
1924 Does the First Epistle of St. Peter Throw Any Light on the Johannine Problem? *Exp* 9/1:221–29.

Riggenbach, B.
1889 Die Poimenik des Apostles Petrus (I Petri 5,1–5) nach ihrer geschichtlichen und praktischen Bedeutung. *Schweizerische Theologische Zeitschrift* 7:185–95.

Rimoldi, A.
1955 L'Apostolo Pietro nella letteratura apocrifa dei primi 6 secoli. *La Scuola Cattolica* 83:196–224.
1958 *L'Apostolo San Pietro, fondamento della Chiesa, principe degli apostoli ed ostiario celeste nella Chiesa primitiva dalle origini al concilio di Calcedonia*. Analecta Gregoriana 96. Series Facultatis Historiae Ecclesiasticae, section B, 18. Rome: Gregorian University.

Rinaldi, G., and P. de Benedetti, eds.
1961 Pages 816–24 in *Introduzione al Nuovo Testamento*. Il Nuovo Testamento Commentato 10. Brescia: Morcelliana.

Robertson, A. T.
1933 *Epochs in the Life of Simon Peter*. New York: Scribner's.

Robertson, P. E.
1982 Is 1 Peter a Sermon? *Theological Educator* 13:35–41.

Robinson, A.
1949 Saints Peter and Paul in the New Testament. *Scripture* 4:120–27.

Robinson, D. F.
1945 Where and When Did Peter Die? *JBL* 64:254–67.

Robinson, J. A. T.
1976 *Redating the New Testament*. Philadelphia: Westminster.

Robinson, M.
1990 The First and Second Epistles General of Peter. Pages 303–15 in *Incarnation: Contemporary Writers on the New Testament*. Edited by A. Corn. New York: Viking.

Robinson, P. J.
1989 Some Missiological Perspectives from 1 Peter 2:4–10. *Missionalia* 17: 176–87.

Rodgers, P. R.
1981 The Longer Reading of 1 Peter 4:14. *CBQ* 43:93–95.

Rolston, H.
1977 *The Apostle Peter Speaks to Us Today*. Atlanta: John Knox.

Romo, C. L.
1977 *La Salvacion en I Pe.1,1–2,10. Vocabulario, estructura, sentido Teológico*. Licentiate Thesis, Pontifical Gregorian University, Rome.

Rosa, G. de
1972 Il sacerdozio comune dei fedeli nel Nuovo Testamento. *Civiltà Cattolica* 123:350–57.

Rousseau, J.
1986 *A Multidimensional Approach towards the Communication of an Ancient Canonized Text: Towards Determining the Thrust, Perspective and Strategy of 1 Peter*. Doctoral Dissertation, University of Pretoria.

Rousseau, O.
1951–1952 La descente aux infers, fondement sotériologique du baptême chrétien. *RSR* 40:273–97.

Ru, G. de
1966 De Heilige Doop: Gebed of gave? (1 Pt 3, 20b.21). *NedTT* 20:255–68.

Rubinkiewicz, R.
1982 “Duchy zamknięte w wiezięniu”: Interpretacja 1 P 3,19 w świetla Hen 10,4.12 (“The Spirits in Prison”: Interpretation of 1 Pet 3:19 in the Light of 1 Enoch 10:4, 12). *RocTKan* 28:77–86.

Rudrauf, K.
1685 *Disputatio theologica inauguralis ad oraculum I. Petri III.18.19*. Giessen: H. Muller.

Russell, R.
1975 Eschatology and Ethics in 1 Peter. *EvQ* 47:78–84.

Ryan, T. J.
1973 *The Word of God in First Peter: A Critical Study of 1 Peter 2:1–3*. S.T.D. Dissertation, Catholic University of America.

Sakkos, S. N.
1989 *Hê martyria tês Kainês Diathêkês*. Volume 1 of *Ho Petros kai hê Rômê*. Thessalonica: Sakkos.

Salmon. P.

1951 Le texte Latin des épîtres de S. Pierre, S. Jean et S. Jude dans le MS 6 de Montpellier. *JTS* 2:170–77.

Salvoni, F.

1971 Cristo andò nello spirito a proclamare agli spiriti in carcere (1 Pietro 3,18–20 e 4,6). *Ricerche Bibliche e Religiose* 6:57–86.

Sander, E. T.

1966 *PYROSIS and the First Epistle of Peter 4:12*. Ph.D. Dissertation, Harvard University.

Sandevoir, P.

1980 Un royaume de prêtres? Pages 219–29 in *Études sur la première lettre de Pierre*. LD 102. Paris: Cerf.

Scharfe, E.

1889 Die schriftstellerische Originalität des ersten Petrusbriefs. *TSK* 62:633–70.

1893 *Die petrinische Strömmung in der neutestamentlichen Literatur: Untersuchungen über die schriftstellerische Eigentümlichkeit des ersten Petrusbriefes, des Marcusevangeliums und der petrinischen Reden der Apostelgeschichte*. Berlin: Reuter & Reichard.

Scharlemann, M. H.

1959 Why the "Kuriou" in 1 P 1:25? *CTM* 30:352–56.

1975 An Apostolic Salutation: An Exegetical Study of 1 Peter 1:1–2. *Concordia Journal* 1:108–18.

1976a An Apostolic Descant: An Exegetical Study of 1 Peter 1:3–12. *Concordia Journal* 2:9–17.

1976b Exodus Ethics: Part One—I Peter 1:13–16. *Concordia Journal* 2:165–70.

1989 He Descended Into Hell: An Interpretation of 1 Peter 3:18–20. *CTM* 27 (1956):81–94. Reprinted in *Concordia Journal* 15:311–22.

Schattenmann, J.

1954–55 The Little Apocalypse of the Synoptics and the First Epistle of Peter. *TToday* 11:193–98.

Schelkle, K. H.

1961 Das Leiden des Gottesknechtes als Form christlichen Lebens (nach dem ersten Petrusbrief). *BK* 16:14–16.

1963 Petrusbriefe. Pages 385–87 in vol. 8 of *LTK*.

1968 Petrus in den Briefen des Neuen Testaments. *BK* 23:46–50.

1969 Petrusbriefe. Pages 1136–40 in vol. 3 of *Sacramentum Mundi*. Freiburg: Herder.

Schembri, G.

1967 Il messaggio pastorale di S. Pietro nella sua prima Epistola. *Antonianum* 42:376–98.

Schertz, M. H.

1992 Nonretaliation and the Haustafeln in 1 Peter. Pages 258–86 in *The Love of Enemy and Nonretaliation in the New Testament*. Edited by W. H. Swartley. Louisville: Westminster John Knox.

Schider, J.

1939 *". . . viel Gnade und Frieden!" 1 Peter 1,2*. Munich: Kaiser.

Schierse, F. J.

1976 Ein Hirtenbrief und viele Bücher: Neue Literatur zum Ersten Petrusbrief. *BK* 33:86–88.

Schlatter, A.

1937 *Petrus und Paulus nach dem I. Petrusbrief*. Stuttgart: Calwer.

Schlier, H.

1968 Eine Adhortatio aus Rom: Die Botschaft des ersten Petrusbriefes. Pages 59–80, 369–71 in *Strukturen Christlicher Existenz: Beiträge zur Erneuerung des geistlichen Lebens*. Edited by H. Schlier et al. Würzburg: Echter.

1972 Die Kirche nach dem 1. Petrusbrief. Pages 195–200 in vol. 4/1 of *Mysterium Salutis*. Edited by J. Feiner and M. Löhrer. Einsiedeln: Benzinger.

Schlosser, J.

1980 Ancien Testament et Christologie dans la Prima Petri. Pages 65–96 in *Études sur la première lettre de Pierre*. LD 102. Paris: Cerf.

1983 1 Pierre 3,5b–6. *Bib* 64:409–10.

Schmalz, W. M.

1952 Did Peter Die in Jerusalem? *JBL* 71:211–16.

Schmauch, W.

1967 1 Pt 4:8–11. Pages 100–104 in *Zu Achten auf des Wort*. Göttingen: Vandenhoeck & Ruprecht.

Schmid, J.

1928 Der Epheserbrief und I Petr. Pages 333–62 in *Der Epheserbrief des heiligen Paulus*. BibS(F) 22/3.4. Freiburg: Herder.

1960 Petrus der "Fels" und die Petrusgestalt der Urgemeinde. Pages 347–59 in *Begegnung der Christen: Studien evangelischer und katholischer Theologen*. Edited by M. Roesle and O. Cullmann. 2d ed. Stuttgart: Evangelisches.

Schmidt, D. H.

1972 I Peter. Pages 19–74, 206–19 in *The Peter Writings: Their Redactors and Their Relationships*. Ph.D. Dissertation, Northwestern University.

Schmidt, P.

1908 Zwei Fragen zum ersten Petrusbrief. *ZWT* 50:24–52.

Schmiedel, P. W.

1899–1903 Simon Peter. Pages 4559–67 in vol. 4 of *EncBib*. Edited by T. K. Cheyne and J. S. Black. London: Black.

Schnackenburg, R.

1971 Das Petrusamt: Die Stellung des Petrus zu den anderen Aposteln. *Wort und Wahrheit: Zeitschrift für Religion und Kultur* 26:206–16.

Scholer, D. M.

1980 Woman's Adornment: Some Historical and Hermeneutical Observations on the New Testament Passages [1 Tim 2:9–10, 1 Pet 3:3–4]. *Daughters of Sarah* 6:3–6.

Schroeder, D.

1990 Once You Were No People. . . . Pages 37–65 in *The Church as Theological Community*. D. Schroeder Festschrift. Edited by H. Huebner. Winnipeg: Canadian Mennonite Bible College.

Schroeder, R.

1954 *The Babylon of I Peter 5:13*. B.D. Thesis, Concordia Seminary.

Schröger, F.
1976 Die Verfassung der Gemeinde des ersten Petrusbriefes. Pages 239–52 in *Kirche im Werden, Studien zum Thema Amt und Gemeinde im Neuen Testament*. Edited by J. Hainz. Munich: Schöningh.
1979 "Lasst euch auferbauen zu einem geisterfüllten Haus" (1 Petr 2,4.5): Eine Überlegung zu dem Verhältnis von Ratio und Pneuma. Pages 138–45 in *Theologie-Gemeinde-Seelsorge*. Edited by W. Friedberger and F. Schnider. Munich: Kösel.
1981a Ansätze zu den modernen Menschenrechtsforderungen im 1. Petrusbrief. Pages 179–91 in *Der Dienst für den Menschen in Theologie*. A. Brehms Festschrift. Edited by R. M. Hübner et al. Regensburg: Pustet.
1981b *Gemeinde im 1. Petrusbrief: Untersuchungen zum Selbstverständnis einer christlichen Gemeinde an der Wende vom 1. zum 2. Jahrhundert*. Schriften der Universität Passau: Katholische Theologie 1. Passau: Passavia Universitätsverlag.
1985 Gemeinde im 1. Petrusbrief. *BK* 41:15–20.

Schückler, G.
1967 Wandel im Glauben als missionarisches Zeugnis. *Zeitschrift für Missionswissenschaft und Religionswissenschaft* 51:289–99.

Schütz, H. G.
1964 *"Kirche" in spät-neutestamentlicher Zeit: Untersuchungen zum Selbstverständnis des Urchristentums an der Wende vom 1. zum 2. Jahrhundert an Hand des 1. Petr., des Hebr., und der Pastoralbriefe*. Doctoral Dissertation, Bonn.

Schulze, J. D.
1802 *Der schriftstellerische Charakter und Werth des Petrus, Judas, und Jakobus zum Behuf der Specialhermeneutik ihrer Schriften*. Weissenfels: Bösesche.

Schulze-Kadelbach, G.
1956 Die Stellung des Petrus in der Urchristenheit. *TLZ* 81:cols 1–14.

Schutter, W. L.
1987 I Peter 4.17, Ezekiel 9.6, and Apocalyptic Hermeneutics. Pages 276–84 in *SBL 1987: Seminar Papers*. SBLSP 26. Atlanta: Scholars Press.
1989 *Hermeneutic and Composition in First Peter*. WUNT 2/30. Tübingen: Mohr (Siebeck).

Schwank, B.
1960 Wie Freie—aber als Sklaven Gottes (1 Petr. 2,16): Das Verhältnis der Christen zur Staatsmacht nach dem ersten Petrusbrief. *Erbe und Auftrag* 36:5–12.
1962a Diabolus tamquam leo rugiens (1 Petr. 5:8). *Erbe und Auftrag* 38:15–20.
1962b Das Problem der Pseudepigraphie im Neuen Testament: Zum Kommentar von K. H. Schelkle über die Petrusbriefe und den Judasbrief. *Erbe und Auftrag* 38:133–36.
1966 Lecture chrétienne de la Bible (1 Pierre 3:8–15). *AsSeign* 59:16–32.
1973a Le "chrétien normal" selon le Nouveau Testament. 1 P 4,13–16. *AsSeign* 29:26–30.
1973b Des éléments mythologiques dans une profession de foi: 1 P 3,18–22. *AsSeign* 14:41–44.

Schweizer, A.
1868 *Hinabgefahren zur Hölle als Mythus ohne biblische Begründung durch Auslegung der Stelle 1 Petr. 3, 17–22 nachgewiesen*. Zurich: Schultness.

Schweizer, E.
1952 I Petrus 4:6. *TZ* 8:152–54.
1968 *Pneuma*: V.3.b. 1 Peter. Pages 447–48 in vol. 6 of *TDNT*.
1992 The Priesthood of All Believers: 1 Peter 2:1–10. Pages 285–93 in *Worship, Theology, and Ministry in the Early Church*. R. P. Martin Festschrift. JNTSSup 87. Sheffield: JSOT Press.

Scott, C. A.
1905 The "Sufferings of Christ": A Note on 1 Peter 1:11. *Exp* 6/12:234–40.

Seethaler, P.
1972 *Hoffnung im Leiden: Die Petrusbriefe, der Judasbrief*. Stuttgart.

Seim, T. K.
1990 Hustavlen 1 Pet 3. 1–7 og dens tradisjonhistoriske sammenhang. *NTT* 91:101–14.

Seland, T.
1995 The "Common Priesthood" of Philo and 1 Peter: A Philonic Reading of 1 Peter 2.5,9. *JSNT* 57:87–119.

Selwyn, E. G.
1947–48 Unsolved New Testament Problems: The Problem of the Authorship of I Peter. *ExpTim* 59:256–58.
1950 The Persecutions in I Peter. *Bulletin of the Society for New Testament Studies* 1:39–50.
1954 Eschatology in 1 Peter. Pages 394–401 in *The Background of the New Testament and Its Eschatology*. C. H. Dodd Festschrift. Edited by W. D. Davies and D. Daube. Cambridge: Cambridge University Press.

Senior, D.
1982 The Conduct of Christians in the World ([1 Pet.] 2:11–3:12). *RevExp* 79:427–38.
1984 The First Letter of Peter. *TBT* 22:5–12.

Seufert, W.
1874 Das Abhängigkeitsverhältnis des I. Petrusbriefs vom Römerbrief. *ZWT* 17:360–88.
1881 Das Verwandschaftsverhältnis des ersten Petrusbriefes und Epheserbriefs. *ZWT* 24:178–97, 332–80.
1885a Der Abfassungsort des ersten Petrusbriefes. *ZWT* 28:146–56.
1885b Titus, Silvanus (*SILAS*) und der Verfasser des ersten Petrusbriefes. *ZWT* 28:350–71.

Seyler, G.
1832 Über die Gedankenordnung in den Reden und Briefen des Apostels Petrus. *TSK* 5:44–70.

Shimada, K.
1966 *The Formulary Material in First Peter: A Study according to the Method of Traditionsgeschichte*. Th.D. Dissertation, Union Theological Seminary, New York.
1979 The Christological Credal Formula in I Peter 3,18–22: Reconsidered. *AJBI* 5:154–76.
1981 A Critical Note on I Peter 1,12. *AJBI* 7:146–50.

1985 Is I Peter a Composite Writing? *AJBI* 11:95–114.

1991 Is I Peter Dependent on Ephesians?: A Critique of C. L. Mitton. *AJBI* 17:77–106.

1993 Is I Peter Dependent on Romans? *AJBI* 19:87–137.

Shroeder, D.

1990 Once You Were No People. Pages 37–63 in *The Church as Theological Community*. Edited by H. Huebner. Winnipeg: CMBC.

Sieffert, E. A.

1875 Die Heilsbedeutung des Leidens und Sterbens Christi nach dem ersten Briefe des Petrus. *Jahrbücher für Deutsche Theologie* 20:371–440.

Sieffert, F.

1950 Peter the Apostle: His Writings. Pages 482–84 in vol. 8 of *The New Schaff-Herzog Encyclopedia of Religious Knowledge*. Edited by S. M. Jackson. Grand Rapids: Baker.

Silvola, K.

1978 "Kristuksen kärsimysten todistaja" 1 Pt 5:1 (The Witness of the Sufferings of Christ). *TAik* 83:416–23.

Sisti, A.

1965 La vita cristiana nell' attesa della Parusia (1 Piet. 4,7b-11). *BeO* 7:123–28.

1966a Il cristiano nel mondo (1 Pt. 2:11–19). *BeO* 8:70–79.

1966b Testimonianza di virtù cristiane (1 Piet. 3,8–15). *BeO* 8:117–26.

1968 Sulle orme di Gesù sofferente (1 Piett 2:21–25). *BeO* 10:59–68.

Skilton, J. H.

1996 A Glance at Some Old Problems in First Peter. *WTJ* 58:1–9.

Skinner, M.

1962 The Ministry of the Layman in the Church (1 Peter). *London Quarterly and Holburn Review* 31:8–13.

Skrade, C. E.

1966 *The Descent of the Servant: A Study of I Peter 3:13–4:6*. Th.D. Dissertation, Union Theological Seminary, Richmond, Virginia.

Slaughter, J. R.

1995 The Importance of Literary Argument for Understanding 1 Peter. *BSac* 152:72–91.

1996a Sarah as a Model for Christian Wives (1 Pet 3:5–6). *BSac* 153:3257–65.

1996b Submission of Wives (1 Pet. 3:1a) in the Context of 1 Peter. *BSac* 153: 63–74.

1996c Winning Unbelieving Husbands to Christ (1 Pet 3:1b–4). *BSac* 153:199–211.

Sleeper, C. F.

1968 Political Responsibility according to I Peter. *NovT* 10:270–89.

1969 The Structure of Christian Existence in I Peter. Pages 109–17 in *Black Power and Christian Responsibility*. Edited by C. F. Sleeper. Nashville: Abingdon.

Sly, D. I.

1991 1 Peter 3:6b in the Light of Philo and Josephus. *JBL* 110:126–29.

Smalley S. S.

1961 The Imitation of Christ in I Peter. *Churchman* 75:172–78.

Smith, M. L.

1912 1 Peter 3:21: *Eperôtêma*. *ExpTim* 24:46–49.

Smith, T. V.

1985 *Petrine Controversies in Early Christianity: Attitudes towards Peter in Christian Writings of the First Two Centuries*. WUNT 2/15. Tübingen: Mohr (Siebeck).

Smothers, E. R.

1926–27 A Letter from Babylon. *Classical Journal* 22:202–29, 418–26.

Snodgrass, K. R.

1977 I Peter II.1–10: Its Formation and Literary Affinities. *NTS* 24:97–106.

Snyder, G. F.

1969 Survey and "New" Thesis on the Bones of Peter. *Biblical Archaeologist* 32 (1969) 2–24.

Snyder, S.

1991 1 Peter 2:17: A Reconsideration. *Filología Neotestamentaria* 4:211–15.

1995 Participles and Imperatives in 1 Peter: A Re-examination in the Light of Recent Scholarly Trends. *Filología Neotestamentaria* 8:187–98.

Soards, M. L.

1988 1 Peter, 2 Peter, and Jude as Evidence for a Petrine School. *ANRW* 2.25.5:3827–49.

Soden, H. von

1883 Der erste Petrusbrief. *Jahrbücher für protestantische Theologie* (1883): 461–508.

Söding, T.

1990 Widerspruch und Leidensnachfolge: Neutestamentliche Gemeinden im Konflikt mit der paganen Gesellschaft. *MTZ* 41:137–55.

Soltau, W.

1905 Die Einheitlichkeit des ersten Petrusbriefes. *TSK* 78:302–15.

1906 Nochmals die Einheitlichkeit des ersten Petrusbriefes. *TSK* 79:456–60.

Souček, J. B.

1960 Das Gegenüber von Gemeinde und Welt nach dem ersten Petrusbrief. *Communio Viatorum* 3:5–13.

Spicq, C.

1932 Saint Pierre, apôtre de l'espérance. Pages 99–157 in *La révélation de l'espérance dans le Nouveau Testament*. Avignon: Aubanel / Paris: Dominicaine.

1965 Agape and Agapan in SS. Peter and Jude. Pages 342–83 in vol. 2 of *Agape in the New Testament*. St. Louis: Herder.

1966b L'Épître de Pierre: Prière, charité, justice . . . et fin des Temps (1 Pierre 4:7–11). *AsSeign* 50:15–29.

1966c La I[a] Petri et le témoignage évangélique de Saint Pierre. *ST* 20:37–61.

Spitta, F.

1890 *Christi Predigt an die Geister (1 Petr. 3,19ff.): Ein Beitrag zur neutestamentlichen Theologie*. Göttingen: Vandenhoeck & Ruprecht.

Spivey, R. A., and D. M. Smith

1982 Pages 395–400, 425 in *Anatomy of the New Testament: A Guide to Its Structure and Meaning*. 4th ed. New York: Macmillan.

Spörri, T.

1925 *Der Gemeindegedanke im ersten Petrusbrief. Ein Beitrag zur Struktur des urchristlichen Kirchenbegriffs*. Neutestamentliche Forschungen 2/2. Gütersloh: Bertelsmann.

Spoto, D. M.
1971 *Christ's Preaching to the Dead: An Exegesis of I Peter 3,19 and 4,6*. Ph.D. Dissertation, Fordham University.
Stegmann, A.
1917 *Silvanus als Missionar und "Hagiograph": Eine exegetische Studie*. Rottenburg: Bader.
Stemmler, G. W.
1894 Het verband van 1 Peter 3,8–4,6. *Theologische Studien* (1894):409–13.
Steuer, A.
1938 1 Petr. 3,17–4,6. *Theologie und Glaube* 30:675–78.
Steuernagel, V. R.
1986 An Exiled Community as a Mission Community: A Study Based on 1 Peter 2:9, 10. *Evangelical Review of Theology* 10:8–18.
Stevick, D. B.
1988 A Matter of Taste: 1 Peter 2:3. *Review for Religious* 47:707–17.
Stibbs, A. M.
1959 Bible Book of the Month, 1 Peter. *Christianity Today* 3:22–24.
Stimpfli, J.
1951 *Das christliche Leben als Verherrlichung Gottes nach dem ersten Brief des heiligen Petrus*. Doctoral Dissertation, Pontifical Gregorian University, Rome.
Stöger, A.
1954 *Bauleute Gottes: Der 1. Petrusbrief als Grundlegung des Laienapostolats*. Lebendiges Wort 3. Munich: Pfeiffer.
Stolt, J.
1981 Isagogiske problemer vedroren de 1 Petersbrev. *Dansk Teologisk Tidsskrift* 44:166–73.
Strahan, J.
1918 Silas or Silvanus. Pages 492–93 in vol. 2 of *HDAC*.
Strathmann, H.
1943 Die Stellung des Petrus in der Urkirche: Zur Frühgeschichte des Wortes an Petrus Mt. 16,17–19. *ZST* 20:223–82.
Streeter, B. H.
1929 The Church in Asia: The First Epistle of St. Peter. Pages 115–36 in *The Primitive Church*. New York: Macmillan.
Strobel, A.
1963 Macht Leiden von Sünden frei?: Zur Problematik von 1 Petr. 4,1f. *TZ* 19:412–25.
Suparschi, M.
1956 Idei moral-sociale în epistolele sf. Ap. Petru. *Studii Teologice* n.s. 8:167–79.
Swigchem, D. van
1955 *Het missionar karakter van de christelijke gemeinte volgens de brieven van Paulus en Petrus*. Kampen.
Sylva, D.
1980 1 Peter Studies: The State of the Discipline. *BTB* 14:155–63.
1983 Translating and Interpreting 1 Peter 3:2. *BT* 34:144–47.
1986 A 1 Peter Bibliography. *JETS* 25 (1982):75–89. Reprinted and expanded: The Critical Exploration of 1 Peter. Pages 17–36 in *Perspectives on First Peter*. Edited by C. H. Talbert. Macon, Georgia: Mercer University Press.

Synge, F. C.
1971 I Peter 3.18–21. *ExpTim* 82:311.

Sywulka, P.
1991 El sufrimiento de Cristo como patrón para el creyente en 1 Pedro. *Kairós* (Guatemala City) 8:53–66.

Talbert, C. H.
1986a Once Again: The Plan of 1 Peter. Pages 141–51 in *Perspectives on First Peter.* NABPR Special Study Series 9. Macon, Georgia: Mercer University Press.
1991 The Educational Value of Suffering in 1 Peter. Pages 42–57 in *Learning through Suffering: The Educational Value of Suffering in the New Testament and in Its Milieu.* Collegeville, Minnesota: Liturgical/Glazier.

Talbert, C. H., ed.
1986b *Perspectives on First Peter.* National Association of Baptist Professors of Religion Special Study Series 9. Macon, Georgia: Mercer University Press.

Tatum, S. L.
1982 Preaching From I Peter. *SwJT* 25:46–57.

Taylor, V.
1959 The First Epistle of St. Peter. Pages 80–88 in *The Person of Christ in New Testament Teaching.* London: Macmillan.

Teichert, H.
1949 1 Petrus 2,13: Eine crux interpretum? *TLZ* 74:303–4.

Tenney, M. C.
1974 Some Possible Parallels Between 1 Peter and John. Pages 370–77 in *New Dimensions in New Testament Study.* Edited by R. N. Longenecker and M. C. Tenney. Grand Rapids: Zondervan.

Testa, E.
1967 S. Pietro nel pensiero dei giudeo-cristiani. Pages 459–500 in *San Pietro: Atti della XIX Settimana Biblica.* Edited by A. Bea et al. Brescia: Paideia.

Thiede, C. P.
1986 *Simon Peter: From Galilee to Rome.* Exeter: Paternoster. [American ed., Grand Rapids: Zondervan, 1988]
1987a Babylon, der andere Ort: Anmerkungen zu 1 Petr 5,13 und Apg. 12,17. *Bib* 67 (1986):532–38. Reprinted pp. 221–29 in *Das Petrusbild in der neueren Forschung.* Edited by C. P. Thiede. Wuppertal: Brockhaus.

Thiede, C. P., ed.
1987b *Das Petrusbild in der neueren Forschung.* TVG 316. Wuppertal: Brockhaus.

Thiele, W.
1958 *Epistulae Catholicae: Epistula I Petri.* Vetus Latina 26/2. Freiburg: Herder.
1965 *Die lateinischen Texte des 1. Petrusbriefes.* Vetus Latina 5. Freiburg: Herder.

Thils, G.
1943 *L'enseignement de S. Pierre.* Ebib. Paris: Lecoffre.

Thomas, J.
1968 Anfechtung und Vorfreude: Ein biblisches Thema nach Jakobus 1,2–18, im Zusammenhang mit Psalm 126, Röm 5,3–5 und 1 Petr. 1,5–7, formkritisch untersucht und parakletisch ausgelegt. *KD* 14:183–206.

Thomas, W. H. G.
1946 *The Apostle Peter*. Grand Rapids: Eerdmans.
Thompson, J.
1990 *The Church in Exile: God's Counter Culture in a Non-Christian World*. Abilene, Texas: Abilene Christian University Press.
Thompson, J. W.
1966 Be Submissive to Your Masters: A Study of I Peter 2:18–25. *ResQ* 9:66–78.
1994 The Rhetoric of 1 Peter. *ResQ* 36:237–50.
Thornton, T. C. G.
1961 1 Peter, a Paschal Liturgy? *JTS* 12:14–26.
Thurén, L.
1990 *The Rhetorical Strategy of 1 Peter with Special Regard to Ambiguous Expressions*. Åbo: Åbo Academy Press.
1995 *Argument and Theology in 1 Peter: The Origins of Christian Paraenesis*. JSNTSup 114. Sheffield: Sheffield Academic Press.
Thurston, R. W.
1974 Interpreting First Peter. *JETS* 17:171–82.
Tiede, D. L.
1984 An Easter Catechesis: The Lessons of 1 Peter. *Word and World* 4:192–201.
Tigert, J. J.
1898 The Paulinism of First Peter. *Methodist Quarterly Review* 47:426–35.
Tite, P. L.
1996 The Compositional Function of the Petrine Prescript: A Look at 1 Pet 1:1–3. *Journal of the Evangelical Society* 39:47–56.
1997 *Compositional Transitions in 1 Peter: An Analysis of the Letter-Opening*. Bethesda, Maryland: International Scholars.
Toynbee, J., and J. W. Perkins
1956 *The Shrine of St. Peter and the Vatican Excavations*. London: Longmans.
Trilling, W.
1971 Zum Petrusamt im Neuen Testament: Traditionsgeschichtliche Überlegungen anhand von Matthäus, 1 Petrus und Johannes. *TQ* 151:110–33.
Trimmaille, M.
1983 Les Épîtres catholiques. Pages 249–63 in *Les Lettres de Paul, de Jacques, de Pierre et de Jude*. Paris: Cerf.
Tripp, D. H.
1981 Eperôtêma (I Peter 3:21): A Linguist's Note. *ExpTim* 92:267–70.
Tuñi, J. O.
1987 Jesus of Nazareth in the Christology of 1 Peter. *HeyJ* 28:292–304.
Turner, C. H.
1926 St. Peter in the New Testament. *Theology* 13:66–78.
Uhlig, S.
1974 Die typologische Bedeutung des Begriffes Babylons. *AUSS* 12:112–25.
Underhill, F. L.
1938 *Saint Peter*. New York: Longmans, Green.
Unnik, W. C. van
1954–55 The Teaching of Good Works in 1 Peter. *NTS* 1:92–110. [Pages 83–105 in part 2 of *Sparsa Collecta*, 1980.]
1955–56 A Classical Parallel to 1 Peter 2:14 and 20. *NTS* 2:198–202. [Pages 106–10 in part 2 of *Sparsa Collecta*, 1980.]

1956–57 Christianity according to I Peter. *ExpTim* 68:79–83. [Pages 111–20 in part 2 of *Sparsa Collecta*, 1980.]

1962a Peter, First Letter of. Pages 758–66 in vol. 3 of *IDB* 3.

1962b Petrusbriefe. Pages 1431–34 in vol. 3 of *BHH*.

1969 The Critique of Paganism in 1 Peter 1:18. Pages 129–42 in *Neotestamentica et Semitica*. M. Black Festschrift. Edited by E. E. Ellis and M. Wilcox. Edinburgh: T. & T. Clark.

1973 Peter, Epistles of Saint. Pages 743–45 in vol. 17 of *EncBrit*.

1973–83 *Sparsa Collecta: The Collected Essays of W. C. van Unnik*. Edited by J. Reiling, G. Mussies, and P. van der Horst. 3 parts in 3 vols. NovTSup 29. Leiden: Brill.

1979 Le rôle de Noé dans les épîtres de Pierre. Pages 207–39 in *Noé, L'homme universel*. Colloque de Louvain 1978. Institutum Judaicum Bruxelles 3. Brussels.

1980 The Redemption in I Peter I 18–19 and the Problem of the First Epistle of Peter. Pages 3–82 in part 2 of *Sparsa Collecta*. [ET of *De verlossing I Petrus 1:18–19 en het problem van den eersten Petrusbrief*. Mededeelingen der Nederlandsche Akademie van Wetenschappen: Afdeeling Letterkunde, Nieuwe Reeks 5/1. Amsterdam, 1942]

Usteri, J. M.

1886 *"Hinabgefahren zur Hölle": Eine Wiedererwägung der Schriftstellen 1 Petr. 3,18–22 und Kap. 4, Vers 6*. Zurich: Höhr.

Vallauri, E.

1982 Succinti lumbros mentis vestiae (1 Piet 1,13): Nota per una introduzione. *BeO* 131:19–22.

Vanhoye, A.

1964 La maison spirituelle (1 Pt 2:1–10). *AsSeign* 43:16–29.

1973 La foi qui construit l'Église (1 Pe 2,4–9). *AsSeign* 26:12–17.

1975 La Chiesa come casa spirituale secondo la prima lettera di S. Pietro. Pages 89–104 in vol. 6 of *Sinodo Documentazione*. Verona.

1980 1 Pierre au carrefour des théologies du Nouveau Testament. Pages 97–128 in *Études sur la première lettre de Pierre*. LD 102. Paris: Cerf.

Vanni, U.

1979–81 Linee antropologiche nelle lettere di Pietro e Giacomo. Pages 789–816 in *L'antropologia biblica*. Edited by G. De Gennaro. Naples: Dehoniane.

1980 Giustizia ed amore: Prospettiva ecclesiale, sociale e politica in Pietro. Pages 515–59 in *Amore-Giustizia*. Edited by G. De Gennaro. Naples: Dehoniane.

1987 La promozione del regno come responsabilità sacerdotale dei cristiani secondo l'Apocalisse e la Prima Lettera di Pietro. *Greg* 68:9–56.

Vidigal, J. R.

1981 Catequese Baptismal na Primeira Carta de Sao Pedro. *Revista de cultura biblica* 5:76–84.

Vielhauer, P.

1975 Pages 580–89 in *Geschichte der urchristlichen Literatur: Einleitung in das Neue Testament, die Apokryphen und die Apostolischen Väter*. Berlin: de Gruyter.

Villiers, J. L. de

1975 Joy in Suffering in 1 Peter. *Neot* 9:64–86.

Vitti, A. M.
1927 Descensus Christi ad inferos ex 1 Petri 3, 19–20; 4:6. *VD* 7:111–18.
1931 Eschatologia in Petri epistula prima. *VD* 11:298–306.
Vögtle, A.
1964 Petrus, Apostel. Pages 334–40 in vol. 8 of *LTK*.
Völkl, R.
1961 Der erste Petrusbrief. Pages 370–80 in *Christ und Welt nach dem Neuen Testament*. Würzburg: Echter.
Völter, D.
1906 *Der erste Petrusbrief: Seine Entstehung und Stellung in der Geschichte des Urchristentums*. Strassburg: Heitz & Mündel.
1908 Bemerkungen zu I. Pt. 3 und 4. *ZNW* 9:74–77.
Vogels, H.-J.
1976 *Christi Abstieg ins Totenreich und das Läuterungsgericht an den Toten*. FTS 102. Freiburg: Herder.
Volf, M.
1994 Soft Difference: Theological Reflections on the Relation between Church and Culture in 1 Peter. *Ex Auditu* 10:15–30.
Volpi, I.
1984 Approcio di struttura su I Piet. II,11–V,14. Pages 153–72 in *Gesù Apostolo e Sommo Sacerdote*. Studi Biblici in memoria di P. T. Ballerini. Edited by L. Provera. Rome: Marietti.
1988 *Battesimo e diluvio: Ricerca su 1 Pt 3,20b–21 nel contesto di 3,18–21*. Doctoral Dissertation, Pontifical Biblical Institute.
Voorwinde, S.
1987 Old Testament Quotations in Peter's Epistles. *Vox Reformata* 49:3–16.
Vorster, W. S.
1979 *Aischynomai en stamverwante woorde in die Nuwe Testament*. Pretoria: Universiteit van Suid-Afrika.
Vowinkel, E.
1899 *Die Grundgedanken des Jakobusbriefes verglichen mit den ersten Briefen des Petrus und Johannes*. BFCT 2/6. Gütersloh: Bertelsmann.
Walsh, J. E.
1982 *The Bones of St. Peter: The First Full Account of the Search for the Apostle's Body*. Garden City, New York: Doubleday.
Walsh, W. T.
1948 *Saint Peter the Apostle*. New York: Macmillan.
Wand, J. W. C.
1955 The Lessons of First Peter: A Survey of Recent Interpretation. *Int* 9: 387–99.
Warden, D.
1989 The Prophets of 1 Peter 1:10–12. *ResQ* 31:1–12.
1991 Imperial Persecution and the Dating of 1 Peter and Revelation. *JETS* 34:203–12.
Warden, P. D.
1986 *Alienation and Community in 1 Peter*. Ph.D. Dissertation, Duke University.
Watson, D. L.
1970 *The Implications of Christology and Eschatology for a Christian Attitude toward the State in I Peter*. Th.D. Dissertation, Hartford Seminary.

Webb, R. L.
1986 *The Apocalyptic Perspective of First Peter.* Th.M. Thesis, Regent College.

Wehr, L.
1996 *Petrus und Paulus, Kontrahenten und Partner: Die Beiden Apostel im Spiegel des Neuen Testaments, der Apostolischen Väter und früher Zeugnisse ihrer Verehrung.* NTAbh n.s. 30. Münster: Aschendorff.

Weiss, B.
1855 *Der Petrinische Lehrbegriff: Beiträge zur biblischen Theologie sowie zur Kritik und Exegese des ersten Briefes Petri und der petrinischen Reden.* Berlin: Schultze.
1906 *Der erste Petrusbrief und die neuere Kritik.* Biblische Zeit- und Streitfragen 2/9. Berlin: Runga.

Wells, P.
1973 Les images bibliques de l'Église dans 1 Pierre 2,9–10. *Études Évangéliques* 33:20–25, 53–65.

Wendland, H.-D.
1970 Der erste Petrus-Brief: Christus, das Urbild des Lebens und Leidens. Pages 101–4 in *Ethik des Neuen Testaments. Eine Einführung.* Grundrisse zum Neuen Testament 4. Göttingen: Vandenhoeck & Ruprecht.

Wenham, J.
1972 Did Peter Go to Rome in AD 42? *TynBul* 23:94–102.

Whelan, J. B.
1965 The Priesthood of the Laity (1 Pt 2:9). *Doctrine and Life* 15:539–46.

Wifstrand, A.
1948 Stylistic Problems in the Epistles of James and Peter. *ST* 1:170–82.

Wikenhauser, A.
1963a The First Epistle of St. Peter. Pages 497–509 in *New Testament Introduction.* New York: Herder & Herder.
1963b The Life of St. Peter the Apostle. Pages 493–97 in *New Testament Introduction.* New York: Herder & Herder.

Wilhelm-Hooijbergh, A. E.
1980 The Martyrdom of Peter Was before the Fire in Rome. Pages 431–33 in *Papers on Paul and Other New Testament Authors.* StudBib 3. JSNTSup 3. Sheffield: JSOT Press.

Wilkes, C. G.
1985 *The Synoptic Tradition in 1 Peter: An Investigation into Its Forms and Development.* Th.D. Dissertation, Southwestern Baptist Theological Seminary.

Willis, W. H.
1964 An Unrecognized Fragment of First Peter in Coptic. Pages 265–71 in *Classical, Mediaeval and Renaissance Studies in Honor of B. L. Ullman.* Edited by C. Henderson, Jr. Storia e Letteratura 93. Rome.

Wilson, J. P.
1942–43 In the Text of I Peter II.17 is *pantas timêsate* a Primitive Error for *panta poiêsate*? *ExpTim* 54:193–94.

Winberry, C. L.
1982a Ethical Issues in 1 Peter. *Theological Educator* 13:63–71.
1982b Introduction to the First Letter of Peter. *SwJT* 25:3–16.

Windisch, H.
1908 Der entsündigte Christ im 1. Petrusbriefe. Pages 227–43 in *Taufe und Sünde im ältesten Christentum bis auf Origenes: Ein Beitrag zur altchristlichen Dogmengeschichte*. Tübingen: Mohr.

Winter, B. W.
1988a The Public Honouring of Christian Benefactors: Romans 13.3–4 and 1 Peter 2.14–15. *JSNT* 34:87–103.
1988b Seek the Welfare of the City: Social Ethics according to 1 Peter. *Themelios* 13:91–94.
1994 *Seeking the Welfare of the City: Christians as Benefactors and Citizens—First Century Christians in the Graeco-Roman World*. Grand Rapids: Eerdmans.

Wolff, C.
1975 Christ und Welt im 1. Petrusbrief. *TLZ* 100:333–42.

Woychuck, N. A.
1953 *The Faith of Experience: Devotional Exposition of I Peter 1:3–8*. Grand Rapids: Eerdmans.

Wrede, W.
1900 Miscellen 3: Bemerkungen zu Harnacks Hypothese über die Adresse des I. Petrusbriefes. ZNW 1:75–85.

Wuest, K. S.
1942 *First Peter in the Greek Testament for the English Reader*. Grand Rapids: Eerdmans.

Yates, T.
1933–34 The Message of the Epistles: The First Epistle of Peter. *ExpTim* 45:391–93.

Zahn, T.
1909 The Epistles of Peter and Jude, and the Epistle to the Hebrews. Pages 134–366 in vol. 2 of *Introduction to the New Testament*. Edinburgh: T. & T. Clark. [Pages 134–94 on 1 Peter]

Załęski, J.
1984 Posłuszeństwo władzy świeckiej według 1 [P]t 2,13–17. *Collectanea Theologica* 54:39–50.
1985 L'obbedienza al potere civile in 1 Pt 2, 13–17. *Collectanea Theologica* 55 (special issue):153–62.

Zampini, S.
1922 *San Pietro, a cui nostro Signor lasciò le chiave e le sue Epistole*. Milan: Hoepli.

Zeilinger, F.
1987 Das "zweite Petrusbekenntnis": Zur Rezeption von 1 Cor 15,3ff in 1 Petr 3,18–22. Pages 81–99 in *Anfänge der Theologie*. J. B. Bauer Festschrift. Edited by N. Brox, A. Felber, and W. Gombocz. Vienna: Styria.

Zeller, E.
1876 Zur Petrusfrage. *ZWT* 19:34–56.

Zerbe, G. M.
1993 Non-retaliation in 1 Peter: A Pragmatic or a Christological Ethic? Pages 270–91 in *Non-retaliation in Early Jewish and New Testament Texts: Ethical Themes in Social Contexts*. JSPSup 13. Sheffield: JSOT Press.

Zezschwitz, C. A. G.
1857 *Petri Apostoli de Christi ad inferos descensu sententia ex loco nobilissimo, I: Ep. III, 19 eruta exacta ad epistolae argumentum*. Leipzig: Ackermann & Glaser.

3. OTHER LITERATURE

◆

A. PRIMARY TEXTS

Aland, K., ed.
1976 *Synopsis Quattuor Evangeliorum*. Stuttgart: Württembergische Bibelanstalt.

Aland, K., B. Aland, J. Karavidopoulos, C. Martini, and B. Metzger, eds.
1993 *Novum Testamentum Graece*. 27th ed. Stuttgart: Deutsche Bibelgesellschaft. [Equivalent to *GNT*[4] (1994).] 26th ed., 1979. [Cited as *NTG*]

Aland, K., M. Black, C. M. Martini, B. M. Metzger, and A. Wikgren, eds.
1994 *Greek New Testament*. 4th ed. New York: United Bible Societies. [Equivalent to *NTG*[27] (1993)]

Kittel, R., and P. Kahle, eds.
1951 *Biblia Hebraica*. 9th ed. Stuttgart: Privilegierte Württembergische Bibelanstalt.

Rahlfs, A., ed.
1952 *Septuaginta, id est Vetus Testamentum graece iuxta LXX interpretes*. Stuttgart: Privilegierte Württembergische Bibelanstalt.

Septuaginta: Vetus Testamentum Graecum auctoritate Societatis Gottingensis editum. Göttingen: Vandenhoeck & Ruprecht, 1931–.

B. PARABIBLICAL TEXTS AND TRANSLATIONS

Black, M., ed.
1970 *Apocalypsis Henochi Graece*. Vol. 3 of *Pseudepigrapha Veteris Testamenti Graece*. Edited by A. M. Denis and M. de Jonge. Leiden: Brill.

Charles, R. H., ed.
1908 *The Greek Versions of the Testaments of the Twelve Patriarchs*. Oxford: Oxford University Press.
1913 *The Apocrypha and Pseudepigrapha of the Old Testament*. 2 vols. Oxford: Clarendon.

Charlesworth, J. H., ed.
1993 *The Old Testament Pseudepigrapha*. 2 vols. Garden City, New York: Doubleday.
1994 *The Dead Sea Scrolls. Hebrew, Aramaic, and Greek Texts with English Translations*. Tübingen: Mohr (Siebeck) / Louisville: Westminster John Knox.

Elliott, J. K.
1993 *The Apocryphal New Testament. A Collection of Apocryphal Christian Literature in an English Translation*. Oxford: Clarendon.

García Martínez, F.
1996 *The Dead Sea Scrolls Translated: The Qumran Texts in English*. 2d rev. ed. Leiden: Brill / Grand Rapids: Eerdmans.
Gaster, T. H.
1976 *The Dead Sea Scriptures*. 3d ed. Garden City: Doubleday.
Hennecke, E., and W. Schneemelcher, eds.
1992 *New Testament Apocrypha*. 2 vols. 2d ed. Philadelphia: Westminster. [1st ed., 1963]
Josephus
1926– *Josephus*. 9 vols. Translated by H. St. J. Thackeray, R. Marcus, A. Wikgren, and H. Feldman. LCL. Cambridge: Harvard University Press.
Lohse, E., ed.
1971 *Die Texte aus Qumran. Hebräisch und Deutsch*. 2d ed. Darmstadt: Wissenschaftliche.
Milik, J. T.
1976 *The Books of Enoch. Aramaic Fragments from Qumrân Cave 4*. Oxford: Oxford University Press.
Philo
1896–1930 *Opera quae supersunt*. 7 vols. Edited by L. Cohn and P. Wendland. Berlin: de Gruyter.
1929–1953 *Philo*. 10 vols. Translated by F. H. Colson, G. H. Whittaker, J. W. Earp, and R. Marcus. 2 sup. vols. by R. Marcus. LCL. Cambridge: Harvard University Press.
Vermes, G.
1987 *The Dead Sea Scrolls in English*. 3d ed. New York: Penguin.

C. General Literature

Aalen, S.
1951 *Die Begriffe "Licht" und "Finsternis" im Alten Testament, im Spätjudentum und im Rabbinismus*. Oslo: Dybwad.
1962 "Reign" and "House" in the Kingdom of God in the Gospels. *NTS* 8:215–40.
Abu-Lughod, L.
1985 A Community of Secrets: The Separate World of Bedouin Women. *Signs: Journal of Women in Culture and Society* 10:637–57.
1986 *Veiled Sentiments: Honor and Poetry in a Bedouin Society*. Berkeley: University of California Press.
Adinolfi, M.
1983 *Il sacerdozio commune dei fedeli*. Rome: Antonianum.
Agnew, F. H.
1986 The Origin of the New Testament Apostle Concept: A Review of Research. *JBL* 105:75–96.
Aguirre, R.
1985 Early Christian House Churches. *TD* 32:151–55. [English summary of La casa como estructura base del cristianismo primitivo: Las iglesias domesticas. *Estudios Eclesiásticos* (Madrid) 59/228 (1984) 27–51]

Aharoni, Y., and M. Avi-Yonah
1968 *The Macmillan Bible Atlas*. New York: Macmillan.

Aland, K.
1965 The Problem of Anonymity and Pseudonymity in Christian Literature of the First Two Centuries. Pages 1–13 in *The Authorship and Integrity of the New Testament*. Edited by K. Aland et al. Theological Collections 4. London: SPCK.

Aland, K., and B. Aland
1989 *The Text of the New Testament*. Translated by E. F. Rhodes. 2d rev. and enlarged ed. Grand Rapids: Eerdmans / Leiden: Brill.

Aland, K., et al.
1965 *The Authorship and Integrity of the New Testament*. Theological Collections 4. London: SPCK.

Albright, W. F.
1964 Gerhard Kittel and the Jewish Question in Antiquity. Pages 229–40 in *History, Archaeology and Christian Humanism*. New York: McGraw-Hill.

Alföldi, G.
1984 *Römische Sozialgeschichte*. 3d ed. Wiesbaden: Steiner.

Allenbach, J., et al., eds.
1975–82 *Biblia Patristica: Index des citations et allusions bibliques dans la littérature patristique*. 2 vols. and supplement. Paris: Éditions du Centre National de la Recherche Scientifique.

Allison, D. C., Jr.
1994 A Plea for Thoroughgoing Eschatology. *JBL* 113:651–68.

Allmen, D. von
1981 *La Famille de Dieu: La symbolique familiale dans le Paulinisme*. OBO 41. Göttingen: Vandenhoeck & Ruprecht.

Althaus, P.
1942 Niedergefahren zur Hölle. *ZST* 19:365–84.

Altmann, P.
1964 *Die Erwählungstradition und der Universalismus im Alten Testament*. BZAW 92. Berlin: Alfred Töpelmann.

Amphoux, C.-B., and B. Outtier, eds.
1996 *La Lecture liturgique des Épîtres Catholiques dans l'Église ancienne*. Histoire du Texte Biblique 1. Lausanne: Éditions du Zèbre.

Andresen, C.
1965 Zum Formular frühchristlicher Gemeindebriefe. ZNW 56:233–59.

Applebaum, S.
1974a The Legal Status of the Jewish Communities in the Diaspora. Pages 420–63 in vol. 1 of *The Jewish People in the First Century*. Edited by S. Safrai and M. Stern. CRINT Section 1. Philadelphia: Fortress.
1974b The Organization of the Jewish Communities in the Diaspora. Pages 464–503 in vol. 1 of *The Jewish People in the First Century*. Edited by S. Safrai and M. Stern. CRINT Section 1. Philadelphia: Fortress.

Archer, L. J.
1990 *Her Price Is beyond Rubies: The Jewish Woman in Graeco-Roman Palestine*. Sheffield: JSOT Press.

Arndt, W.
1948 A Royal Priesthood. *CTM* 19:241–49.

Arthur, M.
1977 Liberated Women: The Classical Period. Pages 60–89 in *Becoming Visible: Women in European History*. Edited by R. Bridenthal and C. Koonz. Boston: Houghton Mifflin.

Aseltine, G. A. van
1979 Dispersion. Pages 962–68 in vol. 1 of *ISBE*.

Asmussen, H.
1946 *Das Priestertum aller Gläubigen*. Stuttgart: Quell.

Asting, R.
1930 *Die Heiligkeit im Urchristentum*. Göttingen: Vandenhoeck & Ruprecht.

Attridge, H. W.
1989 *The Epistle to the Hebrews*. Hermeneia. Philadelphia: Fortress.

Augsburger, D. W.
1986 *Pastoral Counseling across Cultures*. Philadelphia: Westminster.

Aune, D. E.
1992 Eschatology: Early Christian Eschatology. Pages 594–609 in vol. 2 of *IDB*.

Aune, D. E., ed.
1988 *Greco-Roman Literature and the New Testament*. SBL Sources for Biblical Study 21. Atlanta: Scholars Press.

Avi-Yonah, M.
1978 *Hellenism and the East: Contacts and Interrelations from Alexander to the Roman Conquest*. Jerusalem: Institute of Languages, Literature and the Arts, The Hebrew University.

Bachmann, E. T., ed. and trans.
1960 *Word and Sacrament*. Volume 35 of *Luther's Works*. Philadelphia: Muhlenberg.

Bailey, L. R.
1978 *Where is Noah's Ark? Mystery on Mt. Ararat*. Nashville: Abingdon.
1989 *Noah: The Person and the Story in History and Tradition*. Columbia: University of South Carolina Press.
1992 Noah's Ark. Pages 1131–32 in vol. 4 of *ABD*.

Baker, J.
1966 Priesthood of All Believers. *Theology* 69:60–65.

Balch, D. L.
1977 Household Ethical Codes in Peripatetic, Neopythagorean and Early Christian Moralists. Pages 397–404 in *SBL 1977: Seminar Papers*. SBLSP 16. Missoula, Montana: Scholars Press.
1982 Two Apologetic Encomia: Dionysius on Rome and Josephus on the Jews. *JSJ* 13:102–22.
1988 Household Codes. Pages 25–50 in *Graeco-Roman Literature and the New Testament*. Edited by D. E. Aune. SBL Sources for Biblical Study 21. Atlanta: Scholars Press.
1992 Household Codes. Pages 318–20 in vol. 3 of *ABD*.

Balsdon, J. P. V. D.
1962 *Roman Women: Their History and Habits*. London: Bodley Head.

Baltensweiler, H.
1967 *Die Ehe im Neuen Testament: Exegetische Untersuchungen über Ehe, Ehelosigkeit und Ehescheidung*. Zurich: Zwingli.

Balthasar, H. U. von

1969a *Herrlichkeit: Eine theologische Ästhetik*. Part 2: *Neuer Bund*, of vol. 3 of *Theologie*. Einsiedeln: Johannes.

1969b *Theologie der drei Tage*. Einsiedeln: Benzinger.

1970 Abstieg zur Hölle. *TQ* 150:193–201.

Baltzer, K.

1971 *The Covenant Formulary in Old Testament, Jewish, and Early Christian Writings*. Philadelphia: Fortress.

Balz, H., and G. Wanke

1974 "*phobeô* etc." Pages 189–219 in vol. 9 of *TDNT*.

Banks, R.

1994 *Paul's Idea of Community: The Early House Churches in Their Cultural Setting*. Peabody, Massachusetts: Hendrickson.

Barbaglio, G.

1988a Rassegna di studi di storia sociale e di ricerche di sociologia sulle origini cristiane: I. *RivB* 36:377–410.

1988b Rassegna di studi di storia sociale e di ricerche sociologia sulle origini cristiane: II. *RivB* 36:495–520.

Barclay, J. M. G.

1991 Paul, Philemon and the Dilemma of Christian Slave Ownership. *NTS* 37:161–86.

Barnard, L. W.

1964a Clement of Rome and the Persecution of Domitian. *NTS* 10:251–60.

1964b The Testimonium concerning the Stone in the NT and in the Epistle of Barnabas. *SE* 3:306–13.

Barnes, T. D.

1968 Legislation against the Christians. *JRS* 58:32–50.

Barnett, A. E.

1941 *Paul Becomes a Literary Influence*. Chicago: University of Chicago Press.

Barnikol, E.

1931 Personen-Probleme der Apostelgeschichte: Johannes Markus, Silas, und Titus. Pages 1–32 in *Forschungen zur Entstehung des Urchristentums, des Neuen Testaments und der Kirche*. Kiel.

Barrett, C. K.

1970 The Interpretation of the Old Testament in the New. Pages 377–411 in *From the Beginnings to Jerome*. Edited by P. R. Ackroyd and C. F. Evans. Volume 1 of *The Cambridge History of the Bible*.Cambridge: Cambridge University Press.

Bartchy, S. S.

1973 Mallon Chrêsai: *First-Century Slavery and the Interpretation of 1 Corinthians 7:21*. SBLDS 11. Missoula, Montana: Scholars Press.

1988a Servant, Slave (NT). Pages 420–21 in vol. 4 of *ISBE*.

1988b Slavery (NT). Pages 543–46 in vol. 4 of *ISBE*.

1992 Slavery: New Testament. Pages 65–73 in vol. 6 of *ABD*.

Barth, H. M.

1990 *Einander Priester Sein: Allgemeines Priestertum in ökumenischer Perspektive*. Kirche und Konfession 29. Göttingen: Vandenhoeck & Ruprecht.

Barth, M.

1984 Traditions in Ephesians. *NTS* 30:3–25.

Barton, S. C.
1991 *Discipleship and Family Ties in Mark and Matthew*. SNTSMS 80. New York: Cambridge University Press.

Bauckham, R. J.
1983 *Jude, 2 Peter*. WBC 50. Waco, Texas: Word.
1988b 2 Peter: An Account of Research. *ANRW* 2.25.5:3713–52.
1988c Pseudo-apostolic Letters. *JBL* 107:469–94.
1990 Early Jewish Visions of Hell. *JTS* 41:355–85.
1992c Descent to the Underworld. Pages 145–59 in vol. 2 of *ABD*.

Baudissin, W. W.
1889 *Die Geschichte des alttestamentlichen Priesterthums*. Leipzig: S. Hirzel.

Bauer, J. B.
1958 Könige und Priester, ein heiliges Volk (Ex. 19,6). *BZ* 2:283–86.
1965 The Picture of the Apostle in Early Christian Tradition. Pages 35–87 in vol. 2 of *New Testament Apocrypha*. Edited by E. Hennecke and W. Schneemelcher. Philadelphia: Westminster. [On Peter, esp. pp. 45–50]
1971 *Orthodoxy and Heresy in Earliest Christianity*. Translated and ed. by R. A. Kraft and G. Krodel from the 2d German ed. Philadelphia: Fortress.

Bauernfeind, O.
1971 "*strateuomai* etc." Pages 701–14 in vol. 7 of *TDNT*.

Baumbach, G.
1992 Die Funktion des Bösen in neutestamentlichen Schriften. *EvT* 52:23–42.

Baumgärtel, F.
1971 "*sarx*." Pages 105–8 in vol. 7 of *TDNT*.

Baus, K.
1940 *Der Kranz in Antike und Christentum*. Bonn: Hanstein.

Bean, G. E.
1971 *Turkey beyond the Maeander: An Archaeological Guide*. Totowa, New Jersey: Rowman & Littlefield.

Beasley-Murray, G. R.
1963 *Baptism in the New Testament*. London: Macmillan / New York: St. Martin's.

Beaujeu, J.
1960 L'incendie de Rome en 64 et les Chrétiens. *Latomus* 19:65–80, 291–311.

Beck, I.
1968 Sakrale Existenz: Das gemeinsame Priestertum des Gottesvolkes als kultische und ausserkultische Wirklichkeit. *MTZ* 19:17–34.

Behm, H.
1912 *Der Begriff des allgemeinen Priestertums*. Schwerin: Bahn.
1965 "*kardia* etc." Pages 605–14 in vol. 3 of *TDNT*.
1967 "*neos* etc." Pages 896–901 in vol. 4 of *TDNT*.

Bell, A. A., Jr.
1978 The Date of John's Apocalypse: The Evidence of Some Roman Historians Reconsidered. *NTS* 25:93–102.

Bengston, H.
1979 *Die Flavier: Vespasian, Titus, Domitian. Geschichte eines römischen Kaiserhauses*. Munich: Beck.

Benko, S.
1980 Pagan Criticism of Christianity during the First Two Centuries A.D. *ANRW* 2.23.2:1055–1118.

1985a The Kiss. Pages 79–102 in *Rome and the Early Christians*. Bloomington: Indiana University Press.

1985b The Name and Its Implications. Pages 1–29 in *Rome and the Early Christians*. Bloomington: Indiana University Press.

Benko, S., and J. J. O'Rourke, eds.

1971 *The Catacombs and the Colosseum: The Roman Empire as the Setting of Primitive Christianity*. Valley Forge: Judson.

Benoît, A., and C. Munier

1994 *Le Baptême dans l'Église ancienne (Ier–IIIe siècles)*. Traditio Christiana 9. Bern: Lang.

Benoit, P.

1949 L'Ascension. *RB* 55:161–203.

Berger, A.

1953 *Encyclopedic Dictionary of Roman Law*. Transactions of the American Philosophical Society 43/2. Philadelphia: American Philosophical Society.

Berger, K.

1971 Zum traditionsgeschichtlichen Hintergrund christologischer Hoheitstitel. *NTS* 17:391–425.

1974 Apostelbrief und apostolische Rede: Zum Formular frühchristlicher Briefe. *ZNW* 65:190–231.

1977 *Exegese des Neuen Testaments*. Heidelberg: Quelle & Meyer.

1984a *Formgeschichte des Neuen Testaments*. Heidelberg: Quelle & Meyer.

1984b Hellenistische Gattungen im Neuen Testament. *ANRW* 2.25.2:1031–1432, 1831–35.

1988 Henoch. Pages 473–545 in vol. 14 of *RAC*.

1993 "*charisma*." Pages 460–61 in vol. 3 of *EDNT*.

Bergmeier, R.

1995 Erfüllung der Gnadenzusagen an David. *ZNW* 86:277–86.

Bernstein, A. E.

1993 *The Formation of Hell: Death and Retribution in the Ancient and Early Christian Worlds*. Ithaca, New York: Cornell University Press.

Bertram, G.

1971 "*strephô, anastrephô* etc." Pages 714–29 in vol. 7 of *TDNT*.

Bertram, G., et al.

1974 "*psychê* etc." Pages 604–66 in vol. 9 of *TDNT*.

Bertram, G., and W. Grundmann

1965 "*kalos*." Pages 536–56 in vol. 3 of *TDNT*.

Beskow, P.

1970 Mission, Trade and Emigration in the Second Century. *SEÅ* 35:104–14.

Betz, H. D.

1967 *Nachfolge und Nachahmung Jesu Christi im Neuen Testament*. BHT 37. Tübingen: Mohr (Siebeck).

1978 De fraterno amore (*Moralia* 478a–492d). Pages 106–34 in *Plutarch's Ethical Writings and Early Christian Literature*. Edited by H. D. Betz. Studia ad Corpus Hellenisticum Novi Testamenti 4. Leiden: Brill.

Betz, O.

1957 Felsenmann und Felsengemeinde: Parall. zu Mt. 16:17–19 in den Qumranpsalmen. *ZNW* 48:49–77.

1958–59 Die Proselytentaufe der Qumransekte und die Taufe im Neuen Testament. *RQ* 1:213–34.

Beutler, J.
1991a "*martyreô* etc." Pages 389–91 in vol. 2 of *EDNT.*
1991b "*martyria.*" Pages 391–93 in vol. 2 of *EDNT.*
1991c "*martys.*" Pages 393–95 in vol. 2 of *EDNT.*

Beyer, H. W.
1964 "*episkeptomai* etc." Pages 599–623 in vol. 2 of *TDNT.*

Beyer, H. W., and H. Karpp
1954 Bischof. Pages 394–407 in vol. 2 of *RAC*.

Beyerlin, W.
1961 *Herkunft und Geschichte der ältesten Sinai-Traditionen.* Tübingen: Mohr (Siebeck).

Bickerman, E. J.
1968 Trajan, Hadrian and the Christians. *Rivista di filologia e di istruzione classica* 96:290–315.

Bickermann, E.
1949 The Name of Christians. *HTR* 42:109–24. [Reprinted pp. 139–51 in vol. 3 of *Studies in Jewish and Christian History.* AGJU 9/3. Leiden: Brill, 1986]

Bieder, W.
1949 *Die Vorstellung von der Höllenfahrt Jesu Christi: Beitrag zur Entstehungsgeschichte der Vorstellung vom sog[enannten] Descensus ad inferos.* ATANT 19. Zurich: Zwingli.

Bietenhard, H.
1951 *Die himmlische Welt im Urchristentum und Spätjudentum.* Tübingen: Mohr.

Billerbeck, P. (and H. L. Strack)
1926–61 *Kommentar zum Neuen Testament aus Talmud und Midrasch.* 6 vols. Munich: Beck.

Bird, P. A.
1992 Women: Old Testament. Pages 951–57 in vol. 6 of *ABD.*

Birkey, D.
1988 *The House Church: Restructuring for the Renewal.* Scottsdale: Herald.

Biser, E.
1959 Abgestiegen zu der Hölle. *MTZ* 9:205–12, 283–93.

Bitter, R. A.
1982 *Vreemdelingschap bij Philo van Alexandrië: Een onderzoek naar de betekenis van* paroikos. Dissertation, Utrecht..

Bjerkelund, C. J.
1967 Parakalô: *Studien zu Form, Funktion und Sinn der* parakalô-*Sätze in den paulinischen Briefen.* Bibliotheca Theologica Norwegica 1. Oslo: Universitetetsforlaget.

Blanchetière, F.
1974 Juifs et non juifs: Essai sur la diaspora en Asie-Mineure. *RHPR* 54: 367–82.

Blank, J.
1973 The Person and Office of Peter in the New Testament. Pages 42–55 in *Truth and Certainty.* Concilium 83. New York: Herder & Herder.

Blank, S.
1962 Kiss. Pages 39–40 in vol. 3 of *IDB*.

Blech, M.
1982 *Studien zum Kranz bei den Griechen*. RVV 38. Berlin: de Gruyter.

Block, D. I.
1986 Sojourner; Alien; Stranger. Pages 561–64 in vol. 4 of *ISBE*.

Blue, B.
1994 Acts and the House Church. Pages 119–222 in *The Book of Acts in Its Graeco-Roman Setting*. Edited by D. W. J. Gill and C. Gempf. Volume 2 of *The Book of Acts in Its First Century Setting*. Grand Rapids: Eerdmans.

Blum, G. G.
1963 *Tradition und Sukzession: Studien zum Normbegriff des Apostolischen von Paulus bis Irenäus*. Arbeiten zur Geschichte und Theologie des Luthertums 9. Berlin: Lutherisches.

Böcher, O.
1972 *Das Neue Testament und die dämonischen Mächte*. SBS 58. Stuttgart: Katholisches.
1990 "*ho diabolos*." Pages 297–98 in vol. 1 of *EDNT*.
1993 "*ho satanas*." Page 234 in vol. 3 of *EDNT*.

Bömer, F.
1957 Über die Brüderlichkeit in religiösen Gemeinschaften. Pages 172–79 in *Untersuchungen über die Religion der Sklaven in Griechenland und Rom*. Volume 1 of Akademie der Wissenschaften und der Literatur: Abhandlung der Geistes- und Sozialwissenschaftlichen Klasse 10. Mainz: Akademie der Wissenschaften.
1957–63 *Untersuchungen über die Religion der Sklaven in Griechenland und Rom*. 4 vols. Akademie der Wissenschaften und der Literatur: Abhandlung der Geistes- und Sozialwissenschaftlichen Klasse 10. Mainz: Akademie der Wissenschaften.

Boer, I.
1994 Das ius talionis im Neuen Testament. *NTS* 40:1–21.

Boismard, M.-É.
1956 Baptême et renouveau. *Lumen Vitae* 27:103–18.

Bolchazy, L.
1977 *Hospitality in Early Rome*. Chicago: University of Chicago Press.

Bolkestein, H.
1939 *Wohltätigkeit und Armenpflege im vorchristlichen Altertum*. Utrecht: Oosthoeck.

Bonhoeffer, D.
1948 *The Cost of Discipleship*. New York: Macmillan.

Bonnardière, A.-M. de la
1980 La prédication du Christ aux esprits en prison d'après l'interpretation de S. Augustin. Pages 247–67 in *Études sur la première lettre de Pierre*. LD 102. Paris: Cerf.

Bonner, C.
1940 *The Homily of the Passion by Melito Bishop of Sardis with Some Fragments of the Apocryphal Ezekiel*. London: Christophers / Philadelphia: University of Pennsylvania Press.

Borg, M. J.

1984 *Conflict, Holiness and Politics in the Teaching of Jesus.* Studies in the Bible and Early Christianity 5. New York: Edwin Mellen.

Boring, M. E.

1985 Criteria of Authenticity: The Lucan Beatitudes as a Test Case. *Forum* 1:3–38.

Boring, M. E., K. Berger, and C. Colpe, eds.

1995 *Hellenistic Commentary to the New Testament.* Nashville: Abingdon.

Borleffs, J. W. P.

1952 Institutum Neronianum. *VC* 6:129–45. [Reprinted pp. 217–34 in *Das frühe Christentum im römischen Staat.* Edited by R. Klein. 2d ed. Wege der Forschung 267. Darmstadt: Wissenschaftliche, 1982]

Bornhauser, K.

1921 Jesu Predigt für die Geister. *Allgemeine Evangelisch-Lutherische Kirchenzeitung* 54:322–24.

Bornkamm, G.

1968 "*presbys* etc." Pages 651–83 in vol. 6 of *TDNT.*

Bosetti, E.

1986 Quale etica nei codici domestici ("Haustafeln") del NT? *Rivista di Teologia Morale* 72:9–31.

1987 Codici familiari: Storia della ricerca e prospettive. *RivB* 35:129–79.

Botha, J.

1994 *Subject to Whose Authority?: Multiple Readings of Romans 13.* Emory Studies in Early Christianity 4. Atlanta: Scholars Press.

Botterweck, J.

1960 Hirt und Herde im Alten Testament und im Alten Orient. Pages 339–52 in *Die Kirche und ihre Ämter und Stände.* J. Kardinal Frings Festschrift. Edited by W. Corsten et al. Cologne: Bachem.

Bourdieu, P.

1966 The Sentiment of Honour in Kabyle Society. Pages 191–241 in *Honour and Shame: Values of Mediterranean Society.* Edited by J. G. Peristiany. Chicago: University of Chicago Press.

Bourguignon, E., ed.

1980 *A World of Women: Anthropological Studies in the Societies of the World.* Brooklyn: Praeger.

Bourke, M. M.

1970 The Petrine Office in the New Testament. Pages 1–12 in *Proceedings of the 25th Annual Convention of the Catholic Theological Society of America.* Yonkers, N.Y.: St. Joseph's Seminary.

Bousset, W.

1919–20 Zur Hadesfahrt Christi. *ZNW* 19:50–66.

Bowersock, G. W.

1965 *Augustus and the Greek World.* Oxford: Clarendon.

1995 *Martyrdom and Rome.* Cambridge: Cambridge University Press.

Bowman, J. W.

1962 Eschatology of the NT. Pages 135–40 in vol. 2 of *IDB.*

Bradley, K.

1987 *Slaves and Masters in the Roman Empire.* New York: Oxford University Press.

Brady, C.
1961 *Brotherly Love: A Study of the Word* Philadelphia *and its Contribution to the Biblical Theology of Brotherly Love.* Doctoral Dissertation, Fribourg University.

Brandt, W.
1931 *Dienst und Dienen im Neuen Testament.* Gütersloh: Gütersloher.

Branick, V. P.
1989 *The House Church in the Writings of Paul.* Wilmington, Delaware: Glazier.

Brattgard, H.
1963 *God's Stewards: A Theological Study of the Principles and Practices of Stewardship.* Minneapolis: Augsburg.

Braumann, G.
1962 *Vorpaulinische Christliche Taufverkündigung bei Paulus.* Stuttgart: Kohlhammer.

Braun, H.
1962 Vom Erbarmen Gottes über die Gerechten: Zur Theologie der Psalmen Salomos. Pages 8–69 in *Gesammelte Aufsätze zum Neuen Testament und seiner Umwelt.* Tübingen: Mohr.
1966 *Qumran und das Neue Testament.* 2 vols. Tübingen: Mohr (Siebeck).
1970 Das himmlische Vaterland bei Philo und im Hebräerbrief. Pages 319–27 in *Verborum Veritas.* G. Stählin Festschrift. Edited by O. Böcher and K. Haacker. Wuppertal: Brockhaus.

Bravo, F.
1964 *El Sacerdocio común de los creyentes en la teología de Lutero.* Vitoria.

Brayer, M.
1986 *The Jewish Woman in Rabbinic Literature.* 2 vols. New York: KTAV.

Brenner, A.
1985 *The Israelite Woman: Social Role and Literary Type in Biblical Narrative.* Biblical Seminar 2. Sheffield: JSOT Press.

Brettler, M. Z.
1989 *God Is King: Understanding an Israelite Metaphor.* JSOTSup 76. Sheffield: JSOT Press.

Breytenbach, C.
1993 Versöhnung, Stellvertretung und Sühne: Semantische und Traditionsgeschichtliche Bemerkungen am Beispiel der paulinischen Briefe. *NTS* 39:59–79.

Bristow, J. T.
1988 *What Paul Really Said about Women.* New York: Harper & Row.

Brixhe, C.
1987 *Essai sur le grec anatolien au début de notre ère.* 2d ed. Nancy: Presses Universitaires de Nancy.

Bromiley, G. W.
1979 Descent into Hell (Hades). Pages 926–27 in vol. 1 of *ISBE.*

Brooten, B.
1982 *Women Leaders in the Ancient Synagogue: Inscriptional Evidence and Background Issues.* Brown Judaic Studies 36. Chico, California: Scholars Press.

1985 Early Christian Women and Their Cultural Context: Issues in Method and Historical Reconstruction. Pages 65–91 in *Feminist Perspectives on Biblical Scholarship*. Edited by A. Yarbro Collins. Chico, California: Scholars Press.

1986 Jewish Women's History in the Roman Period: A Task for Christian Theology. *HTR* 79:22–30.

Broughton, T. R. S.

1938 Roman Asia Minor. Pages 499–918 in vol. 4 of *An Economic Survey of Ancient Rome*. Edited by T. Frank. Baltimore: Johns Hopkins University Press.

Brown, J. P.

1963 Synoptic Parallels in the Epistles and Form-History. *NTS* 10:27–48.

Brown, P.

1988 *The Body and Society: Men, Women, and Sexual Renunciation in Early Christianity*. New York: Columbia University Press.

Brown, R. E.

1970 *Priest and Bishop: Biblical Reflections*. New York: Paulist.

1984 *The Churches the Apostles Left Behind*. New York: Paulist.

1990 Further Reflections on the Origins of the Church of Rome. Pages 98–115 in *The Conversation Continues: Studies in Paul and John*. J. L. Martin Festschrift. Edited by R. T. Fortna and B. R. Gaventa. Nashville: Abingdon.

1994 *The Death of the Messiah—From Gethsemane to the Grave: A Commentary on the Passion Narratives in the Four Gospels*. 2 vols. Garden City, New York: Doubleday.

Brown, R. E., and J. P. Meier

1983 *Antioch and Rome: New Testament Cradles of Catholic Christianity*. New York: Paulist.

Brown, R. E., and S. M. Schneiders

1990 Hermeneutics. Pages 1146–65 in *NJBC*.

Brox, N.

1961 *Zeuge und Märtyrer: Untersuchungen zur frühchristlichen Zeugnis-Terminologie*. SANT 5. Munich: Kösel.

1973 Zum Problemstand in der Erforschung der altchristlichen Pseudepigraphie. *Kairos* 15:10–23.

1975b *Falsche Verfasserfragen: Zur Erklärung der frühchristlichen Pseudepigraphie*. SBS 79. Stuttgart: Katholisches.

Brox, N., ed.

1977b *Pseudepigraphie in der heidnischen und jüdisch-christlichen Antike*. Darmstadt: Wissenschaftliche.

Bruce, F. F.

1976 Elect, NT. Pages 258–59 in *IDBSup*.

Brunotte, W.

1959 *Das geistliche Amt bei Luther*. Berlin: Evangelische.

Bruns, J. E.

1969 The Roman Primacy in Recent Study. *Ecumenist* 7:65–67.

Brunt, P. A.

1980 Evidence Given under Torture in the Principate. *Zeitschrift der Savigny-Stiftung für Rechtsgeschichte* 97:256–65.

Brusten, C.
1897 *La descente du Christ aux enfers d'après les apôtres et d'après l'église.* Paris: Fischbacher.

Buber, M.
1967 *Kingship of God.* 3d ed. New York: Harper & Row.

Buchanan, E. S.
1911 An Old-Latin Text of the Catholic Epistles. *JTS* 12:487–534.

Büchler, A.
1967 *Studies in Sin and Atonement in the Rabbinic Literature of the First Century.* New York: KTAV.

Büchsel, F.
1964 "*artigennêtos, anagennaô.*" Pages 672–75 in vol. 1 of *TDNT.*

Bultmann, C.
1992 *Der Fremde im antiken Juda: Eine Untersuchung zum sozialen Typenbegriff* gêr *und seinem Bedeutungswandel in der alttestamentlichen Gesetzgebung.* FRLANT 153. Göttingen: Vandenhoeck & Ruprecht.

Bultmann, R.
1964 "*aischynô* etc." Pages 189–91 in vol. 1 of *TDNT.*

Burck, E.
1969 *Die Frau in der Antike.* Darmstadt: Wissenschaftliche.

Burgess, A.
1965 *A History of the Exegesis of Matthew 16,17–19 from 1781 to 1965.* Ann Arbor: Ann Arbor Microfilms.

Burke, D. G.
1979 Cross; Crucify. Pages 825–30 in vol. 1 of *ISBE.*

Buschmann, G.
1995 *Christou koinônos* (*MartPol* 6,2), das Martyrium und der ungeklärte *koinônos*-Titel der Montanisten. *ZNW* 86:243–64.

Cadbury, H. J.
1979 Note XXX: Names for Christians and Christianity in Acts. Pages 375–92 in vol. 5 of *The Acts of the Apostles.* Edited by K. Lake and H. J. Cadbury. Part 1 of *The Beginnings of Christianity.* London: Macmillan, 1933. Reprinted Grand Rapids: Baker.

Caird, G. B.
1956 *Principalities and Powers.* Oxford: Clarendon.

Calder, W. M., and J. Keil, eds.
1939 *Anatolian Studies Presented to William Hepburn Buckler.* Manchester: Manchester University Press.

Cambier, J.
1963 La bénédiction d'Eph 1, 3–14. *ZNW* 54:58–104.

Cameron, A., and A. Kuhrt, eds.
1983 *Images of Women in Antiquity.* Detroit: Wayne State University Press.

Camp, C.
1991 Understanding a Patriarchy: Women in Second Century Jerusalem through the Eyes of Ben Sira. Pages 1–39 in *"Women like This": New Perspectives on Jewish Women in the Greco-Roman World.* Edited by M. J. Levine. SBL: Early Judaism and Its Literature 1. Atlanta: Scholars Press.

Campbell, J. Y.
1932 *Koinonia* and Its Cognates in the New Testament. *JBL* 51:352–80.

Campbell, R. A.
1993 The Elders of the Jerusalem Church. *JTS* 44:511–28.
1994 *The Elders: Seniority within Earliest Christianity*. Edinburgh: T. & T. Clark.

Campenhausen, H. von
1964 *Die Idee des Martyriums in der alten Kirche*. 2d ed. Göttingen: Vandenhoeck & Ruprecht.
1968 The Origins of the Idea of Priesthood in the Early Church. Pages 217–30 in *Tradition and Life in the Church: Essays and Lectures in Church History*. Philadelphia: Fortress.
1969 *Ecclesiastical Authority and Spiritual Power in the Church of the First Three Centuries*. Stanford: Stanford University Press.

Canfield, L. H.
1913 *The Early Persecutions of the Christians*. Studies in History, Economics, and Public Law 55/2. New York: Columbia University Press. [Reprinted AMS Press, 1968]

Cantarella, E.
1987 *Pandora's Daughters: The Role and Status of Women in Greek and Roman Antiquity*. Translated by M. B. Fant. Baltimore: Johns Hopkins University Press.

Caragounis, C. C.
1990 *Peter and the Rock*. BZAW 58. Berlin: de Gruyter.

Carcopino, J.
1971 *Daily Life in Ancient Rome*. Edited by H. T. Rowell. New York: Bantam.

Cardellini, I.
1992 Stranieri ed "emigrati-residenti" in una sintesi di teologia storico-biblica. *RivB* 40:129–81.

Carder, M. M.
1970 A Caesarean Text in the Catholic Epistles? *NTS* 16:252–70.

Carr, A. W.
1981 *Angels and Principalities: The Background, Meaning and Development of the Pauline Phrase* Hai Archai kai Hai Exousiai. SNTSMS 42. Cambridge: Cambridge University Press.

Carrington, P.
1940 *The Primitive Christian Catechism: A Study in the Epistles*. Cambridge: Cambridge University Press.

Carter, W.
1994 *Households and Discipleship: A Study of Matthew 19–20*. JSNTSup 103. Sheffield: JSOT Press.

Castelli, E. A.
1994 Heteroglossia, Hermeneutics, and History: A Review Essay of Recent Feminist Studies of Early Christianity. *Journal of Feminist Studies in Religion* 10/2:73–98.

Cecchelli, C.
1955 Il Nome e la "Setta" dei Cristiani. *Rivista di Archeologia Cristiana* 32:55–73.

Chaine, J.
1934 Descente du Christ aux enfers. Columns 395–431 in vol. 2 of *DBSup*.

Charlesworth, J. H.
1992a Pseudepigrapha, OT. Pages 537–40 in vol. 5 of *ABD*.
1992b Pseudonymity and Pseudepigraphy. Pages 540–41 in vol. 5 of *ABD*.

Chilton, B.
1992 Jews in the NT. Pages 845–48 in vol. 3 of *ABD*.

Chryssavgis, J.
1987 The Royal Priesthood. *Greek Orthodox Theological Review* 32:373–77.

Clark, E. A.
1983 *Women in the Early Church*. Message of the Fathers of the Church 13. Wilmington: Glazier.
1990 Early Christian Women: Sources and Interpretation. Pages 19–35 in *The Gentle Strength: Historical Perspectives on Women in Christianity*. Edited by L. Coon et al. Charlottesville: University of Virginia.
1994 Ideology, History, and the Construction of "Woman" in Late Ancient Christianity. *JECS* 2:155–84.

Clark, E. A., and H. Richardson, eds.
1977 *Women and Religion: A Feminist Sourcebook of Christian Thought*. New York: Harper & Row.

Clemen, C.
1900 *"Niedergefahren zu den Toten": Ein Beitrag zur Würdigung des Apostolikums*. Giessen: Ricker.

Clines, D. J. A.
1976 *I, He, We and They: A Literary Approach to Isaiah* 53. JSOTSup 1. Sheffield: JSOT Press.

Cludius, H. H.
1808 *Uransichten des Christenthums nebst Untersuchungen über einige Bücher des neuen Testaments*. Altona.

Cody, A.
1964 When Is the Chosen People Called a Goy? *VT* 14:1–6.
1969 *A History of Old Testament Priesthood*. Analecta Biblica 35. Rome: Pontifical Biblical Institute.

Coenen, L.
1972 Presbyter. Pages 1003–10 in vol. 3 of *TBNT*.

Coleman-Norten, P. R.
1966 Appendix on Persecutions. Pages 1179–96 in vol. 3 of *Roman State and Christian Church: A Collection of Legal Documents to AD 535*. London: SPCK.

Collins, J. N.
1990 *Diakonia: Re-interpreting the Ancient Sources*. New York: Oxford University Press.

Collins, R. F.
1992 Marriage, New Testament. Pages 569–72 in vol. 4 of *ABD*.

Colpe, C.
1991 Höllenfahrt. Pages 1015–23 in vol. 15 of *RAC*.

Colpe, C., ed.
1977 *Die Diskussion um das "Heilige."* Wege der Forschung 305. Darmstadt: Wissenschaftliche.

Colpe, C., et al.
1995a Jenseits. Pages 246–407 in vol. 17 of *RAC*.

1995b Jenseitsfahrt I (Himmelfahrt). Pages 407–66 in vol. 17 of *RAC*.
1995c Jenseitsfahrt II (Unterwelts- oder Höllenfahrt). Pages 466–89 in vol. 17 of *RAC*.

Colpe, C., and P. Habermehl
1995 Jenseitsreise (Reise durch das Jenseits). Pages 490–543 in vol. 17 of *RAC*.

Colson, J.
1966 *Ministère de Jésus-Christ ou le Sacerdoce de l'Évangile: Étude sur la Condition Sacredotale des Ministres Chrétiens dans l'Église Primitive*. Théologie Historique 4. Paris: Beauchesne.
1972 Ecclesial Ministries and the Sacral. *Concilium* 80:64–74.

Colwell, E. C.
1970 Popular Reactions against Christianity in the Roman Empire. Pages 53–71 in *Environmental Factors in Christian History*. Shirley Jackson Case Festschrift. Edited by J. T. McNeill, M. Spinka, and H. R. Willoughby. Chicago: University of Chicago Press, 1939. Reprinted New York: Kennikat.

Congar, Y. M.-J.
1957 *Lay People in the Church: A Study for a Theology of Laity*. London: Chapman.
1962 *The Mystery of the Temple or the Manner of God's Presence to His Creatures from Genesis to the Apocalypse*. Westminster: Newman.

Conzelmann, H.
1974a "*charisma*." Pages 402–6 in vol. 9 of *TDNT*.
1974b "*phôs* etc." Pages 310–58 in vol. 9 of *TDNT*.

Conzelmann, H., and W. Zimmerli
1974 "*chairô, chara* etc." Pages 359–415 in vol. 9 of *TDNT*.

Coppens, J.
1928 Baptême. Columns 852–924 in vol. 1 of *DBSup*.

Coppens, J.
1971 Le sacerdoce Chrétien: Ses origines et son développement. Pages 49–101 in *Sacerdoce et Célibat: Études historiques et théologiques*. Edited by J. Coppens. BETL 28. Gembloux: Duculot / Louvain: Peeters.

Corley, K. E.
1993 *Private Women, Public Meals: Social Conflict and Women in the Synoptic Tradition*. Peabody, Massachusetts: Hendrickson.

Cornell, T., and J. Matthew
1982 *Atlas of the Roman World*. New York: Facts on File.

Coultre, J. le
1907 De l'étymologie du mot "Chrétien." *RTP* 40:188–96.

Counelis, J. S.
1953 *To basileion ierateuma kata tên synchronon didaskalian tês rômaiokatholikês ekklêsias*. Athens: Trempela.

Countryman, L. W.
1988 *Dirt, Greed and Sex: Sexual Ethics in the New Testament and Their Implications for Today*. Philadelphia: Fortress.

Cramer, J. A.
1971 *A Geographical and Historical Description of Asia Minor*. Amsterdam: Hakkert. [Reprint of 1832 ed.]

Cramer, J. A., ed.
1967 Pages 41–83 in *Catena in Epistolas Catholicas*. Volume 8 of *Catenae Graecorum Patrum in NT.* Oxford: Oxford University Press, 1840. Reprinted, Hildesheim: Olms.

Crehan, J.
1950 *Early Christian Baptism and the Creed*. London: Burn, Oates & Washbourne.

Crook, J. A.
1986 Women in Roman Succession. Pages 56–82 in *The Family in Ancient Rome: New Perspectives*. Edited by B. Rawson. Ithaca, N.Y.: Cornell University Press.

Crosby, M. H.
1988 *House of Disciples: Church, Economics, and Justice in Matthew*. Maryknoll, New York: Orbis.

Cross, F. M., Jr.
1961 *The Ancient Library of Qumran and Modern Biblical Studies*. Garden City, N.Y.: Doubleday.

Crouch, J. E.
1972 *The Origin and Intention of the Colossian Haustafeln*. FRLANT 109. Göttingen: Vandenhoeck & Ruprecht.

Cullmann, O.
1943 *Les premières confessions de foi Chrétienne*. Paris.
1959 *The Christology of the New Testament*. Rev. ed. Philadelphia: Westminster.
1968a "*petra*." Pages 95–99 in vol. 6 of *TDNT.*
1968b "*Petros, Kêphas*." Pages 100–112 in vol. 6 of *TDNT.*

Curren, C. E., and R. A. McCormick, eds.
1984 *The Use of Scripture in Moral Theology*. Readings in Moral Theology 4. New York: Paulist.

Dabin, P.
1941 *Le sacerdoce royal des fidèles dans les livres saints*. Paris: Bloud & Gay.
1950 *Le sacerdoce royal des fidèles dans la tradition ancienne et moderne*. Museum Lessianum, section théologie 48. Brussels: L'édition Universelle / Paris: Desclée de Brouwer.

Dahl, M. E.
1962 *The Resurrection of the Body*. SBT 36. London: SCM.

Dahl, N. A.
1941 *Das Volk Gottes: Eine Untersuchung zum Kirchenbewusstsein des Urchristentums*. Skrifter utgitt av Det Norske Videnskaps-Akademi i Oslo, II: Historisk-Filosofisk Klasse 2. Oslo.
1951 Adresse und Proömium des Epheserbriefes. *TZ* 7:241–64.

Danielou, J.
1947 Déluge, Baptême, Jugement. *Dieu Vivant* 8:97–112.
1950 *Sacramentum futuri: Études sur les origines de la typologie biblique*. Études de théologie historique 19. Paris: Beauchesne.
1956 *The Bible and the Liturgy*. University of Notre Dame Liturgical Studies 3. Notre Dame: University of Notre Dame Press.
1961 *The Ministry of Women in the Early Church*. London: Faith.
1964 *The Theology of Jewish Christianity*. Vol. 1 of *The Development of Christian Doctrine before the Council of Nicaea*. Chicago: Regnery.

Danker, F. W.
1982 *Benefactor: Epigraphic Study of of a Graceo-Roman and New Testament Semantic Field*. St. Louis: Clayton.
1992 Associations, Clubs, Thiasoi. Pages 501–3 in vol. 1 of *ABD*.
Dassmann, E.
1984 Hausgemeinde und Bischofsamt. Pages 82–97 in JAC Ergänzungsband 11. Edited by J. Engemann. Münster: Aschendorff.
Daube, D.
1947 *Kerdainô* as a Missionary Term. *HTR* 40:102–20.
1963 *The Exodus Pattern in the Bible*. Oxford: All Souls.
1966 Haustafeln. Pages 90–105 in *The New Testament and Rabbinic Judaism*. London: Athlone.
Dautzenberg, G.
1983 Zur Stellung der Frauen in den paulinischen Gemeinden. Pages 182–224 in *Die Frau im Urchristentum*. QD 95. Freiburg: Herder.
Davidson, R. M.
1981 *Typology in Scripture: A Study of Hermeneutical typos Structures*. Andrews University Seminary Doctoral Dissertation Series 2. Berrien Springs, Michigan: Andrews University Press.
Davies, G. H.
1962 Elder in the OT. Pages 72–73 in vol. 2 of *IDB*.
Davies, J. G.
1958 *He Ascended into Heaven: A Study in the History of Doctrine*. London: Lutterworth.
Davies, S. L.
1980 *The Revolt of the Widows: The Social World of the Apocryphal Acts*. Carbondale: Southern Illinois University Press.
Davies, W. D.
1967 *Paul and Rabbinic Judaism: Some Rabbinic Elements in Pauline Theology*. Rev. ed. New York: Harper & Row.
Davies, W. D., and D. Daube, eds.
1954 *The Background of the New Testament and Its Eschatology*. C. H. Dodd Festschrift. Cambridge: Cambridge University Press.
Davis, J.
1977 *People of the Mediterranean*. London: Routledge & Kegan Paul.
1984 The Sexual Division of Labour in the Mediterranean. Pages 17–50 in *Religion, Power, and Protest in Local Communities: The Northern Shore of the Mediterranean*. Edited by Eric Wolf. New York: Moulton.
Dean-Jones, L.
1991 The Cultural Construct of the Female Body in Classical Greek Science. Pages 111–37 in *Women's History and Ancient History*. Edited by S. B. Pomeroy. Chapel Hill: University of North Carolina Press.
Deichgräber, R.
1967 *Gotteshymnus und Christushymnus in der frühen Christenheit: Untersuchungen zu Form, Sprache und Stil der frühchristlichen Hymnen*. SUNT 5. Göttingen: Vandenhoeck & Ruprecht.
1980 Benediktionen, II: Neues Testament. Pages 562–64 in vol. 5 of *TRE*.
Deissmann, A.
1901 *Bible Studies*. Translated by A. Grieve. Edinburgh: T.& T. Clark.

1923 *Licht vom Osten: Das Neue Testament und die neuentdeckten Texte der hellenistisch-römischen Welt*. 4th ed. Tübingen: Mohr (Siebeck).

Delany, C.
1987 Seeds of Honor, Fields of Shame. Pages 35–48 in *Honor and Shame and the Unity of the Mediterranean*. Edited by D. D. Gilmore. Washington, D.C.: American Anthropological Association.

Dell, A.
1914 Matthäus 16,17–19. *ZNW* 15:1–49.

Delling, G.
1931 *Paulus' Stellung zu Frau und Ehe*. Stuttgart: Kohlhammer.
1962 *Worship in the New Testament*. Philadelphia: Westminster.
1965 Zur Taufe von "Häusern" im Urchristentum. *NovT* 7:285–311.
1970 Die Bezugnahme vom neutestamentlichen *eis* auf Vorgegebenes. Pages 211–23 in *Verborum Veritas*. G. Stählin Festschrift. Edited by O. Böcher and K. Haacker. Wuppertal: Brockhaus.
1972a "*tassô* etc." Pages 27–48 in vol. 8 of *TDNT*.
1972b "*telos* etc." Pages 49–87 in vol. 8 of *TDNT*.
1978 Geschlechter, Geschlechtstrieb, Geschlechtsverkehr. Pages 780–829 in vol. 10 of *RAC*.
1987 *Die Bewältigung der Diasporasituation durch das Hellenistische Judentum*. Göttingen: Vandenhoeck & Ruprecht.

Delorme, J.
1956 Le practique du baptême dans le judaisme contemporain des origines chrétiennes. *Lumen Vitae* 26:21–60.

Delorme, J., ed.
1974 *Le Ministère et les Ministères selon le Nouveau Testament*. Parole de Dieu 10. Paris: Seuil.

DeRidder, R. R.
1971 *The Dispersion of the People of God*. Kampen: Kok.

Derrett, J. D. M.
1978 *Midrash in Action and as a Literary Device*. Volume 2 in *Studies in the New Testament*. Leiden: Brill.

Deubner, L.
1933 Die Bedeutung des Kranzes im klassichen Altertum. *AR* 30:70–104.

De Vos, C. S
1993 "Kai O OIKOS . . .": *The Nature and Religious Practices of Graeco-Roman Households as the Context for the Conversion and Baptism of Households in the Acts of the Apostles*. Ph.D. Thesis, Flinders University, Adelaide.

Dewdney, J. C.
1971 *Turkey: An Introductory Geography*. New York: Praeger.

Dexinger, F.
1982 Erwählung, II: Judentum. Pages 189–92 in vol. 10 of *TRE*.

Dibelius, M.
1942/1956 Rom und die Christen im ersten Jahrhundert. *Sitzungsberichte der Heidelberger Akademie der Wissenschaften, Phil.-hist. Kl.* 2 (1942). Reprinted pp. 177–228 in vol. 2 of *Botschaft und Geschichte: Gesammelte Aufsätze*. Tübingen: Mohr (Siebeck), 1956.
1953 Pages 48–50, 93–96 in *An die Kolosser, an die Epheser, an Philemon*. HNT 12. Tübingen: Mohr (Siebeck). [1st ed., 1913]

1955 *Die Pastoralbriefe*. HNT 13. Tübingen: Mohr (Siebeck).

Dickey, S.
1928 Some Economic and Social Conditions of Asia Minor Affecting the Expansion of Christianity. Pages 393–416 in *Studies in Early Christianity*. F. C. Porter and B. W. Bacon Festschrift. Edited by S. J. Case. New York: Century.

Dickie, J.
1979 Christian. Page 657 in vol. 1 of *ISBE*.

Dietelmair, J. A.
1762 *Historia dogmatis de descensu Christi ad inferos literaria*. Altdorf: Schupfell.

Dihle, A.
1988 Heilig. Pages 1–63 in vol. 14 of *RAC*.

Dihle, A., B. Studer, and F. Rickert
1991 Hoffnung. Pages 1159–1250 in vol. 15 of *RAC*.

Dill, S.
1925 *Roman Society from Nero to Marcus Aurelius*. 2d ed. London: Macmillan.

Dillon, M., and L. Garland
1994 *Ancient Greece: Social and Historical Documents from Archaic Times to the Death of Socrates (c. 800–399 BC)*. London: Routledge.

Dimant, D.
1978 1 Enoch 6–11: A Methodological Perspective. Pages 323–39 in vol. 1 of *SBL 1978: Seminar Papers*. SBLSP 17. Missoula, Montana: Scholars Press.

Dinkler, E.
1971 Die Taufaussagen des Neuen Testaments. Pages 60–153 in *Zu Karl Barths Lehre von der Taufe*. Edited by F. Viering. Gütersloh.

Dixon, S.
1984 *Infirmitas Sexus*: Womanly Weakness in Roman Law. *Tijdschrift voor Rechtsgeschiedenis* 52:343–71.

Doberstein, J. W.
1954 Introduction to Dietrich Bonhoeffer, *Life Together*. New York: Harper.

Doblhofer, E.
1987 *Exil und Emigration: Zum Erlebnis der Heimatferne in der römischen Literatur*. Impulse der Forschung 51. Darmstadt: Wissenschaftliche.

Dockx, S.
1984a Essai de chronologie de la vie de saint Marc. Pages 179–98 in *Chronologies néotestamentaires et Vie de l'Église primitive: Recherches exégétiques*. Leuven: Peeters.
1984b Silas a-t-il été le compagnon de voyage de Paul d'Antioche à Corinthe? Pages 97–101 in *Chronologies néotestamentaires et Vie de l'Église primitive: Recherches exégétiques*. Leuven: Peeters.

Dodd, C. H.
1953 *According to the Scriptures: The Sub-structure of New Testament Theology*. Digswell Place, Welwyn, Herts: Nisbet.
1959 The Primitive Catechism. Pages 106–18 in *New Testament Essays*. T. W. Manson Festschrift. Edited by A. J. B. Higgins. Manchester: Manchester University Press.

Doehler, G.
1975 Descent into Hell. *The Springfielder* 39:2–19.

Donfried, K. P., ed.
1991 *The Romans Debate*. Rev. ed. Peabody, Massachusetts: Hendrickson.

Donohue, J. R.
1993 The Challenge of the Biblical Renewal to Moral Theology. Pages 59–80 in *Riding Time like a River: The Catholic Moral Tradition since Vatican II*. Edited by William J. O'Brien. Washington, D.C.: Georgetown University Press.

Doty, W. G.
1969 The Classification of Epistolary Literature. *CBQ* 31:183–99.
1973 *Letters in Primitive Christianity*. Philadelphia: Fortress.

Douglas, M.
1973 *Purity and Danger: An Analysis of Concepts of Pollution and Taboo*. London: Routledge & Kegan Paul.
1982 *Natural Symbols*. New York: Pantheon.

Downey, G.
1961 *A History of Antioch in Syria, from Seleucus to the Arab Conquest*. Princeton: Princeton University Press.

Droge, A. J., and J. D. Tabor
1992 *A Noble Death: Suicide and Martyrdom among Christians and Jews in Antiquity*. San Francisco: HarperSanFrancisco.

Dubisch, J., ed.
1986 *Gender and Power in Rural Greece*. Princeton: Princeton University Press.

Duling, D. C., and N. Perrin
1994 *The New Testament: Proclamation and Parenesis, Myth and History*. Fort Worth: Harcourt Brace.

Dumas, A.
1970 La soumission mutuelle dans les épîtres. *Communion: Verbum Caro* 24:4–19.

Dunn, J. D. G.
1970 *Baptism in the Holy Spirit*. SBT 15. London: SCM.
1980 *Christology in the Making*. Philadelphia: Westminster.
1995 Judaism in the Land of Israel in the First Century. Pages 229–61 in *Judaism in Late Antiquity, Part Two: Historical Syntheses*. Edited by J. Neusner. Leiden: Brill.

Dupar, K. W.
1971 *A Study of the New Testament Haustafeln*. Edinburgh: New College Library.

Duplacy, J.
1962 Critique Textuelle du Nouveau Testament. *RSR* 50:242–62.
1969–70 "Le Texte Occidentale" des Épîtres Catholiques. *NTS* 16:397–99.

du Toit, A. B.
1979 Die Charismata. *Nederduitse Gereformeerde Teologiese Tydskrif* 20:189–200.

Eastwood, C.
1962 *The Priesthood of All Believers: An Examination of the Doctrine from the Reformation to the Present Day*. Minneapolis: Augsburg.
1963 *The Royal Priesthood of the Faithful: An Investigation of the Doctrine from Biblical Times to the Reformation*. Minneapolis: Augsburg.

Eck, O.
1940 *Urgemeinde und Imperium: Ein Beitrag zur Frage nach der Stellung des Urchristentums zum Staat*. BFCT 42. Gütersloh: Bertelsmann.
Eckert, J.
1982 Erwählung, III: Neues Testament. Pages 192–97 in vol. 10 of *TRE*.
Eddy, S. K.
1961 *The King Is Dead: Studies in the Near Eastern Resistance to Hellenism, 334–331 B.C.* Lincoln: University of Nebraska Press.
Edwards, D. R.
1992 Dress and Ornamentation. Pages 232–38 in vol. 2 of *ABD*.
Eilberg-Schwartz, H.
1990 *The Savage in Judaism*. Bloomington: Indiana University Press.
Eisenstadt, S. N., ed.
1968 *Max Weber on Charisma and Institution Building: Selected Papers*. Chicago: University of Chicago Press.
Ellington, J.
1990 Kissing in the Bible: Form and Meaning. *BT* 41:409–16.
Elliott, J. H.
1969 The Particularity of the Gospel: Good News for Changing Times. *CTM* 40:369–78.
1984 Philemon and House Churches. *TBT* 22:145–50.
1987 Patronage and Clientism in Early Christian Society: A Short Reading Guide. *Forum* 3:39–48.
1988 The Fear of the Leer: The Evil Eye from the Bible to Li'l Abner. *Forum* 4:42–71.
1990 Paul, Galatians and the Evil Eye. *CurTM* 17:262–73.
1991 Temple versus Household in Luke–Acts: A Contrast in Social Institutions. Pages 211–40 in *The Social World of Luke–Acts: Models for Interpretation*. Edited by J. H. Neyrey. Peabody, Massachusetts: Hendrickson, 1991. Published also in *Hervormde Teologiese Studies* 47 (1991):88–120.
1992c Matthew 20:1–15: A Parable of Invidious Comparison and Evil Eye Accusation. *BTB* 22:53–66.
1993b The Epistle of James in Rhetorical and Social-Scientific Perspective: Holiness-Wholeness and Patterns of Replication. *BTB* 23:71–81.
1993c *What Is Social-Scientific Criticism?* Guides to Biblical Scholarship. Minneapolis: Fortress.
1995b The Jewish Messianic Movement: From Faction to Sect. Pages 75–95 in *Modelling Early Christianity: Social-Scientific Studies of the New Testament in its Context*. Edited by P. Esler. London: Routledge.
1996 Patronage and Clientage. Pages 144–56 in *The Social Sciences and New Testament Interpretation*. Edited by R. L. Rohrbaugh. Peabody, Massachusetts: Hendrickson.
Elliott, J. H., ed.
1986b *Semeia* 35 (*Social-Scientific Criticism of the New Testament and Its Social World*). Atlanta: Scholars Press.
Ellis, E. E.
1957 *Paul's Use of the Old Testament*. Edinburgh: Oliver & Boyd.
1971 Paul and his Co-workers. *NTS* 17:437–52.

1992 Pseudonymity and Canonicity of New Testament Documents. Pages 212–24 in *Worship, Theology and Ministry in the Early Church*. Ralph P. Martin Festschrift. JSNTSup 87. Sheffield: Sheffield Academic Press.

Ellis, R. R.
1988 *An Examination of the Covenant Promises of Exodus 19:5–6 and Their Significance for Israel*. Th.D. Dissertation, Southwestern Baptist Theological Seminary.

Engelken, K.
1990 *Frauen im Alten Israel: Eine begriffsgeschichtliche und sozialrechtliche Studie zur Stellung der Frau im Alten Testament*. BWANT 130. Stuttgart: Kohlhammer.

Engemann, J.
1991 Hirt. Pages 577–607 in vol. 15 of *RAC*.

Esler, P., ed.
1995 *Modelling Early Christianity: Social-Scientific Studies of the New Testament in Its Context*. London: Routledge.

Euler, K. F.
1934 *Die Verkündigung vom leidenden Gottesknecht in der griechischen Bibel*. BWANT 4. Stuttgart: Kohlhammer.

Fanthan, E., et al.
1994 *Women in the Classical World: Image and Text*. New York: Oxford University Press.

Fascher, E.
1954 Theologische Beoachtungen zu *dei*. Pages 228–54 in *Neutestamentliche Studien für Rudolf Bultmann*. BZNW 21. Berlin: Alfred Töpelmann.
1958 *Jesaia 53 in Christlicher und Jüdischer Sicht*. Berlin: Evangelische.
1966 Erwählung. Pages 409–36 in vol. 6 of *RAC*.

Feldman, L. H.
1993 *Jew and Gentile in the Ancient World: Attitudes and Interactions from Alexander to Justinian*. Princeton: Princeton University Press.

Ferguson, E.
1980 Spiritual Sacrifice in Early Christianity and its Environment. *ANRW* 2.23.2:1151–89.
1984 *Demonology of the Early Christian World*. Symposium Series 12. New York: Edwin Mellen.

Fiedler, M. J.
1970 *Dikaiosyne* in der diaspora-jüdischen und intertestamentarischen Literatur. *JSJ* 1:120–43.

Fiedler, P.
1986 Haustafel. Pages 1063–73 in vol. 13 of *RAC*.

Filson, F. V.
1939 The Significance of the Early House Churches. *JBL* 58:105–12.
1962 Pontus. Pages 841–42 in vol. 3 of *IDB*.

Finegan, J.
1981 *The Archeology of the New Testament: The Mediterranean World of the Early Christian Apostles*. Boulder, Colorado: Westview.

Fink, J.
1955 *Noe der Gerechte in der frühchristlichen Kunst*. Beihefte zum Archiv für Kulturgeschichte 4. Münster/Cologne: Bolau.

Finley, M. I.
1968 *Aspects of Antiquity*. New York: Viking.
1980 *Ancient Slavery and Modern Ideology*. New York: Viking.
Finley, M. I., ed.
1987 *Classical Slavery*. Totowa, New Jersey: Cass.
Fischer, K. M.
1973 *Tendenz und Absicht des Epheserbriefes*. FRLANT 111. Göttingen: Vandenhoeck & Ruprecht.
1976 Anmerkungen zur Pseudepigraphie im Neuen Testament. *NTS* 23:76–81.
Fitzgerald, J. T.
1992 Virtue/Vice Lists. Pages 857–58 in vol. 6 of *ABD*.
Fitzmyer, J. A.
1957 4Q Testimonia and the New Testament. *TS* 18:513–37.
1960–61 The Use of Explicit Old Testament Quotations in Qumran Literature and in the New Testament. *NTS* 7:297–333.
1975 *The Dead Sea Scrolls: Major Publications and Tools for Study*. SBL Sources for Biblical Study 8. Missoula, Montana: Scholars Press.
1981 Aramaic *Kephâ'* and Peter's Name in the New Testament. Pages 112–24 in *To Advance the Gospel*. New York: Crossroad.
1993 *Romans*. AB 33. New York: Doubleday.
Flusser, D.
1958 The Dead Sea Sect and Pre-Pauline Christianity. Pages 215–66 in *Aspects of the Dead Sea Scrolls*. Edited by C. Rabin and Y. Yadin. ScrHier 3. Jerusalem: Magnes.
Foakes-Jackson, F. J., and K. Lake, eds.
1979 Volume 5 of *The Beginnings of Christianity, Part 1: The Acts of the Apostles*. Edited by K. Lake and H. J. Cadbury. Grand Rapids: Baker.
Foerster, W.
1971 "*sebomai, asebês*, etc." Pages 168–96 in vol. 7 of *TDNT*.
Foerster, W., and G. Fohrer
1971 "*sôizô* etc." Pages 965–1024 in vol. 7 of *TDNT*.
Foerster, W., and K. Schäferdiek
1971 "*satanas*." Pages 151–65 in vol. 7 of *TDNT*.
Foerster, W., and G. von Rad
1964 "*diabolos*." Pages 72–81 in vol. 2 of *TDNT*.
Fohrer, G.
1963 Priesterliches Königtum. *TZ* (1963):359–62.
Forbes, C. A.
1933 *Neoi: A Contribution to the Study of Greek Associations*. Philological Monographs published by the American Philological Association 2. Middleton, Connecticut: American Philological Association.
Foster, G. M.
1965 Peasant Society and the Image of Limited Good. *American Anthropologist* 67:293–315.
1972 The Anatomy of Envy: A Study in Symbolic Behavior. *Current Anthropology* 13:165–202.
Foucault, M.
1985 *The Use of Pleasure*. Volume 2 of *The History of Sexuality*. New York: Pantheon.

Fraeyman, M.
1947 La spiritualisation de l'idée du temple dans les épîtres pauliniennes. *ETL* 33:378–412.

Frend, W. H. C.
1958 The Persecutions: Some Links between Judaism and the Early Church. *JEH* 9:141–58.
1967 *Martyrdom and Persecution in the Early Church: A Study of a Conflict from the Maccabees to Donatus*. Garden City, New York: Doubleday.
1980 Bekehrung, I: Alte Kirche und Mittelalter. Pages 440–42 in vol. 5 of *TRE*.
1984 *The Rise of Christianity*. Philadelphia: Fortress.

Freudenberger, R.
1969 *Das Verhalten der römischen Behörden gegen die Christen im 2. Jahrhundert, dargestellt am Brief des Plinius an Trajan und den Reskripten Trajans und Hadrians*. 2d ed. MBPF 25. Munich.

Freyne, S.
1985 Vilifying the Other and Defining the Self: Matthew's and John's Anti-Jewish Polemic in Focus. Pages 117–43 in *"To See Ourselves as Others See Us": Christians, Jews, "Others" in Late Antiquity*. Edited by J. Neusner and E. S. Frerichs. Chico, California: Scholars Press.

Friedrich, G.
1964 "*euaggelizomai*, etc." Pages 707–37 in vol. 2 of *TDNT*.

Fuchs, H.
1950 Tacitus über die Christen. *VC* 4:65–93.
1964 *Der geistige Widerstand gegen Rom in der antiken Welt*. 2d ed. Berlin: de Gruyter.

Füglister, N.
1963 *Die Heilsbedeutung des Pascha*. Munich: Kösel.

Fuller, D. P.
1988 Satan. Pages 340–44 in vol. 4 of *ISBE*.

Gärtner, B.
1965 *The Temple and the Community in Qumran and the New Testament: A Comparative Study in the Temple Symbolism of the Qumran Texts and the New Testament*. SNTSMS 1. Cambridge: Cambridge University Press.

Gager, J.
1971 Religion and Social Class in the Early Roman Empire. Pages 99–120 in *The Catacombs and the Colosseum: The Roman Empire as the Setting of Primitive Christianity*. Edited by S. Benko and J. J. O'Rourke. Valley Forge: Judson.

Galanté, A
1937–39 *Histoire des juifs d'Anatolie*. 2 vols. Istanbul: Babok.

Galling, K.
1928 *Die Erwählungstradition Israels*. BZAW 48. Giessen.

Galling, K., and B. Altaner
1950 Babylon. Pages 1118–34 in vol. 1 of *RAC*.

Gammie, J. G.
1989 *Holiness in Israel*. Minneapolis: Fortress.
1990 Paraenetic Literature: Toward the Morphology of a Secondary Genre. *Semeia* 50 (*Paraenesis: Act and Form*):41–77.

Ganschinietz, R.
1919 Katabasis. Columns 2359–2449 in vol. 10/2 of *PW.*
Gardner, J. F.
1991 *Women in Roman Law and Society.* London: Croom Helm, 1986. Reprinted Bloomington: Indiana University Press.
Garnsey, P., and R. Saller
1987 *The Roman Empire: Economy, Society, and Culture.* Berkeley: University of California Press.
Garrett, J. L.
1979 The Pre-Cyprianic Doctrine of the Priesthood of All Christians. Pages 45–61 in *Continuity and Discontinuity in Church History.* G. W. Williams Festschrift. Edited by F. Forrester Church and T. George. Leiden: Brill.
Gaster, T. H.
1962 Satan. Pages 224–28 in vol. 4 of *IDB.*
Gaudemet, J., and E. Fascher
1972 Fremder. Pages 306–47 in vol. 8 of *RAC.*
Gauthier, P.
1988 Métèques, perièques et paroikoi: Bilan et Points d'interrogation. Pages 23–46 in *L'Étranger dans le monde grec.* Edited by R. Lonis. Actes du colloque organisé par l'Institut d'Études Anciennes Nancy, mai 1987. Nancy: Presses Universitaires de Nancy.
Gaventa, B. R.
1986 *From Darkness to Light: Aspects of Conversion in the New Testament.* Philadelphia: Fortress.
Gennrich, P.
1907 *Die Lehre von der Wiedergeburt, die christliche Zentrallehre in dogmengeschichtlicher und religionsgeschichtlicher Beleuchtung.* Leipzig: Deichert.
George, A., ed.
1964 *Baptism in the New Testament.* Baltimore: Helicon.
Georgi, D.
1971 Predigt. *EvT* 31:187–92.
Gercke, A.
1911 Der Christenname ein Scheltname. Pages 360–73 in *Festschrift zur Jahrhundertfeier der Universität Breslau.* Edited by T. Siebs. Breslau: M. & H. Marcus.
Gielen, M.
1986 Zur Interpretation der paulinischen Formel *hê kat' oikon ekklêsia.* ZNW 77:109–25.
1990 *Tradition und Theologie neutestamentlicher Haustafelethik: Ein Beitrag zur Frage einer christlichen Auseinandersetzung mit gesellschaftlichen Normen.* Athenäums Monographien, Theologie. BBB 75. Frankfurt: Hain.
Giesen, H.
1982 *Christliches Handeln: Eine redaktionsgeschichtliche Untersuchung zum* dikaiosynê*-Begriff im Matthäus-Evangelium.* Europäische Hochschulschriften 181. Frankfurt am Main: Lang.
Gignac, F. T.
1976 *Phonology.* Volume 1 of *A Grammar of the Greek Papyri of the Roman and Byzantine Periods.* Milan: Istituto Editoriale Cisalpino—La Goliardica.

Gill, D. W. J., and C. Gempf, eds.
1994 *The Book of Acts in Its First Century Setting*. Volume 2 of *The Book of Acts in Its Graeco-Roman Setting*. Grand Rapids: Eerdmans.
Gillman, J.
1992 Silas. Pages 22–23 in vol. 6 of *ABD*.
Gilmore, D.
1982 Anthropology of the Mediterranean Area. *Annual Review of Anthropology* 11:175–205.
Gilmore, D., ed.
1987 *Honor and Shame and the Unity of the Mediterranean*. American Anthropological Association Special Publication 22. Washington, D.C.: American Anthropological Association.
Gnilka, J.
1980 *Der Kolosserbrief*. HTKNT 10/1. Freiburg: Herder.
1983 Die neutestamentliche Hausgemeinde. Pages 229–42 in *Freude am Gottesdienst: Aspekte ursprünglicher Liturgie*. J. Plöger Festschrift. Edited by J. Schreiner. Stuttgart.
Goldie, R.
1979 Laity: A Bibliographical Survey of Three Decades. *The Laity Today* 26:107–43.
Gomez, M. G.
1962 *Episcopos y Presbyteros: Evolución semántica de los terminos episkopos-presbyteros, desde Homero hasta el siglo segundo después de Jesucristo*. Publicaciones de la Facultad Teologica del Norte de España. Burgo: Aldecoa.
Goodspeed, E.
1942 *A History of Early Christian Literature*. Chicago: University of Chicago Press.
Goppelt, L.
1968 Der Staat in der Sicht des Neuen Testaments. Pages 190–207 in *Christologie und Ethik: Aufsätze zum Neuen Testament*. Edited by L. Goppelt. Göttingen: Vandenhoeck & Ruprecht.
1970 *Apostolic and Post-apostolic Times*. New York: Harper & Row.
1972 "*typos, antitypos* etc." Pages 246–59 in vol. 8 of *TDNT*.
1973 Jesus und die "Haustafel"-Tradition. Pages 93–106 in *Orientierungen an Jesus: Zur Theologie der Synoptiker*. Josef Schmid Festschrift. Edited by P. Hoffmann, N. Brox, and W. Pesch. Freiburg: Herder.
1981 *Typos: The Typological Interpretation of the Old Testament in the New Testament*. Translated by D. H. Madvig. Grand Rapids: Eerdmans.
Gottwald, N. K.
1967 *The Church Unbounded: A Human Church in a Human World*. Philadelphia: Lippincott.
Gouldner, A. W.
1969 *The Hellenic World: A Sociological Analysis*. New York: Harper & Row.
Grant, M.
1971 *Ancient History Atlas*. New York: Macmillan.
Grant, R. M.
1988 *Greek Apologists of the Second Century*. Philadelphia: Westminster.

Green, G. L.
1990 The Use of the Old Testament for Christian Ethics in 1 Peter. *TynBul* 41:276–89.

Greeven, H.
1964 "*eperōtēma*." Pages 688–89 in vol. 2 of *TDNT*.

Grégoire, H.
1964 *Les persécutions dans l'empire romain*. 2d ed. Brussels: Palais des Académies.

Grelot, P.
1956 Notes sur le Testament Araméen de Levi (Fragment de la Bodleian Library, colonne a). *RB* 63:391–406.
1958 La légende d'Hénoch dans les apocryphes et dans la Bible. *RevScRel* 46:5–26, 181–210.
1990 Le ministère chrétien dans sa dimension sacerdotale. *NRTh* 112:161–82.

Grillmeier, A.
1957 Höllenabsteig Christi. Pages 450–55 in vol. 5 of *LTK*.
1975 Der Gottessohn im Totenreich: Soteriologische und christologische Motivierung der Descensuslehre in der älteren christlichen Überlieferung. *ZKT* 71 (1949) 1–53, 184–203. Reprinted pp. 76–174 in *Mit Ihm und in Ihm: Christologische Forschungen und Perspektiven*. Freiburg: Herder.

Grundmann, W.
1959 Die *nêpioi* in der urchristlichen Paränese. *NTS* 5:188–205.
1964a "*agathos* etc." Pages 10–18 in vol. 1 of *TDNT*.
1964b "*dêmos* etc." Pages 63–65 in vol. 2 of *TDNT*.
1965 "*kakos* etc." Pages 469–87 in vol. 3 of *TDNT*.
1971a "*stêkô, istêmi*." Pages 636–53 in vol. 7 of *TDNT*.
1971b "*stephanos* etc." Pages 615–36 in vol. 7 of *TDNT*.
1972 "*tapeinos* etc." Pages 1–26 in vol. 8 of *TDNT*.

Grundmann, W., and G. Bertram
1965 "*kalos*." Pages 536–56 in vol. 3 of *TDNT*.

Grundmann, W., et al.
1974 "*chriô* etc." Pages 493–580 in vol. 9 of *TDNT*.

Güder, E.
1853 *Die Lehre von der Erscheinung Christi unter den Toten, in ihrem Zusammenhang mit der Lehre von den letzten Dingen*. Bern: Jent & Reinert.

Gülzow, H.
1969 *Christentum und Sklaverei in den ersten drei Jahrhunderten*. Bonn: Habelt.
1974 Soziale Gegebenheiten der altkirchlichen Mission. Pages 189–226 in *Die Alte Kirche*. Edited by H. Frohnes and U. W. Knorr. Volume 1 of *Kirchengeschichte als Missionsgeschichte*. Edited by H. Frohnes, H. W. Gensichen, and G. Kretschmar. Munich: Kaiser.

Guerra, M.
1969 Problematica del sacerdocio ministerial en las primeras communidades cristianas. Pages 11–91 in *Theologia del Sacerdocio: Orientaciones Metodologicas*. Burgos: Aldecoa.

Guinan, M. D.
1992 Mosaic Covenant. Pages 905–9 in vol. 4 of *ABD*.

Guterman, S. L.
1951 *Religious Toleration and Persecution in Ancient Rome*. London: Aiglon.
Guthrie, D.
1965 The Development of the Idea of Canonical Pseudepigrapha in New Testament Criticism. Pages 14–39 in *The Authorship and Integrity of the New Testament*. Theological Collections 4. London: SPCK.
Haag, H.
1980 *Teufelsglaube*. 2d ed. Tübingen: Mohr (Siebeck).
1985 *Der Gottesknecht bei Deuterojesaja*. Erträge der Forschung 233. Darmstadt: Wissenschaftliche.
Haas, P. J., ed.
1992 *Recovering the Role of Women: Power and Authority in Rabbinic Jewish Society*. South Florida Studies in the History of Judaism 59. Atlanta: Scholars Press.
Haenchen, E.
1971 *The Acts of the Apostles: A Commentary*. Philadelphia: Westminster.
Haendler, G.
1981 *Luther: On Ministerial Office and Congregational Function*. Philadelphia: Fortress.
Hahn, F.
1973 *The Worship of the Early Church*. Philadelphia: Fortress.
1974 Der Apostolat im Urchristentum. *KD* 20:54–77.
Hainz, J.
1991 "*koinônia* etc." Pages 303–5 in vol. 2 of *EDNT*.
Hall, S. G.
1979 *Melito of Sardis On Pascha and Fragments*. Oxford: Clarendon.
Hallett, J. P.
1984 *Fathers and Daughters in Roman Society: Women and the Elite Family*. Princeton: Princeton University Press.
Hamerton-Kelly, R.
1979 *God the Father: Theology and Patriarchy in the Teaching of Jesus*. Philadelphia: Fortress.
Hamilton, V. P.
1992a Marriage, Old Testament and Ancient Near East. Pages 559–69 in vol. 4 of *ABD*.
1992b Satan. Pages 985–89 in vol. 5 of *ABD*.
Hamlin, E. J.
1962 Nations. Pages 515–23 in vol. 3 of *IDB*.
Hammond, N. G. L.
1981 *Atlas of the Greek and Roman World in Antiquity*. Park Ridge, New Jersey: Noyes.
Hamp, V.
1990 Das Hirtenmotiv im Alten Testament. Pages 186–201 in *Weisheit und Gottesfurcht: Aufsätze zur alttestamentlichen Einleitung, Exegese und Theologie*. Vinzenz Hamp Festschrift. Edited by G. Schmuttermayr. St. Ottilien: EOS.
Hands, A. R.
1968 *Charities and Social Aid in Greece and Rome*. London: Thames & Hudson.

Hanson, A. E.
1991 Continuity and Change: Three Case Studies in Hippocratic Gynecological Therapy and Theory. Pages 73–110 in *Women's History and Ancient History*. Edited by S. B. Pomeroy. Chapel Hill: University of North Carolina Press.

Hanson, A. T.
1980 The Scriptural Background to the Doctrine of the "Descensus ad Inferos" in the New Testament. Pages 122–56 in *The New Testament Interpretation of Scripture*. London.

Hanson, K. C.
1996 How Honorable! How Shameful!: A Cultural Analysis of Matthew's Makarisms and Reproaches. *Semeia* 68 (*Honor and Shame in the World of the Bible*):81–111.

Hanson, K. C., and S. S. Bartchy
1988a Servant; Slave. Pages 419–21 in vol. 4 of *ISBE*.
1988b Slavery. Pages 539–46 in vol. 4 of *ISBE*.

Hanson, P. D.
1977 Rebellion in Heaven, Azazel, and Euhemeristic Heroes in 1 Enoch 6–11. *JBL* 96:383–405.

Hanson, R. P. C.
1970 Biblical Exegesis in the Early Church. Pages 412–53 in *From the Beginnings to Jerome*. Edited by P. R. Ackroyd and C. F. Evans. Volume 1 of *The Cambridge History of the Bible*. Cambridge: Cambridge University Press.
1980 The Christian Attitude to Pagan Religions up to the Time of Constantine the Great. *ANRW* 2.23.2:910–73.

Harder, G.
1971 "*stêrizô* etc." Pages 653–57 in vol. 7 of *TDNT*.

Harnack, A. von
1897 *Die Chronologie der altchristlichen Litteratur bis Irenäus*. 2d ed. Volume 1 of *Geschichte der altchristlichen Litteratur bis Eusebius*. 2 vols. Leipzig: Hinrichs.
1908 *The Mission and Expansion of Christianity in the First Three Centuries*. 2 vols. 2d rev. ed. London: Williams & Norgate / New York: Putnam's. [Volume 1 reprinted New York: Harper, 1962]

Harris, J. R.
1916–20 *Testimonies*. 2 vols. Cambridge: Cambridge University Press.

Harrisville, R. A.
1987 *Ministry in Crisis: Changing Perspectives on Ordination and the Priesthood of All Believers*. Minneapolis: Augsburg.

Hartman, L.
1988 Some Unorthodox Thoughts on the Household-Code Form. Pages 219–34 in *The Social World of Formative Christianity and Judaism*. H. C. Kee Festschrift. Edited by J. Neusner et al. Philadelphia: Fortress.
1992 Baptism. Pages 583–94 in vol. 1 of *ABD*.

Harvey, A. E.
1974 Elders. *JTS* 25:318–32.

Harvey, G.
1996 *The True Israel: Use of the Names Jew, Hebrew, and Israel in Ancient Jewish and Early Christian Literature*. AGJU 35. Leiden: Brill.

Haselhurst, R. S. T.
1926 Mark, My Son. *Theology* 13:34–36.

Haubeck. W.
1985 *Loskauf durch Christus: Herkunft, Gestalt und Bedeutung des paulinischen Loskaufmotivs*. Giessen: Brunnen / Witten: Bundesverlag.

Hauck, F.
1965 "*koinos* etc." Pages 789–809 in vol. 3 of *TDNT*.

Hauck, F., and G. Bertram
1967 "*makarios* etc." Pages 362–70 in vol. 4 of *TDNT*.

Haufe, C.
1959–60 Die antike Beurteilung des Sklaven. Pages 603–16 in *Wissenschaftliche Zeitschrift der Karl-Marx-Universität Leipzig* 9/4.

Hauschild, W.-D., ed.
1974 *Der römische Staat und die frühe Kirche*. Texte zur Kirchen- und Theologiegeschichte 20. Gütersloh: Gütersloher/Mohn.

Hay, D. M.
1973 *Glory at the Right Hand: Psalm 110 in Early Christianity*. SBLMS 18. Nashville: Abingdon.

Heiler, F.
1958 *Prayer: A Study in the History and Psychology of Religion*. Translated and ed. by S. McComb. New York: Oxford University Press.

Heiligenthal, R.
1983 *Werke als Zeichen: Untersuchungen zur Bedeutung der menschlichen Taten im Frühjudentum, Neuen Testament und Frühchristentum*. WUNT 9/2. Tübingen: Mohr (Siebeck).

Heine, S.
1987 *Women and Early Christianity: A Reappraisal*. Minneapolis: Augsburg.

Heinemann, I.
1921 Das Ideal der Heiligkeit im hellenistischen und rabbinischen Judentum. *Jeschurun* 8:99–119.

Helfgott, B. W.
1954 *The Doctrine of Election in Tannaitic Literature*. New York: Columbia University—King's Crown Press.

Helgeland, J.
1978 Roman Army Religion. *ANRW* 2.16.2:1470–1505.

Hellholm, D., ed.
1983 *Apocalypticism in the Mediterranean World and the Near East*. Proceedings of the International Colloquium on Apocalypticism. Tübingen: Mohr (Siebeck).

Hemer, C. J.
1979 Asia Minor. Pages 322–29 in vol. 1 of *ISBE*.

Hengel, M.
1974 *Judaism and Hellenism*. 2 vols. Philadelphia: Fortress.
1977 *Crucifixion in the Ancient World and the Folly of the Message of the Cross*. Philadelphia: Fortress.

1981 *The Atonement: A Study of the Origin of the Doctrine in the New Testament*. London: SCM Press.
1986 *The Cross of the Son of God*. London: SCM.

Henning, R.
1978 "Familiensoziologisches" im Neuen Testament. *JCSW* 19:67–82.

Herr, T.
1978 Die sozialethische Bedeutung der neutestamentlichen Haustafeln. *JCSW* 19:67–82.

Herron, T. J.
1988 *The Dating of the First Epistle of Clement to the Corinthians: The Theological Basis of the Majoral View*. Dissertation, Pontifical Gregorian University, Rome.

Herzog, W. R.
1981 The "Household Duties" Passages: Apostolic Traditions and Contemporary Concerns. *Foundations* 7:33–38.

Hiers, R. H.
1992 Day of Judgment. Pages 79–82 in vol. 2 of *ABD*.

Hillers, D. R.
1969 *Covenant: The History of a Biblical Idea*. Baltimore: Johns Hopkins University Press.

Hiltbrunner, O., et al.
1972 Gastfreundschaft. Pages 1061–1123 in vol. 8 of *RAC*.

Himmelfarb, M.
1983 *Tours of Hell: An Apocalyptic Form in Jewish and Christian Literature*. Philadelphia: University of Pennsylvania Press.
1993 *Ascent to Heaven in Jewish and Christian Apocalypses*. New York: Oxford University Press.

Hobbs, H. H.
1991 *You Are Chosen: The Priesthood of All Believers*. San Francisco: Harper.

Hodgson, R., Jr.
1979 The Testimony Hypothesis. *JBL* 98:361–78.

Hoffmann, P.
1979 Auferstehung, I/3: Neues Testament. Pages 450–67 in vol. 4 of *TRE*.

Hofius, O.
1971 Erwählt vor Grundlegung der Welt (Eph 1,4). *ZNW* 62:123–28.
1993 Das vierte Gottesknechtlied in den Briefen des neuen Testaments. *NTS* 39:414–37.

Hofmann, K. M.
1938 *Philema Hagion*. BFCT 2/38. Gütersloh: Bertelsmann.

Holmberg, B.
1980 *Paul and Power: The Structure of Authority in the Primitive Church as Reflected in the Pauline Epistles*. Philadelphia: Fortress.

Holtz, G.
1971 *Die Parochie: Geschichte und Problematik*. Berlin: Evangelische.

Holtzmann, H. J.
1885 *Lehrbuch der historisch-kritischen Einleitung in das Neue Testament*. Freiburg im Breisgau: Mohr.
1908 Höllenfahrt im Neuen Testament. *AR* 11:285–97.

Holzmeister, U.
1949 Vocabularium secundae Epistolae S. Petri erroresque quidam de eo divulgati. *Bib* 30:339–55.

Hommes, N. J.
1935 *Het Testimoniaboek: Studien over O. T. Citaten in het N. T. en bij de Patres, met critische Beschouwingen over de Theorieën van J. Rendel Harris en D. Plooy.* Doctoral Dissertation, Amsterdam.

Hooker, M. D.
1959 *Jesus and the Servant: The Influence of the Servant Concept of Deutero-Isaiah in the New Testament.* London: S.P.C.K.

Hooyman, R. P. J.
1958 Die Noë-Darstellung in der frühchristlichen Kunst. *VC* 12:113–36.

Hopkins, K.
1978 *Conquerors and Slaves.* Sociological Studies in Roman History 1. Cambridge: Cambridge University Press.

Horbury, W., and B. McNeil, eds.
1981 *Suffering and Martyrdom in the New Testament.* Cambridge: Cambridge University Press.

Horner, T. M.
1960 Changing Concepts of the "Stranger" in the OT. *AThR* 42:49–53.

Horsley, G. H. R.
1981–89 Volumes 1–5 of *New Documents Illustrating Early Christianity.* North Ryde, New South Wales: Macquarie University, Ancient History Documentary Research Center.
1992 Names, Double. Pages 110–17 in vol. 4 of *ADB*.

Hoyer, G. W.
1967 Christianhood, Priesthood, and Brotherhood. Pages 148–98 in *Accents in Luther's Theology.* Edited by H. O. Kadai. St. Louis: Concordia.

Huidekopper, F.
1854 *The Belief of the First Three Centuries concerning Christ's Mission to the Underworld.* New York: Francis. [8th ed., 1890]

Hunter, A. M.
1962 *Paul and His Predecessors.* 2d ed. Philadelphia: Westminster.

Ittig, T.
1730 *Ob denen Todten das Evangelium soll verkundet werden.* Jena: Ritterum.

Jacobs-Malina, D.
1993 *Beyond Patriarchy: The Images of Family in Jesus.* New York: Paulist.

Janowski, B.
1995 Dem Löwen gleich, gierig nach Raub: Zum Feindbild in den Psalmen. *EvT* 55:155–73.

Janowski, B., and P. Stuhlmacher, eds.
1996 *Der leidende Gottesknecht: Jesaja 53 und seine Wirkungsgeschichte mit einer Bibliographie zu Jes 53.* Forschungen zum Alten Testament 14. Tübingen: Mohr (Siebeck).

Jaubert, A.
1963 *La notion d'alliance dans le Judaïsme aux abords de l'ère chrétienne.* Paris: du Seuil.

Jay, E. G.
1981 From Presbyter-Bishops to Bishops and Presbyters: Christian Ministry in the Second Century—A Survey. *The Second Century* 1:327–38.

Jeffers, J. S.
1991 *Conflict at Rome: Social Order and Hierarchy in Early Christianity.* Minneapolis: Fortress.

Jefford, C. N.
1992 Mark, John. Pages 557–58 in vol. 4 of *ABD.*

Jenni, E.
1962 Eschatology of the OT. Pages 126–33 in vol. 2 of *IDB.*

Jensen, P. J.
1903 *Laeren om Kristi Nedfart til de Doede: En Fremstilling of Laerepunktets Historie tilligemed et Indloeg i dette.* Copenhagen.

Jeremias, J.
1925 Der Eckstein. *Angelos* 1:65–70.
1926 Golgatha und der heilige Felsen: Eine Untersuchung zur Symbolsprache des Neuen Testamentes. *Angelos* 2:74–128.
1930 *Kephalê Gônias—Akrogôniaios.* ZNW 29:254–80.
1937 Eckstein—Schlusstein. ZNW 36:154–57.
1964 "*gônia, akrogôniaios, kephalê gônias.*" Pages 791–93 in vol. 1 of *TDNT.*
1966a *ABBA: Studien zur neutestamentlichen Theologie und Zeitgeschichte.* Göttingen: Vandenhoeck & Ruprecht.
1966b Das Lösegeld für Viele (Mk. 10,45). *Judaica* 3 (1947–1948):249–64. Reprinted pp. 216–29 in *ABBA: Studien zur neutestamentlichen Theologie und Zeitgeschichte.*
1966c Die missionarische Aufgabe in der Mischehe (1 Kor. 7,16). Pages 255–60 in *Neutestamentliche Studien für Rudolf Bultmann.* R. Bultmann Festschrift. Edited by W. Eltester. BZNW 21. Berlin: Alfred Töpelmann, 1954. Reprinted pp. 292–98 in *ABBA: Studien zur neutestamentlichen Theologie und Zeitgeschichte.*
1966d *Pais (theou)* im Neuen Testament. Pages 191–216 in *ABBA: Studien zur neutestamentlichen Theologie und Zeitgeschichte.* [Rev. ed.: "*pais theou:* D." Pages 700–717 in vol. 5 of *TDNT* (1967)]
1967 "*lithos, lithinos.*" Pages 268–80 in vol. 4 of *TDNT.*
1968 "*poimên, archipoimên* etc." Pages 485–502 in vol. 6 of *TDNT.*
1969 *Jerusalem at the Time of Jesus: An Investigation into Economic and Social Conditions during the New Testament Period.* Philadelphia: Fortress.

Jocz, J.
1958 *A Theology of Election: Israel and the Church.* New York: Macmillan.

Joest, W.
1959 Allgemeines Priestertum der Gläubigen. *EKL* 3:330–32.

Johnson, L. T.
1982 The Use of Leviticus 19 in the Letter of James. *JBL* 101:391–401.
1987 *1 Timothy, 2 Timothy, Titus.* Atlanta: John Knox.
1989 The New Testament's Anti-Jewish Slander and the Conventions of Ancient Polemic. *JBL* 108:419–41.
1995 *The Letter of James.* AB 37A. Garden City, New York: Doubleday.

Johnson, S. E.
1958 Early Christianity in Asia Minor. *JBL* 77:1–17.

1972 Unresolved Questions about Early Christianity in Anatolia. Pages 181–93 in *Studies in New Testament and Early Christian Literature*. Allen P. Wikgren Festschrift. Edited by D. E. Aune. Leiden: Brill.

1975 Asia Minor and Early Christianity. Pages 77–145 in *Early Christianity*. Part 2 of *Christianity, Judaism and Other Greco-Roman Cults*. Morton Smith Festschrift. Edited by J. Neusner. Studies in Judaism and Late Antiquity 12. Leiden: Brill.

Johnston, G.

1964 *Oikoumenê* and *Kosmos* in the New Testament. *NTS* 10:352–60.

Jones, A. H. M.

1940 *The Greek City from Alexander to Justinian*. Oxford: Oxford University Press.

1971 *The Cities of the Eastern Roman Provinces*. Rev. ed. Oxford: Clarendon.

Jones, B. W.

1979 *Domitian and the Senatorial Order: A Prosopographical Study of Domitian's Relationship with the Senate, A.D. 81–96*. American Philosophical Society 132. Philadelphia: American Philosophical Society.

1992 *The Emperor Domitian*. London: Routledge.

Jones, D. L.

1982 The Title *Pais* in Luke–Acts. Pages 217–26 in *SBL 1982: Seminar Papers*. SBLSP 21. Chico, California: Scholars Press.

Jonge, M. de

1988 Jesus' Death for Others and the Death of the Maccabean Martyrs. Pages 142–51 in *Text and Testimony: Essays on the New Testament and Apocryphal Literature*. A. J. Klijn Festschrift. Edited by T. Baarda et al. Kampen: Kok.

Jost, W.

1939 Poimen: *Das Bild vom Hirten in der biblischen Überlieferung und seine christologische Bedeutung*. Giessen: Kindt.

Jowett, J. H.

1921 *The Redeemed Family of God*. 4th ed. London: Hodder & Stoughton.

Jowkar, F.

1986 Honor and Shame: A Feminist View from Within. *Feminist Studies* 10:45–65.

Judge, E. A.

1960 *The Social Pattern of the Christian Groups in the First Century: Some Prolegomena to the Study of New Testament Ideas of Social Obligation*. London: Tyndale.

Junack, K., and W. Grunewald

1986 *Die Katholischen Briefe*. Volume 1 of *Das Neue Testament auf Papyrus*. Arbeiten zur neutestamentlichen Textforschung 6. Berlin: de Gruyter.

Junker, H.

1947 Das allgemeine Priestertum des Volkes Israel nach Ex 19:6. *TTZ* 56: 10–15.

Juster, J.

1914 *Les juifs dans l'empire romain: Leur condition juridique, économique et sociale*. 2 vols. Paris: Geuthner.

Kähler, E.

1959 Zur "Unterordnung" der Frau im Neuen Testament. *Zeitschrift für evangelische Ethik* (1959):1–13.

1960 *Die Frau in den paulinischen Briefen: Unter besonderer Berücksichtigung des Begriffs der Unterordnung.* Zurich: Gotthelf.

Käsemann, E.
1942 Die Legitimität des Apostels: Eine Untersuchung zu II Korinther 10–13. ZNW 41:33–71.

Käser, W.
1970 Beobachtungen zum alttestamentlichen Makarismus. *ZAW* 82:225–50.

Kamlah, E.
1964 *Die Form der katalogischen Paränese im Neuen Testament.* WUNT 7. Tübingen: Mohr (Siebeck).
1970 *Hypotassesthai* in den neutestamentlichen "Haustafeln." Pages 237–43 in *Verborum Veritas.* G. Stählin Festschrift. Edited by O. Böcher and K. Haacker. Wuppertal: Brockhaus.

Kanjuparambil, P.
1983 Imperatival Participles in Rom 12:9–21. *JBL* 102:285–88.

Karpp, H.
1954 Christennamen. Pages 1114–38 in vol. 2 of *RAC.*

Karrer, M.
1990 Das urchristliche Ältestenamt. *NovT* 32:152–88.
1991 *Der Gesalbte: Die Grundlagen des Christustitels.* FRLANT 151. Göttingen: Vandenhoeck & Ruprecht.

Kasser R., ed.
1961 *Papyrus Bodmer XVII.* Geneva: Bodmeriana.

Kehnscherper, G.
1957 *Die Stellung der Bibel und der alten Christlichen Kirche zur Sklaverei.* Leipzig.

Kelly, H. A.
1968 *The Devil: Perceptions of Evil from Antiquity to Primitive Christianity.* Garden City, N.Y.: Doubleday.

Kelly, J. N. D.
1960 *Early Christian Creeds.* 2d ed. London: Longmans.

Kennedy, H. A. A.
1915 The Significance and Range of the Covenant-Conception in the New Testament. *Exp* 10:385–410.

Keresztes, P.
1973 The Jews, the Christians, and Emperor Domitian. *VC* 27:1–18.
1979 The Imperial Roman Government and the Christian Church, I: From Nero to the Severi. *ANRW* 2.23:247–315.
1984 Nero, the Christians and the Jews in Tacitus and Clement of Rome. *Latomus* 43:404–13.
1989 Volume 1 of *Imperial Rome and the Christians: From Herod the Great to about 200 AD.* Lanham, Maryland: University Press of America.

Kertelge, K.
1970 Das Apostelamt des Paulus, sein Ursprung und seine Bedeutung. *BZ* 14:161–81.

Kikawada, I. M.
1992 Noah and the Ark. Pages 1123–31 in vol. 4 of *ABD.*

Kinder, E.
1953 *Das allgemeine Priestertum im N.T.* Schriften des Theologischen Konvents Augsburgischen Bekenntnisses 5. Berlin: Lutherisches.
Kittel, G.
1967 "*logikos*." Pages 142–43 in vol. 4 of *TDNT.*
Kitzberger, I.
1986 *Bau der Gemeinde: Das paulinische Wortfeld* oikodome/oikodomein. Forschung zur Bibel 53. Würzburg: Echter.
Klassen, W.
1992a Kiss (NT). Pages 89–92 in vol. 4 of *ABD.*
1992b Love: NT and Early Jewish Literature. Pages 381–96 in vol. 4 of *ABD.*
1992c Peace. Pages 206–12 in vol. 5 of *ABD.*
1993 The Sacred Kiss in the New Testament: An Example of Social Boundary Lines. *NTS* 39:122–35.
Klauck, H.-J.
1981a Die Hausgemeinde als Lebensform im Urchristentum. *MTZ* 32:1–15.
1981b *Hausgemeinde und Hauskirche im frühen Christentum.* Stuttgarter Bibelstudien 103. Stuttgart: Katholisches.
1982 Neue Literatur zur urchristlichen Hausgemeinde. *BZ* 26:288–94.
1992 *Gemeinde zwischen Haus und Stadt. Kirche bei Paulus.* Freiburg: Herder.
Klausner, S. Z.
1991 Diaspora in Comparative Perspective. Pages 194–221 in *Eretz Israel, Israel and the Jewish Diaspora. Mutual Relations.* Edited by M. Mor. Studies in Jewish Civilization 1. Lanham, Maryland: University Press of America.
Klein, G.
1909 *Der älteste Christliche Katechismus und die Jüdische Propaganda-Literatur.* Berlin: Reimer.
Klein, G.
1961 *Die zwölf Apostel. Ursprung und Gehalt einer Idee.* FRLANT n.s. 59. Göttingen: Vandenhoeck & Ruprecht.
Klein, R., ed.
1982 *Das frühe Christentum im römischen Staat.* 2d ed. Wege der Forschung 267. Darmstadt: Wissenschaftliche.
Kleinknecht, K. T.
1984 *Der leidende Gerechtfertigte.* WUNT 2/13. Tübingen: Mohr (Siebeck).
Klinzing, G.
1971 *Die Umdeutung des Kultus in der Qumrangemeinde und im Neuen Testament.* SUNT 7. Göttingen: Vandenhoeck & Ruprecht.
Kloppenborg, J. S.
1986 Blessing and Marginality: The "Persecution Beatitude" in Q, Thomas, and Early Christianity. *Forum* 2:36–56.
Kluge, O.
1906 *Die Idee des Priestertums in Israel-Juda und im Urchristentum.* Leipzig: Deichert-Böhme.
Koch, D.-A.
1980 Beobachtungen zum christologischen Schriftgebrauch in den vorpaulinischen Gemeinden. ZNW 71:171–91.
Koch, K.
1955 Zur Geschichte der Erwählungsvorstellung in Israel. ZAW 67:205–26.

1961 Priestertum in Israel. Pages 574–78 in vol. 5 of *RGG*[3].
1976 Pseudonymous Writing. Pages 712–14 in *IDBSup*.

Koenig, J.
1978 *Charismata: God's Gifts for God's People*. Philadelphia: Westminster.
1985 *New Testament Hospitality: Partnership with Strangers as Promise and Mission*. Philadelphia: Fortress.
1992a Hospitality. Pages 299–301 in vol. 3 of *ABD*.
1992b *Rediscovering New Testament Prayer: Boldness and Blessing in the Name of Jesus*. San Francisco: HarperSanFrancisco.

König, J. L.
1942 *Die Lehre von Christi Höllenfahrt nach der heiligen Schrift, der ältesten Kirche, den christlichen Symbolen und nach ihrer vielumfassenden Bedeutung dargestellt*. Frankfurt: Zimmer.

Koerber, J.
1860 *Die katholische Lehre von der Höllenfahrt Jesu Christi*. Landshut: Wolfe.

Koester, H.
1982b *Introduction to the New Testament*. 2 vols. Philadelphia: Fortress.

Kötzsche-Breitenbach, L.
1976 *Die neue Katakombe an der Via Latina in Rom: Untersuchungen zur Ikonographie der alttestamentlichen Wandmalereien*. JAC Ergänzungsband 4. Münster: Aschendorff.

Kooy, V. H.
1962 Hospitality. Page 654 in vol. 2 of *IDB*.

Koskenniemi, H.
1956 *Studien zur Idee und Phraseologie des griechischen Briefes bis 400 n. Chr.* Helsinki: Akateeminen Kirjakauppa.

Kosmala, H.
1959 *Hebräer-Essener-Christen*. Studia Post-Biblica 1. Leiden: Brill.

Kraemer, H.
1958 *A Theology of Laity*. London.

Kraemer, R. S.
1983 Women in the Religions of the Greco-Roman World. *RSR* 9:127–39.
1986 Hellenistic Jewish Women: The Epigraphical Evidence. Pages 183–200 in *SBL 1987: Seminar Papers*. SBLSP 26. Decatur, Georgia: Scholars Press.

Kraemer, R. S., ed.
1988 *Maenads, Martyrs, Matrons, Monastics: A Sourcebook on Women's Religions in the Greco-Roman World*. Philadelphia: Fortress.

Kraft, T.
1994 "Hoy la salvación ha llegado a esta casa" (La familia en el Nuevo Testamento). *Revista Teológica Limense* 28:146–65.

Kränkl, E.
1972 *Jesus der Knecht Gottes: Die heilsgeschichtliche Stellung Jesu in den Reden der Apostelgeschichte*. Biblische Untersuchungen 8. Regensburg: Pustet.

Kredel, E. M.
1956 Der Apostelbegriff in der neueren Exegese: Historisch-kritische Darstellung. *ZKT* 78:169–93, 257–305.

Krentz, E. M.
1989 God in the New Testament. Pages 75–90 in *Our Naming of God*. Edited by C. E. Braaten. Minneapolis: Fortress.
1993 Military Language and Metaphors in Philippians. Pages 105–27 in *Origins and Method: Towards a New Understanding of Judaism and Christianity*. John C. Hurd Festschrift. Edited by B. H. McLean. JSNTSup 86. Sheffield: Sheffield Academic Press.

Krodel, G.
1971 Persecution and Toleration of Christianity until Hadrian. Pages 255–67 in *The Catacombs and the Colosseum: The Roman Empire as the Setting of Primitive Christianity*. Edited by S. Benko and J. J. O'Rourke. Valley Forge: Judson.

Kroll, J.
1963 *Gott und Hölle: Der Mythos vom Descensuskampfe*. Studien der Bibliothek Warburg 20. Leipzig: Teubner, 1932. Reprinted Darmstadt: Wissenschaftliche.

Kroll, W.
1931 Kiss. Pages 511–20 in vol. 5 of PWSup.

Kübler, B.
1937 Peregrinus. Pages 639–55 in vol. 19 of *PW*.

Kümmel, W. G.
1975 *Introduction to the New Testament*. Rev. ed. Nashville: Abingdon.

Küng, H.
1967 The Priesthood of All Believers. Pages 363–87 in *The Church*. New York: Sheed & Ward.
1976 *On Being a Christian*. New York: Pocket.

Kürzinger, J.
1962 Höllenfahrt Christi. Pages 670–75 in *Bibeltheologisches Wörterbuch*. 2d ed. Edited by J. B. Bauer. Graz: Styria.

Kuhli, H.
1991 "*Ioudaios*." Pages 193–97 in vol. 2 of *EDNT*.

Kuhn, K. G.
1952 *Peirasmos-hamartia-sarx* im Neuen Testament und die damit zusammenhängenden Vorstellungen. *ZTK* 49:200–222.
1964 "*Babylôn*." Pages 514–17 in vol. 1 of *TDNT*.
1968 "*prosêlytos*." Pages 727–44 in vol. 6 of *TDNT*.

Kuhn, K. G., and W. Gutbrod
1965 "*Israêl* etc." Pages 359–91 in vol. 3 of *TDNT*.

Kuhn, K. G., and H. Stegemann
1962 Proselyten. Pages 1248–83 in vol. 9 of PWSup.

Kuss, O.
1963 Zur paulinischen und nachpaulinischen Tauflehre im Neuen Testament. *TGl* 42(1952): 401–25. Reprinted pp. 121–50 in vol. 1 of *Auslegung und Verkündigung*. Regensburg: Pustet.

Kutsch, E.
1981 Bund I: Altes Testament; II: Frühes Judentum; III: Neues Testament und frühe Kirche. Pages 397–410 in vol. 7 of *TRE*.

Kyrtatas, D. J.
1987 *The Social Structure of the Early Christian Communities*. New York: Verso.

Labriolle, P. de
1928 Paroecia. *RSR* 18:60–72.
1929–30 Christianus. *Archivum Latinitatis Medii Aevi* 5:69–88.

Lampe, P.
1989 *Die stadtrömischen Christen in den ersten beiden Jahrhunderten*. 2d ed. WUNT 2/18. Tübingen: Mohr (Siebeck).
1991 The Roman Christians of Romans 16. Pages 216–30 in *The Romans Debate*. Edited by K. P. Donfried. Rev. ed. Peabody, Massachusetts: Hendrickson.
1992 "Family" in Church and Society of New Testament Times. *Affirmation* (Richmond, Virginia) 5:1–20.

Landvogt, P.
1908 *Epigraphische Untersuchungen über den OIKONOMOS: Ein Beitrag zum hellenistischen Beamtenwesen*. Strassbourg: Schauberg.

Lane Fox, R.
1986 *Pagans and Christians*. New York: Knopf.

Langton, E.
1949 *Essentials of Demonology: A Study of Jewish and Christian Doctrine, Its Origin and Development*. London: Epworth.

La Piana, G.
1927 Foreign Groups in Rome during the First Centuries of the Empire. *HTR* 20:183–403.

Larrañaga, V.
1938 *L'Ascension de Notre-Seigneur dans le Nouveau Testament*. Scripta Pontificii Instituti Biblici 50. Rome: Pontifical Biblical Institute.

Larsson, E.
1964 *Christus als Vorbild*. Lund: Gleerup.

Last, H.
1954 Christenverfolgung. Pages 1208–28 in vol. 2 of *RAC*.

Lattke, M.
1991 "*oneidos* etc." Pages 517–18 in vol. 2 of *EDNT*.

Laub, F.
1982 *Die Begegnung des frühen Christentums mit der antiken Sklaverei*. SBS 107. Stuttgart: Katholisches.
1986 Sozialgeschichtlicher Hintergrund und ekklesiologische Relevanz der neutestamentlich-frühchristlichen Haus- und Gemeinde-Tafelparänese: Ein Beitrag zur Soziologie des Frühchristentums. *MTZ* 37:249–71.

Laurentin, R.
1978 Charisms: Terminological Precision. Pages 3–12 in *Charisms in the Church*. Concilium 109. New York: Seabury.

Lauterburg, M.
1900 Höllenfahrt Christi. Pages 199–206 in vol. 7 of *RE*.

Lea, T. D.
1988 The Priesthood of All Christians according to the New Testament. *SwJT* 30:15–21.

Le Coultre, J.
1907 De l'étymologie du mot "Chrétien." *RTP* 40:188–96.

Lécuyer, J.
1949 Le sacerdoce royal des chrétiens selon saint Hilaire de Poitiers. *L'Année Théologique* 10:302–25.
1970 Sacerdoce des fidèles et sacerdoce ministériel chez Origène. *Vetera Christianorum* 7:253–64.
Lee, E. K.
1962 "Words Denoting Pattern" in the New Testament. *NTS* 8:166–73.
Leeuw, G. van der
1963 *Religion in Essence and Manifestation*. 2 vols. New York: Harper & Row.
Lefkowitz, M. R., and M. B. Fant
1982 *Womens' Life in Greece and Rome: A Source Book in Translation*. Baltimore: Johns Hopkins University Press.
Legido Lopez, M.
1982 *Fraternidad en el mundo: Un estudio de ecclesiologia paulina*. Biblioteca de Estudios Bíblicos 34. Salamanca: Sigueme.
Leipoldt, J.
1955 *Die Frau in der antiken Welt und im Urchristentum*. Leipzig: Koehler & Amelang, 1954. 2d ed. Gütersloh: Gütersloher/Mohn.
1966 Aus Kleinasien. Pages 26–31 and plates 80–104 in *Umwelt des Urchristentums*. Edited by J. Leipoldt and W. Grundmann. Volume 3 of *Bilder zum neutestamentlichen Zeitalter*. Berlin: Evangelische.
Leivestad, R.
1954 *Christ the Conqueror: Ideas of Conflict and Victory in the New Testament*. London: SPCK.
Lemaire, A.
1971 *Les Ministères aux origines de l'Église—Naissance de la hiérarchie triple: Évêques, presbytres, diacres*. LD 68. Paris: Cerf, 1971.
Lenski, G., P. Nolan, and J. Lenski
1995 *Human Societies: An Introduction to Macrosociology*. 7th ed. New York: McGraw-Hill.
Leonardi, C.
1970 Rapporti tra sacerdozio dei fedeli e ministeri nel Nuovo Testamento. *Presbyteri* 19–20:342–57.
Le Roux, J. H.
1984 A Holy Nation Was Elected (the Election Theology of Exodus 19:5–6). In *The Exilic Period: Aspects of Apocalypticism*. Edited by W. C. Van Wyk. Ou testamentiese werkgemeenskap in Suid-Afrika 25–26. Pretoria.
Lerner, Gerda.
1986 *The Creation of Patriarchy*. New York: Oxford University Press.
Levick, B.
1985 *The Government of the Roman Empire. A Sourcebook*. London: Croom Helm.
Levine, A.-J., ed.
1991 *"Women like This": New Perspectives on Jewish Women in the Greco-Roman World*. SBL: Early Judaism and Its Literature 1. Atlanta: Scholars Press.
Levy, E.
1988 Métèques et droit de residence. Pages 47–67 in *L'Étranger dans le monde grec*. Edited by R. Lonis. Actes du colloque organisé par l'Institut d'Etudes Anciennes Nancy, mai 1987. Nancy: Presses Universitaires de Nancy.

Lewis, J. P.
1968 *A Study of the Interpretation of Noah and the Flood in Jewish and Christian Literature*. Leiden: Brill.
1984 Noah and the Flood in Jewish, Christian and Muslim Tradition. *BA* 47:224–39.
1992 Flood. Pages 798–803 in vol. 2 of *ABD*.
Lewis, T.
1918 Persecution. Pages 168–86 in vol. 2 of *HDAC*.
Lewis, T. J.
1992 Dead, Abode of. Pages 101–5 in vol. 2 of *ABD*.
Lichtenberger, H.
1993 "*pyr*." Pages 197–200 in vol. 3 of *EDNT*.
Lietzmann, H.
1966 *Symbolstudien I–XIV*. Libelli 136. Berlin: Akademie.
Lifschitz, B.
1962 L'origine du nom des Chrétiens. *VC* 16:65–70.
Lillie, W.
1974–75 The Pauline House-Tables. *ExpTim* 86:181–83.
Limberis, V.
1991 The Eyes Infected by Evil: Basil of Caesarea's Homily, *On Envy*. *HTR* 84:163–84.
Lindars, B.
1961 *New Testament Apologetic: The Doctrinal Significance of the Old Testament Quotations*. Philadelphia: Westminster.
1981 Enoch and Christology. *ExpTim* 92:295–99.
Lindboe, I. M.
1990 *Women in the New Testament: A Select Bibliography*. University of Oslo, Faculty of Theology, Bibliography Series 1. Oslo: Faculty of Theology, University of Oslo.
Lindemann, A.
1979 *Paulus im ältesten Christentum: Das Bild des Apostels und die Rezeption der paulinischen Theologie in der frühchristlichen Literatur bis Marcion*. BHT 58. Tübingen: Mohr (Siebeck).
Ling, T.
1961 *The Significance of Satan*. Biblical Monographs 3. London: S.P.C.K.
Lips, H. von
1991 Paulus und die Tradition: Zitierung von Schriftworten, Herrenworten und urchristlichen Traditionen. *VF* 32:27–49.
1994 Die Haustafel als "Topos" im Rahmen der urchristlichen Paränese: Beobachtungen anhand des 1. Petrusbriefes und des Titusbriefes. *NTS* 40:261–80.
Littell, F.
1976 *The Macmillan Atlas History of Christianity*. New York: Macmillan.
Llewelyn, S. R., and R. A. Kearsley, eds.
1992–94 Volumes 6–7 of *New Documents Illustrating Early Christianity*. Macquarie University, New South Wales: The Ancient History Documentary Research Centre.
Lövestam, E.
1963 *Spiritual Wakefulness in the New Testament*. Lund: Gleerup.

Löw, E.
1967 Der Kuss. Pages 641–76 in vol. 2 of *Wissenschaft des Judentums im deutschen Sprachbereich: Ein Querschnitt*. Edited by K. Wilhelm. Schriftenreihe wissenschaftlicher Abhandlungen des Leo Baeck Institutes 16/2. Tübingen: Mohr (Siebeck).

Loewe, R.
1966 *The Position of Women in Judaism*. London: SPCK.

Lohfink, G.
1984 *Jesus and Community: The Social Dimension of Christian Faith*. Philadelphia: Fortress.

Lohmeyer, E.
1927 Probleme paulinischer Theologie, I: Briefliche Grussüberschriften. ZNW 26:158–73.
1937 Vom urchristlichen Abendmahl. *TRu* 9:168–228, 273–312.

Lohse, E.
1963 *Märtyrer und Gottesknecht: Untersuchungen zur urchristliche Verkündigung vom Sühnetod Jesu Christi*. 2d ed. FRLANT 64. Göttingen: Vandenhoeck & Ruprecht.
1967 *History of the Suffering and Death of Jesus Christ*. Philadelphia: Fortress.
1980 Die Entstehung des Bischofsamtes in der frühen Christenheit. ZNW 71:58–73.

Long, B. O.
1980 Berufung, I. Altes Testament. Pages 676–84 in vol. 5 of *TRE*.

Lonis, R., ed.
1988 *L'Étranger dans le monde grec*. Actes du colloque organisé par l'Institut d'Études Anciennes Nancy, mai 1987. Nancy: Presses Universitaires de Nancy.

Lorenzen, T.
1987 Die Christliche Hauskirche. *TZ* 43:333–52.

Luck, U.
1971 "*sôphrôn* etc." Pages 1097–1104 in vol. 7 of *TDNT*.

Lührmann, D.
1975 Wo man nicht mehr Sklave oder Freier ist: Überlegungen zur Struktur frühchristlicher Gemeinden. *Wort und Dienst* 13:53–83.
1980 Neutestamentliche Haustafeln und antike Ökonomie. *NTS* 27:83–97.
1986 *Superstitio*: Die Beurteilung des frühen Christentums durch die Römer. *TZ* 42:193–213.

Lumpe, A., and H. Bietenhard
1991 Himmel. Pages 173–212 in vol. 15 of *RAC*.

Lundberg, P.
1942 *La typologie baptismale dans l'ancienne Église*. ASNU 10. Leipzig: Lorentz / Uppsala: Lundquistska.

Luther, M.
1883– *D. Martin Luthers Werke*. Kritische Gesamtausgabe. Weimar. [Abbreviated WA (*Weimarer Ausgabe*)]
1955–86 *Luther's Works*. 55 vols. General eds. J. Pelikan and H. T. Lehmann. St. Louis: Concordia / Philadelphia: Muhlenberg/Fortress. [Abbreviated *LW*]

Luz, U.

1989 *Matthew 1–7: A Commentary*. Translated by W. C. Linss. Minneapolis: Augsburg.

1990 *Das Evangelium nach Matthäus*. EKKNT 1/2. Zurich: Benzinger / Neukirchen-Vluyn: Neukirchner.

Lyonnet, S.

1961 La bénédiction de Eph 1.3–14 et son arrière-plan judaïque. Pages 341–52 in *A la rencontre de Dieu*. A. Gelin Festschrift. Edited by Facultés catholiques, Lyon. Paris: Mappus.

Maas, W.

1979 *Gott und die Hölle: Studien zum Descensus Christi*. Einsiedeln: Johannes.

MacCullough, J. A.

1930 *The Harrowing of Hell*. Edinburgh: T. & T. Clark.

MacDonald, M. Y.

1988 *The Pauline Churches: A Socio-historical Study of Institutionalization in the Pauline and Deutero-Pauline Writings*. SNTSMS 60. Cambridge: Cambridge University Press.

MacGregor, G. H. C.

1954–55 Principalities and Powers: The Cosmic Background of Paul's Thought. *NTS* 1:17–28.

MacMullen, R.

1966 *Enemies of the Roman Order: Treason, Unrest, and Alienation in the Empire*. Cambridge: Harvard University Press.

1974 *Roman Social Relations 50 B.C. to A.D. 284*. New Haven: Yale University Press.

1980 Women in Public in the Roman Empire. *Historia* 29:208–18.

Magie, D.

1950 *Roman Rule in Asia Minor to the End of the Third Century after Christ*. 2 vols. Princeton: Princeton University Press.

Maiburg, U.

1983 "Und bis an die Grenzen der Erde . . .": Die Ausbreitung des Christentums in den Länderlisten und deren Verwendung in Antike und Christentum. *JAC* 26:38–53.

Malherbe, A. J.

1977 The Inhospitality of Diotrephes. Pages 222–32 in *God's Christ and His People*. N. A. Dahl Festschrift. Edited by J. Jervell and W. A. Meeks. Oslo: Universitetsforlaget.

1983 House Churches and Their Problems. Pages 60–91 in *Social Aspects of Early Christianity*. Edited by A. J. Malherbe. 2d enlarged ed. Philadelphia: Fortress.

1986 *Moral Exhortation: A Greco-Roman Sourcebook*. Philadelphia: Westminster.

1992 Hellenistic Moralists and the New Testament. *ANRW* 2.26.1:267–333.

Malina, B. J.

1979 The Individual and the Community: Personality in the Social World of Early Christianity. *BTB* 9:126–38.

1985 Hospitality. Pages 408–9 in *HBD*.

1986a *Christian Origins and Cultural Anthropology: Practical Models for Biblical Interpretation*. Atlanta: John Knox.

1986b The Received View and What It Cannot Do: III John and Hospitality. *Semeia* 35 (*Social-Scientific Criticism of the New Testament and Its Social World*):171–89.

1986c "Religion" in the World of Paul: A Preliminary Sketch. *BTB* 16:92–101.

1988a Patron and Client: The Analogy behind Synoptic Theology. *Forum* 4:2–32.

1989 Dealing with Biblical (Mediterranean) Characters: A Guide for U.S. Consumers. *BTB* 19:127–41.

1992 Is There a Circum-Mediterranean Person? Looking for Stereotypes. *BTB* 22:66–87.

1993a Hospitality. Pages 104–7 in *Biblical Social Values and Their Meaning: A Handbook*. Edited by J. J. Pilch and B. J. Malina. Peabody, Massachusetts: Hendrickson.

1993b Humility. Pages 107–8 in *Biblical Social Values and Their Meaning: A Handbook*. Edited by J. J. Pilch and B. J. Malina. Peabody, Massachusetts: Hendrickson.

1993c Love. Pages 110–14 in *Biblical Social Values and Their Meaning: A Handbook*. Edited by J. J. Pilch and B. J. Malina. Peabody, Massachusetts: Hendrickson.

1993d *The New Testament World: Insights from Cultural Anthropology*. 2d ed. Atlanta: Westminster John Knox.

1994 "Let Him Deny Himself" (Mark 8:34 & Par.): A Social Psychological Model of Self-Denial. *BTB* 24:106–19.

Malina, B. J., and J. H. Neyrey

1988 *Calling Jesus Names: The Social Value of Labels in Matthew*. Sonoma, California: Polebridge.

1991a Conflict in Luke–Acts: Labelling and Deviance Theory. Pages 97–122 in *The Social World of Luke–Acts: Models for Interpretation*. Edited by J. H. Neyrey. Peabody, Massachusetts: Hendrickson.

1991b First-Century Personality: Dyadic, Not Individual. Pages 67–96 in *The Social World of Luke–Acts: Models for Interpretation*. Edited by J. H. Neyrey. Peabody, Massachusetts: Hendrickson.

1991c Honor and Shame in Luke–Acts: Pivotal Values of the Mediterranean World. Pages 25–65 in *The Social World of Luke–Acts: Models for Interpretation*. Edited by J. H. Neyrey. Peabody, Massachusetts: Hendrickson.

1996 *Portraits of Paul: An Archeology of Ancient Personality*. Louisville: Westminster John Knox.

Malina, B. J., and J. J. Pilch, eds.

1993 *Biblical Social Values and Their Meaning: A Handbook*. Peabody, Massachusetts: Hendrickson.

Malina, B. J., and R. L. Rohrbaugh

1992 *Social-Science Commentary on the Synoptic Gospels*. Minneapolis: Fortress.

Malmede, H. H.

1986 *Die Lichtsymbolik im Neuen Testament*. Studies in Oriental Religions 15. Wiesbaden: Harrassowitz.

Manley, G. T.

1944 Babylon on the Nile. *EvQ* 16:138–46.

Manson, W.
1952 Principalities and Powers. *Studiorum Novi Testamenti Societas* 3:7–17.
Mansoor, M.
1964 *The Dead Sea Scrolls*. Grand Rapids: Eerdmans.
Mantey, J. R.
1923 Unusual Meanings for Prepositions in the Greek New Testament. *Exp* 25:453–60.
1951a The Causal Use of *eis* in the New Testament. *JBL* 70:45–48.
1951b On Causal *eis* Again. *JBL* 70:309–11.
1952 The Elusive Causal *eis*. *JBL* 71:43–44.
Marney, C.
1993 *Priests to Each Other*. Macon, Georgia: Mercer University Press.
Marshall, I. H.
1973 Palestinian and Hellenistic Christianity: Some Critical Comments. *NTS* 19:271–87
Martin, C. L.
1991 The Haustafeln (Household Codes) in African American Biblical Interpretation: "Free Slaves" and "Subordinate Women." Pages 206–31 in *Stony the Road We Trod: African American Biblical Interpretation*. Edited by C. H. Felder. Philadelphia: Fortress.
Martin, D. B.
1990 *Slavery as Salvation: The Metaphor of Slavery in Pauline Christianity*. New Haven: Yale University Press.
Martin, R. P.
1979 *The Family and the Fellowship: New Testament Images of the Church*. Grand Rapids: Eerdmans.
1982 Gospel. Pages 529–32 in vol. 2 of *ISBE*.
1986 Mark, John. Pages 259–60 in vol. 4 of *ISBE*.
1992 Gifts, Spiritual. Pages 1015–18 in vol. 2 of *ABD*.
Martin-Achard, R.
1971 "*gur*." Pages 409–12 in vol. 1 of *THAT*.
1992 Resurrection: Old Testament. Pages 680–84 in vol. 5 of *ABD*.
Massaux, E.
1950 *Influence de l'Évangile de Saint Matthieu sur la littérature chrétienne avant Saint Irénée*. Gembloux: Duculot.
Matson, D. L.
1995 *Household Conversion Narratives in Acts: Patterns and Interpretation*. JSNTSup 123. Sheffield: Sheffield Academic Press.
Matthews, V. H., and D. C. Benjamin
1993 *The Social World of Early Israel 1250–587* BCE. Peabody, Massachusetts: Hendrickson.
Matthews, V. H., and D. C. Benjamin, eds.
1996 *Semeia* 68 (*Honor and Shame in the World of the Bible*). Atlanta: Scholars Press.
Mattingly, H. B.
1958 The Origin of the Name Christiani. *JTS* 9:26–37.
Mauch, T. M.
1962 Sojourner. Pages 397–99 in vol. 4 of *IDB*.

Maurer, C.
1971 "*skeuos*." Pages 358–67 in vol. 7 of *TDNT.*
May, H. G., ed.
1984 *Oxford Bible Atlas*. 3d ed. New York: Oxford University Press.
Mayer, G.
1986 *Die jüdische Frau in der hellenistisch-römischen Antike*. Stuttgart: Kohlhammer.
Mayer-Schärtel, B.
1995 *Das Frauenbild des Josephus*. Stuttgart: Kohlhammer.
Mayor, J. B.
1907 *The Epistle of St. Jude and the Second Epistle of St. Peter.* London: Macmillan. Reprinted, Grand Rapids: Baker, 1965.
McCabe, H.
1963 What Is the Church? VII: A Royal Priesthood. *Life of the Spirit* 18: 162–74.
McCarthy, D. J.
1963 *Treaty and Covenant: A Study in Form in the Ancient Oriental Documents and in the Old Testament*. AnBib 21. Rome: Pontifical Biblical Institute.
1972 *Old Testament Covenant: A Survey of Current Opinions*. Atlanta: John Knox.
McDermott, M.
1975 The Biblical Doctrine of *Koinônia*. *BZ* n.s. 19:64–77.
McDonald, J. I. H.
1980 Kerygma *and* Didache: *The Articulation and Structure of the Earliest Christian Message*. SNTSMS 37. Cambridge: Cambridge University Press.
1993 *Biblical Interpretation and Christian Ethics*. Cambridge: Cambridge University Press.
McGinn, B.
1994 *Antichrist: Two Thousand Years of the Human Fascination with Evil*. San Francisco: HarperSanFrancisco.
McGuire, A.
1990 EQUALITY AND SUBORDINATION IN CHRIST: Displacing the Powers of the Household Code in Colossians. Pages 65–85 in *Religion and Economic Ethics*. Edited by Joseph F. Gower. Lanham, Maryland: University Press of America.
McGuire, M. R. P.
1960 Letters and Letter Couriers in Christian Antiquity. *Classical World* 53:148–53.
McKelvey, R. J.
1962 Christ the Cornerstone. *NTS* 8:352–59.
1969 *The New Temple: The Church in the New Testament*. Oxford: Oxford University Press.
McNamara, M.
1972 *Targum and Testament—Aramaic Paraphrases of the Hebrew Bible: A Light on the New Testament*. Grand Rapids: Eerdmans.
Meade, D. G.
1986 *Pseudonymity and Canon: An Investigation into the Relationship of Authorship and Authority in Jewish and Earliest Christian Tradition*. Grand Rapids: Eerdmans.

Meecham, H. G.
1947 The Use of the Participle for the Imperative in the New Testament. *ExpTim* 58:207–8.

Meeks, W. A.
1983 *The First Urban Christians: The Social World of the Apostle Paul.* New Haven: Yale University Press.
1986 *The Moral World of the First Christians.* Philadelphia: Westminster.
1993 *The Origins of Christian Morality: The First Two Centuries.* New Haven: Yale University Press.

Meier, J. P.
1991 *The Problem and the Person.* Volume 1 of *A Marginal Jew: Rethinking the Historical Jesus.* Garden City, New York: Doubleday.
1994 *Mentor, Message and Miracles.* Volume 2 of *A Marginal Jew: Rethinking the Historical Jesus.* Garden City, New York: Doubleday.

Meiselman, M.
1978 *Jewish Women in Jewish Law.* New York: KTAV.

Mellink, M. J.
1962a Bithynia. Page 443 in vol. 1 of *IDB.*
1962b Galatia. Pages 336–38 in vol. 2 of *IDB.*

Menard, J. E.
1979 Pseudonymie. Pages 245–52 in vol. 9 of *DBSup.*

Mendenhall, G. E.
1955 *Law and Covenant in Israel and in the Ancient Near East.* Pittsburgh: Presbyterian Board of Colportage of Western Pennsylvania.
1962 Covenant. Pages 714–23 in vol. 1 of *IDB.*

Mendenhall, G. E., and G. A. Herion
1992 Covenant. Pages 1179–1202 in vol. 1 of *ABD.*

Merkelbach, R., and S. Sahin
1988 Die publizierten Inschriften von Perge. *Epigraphica Anatolica* 11:97–170.

Metzger, B. M.
1963 *Chapters in the History of New Testament Textual Criticism.* Grand Rapids: Eerdmans.
1968 *The Text of the New Testament: Its Transmission, Corruption, and Restoration.* 2d ed. New York: Oxford University Press.
1971 *A Textual Commentary on the Greek New Testament: A Companion Volume to the United Bible Societies' Greek New Testament.* London: United Bible Societies.

Meyendorff, J., and R. Tobias, eds.
1992 *Salvation in Christ: A Lutheran-Orthodox Dialogue.* Minneapolis: Augsburg.

Meyer, A.
1930 *Das Rätsel des Jakobusbriefes.* BZNW 10. Berlin: Alfred Töpelmann.

Meyer, B. F.
1992 Christus Faber: *The Master Builder and the House of God.* Princeton Theological Monograph Series 29. Allison Park, Pennsylvania: Pickwick.

Meyer, M. A.
1981 Concerning D. R. Schwartz, "History and Historiography": "A Kingdom of Priests" as a Pharisaic Slogan. *Zion* 46:57–58. [Hebrew]

Meyers, C.
1978 The Roots of Restriction: Women in Early Israel. *BA* 41:91–103.
1988 *Discovering Eve: Ancient Israelite Women in Context*. New York: Oxford University Press.
1992 Everyday Life: Women in the Period of the Hebrew Bible. Pages 244–51 in *The Women's Bible Commentary*. Edited by C. A. Newsom and S. H. Ringe. Louisville: Westminster John Knox.
Michaelis, W.
1953 *Das Ältestenamt der christlichen Gemeinde im Lichte der Heiligen Schrift*. Bern: Haller.
1967a "*leôn*." Pages 251–53 in vol. 4 of *TDNT*.
1967b "*parakyptô*." Pages 814–16 in vol. 5 of TDNT.
1967c "*paschô* etc." Pages 904–39 in vol. 5 of *TDNT*.
Michalski, M.
1996 *The Relationship between the Universal Priesthood of the Baptized and the Ministerial Priesthood of the Ordained in Vatican II and in Subsequent Theology*. Lewiston, New York: Edwin Mellen.
Michel, O.
1967 "*oikos* etc." Pages 119–59 in vol. 5 of *TDNT*.
Milgrom, J.
1974 The Compass of Biblical Sancta. *JQR* 65:205–16.
Millburn, R. L. P.
1945 The Persecution of Domitian. *Church Quarterly Review* 139:154–64.
Miller, D. L.
1981 The Two Sandals of Christ: Descent into History and into Hell. *ErJb* 50:147–221.
Milligan, G.
1910 *Selections from the Greek Papyri*. Cambridge: Cambridge University Press.
Minear, P. S.
1960 *Images of the Church in the New Testament*. Philadelphia: Westminster.
Mitchell, S.
1993 *Anatolia: Land, Men, and Gods in Asia Minor*. 2 vols. Oxford: Clarendon.
Mitton, C. L.
1951 *The Epistle to the Ephesians*. Oxford: Clarendon.
Moe, O.
1949 Der Gedanke des allgemeinen Priestertums im Hebräerbrief. *TZ* 5: 161–69.
Mommsen, T.
1909 *The Provinces of the Roman Empire from Caesar to Diocletian*. 2 vols. New York: Macmillan.
Monnier, J.
1904 *La descente aux enfers: Étude de pensée religieuse, d'art et de littérature*. Paris: Fischbacher.
Montefiore, C. G., and H. Loewe
1963 A *Rabbinic Anthology*. New York: World / Philadelphia: Jewish Publication Society of America.
Montagu, A.
1973 *The Natural Superiority of Women*. Rev. ed. New York: Macmillan/ Collier.

Monumenta Asiae Minoris Antiqua
1928–37 5 vols. Publications of the American Society for Archeological Research in Asia Minor. Manchester: Manchester University Press.

Moran, W. L.
1962 A Kingdom of Priests. Pages 7–20 in *The Bible in Current Catholic Thought*. Edited by J. L. McKenzie. New York: Herder & Herder.

Moreau, J.
1950 Le nom des Chrétiens. *La Nouvelle Clio* 4:190–92.
1971 *Die Christenverfolgung im römischen Reich*. Die Welt der Religion n.s. 2. 2d ed. Berlin: de Gruyter.

Morgenstern, J.
1961 The Suffering Servant: A New Solution. *VT* 11:292–320, 406–31.

Morris. L.
1965 *The Cross in the New Testament*. Grand Rapids: Eerdmans.

Morrison, C. D.
1960 *The Powers That Be: Earthly Rulers and Demonic Powers in Romans 13:1–7*. Studies in Biblical Theology 29. Naperville: Allenson.

Motyer, S.
1989 The Relationship between Paul's Gospel of "All One in Christ Jesus" (Galatians 3:28) and the Household Codes. *Vox Evangelica* 19:33–48.

Moule, C. F. D.
1961 *Worship in the New Testament*. Richmond: John Knox.
1960 *An Idiom-Book of the New Testament Greek*. 2d ed. Cambridge: Cambridge University Press.
1982 *Essays in New Testament Interpretation*. Cambridge: Cambridge University Press.

Moule, C. F. D., ed.
1968 *The Significance of the Message of the Resurrection for Faith in Jesus Christ*. SBT Second Series 8. London: SCM.

Moulton, J. H., et al.
1908–76 *A Grammar of New Testament Greek*. 4 vols. Edinburgh: T. & T. Clark.

Moxnes, H.
1988a Honour and Righteousness in Romans. *JSNT* 32:61–78.
1988b Honor, Shame, and the Outside World in Paul's Letter to the Romans. Pages 207–18 in *The Social World of Formative Christianity and Judaism*. Howard Clark Kee Festschrift. Edited by Jacob Neusner et al. Philadelphia: Fortress.

Mühlhaupt, E.
1963 *Allgemeines Priestertum oder Klerikalismus*. Calwer Hefte 65. Stuttgart: Calwer.

Müller, F.
1955 Berufung und Erwählung. *ZST* 24:38–71.

Müller, H.-P.
1976 "*qds*." Pages 589–609 in vol. 2 of *THAT*.

Müller, K.
1983 Die Haustafel des Kolosserbriefes und das antike Frauenthema: Eine kritische Rückschau auf alte Ergebnisse. Pages 263–319 in *Die Frau im Urchristentum*. QD 95. Freiburg: Herder.

Müller, U. B.
1976 *Zur frühchristlichen Theologiegeschichte: Judenchristentum und Paulinismus in Kleinasien an der Wende vom ersten zum zweiten Jahrhundert n. Chr.* Gütersloh: Gütersloher.
Muilenburg, J.
1959 Covenantal Formulations. *VT* 9:343–65.
1962 Holiness. Pages 616–25 in vol. 2 of *IDB*.
Mullins, M.
1991 *Called to Be Saints: Christian Living in First-Century Rome*. Dublin: Veritas.
Muntingh, L. M.
1962 Die Begrip *gêr* in die OT. *Nederduitse Gereformeerde Teologiese Tydskrif* 3:34–58.
Murphy O'Connor, J.
1993 Co-authorship in the Corinthian Correspondence. *RB* 100:562–79.
Murray, G.
1955 *The Five Stages of Greek Religion*. Garden City, New York: Doubleday.
Mussies, G.
1972 *Dio Chrysostom and the New Testament*. Studia ad Corpus Hellenisticum Novi Testamenti 2. Leiden: Brill.
Musurillo, H.
1972 The Christian Persecutions. Pages lvii–lxii in *The Acts of the Christian Martyrs*. Edited by H. Musurillo. Oxford: Clarendon.
Nauck, W.
1958 Das *oun*-paräneticum. *ZNW* 49:134–35.
Neal, J.
1885 *Kissing: Its Curious Biblical Mentions*. London: Simpkin, Marshall.
Neill, S.
1964 *The Interpretation of the New Testament 1861–1961*. London: Oxford.
Nelson, R. D.
1993 *Raising Up a Faithful Priest. Community and Priesthood in Biblical Theology*. Louisville: Westminster John Knox.
Nestle, D.
1972 Freiheit. Pages 269–306 in vol. 8 of *RAC*.
Nestle, W.
1990 Die Haupteinwände des antiken Denkens gegen das Christentum. Pages 17–80 in *Christentum und antike Gesellschaft*. Edited by J. Martin and B. Quint. Darmstadt: Wissenschaftliche.
Neubauer, A.
1969 *The Fifty-Third Chapter of Isaiah according to the Jewish Interpreters*. 2 vols. New York: KTAV.
Neusner, J.
1964 *A History of the Jews in Babylonia*. Leiden: Brill.
1973 *The Idea of Purity in Ancient Judaism*. Leiden: Brill.
1979a Geschichte und rituelle Reinheit im Judentum des 1. Jahrhunderts n. Chr. *Kairos* 21:119–32.
1979b *The Tosefta: The Order of Women*. New York: KTAV.
1981 *Judaism: The Evidence of the Mishnah*. Chicago: University of Chicago Press.

1987 *What Is Midrash?* Guides to Biblical Scholarship. Philadelphia: Fortress.
1989 *Judaism and Its Social Metaphors*. Cambridge: Cambridge University Press.

Neusner, J., and E. S. Frerichs, eds.
1985 *"To See Ourselves as Others See Us": Christians, Jews, "Others" in Late Antiquity*. Chico, California: Scholars Press.

Newsom, C. A., and S. H. Ringe, eds.
1992 *The Women's Bible Commentary*. London: SPCK.

Newton, M.
1985 *The Concept of Purity at Qumran and in the Letters of Paul*. SNTSMS 53. Cambridge: Cambridge University Press.

Neyrey, J. H.
1986 The Idea of Purity in Mark's Gospel. *Semeia* 35 (*Social-Scientific Criticism of the New Testament and Its Social World*):91–128.
1988 Unclean, Common, Polluted, and Taboo: A Short Reading Guide. *Forum* 4:72–82.
1990 *Paul, in Other Words: A Cultural Reading of His Letters*. Louisville: Westminster John Knox.
1993 *2 Peter, Jude*. AB 37C. New York: Doubleday.

Neyrey, J. H., ed.
1991 *The Social World of Luke–Acts: Models for Interpretation*. Peabody, Massachusetts: Hendrickson.

Nicholson, E. E.
1973 *Exodus and Sinai in History and Tradition*. Richmond: John Knox.

Nickelsburg, G. W. E.
1972 *Resurrection, Immortality and Eternal Life in Intertestamental Judaism*. HTS 26. Cambridge: Harvard University Press.
1977 Apocalyptic and Myth in 1 Enoch 6–11. *JBL* 96:383–405.
1981a Enoch, Levi, and Peter: Recipients of Revelation in Upper Galilee. *JBL* 100:575–600.
1981b *Jewish Literature between the Bible and the Mishnah*. Philadelphia: Fortress.
1990 Two Enochic Manuscripts: Unstudied Evidence for Egyptian Christianity. Pages 251–60 in *Of Scribes and Scrolls: Studies on the Hebrew Bible, Intertestamental Judaism, and Christian Origins*. John Strugnell Festschrift. Edited by H. W. Attridge et al. College Theology Society Resources in Religion 5. Lanham, Maryland: University Press of America.
1992a Enoch, First Book of. Pages 508–16 in vol. 2 of *ABD*.
1992b Eschatology: Early Jewish Literature. Pages 579–94 in vol. 2 of *ABD*.
1992c Resurrection (Early Judaism and Christianity). Pages 684–91 in vol. 5 of *ABD*.

Niebecker, E.
1936 *Das allgemeine Priestertum aller Gläubigen*. Paderborn: Schöningh.

Niebuhr, H. R.
1956 *Christ and Culture*. New York: Harper.

Nocent, A.
1970 Il sacerdozio dei fedeli secondo Giovanni Crisostomo. *Vetera Christianorum* 7:305–24.

Nötscher, F.
1959–60 Heiligkeit in den Qumranschriften. *RQ* 2:163–81, 315–44.
Noll, R. R.
1993 *Christian Ministerial Priesthood: A Search for Its Beginnings in the Primary Documents of the Apostolic Fathers*. San Francisco: Catholic Scholars Press.
Nordblad, C.
1912 *Föreställningen om Kristi hadesförd undersoekt till sitt ursprung: En religionshistorisk studie*. Uppsala.
North, C. R.
1948 *The Suffering Servant in Deutero-Isaiah: An Historical and Critical Study*. London: Oxford University Press.
North, R.
1963 Anatolia. Columns 472–83 in vol. 1 of *Enciclopedia de la Biblia*. Barcelona: Garriga.
Nyrop, C.
1901 *The Kiss and Its History*. London: Sand.
O'Brien, P. T.
1977 *Introductory Thanksgivings in the Letters of Paul*. NovTSup 49. Leiden: Brill.
1978 Ephesians 1: An Unusual Introduction to a New Testament Letter. *NTS* 25:504–16.
Odeberg, H.
1944 Nederstigen till dodsriket. *Bibelsk Månadshefte* 18/12:357–59.
Oden, R. A., Jr.
1987 The Place of the Covenant in the Religion of Israel. Pages 429–47 in *Ancient Israelite Religion*. F. M. Cross Festschrift. Edited by P. D. Miller et al. Philadelphia: Fortress.
1992 Cosmogony, Cosmology. Pages 1162–71 in vol. 1 of *ABD*.
Oepke, A.
1964 "*gynê*." Pages 776–89 in vol. 1 of *TDNT*.
Oertel, F.
1921 "*katoikoi*." Pages 1–26 in vol. 11/1 of *PW*.
Ogletree, T. W.
1983 *The Use of the Bible in Christian Ethics: A Constructive Essay*. Philadelphia: Fortress.
1985 *Hospitality to the Stranger: Dimensions of Moral Understanding*. Philadelphia: Fortress.
Ohly, F.
1986 Haus III (Metapher). Pages 905–1063 in vol. 13 of *RAC*.
Oliver, W. H., and A. G. van Aarde
1991 The Community of Faith as Dwelling-Place of the Father: *Basileia tou theou* as "Household of God" in the Johannine Farewell Discourse(s). *Neot* 25:379–400.
Ollenburger, B. C.
1987 *Zion, City of the Great King*. JSOTSup 41. Sheffield: Sheffield Academic Press.
Olofsson, S.
1990 *God Is My Rock: A Study of Translation Technique and Theological Exegesis in the Septuagint*. ConBOT 31. Stockholm: Almqvist & Wiksell.

Ordonez, V.
1956 El Sacerdocio de los Fideles (Sentido escrituristico textual). *Revista Española de Teologia* 64:359–79.
Orlinsky, H. M.
1967 The So-Called "Servant of the Lord" and "Suffering Servant" in Second Isaiah. Pages 1–33 in *Studies on the Second Part of the Book of Isaiah*. Edited by G. W. Anderson et al. VTSup 14. Leiden: Brill.
Ortner, S. B.
1974 Is Female to Male as Nature Is to Culture? Pages 67–88 in *Woman, Culture, and Society*. Edited by M. Z. Rosaldo and L. Lamphere. Stanford: Stanford University Press.
Osborne, K. B.
1988 The Meaning of Lay, Laity and Lay Ministry in the Christian Theology of Church. *Antonianum* 53:227–58.
1993 *Ministry. Lay Ministry in the Roman Catholic Church: Its History and Theology*. New York: Paulist.
Osburn, C. D., ed.
1993 *Essays on Women in Earliest Christianity*. Joplin, Missouri: College Press.
Osiek, C.
1992 Slavery in the Second Testament World: BTB Readers Guide. *BTB* 22: 174–79.
1996 The Family in Early Christianity: "Family Values" Revisited. *CBQ* 58: 1–24.
Osten-Sacken, P. von der
1964 Bemerkungen zur Stellung des *Mebaqqêr* in der Sektenschrift. ZNW 58:18–26.
Oster, R. E., Jr.
1992 Christianity in Asia Minor. Pages 938–54 in vol. 1 of *ABD*.
Otto, R.
1958 *The Idea of the Holy: An Inquiry into the Non-rational Factor in the Idea of the Divine and Its Relation to the Rational*. Translated by J. W. Harvey. New York: Oxford University Press.
Overman, J. A., and W. S. Green
1992 Judaism: Judaism in the Greco-Roman Period. Pages 1037–54 in vol. 3 of *ABD*.
Page, S. H. T.
1995 *Powers of Evil: A Biblical Study of Satan and Demons*. Grand Rapids: Baker.
Pagels, E.
1991 The Social History of Satan, the "Intimate Enemy": A Preliminary Sketch. *HTR* 84:1–23.
1992 The Social History of Satan, Part 2: The Human Face(s) of Satan in the Gospel. Pages 320–45 in *SBL 1992: Seminar Papers*. SBLSP 31. Atlanta: Scholars Press.
Panikulam, G.
1979 KOINÔNIA *in the New Testament: A Dynamic Expression of Christian Life*. AB 85. Rome: Pontifical Biblical Institute.

Parson, M. C.
1987 *The Departure of Jesus in Luke–Acts: The Ascension Narratives in Context.* JSNTSup 21. Sheffield: JSOT Press.
Patai, R.
1959 *Sex and Family in the Bible and the Middle East.* Garden City, New York: Doubleday.
1983 The Realm of Sex. Pages 118–42 in *The Arab Mind.* Rev. ed. New York: Scribner's.
Patrick, D.
1992 Election. Pages 434–41 in vol. 2 of *ABD.*
Patrologiae cursus completus: Series Graeca
1857–68 Edited by J.-P. Migne. Paris: Migne.
Patrologiae cursus completus: Series Latina
1844–55 Edited by J.-P. Migne. Paris: Migne. [1958–1975]
Peel, M.
1969 *The Epistle to Rheginos.* Philadelphia: Westminster.
Peel, M., and J. Zandee
1972 "The Teaching of Silvanus" from the Library of Nag Hammadi (CG VII:84,15–118,7). *NovT* 14:294–311.
Pellend, L.
1949 Le sacerdoce des fidèles. *ScEccl* 2:5–26.
Pellett, D. C.
1962a Asia. Pages 257–59 in vol. 1 of *IDB.*
1962b Cappadocia. Pages 534–35 in vol. 1 of *IDB.*
Peradotto, J., and J. P. Sullivan, eds.
1984 *Women in the Ancient World: The Arethusa Papers.* Albany: State University of New York Press.
Percy, E.
1946 *Die Probleme der Kolosser- und Epheserbriefe.* Lund: Gleerup.
Perdue, L. G., and J. G. Gammie
1990 *Semeia* 50 (*Paraenesis: Act and Form*). Atlanta: Scholars Press.
Perella, N. J.
1969 *The Kiss, Sacred and Profane.* Berkeley: University of California Press.
Peristiany, J. G., ed.
1966 *Honour and Shame: The Values of Mediterranean Society.* London: Weidenfeld & Nicolson, 1965. Reprinted Chicago: University of Chicago Press.
Perkins, P.
1984 *Resurrection: New Testament Witness and Contemporary Reflection.* New York: Doubleday.
Perler, O.
1966 *Méliton de Sardes sur la Pâque et Fragments.* SC 123. Paris: Cerf.
Perlitt, L.
1969 *Bundestheologie im Alten Testament.* WMANT 36. Neukirchen-Vluyn: Neukirchner Verlag.
Perrot, C.
1969 La descente du Christ aux enfers dans le Nouveau Testament. *Lumière et Vie* 87:5–29.

Pesch, R.
1976–77 *Das Markusevangelium*. 2 vols. HTKNT 2. Freiburg: Herder.
Pesch, W.
1970 Zu Texten des Neuen Testaments über das Priestertum der Getauften. Pages 303–15 in *Verborum Veritas*. Gustav Stählin Festschrift. Edited by O. Böcher and K. Haacker. Wuppertal: Brockhaus.
Peters, F. E.
1970 *The Harvest of Hellenism: A History of the Near East from Alexander the Great to the Triumph of Christianity*. New York: Simon & Schuster.
Petersen, D. L.
1992 Eschatology: Old Testament. Pages 575–79 in vol. 2 of *IDB*.
Peterson, E.
1982 Christianus. Pages 355–72 in *Miscellanea Giovanni Mercati I*. Studi e Testi 121. Vatican City, 1946. Reprinted pp. 64–87 in *Frühkirche, Judentum und Gnosis: Studien und Untersuchungen*. Darmstadt: Wissenschaftliche.
Pfammatter, J.
1960 *Die Kirche als Bau*. Analecta Gregoriana 110. Rome: Gregorian Pontifical University.
Pfitzner, V. C.
1967 *Paul and the Agon Motif*. NovTSup 16. Leiden: Brill.
1970 The Biblical Concept of Truth. *Lutheran Theological Journal* 4:1–15.
1971 "General Priesthood" and Ministry. *Lutheran Theological Journal* 5:97–110.
Piepkorn, A. C.
1971 Charisma in the New Testament and the Apostolic Fathers. *CTM* 42: 369–89.
Pierce, C. A.
1955 *Conscience in the New Testament*. SBT 15. London: SCM.
Pietri, C.
1976 *Roma christiana: Recherches sur l'Eglise de Rome, son organisation, sa politique, son idéologie de Miltiade a Sixte III (311–440)*. 2 vols. Bibliotheque des écoles françaises d'Athènes et de Rome 224. Rome: École française de Rome.
Pilch, J. J.
1991b *Introducing the Cultural Context of the New Testament*. Hear the Word 2. New York: Paulist.
1991c *Introducing the Cultural Context of the Old Testament*. Hear the Word 1. New York: Paulist.
1993 "Beat His Ribs While He Is Young" (Sir 30:12): A Window on the Mediterranean World. *BTB* 23:101–13.
1995 Death with Honor: The Mediterranean Style Death of Jesus in Mark. *BTB* 25:65–70.
Pilch, J. J., and B. J. Malina, eds.
1993 *Biblical Social Values and Their Meaning: A Handbook*. Peabody, Massachusetts: Hendrickson.
Pilhofer, P.
1990 PRESBYTERON KREITTON: *Der Altersbeweis der jüdischen und christlichen Apologeten und seine Vorgeschichte*. WUNT 2/39. Tübingen: Mohr (Siebeck).

Piper, J.
1979 *"Love Your Enemies": Jesus' Love Command in the Synoptic Gospels and in the Early Christian Paraenesis. A History of the Tradition and Interpretation of Its Uses.* SNTSMS 38. Cambridge: Cambridge University Press.

Pitt-Rivers, J.
1968 Pseudo-Kinship. Pages 408–13 in vol. 8 of *International Encyclopedia of the Social Sciences.* Edited by D. L. Sills. New York: Macmillan/Free.
1977 *The Fate of Shechem or the Politics of Sex: Essays in the Anthropology of the Mediterranean.* New York: Cambridge University Press.
1992 Postscript: The Place of Grace in Anthropology. Pages 215–46 in *Honor and Grace in Anthropology.* Edited by J. G. Peristiany and J. Pitt-Rivers. Cambridge Studies in Social and Cultural Anthropology. Cambridge: Cambridge University Press.

Plamer, P. F.
1947 The Lay Priesthood: Real or Metaphorical? *TS* 8:574–613.

Plevnik, J.
1993 Honor/Shame. Pages 95–104 in *Biblical Social Values and Their Meaning: A Handbook.* Edited by J. J. Pilch and B. J. Malina. Peabody, Massachusetts: Hendrickson.

Plooy, D.
1932 *Studies in the Testimony Book.* Verhandelingen der Koninklijke Akademie van Wetenschappen te Amsterdam: Afdeling Letterkunde n.s. 32/2. Amsterdam.

Plümacher, E.
1987 *Identitätsverlust und Identitätsgewinn: Studien zum Verhältnis von kaiserzeitlicher Stadt und frühem Christentum.* Biblisch-Theologische Studien 11. Neukirchen-Vluyn: Neukirchner Verlag.

Plumptre, E. H.
1885 "The Spirits in Prison" and "The Descent into Hell." In *The Spirits in Prison and Other Studies on the Life after Death.* 2d ed. London: Isbister.

Pobee, J. S.
1985 *Persecution and Martyrdom in the Theology of Paul.* JSNT 6. Sheffield: JSOT Press.

Pomeroy, S. B.
1975 *Goddesses, Whores, Wives and Slaves: Women in Classical Antiquity.* New York: Schocken.
1984a Selected Bibliography on Women in Classical Antiquity. Pages 315–72 in *Women in the Ancient World: The Arethusa Papers.* Edited by J. Perradotto and J. P. Sullivan. Albany: State University of New York Press.
1984b *Women in Hellenistic Egypt from Alexander to Cleopatra.* New York: Schocken.

Pomeroy, S. B., ed.
1991 *Women's History and Ancient History.* Chapel Hill: University of North Carolina Press.

Pontifical Biblical Commission
1993 *The Interpretation of the Bible in the Church.* Vatican City: Libreria Editrice Vaticane.

Popkes, W.
1976 Gemeinschaft. Pages 1000–1145 in vol. 9 of *RAC.*

Potter, D. S.
1992 Persecution of the Early Church. Pages 231–35 in vol. 5 of *ABD*.
Powell, D.
1975 Ordo Presbyterii. *JTS* 26:290–328.
Prenter, R.
1961 Allgemeines Priestertum. Pages 581–82 in vol. 5 of *RGG*[3].
Price, S. R. F.
1986 *Rituals and Power: The Roman Imperial Cult in Asia Minor*. New York: Cambridge University Press.
Prigent, P.
1959 Quelques Testimonia messianiques. *TZ* 15:419–30.
1961 *Les Testimonia dans le Christianisme primitif: L'Épître de Barnabé I–XVI et ses Sources*. Études Bibliques. Paris.
Procksch, O., and K. G. Kuhn
1964 "*hagios* etc." Pages 88–115 in vol. 1 of *TDNT*.
Prümm, K.
1935 *Der Christliche Glaube und die altheidnische Welt*. 2 vols. Leipzig: Hegner.
Przbylski, B.
1980 *Righteousness in Matthew and His World of Thought*. SNTSMS 41. Cambridge: Cambridge University Press.
Putzger, F. W.
1961 *Historischer Weltatlas*. 85th ed. Bielefeld: Velhagen & Klasing.
Quell, G.
1967 Election in the Old Testament. Pages 145–68 in vol. 4 of *TDNT*.
Quilliet, H.
1911 Descente de Jésus aux Enfers. Columns 565–619 in vol. 4 of *Dictionnaire de théologie catholique*. Paris: Letouzey et Ané.
Quinn, J. D.
1970 Ministry in the New Testament. Pages 69–100 in *Lutherans and Catholics in Dialogue, IV: Eucharist and Ministry*. Edited by P. C. Empie and T. A. Murphy. New York: U.S.A. National Committee of the Lutheran World Federation / Washington, D.C.: Bishop's Committee for Ecumenical and Interreligious Affairs.
Rad, G. von, K. G. Kuhn, and W. Gutbrod
1965 "*Israêl* etc." Pages 356–91 in vol. 3 of *TDNT*.
Rade, M.
1918 *Das königliche Priestertum der Gläubigen und seine Forderung an die Evangelische Kirche unserer Zeit*. Tübingen: Mohr (Siebeck).
Ramsay, W. M.
1904 *The Church in the Roman Empire before A.D. 170*. 8th ed. London: Hodder & Stoughton.
1972 *The Historical Geography of Asia Minor*. London: Murray, 1890. Reprinted Totowa, New Jersey: Cooper Sq.
Rausch, T. P.
1976 *Priesthood and Ministry: From Küng to the Ecumenical Debate*. 2 vols. Ph.D. Dissertation, Duke University.
Reese, J. M.
1978 The Principal Model of God in the New Testament. *BTB* 8:126–31.

Reeves-Sanday, P.
1981 *Female Power and Male Dominance: On the Origins of Sexual Inequality.* Cambridge: Cambridge University Press.

Reicke, B.
1951 *Diakonie, Festfreude und Zelos in Verbindung mit der altchristlichen Agapenfeier.* Uppsala Universitets Årsskrift 1951/5. Uppsala: Lundquistska.
1959 Höllenfahrt Christi, I. Pages 408–10 in vol. 3 of *RGG*[3].
1968 *The New Testament Era: The World of the Bible from 500 B.C. to A.D. 100.* Philadelphia: Fortress.

Reijners, G. Q.
1965 *The Terminology of the Holy Cross in Early Christian Literature as Based upon Old Testament Typology.* Graecitas Christianorum Primaeva 2. Nijmegen: Dekker & van de Vegt.

Reitzenstein, R.
1927 *Die hellenistischen Mysterienreligionen nach ihren Grundgedanken und Wirkungen.* 3d ed. Leipzig: Teubner.

Rengstorf, K. H.
1953 Die neutestamentlichen Mahnungen an die Frau, sich dem Manne unterzuordnen. Pages 131–45 in *Verbum Dei Manet in Aeternum.* O. Schmitz Festschrift. Edited by W. Foerster. Witten: Luther.
1954 Pages 7–52 in *Mann und Frau im Urchristentum.* Arbeitsgemeinschaft für Forschung des Landes Nordrhein Westfalen 12. Cologne: Opladen.
1962 Old and New Testament Traces of a Formula of the Judean Royal Ritual. *NovT* 5:229–44.
1964a "*apostellô* etc." Pages 398–447 in vol. 1 of *TDNT.*
1964b The Idea of New Birth by Conversion to the True Religion in Later Judaism. Pages 665–68 in vol. 1 of *TDNT.*

Rensburg, S. P. J. J.
1970 Sanctification according to the New Testament. *HTR* 26:18–28.

Repo, E.
1951–54 *Der Begriff "Rhema" im Biblischgriechischen: Eine Traditionsgeschichtliche und semiologische Untersuchung.* 2 vols. Annales Academiae Scientiarum Fennicae B 75/2, 88/1. Helsinki: Akateeminen Kirjakauppa.

Reumann, J.
1957 *The Use of* Oikonomia *and Related Terms in Greek Sources to about A.D. 100 as a Background for Patristic Applications.* Ph.D. Dissertation, University of Pennsylvania.
1958 "Stewards of God": Pre-Christian Religious Application of *oikonomos* in Greek. *JBL* 77:339–49.
1959 *Oikonomia*–"Covenant": Terms for Heilsgeschichte in Early Christian Usage. *NovT* 3:282–99.
1966–67 *Oikonomia* Terms in Paul in Comparison with Lucan Heilsgeschichte. *TS* 13:147–67.
1970 Ordained Minister and Layman in Lutheranism. Pages 227–82 in *Eucharist and Ministry.* Lutherans and Catholics in Dialogue 4. Edited by P. C. Empie and T. Austin Murphy. New York: U.S.A. National Committee of the Lutheran World Federation.

1985 The "Righteousness of God" and the "Economy of God": Two Great Doctrinal Themes Historically Compared. Pages 615–37 in *Analypo*. Archbishop Methodius of Thyatira Festschrift. Athens.

1992 Righteousness: Early Judaism, Graeco-Roman World, New Testament. Pages 736–73 in vol. 5 of *ABD*.

Reviv, H.

1989 *The Elders in Ancient Israel: A Study of a Biblical Institution*. Jerusalem: Magnes.

Richards, E. R.

1991 *The Secretary in the Letters of Paul*. WUNT 2/42. Tübingen: Mohr (Siebeck).

Richards, W. L.

1974 Textual Criticism on the Greek Text of the Catholic Epistles: A Bibliography. *AUSS* 12:103–11.

1975 The Present Status of Text Critical Studies in the Catholic Epistles. *AUSS* 13:261–72.

1976 The New Testament Greek Manuscripts of the Catholic Epistles. *AUSS* 14:301–11.

Richardson, P.

1969 *Israel in the Apostolic Church*. SNTSMS 10. Cambridge: Cambridge University Press.

Riemann, P. A.

1976 Covenant, Mosaic. Pages 192–97 in *IDBSup*.

Riesenfeld, H.

1950 La descente dans la Mort. Pages 207–17 in *Aux Sources de la Tradition Chrétienne*. M. Goguel Festschrift. Neuchâtel: Delachaux & Niestle.

Rigaux, B.

1956 *Saint Paul: Les Épîtres aux Thessaloniciens*. Paris: Gabalda.

Ringger, J.

1960 Das Felsenwort: Zur Sinndeutung von Mt 16, 18, vor allem im Lichte der Symbolgeschichte. Pages 271–347 in *Begegnung der Christen: Studien evangelischer und katholischer Theologen*. 2d ed. Edited by M. Roesle and O. Cullmann. Stuttgart: Evangelisches.

Ringgren, H.

1948 *The Prophetical Conception of Holiness*. Uppsala Universitetsårsskrift 12. Uppsala.

Rist, M.

1961 Eschatology of Apoc[rypha] and Pseud[epigrapha]. Pages 133–35 in vol. 2 of *IDB*.

Robbins, V. F.

1991 The Social Location of the Implied Author of Luke–Acts. Pages 305–32 in *The Social World of Luke–Acts: Models for Interpretation*. Edited by J. H. Neyrey. Peabody, Massachusetts: Hendrickson.

Robertson, A. T.

1919 *A Grammar of the Greek New Testament in the Light of Historical Research*. 3d. ed. New York: Hodder & Stoughton, George H. Doran.

Robinson, J. A. T.

1962 Resurrection in the NT. Pages 43–53 in vol. 4 of *IDB*.

1976 *Redating the New Testament*. Philadelphia: Westminster.

Robinson, J. M.
1964 Die Hodajot-Formel in Gebet und Hymnus des Frühchristentums. Pages 194–325 in *Apophoreta*. Ernst Haenchen Festschrift. Edited by W. Eltester and F. H. Kettler. BZNW 30. Berlin: Alfred Töpelmann.

Rödding, G.
1970 Descendit ad inferna. Pages 95–102 in *Kerygma und Melos*. C. Mahrenholz Festschrift. Edited by V. W. Blankenburg et al. Kassel: Bärenreiter.

Rogers, S. C.
1975 Female Forms of Power and the Myth of Male Dominance: A Model of Female/Male Interaction in Peasant Society. *American Ethnologist* 2:727–56.

Rohde, J.
1993 "*presbyteros*." Pages 148–49 in vol. 3 of *EDNT.*

Roheim, J. M.
1958 The Common Human Pattern (Origin and Scope of Historical Theories). *Journal of World History* 4:449–63.

Rohrbaugh, R. L.
1993 The Social Location of the Marcan Audience. *BTB* 23:114–27.

Roller, O.
1933 *Das Formular der paulinischen Briefe: Ein Beitrag zur Lehre vom antiken Briefe*. BWANT 4/6. Stuttgart: Kohlhammer.

Roloff, J.
1965 *Apostolat—Verkündigung—Kirche*. Gütersloh: Gütersloher/Mohn.
1978 Amt/Ämter/Amtsverständnis IV: Im Neuen Testament. Pages 509–33 in vol. 2 of *TRE*.

Rosa, G. de
1972 Il sacerdozio commune dei fedeli nel Nuovo Testamento. *Civiltà Cattolica* 123/2938:350–57.

Rosaldo, M. Z.
1974 Woman, Culture, and Society: A Theoretical Overview. Pages 17–42 in *Women, Culture, and Society*. Edited by M. Z. Rosaldo and L. Lamphere. Stanford: Stanford University Press.

Rostovtzeff, M. I.
1953 *The Social and Economic History of the Hellenistic World*. 3 vols. Oxford: Clarendon.
1957 *The Social and Economic History of the Roman Empire*. 2 vols. 2d rev. ed. Edited by P. M. Fraser. Oxford: Clarendon.

Rousseau, O.
1951–52 La descente aux enfers, fondement sotériologique du baptême chrétien. *RSR* 40:273–97.

Rowley, H. H.
1964 *The Biblical Doctrine of Election*. London: Lutterworth.

Ruppert, L.
1972a *Jesus als der leidende Gerechte? Der Weg Jesu im Lichte eines alt- und zwischentestamentlichen Motivs*. SBS 59. Stuttgart: Katholisches Bibelwerk.
1972b *Der leidende Gerechte: Eine motivgeschichtliche Untersuchung zum Alten Testament und zwischentestamentlichen Judentum*. FB 5. Würzburg: Echter.

1973 *Der leidende Gerechte und seine Feinde: Eine Wortfelduntersuchung.* Würzburg: Echter.

Rusam, D.

1993 *Die Gemeinschaft der Kinder Gottes: Das Motiv der Gotteskindschaft und die Gemeinden der johanneischen Briefe.* BWANT 133. Stuttgart: Kohlhammer.

Russell, J. B.

1977 *The Devil: Perceptions of Evil from Antiquity to Primitive Christianity.* Ithaca, New York: Cornell University Press.

1981 *Satan: The Early Christian Tradition.* Ithaca, New York: Cornell University Press.

1988 *The Prince of Darkness: Radical Evil and the Power of Good in History.* Ithaca, New York: Cornell University Press.

Ryan, L.

1962 Patristic Teaching on the Priesthood of the Faithful. *ITQ* 29:26–51.

Sänger, D.

1994 "Verflucht ist jeder, der am Holze hängt" (Gal 3,13b): Zur Rezeption einer frühen antichristlichen Polemik. ZNW 85:279–85.

Safrai, S.

1974 Relations between the Diaspora and the Land of Israel. Pages 184–215 in vol. 1 of *The Jewish People in the First Century.* Edited by S. Safrai and M. Stern. CRINT Section 1. Philadelphia: Fortress.

Safrai, S., and M. Stern, eds.

1974–76 *The Jewish People in the First Century.* 2 vols. CRINT Section 1. Philadelphia: Fortress.

Sahin, S., E. Schwertheim, and J. Wagners, eds.

1978 *Studien zur Religion und Kultur Kleinasiens.* 2 vols. Karl Friedrich Dörner Festschrift. Études Préliminaires aux Religions Orientales dans l'empire romain 66. Leiden: Brill.

Salmon, A. P.

1963 The Imperatival Use of the Participle in the New Testament. *Australian Biblical Review* 11:41–49.

Sampley, J. P.

1971 *"And the Two Shall Become One Flesh": A Study of Traditions in Ephesians* 5:21–33. SNTSMS 16. Cambridge: Cambridge University Press.

Sanders, E. P.

1977a The Election and the Covenant. Pages 84–107 in *Paul and Palestinian Judaism: A Comparison of Patterns of Religion.* Philadelphia: Fortress.

1977b *Paul and Palestinian Judaism: A Comparison of Patterns of Religion.* Philadelphia: Fortress.

Sanders, J. A.

1955 *Suffering as Divine Discipline in the OT and Post-biblical Judaism.* Rochester, New York: Colgate Rochester Divinity School.

1962 Dispersion. Pages 854–56 in vol. 1 of *IDB.*

Sanders, J. T.

1962 The Transition from Opening Epistolary Thanksgiving to Body in the Letters of the Pauline Corpus. *JBL* 81:348–62.

1975 *Ethics in the New Testament: Change and Development.* Philadelphia: Fortress.

Schaefer, H.
1949 "*Paroikoi*." Pages 1675–1707 in vol. 18/4 of *PW*.
Schäfer, K.
1989 *Gemeinde als "Bruderschaft": Ein Beitrag zum Kirchenverständnis des Paulus*. Europäische Hochschulschriften 23: Theologie 333. Frankfurt: Lang.
Schäfer, P.
1980 Benediktionen, I: Judentum. Pages 560–62 in vol. 5 of *TRE*.
Schelkle, K. H.
1950a "*Akrogōniaios*." Pages 233–34 in vol. 1 of *RAC*.
1950b Jerusalem und Rom im Neuen Testament. *TGl* 40:77–119.
1954 Bruder. Pages 631–40 in vol. 2 of *RAC*.
Schenk, W.
1967 *Der Segen im Neuen Testament*. Berlin: Evangelische.
Schenke, L.
1971 Zur sogenannten "*Oikos*-formel" im Neuen Testament. *Kairos* 13: 226–43.
Schille, G.
1962 *Frühchristliche Hymnen*. Berlin: Evangelische.
Schillinger-Häfele, U.
1979 Plinius ep. 10,96 u[nd]. 97: Eine Frage und ihre Beantwortung. *Chiron* 9:383–92.
Schlier, H.
1958 *Der Brief an die Epheser: Ein Kommentar*. 2d ed. Düsseldorf: Patmos.
1961 *Principalities and Powers in the New Testament*. New York: Herder & Herder.
1964 "*gala*." Pages 645–47 in vol. 1 of *TDNT*.
1969 Grundelemente des priesterlichen Amtes im Neuen Testament. *Theologie und Philosophie* 44:161–80.
Schmidt, B.
1906 *Die Vorstellungen von der Höllenfahrt Christi in der alten Kirche*. n.p.
Schmidt, C.
1919 Exkurs II: Der *Descensus ad Inferos* in der Alten Kirche. Pages 453–76 in *Gespräche Jesu mit seinen Jüngern nach der Auferstehung*. Edited by P. Lacau, C. Schmidt, and I. Wajnberg. Leipzig: Hinrichs. Reprinted Hildesheim: Olms, 1967.
Schmidt, K. L.
1945 Israels Stellung zu den Fremdlingen und Beisassen und Israels Wissen um seine Fremdlings- und Beisassenschaft. *Judaica* 1:269–96.
Schmidt, K. L., M. A. Schmidt, and R. Meyer
1967 "*paroikos* etc." Pages 841–53 in vol. 5 of *TDNT*.
Schmidt, P.
1978 *Vater-Kind-Bruder: Biblische Begriffe in Anthropologischer Sicht*. Düsseldorf: Patmos.
Schmidt, W.
1961 *Königtum Gottes in Ugarit und Israel*. BZAW 80. Berlin: Alfred Töpelmann.
Schmidthals, W.
1969 *The Office of Apostle in the Early Church*. Nashville: Abingdon.

Schmitt, J.
1955 Les écrits du Noveau Testament et les textes de Qumran [Part 1]. 29:381–401.
1956 Les écrits du Noveau Testament et les textes de Qumran [Part 2]. 30: 55–74, 261–82.

Schmitt Pantel, P., ed.
1993 *Antike*. Volume 1 of *Geschichte der Frauen*. Edited by G. Duby and M. Perrot. Frankfurt: Campyrus.

Schmitz, O.
1910 *Die Opferanschauungen des späten Judentums und die Opferaussagen des Neuen Testaments*. Tübingen: Mohr.

Schnackenburg, R.
1949 *Episkopos* und Hirtenamt. Pages 66–88 in *Episkopus: Studien über das Bischofsamt*. M. Kardinal von Faulhaber Festschrift. Regensburg: Pustet. Reprinted pp. 246–67 in R. Schnackenburg, *Schriften zum Neuen Testament*. Munich: Kösel, 1971.
1977 Die grosse Eulogie Eph. 1, 3–14. *BZ* 21:67–87.

Schneider, Jane
1971 Of Vigilance and Virgins: Honor, Shame and Access to Resources in Mediterranean Societies. *Ethnology* 10:1–24.

Schneider, Jane, and P. Schneider
1976 *Culture and Political Economy in Western Sicily*. New York: Academic.

Schneider, Johannes
1959 Erwählung im NT. Pages 613–14 in *RGG*[3].
1964 "*proserchomai*." Pages 683–84 in vol. 2 of *TDNT*.
1972 "*timê, timaô*." Pages 169–80 in vol. 8 of *TDNT*.

Schnider, F., and W. Stenger
1987 *Studien zum Neutestamentlichen Briefformular*. NTTS 11. Leiden: Brill.

Schniewind, J.
1927–31 Euaggelion: *Ursprung und erste Gestalt des Begriffs Evangelium*. BFCT 2/13, 25. Gütersloh: Bertelsmann.
1964 "*aggelia* etc." Pages 56–73 in vol. 1 of *TDNT*.

Schöllgen, G.
1988 Hausgemeinden, *oikos*-Ekklesiologie und Monarchischer Episkopat: Überlegungen zu einer neuen Forschungsrichtung. *JAC* 31:74–90.

Schoeps, H.-J.
1950a I, Haggadisches zur Auserwählung Israels: Eine Studie zur midraschischen Theologie. Pages 184–200 in *Aus frühchristlicher Zeit: Religionsgeschichtliche Untersuchungen*. Tübingen: Mohr (Siebeck).
1950b II, Weiteres zur Auserwählung Israels. Pages 201–10 in *Aus frühchristlicher Zeit: Religionsgeschichtliche Untersuchungen*. Tübingen: Mohr (Siebeck).

Scholer, D. M.
1980 Women's Adornment: Some Historical and Hermeneutical Observations on the New Testament Passages. *Daughters of Sarah* (Chicago) 6/1:3–6.

Schottroff, L.
1978 Non-violence and the Love of One's Enemies. Pages 9–39 in *Essays on the Love Commandment*. Edited by R. H. Fuller. Philadelphia: Fortress.

Schrage, W.
1974–75 Zur Ethik der neutestamentlichen Haustafeln. *NTS* 21:1–22.

Schrenk, G.
1964 "*graphê*." Pages 749–61 in vol. 1 of *TDNT.*
1965a "*hierateuma*." Pages 249–51 in vol. 3 of *TDNT.*
1965b "*hieros* etc." Pages 221–83 in vol. 3 of *TDNT.*
1967 "*patêr* etc." Pages 945–1022 in vol. 5 of *TDNT.*
Schrenk, G., and G. Quell
1967 "*eklegomai, eklogê, eklektos*." Pages 144–92 in vol. 4 of *TDNT.*
Schroeder, D.
1959 *Die Haustafeln im Neuen Testament: Ihre Herkunft und ihr theologischer Sinn*. Doctoral Dissertation, Hamburg.
Schröer, H., and G. Müller
1982 *Von Amt des Laien in Kirche und Theologie*. Berlin: de Gruyter.
Schubert, P.
1939 *Form and Function of the Pauline Thanksgiving*. Berlin: Alfred Töpelmann.
Schürer, E.
1904 Diaspora. Pages 91–109 in vol. 5 of *HDB*.
1973–87 *The History of the Jewish People in the Age of Jesus Christ*. New English version rev. and ed. G. Vermes et al. 3 vols. Edinburgh: T. & T. Clark.
Schüssler Fiorenza, E.
1972 *Priester für Gott: Studien zum Herrschafts- und Priestermotiv in der Apokalypse*. NTAbh n. s. 7. Münster: Aschendorff.
1976a Cultic Metaphors in Qumran and in the New Testament. *CBQ* 38: 159–77.
1976b Eschatology of the NT. Pages 271–77 in *IDBSup*.
1983a *In Memory of Her: A Feminist Reconstruction of Christian Origins*. New York: Crossroad.
1983b The Phenomenon of Early Christian Apocalyptic: Some Reflections on Method. Pages 295–316 in *Apocalypticism in the Mediterranean World and the Near East*. Edited by D. Hellholm. Proceedings of the International Colloquium on Apocalypticism. Tübingen: Mohr.
Schütz, J.
1975 *Paul and the Anatomy of Apostolic Authority*. SNTSMS 26. Cambridge: Cambridge University Press.
Schulz, A.
1962 *Nachfolge und Nachahmen: Studien über das Verhältnis der neutestamentlichen Jüngerschaft zur urchristlichen Vorbildethik*. SANT 6. Munich: Kösel.
Schweizer, E.
1960 *Lordship and Discipleship*. SBT 28. London: SCM.
1961 *Church Order in the New Testament*. SBT 32. London: SCM.
1977 Die Weltlichkeit des Neuen Testaments: Die Haustafel. Pages 397–413 in *Beiträge zur alttestamentlichen Theologie*. Walter Zimmerli Festschrift. Edited by H. Donner et al. Göttingen: Vandenhoeck & Ruprecht.
1979 Traditional Ethical Patterns in the Pauline and Post-Pauline Letters and Their Development (Lists of Vices and House-Tables). Pages 195–209 in *Text and Interpretation*. M. Black Festschrift. Edited by E. Best and R. McL. Wilson. Cambridge: Cambridge University Press.
Schweizer, E., et al.
1971 "*sarx, sarkikos, sarkinos*." Pages 98–151 in vol. 7 of *TDNT.*

Scott, R. B. Y.
1950 A Kingdom of Priests (Ex 19:6). *OtSt* 8:213–19.
Scott, W. F. M.
1957 Priesthood in the New Testament. *SJT* 10:399–415.
Searle, J. D.
1975–76 Christian: Noun, or Adjective? *ExpTim* 87:307–8.
Sedlaczek, H.
1894 *Philadelphia* nach den Schriften des heiligen Apostel Paulus. *TQ* 76:272–95.
Seeberg, A.
1960 *Der Katechismus der Ur-Christenheit*. Leipzig: Deichert, 1903. Reprinted, with an introduction by F. Hahn. TB 26. Munich: Kaiser.
Seeley, D.
1990 *The Noble Death: Graeco-Roman Martyrology and Paul's Conception of Salvation*. JSNTSup 28. Sheffield: JSOT Press.
Seesemann, H.
1933 *Der Begriff* Koinonia *im Neuen Testament*. BZNW 14. Berlin: Alfred Töpelmann.
Segal, A. F.
1980 Heavenly Ascent in Hellenistic Judaism, Early Christianity and Their Environment. *ANRW* 2.23.2:1333–94.
Segal, J. B.
1979 The Jewish Attitude towards Women. *Journal of Jewish Studies* 30:121–37.
Seidensticker, P.
1954 *Lebendiges Opfer (Röm. 12.1)*. NTAbh 20 1/3. Münster: Aschendorff.
Sertima, I. van, ed.
1985 *Black Women in Antiquity*. London. [1st pub. *Journal of African Civilization* 6/1 (1984)]
Sevenster, G.
1958 Het Koning- en Priesterschap der Gelovigen in het Nieuwe Testament. *NedTT* 13:401–17.
Severus, E. von, et al.
1972 Gebet [Part 1]. Pages 1134–1258 in vol. 8 of *RAC*.
1976 Gebet [Part 2]. Pages 1–36 in vol. 9 of *RAC*.
Sheils, W. J., and D. Wood
1989 *The Ministry: Clerical and Lay*. Oxford: Blackwell.
Sheldon, C. M.
1967 *In His Steps*. Grand Rapids: Zondervan. [Originally pub., 1896]
Shepherd, M. H., Jr.
1962 Ministry, Christian. Pages 386–92 in vol. 3 of *IDB*.
Sherwin-White, A. N.
1952 The Early Persecutions and Roman Law Again. *JTS* 3:199–213. Appendix V: The Early Persecutions and Roman Law. Pages 772–87 in *The Letters of Pliny: A Historical and Social Commentary*. Oxford: Clarendon, 1966. [Reprint with modifications]
1966 *The Letters of Pliny: A Historical and Social Commentary*. Oxford: Clarendon.
1963 *Roman Society and Roman Law in the New Testament*. Oxford: Clarendon.

1964 Why Were the Early Christians Persecuted? An Amendment. *Past and Present* 27:23–27.

Shogren, G. S.
1992a Election (New Testament). Pages 441–44 in vol. 2 of *ABD.*
1992b Redemption (New Testament). Pages 654–57 in vol. 5 of *ABD.*

Shurden, W. B., ed.
1993 *Proclaiming the Baptist Vision: The Priesthood of All Believers.* Macon, Georgia: Mercer University Press.

Sigal, P.
1984 Early Christian and Rabbinic Liturgical Affinities: Exploring Liturgical Acculturation. *NTS* 30:63–90.

Sjöberg, E.
1951 Wiedergeburt und Neuschöpfung im palästinischen Judentum. *ST* 4:44–85.
1955 Neuschöpfung in den Toten-Meer-Rollen. *ST* 9:131–36.

Sly, D.
1990 *Philo's Perception of Women.* Atlanta: Scholars Press.

Smalley, S. S.
1961–62 The Christology of Acts. *ExpTim* 73:358–62.
1973 The Christology of Acts Again. Pages 79–93 in *Christ and Spirit in the New Testament.* C. F. D. Moule Festschrift. Edited by B. Lindars and S. S. Smalley. Cambridge: Cambridge University Press.

Smallwood, E. M.
1970 *Philonis Alexandrini: Legatio ad Gaium.* 2d ed. Leiden: Brill.
1976 *The Jews under Roman Rule.* Leiden: Brill.

Smits, C.
1952–63 *Oud-Testamentische Citaten in het Nieuwe Testament.* Collectanea Franciscana Neerlandica 8/1–4. 's-Hertogenbosch: Malmberg.

Smyth, H. W.
1980 *Greek Grammar.* Cambridge: Harvard University Press.

Snyder, G. F.
1977 The *Tobspruch* in the New Testament. *NTS* 23:117–20.
1985 *Ante Pacem: Archaeological Evidence of Church Life before Constantine.* Macon, Georgia: Mercer University Press.
1992 Christianity at Rome. Pages 968–70 in vol. 1 of *ABD.*

Soares-Prabhu, G. M.
1992 Christian Priesthood in India Today: A Biblical Reflection. *Vidyajyoti* 56:61–88.

Sobosan, J. G.
1974 The Role of the Presbyter. *SJT* 27:129–46.

Soden, H. von
1964 "*adelphos* etc." Pages 144–46 in vol. 1 of *TDNT.*

Sohn, S.-T.
1991 *The Divine Election of Israel.* Grand Rapids: Eerdmans.

Sommerlath, E.
1953/1954 Amt und allgemeines Priestertum. Pages 40–89 in vol. 5 of *Schriften des Theologischen Konvents Augsburgischen Bekenntnisses.* Berlin, 1953. [Reprinted as separate volume under same title, Berlin: Lutherisches, 1954]

Sordi, M.
1994 *The Christians and the Roman Empire*. London: Routledge.
Speyer, W.
1963 Zu den Vorwürfen der Heiden gegen die Christen. *JAC* 6:129–35.
1969 Fälschung, literarische. Pages 236–77 in vol. 7 of *RAC*.
1971 *Die literarische Fälschung im heidnischen und christlichen Altertum: Ein Versuch ihrer Deutung*. Munich: Beck.
1977 Religiöse Pseudepigraphie und literarische Fälschung im Altertum. Pages 195–263 in *Pseudepigraphie in der heidnischen und jüdisch-christlichen Antike*. Edited by N. Brox. Darmstadt: Wissenschaftliche.
Spicq, C.
1938 La conscience dans le Nouveau Testament. *RB* 47:50–80.
1947 L'origine des catalogues de devoirs individuels. Pages 257–61 in *Les Épîtres Pastorales*. Paris.
1961 Ce que signifie le titre de chrétien. *ST* 15:68–78.
1969 La place ou le rôle des jeunes dans certaines communautés néotestamentaires. *RB* 76:508–27.
1978 Le Vocabulaire de l'esclavage dans le Nouveau Testament. *RB* 85: 201–26.
Spohn, W. C.
1995 *What Are They Saying about Scripture and Ethics?* Rev. and expanded ed. New York: Paulist.
Staab, K.
1924 Die griechischen Katenenkommentare zu den katholischen Briefen. *Bib* 5:296–353.
Stählin, G.
1930 *SKANDALON: Untersuchung zur Geschichte eines biblischen Begriffes*. BFCT 2/24. Gütersloh: Bertelsmann.
1968 "*proskoptô* etc." Pages 745–58 in vol. 6 of *TDNT*.
1971 "*skandalon, skandalizô*." Pages 339–58 in vol. 7 of *TDNT*.
1975 "*phileô* etc." Pages 112–69 in vol. 9 of *TDNT*.
Stagg, E., and F. Stagg
1978 *Women in the World of Jesus*. Edinburgh: Saint Andrews / Philadelphia: Westminster.
Stalder, K.
1971 Episkopos. *Internationale kirchliche Zeitschrift* 61:200–232.
Stanley, D. M.
1954 The Theme of the Servant of Yahweh in Primitive Christian Soteriology, and Its Transposition by St. Paul. *CBQ* 16:385–425.
1965 Paul and the Christian Concept of the Servant of God. Pages 312–51 in *The Apostolic Church in the New Testament*. Westminster: Newman.
Stauffer, E.
1943 Zur Vor- u[nd] Frühgeschichte des Primatus Petri. *ZKG* 62:3–34.
Ste. Croix, G. E. M. de
1963 Why Were the Early Christians Persecuted? *Past and Present* 26:6–31.
1964 Why Were the Early Christians Persecuted?: A Rejoinder. *Past and Present* 27:28–33.
1981 *The Class Struggle in the Ancient Greek World from the Archaic Age to the Arab Conquests*. Ithaca, New York: Cornell University Press.

Stelzenberger, J.
1961 *Syneidesis im Neuen Testament.* Abhandlungen zur Moraltheologie 1. Paderborn: Schöningh.

Stendahl, K.
1953 The Called and the Chosen: An Essay on Election. Pages 63–80 in *The Root of the Vine: Essays in Biblical Theology.* Edited by A. Fridrichsen et al. Westminster: Dacre.
1966 *The Bible and the Role of Women: A Case Study in Hermeneutics.* Facet Books 15. Philadelphia: Fortress.

Stenger, W.
1979 Beobachtungen zur sogenannten Völkerliste des Pfingstwunders (Apg 2.7–11). *Kairos* 2–3:206–14.

Sterling, G. E.
1993 Women in the Hellenistic and Roman Worlds (323 BCE–138 CE). Pages 41–93 in *Women in the Church: Refocusing the Discussion.* Edited by C. D. Osburn. Joplin, Missouri: College Press.

Stern, M.
1974 The Jewish Diaspora. Pages 117–83 in vol. 1 *The Jewish People in the First Century.* Edited by S. Safrai and M. Stern. CRINT Section 1. Philadelphia: Fortress.

Storck, H.
1953 *Das Allgemeine Priestertum bei Luther.* Theol. Existenz heute n.s. 37. Munich: Kaiser.

Stowers, S. K.
1986 *Letter Writing in Greco-Roman Antiquity.* Philadelphia: Westminster.

Strathmann, H.
1967 "*martys* etc." Pages 474–514 in vol. 4 of *TDNT.*

Strathmann, H., and R. Meyer
1967 "*laos.*" Pages 29–57 in vol. 4 of *TDNT.*

Strecker, G.
1989 Die neutestamentlichen Haustafeln (Kol 3,18–4,1 und Eph 5,22–6,9). Pages 349–75 in *Neues Testament und Ethik.* Rudolf Schnackenburg Festschrift. Edited by H. Merklein. Freiburg: Herder.
1991 "*euaggelizô* etc." Pages 69–74 in vol. 2 of *EDNT.*

Strobel, A.
1965 Der Begriff des "Hauses" im griechischen und römischen Privatrecht. ZNW 56:91–100.

Strynkowski, J. J.
1972 *The Descent of Christ among the Dead.* Doctoral dissertation, Pontifical Gregorian University, Rome.

Studer, B.
1970 Il sacerdozio dei fedeli in sant'Ambrogio di Milano: Rassegna bibliographica 1969–1970. *Vetera Christianorum* 7:325–40.

Stuhlmacher, P.
1968 *Das Paulinische Evangelium, I: Vorgeschichte.* FRLANT 95. Göttingen: Vandenhoeck & Ruprecht.

Stuiber, A.
1957 Diaspora. Pages 972–82 in vol. 3 of *RAC.*

Sundberg, A. C.
1959 On Testimonies. *NovT* 3:268–81.

Sutcliffe, E. F.
1953 *Providence and Suffering in the Old and New Testaments*. London: Nelson.

Swartley, W. H., ed.
1992 *The Love of Enemy and Nonretaliation in the New Testament*. Louisville: Westminster John Knox.

Swidler, L.
1976 *Women in Judaism: The Status of Women in Formative Judaism*. Methuen, New Jersey: Scarecrow.

Tabor, J. D.
1992 Heaven, Ascent To. Pages 91–94 in vol. 3 of *ABD*.

Tachau, P.
1972 *"Einst" und "Jetzt" im Neuen Testament: Beobachtungen zu einem urchristlichen Predigtsthema in der neutestamentlichen Briefliteratur und zu seiner Vorgeschichte*. Göttingen: Vandenhoeck & Ruprecht.

Talbert, C. H.
1991 *Learning through Suffering: The Educational Value of Suffering in the New Testament and Its Milieu*. Collegeville, Minnesota: Liturgical.

Taylor, J.
1994 Why Were the Disciples First Called "Christians" at Antioch? (Acts 11, 26). *RB* 101:75–94.

Taylor, V.
1958 *The Atonement in New Testament Teaching*. 3d ed. London: Epworth.

Tcherikover, V.
1974 *Hellenistic Civilization and the Jews*. New York: Atheneum.

Temporini, H., and W. Haase, eds.
1972– *Aufstieg und Niedergang der römischen Welt*. Berlin: de Gruyter. [Cited as *ANRW* n.s.]

Testuz, M.
1959 *Papyrus Bodmer VII–IX, VII: L'Épître de Jude; VIII: Les deux Épîtres de Pierre; IX: Les Psaumes 33 et 34*. Geneva: Bodmeriana.

Thébert, Y., and P. Veyne
1987 Private Life and Domestic Architecture in Roman Africa. Pages 313–409 in *A History of Private Life, I: From Pagan Rome to Byzantium*. Edited by P. Veyne. Cambridge: Belknap.

Theissen, G.
1992 Nonviolence and Love of Enemies (Matthew 5:38–48; Luke 6:27–38). Pages 115–56 in *Social Reality and the Early Christians: Theology, Ethics, and the World of the New Testament*. Minneapolis: Fortress.

Thiering, B. E.
1980 Inner and Outer Cleansing at Qumran as a Background to New Testament Baptism. *NTS* 26:266–77.

Thomas, J.
1968 Anfechtung und Vorfreude: Ein biblisches Thema nach Jakobus 1, 2–18, im Zusammenhang mit Psalm 126, Röm 5,3–5, und 1 Petr. 1,5–7 formkritisch untersucht und parakletisch ausgelegt. *KD* 14:183–206.

Thompson, J. W.
1966 Be Submissive to Your Masters: A Study of I Peter 2,18–25. *ResQ* 9:66–78.

Thompson, L. L.

1986 A Sociological Analysis of Tribulation in the Apocalypse of John. *Semeia* 36 (*Early Christian Apocalypticism*):147–74.

1990 *The Book of Revelation: Apocalypse and Empire*. New York: Oxford University Press.

Thraede, K.

1968–69 Ursprünge und Formen des "heiligen Kusses" im frühen Christentum. *JAC* 11–12:124–80.

1972a Frau. Pages 197–269 in vol. 8 of *RAC*.

1972b Friedenskuss. Pages 505–19 in vol. 8 of *RAC* 8.

1977a Ärger mit der Freiheit: Die Bedeutung von Frauen in Theorie und Praxis der alten Kirche. Pages 35–182 in *"Freunde in Christus werden . . .": Die Beziehung von Mann und Frau als Frage an Theologie und Kirche*. Gelnhausen: Burckhardthaus.

1977b Frauen im Leben frühchristlicher Gemeinden. *Una Sancta* 32:286–99.

1980 Zum historischen Hintergrund der "Haustafeln" des Neuen Testaments. Pages 359–68 in *Pietas*. B. Kötting Festschrift. Edited by E. Dassmann and K. S. Frank. JAC Ergänzungssband 8. Münster: Aschendorf.

1992 Homonoia (Eintracht). Pages 176–289 in vol. 16 of *RAC*.

Thurston, B. B.

1989 *The Widows: A Women's Ministry in the Early Church*. Philadelphia: Fortress.

Tillard, J. M. R.

1973 What Priesthood Has the Ministry? *One Christ* 9:237–69.

1992 *Church of Churches: The Ecclesiology of Communion*. Collegeville, Minnesota: Liturgical/Glazier.

Tischendorf, C., ed.

1872 *Novum Testamentum Graece*. 8th ed. Editio octava critica maior. Leipzig: Giesecke & Devrient.

Tooley, W.

1964–65 The Shepherd and Sheep Image in the Teaching of Jesus. *NovT* 7:15–25.

Torjesen, K. J.

1993 *When Women Were Priests: Women's Leadership in the Early Church and the Scandal of Their Subordination in the Rise of Christianity.* San Francisco: HarperSanFrancisco.

Torrance, T. F.

1993 *Royal Priesthood*. Scottish Journal of Theology Occasional Papers 3. Edinburgh: Oliver & Boyd, 1955. Reprinted Edinburgh: T. & T. Clark.

Trebilco, P. R.

1991a *Jewish Communities in Asia Minor.* SNTSMS 69. Cambridge: Cambridge University Press.

1991b The Prominence of Women in Asia Minor. Pages 104–26 in *Jewish Communities in Asia Minor.* Cambridge: Cambridge University Press.

Treggiari, S.

1991 *Roman Marriage:* Iusti Coniuges *from the Time of Cicero to the Time of Ulpian*. New York: Oxford University Press.

Trites, A. A.

1977 *The New Testament Concept of Witness*. SNTSMS 31. Cambridge: Cambridge University Press.

Turmel, J.
1908 *La descente du Christ aux enfers*. Paris: Bloud.

Unnik, W. C. van
1964 Die Rücksicht auf die Reaktion der Nicht-Christen als Motiv in der altchristlichen Paränese. Pages 221–34 in *Judentum, Urchristentum, Kirche*. J. Jeremias Festschrift. Edited by W. Eltester. BZNW 26. Berlin: Alfred Töpelmann.
1979 Le rôle de Noé dans les épîtres de Pierre. Pages 207–39 in *Noé, L'homme universel*. Colloque de Louvain 1978. Institutum Judaicum Bruxelles 3. Brussels.
1983a "Diaspora" and "Church" in the First Centuries of Christian History. Pages 95–105 in part 3 of *Sparsa Collecta: The Collected Essays of* W. C. *van Unnik*. Edited by J. Reiling, G. Mussies, and P. van der Horst. Three parts in 3 vols. NovTSup 31. Leiden: Brill.
1983b An Unusual Formulation of the Redemption in the Homily on the Passion by Melito of Sardis. Pages 148–60 in part 3 of *Sparsa Collecta: The Collected Essays of* W. C. *van Unnik*. Edited by J. Reiling, G. Mussies, and P. van der Horst. Three parts in 3 vols. NovTSup 29. Leiden: Brill.
1993 *Das Selbstverständnis der jüdischen Diaspora in der hellenistisch-römischen Zeit*. Edited by P. W. van der Horst. AGJU 17. Leiden: Brill.

Vajta, V.
1950 Der Christenstand als königliches Priestertum. Pages 350–73 in *Welt-Luthertum von Heute*. A. Nygren Festschrift. Stockholm: Svenska Kyrkans Diakonistryrelses.

Vander Broek, L.
1985 Women and the Church: Approaching Difficult Passages. *Reformed Review* 38:225–31.

VanderKam, J.
1984 *Enoch and the Growth of an Apocalyptic Tradition*. CBQMS 16. Washington, D.C.: Catholical Biblical Association.

Vanhoye, A.
1986 *Old Testament Priests and the New Priest according to the New Testament*. Translated by J. B. Orchard. Petersham, Massachusetts: St. Bede's.

Vermeulen, A. J.
1981 Gloria. Pages 196–225 in vol. 11 of *RAC*.

Verner, D. C.
1983 *The Household of God: The Social World of the Pastoral Epistles*. SBLDS 71. Chico, California: Scholars Press.

Veyne, P., ed.
1987 *A History of Private Life, I: From Pagan Rome to Byzantium*. Cambridge: Belknap.

Vielhauer, P.
1940 OIKODOME: *Das Bild vom Bau in der christlichen Literatur vom Neuen Testament bis Clemens Alexandrinus*. Karlsruhe: Tron.

Vielliard, R.
1959 *Recherches sur les origines de la Rome chrétienne*. 2 vols. Rome: Edizioni di Storia e Letteratura.

Vittinghoff, F.
1984 "Christianus sum": Das "Verbrechen" von Aussenseitern der römischen Gesellschaft. *Historia* 33:331–57.
Vögtle, A.
1936 *Die Tugend- und Lasterkataloge im Neuen Testament, exegetisch, religions- und formgeschichtlich untersucht*. NTAbh 16, 4/5. Münster: Aschendorff.
Völkl, R.
1961 *Christ und Welt nach dem Neuen Testament*. Würzburg: Echter.
Vogler, W.
1982 Die Bedeutung der urchristlichen Hausgemeinde für die Ausbreitung des Evangeliums. *TLZ* 107:786–94.
Vogt, H. J.
1982 Zum Bischofsamt in der frühen Kirche. *TZ*:221–36.
Vogt, J.
1954 Christenverfolgung I (historisch). Pages 1159–1208 in vol. 2 of *RAC*.
Volkmar, G.
1861 Über die katholischen Briefe und Henoch [Part 1]. *ZWT* 4:427–36.
1862 Über die katholischen Briefe und Henoch [Part 2]. *ZWT* 5:46–75.
Vorgrimmler, H.
1966 The Significance of Christ's Descent into Hell. *Concilium* 11:147–59.
Vorster, W. S.
1974 *Aischunomai en stamverwante woorde in die Nuwe Testament*. Pretoria: Universiteit van Suid-Afrika.
Vriezen, T. C.
1953 *Die Erwählung Israels nach dem Alten Testament*. ATANT 24. Zurich: Zwingli.
Wachtel, K.
1995 *Der Byzantinische Text der Katholischen Briefe: Eine Untersuchung zur Entstehung der Koine des Neuen Testaments*. Arbeiten zur Neutestamentlichen Textforschung 24. Berlin: de Gruyter.
Wagner, F.
1980 Berufung, II: Neues Testament. Pages 684–88 in vol. 5 of *TRE*.
Wagner, U.
1994 *Die Ordnung des "Hauses Gottes": Der Ort von Frauen in der Ekklesiologie und Ethik der Pastoralbriefe*. WUNT 2/65. Tübingen: Mohr (Siebeck).
Wahl, C. A., and J. B. Bauer
1972 *Clavis Librorum Veteris Testamenti Apocryphorum Philologica*. Graz: Akademische. [Reprint of 1853 ed.]
Walcot, P.
1978 *Envy and the Greeks: A Study of Human Behavior*. Warminster: Aris & Phillips.
Wall, R. W.
1992 Community: New Testament *Koinônia*. Pages 1103–10 in vol. 1 of *ABD*.
Wambacq, B. N.
1975 Le mot charisme. *NRTh* 97:345–55.
Wanamaker, C. A.
1990 *The Epistles to the Thessalonians*. NIGTC. Grand Rapids: Eerdmans.
Watson, D. F.
1992 Gehenna. Pages 926–28 in vol. 2 of *ABD*.

Webb, R. L.
1992 Epistles, Catholic. Pages 569–70 in vol. 2 of *ABD*.

Weber, M.
1952 *Ancient Judaism*. Glencoe, Illinois: Free.
1978 *Economy and Society: An Outline of Interpretive Sociology*. 2 vols. Edited by G. Roth and C. Wittich. Berkeley: University of California Press.

Wegner, J. R.
1988 *Chattel or Person?: The Status of Women in the Mishnah*. New York: Oxford University Press.
1991 Philo's Portrayal of Women: Hebraic or Hellenic? Pages 41–66 in *"Women like This": New Perspectives on Jewish Women in the Greco-Roman World*. Edited by M. J. Levine. SBL: Early Judaism and Its Literature 1. Atlanta: Scholars Press.

Weidinger, K.
1928 *Die Haustafeln: Ein Stück urchristlicher Paränese*. UNT 14. Leipzig: Hinrichs.

Weigandt, P.
1963 Zur sogenannten "Oikosformel." *NovT* 6:49–74.

Weinfeld, M.
1971 Covenant. *EJ* 5:1011–22.

Weiss, J.
1901/ 1951 Asia Minor in the Apostolic Time. Pages 314–18 in vol. 1 of *The New Schaff-Herzog Encyclopedia of Religious Knowledge*. Edited by S. M. Jackson.Grand Rapids: Baker. [Abbreviated ET of Kleinasien. Pages 535–63 in vol. 10 of *Realencyclopädie für Protestantische Theologie und Kirche*. 3d ed., 1901.]

Wendland, H.-D.
1958 Zur sozialethischen Bedeutung der Neutestamentlichen Haustafeln. Pages 34–46 in *Die Leibhaftigkeit des Wortes*. Adolf Köberle Festschrift. Edited by O. Michel and U. Mann. Hamburg: Furche.

Wenger, A.
1957 *Huit Catéchèses Baptismales*. SC 50. Paris: Cerf.

Wengst, K.
1974 *Christologische Formeln und Lieder des Urchristentums*. SNT 7. 2d ed. Gütersloh: Gütersloher/Mohn.
1987 *Pax Romana and the Peace of Jesus Christ*. Philadelphia: Fortress.
1988 *Humility—Solidarity of the Humiliated: The Transformation of an Attitude and Its Social Relevance in Graeco-Roman, Old Testament-Jewish, and Early Christian Tradition*. Philadelphia: Fortress.

Wenschkewitz, H.
1932 *Die Spiritualisierung der Kultusbegriffe Tempel, Priester und Opfer im Neuen Testament*. Angelos 4. Leipzig: Pfeiffer.

Westermann, W. L.
1935 Sklaverei. Pages 894–1068 in vol. 6 of PWSup.
1955 *The Slave Systems of Greek and Roman Antiquity*. Philadelphia: American Philosophical Society.

Wettstein, J. J.

1962 Volume 2 of *Novum Testamentum Graece*. Graz: Akademische. [1st ed. Amsterdam: Dommerian, 1752]

White, J. L.

1972 *The Form and Function of the Body of the Greek Letter*. SBLDS 2. Missoula, Montana: Scholars Press.

1983 Saint Paul and the Apostolic Letter Tradition. *CBQ* 45:433–44.

1986 *Light from Ancient Letters*. Philadelphia: Fortress.

White, L. M.

1982 *Domus Ecclesiae-Domus Dei*. Ph.D. dissertation, Yale University.

Wibbing, S.

1959 *Die Tugend- und Lasterkataloge im Neuen Testament und ihre Traditionsgeschichte unter besonderer Berücksichtigung der Qumran-Texte*. BZNW 25. Berlin: Alfred Töpelmann.

Wichmann, W.

1930 *Die Leidenstheologie: Eine Form der Leidensdeutung im Spätjudentum*. BWANT 4/2. Stuttgart: Kohlhammer.

Wicker, K.

1975 First Century Marriage Ethics: A Comparative Study of the Household Codes and Plutarch's Conjugal Precepts. Pages 141–53 in *No Famine in the Land: Studies in Honor of John L. McKenzie*. Edited by J. W. Flanagan and A. Weisbrod Robinson. Missoula, Montana: Scholars Press.

Wiedemann, T.

1981 *Greek and Roman Slavery*. Baltimore: Johns Hopkins University Press.

Wiefel, W.

1991 The Jewish Community in Ancient Rome and the Origins of Roman Christianity. Pages 85–101 in *The Romans Debate*. Edited by K. P. Donfried. Rev. ed. Peabody, Massachusetts: Hendrickson.

Wikan, U.

1982 *Behind the Veil in Arabia*. Baltimore: Johns Hopkins University Press.

1984 Shame and Honor: A Contestable Pair. *Man* 19:635–52.

Wilcox, M.

1975 A Foreword to the Study of the Speeches in Acts. Pages 206–25 in *New Testament*. Edited by J. Neusner. Part 1 of *Christianity, Judaism and Other Greco-Roman Cults*. M. Smith Festschrift. Leiden: Brill.

1977 "Upon the Tree": Deut 21:22–23 in the New Testament. *JBL* 96:85–99.

Wildberger, H.

1960 *Jahwes Eigentumsvolk*. ATANT 37. Zurich: Zwingli.

Wilhelm, F.

1915 Die Oeconomica der Neupythagoräer, Bryson, Kallikratidas, Periktione, Phintys. *Rheinisches Museum* n.s. 70:161–223.

Wilken, R. L.

1984 *The Christians as the Romans Saw Them*. New Haven: Yale University Press.

Wilkins, M. J.

1992 Christian. Pages 925–26 in vol. 1 of *ABD*.

Williams, G. H.

1958 The Role of the Layman in the Ancient Church. *Greek, Roman and Byzantine Studies* 1:9–42.

Williger, E.
1922 Hagios. *Untersuchungen zur Terminologie des Heiligen in den hellenisch- und hellenistischen Religionen*. RVV 19/1. Giessen: Alfred Töpelmann.

Wilson, J. C.
1993 The Problem of the Domitianic Date of Revelation. *NTS* 39:587–605.

Windisch, H.
1908 *Taufe und Sünde im ältesten Christentum bis auf Origenes: Ein Beitrag zur altchristlichen Dogmengeschichte*. Tübingen: Mohr (Siebeck).

Winckler, J. J.
1990 *The Constraints of Desire: The Anthropology of Sex and Gender in Ancient Greece*. New York: Routledge.

Wink, W.
1984 *Naming the Powers: The Language of Power in the New Testament*. Philadelphia: Fortress.
1986 *Unmasking the Powers: The Invisible Forces That Determine Human Existence*. Philadelphia: Fortress.

Wire, A. C.
1990 *The Corinthian Women Prophets: A Reconstruction through Paul's Rhetoric*. Minneapolis: Fortress.

Witherington, B.
1984 *Women in the Ministry of Jesus*. Cambridge: Cambridge University Press.
1988 *Women in the Earliest Churches*. SNTSMS 59. Cambridge: Cambridge University Press.
1992 Women: New Testament. Pages 957–61 in vol. 6 of *ABD*.

Wlosok, A.
1959 Die Rechtsgrundlagen der Christenverfolgung der ersten zwei Jahrhunderte. *Gymnasium* 66:14–32. Reprinted pp. 275–301 in *Das frühe Christentum im römischen Staat*. Edited by R. Klein. Wege der Forschung 267. Darmstadt: Wissenschaftliche, 1982.

Wolff, H. W.
1950 *Jesaja 53 im Urchristentum*. 2d ed. Berlin.

Wolter, M.
1990 Der Apostel und seine Gemeinden als Teilhaber am Leidensgeschick Jesu Christi: Beobachtungen zur paulinischen Leidenstheologie. *NTS* 36:535–57.

Wood, A. S.
1979 Creeds and Confessions. Pages 805–12 in vol. 1 of *ISBE*.

Wordelman, A. L.
1992 Everyday Life: Women in the Period of the New Testament. Pages 390–96 in *The Women's Bible Commentary*. Edited by C. A. Newsom and S. H. Ringe. Louisville: Westminster John Knox.

Workman, H. B.
1980 *Persecution in the Early Church*. Oxford: Oxford University Press. [Reprint of the original 1906 ed.]

Woschitz, K. M.
1979 *Elpis-Hoffnung: Geschichte, Philosophie, Exegese, Theologie eines Schlüsselbegriffs*. Freiburg: Herder.

Wright, D. P., and R. Hodgson, Jr.
1992 Holiness. Pages 237–49 in vol. 3 of *ABD*.

Wright, G. E.
1958 Erwählung im AT. Pages 610–12 in vol. 2 of *RGG*[3].
1962 *Biblical Archaeology*. Rev. ed. Philadelphia: Westminster.
Yarbro-Collins, A.
1985 Insiders and Outsiders in the Book of Revelation and Its Social Context. Pages 187–218 in *"To See Ourselves as Others See Us": Christians, Jews, "Others," in Late Antiquity*. Edited by J. Neusner and E. S. Frerichs. Chico, California: Scholars Press.
Yarbro-Collins, A., ed.
1985 *Feminist Perspectives on Biblical Scholarship*. Atlanta: Scholars Press.
Yarbrough, O. L.
1985 *Not like the Gentiles: Marriage Rules in the Letters of Paul*. SBLDS 80. Atlanta: Scholars Press.
Yoder, J. H.
1994 Revolutionary Subordination. Pages 162–92 in *The Politics of Jesus*. 2d ed. Grand Rapids: Eerdmans.
Young, F. M.
1973 Temple Cult and Law in Early Christianity: A Study in the Relationship between Jews and Christians in the Early Centuries. *NTS* 19:325–38.
Ysebaert, J.
1962 *Greek Baptismal Terminology: Its Origins and Early Development*. Nijmegen: Dekker & van de Vegt.
1994 *Die Amtsterminologie im Neuen Testament und in der Alten Kirche: Eine lexikographische Untersuchung*. Breda: Eureia.
Zeiller, J.
1949 Legalité et arbitraire dans les persécutions contre les chrétiens. Pages 49–54 in vol. 1 of *Mélanges Peeters*. AnBoll 67. Brussels: Société des Bollandistes.
Zerbe, G. M.
1993 *Non-retaliation in Early Jewish and New Testament Texts: Ethical Themes in Social Contexts*. JSPSup 13. Sheffield: JSOT Press.
Zerwick. M.
1963 *Biblical Greek*. Rome: Pontifical Biblical Institute.
Zisioulas, John D.
1983 Episkope et Episkopos dans l'Église primitive: Bref inventaire de la documentation. *Irenikon* 56:484–501.
Zobel, H.-J.
1968 Ursprung und Verwurzelung des Erwählungsglaubens Israels. *TLZ* 93:1–12.
Zucker, F.
1928 *Syneidêsis—Conscientia: Ein Versuch zur Geschichte des sittlichen Bewusstseins im griechischen und im griechisch-römischen Altertum*. Jena: Fischer.
Zuurmond, R.
1991 The Flood according to Enoch in Early Christian Literature. Pages 766–72 in *SBL: Seminar Papers 1991*. SBLSP 30. Atlanta: Scholars Press.

TRANSLATION, NOTES AND COMMENTS

◆

1 PETER

◆

EPISTOLARY PRESCRIPT (1:1–2)

1:1 Peter, an apostle of Jesus Christ,
1b to the elect strangers of the Diaspora in
Pontus, Galatia, Cappadocia, Asia, and Bithynia,
2a [elect] according to the foreknowledge of God the Father,
2b through the sanctifying action of the Spirit,
2c because of the obedience and the sprinkling of the blood
of Jesus Christ
2d May you enjoy abundant grace and peace!

INTRODUCTION

1 Peter opens (1:1–2), as it closes (5:12–14), with the typical features of a conventional letter.[1] The prescript and postscript frame the body of the letter proper (1:3–5:11) and provide personal information about the sender(s) and intended recipients. Verses 1:1–2, embodying the customary formula of an epistolary prescript ("A to B + greetings"), indicate (a) the person in whose name and authority the letter is composed and sent (*superscriptio* [sender's name] plus *intitulatio* [title]); (b) the addressees (*adscriptio*), their condition, geographical location, and three characteristics of their elected status; and conclude with (c) a salutation (*salutatio*). The qualifications of the addressees (vv. 1b–2c) announce concepts and themes that will be developed in 1:3–12 as well as in further sections of the letter and clarify the commonalities binding recipients (1:1b–2c) and senders (1:1a; 5:12–14; cf. 5:1). In contrast to the letters of Paul, 1 Peter is addressed to a far wider expanse of communities who are located not in a single city but throughout four Roman provinces of Asia Minor. For this reason it has been classified as a "general" or "catholic" letter. In addition to this general address, other features of the prescript and of the writing as a whole also distinguish this letter from those of Paul (cf. Goppelt 1993, 62–64).

[1] On ancient letters and their formal characteristics see Roller 1933; Andresen 1965; Doty 1973; White 1972, 1986; K. Berger 1974; Stowers 1986; Schnider and Stenger 1987; R. P. Martin 1992, 41–79.

NOTES

1:1a. *Peter, an apostle of Jesus Christ* (*Petros apostolos Iēsou Christou*). These initial words of the prescript identify the implied author of the letter or, more accurately, the chief authority in whose name the letter has been composed and dispatched. 1 Peter, as explained more fully in the GENERAL INTRODUCTION, 7. Authorship, is a letter from one branch of the worldwide Christian brotherhood (5:9) residing in Rome (including Silvanus and Mark, 5:12–13) to another branch of the brotherhood residing in parts of Asia Minor. It is written in the name and apostolic authority of this Roman group's most renowned leader, the Apostle Peter. Peter's own apostolic ministry as "witness" to and "sharer" in the "sufferings" and "glory" of the Christ (5:1; cf. 1:11) constitutes both an experiential bond with the "sufferings" and "glory" of the addressees (4:13–14) and an authoritative basis for this epistolary affirmation of divine grace and joy in the face of innocent Christian suffering (5:10, 12).

Peter is the anglicized version of *petros*, a masculine Greek term for "rock" or "stone" similar to the feminine Greek term, *petra*, with the same meaning. *Petros*, in turn, translates the Aramaic *Kêpāʾ* (rendered *Kēphas* in Greek) also meaning "rock," "stone," "crag" (Fitzmyer 1981; cf. Heb. *kêpim* ["rocks"] in Job 3:6; Jer 4:29, which LXX translates *petrai*). Neither *kêpāʾ* nor *petros* was a personal name in its respective language. Rather, the two names represent versions of an epithet, nickname, or surname that Jesus was said to have given to Symeōn Bar-Jonah, Simon son of Jonah/John (J. K. Elliott 1972; R. Pesch 1993), on an occasion about which there is a divided witness in the tradition (R. Pesch 1993). According to Matthew, this name-giving occurred at Caesarea Philippi in Galilee at the end of Jesus' ministry in conjunction with his departure for Jerusalem and his death (Matt 16:13–28). In response to the statement of "Simon Peter" (Matthew's narrative identification) declaring Jesus to be "the Christ, the Son of the living God" (16:16), Jesus responds: "Blessed are you, Simon Bar-Jonah (*Simōn Bariōna*). . . . You are *Petros* and on this rock (*petra*) I will build my church . . ." (16:17, 18). According to John, the nicknaming took place instead in Judea at the outset of Jesus' ministry and in conjunction with Andrew, "Simon Peter's brother" (John's narrative identification), inviting his brother Simon to cease following John the Baptist and to follow Jesus, the Messiah (John 1:35–42). Jesus then "looked at him and said, 'You are Simon the son of Jonah (*Simōn, ho hyios Iōna*); you shall be called *Kēphas*, which [the Johannine author clarifies] means *Petros*' "(1:42); cf. also Matt 10:2/Mark 3:16/Luke 6:14 ("Simon whom he surnamed Peter") and John 21:15–17 ("Simon Peter" and "Simon, son of Jonah/John," 3×). Thus, "Peter" initially was not a proper name but an epithet or surname used with Simon (Simon "Rock") or absolutely ("Rock/Rocky"). Eventually, however, *Kēphas* and *Petros* (both used absolutely) were employed as proper names (analogous to the development of the nomenclature Jesus/Jesus the Christ/Christ), with *Petros* preferred in Greek-speaking Christianity. Although it occasionally has been postulated that the names Cephas and Peter referred to different persons (Ehrman 1990, rehearsing earlier arguments), a far stronger case can be made for their identification (Allison 1992). The symbolic implications of the surname *Kēphas/Petros* (firmness, immovability, a rock like Abraham from which Israel was hewn [Isa 51: 1–2], etc.), the possible Greek wordplay on *petra/Petros* in Matt 16:17–19, and the theological and ecclesiological significance of the name in this key Matthean text have been the subject of a large body of research and debate.[2]

According to the NT witness, Simon Peter occupied a position of priority and primacy among the early followers of Jesus, however individual authors nuanced this role and his portrait in general (cf. R. E. Brown, Donfried, and Reumann, eds. 1973). He was the first to be called as a disciple (Matt 4:18–20/ Mark 1:16–18; compare John 1:40–42), the first to confess Jesus as the Christ (Matt 16:13–23 par.), the first to deny his Lord (Matt 26/Mark 14/Luke 22), the first to witness the empty tomb (John 20:6–7), and the first to whom the resurrected Christ appeared (1 Cor 15:5; but contrast John 20:14–17). It was especially this experience of the risen Christ that established his primacy in the post-Easter community. And it was God's raising Jesus from death to life that formed the fundamental emphasis of the speeches attributed to Peter in Acts (2:14–36; 3:12–26; 4:8–12; 10:34–43) as it does in 1 Peter (1:3, 21; 3:18, 22). He is remembered in Acts as the first leader of the post-Easter community (1:15–5:42; 9:32–43), a fervent supporter of the mission to the Gentiles (Acts 10:1–11:18; 15:7–11), and among the first members arrested (12:2–19). In Jerusalem he had close contact with John Mark (12:12–17) and Silvanus (15:1–32), two figures who are mentioned in 1 Peter and who apparently had rejoined the apostle years later in Rome as well (see the NOTES on 5:12, 13).

This final phase of his ministry in Rome is attested voluminously in post-NT tradition from Clement of Rome (ca. 96 CE) onwards (*1 Clem.* 5:1–4; Ign. *Rom.* 4:3; cf. Eusebius, *Hist. eccl.* 2.14.6; 2.15.6; 2.17.1; 4.1), as is his association with Mark, his assistant and interpreter (Eusebius, citing Papias, Irenaeus, and Clement of Alexandria; cf. *Hist. eccl.* 2.15; 3.11; 3.39.15; 5.8.2–3; 6.14.5–7; cf. also the NOTE on 5:13). This tradition also records Rome as the site of his death sometime after the devasting fire of 64 CE and Nero's pogrom against the Christians, whom he held responsible. His death may be placed somewhere between late 64 and 67 CE and is commemorated, along with Paul's, in the Church's calendar on June 29.

In the reflection of the early Church, the memory of Peter as proto-disciple, proto-apostle, and proto-eyewitness of Jesus Christ remained vibrant. Eventually he became the focus of an extensive Petrine tradition, already apparent in the NT, as the one who, because of his personal association with Jesus and his witness of Jesus' death and resurrection, provided an historical link with the very beginning of Jesus' ministry and served as an eyewitness of the authenticity of

[2] See Dell 1914; Goetz 1927; Strathmann 1943; Clavier 1954; Ludwig 1952; Geyser 1959; Ringger 1960; Schmid 1960; Cullmann 1958, 1968; R. E. Brown, Donfried, and Reumann, eds. 1973; Lampe 1979; Caragounis 1990; Luz 1990, 450–83.

the Jesus tradition. On Peter, his name, and his role in the NT and early church, see the DETAILED COMMENT.

apostle of Jesus Christ (apostolos Iēsou Christou). The same apostolic identification (*intitulatio*) is employed by Paul in his first letter to the Corinthians ("Paul called an apostle of Jesus Christ," 1:1). More frequently in the Pauline and Deutero-Pauline letters, however, is the form "apostle of Christ Jesus" (2 Cor 1:1; Eph 1:1; Col 1:1; 1 Tim 1:1; 2 Tim 1:1; Titus 1:1). Elsewhere in the NT, Peter's role (rather than "office") as apostle is amply noted (Matt 10:2/ Luke 6:13–14; Luke 22:8/14; Acts 2:37, 42, 43; 5:2–3, 12–16, 17–32, 40; 8:14–24; 11:1–2; 15:1–35; Gal 1:17–19; 2 Pet 1:1) and is also implied in general references to the apostles (as in Mark 3:14; 6:30/Luke 9:10; Luke 17:5; 22:14; 24:10; Acts 1:2, 26; 4:33–37; 6:6; 8:1; 9:27; 16:4).

An *apostle* is one who has been delegated and dispatched by one or more persons in authority and who represents the full authority of the sender. The Israelite institution of the *shaliach*, the representive of the Jerusalem Temple sent annually to Israelite communities throughout the Mediterranean world to collect the obligatory Temple tithes, may have served as the immediate historical model for the Christian apostle (Rengstorf 1964a, 407–45, esp. 414–24; Agnew 1986). But the Christian concept of *apostle* is linked essentially and theologically with a personal encounter with, and commissioning by, Jesus the resurrected Christ (1 Cor 15:3–11; Matt 28:16–20; Rom 1:1; Gal 1:1). According to the ancient pre-Pauline tradition preserved in 1 Cor 15:3–8, Peter (Cephas) was the first such privileged witness of Christ's resurrection (see also Luke 24:34), and it was this privilege that established his priority, authority, and leading role among the first followers of Jesus as portrayed retrospectively in the Gospels. The preeminent status ascribed to these apostles is likewise evident in the lists of community leaders contained in 1 Cor 12:28 ("and God has appointed in the church first apostles . . .") and Eph 4:1. The weight attributed to the apostle in the early church as one commissioned and "sent forth" to witness to Christ's resurrection and its saving effects underlines the community's conception of itself as a *missionary* movement and accords with its rapid geographical expansion from one end of the Mediterranean to the other.

The fullest articulation of the developing Christian concept of *apostle* occurs in the Pauline (Rom 1:1–6; 1 Cor 9; 15:7–11; Gal 1:1–2:10; 2 Corinthians) and Deutero-Pauline writings (Eph 2:20; 3:1–3; 4:11–16), often when Paul feels called upon to defend his apostolic credentials against his detractors. In 1 Peter, by contrast, no such attempt at apostolic self-legitimation is evident. No further qualification of "apostle" is offered in 1:1. In 5:1 the author, in addressing the presbyters, appeals not to his apostolic authority but to his collegial role as "co-elder" (*sympresbyteros*).[3]

---

[3] For studies on the subject of apostle and its history of interpretation see Käsemann 1942; Kredel 1956; G. Klein 1961; Blum 1963; Bauer 1965; Roloff 1965; Schmidthals 1969; Kertelge 1970; Hahn 1974; Schütz 1975.

of Jesus Christ. The identity, status, and union of author and addressees is conditioned by their relation to Jesus Christ, reference to whom frames 1:1–2e. Peter is an apostle of Jesus Christ and the addressees are elect, among other reasons (v 2a, b), "because of the obedience and the sprinkling of the blood of Jesus Christ" (v 2c).

Christ (from the Greek *christos*, translating the Hebrew *māšîaḥ* [messiah]) is an appellation of faith declaring Jesus of Nazareth to be God's awaited "anointed one" (the literal meaning of *māšîaḥ* and *christos*), whose advent was to inaugurate the end (*to eschaton, telos*) of the age(s), the rule of God, and the judgment of the world. Elements of this constellation of beliefs are contained especially in the kerygmatic, creedal, and hymnic formulations of early Christianity and abound in 1 Peter as well (1:2, 7–9, 10–11, 19–21; 2:2, 4, 6–8, 21–25; 3:15, 18, 22; 4:1, 6, 7, 13, 17–18; 5:1). The movement to which the addressees of 1 Peter belonged had its beginnings as a messianic faction and then messianic sect of Israel that at the time of the letter's composition was in the process of dissociating from the parent body of Israel both ideologically and socially (Elliott 1995b). From the title "Christ," Gentile opponents of the messianic sect constructed the opprobrious label "Christian" (lit., "partisan of Christ" in the derogatory sense of "Christ-lackey"), a label later mentioned in 4:16; see the NOTE on 4:16 for further discussion.

Paul also uses the appellation "apostle of Jesus Christ" (1 Cor 1:1; cf. Titus 1:1), but the more frequently occurring designation is "apostle of Christ Jesus" (2 Cor 1:1; cf. also Eph 1:1; Col 1:1; 1 Tim 1:1; 2 Tim 1:1). Elsewhere in 1 Peter our author uses the formulations "Jesus Christ" (1:1, 2, 3 [2×], 7, 13; 2:5; 3:21; 4:11), "Christ" (1:11 [2×], 19; 2:21; 3:15, 16, 18; 4:1, 13, 14; 5:1, 10, 14), with the single occurrence of "Christ Jesus" (5:10) constituting a likely secondary variant.

Although the letter is specifically ascribed to Peter as the chief apostolic authority behind this letter, Silvanus (5:12) and Mark (5:13), along with "the co-elect" ("brotherhood," *adelphotēs*; cf. 2:17 and 5:9) also belong to the group from which this letter emanates. Silvanus and Mark, along with Peter, were important figures of the early Palestinian and Antioch phases of the Jesus movement (see Acts 12, 15). The association of these persons now in Rome indicates the global spread of the movement from the eastern to western borders of the Mediterranan world. On these persons and the Petrine circle in Rome, see Elliott (1980; 1981/1990, 267–95), the NOTES on 5:12 and 13, and the discussion in the GENERAL INTRODUCTION, 7.1. Authorship.

At several points in the letter, especially its kerygmatic formulations, the author includes himself and his co-senders among the beneficiaries of God's grace. Thus God is praised as the "Father of *our* Lord Jesus Christ" (1:3a), who has caused "us" (1:3b) to be reborn. As a result of Jesus Christ's vicarious death, senders and recipients share together the ethical consequences of the experience of sin's termination and a life of righteousness (2:24, "our," "we"). Senders and addressees likewise share membership in the household of God, with whom ("us") judgment commences (4:17; cf. 2:5), and in the worldwide suffering

Christian brotherhood (5:9). Together they are united by the affection of brotherly (and sisterly) love (1:22; 3:8; 4:8) typical of this family of God and so address one another as "beloved" (2:11; 4:12). Finally, in three instances (2:11; 5:1; and 5:12) the implied author, Peter, speaks in the first-person singular of his "exhorting" (2:11, 5:12) and "bearing full witness to the true grace of God" in this letter (5:12). In 5:1 he addresses the community elders as a "co-elder," a "witness" of the sufferings of the Christ, and a "sharer" in the glory [of the Christ] about to be revealed. In 5:12 he personally commends Silvanus, the courier of the letter: "the faithful brother, as I regard him."

The senders do not include themselves among those who *first* proclaimed the good news to the recipients (1:12, 25). However, all of these instances of self-reference link fundamental theological, ecclesiological, and ethical accents of the letter (divine mercy, Christ's resurrection, divine rebirth, hope, inheritance, salvation, termination of sin, righteousness of life, membership in the household of God and brotherhood of faith, and sharers in the suffering and glory of Christ and the grace of God) to the apostolic figure and memory of Peter in early Christianity. They likewise underscore the bonds of experience, faith, and hope that unite the brotherhood in the Diaspora of Babylon-Rome with the brotherhood in the Diaspora of Asia Minor.

1b. *to the elect strangers of the Diaspora* (*eklektois parepidēmois diasporas*). This initial designation of the addressees expresses at the letter's outset their paradoxical situation: they are *strangers* in society, yet *elected* by God.

"Strangers" translates *parepidēmois* and is closely related in its import to the following qualifying expression "of the Diaspora" and the terms *paroikoi* (2:11) and *paroikia* (1:17). *Parepidēmoi* (lit., "visiting stranger") recurs in tandem with *paroikoi* ("resident aliens") in 2:11. Both terms signal the precarious social condition of the addressees in the midst of an alien, Gentile society. Both terms denote persons who were "by-dwellers" (*par-epidēmos*, *par-oikos*) living in locales different from their place of origin. *Parepidēmos*, however, particularly denotes the *transient stranger* visiting *temporarily* in a given foreign locale. The related verb *epidēmeō* ("stay in a place as a stranger or visitor") is used in Acts of persons from Rome, both Judeans and proselytes, visiting in Jerusalem for the Passover festival (Acts 2:11), of foreigners (*xenoi*) visiting in Athens (17:21), of some Corinthians visiting in Athens (Acts 18:27 Codex D), and of Paul visiting in Achaia (Acts 18:27 D). The term *paroikos*, on the other hand, bearing more political and legal overtones, designates the "resident alien" who dwelled *permanently* in a foreign locale, and one who was permitted only limited political, economic, and social rights and status (see Elliott 1981/1990, 24–37; Pilch 1991; and the NOTE on 2:11 for further detail and documentation).

The correct but antiquated translation "sojourners" or the term "foreigners" captures the provisional connotation of these terms and the condition of social alienation that they imply (see also *paroikia*, "residence as aliens," in 1:17). But other renditions of the terms in 1:1; 1:17; and 2:11 (listed and compared in Elliott 1981/1990, 39–41), such as "exiles" (RSV, NRSV), "pilgrims" (Luther, KJV, NKJV, JB) or "refugees" (TEV) introduce concepts not associated with their basic meanings or usages. Goppelt (1993, 66–70), while noting that *parepidēmoi* conveys "the sociological effect of being a foreigner" (1993, 67), assumes without conclusive evidence that it is their divine election alone that transformed the addressees into such social foreigners. This notion, shared by many commentators, assumes that "strangers" (1:1; 2:11), "alien residence" (1:17), and "strangers and resident aliens" (2:11) are employed solely as theological metaphors descriptive of the condition of the addressees following their conversion. There is no necessity or cogent grounds, however, for this assumption. Taken in their conventional sense as evident in the LXX and popular usage, these terms indicate the actual social condition of the addressees as strangers and aliens in Asia Minor society. They likewise intimate key aspects of their precarious social circumstances as "strangers in a strange land," dislocated from their actual place of origin and belonging, disenfranchised, and subject to the ignorance, slander, and hostility of a local populace suspicious of their pedigrees, intentions, and allegiances. Such was the perennial predicament of strangers in the ancient, xenophobic world.

It is the designation of these strangers as "elect" (discussed below) that defines their specific Christian character, a designation the implications of which are spelled out more fully in 2:4–10. For further discussion of these terms, see the NOTES on 1:17 and 2:11 and the DETAILED COMMENT on 2:11.

of the Diaspora (*diasporas*). *Diaspora* is an English transliteration of a Greek term formed etymologically from *dia* + *spora* (lit., "scattering of seed") and means "dispersion." In the LXX and related Israelite literature, *diaspora* became a technical term denoting the "dispersion" of Israelites among the Gentiles beyond the borders of the Holy Land (Deut 28:25; 30:4; Jer 15:7; 41:17 LXX; *Pss. Sol.* 8:28; 9:2; *T. Ash.* 7:2) as a result of war, exile, forced dislocation, or voluntary resettlement due to commerce and trade. The term could denote either (a) "the *persons* who were dispersed" (Isa 49:6; Ps 146[147]:2; 2 Macc 1:27; *Pss. Sol.* 8:28; 9:2; John 7:35) or (b) the "*place* where the dispersed were located" (Jdt 5:19; *T. Ash.* 7:2; Philo, *Praem.* 115). Since Israelites of the Diaspora were not usually permitted citizenship in the cities they inhabited, living in the Diaspora always entailed some form of alien status. The misery this could also entail is evident in the words of the *Testament of Asher* (7:2): "You will be scattered to the four corners of the earth; in the Diaspora [or dispersion] you shall be despised as worthless, like useless water, until such time as the Most High visits the earth."

In continuity with this Israelite usage, the messianic sect employed the term to denote the location or population of God's people scattered beyond the original Palestinian homeland (John 7:35; Jas 1:1; 1 Pet 1:1). By the first century CE, out of an estimated Israelite population of 4–4.5 million (ca. 7% of a total Mediterranean population of 50–60 million), the vast majority of Israel (ca. 4 million) lived in the Diaspora (Philo, *Legat.* 36; Josephus, *Ant.* 14.7.2; *Sib. Or.* 3:271). Particularly heavy concentrations of Israelites outside of Palestine were located not only in Mesopotamia and Egypt but also Asia Minor (Philo, *Legat.* 245, 281; Josephus, *Ant.* 14.185–267; 16.160–78; Schürer 1986, 17–35; Trebilco

1991a; see also the maps in J. A. Sanders 1962 and M. Grant 1971, 81). It was also especially in Asia Minor that the early messianic movement made its greatest headway. Reicke (1968, 302–4) estimates a Christian population there of approximately 80,000 by the end of the first century. This network of Christian households and communities comprised a mixed constituency of former Israelites and Gentiles; see GENERAL INTRODUCTION, 5. Addressees.[4]

In 1 Peter, the precise identification of the location of the Diaspora in Asia Minor (Pontus, Galatia, Cappadocia, Asia, Bithynia, 1:1) indicates that the term *Diaspora* here has a customary literal (geographical) rather than figurative force. As a metaphor for a "scattered existence *in the world*" in contrast to "a heavenly home" (as proposed by BAGD 188; T. W. Martin 1992a, 144–61; and others), it would be without parallel in both the LXX and NT. Nor does 1 Peter present any ideology of Diaspora, as is found in writings of the House of Israel, an ethnic population separated from but inseparably linked in its history, ethnic identity, and political and cultural loyalies to "the land of Israel," with the hope of an eventual return of all of the dispersed persons (see the six defining characteristics of "Diaspora populations" in Klausner 1991, 195). The term, as employed here, expresses simply the physically dispersed situation of the addressees in *regions beyond the traditional Israelite "Land of inheritance"* (see NOTE on v 4) and the historical continuity of the elect strangers with the frequent condition of Israel as a vulnerable minority in foreign and hostile regions. See Origen (*Comm. Gen.*, cited in Eusebius, *Hist. eccl.* 3.1.2) and Eusebius (*Hist. eccl.* 3.4.2), who also take *Diaspora* in this geographical sense. Thus van Unnik (1983, 102) prefers the translation, "those of the Diaspora (of the Jews) who lodge. . . ."

For the early Christian movement, living as an alien people scattered in territories once beyond the borders of the traditional homeland posed the perennial problem encountered by Diaspora Israel and all displaced, dispossessed, and disenfranchised peoples: the maintenance of a distinctive communal identity, social cohesion, and commitment to group values, traditions, beliefs, and norms in the face of constant pressures urging assimilation and conformity to the dominant values, standards, and allegiances of the broader society. Moreover, as the history of Israel residing in the Diaspora so frequently attests, aliens of the House of Israel, called "Judeans" by their Gentile neighbors because of their allegiance to Judea and the Jerusalem Temple, could always be forced out of the cities where they had taken up residence, as in the expulsion of Judeans from Rome under Tiberius (Tacitus., *Ann.* 2.85.4) and again later under Claudius (Suetonius, *Claud.* 25.4), an expulsion that prompted the Chris-

[4] On Israel of the Diaspora, the concept of "Diaspora," and the conditions and strategies of Diaspora existence, see Stuiber 1957; J. A. Sanders 1962; Applebaum 1974a–b, 420–63, 464–503; Hengel 1974; Safrai 1974; Stern 1974; Schürer 1986, 1–149; Delling 1987; Lamau 1988, 87–93. On the Israelite Diaspora in Asia Minor, see Trebilco 1991a and Feldman 1993, 69–74; and on the dispersed addressees of 1 Peter, Lamau 1988, 81–87, 93–105. On the Christian usage of the term as a geographical pointer and not as a symbol for the church, see van Unnik 1983a.

tians Aquila and Priscilla to emigrate from Italy to Corinth (Acts 18:2). Feldman (1993, 69–74), commenting on the minority status of the "Jewish" Diaspora in Asia Minor, suspects that the peculiarities of Judean life there may even have facilitated conversion to Christianity: "The relative lack of contact between the Jews of Asia Minor and the fountainhead in the Land of Israel may explain why Christianity seems to have made relatively great progress in Asia Minor, presumably among Jews, by the beginning of the second century" (Feldman 1993, 73).

It was precisely this condition of vulnerable existence that lay behind the hostility and suffering experienced by the addressees of 1 Peter and that motivated the letter's response. This predicament, shared by both the addressees in Asia Minor and the senders in Babylon/Rome, is dramatically emphasized at the letter's outset (1:1) and close (5:13) and thus provides a framing scenario for the letter as a whole.

elect (*eklektois*). There is superior manuscript support for regarding *eklektois* as an adjective modifying *strangers* rather than as a substantive joined to *strangers* by an added "and" (only in Codex א*). *Eklektos* means "elect," "select," or "chosen" in 1 Peter, the LXX and NT generally, with God as the implied electing agent. This venerable honorific designation of God's people is rooted in the memory of God's election of and covenant with the house of Jacob at Mt. Sinai (Exod 19:3–8) and is further associated with the concepts of "sanctification-holiness" (1:2b, 15–16, 19, 22; 2:5, 9; 3:5, 15) and divine "calling" to a new and holy way of life (1:15; 2:9, 21; 3:9; 5:10). Each of these three related concepts conveys both divinely conferred dignity and honor on the one hand and distinction/demarcation from other peoples on the other. Members of the Christian brotherhood are described as "elect" at both the opening and close of the letter (5:13, *syneklektē*, "co-elect") so that the concept of election provides a thematic inclusion for the letter as a whole. In 2:4–10 this theme of divine election receives its fullest articulation as a quality linking the elect believers with both God and their elect Lord.

The expression *elect strangers* is a paradoxical one (Rousseau 1986), articulating on the one hand the vulnerable condition and lowly status of the brotherhood *in society* and on the other its elevated and elite ("elite" derives from *eklektos*) status *with God*. The community shares this paradoxical condition with its Lord, who was also "rejected by humans but elect, honored in God's sight" (2:4). This polar contrast between the condition of the suffering Christians in society on the one hand and their election and vocation by God on the other frames (1:1; 5:13) and animates the letter as a whole (Elliott 1966b; Chevallier 1971). As Rousseau (1986, 264–65, 272–73, 383) has aptly noted, this oxymoronic expression constitutes a "pre-signal" of the thrust of the entire communication.

1c. *of Pontus, Galatia, Cappadocia, Asia and Bithynia* (*Pontou, Galatias, Kappadokias, Asias kai Bithynias*). The overwhelming weight of the manuscript evidence supports this longer textual reading over the variants that either add an "and" before Asia (614 1243 1505 etc.), omit "Asia" (א* 048, other MSS,

Vulg., and some Lat. citations in Eusebius), omit "Bithynia" (B*), or omit the "and" joining "Asia" and "Bithynia" (a few Gk. MSS, Aug.). The omissions were most likely inadvertent instances of haplography prompted by the similar endings of the place-names.

The geographical location of the Christian Diaspora in Asia Minor addressed in this letter comprises four Roman provinces north of the Taurus Mountains, which extended East West across southern Asia Minor. See MAP 1 (above, p. 85). A detailed description of these Roman provinces is given in the GENERAL INTRODUCTION, 5.1. The Geographical Location of the Addressees.

The populations of these provinces included a variety of native ethnic groups, free citizens outnumbered by a vast number of slaves, a small number of Romans on administrative or military missions, many Israelites (1 Macc 15:22; Philo, *Legat.* 280–81; Acts 2:9; Josephus, *Ant.* 14.223–30, 234–55, 259–64; cf. Stern 1974, 143–55; Trebilco 1991a), and numerous types of resident aliens (travelers engaged in trade and commerce, itinerant scholars, and native farmers alienated from their ancestral lands and recategorized as "resident aliens"), as well as streams of temporary strangers just passing through. Acts, Galatians, Deutero-Pauline letters (Ephesians, Colossians, 1–2 Timothy), and Revelation attest the presence of Israelites and followers of Jesus in Asia, Galatia, Pontus, and Cappadocia, but in the case of the latter two provinces and Bithynia the information is sparse. Philo (*Legat.* 36) mentions Israelites in Pontus. According to Acts, Israelites from Pontus were present at the Pentecost festival in Jerusalem (Acts 2:9), where through Peter's proclamation 3,000 persons were said to have been won to the faith (Acts 2:1–42). Here Pontus is also mentioned as the birthplace of Aquila (Acts 18:2). Second-century witness to the presence of Christians in Pontus is found in the letters of Pliny the Younger (*Ep.* 10.96–97) and Dionysius of Corinth (in Eusebius, *Hist. eccl.* 4.23.6). Sinope of Pontus was the birthplace of Marcion, son of a bishop and wealthy ship-builder (early second century CE).

Of the four provinces addressed in 1 Peter, only Galatia and Asia were certain sites of a Pauline mission. The only NT reference to Bithynia outside of 1 Pet 1:1 notes expressly that Paul was prevented by the Spirit of Jesus from entering Bithynia (Acts 16:7). The absence of any record of Pauline activity in Bithynia-Pontus and Cappadocia weighs heavily against the supposition that 1 Peter was addressed primarily to Pauline churches (against Goldstein 1975 and others).

How Christianity reached these several provinces remains uncertain. The cases of Aquila (not a Pauline convert) and the Pontic Pentecost pilgrims (possibly converted by Peter), however, point to the activity of other missionaries in addition to Paul. The vast scope of the areas mentioned, comprising approximately 129,000 square miles, much of it rural territories and regions untouched by the Pauline urban mission, requires a date for 1 Peter significantly later than Paul's missionary journeys in the 50s in order to allow for the extensive spread of the Christian movement throughout this region as presupposed by this letter.

Its address to "strangers of the Diaspora" (1:1b) identifies 1 Peter as a Diaspora letter, which, like that of James ("to the twelve tribes in the Diaspora," 1:1), was modeled after similar Israelite Diaspora letters (see NOTE on 1:2d). This contrasts sharply with the letters of Paul which, except for Galatians, were directed to churches or individual households in specific cities.

The sequence in which the provinces are named is curious, with Pontus mentioned first and separate from Bithynia, with which it had formed a single province since 25 BCE. This sequence, however, may well suggest the *route* intended to be taken by Silvanus, the letter's courier.[5] Why someone bearing a letter from the Apostle Peter should begin his journey in remote northern Asia Minor is difficult to imagine, since there is no evidence of Peter's personal presence there. Ships, however, made their way there from ports to the west, including Rome. A courier's having arrived at Pontus on a ship bound from Rome would provide an explanation, especially in view of the likelihood that 1 Peter was written in and dispatched from Rome, signified as "Babylon" in 5:13. The speediest and safest route to Asia Minor from Rome would have been by sea, with the voyage eastward passing through Greece and then northward through the Aegean and the Bosporus into the Black Sea and ending at some seaport in Pontus, such as Sinope (so Hort 1898) or Amisus (so Hemer 1979), where the land journey would begin. From Pontus, the courier Silvanus (5:12) would have traveled along the main routes leading first south through the northern tip of Galatia, then to Cappadocia, then eastward through Galatia again (since Cappadocia is not contiguous with Asia), further eastward to Asia, and then northward to Bithynia; see MAP 3 (p. 93); cf. also the map sketched by Hemer (1978, 239).

Along his route, Silvanus would have been received and hosted by local house churches, an essential form of the hospitality and love urged in 4:8. He, in turn, would have supplemented the contents of the letter with remarks of his own; hence his commendation as a faithful and reliable brother (5:12). Having commenced his journey in Pontus, he would conclude it in Bithynia, the western half of the province of Bithynia-Pontus. From a Bithynian port such as Nicomedia, he would then return by ship to Rome. (See MAP 3.) If we take this scenario to be plausible, 1 Peter can be characterized not simply as a "general" but as an *encylical* or "circular" Diaspora letter.

In v 2a–c, three prepositional phrases describe the origin, instrumentality, and cause of the addressees' elect status. To indicate this relation in English, the term "elect" is repeated and put in brackets. Here and throughout the translation, terms in brackets indicate words not explicitly occurring in the Greek but semantically or syntactically implied.

2a. *according to the foreknowledge of God the Father* (*kata prognōsin theou patros*). This first qualification of the believers roots their election in the foreknowledge of God. The preposition *kata* ("according to," "in accord with")

[5] So Hort 1898, 167–84; Selwyn 1947, 119; and Hemer 1978, with modifications. For further discussion see the GENERAL INTRODUCTION, 5.1. Addressees.

occurs frequently in 1 Peter to indicate qualities, action, or conduct that are consonant with God's foreknowledge (1:2), mercy (1:3), holy nature (1:15), or will (4:6, 19; 5:2); see also 1:17; 2:11; 3:7; 4:6.

The symbolization of the chief deity as "Father" (*patēr*) was traditional in Israelite, Christian, and Greco-Roman (Father Zeus, Father Jupiter) patriarchal cultures, and "Father" is the principal metaphor for God in the NT (Reese 1978). The metaphor recurs in 1:3 and 1:17 and is linked conceptually with the images of Christian conversion as "rebirth" (1:3, 23; cf. 2:2) through the agency of God as procreator (1:3, 23), the believers as "children" of God (1:14) and hence loving "brothers (and sisters)" one with another (1:22; 3:8; 5:12, 13), and the dominant corporate image of the Christian community as "brotherhood" (2:17; 5:9) and family or "house(hold)" of God (2:4–10; 4:17).

The term *prognōsis* ("foreknowledge") occurs in the NT only here and in Peter's Pentecost address referring to "Jesus delivered according to the definite plan and foreknowledge of God" (Acts 2:23); for its only LXX occurrence, see Jdt 9:6. However, the concept of divine foreknowledge recurs in the Christological tradition cited in 1 Pet 1:20, "Christ foreknown (*proegnōsmenou*) (by God) before the foundation of the world." The word *prognōsis* denotes God's predetermining knowledge, a notion also expressed with other terms in Amos 3:2; Hos 5:3; and Jer 1:5. Earlier the Qumran community had affirmed concerning the righteous "sons of light" that "from the God of knowledge comes all that is and shall be. Before ever they existed He established their whole design, and when, as ordained for them, they come into being, it is in accord with His glorious design that they fulfill their work" (1QS III 15–16; cf. 1QH[a] I 23–25; IX 26–36). Divine election and foreknowledge are linked here in 1 Pet 1:2, as they are by Paul and his disciples (Rom 8:28–30), who also speak assuringly of believers' being "called" (*klētois*; cf. 1 Pet 1:25; 2:9, 21; 3:9; 5:10) according to God's prior purpose (*prothesin*) and their being preestablished (*proōrisen*) for conformity with the image of God's son (cf. Eph 1:4–5; 3:13; 2 Thess 2:13). For our author, as for early Christianity in general, foreknowledge and election are Christologically oriented (v 2c, 20; 2:4–10). Voluntary identification with Jesus Christ is the means of salvation foreknown by God, and solidarity with him, the "elect stone," is the basis for sharing in his election and honor, as the author will soon indicate (2:4–10). Here in 1:2 the election of creatures for salvation first of all is depicted as a consequence of the eternal foreknowledge and saving purpose of God the creator and father (see also the NOTE on 2:8). This forms one of the chief reasons that suffering believers can confidently "entrust their lives to a faithful Creator" (4:19; cf. 5:7, 10).

2b. *through the sanctifying action of the Spirit* (*en hagiasmōi pneumatos*). This second qualification of "elect," introduced with the preposition *en* used instrumentally, describes the believers' election as effected *through* the sanctifying action (*hagiasmōi* as noun of action) of the (Holy) Spirit of God who hallows, purifies, consecrates, and sets apart (Rom 15:16; 1 Thess 5:23; cf. 1 Cor 6:11; Heb 2:11; 10:10). 2 Thessolonians 2:13 contains the same unusual phrase in a similar complex of ideas. The combination of *sanctifying action* with *Spirit*, together with the triadic form of 1:2a–c, suggests the influence here of primitive Christian baptismal tradition (Rom 6:1–11, 19, 22; Matt 28:19; cf. 1 Cor 6:11). The more traditional expression for the divine Spirit, "Holy Spirit," occurs in 1 Peter only at 1:12; compare "Spirit of God," 4:14; "Spirit of Christ," 1:11; "spiritual," "of the Spirit," 2:5. Electedness and holiness were traditionally correlated qualities of the people of God (see NOTES and COMMENT on 2:4–10) that marked it as a covenant community selected and set apart by God from other peoples. "Holiness," as a quality conferred by the divine Spirit, is stressed frequently throughout the letter, together with purity (1:19 *amōmos, aspilos,* of Christ; *hagnizō* 1:22; *katharos* 1:22), as a preeminent distinguishing feature of Christian identity and conduct (1:15, 16; 2:5, 9; 3:15), as it was of the holy matriarchs (3:5) and the covenant community of Israel (Exod 19:6 cited in 2:5, 9).

2c. *because of the obedience and the sprinkling of the blood of Jesus Christ* (*eis hypakoēn kai rhantismon haimatos Iēsou Christou*). This final prepositional phrase roots the *cause* of Christian election in Jesus Christ's obedience to the Father's will and his suffering and death (involving the shedding of his blood; cf. 1:11, 19; 2:21–24; 3:18; 4:1, 13; 5:1). The translation takes the initial preposition *eis* to indicate cause ("because of"), as argued persuasively by Agnew (1983) and Mantey (1923, 1951a, 1951b, 1952; cf. also BDF §207), rather than purpose ("for"), and "of Jesus Christ" (*Iēsou Christou*) as a subjective rather than objective genitive. The preposition *eis* has the value of purpose elsewhere in 1 Peter (1:3, 4a, 5, 7, 22; 2:5, 7, 8, 9, 14, 21; 3:7, 9; 4:2, 7), and occasionally Jesus Christ is the object of Christian love and faith (1:8; 3:15), though never of obedience. But other factors favor the choices proposed here. The preposition *eis* controls both "obedience" and "sprinkling of blood" (*hypakoēn kai rhantismon haimatos*). If indicating purpose, it would make sense with the first noun ("elect . . . for [believers'] obedience to Jesus Christ") but not the second ("elect . . . for [believers'] sprinkling the blood of Jesus Christ"). According to our author (1:18), the *precious blood of Christ* (i.e., blood that Christ, *as subject*, shed) is, rather, the price and *cause* of redemption, a concept that belongs to the general theme of Christ's obedience to God's will and his suffering, death, and resurrection as the basis and motivation for Christian hope and conduct (1:3, 11–13, 21; 2:18–25; 3:13–4:6; 4:1, 13–16; 5:1, 10). This is reason for regarding *Jesus Christ* as a subjective genitive here in 1:2c as well and thus the subject of both active nouns ("obedience," "sprinkling"). Moreover, with *Jesus Christ* as subjective genitive, the three phrases of v 2a–c assume a balance in which God, Spirit, and Jesus Christ each is assigned an active role in Christian election, its origin, mediation, and cause. Taking *eis* to indicate purpose and assuming the elect believers to be the subject of *obedience* but Jesus Christ as the subject of *sprinkling*, on the other hand, results in an awkward syntactical construction (Agnew 1983, 69) that obscures the balance of these three phrases, which appear to focus exclusively on the action of God, Spirit, and Jesus Christ.

Jesus Christ's obedience and submission to God's will are a common theme of early Christian tradition (Mark 14:36/Matt 26:39/Luke 22:42; Rom 5:19;

Phil 2:8; Heb 5:8; cf. Justin Martyr, *Dial.* 99.2). In 1 Peter, Christ's subordination to God's will (2:22–23; 3:18) will serve as a model for the obedience enjoined upon his followers (1:14, 17, 22; 2:15, 17, 18–25; 3:14, 16; 5:2, 6). On the prominence of the theme of obedience in 1 Peter, see F. S. Carter 1975 and on the theme of Jesus as model of Christian obedience and submission see the NOTES on 2:18–25 and 3:18–22.

sprinkling of the blood of Jesus Christ (*rhantismon haimatos Iēsou Christou*). The phrase is unique in the NT, and *rhantismos haimatos* occurs nowhere in the OT. The description of the sin offering for atonement in Lev 6:24–30 with its reference to the "blood" (of the sin offering) "sprinkled on a garment" (6:27) offers no real parallel. The closest equivalent is the only other instance of the combination of "sprinkling" and "blood"—namely, Heb 12:22–24 ("you have come . . . to Jesus the mediator of a new covenant and to the sprinkled blood [*haimati rhantismou*]"). This expression appears to allude to a motif derived from Exod 24 and its reference to the "blood of the covenant" by which the covenant between God and Israel was sealed (24:8; cf. also Heb 10:29 and *Barn.* 5:1). In 1 Peter, a similar association of election and covenant is later explicated in 2:4–10 through the use of the covenant formula of Exod 19:6 to affirm the election of the Christian community.

Goppelt (1993, 70–72) claims a "conspicuous similarity" between this verse and a text of the *Rule of the Community* at Qumran (1QS III 6–8), in which it is said of the initiant: "He shall be cleansed from all his sins by the spirit of holiness uniting him to His truth . . . And when his flesh is sprinkled with purifying water and sanctified by cleansing water, it shall be made clean by the humble submission of his soul to all the precepts of God." The similarity of these motifs with those of the Christian initiatory rite of baptism suggests, in his view, the possibility that "I Pet 1:2 derives perhaps from a Palestinian-Syrian baptismal catechesis prompted by Essene precedents," a catechesis known to the Roman church (cf. Heb 10:22; 13:24). While this is conceivable, particularly because of the explicit concern of the Petrine author with baptism (3:21) and because of the frequent allusions throughout to Christian baptismal tradition, it is the theme of election rather than the process of baptism that is the focus here, as Goppelt also acknowledges (1993, 72).

This final phrase, in effect, introduces at the letter's outset two major themes to be developed subsequently: first, the suffering of Christ including his shedding of blood (1:11, 19; 2:21, 23, 24; 3:18; 4:1, 13; 5:1), and second, the fact that Christian election (2:4–10), holiness (1:14–16), and obedience to God in the face of innocent suffering (1:6: 2:19–20; 3:14–17; 4:1, 13, 15, 19; 5:9, 10) are rooted in the election (2:4), holiness (1:19), and obedience (2:21–24; 3:18) of the Christ who serves as both the enabler and example of the believing community. Cervantes Gabarrón (1991a) offers an excellent study of the theme of the passion of Jesus Christ in 1 Peter, (on 1:2 in particular, see 1991a, 319–28).

2d. *May you enjoy abundant grace and peace* (*charis hymin kai eirēnē plēthyntheiē*). The Greek reads literally: "may grace and peace be multiplied to you." In wishing an abundance of "grace" (*charis*) and "peace" (*eirēnē*) to the recipients, the author employs a stock phrase found in virtually all NT letters.[6] *Charis* ("grace," "favor" [of God]; cf. NOTE on 1:10) is a Christian variation on the conventional term *chairein* "greeting!" used in Greek letters (e.g., Acts 15:24; 23:26; Jas 1:1) and is combined with "peace," a conventional Israelite greeting (*šālôm lākem*, "peace to you," Judg 6:22; 19:20; 1 Sam 25:6; Dan 10:19; Luke 10:5–6; John 20:19, 21, 26). In 1 Peter, "peace" (*eirēnē*) is mentioned also in 3:11 and 5:14, but it is the concept of *grace*, divine favor, which confers a privileged condition and status with God, that receives special stress in 1 Pet (1:2, 10, 13; 3:7; 4:10; 5:5, 10, 12; cf. 2:19, 20). This Greek term expresses a celebrated quality of generous benefactors and patrons (Deissmann 1923, 311; Danker 1982). As God is portrayed by Christians as the heavenly benefactor par excellence (Danker 1982, 489–93; Malina 1988a), "grace," like "mercy" (1:3), denotes the favor and generosity that a heavenly father conferred on his children and "clients." Such beneficence on God's part called for expressions of gratitude and praise on the part of his beneficiaries (cf. 1:3; 4:11; 5:11) and the public extolling of his noble virtues (cf. 2:9; Danker 1982, 452–53).

Use of the verb *plēthyntheiē* here in the inscript distinguishes 1 Peter from the letters of Paul, where the term never occurs; compare Paul's standard epistolary greeting: "Grace to you and peace from God our Father" (Rom 1:7; 1 Cor 1:3; 2 Cor 1:2; Gal 1:3; Eph 1:2; Phil 1:2; Col 1:2; Phlm 3; cf. 2 Thess 1:2; Titus 1:4). Perhaps under the influence of 1 Peter it is employed also in the epistolary salutations of 2 Peter (2:1) and Jude (v 2) as well as in the inscripts of *1 Clement*, Polycarp, *To the Philippians*, and the *Martyrdom of Polycarp*. Prior to 1 Peter, the verb is employed in an earlier encyclical letter of the Persian king Darius concerning Diaspora "Jews" under his reign ("peace be multiplied to you," Dan 6:26 LXX (Theod.); cf. LXX 4:1, 37c) as well as in Israelite Diaspora letters (Syr. *Bar* 78:2; *b. Sanh.* 11b ["to our brothers, dwellers in the Babylonian Diaspora . . . may peace be multiplied to you"]). Thus, this feature too underlines the character of 1 Peter as a Diaspora letter.

The accent on "grace" and "peace" with which the letter opens is sounded again at the letter's conclusion (5:10, 11)

GENERAL COMMENT

These initial verses form the prescript of the letter. However, in advance of 1:3–12, the actual prologue of the letter, they also announce several terms and themes that figure prominently in the body of the letter to follow:

- *elect*: see 2:4–10 (Jesus Christ and believers as *elect*); 5:13 (*co-elect* [brotherhood] *in Babylon*); and the link between *elect* and (divine) *call* (1:15; 2:9, 21; 3:9; 5:10)

[6] Rom 1:7; 1 Cor 1:3; 2 Cor 1:2; Gal 1:3; Eph 1:2; Phil 1:1; Col 1:2; 1 Thess 1:1; 2 Thess 1:2; Titus 1:4; Phlm 3; 2 Pet 1:2; cf. 1 Tim 1:2 and Rev 1:4.

- *visiting strangers*: see 2:11 and 1:17 and Sarah, the stranger in a strange land, as model (3:6)
- *Diaspora*: see 5:13 (*Babylon*) and 1:17 (*alien residence*)
- *sanctifying action of the Spirit*: see 1:12 (*Holy Spirit*), 3:15 (*sanctify*) and the stress on *holiness* (1:15, 15; 2:5, 9; 3:5), *purity* (1:22), *purification* (1:22), and *spotlessness* (1:19)
- *obedience-disobedience*: see 1:14, 22; 2:8; 3:1, 6, 20; 4:17 and the *will of God* (2:15; 3:17; 4:2, 19; 5:2) or *mindfulness of God* (2:19; 3:16, 21) as norm
- *sprinkling of the blood of Jesus Christ*: see 1:19 (*blood of Christ*) and stress on Christ's suffering and death (1:11; 2:21–24; 3:18; 4:1, 13; 5:1)
- *grace*: see 1:10, 13; 3:7; 4:10; 5:5, 10, 12
- *peace*: see 3:11; 5:14

These numerous links among the prescript, body, and subscript of the letter speak decisively against the theory (von Harnack 1897; Beare 1970; Marxsen 1979) that 1:1–2 and 5:12–14 were not part of the original composition but were, rather, secondary additions to 1:3–5:11 by a later redactor in order to transform a purported homily (1:3–5:11) into a letter (see GENERAL INTRODUCTION, 1. Genre, for fuller discussion). The fatal flaw in this theory is the fact that the vocabulary, style, and thematic content of 1:1–2 and 5:12–14 are fully consistent with that of 1:3–5:11. As original integral elements of the composition, 1:1–2 and 5:12–14 are key indicators of the original epistolary character of 1 Peter.

It has been suggested that the Qumran community provides the closest analogy to the notion of "elect strangers" and the related motifs of 1:3–2:10 (cf. also Acts 7; 13:7; and Heb 11; Goppelt 1993, 68–70, citing CD III 21–IV 6; VI 4–5 and 1QM I 2–3 as examples). But in addition to the traditional character of the motifs cited (exodus, exile, tribulation, true Israel, repentance), several features also distinguish the thought of 1 Peter from that of Qumran: the "elect" in Qumran comprise not the entire community but only the sons of Zadok; the Diaspora of 1 Peter is in Asia Minor not "Damascus"; the Petrine author, as Goppelt concedes, speaks not of repentance but of "rebirth" (1:3, 22) and employs the language of the LXX and Hellenistic Israel. This amounts to not simply a Petrine modification of the content of the Qumran texts cited (as Goppelt claims) but a totally different frame of reference (see NOTES at 1:17 and 2:11). Moreover, in contrast to the physical and social isolation undertaken by the Qumran community, the Petrine author advocates not withdrawal from but engagement with society, but in a holy and nonconformist mode (see 1:14–17 and NOTE).

There is also no necessity or textual basis for regarding the terms *strangers* and *Diaspora* (cf. also *paroikia*, *paroikoi*; *Babylon*) as indications that 1 Peter offers a "pilgrim theology" for strangers here on earth yearning for their heavenly home (e.g., Furnish 1975; and his notes on 1 Peter in the Oxford Study Edition of the NEB; and more recently Feldmeier 1992, representing a widely held view of 1 Peter in both academic and popular circles; for a critique of this view, see Elliott 1981/1990, 129–32 and pp. 101–64 on the sectarian strategy of 1 Peter in general). The distinctions in 1 Peter are not cosmological (earth-heaven), as in Hebrews, but social: believers who form a minority of strangers in their society versus a dominant and hostile society of nonbelievers (cf. the contrasts between believers-nonbelievers in 2:4–10, 11–12; 3:13–17; 4:1–6, 12–19). With these terms the author acknowledges their inferior and vulnerable social status but subsequently affirms that these strangers in society have a place of belonging in the family or household of God. Their behavior in society then must be a reflection of their union with God, Christ, and one another in the brotherhood of faith (see Elliott 1981/1990, 129–32, and GENERAL INTRODUCTION, 6. Aim, Strategy).

There is also no manuscript support or compelling evidence for the egregious conjecture that in 1:1 the name *Peter* was a secondary replacement for an original *Paul* (Fischer 1973, 15). This represents a desperate effort to turn 1 Peter into a Pauline composition "by hook or by crook." As the commentary will show in numerous instances, this letter has many features that distinguish it from Pauline style, thought, and theology. 1 Peter is best viewed as a composition written independently of Paul and the Pauline circle, though similar to the Pauline and Deutero-Pauline letters through the common use of a common reservoir of tradition. Differences from Pauline practice already apparent in these opening verses include its address not to a single "church" (the term *ekklesia* is not used in 1 Peter) in a particular city (Paul's arena of activity) but to *strangers of the Diaspora* (nowhere used by Paul) in Asia Minor provinces where Paul was not present (Bithynia-Pontus, Cappadocia) and a form of salutation (1:2d) not employed by Paul.

These initial verses thus mark the composition as a personal letter, link its message to the Apostle Peter, acknowledge the paradoxical condition of its intended recipients (strangers in the Diaspora yet elect and holy before God), and thereby announce themes to be subsequently developed. The triadic structure of v 2 in particular anticipates a similar triadic structure in the immediately following unit, 1:3–12, which also expands on the roles of God the Father, Jesus Christ, and Holy Spirit and elaborates further on the privileges of the elect people of God.

DETAILED COMMENT: PETER, HIS NAME, AND HIS ROLE IN THE NEW TESTAMENT AND EARLY CHURCH

The NT contains 188 references to this leading and most-often-named follower of Jesus in the primitive church under the names *Symeōn* (Greek transliteration of the Hebrew name *Šimĕʿôn*, Acts 15:14) or *Simōn* (a genuine Greek name but probably a grecized form of *Šimĕʿôn*, 22×), generally used by Jesus (e.g., Matt 17:25; Mark 14:37; Luke 22:31) and employed absolutely; *Symeōn*

Petros (2 Pet 1:1); or *Simōn Petros*, or "Simon, called Peter" (27×); *Kēphas* (Greek transliteration of Aramaic *Kêpā'*, absolutely, 9×); and *Petros* (absolutely, 128×). In the Syriac versions of the Gospels and Acts, the common designation for the apostle is *Simon Kephas*. Neither *Kêpā'* in Aramaic nor *Petros* in Greek was a normal proper name. According to the tradition, the former was assigned to Simon by Jesus (John 1:43; cf. Mark 3:16; Matt 16:18) as a surname or nickname ("Rocky"), implying something about Simon's character or career; see also *Gos. Eb.* 1 (in Epiphanius, *Pan.* 30.13.2–3): "Simon whose surname was Peter." On "Simon Peter" and the custom of double names, see Horsley (1992, 1011–17); on the names of Peter see also Hort 1898, 151–53. His father was Jonah (*Iōnas*, Matt 16:17 and textual variants in John 1:42 and 21:15–17; compare the less likely John [*Iōannēs*, John 1:42; 21:15–17]), and his brother was Andrew (Mark 1:16/Matt 4:18; Mark 1:29; Matt 10:2; Luke 6:14; John 1:40, 45). The names of his wife (1 Cor 9:5; Eusebius, *Hist. eccl.* 3.30.1–2) and mother-in-law (Mark 1:30; Matt 8:14; Luke 4:38) are not recorded. The Greek name *Andreas* ("manly"), conferred on his younger brother by his parents, suggests a family open to Greek as well as Israelite culture. His Galilean home was the cosmopolitan town of Bethsaida (John 1:44), and he spoke his native tongue with a recognizable Galilean accent (Mark 14:70; Matt 26:73). Later he resided at Capernaum (Matt 8:14), a port on the northwest shore of the Sea of Galilee. His occupation, like that of his father, brother, and partners, James and John (the sons of Zebedee), was that of a fisherman (Mark 1:16–20/Matt 4:18–22; Luke 5:1–11; cf. John 21:3). It was in Galilee, according to the Synoptic authors that he was called to be a disciple of Jesus at the outset of Jesus' public ministry (Mark 1:16–20/Matt 4:18–22; Luke 5:1–11; contrast John 1:28, 35–42). In the view of representatives of the Sanhedrin (Acts 4:13), he and his companion John were untrained in the finer points of the Mosaic Law (*agrammatoi kai idiōtai*). In the NT sources he is presented as a complex figure and is portrayed variously as impetuous (Mark 14:29–31; John 18:10) and unclear regarding many things (Mark 9:5–6; Matt 16:22–24; Luke 22:33-34; John 13:8–10; Acts 10:14; 12:9) yet also firm and loyal (John 21:15–17); cowardly (Mark 14:66–72 par.) and vacillating (Gal 2:11–14) as well as resolute (Acts 4:10; 5:1–10; 11:2–17; 12:11; 15:7–11).

Important features of the diverse portrait of Peter in the NT that illustrate and underline his leading role in the early Church include his priority as first-called (Mark 1:16–18/Matt 4:18–20; compare John 1:40–42) and first-named (Matt 10:1–4 par.; Acts 1:13) among the disciples; his representative role as the disciples' spokesperson (Matt 15:15; Luke 8:45,12:41) and, with James and John, his privileged witness of Jesus' raising of Jairus' daughter (Mark 5:37; Luke 8:51), Jesus' transfiguration (Matt 17:1 par.; 2 Pet 1:16–18), and his experience in Gethsemane (Mark 14:33/Matt 26:37); his individual experience of Jesus' benefactions (Luke 5:1–11; Mark 1:29–31; Matt 14:28–32; 17:24–27); his confession of Jesus as Messiah (Matt 16:13–23 par.); his test of faith, denial of Jesus, and turning again to strengthen the brothers (Luke 22:31–34, 54–62 and par.); his witness of the empty tomb (John 20:6–7); his priority among those to whom the risen Christ appeared (1 Cor 15:5; cf. Luke 24:34); his postresurrection charge to feed Christ's sheep (John 21:15–19); his sermons focusing on the passion, death, and resurrection of Jesus as God's suffering servant (Acts 2–4); his ministry to both Israelites (Acts 1–5; Gal 2:7–8) and Gentiles (Acts 10–11 and 15:7–11); his leadership among the "pillars" of the Jerusalem community (Acts 1–5; Gal 1–2); his mission to the Gentiles (Acts 10–11:18); his suffering and arrest under Herod Agrippa (Acts 12:1–17); his support of the Gentile mission at the so-called Apostolic Council (Acts 15); and his constrained death by which he glorified God (John 21:19; cf. 1 Pet 5:1).

The history of his apostolic activity from the death of Jesus until his own death is one of the most discussed and controverted issues of early Church history. Information on Peter and his career following the resurrection, except for Acts, is fragmentary (knowledge of Peter/Cephas at Corinth [1 Cor 9:5, 15:5] and his possible linkage with a Cephas party [1 Cor 1:12, 3:22]) or filtered through Paul's own theological perspective (Gal 1–2, especially 2:7–8) and Paul's one-sided account of his encounter with Peter at Antioch (2:11–14). Acts, reflecting in turn Luke's theological program ascribes to Peter a key role in the spread of an inclusive Christian gospel from "Jerusalem, Judea, and Samaria to the end of the earth" (1:8). Here Peter's movements are traced from Jerusalem and Judea (chs. 1–9) to Samaria and his conversion of the Gentile Cornelius and his family in Caesarea Maritima (chs. 10–11), to Jerusalem where he confronted the "circumcision party" (11: 1–18) and was arrested and imprisoned by King Herod Agrippa I (12:1–5). The subsequent story of his divine deliverance from prison (12:6–11) and his receiving refuge at the home of Mary, the mother of John Mark (12:12–17), ends with the tantalizing observation, "then he departed and went to another place" (12:17), an event occurring shortly before the death of Herod in 44 CE (Acts 12:20–23; Josephus, *Ant.* 19.343–52).

The account of the so-called Apostolic Council in Jerusalem (Acts 15) contains the last mention of Peter in Acts. Here it is recounted that Paul and Barnabas and some others representing the community in Antioch met in Jerusalem with the apostles and elders, among whom are included Peter and James, the Lord's brother. The point of discussion was the insistence of some believers belonging to the Pharisaic party that circumcision and observance of the Mosaic Law must be retained. In this debate Peter is portrayed as recalling his experience of God's eliminating the ethnic distinction between Israelite believers at Caesarea and the Spirit's cleansing of the latter through faith (15: 7–9), and supporting the principle of salvation solely through the grace of the Lord Jesus (15:10–11). James (15:13–21) concurs with this word of "Symeon" (Peter's Aramaic personal name, 15:14). The leaders of the Jerusalem community thereupon send a letter to the Gentile brothers in Antioch, Syria, and Cilicia (15:22–29) commending Paul and Barnabas and stating four minimal requirements of abstention (15:29) to be observed there. Judas Barsabbas and Silas, "leading men among the brothers" in Jerusalem, are elected to serve as the letter's emissaries. The historical basis of this account has met with no small degree of skepticism among scholars who see here the heavy hand of Luke. The jury, however, is still out on this issue. Of particular significance for 1 Peter is the memory of Peter's theological position, which this episode (along with Acts 10:1–11:14) records, as well as his personal association in Jerusalem with Silas (with great likelihood the same person known as Silvanus in Paul's letters and 1 Peter [5:12] and earlier with John Mark [Acts 12:12–17]). These same two names occur in the postscript of 1 Peter (5:12–13) as associates of Peter in Rome, with Silvanus identified as courier of this letter (see NOTE on 5:12).

According to early and later post-NT evidence, Peter's mission eventually took him to Rome (*1 Clem.* 5:1–4; Ign. *Rom.* 4:3; cf. Eusebius, *Hist. eccl.* 2.14.6; 2.15.6; 2:17.1; 4.1). There he proclaimed the gospel accompanied by Mark (according to the early elders, Papias, Irenaeus, and Clement of Alexandria (Eusebius, *Hist. eccl.* 2.15; 3.11; 3.39.15; 5.8.2–3; 6.14.5–7; cf. also *Hist. eccl.* 2.17.1 and the NOTE on 5:13). In the aftermath of the great fire of Rome (64 CE) and Nero's execution of the Christians held responsible for it, he, along with Paul, experienced a martyr's death (*1 Clem.* 5:4; Eusebius, *Hist. eccl.* 2.25.4–8 [citing Tertullian, Gaius, and Dionysius of Corinth]; 3.1.2; cf. John 21:18–19; 1 Pet 5:1; see also the NOTE on 5:13).

Later tradition varies as to the specific place of his burial (at the catacombs of San Sebastiano on the Via Appia outside Rome or at Vatican Hill [Eusebius, *Hist. eccl.* 2.25.6–7]; cf. Toynbee and Perkins 1956; Cullmann 1958; de Marco 1964; D. W. O'Connor 1969, 1975; see also the NOTE on 5:13).[7]

1 and 2 Peter were the first in a long line of Christian compositions attributed to this foremost figure of the primitive church (Eusebius, *Hist. eccl.* 3.1.3–4; 3.4:2; 3.25.1–7). Subsequent writings from the second century onward that are ascribed to or focus upon Peter include the *Gospel of Peter*, the *Apocalypse of Peter* (Ethiopic and Greek), the *Preaching of Peter* (*Kerygma Petrou*), the *Acts of Peter* (including the *Martyrdom of Peter*); the *Acts of Peter and Paul*, the *Acts of Peter and Andrew*, the *Acts of Peter and the Twelve Apostles*, the *Passion of Peter*, the *Passion of Peter and Paul*; the Gnostic *Revelation of Peter* (Coptic); the *Epistle of Peter to Philip*, and the *Epistle of Peter to James*. In these "Petrine" writings, or texts where Peter figured prominently, as also in the Pseudo-Clementine writings, Peter appears as the apostolic guarantor of the truth of their contents whether in opposition to heretical factions or as recipient of higher gnostic wisdom. This truth is guaranteed by the weight of antiquity and the personal connection of Peter with the birth of the messianic movement and his eyewitness experience of Jesus, his ministry and teaching, suffering, death, and resurrection. In regard to 1 Peter, the significance of the NT portrait

[7] On the chronology of the life of Peter in the biblical and postbiblical tradition see Chase 1900a; Heussi 1955; Finegan 1964; Martimort 1972; R. E. Brown, Donfried, and Reumann, eds. 1973; R. E. Brown 1976; Dockx 1984; Donfried 1992; Ghiberti 1992; P. Perkins 1994, 18–51, 168–81.

of Simon Peter lies in its representation of various themes clustering around the figure of Peter that also appear in this letter.[8]

For studies on 1 Pet 1:1–2, see Agnew 1983; Arndt 1934; Chevallier 1971; Dupont-Roc 1995; Elliott 1980, 1981/1990, 1982; Feldmeier 1992; Furnish 1975; Geyser 1959; Goldstein 1975; Grosheide 1960; Hemer 1978; Hiebert 1980a; Holzmeister 1922; Hort 1898, 151–84; LaVerdiere 1969; Mantey 1923, 453–60; 1951a, 1951b, 1952; T. W. Martin 1992a; Nestle 1898–99; Pilch 1991a; Romo 1977; J. Rousseau 1986; Scharlemann 1975; Schider 1939; Schnider and Stenger 1987.

---

[8] On the portrait of Peter and Petrine tradition in the NT, see Chase 1900a, 756–67; Elert 1911; Foakes-Jackson 1927b; Holzmeister 1937, 1–77; Fascher 1938; Leclerq 1939; Stauffer 1943; Strathmann 1943; Lowe 1956; Schulze-Kadelbach 1956; Cullmann 1958; Gaechter 1958; Rimoldi 1958; Schmid 1960; Finegan 1964; Vögtle 1964; Rigaux 1967; Testa 1967; Pesch 1971, 1980; Trilling 1971; R. E. Brown, Donfried, and Reumann, eds. 1973; Mees 1973; R. E. Brown 1976; 1984, 75–83; Bruce 1979; D. W. Perkins 1982; R. E. Brown and J. P. Meier 1983, 128–39; T. V. Smith 1985, 143–214; R. P. Martin 1986a; Thiede 1986, 1987b; M. Karrer 1989; Donfried 1992; Grappe 1992; D. W. O'Connor 1992; P. Perkins 1994, 52–130. On the reputation, prestige, and figure of Peter in postbiblical tradition, see von Harnack 1897, 240–43, 450–65, 703–10; Chase 1900a, 767–817; Goetz 1927; Dinkler 1939, 1966; Stauffer 1943; Heussi 1955; Rimoldi 1955; Bauer 1965, 2:45–50; Danielou 1967; Testa 1967; D. H. Schmidt 1972; R. E. Brown, Donfried, and Reumann, eds. 1973; Mees 1973; R. Pesch 1980; T. V. Smith 1985, 1–142; P. Perkins 1994, 131–81.

I. By God's Mercy Believers Are Reborn an Elect and Holy People (1:3–2:10)

◆

I. A. Praise to God for the Saving Benefits of His Mercy (1:3–12)

1:3a Blessed [is] the God and Father of our Lord Jesus Christ
3b who in accord with his lavish mercy
has caused us to be born again
3c for a living hope through the resurrection of
Jesus Christ from the dead,
4a for an inheritance [that is]
imperishable,
undefiled, and
unfading,
4b kept in the heavens for you,
5a who by God's power are guarded through faith,
5b for a salvation ready to be revealed in the last propitious time.
6a Consequently you exult with joy,
6b while now for a brief time, if it must be,
you are afflicted by various testings,
7a so that the tested genuineness of your faith,
7b which is more precious than perishable gold tested by fire,
7c may be found worthy of praise and
glory and
honor
at the revelation of Jesus Christ.
8a Without having seen [him], you love him;
8b without now seeing [him], yet trusting in him,
8c you nevertheless exult with unutterable and glorious joy,
9 receiving for yourselves as the final outcome of your faith
the salvation of [your] lives.
10 Concerning this salvation, prophets,
who prophesied of the grace intended for you,
searched and investigated,

11a investigating to what sort of person or propitious time
the spirit of Christ within them was referring,
11b bearing prior witness to the sufferings [destined] for Christ
and the glories after these [sufferings].
12a To them it was revealed that they were serving not themselves
but rather you in these things,
12b [things] that now have been announced to you
by those who proclaimed good news to you
through the Holy Spirit sent from heaven,
12c [things] into which angels yearn to gain a glimpse.

INTRODUCTION

The body of the letter opens (1:3–12), as it closes (5:10–11), on a worshipful note of blessing and praise. This benediction, praising God for the several effects of divine mercy, forms the first part of a stirring declarative affirmation of the divinely conferred dignity and distinctive identity of the believing community (1:3–2:10). Praise of God (1:3–12) and his wondrous deeds (2:9), along with emphasis on the transforming experience of divine *mercy* (1:3; 2:10), forms an inclusion marking the beginning and end of this first major unit of the letter. The subunits of this section, 1:3–12, 13–21, 22–25, 2:1–3, 4–10, while articulating various aspects of this dignity and identity, are integrated by a progression of thought tracing the course of the believers' new life from their rebirth, their hope and holiness as the children of God, their brotherly love, their nourishment and growth through the word by which they were reborn, to their union with Jesus Christ and consolidation as the household of God. This initial declaration of the benefits of spiritual rebirth—hope, inheritance, salvation, separation from a former ungodly way of life, union with God and Christ, and membership in the elect and holy family of faith—provides the foundation for the moral exhortation that follows in the remainder of the letter.

The blessing with which this unit begins formally embraces vv 3–5. With v 6 the focus shifts from praise of God's action to the behavior of the believers (vv 6–9, prepared for by vv 4b–5) and the prophets (vv 10–12). On the whole, 1:3–12 comprises one extended period or single sentence with relative clauses (*en hoi*, v 6; *peri hēs*, v 9) and the link-word *salvation* (vv 9, 10) marking and joining its subunits. Its conclusion in v 12 is indicated by the new section beginning at 1:13, which shifts from the indicative to imperative mood and employs the inferential particle *dio* ("therefore," v 13) to introduce the imperatives that follow. The triadic structure of vv 3–12, focusing on God the Father (vv 3–5), Jesus Christ (vv 6–9), and Holy Spirit (vv 10–12), echoes in modified sequence the similar triadic structure of v 2 (God-Spirit-Jesus Christ). Link-words joining its subunits (*you*, *your*, 1:4–5/6–8; *salvation*, 1:5/9/10) and repeated terms ([*Jesus*] *Christ*, 1:3, 7, 11; *heaven*, 1:4, 12; *revealed*, 1:5, 7, 12; *propitious time*, 1:5, 11; *suffer/sufferings*, 1:6, 11; *glory*, 1:7, 11) likewise provide a syntactic and thematic coherence to the unit. The blessing (vv 3–5) grounds the indicative statements that follow in the saving action of God and sounds a note of confidence and praise that pervades the letter as a whole. This opening section in its entirety serves here, as in other NT letters, to announce themes receiving accentuation in the remainder of the writing (Kendall 1986).

NOTES

Verses 3–5, comprising the first of three subunits of this section, declare God *blessed* for three specific transforming benefits that believers have received as a result of God's great mercy and regenerating action: a living hope, an imperishable inheritance, and a salvation about to be revealed.

1:3a. *Blessed [is] the God and Father of our Lord Jesus Christ* (*Eulogētos ho theos kai patēr tou kyriou hēmōn Iēsou Christou*). Exactly the same phrase occurs in the opening sections of 2 Corinthians (1:3) and Ephesians (1:3), where an implied indicative "is" is also preferable to an implied Greek optative translated "be" (see Furnish 1984, 108). The formula *and Father of our Lord Jesus Christ* (cf. also Rom 15:6) represents a Christian expansion of the traditional Israelite *berakah* or benediction (from Latin *benedictus*) which, like similar expressions of praise, thanksgiving, and doxology, had its home in public and private Israelite worship (Deichgräber 1967, 40–43, 64–87; 1980; Schäfer 1980).

The formula of praise, "blessed is God," "blessed is the Lord God who . . . ," with *eulogētos* translating the Hebrew *barak*, occurs frequently in the LXX.[9] The formula is often followed, as in 1 Pet 1:3–5, with a statement extolling God's attributes or benefactions.[10] In the NT, similar eulogistic blessings of God are found in Luke 1:68; Rom 1:25, 9:5; 2 Cor 11:31, in addition to 2 Cor 1:3 and Eph 1:3.

This introductory *eulogia* is closest in mood and function to those of 2 Cor 1:3–11 and Eph 1:3–14 among all the introductory thanksgivings of the Pauline and Deutero-Pauline letters. Employing the blessing formulas of Israelite worship (see **NOTES** on 1:3) and letters (2 Chr 2:11), the early Christians began their letters with praise and thanks for benefits received and in these initial indicative statements of the letters introduced themes developed later in the writing. Such eulogies (from *eulogeō*, lit., "speak well of"), like doxologies (declarations of glory [*doxa*]; cf. 4:11; 5:11) and aretologies (recitals, wondrous deeds [*aretai*]; cf. 2:9), are public declarations of the honor and praiseworthiness of the one celebrated.

In later Israel this "quintessential proto-rabbinic liturgical form" (Sigal 1984, 71) eventually became the subject of an entire tractate of the Mishna and Tal-

---

[9] E.g., 1 Kgdms (1 Sam) 25:32; 3 Kgdms (1 Kgs) 5:21; 8:15, 56; 1 Esd 4:40; Pss 40[41]:13; 65[66]:20; 67[68]:19; 105[106]:48.

[10] E.g., Gen 14:20; Exod 18:10; 2 Chr 2:11; 6:4; 1 Esd 8:25; Pss 65[66]:20; 71[72]:18; 123[124]:6; 134[135]:21; 143[144]:1; Dan 3:26, 52–90, 95; Tob 11:17; 13:1; cf. *Pss Sol*. 2:33, 37.

mud (*Berakot*). To "speak well" of God (in a "blessing" or benediction or *eulogia*) is to publicly declare God's honor (cf. 2:9)—the expected behavior of a client vis-à-vis his or her patron and benefactor.[11]

The term "father" (*patēr*) repeats the traditional epithet for God used in 1:2 and expresses the intimate, familial relation of God to both "our Lord Jesus Christ" and to God's believing "children" (1:14; 2:2), who call upon God as "Father" (1:17). Since in antiquity males were thought to bear in their semen the entire human being (*homunculus*, the "tiny human") with which they impregnated women, male-gendered deities could be thought of similarly as progenitors. Thus the metaphor of God as father is likewise consonant with the recurrent theme of rebirth (1:3, 23; 2:2) that implies God as progenitor and the believing community as God's family or household (2:5; 4:17) and "brotherhood" (2:17; 5:9; see the NOTE on 1:2 and Elliott 1990, 165–266). On God as father, see also the NOTE on 1:17.

3b. *who in accord with his lavish mercy* (*ho kata to poly autou eleos*). The stress on divine *mercy* recurs in 2:10 and serves as an inclusion marking the beginning and end of the letter's first major section, 1:3–2:10. *To eleos*, meaning "mercy," "compassion," "pity," "clemency," in the OT is a prominent characteristic of God's goodness toward His people (e.g., Ps 31:10; 32:5, 22; 85:13). It is often seen as manifested in the covenant between God and Israel (Exod 20:6; 34:6, 10; Deut 5:2, 9–10; Hos 2:20). In Hosea, as in 1 Peter, which alludes to Hos 1–2 in 2:10, "mercy" is an expression of the intimate relationship between God and Israel symbolized by fidelity and family. The fulsome Greek phrase, which reads, literally, "in accord with the greatness of his mercy," is unique in the NT (but occurs in Sir 16:12 and *T. Naph.* 4:3) and underlines the magnitude attributed to this quality of divine generosity, another of the several features of God's honor that the author celebrates (cf. also grace/favor, glory, power, nobility, etc.).

has caused us to be born again (*anagennēsas hēmas*). The verb *anagennaō* ("cause to be born again," "beget again") occurs only here and in 1:23 in the NT; cf. also the related *artigennēta* ("newborn" [babies]) in 2:2. It serves as a dramatic metaphor for the decisive transformation of life that believers have experienced through God's mercy. God has honored the readers by "rebirthing" them (see also 1:23) as his "children" (1:14) and "newborn babies" (2:2) and incorporating them into his family (2:4–10). This radical transformation

[11] On the eulogistic formula in 1 Pet 1:3–4 (5), see Shimada 1966, 139–59; and Deichgräber 1967, 77–78. On the Israelite blessing and its Christian epistolary employment, see Delling 1962, 61–68; J. T. Sanders 1962; J. M. Robinson 1964; Deichgräber 1967, 40–43, 64–87; Doty 1973, 31–33; O'Brien 1977, 1978; Schäfer 1980; Schnider and Stenger 1987, 42–49. On Hellenistic public praise of the qualities and benefactions of gods and mortals, see Danker 1982. On 2 Cor 1:3–11, Eph 1:3–14, and their relation to 1 Pet 1:3–12, see Mitton 1950; Dahl 1951; Coutts 1957; Schnackenburg 1977. On the function of introductory blessings/thanksgivings in epistles, see Schubert 1939; and on 1 Pet 1:3–12, in particular Kendall 1986.

from a dead-ended existence to new life (cf. 2:5, 24bc), enacted in baptism (3:21), involves entry into a new kinship-like relation with God, Christ, and one another. Thus baptism is logically likened to rebirth, since one can only become kin through birth. Subsequent references to the believers' passage from "darkness to light" (2:9), and to their former and present phases of existence (2:10, 25; 4:2–4; cf. 1:18–19), further emphasize this transition. Such transition and transformation also entails deliberate severance from previous futile modes of living and deadly social alliances (1:14–16, 18; 2:1, 11; 4:2–4).

The absence of the verb *anagennaō* elsewhere in the NT and LXX (one instance is an improbable variant of *paragennētheis* in the Prologue of Sirach, 28), coupled with the relative rareness of the concept of regeneration (with God as subject and humanity as object) in OT and NT (cf. *palingenesia* in Matt 19:28; Titus 3:5) and contemporary literature (Büchsel 1964, 673–75) accentuates all the more its prominence in 1 Peter. In the OT, God occasionally is depicted as the one who figuratively "begets" (*gennaō*) Israel (Deut 32:18), David as adopted king (Ps 2:7, cited in Acts 13:33; Heb 1:5; 5:5), or Wisdom (Prov 8:25) but never as one who causes to be "born again." This also holds true for Philo's discussion of the Stoic doctrine of the regeneration of the world (*Aet.* 89–103; see *Leg.* 3.219 regarding divine creating as begetting). Josephus uses the term once of ashes "reproduced" (*anagennōmenēn*) in the fruits visible after Sodom's destruction (*J.W.* 4.484.). Likewise in the NT, the simple verb *gennaō* ("give birth to," "beget") is used figuratively of believers who have been "born" of God (John 1:13; 3:3; 1 John 2:29; 3:9 [2×]; 4:7; 5:1 [3×]; 5:4; 5:18 [2×]) but, except for 1 Peter, never the composite verb *anagennaō*. The term's derivation from the Mystery Religions, as proposed by Perdelwitz (1911, 16), is highly unlikely due to its singular appearance in a passage of Sallust (*De Deis* 4), postdating 1 Peter, and due to differing conceptions of regeneration. For the texts and discussion of the essential differences between 1 Peter and the Mysteries on the theme of rebirth, see Büchsel 1964, 669–70, 672–75, 686–89; Selwyn 1947, 305–11; Schelkle 1976, 28–31.

Postbiblical Israelite tradition, on the other hand, offers striking analogies. One example involves a midrash on the Song of Songs (*Midr. Cant. Rab.* on 8:2), which depicts Israel as a newborn babe born at Sinai through its covenant with God (Sjöberg 1951, 51–52). Our author focuses on this same covenant in 2:5 and 9 at the conclusion of this section on rebirth (1:3–2:10), thereby suggesting the association in his mind of covenant and rebirth. An even closer analogy to the apparent synonymous sense of *anagennaō* ("beget anew") and *artigennētos* ("newly born," 2:2) in 1 Peter as terms for transformation is the rabbinic comparison of conversion to Israel as a "new birth." This is exemplified by a midrash on the same Song of Songs (1:3; *Cant. Rab.* 1), which reads: "When someone brings a creature (i.e., a person) under the wings of the Shekinah (i.e., wins him to Israel, according to *Cant. Rab.* 1 on 1:1), then it is counted to him (i.e., by God) as though he had created and fashioned and formed him (i.e., as empowered by God the creator and procreator)." Similarly, a Talmudic passage, *b. Yebam.* 22a (citing a saying of R. Jose, ca. 150 CE), asserts: "A proselyte just converted is like a newly-born child." Although the *literary* attestation of this Israelite association of conversion and new birth postdates the composition of 1 Peter, the influence of earlier oral tradition is conceivable, especially given the author's familiarity with further elements of Israelite thought and practice including proselyte baptism (van Unnik 1980, 3–82). The similarity is particularly compelling given the author's obvious use of rebirth/new birth as a metaphor for baptismal conversion (Gaventa 1986, 130–45; one of the earliest *explicit* identifications of baptism as rebirth occurs in Justin, *1. Apol.* 61.3). A noteworthy difference, however, as Francis (1980) has noted, is that, whereas the rabbis speak of divine "begetting" but never of divine "regeneration," our author repeatedly employs only the latter concept (1:3, 23; 2:2a). It is the rebirth of the believers and their identification as the "obedient children" of God (1:14) that serves as the ground of the imperatives that they be holy (1:15) and hunger for the "guileless milk of the word" (2:2a).

The image of new birth and regeneration appears elsewhere in the NT as a metaphor for conversion in contexts suggesting its role in the baptismal catechesis of the early Church (John 3:3–8; Rom 6:4; 2 Cor 5:17; Titus 3:5–6; Jas 1:18; 1 John 3:9–10; 5:1–5; cf. the related image of adoption as God's children in Rom 8:9–30; Gal 4:4–7; Eph 1:5). This baptismal tradition appears to be the source of the image here as well. The theme of rebirth/new birth permeates the first section of the letter as a metaphor for the radical transformation of the believer's relation to God, Jesus Christ, one another, and society. This transformation of relationship and status was inaugurated in their baptismal conversion, as later explicated in 3:21. The source of this transformation was God as a merciful Father (1:3) and His word (1:23; cf. 2:2a, 8), the good news about the Lord Jesus Christ (1:25; cf. 1:12) and his resurrection (1:3, 21). For their further growth toward salvation, it is imperative, on the one hand, that as newborns they continue to draw sustenance from this milk of the word (2:2–3). On the other hand, their rebirth also requires a decisive break with their former life and its ungodly desires (1:17; 2:11; 4:2), loyalties (1:18; 4:3). and behavior (2:1; 4:15). For they are now the holy children of God (1:14–17), redeemed by the holy Christ (1:18–19), and children whose trust and hope are now in God (1:21).[12]

3c. *for a living hope through the resurrection of Jesus Christ from the dead* (*eis elpida zōsan di' anastaseōs Iēsou Christou ek nekrōn*). This is the first of three successive *eis* ("for") phrases (vv 3a, 4a, 5b) identifying three related results or benefits of God's regenerating action (see BDF §21 for this syntactical use of the preposition *eis*). This triad of benefits is consistent with the triads (vv 4a, 7c) and triadic patterns (v 2abc, vv 3–5, 6–9, 10–12) throughout vv 1–12. The expression "living hope" (*elpida zōsan*) has earlier and superior manuscript support than its variant "hope *of life*" (*elpida zōēs*, 1505 1852 2495 syr cop^{bo} and

[12] On the concept of rebirth/regeneration/new birth, see also Sjöberg 1951, 1955; Rengstorf 1964b, 665–68; Schelkle 1976, 28–31; Parsons 1978; and on its role in 1 Peter (and related NT texts), Shimada 1966, 159–98; Parsons 1978; Gaventa 1986, 130–45. On the early Christian baptismal tradition reflected in vv 3–5, see the GENERAL COMMENT.

later Fathers); the adjective recurs in 1:23; 2:4, 5. Reference to *hope* in the NT often occurs in the triadic expression "faith-love-hope" (1 Cor 13:13; Col 1: 4–5; 1 Thess 1:3; 5:8), indicating both the association of these concepts and their overlapping meanings. All three terms appear also here in 1 Peter, though separately (vv 3, 5, 7, 8, 9); the combination *faith* and *hope* occurs in 1:21. Though faith and love are prominent emphases of 1 Peter (faith: 1:5, 7, 8, 9, 21; 2:6, 7; 5:9; cf. 4:19; 5:12; and faith's antithesis, unbelief in 2:8; 3:1, 10; 4:17; love and its paronyms: 1:8, 22; 2:11, 17; 3:10; 4:8; 5:11, 14), it is its stress on hope as enduring trust in God despite affliction and suffering that particularly characterizes this writing; cf. Cothenet 1980–1981; Küschelm 1983.

Here in v 3 *hope* as a lively (*living*) confidence in the power of God is cited as the first benefit of divine rebirth. Similarly, as the first exhortation of the following section of the letter (1:13–21), the readers are urged to "set your hope upon the grace that is coming to you at the revelation of Jesus Christ" (1:13). A stress on *trust and hope in God* likewise concludes this section (1:21). In 3:5 the holy matriarchs "who hoped in God" are held up as a model for Christian wives and all the readers. And where the vexing issue of suffering for righteousness' sake is addressed (3:13–17), again the readers are encouraged to "always be prepared to offer a defense for the hope that fills you" (3:15). Hope was a rare commodity in an age suffering "a failure of nerve" (G. Murray) in the face of the collapse of old institutions and the emergence of new, uncertain alignments of political power. Hope clearly differentiated adherents of the Jesus movement from Gentile outsiders who were "without hope and without God in the world" (Eph 2:12). It is especially their hope in the face of abuse and suffering and opposition that made the Christians stand out from their anxious contemporaries (3:15). Moreover, the hope and holiness (1:13–21; 3:1–6) that distinguished their conduct represented unusual and superior qualities that could even move detractors and unbelievers to join the Christian cause (2:12; 3:2).

through the resurrection of Jesus Christ from the dead (*di' anastaseōs Iēsou Christou ek nekrōn*). At the very outset and then throughout the letter, God's resurrection of Jesus Christ from the dead is set forth as the quintessential demonstration of God's animating and saving power and the basis for hope and trust in God despite all adversity. In his focus on the resurrection of Jesus Christ the author reflects the central role that this belief had in the early Christian kerygma (J. A. T. Robinson 1962; Hoffmann 1979; Perkins 1984; Nickelsburg 1992c) and in his terminology draws heavily on these kerygmatic formulations; for *anastasis* of Christ's resurrection, see also 3:21d; Acts 1:22; 2:31; 4:33; Rom 14; 6:5; Phil 3:10, 11 (*exanastatis*); *1 Clem.* 42:3; Ign. *Smyrn.* 3:1, 3; cf. also Acts 17:18. At the same time, however, he expands on this theme in new and creative ways. The phrase "through the resurrection of Jesus Christ" is linked most immediately with "living hope," thereby explaining the basis for and enlivened quality of Christian hope; see also Rom 8; 1 Cor 15. It states the basis, however, for the adjoining thoughts as well. It is also through the resurrection of Jesus Christ that the believers have been reborn by God (1:3b), made heirs of an incorruptible inheritance (1:4), and set on the course of salvation (1:5) through their baptism that saves "through the resurrection of Jesus Christ" (3:21a). It is through trust in the raised "living," "elect" stone (2:4, 6), the Christ who has been made alive (3:18e), that believers are themselves "living stones" (2:5), the "elect" of God (2:9–10) and heirs of the "grace of life" (3:7). As he has been made alive with respect to his spirit (3:18e), so they too shall live in the spirit (4:6). His resurrection and elevation to God's right hand of honor and power (3:22) assure believers that he can lead them also to the presence of God (3:18c). It is his superiority, as the resurrected one, over "angels, authorities, and powers" (3:22c) that consoles the suffering addressees that no harm can come to them (3:13). It is in his glory as the suffering yet resurrected one (1:11, 21; 3:22; 4:13; 5:1) that his faithful followers will also share (1:7; 4:13–14; 5:4, 10). And as vindication of his obedience of God's will despite suffering (1:2; 2:21–24; 3:18, 22), the resurrection of the living Lord serves as motivation for a similar obedience on the part of the suffering believers, for in their faithfulness they too will be vindicated by God (3:13–22; 4:6, 13–14; 5:10).

4a. *for an inheritance [that is] imperishable, undefiled, and unfading* (*eis klēronomian aphtharton kai amianton kai amaranton*). The second benefit of rebirth is an inheritance "in perpetuity," as it were. To be reborn children of God entails the right of inheritance (cf. Gal 4:7).

In the OT, the land of Canaan was regarded as an "inheritance" (*klēronomia*) bequeathed by God, who owned the land (Lev 25:23; Josh 22:19; Isa 14:2), to the patriarchs and their progeny (Gen 12:7; 50:24; Deut 34:4). In Israel's undulating history, that inheritance, however, was often defiled and lost-gained-lost as the result of its domestic idolatries, foreign invasions, and deportations (Deut 30:1–10; Jer 2:7). For the vast majority of Israelites, those resident in the Diaspora, that territorial inheritance was a distant memory and a future hope rather than a present reality (Lam 5:2; Jdt 8:22; 2 Macc 1:27–29 and 2:18).

The three Greek adjectives modifying "inheritance," namely *aphtharton* ("imperishable"), *amianton* ("undefiled"), and *amaranton* ("unfading"), form an alliterative triad of terms (all beginning with an *alpha*-privative). Such alliterations occur frequently in this letter and are one example of the author's literary refinement; see also 1:6, 9–11a, 19; 2:12, 15, 18–20, 21; 3:17; 4:4. Of these adjectives, *aphthartos* recurs in 1:23 and 3:4 ("imperishable seed, jewel") and *amarantinos*, a paronym of *amarantos*, in 5:4 ("unfading crown of glory")—both emphasizing permanence in contrast to transitoriness. The idea of undefilement and its cultic overtones reappears in 1:18–19, where the precious blood of Christ, "as a flawless and faultless (*amōmou kai aspilou*) lamb," is contrasted to "corruptible things" (*phthartois*) as the price of redemption.

This nonterritorial concept of inheritance (cf. also 3:7) distinguishes the Christian sect from Israel, its parent body, in at least four important ways:

(1) The Christian focus of hope is no longer on the reacquisition of the land of Israel from its colonial overlords and the restoration of its political autonomy.

(2) Christians are not defined by their belonging to this land or for that matter to any particular locality. Christianity is a worldwide phenomenon (5:9) with a worldwide mission (as the book of Acts affirms).

(3) The notion of a holy land is superseded by that of a holy community (2:4–10). The Christian brotherhood, wherever it exists (2:17; 5:9), provides a new place of identity and belonging for the reborn children of God.

(4) The inheritance of Christians, in contrast to the inheritance of the Holy Land, is one that cannot perish, be defiled, or fade, as the following words explain.

4b. *kept in the heavens for you* (*tetērēmenēn en ouranois eis hymas*). The Christian inheritance is imperishable, undefiled, and unfading because it is not a material but a transcendent reality. It is "kept" (*tetērēmenēn*, "reserved," "guarded") by God (this participle being one of numerous passives implying God as agent) "in the heavens" (*en ouranois*, lit., "in heavens"), that is, God's dwelling place. See Col 1:5 for a comparable concept of "hope laid up for you in the heavens" (*en tois ouranois*). The plural "heavens," preferred to the singular "heaven" (only א), reflects the Hellenistic and Israelite notion of a plurality of heavens, with God often conceived as residing in the seventh heaven; "heaven" in the singular (1:12 and 3:22) most likely implies this ultimate heavenly sphere. The phrase *en ouranois* (without the article; cf. Matt 5:45; 12:50; 18:10, 14, 19; 19:21; Mark 11:26; 12:2; Heb 12:23) appears to have been equivalent to *en tois ouranois* (Matt 6:1; 7:11, 21; 10:32, 33; 16:17; 19:2; Mark 11:25; 2 Cor 5:1; Heb 8:1; 9:23). For further information on this point, see the NOTE and DETAILED COMMENT on 3:19.

This transcendentalized notion of inheritance occurs in the later OT and Israelite writings (Dan 12:13; *Pss. Sol.* 14:17; 1QS XI 7) as well as in the NT, where it denotes the inheritance of "eternal life" (Mark 10:17; Titus 3:7), "the kingdom of God" (Matt 25:34; 1 Cor 6:9–10; Gal 5:21; Jas 2:5), "imperishability" (1 Cor 15:50), "glory" (Rom 8:17–18), or the eschatological gift of salvation in general (Col 3:3; Heb 1:14). According to our author, the permanent inheritance is that believers are established by God as heirs of salvation and "coheirs (*sygklēronomoi*) of the grace of life" (3:7) and have been "called to inherit (*klēronomēsēte*) a blessing" (3:9). Regaining the geographical land of Israel as an inheritance is no longer an issue for these strangers in the Diaspora, for perishable turf has now been replaced with something transcendent and permanent—salvation assured by the power of God. For strangers and resident aliens who would also be ineligible to inherit land where they currently reside, this promise of an inheritance preserved in heaven thus had a double appeal.

for you (*eis hymas*). At this point the focus shifts from the inclusive "our" (3a), "us" (3b) to the addressees as the specific recipients of and responders to God's saving action, and this focus dominates throughout the remainder of the letter (*you*; *to, for you* [obj.]: 29×; *you* [subj.]: 2×; *your*: 21×; 2d-person pl. verbs and participles: 91×). This consistent stress upon the "for-you-ness" of the letter's good news is one of the most typical and noteworthy features of its encouragement and exhortation.

5a. *who through faith are guarded by God's power* (*tous en dynamei theou phrouroumenous dia pisteōs*). This phrase modifies the preceding *you* (v 4b) and affirms that the believers, like their inheritance (v 4a), are also under God's protection. Verses 4 and 5 in fact form a minor chiasm: A: *eis klēronomian* . . . ; B: *tetērēmenēn* . . . *eis hymas*; B′: *tous* . . . *phrouroumenos*; A′: *eis sōtērian* in which both the verbs of protection and the nouns "inheritance" and "salvation" complement each other.

The picturesque participle *phrouroumenous* ("guarded") is related linguistically to the term *phrouria* denoting the numerous "forts" or "fortifications" dotting the rural areas of Pontus, Cappadocia, and Galatia (Strabo, *Geogr.* 12.3.28; 12.4.6; 12.5.2, 6.1) and used by local rulers and later Roman garrisons for securing the villages and countryside (Broughton 1938, 629, 635). The related noun *phroura* occurs with the verb "keep" (cf. 4b) in 1 Macc 6:50 of a "garrison" deployed to "keep" (*tērein*) the city of Bethsura, illustrating the military usage of both terms.

faith (*pistis*), mentioned repeatedly in this section (vv 5, 7, 9; cf. also 1:21; 5:9), is exclusive commitment to God (1:7a; 5:9) and trust in God's power (*dynamei theou*) to save (1:9, 21); see also the NOTE on 1:7a. The certainty of God's protection is particularly reassuring for believers not only harassed by their neighbors (3:13–4:19) but also menaced by their arch-adversary, the Devil (5:8–9). For our author, the chief evidence of God's power (*dynamis*) and the basic reason for trust is God's raising and glorification of Jesus Christ (1:21; 3:18, 22; cf. 1:3).

5b. *for a salvation ready to be revealed in the last propitious time* (*eis sōtērian hetoimēn apokalyphthēnai en kairōi eschatōi*). The last of the triad of benefits of God's regenerating action is "salvation" (*sōtēria*). On the syntax of vv 4–5, see most recently Parker 1994, 27–28. With its related terms "savior" (*sōtēr*), "save" (*sōzō*), and so on, "salvation" figures prominently in biblical and extrabiblical literature to denote rescue from a perilous situation through both human and divine benefactors. Physicians, generous nobles, emperors, as well as the god Aesclepius, the God of Israel, and Jesus were all acclaimed by their grateful beneficiaries for their acts of deliverance or healing in times of public or personal peril (see Danker 1982 for texts). In the NT, the appearance of Jesus as Messiah and mediator of God's saving activity is heralded as the definitive sign of the end time (Luke 1:69, 71, 77; Acts 4:12, 5:9–10; Rom 1:16; 1 Thess 5:9–10; etc.). This acclamation of Jesus as Messiah/Christ distinguished the Jesus group from other Israelite factions (Hasidim, Essenes, John the Baptist group), whose members were also convinced of living in the end time, and won for the messianic movement its distinctive label "Christian" (cf. 4:16).

In 1 Peter, salvation as a key focus of Christian proclamation has both a present and future aspect (cf. D. G. Miller 1955). Here, as throughout the NT, both salvation and the final propitious time of divine deliverance and judgment are conceived as inaugurated but not yet completed. Commenting further on salvation as the goal of faith (1:9), our author states in vv 10–12 that the subject of salvation was a preoccupation of the prophets of old, but its reality only became known to the believers through their hearing of the good news of Christ's suffering and glorification. So far, the salvation inaugurated by Jesus Christ and his resurrection are a present reality to which believers have access through faith and through baptism that "now saves you" (3:21). However, the *culmination* of this process of divine rescue and deliverance awaits the future, when the glorified Christ will be revealed (1:7, 13; 4:13; 5:1, 4) and the goal of faith will be attained (1:9). Life in the interim, therefore, is marked by hope (1:13, 21; 3:15) and calls for constant nourishment on the word of the gospel (2:2–3), commitment to Christ (1:8; 2:4–8; 3:15; 4:1, 13–14), and trust in God's guarding power (1:5a; 5:6–11).

Here and elsewhere in the letter it is evident that 1 Peter expresses the common eschatological conviction of the early Church (Bowman 1962; Aune 1992) that with the revelation of Jesus as Messiah (1:10–12, 20) the last of the ages is at hand (1:20; 4:7 and respective NOTES), that the final judgment of God is commencing (4:17–18; cf. 1:17; 4:5), and that therefore Christians are to entrust themselves in confidence and obedience to a faithful Creator (1:21; 4:19). In this letter, with the sole exception of 1:12, the verb *apokalyptō* (1:5; 5:1) and its related noun *apokalypsis* (1:7, 13; 4:13) refer to the future and final revelation (of Jesus Christ, salvation, or glory).

eschatos (*last*), here modifying *kairos*, appears again in the formula of 1:20b declaring that Christ "was made manifest at the last (*eschatou*) of the ages (*chronōn*)." Both *chronos* and *kairos* refer to aspects of time. Whereas *chronos* refers to time in its durative sense ("age," "period of time"; cf. its absolute use in 1:17; 4:2, 3), *kairos* designates a specific propitious point in time, a critical moment in the passage of time. Elsewhere in the letter, *kairos* is used absolutely in reference to the advent of the Messiah/Christ (1:11), the beginning of divine judgment (4:17), or the occasion of God's ultimate exaltation of the faithful (5:6). Here *en kairōi eschatōi* refers to that final propitious point in time when, as envisioned in 5:6, the salvation of the faithful will take place. Both terms, along with *apokalyptō*, *apokalypsis*, and *telos* (4:7) and the statements in which they occur, illustrate the pervasive eschatological perspective of this letter (Selwyn 1956). It is *eschatos* in particular that underlies the theological term "eschatology" that encompasses the complex of ideas concerning the final period of history and existence (Jenni 1961; Rist 1962; Bowman 1962). In temporal perspective vv 3–5 thus describe the totality of reborn Christian existence from its inception to its final outcome.

Verses 6–9 constitute the second subunit of this section, with attention now shifting from the praise of God to the consolation and joy of the believers. Their current affliction is described as a test of faith and even an occasion for rejoicing in view of their confidence in Christ's final appearance and their certain experience of salvation.

6a. *Consequently you exult with joy* (*en hōi agalliasthe*). The Greek prepositional phrase *en hōi* ("consequently," lit., "in this") links this unit with the foregoing, but the precise antecedent of the relative pronoun is uncertain (cf. also 2:12; 3:16, 19; 4:4). Although it could refer grammatically to "last propitious time" (v 5b), the repeated use of this phrase elsewhere in the letter (cf. P. R. Fink 1967) as a temporal or circumstantial conjunction with the sense of "in this connection," "in which case or circumstance when," "on which occasion" (2:12; 3:16, 19; 4:4) argues for a similar use here. Taken in this manner, the phrase refers to the entire thought expressed in vv 3–5 and, rendered "consequently," introduces joy as the consequential response to God's merciful action.

The verb "exult with joy" or "shout for joy" (*agalliasthe*) occurs also in v 8c and 4:13. Here and in v 8 its present tense has superior manuscript support. Selwyn (1947, 258–59) recognizes this, yet argues, unconvincingly, for the future tense in v 8. T. W. Martin (1992a, 59–64; 1992b) and Goppelt (1993, 88) see here a present tense used to refer to the future; but the recurrence of "exult" (*agalliōmenoi*) with the force of a present tense in 4:13 favors a focus on the present and not simply the future here as well. The distinction, however, is not crucial. As with many concepts presented in this letter (grace, salvation, glory, and their semantic fields), so in the case of rejoicing, present and future realities tend to intersect and overlap. The exultation or exuberant demonstration of gladness spoken of in v 6 is the joyous response to the threefold benefactions enumerated in vv 3–5. In v 8, future exaltation (salvation) is the reason for present exultation.

The jubilation of believers, however, is tempered by the fact that they are currently faced with the reality of suffering for their commitment to Jesus Christ (1:6b). Once again, as in the paradoxical phrase *elect strangers* (1:1b), the letter notes at the outset a further and related paradoxical feature of Christian existence; namely, rejoicing despite, or even because of, suffering (cf. 4:13).

6b. *while now for a brief time, if it must be, you are afflicted by various trials* (*oligon arti ei deon estin lypēthentes en poikilois peirasmois*). At this point the critical problem of affliction, pain, and suffering is introduced, an issue that dominates the letter as a whole (suffering of Christians from social harassment: 2:19–20; 3:13–17; 4:1, 12–19; 5:8–9, 10; suffering of Christ: 1:11; 2:4, 7; 2:21–24; 3:18; 4:1, 13; 5:1).

you are afflicted by various testings (*lypēthentes en poikilois peirasmois*). *Lypēthentes* (a nominative participle preferred to the variants *lypēthentas* [accusative] and *lypēthēnai* [infinitive]) is the aor. pass. part. of *lypeō* ("feel afflicted; feel grief, pain, sorrow"); literally, "having been afflicted." The equation of "afflictions" (*lypai*) and "unjust suffering" (*lypas paschōn adikōs*) is clear in 2:19 and the portrayal of suffering as a divine "testing" of faith reappears in 4:12.

Three qualifications of Christian suffering and grief serve to cast a potentially demoralizing experience in a positive light. Suffering affliction for the faith from hostile outsiders, first of all, is a *potentiality* of Christian experience, since believers share the experience of their suffering Lord (2:21; 3:18; 4:1, 13). But suffering is *not a necessity,* as the qualifier "if it must be" (*ei deon* [*estin*]) makes clear. Elsewhere in the NT, *dei, deon* ("must") are used frequently in reference to God's will concerning the suffering of Jesus (Mark 8:31 par.; Luke

17:25; 24:7, 26; John 3:14; 12:34; Acts 3:21; 17:3) and his followers (Acts 14:22) or of events that "must" take place (Mark 13:7; Rev 1:1; 4:1; 22:6; see Fascher 1954). The conditional formulation here ("if"), similar in sense and usage to the analogous conditional qualification of suffering in 3:17 (*ei theloi to thelēma theou*, "if this should be God's will"), indicates the *possibility* of innocent suffering (cf. also 3:14) rather than its necessity. As is later indicated, Christians are "called" by God not to suffer as such but primarily to be obedient to God's will even in the face of innocent suffering (2:21 following 2:19–20; 4:19; cf. 1:14; 2:15; 4:2), to "inherit a blessing" for doing good (3:9), and, following a brief period of suffering, to share in God's glory (5:10).

Second, the suffering of affliction (caused by hostile nonbelievers, 2:12, 19–20; 3:14; 4:14) is not a permanent but only a *temporary situation*. It is only *for a brief time*, a little while (*oligon*), a point reiterated in the parallel formulation of 5:10c; compare *oligon . . . lypēthentes* and *oligon pathontas*.

Third, affliction and suffering should be regarded as "various testings" from God (*poikilois peirasmois* forming another alliteration; cf. the singular *peirasmos* in 4:12), the purpose of which is *the testing of your faith* and its praiseworthy outcome (*hina* clause, v 7). The positive value of innocent suffering is stressed again in 4:1 and esp. 4:12–19; see the related NOTES.

7a. *so that the tested genuineness of your faith* (*hina to dokimion hymōn tēs pisteōs*).

the tested genuineness (*to dokimion*). The same Greek root is shared by the neuter substantive *to dokimion* ("the tested genuineness," "purity," v 7a; [𝔓[72], 𝔓[74], and a few minuscules read *to dokimon*]) and the pres. pass. part. *dokimazomenou* ("tested," v 7b), the former representing the result of the latter (cf. *apodokimazō* ["reject," as a result of testing] in 2:4, 7). On the semantic affinity of *peirasmos* and *dokimion, dokimazō*, see the NOTE on 4:12.

of your faith. *Pistis* in the NT and the Greco-Roman world generally denotes "faithfulness, reliability" (BAGD s.v. 1.a.) in a relationship. In the ancient world, where attention focuses chiefly on external social behavior and relations, "faith," "having or demonstrating faith" is the social, externally manifested behavior of loyalty and commitment to another person or group or deity. This contrasts to its meaning in modern society, where attention focuses on individuals and their internal or psychological states of being and where "faith" or "belief" usually means individual cognitive and affective assent of mind to truth or teaching. In 1 Peter, "faith" (*pistis, pisteuō, pistos*) entails maintaining trust, loyalty, and commitment toward Jesus Christ (1:8, 9?; 2:6, 7) but primarily toward God (1:21 [2×]; also implied in 1:5, 9?; 5:9). Similarly, the adjective *pistos* describes the readers as "trusting in God" (1:21) and denotes both God (4:19) and Silvanus (5:12) as "faithful," because both God the Father (1:3) and "brother" Silvanus are loyal to the Christian brotherhood. The later concept of *faith* as a body of transmitted beliefs, the "faith which is believed" (1 Tim 3:9; 5:8; 2 Tim 4:7; Titus1:13; 2 Pet 1:1; Jude 3, 20; Rev 2:13), does not occur in 1 Peter. For a similar stress on the testing of faith/loyalty and accompanying joy at its positive outcome, see Jas 1:3–4, 12.

7b. *which is more precious than perishable gold tested by fire* (*polytimoteron chrysiou tou apollymenou dia pyros de dokimazomenou*). Here, as later in 4:12, the testing of Christian loyalty is compared with the testing and refining of gold ore through "fire" (*pyr*; cf. *pyrosis*, 4:12). The metallurgic process is a familiar one for producing precious metals for jewelry, coins, and gilded artifacts in Asia Minor and elsewhere (Broughton 1938, 62–26, 693–95); cf. Ps 11:7 [MT 12:6]: "silver refined in a fire (*argyrion pepyrōmenon dokimion*). *Faith* (*loyalty, commitment*), however, is declared even "more precious" ("worthy," "honorable") than the rare commodity of "gold" (note a similar comparison in 1:18–19 between *perishable silver and gold* and *Christ's precious blood*). Moreover, as gold is refined only through a fire's heat, so commitment is refined and purified in the furnace of affliction. Seneca (*Prov.* 5.10) notes: "Fire proves gold; misfortune, a man." It is likely, however, that our author is drawing on biblical imagery as found in such texts as Zech 13:9, "I will put one-third [of the people] into the fire (*pyr*) and refine them as one refines silver, and test (*dokimō*) them as gold is tested (*hōs dokimazetai to chrysion*)" (cf. also Isa 43:2; Mal 3:2), and in the depiction of the Babylonian Exile as a purifying fire.[13] The consolation of the socially afflicted in Wis 3:4–6 is especially apposite: "For though in the sight of men they [the righteous] were punished, their hope is full of immortality. Having been disciplined a little, they will receive great good, because God tested them and found them worthy of himself; like gold in the furnace he tried them." Sirach 2:1–9 also contains terms and themes echoed here:

> My son, if you come to serve the Lord God, prepare yourself for testing (*peirasmon*) . . . cleave to him and do not turn away so that you may be increased at your last end (*eschatōn*). Whatever is brought upon you take cheerfully . . . for gold is tested in fire (*en pyri dokimazetai chrysos*) and acceptable men, in the furnace of adversity. Trust (*pisteuson*) him and he will help you. . . . You that fear the Lord, trust him . . . hope for good, and for everlasting joy and mercy.

The linked motifs of suffering, joy, and testing found here, in 4:12–13, and in other Israelite and Christian texts in fact are reflective of an ancient Israelite and Christian tradition in which adversity is portrayed as an occasion of testing of trust in God and a reason for joy (see Selwyn 1947, 439–58; Nauck 1955; J. Thomas 1968; de Villiers 1975; and the NOTES on 4:12–13). In 1 Peter this thought figures prominently as a means to console and encourage the faithful in the face of social harassment and affliction.

7c. *may be found worthy of praise and glory and honor at the revelation of Jesus Christ* (*heurethē eis epainon kai doxan kai timēn en apokalypsei Iēsou*

---

[13] Ps 65[66]:10, 12; Isa 48:10; see also Ps 16[17]:3; Prov 17:3; Sir 2:1–6; 1QS VIII 4; 1 Cor 3:13–15; Rev 3:18; *Did.* 16:5.

Christou). Yet another triad of terms is used to express the positive final outcome of affliction-as-testing (cf. Jas 1:2–4, 12). *May be found worthy of* translates the Greek aor. pass. subj. *heurethē* + *eis*, literally, "may be found for." The formulation is a divine passive indicating God as subject (cf. 2:22; 1 Cor 15:15; Phil 3:9); for the passive + *eis*, see also Rom 7:10; and BAGD s.v. for *heuriskō* of judicial assessment).

at the revelation of Jesus Christ. Apokalypsis ("revelation"), here and elsewhere in the letter (1:13; 4:13), like the verb *phaneroō* in 5:4, refers to the final revelation of Jesus Christ at the end of time. While this same usage is found in Paul (Rom 8:19; 1 Cor 1:7; cf. 2 Thess 1:7), Paul more frequently employs the term *parousia* ("coming," 1 Cor 15:23; 1 Thess 2:19; 3:13; 4:15; 5:23; 2 Thess 2:1, 8), which is never employed in 1 Peter. At this final revelation, notes the Petrine author, the assessed probity of the believers' loyalty will be the basis of their share (2:7; 4:13; 5:1) in the "praise" (*epainon*), "glory" (*doxan*), and "honor" (*timēn*) already ascribed to God (4:11; 5:11; cf. 2:12) and Jesus Christ (1:11, 21; 2:4, 6, 5:1). As the letter unfolds, the present honor of the believers before God (2:4–10) and their honorable conduct in society (2:11–5:11) will receive extended attention.

Verses 8–9. The Greek syntax of these verses requires some unraveling in English. The relative pronouns *hon* of v 8a and 8b (lit., "whom") have *Jesus Christ* (v 7c) as their antecedent.The thoughts of v 8a and 8b, virtually parallel in form (*whom not having seen, you love; whom not now seeing, you trust,* although *love* is a finite verb and *trust,* a participle), qualify the nature of the addressees' relation to Jesus Christ: love and trust despite the lack of any physical contact with him in either the past or the present. At the same time v 8b also modifies the main verb of vv 8c–9, *you exult* (v 8c), as the phrase *without having seen* [*him*] modifies *you love him* in v 8a, though the parallel here is more formal than material. In any case, it is the addressees' relation to Jesus Christ that forms the basis for their joyous exultation and confidence concerning the outcome of their faith.

8a. *Without having seen* [*him*], *you love him* (*hon ouk idontes agapate*). Some manuscipts (A K Ψ, majority of later minuscules, Clem. Alex.) read "knowing" (*eidotes*) in place of "having seen" (*idontes*). But *eidotes* is clearly a scribal error, whereas *ouk idontes* ("not having seen") is balanced by *mē horōntes* ("not now seeing," v 8b). The aor. act. part. *ouk idontes* ("not having seen," v 8a) and the pres. act. participle *arti mē horōntes* ("not now seeing," v 8b), along with their accompanying verbs *love* and *yet trusting,* lay double stress on the fact that the love and trust that believers have toward Jesus Christ is not a commitment based on sight or eyewitness experience. The point is concessive and appropriate for believers of the postapostolic period who had learned of Jesus only through the proclamation of the good news (1:12, 25; 4:17) but had never seen Jesus personally (cf. John 20:29; Pol., *Phil* 1:3 [quoting 1 Pet 1:8a]). For the reassuring notion that trust and commitment do not require physical contact with the historical Jesus or "things seen," see also John 20:29; 1 Cor 2:9; 2 Cor 4:18; 5:7; and Heb 11:1, 3.

8b. *without now seeing [him], yet trusting in him (eis hon arti mē horōntes, pisteuontes).* In the parallelism of v 8a and v 8b, the verbs "love" (*agapate*) and "trust" (*pisteuontes*) are virtually synonymous in sense and indicate the loyalty toward and reliance on Jesus Christ, despite not having seen him, that characterize distinctly Christian existence and that make joyous exultation possible. In 1 Peter, the verb *pisteuō* ("trust," "believe"), like the noun *pistis* (cf. v 7), denotes fidelity toward and confidence and trust in God (1:5, 7, 21; 5:9) and Jesus Christ (1:8; 2:6, 7), which also demarcate Christians from nonbelievers, Israelites and Gentiles alike (cf. 2:8; 3:1, 20; 4:17). "Love" (*agapaō, apapē*; cf. *agapētos*), the act of emotional commitment, is more often encouraged toward fellow-believers (1:22; 2:17; 4:8; 5:14; cf. 2:11, 4:12) as an expression of familial affection and a manifestation of loyalty and support. See the NOTE on 1:22. Both v 8a and 8b lay the basis for the thought (and the main verb) that follows.

8c. *you nevertheless exult with unutterable and glorious joy (de agalliasthe charai aneklalētōi kai dedoxasmenēi).* The second subunit concludes, as it began (v 6), on the note of joy, now in heightened form with a repeated *exult* joined by *unutterable and glorious joy.*

"Exult" (*agalliasthe*) is the main verb of vv 8b–9, as it is in vv 6–7. Despite the believers' possible experience of affliction (v 6), and despite their not having ever seen Jesus personally, exultation *nevertheless* (*de*) is possible and appropriate because of their union with Jesus Christ (v 8ab) and the prospect of their eventual salvation (1:9). Although the verb *agalliaomai* ("exult," "be glad," "be overjoyed") is unattested outside the Bible and the Christian literature, it is used frequently in the Psalms (41×) to express the jubilation of the individual or the worshiping community over the experience of God's goodness and mercy. The sense of joy in the face of suffering and in the midst of an alien residence (*paroikia*, cf. 1:17) seems to echo that of the prophet Habakkuk who in his alien residence (*paroikia*) prays: "Yet I will exult (*agalliasomai*) in the Lord; I will rejoice (*charēsomai*) in God my savior" (3:18); cf. also LXX Ps 12:6; 13:7. In the NT, the births of John the Baptist and Jesus were greeted with exultation and joy (Luke 1:14, 44, 47). Jesus, moreoever, invited his followers to "rejoice and exult" in the face of persecution (Matt 5:11–12; cf. Rev 19:7), and the Pentecost community broke bread and shared food with "exulting and generous hearts" (Acts 2:46). Similarly, the exultation and joy of which our author speaks is a present reality (1:6, 8; 4:13b) as well as a future prospect (4:13c); on the verb and its variants see Selwyn 1947, 258–59. On exultation in early Christian worship, see Reicke 1951.

with unutterable and glorious joy (charai aneklalētōi kai dedoxasmenēi). "Joy" (*chara*) and "rejoicing" (*chairō*, 4:13), like exultation, characterize the present attitude of the believing community. "Unutterable" (*aneklalētōi*, only NT occurrence) and "glorious" (*dedoxasmenēi*) convey the sense of a superlative joy beyond all words and a joy at sharing in the very glory and honor of Jesus Christ and God (*doxa*, 1:7, 11, 21; 4:11, 13–14; 5:1, 4, 10). This phrase is echoed by Polycarp (*Phil* 1:3) in his adaptation of this verse: "in whom, though you did not see him, you believe with unutterable and glorious joy."

The stress on joy in the face of the "testing" of faith/loyalty reappears in 4:12–13. Affinities of this motif with other NT occurrences suggest derivation from a common Israelite and Christian tradition.

9. *receiving for yourselves as the final outcome of your faith the salvation of [your] lives* (*komizomenoi to telos tēs pisteōs hymōn sōtērian psychōn*). This phrase qualifies v 8c and joins v 7c in putting the test of faith and the sense of joy into eschatological perspective. The reading "your" (*hymōn*) with "faith" has far weightier manuscript support than "our" (*hēmōn*) and is consonant with the 2d-person pl. verbs of vv 6–8. Joy and exultation accompany fidelity in the test of suffering in the present (vv 6–8); they are also prompted by the prospect of the surety of salvation in the future (v 9, rephrasing v 7c). It is then that believers "receive" (*komizomenoi*) the "outcome" or "intended end" (*to telos*, cf. 4:17) *of their faith/loyalty*, namely their ("your") *salvation* (cf. 1:5; 2:2). *Komizomenoi*, modifying *you exult*, as a middle form of *komizō* means "receive for yourselves," "obtain as reward," in the NT often of eschatological recompense (cf. 2 Cor 5:10; Eph 6:8; Col 3:25; Heb 10:35; 11:13, 39). The verb is used with similar eschatological overtone in 5:4, where elders are assured that "you will receive for yourselves the unfading crown of glory." Salvation, for 1 Peter, is thus a process of divine deliverance inquired into by the prophets (1:10–11), made known through the proclamation of the good news (1:12), inaugurated in baptism (3:21), and assured to those faithful to God and Jesus Christ (1:6–9; 2:2; 4:18; 5:2–4).

The English term "lives" translates *psychōn* (lit., "souls") and *your* is added according to sense in English. *Psychē* occurs frequently in 1 Peter (1:22; 2:11, 25; 3:20; 4:19) and elsewhere as a Semitism standing for a reflexive pronoun. Here, and in the Bible generally, it denotes not an entity within or distinguishable from the human body but human beings in their entirety as *living beings* animated by the breath of God (Gen 2:7; cf. Bertram et al. 1974). For our author, the total persons, personal selves as living beings and not their "spiritual souls" alone, are the object of divine salvation (cf. Dautzenberg 1964). This holistic sense of the term differs notably from Pauline usage, where *psychē*, *psychikos* can also designate the lower, sensual, and inferior dimension of human personality, a *psychikos anthropos* as contrasted to a *pneumatikos* ("spiritual") person (1 Cor 2:14) or an inferior "physical body" (*sōma psychikon*) in contrast to a superior "spiritual body" (*sōma pneumatikon*; 1 Cor 15:44). The dissimilarity is among the several elements of word usage, thought, and style that distinguish 1 Peter from the writings of Paul.

Verses 10–12, the final subunit of 1:3–12, comment further on the concept of *salvation* (v 9), contrasting the unfulfilled inquiries of Israel's prophets and even of angels concerning salvation to the good news of the Christ and grace that only the believers have experienced. This complex formulation in Greek is held together by a series of relative or intensive pronouns (*hēs*, v 10; *autois*, v 11; *hois*, *ha*, *ha*, v 12) and link-words (*sōtēria*, vv 9, 10; *exēraunēsan*, *eraunōntes*, vv 10, 11).

10. *Concerning this salvation* (*peri hēs sōtērias*). The relative *hēs* ("which," "this") and the link-word *sōterias* ("salvation") join this unit with the foregoing (*sōteria*, v 9; cf. v 5b) and continue the focus on salvation now presented as once foretold and now in the process of fulfillment. This use of relative pronouns, especially in strings of relative pronouns, as well as the use of link-words for extending and integrating lines of thought is typical of the letter's style.[14]

prophets . . . searched and investigated (*exezētēsan kai exēraunēsan prophētai*). The "prophets" (*prophētai*) mentioned here are the spokespersons of God of the OT. However, their "prophesying" (*prophēteusantes*) is characterized here not as addressing the critical word of God to Israel's present circumstances, as was the prophets' primary function. Rather, it is claimed that they diligently "searched" ("sought out," *exezētēsan*) and "investigated" (*exēraunēsan*, occurring only here in the NT) "concerning" (*peri*) something yet to occur in the future. The verb *exeraunaō* occurs only here in the NT and combined with *exezētēsan* illustrates the author's rhetorical sensitivity for assonance; see also 5:2–3 and 5:10. The combination of both compound verbs also occurs in 1 Macc 9:26 regarding foreign authorities who tracked down the friends of Judas Maccabeus.

who prophesied of the grace intended for you (*hoi peri tēs eis hymas charitos prophēteusantes*). In the Greek this phrase is located after the preceding verbs, but, since it modifies *prophets*, it is joined immediately to this term in the translation for the sake of clarity. Here "salvation" (*peri sōtērias*) is equated with "grace" (*peri tēs . . . charitos*) and is stated to be intended specifically for the addressees (*eis hymas*), thereby continuing the focus on the readers that is so prominent in this unit. *Charis* ("grace") is one of the author's preferred terms for denoting the divine favor and beneficence that believers have experienced as a result of their rebirth into the family of God (1:2, 10, 13; 3:7; 4:10; 5:5, 10, 12); see the NOTE on 1:2. In 5:12 it constitutes a one-word summary of the addressees' condition before God and the chief focus of the letter's exhortation and witness.

11a. *investigating* (*eraunōntes*). The pres. act. part. of the simple verb *eraunaō* forms a link-word to the preceding composite verb *exēraunēsan*, thereby joining v 11 to v 10. What follows specifies the object of the prophets' diligent inquiry (v 11b) and the substance of the prior witness of the spirit of Christ (v 11c).

11b. *to what sort of person or propitious time the spirit of Christ within them was referring* (*eis tina ē poion kairon edēlou to en autois pneuma Christou*). The preposition *eis* ("to") is linked with the verb *edēlou* ("was referring"); see BAGD 178. *Tina* (obj. case of the interrogative *tis*) is taken here as an independent substantive ("who, whom?" [cf. Matt 3:7; 16:13], "what sort of person?" [Luke 5:21; John 8:53]) rather than redundantly as an adjective modifying *poion*

[14] For relative pronouns, see 1:5a, 6a, 8a, 12a, 12c, 21; 2:4a, 22a, 23a, 24a, 24d; 3:2, 4b, 6b, 19a, 20d, 21a, 22a; 4:4a, 5a, 11d; 5:9b, 11a; for link-words, see the GENERAL INTRODUCTION, 3.2. Style.

kairon ("what sort of propitious time?"). It anticipates *Christ* in v 11c and together with *propitious time* reflects the traditional association of the coming of the Messiah, salvation, and the eschatological time of favor.[15]

the spirit of Christ within them was referring (*edēlou to en autois pneuma Christou*). The verb *edēlou*, an imperfect active form of *dēloō* ("show, refer to something [with *eis ti*], make clear, reveal, indicate") has weightier manuscript support than the imperfect passive *edēlouto* (L Ψ 049 etc.). It occurs also in Heb 9:8 with the Holy Spirit as subject; cf. also Heb 12:27 and 1 Cor 2:10.

The subject of this verb, *the spirit of Christ*, is a rare phrase, occurring only here and in Rom 8:9 ("Anyone who does not have the spirit of Christ does not belong to him"). Acts 16:7 ("the spirit of Jesus"), Gal 4:6 ("the spirit of his son"), and Phil 1:19 ("the spirit of Jesus Christ") are similar, but all, like Rom 8:9, involve statements concerning the spirit of Christ active in the Christian community, not within the ancient Israelite prophets. This could explain the omission of *of Christ* in Codex Vaticanus. The fact that the association of "the spirit of Christ" with OT prophets (*en autois*) is without parallel was used by Selwyn (1947, 134, 259–68; see also Rigato 1990) to argue for the identification of the prophets of v 10 as *Christian prophets*. However, the succeeding reference to the "prior witness" of these prophets and the contrast between them and the believers (v 12) make this unlikely. *Christou* could refer to either the "Messiah" or "(Jesus) Christ" specifically. In the former case the reference would be to "the spirit of the Messiah," the spirit within the prophets that witnessed to the future sufferings and glories of the Messiah. In the latter case, it would refer to the preexistent spirit of Jesus Christ, which within the prophets witnessed to Jesus Christ's future sufferings and glory. Both ideas are without exact precedent or parallel and either would fit the manner in which our author speaks of "the Messiah/the Christ" (3:15; 4:13; 5:1). It is however conceivable that the two ideas are complementary since, from the author's perspective, Jesus Christ is in fact the long-expected Messiah. The Messiah whose spirit spoke through prophets earlier has now been revealed as Jesus, the Messiah/Christ (1:19–20) who himself was "foreknown before the foundation of the world" (1:20). The notion that OT prophets were moved by Christ or the spirit of prophecy to announce events fulfilled in the Christian era as well as events of their own time is found frequently among second-century Christian writers (Ign. *Magn.* 8:2; *Barn.* 5:6; Herm. *Sim.* 9.12.1–2; 2 *Clem.* 17:4; Justin Martyr *1 Apol.* 31–53; 62.4; *Dial.* 56–57; Irenaeus *Haer.* 4.20.4).

11c. *bearing prior witness to* (*promartyromenon*). The participle modifies *the spirit of Christ* and has as its object *the sufferings and glories of Christ*; namely, the substance of the prophets' prophesying.

The verb *promartyromai* ("bear prior witness to, predict") occurs nowhere else in the NT, the LXX, or contemporary secular Greek. In our letter this prior

---

[15] See 1:5; 5:6; Isa. 49:8–16; 60:22; Jer 3:17–18; Dan 7:21–22; Zeph 3:16–20; 1QpHab VII 1–6; Mark 1:14; 10:30; 2 Cor 6:2; Rev 1:3; 22:10; cf. Kilpatrick 1986.

witness to the sufferings and glories of the Christ on the part of the ancient prophets is balanced by the "*full witness*" to these same sufferings and glories on the part of the author himself (*epimartyrōn*, 5:12; cf. 5:1). That which the prophets inquired into but did not realize Peter confirmed as the grace experienced by Christian believers.

the sufferings [destined] for Christ and the glories after these [sufferings] (*ta eis Christon pathēmata kai tas meta tauta doxas*). This phrase too is unique in both the OT and NT and constitutes a significant indication of our author's Christology, theological focus, and hermeneutical perspective. The term *ta pathēmata* ("the sufferings") is thematically related to the fundamental issue addressed in this letter, the innocent suffering of Christians resulting from their abuse by nonbelieving outsiders. 1 Peter contains one-fourth of the 16 NT occurrences of the term *pathēma* (all pl. except for Heb 2:9) and more than one-fourth (12) of the 40 NT occurrences of the related verb *paschō* ("suffer"). Tackling the problem of the innocent suffering of his readers head-on, the author refers frequently to this experience of Christian suffering (*paschein*: 2:19, 20; 3:14, 17; 4:1c, 15, 19; 5:10; cf. also *lypein*, 1:6; *lypai*, 2:19), repeatedly declaring it to be a sharing in or emulation of the suffering of Christ (2:18–25; 3:13–22; 4:1, 12–16). Apart from the allusion to the suffering of Christ in 1:2 ("sprinkling of the blood of Jesus Christ"), this present verse constitutes the first explicit mention of Christ's suffering. *Ta pathēmata*, a plural of *to pathēma* and a paronym of the verb *paschō*, appears 4 times in this letter in reference to both the sufferings of believers (5:9) and, as here, the sufferings of Christ (see also 4:13; 5:1; for *paschō* used of the suffering of Christ, see 2:21b, 23b; 3:18a; 4:1a). *Ta pathēmata* is used of the sufferings of Christ also elsewhere in the NT (2 Cor 1:5; Phil 3:10; Heb 2:9, 10). The term does not appear in the LXX, however, nor is there any trace in the OT of the concept that the Messiah or Christ was destined to suffer. Thus the expression "the sufferings destined for Christ" reflects a unique Petrine formulation of a concept found nowhere in the OT, with the exception of its intimation in the Suffering Servant song of Isa 52:13–53:12, a passage underlying much of 2:21–25.

The combination of *the sufferings destined for Christ* and *the glories* [*doxas*, plural] *after these* (*sufferings*) is also unique, although the Suffering Servant, his suffering and glorification, again offers a conceptual antecedent. Paul combines the terms *ta pathēmata* and *doxa* (sing.) but in a non-Christological reference to "the sufferings of this present time [that] are not worth comparing to the glory that is to be revealed to us" (Rom 8:18). Hebrews 2:9–10, on the other hand, provides the closest parallel to the Petrine formulation, though here too, as in Rom 8:18, "glory" appears only in the singular: "But we see Jesus, who for a little while was made lower than the angels, crowned with glory and honor because of his suffering of death. . . ." The preceding context (Heb 2:6–8, citing Ps 8:5–7 LXX) makes clear that the formulation of Heb 2:8b–10 is an adaptation of the wording of Ps 8 and that the expression "crowning him with glory and honor" derives from Ps 8:6. Since the linguistic differences between Heb 2:9–10 and 1 Pet 1:11 rule out any direct literary dependence of each on the other, it is likely that both texts are independent formulations of a common Christian tradition succinctly summarizing the two chief foci of Christ's life, his suffering (and death) and his (resurrection and) glorification by God. In juxtaposition with *sufferings*, *glories* (*doxai*) or *glory* in the singular (*doxa*, 4:13; 5:1) denotes, as the larger context indicates, Christ's resurrection or being made alive or enthroned by God (1:3, 21; 3:18e, 22; cf. also "living stone," 2:4b) as well as his being "elected" and "honored" by God after his rejection by humans (2:4; 3:22). In this honored and glorified state he is soon to appear (5:1), and steadfast believers will share in his glory (1:7; 4:13; cf. 5:4), a glory that unites them as well with the glory of God (5:10; cf. 2:12; 4:11, 16). This juxtaposition (also in 4:13 and 5:1) constitutes a Petrine variation on a common early Christian tradition and conception of Jesus Christ's suffering-death-resurrection-glorification-life as a single salvatory event.[16] The unusual plural, *glories*, here in v 11 may have been designed to balance its plural counterpart, *sufferings*.

The expression as a whole thus constitutes a unique Petrine formulation of the kerygmatic tradition that annnounces early on in the letter the experience of Christ, his suffering and glorification, which is to serve as a basis and model for the experience of his faithful followers. Moreover, the author who affirms this association declares himself to be a "witness of the sufferings of Christ and also the sharer in the glory about to be revealed" (5:1).

[*destined*] *for Christ* conveys in English the sense of *eis Christon*, paralleling the phrase *eis hymas* ("intended for you," v 10; cf. 1:4b). "These" (*tauta*, Greek neuter pl. demonstrative pronoun) refers back to "sufferings" (*ta pathēmata*, Greek neuter pl.) as its antecedent.

The phrase *destined for Christ* expresses the common *Christian* conviction that the OT prophets, and the Sacred Scriptures generally, prophesied beforehand concerning Jesus Christ, his suffering, death, and resurrection, his followers, and in general the saving events now come to pass.[17] The reflection of this notion here makes it unnecessary to regard the prophets of v 10 as Christian. The following verse actually constitutes the most serious weakness of the Christian-prophet theory, for the contrast between searching prophets serving not themselves but the believers ("you") to whom the good news was proclaimed could hardly be made with Christian prophets in mind. Concerning specific prophets that the author may have had in mind, Isaiah could have been foremost. This is suggested by the frequent appeal to Isaiah in this letter (approximately 18 citations or allusions; see the GENERAL INTRODUC-

---

[16] See Mark 8:31 par.; 9:31 par.; 10:33–34 par.; Luke 24:26, 46; Acts 2:23–24; 4:10–11; 10:39–40; Rom 8:17–18; 1 Cor 15:3–4; 2 Cor 4:10–11; 13:4; 2 Tim 2:11–12; Heb 2:9–10; Rev 1:9.

[17] See the "fulfillment" texts of Matthew; Luke 24:25–27, 45–46; John 5:39, 46; Acts 1:16; 2.22–36; 3:17–26; 8:27–39; 10:43; 17:2–3; 26:22–23; Rom 1:2; 3:21; 15:4; 16:25–26; 1 Cor 10:11; Heb 2:5–9; 10:15–17; *Barn.* 5:6, 13; Ign. *Magn.* 9:2; *Pre. Pet.* frag. 6 (in Clem. Alex. *Strom.* 6.15.128).

TION, 2. Sources), the similarity of the language of 1:12 and 1:24–25 (citing Isa 40:6–8), and especially by the use of Isa 53 in 2:21–25 in speaking of the innocent and vicarious suffering of Christ. John 12:41 offers an interesting parallel: "Isaiah said this (referring to Isa 6:10 cited in John 12:40), because he saw his (i.e., Jesus') glory and spoke of him."

12a. *To them it was revealed* (*hois apekalyphthē*). "To them" (*hois*, lit., "to whom") likewise refers back to *prophets* (v 10). The passive *was revealed* implies either *spirit of Christ* or God as subject, with the latter being more likely; compare the passive synonym *phanerōthentos* ("made manifest" [by God] in both 1:20 and 5:4).

that they were serving not themselves but rather you in these things (*hoti ouch heautois hymin de diēkonoun auta*). *Serving . . . in these things* embraces all of the prophetic activities enumerated in vv 10–11, now characterized comprehensively as an ongoing act of "ministering" or "serving" (imperf. of the verb *diakoneō*, which takes the dative of its object ["themselves," "you"]; cf. Shimada 1981).

not themselves but rather you (*ouch heautois hymin de*). The phrase stresses the dramatic contrast between the prophets, who were not the beneficiaries of their own searching and investigation, and the believers, who were. For similar contrasts, see *1 En.* 1:2; 16:3; Acts 2:34–35; 13:34–36; Heb 4:6, 10–11; 11:13–16. "You" (*hymin*), as in vv 10, 12a, 12b, is preferable to the variant reading "us" (*hēmin*) (MSS 945 1241 etc.; vg^{ms} [syr^{p}] Jerome).

in these things (*auta*) refers to the services rendered by the prophets, but essentially to their witness to the Messiah's "sufferings and glories." 1 Peter 4:10 contains a similar construction of *diakoneō* and the neuter singular *auto*; (see also 2 Tim 1:18 and BAGD 184, s.v. *diakoneō*, regarding the use of this verb with the dative for those served and accusative for the thing rendered).

12b. [*things*] *that now have been announced to you* (*ha nyn anēggelē hymin*). The formulation [*things*] translates the relative neuter plural pronoun *ha*, referring to the immediately preceding *auta* ("these things"), and introduces a point further stressing the privileged status of the audience ("you"). The verb *anēggelē* ("announced," "disclosed," "proclaimed") is a paronym of the verb *euaggelizomai* ("announce, proclaim good news") immediately following, with both verbs having the same subject. The adverb "now" (*nyn*) emphasizes the contrast between the previous time of the prophets and the current time of salvation, the anticipation and the final proclamation and reception of the good news (cf. similar temporal contrasts in 2:10, 25; 3:20–21). This temporal contrast constitutes a final indication that the prophets mentioned here are those of ancient Israel and not of the present Christian community.

by those who proclaimed good news to you (*dia tōn euaggelisamenōn hymas*). The verb *euaggelizomai* ("proclaim good news") and its noun *euaggelion* (*eu-* ["good"] + *aggelion* ["news, message"]) are two of the most frequently employed terms in the NT (54× and 76×, respectively) for characterizing the Christian proclamation of divine salvation now available to humanity through faith in Jesus Christ, (cf. the related *exaggelō*, 2:9). On the whole, the "gospel" (*euaggelion*) is not simply "news" in general but always "good news" for persons in specific "bad or perilous situations." The specific content of this joyous proclamation therefore varies according to the circumstances addressed (Elliott 1969). According to our author, this *good news* proclaimed previously to the readers, including those who have already died (4:6), originates with God ("good news of God," 4:17) and is the "seed" (1:23) or "word" (1:25) concerning Jesus Christ the Lord by which believers have been born (1:23–25) and the "word-milk" from which they are nourished (2:2–3), as well as the word over which disobedient nonbelievers stumble (2:8; 4:17). In response to the chief issue addressed in this letter, that of the suffering of the innocent, the author will expatiate on this good news by stressing the manner in which the suffering, death, resurrection, glorification, and vindication of Jesus Christ provide the basis for human transformation and new life with God, the model for Christian behavior in the face of innocent suffering, and the ground for trust and hope in God's power to save all who live as his children, his elect and holy people.

The entire phrase (*by those . . . you*) refers to earlier missionaries who first evangelized the addressees. The lack of any identification of these preachers could indicate that their names were not known to the author and that he, putatively Peter, was not among them. However, the fact that believers of Pontus are among the addressees (1:1) and that Israelites from Pontus were among the pilgrims at Pentecost brought to the faith by Peter according to Acts 2:1–42 could mean that some of the addressees had first heard the good news from Peter. The vagueness of the present formulation, however, leaves this only a remote possibility.

through the Holy Spirit sent from heaven (*en pneumati hagiōi apostalenti ap' ouranou*). Proclaimers of the good news spoke under the direction and power of the *Holy Spirit* (in Greek without the article; cf. John 20:22; Acts 8:15, 17).[18] This is the second of three references to the Holy Spirit or Spirit of God in this letter; see also 1:2 and 4:14.

12c. [*things*] *into which angels yearn to gain a glimpse* (*eis ha epithymousin aggeloi parakypsai*). This is a second qualifying phrase referring, like v 12b, back to *things* in v 12a. "To gain a glimpse" translates *parakyptō* ("to bend over" to see something better; colloquially, "steal a peek"; cf. John 20:11 and Michaelis 1967b). The *Epistle to the Apostles* contains a later adaptation of this thought: "Truly I say to you, such and so great a joy has my Father prepared (for you) that angels and powers desired and will desire to view and to see it, but they will not be allowed to see the greatness of my Father" (*Ep. Apos.* 19). Here in 1 Peter the thought heightens the exclusive privilege granted the addressees: not the ancient prophets, not even angels in heaven—despite their efforts or desires—have seen or heard the things proclaimed only to you!

---

[18] See also Luke 12:12; Acts 2:4; 4:8; 6:10; 7:55; 11:12 and passim; 1 Cor 12:3; Eph 3:5; 5:18; 6:18.

GENERAL COMMENT

The body of the letter opens (1:3–12) on a note of blessing, praising God for the gifts of His fatherly mercy (vv 3–5), affirming joy in the midst of suffering (vv 6–9), and stressing the privileged status of the addressees as recipients of the good news of salvation (vv 10–12). Readers are assured at the outset of the divinely conferred honor which is theirs as a result of their incorporation into the family of the reborn.

Beside the eulogy of vv 3–5, further echoes of early Christian tradition are evident here, as throughout the letter. The affinities between vv 3–5, Titus 3:4–7, and Rom 6:16–24; 8:16–24 suggested to Boismard (1956b, 183–91; 1961, 15–56) the use of a liturgical text, probably a "baptismal hymn." While the content of these and related NT texts[19] involves motifs associated with baptism (rebirth/conversion/transformation, hope, inheritance, salvation), the formal as well as material variations in these texts point less to the use of a structured hymn (or prayer [contra Coutts 1957]) than to the influence of a fluid oral tradition. 1 Peter contains only one explicit reference to baptism (3:21), but influence of this common baptismal tradition and its constellation of motifs is evident throughout the letter, as Selwyn's comparative analyses indicate (1947, 369–419; cf. also Lohse 1954/1986; Shimada 1966, 176–98; and Hill 1982, 46–53). These frequent allusions to baptism and conversion highlight the new, divinely conferred dignity of the baptized and the contrast between their former and present allegiances and modes of behavior (1:14–2:3, 9–10, 11–12; 3:13–4:6).

Verses 6–8 (9) in turn make use of an Israelite-Christian persecution tradition calling for joy in the face of suffering (Selwyn 1947–1948, 439–58; Nauck 1955; J. Thomas 1968; Villiers 1975) with possible affinities to the instruction associated with Israelite proselyte baptism and the hardships converts will face (cf. the tractate *Gerim*, and van Unnik 1980, 41–79). In this letter, which is so focused on the dilemma of Christian suffering from start to close, this tradition of joy in suffering (1:6, 4:12–13; cf. 3:14, 4:14) together with stress on solidarity with the suffering Christ (2:18–25; 3:13–4:1; 4:13), the certainty of divine protection (1:4; 5:6–7, 10–11), and conferral of the Spirit (4:14) serve not only to motivate exultation in the face of suffering (1:6; 4:13) but also to remind beleaguered believers of the inevitability and commonality of suffering (4:12; 5:9) and the imminence of judgment (4:17) as well as of the prospect of eventual salvation and glory (1:8–9; 4:14, 16; 5:10) for those who remain steadfast (5:12).

The final subunit of this section, vv 10–12, presents a resounding affirmation of the exclusive privileges of the addressees that make them superior to God's spokespersons of old and even to angels. These verses contain what has rightly been termed "the hermeneutical key" of 1 Peter (Schutter 1989, 100–109; Cervantes Gabarrón 1991b, 106). The reason, however, is not because they reveal

[19] John 3:3–5; Rom 6:3–11; 1 Cor 6:11; Gal 3:23–4:7; Eph 5:26; Col 2:12; Jas 1:18; Heb 5:12–6:20; 1 John 2:29; 4:7; 5:1, 4, 18.

a "*pesher*-like exegesis" that characterizes the letter as a whole (so Schutter) but because they introduce the theme of the sufferings and glories of Jesus Christ, which provides both the fundamental motivation for the exhortation of the letter (Cervantes Gabarrón) and the hermeneutical lens through which the Sacred Scriptures are read and appropriated.

The author of 1 Peter, like the early Church in general, read the prophets and the Sacred Scriptures in their entirety with the conviction that the things announced beforehand had now in these last days come to pass. This conviction the messianic sect shared with their contemporaries, the community of Qumran (e.g., 1QpHab VII 1–5 cited by Schutter 1989, 11; cf. also 1QpHab II 5–10). The fundamental difference between these groups, however, is that, for the Christians, Jesus as suffering and exalted Messiah constituted both the focal object of their interpretation and the prism through which the Sacred Scriptures were read. Accordingly, the Petrine author can claim that as ancient prophets inquired as to the future agent and time of salvation they were informed by "the spirit of Christ" who "bore prior witness to the sufferings and glories destined for the Christ," none of which is stated in the OT.

In addition, he maintains that it was revealed to them by God that, in regard to these things, they were serving not themselves but rather future persons; namely, the present readers. This claim in no way tallies with anything found in the OT or Israelite writings but derives solely from the Christian conviction that in Jesus the Messiah the sacred writings find their culmination and ultimate meaning. Insofar as vv 10–12 illustrate the author's view of both the continuity and differences between the prophetic expectations of the OT and their realization in Jesus Christ, these verses indicate the hermeneutical perspective of the author as it bears on his use of Scripture throughout the letter, as Schutter has indicated (1989, 100–109). However, Schutter's further claims that the author's use of Scripture is similar to the "*pesher*-like exegesis" typical of the Qumran community (1989, 122) and that 1:14–2:9 in particular constitutes a similar form of "homiletic midrash" on specific OT texts (1989, 100, 123–38) are not cogently sustained. Consequently it is difficult to concur with his assertion that vv 10–12 in their entirety represent the "hermeneutical key" (Schutter 1989, 110, 109) to the compositional mode of the letter as a whole.[20]

The double contrast in this opening section between the House of Israel, on the one hand, with its transitory inheritance and unfulfilled hopes, and Christian believers, on the other, who now enjoy an imperishable inheritance (v 4), salvation and divine grace (v 10), and the good news of the Messiah (v 12) is subtle but striking. These verses affirm not only the continuity between the eschatological people of God and ancient Israel (see also 2:4–10) but also the demarcation of Israelites and Christians brought about by faith in or rejection of Jesus as Messiah. What is evident here is not a balance of "promise and ful-

[20] On Qumranic and early Christian interpretation of the OT, see C. K. Barrett 1970; R. P. C. Hanson 1970; on the use of the OT in 1 Peter, see also the GENERAL INTRODUCTION 2. Sources, and the NOTES on 1:24–24; 2:3, 4–10, 17, 21–25; 3:10–12, 19–20, 22; 4:8, 14, 18; 5:5, 7.

fillment" as accentuated in the Gospels, but a decisive contrast between anticipations unrealized by the prophets over against a revelation of grace and good news to contemporary believers alone. Thus the concept of a transcendent inheritance in this context has more social and religious than cosmological overtones. Along with vv 10–12 it distinguishes believers with an imperishable inheritance and an experience of good news from persons still tied to a perishable land of inheritance and still awaiting a Messiah to come. On the whole, however, 1 Peter, in contrast to Paul (e.g., Galatians and Romans), broaches this subject of Israelite-Christian relations only obliquely, as here and in 2:4–8, where faith in Jesus, God's "elect stone," distinguishes believers from *all* nonbelievers, Israelites and Gentiles alike. The central relationship with which this letter is concerned is not that of "Church" and "Synagogue" but followers of Jesus Christ vis-à-vis all others.

As noted by Schnider and Stenger (1987, 64–68), these concluding verses of the introduction also have a legitimating function. The author himself, as a "witness of the sufferings of the Christ" (5:1) and composer of a letter bearing "full witness to the true grace of God" (5:12), stands in continuity with both the prophetic witnesses of old (1:10–11) and those who under the Holy Spirit's aid first proclaimed the good news to the addressees (1:12). This establishes an authoritative basis for the exhortation to follow.

One of the most typical and remarkable features of 1 Peter as a letter of encouragement and exhortation is its constant stress on the "for-you-ness" of the gospel. This is not a writing of theological generalities "to whom it may concern" but a specific communication of "good news" for suffering believers in a "bad situation." Consequently, the addressees are constantly assured that they are the direct recipients of the good news about all that God has accomplished through Jesus Christ.

The unit as a whole (1:3–12) thus has a fourfold epistolary, didactic, parenetic, and legitimating function, similar for the most part to that of Eph 1:3–14 (O'Brien 1978, 512, 514–15). It sets a doxological tone for the letter as a whole and as a prologue introduces several of its major themes (cf. Kendall 1984, 1986). It reminds the vulnerable Christian strangers in Asia Minor of the blessings from God that have transformed them and marked them as the reborn children of God, both religiously and socially, while simultaneously stressing that saving grace involves the movement from present suffering to future glory (Kendall 1986, 116–17). It establishes this writing as continuous with the authoritative prophetic witness to the sufferings and glory of Christ. And it provides a theological basis for the following exhortation (1:13–21, 22–25; 2:1–3) which will expand on these ideas and detail their theological, Christological, moral, and social implications.

For studies on 1 Pet 1:3–12, see Barth 1966; Boismard 1961; Calloud 1980; Cervantes Gabarrón 1991a; Cipriani 1986; Cothenet 1971, 1980–1981; Coutts 1957; Dalton 1982a; Dautzenberg 1964; Deichgräber 1967, 61–87; Delling 1973; Dupont-Roc 1995; du Toit 1974; Elliott 1982; P. R. Fink 1967; Grosheide 1954, 1960; Hiebert 1980b; Hill 1976; Kendall 1984, 1986, 1987;

G. D. Kilpatrick 1986; Küschelm 1983; Lamparter 1960; Margot 1979; T. W. Martin 1992a; D. G. Miller 1955, 1995; Mitton 1950; Nauck 1955; Parker 1994; Parsons 1978; Rigato 1990; Romo 1977; Scharlemann 1976a; Schnider and Stenger 1987; Scott 1905; Selwyn 1947, 250–268, 305–311; 1956; Shimada 1966, 1981; J. Thomas 1968; Villiers 1975; D. Warden 1989.

I. B. THE HOPE AND HOLY CONDUCT OF THE CHILDREN OF GOD (1:13–21)

1:13a Therefore having "girded" your minds for action and remaining alert,
13b set your hope ultimately upon the grace being brought to you
with the revelation of Jesus Christ.
14a As obedient children,
14b do not allow yourselves to be molded by the cravings
of your former ignorance,
15a but, in conformity with the Holy One who called you,
15b you too be holy in all [your] conduct;
16a for it is written that
16b "You shall be holy, because I am holy."
17 And since you call upon a Father who judges impartially
according to each one's deeds,
17b conduct yourselves with reverence throughout the time
of your residence as aliens,
18a knowing that you were ransomed from the futile conduct
inherited from your ancestors,
18b not with corruptible things [such as] silver or gold,
19 but with the precious blood of Christ,
19b as a lamb flawless and faultless;
20a he was foreknown before the foundation of the world
20b [and] was made manifest at the last of the ages
20c for the sake of you,
21a who through him trust in God,
21b who raised him from the dead and gave him glory,
21c so that your trust may also be [your] hope in God.

INTRODUCTION

Following an opening blessing of God and an assurance to the believers of their favor with God as cause for rejoicing (1:3–12), our author now shifts from declaration to exhortation. Expanding on themes of the foregoing sections 1:1–2 and 1:3–12, he now draws out a first set of behavioral consequences.

Emphasis on "hope" in v 13b and v 21c forms an inclusion marking the opening and closing of the unit. Two internal subunits have "holiness" as their unifying theme: the holiness of the believers, which models that of the holy God who called them (vv 14–16) and the holiness of Christ through whom their redemption was secured (vv 17–21b). The unit as a whole thus has a chiastic structure uniting the themes of hope and holiness as hallmarks of the reborn children of God:

A. Hope (v 13)
  B. Holiness (vv 14–16)
  B′. Holiness (vv 17–21b)
A′. Hope (v 21c)

The section is joined to what immediately precedes it by the particle *dio* ("therefore," v 13), introducing inferences drawn from the foregoing, and by the linkword *grace* (v 13b; cf. 1:10; 1:2). More generally, these verses expand on at least four preceding related strands of thought: (1) setting *hope* firmly on the grace (1:13; cf. 1:10) coming with the revelation of Jesus Christ (v 13; cf. 1:5, 6, 9); (2) the *obedience* that *children* of God owe the *Father* from whom they have been *reborn* (1:14, 17; cf. 1:3); (3) the *holiness* of the believers, which should be consistent with the holy God who has called them (1:15), a holiness also consonant with their *sanctification by the Spirit* (1:2b) and their redemption through the blood of Christ (1:18–19; cf. 1:2c), the holy lamb (1:19); and (4) the *reverent* conduct, nonconformist behavior, and hope appropriate for strangers of the Diaspora during the time of their alien residence (1:17b; cf. 1:lb).

Thus 1:13 does not introduce an entirely new or different section of the letter but commences an exposition of the moral implications of what has been previously stated (for a contrary view see, most recently, Cervantes Gabarrón 1991a, 55–56, 110, 423 and T. W. Martin 1992a, 69–79, 161–88).

NOTES

1:13a. *Therefore* (*Dio*). As noted above, the particle *dio* (also "so then," "for this reason") introduces a new section that is imperative in mood and joined to the foregoing indicative statement (1:3–12) in terms of condition followed by consequence. The main verb of the verse is "set your hope" (*elpisate*), modified by the preceding participles, *anazōsamenoi* and *nēphontes*. Although our author often uses participles as imperatives (see the NOTE on 1:14b), this is not the case here, where both participles are subordinate to a proximate finite verb that follows, *elpisate* ("set your hope on"); so also S. Snyder (1995, 189–190).

having "girded" your minds for action (*anazōsamenoi tas osphyas tēs dianoias hymōn*); literally "having girded up (*anazōsamenoi*) the loins (*tas osphuas*) of your mind" (*tēs dianoias hymōn*). "Having rolled up the sleeves of your mind" would represent an idiomatic English equivalent. The verb *anazōsamenoi* (aor.

middle participle) occurs nowhere else in the NT, but the related verb *perizōnnymi* (with *osphyas*; "gird the loins") appears in Luke 12:35 and Eph 6:14; cf. *Did.* 16:1. This action of "girding the loins" was customary in Levantine cultures, where persons wearing long robes needed to secure them and "hike them up" in preparation for strenuous activity. To "gird the loins" was thus to get ready for action (Nah 2:1; Job 38:3; 40:7; Prov 31:17; Philo, *Sacr.* 63). An important ritual instance of the girding of loins in Israel took place in conjunction with the Passover festival commemorating God's liberation and redemption of his people from Egyptian bondage: "In this manner you shall eat it: your loins girded (*periezōsmenai*), your sandals on your feet, and your staff in your hand; and you shall eat in haste. It is the Lord's passover" (Exod 12:11). The figurative Petrine construction implies "getting mentally prepared for action," but the verb recalls the Passover and the saving event it commemorated, a fact that the translation *girded* in quotation marks seeks to make clear. "Girding up the loins *of the mind* (*dianoia*)" is a metaphorical extension of this expression (cf. Vallauri 1982) accentuating the present need for *mental* preparedness (cf. *knowing*, 1:18a and contrast *agnoia*, "ignorance," 1:14) for both the final revelation of Jesus Christ (v 13b) and the readers' moral responsibility in the meantime (vv 14–16). Allusions to the Passover also recur in 1:17–19 and 2:4–10. In later time the Passover continued to be a focus of Christian attention, as is illustrated by the eloquent second-century *Passover Homily* (*Peri Pascha*) of Melito of Sardis, which links the Passover and the passion of Christ (cf. 1 Pet 1:13 and *Peri Pascha* 13).

and remaining alert (*nēphontes*). This pres. act. participle, as in 4:7 and 5:8 and elsewhere in the NT, denotes the mental and spiritual alertness, sobriety, freedom from spiritual stupor or "drunkenness," and self-control called for in the critical hour (1 Thess 5:6, 8; 2 Tim 4:3–5; cf. Luke 12:35–40; Eph 5:17–18; *Did.* 16:1). The three occurrences of this verb in 1 Peter constitute half of its NT appearances, and all three are eschatologically conditioned.

13b. *set your hope ultimately* (*teleiōs elpisate*). The main verb of this verse, an aor. act. imperative, resumes the theme of hope (i.e., enduring trust) introduced in 1:3 and with 1:21 (*hope in God*) forms an inclusion embracing the entire section. Hope, according to our author, is awakened by God's raising Jesus Christ from the dead (1:3, 21b; cf. 3:18e, 21d) and is focused on God (1:21) and the grace that God confers (1:13; cf. 1:10). On the theme of hope in 1 Peter, see Cothenet 1981. The adverb *teleiōs* (only NT occurrence), meaning either "completely" or *ultimately*, modifies either the preceding participle (*remaining completely alert*; see similar syntactic constructions in 1:22; 2:19; 2:23) or the following verb. The latter is favored by the sense of the clause (hope looking forward to ultimate blessing) and by the similar future orientation evident in 1:9; 4:17; and 5:4.

upon the grace being brought to you with the revelation of Jesus Christ (*epi tēn pheromenēn hymin charin en apokalypsei Iēsou Christou*). The phrase identifies the foundation and focus of Christian hope, the divine grace (*charis*) that is brought or "borne" (*pheromenē*) to believers ("you," *hymin*) with (*en*) the revelation of Jesus Christ (*apokalypsei Iēsou Christou*). Two temporal revelations of Jesus Christ are mentioned in this letter, his initial manifestation in human history (1:20; cf. 2 Cor 12:1; Gal 1:12), and his final appearance at the end of time (1:5, 7; 4:13; 5:4; cf. Luke 17:30; 1 Cor 1:7; 2 Thess 1:7; 2:8). The phrase here could refer to either. The future orientation of *hope* could favor the latter case, but the former option is perhaps preferable. In this case, the phrase would be alluding to the reception of the good news of Christ just mentioned in 1:10–12 and would be consistent with the fact that believers are said to already experience God's grace (4:10; 5:5, 10, 12) through faith in the crucified and resurrected Jesus Christ. In this sense, the experience of the grace conferred with the revelation of Jesus Christ would be the basis of hope, and the goal of hope would be its final confirmation. In either case, the original manifestation of Jesus as Messiah and his final revelation in glory mark the boundaries of the endtime and of the period of lively hope.

14a. As (*hōs*). The repeated use of the comparative particle *hōs* is a stylistic characteristic of 1 Peter, occurring more often here (27×) than in any other NT writing (1:14, 19, 24 [2×]; 2:2, 5, 11, 12, 13, 14, 16 [3×], 25; 3:6, 7 [2×]; 4:10, 11 [2×], 12, 15 [2×], 16; 5:3, 8, 12). It serves not simply to introduce a comparison but often to mark an essential quality of the term or phrase that it precedes; see BAGD 898 III.1. Here, as elsewhere, the *hōs* phrase states the qualifying condition for the accompanying imperative: "since you are obedient children . . ." (cf. also 2:2, 11, 13, 14, 16 [3×]: 3:7 [2×], 4:10, 11 [2×], 12, 15, 16: 5:3; see Puig Tarrech 1980, 393–95).

obedient children (*tekna hypakoēs*). Depicting believers as the *obedient children* (of God) extends the metaphor of their divine rebirth (1:3) and states the basis for the imperatives that follow (vv 14–15), as well as the grounds for their invoking God as Father (v 17). In this Semitic construction, the qualifying term *of* "obedience" (*hypakoēs*) serves as a modifier of "children" (*tekna*). The expression "children of X," like "sons of X," identifies an essential quality or power by which its referent is controlled (cf. Hos 10:9; Isa 57:4; 1 Macc 2:47; *1 En.* 91:3; Luke 16:8; Eph 2:2, 3; 5:6; Col 3:6; 2 Thess 2:3; 2 Pet 2:14; see Deissmann 1901, 161–66). *Hypakoē* (*hypo* + *akouō*) is related to *akouō* ("hear"), which can also have the sense of "hear-and-heed," that is, "obey" (Deut 4:1; 5:1; 9:1; etc.). The theme of obedience to God and good conduct consonant with the will of God is fundamental to the exhortation of 1 Peter and pervades the letter as a whole.[21] In this exhortation, it is the obedience of Jesus Christ (1:2c; cf. 2:21–24; 3:18b) that provides the paramount basis and model for the obedience of the believers and their subordination to God's will.

14b. *do not allow yourselves to be molded* (*mē syschēmatizomenoi*) or "be no longer conformed to." The translation seeks to convey the sense of the middle voice of the participle *syschēmatizomenoi* as well as its imperatival force. Similar

[21] 1 Peter 1:2, 14–17, 22; 2:1, 8; 2:11–12; 2:13–17, 18–20; 3:1–6, 13–17; 4:1–6, 13–19; 5:1–11; cf. Carter 1975.

imperatival participles are employed frequently in 1 Peter (see 2:1, 18; 3:1, 7, 9; 4:8, 10; cf. also Rom 12:9–21 [17×]; 13:11; Eph 4:2–3; 5:21; Col 3:12–17; Heb 13:5). Daube (in Selwyn 1947, 467–88) saw an analogy in the rabbinic (Tannaitic) employment of Hebrew participles to express rules of conduct and religious precepts included in ethical codes (as illustrated in the Mishna, Tosephta, and Talmud). Lohse (1986, 45–47) and Kanjuparambil (1983) noted earlier instances in the Qumran literature (e.g., 1QS V 1–7), that suggest a Palestinian origin of this usage (see also Meecham 1947 and Gielen 1990, 478–83; pp. 481–82 for examples from Koine Greek). S. Snyder (1995) presented generally sound criteria for distinguishing circumstantial or adverbial participles from those with imperatival or "commanding" force but failed to include among these criteria a possible influence of Christian hortatory tradition. This criterion pertains here and to other participles employed in 1 Peter (see 2:1; 3:9a, 3:9c; 4:8, 10b), since an imperatival form of *syschēmatizō* occurs in the closely related passage of Rom 12:2, its only other NT occurrence: "Do not be conformed (*mē syschēmatizesthe*) to this world, but be transformed by the renewal of your mind (*noos*; cf. *dianoias*, 1 Pet 1:13), that you may prove what is the will of God, what is good and acceptable and perfect."

In both cases, moreover, the imperative is used negatively as an antithesis to positive action; and in both instances the issue is the same: nonconformity to evil in contrast to conformity to the holiness of God (1 Peter) or God's will (Romans). The similarities of these texts, their appositeness for explicating the implications of baptism and conversion, and their further formal and material affinities with other NT exhortation related to baptism suggested to Selwyn (1947, 400–407) their indebtedness to early Christian baptismal catechesis based on the Holiness Code of Lev 17–26 (see GENERAL INTRODUCTION, 2.4.). Earlier, the Qumran community made separation from evil and evil persons a requirement for entrance into the community (1QS V 1, 10–13, 15–20; VII 24–25; VIII 11; CD VI 14–15). For Christians also, rebirth into the new entails renunciation of the old. Union with God and the suffering Christ involves "dying with respect to sinning/wrongdoing" and "living for doing what is right" (2:24; cf. 4:1–3); see also the related baptismal image, "put off the old—put on the new" (Rom 13:12–14; Col 3:5–17; Eph 4:22–32; cf. Gal 3:27).

by the cravings (*tais . . . epithymiais*). The term *epithymia* can denote simple desire in a neutral or positive sense. However, when weighted negatively, it denotes desire that has degenerated into insatiable craving (cf. Büchsel 1964). With this negative connotation, as in the NT and throughout 1 Peter (1:14; 4:2, 3), it denotes a vice universally decried in Greco-Roman, Israelite, and Christian circles, with various shades of overlapping meanings: insatiable craving, selfish yearning, sexual lust, uncontrolled passion (in contrast to reason), coveting, compulsive ambition, self-indulgence. In 1 Peter, *epithymia* is presented as a vice typical of nonbelievers identified as "Gentiles" (4:2–4; cf. 2:11–12). Here it describes the control that insatiable craving and self-indulgence had over the believers prior to their conversion.

of your former ignorance (*proteron en tēi agnoiai hymōn*). The phrase *cravings of your former ignorance* characterizes the moral condition of the addressees prior to their conversion and rebirth. In Israelite parlance, "ignorance" (*agnoia*) typified the condition of the Gentiles (i.e., non-Israelites), who lacked knowledge of the true God and His law (Wis 13;1, 14:18, 22; 15:11). From the Christian vantage point, however, ignorance could be attributed to all persons, Israelites as well as non-Israelites, who lacked knowledge of God as revealed in Jesus the Christ (Acts 2:36; 3:14, 17; 17:30–31; Gal 4:8–10; Eph 4:18). The case is similar if one redefines the term "Gentile" to designate not simply "non-Israelites" but all nonbelievers (see NOTE on 2:12). As a consequence of this shift in the meaning of terms used to label outsiders, the phrase "former ignorance," like the related phrase of 1:17, "ransomed from the futile ways inherited from your fathers," describes the pre-Christian condition of the believers, whether former Israelites or Gentiles. Through their rebirth and calling by God (1:3, 15, 23; 2:9, 21; 3:9; 5:10), believers have now been liberated from the ignorance and pollution that typifies their surrounding society (2:15; 3:15; 4:2–3), and as people made holy they know and obey the truth (1:13, 22; 5:12).

This injunction is repeated twice elsewhere in the letter. In 2:11 the addressees are again urged to distance themselves from "deadly cravings that wage war against life" and to "maintain honorable conduct among the Gentiles." Likewise in 4:2–3 they are exhorted to have nothing more to do with the "cravings" of their past and other vices typical of the Gentiles, which are incompatible with fidelity to the will of God. These three related passages, together with further encouragements to avoid evil (2:1, 16, 20; 3:9; 4:15), to "resist" the Devil (5:8–9), and to "stand fast" in grace (5:12) manifest the author's consistent stress on the necessary, conscious, and definitive break that believers must make with former allegiances and alliances and the immorality that these associations entail.[22]

Verse 15 presents the positive alternative to the preceding negative statement, a construction typical of the exhortation of 1 Peter (see the NOTE on 2:11). The *positive* aspect of "obedience" (v 14a) is clarified; v 15a, like v 14a, introduces the basis for the imperative that follows (v 15b); and this imperative is then supported by a citation from Scripture (v 16).

15a. *but* (*alla*). The adversative particle *alla* ("but," "rather," "instead") introduces a difference from or contrast to what precedes it and occurs in many of the numerous antitheses of 1 Peter (1:18/19, 23b/c; 2:16b/c, 2:18c/d, 2:20bc/d, 2:25a/b; 3:13/14, 3:15/16, 3:21b/c; 4:2b/c, 4:12/13; 5:2c/d, 5:2e/f; 5:3a/b).

in conformity with (or "in accord with," *kata*). The preposition *kata* often serves to introduce the norm that governs behavior ("according to, in accordance with, corresponding to X") or the example with which something should

[22] On the theme of renunciation of past behavior and loyalties integral to conversion, see also *Jos. Asen.* 10:2–17:10; 1QS I 24–26; 2 Cor 6:14–7:1; 1 Thess 4:3; and Just. Mart., *1 Apol.* 14, 39.

conform ("as X, so Y") or the reason for something (BAGD). *Kata* phrases are used repeatedly in this letter to indicate God as the source and norm of Christian blessings and behavior (1:2, 3, 15; 4:6, 19; 5:2) and thus mark the theological as well as Christological orientation of the letter.

the Holy (One) (*ton . . . hagion*). This use of *ho hagios* as a designation for God is unique in the NT, but has much OT precedence. "The Holy One (of Israel)" as a designation (reverential circumlocution) for Yahweh, the God who has covenanted with Israel, occurs frequently in Isaiah (1:4; 5:19, 24; 10:20;), Second Isaiah (40:25; 41:14, 16, 20; 43:3, 14–15), and elsewhere.[23] With various shades of meaning and in conjunction with other terms, it expresses a sense of God's "awesomeness," "power," "majesty," "glory," "wondrousness," "distinctiveness," and "separateness" from and "intolerance" of all that is evil, impure, unclean, polluted, and profane (Muilenburg 1962). The holiness of God is cited here in v 15a as the basis and model for the holy behavior of God's obedient children enjoined in v 15b.

who called you (*kalesanta hymas*). In biblical parlance, to "call" (*kaleō*) means that someone in authority, especially God, selects and summons a person or group for a particular task or status (e.g., Moses, Samuel, Jeremiah as prophets, Exod 19:3; 1 Kgdms 3:1–21; Jer 1:5). Israel, as a people, was also "called" by God and since the time of Second Isaiah this calling was virtually synonymous with Israel's divine election and privileged status (Isa 41:8–9; 42:6; 43:1; 45:3; 46:11; 48:12, 15; cf. Long 1980). In the NT disciples, apostles, and believers generally are called to salvation, discipleship, and witness.[24] The notion of the believers' having been "called" (*kaleō*) by God recurs throughout 1 Peter both as an affirmation of their special elect status before God (2:9; 5:10) and as a reason for their behavior (1:15; 2:21; 3:9; see F. Müller 1955; F. Wagner 1980).

15b. *you too be holy in all* [*your*] *conduct* (*kai autoi hagioi en pasēi anastrophēi genēthēte*). Here holy conduct constitutes the positive counterpart to the preceding negative injunction of v 14b (similar to the contrasts in 2:1/2–3, 11/12; 2:16b/c; 2:24b/c; 3:3/4; 3:9b/c, 14/15; 4:15/16; 5:2–3).

In the ancient world, holiness, conceived as a mysterious radiating power with a force field both constructive and destructive in its potency (analogous today to electric current or atomic energy) was associated everywhere with divinity, the gods, and their cults. In the Bible, Yahweh was "the Holy One" par excellence, and all that was dedicated, consecrated, or set apart for God and for use in cultic worship was considered holy (*qdš, hagios*), including the sanctuary (tent or temple), the holy priests, and the sacrifices (Lev 27 and passim). The covenant that Yahweh, the Holy One, made on the holy mountain of Sinai with the Israelites made of them a "holy people" (Exod 19:6; cf. the stress on holiness throughout Exod 19; see also Deut 7:6–13). The prophets

---

[23] Hab 3:3; Job 6:10; Sir 4:14; 23:9; 43:10; 47:8; 48:20; Bar 4:22, 37; 5:5; Tob 12:12, 15; *1 En.* 1:3; 10:1; 12:3; etc.

[24] Matt 20:16; 22:14; Rom 1:1–17; Gal 1:15; 1 Cor 1:2, 9; 7:14–24; Eph 1:18; 4:1, 4; 2 Thess 1:11; 2 Tim 1:9; 2 Pet 1:3, 10.

laid stress on the ethical implications of both God's holiness and the people's (Isa 1:4; 5:6; Ezek 36:20–32; cf. also Deut 7:6–13; 14:1–15:23; 26:18–19; 28:9). This is an emphasis that is programmatically developed in the Holiness Code of Leviticus (chs. 17–26) with its recurrent refrain that "you shall be holy as I the Lord your God am holy" (19:2; 20:7, 26; cf. 11:44–45). Here God's holiness and his mighty liberation of Israel from Egypt are given as the motivating reasons for Israel's holy obedience to the covenant commands and its social and moral "separateness" from the polluted ways of Israel's neighbors (Lev 18:1–5, 24; 20:23).

From the postexilic period onward, appeal to the required holiness and purity of God's people served as a fundamental social stratagem for enforcing clear social boundaries between the holy people of God and their unholy neighbors (Lev 17–26; Ezra 6:21; 9:1–2, 11, 14; 10:2; Neh 10:28, 30–31); or, as later in the case of Qumran, between the Qumranite sectarians and wicked Israelites of uncircumcised lips and hearts (1QH^{a} II 18–19; 1QpHab XI 13). As a restored Temple, priesthood, and cult became the chief symbol of Israel's national identity and its political, economic, social, and cultural nerve center, an elaborate system of cultic purity and moral holiness was developed by the Temple elites that regulated both the internal social stratification of Israel and controlled its boundaries vis-à-vis Gentiles. Concern about and contention over holiness/purity regulations figured prominently in the inner-Israel disputes involving the Qumran community, Sadducees, Pharisees, and the Jesus movement. The Jesus movement continued to conceive of holiness as an essential quality both of God and of God's people, but now regarded Jesus as "the holy one" (Mark 1:24; Luke 4:34; John 6:69; Acts 3:14; 4:27, 30; 1 John 2:20; Rev 3:7), who provided all people, Israelites and Gentiles alike, with access to the holy God. It saw itself as the community animated by the Holy Spirit (John 20:22; Acts 2:4, 17, 38; 4:8; Rom 5:5; 8:1–27; etc.).[25]

In 1 Peter, holiness is stressed as a paramount quality uniting believers with God and Jesus Christ and distinguishing them from nonbelievers. It is noteworthy how many of the terms cited by Louw-Nida (1:745–46) as constituting the semantic field of "holy, pure" are employed here (cf. also Danker 1982, 354–59). "Holy" (*hagios* 1:12, 15, 16; 2:5, 9; 3:5), its paronyms (terms from the same root, such as "sanctify" [*hagiazo* 3:15]; "sanctification" [*hagiasmos* 1:2]) and synonyms ("purify" [*hagnizō* 1:22]; "pure" [*hagnos* 3:2]; "unblemished" [*amōmos* 1:19]; "spotless" [*aspilos* 1:19]; "pure" [*katharos* 1:2]; cf. also "sprinkling" [*rhantismos* 1:2]) connote here both consecration to God and separation

[25] On the phenomenon of the sacred and the concept of holiness in general, see Otto 1958; van der Leeuw 1963; Colpe 1977; for the biblical terms and concept, see Asting 1930; Ringgren 1948; Muilenburg 1962; Procksch and Kuhn 1964; Rensburg 1970; H. P. Müller 1976; Dihle 1988; Milgrom 1974; Gammie 1989; D. P. Wright and R. Hodgson, Jr., 1992; on holiness in the Greco-Roman world, see Williger 1922; Dihle 1988; on holiness and purity-pollution strategies in Israel and early Christianity, see Heinemann 1921; Nötscher 1959–1960; Neusner 1973, 1979a; Borg 1984; Newton 1985; Neyrey 1986; Neyrey, ed. 1991, 271–304; Countryman 1988, 11–143; Elliott 1991, 211–40; Malina 1993f, 149–83.

from all that is impure, unclean, and polluted. This holiness of the believers is a result of their election by God (1:1; 2:4–10; 5:13), their sanctification by the Holy Spirit (1:2), their call by God, the Holy One (1:15), and their redemption through the blood of Christ, the holy lamb (1:18–19; 1:2c).

As 1:14–16 indicates, a holy identity requires holy conduct: conduct in conformity with God's holiness and obedience to his will (1:14–16, 17); love of brothers and sisters with pure hearts (1:22; 3:2); and sanctifying the Christ as Lord amidst suffering (3:14–15). It likewise entails a holy nonconformity to Gentile values and to all forms of behavior contrary to the will of God (1:14; 2:11, 16; 4:2–3). Holiness as a distinguishing feature of the identity and behavior of the baptized believers is a theme found throughout the NT.[26] The association of holiness and obedience, moreover, finds its classic Israelite expression in the words of the Shema, Israel's "confession of faith," prayed twice daily: "Hear, O Israel, the Lord our God is one Lord. . . . So shall you remember and do all my commandments, and be holy to your God" (Deut 6:4; Num 15:40). In 1 Peter, the holiness of the believing community is underscored again in 2:4–10, which helps lay the basis for the exhortation that follows from 2:11 onward.

conduct. The focus upon good and honorable conduct (*anastrophē*) is a central feature of 1 Peter, which contains virtually half (six) of the thirteen NT occurrences of this term. The noun and its verb *anastrephō* denote in their figurative sense human "behavior, conduct, way of life," as illustrated by extrabiblical Greek usage (Deissmann 1901, 88, 194; 1923, 264–65; MM; BAGD s.v.), the OT (Tob 4:14; 2 Macc 6:23), and the NT (*anastrophē*: Gal 1:13; Eph 4:22; 1 Tim 4:12; Heb 13:7; Jas 3:13; 2 Pet 2:7; 3:11; *anastrephō*: e.g., 2 Cor 1:2; Eph 2:3; 1 Tim 3:15; Heb 13:18; 2 Pet 2:18). Their heavy use in 1 Peter (1:15, 17, 18; 2:12; 3:1, 2, 16) in connection with "good deeds" here (1:15, 17) and in 2:12 illustrates the profoundly ethical orientation of this letter and its emphasis upon a way of life that is "holy" (1:15; 3:1, 2), "reverent" (3:2), "good" (3:16), and reckoned as honorable and attractive (*kalos*) even by nonbelievers (2:12; cf. 3:1–2, 16). This conduct is later specified by another key word group of the letter as "doing what is right" (*agathopoieō, agathopoiia, agathopoios, agathos*: 2:14, 15, 20; 3:6, 17; 4:19; cf. 3:10–12, 16, 21) as opposed to "doing what is wrong" (*kakopoieō, kakapoios, kakos, kakia*: 2:1, 12, 14, 16; 3:9, 10–12, 17; 4:15). The believers' present "holy way of life" manifested in "doing what is right" marks believers' conversion from the "futile way of life" inherited from their ancestors (1:17) and now serves as a means of socially and morally distinguishing believers from nonbelievers. This conduct complements their verbal witness to God (2:9) with concrete deeds that can silence their accusers (2:13–16) and eventually even win the latter for the faith (2:12; 3:1–2). On *anastrophē* in secular Greek and the NT, see Danker 1982, 358–59; on its significance in

[26] Rom 1:7; 1 Cor 1:2; 2 Cor 1:1; Eph 1:1; Phil 1:1; Col 1:1, 4, 12, 22; 3:12; 1 Thess 3:13; 4:3–8; 2 Thess 1:10; Phlm 5, 7; Heb 13:14; Jas 1:27; 4:8; Jude 3; Rev 22:11.

1 Peter, see Brandt 1953; on the relation of *anastrophē* and *agathopoiia* and other similar words in 1 Peter, see Elliott 1966b, 179–81.

16a. *for it is written that* (*dioti gegraptai hoti*). The conjunction *dioti* ("for"), used in place of the causal *hoti* (BAGD s.v.) here as in 1:24 and 2:6, along with "it is written" (*gegraptai*) introduces an explicit citation of Scripture that provides authoritative substantiation of the foregoing statement. The presence of the similar terms *dioti* and *hoti* (twice) in this verse apparently led some scribes to favor *dio* in place of *dioti* (א C), omit the first *hoti* as redundant (𝔓[72] א A C P 𝔐, latt), substitute *dioti* for the second *hoti* (𝔓[72] א 81), or omit *dioti gegraptai* altogether (33 1243). However, the use of *dioti* to introduce quotations (1:24; 2:6) and the causal sense of the second *hoti* (cf. 3:15, 21; 3:12, 18; 4:8, 14, 17; 5:7) are consistent with the author's style throughout the letter.

16b. *"You shall be holy, because I am holy"* (*hagioi esesthe hoti egō hagios eimi*). Quotation marks are added to indicate a relatively certain scriptural quotation, as in 1:17b, 24; 2:3, 4–10, 22–25; 3:10–12, 14c, 15a; 4:8b, 18ab; 5:5c, 7a, 8b. Similar wording is found in Lev 11:44–45; 20:7, 26; and 19:2, but affinity with Lev 19:2 is closest: "Say to all the congregation of the people of Israel, You shall be holy, because I the Lord your God am holy." The absence of *eimi* ("am") in Lev 19:2 may explain its absence in some manuscripts of 1 Peter (א A* B etc.), but no difference in meaning is involved. *Genesthe* (K P etc.) and *ginesthe* (majority of later witnesses), semantic equivalents of *esesthe*, were perhaps substitutions for this verb prompted by the preceding *genēthēte* of v 15. The section of Leviticus (ch. 19) that contains these words occupies the central position in Leviticus and therefore in the Pentateuch. The Rabbis rightly regarded it as the kernel of the Law and declared that "the essentials of the Torah . . . are summarized therein (*Sipra*)" (Hertz 1990, 497). The command regarding holiness articulates the fundamental principle underlying the legislation of the Holiness Code (Lev 17–26): Israel's sanctification by and union with the holy God who delivered this people from Egypt (19:36; 22:33) and its separation from the contagious pollution of the Gentiles (18:1–5; 20:23). This principle of the Levitical Holiness Code—association with and imitation of the holiness of God the Holy One—also entails dissociation from all who are unholy. It thus has social as well as religious significance in 1 Peter as in Leviticus, and in 1 Peter undergirds the dissociative stance implied in conversion and advocated in v 15 as well as 4:2–4.

References to Lev 19 are found in both Israelite (*Ps.-Phoc.* 9–21) and Christian ethical exhortation (Jas 2:1, 8, 9; 5:4, 9, 12, 20 [on which, see L. T. Johnson 1982]; cf. also Matt 5:33; 18:15), particularly to Lev 19:18 (love of neighbor as of self), cited by Jesus as the second half of the great commandment (Matt 22:37–39 par.; cf. Matt 19:19; Rom 12:19; 13:9; Gal 5:14; Jas 2:8). Selwyn (1947, 369–75) compared NT texts stressing this holiness as enjoined in Lev 19 and related virtues (renunciation of evil, love) and followed Carrington (1940) in proposing that the NT affinities are due to common use of an early baptismal pattern of instruction for Christian converts. The prominence of Lev 19 in this instruction suggested to Selwyn "a conception of the Church as a 'neo-Levitical' or priestly community" (1947, 374), an image he also finds articulated in 1 Pet 2:1–10. While holiness is clearly a prominent theme of Christian baptismal tradition, neither the scheme nor the content of the proposed catechism nor the notion of "neo-Levitical community" have stood up under close scrutiny. Moreover, none of the NT texts citing or alluding to Lev 19 develops a notion of the Church as a "neo-Levitical" community, and in 1 Pet 2:4–10 the stress is on the recurrent theme of the holiness and election of the community rather than on its "priestly" quality (see NOTES and COMMENT on 2:4–10 and Elliott 1966b, 207–13). There are thus no cogent grounds for imagining that our author is "addressing his readers in distinctly priestly terms" (against Michaels 1988, 60), or as a "neo-Levitical community" (against Selwyn 1947, 374, 459–60). Leviticus 19:2 is cited here in v 16 to support the imperative of holy obedience in conformity with the holiness of God; the focus is on holiness, not priestliness. The passage illustrates the author's vital concern for communal holiness and separation from society's pollution, a concern characteristic of the NT in general.[27] For the notion of sharing in God's holiness, see also Heb 12:10, and for God as model, Matt 5:48; Eph 5:1.

Verses 17–21b comprise a second unit on holiness paralleling vv 14–16, indicating how the holiness of God's children is manifested in reverent conduct during their residence as aliens and how this is consonant with the fact of their redemption through the sacrifice of Christ, the holy lamb.

17a. *And since you call upon a Father* (*kai ei patera epikaleisthe*). The particle *ei* here, as elsewhere (2:3; 4:14, 17, 18), has the force of "since" rather than "if," since it introduces a given reality as the premise on which the following injunction (v 17b) is based; on the traditional character of v 17a, see Shimada 1966, 199–229. The Jesus movement, like Israel and the ancients in general, conceptualized and called upon God as "father" (*patera*) in accord with the prevailing patriarchal world view of their male-dominated, patriarchal culture (Schrenk 1967; Hamerton-Kelly 1979; Reese 1978; Krentz 1989). Applied to God, the metaphor implied God's progenerating or bringing his human "children" into existence (Isa 45:9–10; 64:8; 2 Sam 7:14; Pss 2:7; 89:26), his authority over them (Deut 14:1), his paternal affection, protection, and care for them (Ps 103:13; Isa 63:16; Jer 3:19; Hos 11:1), and his function as the "father of the fatherless" (Ps 68:5). Jesus characteristically thought of Yahweh as "father" (Matt 6:1–18, 25–34; 10:33; 18:10–14; 23:9; Mark 14:36 par.; Luke 10:21; John 5:18, cf. 19:7), and his followers thought of him as God's particularly favored son (Mark 1:11 par.; 9:7 par.; Rom 1:3–4; 8), who had made the Father known (John 1:18; 14:9). Jesus taught his followers to pray to God as "father" (*abba, patēr*; Matt 6:9; Luke 11:1), and this practice was continued after his death (Rom 8:15; Gal 4:6; 1 Pet 1:17). The Israelite Kaddish prayer and the Shemoneh Esreh illustrate the similar Israelite invocation of God as father. On God as father, see also the NOTE on 1:3a.

[27] Acts 15:20, 29; 1 Cor 3:17; 6:18–20; 2 Cor 6:14–7:1; Eph 5:1–13, 27; Col 1:22; 1 Thess 3:13; 4:3–8; 2 Pet 3:11; 1 John 3:3; Rev 22:12, 14–15.

It is therefore likely that the verb *epikaleisthe* (containing the preposition *epi*, "upon") has the sense of "calling upon" God the father in prayer (as in the "Our Father" [Matt 6:9; cf. Luke 11:2; see also Acts 2:21; Rom 10:13) rather than "calling" God "father" (contrast the variant *kaleite* [𝔓[72]]), although the two acts are certainly congruent. The metaphor of God as "father" echoes 1:2 and 3, corresponds to the metaphor of the believers as "obedient children" (1:14), and continues further the metaphor of the believing community as the "household" or "family" of God.

who judges impartially according to each one's deeds (*ton aprosōpolēmptōs krinonta kata to hekastou ergon*). Paternal authority includes the right and responsibility of judging and disciplining the behavior of family members. The notion of God as judge is a biblical commonplace and recurs elsewhere in 1 Peter (2:23; 4:5, 6, 17; cf. 2:12). The adverb *aprosōpolēmptōs* (*impartially*) occurs only here in the NT (cf. *1 Clem.* 1:3; *Barn.* 4:12), but the idea of divine impartiality in judgment (*aprosōpolēmpsia*; lit., "not regarding someone's face"), focusing not on appearance or status but behavior, likewise is a commonplace of Israelite and Christian teaching.[28] In the NT instances, this divine impartiality generally is related to God's unbiased favor shown to Gentiles as well as Israel, thus serving as an authorization for the Church's mission to the Gentiles, a point also made by the Apostle Peter, according to Acts (10:1–11:18). Here in 1 Peter, mention of God's impartial judgment *according to each one's deeds* (*ergon*, sing. used collectively for "behavior," as in 1 Cor 3:13; Gal 6:4; Rev 20:12–13, 22:12; cf. 2:12 [pl. *erga*]) removes the possibility of fatherly favoritism and thus prepares the ground for v 17b. The idea of judgment according to one's deeds is traditional (Prov 24:12; Ps 18:25; 28:4; 62:13; Jer 16:18; Sir 17:23; 35:22; *4 Ezra* 7:35; Rom 2:1–11; 1 Cor 3:13; 2 Cor 5:10; Jas 2:14–26; Rev 2:23; 20:12). The thought recalls Jesus' stress on the moral actions according to which humans will be judged (Matt 5:21–7:28; 12:33–37; 25:31–46).

17b. *conduct yourselves with reverence*. The translation renders the terms *anastraphēte* ("conduct yourselves") and *en phobōi* ("with reverence"), which in the Greek are related verb and modifier but appear for emphasis at the end and beginning of this clause, respectively. Regarding the verb and its noun *anastrophē*, see the NOTE on 1:15. The noun *phobos* and its verb *phobeō* can denote either the feeling of "fear" or "fright" in the negative sense, or, as here and generally in relation to God or deities, the positive feeling of "awe" and "reverence" as a response to the numinous (cf. Balz and Wanke 1974). In the Bible, *phobos* and *phobeō* denote an elemental reaction of awe-dread-reverence, "fear and trembling," at manifestations of the holiness, majesty, mercy, and power of God and his awesome (*phoberos*) actions (Ps 65[66]:3–7; 88:6–8 LXX; 89:5–7 MT; 98[99]:3; 110[111]:9; 144[145]:6; Luke 1:12; 7:16; Acts 2:43; Phil 2:12). Awe/fear of God is likewise a motive for keeping his commandments

[28] See Deut 10:17; 2 Chr 19:7 (linked with not taking bribes); *Jub.* 33:8; *2 Bar.* 13:2; *Pss. Sol.* 2:18–19; Acts 10:34, 42b; 15:8–9; Rom 2:11; Gal 2:6; Eph 6:9; Col 3:25; cf. Jas 2:1–13.

(Exod 20:20; 2 Kgdms 23:3; 2 Chr 19:9; 2 Esd [Neh] 5:9, 25; Ps 2:1; 33[34]:11; Prov 8:13; 2 Cor 7:1, 15) and is the beginning of wisdom (Ps 110[111]:10; Prov 1:7), which sets the faithful apart from the ignorant Gentiles (Rom 3:18). See the discussion of the word "holy" in the NOTE on v 15a. The context is generally determinative. 1 Peter 2:17 clearly exhorts the readers to "revere God" (in contrast to "honoring" the emperor and all persons) and the contexts of 1:17; 2:18; 3:2 (*phobos* + *anastrophē*); 3:16 (*syneidēsin* meaning "a sound knowledge" [of God and God's will]) indicate *reverence* toward God as a motive for behavior. On the other hand, in 3:6 and 3:14 (both OT allusions) the verb *phobeō* refers to "fear" of humans, which is not appropriate for the believers who do what is right and *fear/revere* God alone.

throughout the time (*ton . . . chronon*). *Chronos*, "time," in the durative sense, contrasts with *kairos*, which denotes a particular *critical point in time, a propitious time* (1:5, 11; 4:17; 5:6). Here and in 4:2 ("the remaining time in the flesh"), *chronos* denotes the remaining period of the believers' lives, while in 4:3 ("the time that is past"), it refers to the period prior to the believers' conversion.

of your residence as aliens (*tēs paroikias hymōn*). This significant phrase describes the present estranged social situation in which the addressees find themselves. The noun *paroikia* ("residence as aliens, alien residence"), together with its related terms *paroikoi* (2:11) and *parepidēmoi* (1:1; 2:11), highlight the precarious condition of the believers as aliens and "outsiders" in Asia Minor society.

The noun *paroikia* occurs only one other time in the NT (Acts 13:17), where Paul reminds the Israelites and godfearers of Pisidian Antioch that "the God of this people Israel chose our fathers and made this people great during their *residence as aliens* in the land of Egypt and with uplifted arm he led them out of it." Here the term refers to the political and social situation of Israel's ancestors living as displaced aliens (from Canaan) in the host country of Egypt prior to their exodus (as narrated in Gen 46:1–Exod 12:28). This OT narrative recounts in detail the drastic change in Israel's status and treatment as a result of new political leadership, their enslavement and forced labor, the hatred directed against them by the native Egyptians, and their yearning for freedom and return to Canaan—all features of vulnerability, exploitation, and animosity typical of Israel's existence among foreigners as "resident aliens."

In the LXX, *paroikia* is also used of Israel's *residence as aliens* in the land of Egypt (Wis 19:10; cf. *T. Levi* 11:2) as well as of its earlier ancestors in Mesopotamia (Jdt 5:9) and its later successors in Babylon (Lam 2:22; 1 Esd 5:7; 2 Esd 8:35), and still later in Egypt under the rule of the Ptolemies (Sir Prologue 23; 3 Macc 6:36; 7:19; cf. also of Lot in Sodom, Sir 16:8). It is used only once to translate the Hebrew term *gôlâ* ("exile," 2 Esd 8:35), which is otherwise rendered by the terms *aichmalōsia* (12×) *apoikesia* (6×), *apoikia* (15×), *apoikismos* (2×), and *metoikesia* (4×). Occasionally it is also used in reference to the adverse circumstances of strangers in general (Ps 33:5; 118[119]:54; 119[120]:5; Hab 3:16; Sir 41:5; 44:6). Terms of the *paroik-* family likewise feature prominently in the recitals of Israel's history (Deut 26:5–9; 1 Chr 16:8–36; Pss 104[105], 105[106]; Jdt 5:5–21).

In *T. Levi* 11:2, Levi explains that while in Canaan he had a son whom he named "Gersam," "for we were in a land of alien residence" (*paroikia*), the name in Hebrew consisting of *ger*, meaning "stranger" (*paroikos*), and *šam*, meaning "there;" for a similar explanation of naming, see Exod 2:22. Its use in *Pss. Sol.* 17:19 is particularly instructive, for here it denotes a community of Judeans residing as strangers in the Diaspora, a situation closely akin to that envisioned for the addressees of 1 Peter.

3 Maccabees 7:19 offers an even closer parallel to both the meaning of *paroikia* in 1 Pet 1:17 and the phrase in which it is employed. As 3 Maccabees narrates, Judeans "residing as aliens" (*paroikia*, 6:36) in Egypt during the reign of Ptolemy Philopater (ca. 217 BCE) were rounded up as suspected traitors and threatened with execution. Their priest, Eleazar, prayed for the divine deliverance of these defenseless "strangers in a strange land" (3:3). The king as a result of heavenly intervention eventually relented and the Judeans were spared. In thanksgiving they vowed to observe these days as days of joy "during the time of their residence as aliens" (*ton tēs paroikias autōn chronon*; cf. the virtually identical phrase in 1 Pet 1:17b). In later time Epiphanius (*Pan.* 25.190.15) employs a similar construction when he refers to "the sons of Israel in the land of Egypt . . . where occurred the time of their residence as aliens." The precarious political and social situation of these Diaspora Judeans and their vulnerability to social hostility likewise provide an analogy for the *paroikia* of the Christians in Asia Minor under similar hostile circumstances.

In Ps 118[119], the Psalmist recounts the various afflictions experienced by one who was a "resident alien in the land" (*paroikos . . . en tēi gēi*, v 19) and sought God's protection "in the place of my alien residence" (*paroikias*, v 54). In the Greek parlance of the period the term *paroikia* denoted the condition of "living as aliens (*paroikoi*) for an extended period of time in a place which was not one's homeland." *Paroikoi* and *parepidēmoi* are strangers or aliens who literally dwell "beside" (*par-*) others to whose home and homeland (*oikos*, *oikia*) they have no relation by blood, ethnic ties, religion, history, or culture. For further discussion of this family of terms, see the NOTES on 1:1 and 2:11 (and its DETAILED COMMENT).

Bible translations, which include "sojourning," "pilgrimage," "stay," often obscure the meaning and social implications of this term by assuming and attributing a "spiritual" meaning (spiritual "pilgrimage" or "exile" on earth), especially through the occasional addition of the words "here on earth" (NEB; TEV; Phillips; Beare: "earthly") not present in the original Greek text. Such renditions presume without warrant that *paroikia* and *paroikos* (2:11) imply a temporary "pilgrimage" or "exile" "on earth" in contrast to a future home or abode "in heaven." This cosmological contrast, however, is not indicated by the term *paroikia* itself or by its biblical usage or by the context of 1 Peter.

On the whole, *paroikia*, like its related terms *paroikos* and *paroikeō* (see NOTE and DETAILED COMMENT on 2:11), means neither "exile" (see rather *apoikia*, Jer 36[29]:4; 37[30]:3; *metoikesia*, Matt 1:11, 12, 17; cf. Acts 7:4, 43) nor "pilgrimage" (on earth). The term rather denotes the precarious social situation of the people of God among foreigners at various stages of its history and bears this meaning here in 1 Pet 1:17 as well (Elliott 1981/1990, 37–49; for an alternative view, see Michaels 1988, 62). The messianic sect finds itself in a situation of *paroikia* similar to that experienced by Israel and its ancestors from its earliest history onward (see also the evidence in NOTE and COMMENT on 2:11). Acknowledging this precarious situation of the addressees and the suffering they are experiencing, our author's aim is to encourage them, nevertheless, to trust fully in God's protection and to conduct themselves reverently in accord with his will, for in the suffering but vindicated Christ they have both an example and an enabler.

The use of *paroikia* in reference to Christians' residence as aliens *in this world* occurs for the first time in the second-century CE writing of 2 *Clem.* 5:1: "Let us forsake our alien residence in this world (*paroikian tou kosmou touto*), and let us not fear to go forth from this world . . . our visit (*hē epidēmia*) in this world in the flesh is a little thing and lasts a short time, but the promise of Christ is great and wonderful, and brings us rest in the kingdom which is to come and in everlasting life" (5:1, 5). This use of *paroikia* and its accompanying dualistic contrast of "this world" and "kingdom to come" (5:5; cf. 6:3–9; 8:1, 3, 6; 12:1, 60) is far removed from the language and perspective of 1 Peter and illustrates a development of thought along Platonic-Hellenistic lines (cf. similarly Philo, *Conf.* 80; CIG 9474; IG 14 [Sic. It.] 531.7). Also subsequent to the time of 1 Peter, the verb *paroikeō* was employed as part of an epistolary formula referring to "the church . . . which resides as an alien in . . ." (*1 Clement inscr.*; Polycarp, *To the Philippians inscr.*; *Martyrdom of Polycarp inscr.*; Dionysius of Corinth in Eusebius, *Hist. eccl.* 4.23.5, 6) and, in an analogous later development, *paroikia* (from which "parish" derives) came to designate a community of Christians organized as a geographical unit—that is, as a diocese, province, or parish (Eusebius, *Hist. eccl.* 1.1.1, etc.; see *PGL* s.v. for further patristic references and Holtz 1971 on the history of *paroikia*/parish).

The word *paroikia*, therefore, is best taken here, as in the LXX, as a designation of the addressees' actual social situation of "alien residence" or "residing as aliens" in a land and among people not their own. In this condition of residence as aliens, the addressees are exposed, as was ancient Israel in its several instances of residing as aliens on foreign soil, to all the various forms of suspicion, hostility, and suffering that strangers living in a foreign land always had to endure. Living among hostile natives who are ignorant of their origins, their families, and their history, and who are suspicious of their commitments and conduct (2:12, 15; 3:1–4, 9, 13–17; 4:2–5, 14–16), they are nevertheless exhorted not to conform to prevailing social patterns of behavior but to be holy as God is holy and to conduct themselves with reverence toward the one who called and regenerated them as children of his family. Our author draws no cosmological contrast between residence as aliens "on earth" and an eventual home "in heaven." The contrast here is rather a *temporal* one distinguishing present holy from past unholy phases of the believers' lives (1:14–16; cf. 2:10).

This temporal distinction, as in 4:2–4, also underlines the *social and religious differences* demarcating the believers from their nonbelieving neighbors.

Verses 18–21 consist of a series of subordinate clauses, which describe facts that are "known" to the believers and thus serve as motivation for the foregoing imperative concerning holy and reverent conduct (vv 14–16, 17). Verse 21c ("your hope"), like vv 20c, 21a, applies these facts directly to the readers ("you") and with v 13 ("hope") forms the final half of the inclusion bracketing vv 13–21. Here, as again in 2:21–25 and 3:18–22, exhortation concerning Christian behavior (1:13–17; 2:18–20; 3:13–17) is given Christological substantiation and motivation.

18a. *knowing that* (*eidotes hoti*). "Knowing" (*eidotes*, perf. act. part. of *oida*) modifies the "you" of v 17. The phrase *eidotes hoti* (cf. 5:9), as elsewhere in the NT, introduces material, frequently elementary Christian teaching, providing the reason or reasons for a preceding imperative (1 Cor 15:58; Eph 6:8, 9; Col 3:24, 4:1; Jas 3:1; cf. 2 Tim 2:23; 3:14; Titus 3:11; and 1 Pet 5:9; on the tradition behind vv 18–19, see Shimada 1966, 230–61). 1 Peter 1:12 (cf. 1:25 and 4:17) indicates that this common information was contained in and had been mediated through the proclamation of the "good news."

you were ransomed (*elytrōthēte*). The translation reverses the sequence of the Greek, which reads, literally, "not with corruptible things, silver or gold, were you ransomed . . . but with . . ." for a clearer expression of the contrast in English. The verb *lytroō* ("free by paying a ransom," "redeem"; generally, "set free, redeem, rescue") occurs in the NT only here and in Luke 24:21 and Titus 2:14. Its combination with "blood of Christ" is singular in the NT. However, the NT writings employ various paronyms of the "ransom/redeem" word field (*lyō, apolyō; lytron; lytrōsis; lytrotēs; apolytrōsis*; cf. also *agorazō, exagorazō*) and some combined with "blood of Christ" (Rom 3:24–25; Eph 1:7; Heb 9:12). Thus the concept of ransom/redemption through the blood of Christ is a widespread and early metaphor for salvation in the early Church, and conceivably a development of words of Jesus concerning the shedding of his blood (Mark 14:24 par.; 1 Cor 11:24) and his death as ransom (*lytron*) for many (Mark 10:45). This soteriological metaphor in part has its origin in the OT (LXX), where the verb *lytroō* is frequently employed in reference to God's ransoming/redeeming/rescuing Israel from its enslavement in Egypt (Exod. 6:6; 15:13; Deut 7:8; 9:26; 15:15; 21:8; 24:18; 2 Kgdms 7:23; cf. *m. Pesaḥ*. 10:5, 6) and its exile in Babylon (Isa 45:13; Isa 52:3). But of these texts only Isa 52:3 employs the verb in the specific sense of "ransom" in conjunction with a "price" but in a statement quite the opposite of 1 Peter: "For thus says the Lord: 'You were sold for nothing and you shall be ransomed/redeemed *without money*.'" Whereas Isaiah refers to a ransom without a price, 1 Pet 1:18–19 speaks of a ransom with a price even more costly than that of silver and gold, namely "the precious blood of Christ." The ancient world knew the practice of redeeming with a payment of money those who had been captured in war and held as hostages for a ransom, or those free persons who because of unpayable debts had sold themselves into slavery (Lev 25:47–54), as well as the process of sacral manumission of slaves (involving a fictive "sale" to a deity, return of the price to the owner, and freedom for the slave [e.g., SIG[3] 845; cf. Deissmann 1923, 273–84; Horsley 1982, 90; 1983, 72–75]). This could explain the association of redemption and price made here. However, the fact that the "blood of Christ" is cited here as the means of redemption points to the influence of a specifically Christian tradition in which the thought of Jesus as vicarious ransom for all (Mark 10:45) was developed through the use of Isa 53, which spoke of the vicarious suffering of the servant of God (Wolff 1950; Jeremias 1966b, 216–29; Lohse 1963, 113–46). Here in 1 Peter the passive voice of the verb again implies that it is God who has redeemed the believers.

from the futile conduct inherited from your ancestors (*ek tēs mataias hymōn anastrophēs patroparadotou*). The rendering of *anastrophē* as "conduct" displays in English the connection of this verse with vv 15 (*anastrophē*) and 17 (*anastraphēte*). However, the term implies not merely behavior but also the values, norms, and commitments that constitute an entire "way of life." This way of life from which the believers have been redeemed was previously described as their "former ignorance" (v 14) and contrasts directly to their holy and reverent *conduct* or "way of life" enjoined in vv 15–17.

The adjective *mataios* ("futile") and its paronyms are regularly used by Israelites and Christians to condemn the idolatrous ways of the pagans as "empty," "useless," "worthless," "lacking in honor" (Jer 2:5; 8:19; Esth 4:17; 3 Macc 6:11; Acts 14:15; Rom 1:21; Eph 4:17).

The second adjective, *patroparadotos* (lit., "handed down from the fathers"), occurs nowhere else in the NT or LXX. But in Greco-Roman literature and inscriptions it designates the positive sense of values, traditions, and customs that are rooted in the past and transmitted by the fathers as a worthy heritage.[29] Here in 1 Peter, however, in conjuction with *mataios*, it is employed in a negative sense of conduct encouraged by the fathers that was empty and aimless, conduct from which the believers have now been liberated. Both adjectives, especially since they are used in conjunction with *former ignorance* (of God, v 14b), suggest that our author has in mind here readers of pagan origin. For an Israelite example, however, of the renunciation of the ways of one's fathers upon entrance to the community, see 1QS I 24–26; cf. II 9.

In ancient society, the antiquity of something, a people or a practice, established its worth. A fundamental axiom of evaluation was "older is better, oldest is best." Thus Fronto (*Ep.* 162.9) observes: "that which is preferable is commonly called senior" (*antiquius*; cf. also Cicero, *Inv.* 1.142; *Pomp.* 60 and Josephus' appeal to the antiquity of Israel's history and law in his defense of Israel [*Ant.*; *Ag. Ap.*]). In later time, the Christian apologetes effectively used this principle in asserting the antiquity and hence prestige of the Israelite and Christian

[29] See, e.g., inscriptions from Pergamon (I. Perg. 28.49) and elsewhere (I. Eph. 1a.21 [= 6.2019]; OGIS 331.49; IG 12/5.860.4) and Dionys. Hal., *Ant. rom.* 5.48.2; Diod. Sic., *Hist.* 4.8.5; 15.74.5; 17.2.2, 4.1.

people of God and their Scriptures (e.g., Theoph., *Autol.* 3.17–29; on the prevalence of the principle "older is better," see Pilhofer 1990). Accordingly, living in conformity with ancestral customs and the conventional wisdom of the past was the mark of a wise and moral person. The pagan Porphyry (ca. 232–303), writing to his wife Marcella (*Marc.* 14), expresses what is typical of ancient sentiment on the whole: "The greatest fruit of piety is to worship the gods according to the traditions of our ancestors." Neglect of one's ancestors and disavowal of one's ancestral roots and religion were signs of gross disrespect and "impiety" and cause for social disdain and alienation (Cicero, *Leg.* 2.7.19–27; Plut., *Am. Prol.* 756; Dio Cassius 52.36; see van Unnik 1969; Talbert 1986, 145).

Nevertheless, conversion to Christianity, our author asserts, entails a divine liberation from these futile ways of the past and continued separation from those who practice them (1:14; 2:11; 4:2–4). Moreover, this liberation, as soon to be noted (v 20a), was accomplished by one already "foreknown before the foundation of the world" and thus older and superior to even human ancestral custom. In place of ancient pagan wisdom and ancestral traditions, early Christianity offered to Gentile converts the antiquity of the Christ, the antiquity of its ancient Scriptures (older than secular wisdom, so its apologists claimed, and cited so frequently in 1 Peter), and inclusion in the history and privileges of ancient Israel (1:4; 2:4–10; 3:5–6, 20–21).

This radical break with previous loyalties and revered traditions undoubtedly contributed to the animosity that Christian converts experienced from their former cronies and prompted Gentile pressures urging social conformity (Talbert 1986, 145). Conservative antipathy to the forsaking of ancestral custom is reflected in the advice given by "Maecenas" to "Augustus" in Cassius Dio's *Roman History*:

> Therefore, if you desire to become in very truth immortal, act as I advise; and furthermore both yourself worship the Divine Power everywhere and in every way in accordance with the traditions of our fathers and compel all others to honor it. Those who attempt to distort our religion with strange rites you should abhor and punish, not merely for the sake of the gods, but because such men, by bringing in new divinities in place of the old, persuade many to adopt foreign practices, from which spring up conspiracies, factions and cabals, which are far from profitable to a monarchy. Do not, therefore, permit anybody to be an atheist or a sorcerer. (52.36)

The text is from the early third century CE but reflects long-standing sentiments. It was these conservative sensibilities that Christianity, in the period after 1 Peter, eventually would be charged with violating. Our author reckons with the problem that the renouncing of these customs poses for the addressees (cf. 2:11; 4:2–4) and therefore reminds them of the still more ancient pedigree of their redeemer: he "was known before the foundation of the world" (v 20a).

Verses 18b–19b constitute an antithetical parallelism contrasting the medium of redemption (not money but blood) and its quality (not corruptible but costly, holy). As the dative *corruptible things* (v 18b) is implicitly exemplified by the phrase *silver or gold* (v 18c), so *Christ* in the dative phrase *the precious blood of Christ* (v 19a) is explicitly (*hōs*) exemplified by the phrase *as a flawless and faultless lamb* (v 19b), which is interposed in the Greek between *blood* and *of Christ*.

18b. *not with corruptible things* (*ou phthartois*). The term *phthartois* (dat. pl. of the neuter *phtharton*) can mean "perishable, subject to decay or destruction" (1 Cor 9:24; 1 Pet 1:23) or "mortal" when applied to living creatures (Rom 1:23; 1 Cor 15:53–54). But in vv 18–19 the contrast with "the precious blood of Christ as a flawless (*amōmos*) and faultless lamb" is not that of perishable versus imperishable or mortal versus immortal but rather corruptible or defective in contrast to something unblemished and spotless, as in the cultic sphere. This is precisely the sense of *aphthartos* in Lev 22:17–25, which lists the requirements pertaining to acceptable sacrifices. Only those sacrifices of a lamb (*probaton*), bull, or goat are acceptable to the holy God that are themselves "flawless" (*amōmos*)—that is, complete, unmutilated, lacking any blemish or defect (*mōmos*; Lev 22:19, 20, 21, 25). And, as Lev 22:25 makes clear, that which is "corrupted" (*phtharta*) is unacceptable because it is flawed, defective (*mōmos*). *Phthartos* thus functions as a synonym of *mōmos* and antonym of *amōmos* as van Unnik (1980c, 27–28, 37–40) has cogently argued. The Passover ceremony in particular (Num 28:16–25) involved the sacrifice of lambs (*amnoi*) that were flawless (*amōmoi*). This sense and use of *phthartos* and *amōmos* seem to be implied here in 1 Peter as well, an interpretation that clarifies the logic of their contrast. Thus, elements of Israelite cultic practice along with tradition pertaining to Israel's redemption from Egypt and the ransom of slaves have been creatively interwoven here to describe the liberation gained through Christ and its continuity with the patterns of Israel's history, institutions, and worship.

18c. [*such as*] *silver or gold* (*argyriōi ē chrysiōi*). *Silver or gold* stands in apposition to *corruptible things*, which they illustrate. These are precious metals that actually defy decay and hence would not provide a logically apposite illustration of things "perishable." But they do provide a negative example of things that, though of great value (especially in the ransom process), are nevertheless "defective" and inferior when compared with the precious blood of Christ, the flawless lamb. Psalm 104[105], in rehearsing God's deliverance of Israel from its Egyptian "alien residence" (v 23), recalls that God "led forth Israel with silver and gold" (v 37). But no allusion to or contrast with this thought seems intended here, since the silver and gold of the Exodus passage were not a redemption price but a gift of the Egyptians (cf. Exod 12:35–36). The closest OT affinity is, rather, with Isa 52:3, alluding to Israel's alien residence in Egypt (52:4) and its redemption from Babylon as from Eygpt: "You were sold for nothing, and you shall be redeemed (*lytrōthēsesthe*) without silver." However, our author takes this thought in a different direction by declaring the blood of Christ to be the price of Christian redemption and comparing Christ with an innocent lamb (v 19), a comparison suggested by the continuing text of Isaiah

(53:7). The added words *such as* express the implied comparison here, which is balanced by the explicit comparison in v 19b.

19a. *but with the precious blood of Christ* (*alla timiōi haimati . . . Christou*). This phrase echoes the thought of 1:2 and sounds again the theme of Christ's suffering and death that pervades the entire letter; see the NOTE on 1:11b and Cervantes Gabarrón 1991b, 328–39 on 1:18–19. For the ancients, blood (*haima*) was the life of a living being (Gen 9:4; Deut 12:23), and in Israel's sacrificial cult, blood represented the life that was symbolically offered to God. The blood of flawless animals sacrificed to make atonement for sins was thrown against the altar (Lev 1:5), sprinkled before the sanctuary (Lev 4:6), and smeared on the horns of the altar (Lev 4:25). In Egypt, the blood of the Passover lamb, which the Israelites smeared on their doorposts, protected them from the angel of death (Exod 12:7, 13), and in the covenant ritual, the blood of sacrificed animals was sprinkled on both the altar (representing God) and on the people, signifying that the covenant partners shared a mutual commitment and a common life (Exod 24:3–8). For the followers of Jesus this conception of blood and its role in Israelite history and cult provided the means for interpreting the saving and atoning power of Jesus' suffering and death. Thus Jesus is portrayed as "our Passover lamb" (1 Cor 5:7), "the lamb of God who takes away the sins of the world" (John 1:29), the one whose blood confers life and effects a new and everlasting covenant between God and humanity (Mark 14:24 par.; John 6:53–56; 1 Cor 11:25; Heb 9–10; 13:20), whose blood redeems (Rom 3:24–25; Eph 1:7; Rev 1:5), makes righteous (Rom 5:9), purifies (1 John 1:7; *Barn.* 5:1), brings near to God (Eph 2:13), and makes peace (Col 1:20). The Petrine author draws on this Christological tradition and its OT roots to provide a Christological as well as a theological (vv 15–16) warrant for his exhortation to holiness.

Christ's blood is declared *timios* ("precious," "costly," "of great value"), and the comparison and contrast with *silver and gold* recall a similar contrast made earlier between valuable gold and the greater preciousness (*polytimoteron*) of genuine Christian faith (1:7). Later in 2:4–7, related terms are used to portray Christ as the "precious, honored" (*entimon*) stone elected by God (2:4, 6) and those who believe in him as sharing in this "honor" (*timē*, 2:7). An early echo of this phrase is contained in *1 Clement*, a writing of the church at Rome (ca. 96 CE) with numerous reminiscences of 1 Peter: "Let us look intently on the blood of Christ and know that it is precious (*timion*) to his father because, poured out for our salvation, it brought the grace of repentance to the entire world" (7:4; cf. also Melito, *Peri Pascha* 44).

19b. *as a lamb flawless and faultless* (*hōs amnou amōmou kai aspilou*). In the Greek this phrase is interposed between *with the precious blood* and *of Christ* and modifies the latter. This construction places *Christ* at the conclusion of vv 18–19, thereby clarifying the term to which the participles of v 20 refer. The use of *amnos* ("lamb") to symbolize Jesus Christ is infrequent in the NT (John 1:19, 36; Acts 8:32–35; cf. 28 occurrences of the related term *arnion* ["lamb"] in reference to Christ in Revelation; cf. also 1 Cor 5:7). In 1 Peter this usage is most likely prompted by the figure of the suffering servant as a lamb in Isa 53:7, since Isa 52:3 is alluded to in 1:18, and further terminology from Isa 53 is also employed in the Christological statement of 2:22–25. The modifying adjectives "flawless" (*amōmos*) and "faultless" (*aspilos*), however, do not derive from Isaiah but represent an original Petrine blending of independent concepts. The image of the lamb used in Isa 53 as a metaphor for the suffering servant of God is now applied to Christ. To underline the *holiness* of Christ the lamb, the adjective describing flawless and therefore acceptable sacrifices in Israel's cult, *amōmos*, is used as modifier (cf. Heb 9:14), together with *aspilos*, a term of secular provenance (no LXX occurrences) meaning "faultless" in either a physical or moral sense (see BAGD for examples). On the required use of "flawless lamb(s)" for sacrifice, see Lev 9:3; 12:6; 14:10; 23:18; Num 6:14; 7:69; 28:3, 9, 11, 27; 29:2, 17, 20, 23, 26, 29, 32, 36; Ezek 46:13.

Hebrews 9:12–14, a passage with striking linguistic similarities to 1 Pet 1:18–19 and its context, also speaks of the "redemption" secured through the "blood of Christ," applies *amōmos* to Christ, and indicates the association of *amōmos* with holiness:

> He [Christ] entered once for all into the holy place, taking not the blood of goats and calves but his own blood, thus securing an eternal redemption (*lytrōsin*). For if the sprinkling (*rhantizousa*; cf. 1 Pet 1:2) of defiled persons with the blood of goats . . . sanctifies (*hagiazē*; cf. 1 Pet 1:15–16) for the cleansing (*katharotēta*; cf. 1 Pet 1:22) of the flesh, how much more shall the blood of Christ, who through the eternal Spirit offered himself flawless (*amōmos*) to God, cleanse your conscience from dead works (*ergōn*; cf. 1 Pet 1:17) to serve the living God.

Although the passages differ sufficiently in formulation and thought to rule out literary dependency, they illustrate the degree to which motifs drawn from Israel's history and cult shaped the Christological formulations of the early Church. In the following century, Melito of Sardis (Asia Minor) in his Passover Homily (*Peri Pascha*) celebrated Christ as the Christian Passover and attributed a variation of this formulation of 1 Peter (*aspilon amnon kai amōmon*) retrospectively to the Passover lamb of the exodus (*Peri Pascha* 12), while also linking this lamb to that of Isa 53 (*Peri Pascha* 4, 64, 67; cf. also Iren., *Epid*. 25). At this time Christian interpolations in the *T. Jos*. (19:8) and *T. Benj*. (3:8) also employ the phrase "flawless lamb" with reference to Christ. The following references to Christ being "foreknown," and finally "manifest," likewise recall Israelite and Christian traditions concerning the ram sacrificed as a replacement for Isaac (Gen 22) and the association of the blood of this sacrifice with the blood of the Passover lamb (*Mekilta* on Exod 12:13; cf. le Déault 1961; Michaels 1988, 66).

The result of this blending in 1 Peter is a statement that is both rhetorically attractive and theologically impressive. Rhetorically, the phrase *amnos amō-*

mos kai aspilos illustrates the author's refined appreciation of alliteration (as in 1:4: *aphtharton kai amianton kai amaranton*; cf. also 2:12, 15, 18–20, 21; 3:17; 4:4). This stylistic feature is captured in part by the English "flawless and faultless," which I patterned after Michaels' felicitous translation. In contrast to Michaels, however, I render *amōmos* "flawless" (in the light of Lev 17:22–25) and *aspilos* "faultless" (because of its moral usage; cf. 1 Tim 6:14; Jas 1:27; 2 Pet 3:14).

The association of sacrifice (1:18–19) and conversion from one way of life to another (1:14–15) was prompted, van Unnik has suggested (1980, 41–79), by the ritual of Israelite proselyte conversion. Here, too, conversion was accompanied by a sacrifice that, along with baptism and circumcision, comprised one of the three essential elements of the rite. The blood (of the sacrifice) is "precious," according to van Unnik because it "delivers" (*lytroō*) from Gehenna. Given the further traces of motifs of Israelite proselytism in 1 Peter (van Unnik [1980c, 53–68] lists 15 examples), the proposal is plausible though not probative, since the supporting evidence (*m. Ker.* 2:1; *b. Ker.* 9a) is later than 1 Peter. This problem, however, is mitigated by the fact that the practice of sacrifice in conjunction with the rite presumes a time prior to the destruction of the Temple in 70 CE and therefore before 1 Peter. On the whole, van Unnik's study argues a compelling case for the similarity of the conversion process and associated motifs in Israel and early Christianity, as attested in 1 Peter.

Theologically, vv 18–19 in their entirety represent a fabric of thought interwoven from several strands of OT and early Christian tradition. The result is a portrayal of the redemption accomplished through Christ that evokes memory of the historic deliverance of Israel from Egypt, the sacrificial system through which atonement between God and Israel was achieved, and the poignant depiction of the Suffering Servant of Isaiah. The readers are hereby provided with a rationale for their holy and distinctive conduct, which is based on both the holiness of God and the holiness of Christ. On vv 18–19 and the "blood of Christ" in 1 Peter, see Cervantes Gabarrón 1991b, 319–39; Lohse 1963, 138–45, 182–87. Clement of Alexandria (*Paed.* 3.12.85), in a summary about Christian morality, cites 1 Pet 1:17–19 (and 4:3) and then alludes to baptism (*anagennēthentes*), thereby illustrating the role of these verses in the baptismal catechesis of the early Church.

Verses 20–21 continue without interruption the proximate statement begun in v 17 and, with a series of subordinated formulations, conclude the line of thought initiated in v 13. Verse 20ab contains a pair of parallel participial phrases modifying *Christ* (v 19b); vv 20c–21a apply the foregoing to the readers (*for your sake, you who trust in God*); v 21b (*who raised him from the dead and gave him glory*) modifies *God* (vv 21a); and v 21c, pertaining again to the readers, concludes the unit of vv 13–21 by returning to the stress on *hope* with which this section began (v 13b).

20a. *he was foreknown before the foundation of the world* (*proegnōsmenou men pro katabolēs kosmou*). This participial genitival phrase and the one that follows (v 20b) form a carefully balanced couplet modifying *Christ* (v 19). The couplet is marked by a parallelism of terms and the contrastive particles *men* and *de*, akin to the similarly constructed couplet modifying *Christ* in 3:18de. As a unit they relate *Christ* (*he*) to both the commencement and close of God's action in history:

> (he, i.e., Christ)
> was foreknown before the the foundation of the world (and)
> was manifested at the last of the ages.

was foreknown. The participle *proegnōsmenou* (with the passive implying God as agent) recalls the phrase "foreknowledge of God" (*prognōsin theou*) in 1:2a and indicates that Christ, like the election of the addressees, was the focus of God's foreknowledge and intention. Both of these texts bear an affinity to words of Peter recorded in Acts 2:23: "this Jesus, delivered up according to God's ordained plan and foreknowledge (*prognōsei*)." Acts 2:23 and 1 Pet 1:2a contain the only NT uses of *prognōsis* and similarly regard Christ or his death (cf. 1 Pet 1:19) as foreknown and foreordained by God. The more general notion that the passion took place in accord with God's intention was an element of the primitive Christian kerygma (Acts 4:27–28; 13:32–33; Rom 1:1–4; 1 Cor 15:3–4; cf. Mark 8:31; Luke 22:22; 2 Tim 1:9–10).

before the foundation of the world (*pro katabolēs kosmou*). This phrase (also in John 17:24 and Eph 1:4) or "from (*apo*) the foundation of the world" (*As. Mos*. 12:4; Matt 13:35; 25:34; Luke 11:50; Rev 13:8; 17:8; *Barn*. 5:5; *Odes Sol*. 41:14) is a conventional expression that relates the subject it qualifies to the farthest imaginable reaches of past time, to the primordial period before or beginning with God's creation of the world. Here, as in John 17:24 (cf. 17:5) and *Barn*. 5:5, it is the Messiah/Christ (cf. *Odes Sol*. 41:14: "the anointed") who is said to be the focus of God's prehistoric foreknowledge and salvific intention. The combination of "before the foundation of the world" and "end of time" circumscribes the entire scope of world history from start to close. The implied founder of creation is God, who in another context but similar sense is described as "the Alpha and Omega, the first and the last, the beginning and the end" (Rev 22:13; cf. 1:8; 21:6).

The word *kosmos* here as in 5:9 refers simply to the inhabited world, the orderly universe (Matt 4:8; 5:14; 13:38; Mark 14:9; 16:15; Luke 12:30; Acts 17:14; Rom 1:8; Eph 1:4; etc.) with no negative valuation, as found for instance in Paul and the Johannine writings; see the NOTE on 5:9. In 3:3, on the other hand, it appears in its other sense of "adorning" in reference to women's attire.

20b. [*and*] *was made manifest at the last of the ages* (*phanerōthentos de ep' eschatou tōn chronōn*). The second half of the couplet refers to Christ's manifestation by God's ushering in the last of the ages. Like the preceding passive verb *proegnōsmenou*, the passive participle *was made manifest* (*phanerōthentos*) likewise implies God as agent. The verb recurs in 5:4 with reference to the divine manifestation of Christ the chief shepherd at the conclusion of history, the same point in time to which the synonymous terms for "revelation" (*apokalyptō* and *apokalypsis*) refer in 1:5, 7; 4:13; and 5:1. Here, however, it refers to the first advent of the Christ in human history (cf. also "revelation" in 1:13) as agent of redemption (cf. Rom 3:21; 1 Tim 3:16; 2 Tim 1:9–10; 1 John 1:2; 3:5, 8). This verb, like *apokalyptō*, implies that something hidden or unknown has been disclosed (cf. 1:10–12). This was a popular motif of Israelite apocalyptic writings, where the agent of salvation was portrayed as "concealed" in the presence of God before the creation of the world and then "revealed" to the elect and holy ones at the end of the ages (*1 En.* 48:6; 62:7; *4 Ezra* 12:32; 13:52; *2 Bar.* 3:1–5). This same motif characterized the outlook of early Christianity, which maintained that the hidden Messiah or mystery of salvation has been revealed in Jesus (Rom 16:25–26; 1 Cor 2:7–13; Eph 3:4–6, 9–10 [cf. 1:4]; Col 1:26; 2 Tim 1:9–10; Titus 1:2–3; Ign. *Magn.* 6:1; *2 Clem.* 14:2; Herm. *Sim.* 12.2–3). Of these texts, Rom 16:25–26 and 2 Tim 1:9–10 also employ the contrasting schema "ages ago"–"now manifested" (cf. also Heb 9:26–27, "from the foundation of the world"–"now appeared" [*pephanerōtai*]).

last of the ages (*eschatou tōn chronōn*). This phrase has stronger manuscript support ($\aleph^2$ A B C etc.) than its alternatives ("last of the days" [69 and a few other MSS]; "end of the age" [$\aleph^*$ Ψ]), with "last" (*eschatou*) serving as a substantive in the singular modified by "of the ages" (*tōn chronōn*; cf. Acts 1:7; 3:21; 17:30; Rom 16:25; Titus 1:2). The phrase, as in apocalyptic texts of Israel (*4 Ezra* 3:14; 12:9; *2 Bar.* 13:3; 21:8; 27:15; 29:8; 30:3; 59:4; 76:2; cf. Dan Theod. 2:28; Heb 1:2; 2 Pet 3:3; Jude 18), alludes to the end time, the last of the ages or periods (*chronoi*) of human history, with its accompanying events (final tribulation [*2 Bar.* 27:15], advent of the Messiah [*2 Bar.* 29:8], and divine judgment [*2 Bar.* 13:3]). The Petrine author also distinguishes two periods in the lives of the addressees, one prior to their conversion and the other after it (1:14–19; 4:2–3). Here, however, the *ages* are the periods of human history circumscribed by God's prior foreknowledge of Christ and God's final manifestation of the Christ at the end time. The term may also be implied in 4:7 ("the end of all [ages] is at hand"). For our author, as for early Christianity in general, the initial (1:19, 20b) and final (5:4; cf. 1:7; 5:1) appearances of Jesus Christ mark the boundaries of the end time. The expression illustrates the pronounced eschatological perspective of 1 Peter (cf. also 4:7, 17–19).

On the whole, this formalized couplet and its content appear to have been derived from early Christian apocalyptic Christological tradition. It refers not to the preexistence and incarnation of the Christ/Messiah but to his *role* in the divinely established course of salvation (cf. God's "establishing" or "setting" of the stone [Christ] as the object of belief and means of Christian election [2:6–8]). Le Déault (1961) saw the couplet as part of a midrashic comment on Gen 22:8 that began in vv 18–19, a conjecture at best, since interest in Gen 22:8 here is hardly pronounced. More influential is the theory of R. Bultmann (1947, 293, 297), who regarded the couplet as a dislocated fragment of an early Christian hymn, elements of which also were adopted and adapted in 3:18–19, 22; so also Boismard 1961, 60–67 and others. The reason for the assumed fragmentation of the "hymn," however, and for use of only one unit thereof, Bultmann left unexplained. While its original place in an early Christian hymn or creed is highly questionable, the couplet's reflection of Christian christological tradition is recognized by all commentators. (On the use of formulary material in vv 18–20, see Shimada 1966, 230–302; and Deichgräber 1967, 169–70). The manner in which the couplet is merged here with other traditions and themes is indicative of the author's rhetorical competence (Lash 1982) and of his idiosyncratic blending of various traditions and themes elsewhere in the letter (e.g., 2:4–10, 21–25; 3:18–22; cf. the DETAILED COMMENT on 3:18–22).

20c. *for the sake of you* (*di' hymas*). Here, as previously (1:4–5, 6–9, 10–12; see NOTE on 1:4), the author stresses the "for-you-ness" of the gospel by relating the preceding Christological formulation directly to the readers. Distinguished from the parallelism, rhythm, and christological content of the couplet, vv 20c–21 in their entirety represent the distinctive hand and pastoral focus of the Petrine author.

21a. *who through him trust in God* (*tous di' autou pistous eis theon*). The focus that has shifted to the readers in v 20c continues (with *tous* ["who"] having "you" as its antecedent), but the phrase *through him* makes it clear that the Christ foreknown and manifested by God is the one who mediates their "trusting in" (*pistous* used as a verbal adj.) and their relationship with God (cf. also "through [*dia*] Jesus Christ" in 1:3; 2:5; 4:11). In regard to the meaning of *pistos* as "trusting" rather than "believing" when applied to the readers, see the NOTE on 1:7 (*pistis*).

21b. *who raised him from the dead and gave him glory* (*ton egeiranta auton ek nekrōn kai doxan autōi donta*). This phrase modifies *God* and now shifts the focus to God's exaltation of the Christ as the ultimate basis for Christian trust and hope. The conviction that God raised Jesus from the dead is a central and recurrent element of Christian proclamation and a stable element of early Christian tradition (Acts 13:30, 32, 34, 37; 17:31; Rom 4:24; 8:11; 10:9; 1 Cor 6:14; 15:4, 12–28; 2 Cor 4:14; Gal 1:1; Eph 1:20; Col 2:12; 1 Thess 1:10; 2 Tim 2:8; cf. Mark 8:31 par.; 9:31 par.; 10:34 par.; 14:28 par.; Matt 28:7; Luke 24:7; John 21:14); for a comparative table of NT usage, see Dahl 1962, 98–99. It also figures prominently in the preaching associated with Peter in particular (Acts 2:24, 32; 3:13, 15; 4:10; 5:30; 10:40) as well as in this letter attributed to him (1:3, 21; 3:21). The Gospel of John speaks of God's glorifying the Son (12:23; 13:31–32; 17:1, 5) and "giving him glory" (17:22) in the context of Jesus' passion and resurrection (chs. 13–20, 21).

However, this formulation of 1 Peter, which combines *who raised him from the dead* with *and gave him glory*, is unique in the NT, though it succinctly formulates similar words by Peter in Acts: "(God) glorified his servant Jesus . . . whom God raised from the dead" (3:13, 15, recalling Isa 52:13 LXX: "Behold, my servant shall prosper and shall be exalted and greatly glorified [*doxasthēsetai*]). Emphasis upon "glory" (*doxa*) and "glorify" (*doxazō*) is a hallmark of 1 Peter (Selwyn 1947, 253–58, and the NOTE on 2:11), as is the combined mention of "suffering(s)" and "glory (glories) of Christ" (1:11; 4:13; 5:1; see NOTE on 1:11). Likewise in 1 Peter, Jesus' resurrection and glorification is a demonstration of his acceptance, honoring, and vindication by God despite human rejection (cf. 2:4, 6–8; 3:18, 22). This honor and glory of the suffering Christ is thus a surety of the glory and honor in store for believers who remain faithful in adversity (1:7; 4:13–16; 5:1; cf. 2:4–5, 7a). On the traditions behind 1:18–19, 20, see Shimada 1966; on their relation to the theme of suffering in general see Cervantes Gabarrón 1991b, 328–39.

The formulaic features of vv 20 and 21b (parallelism, rhythm, kerygmatic content) have led several commentators to suspect influence of early Christian confessional or hymnic tradition here as in 2:21–24 and 3:18–22 (Shimada 1966, 230–302) with some, but not all, accepting Bultmann's membra disiecta theory. The function of this kerygmatic tradition here and throughout the letter is to provide support, rationale, and motivation for the foregoing ethical injunctions (Lohse 1986, 55–59).

Polycarp, bishop of Smyrna (martyred ca. 155 CE), who frequently cites 1 Peter in his *Letter to the Philippians*, combines in an exhortation to a virtuous life (*Phil.* 2:1–3) several expressions reminiscent of 1 Pet 1:13–21:

> Therefore having girded your loins (cf. 1 Pet 1:13), serve God in reverence (cf. 1 Pet 1:17) and truth, putting aside empty futile speaking (cf. 1 Pet 1:18a) and common error, trusting in the one who raised our Lord from the dead and gave him glory (cf. 1 Pet 1:21a, 21b), and a throne on his right hand (cf. 1 Pet 3:22a), to whom are subject all things in heaven and earth (cf. 1 Pet 22c), whom all breath serves, who is coming as the judge of the living and the dead (cf. 1 Pet 4:5), whose blood (cf. 1 Pet 1:19a; 1:2) God will require from those who disobey him (cf. 1 Pet 2:7b, 8b). (Polycarp, *Phil.* 2:1)

21c. *so that your trust may also be* [*your*] *hope in God* (*hōste tēn pistin hymōn kai elpida eis theon*). This clause, involving *hōste* ("so that") and the infinitive *einai* ("may be"), states the intended personal result (BDF §393.3) of Christ's eschatological manifestion, resurrection, and glorification by God; namely, the believers' hopeful trust in God (cf. Selwyn 1947, 147–48). *Pistis* here, as elsewhere (1:5, 7, 9; 5:9; cf. *pisteuō*, 1:8; 2:6, 7), means unshakable and unswerving trust in God evoked by God's raising Jesus from the dead and giving him glory. The entire Greek formulation involving *trust* and *hope* is ambiguous and can be rendered in one of two ways: (a) "so that your trust and hope may be directed to God" or (b) "so that your trust may also be your hope in God." This latter option is supported by the use of the definite article only with *pistin* (viewing the article of $\mathfrak{P}^{72}$ as a secondary addition) and the location of *hymōn* immediately following *pistin*. Since the first option would merely repeat the point of v 21a, the second option, as proposed by Dalton (1974, 272–74), is preferable. This qualification of trust as hope underlines the enduring and eschatological nature of trust; believers confidently trust and entrust themselves to God (4:19), not only in the present but until life's end. The location of *hope* in the final position of the Greek clause makes it emphatic and climactic.

This statement thus constitutes a fitting conclusion to a line of thought calling for hope and holiness on the part of the believers during their alien residence as a consequence of their calling by God and their redemption by Christ. Moreover, this stress on hope, which concludes the unit, balances a similar emphasis on hope at the outset (v 13) and thus forms a deft rhetorical inclusion demarcating and framing the entire passage.

GENERAL COMMENT

Drawing out the first implications of the addressees' conversion, symbolized as "rebirth by God," these verses affirm that as "children" of God they have reason for hope and motive for a holy conduct that distinguish them from nonbelievers. This combined stress on hope and holiness is evident from both the content and the chiastic structure of these verses.

The inclusive stress on "hope" in this set of verses expands on the idea of hope as one of the results of God's "rebirthing" the believers (1:3) and maintains the focus on the enduring trust that believers can place in God (3:15; cf. 4:19; 5:10) as a result of their election, rebirth, sanctification, and redemption. Despite the fact that the family of God finds itself in an "alien" environment, as was so often the case for Israel in the past, it has reason for hope—that is, sustained trust in God; for the One who once liberated his people in Egypt and Babylon has at the end of the ages once more redeemed his own through the blood of the suffering, raised, and glorified Christ. This characteristic quality of hope and trust in God unites the Christian community with the hopeful matriarchs of old (see 3:5), but is animated by a sense of union with the Messiah already revealed and soon to appear one final time. This lively hope also distinguishes the faithful from all present nonbelievers (see 3:15).

The related stress on holiness similarly situates the addressees within the history of Israel, anchors holiness in union with Christ as well as God, and demarcates holy insiders from unholy outsiders, and unholy life prior to rebirth from holy conduct following conversion. Like holy Israel of old living in *paroikia*, the addressees are urged not to conform to Gentile standards of conduct but to obey God and be distinctively holy, as the One who called them is holy. Their holiness is grounded in the holiness of the God who called them and that of Christ, the holy lamb by whose blood they were redeemed. This holiness has both a moral and a social aspect. Holy conduct is obedience, which the children of God owe their divine Father and Judge, an obedience consistent with that of Jesus Christ (1:2). At the same time, the holiness that unites them with God and Christ distinguishes them from impure nonbelievers. Holiness of calling and conduct marks the collective identity of the children of God and is the social boundary demarcating them from unholy outsiders and from their own former past in all of its ignorance and aimlessness.

Several other motifs from Israel's history and strands of early Christian tradition have also been woven together here in a manner typical of the letter as a whole: elements from the Exodus tradition (girded loins [1:13]; redemption [1:17]; blood of the lamb [1:19]; separation and sanctification [1:14–17]; cf. Leaney 1964; Adinolfi 1967b, 319–36); the imperative of the Holiness Code (1:14–16) and features of the sacrificial cult (1:18–19); Israel's experience of *paroikia* (1:17); the suffering servant song of Isaiah (1:19, 21); and primitive Christian hortatory, kerygmatic, and Christological tradition (1:13, 14–15, 17, 18, 19, 20, 21).

Reference to the believers' situation as one of "alien residence," repeated again in 2:11 (cf. also "strangers" and "Diaspora" in 1:1 and "Babylon" in 5:13) underscores the letter's acknowledgement of the Christian brotherhood as a strange and endangered minority, vulnerable to the suspicions and accusations of their neighbors (see also the NOTE and COMMENT on 2:11). This situation and the suffering it provoked is kept firmly in view throughout the letter and constitutes the set of circumstances that 1 Peter is designed to address from 2:11 onward.

Thus in 1:13–21 our author expands on further aspects of God's "rebirthing" action and its implications in terms of hope and holiness, while also laying ground for what follows. In so doing, he advances and develops the line of thought extending from 1:3–2:10, while also preparing for the exhortation of 2:11–5:11. In the unit that immediately follows (1:22–25), he will refer specifically to the holiness or "purity" of the believers (1:22; cf. 1:14–16) and their "obedience" (1:22; cf. 1:14a) as the precondition and impetus for a brotherly and sisterly love with pure hearts (1:22–23) and maintenance of familial solidarity.

For studies on 1 Pet 1:13–21, see Botha 1988; Brandt 1953; Bultmann 1947; Carter 1975; Cervantes Gabarrón 1991a; Cothenet 1980–1981; Dalmer 1898–1899; Dalton 1974; Deichgräber 1967; Elliott 1982; Gatzweiler 1970; Harris 1929–1930; Lash 1982; le Déaut 1961; Meecham 1947; Rasco 1981; Shimada 1966; van Unnik 1969; 1980; Vallauri 1982.

I. C. FAMILIAL LOVE AND REBIRTH THROUGH THE WORD OF THE GOSPEL (1:22–25)

1:22a Having purified yourselves by [your] obedience to the truth
for an unhypocritical brotherly [and sisterly] love,
22b with a pure heart love one another constantly,
23a since you have been born again
not from perishable
but from imperishable seed,
23b through the living and enduring word of God;

24a for
"All humanity [is] as grass
24b and all its glory as the flower of grass;
24c the grass withers,
24d and the flower falls,
25a but the word of the Lord abides for ever."
25b This "word" is the good news that was proclaimed to you.

INTRODUCTION

Expanding further on the image of the believers as the reborn holy children of God (1:3, 14–19), our author now calls for a constant exercise of familial-like love/loyalty essential for the internal cohesion of the family of God, with v 22b serving as the main imperatival clause of this unit. Though distinct from 1:13–21, which is marked by a chiastic structure and an inclusion (vv 13, 21), vv 22–25 are linked with the preceding in a variety of ways. "Purified, pure" (v 22a,b) continue the accent on holiness (1:14–16, 19; cf. 1:2). "Obedience" (v 22a) recalls "children of obedience" (1:14; cf. 1:2), and "born again" (v 23a) resumes the theme of "rebirth" introduced in 1:3. The antithesis of "perishable-imperishable" (v 23b/c) recalls a similar contrast in 1:18–19 and one implied still earlier in 1:4. The concluding statement concerning the "good news" preached to the believers (v 25b) echoes the words of v 12 that similarly concluded vv 3–12. Structurally, vv 24–25 mark the end of this subunit in two ways: (1) here, as elsewhere in the letter, a scriptural quotation grounds and concludes a line of thought (cf. 1:16; 2:3; 2:4–10 concluding 1:3–2:10; 2:17; 3:10–12; 5:5c); (2) reference to the "good news" concludes this unit as it does 1:3–12 (cf. also 4:17). Thus, though a formal subunit, vv 22–25 also serve to maintain and extend the general line of thought begun in 1:3.

At this point in the section of thought extending from 1:3 to 2:10, it is the readers' behavior within the family of the reborn that is in view. An insistence upon the constancy of their love for one another as brothers and sisters (v 22b) is preceded by a statement concerning the basis and goal for this action (v 22a); v 23 further explains this basis; vv 24–25a provide scriptural substantiation (Isa 40:6–8) concerning the permanence of the word of God by which the believers have been reborn; and v 25b clarifies this word of God as that which has been proclaimed to the believers as "good news."

NOTES

22a. *Having purified yourselves by* [*your*] *obedience to the truth* (*Tas psychas hymōn hēgnikotes en tēi hypakoēi tēs alētheias*). This initial phrase recalls 1:14–16 and describes the active role that the addressees played in the process of their conversion from Gentile pollution. The verb *hagnizō*, "purify," in the LXX and NT often denotes ceremonial purification of objects (Num 31:23) or people

(Exod 19:10; 2 Chr 31:18; John 11:35; Acts 21:24, 26; 24:18). But here, as in Jas 4:8 and 1 John 3:3, it denotes moral purification, as the reference to "obedience" makes clear. Thus, the verb functions as a synonym of "being holy" (1:15–16) and, with the adjective "pure" (*katharas*) of v 23, belongs to the letter's broader semantic field of "holiness" (1:2, 12, 15–16, 19; 2:5, 9; 3:5, 15), stressing union with God and separation from former impurity. The verb's perfect tense (*hēgnikotes*), like that of "having been reborn" in v 23, indicates the completed state that now makes the imperative of v 22b possible. Both verbs, along with "obedience to the truth," express aspects of the Christians' completed baptismal conversion, the moral implications of which are now to be explicated in 1:22–2:3.

yourselves translates *tas psychas hymōn* (lit., "your souls"; see the NOTE on 1:9). These words are accentuated in the original Greek through their location at the head of the statement and contrast to "one another" (*allēlous*) in the latter part of the verse, as Hort (1898, 87) has observed. Self-purification and commitment to the truth are a prerequisite for a love of others, but the former are incomplete without the latter.

by [your] obedience to the truth (*en tēi hypakoēi tēs alētheias*) identifies the means of the believers' purification. "Obedience" (*hypakoē*) has already been mentioned as a quality of the "obedient children" (of God), which is consistent with the obedience of Jesus Christ (1:2). In 1:14–16, "obedience" is linked with "holiness" and here with "purification" as the action that distinguishes the believers from their former, preconversion style of life. It belongs to the larger semantic field of terms used in 1 Peter to urge continued submission and fidelity to the will of God (*hypakouō*, 3:6; "will of God," *thelēma* [*tou theou*], 2:15; 3:17; 4:2, 19; "must be," *deon*, 1:16; "be subordinate," *hypotassō*, 2:13, 18; 3:1, 5, 22; 5:5; cf. also 5:2, "in accord with God," *kata theon*; contrast "disobey," *apeitheō*, 2:8; 3:1, 20; 4:17).

The term "truth" (*alētheia*) occurs only here in 1 Peter, but in 5:12 its adjective, *alēthēs*, is used to accentuate "the grace of God" as "true." "Truth," in contrast to lie or falsehood, is that which corresponds exactly to reality. In Christian conceptuality, God is the "father of truth" (2 *Clem*. 3:1; 20:5), whose word is truth (John 17:1) and who has spoken "the word of truth" in Jesus Christ and the gospel (Col 1:5; Eph 1:13; 4:20). Thus, to become a Christian is to be "brought forth by the word of truth" (Jas 1:18) or "to come to the knowledge of the truth" (1 Tim 2:4; 2 Tim 3:7; Heb 10:26; cf. 1 Tim 4:3; 2 John 1) and to be given the responsibility of "obeying the truth" (Gal 5:7; cf. Pfitzner 1970).

In 1 Peter, "truth," like "grace" (cf. 5:12), summarizes in a single term that to which Christian believers have been introduced as a result of their rebirth and that reality by which their actions are controlled. For children born of God and the word of good news, truth has replaced "former ignorance" (1:14; cf. 2:15), and believers, now grounded in the truth, are henceforth to love one another with sincerity (v 22a) and purity of heart (v 22b) and to rid themselves of insincerity or hypocrisy (2:1). Thus, "truth" in this context is synonymous with the "word of God" (vv 23–25). "Obeying the truth," like "obeying the word" (cf. 2:7–8), is a marked feature of the obedient children of God (1:14).

Our translation omits the phrase "through the Spirit" (*dia pneumatos*) found at this point in numerous later manuscipts. Its absence in the earlier and superior manuscipts (𝔓[72] ℵ A B C Ψ etc.) and most ancient versions suggests that this was a later addition inserted to affirm the Spirit's role in the conversion process (cf. 1:2).

for an unhypocritical brotherly [*and sisterly*] *love* (*eis philadelphian anhypokriton*). Rebirth in God's family brings with it familial obligations. Genuine love of one's fellow believers as brothers and sisters in the family of God is indicated as an important goal ("for," *eis*) of purification and conversion.

philadelphian. In Greco-Roman society, the love of blood-brothers and siblings for one another was a highly celebrated virtue as a sign of a harmonious and mutually supportive household/family and a signal of its honorable character and public reputation (Xen., *Mem.* 2.3.19; Plut., *Peri Philadelphias* [*De Fraterno Amore*]; Epict., *Diatr.* 1.11; 2.10.7–9; Mus. Ruf. 15; Lucian, *Dial. d.* 26.2). In Israel, such fraternal affection and familial solidarity was no less prized (see esp. 4 Macc 13:19–4:1; also *T. Gad* 6:1–2; Philo, *Virt.* 192; *Mos.* 1.150; *Legat.* 12). Moreover, the "fraternal" love denoted by *philadelphia* actually included not only brothers (*adelphoi*) but also sisters (*adelphai*), for in this patriarchal society all females were "embedded," as anthropologists put it, in the households of some dominant male (Malina 1993d, 28–62, 117–48). What is said about the family in regard to its male representatives in public life also pertains to its females within the household; see Luke 21:16, where "there is no doubt that *adelphoi = brothers and sisters*" (BAGD s.v.). Thus *philadelphia* properly implies the affection and support shared by sisters as well as brothers of the same kin or surrogate kin group (see, e.g., Ptol., *Apotel.* 3.6, where the topic *peri adelphōn* treats of both males and females). Our present translation adds "and sisterly" in brackets in order to express this fact for contemporary readers. An earlier Israelite extolling of *philadelphia*, 4 Macc 13:9–14:1, contains a juxtaposition of terms describing the affection and loyalty of seven brothers facing martyrdom (*adelphikōs, adelphoi, adelphotēs, philadelphoi, philadelphia*). But there it is the brotherly love of blood siblings that is in view.

In the teaching of Jesus, however, the notion of kin group and family (*oikos*) and thus of "brotherly love" was radically altered. In Greco-Roman society, kinship by blood legally determined who was "sister" and "brother." But the terms could also be used in the figurative sense to identify compatriots (Plato, *Menex.* 239A), friends (Xen., *Anab.* 7.2.25), or members of a religious society (Vet. Val. 4.1; von Soden 1964, 146). In Israel also, these terms were applied not only to natural siblings but to co-religionists who had converted and observed the Mosaic Law according to its contemporary interpretation.[30] Thus, Jesus and

[30] Lev 25:35–36; Deut 15:3, 12; 23:19; 2 Macc 15:14; 1QS VI 22; 1QM XIII 1; XV 4, 7; CD VIII 17, 19; IX 16; Philo, *Spec.* 2.79–80.

his followers spoke of their fellow Israelites as "brothers" (Matt 5:22–24, 47; 7:3–5; 18:15; Acts 2:29; 3:17, 22; 7:2, 37; etc.). Such usage formed a general precedent for similar Christian usage. On the whole, however, the prevailing principle in Israel was that kinship and descent determined community.

With Jesus this principle is reversed and community determines kinship. Or put another way, kinship is redefined as the affiliation of those carrying out God's will. For Jesus, natural descent and bloodlines no longer determine one's relation to God and status within Israel. His declaration that "whoever does the will of my father in heaven is my brother, and sister, and mother" (Matt 12:50/Mark 3:35/Luke 8:21; cf. Matt 23:8) established a new and more inclusive notion of family based, not on blood or Torah observance as officially defined, but on fidelity to God's will and loyalty to God's Messiah. Accordingly, the kingdom of God is interpreted as the household of God (Aalen 1962), followers of Jesus are the "children" of the heavenly Father, believers regard and treat one another as "brothers" and "sisters" united by faith and familial loyalty, and the Christian community as a whole is visualized as the family or household (*oikos*) of God (1 Tim 3:15; Heb 3:1–6; 10:21; 1 Pet 2:5; 4:17; cf. "household of faith," Gal 6:10) or "brotherhood" of the faithful (*adelphotēs*, 1 Pet 2:17; 5:9). Thus in the NT, "brother" (343×) and "sister" (26×) most frequently denote fellow-believers.

Within this family of God, believers are to practice brotherly and sisterly love as well as the good order typical of natural honorable families. This involves nurturing the bonds of affection, being generous and unstinting in the material and emotional support of fellow believers, being respectful of those in authority, avoiding familial strife, maintaining the solidarity of the household, offering hospitality, and conduct in the public arena that will bring honor to both the family and its heavenly father.

While this familial ethos and ethic is evident in virtually all of the NT writings, in 1 Peter it receives an especially accented expression. Here, more than in any other writing of the NT, the themes of God's fatherhood, the rebirth of the believers, their identity as children of God, the community as brotherhood and household of God, and the ethic of the household, its proper order, and the behavior contributing to its cohesion and reputation, are unified in one concerted message concerning the dignity and honor of the household of God (Elliott 1981/1990, 165–266; see also GENERAL INTRODUCTION, 6. Aim and Strategy).

Brotherly and sisterly love was urgently promoted in early Christianity (Rom 12:9–10; 1 Thess 4:9; Heb 13:1; 2 Pet 1:7; cf. Sedlaczek 1894). Its Christian accentuation reflects not only the importance attributed to action that assured the cohesion of the community but also the movement's understanding of itself as a new family of God. In 1 Peter, *philadelphia* and its related terms *philadelphoi* ("loving of brothers [and sisters]," 3:8), *philoxenoi* ("hospitable," 4:9), and *philēma* ("kiss," sign of familial affection) express the behavior that, like love (1:22b; 2:17; 4:8; 5:14), compassion (3:8), mutual respect (3:8; 5:6), and mutual service (4:8–11), is encouraged to enforce the emotional and social bonds within the "brotherhood" (*adelphotēs*, 2:17; 5:9) or "household of God" (2:5; 4:17). See Elliott 1981/1990, 75, 83, 139, 145, 202 and the COMMENT for elaboration of these points.

1 Clement 47:5 notes that the Christians of Corinth were famous for their "brotherly love" (cf. also 48:1 and 1 Cor 13, which may have inspired this thought). Brotherly love was even a Christian mark of distinction in the eyes of pagan adversaries. When in the following century Christians were rounded up to die in the arena, R. Lane Fox observes (1986, 324), "the crowds, said Tertullian, would shout 'Look how these Christians love one another.'" Such Christian love, Lane Fox goes on to note, "was public knowledge and must have played its part in drawing outsiders to the faith."[31]

unhypocritical (*anypokriton*) marks a brotherly love that is genuine, authentic, sincere, without dissimulation (Rom 12:9; 2 Cor 6:6), and in accord with the "truth." Thus, it anticipates the sense of "pure heart" (v 22b) and contrasts with "insincerity" (*hypokrisis*, 2:1), which is to be avoided.

22b. *with a pure heart love one another constantly* (*ek katharas kardias allēlous agapēsate ektenōs*). This imperative constitutes the main clause of vv 22–23 and follows logically from the preceding. The command to "love one another" (*allēlous agapēsate*) spells out the implications of "for brotherly love," and "with a pure heart" (*ek katharas kardias*) rephrases "unhypocritical"; for the expression "pure of heart," see also Matt 5:8. That Christians should love and cherish one another, as the author repeatedly enjoins them to do (see also 2:17; 3:8; 4:8; 5:14; and respective NOTES), would not only be consonant with the command of their Lord (Matt 22:36–39 / Mark 12:30–31 / Luke 10:27; John 13:34–35; 15:12–17); it is also essential to their cohesion and survival as a social movement. On love in 1 Peter with stress on its "fraternal" character, see also Spicq 1965, 2:342–65.

In contrast to modern individualistic notions of love and romantic sentimentality, "love" (*agapē, agapeō*) for the ancients denoted devoted attachment and loyalty to one's group and its significant figures (Malina 1993c, 110–14). This was a consequence of the fact that the ancients were oriented primarily not to *individuals* but to their primary *group* (Malina 1993d, 63–89). Their experience had taught them that a meaningful existence required total reliance on the group in which one was embedded, be it kin group, surrogate kin group, village group, or any other association one might join. For Christians, that primary group was the community of the faithful, however it might be named. "Love" within this conceptual framework entailed both an inward feeling of attachment expressed in an outward manifestation of loyalty to God, Jesus, and fellow group members and an unrelenting commitment to this group's

---

[31] On the use of the terms "brother" and "sister" as designations for fellow-believers, see Schelkle 1954 and von Soden 1964; on the factors contributing to the shift from natural to surrogate kinship in Israel, see Eilberg-Schwartz 1990, 195–216; on *philadelphia* and related terms, see Sedlaczek 1894; von Soden 1964; Brady 1961. See also the NOTES and COMMENTS on 2:17 (*adelphotēs*); 3:8 (*philadelphoi*); 4:8 (*agapē*); and 5:12 (*adelphos*).

values and beliefs. For the early Christians facing a hostile society, such commitment was essential for the very survival of the movement. Thus love and other expressions of commitment and mutual support figure prominently as imperatives of Christian behavior, not only in 1 Peter, but throughout the early Christian literature. Even among Christians' adversaries, brotherly love became a hallmark of Christian identity (Laue Fox 1986, 323–25). The reciprocal pronoun "one another" (*allēlous*) explicitly expresses the reciprocal character of this internal bond in 1 Peter (cf. also 4:9; 5:5b, 14) and throughout the NT, where it occurs some one hundred times (see Lohfink 1984, 99–106).

with a pure heart (*ek katharas kardias*). These words describe the internal origin of this commitment. The adjective *kathara* ("pure") was omitted in some important manuscripts (B A etc.) but was included in other weighty manuscripts ($\mathfrak{P}^{72}$ ℵ* C P Ψ 𝔐 etc.). Its omission was possibly a case of double homoeoarcton involving the terms *katharas* and *kardias*. The heart (*kardia*; cf. also 3:4, 15) was viewed as the seat of rational thought, disposition, and volition, as well as of emotion (cf. Behm 1965). A "pure heart" or "purity of heart" meant singleness of purpose (*T. Naph*. 3:1; *T. Jos*. 4:6; Matt 5:8; 2 Tim 2:22; cf. Acts 15:9: "purify your hearts"). Love proceeds from the heart (*T. Sim*. 4:6–7; *T. Dan* 5:3), and a love "from a pure heart" denoted love that was genuine and "without hypocrisy" (1 Tim 1:5). Virtually identical expressions are contained in *T. Gad* 6:3, "Love one another from the heart" (*agapēsate allēlous apo kardias*—in contrast to "guile," *dolos*; cf. 1 Pet 2:1) and 7:7, "love one another with singleness of heart" (*agapēsate allēlous en euthytēti kardias*—in contrast to "envy," 7:2, 4, 6; cf. *T. Sim*. 4:7; and 1 Pet 2:1). Loving one another with a *pure* heart, like *sincere* brotherly love, is consistent with obedience to the *truth* (v 21a) and contrasts with "guile" and the other vices condemned in 2:1.

constantly (*ektenōs*). While the notion of loving one another "with a pure heart" is conventional, the additional qualification given by the adverb *ektenōs* is not. Our author makes a similar appeal in 4:8, "maintain constant (*ektene*) love toward one another." The RSV renders *ektenōs* "earnestly" and the NRSV, "deeply." But the following verses, which elaborate on the implications of this term, are concerned with the issue of imperishability, permanence, and endurance, a note also sounded in 1:4, 18–19 and 5:4 (cf. Evang 1989). Thus, in this context, "it is not so much warmth or intensity of love that *ektenōs* expresses, as strenuousness and steady earnestness in it as opposed to fitfulness and caprice. . . . Love of the brethren was not to be such as would shew itself in casual bursts of emotion, but in a deliberate principle of life" (Hort 1898, 91, 93). "Unremittingly" (Hort 1898, 93; Michaels 1988, 76) also captures this sense and points to a love that in the face of adversity must remain constant and enduring.

The reflection here of baptismal tradition is suggested by the similar thought of Heb 10:22–24: "let us draw near with a true heart in full assurance of faith, with our hearts sprinkled clean from an evil conscience and our bodies washed with pure water . . . and let us consider how to stir up one another to love and good works."

Verses 23–25 attach directly to the foregoing verse (1 Pet 1:22) and provide further logical and scriptural substantiation for the necessary "constancy" of brotherly love (cf. the antithesis of "perishable-imperishable" and the verb "endure," vv 23, 25). They pose, however, several questions concerning word usage and train of thought that require clarification. These include the meaning of the term *spora* (v 23a); the logic of the comparison between "imperishable" and "perishable" *spora* and "word of God" (v 23bc); the point of the contrast between perishing humanity or grass (v 14abc), on the one hand, and the enduring word of the Lord (v 25a), on the other; the reason for the identification of this word with the good news proclaimed (v 25b; cf. 1:12); and finally, the thematic significance of the continued accentuation on "word" here, in 2:2 (*logikos*), and in 2:8. The interweaving of images and sources in the elaboration of an overall line of thought, as we find it here, is typical of the author's style and artistry, as 1:18–21; 2:4–10, 21–25; and 3:18–22 also illustrate. A settling of particular linguistic issues, therefore, requires attention to context and broader themes under development.

23a. *since you have been born again* (*anagegennēmenoi*). The image of conversion as a "rebirth," with which the letter began (1:3), reappears, rather logically, in a context dealing with brotherly love and familal relations. At this point, the perfect passive plural participle *anagegennēmenoi* with "you" as the subject balances the preceding perfect participle *hegnikotēs* (v 22a) and likewise introduces a condition of Christian conversion—now its divine origin (cf. John 1:13; 3:3;1 John 3:9; 4:7–8). Both participles are subordinate to and modify the main verb *agapēsate*. Earlier, God the Father was praised as the divine agent of Christian rebirth (*anagennēsas*, 1:13). Here the verb is repeated in a statement describing God's living and enduring word as the "seed" or "sowing" that has produced new birth.

23b. *not from perishable but from imperishable seed* (*ouk ek sporas phthartēs alla aphthartou*). This phrase and the following phrase, *through the living and enduring word of God*, qualify the preceding participle *since you have been born again*. This juxtaposition indicates a relation between the two phrases and between "seed" and "word" (*logos*) in particular. It also indicates an equivalency between the "living and enduring" quality of the word (cf. also v 25), on the one hand, and "imperishable" seed, on the other. Emphasized here is the enduring quality that brought the believers into being. But questions concerning the specific meaning of *spora*, what kind of *spora* could be either perishable or imperishable, and what weight is to be given to the fact that different prepositions are used to introduce each phrase ("from" [*ek*] and "through" [*dia*]) require clarification.

The feminine noun *hē spora* (only NT occurrence) can denote the activity of "sowing" (4 Kdgms 19:29; and in a figurative sense, "procreation"), that which is "sown," or the "seed" sown (1 Macc 10:30). It is a paronym of the masculine noun *ho sporos*, which can also mean "sowing" or "seed" (BAGD s.vv.). Both nouns are related to the verb *speirō* ("sow seed"), *to sperma* ("seeds," male semen, or progeny), and the noun *diaspora* (lit., "scattering [of seed]"). The specific meaning of *hē spora*, like that of its paronyms, is generally determined by its context. The variant reading "from perishable perishing" (א A C) is no doubt the result of scribal auditory error.

In its present context, *spora* could denote either "seed" or "sowing." If taken as "seed," "perishable seed" (*spora phthartēs*; cf. the same adjective in 1:18) would be illustrated by the "flower" of grass (containing the seed) mentioned in v 24 (quoting Isa 40:6–8). As this flower falls (and dies), so some seed is "perishable." "Imperishable seed" (*sporas aphthartou*), on the other hand, is like the "living and enduring word of God," for it continues to be the source of new life. In this sense, the equation of "seed" (*hē spora*) with the word of God would parallel a similar equation of "seed" (*ho sporos*) and word of God in the parable of the sower (Luke 8:11; cf. Mark 4:14; Kokot 1974). The sense of *spora* as an action ("sowing") is preferred by Michaels (1988, 76), but his translation "not from the planting of perishable seed but from imperishable" is awkward and states more than the original Greek contains. The shift of prepositions from *ek* ("from") to *dia* ("through") in the related phrases perhaps is due not so much to the reference of *spora* "to the process of sowing" (so Michaels) as to the distinction being made between the *source* of regeneration ("imperishable seed") and the *instrument* of its communication ("God's living and enduring word"), as Selwyn (1947, 150–51) suggests. While *ek* is used with the verb for birth (*gennaō*) to indicate its *source* (Matt 1:3, 5; John 1:13; 1 John 3:9), *dia* is employed in 1 Peter to express the *means* of rebirth ("through the resurrection of Jesus Christ from the dead," 1:3), as well as the *means* of the proclaiming of the good news (1:12), a motif reiterated later in the same context (v 25b). The two phrases thus express the double aspect of the word of God as seed: it is both the imperishable source and the enduring means of Christian rebirth (and continuing nourishment, 2:2).

23c. *through the living and enduring word of God* (*dia logou zōntos theou kai menontos*). This phrase identifies the "imperishable seed" through which (*dia*) the believers were reborn as *the living and enduring word of God*. The adjectival participles "living" (*zōntos*) and "enduring" (*menontos*) are used to describe God in Dan 6:26 (cf. 1 Thess 1:9, "living and true God"), but here they modify God's word (*logou*), which is the chief focus of attention (cf. Heb. 4:12; 1 John 1:1; 2:14; LaVerdiere 1974). In all likelihood, "enduring" (*menontos*) has been suggested by the terminology of the Isaiah text about to be quoted (*menei*, v 25a). The expression "forever" (*eis ton aiōna* or *eis tous aiōnas*), modifying "enduring" in several manuscripts, has weak support and appears to be prompted by the phrase "endure forever" in v 25a. The double appearance of the verb "endure" (vv 23, 25) establishes the grounds for the "constant" practice of brotherly love (v 22). The association of this living and enduring word with the "good news" of Jesus' suffering and glorification becomes evident in the interpretation given to "word of the Lord" in vv 24–25, as discussed below.

In vv 24–25, scriptural substantiation for the imperishability of the regenerative word is supplied by a quotation from Isa 40:6–8, where human impermanence is compared with perishable grass and contrasted to the permanence of God's word. Petrine minor and inconsequential deviations from the LXX Isaiah text (except for "Lord" for "our God") may be due to use of a text varying in minor points from that of modern critical editions (see the Petrine insertion of *hōs* ["as"] before "grass;" substitution of *autēs* for *anthrōpou* and of *kyriou* for *tou theou hēmōn*). Variant readings in the manuscripts appear to have arisen from scribal attempts to conform the text of 1 Peter to that of the LXX. The portion of the quotation cited in v 24 (Isa 40:6–7) illustrates the nature of impermanence and perishability characteristic of "perishable seed" (v 23b), while Isa 40:8 cited in v 25a illustrates the enduring quality of the divine word mentioned in v 23c. The fuller force of this Isaian text and its significance for the message of 1 Peter in general becomes evident when its broader context is taken into consideration. This prophecy opens Deutero-Isaiah, the book of the consolation of Israel (Isa 40–55) addressed to an exiled and oppressed people living as strangers in the strange land of Babylon. It offers them comfort, "good news," and the prospect of salvation. Both the situation and the message are particularly apposite to that of 1 Peter and this, in turn, suggests why 1 Peter displays such an interest in this particular OT writing.

24ab. *for "All humanity* [*is*] *as grass and all its glory as the flower of grass"* (*dioti pasa sarx hōs chortos kai pasa doxa autēs hōs anthos chortou*). The quotation is introduced with the conjunction "for" (*dioti*), as in the scriptural citations in 1:16 and 2:6 ("for it is written"). The formulation is elliptical, with an "is" implied. The first occurrence of the comparative *hōs* ("as," "like") is not present in the Isaiah text (and several MSS) and transforms the original metaphor ("all humanity is grass") into a simile. This could well be an addition of our author, for the frequent use of this comparative (27×) is a special feature of the letter (see the NOTE on 4:10c). The couplet is a synonymous parallelism with the sense of its first half further expanded in its latter half. The expression *pasa sarx* (literally, "all flesh") is a conventional phrase meaning humanity in its totality (Baumgärtel 1971, 106) and is likened to grass (*chortos*), its flower (*anthos*) and splendor or glory (*doxa*). The ordinary "glory" and honor of mortals is no more permanent than the glory of perishing grass.

24cd. *"the grass withers, and the flower falls"* (*exēranthē ho chortos kai to anthos exepesen*). The first line of the citation (v 24ab) states the terms of the comparison. The second line (v 24cd) expresses its sobering implications: all humanity, like grass, is finite, and its glory, short-lived and perishing. *Sic transit gloria mundi*.

25a. *"but the word of the Lord endures forever"* (*to de rhēma kyriou menei eis ton aiōna*). The final line of these Isaian verses expresses a dramatic yet consoling contrast: human beings perish, but (*de*) the word of the Lord persists. The fact of the permanence of God's word in contrast to the transitoriness of human life has, for both Isaiah and 1 Peter, social as well as personal implications. At the outset of Deutero-Isaiah's consoling message of "good news" (40:9), this fact implied God's continuing control over history and the wars of nations (40:1–2), his power to reverse the degraded state of his people, and as a shepherd to lead them home (40:3–5, 9–11). In the immediate context of our letter, the certain endurance of God's word provides motivation for the necessary endurance of Christian brotherly love. James (1:10–11), on the other hand, uses Isa 40:6–7 to contrast the exalting of the humble and the passing of the wealthy. The resonance that further aspects of Isaiah's good news find in 1 Peter indicates the accuracy of C. H. Dodd's observation (1953, 126) that citations of specific OT verses in the NT generally serve as "pointers" to more encompassing "total context[s]." Our author's use of Isaiah and Ps 33[34] is especially illustrative of this fact. See GENERAL INTRODUCTION 2.1. for Petrine citations of and allusions to these OT texts.

The term for "word" (v 25 ab) is *rhēma*, a term akin to *logos* ("word") occurring in v 23; it denotes the *activity* of "speaking" as well as the words uttered (BAGD s.v.; Repo 1951). The reading of *kyriou* ("of the Lord") in place of *tou theou hēmōn* ("of our God") is the most significant variation from the LXX text. This could indicate either the use of a variant LXX text or a quotation from memory or an assumed equation of *kyrios* and *theos* (see Isa 40:3, where they are synonymous). The Petrine context, however, makes it likely that the change was deliberate. Verse 25b contains the author's own clarification of the word spoken of in the Isaian text and its import for the readers. This verse ("this 'word' is the good news that was proclaimed to you") relates the "word" of v 25a to the previous statement of vv 10–12 concerning the good news regarding Christ (v 11b) that was proclaimed to the addressees (v 12b). Thus, for our author the "good news" of the word concerns Jesus Christ, and this association prompted the substitution of "Lord" (referring to Jesus Christ) for "God" in v 25a.

This reason for the alteration is further confirmed by the identification of "Lord" (*kyrios*) in 2:2 (quoting Ps 33:9[34:8]) with Jesus Christ in the verses that follow (2:4–5) and by the regular Petrine identification of Jesus as *kyrios* (1:3; 2:13; 3:15), with the reservation of *theos* for God the Father (1:2, 3, 5, 21, 23, etc.), except in an OT citation (3:12). The Isaian phrase *rhēma tou theou hēmōn* is a subjective genitive construction (the word that our God speaks). But our author's substitution of "Lord" for "God," along with the echo of vv 10–12 in vv 24–25, suggest that he intended this as an objective genitive construction: the word *about* the Lord. From his perspective, the word that endures forever is the word about Jesus Christ, his suffering, and glorification. This constitutes the heart of the good news for his suffering audience and the word from which they are to draw constant nourishment (2:3). According to this same equation of good news about the Christ and word of the Lord, the "word" through which they have been reborn (v 23) likewise implies the proclamation of the good news of Jesus' suffering and glorification and thereby provides a Christological and evangelical motivation for brotherly love. The point made here is analogous to that of 1:18–21. As believers were redeemed by a superior means (Christ's precious blood, 1:18), so they were born anew from a superior eternal seed. Both statements are designed to convince the readers of the superior quality of their new life as children of God.

25b. *This "word" is the good news that was proclaimed to you* (*touto de estin to rhēma to euaggelisthen eis hymas*). This clause constitutes the author's clarification of the preceding phrase, "word of the Lord" (v 25a), and its implications for the readers. The aorist passive participle *euaggelisthen* ("that was proclaimed as good news") recalls the thought of vv 10–12, where the "proclaiming of good news" (*euaggelisamenōn*, v 12b) concerns the sufferings and glorification of the Christ (v 11). By explicitly identifying the "word" (*rhēma*) of the Isaiah citation as the "good news" (cf. Isa 40:9) proclaimed to the readers, and by linking this word with Jesus Christ (*kyrios* substituted for *theos*), the author interprets his source Christologically (cf. also "through Jesus Christ," 1:3, 21; 2:5; 3:21; 4:11) and links the enduring word of God (v 25a) as the means (*dia*) of rebirth (v 23) with the "good news" (v 12b) through (*dia*) which the readers have been reborn (1:3). Accordingly, "the word that was preached to you as good news" (v 25b) interprets "the word of the Lord" in the Isaiah text, which in turn illustrates the permanent character of the "the living and enduring word" symbolized as "imperishable seed" through which the believers have been reborn (v 22b). The interpretation of *rhēma* as Christian proclamation occurs also in Rom 10:8 (citing Deut 30:17). Similarly, the equation of "word" (*logos*) with "seed" as a symbol of the gospel that is preached recalls the allegorized interpretation of the sower parable in Mark 4:1–9, 13–20 par. and the metaphor of "sowing" for evangelical proclamation (Matt 13:24–30; 1 Cor 9:11). On the use of Isa 40:6–8 here, see also Schutter 1989, 124–29.

The phrase "to you" (*eis hymas*), located last for emphasis, once again illustrates the stress placed in this letter on the "for-you-ness" of the good news (see NOTE on 1:4). Their privileged reception of this good news marks the divinely conferred dignity of the believers in contrast to their public demeaning, and the enduring power of this good news provides the strength for their familial solidarity. This subunit concludes, as does 1:3–12 and 4:12–19, on an encouraging note of good news.

GENERAL COMMENT

These verses, on the whole, continue the general line of thought introduced in 1:3 by clarifying the source and instrumentality of the believers' rebirth (1:3, 23), the word of God preached as good news concerning Jesus Christ (vv 23–25), and by underlining the necessity of brotherly and sisterly love by which the internal solidarity of the household of God is secured (v 22). The terminology and images ("purified," "obedience to the truth," "reborn . . . through the living and enduring word of God") are obvious allusions to the event of baptism, through which believers have become children of God and members of the family of God (Scharlemann 1959; Goppelt 1993, 126). Other traces of early Christian baptismal tradition in 1 Peter (Selwyn 1947, 369–439), along with the explicit reference to baptism in 3:21, indicate the extent to which the letter as a whole is an explication of the dignity and responsibility conferred by baptism (Brooks 1974). These frequent allusions to baptism and its moral implications, however, offer no cogent reason for assuming that the letter as a whole constituted an original baptismal homily or portion of a baptismal liturgy, as has often been suggested (see GENERAL INTRODUCTION, Genre). Nor is there any compelling support for the conjecture (Windisch and Preisker 1951, 156–60) that these verses presume that an actual baptism had taken place between v 20 and v 21 of the preceding unit because of the shift to the present tense in v 21 and perfect tense verbs in vv 22–23. The genre of this writing is, rather, that of a genuine letter and is addressed to persons who from the outset of the writing are regarded as elect (1:1), sanctified (1:2), reborn (1:3), and children (of God) (1:14). Verses 22–25, like vv 14–16, instead recall that baptismal experience and elaborate its implications for behavior within the Christian community.

Through baptism and rebirth, believers have become not only children of God but also brothers and sisters one of another. This new identity entails the responsibility of familial love and loyalty to fellow believers. This love is to be constant and enduring because the word through which they have been reborn, the gospel, is itself enduring and makes love's constancy possible.

In regard to the citation from Isaiah 40:6–8, which is employed to substantiate the enduring nature of the word of God by which they have been reborn, the broader context of this Isaian passage indicates its particular relevance for the whole of this letter (see also Hort 1898, 94; Selwyn 1947, 152). In fact, it could well have been the similarity of the precarious situations faced by both authors and the power of Isaiah's response that inspired our author's frequent use of this writing. As Isaiah addressed Judean exiles in Babylon (43:14; 47:1; 48:14, 20) as a people reproached, reviled (51:7; 53:1–12), and refined by fire (48:10), so our author from his Babylon (5:13) addresses strangers and resident aliens (1:1, 17; 2:11), harried and abused in their society (2:12; 3:9, 13–17; 4:4, 12–19; 5:9), and likewise tested in the fire of affliction (1:6; 4:12). As the exodus and God's redemptive liberation of his people from darkness to light provided a model for Isaiah (40:3–5; 42:6, 7, 13, 16; 43:1–21; 52:3, 9), so also for 1 Peter (1:13, 18–19; 2:9). As the covenant and Israel's divine election were for Isaiah's message grounds for confidence, hope, and praise (41:8, 9; 42:1, 10–13; 43:10, 21; 44:1–2; 49:7; 54:10), so too for 1 Peter (1:1; 2:4–10). Isaiah's optimistic appraisal, to all appearances, of a dire situation likewise is matched by that of the Petrine author. As Isaiah celebrates the glory of God (40:5; 41:16; 42:8, 12, etc.), so too our author (2:12; 4:11, 13, 14; 5:10). And as Isaiah's proclamation of good news (40:9; 52:7) and encouragement (40:1; 42:10–13) is permeated by a note of joy and exultation (41:16; 49:13; 51:3, 11; 54:1–17; 55:1–13), so too the message of 1 Peter (1:6–8; 2:9; 4:13).

The point in noting these similarities is not to suggest extensive literary dependency, however much the terminology of 1 Peter resembles that of Isaiah. These affinities rather illustrate a common mood and outlook permeating 2 Isaiah and 1 Peter and a similar manner of assessing present and future possibilities in the light of past events. While the Petrine author directly quotes from 2 Isaiah on several occasions and alludes to its formulations and motifs in other instances, it is the generally confident and consoling tone of the prophet, despite adverse conditions, that so typically permeates the letter as well. The relation of 1 Peter to Ps 33[34] can be seen in the same light. Our author's final comment on this Isaian passage (v 25) specifically identifies the word concerning the Lord as the good news proclaimed *to you*, once again underlining the "for-you-ness" of the good news.

The theme of rebirth does not end with these verses. The following subunit, 2:1–3, continues to expand on this theme (2:2) as well as on the notion of the word (1:23, 25) as source of nourishment (2:2–3). Moreover, the negative imperative of 2:1 contrasts to the preceding positive imperative of 1:23 (see Elliott 1966b, 199–218 on the developing line of thought). Positively, the obedience to the truth and sincerity of brotherly love require an end to insincerity and guile (2:1). And the word through which they have been reborn is the same word on which they are to continue to feed in their growth toward salvation.

For studies on 1 Pet 1:22–25, see Bishop 1953; Blendinger 1967; Danker 1967b; Elliott 1982; Evang 1989; Kokot 1974; LaVerdiere 1974; Parsons 1978; Scharlemann 1959.

I. D. Renunciation of Evil; Nourishment and Growth of the Reborn through the Word (2:1–3)

2:1 Therefore rid yourselves of all evil and
all guile and
hypocrisy and
envying and
all slandering.
2a As newborn babies,
hunger for the guileless milk of the word,
2b so that by it you may grow up toward salvation,
3 since
"you have tasted that the Lord is good."

INTRODUCTION

While extending the foregoing line of thought, 2:1–3 constitutes a specific subunit. Its structure is similar to that of 1:14–16 (and with minor differences, 1:22–25). An initial negative injunction (v 1) is followed by a positive one (v 2), and the thought is concluded with a substantiating biblical quotation (v 3). Our author expands on his preceding remarks in two chief ways. First (v 1), he calls for the renunciation of all types of evil and hypocrisy that undermine the internal solidarity of the community and inhibit the unhypocritical practice of brotherly and sisterly love (1:22). Second, as a positive counterpart to this renunciation of guile and wrongful behavior, he urges the addressees as "newborn babies" to yearn eagerly for the guileless milk of the word that will fortify their growth toward salvation (v 2). The phrase "newborn babies" continues the theme of rebirth (1:3, 22); the previous metaphor of word-as-seed (means of rebirth) is balanced by the metaphor of word-as-milk (means of nourishment); and the focus now advances from the origin of Christian life to the process of its growth. Finally, the imperative of v 2 is substantiated in v 3 with a citation of Scripture (Ps 33[34]:9), a use of Scripture already noted in 1:16 and 1:24–25a. On the development of this "rebirth-word-growth" theme from 1:3 onward, see Elliott 1966b, 199–207.

NOTES

2:1. *Therefore rid yourselves of all evil and all guile and hypocrisy and envying and all slander* (*Apothemenoi oun pasan kakian kai panta dolon kai hypokriseis kai phthonous kai pasas katalalias*).

Therefore (*oun*). *Oun* is an inferential conjunction that serves here and elsewhere in 1 Peter (4:1, 7; 5:1, 6) to introduce an imperatival inference being drawn with reference to the foregoing. It appears often in and signals the use of parenetic tradition (Nauck 1958). Here it indicates the connection of 2:1–3 with the preceding verses and the imperatival force of the aor. middle part. *apothemenoi* ("rid yourselves") that it accompanies.

rid yourselves of (*apothemenoi*). The plural participle (with "you" as implied subject) is unaccompanied by a finite verb and has imperatival force, a use of the participle typical of this letter; see the NOTE on 1:14b. The verb *apotithēmi* can denote the "taking off" of clothes (2 Macc 8:35; Josephus, *Ant*. 8.266; Acts 7:58; *Mart. Pol*. 13:2). More frequently it has the figurative sense of "laying aside," "abandoning," "renouncing," or "ridding oneself" of something, with the preposition *apo-* having separative force ("put *off*"; cf. *apo-dokimazō* ["reject, dis-miss"], 2:4, 7; *ap-echō* ["ab-stain, stay *away from*"], 2:11). In the NT it is used, as here, to urge ridding oneself of wicked dispositions and forms of behavior typical of life prior to baptismal conversion (Rom 13:12–14; Eph 4:22–32; Col 3:8–10; Heb 12:1–2; Jas 1:21). All of these texts, as also 1 Pet 2:2, combine a negative command of renunciation with a positive command of "putting on" or engaging in behavior appropriate to the new life. That this reflects features of traditional baptismal catechesis is likely (Selwyn 1947, 393–400; Kamlah 1964, 34–38, 183–89), especially in the light of 3:21, where the related noun "putting off" (*apothesis*) is used in conjunction with "baptism" (*baptisma*). A further development of this tradition is evident in later baptismal liturgies, where the candidate puts off old clothing before descending into the pool and dons new attire upon emerging from the water, thereby symbolizing the abandonment of old ways and adoption of a new life of innocence (J. N. D. Kelly 1969, 83–84; cf. Hipp., *Apost. Trad*. 21; Cyril of Jerusalem, *Myst. Cat*. 2.2; *Procat*. 4). From this later tradition Kelly concluded that *apothemenoi* should be regarded not as an imperative but as a true aorist participle, which indicates an action that has already taken place at baptism. In this case, "having put off" would recall "having purified yourselves" in 1:22a and would provide, as this earlier participle does, the basis for the imperative that follows (1:22b; 2:2). However, later exhortation to abstain from "fleshly desires" (2:11; 4:2–3) indicates that the renunciation in baptism is not regarded as a once-for-all occurrence but requires continual reenactment of a one-time commitment.

What follows is a general list of vices to be avoided as barriers to the practice of "unhypocritical brotherly and sisterly love" (1:22; cf. further lists in 4:3, 15). The vices are those generally condemned in Greco-Roman and Israelite cultures as well (Vögtle 1936; Wibbing 1959). Christians adopted such conventional lists to illustrate traits and actions that were incompatible with the new life conferred by God and destructive of communal solidarity.[32]

all. The threefold use of "all" (*pas*), modifying "evil," "guile," and "slander," conveys the sense of totality and inclusiveness (no exceptions!) and frames this list.

evil. The Greek term *kakia* that heads this list is the most generic of the vices mentioned, embracing virtually all that follow. It can denote "trouble" or "misfortune" (1 Kdgms 6:9; Eccl 7; 12:1; Sir 19:6; Matt 6:34) but is used more often in the moral sense of "wickedness," "malice," "ill-will," and of disposition and behavior ("wrongdoing") contrary to conventional morality. In 1 Peter it belongs to a field of terms ("wrong" [*kakos*, 3:9, 10–12]; "do what is wrong" [*kakopoieō*, 3:17]; "wrongdoer" [*kakopoios*, 2:12, 14; 4:15]; "harm," "do wrong to" [*kakoō*, 3:13]), some instances of which concern wrongdoing to be avoided and other instances, wrongdoing falsely ascribed to the believers by their adversaries. This suggests that while evil/wrongdoing in 2:1 is mentioned in the same breath with other terms clearly the counterpart of "brotherly love" in 1:22, the author already may be thinking of these charges of wrongdoing and exhorting the readers to avoid giving outsiders any basis for their accusations (cf. esp. 2:14, 16; 3:10–12; 4:15). As our author later makes clear, doing what is wrong is contrary not simply to societal norms but to the will of God, which is the ultimate criterion for distinguishing doing what is wrong from doing what is right (2:12, 16; 3:8–12, 17; 4:15–16, 19).

guile. *Dolos* ("guile," "deceit," "cunning," "treachery") occurs in lists of proscribed vices (Mark 7:22; Rom 1:29; *Did*. 5:1; *Barn*. 20:1) but in this context also represents the counterpart to the "truth" (1:22a) and "pure heart" (1:22b) mentioned in the previous unit. Ridding yourselves of all guile (*dolos*) likewise forms the pendant to "hunger for the guileless (*adolon*) milk of the word" (2:2a). Since cohesive family relations are built on truth and genuineness, guile/deceit is intolerable within the brotherhood. Similarly, the practice of guile/deceit would be incompatible with yearning for the unadulterated and guileless milk

---

[32] See the texts listed in the NOTE on 4:3. On the parenetic character of this motif and its baptismal setting, see Selwyn 1947, 393–400; and Kamlah 1964, 183–89.

of the word. "Speaking guile" (i.e., deceitfully) is later condemned in 3:10–11 (quoting Ps 33[34]:14) as an example of doing what is wrong (*kakon*) in contrast to doing what is right (*agathon*). Christ, on the other hand, is characterized as free from guile in 2:22b (echoing Isa 53:9), and his depiction there as a model for the believers (2:21–23) would, in retrospect, apply here as well.

hypocrisy. The Greek plural of this term (*hypokriseis*) and *katalalias* ("slandering") is preferred, as conforming with the plural *phthonous* ("envying"), over the manuscripts that support the singular for the first (B א[1] some Old Latin versions) and last (א*) of these final three vices. The plurals (translated with singular terms) cover the varied forms by which all three vices are manifested. "Hypocrisy" is "playing a part," "pretense," or "outward show," which generally involves insincerity and deceitful intention (Matt 23:28; Mark 12:15; Luke 12:1; Gal 2:13; 1 Tim 4:2). Like "guile," it is the opposite of "truthfulness" and "genuineness" and characterizes persons lacking integrity (as in Jesus' condemnation of his opponents as "hypocrites" whose actions do not match their words, Matt 6:2, 5, 16; 23:13–15; Mark 7:6; Luke 13:15). Hypocritical forms of behavior are the precise opposite of the exercise of "unhypocritical" brotherly love (1:22a) and, like "guile," are incompatible with loving with a "pure" heart (1:22b).

envying, literally, "envies" (*phthonous*). Envy (*phthonos*), the displeasure at the success or health or possessions of another and the malevolent desire to see these things destroyed, was regarded by the ancients as one of the most pernicious of all the vices[33] and was associated especially with the malicious "evil eye" (Elliott 1988, 1990, 1991, 1992c, 1994; Limberis 1991). In the conflict-ridden society of antiquity, where all the resources of life were regarded as limited in quantity, any advance on the part of some was regarded as a diminishment of the status of others (Foster 1965, 1972; Malina 1993d, 90–116). In this zero-sum game and agonistic context, envy and the evil eye were symptomatic of the constant struggle between the "haves" and the "have-nots." Envy and the evil eye were associated with greed, miserliness, and the refusal to share one's goods with those in need. The history of Israel is replete with stories of envy and its disastrous results (Cain and Abel, Sarah and Hagar, Joseph and his brothers, Saul and David). According to popular wisdom, "an envious evil-eyed person begrudges bread and it is lacking at his table" (Sir 14:10; cf. 18:18; Deut 28:54–57; Prov 23:6–8). Envy "blinds the mind" (*T. Sim.* 2:6–7), and "the gift of a begrudging evil-eyed person makes the eyes dim" (Sir 18:18). "What has been created more evil than the envious evil eye? It sheds tears from every face" (Sir 31:13). The spirit of envy, notes one Israelite treatise on the subject, "makes the soul savage and corrupts the body; it foments anger and war in the mind, excites the shedding of blood, drives the mind to distraction, arouses tumult in the soul, and trembling in the body" (*T. Sim.* 4:8).

---

[33] See Arist., *Rhet.* 2.10.1387B–88A; Cyprian, *De Zelo et Livore*; Basil, *Homily 11 on Envy*; Walcott 1978.

As the Torah warned against envy and the evil eye (Deut 15:7–11; cf. Tob 4:5–11, 14–19), so too did Jesus (Matt 6:22–23/Luke 11:33–36; Matt 20:1–15; Mark 7:22) and his followers. In these warnings, envy (*phthonos* or its synonym *zēlos*) is frequently combined with other vices, such as theft, murder, deceit (Mark 7:22), hatred (Titus 3:3), communal strife (Rom 1:29; Phil 1:5), enmity and dissension (Gal 5:2–21; 1 Tim 6:4), all actions whose social divisiveness is readily apparent. Envy, in fact, was considered the cause of Jesus' betrayal (Matt 27:18/Mark 15:10) and of early opposition to his followers (Acts 15:7; 13:45). It is therefore hardly surprising that *envying* should be listed here in 1 Peter among the vices detrimental to brotherly love and communal cohesion.

slandering, literally, "slanderings" (*katalalias*). This vice of the tongue, speech (cf. Wis 1:11), and insulting language is the practice of "disparaging," "putting down," "bad mouthing" others and insulting their honor (*1 Clem.* 31:1; 35:5; Herm. *Mand.* 2.2–3, 8.3; Herm. *Sim.* 9.15.3, 9.23.2–3; *Barn.* 20:2; Pol. *Phil* 2:2; 4:3). The readers themselves, as later indicated, are victims of such verbal abuse from their nonbelieving neighbors, who out of ignorance (2:15) slander (*katalalousin*) them as "wrongdoers" (2:12). Here, as in its other NT occurrence in 2 Cor 12:20, it is the slandering of fellow-believers that is in view. Such slanderous speech is specifically inconsistent with the word through which the believers themselves have been born anew (1:23, 25b), the truth that they obey (1:22), and the love that binds them together (1:22).

All of these forms of behavior were widespread in a society marked by factional rivalries and intense social competition and conflict. See Gouldner 1969 for a sociological description of the contest system and the competitive patterns that characterized Greco-Roman culture. It is for this reason that they appear so frequently in catalogues of proscribed vices (Vögtle 1936; Wibbing 1959). Their proscription here is especially appropriate in a letter addressed to mixed communities involving groups of different ethnic origins or social levels. Involvement in such socially divisive behavior within the Christian community would not only be a violation of brotherly love (1:22) but would seriously undermine the brotherhood's social cohesion and stunt the movement's growth (2:3).

2a. As *newborn babies, hunger for the guileless milk of the word* (*hōs artigennēta brephē to logikon adolon gala epipothēsate*). The accent shifts now from negative (v 1) to positive (vv 2–3), a characteristic sequence in 1 Peter.[34]

As. Once again the particle *hōs,* so typical of our author's style (see the NOTE on 1:14a), is used to mark the essential quality of the noun it accompanies: "as the newborn babies that you are. . . ."

newborn babies (*artigennēta brephē*). A *brephos* is a "neonate," a newly-born baby; the term is used of the newly-born Jesus (Luke 2:12, 16) and as a metaphor for believers (1 Thess 2:7). The accompanying adjective *artigennētos*

[34] See 1:14/15–16; 1:18/19–21; 2:4, 10, 11/12, 16; 3:3/4, 11, 14/15, 18, 21; 4:2, 6, 12/13–14, 15/16; 5:2 (3×), 5b.

("newly [*arti-*] born"), combined with *brephos* also in Lucian (*Dial. meretr.* 12.1), occurs only here in the NT. Although the expression is technically redundant, *artigennēta* is related to the foregoing term *anagennēmenoi* (1:23; cf. 1:3) so that the phrase as a whole resumes and extends the foregoing birth metaphor and serves as a further means for linking 2:1–3 with 1:22–25. Beare (1970, 114) regards this expression as "appropriate to the condition of converts who have just been received into the Church by baptism" and cites Augustine, who quotes 1 Pet 2:1–3 in an address to those "fresh in the infancy of spiritual regeneration" (*Sermon* 353). The expression, however, belongs to a broader semantic field in which aspects of birth, rebirth, and infancy are common metaphors of baptismal catechesis (see Grundmann 1959 and the NOTE on 1:3). Moreover, the point of the comparison, as the following words make clear, is not the recentness of the believers' new birth but the fact that they, as new born babies, should "hunger for" the milk of the word, just as sucklings yearn for mother's milk. On the metaphor of rebirth, see the NOTES on 1:3 and 23.

hunger for. The main verb of this verse, *epipothēsate* (a 2d-person pl. aor. act. imperative), "fervently desire," "long intensely for," is a composite verb containing the preposition *epi*, indicating intensity. Paul employs it in the sense of "yearning eagerly" but with no reference to a figurative nursing (Rom 1:11; 2 Cor 5:2; 9:14; Phil 1:8; 2:26; 1 Thess 3:6; cf. 2 Tim 1:4; see Ps 118[119]:20 with respect to yearning for the ordinances of the Lord). The metaphor of newborn sucklings who nurse eagerly at mother's breast suggests the translation "hunger for" (cf. Arichea and Nida 1980, 51: "always be thirsty for").

the guileless milk of the word (*to logikon adolon gala*). The phrase is "unquestionably difficult" (Hort 1898, 100) but in the light of its context refers to "the divinely-given nourishment supplied by the Gospel" (Selwyn 1947, 154).

milk (*gala*). As the object of hunger, milk fits naturally with the depiction of the believers as newborn sucklings. Beare (1970, 115), following Perdelwitz (1911; cf. also Reitzenstein 1927, 329–30), finds here "a direct reference to the cup of milk which was given to initiates in the mystery cults." However, as other scholars (Selwyn 1947, 154–55; Grundmann 1959; Danker 1967b, 94–95; Goppelt 1993, 128–30) have pointed out, "milk" here is figurative not literal, and the images of milk and nursing are familiar metaphors (often of elementary instruction) in Israel and early Christianity.[35] For patristic texts and a discussion of the later administration of milk and honey to the newly baptized, see Selwyn (1947, 154–55, 308–9) and Beare (1970, 117). There is little to indicate, however, that this later practice is implied here, as Goppelt (1993, 130) correctly notes. The linking of nursing or milk metaphors with the word of the good news in 1 Thess 2:7; Heb 5:12–13/6:5; and *Barn.* 6:17 suggests that this is the association implied here as well. And in fact the modification of *milk* by *logikon* makes this certain.

---

[35] Philo, *Agr.* 9; 1QH^{a} VII 20–22; XI 34–36; 1 Cor 3:1–3; 1 Thess 2:7; Heb 5:12–6:7; cf. later, Clem. Alex., *Paed.* 5–6 and *Strom.* 5.10 (citing 1 Pet 2:1–3 and Ps 33:9, respectively); *Odes Sol.* 8:15–18; 19:1–5.

The concept of newborn babies desiring milk is a natural figure. This is not the case, however, with the two adjectives modifying *milk*. Their sense becomes clear from the fact that each involves a wordplay relating the phrase to its preceding context.

While mother's milk would normally be characterized as "pure" or "unadulterated," here milk is described in an unusual way as "guileless," "without deceit" (*adolon*, its only NT occurrence). Its choice, like that of *logikon*, appears prompted by the context. "Guileless" (*adolon*) provides an exact contrast to *dolos* (2:1), the "guile" that believers are to renounce. Such guile and deceit, as already indicated, are inconsistent with the "obedience to the *truth*" and the "*pure* heart" mentioned in 1:22. Thus *guileless milk* is milk free of deception and impurity, and the phrase indicates that the thought of 2:1–3 continues and expands upon that of 1:22–25. This fact also determines the sense of the second adjective, *logikon*.

of the word. This translation of *logikon* is found in the KJV and NASB and is favored by scholars noting the relation of *logikon* to the foregoing *logos* of 1:23. This rendering has been contested by Hort (1898, 100) on the grounds that "the qualitative adjective *logikon* could never stand for the definite genitive *tou logou*." Of the two chief senses of *logikos* in profane Greek, one was "belonging to reason" (where *logos* meant "reason"). The Stoics, for instance, regarded the human being principally as a "rational creature" (*logikon zōon*). This sense of *logikos* may explain the preference for "rational" on the part of the Latin versions of this verse (*rationabile, rationale*). But the expression "rational milk" has little sense in this context, for rationality and irrationality are not at issue. Moreover, even those who favor "rational" note that this sense is too narrow, "for *logos* is not equivalent to *ratio*" (Beare 1970, 115). The only other biblical occurrence of *logikos* is in Rom 12:1, where it modifies "worship" (*latreia*) and could have the sense of either "reasonable" or "spiritual." Those preferring the latter sense here suggest that *logikon* is then equivalent to *pneumatikos* ("spiritual") used twice in 2:5 (Selwyn 1947, 155; Beare 1970, 115). Still others prefer the translation "metaphorical" (see MM for examples), suggesting that in this sense *logikos* underscores the fact that *milk* is not intended literally but metaphorically (BAGD 476; Michaels 1988, 870; see Selwyn 1947, 155, however, for a cogent critique).

A consideration of two facts provides a reasonable solution to this controverted issue. First, a second chief sense of *logikos* in profane Greek is "belonging to speech" (Hort 1898, 100); compare Plut., *Cor.* 38, "not even a god can utter meaningful speech without a body containing speech organs (*meresi logikois*)." McCartney (1991, 132), on the basis of a comprehensive computer search of the term, concludes that "the use of *logikos* in Hellenism, while its contexts may frequently stress the aspect best expressed by our term 'reason,' clearly involves the idea of verbal communication." Verbal communication is precisely the focus of attention in 1 Pet 1:23–25 and 2:1.

Second, this translation makes more sense than any other *in this particular context*. Here, *logikos*, like *adolon*, has been prompted by the foregoing thought and its particular terminology. Both adjectives are unusual modifiers of milk, and are chosen to integrate the metaphor of *milk* as object of desire into a broader line of thought involving the divine means of rebirth and its moral implications. *Logikos* recalls the "word" (*logos*) of 1:23, its synonym *rhēma* (2:24, 25a), and its interpretation as the "good news" in 1:25b—all portraying the means of Christian rebirth. In addition, it anticipates the further reference to this same "word" (*logos*) in 2:8, where obedience-disobedience to the word is the point.

The unusual expression "guileless milk of the word" captures the attention of the readers and alerts them to the relation of the word through which they have been born and the word on which they are to continue to feed for nourishment and growth. As Francis (1980) has observed, two distinct though related images are combined here: regeneration through the word (1:23; cf. Jas 1:18; Titus 3:5; John 3:3–12) and continued nourishment on the word-milk. In both instances this word-milk is the proclamation of the good news concerning Jesus as Lord (1:25b). This identification was sensed also by Clement of Alexandria (*Paed.* 1.6) who, when citing 1 Pet 2:1–3, associates the "milk of the word" with the "milk of the Father," Jesus Christ, and good news. For a survey of translations and commentary on *logikos* and a similar interpretation, see McCartney (1991).

This Petrine verse supplied the first line of the traditional introit of the liturgy for the first Sunday after Easter, hence the name *Quasimodogenti*, "As newborn babies," for this Sunday.

2b. *so that by it you may grow up toward salvation* (*hina en autōi auxēthēte eis sōtērian*). Eager nursing on the word has growth toward salvation as its ultimate goal.

so that. The conjunction *hina* (also "that," "in order that") serves here to introduce a statement indicating the purpose or goal of the preceding imperative (v 2a). For other *hina* clauses in 1 Peter, see 1:7; 2:12, 21, 24; 3:1, 9, 16, 18; 4:6, 11, 13; 5:6.

by it. The formulation *en hōi* is an instrumental dative, with the pronoun *hōi* referring specifically to *milk* but encompassing in sense the entire action of craving the guileless milk of the word.

you may grow up (*auxēthēte*). The idea of growth proceeds naturally from the foregoing notion of nursing and nourishment. The line of thought now moves from rebirth and feeding to growth. The verb *auxēthēte* is a 2d-person pl. aor. pass. subjunctive of *auxanō*, which in the passive is used literally of the growth of children (Gen 21:8; 25:27) and figuratively of the growth of the gospel (Col 1:6), faith (2 Cor 10:15), or of believers growing in knowledge (Col 1:10). In the active voice it also denotes, literally, Jesus' growing and maturing as a child (Luke 1:80; 2:40), the increase of Israel in Egypt (Acts 7:17), or figuratively, the growing of the word of God/Lord (Acts 6:7; 12:24). The theme of correlated personal and communal growth in the faith is a major accent of Eph 4:11–16 (cf. Col 2:19), and a related passage on this same theme (Eph 2:11–22) contains both similarities to and differences from the accent on familial integration in 1 Pet 2:4–10. For discussion, see the NOTES and COMMENT on 2:4–10. Here in 1 Peter also, as 2:4–10 indicates, the growth pertains not simply to that of individual believers but to their maturation and integration within the family of the reborn (Grundmann 1959, 194, 205).

toward salvation (*eis sōterian*). These words are omitted in the Majority Text, but their inclusion has far weightier manuscript support (𝔓[72] ℵ A B C K P Ψ etc.). Omission of the phrase was likely the result of haplography (cf. *eis* [*sōtērian*] and *ei* constituting a double homoeoarcton). The *salvation* of the believers is the ultimate goal of God's rebirthing and redemptive action (as in 1:5, 9, 10; cf. 3:21; 4:18). A passage of James (1:18, 21) offers a close parallel to the thought and terminology of 1 Pet 2:1–2 and its context: "Of his [God's] own will he brought us forth by the word of truth (*logōi alētheias*). . . . Therefore rid yourselves (*apothemenoi*) of all (*pasan*) filthiness and excess of evil (*kakias*) and receive with humility the implanted word (*emphyton logon*) which is able to save (*sōsai*) your lives." Baptism has set the addressees on the course of salvation (3:21), but salvation itself, as this notion of growing up toward (*eis*) the goal of salvation makes clear, is an ongoing process. Its final realization is still anticipated and hoped for (1:5, 9, 10; 4:18), a thought consistent with the typically eschatological orientation of this letter. As the metaphor of rebirth through the word signifies the commencement of this process of new life, feeding on the milk of the good news signifies its implementation, and salvation, its goal.

3. *since "you have tasted that the Lord is good"* (*ei egeusasthe hoti chrēstos ho kyrios*). The metaphor of rebirth and nourishment through the word/good news/milk is extended by an identification of the chief subject of that word—the Lord Jesus Christ. The language of the statement is derived from Ps 33:9[34:8]. Here, as elsewhere in the letter, a scriptural citation is used to substantiate and conclude the foregoing (cf. 1:16; 1:24–25; 2:6; 3:10–12; 5:5c; cf. 2:17; 4:18).

since. *Ei* (with better MS support than *eiper*) can serve as a conditional particle ("if"), but here introduces a causal clause with the positive force of "since," "because," "seeing that" (cf. similarly, 1:17; 4:14, 17, 18; and Matt 6:30 / Luke 12:28; Matt 7:11; John 11:23; Rom 6:8; etc.). With the aorist verb *egeusasthe*, "you have tasted," the clause alludes to a prior experience of the readers as a motivation for the imperative "hunger for."

"you have tasted that the Lord is good" (*egeusasthe hoti chrēstos ho kyrios*). These words are a citation of Ps 33:9 LXX (MT 34:8, "taste and see that the Lord is good"), with noteworthy modifications and shifts of meaning. This psalm holds special significance for the author as a consolatory song concerning "resident aliens" (Ps 33:5). Later in the letter he quotes from it extensively (1 Pet 3:10–12 = Ps 33:13–17). In the immediate context of our verse, the term *proserchomenoi* in 2:4 may also have been inspired by Ps 33:6. The similarities of language and tone between 1 Peter and Ps 33[34] in general have been noted by W. Bornemann (1919–1920). He claims to have found no fewer than 51

direct references or indirect allusions to the psalm. This led him to envision 1 Peter as a baptismal homily based on this psalm. This hypothesis has been cogently critiqued by W. Schutter (1989, 44–49) as an exaggeration of the evidence; but the Psalm's importance for 1 Peter remains incontestable (Danker 1967b, 94–95; J. N. D. Kelly 1969, 87; Snodgrass 1977, 102–3).[36] In later time Ps 33:9, perhaps mediated through 1 Peter, was employed in the eucharistic liturgy, and "Lord" was identified as the "eucharistic Christ."[37] This later liturgical usage, however, provides no proof that the psalm already had a "eucharistic sense" in our author's time, or that it was cited to remind the readers of "the blessings they have received through sacramental fellowship," as J. N. D. Kelly (1969, 87) claims. As the present context (1:22–2:3) makes clear, it is the *inception* of renewed life that is in view and thus the experience of baptism, not of the eucharist.

Here in 2:3 the psalm's metaphor of "tasting the goodness of the Lord" admirably suits the Petrine context, where nursing on milk is the image. However, the words and the sense of the original have been modified to serve a new purpose. The psalm's aorist imperative (*geusate*, "taste") is changed to an aorist indicative and is preceded by a "since" (*ei*) added by our author. Furthermore, the psalmist's words "and see" following "taste" are omitted (contrast their secondary inclusion in a few MSS and the Syriac Peshitta), thereby creating the unusual construction "taste that. . . ." In place of the omitted words, the scribe of 𝔓[72] substituted "you believed" (*episteusate*), possibly for better sense: "you believed that . . . " (Quinn 1965, 243–44; Michaels 1988, 90). The chief effect of these modifications is that the psalm's words now serve to describe the *past* experience of the believers, when they first heard the good news of the Lord.

"Lord" (*kyrios*), moreover, in the Petrine context no longer refers to God as it did in the psalm but to Jesus Christ. This shift in meaning is evident from both the intentional substitution of *kyrios* ("Lord") for *theos* ("God") in 1:25a (and the interpretation of "word" as the "good news" concerning Jesus Christ [1:25b relating to 1:10–12]) and the following words of 2:4, where the pronoun "him" refers back to *kyrios* and forward to Jesus Christ (vv 5–6).

good. The Greek term translated "good," *chrēstos*, likewise is now associated with Jesus Christ in a twofold manner. As an adjective it describes something as "good" or someone as "kindly," "benevolent," or "honorable" (cf. Danker 1982, 325–27); for the identification of God (*kyrios*) as "good" (*chrēstos*), see also Ps 24[25]:8; 85[86]:5; 99[100]:5; 118[119]:68; 135[136]:1; Dan 3:89. In this sense it would imply the kindly reception believers have received from the Lord (see Matt 11:29–30, "Take my yoke upon you and learn from me; for I am gentle and humble in heart. . . . For my yoke is kindly [*chrēstos*], and my

---

[36] On citations of and allusions to Ps 33[34], see the GENERAL INTRODUCTION, 2. Sources, and the NOTE on 3:10–12.

[37] Clem. Alex., *Paed.* 1.6; cf. *Strom.* 5.10; *Apost. Const.* 8.13.16; Cyril of Jerusalem, *Myst. Cat.* 5.20; Jerome, *Epist.* 71.6; Liturgy of St. James; Mozarabic Liturgy.

burden is light"). In contemporary pronunciation, however, where the Greek vowel *ēta* (*ē*) was often pronounced in the same manner as *iota* (*i*), *chrēstos* could be both spoken and heard as *christos* (cf. BDF §§22–27). This may account for the variant reading *Christos* (𝔓[72] K L and others) here and the inverse reading *Chrēstianos* (for *Christianos*) in 4:16 and Acts 26:28 in the original hand of Codex Sinaiticus. Tertullian (*Apol.* 5 and *Nat.* 3) calls attention to this confusion (cf. also Justin, *1 Apol.* 4) and in Clement of Alexandria the alternative is explicit: *Paed.* 1.6, "since you have tasted that the Lord is Christ" and *Strom.* 5.10, "Taste and see that the Lord is Christ," a reading that is quite close to that in 𝔓[76], which substitutes the *nomen sacrum* or abbreviation *XPC* for *chrēstos*. If *chrēstos* here in 1 Peter were written, spoken, or heard as *Christos*, the sentence would change from a description of the Lord as good to a confession of the Lord as Christ (cf. 3:15). While this would be consistent with the Christological sense of this passage, the reading *chrēstos* meaning "good" has superior manuscript support (א A B C Ψ 𝔐) and is more compatible with the image of tasting.

On the whole, v 3 with these modifications now constitutes a metaphor still appropriate to the image of nursing but indicative of the believers' initial experience of rebirth through the hearing of the good news concerning Jesus Christ. The experience of having initially tasted the goodness of the Lord is the basis for their continuing to crave this word as a source of ongoing sustenance.

As a metaphor for the initial stage of Christian conversion, the entire expression is similar to the imagery of Heb 5–6 but makes a different point. Hebrews 5:12 states that "You need someone to teach you again the first principles of God's word. You need milk (*galaktos*), not solid food; for every one who lives on milk (*galaktos*) is unskilled in the word of righteousness, for that one is a child." Then 6:4–5 continues, "for it is impossible to restore again to repentance those who have once been enlightened, who have tasted (*geusamenous*) the heavenly gift . . . and have tasted the goodness of the word of God (*kalon geusamenous theou rhēma*)." The point of our author, on the other hand, is not a contrast between the beginning and more mature stages of faith or the impossibility of restoration but solely that hearing the good news of Jesus Christ is equivalent to having tasted as sucklings the goodness of the Lord, the word-milk. The milk metaphor (cf. also 1 Cor 3:1–2; *Odes Sol.* 8:13–16; 19:1–2), like the reference to the "implanted word that is able to save you" (Jas 1:21), probably belonged to the catechetical tradition upon which Christian authors drew. Our author employs the metaphorical language of Ps 33:9 in a unique manner to identify Jesus as the word-milk by whom believers have been reborn and fed and to prepare for further commentary on the relation between the Lord and his followers in the verses that follow.

GENERAL COMMENT

The immediate significance of 2:1–3 lies in the manner in which these verses build directly on 1:22–25 and prepare for the verses that follow, 2:4–10 (Elliott

1966b, 203–7; Schutter 1989, 57–58). They also play a vital role, however, in the larger line of thought extending from 1:3 to 2:10.

In the immediately foregoing unit (1:22–25), the readers have been urged to love and be loyal to one another constantly as befitting their baptismal purification and obedience (v 22). The reason for such constancy is the enduring nature of the word of God through which they have been reborn—that is, the good news of the Lord Jesus Christ (vv 23–25). Maintaining familial solidarity, however, requires actions both negative and positive in nature. Negatively (2:1), the believers must rid themselves of all hypocritical attitudes and behavior that are inconsistent with the truth (v 22) to which their baptism committed them and which could impair or undermine unhypocritical familial commitment (v 22b). On the other hand, for positive growth to take place (vv 2–3), it is urgent that the reborn readers nurse constantly on the *guileless* (contrast v 1) milk of the word, drawing nourishment from the same word through which they were brought to new life (vv 23–25). This they should find a welcome task, for at their initial hearing of the good news they discovered the goodness of the Lord Jesus Christ.

In this development of thought we find not only wordplays ("unhypocritical"–"hypocrisy," "guile"–"guileless," *logos/logikos*) but also merged metaphors ("word" as "seed," as "speaking" [*rhēma*], as "good news," and as "milk"; "milk of the word" and "Lord" as objects of "hunger"/"tasting"). These metaphors are consistent with imagery employed in early Christian tradition for proclaiming the good news and illustrating the nature of Christian baptism. Such blendings of images and traditions are typical of this letter and are found elsewhere in 1:13–21; 2:4–10, 21–25; 3:18–22; and 4:12–19. Both wordplays and metaphors, moreover, serve to integrate these verses into a coherent line of thought.

Within the broader development of thought commencing at 1:3, these verses resume and advance the metaphor of rebirth (1:3, 23; 2:2) and its related idea of the reborn constituting a family of God. In this family, brought into being by the seed-word of God, fraternal affection is its bond, and nourishment from the milk of the word, its means of growth. Finally, these verses extend the image of rebirth and family by advancing the focus from birth to growth toward salvation, an idea with both personal and communal implications. This development finds its conclusion in the following section (2:4–10), where the focus moves one step further from rebirth and growth to consolidation and upbuilding of the family of God. The implied identification of "Lord" in 2:3 with Jesus Christ and the syntactic and semantic links of this verse with 2:4–10 indicate the manner in which 2:3 in particular prepares for what follows and, thus, how 2:1–3 forms yet another unit in the progress of thought extending from 1:3–2:10.

For studies on 1 Pet 2:1–3, see Arichea and Nida 1980; Elliott 1966b, 1982; Francis 1980; Hillyer 1969b; McCartney 1991; Parsons 1978; Perdelwitz 1911; Quinn 1965; T. J. Ryan 1973; Snodgrass 1977; Stevick 1988.

I. E. ELECTION AND REJECTION: CHRIST, BELIEVERS, NONBELIEVERS—THE CONSOLIDATION AND HONOR OF THE HOUSEHOLD OF GOD (2:4–10)

2:4a Continuing to come to him,
4b a living "stone,"
4c "rejected" by humans
4d but "elect, honored" in God's sight,
5a you, yourselves, also
5b as living stones,
5c are being built up;
5d [you are] a house(hold) of the Spirit
5e to be a holy "priestly community"
5f to offer spiritual sacrifices
acceptable to God through Jesus Christ;
6a for it stands in Scripture:
6b "Behold, I am setting in Zion a stone,
a cornerstone,
elect,
honored,
6c and whoever believes in him will not be shamed."
7a To you therefore who "believe" belongs this "honor";
7b but for those who do not "believe,"
7c "the very stone that the builders rejected
7d has become the head of the corner,"
8a and "a stone of stumbling"
and "a rock of offense";
8b they "stumble" by disobeying the word,
8c as they were set to do.
9a But you [are] an "elect stock,"
9b a "royal residence,"
9c a "priestly community,"
9d a "holy people,"
9e a "people for [God's] possession,"
9f that you may "declare the praises" of him
who "called" you out of darkness into his marvelous light.
10a Once you [were] "Not-people,"
10b but now [you are] "God's-people";
10c [once] you [were] "Not-shown-mercy,"
10d but now [you are] "Those-shown-mercy."

INTRODUCTION

These verses bring to a resounding climax the line of thought begun in 1:3 (cf. Elliott 1966b, 199–218). This first major section of the letter (1:3–2:10) ends, as it began, on the note of God's lavish mercy (1:3; 2:10) and traces the course of Christian life from "rebirth" (1:3, 23; 2:2) through "growth" (2:1–3) to the "consolidation" of the Christian community as the elect and holy household of God (2:4–10). This final unit reiterates and ties together several foregoing motifs: (1) rebirth as a process of regeneration, growth, and familial incorporation; (2) the divine word of the good news as "seed" and medium of rebirth; (3) the holy union with God and Jesus Christ; (4) the distinction between believers and nonbelievers, who reject Jesus as Lord; (5) the identification with Jesus Christ, both in his rejection by humans and in his divine election; and (6) behavior indicative of the believers' divine calling and election in the midst of their alien residence. Particular accent in this concluding unit is given to the union of believers with Jesus Christ, their distinction from the disobedient, and the high privileges and great responsibilities that are theirs as God's covenant community and household.

This passage is connected with its immediately preceding context by the introductory phrase *continuing to come to him* (v 4a), in which "him" has as its antecedent "Lord" in v 3, and to earlier units by several elements, including the reiterated reference to holiness (vv 5e, 9cd; cf. 1:15–16, 19, 22), "believe, faith, trust" (2:6c, 7a; cf. 1:7, 8, 9, 21), "obedience, disobedience" (2:8b; cf. 1:14, 22), "word" (v 8b; cf. 2:2a and 1:23c), divine "calling" (v 9f; cf. 1:15), and "mercy" (v 10cd; cf. 1:13).

At the same time it constitutes a coherent and self-contained unit embracing vv 4–10. The *unity and structure* of this complex unit are marked by terms bracketing the passage ("elect," vv 4, 6, 9; "priestly community," vv 5, 9; "holy," vv 5, 9; "God," vv 4, 10) and forming a structural inclusion of vv 4–10. Terminological-conceptual correspondences and link-words give it its internal unity ("stone[s]," vv 4, 5b, 6–8; "reject," vv 4, 7; "honored/honor," vv 4, 6, 7a; "cornerstone/head of corner," vv 6, 7; "believe," vv 6, 7; "stumbling," v 8a, b); see also the repeated antitheses ("humans-God," v 4; "believers-nonbelievers," vv 7a/7b–8/9–10; "honor-shame," vv 4c/d, 6, 7a/7b–8/9–10; v 7c/d; "once-now," v 10a/b, c/d).

The content consists of an extensive catena of OT citations and allusions together with their redactional interpretation and application to Jesus Christ, believers, and nonbelievers. Three discernible blocks of material shape the threefold structure of this unit: two distinct subunits of OT citations (vv 6–8 and vv 9–10) introduced and integrated by vv 4–5 (see Elliott 1966b, 16–49).

(1) Verses 6–8 involve one group of related OT texts (Isa 28:16; Ps 117 [118]:22; Isa 8:14) concerning a "stone," which in both Israelite and Christian tradition had been viewed as an image of the Messiah (as discussed in the NOTES). Redactional comments in vv 7–8 use these "stone" texts to contrast believers (v 7a) and nonbelievers (vv 7b–8). An inclusion ("I am setting" [*tithēmi*], v 6a; "they were set" [*etethēsan*], v 8c) frames this subunit.

(2) Verses 9–10 involve another collage of OT texts and allusions (Exod 19:5–6; Isa 43:20–21; 42:6–9; 63:7–9; Hos 1:6, 9; 2:23) constituting honorific predicates of ancient Israel as the elect and holy people of God, predicates now applied to the community of the reborn.

(3) Verses 4–5 form an introductory pair of parallel verses that introduce, combine, and apply to Jesus Christ (v 4) and the believers (v 5) elements of the material that follows (vv 4b–5a pertaining to vv 6–8, and the remainder of v 5 pertaining to vv 9–10). Pervading and uniting this complex passage is the concept of the *election and holiness* of God's people (vv 4, 5, 6, 9), which in turn links this passage to a dominant emphasis of the letter as a whole (election, 1:1 and 5:13; holiness, 1:2, 12, 14–16, 19, 22; 3:5, 15).

The structure of these verses may be schematized as follows:

Verses 4–5	*Verses 6–8, 9–10*
v 4	vv 6–8
Jesus Christ, the rejected-elect stone	belief-nonbelief in Jesus the stone believers (v 7a) contrasted to nonbelievers (vv 7b–8)
v 5	vv 9–10
believing community, elect and holy	people of God, elect and holy
house(hold) of the Spirit	royal residence
holy priestly community	priestly community
offer spiritual sacrifices	declare the praises of God believers (vv 9–10) again contrasted to nonbelievers (vv 7b–8)

More specifically:

Verse 4	*Verses 6–8*
(Jesus Christ, "him")	
stone	
"living" (cf. 3:18d)	
"rejected" by humans	v 7b (Ps 117:22); cf. 2:8 (Isa 8:14)
"elect"	v 6 (Isa 28:16)
"honored" in God's sight	v 6 (Isa 28:16); cf. 2:7a (believers)
Verse 5	*Verse 9*
(believers, "you")	
stones	
living (cf. 1:3)	
are being built up (cf. 5:10)	
[you are]	
a house(hold) of the Spirit	royal residence (Exod 19:6)
to be a "holy priestly community"	priestly community, holy nation (Exod 19:6)
to offer spiritual sacrifices	declare the praises

NOTES

2:4a. *Continuing to come to him (pros hon proserchomenoi).* This phrase extends the thought of 2:2–3 regarding continued fidelity to the Lord and introduces a unit (vv 4–10) that compares believers with their elect Lord and contrasts these elect believers and their honor with rejecting nonbelievers and their shame. The relative "him" (*hon*) has as its antecedent "the Lord" (i.e., Jesus Christ, 2:3; cf. 2:5). The pl. pres. part. *proserchomenoi* ("continuing to come to him") does not have imperatival force but continues the indicative mood of 2:3 ("for you have tasted that the Lord is good") and expresses, as do all verbs of this unit, the indicative mood and descriptive function of vv 4–10 as a whole (Cervantes Gabarrón 1991b, 343–44). The construction of an initial participle followed by a finite indicative verb (*proserchomenoi . . . oikodomeisthe*) occurs frequently in this letter (1:8a, 8bc, 13, 22ab; 2:12cd, 20 [2×], 23 [2×]; 3:18de–19b). The phrase may have been prompted by the language of Ps 33:6 (*proselthate pros auton*, "come to him"), since v 9 of this same psalm is cited in the foregoing verse (2:3) and since the author cites from the psalm again in 3:10–12. However, the verb *proserchō* also is linguistically related to the Greek term for "proselyte," *prosēlytos* (one who has approached or drawn near to a group in order to join it or one who "has drawn near to God").[38] In this light the term appropriately describes the continued solidarity of Christian converts and proselytes with their Lord as the precondition for communal consolidation and action (2:5, 9).

4b. *a living "stone" (lithon zōnta).* The Lord whom the believers approach in faith is now depicted by a new metaphor, *living stone*, which in the following verse is applied to the believers as well. The terms "stone" (*lithos*) and "rejected" (*apodedokimasmenos*, v 4c) derive from and anticipate the language of Ps 117[118]:22, cited in 1 Pet 2:7cd. This psalm verse formed part of a complex of OT "stone" passages cited in v 6 (Isa 28:16), v 7cd and v 8a (Isa 8:14). In Israelite tradition prior to 1 Peter, at least one of these texts (Isa 28:16) had already been interpreted messianically (LXX addition of the words "in him" [*ep' autōi*] in Isa 28:16 and possibly the Targumic interpretations of Isa 28:16), or it had been applied eschatologically to the Qumran community (1QS VIII 7–8; cf. as possible allusions 1QS V 5; 4QpIsa[d] 1; 1QH[a] VI 26–27; VII 8–9). Moreover, in both the NT (Mark 12:1–2/Matt 21:33–46/Luke 20:9–19; Acts 4:8–12; Rom 9:33; Eph 2:11–22) and later Christian literature (*Barn.* 6:2–4; *Gos. Thom.* 65–66), elements of these OT "stone" passages were variously employed in Christological formulations. Influence of this interpretive tradition is evident here also; however, the "stone" texts are used in a distinctive way to underscore the divine honoring of Christ and believers on the one hand, and their distinction from the divinely shamed nonbelievers, on the other.

---

[38] See Isa 54:15 (*prosēlytoi proseleusontai soi* ["proselytes will draw near to you"]); Philo, *Spec.* 1.51; 1.309; *Praem.* 152; Heb 4:16; 7:25; 11:6; and for the Hebrew equivalent, *qrb*, see 1QS VI 16, 19, 22; VII 21; IX 19; 1QH[a] XIV 13–14, 18; cf. Kuhn and Stegemann 1962; Kuhn 1968.

In expressions such as "living stone" or "living water," the adjective describes an object in its natural state as rooted in the earth or flowing water (Plumpe 1943). In this Petrine context, however, the adjective "living" (*zōnta*) clearly corresponds to the qualifiers "elect," "honored" in v 4d and represents the author's interpretation of the stone (Christ) as "made alive" (*zōiopoiētheis*, 3:18) and "raised" (to life) by God (cf. 1:3; 3:22; Luke 24:5; Acts 1:3; Rev 1:18). Made alive by God, this living stone mediates life for believers who are reborn through his resurrection (1:3), who now "live" (*zēsōmen*) in righteousness (2:24) and who possess a "living (*zōsan*) hope" (1:3).

4c. *"rejected" by humans (hypo anthrōpōn men apodedokimasmenon)*. Verses 4c and 4d form an antithetical (*men, de*) pair of phrases that modify *stone* with language drawn from Ps 117[118] and Isa 28 cited in vv 6–7 and contrast human and divine assessments of the "stone" (Jesus Christ). The term "rejected" (*apodedokimasmenon*) derives from Ps 117[118]:22 (cf. 2:7c), in which the psalmist compares his rejection and oppression by his enemies (117:10–13) to a stone that was rejected by the "builders" (*hoi oikodomountes*). In Jesus' parable of the vineyard (Mark 12:1–12/Matt 21:33–46/Luke 20:9–18/*Gos. Thom.* 65–66; cf. Herm. *Sim.* 5.2.1–8), this psalm text is quoted *in extenso* and applied to the son who is rejected, and implicitly to Jesus as rejected by his Jerusalem opponents (Matt 21:42, 45/Mark 12:10, 12/Luke 20:17, 19). The tradition of Jesus' passion also employs the verb *apodokimazō* to describe Jesus' rejection (Mark 8:31/Luke 9:22; 17:25). In Peter's speech before the Jerusalem Sanhedrin (Acts 4:8–12), this same psalm text is cited in modified form and applied directly both to Jesus Christ ("whom you crucified") and to the rulers, elders, and scribes themselves: "This is the stone that was rejected by *you* builders" (4:11; cf. 3:14–15; 4:10; 5:30–31; 13:27–30).

Here in 1 Peter, however, "builders," is replaced with the more inclusive term "humans" (*anthrōpōn*). This modification shifts the focus from anti-Judean polemic in particular to a universalizing indictment of *all nonbelievers* who reject Jesus Christ (cf. 2:7b and also the contrast of humans-God in 4:2). In regard to the minor textual variant, the preposition *hypo* ("by") has better manuscript support than the variants *hyper* (aural confusion with *hypo*) and *apo* (possibly influenced by *apodedokimasmenon*).

4d. *but "elect, honored" in God's sight (para de theōi eklekton entimon)*. This second member of the antithesis containing the adversative particle *de* contrasts the positive assessment of the "stone" by God to the negative rejection by humans. The Greek preposition *para* followed by the dative denotes "in the sight or judgment of someone." For the construction *para* (*tōi*) *theōi*, see also 2:20 and 1 Cor 3:19; Gal 3:11; 2 Thess 1:6; Jas 1:27; 2 Pet 3:8 (cf. also 1 Pet 3:4, *enōpion tou theou*). 1 Peter 4:2–6 contains further contrasts between humans (Gentiles) and God.

The terms "elect" (*eklektos*) and "honored" (*entimos*) derive not from Ps 117 but from Isa 28:16, which is cited in v 6. They are adjectives describing the honor conferred by God upon Jesus, in contrast to his rejection by humans. Thus "elect" and "honored" serve as our author's equivalents of the more traditional concepts of "resurrected" and "glorified" (cf. 1:11, 21; 3:18de; 5:1; Rom 1:4; John 11:4; 12:23; 1 Cor 15:3–4). On the whole this antithesis between the Lord's rejection by humans and election by God is a succinct and peculiar formulation on the part of our author of the traditional crucifixion/resurrection kerygma (Mark 8:31 par.; 9:31 par.; 10:33; Luke 24:46; Acts 2:23–24; 4:10; 10:39–40; Rom 6:4; 8:34; 1 Cor 15:3–4; Heb 2:9). This kerygma is modified here to emphasize the election and honor (2:4cd, 7a) that bind the rejected, suffering, and yet elect Christ with his rejected, suffering, and elect followers, as further explicated in vv 5–10. For similar linking of Christ and the believers, see 2:18–25; 3:13–22; 4:1, 12–16; and 5:1. Elsewhere in the NT Jesus is designated "elect" only in the crucifixion account of Luke, where he is mocked by his adversaries as "the Christ of God, his elect one" (Luke 23:35), and in variant readings of John 1:34, in which John the Baptist attests that Jesus is "the elect of God" or "elect son of God."

As the Lord Jesus is declared to be the *elect* "stone" in God's sight, so in v 9a the first thing said of those who believe in him is that they constitute an "elect people" (*genos eklekton*, deriving from Isa 43:20). The notion of election is also implied in the further epithets of Israel ascribed to the believing community in vv 5e and 9bc, *royal residence and priestly community* (deriving from the covenant formula of Exod 19:6). Stress on the idea of election thus permeates this unit from start to finish, frames the unit as an inclusion, and represents an integrating theme, according to which the different traditions employed here have been united. The election of both Jesus and believers identifies them as demarcated and dignified, elite and exalted in God's sight. The elect status once claimed by Israel as a concomitant of its exclusive covenant with God is now claimed by those in union with God and God's elect one.

The adjective *entimos* belongs to the family of terms pertaining to "honor," several of which are used in 1 Peter (*timē*, 1:7; 2:7; 3:7; *timaō*, 2:17; *timios*, 1:19; *polytimoteros*, 1:7; *epainos* ["praise"] 1:7; 2:14; *makarios* ["honored"] 3:14; 4:14). "Honor" (*timē*) (one's worth, good name, fame, social rating, and esteem as recognized by others) was a pivotal value of ancient Mediterranean culture (Malina and Neyrey 1991c; Moxnes 1988a, 1988b; Pilch 1991b, 49–70; 1991c, 57–92; Malina 1993d, 28–62; K. C. Hanson 1996). Such honor was connected to and contrasted with "shame" (the actual loss, or sensitivity regarding the loss, of honor), "being shamed," and "being put to shame." Here and elsewhere in 1 Peter, the honor that is conferred by God upon both Jesus Christ (vv 4d, 6b, 7c) and his believers (vv 5, 7a, 9–10) is contrasted to the divine shaming (vv 6c, 7bc, 8ab) of those who have shamed and rejected both Jesus (v 4c) and his followers (4:14–16); see also the related contrast of suffering and reproach caused by human opponents versus honor from God in 3:14 and 4:14. For further discussion of the honor and shame code in the biblical world and of the prominence of the idiom of honor and shame in 1 Peter, see Elliott 1995.

On the whole, v 4 forms with v 5 a couplet linking the divine election and honor conferred upon Jesus (v 4) with that conferred upon the believers (v 5) and introducing terminology and themes derived from OT material cited in vv 6–8 and 9–10 (Elliott 1966b, 17–49). The language of rejection-living/election/honor drawn from the complex of OT "stone" texts succinctly describes the suffering/crucifixion-resurrection/vindication of Christ as prelude for the encouragement of the suffering-vindication of the faithful (Cervantes Gabarrón 1991b, 341–62), a correlation of concepts pervading the letter. As v 4 introduces and interprets terms contained in the OT material cited in vv 6–8, v 5 introduces and interprets terms contained in the OT material cited in vv 9–10.

Verse 5 presents some syntactical, grammatical, and semantic problems that are most likely the result of the combination of originally independent traditions and motifs: (1) a continuation in v 5abc of the "stone" metaphor introduced in v 4 (related to vv 6–8) and (2) material in v 5d–f related to the complex of OT texts cited in v 9. The main problems include the following:

(1) The verb *oikodomeisthe* can be taken as either a middle imperative ("build yourselves up") or a passive indicative ("you are being built up"). The indicative mood of the entire passage and the stress on God's implied action (2:6c, 8d, 9f), however, strongly favor the latter. (The variant *epoikodomeisthe* is virtually synonymous and was possibly influenced by 1 Cor 3:10, 12, 14; Eph 2:20; and Col 2:7.)

(2) The syntactical relation between the verb *oikodomeisthe* and *oikos pneumatikos* (a nominative phrase) is problematic. The latter is clearly not the object of the former (as the misleading translations of the RSV, Goppelt, Michaels, and others suggest: "built into a spiritual house"). Rather, the nominative suggests an implied ellipsis involving the words "you are" (a house[hold] of the Spirit).

(3) The syntax involving *eis hierateuma hagion* also is problematic. This may account for the omission of the preposition *eis* ("for," indicating purpose) in Codex P, the majority of later manuscripts, and the Vulgate. According to this reading, *holy priestly community* would likewise be a nominative and in apposition to *house(hold) of the Spirit*. The preponderance of earlier manuscripts, however, supports the original presence of the preposition, thus making *eis hierateuma hagion* a phrase describing the *purpose* or *function* of *house(hold) of the Spirit* (analogous to the construction of *eis peripoiēsin* modifying *laos* in v 9f). Goppelt (1993, 141 n. 33) proposes that *eis hierateuma*, like *oikos pneumatikos*, is governed by the verb *oikodomeisthe* ("built into a spiritual house, into a holy priesthood"). But conventional usage as well as grammar make this unlikely. The only biblical combination of *oikodomeō* + *eis* is in Sir 48:17, where *eis* describes the purpose for cisterns that Hezekiah built, "for [holding] water." However, the apposition of *basileion* and *hierateuma* in v 9bc makes it likely that their parallels in v 5de have a general appositional relationship as well.

(4) The variant readings regarding the inclusion or exclusion of the definite article preceding *theōi* in v 5f concern style rather than syntax or grammar. Michaels (1988, 93) correctly favors inclusion on the basis of preference for the article in "more formal expressions of praise or virtue offered up to God (e.g., 2:12, 17; 3:4, 18; 4:11, 16)."

(5) Finally, the semantic association between *lithos/lithoi* ("stone[s]") and *oikos* ("house[hold]") requires clarification. Does the term *oikos* (with its polyvalent senses of both "building" and "house[hold]") enable a plausible transition from a "stones/building/construction" metaphor to a focus on *oikos* as community of agents?

In v 5, the believers are described in terms consistent with both v 4 and vv 9–10. The two originally independent traditions and sets of epithets employed in vv 4, 6–8 ("stone") and vv 9–10 ("elect" and "holy people" of God) are combined in such a way that this verse completes the thought begun in v 4 while also anticipating and interpreting vv 9–10.

5ab. *you, yourselves, also as living stones (kai autoi hōs lithoi zōntes)*. By continuing their contact with the living stone, the believers themselves (*autoi*) also (*kai*) share his identity (*lithoi*) and his life (*zōntes*), a metaphorical epithet that is unique in the NT (for "stones," see Ign. *Eph.* 9:1). As the faithful are reborn to a "*living* hope" through the resurrection of Jesus Christ (1:3), so they are *living* stones who "*live* for doing what is right" (2:24), and are "coheirs of the grace of *life*" (3:7). Their sharing in Christ's life provides the basis and motivation for a sharing in his suffering (2:21–25; 3:13–18; 4:1, 12–16; 5:1, 10). The particle *hōs* ("as") here, as elsewhere in 1 Peter (27×), indicates an intrinsic and essential quality of a subject. On the metaphor of "living stones" in classical antiquity, see Plumpe 1943.

5c. *are being built up (oikodomeisthe)*. This verb, the only finite verb and therefore chief verb of vv 4–5c, concludes the thought of vv 4–5c. Formally, it could be taken as a middle or passive imperative ("allow yourselves to be built up," "be built up") or as a passive indicative ("you are being built up"). Either form of such an imperative, however, would be without parallel in both the LXX and the NT and would be inconsistent with the indicative mood of vv 4–10 as a whole. The verb is therefore best taken a passive indicative verb that is consonant with the prevailing indicative mood of vv 4–10 and with biblical usage (Selwyn 1947, 159; Elliott 1966b, 163; Vanhoye 1986, 256). For the passive indicative of *oikodomeō*, often with God as implied agent, see Ps 88[89]:3; Isa 44:28; 54:14; 58:12; Jer 12:16; and for the biblical metaphor of God's salvific "building up" of his people in the sense of uniting and restoring them, see Ps 88[89]:3; Isa 54:11–14; Jer 1:10; 12:16; 38[31]:4, 28; 49[42]:10; cf. also Amos 9:11; Jdt 16:14; and for rabbinic usage, Billerbeck (1926, 1:732–33).

As a divine passive, *oikodomeisthe* expresses semantically the idea of God's construction and consolidation of the living stones into a single unit (see 5:10, where God is the explicit subject of the kindred verb *themeliōsei*, "will establish") and is consonant with the divine passives elsewhere in this context (vv 6c, 7d, 8c, 10c) and frequently throughout the letter.[39] Moreover, as God is the implied agent of Jesus' election and honoring (v 4d) and the subject of

---

[39] See 1:2d, 5b, 7c, 12a, 12b, 13b, 18a, 20 (2×), 23a; 2:21a, 22b, 24d, 25b; 3:9d, 16d, 18e, 20d, 22c; 4:18a, 5:1c, 4a.

tithēmi in v 6b, so here in the parallel to v 4 God is also the implied agent of the community's construction. Linguistically, the verb is related to the following noun *oikos*, "house(hold)." However, this noun is part of an ellipsis beginning a new statement and, with v 5d, the metaphor shifts from "stones" being built up to persons who constitute a "house(hold)" and "priestly community." While the verb and the building-metaphor occur also in Paul,[40] 1 Pet 2:5 represents a unique formulation independent of Pauline influence (Kitzberger 1986, 309–19).[41]

5d. *[you are] a house(hold) of the Spirit (oikos pneumatikos)*. As already noted, *oikos pneumatikos* is a nominative phrase and therefore not the object of the preceding verb, *oikodomeisthe*, as numerous translations would suggest. The phrase *oikos pneumatikos* is, rather, part of an ellipsis, with the verb "you are" implied. Such ellipses occur elsewhere in this context (vv 7a, 9a, 10a, b, c, d) and frequently throughout the letter.[42]

The meaning of *oikos* here and in 4:17 (*oikos tou theou*) is ambiguous and has been the subject of much discussion. The Greek term *oikos*, occurring some 114 times in the NT alone, like its Hebrew equivalent *bayit/bet*, means "house," referring either to (1) a "family" or kin group, or "household" (of kin and non-kin) residing in a given place, or (2) the residence itself, the building in which persons lived (*oikos* as equivalent to *oikia*). The term could also designate (3) an extended family, clan, tribe, realm, or lineage, as in the "house of Jacob," "house of Israel," "house of Pharaoh," or "house of David." In Jesus' day, the people worshiping Yahweh were known as "the house of Israel" (Matt 15:24; cf. Acts 2:36; 7:42) or "the house of Jacob" (Luke 1:33). Jesus and his father were more specifically of the "house of David" (Luke 1:27, 69; 2:4). Metaphorically, *oikos* could refer to a temple, shrine, or sanctury as the "house" or "dwelling-place" of a deity, and in this sense it frequently is used of the Jerusalem Temple. It could also serve to designate a community of people as "household" or "family" of God (see below). More generally it could mean "home" as a place of residence and belonging (Mark 2:1; 2:11/Matt 9:6/Luke 5:24; Mark 3:20a; 5:19/Luke 8:39; Mark 8:26; Matt 12:44/Luke 11:24; 15:6; Acts 2:46; 5:42; 1 Cor 14:34, 35).

In the case of such a polyvalent term, the context of its use generally determines its meaning. The famous text of 2 Sam [2 Kgdms] 7:1–17 (cf. 1 Chr 17:1–15), however, dramatically illustrates an instance in which multiple denotations could occur within a single passage. Whereas King David had planned to build God a house (*oikos*, i.e., a temple), God countered his intention by promising to build him a house (*oikos*, i.e., royal lineage) that would last

---

[40] See 1 Cor 3:9; 8:1, 10; 10:23; 14:3–4, 17; 2 Cor 5:1; 10:8; 12:19; 13:10; Gal 2:18; 1 Thess 5:11; cf. Eph 2:19–22; 4:11–16, 29; Col 2:7.

[41] On the concept of "building" in Pauline usage, see Vielhauer 1940; Pfammatter 1960; Kitzberger 1986; on Eph 2:19–22, see the NOTE on 2:6.

[42] See 1:3a, 4a, 8b; 2:16a, 19a, 20a, 20f; 3:8, 14, 16a; 4:9, 11a (2×), 11b; 4:14b, 16a, 16c, 17a, 17b, 17c; 5:11, 13b.

forever. On the interweaving of Temple and Davidic traditions, see Bergmeier 1995. In later time the Qumran community saw itself as the eschatological realization of this promise to David (4QFlor; 4Q147; Bergmeier 1995). In the NT the polyvalence of *oikos* is especially evident in Acts 7, where *oikos* designates Pharaoh's "realm" (7:10), Moses' father's "house(hold)" (7:20), the "house" of Israel (7:42), the "house" of Jacob (7:46), and Solomon's Temple (7:47; cf. v 49). Certain Israelite apocalyptic texts anticipated the construction of an eschatological dwelling-place of God to last forever, speaking of it as either "a house" built for the Great King (*1 En.* 91:13), "a royal temple of the Great One" (4QEnoch^{g}) or a "sanctuary" that God would build in the midst of his people (*Jub.* 1:17).

In the case of 1 Peter, various reasons have been advanced for regarding *oikos* as an allusion to "Temple": the frequent use of *oikos* for Temple in the LXX; the early Christian conception of the church as the eschatological Temple of God, similar to the self-understanding of the Qumran community; an assumed affinity of *oikos* with the "stone" tradition and the messianic connotations of the Temple foundation-stone or copestone; or the accompanying language in v 5 "(holy priestly community . . . offer sacrifices"), which is thought to give *oikos* a "cultic connotation."[43]

However, the structure of 2:4–10, in which the terms of v 5 (*oikos, hierateuma, hagion*) anticipate those of v 9 (*basileion, hierateuma, hagion*), and the wider context of the letter as a whole favor the rendition "house(hold)."[44]

(1) In the NT, *oikos* can denote "Temple" as the house of God, but only in OT quotations (Mark 11:17/Matt 21:13/Luke 19:46/John 2:16; Acts 7:49) or OT allusions (Mark 2:26 par.; Luke 11:51; Acts 7:47, 49) or their context (John 2:17). If our author had intended to portray the believers as constituting a new "Temple" of God, *naos*, the frequent term for Temple, would have been more appropriate. In the NT, *naos* occurs 18× in reference to the Jerusalem Temple. It also is used metaphorically to designate Jesus' body as "Temple" (John 2:19–21; cf. Rev 21:22) and the Christian community as God's Temple or dwelling-place (1 Cor 3:16–17; 6:19–20; 2 Cor 6:16; Eph 2:21–22; Rev 3:12; cf. *Barn.* 4:11; 16:1–10; Ign. *Eph.* 9:1–2; *Magn.* 7:1–2; *Phld.* 7:2). Under its priestly leadership, the Qumran community also had identified itself as the true Temple and dwelling-place of God in contrast to the allegedly corrupt Jerusalem Temple (1QS V 5–7; VIII 1–10; IX 3–6; CD III 19).

On the other hand, when Christians are portrayed as the "Temple" of God in the NT, *oikos* is never used. The Petrine author speaks of an *oikos*, not a *naos*, and manifests no interest in polemicizing against the Jerusalem Temple and its cult or in claiming its replacement by a new "Temple" served by the Christian equivalent of the "sons of Aaron."

---

[43] So Blinzler 1949, 54–55; Gärtner 1965, 72–79; McKelvey 1969, 128; Best 1971, 101–2; Goppelt 1993, 141; see also Selwyn 1947, 160, 285–91; Congar 1962, 175–80.

[44] See Elliott 1966b, 156–59; 1981/1990, 167–70, 200–37, 240–41; so also J. Rousseau 1986, 343–44, 382; Dalton 1990, 905; cf. Vielhauer 1940, 146–47; Schlatter 1928, 28–29.

(2) Elsewhere in the NT, *oikos* designates not only a literal household or family (Acts 10:2; 11:14; 16:15, 31; 18:8; 1 Cor 1:16; 1 Tim 3:4, 5, 12; 5:4; 2 Tim 1:16; 4:19; Titus 1:11; Heb 11:7). It also identifies the Christian community metaphorically as the "household" or "family" of God (1 Tim 3:15; Heb 3:1–6 [alluding to Num 12:7, "My servant Moses . . . is faithful in my entire house," with *oikos* implying Israel]; Heb 10:21; see also Gal 6:10 [*oikeious tēs pisteōs*, "household of faith"]). This metaphor is related to, if not immediately derived from, Jesus' redefinition of his family as "those who do the will of God" (Mark 3:31–35 par.) and represents his fundamental image for describing the eschatological people of God (Elliott 1991); see Aalen (1962) on the association of *oikos* and reign of God, and Michel (1967) on *oikos* and related terms.

(3) In v 5 *oikos* is juxtaposed to *hierateuma*, a term derived from the covenant formula of Exod 19:5–6, cited in v 9. Thus *oikos* here appears to be a Petrine equivalent for *basileion* juxtaposed with *hierateuma* in v 9. In the entire tradition of interpretation of Exod 19:5–6, *basileion* is never interpreted as "Temple" but, rather, as "royal residence" (of God) (Elliott 1966b, 50–128).

(4) An identical interpretation of *basileion* as *oikos* is given by the near contemporary, Philo, in a text in which he too cites LXX Exod 19:6, namely *De sobrietate* 66. Philo cites the Exodus formula in his comment on Gen 9:27, "God enlarge Japheth and may he dwell in the houses (*oikous*) of Shem":

> Once more Jacob is the source of the twelve tribes, of whom the oracles say that they are "the royal residence and priestly community (*basileion kai hierateuma*) of God," thus following in due sequence the thought originated in Shem, in whose houses (*oikous*) it was prayed that God might dwell. For surely by "royal residence" (*basileion*) is meant the King's house (*ho basileōs . . . oikos*), which is holy indeed and the only inviolable sanctuary.

Here Philo not only explicitly explains the *basileion* of Exod 19:6 as "the King's house (*ho basileōs . . . oikos*) but sees this identification of *basileion* as *oikos* of God as being consistent with the thought that the "twelve tribes" and the "houses" (*oikous*) of Shem are the dwelling-place of God. It is the "house of Jacob" (cf. Exod 19:3), the "houses" of Shem (i.e., the people of God), which as God's *basileion* are God's dwelling place. Nothing is said here of Israel as "the Temple of God," an invalid claim that Seland (1995, 109) bases on his premise that "the only place where God can be 'housed' is the Temple." Indeed, Philo again uses *basileion* and *oikos theou* synonymously (*Praem*. 123) in describing the mind of a wise man: "for in truth the wise man's mind is a royal residence and house of God (*basileion kai oikos theou*)," which is declared to "possess personally the God who is the God of all," similar to "the chosen people . . . of the one and only true ruler, a people holy even as He is holy."

There are no grounds for supposing literary dependence here, for the contexts and lines of thought in 1 Peter and Philo are quite dissimilar. Both authors, rather, reflect a traditional understanding of the Exodus formula, in which *basileion* is regarded as a substantive with the sense of *oikos* or divine dwelling place. They likewise concur in employing the Exodus formula to demonstrate God's dwelling within the covenant people (the house [*oikos*] of Jacob, the houses [*oikoi*] of Shem, or the house [*oikos*] of the believing Christians) by intepreting *basileion* as the *human community* in which God dwells as king.

(5) The immediate Petrine context also favors this alternative.

First, the structure of vv 4–10 involves a correspondence of vv 5 and 9; see also the NOTE on 2:9. As v 5 announces and interprets elements of v 9, and as *hierateuma* and *hagion* of v 9 are anticipated in *hierateuma hagion* in v 5, so *oikos* anticipates and interprets the term *basileion*, which accompanies *hierateuma* in v 9 (see further detail in NOTE on 2:9). Moreover, in Exod 19:6, which is cited in 2:9, *basileion* is an epithet applied to the "house (*oikos*) of Jacob" (Exod 19:3) not as "Temple" but as the *people* over whom God rules and with whom God dwells ("royal residence"). In 2:5d, *oikos* also corresponds to *basileion* (2:9b) but, as in 2:9b, this epithet for the house of Jacob is applied to the house(hold) of the faithful as constituting the eschatological community of the elect.

Second, *oikos pneumatikos* introduces in v 5 new material (anticipating v 9) that originally had no connection with the "stone" metaphor (v 4) and its tradition (vv 6–8). This "stone" tradition cannot be used, as Goppelt attempts to do (1993, 141), for determining the meaning of *oikos* as "Temple." Although Isa 28:16 (cited in 2:6) and Ps 117[118]:22 (cited in 2:7) imply references to the Temple in Jerusalem, the Petrine use of these texts restricts attention to their *Christological* implications (Jesus Christ as *lithos*) and the distinction between honored believers and shamed nonbelievers.

Third, because of the polyvalence of the term *oikos* (meaning either *house-as-building* or *house-as-people*), the phrase *oikos pneumatikos* is admirably suited to facilitate the shift in v 5 from the notion of believers-as-stones being built up (*oikodomeisthe*) to their identification as *house(hold) of the Spirit*.

Fourth, as an appositive to "holy priestly community" in 2:5, *oikos* as "household" rather than as "Temple" makes better sense: a household of persons, like a priestly community, can offer sacrifices, but a Temple cannot. A priestly community might be thought of as serving within a Temple, but then it cannot also simultaneously constitute the Temple itself.

Fifth, the more remote context of 1 Peter also emphatically favors this alternative. In 4:17 the phrase *oikos tou theou* reformulates *oikos pneumatikos* (*tou theou* = *pneumatikos*), and the contrast between the household of God, identified as a community ("us," 4:17b), and the "disobedient" (4:17b) replicates the same contrast in 2:7a/7b–8. Moreover, the sense of *oikos* as "house(hold)" or "family" of God rather than as "Temple" in both instances is consistent with the depiction of the believing community in familial metaphors throughout the letter. The believers are "caused to be reborn" as "children" of God's holy family (1:3, 14–16, 23; 2:2–3). They form a "brotherhood" of faith (2:17; 5:9). Throughout the letter, additional familial terms and imagery are employed to depict the unity of the believers with God and one another and the intimacy of that relationship. God, their heavenly "Father" (1:2, 3, 17), has not only caused them to be reborn but nourishes (2:2) and consolidates them (2:5c; 5:10) into a household or family (2:5; 4:17). As God's children, they are subordinate to their heavenly father's will (2:15; 3:17; 4:2, 19) and owe him reverence (1:17; 2:17, 18; 3:2, 16) and honor (2:5f, 9; 4:11, 16; 5:11). As brothers and sisters, through faith in Jesus Christ they constitute a brotherhood whose intimate integrity is maintained through brotherly love (1:22; 2:17; 3:8; 4:8; cf. 2:11; 4:12) and related actions of familial solidarity (3:8; 4:8–11; 5:5b–7; cf. 2:18–20; 3:1–7; 5:1–5a). In this household of faith, household slaves (*oiketai*) are the examples of all (2:18–25), husbands and wives live together (*synoikein*) in domestic harmony (3:7), younger members respect the elders (5:5a), co-senders are regarded as "brother" (5:12) and "son" (5:13), and all serve one another as "household servants of the varied grace of God" (4:10). Familial imagery pervades this composition from beginning to end, and the model of household/family serves as the dominant ecclesial metaphor through which its consolation and exhortation are integrated. *Oikos pneumatikos* (*oikos tou theou*) constitutes the root metaphor for Christian community in 1 Peter, the fundamental concept that identifies the collective identity of the Christians, their relation to God and to one another, and the basis of their behavior as a family or brotherhood (Elliott 1981/1990, 200–37). On the role of house(hold) and family of God in the strategy of 1 Peter, see also the GENERAL INTRODUCTION, 6. Aim, Strategy.

The adjective *pneumatikos* ("of the Spirit" [*pneuma*], "spiritual") can indicate the inner dimension of a human being (1 Pet 3:4), but "in the great majority of cases it refers to the divine *pneuma*: 'caused by or filled with the (divine) Spirit'" (BAGD 678). Accordingly, the adjective here recalls the divine Spirit by whom the believers were sanctified (1:2; cf. 2:5, 9) and anticipates reference to the "divine Spirit of glory" resting upon them (4:14). The function of *pneumatikos*, which modifies both "house(hold)" (v 5d) and "sacrifices" (v 5f), is not to identify these entities as "figurative" or "immaterial" (in contrast to material realities) or as contrasted to Israelite physical cultic sacrifices, but as entities that are controlled and animated by God's sanctifiying Spirit. In the phrase "a house(hold) of the Spirit," the author interprets the term "royal residence" (*basileion*) in v 9b and identifies the divine King of the residence as God, by whose Holy Spirit the community was sanctified and brought into being. On *pneumatikos* in 2:5, see also Selwyn 1947, 281–85.

5e. *to be a holy "priestly community" (eis hierateuma hagion)*. The uncertain syntactical relation of this phrase to the foregoing is reflected in the textual variants. Some manuscripts omit the preposition *eis* (𝔐, later uncials [K L P], most minuscules, vg), perhaps regarding this phrase as nominative in apposition to *oikos pneumatikos* (as *basileion* is to *hierateuma* in v 9bc) and likewise controlled by the ellipsis *you are* (*you are a house*[*hold*] *of the Spirit, a holy priestly community*). Inclusion of the preposition, however, has earlier and superior attestation ($\mathfrak{P}^{72}$ ℵ A B C and others). In this preferred reading, *eis hierateuma* is subordinate to and qualifies "household of the Spirit" by indicating its purpose: "[you are] a house(hold) of the Spirit to be a holy 'priestly community' to offer spiritual sacrifices . . ."). Similar *eis* constructions expressing purpose occur in the immediate context (2:7d, 8c, 9c) and elsewhere (1:3c, 4a, 5b, 7c, 22a; 2:14b, 21a; 3:7f, 9a; 4:2a, 7b). The Semitic character of this construction is demonstrated by Wis 14:11; Bar 2:23; Jdt 5:10, 18, 21, 24; Sir 31:10; Matt 19:5; Luke 3:5; 2 Cor 6:18; Heb 1:5; 8:10.

The word *hierateuma* here and in v 9 is unique in the NT. Its absence in secular Greek and its occurrence elsewhere only in LXX Exod 19:6 (repeated in Exod 23:22 LXX but not in the MT) decisively indicates its derivation from LXX Exod 19:6. Exodus 19:5–6 comprises part of the ancient formulation of the covenant established by God with the house of Jacob on Mt. Sinai (Exod 19:3–8):

> Thus you shall say to the house of Jacob and tell the people of Israel: "You have seen what I did to the Egyptians, and how I bore you on eagle's wings and brought you to myself. Now therefore, if you will obey my voice and keep my covenant, you shall be my own possession among all peoples; for all the earth is mine; and you shall be to me a kingdom of priests and a holy people (*mamleket kōhănîm wĕgôy qādôš / basileion hierateuma kai ethnos hagion*)."

This covenant established the basis of Israel's union with God as its exclusive kingly ruler, its collective identity as God's special elect and holy people, its rights and particular obligations, and its demarcation from all other nations. The history of the subsequent references to this covenantal formulation of Exod 19:5–6 prior to 1 Peter (*Jub.* 16:18, 33:20; Greek Frg. of *T. Levi* 11:4–6; 2 Macc 2:17; Philo, *Sobr.* 66; *Abr.* 56) indicates that this text was consistently employed to affirm not aspects of Israel's kingship or priesthood in particular but Israel's collective identity as *the elect and holy people of God the king* (Elliott 1966b, 50–128).[45]

In 1 Pet 2:4–10, a pronounced emphasis upon election (*eklektos*, vv 4d, 9a) frames these verses. Moreover, the combined use of Exod 19:5–6 and Isa 43:2–21 in v 9 indicates that the terms of the Exodus text employed in vv 5 and 9 have the same import as in earlier tradition generally and are intended to designate the believing community collectively as the elect and holy covenant people of God. Here, cardinal identifying features of ancient Israel, the house of Jacob covenanted with God at Sinai, are employed to affirm the elect and holy character of the community of the reborn, the family of God.

---

[45] In regard to Philo in particular, the term *hierateuma* occurs only in *Sobr.* 66 and *Abr.* 56. Seland (1995, 110–12) refers to Philonic passages speaking of Israel's corporate functioning as priests (e.g., at Passover; cf. *Mos.* 2.224–25; *Spec.* 2.145; *QE* 1.10 and further *Spec.* 1.243; 2.164). But they have no direct bearing on the meaning of *hierateuma* in *Sobr.* 66 and *Abr.* 56.

The unique term *hierateuma*, moreover, is a collective term analogous to other collective terms with the *-euma* suffix (e.g., *bouleuma* ["council session"], *politeuma* ["corporate civil body"], *presbeuma* ["embassy, delegation"], *techniteuma* ["body of craftsmen"], *strateuma* ["army"]; cf. Elliott 1966b, 64–70). Like these analogous terms, *hierateuma* identifies a (1) collectivity of (2) persons (3) exercising a specific function. Thus, like its accompanying term *oikos* and the other collective terms of vv 9–10, it denotes not individuals, not "priests" (*hiereis*), not even an abstract "priesthood" (*hierateia*), but a "body of priests," *a community of holy persons enjoying, like priests, direct access to God and functioning in this capacity* (see also the NOTE on v 9). This is its sense in LXX Exod 19:6 as well as 1 Peter, with the decisive difference that in 1 Peter this term of the ancient covenant formula is now applied exclusively to the children of God who have been reborn in Christ. Christian participation in the historic covenant made between God and Israel at Sinai is the point of this Petrine passage, and its focus is the election and holiness of God's eschatological people.

The Petrine author shows no interest elsewhere in the letter in developing a notion of Christians as priests. The term *hierateuma*, like *basileion*, was derived from a covenantal formula (Exod 19:6) expressing the privileged status and the elect and holy character of God's people. This is the sense in which the formula was interpreted before 1 Peter, and this is its sense in this letter as well. Thus, *hierateuma* is related conceptually to the letter's stress on the holiness, purity, and election of the Christian community but not to any notion of Christian "priestliness." Nor is any connection made between this term and the passages that deal with the mutual ministries within the community (4:8–10) or congregational authority and order (5:1–4). Later attempts in Christian history to see in this text and the term *hierateuma* in particular a basis for a general priesthood of all believers, in which all of the baptized (and not just the clergy) have the authority and status of priests and kings (e.g., Tertullian, Luther, and post-Reformation theology) have seriously misconstrued the actual focus of 2:4–10. In attempting to exploit this text for dealing with issues of authority and ecclesial order, they have distorted the collective sense of *hierateuma*, isolated it from its covenantal context, and ignored the function of this convenantal formulation as an emphasis on the election and holiness of the people of God. For further discussion of the Exodus text and its interpretive history, see Elliott 1966b, 50–128.[46]

The phrase "holy people" (*ethnos hagion*) stands in apposition to the terms "royal residence" (*basileion*) and "priestly community" (*hierateuma*) in v 9 (citing Exod 19:6). Similarly, in v 5, which anticipates v 9, *holy* modifies "priestly community" and further underlines the essentially sacred nature of "priestly community"—namely, its proximity to God, the Holy One (1:15a). This stress

[46] For discussion of the idea of the priesthood of all believers, see the DETAILED COMMENT.

on the holiness of the covenant people and its implication of separation from the unholy Gentiles is consonant with earlier references to Exod 19:6, especially in *Jub.* 16:17–18 and 33:20.[47] Accentuation of the *holy* nature of the believing community likewise reinforces earlier stress on the believers' sanctification (1:2, 22), their union with a holy God and divine calling to holy conduct (*anastrophē*, 1:15–16), their redemption through the blood of Christ the holy lamb (1:18–19), and their purity (1:22). It thus forms part of a fundamental stress on the holiness of the community, which in turn undergirds the following exhortation concerning the community's holy and honorable conduct in society (2:11–5:11). Holiness, for 1 Peter, is a concept with social and ethical, rather than cultic, implications.

5f. *to offer spiritual sacrifices (anenegkai pneumatikas thysias)*. The members of this spiritual house(hold) and holy priestly community offer "spiritual sacrifices" (*pneumatikas thysias*); that is, sacrifices prompted by the Holy Spirit. The phrase "to offer sacrifices" (*anenegkai . . . thysias*) recalls the Levitical sacrificial system (Lev 17:5; Isa 57:6; 1 Esd 5:49; 2 Macc 1:18; Heb 7:27) but is also used with reference to offering sacrifices of praise (Heb 13:15; cf. 2 Chr 29:31). Since this phrase anticipates and interprets the expression in v 9, "that you may 'declare the praises' of him who 'called' you out of darkness into his marvelous light," it is clearly the offering of praise and thanksgiving that is suggested here. The use of the term "sacrifices" is consonant with the depiction of the believers as a "priestly community" and spells out its proper priestly function. Nowhere else in the letter, however, is there any elaboration of the concept of the believers as a priestly community. Nor is there any suggestion that believers as a priestly community or with their sacrifices share in the sacrifice of Christ or in his priesthood (against Feuillet 1974; also against Luther, who takes this as a teaching that the believers, "like true priests [are] to sacrifice themselves to God as Christ sacrificed himself," *LW* 35:391). In 1 Peter, Christ is nowhere depicted as a priest; it is as living stones, as the elect of God, and as sharers of his suffering and glory through faith that believers are united with their suffering and resurrected Lord, the elect and living stone.

The nature of the sacrifices is instead determined by tradition as well as context. Since the time of the prophets, thanksgiving and righteous conduct were

---

[47] *Jubilees* 16:17–18: "But from the sons of Isaac one (Jacob) would become a *holy* seed and he would not be counted among the nations because he would become the portion of the Most High and all his seed would fall (by lot) into that which God will rule so that he might become *a kingdom and priests and a holy nation*." See also Abraham's blessing of Jacob: "May he *elect* you and your seed so that you become a people for him who always belong to his inheritance according to his will (*Jub.* 22:10) . . . in order to be a *holy people* (*Jub.* 22:12)." The context of *Jub.* 33:20 (33:18–20) recounts Moses' being directed to warn the people of sexual defilement as incompatible with Israel's holiness and concludes (v 20): "And there is no greater sin than the fornication that they [the defiled] commit upon the earth, for Israel is a *holy people* to the Lord his God, and a people of inheritance, and *a priestly and royal people*, and a (special) possession. And there is nothing that appears, that is as defiled as this among the *holy people*."

considered equivalent, and in some instances superior, to animal sacrifices.[48] Among Israelites of the Diaspora for whom sacrifice at the Jerusalem Temple was not always possible, the equation of praise and moral conduct with such sacrifices was particularly welcomed (Sir 35:1; Jdt 16:16; 2 *En*. 45:3; *Let. Aris*. 234). In similar fashion, the sacrifices of which our author speaks involve the glorification of God through praise (2:9; cf. 2:12; 4:11d; 5:11; cf. Ps 115[116]:8; Heb 13:15) and honorable and holy conduct (*anastrophē*, 2:12; 4:11c; cf. 1:15; 3:2, 15–16), the doing of good in accord with God's will (2:14, 15, 20; 3:6, 10–12, 13, 16, 17, 21), and upright behavior (*dikaiosynē*, 2:24c; 3:14; cf. Ps 4:6 ["offer the sacrifice of righteousness and hope in the Lord"]; and Elliott 1966b, 174–85). In his letter to the Romans, Paul likewise exhorted the readers to "present your bodies as a living sacrifice, holy and acceptable to God, which is your spiritual service" (12:1, followed by references to moral conduct in 12:3–15:13). He further employed the cultic metaphor in speaking of his ministry as a "priestly serving" (*hierourgounta*) of the gospel of God and of the Gentiles as his "offering" (*prosphora*) to God (15:16; cf. Phil 2:17; 2 Tim 4:6). The letter to the Hebrews entails the broadest NT use of the cultic metaphor in its description of Christ as both priest and victim (4:14–5:10; 6:20–10:31; cf. Eph 5:2); for a subsequent development, see also *1 Clem*. 40, 43; 44:1–4. In 1 Peter, by contrast, cultic metaphors are minimal ("sprinkling," 1:2 and "blood," 1:19; cf. "bring us to God," 3:18c), and it is chiefly moral action by which the holiness of the believers is to be demonstrated.[49] Although it is conceivable that these offerings of thanksgiving might include the eucharist,[50] there is no certain evidence of this in our text or its context.

spiritual (pneumatikas). In this context, "spiritual" approximates the notion of "holy" ("holy priestly community"); holiness and sanctification, in turn, are marks of the Holy Spirit (1:2; cf. 1:11, 12; 4:14). Thus, in tandem with the house(hold) governed by the Spirit, "spiritual" qualifies the sacrifices as "motivated by the Holy Spirit." Selwyn (1947, 161) and Moule (1950, 34–35) suspect in the qualifier "spiritual" a contrast to and implied criticism of the animal sacrifices of the Israelite cult. On the other hand, Danker (1967b, 330), noting the influence of Isa 43 on 1 Pet 2:4–10 (Isa 43:20–21, cited in 2:9), sees in the expression "spiritual sacrifices acceptable to God" not a polemic against the cult in particular but a contrast to the sacrifices of Israel that failed to honor God (Isa 43:23). In view of 2:7b–8 with its critique of all nonbelievers, Israelites and pagans alike, such a contrast is conceivable but at best implicit. Within the present and more remote context of 1 Peter, the sacrifices moti-

---

[48] See Hos 6:6, cited by Jesus (Matt 9:13; 12:7); Isa 1:10–17; Ps 49[50]:13–23; 50[51]:17–19; Amos 5:23–24; Mic 6:6–8; cf. 1QS VIII 8; 9.4–6; X 6; Philo, *Spec*. 1.272; *Barn*. 2:1–10.

[49] On the metaphorical use of cultic concepts in Israel and Christianity, see Schmitz 1910; Wenschkewitz 1932; Seidensticker 1954; Best 1960; Elliott 1966b, 154–56; Klinzing 1971; Feuillet 1974; Schüssler Fiorenza 1976a; Ferguson 1980; Hill 1982.

[50] So Selwyn 1947, 160–61, 294–98, following Lohmeyer 1937; Dacquino 1967; J. N. D. Kelly 1969, 91–92; Hill 1982, 63; cf. *1 Clem*. 44:4; Ign. *Eph*. 5:2; *Phld*. 4; also *Did*. 14:1–3.

vated by the Spirit are best seen as encompassing the praise of God (2:9; 4:11d; 5:11) and a holy, righteous, and honorable way of life lived to the glory of God.[51]

acceptable to God through Jesus Christ (euprosdektous [tōi] theōi dia Iēsou Christou). This phrase modifies spiritual sacrifices. The sacrifices are acceptable or "well-pleasing" to God (*euprosdektous* [*tōi*] *theōi*) because they are motivated by the Holy Spirit and offered through the mediation of Jesus Christ (*dia Iēsou Christou*). For *acceptable to God* (with varying Greek terms), see also Rom 15:16; 2 Cor 8:12; Phil 4:18; Heb 12:28; 13:15–16; 1 Tim 2:3.

through Jesus Christ expresses the mediatorial role of Jesus Christ here, as elsewhere in the letter (1:3; 3:21; 4:11). The words *Jesus Christ* likewise make it clear that it is *he* that is the "Lord" (v 3) to whom the believers have come (v 4), the "elect" and "living stone" whose attributes believers share, as well as the "stone" whom the nonbelievers have rejected and the object of the "word" that they have disobeyed (v 8b). The combination of Spirit (*spiritual*), God, and Jesus Christ recalls the triadic formulations of 1:2 and 1:3–12.

6a. *for it stands in Scripture (dioti periechei en graphēi).* This expression (unique in the NT) initially introduces a citation of Isa 28:16 (v 6bc), a text that has supplied the "stone" image of v 4 and its accompanying adjectives "elect" and "honored." This OT text is combined by the author with two other "stone" texts (Ps 117[118]:22a in v 7cd; Isa 8:14 in v 8a), and this complex of OT citations is followed in vv 9–10 by another group of OT quotations or allusions. In its entirety this constitutes one of the most extensive chains of OT citations in the NT.

The formulation *periechei en graphēi* means "it is contained in writing" or "it stands in writing" (Hort 1898, 114–15); compare the variant readings in *T. Levi* 10:5 (*periechei hē biblos Enōch* [Greek MSS]; *gegraptai in biblois* [Armenian Version]). In the NT, however, *hē graphē* (*hai graphai*) frequently refers to the sacred writings of the OT.[52] In view of this usage, the explicit OT citations in vv 6–10, and the use of *dioti* in 1:16, 24 to introduce scriptural citations, *graphē* despite its lack of the definite article is best taken as a reference to Sacred Scripture rather than to a less definite "writing" or, more specifically, a written collection of OT "testimonies"[53] or a hymn (against Selwyn 1947, 273–77; cf. Elliott 1966b, 133–38; Snodgrass 1977, 105).

This introductory clause thus introduces two complexes of OT passages concerning a stone (vv 6–8) and the people of God (vv 9–10) and thereby identifies

---

[51] See 1:15; 2:12, 13–17, 18–20, 24c; 3:1–4, 7, 8–12, 13–17; 4:1–4, 7–11, 12–19; 5:2–4, 5–9; cf. Elliott 1966b, 174–85.

[52] See Mark 12:10; Luke 4:21; John 7:38, 42; Acts 8:35; Rom 4:3; 9:17; 10:11; 11:2; Gal 3:8; 4:30; 2 Tim 3:16; Jas 4:5; cf. Stephenson 1902–3.

[53] J. R. Harris (1916–1920) found in the Testimonia collection edited by Cyprian in the third century examples of a use of OT testimonies, which he thought could be traced back to the NT period. His conclusion that the "stone" passages of Peter and Paul reflected use of some such Testimonia source was accepted by Plooy (1932) and a few others (listed in Elliott 1966b, 131) but was generally rejected (Hommes 1935; Smits 1952–1963; Dodd 1953, 24–27; Elliott 1966b, 130–33; cf. also Ellis 1957, 98–113; Sundberg 1959; Barnard 1964b; Snodgrass 1977, 105–6; Hodgson 1979).

the scriptural sources and sacred warrant for vv 4–5. At the same time, vv 6–8 and 9–10 also contain the author's glosses on these OT texts (vv 7ab, 8bc, 9a, 9f, 10), which expatiate further on the Christological and ecclesiological implications and applications of this OT material.

6b. *"Behold, I am setting in Zion a stone" (idou tithēmi en Siōn lithon)*. The OT text cited is Isa 28:16, a verse from a passage indicting Jerusalem's lying leaders, who have covenanted with death (vv 14–15), and announcing that God will set in Zion a stone for a sure foundation of justice and deliverance (vv 16–22). Isaiah probably conceived of the stone as a reference to the kingdom founded on David (so Hort 1898, 117); compare Ps 2:6 ("I have established my king on Zion my holy mountain") and Ps 110:2. The adjectives accompanying "stone" describe the preeminence and national strength and security provided by this kingdom. The earliest interpretation of "stone" in this Isaian passage explicitly identifies it with the (messianic) king whom God will establish for Judah's security: "Behold, I will appoint in Zion a king, a strong king, powerful and terrible" (*Isaiah Targum*).

This association of the stone with a *human being* is already presumed in the LXX, which in the second half of the verse adds the words "in him" following "believe" (lacking in the Hebrew text). At a later point, the Qumran community applied Isa 28:16 to itself as a firm foundation for the house of Israel (1QS VIII 7, with further possible allusions in 1QS V 5; 4Q164; 1QH[a] VI 26–27; VII 8–9). This Israelite interpretive tradition prepared the way for the association of Isa 28:16, and "stone" in particular, with Jesus as the Messiah (Jeremias 1967, 272–73; cf. also Snodgrass 1977). As Paul (Rom 9:32–33; 10:11) and 1 Peter illustrate, the messianic sect continued and expanded on this understanding.

The Petrine version entails certain variations from that of the LXX, which reads: "Behold I (*egō*) am laying for the foundations (*embalō eis ta themelia*) of Zion a stone, costly (*polytelē*), elect, a cornerstone, honored, for its foundations (*eis ta themelia autēs*), and whoever believes in him is not shamed." The variant *tithēmi* (for *emballō*) both here and in Rom 9:33, the omission of "costly" and "for the/its foundations" in both, and the different verb form in Paul ("will not be shamed" [*kataischynthēsetai*, Rom 9:33; 10:11]; contrast *kataischynthēi* in 1 Peter) all suggest varying Greek text forms underlying the citation of this Isaian verse by Paul and the Petrine author. The verb *tithēmi* ("I am setting") here and in v 8d (*etethēsan*, "they were set") refers to God's activity and forms an inclusion framing the "stone" texts of vv 6–8.

in Zion (en Siōn). "Zion" here and in Isa 28:16 is a metonymy (a part used for the whole) for Israel or Jerusalem but refers specifically to the mount on which the royal palace and the Jerusalem Temple were located (cf. Isa 30:29, "go to the mountain of the Lord, to the rock of Israel"). The cosmic, historical, and theological associations of Zion and the stone on which the Temple was situated (navel of the universe, site of Adam's creation and abode, stone altar on which Melchizedek and Abraham sacrified, association with Golgotha, intersection point of heaven and hell) are discussed by Jeremias (1926; cf. also

McKelvey 1969, 188–92). On the Zion tradition, its Davidic origins, and later developments, see Betz 1967; Ollenburger 1987.

a stone (lithon). "Stone," understood messianically by the Petrine author in accord with earlier Israelite tradition, supplied the term *lithos* as a metaphor for Jesus Christ in v 4b. It also constitutes the link-word joining this verse with vv 7b and 8a, where further OT "stone" passages are cited. The term *lithos* often designated a cut stone (building stone, millstone, gemstone) in contrast to *petra*, a rock that is still part of the natural environment. The accompanying modifiers declare this stone to be an eminent stone, an elect and honored cornerstone.

a cornerstone (akrogōniaion). This term is actually an adjective marking *lithon* as a special stone set at the extreme (*akro-*) corner (*gōnias*) of a building. It is attested only in the Bible, appearing only in Isa 28:16; 1 Pet 2:6; and Eph 2:20 (cf. *Barn.* 6:2). A similar expression, *lithos gōniaios* (Job 38:6), refers to the cornerstone of the foundation of the earth. The formulation *kephalēn gōnias* (v 7d) represents an equivalent. Jeremias (1925, 65–70; 1926, 11; 1937; 1964, 792; 1967, 274) favored viewing *lithos akrogōniaios* as the "keystone" or "capstone" that is set above the entrance of a building (as indicated in *Test. Sol.* 22:7–9; 23:1–4; see NOTE on 2:7b). But the Isaian text speaks of a stone "for the foundations" (*eis ta themelia*) and clearly implies a cornerstone for the base or foundation of a structure (so McKelvey 1962). "Since this stone was the one that gave the line of the building, it was carefully selected, dressed, squared, and tested" (McKelvey 1969, 198). This sense of *akrogōniaios* as pertaining to a foundation stone likewise fits the contexts of Isa 28; 1 Peter; and Eph 2:20–22 and is so presumed in later Israelite exegesis (McKelvey 1962; 1969, 188–92). Ephesians 2:20–22 alludes to, rather than quotes, Isa 28:16 (*akrogōniaios, themelia*). The description of Christ Jesus as "cornerstone" is used to develop the metaphor of the church as a building (*oikodomē*, v 21) built upon the foundation of the apostles and prophets, with Christ Jesus serving as the cornerstone and base stone through which the entire edifice is joined together and supported.[54]

The order of the adjectives modifying "stone" in 1 Peter is one of its several variations from the LXX (where *akrogōniaion* separates *eklekton* and *entimon*) but is supported by superior witnesses. The combination and sequence of *eklekton* and *entimon* in v 4d thus is identical to that in v 6b, and it is these lat-

[54] Besides *akrogōniaios*, Ephesians and 1 Pet 2:5 have in common further building terminology (Ephesians: *epoikodomēthentes* ["built upon"], *themeliōi* ["foundation"], *oikodomē* ["structure"], *synoikodomeisthe* ["you are built together"], *katoiktērion* ["dwelling place"]; 1 Peter: *oikodomeisthe* ["you are being built up"]), household imagery (Ephesians: *oikeioi* ["members of the household"]; 1 Peter: *oikos* ["household"]), and the theme of unification or consolidation. But Ephesians contains no parallel to the use of the OT "stone" texts in 1 Peter, and the unification it discusses concerns not the consolidation of the reborn, as in 1 Peter, but the integration of Israelite and Gentile believers in the church of Christ. The differences rule out the possibility of literary dependency, while the similiarities indicate common but divergent use of a messianically interpreted OT text; see McKelvey 1969, 195–204; Elliott 1990, 255.

ter two adjectives rather than *akrogōniaios* (omitted in v 4d) that form the basis of the author's comments in v 4 and vv 7–8.

elect (eklekton). The stone is specially selected (*eklekton*) to serve its special function as cornerstone, requiring appropriate size, strength, and beauty. The adjective *elect* in this Isaian verse (describing the Messiah) supplied the *elect* in v 4d describing Jesus. These references to election are balanced by the description of the believing community in v 9a as an "elect stock." Thus it is evident that it is the theme of election that pervades and unifies the three segments of vv 4–10. As the Messiah of Israel is elect, so Jesus Messiah/Christ is elect, and so the household of God is elect. An unrelated phrase, "elect stones" (*lithous eklektous*), appears in Isaiah's forecast of the rebuilding of Jerusalem and its walls after its destruction by the Babylonians (Isa 54:11–12; see also LXX Jer 38[MT 31]:39).

honored (entimon). This adjective can denote something as "precious" (e.g., blood, 1:19), but in this context, where "shame" (v 6c) is also mentioned, *honored*, the logical pendant to "shamed," is its implied sense. This term of the Isaian citation supplied the *entimon* of v 4d.

This image of Christ the honored cornerstone eventually became a staple of Christian hymnody, as illustrated by the following seventh-century Latin hymn:

> Christ is made the sure foundation,
> Christ the head and cornerstone;
> chosen of the Lord and precious
> binding all the church in one;
> holy Zion's help for ever,
> and her confidence alone.
> (trans. John Mason Neale, in *Hymns Ancient and Modern*, 1861)

6c. *and whoever believes in him (kai ho pisteuōn ep' autou)*. In the Isaian text, the participle *pisteuōn* has the sense of "trust" rather than "believe." In the NT, the verb *pisteuō* and the noun *pistis* also frequently denote belief in the sense of trust (cf. the NOTES on 1:6, 8). However "believe" in the Petrine context indicates the act that identifies the acceptance of and trust in Jesus as the living stone, which separates those who "believe" (v 7a) from nonbelievers (*apistousin*, v 7b), who "disobey" (*apeithentes*) the word (v 8b).

in him. The phrase *ep' autōi* is absent in the Hebrew text (and LXX Codex B) but was added in Codex A of the LXX. This addition had the effect of making the *stone* rather than God the object of trust and implying that "stone" refers to a person. This addition and its personal implication is also presumed in the *Isaiah Targum*: "Behold I set in Zion a king, a mighty king, mighty and terrible, whom I will uphold and strengthen; the prophet says: And the righteous in whom is confidence shall not tremble when affliction comes." Our author likewise regards this verse messianically and applies it to Jesus Christ; hence, the present context requires the translation *in him*.

will not be shamed (ou mē kataischynthēi). Still part of the Isaiah citation, the aor. pass. subj. *kataischynthēi* functions as a prospective subjunctive stating the outcome of belief (BDF §363), and the passive implies God's action (as in vv 5c, 8c, 10d; cf. also 3:16). According to Israelite and early Christian theology, it is God who ultimately shames, exposes, humiliates, and condemns the unfaithful and the opponents of God's people (Ps 30[31]:2, 18; 118[119]:31, 78, 116; Isa 47:3; Jer 23:40; Ezek 16, 23; LXX Dan 3:41; 1 Cor 1:27). Shame (cf. also 3:16; 4:16; 5:2) is the negative counterpart of honor (timē, v 7a; cf. 1:7; 3:7). The composite idea of belief/trust and not being put to shame occurs in Sir 2:10: "Whoever trusted in the Lord and was shamed?" (*tis enepisteusen kyriōi kai katēischynthē*). Honor and shame were fundamental, central values of the cultural system of the ancient Mediterranean. "Honor" concerned the positive social standing, reputation, and status rating of individuals and groups in the opinion of others and of God. "Shame" (*aischynē*; see also *aischynomai* ["feel shamed," 4:16]; *kataischynō* ["put to shame," 2:6; 3:16]; *aischrokerdōs* ["for shameful gain," 5:2]) entailed sensitivity regarding loss of honor or the actual loss of honor. The Bible is replete with honor and shame language[55] that reflects the centrality of these values in ancient Mediterranean culture,[56] and here it is God who is regarded as the ultimate conferrer or adjudicator of honor or shame. The idiom of honor and shame pervades 2:4–10 as the author contrasts the shameful rejection of Christ to his honor before God (v 4) and the divine shaming and condemnation of nonbelievers (vv 7b–8) to the honor conferred by God upon believers (vv 4, 9–10). Indeed the language of honor and shame, praise and blame, pervades the entire letter, as the public shaming to which Christians are exposed is contrasted to the honor that is theirs as God's elect and holy family of faith (2:12, 13–17, 18–25; 3:1–7, 8, 13–17; 4:1–6, 12–16; 5:10–11; see Elliott 1995a). Later in the letter the author returns to this theme of divine shaming when he notes how, on the one hand, those who disparage the good conduct of the believers will be put to shame (3:16) and, on the other, how suffering for being a Christian is no cause for shame but an opportunity for giving God glory/honor (4:16).

In vv 7–8, believers (v 7a) and nonbelievers (vv 7b–8) are contrasted in respect to their differing responses to Jesus as the "stone" established by God. The honor of the former, moreover, is contrasted to the shame of the latter. Much of the terminology derives from Isa 28:16 (v 7a); Ps 117[118]:22 (v 7bcd); and Isa 8:14 (v 8).

7a. *To you therefore who "believe" belongs this "honor" (hymin oun hē timē tois pisteouousin)*. The addressees, as believers (*tois pisteuousin*; cf. *pisteuōn*, v 6c from Isa 28:16), share in the honor (*timē*) of the messianic "stone" (cf.

[55] See Harrelson 1962; Vorster 1979; Malina and Neyrey 1991c; Plevnik 1993.

[56] See Vermeulen 1981; Malina 1993d, 28–62; cf. also Peristiany 1966; Gilmore, ed. 1987.

entimon, v 6b from Isa 28:16), just as they resemble Jesus Christ as "living stones" (vv 4–5).

7b. *but for those who do not "believe" (apistousin de)*. In contrast (*de*) to the honored believers, *those who do not believe* or disobey (*apistousin* [preferred over *apeithousin*, which the scribes assimilated to *apeithountes* in v 8b]) are those who have "rejected" Jesus as God's living stone (v 4c), as v 7cd makes clear. The substantive *hoi apistountes*, like the related *hoi apistoi* (1 Cor 6:6; 7:12, 13, 14, 15; 10:27; 14:22, 23, 24; 2 Cor 4:4; 6:14; 1 Tim 5:8; Titus 1:15; Rev 21:8) denotes all nonbelieving outsiders and in 1 Peter is synonymous with the expressions "those who disobey" (*apeitheō*, 2:8; 3:1; 4:17), "Gentiles" (*ta ethnē*, 2:12; 4:3), and "impious and sinner" (*asebēs kai hamartōlos*, 4:18). This is the first of several such contrasts between "us" and "them," believers and nonbelievers, throughout the letter (2:12, 15, 18; 3:1–2; 18–20; 3:13–17; 4:2–4; 4:14–18).

7c. *"the very stone that the builders rejected" (lithos hon apedokimasan hoi oikodomountes)*. These words derive from Ps 117[118]:22, a fragment of which was already employed in v 4c ("rejected," *apedokimasan*). The word *very* is added in the translation to express the antithesis between v 7c and v 7d, thus eliminating the need to translate the demonstrative pronoun *houtos* ("it") initiating v 7d.

Psalm 117[118] was one of the Hallel psalms (Pss 113–18) sung by the Levites at Passover during the slaughtering of the lambs (*m. Pesaḥ*. 5:7; 9:3; 10:5, 6). Mark 12:1–12 and parallels also seem aware of the connnection between this psalm and the Passover; see the Passover setting and the citation of Ps 117[118] in Mark 12:10–11/Matt 21:42/Luke 20:17. The psalmist may have been assumed to be David (Derrett 1978, 61) or some king who praises God for deliverance from affliction (Ps 117[118]:5–18, 21–25, 28–29). Verses 19–20, 26–27 suggest that the site of this praise was the Jerusalem Temple. The psalmist describes himself in his affliction by those who hate him (cf. v 7) as a "stone that the builders have rejected." But through God's deliverance (vv 15–18, 21), he, the rejected stone, "has become the head of the corner." According to Derrett (1978), the psalm is clearly "about David and therefore inferentially about the Messiah" (1978, 61). David is an instance of the "junior" and unlikely one whom God has chosen for his purpose (Derrett 1978, 62). In rabbinic teaching, this text was associated with either Abraham, Jacob, David, or the Messiah (Billerbeck 1926, 1:875–77) and, in Christian circles, with Jesus as Messiah.

According to the Evangelists, Jesus in debate with the Temple authorities cited this text at the conclusion of his parable of the wicked vineyard keepers (Matt 21:33–46/Mark 12:1–12/Luke 20:9–19; cf. *Gos. Thom*. 65–66), a parable that his opponents perceived to be directed against them (Matt 21:45/Mark 12:12) because they were rejecting Jesus as the tenants rejected and killed the son in the parable. Acts 4:11 (within Peter's speech to the Jerusalem authorities, vv 8–12) also shows that Ps 117[118] had become an early Christian prooftext for the death and resurrection of Jesus Christ, as it is in 1 Peter (2:4cd); compare also *Barn*. 6:4 (Ps 117[118]:22–23 combined with Isa 28:16 in 6:2).

The Petrine use of Ps 117[118] here differentiates 1 Peter from Paul, who makes no reference to this psalm in his citations of Isa 28:16 and Isa 8:14 (Rom 9:32–33), so that the Petrine formulation cannot be judged to be literarily dependent upon Paul.

builders (hoi oikodomountes). In the context of the psalm, the *builders* are the psalmist's oppressing enemies. Later, the Qumran sectarians criticized the Jerusalem establishment as "builders of a rickety wall" (CD IV 19, alluding to Ezek 13:10) or as "those who build the wall and cover it with whitewash" (CD VIII 12; cf. CD VIII 18, "God hates the builders of the wall"). Subsequent rabbinic tradition used the term as a positive designation for the Sages as "builders" of Israel through their Torah instruction (*b. Šabb.* 114a; *b. Ber.* 64a; *Midr. Cant. Rab.* 1:5). Paul also described himself as a "wise master builder" (*sophos architektōn*, 1 Cor 3:10). Here in 1 Peter, the psalm's negative implication of builders as the enemies of God's favored stone is retained.

7d. *"has become the head of the corner" (houtos egenēthē eis kephalēn gōnias).* The expression "head of the corner" (*kephalēn gōnias*) from Ps 117[118]:22 is equivalent to the term *akrogōniaion* in Isa 28:16, cited in v 6. In both OT passages, so Jeremias has argued (see the NOTE on 2:6), this cornerstone did not function as a foundation stone but rather as a keystone belonging to the elevated portal of a building (so also Derrett 1978, 61, 64). His chief witness is a passage from the *Testament of Solomon* (22:7–9; 23:1–4) that describes Solomon's erection of the Temple and use of a cornerstone at the top of the building: "And there was a great cornerstone (*lithos akrogōniaios*) that I wished to put at the head of the corner (*eis kephalēn gōnias*) crowning the Temple of God. And all the tradesmen and all the spirits who labored on it came together to bring the stone and set it on the pinnacle of the Temple (*eis to pterygion tou naou*)" (22:7–9). In conclusion, Solomon rejoices: "truly the Scripture is now fulfilled that said: 'The stone that the builders rejected has become the head of the corner (*kephalēn gōnias*)'" (23:4).

It is by no means clear, however, that this passage in the *Testament of Solomon* reflects the psalmist's understanding of the stone's function. The term *kephalē* (*gōnias*) designates the "tip" or outermost edge of the corner (either horizontal or vertical). Its Hebrew equivalent, *rōʾš*, can also indicate the place where a street begins (Ezek 16:25, 31). Thus *kephale gonias* can designate the outermost corner of a stone at the horizontal level. As a hewed squared stone, it was not sunk deeply into the ground but nevertheless firmly fixed the site of the building and determined its direction. The similarity between *kephalē gōnias* and *akrogōniaios* in the context of 1 Peter (cf. also the parallelism of *lithon eis gōnian* and *lithon eis themelion* in Jer 28[51]:26) favors their similar designation of *foundation* stones set at the farthest (and foremost) corner with which a building is begun. This fact is also conceded by Jeremias (1964, 793), although his reasoning is not cogent, since, as noted below, the "stones" mentioned in Isa 28:16 and Ps 117[118]:22 are of a different type from the stones in Isa 8:14, and the latter verse does not determine the meaning of the former. Ultimately, however, the issue is not crucial, for our author, unlike the writer of Eph 2:20–22, shows no interest in building details in vv 6–8 and employs a combination of OT texts that is not found in Ephesians. Goppelt's notion of Jesus as "foundation of the universal edifice" (1993, 146) pertains to Ephesians rather than to 1 Peter. In 1 Peter, the OT "stone" passages instead serve primarily as a means for contrasting the acceptance or rejection of Jesus Christ as God's living stone and for demarcating believers and nonbelievers.

8a. *and "a stone of stumbling" and "a rock of offense" (kai lithos proskommatos kai petra skandalou)*. Fragments of another OT "stone" text (Isa 8:14) are now joined by the copulative *kai* ("and") to the stone text (Ps 117[118]:22) of the preceding verse (v 7cd) in order to expand on the theme of the nonbelievers' rejection of the stone and the consequences of rejecting. The two conflated phrases (*lithos proskommatos, petra skandalou*), occurring only in 1 Pet 2:8 and Rom 9:33 in the NT, are derived from some Greek version of Isa 8:14. The LXX, which our author normally follows, reads, "And if you trust in him [lacking in the MT], he [the Lord] shall be to you for a sanctuary and you shall not come against (him) as a stone of stumbling or as a rock of offense [*ouch hōs lithou proskommati synantēsesthe autōi oude hōs petras ptōmati*]; but the houses of Jacob are in a snare and the dwellers of Jerusalem in a pit." This diverges from the MT, which reads: "And he [i.e., the Lord of hosts] will become a sanctuary, and a stone of offense and a rock of stumbling to both houses of Israel, a trap and a snare to the inhabitants of Jerusalem." The translation of Aquila reads *kai estai eis hagiasma kai eis lithon proskommatos* (so also Theodotion) *kai eis stereon skandalou* (Theodotion: *kai eis petran ptōmatos*); Symmachus reads *kai estai eis hagiasma eis de lithon proskommatos kai eis petran ptōmatos* (*skandalou*, Eus. frag.); compare 8:14c: *tois dysin oikois Israēl eis pagida kai eis skandalon* (Aquila, Symmachus, Theodotion). The variants signal a fluid textual tradition. The identical wording in both Rom 9:33b and 1 Pet 2:8a appears to reflect a form of the Isaiah text closest to that of the translations of Aquila, Symmachus, and Theodotion.

Whereas the "stone" in Isa 28 and Ps 117[118] may refer to the kingdom of David as the firm foundation established and chosen by God, this is not the case with the "stone" in Isa 8:14. Here it is God who is (MT) or will not be (LXX) a stone over which Israel stumbles and falls (Isa 8:13–15).

Thus the "stone" spoken of in 1 Pet 2:8a is not a foundation stone but a freestanding stone or rock over which persons can stumble and fall. The noun *proskomma* can mean "snare" (Exod 23:33; 34:12; Isa 29:21), "offense" (Jdt 8:22; Rom 13:13, 20; 1 Cor 8:9), or "obstacle" (Sir 39:24), but the meaning "stumbling" (Sir 31[34]:7, 16, 30) fits well with "stone." Its related verb *proskoptō*, besides denoting the taking of offense (Rom 14:21) or giving of offense (Sir 31:17), can also mean "stumble" (Prov 3:23; Jer 13:16; Tob 11:10; Rom 9:32) or "striking" one's foot against a stone (Ps 90[91]:12, cited in Matt 4:6/ Luke 4:11). The phrase *lithos proskommatos* thus refers to a stone over which one stumbles, a stone which leads to a fall (Stählin 1968, 746).

Both Paul and the Petrine author ignore the promise in Isa 8:14 ("if you believe in him, you will *not* come against him as a stumbling stone or as a rock of offense") and instead use the selected terms from this verse to make a *negative* statement about nonbelievers. Although both authors cite Isa 28:16 and Isa 8:14 in close proximity, there is no literary dependence of one author upon the other. Paul interweaves both Isaian texts as though they were one passage: "Behold I am setting in Zion [Isa 28:16a] a stone of stumbling and a rock of offense [Isa 8:14], and whoever believes in him shall not be put to shame [Isa 28:16b]." By contrast, our author cites these Isaian texts separately in vv 6 and 8 and adds an intermediate citation of Ps 117[118]:22 in v 7bcd. Paul, moreover, uses Isa 8:14 in combination with Isa 28:16 to underscore Israel's stumbling over Christ the stone (Rom 9:31–33). Our author, on the other hand, applies it not simply to unbelieving Israelites but to all "humans" (*anthrōpōn*) who reject Jesus as God's living stone (v 4c). In Luke's version of the Vineyard parable (Luke 20:9–18), which also cites Ps 117:22 (Luke 20:17), the added allusion to Dan 2:34–35, 44–45 in Luke 20:18 ("everyone who falls on that stone will be broken to pieces and when it falls on any one it will crush him") entails a similar stress on falling and judgment, though with no reference to Isa 8:14. These variations eliminate the possibility of mutual influence or literary dependency[57] and instead represent diverse Christian usage of a traditional combination of "stone" texts applied to Jesus and employed to distinguish Christian believers from either the house of Israel or all nonbelievers.

The combination of all three OT "stone" texts is unique to 1 Peter, and with these texts differing points are made. The sole connection is the term *lithos* and in the case of Isa 28:16 and Isa 8:14 the factor of belief or nonbelief in this stone. The thought of the Christian *Sib. Orac.* 1:344–47 ("from the land of Egypt shall come, safeguarded, a precious stone; upon it the people of the Hebrews shall stumble, but the Gentiles shall gather by his guidance," ca. 150 CE) is closer to the interpretation of Paul than to that of our author.

and "a rock of offense" (kai petra skandalou). It is impossible to determine whether the copulative "and" (*kai*) that joins the two phrases "stone of stumbling" and "rock of offense" was already present in the tradition or was added by our author, especially since the versions of Aquila, Symmachus, and Theodotion all include *kai*.

The phrase *petra skandalou* (only in Isa 8:14 [Aquila, Symmachus, Theodotion]; Rom 9:33; and 1 Pet 2:8) functions as an appositive to *stone of stumbling*, to which it is joined by the copulative *kai*. The combined phrases from Isa 8:14 have virtually the same meaning. Paul views *proskomma* and *skandalon* as appositives in Rom 14:13, as well as in 9:33.

Although *petra* and *lithos* can be used synonymously (Wis 11:14), *petra*, in contrast to *lithos* (a hewn or crafted stone), generally denotes a large and solid rock that is still part of its natural environment (Exod 17:6 and Num 20:8, 10 [cf. 1 Cor 10:4]; Ps 80[81]:16; Matt 7:24, 25; 27:51; Luke 6:48; 8:6, 13; Rev 6:15,

[57] The theory of literary dependency has been cogently rejected by Dodd 1953, 41–43; Selwyn 1947, 268–78; Hillyer 1971; Snodgrass 1977, 98–101; and Shimada 1993, 113–16.

16; see especially the distinction between *petra* and *lithos* in Mark 15:47/Matt 27:60. For *petra* used of God in a positive sense, see 2 Kgs 22:2 [God as David's rock and fortress]).

In the LXX, the meaning of *to skandalon* is generally nuanced by its context. It can denote a "stumbling block" in the way of the blind (Lev 19:14) or the righteous (Ps 118[119]:165; Sir 7:6; cf. 27:23); offense against the law caused by involvement with foreign gods (Judg 2:3, 8:27; Ps 105[106]:36; Hos 4:17; Wis 14:11; Jdt 12:2); a person as stumbling block (1 Kgdms 18:20–21, of Michal, Saul's daughter as wife for David); an action (1 Kgdms 25:31, David's shedding of blood not a stumbling block); offense against a family member (Ps 49[50]:20); battle impediments (Jdt 5:1; 1 Macc 5:4) or "downfall" (Jdt 5:20). The terms *skandalon* and *pagis* ("snare") are combined in a statement in Josh 23:13 concerning the surrounding nations that shall be for Israel "snares and stumbling blocks (*eis pagidas kai eis skandala*), nails in your heels and darts in your eyes until you are destroyed off this good land."[58] For the use of the verb in an antithesis akin to 1 Pet 2:7a/7b–8, see Sir 35[32]:15, "he that seeks the law will be filled with it; but the hypocrite will be offended (*skandalisthēsetai*) by it."

In the NT, the verb *skandalizō*, like *proskoptō*, can denote "being offended" (Matt 15:12), "taking offense" (at Jesus: Mark 6:3/Matt 13:57; Matt 11:6/Luke 7:23; Matt 15:12; John 6:61); "giving or causing offense" in the sense of leading others to sin or lose faith or hindering access to eternal life (Mark 9:42–47/Matt 18:6–9/Luke 17:2; Matt 5:29, 30; 17:27; Rom 14:21 [both verbs]; 1 Cor 8:13; 2 Cor 11:19) or "falling away" (Mark 4:17/Matt 13:21; Mark 14:27, 29/Matt 26:31, 33 [Peter]; Matt 24:10; John 16:1). The noun *to skandalon* (*ta skandala*) is used of offenses against the Mosaic Law (Matt 13:41); Peter as an obstacle to Jesus (Matt 16:23); hindrance to eternal life (Matt 18:7/Luke 17:1); an Israelite feast as a snare and a trap (Rom 11:9, citing Ps 68[69]:23); the Israelite purity code as a stumbling block (Rom 14:13); dissensions as a hindrance to unity (Rom 16:7); hatred of a fellow-believer as a cause of stumbling (1 John 2:10); eating sacrifices to idols as a stumbling block and cause of sin (Rev 2:14); and the crucifixion and cross of Jesus Christ as a stumbling block to Israel (1 Cor 1:23; Gal 5:11).

In general, *skandalon* overlaps in meaning with *proskomma* and denotes some person or action causing social offense, violation of the social or moral code, and thereby undermining the cohesion and commitment of the community. The followers of Jesus acknowledged that Jesus' crucifixion and death were the chief obstacle to his acceptance as Messiah for many in Israel. Our author, however, in contrast to Paul, identifies Jesus Christ as a "stone of stumbling" and "rock of offense" not simply for the House of Israel but for all those who reject Jesus as God's elect stone and who "stumble" over the word con-

[58] See also Ps 68[69]:22 (cited in Rom 11:9); Ps 140[141]:6–10 (*petra, pagis, skandala*, "falling"); Sir 9:3, 5; Wis 14:11; 1 Macc 5:4.

cerning the living Lord. A further Petrine reference to Isaiah 8 (vv 12–13) occurs in 1 Pet 3:14–15.

Moule's suggestion (1955) that a possible connection between the term "rock" (*petra*) and the name of the author (*Petros*; cf. Matt 16:17–18: "You are *Petros* and upon this *petra* I will build my church . . .") could account for the use of the stone tradition in 1 Peter lacks compelling support. The dominant term of the stone tradition and the term linking Isa 28:16; Ps 117[118]:22; and Isa 8:14 is *lithos* not *petra*. The stone here, moreover, is Jesus Christ, not Simon Peter, with no evidence of any pun on the name *Peter* or of any allusion to the saying in Matt 16:17–18. It is worth noting, however, the association in early Christian tradition between the Apostle Peter and two features explicit in this Petrine context: the Petrine speech in Acts 4:8–11 also applying Ps 117[118]:22 to Jesus' death and resurrection and Jesus' censure of Peter as a *skandalon* (Peter's rejection of Christ's suffering as a hindrance to his mission, Matt 16:21–23). These elements form part of a larger body of tradition associated with Peter in the early Church, to which other elements of 1 Peter (5:1, 12–13) also testify.

8b. *they "stumble" by disobeying the word (hoi proskoptousin tōi logōi apeithountes)*. The application of the words from Isaiah to the nonbelievers is now clarified. Those who do not believe (*apistousin*, v 7b) "stumble" (*proskoptousin*) over the stone of stumbling (*proskommatos*) by not obeying the word (*tōi logōi apeithountes*). The textual variants of *apistousin* in v 7b and *apeithountes* in v 8b reflect scribal awareness of the relation of these verbs and the attempt to make them agree exactly.

The verb *apeitheō* ("disobey"; cf. also John 3:36; Acts 14:2; 17:5; 19:9; Rom 2:8; 11:31; 15:31) is used also in 3:1 of husbands who do not obey the word and in 4:17 of those who do not obey the gospel. In 3:19–20 it is also used of the primordial "spirits in prison" who once "disobeyed" in the days of Noah. In the present context it is synonymous with "not believing" (*apistousin*, 2:7b; cf. Heb 3:18–19, where *apeithēsasin* parallels *apistia*) and contrasted to "believing" (*pisteuōn*, *pisteuousin*, 2:6c, 7a).

The object of disobedience, "the word" (*tōi logōi*), as the context indicates, refers either to Jesus Christ or to the good news about Jesus Christ (1:25). By this word (*logos*) believers are reborn (1:23), and by this word-milk (*to logikon gala*) they are nourished (2:2). Thus, identification of the "stone" as the "word" that is not obeyed links this unit with the three preceding references to the word (1:22–25; 2:1–3) and adds a fourth metaphor to the line of thought: (a) enduring word contrasted to perishable seed; (b) word as good news; (c) word as nourishing word-milk; (d) word as stumbling stone.

as they were set to do (eis ho kai etethēsan). The verb "set" (*etethēsan*), another divine passive, repeats the same verb in v 6b, which is also used of God's action in "setting" a stone in Zion. For the construction of *tithēmi* + *eis* describing God's purposeful activity, see also 1 Tim 2:7 ("for this purpose I was appointed [*eis ho etethēn*] a preacher and apostle") and 1 Thess 5:9 ("For God has not set [*etheto*] us for [*eis*] wrath but for [*eis*] the possession of salvation through our Lord Jesus Christ"). This Petrine formulation is no reference to divine predestination of nonbelievers to condemnation (and of believers to salvation). That which is "set" or established by God is the stumbling (*to proskomma*) resulting from not heeding the word, rather than the disobedience itself (Bigg 1902, 126; Beare 1970, 123; cf. the same sense of *keitai* in Luke 2:34, "this child is set [*keitai*] for the fall and rising of many in Israel"). Or to express it differently, it is the *result* of disobedience that is foreordained, not the decision itself (cf. also Spörri 1925, 163–65). That the author presumes free will in accepting or rejecting Jesus as the Christ is evident from 2:12, where he envisions that the honorable behavior of the believers might turn their accusers from slander to the glorifying of God. Similarly, in 3:1, it is anticipated that the holy behavior of wives might win their unbelieving husbands for the Christian faith. The Petrine author thus allows for, indeed, reckons with the holy behavior of believers as having a transformative impact upon the ignorance of the nonbelievers. His hope is not in their condemnation but in their conversion (Feldmeier 1992, 182–83).[59]

In this catena of OT "stone" texts, the focus is not on the texts themselves and their meaning but on the present realities that they are employed to illuminate: Jesus Christ, his human rejection and divine election; the honor of those who believe in him and the shame of those who disobey and reject him. What these OT texts have in common is primarily only the term *lithos* (and "cornerstone"), not other features in their context. Moreover, the three texts involve different types of stones: Isa 28:16 and Ps 117[118]:22, a foundation cornerstone; and Isa 8:14, by contrast, a free-standing stone similar to a rock (*petra*), over which one can stumble and fall. This stone in Isa 8:14 is an attribute of God himself rather than a stone that God establishes (Isa 28:16) or selects (Ps 117[118]:22) and in 1 Peter refers to Jesus Christ. 1 Peter 2:6–8 thus is not "midrash" in the sense that any of these OT texts is the primary focus of attention (against Schutter 1989, 130–38). Verses 6–8 (and the OT texts they cite), rather, supply terminology and scriptural support for the thought of vv 4–5 and material that the author skillfully weaves together to affirm his major themes of Jesus as rejected yet honored stone, faith as the means for sharing in his honor, and the contrast between the honor of believers and the shame of the rejecting nonbelievers.

The verb *tithēmi*, with God as subject, serves as an inclusion framing vv 6–8 and in v 8c marks the conclusion of this subunit.

With vv 9–10, the focus returns again to the addressees as believers (cf. v 7a and v 5). Here the honor conferred by God upon the believers (cf. v 7a) is expanded on and contrasted to the shame experienced by the nonbelievers (vv 7b–8), and the divine election of the believers is correlated with the election of their living Lord (v 4d) and of God's Messiah (v 6b).

9a. *But you [are] (hymeis de)*. The words *hymeis de* occur in Exod 19:6, but in 1 Pet 2:9 they involve an ellipsis, with the verb *are* implied (compare Exod

[59] For a recent interconfessional discussion of predestination and election, see Meyendorff and Tobias 1992, 133–69.

19:6, *esesthe*), similar to the ellipsis in v 5d. They extend the contrast ("but" [*de*]) between believers and nonbelievers begun in v 7a (v 7a, believers; vv 7b–8, nonbelievers) and introduce a complex of honorific epithets of ancient Israel that are now applied to the addressees (*you*). The Petrine ellipsis implies a present tense in contrast to the future tense in LXX Exod 19:6: the earlier promise has now become a present reality and a proclamation of fact (cf. 2:10, "once"-"now").

an "elect stock" (genos eklekton). As Jesus Christ is the "elect stone" (v 4d), as was Israel's Messiah (v 6b), so his followers constitute an "elect people." The phrase *genos eklekton*, unique in the NT, is a contraction of the phrase in Isa 43:20, *to genos mou to eklekton* ("my [God's] elect stock"). It is the first of several honorific epithets of ancient Israel that here are appropriated and applied to the followers of Jesus Christ (P. Richardson 1969, 171–75). These prestigious predicates are derived from Isa 43 and Exod 19 and are arranged so as to give precedence and prominence to the concept of *election* (1 Pet 2:9a [Isa 43:20]; v 9bcd [Exod 19:6]; v 9e [Isa 43:21a]; v 9f [Isa 43:21b]). The divine election of the believers corresponds to that of their elect Lord (2:4d) and contrasts the honor given by God to the faithful (v 7a) with the shame experienced by the nonbelievers (vv 7b–8).

The term *genos* denotes a collectivity of persons, a stock or "line" of persons descended from a common ancestor—in the case of Israel, the stock of Jacob (Isa 43:1; Exod 19:3) or Abraham (Acts 13:26; cf. Gal 3:7–9). Thus, as a designation for Israel,[60] it could function as a synonym for a "house" ("house of Abraham, of Jacob, of David") or "family/kindred" bonded by blood and common lineage (cf. *T. Job* 1:5: Job to his children: "you are a chosen and honored stock [*genos eklekton entimon*] from the seed of Jacob"). In the context of 1 Pet 2:9, it is synonymous with *ethnos* (v 9d) and *laos* (vv 9e, 10ab) as a designation of the *stock* or "people" whom God has elected. However, here, in contrast to Isaiah and Exodus, it is *faith* rather than a biological bloodline that determines inclusion in the "elect stock" of God and that unites the elect people with their elect Lord. Although the believers constitute a *genos eklekton* in God's sight, in the view of some outsiders such as the mob at Rome in Nero's time they were a *genus hominum superstitionis novae ac maleficae* ("a line of persons given to a novel and maleficent superstition," Suetonius, *Nero* 16.2). Such an erroneous opinion the Petrine author will soon encourage his readers to disprove with their honorable behavior (2:12). Only after 1 Peter, however, do Christians refer to themselves as a "*new* stock" (*kainon genos, Diogn*. 1:1); cf. *Mart. Pol*. 16:1, "the *genos* of the righteous") or a "third stock" (*tertium genos*) differentiated from the House of Israel and Gentiles (Tert., *Nat*. 1.8).

9b. *a "royal residence" (basileion)*. Three further honorific epithets of ancient Israel, *basileion* ("royal residence"), *hierateuma* ("priestly community"), and *ethnos hagion* ("holy people"), are mentioned, and all derive from the

---

[60] Esth 3:7, 8, 11; 6:14; Add Esth 8:12f (*eklektou genous*); 3 Macc 1:3; Acts 7:17; Gal 1:14; 2 Cor 11:26; Phil 3:5.

covenantal formulation of LXX Exod 19:6, which reads: "You shall be to me a royal residence, a priestly community, and a holy nation" (*esesthe moi basileion hierateuma kai ethnos hagion*).[61] This OT passage (Exod 19:3–8) has been identified as the "*fons* and *origo* of the many covenantal pericopes which appear throughout the Old Testament" (Muilenburg 1959, 352).[62]

The grammatical form and function of *basileion* (translating the Heb. construct *mamleket*, "kingdom of," "exclusive kingly domain of" [Buber 1967, 129]) is open to debate. In both secular Greek literature and the LXX, *basileion* can serve as either an adjective ("royal," "belonging to the king" [*basileus*]) or a substantive ("kingdom," "royal throne," "royal residence"). Particularly noteworthy is Strabo's mention of such royal residences in Galatia (*Geogr.* 12.5.2, 3) and Cappadocia (*Geogr.* 12.2.7), two provinces where the addressees of 1 Peter reside; cf. also *Geogr.* 14.2.16, 23. Septuagintal usage (23× as a substantive; 4× as adjective), as well as the history of the translation and interpretation of Exod 19:6 (*Jub.* 16:18; 33:20; Targumic versions; 2 Macc 2:17; *T. Levi* 11:6 [Greek Fragment 67]; Philo, *Sobr.* 66; *Abr.* 56; Rev 1:5–6; 5:9–10),[63] strongly favor its substantival usage in both the LXX and 1 Pet 2:9.

Thus in the covenantal formula of LXX Exod 19:6, *basileion* denotes the house of Jacob (Exod 19:3) as the house of God the king, the people among whom God dwells, God's royal residence. In view of the fact that this Greek translation was produced in Alexandrian Egypt under Ptolemaic auspices, this rendition of "kingdom" (Heb. *mamlākâ*) as "royal house" (Gk.) is consistent with the fact that earlier Pharaohs and their successors, the Macedonian Ptolemies, claimed the land of Egypt as their personal possession. "The whole of Egypt was the *oikos* of the king, his private household, which he owned in his character of a living god" (Rostovtzeff 1953, 2:1309). Philo's identification of *basileion* as "*oikos* of the king" (*Sobr.* 66) should also be seen in this light; for the text of *Sobr.* 66, see the NOTE on 2:5d.

---

[61] The phrase *basileion hierateuma* is unique in the NT and obviously derives, along with *ethnos hagion*, from LXX Exod 19:6, its only other biblical occurrence. The Hebrew reads: "You shall be to me a priestly kingdom and a holy nation" (*wĕattem tihyû-lî mamleket kōhănîm wĕgôy qādôš*). The LXX contains a duplication of Exod 19:6 in Exod 23:22, but this is a secondary addition not found in the MT. The paramount significance of these words derives from the fact that they form part of the wording of the ancient covenant between Yahweh and the house of Jacob (*oikos Iakōb*) at Mount Sinai (Exod 19:3–8), the covenant fundamentally determining the identity and obligations of the house of Jacob (Israel) as God's special people.

[62] On the form, setting, and meaning of this OT passage see, in addition to the commentaries, Junker 1947; Scott 1950; Bauer 1958; Wildberger 1960; W. Schmidt 1961; Moran 1962; Fohrer 1963; Cody 1964; Elliott 1966b, 50–59, 63–76; Baltzer 1971; Schüssler Fiorenza 1972, 113–55; Le Roux 1984; R. R. Ellis 1988. On the use of this Exodus formula in 1 Peter, see Cerfaux 1939; Ketter 1947; Blinzler 1949; Elliott 1966b, 1981/1990, 1982; Best 1969; Cothenet 1969; Coppens 1969; Ramos 1970; Schüssler Fiorenza 1972, 51–59, 94–101; Snodgrass 1977; Sandevoir 1980; Schlosser 1980; Balch 1981, 132–36; Schröger 1981b, 55–93; T. D. Osborne 1981b; Manns 1984a; Vanhoye 1986, 243–77; Prigent 1992.

[63] See Cerfaux 1939; Blinzler 1949; Fohrer 1963; Elliott 1966b, 50–128; Schüssler Fiorenza 1972, 78–155; McNamara 1972, 148–59; Muños León 1978.

Most of the modern translations of 1 Pet 2:9 seem to have taken their cue from the original Hebrew formulation of Exod 19:6 or from Jerome's Vulgate. It must be noted, however, that Jerome's translations of Exod 19:6 (*regnum sacerdotale*, "priestly kingdom") and 1 Pet 2:9 (*regale sacerdotium*, "royal priesthood") are inconsistent. The fact that for over a millennium the Vulgate was the Bible of the Church and the source for biblical quotation may account for the widespread but erroneous rendition of 1 Pet 2:9 as "royal priesthood." This translation, in turn, was in part responsible for a misconception of the entire import of 2:4–10 and the term *hierateuma* in particular; see the DETAILED COMMENT.

The sequence of terms in 1 Pet 2:9 (nouns followed by qualifying adjectives) has been cited as a reason for regarding *basileion* as an adjective modifying *hierateuma*. Thus, as *genos* is modified by *eklekton*, *ethnos* by *hagion*, and *laos* by *eis peripoiēsin*, so *hierateuma* by *basileion*. The substantival function of *basileion*, however, as already noted, is supported by superior evidence: (1) Even in the case of MT Exod 19:6, "kingdom" is modified by "priests," not vice versa, as in the alleged case of 1 Peter. Moreover, our author clearly cites not the MT but the LXX. (2) The word order in 1 Peter replicates that of both the MT and the LXX (*mamleket/basileion*, preceding *kōhănîm/hierateuma*), thereby undermining the argument based on the sequence of phrases. (3) The dominant trend of the tradition concerning Exod 19:6 argues most strongly for regarding *basileion* as a substantive here as elsewhere (Elliott 1966b, 50–128). (4) There is an obvious relation between 1 Pet 2:9 and 2:5. The term *hierateuma* occurs in each verse (but nowhere else in the NT), and in v 5 the phrase *oikos pneumatikos* preceding *hierateuma* interprets *basileion* not as an adjective but as a substantive. (5) This Petrine interpretation is identical with that of Philo, who also treats *basileion* in Exod 19:6 as a substantive (*Abr.* 56; *Sobr.* 66) and interprets *basileion* as *oikos* (*Sobr.* 66).

The combined weight of this evidence suggests that our author follows the dominant trend for interpretation of the terms in Exod 19:6 and that *basileion* functions in 2:9 as an independent substantive with the meaning "royal residence." This term, in turn, is interpreted in 2:5 as "house(hold) of the Spirit" (Elliott 1966b, 149–54).[64]

9c. *a "priestly community" (hierateuma)*. This term too, like *basileion*, derives from LXX Exod 19:6, as indicated in the NOTE on v 5e. Its use in 2:5e anticipated its citation here. In both instances it denotes not individual "priests" but rather an active *priestly community*, along with the accompanying collective nouns "stock, people" (*genos*, *ethnos*, *laos*) and "royal residence" (*basileion*). In continuity with the transmission and interpretive history of Exod 19:6, *hierateuma* identifies its subject, here the believing community, as God's particular covenant people, whose intimate relation to God is like that of holy priests.

[64] So also Holzmeister 1937, 248; Selwyn 1947, 165–67; J. N. D. Kelly 1969, 96–97; Dalton 1990, 905. For the contrary view, see Cerfaux 1939, 301; Blinzler 1949, 62; Danker 1967a, 331; Vanhoye 1986, 253–54; Michaels 1988, 108–9; Goppelt 1993, 149.

The holiness implied by this term is stressed by its appositive, "holy people" (*ethnos hagion*, v 9d) and by its modifier *holy* in v 5e ("holy priestly community" [*hierateuma hagion*]). As part of the covenant formula of Exod 19:6, its application to Christian believers affirms that they too stand in continuity with the people of God brought into being at Sinai. Whether formerly pagans or members of the House of Israel, they too now by God's mercy enjoy membership in God's elect and holy people of the end time. For further discussion of this term, see the NOTE on 2:5e.[65]

9d. *a "holy people" (ethnos hagion)*. This pendant phrase stands in apposition to "royal residence" and "priestly community" in the original covenant formula of LXX Exod 19:6. In both Exodus and 1 Peter it makes explicit the *holiness* characteristic of the covenant community and its separation from all who are unholy. The identification of Israel as *ethnos* (MT: *gôy*), however, is unusual, since *laos* (MT: *ʿam*) is the predominant term for Israel in the OT, especially in such important formulations as Deut 7:6; 14:2, 21; 26:19; and 28:9 ("holy people"). However, *gôy* is used of Israel in Deut 4:6; Josh 3:17; 4:1; 10:13; Jer 31:36, and other places (cf. Cody 1964).[66] The expression *gôy qādôš*, it therefore has been suggested, may reflect a subsequent reformulation of *ʿam qādôš* in a *later* period, when Israel was conceived as a political entity or state set apart from other states (*gôyîm*) and declared holy to God (Perlitt 1969, 172–73). On the other hand, the phrase could also reflect a very *early* stage of the tradition when *ʿam* had not yet become the preferred term for Israel, and *gôy* had not yet become a technical term for designating non-Israelite peoples or states ("Gentiles" as enemies; cf. Ezra 6:21; Neh 5:8; Ps 9:6, 16, 20, 21; 10:16; Isa 8:23). Representing this position, Buber (1967, 129, 130) renders *gôy qādôš* "holy tribe." On the dating of the Exodus formula in general, see Elliott 1966b, 56–57 and Schüssler Fiorenza 1972, 136–38. The use of *gôy* and *ʿam* as synonymous terms for Israel, however, may also be typical of classic Hebrew poetry; see their juxtaposition in Isa 1:4. In the context of 1 Pet 2:9, in any case, *ethnos* (*hagion*) identifies the believers not as a politically constituted "nation" or state but rather as a (*holy*) *people* sharing a common historical, cultural, and religious heritage. It is used synonymously with *genos* (*eklekton*, v 9a) and *laos* (*eis peripoiēsin*, vv 9e, 10ab) to denote the believers as members of the covenant people of God. Elsewhere in this letter, the plural of *ethnos*, *ethnē* (2:11, 4:3) denotes nonbelieving outsiders ("Gentiles") in a fashion simi-

[65] In post-NT time, allusions to *basileion* and *hierateuma* in 1 Pet 2:9 are found in Melito, *Peri Pascha* 68 and Just. Mart., *Dial.* 116:2–3. Early citations include: Clem. Alex., *Protr.* 4.59.2–3; *Adumb.* on 1 Pet 2:9 ("That we are a chosen stock by the election of God is abundantly clear. He says 'royal' because we are called to sovereignty and belong to Christ; and 'priesthood' on account of the oblation which is made by prayers and instructions, by which are gained the souls which are offered to God"); Ps.-Ign., *Ep. Spur.* 6.4.3; Ps.-Clem., *Virg.* 1.9.4; Origen, *Cels.* 4.32.34; 5.10.16; 8.19.25; *Comm. Jo.* 10.35.228; *Mart.* 5.13; *Apos. Con.* 2.26.1; 3.16.3; 3.57.20; 5.15.1–2; 8.12.44.

[66] For *ethnos* designating Israel, see also Ps 105[106]:5 (*ethnos sou* = *hoi eklektoi sou*); Ps 32[33]:12 (*ethnos* and *laos*); Wis 17:2 (*ethnos hagion*, of Israel in Egypt); Josephus, *Ant.*19.278 (*to Ioudaiōn ethnos*).

lar to its employment in Israel; see the NOTE on 2:12. On the term and the concept, see Dahl 1941.

9e. *a "people for [God's] possession" (laos eis peripoiēsin)*. The phrase has affinities with both Exod 19:5 and Isa 43:21a. LXX Exod 19:5 (*laos periousios*; cf. Deut 7:6; 14:2; 28:16; Titus 2:14) translates the Hebrew "my own possession [*segullah*] from among all peoples," and Isa 43:21a reads *laon mou, hon periepoiēsamēn*, "my people whom I have acquired for myself." The Petrine formulation, while clearly inspired by Exod 19:5, is closer to Isa 43:21a in that it involves a noun (*peripoiēsin*) of the same root as the Isaian verb (*periepoiēsamēn*), just as 1 Pet 2:9f is reminiscent of Isa 43:21b. The phrase *eis peripoiēsin* indicates purpose ("for"), similar to *eis hierateuma* (v 5e) and occurs also in Mal 3:17; Eph 1:14; 1 Thess 5:9; 2 Thess 2:14; Heb 10:39. The epithet makes clear that the covenant community is God's particular possession from among all the peoples of the earth (cf. Exod 19:5).

9f. *that you may "declare the praises" of him who "called" you out of darkness into his marvelous light (hopōs tas aretas exaggeilēte tou ek skotous hymas kalesantos eis to thaumaston autou phōs)*. As the preceding epithets of v 9 affirm the identity of the believers as God's elect and holy covenant people, this statement clarifies its reponsibility (introduced by the conjunction *hopōs* ["that"] indicating purpose). The language is an amalgam of terms and motifs from Isa 43 and its broader context.

The finite verb *exaggeilēte* ("declare, proclaim publicly"), perhaps influenced by Ps 9:15 (*hopōs an exaggeilō pasas tas aineseis sou*, "that I might proclaim your praises") occurs only here and in the *conclusio brevior* of Mark. It substitutes for the infinitive *diēgeisthai* of Isa 43:22, which has the same basic meaning (cf. Sir 39:10; 44:15; Ps 9:2; 49[50]:16; 70[71]:15; 73[74]:3). Like its synonym, *exaggellō* is used for public declarations of praise (Ps 9:15; 70[71]:15; 72[73]:28, 78[79]:13; 106[107]:22; Sir 18:4; 39:10; 44:15; *T. Levi* 2:10; *T. Jos.* 5:2, 3) and aretologies (Ael. Arist., *Or. Sac.* 2.20–21).

The noun *aretai*, plural of *aretē*, can mean either "wondrous, praiseworthy deeds," "manifestations of divine power and glory" (Isa 63:7; Philo, *Spec.* 1.209; Josephus, *Ant.* 17.56), or the "praises" that such manifestations of glory elicit on the part of the recipients and witnesses (Isa 42:8, 12; 43:21). In the Greek world, *aretē* is frequently combined with *doxa* (Paus., *Descr.* 52.6; Dionys. Hal., *Ant. rom.* 5.62.4; Diodorus Siculus 2.45.2; 3.70.5; cf. Isa 42:8; 2 Pet 1:3) in the acknowledgment of the "excellence and honor" of public benefactors and saviors (Danker 1982, 318, 348–51). In continuity with the idiom of honor and shame (vv 6–8), the believers are portrayed as recipients of divine favor who are now obligated to pubicly praise the excellencies of the God (*autou*) who has elected them and made them his own. The generous conferral of honor obligates beneficiaries to the grateful acknowledgment thereof. The venue of collective worship would be one natural place for such public praise. But the author's concern with the witness that the believers are to give in society (2:11–5:11) suggests that this proclamation of God's honor is fitting not only within but also *beyond* the boundaries of the

Christian community. Their divine election does not imply or require social isolation into an enclave of the redeemed but, on the contrary, entails a declaration of the power and glory of their regenerating God in all circumstances, private and public.

In the present context, the believers' public praise of God's glory and saving deeds is described as the "spiritual sacrifices" (v 5f) that they offer as his loyal household. In the larger context of 1:3–2:10, this note of praise echoes that with which the body of the letter began (1:3–5). This praise, the author soon notes (2:12; cf. 3:1–2), may well be joined by that of the outsiders, who will glorify God because of the believers' good conduct.

who "called" you out of darkness into his marvelous light (tou ek skotous hymas kalesantos eis to thaumaston autou phōs). The implied subject of the participle *tou . . . kalesantos* is God. The image of God "calling" (*kaleō*) his people is especially prominent in the book of Isaiah (41:9; 42:6; 43:1, 22; 48:12, 15; 49:6; 51:2; 54:6; 65:12; 66:4) and is found frequently in the NT.[67] God's calling, like God's electing, with which "call" is often associated, implies not only an invitation but also a determination of a course of life. It is stressed repeatedly in our letter as a motivation for Christian conduct and a reason for hope (1:15; 2:9, 21; 3:9; 5:10).

out of darkness into his marvelous light (ek skotous . . . eis to thaumaston autou phōs). The salvation of the Christian believers is depicted here in language reminiscent of the terms with which Isaiah portrayed Israel's deliverance from Egypt's darkness and its captivity in Babylon (Isa 42:16; 58:10); see especially Isa 9:2, "The people who walked in darkness have seen a great light; those who dwelt in a land of deep darkness, on them has light shined." In addition, it echoes familiar strains of the Festival Psalms (Pss 77[78], 104[105], 105[106]), recounting the "marvels" (*thaumasia*, Pss 77:4, 11, 12; 104:2, 5; 105:7, 22; *thaumasta*, Ps 97[98]:1; Wis 19:9; cf. Ps 117[118]:22) of God's deliverance of his resident aliens (*paroikoi*, Ps 104:11–12, 23) and elect covenant people (Pss 104:6, 8, 9, 10, 37–43; 105:3, 5, 7–12, 45) from Egypt and from darkness into light (cf. Ps 106[107]:14; Isa 42:16; 58:10; *T. Jos*. 19:3; cf. 20:2). This event was commemorated in the Israelite Passover liturgy (*m. Pesaḥ*. 10:5) in words similar to those of 1 Peter: "In every generation one must so regard oneself as if he/she came forth from Egypt. . . . Therefore we are bound to give thanks, to praise, to glorify, to honor, to exalt, to extol, and to bless him who wrought all these wonders for our fathers and for us. He brought us out from bondage to freedom, from sorrow to gladness, and from mourning to a festival day, and from darkness to a great light . . . so let us sing before him the Hallelujah." Psalm 117 [118], one of the Hallel Psalms sung at Passover and cited previously in v 7, recalls this same Passover tradition.

The alternation of light and darkness regulated the daily round of the ancients. As light and daytime were the period of work and security, so darkness

[67] See Matt 20:16; 22:14; Rom 1:1; 8:30; 1 Cor 1:1, 9; 7:15, 17–24; Gal 1:15; 5:13; Eph 4:1, 4; Col 3:15; 1 Thess 2:12; 4:7; 5:24; 2 Tim 1:9; 2 Pet 1:3; Rev 17:14.

and night were the time of inactivity and insecurity. Accordingly, as symbols, light was associated with life, health, and God; and darkness, on the other hand, with illness (e.g., blindness), death, and the forces of evil (Ps 91:5–6; 104: 22–23; Exod 10:22). Light, created by God, is a symbol of God, a synonym for glory (*doxa*), and an image of divine salvation and deliverance (Ezek 43:2; Isa 9:1; 60:1; Acts 9:3; cf. Aalen 1951 and Malmede 1986, 9–34, 61–135). Thus, movement from darkness to light can signify a transition from death to life, or from alienation to community. It therefore served as a graphic symbol for conversion.[68]

Like the community of Qumran, which distinguished socially and morally between the righteous "Sons of Light" and the unrighteous "Sons of Darkness" (1QS I 9–10; III 17–IV:1; 1QM), so the followers of Christ, the "light of the world" (John 3:19; 8:12; 9:5), saw themselves as "children of the light" (Luke 16:8; John 12:36; 1 Thess 5:5; Eph 5:8) who through baptism were "delivered from the realm of darkness" and "given a share in the inheritance of the sons of light" (Col 1:12–13).

The phrase *from darkness to light* thus not only recalls Israel's momentous deliverance from the darkness that enveloped Egypt prior to the Exodus; in this Petrine context, it also serves as a metaphor for sharing in the glory of God and as an image for salvation as a conversion, transition, and transformation. This concept of transformation is further developed in v 10 and recurs elsewhere in the letter as well (1:14–16; 2:24; 4:1–4).

10. This final verse contains a couplet of antithetical parallelisms fashioned from material drawn from Hosea (1:6, 9; 2:3[MT 2:1], 25) and serves to further undergird the identity of the believers as the *people (laos) of God* while also illustrating the contrast that their conversion has effected.

> *hoi pote ou laos* (v 10a)
>   *nyn de laos theou* (v 10b)
> *hoi ouk ēleēmenoi* (v 10c)
>   *nyn de eleēthentes* (v 10d)

> Once you [were] "Not-people" (v 10a)
>   but now [you are] "God's-people" (v 10b)
> [once] you [were] "Not-shown-mercy" (v 10c)
>   but now [you are] "Those-shown-mercy" (v 10d)

The twofold relative pronouns *hoi* (nominative plurals, lit., "those who") have "you" (v 9a) as their antecedent and consequently are translated "you." The verbs of the ellipses are supplied according to temporal and semantic sense, as is the second "once" in v 10c. The repeated adverbs "once" (*pote*) and "but

[68] *Jos. Asen.* 8:9; 15:13; Philo, *Virt.* 1.179–80; Acts 26:18; 2 Cor 4:6; Eph 5:11–14; Col 1:12–13; 1 Thess 5:4–5; 1 John 2:8–12; *1 Clem.* 36:2, 59:2; *Barn.* 14:5–7; *Odes Sol.* 21:3; 42:16; *Ep. Apos.* 21.

now" (*nyn de*) mark the contrast between the former and present condition of the believers, that is, prior to and following their conversion.

This collation of terms from Hosea actually involves the names of Hosea's children by his harlot wife, Gomer, and the altered relation to God that their change of names signifies. The Hosean context describes the birth and naming of Hosea's three children, *Jezreel*, *Lo-ruḥamah*, and *Lo-ammi*, an incident that symbolized God's dealing with his faithless people Israel (Hos 1:3). As a sign of Israel's infidelity to the covenant, the second and third of Hosea's children were named "Not-shown-mercy" (Heb.: *Lō-ruḥāmâ* / LXX: *Ouk-ēleēmenēn*, 1:6) and "Not-my-people" (Heb.: *Lō-ʿammî* / LXX: *Ou-laos-mou*, 1:9), signifying that God would no longer have mercy on the House of Israel and would no longer regard Israel as his people. Nevertheless Hosea envisions a future reversal, when God will have mercy on his people and claim them as his own. Then the daughter "Not-shown-mercy" will receive mercy (2:23) and will be renamed "She-who-has-received-mercy" (Heb.: *Ruḥāmâ* / LXX: *Eleēmenē*, 2:3[1]) and the son "Not-my-people" will be called "My-People" (Heb.: *ʿAmmî*, 2:1, 23 / LXX: *Laos-mou*, 2:3, 25).

In the NT, elements of this prophetic text are used by Paul as well as by our author. In his letter to the Romans, Paul conflates modified elements of LXX Hos 1:9, 2:25 and 2:1 (Rom 9:25–26, but reading "not loved" and "loved" for the LXX "Not-shown-mercy," "Shown-mercy") in order to prove from Scripture that Gentiles as well as Israelites were "called" by God. This diverges from the original point of Hosea, which contrasts not Israelites and Gentiles but the *different conditions of the same people Israel*, as either rejected or accepted by God. The Petrine author, on the other hand, while also drawing on Hosea, does not cite the text explicitly and fully, but focuses exclusively on the names (presented with minor modifications) and their changes. In 1 Peter it is also less certain than in Romans that "Not-people" and "Not-shown-mercy" (the possessive *mou* in Hosea is omitted in both instances) were meant to identify former Gentiles who then were embraced by God, although this sense is possible given the fact that the addressees involve both former Gentiles and former Israelites (see 1:14–19; 4:2–4; and GENERAL INTRODUCTION, 5.2). These differences between Paul and 1 Peter argue against any literary dependency of one upon the other (Selwyn 1947, 280–81; Dodd 1953, 75; Ellis 1957, 94; Elliott 1966b, 44–47). The Petrine author, rather, uses the Hosean material (1) to supply further scriptural warrant for the identification of the believers as the people of God (*laos theou*; cf. v 9e); (2) to indicate the change ("once/now") that conversion has effected (2:25; cf. 1:3, 10–12, 14–16, 23; 4:1–4), a common feature of early Christian exhortation involving "once-now";[69] and (3) to note again the lavish divine *mercy* (see *eleos*, 1:3) that the believers have experienced as the reborn children of God.

[69] See Rom 1:18–3:20/3:21–8:39; 6:17–22; 7:5–6; 11:30; Gal 3:4–7, 24–27; 4:8–9; Eph 2:1–10, 11–22; 5:8; Col 1:21–22; Titus 3:3–7; cf. Tachau 1972, 16–20.

No reference is made here or elsewhere in 1 Peter to a "*new* people" (in contrast to *Barn.* 5:7 [*ton laos ton kainon*], where the concern was to demarcate followers of Jesus from Israelites). Here in 1 Peter (2:9–10), the point is that, through the mercy of God and their belief in Jesus Christ, the believers are incorporated into God's ancient covenant people and share the heritage of ancient Israel. For this same theme, see 1:10–12 (expectations of the prophets); 1:4a ("inheritance); 3:7 ("coheirs"); and the models of Sarah and the matriarchs (3:5–6) and of Noah and his family (3:20–21). This employment of material from Hosea in v 10 concludes a unit (vv 4–10) with the most extensive combination of OT texts in 1 Peter and in the NT as well.

This use of the OT to substantiate and conclude units of thought is typical of 1 Peter; 3:10–12 similarly concludes a major unit (2:13–3:7), and minor units are concluded with OT quotations or allusions in 1:14–15/16; 1:22–23/24–25a; 2:13–16/2:17; 2:18–20/21–25; 3:1–4/5–6; 4:12–17/18 (19); and 5:5b/c (6–7). The stress on *mercy* in v 10b repeats that of 1:3 and thereby forms an inclusion framing the entire first section of the letter (1:3–2:10).

GENERAL COMMENT

This finely crafted and rhetorically powerful statement provides a resounding conclusion to the first major section of letter (1:3–2:10). Here readers experiencing unjust suffering and social estrangement are assured of the divinely conferred honor that is theirs as a result of their divine rebirth, their faith in Jesus Christ their rejected yet elect Lord, and their incorporation into the household or family of God. This unit comprises a unique combination of OT terms and motifs without parallel in the NT and concludes a section of the letter that itself manifests a remarkable merging of OT themes and early Christian tradition. The interweaving of diverse traditions in 2:4–10 is a unique accomplishment of our author and constitutes a singular contribution to the theology of election and ecclesiology in the early Church. It is likewise one of the several features of this letter that differentiates it clearly from the formulations of Paul and the Pauline circle.

This final subunit of the first major section of the letter completes a line of thought begun in 1:3. The course of Christian conversion and growth is traced from rebirth through the mercy of God (1:3–12) to the hope and holiness characteristic of God's children, who are redeemed by the holy Christ (1:13–21), the familial love expected of those reborn through the word of the Gospel (1:22–25), their nourishment on and continued growth through the word (2:1–3), to their consolidation as the household of God, which constitutes the eschatological covenant people of God (2:4–10). In this depiction of the family of the reborn and its development from birth to growth to consolidation, diverse images and traditions are skillfully united to express the family's divine regeneration, sanctification, and election, its union with God and Jesus Christ, and its distinction from all nonbelievers. The formation of this family of God as a result of God's *mercy* (1:3 and 2:10) provides a grand inclusion framing this first major section of the letter.

Several related themes of this section are designed to provide a basis for the exhortation to follow and to equip the readers for a confident confrontation with the hostility, abuse, and suffering they experience from their social environment. In general, these themes are designed to affirm and foster the communal identity, dignity, cohesion, and commitment of the believers.

(1) Multiple honorary epithets of ancient Israel, all corporate in nature, are employed in 2:9–10 to affirm the communal identity of the believers: "elect stock," "royal residence," "priestly community," "holy people," "people for God's possession," "God's people." They express not the qualities of individuals but rather the special nature of the community as a single cohesive unit with a common origin, character, and purpose (Spörri 1925, 38; Elliott 1966b, 38–48; 166–74). In applying these honorific predicates of Israel to the messianic community, our author affirms the incorporation of believers, former Gentiles as well as former Israelites, into the eschatological people of God. Identified as the "house(hold) of the Spirit," the believing community is linked with the "house of Jacob" (Exod 19:3) as heir of the ancient covenant on Sinai. The communal metaphor, "house(hold) of the Spirit" or "household of God" (4:17), serves as an inclusive root metaphor in the letter's description of the Christian community. Thus it includes the images of God as father and procreator (1:3, 17) and of the believers as his reborn (1:3, 23; 2:2), obedient children (1:14), who are brothers and sisters practicing familial love (1:22; 2:17; 3:8; 4:8), who are growing up toward salvation (2:2–3), and who are knit together as the household or family of God (2:5; 4:17). Their membership in the family of God stands in stark contrast to the predicament of the believers in society, where as "strangers and resident aliens" (*parepidēmoi, paroikoi*, 1:1, 17; 2:11) they have no home (*oikos*) and place of belonging. Awareness of this communal familial identity on the part of the believers dispersed throughout the regions of Asia Minor is an essential element in their coping with the abuse of outsiders and presenting a collective front of resistance. And it is this symbolization of Christian community that will serve as a presupposition for the exhortation of the remainder of the letter.

(2) The communal epithets, which are drawn mainly from Israel's exodus and covenant traditions, identify the believers as members of the covenant community of the end time and sharers in the honor, dignity, and status of God's special people. The election and holiness of Israel were concomitant elements of its special covenantal relationship with God. The concepts of divine election and holiness (sanctification) are closely related in that they both express aspects of selection, separation, special possession, elevation and distinction, particularity and prestige. In Exod 19:3–6 and Isa 43:20–21, various related terms make this evident: the house of Jacob is distinguished as it is delivered from the Egyptians (Exod 19:4); it is declared by God "my own possession from among all nations" (Exod 19:5) or "my elect people whom I have

formed for myself (Isa 43:21). As it is "my elect stock" (Isa 43:20) selected from among the peoples (Exod 19:5) and the entity (*basileion*) within which God dwells as king, so it is a "holy people" (Exod 19:6) sanctified by and united to the Holy One of Israel (Isa 43:14). Israelites thought of themselves as unique among the peoples because of their allegiance to the unique God who had liberated them and with whom they were bound by a unique covenant with its particular regulations.[70] This self-awareness on Israel's part of constituting God's special elect and holy community distinguished from all the other peoples of the earth (Exod 19:5) pervades and informs the entire story of its history—"from the song of Miriam and the Bileam oracle of the Davidic era, and from the sayings of the prophets to the psalms of the era of the dissolution of the Israelite state to the days of the Maccabees" (Galling 1928, 28). Israel's election marks both its particularity and its prestige, its dignity and its distinctiveness.[71] When, in the course of Israel's history, appeal is made to Israel's divine election, that appeal is frequently directed to a minority people or a remnant experiencing spatial dislocation and social alienation. The divine election of these beleaguered communities assured them of God's special protection and favor, oppressive conditions to the contrary notwithstanding, and provided a rationale for resistance to cultural encroachments and for hope amidst adversity. Accordingly, Second Isaiah proclaims: "Thus says the Lord, the Redeemer of Israel and his Holy One, to one deeply despised, abhorred by the nations, the servant of rulers: 'Kings shall see and arise; princes, and they shall prostrate themselves; because the Lord, who is faithful, the Holy One of Israel, has chosen you'" (49:7; cf. also 2 Sam 22:26–28; 1 Chr 16:12–22; LXX Esth 8:12f; Ps 105[106]:4–5; 2 Macc 1:25–26). Only when the claim to divine election is seen in this social light can it assume credibility and be rescued from absurdity.

The concept of election played an important role in the postexilic period within apocalyptic sectarian circles. *1 Enoch*, in particular, contains numerous references to the righteous and holy ones as the "elect": 1:1, 3, 8; 5:7, 8; 25:5; 39:1, 6, 7; 40:5; 48:1, 9; 51:5; 56:3, 4, 6, 8; 58:1, 2, 3; 60:6; 61:4, 12, 13; 62:7, 8, 12, 13, 15; 70:3; 93:2, 10. In addition, frequent reference is made to the special agent of God, designated as the "Elect One" (39:6; 40:5; 41:2; 45:3–6; 48:5; 49:2, 4; 50:5; 51:3, 5; 52:6, 9; 53:6; 55:4; 61:5, 8, 10; 62:1–14). The term is also used collectively of God's people in Tob 8:15; Wis 3:9; 4:15; *Jub.* 15:30; 22:9; *2 Bar.* 48:20; *As. Mos.* 4:2; *4 Ezra* 3:13; 5:23–27. It likewise was employed as a communal self-designation at Qumran: 1QS VIII 6; IX 14; XI 16; 1QM

[70] On the covenant and the covenant formula, see Mendenhall 1955, 1962; Mendenhall and Herion 1992; Jocz 1958; Beyerlin 1961; McCarthy 1963, 1972; Hillers 1969; Perlitt 1969; Baltzer 1971; Weinfeld 1971; Riemann 1976; Kutsch 1981; Oden 1987; Guinan 1992.

[71] On the election of the house and descendants of Jacob/Israel, see Deut 7:6–7; 14:2; 1 Chr 16:13; Esth 8:12f; Ps 32[33]:12; 46[47]:4; 104[105]:6, 43; 105[106]:4–5, 43; 105[106]:5; 134[135]:4; Wis 3:9; 4:15; Sir 46:1; 47:22 Isa 14:1; 40:30; 41:8–9; 42:1; 43:10, 20; 44:1, 2; 45:4; 49:2,7; 65:9, 15, 23; Zech 11:16; 2 Macc 1:25; cf. Deut 4:37; 7:7; 10:15; 2 Kgdms 22:27; 3 Kgdms 3:8.

XII 1; 1QH[a] II 13; XIV 15; 1QpHab V 4; IX 12; X 13; XIV 15; 4Q164 1 3; cf. 1QS I 4; IV 22; XI 7; 1QM X 9; 1QH[a] XV 23; XVI 13; XVII 21; CD VI 2 (the sons of Zadok).

In the NT, the word "elect" (*eklektos, eklektoi*) is used as a designation of (1) Jesus (Luke 23:35; cf. 9:35; John 1:34 *v.l.*; 1 Pet 2:4); (2) the followers of Jesus as the eschatological elect (Matt 20:16; 22:14; 24:22, 24, 31; Mark 13:20, 22, 27; Luke 18:7; Rom 8:33; Col 3:12; 2 Tim 2:10; Titus 1:1; 1 Pet 1:1; 2:9 [cf. "co-elect" (brotherhood), 5:13]; Rev 17:14); (3) certain individuals (Rufus as elect of God [Rom 16:13]; elect lady, sister [2 John 1, 13]); or (4) angels (1 Tim 5:21). God's electing activity is expressed through the verb *eklegomai* (Mark 13:20; Acts 13:17; 1 Cor 1:27–28; Eph 1:4; Jas 2:5). The verb has the more prosaic sense of "choose" in certain cases (Acts 1:24; 6:5; 15:22, 25) but may take on more theological coloration when Jesus' selection/election of his disciples is the subject (Luke 6:13; John 6:70; 13:18; 15:16, 19; Acts 1:2; 15:7 [Peter chosen by God]). The related noun *eklogē* ("choice," "election") is used to denote God's election/selection of ancient Israel (Rom 9:11; 11:28), Paul (Acts 9:15), and believers in Jesus (Rom 11:5, 7; 1 Thess 1:4; 2 Pet 1:10).

On the whole, Old and New Testament material thus indicates that the concept of the election of God's people is an intrinsic element of the Exodus and Sinai covenant traditions, according to which a vulnerable and oppressed people is liberated by God, is taken under this God's special protection, and is obligated to a particular and distinctive social and moral code.[72]

Nowhere in the NT does the theme of election assume the dominating significance that it has in 1 Peter. This was noted years ago by G. Schrenk, who commented: "1 Pet. is the only NT work in which *eklektos* has from the very outset thematic significance. Here everything is worked out in terms of this controlling concept" (Schrenk 1967, 190; original German, 1942). At the letter's outset (1:1–2), the source (God's foreknowledge), medium (sanctification through the Spirit), and cause (the obedience and death of Jesus Christ) of the believers' election are clarified. In the present passage, 2:4–10, this theme of election is elaborated and accentuated in a variety of ways. The elect status of the believers (v 9a) is correlated with the elect status of their resurrected and living Lord (v 4d; cf. v 6b). The scriptural sources of the term "elect" (*eklektos*) that are cited here derive from two disparate and independent traditions: a complex of "stone" texts (Isa 28:16; Ps 117[118]:22, and Isa 8:14) employed in vv 6–8 and a complex of "people-of-God" texts (esp. Isa 43:2–21; Exod 19:6; and Hos 1–2) used in vv 9–10. Terms of Exod 19:6, part of the classic formula of the covenant established on Mt. Sinai expressing the election of Israel as God's

[72] On the subject of election, election tradition (and covenant), see Galling 1928; Schoeps 1950b; Stendahl 1953; Vriezen 1953; Helfgott 1954; K. Koch 1955; Jocz 1958; Wildberger 1960; Altmann 1964; Rowley 1964; Fascher 1966; Schrenk and Quell 1967; Zobel 1968; Bruce 1976; Sanders 1977a; Dexinger 1982; Sohn 1991; Patrick 1992; Shogren 1992a. On the election theme in 1 Peter, see Spörri 1925, 24–26, 163–67; Schrenk 1967, 190–91; Elliott 1966b, passim.

special people, and terms of the echo of this text in Isa 43:20–21 were specifically used by the Petrine author to affirm the divine election of the eschatological people of God. The election and covenant terms *hierateuma* and *hagios* (Exod 19:6b, cited in v 9) supply the terms of v 5e, and the associated election and covenant term *basileion* (Exod 19:6, cited in v 9b) is interpreted in v 5d as "house(hold) of the Spirit." The "elect and honored stone" of Isa 28:16 (cited in v 6) is applied in v 4 to Jesus Christ as the "living stone" who is "elect, honored in God's sight."

The theme of election is highlighted as well by the arrangement of this material. The triple use of "elect" (vv 4, 6, 9) gives shape and focus to this unit. In vv 4–5, which combine motifs of both the "stone" and "people of God" complexes, the adjective "elect" is made the first positive modifier of Jesus Christ (v 4d) just as "elect" is the initial modifier of the believing community in v 9a. Thus in this unit the twin concepts of election and holiness are presented as basic and determining features of the reborn family of God.

(3) Along with other material of this section informed by the exodus and Passover tradition (loins girded, 1:13; living in *paroikia*, 1:17; redeemed by the blood of Christ the lamb, 1:18–19; use of the Hallel Psalm 117[118], 2:7cd; called from darkness to light, 2:9), this stress on the election and holiness of the believers marks them as the heirs of Israel (cf. also 1:4; 3:7, 21) and recipients of the expectations of the prophets (1:10–12). Continuity with OT Israel, rather than anti-Israel polemic, is the theme of this section (Danker 1967b, 99; cf. also P. Richardson 1969, 74–84; Chevallier 1974, 1978; Brox 1981). No attack against the House of Israel is mounted here or, for that matter, anywhere else in the letter. The honorific epithets of ancient Israel are simply appropriated and applied to the messianic community without further comment. The believers are not said to constitute a "new people" but, rather, are declared the eschatological realization of Israel as God's elect and holy people (against Achtemeier 1988, 224–31, who reads the concept of "newness" into terms ["reborn," 1:3, 23; "people of God," 2:9] that in fact do not carry this meaning). However, it is now through faith rather than biological membership in the house of Jacob that admission is gained to the elect and holy people of God. This sense of sharing in the history and destiny of God's ancient covenant will later enable the Christian community to reject any specious charges that they constitute only a "new" phenomenon or "novel superstition" without the validity granted by antiquity of roots (see also the pertinent comments of Beare [1970, 127–28]).

(4) The correlate of believers constituting the special people of God is their separation and distinction from those who are ignorant of God (1:14–17) and who reject Jesus as God's agent of salvation (2:4c, 7b–8). Whereas those who are sanctified (2:5, 9; cf. 1:14–16, 22) and elected (2:5, 9; cf.1:1; 5:13) by God share in the election and honor of the Christ (2:4–5, 6–7a, 9–10), nonbelievers will be put to shame for rejecting the living stone and the word (2:4c, 7b–8; cf. 3:16). This distinction signals the demarcation brought about by baptismal conversion and provides the basis for later exhortation calling for dissociation

from the Gentiles and their immoral way of life (4:1–4; 2:11; cf. 2:1; 5:8–9) and standing firm in the grace of God (5:12).

(5) It is faith in Jesus Christ (in contrast to rejection and disobedience) that constitutes access to the people of God and the line of demarcation between the believers and Gentiles, the honored and the shamed (2:6, 7–8). No predestination to damnation is implied here, for it is the free choice exercised in faith or unbelief, obedience or disobedience, that brings about either honor or shame. Through faith and continued loyalty to Christ, the reborn children of God are nourished by the word (2:2–3), come to the Lord (2:4), and are consolidated into the household of God. Moreover, faith, like solidarity with Jesus Christ, involves solidarity with both his suffering and rejection and his divine vindication. Through faith in Jesus Christ, the living stone of God, believers become the living stones of God (2:4–5). Similarly, as Jesus Christ is God's elect and honored one (2:4), so believers are God's elect and honored people (2:5, 9–10). The fact of God's reversal of human designs in the case of Jesus Christ establishes the basis for Christian confidence in the face of suffering. Thus, as Jesus Christ was rejected and suffered innocently (2:4c, 7c) and yet was vindicated by God, so faithful Christians similarly exposed to rejection and suffering may also look forward to their divine vindication, as the remainder of the letter makes clear.

(6) The task to which the community is called is to declare publicly the praises and excellencies of the God who has led his people from darkness to light, to honor with their lives the One who has so honored them. Specific ways and means for so honoring and glorifying God (2:12; 4:11; 5:11) are the subject of the remainder of the letter.

(7) The accent on the divine *election* of the household of God relates this passage to both the opening and close of the letter, where both addressees and the brotherhood at Rome are described as the "elect" or "co-elect" of God (1:1; 5:13). As applied to an oppressed group of Christians scattered throughout Asia Minor, this concept, rooted in the tradition of Israel's divine deliverance from Egypt and its covenant with God at Sinai, is used to assure beleaguered believers of their elevated status and protection as God's particular people, their distinction from nonbelieving Gentiles, and their obligation to lead lives manifesting their election and holiness. The concept, as elaborated here, is both Christological and ecclesiological in nature. It involves the election and elevation of Jesus, who was rejected by humans, and of those who are similarly rejected and abused by society for aligning themselves in faith with the rejected one. Understood in this light, the election of the rejected ones, rooted in the cross and viewed as an expression of God's reversal of human designs, cannot be conceived as a basis for pride but only as a sign of amazing grace and favor. The formulation "elect strangers" (1:1) effectively expresses the paradox of the believers' estrangement in society, on the one hand, and their union with Jesus Christ and God, on the other. It voices the tension shaping the predicament and assurance of the community from the beginning of this letter to

its close (Spörri 1925, 24–26; Elliott 1966b, 16–49; 1981/1990, 127, 134–35; Rousseau 1986, 141, 383).

(8) Finally, the terms drawn from the prophet Hosea, with which our passage concludes, summarize in succinct and pregnant fashion the grand transformation experienced by the addressees in their divine election and conversion: once estranged from God, they are now God's elect people; once without mercy, they now enjoy mercy in its fullness.

In sum, 2:4–10 brings to a stirring close an opening affirmation of the believers as members of the divinely honored people of God. It completes and concludes the overarching theme of the rebirth-growth-consolidation of the household of God. It establishes the communal identity and divinely conferred honor of the believers as the covenant people of God. And it demarcates the honored believers in solidarity with Jesus Christ from those who have rejected the living stone. Their particular union with both God and Jesus Christ and their experience of God's mercy serve as both consolation in the midst of suffering (Danker 1967b) and basis for the following exhortation concerning the behavior of God's family in society.

DETAILED COMMENT: 1 PETER 2:5, 9 AND THE DOCTRINE OF THE PRIESTHOOD OF ALL BELIEVERS

Since the period of the Reformation, the doctrine of the universal priesthood of believers has been heralded in various ecclesial communions as "the decisive formula of all non-episcopal Christendom" and "one of the basic truths of Catholic ecclesiology" (K. E. Kirk and H. Küng, respectively, cited in Elliott 1966b, 1). One cardinal text seen as the "locus classicus" of this doctrine is 1 Pet 2:4–10, specifically vv 5 and 9. The popularity of this doctrine in modern times is due primarily to the great influence of the sixteenth-century reformer Martin Luther, who gave it a prominent place in his ecclesiology, with an appeal to 1 Peter 2 as its biblical basis.

In response to the monopolization of the means of grace by an official priesthood and the cleavage separating clergy and laity, Luther found it necessary to emphasize the equality before God of all the baptized, laity as well as clergy, as recipients and mediators of the means of grace. Through baptism, he insisted, Christians "altogether are consecrated as priests" ("allesampt durch die tauff zu priestern geweyhet," *WA* 6.407.22–25; cf. also 6.564.6–7), pointing to 1 Pet 2:9 (and Rev 5:10) as biblical confirmation for this thought. Among the features of this doctrine as stressed by Luther were the equivalent dignity and status conferred on all Christians by baptism; the Christian's unobstructed approach to God and his word apart from a mediating clergy; the priestly office of offering oneself to God and service to others; and the commission of proclamation given to every Christian within certain defined areas and occasions

(Brunotte 1959, 200). This priesthood of all believers complements the ministerial priesthood of the officially ordained—itself, according to Luther, a divine institution. Both general and specific priesthoods or ministries, moreover, according to Luther, participate, each in its own fashion, in the priesthood of Christ. For relevant texts, see WA 6.370, 407, 408.32–35, 409.7, 440, 561, 564.6–13; 7.27.17–23; 8.486.27; 11.411.31–413.2; 12.178.26–179.40, 180.17–23; 18.202; 30.2.526–30, 554.2; 38.230.13, 299.19; 41.207.37; 50.632.35–634.15.

The association of this Petrine text with baptism, a general priesthood, the priesthood of Christ, and Christian holiness and service by no means originated with Luther but reflects a developing body of theological thought from the early Fathers onward (see Dabin 1941, 1950, and other works listed in the BIBLIOGRAPHY). From the second century onward, the development of a notion of a special priesthood responsible for the eucharistic sacrifice was paralleled, on occasion, by a notion of the priestly character of all the faithful. Tertullian, Justin Martyr, Origen, and Chrysostom are representative of a small chorus of voices. Tertullian, while acknowledging the former, also gives expression to the latter. Asserting that "they who are chosen into the sacerdotal order must be men of one marriage" (*Exh. cast.* 7.2–3), he observes: "It would be idle for us to suppose (in the case of second marriage) that what is forbidden to priests is allowed to the laity. Are not laymen also priests? The Scripture says: 'He has made us a kingdom and has made us priests for God and his father'" (citing Rev 1:6); for the idea that all believers are priests in respect to prayer and service of God, see also Tertullian, *Mon.* 12; *Or.* 28; *Exh. cast.* 7.3 (cf. Irenaeus, *Haer.* 4.8.3, "All the apostles of the Lord are priests").

Justin (*Dial.* 116) describes the transformation experienced by those "who believe in Christ the High Priest" and, alluding to the language and thought of Hebrews, concludes "we are the true high priestly stock of God (*archieratikon to alēthinon genos*), as even God himself bears witness, saying that in every place among the Gentiles sacrifices are presented to him well-pleasing and pure. Now God receives sacrifices from no one except His priests" (116.3), sacrifices explained as the Eucharist and prayer in ch. 117. Origen, in his *Homily on Leviticus* (9.1), making a similar point, cites 1 Pet 2:9 for support: "Do you not know that the priesthood has been given to you, that is to say, to the whole church of God and to the believing people? Hear Peter say to the faithful: 'an elect people, a royal priesthood, a holy nation, a peculiar people.' You, then, have the priesthood since you are a priestly people, and so you ought to offer to God a sacrifice of praise, a sacrifice of prayers, a sacrifice of mercy, a sacrifice of purity, a sacrifice of sanctity" (cf. also 6.1; 9.9 [believers are made priests through baptism]; and *Mart.* 30). John Chrysostom (*Hom. 1 Cor.* 3.7) roots the laity's participation in the triple role of priest, prophet, and king in their reception of baptism: "In baptism you have become king, and priest, and prophet," with no reference, however, to 1 Peter. The Venerable Bede (*PL* 93,50–51), commenting on 1 Pet 2:9 and representing the harmonizing typical of the Fathers, observes: "They [the believers] are a *royal priesthood* (*regale sacerdo-*

tium) because they are united to the body of Christ, the supreme king and true priest. As sovereign he grants them his kingdom, and as high priest he washes away their sins by the offering of his blood. Peter says they are a royal priesthood; they must always remember to hope for an everlasting kingdom and to offer to God the sacrifice of a blameless life."

As this notion of a priesthood of all believers developed, with or without reference to 1 Peter, it was thus variously associated with direct access to the presence of God; union with the body of Christ, the high priesthood of Christ, and Christ as king (concepts absent from 1 Peter); the Church as a high-priestly stock; the missionary calling of the Church; and the lives of spiritual sacrifice, praise, and holiness expected of all its members. On the whole, however, the idea of a priesthood of all the faithful in the early and medieval church, developed through a harmonizing of various biblical themes and writings and remained an occasional and muted theme.

It was Luther's creative combination and elaboration of these ideas, however, to meet a crisis of his own time that enabled his thought to have a profound and indelible impact upon subsequent thinking concerning the nature of the Church, its ministry, and those who share its priestly character. On Luther's teaching concerning the priesthood of all believers, see Rade 1918; Storck 1953; Brunotte 1959; Prenter 1961; Mühlhaupt 1963; and the works listed in Elliott 1966b, 3. J. Reumann (1970) provides a nuanced summary of the relation of universal priesthood of the baptized and the office of ministry in the Reformation and post-Reformation Lutheran tradition (see also V. Pfitzner 1971). C. Eastwood (1962), in surveying the period from the Reformation to the twentieth century, claims that "the history of the Reformation, the History of Puritanism, and the History of the Evangelical Revival are the story of the extent to which Christians have understood and applied the doctrine of the priesthood of all believers" (Eastwood 1962, 241).

Luther's initial ruminations on this doctrine and his recourse to 1 Pet 2 were prompted more by theological than exegetical concerns, and it must be questioned whether this did not color his reading and use of 1 Pet 2. Until this present century, however, 1 Pet 2:4–10 had not been subjected to an independent and thorough exegetical analysis. This gap eventually was filled by the articles of J. Blinzler (1949), L. Cerfaux (1939), and the monograph of the present author (Elliott 1966b). One of the results of these investigations is the conclusion that 1 Pet 2:4–10 has little, if anything, to do with the idea of the universal priesthood of believers as this notion was expounded by Luther and the theologians who followed his lead (see Elliott 1966b, 6–8, 219–26; W. Pesch 1970). A recollection of the following points makes this patently clear.

(1) As is evident from its structure and content and from the accentuation of the election of both Jesus Christ and the believing community, 1 Pet 2:4–10 is designed as an affirmation of the elect and holy character of the believing community, which, through faith, is one with the elect and holy Christ. *Election rather than priesthood is its central focus.* The theme of election that extends

from the letter's beginning to its end (1:1; 5:13) receives here its most profound articulation. The passage, in fact, constitutes one of the most elaborate statements on Christian election in the entire NT.

(2) The covenant formula of LXX Exod 19:6, which included the terms *basileion* and *hierateuma*, in accord with prior Israelite interpretation of this text was one of several OT texts employed by the Petrine author to explicate the elect and holy character of the covenantal people of God as once affirmed at Sinai and now affirmed of God's people of the end time.

(3) The term *hierateuma*, like the other honorific epithets for Israel with which it is joined here ("elect stock," "holy people," "people of God"), is a *collective* noun designating the believing community as a whole, akin to the collective terms "brotherhood" (2:17; 5:9; cf. 5:13), "flock of God" (5:2), and "household of God" (4:17). It does not mean "priests" (*hiereis*) or "priesthood" (*hierateia*), but "priestly community." The term cannot apply to the believers as individuals, but only to the believing community *as community*, as is true of the other collective terms as well. The substantive *basileion*, "royal residence" (v 9b), likewise is applied to the believing community in its entirety and is interpreted as the "house(hold) of the Spirit" (v 5d).

(4) In both 1 Peter and its source, Exod 19:6, "priestly community" expresses the *holiness* of the covenant community and the immediacy of its relation to God, both of which are distinctive qualities of the believing community that the author stresses throughout the first major section of the letter with other language as well (1:2, 3–5, 14–16, 17–21, 22; 2:5 ["holy priestly community"], 9–10; cf. also 3:5, 15, 18c; 5:7a, 10). The action of the believers as priestly community is to offer "spiritual sacrifices acceptable to God" (2:5f), a cultic image that occurs only here in 1 Peter and that is not elaborated on anywhere else in the letter. Similarly, neither *hierateuma* nor a concept of Christian priesthood occurs elsewhere in 1 Peter and *hierateuma* plays no independent role in the ecclesial thought of the letter. The appearance of *hierateuma* in 2:5 and 9 is due solely to its place in the covenant formula of Exod 19:6, which is used by the Petrine author to affirm the election and holiness of the household of faith.

(5) No mention is made in 2:4–10 of baptism or any baptismal "ordination" or "consecration" to priesthood on the part of the believers.

(6) Nowhere in 1 Peter is there any reference to the priesthood of Christ or any suggestion that believers share in the priesthood of Christ by virtue of their constituting a "priestly community." In the book of Hebrews, on the other hand, Jesus Christ is identified metaphorically as a priest (Heb 7:15, 21; 8:4; 10:21) or high priest (Heb 2:17; 3:1; 4:14–15; 5:5, 10; 6:20; 7:26; 8:1; 9:11). In Revelation, Christians are denoted metaphorically as priests as well (Rev 1:6; 5:10; 20:6). In other NT writings, cultic metaphors occasionally are used to describe the proclamation of the gospel (Rom 15:16), the gift of material support (Phil 4:18), or aspects of salvation (Heb 4:16; 8:1; 9:11–14, 23–28; 10:10, 19–22; 13:10–16). No single NT author, however, makes any attempt to integrate these random images into a unified teaching on Christian priesthood, and this

certainly includes the author of 1 Peter. To attribute these various motifs to 1 Peter is to impute alien notions to this text and to distort its focus (see Elliott 1966b, 219–22; and 1968). In 1 Pet 2:4–10, the association of believers with Christ is that of "living stones," who through faith are one with Christ, the "living stone," and who are "elect" as he was "elect" in God's sight.

In the light of these facts, the claim that 1 Pet 2:5 and 9 provides the biblical basis for a "priesthood of all believers," as put forth by Luther and others, is exegetically unwarranted. Although this text indeed celebrated the dignity and honor of the Christian community before God, Luther fastened on and singled out the term *hierateuma*, inaccurately applied it to individual believers, and exaggerated its role and significance within its context. Consequently, his preoccupation with the concept of priesthood and his individualistic interpretation of the collective term *hierateuma* resulted in a misreading of 2:4–10 that ignored or obscured the actual aim of this text and its stress on the believers' union with Christ, their distinction from nonbelievers, and their consolidation as the elect and holy people of God, the household of the Spirit.

A broader "biblical doctrine" of a priesthood of all believers was constructed by Luther and others only through a harmonization of images and themes from originally distinct and independent sources: Paul's writings, Hebrews, 1 Peter, and Revelation. In respect to Luther, specifically, see his treatises "Concerning the Ministry" (*LW* 40:3–44), "To the Christian Nobility of the German Nation" (*LW* 44:115–217), "The Misuse of the Mass" (*LW* 36:127–230), and his "Sermons on the First Epistle of St. Peter" (*LW* 30:1–145). Paul, however, while speaking of his own ministry in cultic terms, never refers to Christ, himself, or other believers as "priest" or to followers as constituting a "priesthood." The image of the "body of Christ" he employs to affirm the unity of Christ and Christians and the notion of diversity within unity (Rom 12:3–8; 1 Cor 12:4–31) is unique to Paul and appears nowhere in Hebrews, 1 Peter, or Revelation. Hebrews also describes Christian action in the cultic terms of sacrifice, as do the other three documents, while also presenting Christ as priest and high priest. But the point of this writing is that the priesthood of Christ is unique and inimitable. Revelation describes believers metaphorically as priests but focuses primarily on their reigning with Christ, with no suggestion that believers as priests share in the priesthood of Christ, a thought absent in 1 Peter as well. Attention to the *specific* content of all these independent writings makes it clear that no single NT composition presents a notion of a priesthood of all believers as constructed by theologians in later time.

It has long been recognized that the Reformation doctrine of the priesthood of all believers was a product of the ecclesiastical polemics of the sixteenth century and an attempt to affirm the priestly character of *all* the baptized over against the "papist" position that the status and responsiblities of priesthood were reserved exclusively to ordained clergy. This was a time when the primary content and intent of biblical texts were often misconstrued and misapplied in the rush for proof texts used to bolster one theological position or another.

Luther's use of 1 Pet 2:5 and 9 as the biblical basis for his position is a case in point. Following Luther's lead, the Reformation churches in particular have continued to stress the rights, privileges, and authority of each believing Christian and have continued to link these qualities with the text of 1 Pet 2, along with numerous other NT passages. Given the original polemical context in which Luther formulated this doctrine, the affirmation of this teaching by the Roman Catholic bishops of the Second Vatican Council is nothing short of ironic; see the *Dogmatic Constitition on the Church* 9.10.34; the *Constitution on the Holy Liturgy* 14; the *Decree on the Lay Apostolate* 3; the *Decree on the Service and Life of Priests* 2; and the *Decree on the Mission of the Church* 15. Here too, however, though without explicit reference to Luther, one encounters a combination and harmonization of biblical texts from diverse sources in a proof text method that fails to respect their unique content and the function in their own contexts; see the insightful critique of the Roman Catholic exegete H. Frankemölle (1987, 45) and, for a more exegetically nuanced appreciation of 1 Pet 2, the study on the church by Roman Catholic scholar J. M. R. Tillard (1992). For an ecumenical as well as historical perspective on the doctrine since Luther, see H. M. Barth (1990).

However efforts at ecclesial reform and restructuration are to be judged, and whatever other NT texts might support this notion of a priesthood of all believers, any appeal to 1 Pet 2 must be regarded as exegetically unfounded. According to the definition of this doctrine by the Danish Lutheran theologian R. Prenter, "one speaks of a general priesthood (*allgemeines Priestertum*) when *each member* of the people can exercise partial or entire priestly *rights* and functions" (Prenter 1961, 581, italics mine). If Prenter's succinct definition adequately captures the central thrust of this doctrine as currently conceived, then this doctrine and the related doctrine of a Christian ministry of the laity will have to seek biblical support in texts other than 1 Pet 2:4–10, which depicts not the rights and privileges of individuals but the electedness and holiness of the *communal* people of God. This Petrine passage ought not to be enlisted in considerations of the distinction and relation of laity and clergy, the general ministry of the faithful, or the special ministry of the ordained because these issues are foreign to the actual point of this passage.

This is not to question the clear biblical foundation for a theology of the *ministry* of all the faithful, as Luther also stressed. That all baptized Christians are called to serve and minister to one another is a thought abundantly documented in the NT and evident in 1 Peter as well (4:8–11). Among the numerous treatments of ministry in the NT, the essay of J. Quinn 1970 is especially succinct and instructive; for more general observations and the preference for a "ministry of leadership" over "priesthood," see also the apposite remarks of H. Küng 1976, 486–88. This is also not to challenge efforts to formulate a theology of priesthood (in the sense of *universal ministry*) consistent with the entire NT. The point of this comment is only to emphasize that 1 Pet 2:4–10 is not directly relevant to these concerns and to insist upon an appreciation of 1 Pet 2:4–10 on its own terms.[73]

For studies on 1 Peter 2:4–10 see Ambroggi 1947; Balch 1981; Best 1969; Blinzler 1949; Cerfaux 1939; Cipriani 1981; Colecchia 1977; Coppens 1969; Cordero 1959; Cothenet 1969; Dacquino 1967; Dale 1896c; Danker 1967a, 1967b; Deist 1970; Elliott 1966b, 1968, 1981/1990, 1982, 1995; Feuillet 1974; Giesen 1986; Goldstein 1979; Halas 1984; Hill 1982; Hillyer 1969b, 1971; Kayalaparampil 1989; Ketter 1947; LaVerdiere 1969; Manns 1984a; J. S. Marshall 1946; Minear 1982; Mole 1961; Moule 1955–1956; Muñoz León 1978; Oss 1989; Otranto 1970; Pietrantonio 1980; Plumpe 1943; Prigent 1992; Ramos 1970; P. J. Robinson 1989; J. Rousseau 1986; Sandevoir 1980; Schlosser 1980; D. Schroeder 1990; Schröger 1979, 1981b; Schutter 1989, 130–38; E. Schweizer 1992; Seland 1995; Selwyn 1947, 268–98; Snodgrass 1977; Spörri 1925; Steuernagel 1986; Vanhoye 1964, 1973; 1986, 243–67; Vanni 1987; Wells 1973; Whelan 1965.

---

[73] For relevant studies, exegetical and theological, on the priesthood of all believers, see: Luther *LW* 30:1–145 (= *WA* 12:259–399); *LW* 36:3–126 (= *WA* 6:497–573); *LW* 40:3–44 (= *WA* 12:169–95); *LW* 44:115–217 (= *WA* 6:[381] 404–69); Behm 1912; Rade 1918; Botte 1934; Niebecker 1936; Dabin 1941, 1950; Asmussen 1946; Plamer 1947; Arndt 1948; Lécuyer 1949, 1970; Moe 1949; Pellend 1949; Vajta 1950; Counelis 1953; Kinder 1953; Sommerlath 1953/1954; Storck 1953; Torrance 1955; Ordonez 1956; Congar 1957; W. F. M. Scott 1957; Kraemer 1958; Sevenster 1958; G. H. Williams 1958; K. Koch 1961; Prenter 1961; Eastwood 1962, 1963; L. Ryan 1962; Skinner 1962; McCabe 1963; Mühlhaupt 1963; Bravo 1964; Baker 1966; Colson 1966, 1972; Hoyer 1967; Küng 1967, 1976; Beck 1968; Guerra 1969; Schlier 1969; R. E. Brown 1970; Leonardi 1970; Nocent 1970; W. Pesch 1970; Quinn 1970; Reumann 1970; Studer 1970; Coppens 1971; Pfitzner 1971; de Rosa 1972; Tillard 1973, 1992; Rausch 1976; Goldie 1979; Haendler 1981; Schröer and Müller 1982; Adinolfi 1983; Grelot 1990; Brox 1986, 108–10; Chryssavgis 1987; Harrisville 1987; Barth 1988, 1990; Lea 1988; Osborne 1988, 1993; Sheils and Wood 1989; Hobbs 1991; Soares-Prabhu 1992; Marney 1993; Nelson 1993; Shurden 1993; Barilier 1995.

II. Transition: As Aliens and Strangers, Maintain Honorable Conduct among the Gentiles to the Glory of God (2:11–12)

◆

2:11a Beloved, I exhort [you] as resident aliens and visiting strangers
11b to avoid the deadly cravings that wage war against life;
12a maintain honorable conduct among the Gentiles,
12b so that when they slander you
as those who do what is wrong,
12c from observing [your] honorable deeds,
12d they may glorify God on the day of visitation.

INTRODUCTION

Following his opening affirmation of the addressees as the elect and holy household of God with divinely conferred honor and dignity (1:3–2:10), our author now shifts attention to the honorable behavior of this household of God in the larger society. This shift in subject matter and mood is marked by several elements. The audience is now addressed directly ("Beloved," v 11; the same address in 4:12 also opens a new section of the letter); the author speaks directly ("I exhort [you]," 1st-person sing. verb); issues of conduct are introduced; and the mood changes from indicative to imperative as the focus moves from an affirmation of the believers as the family of God to a delineation of their responsibilities in a society where this family of God (*oikos tou theou*) is regarded as a collection of resident aliens and strangers (*paroikoi kai parepidēmoi*). The subject now under consideration is their engagement with outsider "Gentiles" (i.e., nonbelievers), and the manner in which their honor as the elect and holy people of God can be maintained in the face of slander, insult, and suffering—issues taken up throughout the remainder of the letter. The linguistic and thematic links between these verses and what precedes and follows (see DETAILED COMMENT 1) indicate their function as a *transitional statement* in which the moral and social implications of the foregoing (1:3–2:10) are now introduced.

NOTES

2:11. *Beloved (Agapētoi).* The direct address of the recipients as *beloved,* with the substantive *agapētoi* used as a vocative here as in 4:12, is consonant with the author's stress on familial ("brotherly") love (1:22; 2:17; 3:8; 4:8) and expresses the intimate bond uniting author and addressees as joint members of the brotherhood (*adelphotēs,* 2:17; 5:9) and household of God (2:5; 4:17). *Beloved* is a conventional term of Christian address (Rom 1:7; 12:19; 1 Cor 10:14; 2 Cor 7:1; 1 Thess 2:8; 2 Pet 3:1; 1 John 2:7; 4:7), often combined with "brothers" (*adelphoi*), as in 1 Cor 15:58; Phil 4:1; Jas 1:16, 19; 2:5.

I exhort [you] (parakalō). This first instance of the author speaking directly (1st-person sing. of *parakaleō*) introduces a combination of exhortation and encouragement that dominates the remainder of the letter. Exhortation, reflecting early Christian hortatory tradition (2:13–17, 18–20; 3:1–5, 7, 13–17; 4:1–6, 7–11, 12–19; 5:1–5a, 5b, 6a, 7a, 8a, 9a), is supported with encouragement drawn from Christological (2:21–25; 3:18, 22; 4:1a, 13; 5:4), Scriptural (3:6, 10–12; 4:17–18; 5:5c, 7c), and liturgical (4:11; 5:10–11) tradition. The introductory verb *parakalō* (see also 5:1), like *beloved* in 2:11 and 4:12, signals the commencement of a new, hortatory unit. This verb occurs frequently in the NT (109×), often with the overlapping senses of "appeal," "urge," "encourage," "exhort," "comfort," "console" (BAGD 617) and often to introduce traditional hortatory material (e.g., Rom 12:1; Eph 4:1; 1 Thess 4:1, 10; 5:14; 2 Thess 3:12; 1 Tim 6:2; Titus 2:6, 15). According to Bjerkeland (1967), the verb customarily is used to establish a fraternal atmosphere in which to make specific requests in a diplomatic fashion. Its force is somewhat more than "request" but less than "command." Here, and again in 5:1, it introduces the exhortation that follows. At the close of the letter it is employed one final time (5:12) to characterize the thrust of the writing as a whole.

as resident aliens and visiting strangers (hōs paroikous kai parepidēmous). Our author has already referred to his addressees as "elect strangers" (*eklektois parepidēmois*) at the outset of the letter (1:1) and in 1:17 spoke of their "residence as aliens" (*paroikia,* a paronym of *paroikoi*). Now at this transitional point in the letter he returns to the situation of the social estrangement of his audience, to which these terms point, as the context for the exhortation that follows. With the particle *hōs* ("as"), a favorite and characteristic term of 1 Peter (see the NOTE on 1:14a), the addressees are not simply compared to aliens and strangers but are actually identified as such (against Martin 1992, 188–93). For this use of *hōs,* see also 2:13b, 14a, 16a; and 4:16a and elsewhere (Rom 1:21; 1 Cor 4:14; Phlm 16; and esp. Heb 11:9, where *hōs allotrian* ["as a stranger"] explains Abraham's having "dwelled as a resident alien" [*parōikēsen*]). The sense is: "as the resident aliens and strangers that you actually are."

Modern translations of the terms *paroikoi* and *parepidēmoi* vary greatly and often fail to reflect the actual meaning of these terms in the Bible and the Greek-speaking world, so that their meaning here in 1 Peter is frequently obscured (see DETAILED COMMENT 2). Neither term, for instance, means "pilgrims" or "exiles." The Bible contains no particular word for "pilgrim" in either a literal (visitor to a religious shrine) or a figurative sense. Terms for "exile" include *metoikia, apoikia,* or *aichmalōsia* but neither of our two words. Hence, the translation of *parepidēmoi* as "pilgrims" (e.g., KJV, JB, Luther) or "exiles" (RSV, NRSV; cf. NAB; Goodspeed) is misplaced and misleading.

Consistency in translation is a further problem. The term *parepidēmoi* is rendered "strangers" by the KJV in 1:1 but "exiles" in 2:11; see also Jerome, who employs *advenis* at 1:1 but *peregrinos* at 2:11; NAB, which reads "strangers" at 1:1 but "in exile" at 2:11; and Goppelt, who uses "foreigner" for *parepidēmoi* in 1:1 and for *paroikoi* in 2:11. For *parepidēmoi* compare also "people who lodge for a while" (NEB, 1:1), "those living among foreigners" (JB in 1:1 but "pilgrims" in 2:11), "refugees" (TEV in 1:1 and 2:11); "immigrants" (Reicke in 1:1 and 2:11); "sojourners" (Beare in 1:1 and 2:11); "temporary residents" (Phillips); "temporary sojourners" (Kelly). For *paroikoi,* compare "strangers" (KJV, TEV, Phillips), "aliens" (RSV, NRSV, NEB, NAB, Goodspeed, Kelly), "foreigners" (Beare, Goppelt), "visitors" (JB), "pilgrims" (Reicke). For a fuller comparative listing of translations of *parepidēmoi, paroikoi,* and *paroikia* in 1:1; 2:11; and 1:17, see Elliott 1990, 39–41.

In actuality, *paroikoi* and *parepidēmoi* refer to types of strangerhood but have distinguishable connotations (Elliott 1981/1990, 30; Pilch 1991; and the NOTE on 1:1). "Strangers" in general (*xenoi, allotrioi, allogenai*), by definition, are persons located elsewhere than in the place of their birth and hence from the perspective of the natives are "others," who lack roots in the language, customs, culture, and political-social allegiances of the people among whom they dwell. They constitute the fundamental category of "they" compared to the constituency of "we"; alien "outsiders" as distinguished from familiar "insiders." *Paroikoi* and *parepidēmoi* are subsets of these strangers. As the content of the terms indicates, they are persons displaced from their own homes and places of birth and belonging, and live as "by-dwellers" (*par-oikoi, par-epidēmoi*) among the homes (*oikoi*) and countries (*dēmoi*) of others, with whom they share no kinship or cultural ties.

The substantive *parepidēmos* and its verb *parepidēmeō* are used most often of the *temporary visitor*, the *transient* stranger who, as traveler passing through, has no intention or opportunity to establish permanent residence. This sense is richly illustrated in Greek inscriptions and other sources.[74] The substantive occurs only twice in the LXX, in each case combined with *paroikos*: once on the lips of Abraham (Gen 23:4) and once as a self-designation of the psalmist (Ps 38[39]:12). Its NT occurrences are likewise limited. It appears only twice in 1 Peter (1:1; 2:11) and once in Hebrews (11:13, with reference to Abel, Enoch, Noah, Abraham, and Sarah). The related verb *parepidēmeō* is absent in the

---

[74] See IGBR 251; SGDI 103c; I. Crete 4.168; IG 5.1145; PTebt. 782.10; SIG^3 640.5; 707.20; 714.30; OGIS 383.150; 139.4; 268.9; 329.28; 339.29; PPetr. 3; cf. also Calixenus 2; Polyb. *Hist.* 32.6.4.

NT but occurs in 1 *Clem.* 1:2 (of fellow-believers temporarily visiting the Roman community).

The term *paroikos*, on the other hand, is used of the stranger who resides longer or permanently in a place different from that of his or her origin and hence is a *resident alien*. If, as seems likely, this term refers to the same class of persons called *metoikoi* earlier in Greek history, the definition of the latter term suggests that a temporary visitor (*parepidēmos*) became a *paroikos* after a month of residence. "A *metoikos*," according to Aristophanes of Byzantium (ca. 257–180 BCE), "is anyone who comes from a foreign city and lives in the city, paying tax towards certain fixed needs of the city; for a number of days he is called a *parepidēmos* and is free from tax, but if he outstays the time laid down he becomes a metic (*metoikos*) and liable to taxation" (*Frag.* 38). For additional illustrative texts and further discussion, see DETAILED COMMENT 2. In literature and inscriptions, *paroikos* appears more frequently than *parepidēmos*[75] and identifies one who lacks the legal status and privileges of a full citizen. In numerous inscriptional lists of urban constituencies, resident aliens (*paroikoi*, occasionally *metoikoi*, esp. in classical Athens) are identified as forming a stratum of the population distinguished from full citizens (*politai*), who are ranked above them, and strangers (*xenoi*), freed persons (*apeleutheroi*), and slaves (*douloi*), ranked below them (see the evidence assembled by Schaefer 1949). In the rural territories of Asia Minor, native farmers whose lands were gradually annexed to expanding urban territories but who never received the full rights of municipal citizenship were also reckoned among the *paroikoi* (Rostovtzeff 1957, 1:255–57). The process is not dissimilar from instances in the nineteenth and twentieth centuries when native American Indians and native Africans were deprived of their ancestral lands, relegated to "reservations" or "homelands," stripped of self-determination, and treated as strangers in their own lands.

Strangers, whether transients or resident aliens, were accorded only limited political or legal privileges in the localities where they resided, a situation that has prevailed from antiquity down to the present age. They were constantly vulnerable to the suspicion and fear of the local populace that their strangeness and alien ways posed an ongoing threat to the common good and the favor of the local gods (Elliott 1981/1990, 37–49). Discrimination along legal lines was accompanied by countless forms of social discrimination, disparagement, scapegoating, and public shaming—precisely the forms of harassment encountered by the addressees of 1 Peter.

The entire phrase in which these two terms are combined here was undoubtedly inspired by Gen 23:4 LXX, the only other occurrence of this precise phrase in the ancient Greek literature prior to 1 Peter. In this text, Abraham,

[75] Including the LXX (33×) and NT (4×; Acts 7:6, 29; Eph 2:19; 1 Pet 2:11); cf. the verb *paroikeō*, Luke 24:18; Heb 11:9; and the related noun *paroikia*, Acts 13:17 and 1 Pet 1:17.

who is a foreigner residing among the Hittites in the land of Canaan, states of himself: "I am a resident alien and stranger among you" (*paroikos kai parepidēmos egō eimi meth' hymōn*). A later, modified echo of this Abrahamic statement occurs in a psalm attributed to David (Ps 38[39]:13): "I am a resident alien (*paroikos*) in your sight (*v.l.* "in the land") and a stranger (*parepidēmos*) as were all my fathers" (cf. also 1 Chr 29:15). That the Petrine author, however, has Gen 23:4 LXX and Abraham in mind is indicated by both the exactness of the terminological correspondence (with a plural substituted for the original singular according to sense) and the further reference to Abraham and Sarah in 3:6, where the couple and Sarah's conduct in particular are cited as a model for the behavior of the present believers.

The statement of Abraham in Genesis illustrates his material plight as resident alien. As such, he owned no land and therefore was required to purchase from the native Hittites a parcel of earth in which to bury Sarah (Gen 23:1–11), as noted also by Irenaeus (*Haer.* 5.32.2). A later Israelite, writing closer to the time of 1 Peter, the author of the *Testament of Levi*, specifically traces the harassment of Abraham and his family by the Shechemites of Canaan to the fact that he was a stranger:

> They persecuted Abraham our father since he was a stranger (*onta xenon*) and harassed his flocks since the ewes were pregnant and they grossly mistreated Eblaen his kinsman. This is how they treated all strangers (*tois xenois*), seizing their wives (*tas xenas*) and murdering them. (*T. Levi* 6:9–10)

Abraham and Sarah are, for the biblical communities, the prototypical resident aliens, whose own experience of *paroikia* among Gentiles established the pattern repeated so frequently in Israel's subsequent history (see DETAILED COMMENT 2). In describing his addressees with terms derived from Gen 23:4, the Petrine author links their situation of social estrangement to that of their spiritual ancestors Abraham and Sarah.

They too, like Israel of old, are strangers and resident aliens in a foreign and hostile land. Some of them may have been aliens in the lands where they resided prior to their conversion and joined the messianic movement hoping to find here an acceptance and support not available to them in society. While that was indeed what they found, they also soon learned that the community they joined had itself a long history of being strangers and aliens on foreign soil, going all the way back to Abraham and Sarah and the house of Jacob at Sinai. The author has just reminded them that they are part of a community that was divinely called, elected, and set apart from all other peoples as God's special people (2:4–10, describing the current readers in the terms of the covenant made with the house of Jacob at Sinai [Exod 19:3–8]). As God's reborn children, they indeed have a place of acceptance and belonging in God's household (2:5). But this household is distinct from the society at large and must manifest this distinctiveness in its conduct. Consequently, the readers are reminded of their status as strangers and resident aliens in both the religious and social senses of these terms in Israel's history and of the necessity of distancing themselves from the vices typical of Gentile outsiders.

A common misconception is that these terms for strangers imply a strangerhood "on (an evil) earth" in contrast to a "homeland in heaven."[76] Some commentators and translators, in fact, go so far as to add "in this world" or "on earth" where these words do not occur in the original Greek (e.g., TEV, Phillips at 2:11; NEB, TEV, Phillips, Beare 1970, 100 at 1:17). In doing so, however, they introduce and impose an alien cosmological contrast not in the original Greek text and not consistent with the social rather than cosmological orientation of this letter (cf. Elliott 1981/1990, 39–48 for discussion).

This view, moreover, which assumes only a metaphorical sense of *paroikoi* and *parepidēmoi*, further assumes that the addressees had only become "strangers" as a consequence of their affiliation with the messianic movement. Both assumptions, however, are arbitary and open to serious question. On the one hand, the predominant use of both terms in the LXX (*parepidēmos*, 2×; *paroikos*, 33×) is literal, not metaphorical. This is expressly the case in respect to Gen 23:4 LXX, cited in 1 Pet 2:11. Hence, consistent LXX usage requires the assumption of a literal sense unless the context *requires* a metaphorical sense. Since the Petrine context does not make this explicitly clear, those favoring a metaphorical sense resort to a further assumption that the Petrine author regarded the addressees as having become strangers in a metaphorical sense as a result of their conversion. However, nothing is said of this explicitly in 1 Peter, so this remains yet another assumption open to serious question. The most that can be inferred is that the nonconformity with a former way of life that the author encourages (1:14–16; 4:2–4) and the exclusive allegiance to God and Jesus Christ that he stresses, if practiced, would estrange believers socially and religiously from their nonbelieving neighbors.

But this does not deal with the question of whether some of the believers had occupied the social stratum of strangers and resident aliens *prior* to their conversion, a condition of alienation only exacerbated by their conversion. Thus we must allow for the possibility that at least *some* of the believers occupied the stratum of strangers and resident aliens *prior* to their conversion and that it was this precarious condition that led them to seek a place of acceptance and belonging in the messianic movement in the first place. Eventually the estrangement that subsequent adherents of the movement also experienced made it possible for our author to describe the entire brotherhood as a community of strangers and resident aliens. This hypothesis would take into account (1) the large number of actual strangers and resident aliens within this mobile, missionary movement; (2) the attraction to this movement of others who were also actual strangers and aliens where they resided; and (3) the eventual global designation of the entire movement as a community of strangers

[76] For example, Hort 1898, 132; Weiss 1906, 275; Beare 1970, 75, 102, 135; Furnish 1975, 10; Martin 1992, 188; Feldmeier 1992, 175–92; Metzner 1995, 181–83.

and resident aliens in a secondary and extended metaphorical sense, distinguished from and harassed by their nonbelieving neighbors.

As discussed further in DETAILED COMMENT 2, these terms identify the believers as both socially and religiously distinct from their neighbors and as sharing in the history of Israel's repeated estrangement in society. The maintenance of social and religious differentiation, moreover, should not be confused with isolationism or "pie-in-the-sky" escapism. Believers rather are urged, as these and the following verses indicate, to engage with outsiders in a fashion that, while demonstrating their distinctiveness, will allay outsiders' suspicions and even attract their praise. In 1:3–2:10 the author focused on the distinctive communal *identity* of the believers. Now he stresses the distinctive *conduct* by which this distinctive identity is to be manifested in society. Conduct, moreover, is one of the chief factors that distinguishes strangers and aliens from natives.

11b. *to avoid (apechesthai)*. The translation presumes the infinitive *apechesthai* (supported by ℵ, B, Ψ, 049, 𝔐, lat, sa) as the more likely original reading rather than the imperative *apechesthe* (𝔓[72] A C L P and others). While the same preceding verb, "exhort," is used in 5:1 and followed by an imperative in 5:2 (cf. also 1 Cor 4:16; Heb 13:22), the construction of *parakaleō* with an infinitive occurs far more frequently in the NT.[77] The grammatical alternatives, however, involve no difference in semantic meaning.

In the middle voice, as here and in other hortatory contexts, *apechō* has the sense of "hold oneself (*echō*) apart from (*apo*)," "stay away from," "keep clear of," "avoid," with various types of vices as object. Its combination with *epithymia* is known since Plato (*Phaed.* 82C, 83B; *Leg.* 8.835E). In Israelite comments on moral behavior, the verb often is used in conjunction with vices considered typical of Gentile conduct.[78]

Certain NT texts employing this term (Acts 15:20, 29; 21:25; 1 Thess 4:3; and 5:22) suggested to Selwyn (1947, 365–466) the influence of a primitive ethical "holiness code" that was subsequently incorporated into a baptismal catechetical tradition, upon which numerous NT authors drew. This theory, however, and especially the "pattern" of instruction that Selwyn constructed, is not sustained by the evidence. The exhortation initiated in 2:11, therefore, is best seen as drawing on a broad and fluid stream of early Christian tradition associated with baptismal ethical instruction. Similarly unconvincing is Selwyn's attempt (1947, 9–17, 369, 383–84) to use this appearance of the verb *apechomai* to buttress his theory that Silvanus was the actual author of 1 Peter. Noting the occurrence of this verb in texts involving the presence of Silvanus/Silas (Acts 15:20, 29; 1 Thess 4:3; 5:22; 1 Pet 2:11), and claiming similarities in style and content between 1 Thessalonians and 1 Peter, he proposed that

[77] See Rom 12:1; 16:17; 2 Cor 2:8; 6:1; Eph 4:1; Phil 4:2; 1 Thess 3:2; 4:10; 1 Tim 1:3; 2:1; Titus 2:6; Heb 13:19; Jude 3; and 10× in Acts.

[78] See Job 1:1, 8; 2:3; 13:21; 28:28; Isa 54:14; Jer 7:10; Wis 2:6; Mal 3:6; Philo, *Virt.* 163; *Did.* 1:4; Pol. *Phil* 2:2; 6:1; *Diogn.* 3:2; 4:6.

Silvanus authored both documents. The verb *apechomai*, however, is a term of traditional parenesis, as Selwyn himself observed, and 1 Thessalonians is distinctively Pauline in form and content; see the convincing critique of Selwyn's theory by Rigaux (1956, 105–11).

deadly cravings (tōn sarkikōn epithymiōn). The noun *epithymia*, as already noted in conjunction with its occurrence in 1:14b, when used in a negative sense, denotes "insatiable craving," "selfish yearning," "self-indulgence" (cf. also 4:2, 3). According to Plato (*Phaed.* 83B), it was one of the four chief vices to avoid (*Phaed.* 82C; cf. *Leg.* 8.835E). Philo, in his commentary on the tenth commandment (*ouk epithymēseis*), discussed this vice at length (*Spec.* 4.79–131) and described it as "the fount of all evil" (*Spec.* 4.84–85). Elsewhere in the NT, *epithymia* is modified by such adjectives as "foolish" (1 Tim 6:9), "defiling" (2 Pet 2:10), "deceptive" (Eph 4:22), and "godless" (Jude 18). It can include, but is not restricted to, sexual desire ("lust"). Thus, the translation "craving" is preferable to that of "passion," which today is so often associated exclusively with sexual desire.

Although the phrase *sarkikai epithymiai* occurs only here in the NT (cf. *Did.* 1:14 and, less exactly, 4 Macc 1:32), it is close in meaning to the expression "desire(s) of the (our) flesh" (Gal 5:16; Eph 2:3; 1 John 2:16; 2 Pet 2:18; cf. Rom 13:14; Gal 5:24; 2 Pet 2:10).

The adjective *sarkikos* appears elsewhere in the NT only in the Pauline writings (Rom 15:27; 1 Cor 3:3; 9:11; 2 Cor 1:12; 10:4). Like its semantic equivalent *sarkinos* (see 1 Cor 3:1–3, where both terms are used interchangeably), *sarkikos* derives from the noun *sarx* ("physical, mortal body") and qualifies something as physically controlled, mortal, and transitory, or "sinful" (when *sarx* is associated with sin). The specific nuance of *sarkikos* is determined by its use in context. Paul associates *sarkikos* with envy and strife (1 Cor 3:3) and with material or human objects in contrast to spiritual realities (1 Cor 9:11; cf. 1 Cor 3:3; 2 Cor 1:12; 10:3–5).

The importance of separation from insatiable and corrupting craving typical of a former mode of life has already been stressed in 1:14–18, and the point is repeated again in 4:1–4 (cf. also 3:10–12; 4:15). It is in the light of these passages that the phrase *sarkikai epithymiai*, and in fact all of vv 11–12, is best understood. In 1:14–18, believers were urged not to allow themselves to be molded by the "cravings of your former ignorance," that is, by dispositions and actions that governed their life prior to their conversion and from which they have been ransomed by Jesus Christ. In 4:1–4, "cravings" are listed among several vices of excess, debauchery, and idolatry, which are representative of Gentile intentions and from which the believers are to have separated themselves, a point recalling 1:14–18 and 2:11. The association of *sarx* and sin in 4:1cd (a typically Pauline association) could suggest the rendition "sinful desires" here in 2:11. However, the use of *sarx* to designate the mortal human body (4:1a, 1c, 2a, 6b)—with no implication of sin when referring to Christ (4:1a; cf. 3:18 and 2:22)—also suggests the rendition "physical (and ephemeral) desires" as a possibility. On the whole, the definition of *sarkikos* given in

BAGD s.v. covers the variety of connotations that the term has within the context of 1 Peter: "belonging to the realm of the flesh insofar as it is weak, sinful, and transitory, and in these respects is the opp[osite] of the spirit"; for the contrast of flesh and spirit, see 3:18 and 4:6.

For our author, however, an important point concerning these cravings is their association with the corrupt and corrupting behavior of the nonbelieving Gentiles and with a former way of life, from which the baptized believers were to have separated themselves when they became the holy children of God subject to his will (1:14–18; 4:1–3). Thus, in context, the phrase *sarkikai epithymiai* implies cravings that are both *corrupting* and *deadly*. These cravings are morally corrupt in themselves but also have a socially corrupting influence upon others. For this reason it is essential to avoid them and to have done with them. Their "deadly" aspect derives not only from this sense of corruption but also from the manner in which they attack life, as the remainder of this verse makes clear.

that wage war against life (haitines strateuontai kata tēs psychēs). A term from military life, *strateuontai* ("wage war") figuratively depicts the devastating internal effect of Gentile-like desires upon believers. A related military metaphor ("arm yourselves") is similarly employed in 4:1, within a context already shown to be related to this verse. These constitute two of the four military metaphors used in 1 Peter (Puig Tarrech 1980, 360–63, referring also to "guarded" [*phrouroumenous*, 1:5] and "crown" [5:4]). The verb *strateuomai*, used literally, means "serve as a soldier," "do battle," "wage war" (Luke 3:14; 1 Cor 9:7; 2 Tim 2:4 [explaining the metaphor of Timothy as a "good soldier of Christ Jesus," 2:3]). Plato (*Phaed.* 66C; cf. 86C) had already linked actual war with craving (evil desire), noting that *epithymia* is the sole cause of wars and revolutions. James, employing the verb *strateuomai* metaphorically, traces battles and wars within the Christian community to "passions that are at war (*strateuomenōn*) in your members" (4:1; cf. Lucian, *Vit. Auct.* 8). Paul also uses *strateuomai* metaphorically to describe the war he wages with arguments against obstacles to the knowledge of God and obedience to Christ (2 Cor 10:3–6), and in 2 Tim 2:3 Timothy is depicted as a "good soldier (*kalos stratiōtēs*) of Christ Jesus." On military metaphors in Paul and the Pastorals, see Pfitzner 1967, 157–86; Krentz 1993.

Greek and Roman philosophers often employed military metaphors to depict the struggle of the moral life. Hierocles, a second-century CE Stoic, comments:

> On the whole, we must conclude that our lives appear to be a long sort of war which lasts many years, partly because of the nature of things themselves which possess a certain resistant quality, and partly because of the sudden and unexpected incursions of fortune, but especially because of vice itself, which does not abstain from any violence or from guile and evil stratagems (*Duties* 4.27.30a, quoted in Malherbe 1986:95; cf. also Soph., *Electra* 996; *Anthologia Palatina* 5.92).

In the NT, the battle in which believers are engaged can also be viewed as one of cosmic scale (cf. Rom 13:11–14; Eph 6:10–20), but here in 1 Peter it is the corrupting and deadly effect of insatiable cravings on one's personal life that is in view. This Petrine verse, along with Gal 5:17, may have inspired the later exhortation of Polycarp (*Phil* 5:3): "for it is good to be cut off (*anakoptesthai*) from the desires in this world, for every desire wages war against the spirit" (*pasa epithymia kata tou pneumatos strateuetai*). One notable difference, however, is that for our author the attack is directed not against the spirit but against "life."

against life (kata tēs psychēs). The term *psychē*, used elsewhere in 1 Peter in the plural, denotes human beings or personal selves as "lives" or "living beings" who are under God's control and care and destined for salvation (1:9, 22; 2:25; 3:20; 4:19; see NOTE on 1:9). The singular noun, unaccompanied by any personal pronoun such as "your," lends the entire expression the form of a general principle applying to the lives of all persons collectively. By stating that it is *life* that is under attack from compulsive cravings, the author underscores not only the corrupting but also the deadly effect of this vice. In 1 Peter, indulgence in *epithymiai* characterizes a previous and deadened form of existence from which believers have been liberated through their divine rebirth to new life (1:3; cf. 1:22–23; 2:1–2, 5). A return to or compromise with this now alien existence would mean a forfeit of the precious hope of salvation. From a social point of view, this would also entail an undermining of the integrity and cohesion of the community and any positive effect it might have on outsiders (v 12). Thus deadly cravings, which so typically drive the lives of those alienated from God, must be avoided at all costs (cf. also 4:2–3); their effect is personally destructive and socially corruptive.

12. The foregoing negative admonition is now balanced by a positive injunction that concerns the winsome effect Christian conduct can have on even hostile outsiders. This balanced combination of negative and positive injunctions is a compositional feature typical of 1 Peter.[79]

12a. *maintain honorable conduct among the Gentiles (tēn anastrophēn hymōn en tois ethnesin echontes kalēn)*. In this hortatory context, the participle *echontes* ("maintain") has imperatival force (as in 3:16 and 4:8), even though it is not one of the typical parenetic imperatival participles employed elsewhere in 1 Peter (2:18; 3:1, 7, 9; 4:8, 10; see the NOTE on 2:18). With the sense of "maintain" (as in 3:16 and 4:8), it presents the positive counterpart to the preceding verb of the same root *apechesthai* ("avoid"), literally, "hold on to" in contrast to "hold off from."

honorable conduct (tēn anastrophēn . . . kalēn). The believers have already been reminded of their ransom from "the futile conduct (*anastrophē*) inherited from your ancestors" (1:18a) and advised of the necessity of holy (1:15b)

---

[79] See 1:14/15; 2:1/2; 3:3/4, 9ab/c, 11, 14/15; 4:2b/c, 12/13, 15/16; 5:2c/d, 2e/f, 3a/b; cf. also further instances of the negative/positive sequence in 1:8, 10–11/12, 18/19, 23, 24/25; 2:4c/d, 10a/b, c/d, 16b/c, 18, 20, 23a, b, 25a/b; 3:9ab/c, 13, 16, 18d/e, 21b/c; 4:6b/c, 16b/c; 5:5c.

and reverent conduct "throughout the time of your residence as aliens" (1:17b). This thought is now reiterated and introduces a repeated stress on honorable conduct, which continues throughout the remainder of the letter (*kala erga*, 2:12c; *anastrophē* [*kalē*], 3:1, 2, 16; *agathopoios*, 2:14; *agathos*, 3:10, 11; *agathopoieō*, 2:15, 20; 3:6, 17; *agathopoiia*, 4:19; *dikaios*, 3:12, 18; 4:18; *dikaiosynē*, 2:24; 3:14). The adjective *kalos*, modifying both *anastrophe* ("conduct") and (*erga*, v 12c) "deeds," frequently served as a synonym for *agathos* ("good"). The concept of the *kalos kai agathos* played an important role in Greek social life. In contrast to the *dēmos*, or general population, the *kaloi kai agathoi* were the leading and most honored citizens (Thucydides 8.48.6), the aristocratic political leadership (Aristoph., *Eq*. 227; cf. Xen., *Hist. Graec*. 2.13.15; *Cyr*. 4.3.23). However, this concept could also be held up as an ideal for all (Xen., *Oec*. 6.12–17). In the LXX and NT, the expression *to kalon* likewise designates behavior that is honorable in the sight of God (and humans; cf. Deut 6:18; 12:28; Amos 5:14; 2 Cor 13:8; Jas 4:17; cf. Prov 3:4; Isa 1:17). The term *kalos* has an aesthetic as well as a moral connotation. It denotes conduct that is both morally just and aesthetically attractive, thus behavior that is in all senses worthy of honor. This double aspect of the term is obviously important to our author, who notes that honorable behavior and deeds will be "observed" (*epopteuontes*, v 12c) and thereby confirmed from experience as good and honorable. Thus, the author is encouraging the kind of behavior that can prompt the reversal of opinion and action described in the remainder of this verse. On *anastrophē* and the *agathopoiia* family of terms as the ethical aspect of the sacrifices motivated by the Spirit (2:5c), see Elliott 1966b, 179–83.

among the Gentiles (en tois ethnesin). The Greek *ethnē*, which can denote "peoples" or "states," here and in 4:3 is used as a collective term for all nonbelieving "outsiders" as differentiated from the Christian believers (as in 1 Cor 5:1; 12:2; 1 Thess 4:5; 3 John 7; Rev [passim]; cf. Matt 6:7, 32; 24:9; 28:19; and Schmidt 1964, 371). This employment of the term to designate "others," "outsiders" is similar to the use of *barbaroi* ("barbarians") by the Greeks to classify all non-Greeks or *gentiles* by the Romans for all non-Romans. But it is appropriated especially from Israelite usage where "Gentiles" (*ethnē* for Heb. *gōyim* in contrast to *ʿam/laos*) is not merely a neutral term for "peoples" but, especially from the postexilic period onward, designates all non-Israelites, often as enemies (Isa 24–27; Ezek 38–39; Zech 9–14; Dan 3:7, 37; 7:14; 8:22; 9:26; Theodotianic text of Dan 3:4, 37; cf. Hamlin 1962). Christians, as a messianic sect of the house of Israel, appropriated not only the honorary epithets of Israel but also its discriminating terminology. In most of its NT occurrences, the term *ta ethnē* (or *hoi ethnikoi*) continues to denote non-Israelites in contrast to Israelites (e.g., Matt 4:15; 20:19/Mark 10:33; Rom 2:14; Gal 2:2, 15; 3:8; 1 Cor 12:2; Eph 2:11; 1 Thess 4:5).

However, in some cases, as here in 1 Peter, when *ta ethnē/hoi ethnikoi* is a foil to followers of Jesus, it becomes a designation for all non-Christians who "disobey" (2:7; 3:1), who have rejected Jesus as Messiah and malign his followers, including pagans and mainstream Israel alike.[80] Inasmuch as Israelite elites had allied with pagans against Jesus and his followers (Mark 10:33 par.; Acts 4:27; 12:1–5; 14:2; 17:5–9; 18:12–17; 2 Cor 11:26), it was only a matter of time before the sectarians included the Israelite parent body as well in the generic term for "outsiders"; see also the NOTE on 4:3. This is an example of ingroup-outgroup labeling and demarcation so typical of ancient Mediterranean cultures. As followers of Christ called nonbelieving outsiders "Gentiles," so these outsiders labeled members of the messianic sect with the contemptuous label "Christians," "Christ lackeys"; see the NOTE on 4:16.

12b. *so that when (hina en hōi)*. The aim and purpose (*hina*) of the preceding injunction is now indicated. The phrase *en hōi* (lit., "in which") lacks a specific antecedent and functions as a circumstantial or temporal conjunction (as in 1:6; 3:16, 19; 4:4). Here it has the sense of "in the circumstance when," "in a case where," as it does also in 3:16, a closely related passage; so also Fink 1967; Michaels 1988, 117.

they slander you (katalalousin hymōn). The indicative of the verb *katalaleō* is also used in 3:16 and is therefore preferable to the subjunctive variant *katalalōsin* (L P several cursives and vg^{mss}), which makes the action more hypothetical. This verb ("speak evil of," "slander," "malign") is one of several employed in the letter to depict the hostile *verbal abuse* directed against the believers by their neighbors; see also *loidoreō* ("insult"), 2:23; *loidoria* ("insult"), 3:9 (2×); *antiloidoreō* ("insult in return"), 2:23; *blasphēmeō* ("malign"), 4:4; *epēreazō* ("disparage"), 3:16; *oneidizō* ("reproach"), 4:14. Such slander on the part of believers has already been proscribed (2:1). All of these related terms illustrate the kind of oppression to which the nonbelievers subjected the believers: verbal abuse, disparagement, denigration, maligning, insult, contemptuous reproach, public defamation of character and public shaming on the suspicion of their "doing what is wrong." This shaming behavior is in stark contrast to the honor that believers have been accorded by God (2:7a, 9–10 and 1:3–2:10 in general). On the conventions of slander employed throughout the ancient world to demean and discredit those who were different and suspected of deviating from customary norms, see Johnson 1989.

as those who do what is wrong (hōs kakopoiōn). Like strangers everywhere, the Christian believers were suspected of "being up to no good." The substantive *kakopoiōn* ("those who do what is wrong") has the same genitive case as its antecedent *hymōn* ("you"), the object of *katalalousin* (which takes an objective genitive). An adjective used as a substantive, *kakopoios* ("one who does what is wrong, mischievous, harmful or wicked") occurs only in 1 Peter (2:12, 14; 4:15) in the NT, and in the LXX, only twice (Prov 12:4; 24:19). Its related verb, *kakopoieō* ("do what is wrong"), appears in 3:17, where "doing what is right" and

---

[80] See Eph 4:17; 3 John 7; and probably Matt 5:47; 6:7; Matt 6:32/Luke 12:30; Matt 20:25/Mark 10:42/Luke 22:25; Matt 24:9/Mark 13:13/Luke 21:17; 1 Cor 5:1; 12:2; cf. Walter 1990, 383.

"doing what is wrong" are contrasted; compare also Mark 3:4/Luke 6:9 and 3 John 11. As a generic term for "wrongdoer," *kakopoios* can refer to an individual guilty of legally defined crimes (2:14) or to one insensitive to or deviating from custom and conventional standards of morality (Prov 12:4; 24:19). In 4:15 it appears in a list of four vices in which the addressees are specifically warned to have no part: "Let none of you suffer as a murderer or a thief or a wrongdoer or as a meddler in the affairs of others." Whereas the first two terms concern crimes, the latter two involve matters of social deviancy; see the NOTE on 4:15. The content and immediate context of 2:12 suggest that here too *kakopoios* implies some form of social deviancy of which the believers are accused by nonbelievers who "slander" them (rather than bringing formal criminal charges against them).

These Christians, as strangers and aliens with alien customs, beliefs, and ties to a Palestinian Israelite executed by the Romans, and as persons deviating from the ways of their neighbors and their ancestral customs (*mos maiorum*, cf. 1:18), were prime candidates for such a pejorative label as "wrongdoer." As a smear word it also appears in its Latin form (*maleficus*) in Suetonius's description of the Christians of Rome as "a class of persons given to a novel and mischievous superstition" (*superstitionis novae ac maleficae;* Suetonius, *Nero* 16.2); see also Tertullian, *Apol.* 1.11–12 and ch. 7 for malicious rumor as the source of unfounded accusations: infanticide, cannibalism, incest, impure wives, atheism, and so on.[81]

12c. *from observing [your] honorable deeds (ek tōn kalōn ergōn epopteuontes).* This action constitutes an actual experience of the Gentiles that contrasts with their preceding claim (that the believers do what is wrong) and discredits it. At the same time it constitutes the cause for the reversal of behavior described in v 12d. The implied sequence of acts is: slander / observance of good deeds / glorification of God. The translation seeks to render the sense of the somewhat awkward phrase *ek tōn kalōn ergōn epopteuontes*, literally, "from (your) honorable deeds, observing (them)." The present participle "observing" (*epopteuontes*) has iterative force: "continuing to observe," "viewing over a period of time." The variant aorist participle, *epopteusantes* ("having observed," A P Ψ 𝔐 Cl) probably was substituted to clarify the logical priority of observance to the main verb, *glorify* (v 12d). This rare verb, *epopteuō* (only here and 3:2 in the NT; cf. *epoptai*, "eye-witnesses," 2 Pet 1:16), underlines the author's interest in the visual character and impact of honorable deeds. In a culture where such great weight is laid upon vision as the ultimate arbiter of truth, this stress upon the *visibility* of Christian behavior and its empirical apprehension makes eminent sense. Virtuous deeds silence and refute slanderous words (cf. 2:15). In 3:1–2 the same word is used to express a virtually identical thought: honorable behavior, when observed, will win over nonbelievers. Beare (1970, 134)

[81] On popular reactions against Christianity, see Colwell 1939; Benko 1980; Nestle 1990; on their relevance for 1 Peter, see Elliott 1981/1990, 78–84; Feldmeier 1990, 105–32.

proposes the translation "by your excellent deeds attain spiritual insight" and suggests that it is this spiritual insight on the part of the Gentiles that leads to their glorification of God. But this interpretation presumes a reliance of 1 Peter upon the "technical language of the mysteries" (1970, 138; cf. 37–38), an earlier scholarly presumption that has not been demonstrated.

[your] honorable deeds (kalōn ergōn) is synonymous with "honorable conduct" (*anastrophēn kalēn*, v 12a) and likewise forms a contrast to the claim of the Gentiles that the believers were involved in wrongdoing. The pronoun *your*, while originally absent, is implied and was added secondarily by several manuscripts (614 630 945 syr cop) to make this contrast clear. The adjective *kalos* in both instances describes behavior that is good, just, and *honorable* in the sight of both God (cf. 1:17) and society. For Greeks and Romans, honorable deeds involved doing one's duty toward parents, friends, and the state and being helpful to one's fellows (Seneca, *Ben.* 1.6.1; cf. 1.2.4). For Israel, they consisted of works of charity (*gemilūt ḥasidīm*) such as visitation of the sick, hospitality toward strangers, comfort of the mourning, care for the dead, and especially aid to the poor and afflicted (see Tob 1:3–2:8 and Billerbeck 1928, 4:536–58).[82] Stress upon *kala erga* is also found frequently in the Pastorals (1 Tim 5:10, 25; 6:18; Titus 2:7, 14; 3:8, 14) with a similar eye toward their conspicuousness and defensive effect: "Honorable deeds are conspicuous" (1 Tim 5:25); "show yourself in all respects a model of honorable deeds . . . so that an opponent may not put us to shame, having nothing evil to say of us" (Titus 2:7). In 1 Peter, the phrase *kala erga* as well as the general thought of v 12 may well have been inspired by the saying of Jesus recorded in Matt 5:16: "Let your light so shine before people, that they may see your honorable deeds and glorify your father who is in heaven." Such sensitivity concerning the positive impact of behavior on outsiders is typical of the early Christian movement.[83] What these honorable deeds entail for the readers of 1 Peter will be specified in the following series of exhortations: respect for order and authority ("subordination"), conduct recognized as honorable (*agathopoiia*) by both God and society, and behavior illustrative of the believers' holy calling (2:21; 3:9; see van Unnik 1954–55).

The alliterative string of terms beginning with the Greek letters *kappa alpha* (*kalēn . . . katalalousin . . . kakopoiōn . . . kalōn*) is one of a number of indications of the author's rhetorical competence; for other alliterations, see 1:4, 6, 19; 2:15, 16, 18–20, 21; 4:4.

12d. *may glorify God (doxasōsin ton theon).* The positive impact of honorable behavior and deeds is not only the refutation of slander as baseless but the moving of erstwhile detractors to glorify God. This final member of v 12 completes a minor chiasm in which the Gentiles' slandering (A = v 12bα) is

---

[82] On honorable deeds in general, see Bolkestein 1939; Hands 1968; van Unnik 1980e.

[83] See also Matt 5:13, 14; Rom 14:16; 1 Cor 10:32–33; Phil 2:15; Col 4:5–6; 1 Thess 4:11–12; 1 Tim 3:7; 6:1; Titus 2:5, 8; *1 Clem.* 47:6–7; Ign. *Eph.* 10:1–3; Ign. *Trall.* 8:2; Pol. *Phil* 10:2–3; 12:3; *2 Clem.* 13:4; cf. van Unnik 1954–1955, 1964.

balanced by their glorifying God (A′ = v 12d), and the alleged wrongdoing of the believers (B = v 12bβ) is balanced by the observation of their honorable deeds (B′ = v 12c).

The God implied here is the God of the Christians, a fact that 𝔓⁷² makes explicit by adding "your" (God). This pair of verses ends with a thought that links them to their preceding context and that also permeates the letter as a whole—the theme of glory and glorification of God.

"Glory" (*doxa*), "glorify" (*doxazō*), and their synonyms, as the previous COMMENT on 1 Pet 2:4–10 has indicated, belong to an accentuated theme of this letter. Relative to its length, 1 Peter contains more references to glory and glorification than any other writing of the NT. These terms figure prominently as well in the author's honor and shame culture. Glory, praise, and declarations of honor are what indebted clients owe their powerful and generous patrons. In having this glory and honor of their patrons and benefactors acknowledged by all, clients themselves bathe in and share the honor of their benefactors. According to the Petrine author, the glory that belongs to God (4:11, 13; 5:10, 11) and Jesus Christ (1:11, 21; 4:13; 5:1) is enjoyed by the believers as well (1:7; 4:13, 14; 5:4, 10). God's glorious honoring of Jesus Christ and the believers (2:4–10) elicits their praise of his wondrous deeds (2:9; 4:16; cf. 1:3) and their doxologies (4:11; 5:11).

Christians, moreover, not only celebrate God's honor and glory themselves, they are also to live so that others might join them in declaring God's glory. The Israelite roots of this thought are evident in *T. Naph.* 8:4: "If you work that which is good (*to kalon*), my children, both humans and angels will bless you; and God will be glorified among the Gentiles through you, and the devil shall flee from you" (cf. also 1 *En.* 63; *T. Jud.* 25:5; 1QS IV 26, IX 23, X 17–21; *Let. Aris.* 234; Ign. *Eph.* 10:1–3). On a similar optimistic note, our author envisions that the believers' resolute honorable conduct, even in the face of calumny, can have a positive effect. As believers have been honored by God, so their conduct is to be honorable with the prospect that such excellent behavior will even move their slanderers to cease their unfounded accusations and join the believers in the glorification of God; for Gentiles (i.e., non-Israelites) glorifying God, see also Rom 15:9. The thought is repeated in 3:1–2 with respect to the winsome effect that Christian wives in particular can have on their non-believing husbands.

on the day of visitation (en hēmerai episkopēs). The expression occurs only here in the NT (cf. *ton kairon tēs episkopēs sou*, Luke 19:44) but recalls Isa 10:3 (*en tēi hēmerai tēs episkopēs*).[84] The "day of the Lord" as a day of God's "visitation" in judgment was a stock concept of Israelite eschatology (Zeph 1:7, 14–15; 2:2–3; Zech 14:1–20; LXX Mal 3:22[MT 4:1]). The notion of divine visitation is diversified. On the one hand, God visits his people to liberate them from

[84] Cf. also *en kairōi episkopēs* (Jer 6:15; 10:15; Wis 3:7), *en hōra episkopēs* (Sir 18:20), and *en episkopēi psychōn* (Wis 3:13).

Egyptian bondage (Gen 50:21–25; Exod 3:16; 4:31; 13:19) or from Babylonian Exile (Jer 27:22; 29:10; 32:5; cf. Zeph 2:7; Zech 10:3; 1 Esd 6:5) or to save (and destroy) at the end of time.[85] On the other hand, divine visitation can also denote a coming in judgment[86] or a visitation for probation and testing (Ps 17[18]:3; Job 7:18; 31:14; Wis 3:7, 13; Sir 2:14; 18:20; 3 Macc 5:42; Luke 19:44?). The notion of "the day of the Lord" is similarly ambiguous, designating either a day of judgment or a day of deliverance or both, often with reference to the end of time (Amos 5:18–20; Isa 2:12–21; Zech 12–14; Mal 4:1–6 [LXX 3:19–24]; Hiers 1992, 79–83).

The meaning of "day of visitation" in 1 Peter is ambiguous as well, and a decision between two main alternatives is difficult. Unfortunately, the use of the related term *episkopos* ("overseer") of God in 2:25 (and of the verb *episkopeō* of presbyters in 5:2) and the uncertain variant reading in 5:6b (*en kairōi episkopēs*) shed little light here, and the larger context of the letter must be taken into consideration. On the one hand, this phrase may allude to the final eschatological day of judgment (so Goppelt 1993, 160; Michaels 1988, 119–20), since reference is made elsewhere in the letter to this event (1:5, 7, 13; 4:7, 13, 17; 5:1) when the living and the dead are judged (4:5; cf. 1:17). However, the notion expressed in 4:17–18 that at the final judgment there are only the family of God and nonbelievers who remain obdurate sinners rules out any possibility of some of the latter glorifying God at *that* time (cf. also 2:8). Therefore, it is more likely that this phrase refers to God's visitation of individual nonbelievers *as an occasion of testing* when they are confronted with the winsome behavior of the believers and are thereby motivated to join the Christians in their glorification of God (so Selwyn 1947, 171). This alternative is consistent with the notion that the present time is one of testing (1:6–7; 4:12) and is especially supported by the similar thought of 3:1–2, which envisions that the holy behavior of Christian wives can "win" their unbelieving husbands to the Christian faith. Thus, while the author assures the addressees elsewhere of a final condemnation of recalcitrant sinners, here, as in 3:1–2, he impresses upon them the hopeful prospect that honorable behavior on their part will not only demonstrate their innocence but can even prompt the conversion of those who malign them.

GENERAL COMMENT

In the first major section of his letter (1:3–2:10), our author has assured the addressees, as "elect strangers in the Diaspora," of their divinely conferred honor and dignity, their holy union with God and Jesus Christ, and their incorporation through God's mercy into the family of God. Verses 11–12 form a carefully

---

[85] See *T. Levi* 4:4; *T. Jud.* 23:5; *T. Ash.* 7:3; Luke 19:44; cf. 1QS III 14, 18; IV 6, 11, 19, 26; 1QH[a] I 17; XIII 10; CD VII 21; VIII 2–3; XIX 6–12.

[86] See Exod 32:34; Job 6:14; 7:18; Ps 58:6[59:5]; Isa 10:3; Jer 6:15; 8:12; 10:5; Sir 16:18; Luke 19:44?

crafted transition that recalls what was previously stated while simultaneously providing an introduction to the exhortation that follows. Sharing in the history of Israel not only as the elect and holy people of God but also as strangers and resident aliens in society, the addressees are now given two principles that are to inform their interaction with nonbelievers. These two verses succinctly summarize the tenor of the exhortation and admonition that follow in the remainder of the letter.

The "deadly cravings" that they are to avoid concisely circumscribe an entire way of life opposed to the will of God (as in 4:1–3). Such deadly cravings are incompatible with their new life as the elect and holy people of God and their moral transformation as described in 1:3–2:10. This thought bears a noteworthy resemblance to a passage of Philo (*Praem.* 123–24), where a similar point is made with similar terminology. Philo, in commenting on the blessings conferred on a virtuous man, finds an analogy in Israel's liberation from Egypt. The mind of a virtuous man, he remarks, "is a palace and house of God" (*basileion kai oikos theou*; cf. 1 Pet 2:5, 9), which, like the chosen and holy people of God (cf. 1 Pet 2:, 9), once "lay under the yoke of many pleasures and many desires (*epithymiai*) and the innumerable distresses which its vices and desires (*epithymiai*) entail" but which was "redeemed into freedom by God who broke asunder the miseries of its slavery." The similarity of this line of thought and language with 1 Peter (divine liberation and election entail freedom from desire) is striking, though the differences (primarily Philo's allegorical identification of the virtuous one with the chosen people) preclude any likelihood of direct influence. The chief point common to both authors is that divine redemption and election entail liberation from enslaving cravings. From the Petrine author's perspective, such cravings are typical of Gentile behavior and are corruptive as well as deadly. They are to be avoided because they typify a way of life that is unholy, futile, and alienated from God. As is later made clear (4:1–6; cf. also 1:14–16), avoidance of such vices also entails social detachment from people whose life is typified by such immorality. At the same time, believers are to behave honorably among the nonbelievers in the prospect that their honorable conduct will put the lie to Gentile accusations of Christian wrongdoing and even lead these slanderers to glorify God.

On the whole, the content and tenor of these verses are consonant with a broad Israelite and early Christian ethical tradition emphasizing the avoidance of immoral conduct often associated with the Gentiles and the maintenance of an honorable way of life[87] with sensitivity to the reputation of the community in the larger society.[88]

The tense situation in which the addressees of 1 Peter find themselves requires a carefully nuanced strategy. The estrangement and alienation of Chris-

[87] See Rom 13:11–13; Gal 5:16–26; Eph 4:17–5:20; Col 3: 5–17; 1 Thess 4:1–8; Rev 21:8; 22:11, 15; cf. 1 Cor 5:1.

[88] See Rom 14:16; 1 Cor 10:31–32; 14:40; 1 Thess 4:11–12; Col 4:5; 1 Tim 3:7; Titus 2:5, 8; and van Unnik 1964.

tians from their neighbors has prompted accusations of wrongdoing. Rather than attempting to mitigate that estrangement by "doing like the Gentiles," the author insists that they avoid Gentile-like vices and lead an irreproachable way of life consistent with their holy election.

This call to avoid vices typical of the Gentiles echoes 1:14–16 and 2:1 and is repeated in 4:1–4 (cf. also 4:15). The repetition indicates how urgent the matter is from the author's perspective. The behavior of the Christians must be consistent with their distinctive identity as the elect and holy family of God while at the same time providing no actual basis for reproach on the part of their neighbors. Hesitancy in making a clean break from their past ways and ancestral traditions (1:14–16, 18; cf. also 4:1–4) might mitigate any charges that the believers were nonconformist strangers and aliens "up to no good." Such a tactic, however, would deny their transformation and rebirth as the children of God. The author therefore urges that as strangers and aliens they eliminate any moral grounds for reproach by distancing themselves from deadly, Gentile-like cravings while simultaneously engaging in honorable behavior that can lead their slanderers to cease their calumny and join the Christians in their glorification of God. The specifics of this honorable behavior will then be explicated in the remainder of the letter.

The exhortation that vv 11–12 introduce is addressed to the readers who are specifically identified as "resident aliens and visiting strangers." These terms reiterate the designation of the readers at the outset of the letter (*parepidēmoi*, 1:1) and the identification of their situation in 1:17 (*paroikia*). As strangers and aliens who through baptism have become reborn children in the household of God, they are now strangers in a theological as well as a social sense. Their response to the call of God aligns them with Abraham, the *paroikos* par excellence, and the estrangement that he and his descendants experienced is now encountered by the spiritual children of Abraham and Sarah (3:6) as well. In Israel's history, social alienation and oppression had been the regular experience of God's chosen people, commencing with the first ancestors. From this history the Petrine author drew on models and memories of estrangement and community, dispersion and gathering, suffering and deliverance, societal rejection and divine acceptance, so that continuity with the past, along with faith in the present, might serve as an enlivening basis for hope in the future.

While aliens and strangers, the addressees are not urged to be isolationists who withdraw from society as did the community at Qumran. They are, rather, challenged to engage with society and present it a superior form of moral and religious life. This is the only practical strategy appropriate for such a sectarian movement that is intent on gaining new members through conversion while simultaneously preserving its distinctiveness. To accomplish this, it is necessary for the Christian community to embody a way of life that, despite slanderous accusations of wrongdoing, will move even detractors to join them in the glorification of God. This stress on honorable and attractive behavior as a missionizing means for recruitment is made here with respect to all of the believers and again in 3:2 in regard to Christian wives in particular.

The terms *paroikoi* and *parepidēmoi* identify the readers in respect to their social environment, whereas in 2:4–10 *oikos pneumatikos* and the names of the elect and holy community describe them in their relation to God and Jesus Christ. Thus *paroikoi* (and *paroikia*) and *oikos* are correlated not only linguistically (as terms from the same Greek root) but also socially and theologically. Having first been defined as God's reborn children and the household in which the divine Spirit resides, the addressees are now encouraged to live out their identity as God's people in a society where they are treated as strangers and aliens. This contrast of at-home-ness with God versus estrangement in society, replicated in the related contrast of election by God but maligned by humans, epitomizes the tension underlying the entire letter (Chevallier 1975; Elliott 1981/1990) and is paralleled by a similar tension between the human rejection and divine election of the believers' Lord (2:4, 7; 2:21–24; 3:18, 22). Rousseau (1986, 245) rightly sees this tension already captured by the "oxymoron" or "paradoxical" expression "elect visiting strangers" with which the letter begins (1:1) and which constitutes a "presignal" of the thrust of the entire communication (1986, 264–65, 272–73, 383).

At this point in the communication, as Danker (1980, 144) graphically puts it, "theology hits the streets." The author now makes clear how a community of people transformed by God's mercy conducts itself amid social structures of the old, former, untransformed society. Among even those who slander them, our author asserts, the believers are to lead honorable and holy lives consistent with God's will and the behavior of their Lord. In what follows, such honorable behavior is spelled out as an acknowledgment of all in authority, respect for social order, and commitment to the doing of good even in the face of unjust treatment (2:13–4:19). This strikingly positive view of the power of good conduct is remarkable in a document that portrays so graphically the intense social conflict between believers and outsiders. It illustrates both the practical dimension of Christian hope and the supreme confidence of its author in the word of Jesus that good and noble deeds can indeed win others to the essential task of all creatures, namely the glorification of God. In a fundamental sense, this thought of v 12 serves as an eloquent motto for Christian life as portrayed by 1 Peter: to live life to the greater glory of God (*ad maiorem Dei gloriam*).

DETAILED COMMENT 1: 1 PETER 2:11–12 AS A STRUCTURAL TRANSITION

Verses 11–12 contain numerous terms and concepts that occur in both the preceding and following sections of the letter:

agapētoi ("Beloved," 4:12): cf. terms for "love" (*agapaō*, *agapē*) in 1:8, 22; 2:17; 4:8 and "loving of brothers [and sisters]," 3:8

parakaleō ("exhort"): 5:1, 12

paroikoi kai parepidēmoi ("resident aliens and visiting strangers"): 1:1, 17

apechō ("avoid"): cf. "rid yourselves of" (*apothemenoi*, 2:1); "do not allow yourselves to be molded by the cravings of your former ignorance" (1:14b); "keep the tongue from [uttering] what is wrong" (3:10c); "turn away from wrongdoing" (3:11a); "cease from sinning" (4:2)
sarkikai epithymiai ("deadly cravings"): cf. *epithymiai*, 4:2, 3
strateuomai ("wage war"): cf. "arm yourselves" (*hoplisasthe*), 4:1
psychē ("life"): 1:9, 22; 2:25; 4:19
anastrophē ("conduct"): 1:15, 18; 3:1, 2, 16; *anastrephō*, 1:17
ethnē ("Gentiles"): 4:3
katalaleō ("slander," verb): 3:16; *katalalia* ("slander," noun), 2:1; cf. "insult" (*loidoreō*, 2:23; *loidoria*, 3:9); "disparage" (*epēreazō*, 3:16); "malign" (*blasphēmeō*, 4:4); "reproach" (*oneidizō*, 4:14)
kakopoios ("one who does what is wrong"): 2:14; 4:15; cf. "do what is wrong" (*kakopoieō*, 3:17); *kakon*, 3:9, 10, 11, 12; *kakia*, 2:1
kala erga ("honorable deeds"): cf. "do what is right" (*agathopoieō*), 2:15, 20; 3:6, 17; *agathopoios*, 2:14; *agathopoiia*, 4:19; "zealots for what is right (*tou agathou zēlōtai*), 3:13; "honorable household stewards" (*kaloi oikonomoi*), 4:10
epopteuō ("observe"): 3:2
doxazō ton theon ("glorify God"): 4:11, 16; 5:11; cf. 1:3: 2:9.

Structural as well as terminological similarities between 2:11–12 and subsequent verses are also evident in at least two cases:

(1) 2:11–12 and 4:10–11 (Chevallier 1971, 141)

1 Peter 2:11-12	1 Peter 4:10-11
paroikous	*oikonomoi*
kalēn . . . kalōn	*kaloi*
katalalousin	*lalei*
doxazōsin ton theon	*doxazētai ho theos*

(2) 2:12 and 3:16 (Michaels 1988, 115)

1 Peter 2:12	1 Peter 3:16
tēn anastrophēn kalēn	
tēn anastrophēn echontes	*syneidēsin echontes*
kalēn	*agathēn*
hina en hōi	*hina en hōi*
katalalousin	*katalaleisthe*
	tēn agathēn . . . anastrophēn

While vv 11–12 are clearly linked terminologically, thematically, and compositionally with what precedes and follows and thus are "at once resumptive and prefatory" (Selwyn 1947, 169), they are also distinguished from foregoing and following contexts. The direct address ("Beloved"), the voice of the author in the 1st-person sing. ("I exhort") and the shift from an indicative to an imperative mood set these verses off from the foregoing (1:3–2:10). Similarly, the generalizing nature of their exhortation is different from the specific areas of conduct addressed in 2:13–3:6 under the theme of "subordination," whose recurrent term *hypotassō* is not employed in vv 11–12. Given the distinctive foci of all the units from 2:13 to 5:11, it is also unlikely, contrary to various proposals, (1) that 2:11–12 forms a large literary inclusion with either 4:11 (2:11–4:11) or 5:10–11 (2:11–5:11) (marked by stress on glorification) or (2) that 2:11–4:19 forms a major section set off from 5:1–11 by the repeated use of *parakaleō* and direct address in 5:1 (as in 2:11) or (3) that 2:11–3:12 forms a section concluded with a scriptural citation, since biblical citations conclude both units and subunits (1:16, 24; 2:3; 2:17; 2:25; 4:18; 5:5c–6[7]). The claim of Cervantes Gabarrón (1991, 53–56) that 2:11–3:7 forms a subsection distinct from 3:8–22, on the other hand, ignores the function of 3:8–12 as a conclusion to 2:13–3:7.

Accordingly, vv 11–12 are best viewed as constituting a major structural transition related to and yet distinguished from both preceding and following contexts. They articulate a general principle and a chief goal of Christian behavior that is based upon the foregoing affirmation of Christian communal identity and that is concretized in the exhortation that follows throughout the remainder of the letter. This pair of verses, in sum, functions as a major structural hinge of the entire composition.

DETAILED COMMENT 2: "RESIDENT ALIENS AND VISITING STRANGERS"

The meaning of the phrase "resident aliens and visiting strangers" (2:11) and its related terminology (*paroikia*, 1:17; *parepidēmoi*, 1:1) is best clarified through consideration of the meaning and use of these terms in the biblical and nonbiblical writings and their particular employment in 1 Peter. This comment also supplements the NOTES provided on *parepidēmoi* at 1:1 and *paroikia* at 1:17.

Both the Hebrew and Greek texts of the OT employ specific terms for distinguishing the stranger or alien or "outsider" from the native or "insider." In the LXX, the term *parepidēmos* occurs twice (Gen 23:4; Ps 38[39]:13), in each case translating the Hebrew word *tôšāb* ("by-dweller," lacking the status and privileges of natives). The term *paroikos* occurs far more frequently (33×), often also rendering *tôšā*b (10×), but also translating other terms, including gôy (1×), *šākēn* (1×), *gûr* (1×), and most frequently *gēr* (11×, "resident alien," as distinguished from the foreigner in general [*nokrî*, *zār*]). In both Hebrew and Greek, the specific denotations and connotations of these terms fluctuated from one period of history to another. But in general it can be said that, though *parepidēmos* and *paroikos* both translated *tôšāb*, the more generic term for "by-dweller" (transient or permanent), *paroikos*, was the preferred term for rendering *gēr*, since both had the specific meaning of "resident alien." When these terms were applied to Israel itself, the focus was primarily on Israel and its leading figures as "resident aliens" (*gērīm*, *paroikoi*) in foreign territories and the consequently restricted economic and social privileges as well as precarious social and political status that such residence as aliens entailed.[89]

Throughout the biblical record of the history of the children of Abraham, recurrent reference is made to the actual situation of Israel as "resident aliens" (*paroikoi*, *paroikeō*) in foreign territories (cf. Elliott 1981/1990, 27–33). These references include: Abraham, the prototypical resident alien and his seed in the land of Egypt (Gen 12:10; 15:13; Deut 26:5), among the Hittites (Gen 23:4), or in Canaan (Gen 17:8; Ps 104[105]:12); Lot in Sodom (Gen 19:9); a Levite from Bethlehem-Judah in Ephraim (Judg 17:7–9); Elimelech and his family in Moab (Ruth 1:1); Moses and his family in Midian (Exod 2:22); the patriarchs residing in Mesopotamia (Jdt 5:7, 8) or Egypt (Jdt 5:10; Wis 19:10); the Judeans in Babylonian captivity (1 Esd 5:7; Ezra 8:35) or in Egypt during the reign of Ptolemy Philopater (3 Macc 6:36; 7:19); or generally Israelites as resident aliens in a land unnamed (1 Chr 29:15; Ps 38[39]:12; 118[119]:19; cf. 119[120]:5–7). The memory of Abraham and Sarah and their descendants as resident aliens is enshrined in one of Israel's earliest "creeds": "A wandering Aramaean (Jacob) was my father (MT; cf. LXX: "my father left Syria"), and went down into Egypt and lived there as a resident alien (*parōikēsen*), few in number . . . and the Egyptians treated us harshly and afflicted us . . ." (Deut 26:5–6). Israel's own experience as resident aliens in Egypt, moreover, is cited as a reason for just treatment of the aliens residing in its midst (Lev 25:35–40; Deut 23:8).

This use of *paroikos* and paronyms (*paroikia*, *paroikeō*, etc.) in the LXX to identify the resident alien reflected general Greek usage (cf. Elliott 1981/1990, 24–26). Greek inscriptions in particular, which list the various constituencies of cities, mention resident aliens (*paroikoi*) as a stratum of the population ranked below full citizens (*politai*) and above complete strangers (*xenoi*), freed persons, and slaves (Schaefer 1949). In Asia Minor in the Hellenistic period, the term *paroikoi* appears to have been used as an equivalent for the related term *metoikoi*, which had designated the "resident aliens" of Athens. Such *metoikoi* (see Hommel 1932 on the term) and, by association *paroikoi*, were distinguished from "inhabitants" in general (*katoikoi*; on this term, see Oertel 1921; cf. Gauthier 1988 and Levy 1988). These *paroikoi* or *metoikoi* constituted a registered stratum of the population that was distinguished legally and socially from "citizens" (*politai*) and resident "Romans," who were higher on the

[89] On *parepidēmos*, *paroikos*, and related terms in biblical and nonbiblical usage, see Hort 1898, 154–56; Oertel 1921; Labriolle 1928; Hommel 1932; K. L. Schmidt 1945; Schaefer 1949; de Jonge 1956–1957; Horner 1960; Muntingh 1962; Grundmann 1964, 54–65; Schmidt and Meyer 1967, 841–53; Kuhn 1968; Martin-Achard 1971, 409–12; Elliott 1981/1990, 21–58; Puig Tarrech 1980, 101–16; Plümmacher 1987, 39–44; Block 1988; Lamau 1988, 81–87; Chin 1991; Cardellini 1992; Feldmeier 1992. On the concept, condition, and legal standing of the stranger in antiquity, see Clerc 1898; Francotte 1903; Kübler 1937; Berger 1953, 626–27 (*peregrinus*); Adinolfi 1967; Fascher 1971; Gaudemet and Fascher 1972; Levy 1988; Gauthier 1988. On Israel as a "pariah" (from *paroikos*) people, Weber 1952, 356–424.

social ladder, and from total strangers (*xenoi*), freedmen, and slaves, who ranked at the bottom end of the social scale; see the texts listed in Schaefer (1949, 1695–1707) and a fragmentary stele (1st century BCE–1st century CE) erected in the Asia Minor city of Kyme (Llewelyn and Kearsley, eds. 1992–1994, 7:233–41; esp. p. 234, line 17). In contrast to total strangers (*xenoi*) and slaves who possessed no legal rights whatsoever, *paroikoi*, because of their extended residence in a locality, were afforded some degree of protection and privilege to secure their loyalty, though this status could be lost if they proved uncooperative with local undertakings, particularly the military defense of the city. Thus, this *paroikos* status was an uncertain one and constantly vulnerable to political manipulation. Nor were such *paroikoi* ever free of the suspicion, discrimination, and disdain that they, as strangers, constantly experienced from the citizens and natives of the locality. Included among such *paroikoi* were merchants, traders, traveling artisans and teachers whose occupations and interests took them from one locality to another, or even larger populations that were deported and settled elsewhere (as in the case of the Israelites forcibly removed to Babylon or the 2,000 Israelite families deported by Antiochus III from Mesopotamia and Babylonia to Phrygia in Asia Minor ca. 201 BCE Josephus, *Ant.* 12.147).

Among the ranks of the *paroikoi* in Asia Minor, Rostovtzeff has noted (1957, 1:255–57; 2:654–55), there were also native tenant farmers on lands attached or attributed to expanding cities, farmers who were never given the full rights of municipal citizenship. "How to deal with these large numbers of peasants was a serious question for the city aristocracy as was the problem of the city proletariat."[90]

The tenuousness of *paroikos* status is graphically illustrated by the bitter struggle that engulfed Judeans dwelling in Alexandria as resident aliens during the reign of Gaius (ca. 39/40 CE). As Philo reports (*Flacc.* 1–96; *Legat.* 119–77), the Judean population of the city, one million strong (*Flacc.* 43), because of resentment on the part of native aristocrats and Greeks, had been threatened with the loss of their legal status as resident aliens and demotion to the legal position of "complete aliens and foreigners" (*xenous kai epēlydas, Flacc.* 54). Subjected to a cruel pogrom under Flaccus, the Roman prefect of Alexandria and Egypt, they were forced to make a direct appeal to Gaius, the emperor, to protest their treatment and to hinder this threatened reduction of their status and privileges (*Legat.* 178–80; cf. Smallwood 1970, 20). The delegation to Gaius, however, received no justice but only disdain and a deaf ear (*Legat.* 349–73).

Another moving description of the socioeconomic plight and degrading experiences of the *paroikos* is provided by Sirach, writing for the benefit of Israelites residing as aliens in Egypt (ca. 132 BCE):

---

[90] On the village *paroikoi* of Asia Minor, see also S. Dickey 1928, 398–99; Broughton 1938, 628–48, esp. 638–39; Magie 1950, 1:639–40; 2:149–50, 225, 1036–37, 1503.

> The essentials for life are water and bread and clothing and a house (*oikos*) to cover one's nakedness. Better is the life of a beggar (*ptōchos*) under the shelter of his roof than sumptuous food in another man's house (*en allotriois*). Be content with little or much and you will not hear the reproach of your alien residence (*oneidismon paroikias*). It is a miserable life to go from house to house (*oikia*); and where you reside as an alien (*paroikēseis*) you may not open your mouth. You will play the host and provide drink without being thanked, and besides this you will hear bitter words: "Come here, alien (*paroike*), prepare the table, and if you have anything at hand, let me have it to eat." "Give place, alien (*paroike*), to an honored person; my brother has come to stay with me; I need my house." These things are hard to bear for a man who has feeling: scolding about lodging (*oikias*) and the reproach (*oneidismon*) of the moneylender. (Sir 29:21–29)

A rare metaphorical use of *paroikos* and its verb *paroikeō*, on the other hand, is found occasionally in Philo's writings (Feldmeier 1992, 60–72). In one instance he allegorically interprets the references to the alien residence of Abraham in Canaan (Gen 23:4), Jacob in Egypt (Gen 47:9), and Isaac in Gerar (Gen 26:2) as an indication that "the wise man only dwells as an alien (*paroikei*) in the body, which our senses know as a strange land, but dwells in (*katoikei*) and has for his fatherland the virtues known through the mind" (*Conf.* 79–81; cf. also *QG* 4.74). In this same context he observes that "all whom Moses calls wise are represented as resident aliens (*paroikountes*). For their souls are never colonists leaving heaven for a new home; their way is to visit earthly nature as men who travel abroad to see and learn" (*Conf.* 77). On another occasion, in commenting on Lev 25:23 ("but you are strangers and resident aliens [*prosēlytai kai paroikoi*] before me"), Philo explains: "for each of us has come into this world as into a foreign city, in which before our birth we had no part, and in this city one resides as an alien (*paroikei*) until he has exhausted his appointed span of life" (*Cher.* 119–21). This metaphorical usage is consistent with Philo's allegorical mode of interpretation and represents a psychological and dualistic interpretation of human existence in the world typical of the Greek Platonic tradition.

This is in contrast to the usage of the Septuagint, where these terms regularly refer to an actual condition of social estrangement (with the possible exception of Ps 118[119]:19 and its parallel, 2 Chr 29:15, where they allude perhaps to the transitoriness of human life; see Chin 1991). Occasionally the noun *parepidēmia* is used to portray the brevity of life (Pseudo-Plato, *Axiochus* 365b; Pseudo-Hipparchus, *Peri enthymias* [in Stobaeus 4.44.81]; cf. also Marcus Aurelius, *Med.* 2.17 [*xenou epidēmia*] and Feldmeier 1992, 23–38 regarding Greek and Roman concepts of the stranger as a metaphor for human existence). These Philonic texts illustrate the natural affinity of metaphorical usage, allegorical interpretation, and a philosophical framework of cosmic dualism. The fact that such a constellation is rarely, if ever, to be found in the LXX and NT suggests that we should be cautious about claiming that in 1 Peter these terms for strangerhood are metaphors consonant with a "widely held view" (against Feldmeier 1992 and Chin 1992).

Use of these terms in the NT is, on the whole, similar to that of the LXX. In Acts, Luke presents Stephen as recalling that alien residence in foreign territories was the historical course and destiny of God's people from the beginning (Acts 7:2–53). God, after calling Abraham to depart from his homeland in Chaldea (7:2–4), "settled him as a resident alien (*metōikisen*) in the land of Canaan" (7:4) and announced that his posterity would be resident aliens (*paroikos*) in a land belonging to others, who would enslave and mistreat them (7:6, citing Gen 15:13). Moses likewise is said to have been a resident alien (*paroikos*) in the land of Midian (7:29, alluding to Exod 2:11–22). In Acts 13:17, *paroikia* is used to refer to Israel's "residence as aliens" in the land of Egypt. According to the Lukan narrative of the postresurrection appearance of Jesus on the way to Emmaus, Jesus himself was mistaken for a "resident alien" by a certain Cleopas: "Are you only a resident alien (*paroikeis*) in Jerusalem and do not know the things that have happened in these days?" (Luke 24:18). This same verb is used in Heb 11:8–9 with reference to the faith of Abraham: "By faith he resided as an alien (*parōikēsen*) in the land of promise." Finally, in Eph 2:19, in a context replete with political terminology (2:11–12), the Gentile Christian addressees are declared to be "no longer strangers and resident aliens (*xenoi kai paroikoi*) to the people of God but fellow citizens (*sympolitai*) with the saints and members of the household of God (*oikeioi tou theou*)." This metaphorical (yet social) sense of the term *paroikos* is paralleled by a similar (but cosmological) use of *parepidēmos* in Heb 11:13, its only NT occurrence other than 1 Pet 2:11: "All these (descendants of Sarah and Abraham) died in faith, not having received what was promised, but having seen it and greeted it from afar, and having acknowledged that they were foreigners and strangers on earth (*xenoi kai parepidēmoi epi tēs gēs*)."

On the whole, the literal use of these terms for "stranger" and "resident alien" predominates in the NT, as in the LXX and extrabiblical sources. Ephesians 2:19 and Heb 11:13 represent notable exceptions. Hebrews, in particular, is the NT document closest in perspective to the Platonic and dualistic view of Philo. Common to both is (1) a dualistic distinction between heavenly "fatherland" and "city," on the one hand, and "estrangement" on earth, on the other; (2) the support of this dualistic perspective with an allegorizing interpretation of OT texts; and (3) an ascetic concept of the way of faith leading from earth to heaven (so Braun 1970). Hebrews' portrayal of Christian life as a journey from earth to heavenly rest (4:1–13, 14–16; 6:19–20; 10:19–22; 11:13–16) and its clear and repeated cosmological distinction between present earthly existence and the future heavenly city or homeland (8:4–5; 11:14–16; 12:18–29; 13:10–14) involves a perspective so different from that of 1 Peter that Hebrews' and 1 Peter's uses of the term *parepidēmos* must be carefully distinguished, as also noted by Goppelt 1993, 68. For later usage more in accord with the cosmological and allegorical perspective of Philo and Hebrews, see 2 *Clem.* 5:1–5; *Diogn.* 5:1–17; Clem. Alex. *Protr.* 10.108.4; Tertullian, *Apol.* 1; *De Corona* 13.

In regard to 1 Peter, the predominant literal use of the terms *paroikos* and *parepidēmos* in the literature discussed and especially their sense in Gen 23:4 LXX must be the starting point for the determination of their meaning and implication in this letter. The unjustifiable addition of the qualifying words "on earth" or "in this world" found in some commentaries and translations of 2:11 and 1:17 (see the comparative listing in Elliott 1981/1990, 39–41) introduces an earth-heaven distinction found neither in the text of Gen 23:4 nor that of 1 Peter. This interpolation reveals more about the dualistic spirituality of the interpreters than it does about the perspective of the Petrine author. The constant perspective of this document is social not cosmological, and in this context *parepidēmos*, *paroikia*, and *paroikos* describe a condition of *social*, not cosmological, estrangement. It is this condition of social alienation that accounts for the suspicion and hostility on the part of the outsiders and its consequence, the suffering of the believers.

But could the phrase "resident aliens and strangers," though indicating social alienation, still be employed metaphorically rather than literally? One widely held view considers this possible and regards these terms as metaphors describing the social estrangement of believers that has been brought about by their conversion to Christianity. The addressees, it is suggested, became aliens and strangers in a metaphorical sense as a result of their response to God's call and their acceptance of baptism (Chevallier 1974; Furnish 1975; Wolff 1975; Feldmeier 1992, 102; Goppelt 1993, 67–68, representing the majority opinion). On the other hand, it has also been proposed that *some* of these addressees had already been resident aliens and strangers in a *literal* sense prior to their conversion (Elliott 1981/1990, 37–49, 67–84; Puig Tarrech 1980, 101–16). These persons would have included not only itinerant traders, merchants, and traveling artisans who had been attracted to the Christian movement but also and especially many of the village *paroikoi* of the Asia Minor provinces whose land has been annexed to urban settlements but who were restricted from full citizenship and its accompanying rights and protection. In the Christian movement these *paroikoi* then found the home and place of belonging that they lacked as resident aliens and strangers in the larger society.

In actuality, it is neither necessary nor advisable to require an absolute distinction between literal and figurative usage with respect to these Petrine terms. It is conceivable that their usage here reflects an historical process in which the condition of *some* addressees as actual strangers and resident aliens provided the experiential basis for eventually characterizing the condition of *all* Christians in a secular society. Thus, as Paul and his traveling coworkers were actual temporary strangers (passing briefly through several localities) in some instances and resident aliens in others (with longer stays in Corinth or Ephesus, for example), so Paul, on the basis of this experience, could portray the experience of all believers metaphorically as a temporary residence on earth with a permanent "citizenship" (*politeuma*) in heaven (Phil 3:20). The latter metaphor did not eliminate the actual experience of social strangerhood on which it was based (just as the concept of a *politeuma* in heaven did not deny the actual fact of the special Israelite political mode of organization [*politeuma*] on which this concept was based). The case is similar in 1 Peter. The experience of many as actual strangers and resident aliens provided an existential basis for the depiction of all believers as strangers and resident aliens in a metaphorical sense. The discrimination and suspicion, which many encountered prior to their conversion as actual strangers and resident aliens, eventually became the experience of all who pledged an exclusive loyalty to a strange God and a rejected Christ. In continuity with the house of Abraham and the house of Israel, the messianic community as the household of God and the children of Sarah and Abraham (3:6) likewise form a community of resident aliens and strangers in a hostile society (Lamau 1988, 87). However, for the Petrine author, in contrast to Paul and the author of Hebrews, this condition of estrangement and alienation remains *social rather than cosmological* (so also Goppelt 1993, 68–69). The strangers' predicament is contrasted not to having a "home in heaven" but rather to having a home within the Christian community. To attribute cosmological implications to these terms, as do Chin (1991), Feldmeier (1992), Martin (1992) and others, is to ignore or minimize the predominantly social meaning of these terms in Greco-Roman society, the Greek Bible, and Gen 23:4 LXX in particular. And it is at variance with the predominantly social rather than cosmological perspective of 1 Peter. These terms for strangerhood are not part of a "metaphor complex" depicting Christian Diaspora existence on earth; nor is *diaspora* alone, a term occurring only in 1:1, the "controlling metaphor" of 1 Peter (against Martin 1992, 144–61). Rather, *paroikos* and *paroikia*, as descriptions of Christian social existence, constitute both linguistic and social correlates of the dominant ecclesiastical metaphor of *oikos* and the concept of election with which it is associated (Elliott 1981/1990, 165–266). Only when the correlation and contrast of strangerhood in society and at-home-ness with God are clearly grasped does the complete message of this letter become clear: Christian believers are strangers and without a home in society and indeed should remain so; for in the *oikos* of God these *paroikoi* in society have found a home for the homeless. The exhortation that follows indicates what living as elect and holy resident aliens and strangers in society entails.

Following 1 Peter, the verb *paroikeō* appears in the *inscript* of *1 Clement*: "The church of God that makes its alien residence in Rome (*hē paroikousa Rōmēn*) to the church of God that makes its alien residence in Corinth (*tēi paroikousēi Korinthon*)." The proximate verse, *1 Clem.* 1:2, includes the verb *parepidēmeō* in its literal sense: "Who is there who has stayed with you temporarily (*parepidēmas*) that has not attested the virtue and steadfastness of your faith?" This makes it likely that *paroikeō* of the inscript also has a literal sense and refers to believers who have the actual status of resident aliens in Rome and Corinth. If, on the other hand, Clement is employing *paroikeō* metaphorically, he could be expressing the idea that churches of God, wherever they are located, constitute communities distinct from their social environment both socially and religiously. The use of these terms may have been prompted by their presence in 1 Peter, since Clement clearly was familiar with the letter. However, the formulation "the church of God that makes its alien residence in . . ." is new and perhaps is the precedent for similar formulations in later Christian correspondence (see, e.g., *Pol. Phil inscr.*; *Mart. Pol. inscr.*; and the letters of Dionysius of Corinth [Eusebius, *Hist. eccl.* 4.23.5, 6]). On the use of the kindred term *paroikia* subsequent to 1 Peter, see the NOTE on 1:17. The notion that finds expression from the second century onward, that Christians constitute "strangers" and "pilgrims" on earth with a home or city in heaven (e.g., *2 Clem.* 5:1, 5; *Diogn.* 5:2; *Clem.* Alex. *Paed.* 3.41.1; *Protr. hyp.* 10.108; Tert. *Cor.* 13; Augustine, *Conf.* 9.13.37; *City of God* 18.51.2), reflects the influence of Platonic-Hellenistic thought and the conceptuality of Hebrews (and Phil 3:20) rather than that of 1 Peter. On the subsequent history of the theme of Christian strangerhood in Christian theology and spirituality, see Feldmeier 1992, 211–18. In 1 Peter, on the other hand, the issue is the suffering of believers treated as social-cultural strangers and aliens. The encouragement that our author offers is not that the addressees are pilgrims on their way to a heavenly home but that they have already been granted a home in the household of God.

For studies on 1 Pet 2:11–12, see Adinolfi 1967; Balch 1984; Cardellini 1992; Chin 1991; Elliott 1981/1990; Feldmeier 1992; Fink 1967; Goppelt 1982, 161–78; de Jonge 1956–1957; Martin 1992; Meecham 1953; Ogara 1936; Pilch 1991; Puig Tarrech 1980; Senior 1982; Sisti 1966; van Unnik 1954/55, 1964.

III. HONORABLE SUBORDINATE CONDUCT IN CIVIL AND DOMESTIC REALMS (2:13–3:12)

◆

III. A. HONORABLE SUBORDINATE CONDUCT IN THE CIVIL REALM (2:13–17)

2:13a Be subordinate to every human creature because of the Lord,
13b whether to the emperor as supreme,
14a or to governors as sent by him
14b to punish those who do what is wrong
14c or to praise those who do what is right;
15a for thus it is God's will
15b that by doing what is right you silence the ignorant talk of the foolish.
16a [Do this] as free persons,
16b yet not using your freedom as a cover for wrongdoing,
16c but as slaves of God.
17a Honor everyone;
17b love the brotherhood;
17c revere God;
17d honor the emperor.

INTRODUCTION

In the transitional unit of 2:11–12, the focus shifted from an affirmation of the dignity and favored status of the believing community before God (1:3–2:10) to the conduct of the community in society and its interaction with hostile outsiders. The believers, accused of wrongdoing and subjected to suffering, are now encouraged to behave in a manner that will disprove and silence slanderous accusation, demonstrate their innocence and fidelity to God and Jesus Christ despite their suffering, and manifest their honorable character.

With 2:13, a series of exhortations is introduced that apply the general ethical principle stated in 2:11–12 to specific social areas of behavior, civil and domestic, involving the interaction of believers and nonbelievers. The first larger unit of exhortation is contained in 2:13–3:12, although the theme of doing what is right in contrast to accusations of wrongdoing extends from

2:13 through 4:19. Common to the exhortations of 2:13–17, 2:18–25, and 3:1–6 (7) is the idea of subordination (2:13, 18; 3:1, 5). Subordination, however, is an illustration of the larger theme that dominates 2:13–4:19, namely the necessity of doing what is right rather than doing what is wrong (2:14, 15, 20; 3:6, 10–11, 13, 14, 17, 18b; 4:1–4, 15, 18, 19). Instruction of husbands (3:7) is joined to instruction of wives (3:1–6) by the terms "husband" (3:1, 7) and "likewise" (*homoiōs*, 3:6), as 3:1–6 is similarly linked by *homoiōs* and *hypotassomai* to the foregoing exhortation to slaves (2:18–25); 3:8–9 presents a generalizing ("all of you") conclusion (*to de telos*, "finally") concerning the respectful conduct of *all* members of the Christian community and repeats the notion of calling (3:9) found in 2:21a. As elsewhere in the letter, a citation of Scripture (3:10–12) concludes the section (2:13–3:12).

The first hortatory unit (2:13–17) takes up the issue of the honorable conduct (2:12) of free persons (2:16) in the civil sphere (cf. Barr 1961). The thoughts expressed here are similar to traditional Christian teaching on political responsibility[91] but also reveal the particular perspective of the Petrine author. Several of its terms and concepts link this unit with vv 11–12: (1) the doing of what is wrong (*kakopoios*, v 14; *kakia*, v 16; cf. v 12); (2) its positive antithesis, doing what is right (*agathopoios*, *agathopoieō*, vv 14, 15), which relates to *kalē anastrophē* and *kala erga* (v 12) and the showing of respect, honor (*timaō*, v 17); and (3) reference to God's will (v 15a), being "slaves of God" (v 16c), and reverence for God (v 17c), all of which continue the focus on God in 2:12d.

At the same time, 2:13–17 also constitutes a self-contained unit: (1) A new verb, "be subordinate" (*hypotassō*), is introduced (v 13) to explicate honorable behavior (v 12). Its further use in 2:18 and 3:1, 5 thematically unites these three units, 2:13–17; 2:18–25; and 3:1–6 (7), under the general hortatory theme of subordination as an illustration of doing what is right. (2) A defined area of behavior is introduced—conduct in the civil sphere. (3) A specific group, free persons (2:16), is addressed. (4) The words "everyone" (*pas*) and "emperor" (*basileus*) at the beginning and end of this passage (vv 13, 17) create an inclusion that frames this unit. (5) Here, as frequently in the letter, a reference to Sacred Scripture, in this case a modified allusion to Prov 24:21, concludes the unit.

From this point onward in the letter, we encounter language and concepts that are typical of the Greco-Roman environment in which the author and his audience find themselves: the conventional concerns of Hellenistic morality with civil duty and "household management," social order in public and private, respect for authority, the doing of good, honorable versus shameful behavior, reward and punishment, and conduct appropriate to one's social role and status. In 2:13–3:7 (as later in 5:1–5), ideas involved in the Hellenistic moral tradition of "household management" (*oikonomia*) are invoked to address

[91] See Mark 12:13–17 par.; Matt 17:24–27; Rom 13:1–7; 1 Tim 2:1–3; Titus 3:1–3, 8; *1 Clem.* 60:2–61:2.

the subject of social order (*taxis* in Greek) and to illustrate the nature of "honorable conduct" urged in 2:12.

NOTES

13a. *Be subordinate* (*hypotagēte*). This is the first of six occurrences of the verb *hypotassō* (2:13, 18; 3:1, 5, 22; 5:5), a term of thematic significance throughout 1 Peter. The verb is a compound of the preposition *hypo-* (*sub-*, "under") and the verb *tassō* ("order," "place," "station"), which in turn is a derivative of the Greek noun for "order" (*taxis*; cf. *tagma*, "that which has been ordered"). It occurs 31 times in the LXX and 38 times in the NT, especially in contexts of moral instruction.[92] In profane Greek literature, by contrast, it occurs relatively less frequently and more often in reference to political or military subjection than to moral subordination (Kamlah 1970, 238–39). The LXX employs no less than 45 terms of the *tassō* family and the NT, 21. The verb *hypotassō* (including the middle *hypotassomai*, "subordinate oneself to") and its related noun *hypotagē* ("subordination"), like *taxis* and *tagma*, presume a concept and standard of natural and social order prevalent throughout the Greco-Roman world. This cosmic and social order, it was held, generated reciprocal relationships in which one or more parties occupies a superior social position and the other, an inferior position.

The societies of the Greco-Roman period were greatly concerned with the establishment and maintenance of "order" (*taxis*) in all areas of public and private life as a replication of an ordered universe (*kosmos*). The social structure and stratification of society were perceived as manifestations of an order ordained by nature. Superordination and subordination involved the acting out of statuses and roles determined by one's assigned place in the stratified social order. Focus on subordination is a typical feature of collectivist, group-oriented societies such as those of the ancient Circum-Mediterranean (Malina 1992, 1994, summarizing the anthropological research on this issue). In contrast to modern individualist-oriented societies, where the individual is perceived to be in control of and responsible for his/her destiny, members of collectivist societies saw themselves as under the control of superordinate powers such as God or the gods, angels and demons, the emperor and his representatives, local kings and other elites, the local military, the well born, older relatives, parents, and the like. Appropriate and honorable behavior was measured by the manner in which one conducted oneself according to one's allotted rank in the social order.

At the apex of the Roman social order stood the emperor and his retinue. Below the imperial house was the "order" (Latin, *ordo*) of senators, then the equestrians and lesser nobility, then the order of local provincial decurions. From these elites, who constituted from 3% to 5% of the population, was dis-

[92] E.g., Rom 13:1, 5; 1 Cor 14:32; 16:16; Eph 5:21, 22; Col 3:18; Titus 2:5, 9; 3:1; Jas 4:7.

tinguished the remainder of the population, the lower class, ranked in the descending order of urban and rural free plebians (*eleutheroi, liberi*), freed persons (*apeleutheroi, liberti*), slaves (*douloi, servi*), the destitute (*ptōchoi*), and finally the aliens (*xenoi, alieni*) at the very bottom of the pecking order. Within the household, the microcosm of the state, beneath the male heads of the household in their roles as husbands, fathers, and masters/owners, were subordinated the wives, children, and slaves, respectively. The subordination of children to their parents (male and female) and of younger persons to their elders (male and female) rounded out the general picture.[93]

It was this structure of social order, in turn, that established the "playing field" according to which the "game" or script of honor and shame was "played." To behave honorably was to conduct oneself in accord with one's social station and given roles.[94] To behave shamefully was to attempt to rise above one's allotted position or to withhold the respect that was due one's superiors. In his discussion of social duties, Cicero (*Off.* 2.22–23) lists various motives by which people are led to submit to the power and authority of others, including good will, gratitude, another's eminence, hope for gain, fear of coercion, and love.

When the verb *hypotassō* and noun *hypotagē* are used in ethical contexts, they denote recognition of and respect for authority and order, which involve submission, deference to, subjection to, and obedience to superiors, namely God and humans in positions of recognized authority. It is primarily a concept of "order" (*taxis*) that is basic to these terms. This is evident in the Greek (*tass-*, *tag-*) but not always in their modern translations. Since the term "subordinate" conveys in English a sense of the "order" implicit in the Greek verb *hypotassō*, it is therefore preferable in all instances (1 Pet 2:13, 18; 3:1, 5, 22; 5:5) to translations such as "be subject" (RSV, NAB), "subject" or "submit yourselves" (KJV, NEB, Goppelt), "accept the authority of" (NRSV), or "defer" (Michaels). Consistency in English should also reflect that of the Greek, in contrast to the NAB, which prefers "be subordinate" at 3:1 but "be subject" elsewhere.

The meaning and use of the verb *hypotassō* in 1 Peter are consonant with its other NT occurrences and entail a recognition of and respect for order manifested in the acknowledgment of one's subordinate position in relation to those in authority, in showing proper deference, or in "placing oneself at the disposal of others" (Cervantes Gabarrón 1991a, 134–38). It serves as a recurrent motif uniting several units of instruction concerning proper conduct in the civil (2:13–17) and domestic realms (2:18–25; 3:1–6 [7]; 5:1–5a).

---

[93] For a discussion of social structure in agrarian societies in general, see Lenski, Nolan, and Lenski 1995, 175–222; on the structure and stratification of Roman imperial society, see G. Alföldy 1984, 85–132; and Gager 1971; on the social structure of Herodian Palestine, see the charts in Duling and Perrin 1994, 56; and Rohrbaugh 1993.

[94] See Perdue and Gammie 1990 on the social setting and socializing function of paraenesis—that is, traditional hortatory instruction.

Our author's concern for order and domestic harmony matches that of society in general; respect for this order on the part of the addressees, moreover, will secure their reputation as honorable persons. However, it is the will of their God and judge, and the model of their Lord who subordinated himself to God's will as an obedient suffering servant, that serve as the paramount and distinctive motivations for this behavior. This is a thought implied throughout the letter (2:13, 15–16, 18–20, 21–25; 3:2, 12; cf. also 1:2c, 17; 3:18b, 21; 4:5, 17–18; 5:5b), but most fully explicated in 2:21–25.[95]

Subordinate persons		*Superordinate persons*
	2:13–17	
free persons		emperor, governors
	2:18–20 (25)	
household slaves		masters/owners
	3:1–6	
wives		their own husbands
	5:1–5a	
younger persons		elders

In all of these units a conventional notion of social order and stratification is presupposed, which determines the status, roles, and relations of the superordinate and subordinate. Conduct in accord with one's (assumed) allotted position and role in society and the showing of proper deference is encouraged as an important concretization of the "honorable conduct" called for as a general principle in 2:12. In regard to 2:13, several later manuscripts add *oun* ("therefore") to make this implication explicit. In this sense it is also a form of "doing what is right" (2:15b, 19–20, 24c; 3:6, 10–11, 13, 14, 17, 18b; 4:18, 19), of "obedience" (3:6), and of acting in a spirit of modesty (3:4, 16). Subordination, in general, is a manifestion of a humble attitude (Kamlah 1970, 242), and in 3:8 and 5:5b–6 subordination is summed up as the humility expected of all believers. According to our author, all such instances of subordinate and humble behavior are forms of conduct that ultimately demonstrate mindfulness of God (2:19; 3:16), reverence for God (2:17; 3:2, 14, 16), and obedience to God's will (1:2, 14, 22; 2:13, 15, 19–20; 3:4, 17; 5:2; cf. 3:21). In 2:21–24 (cf. 3:18), the subordination of Jesus Christ himself to God's will as God's servant provides the paramount model for Christian subordination.

[95] The concern for order and subordination expressed in various NT writings continued unabated in the writings of the Apostolic Fathers in regard to civil (*1 Clem.* 1:3; 37:3; 61:1; *Mart. Pol.* 10:2), domestic (*Did.* 4:11; *Barn.* 19:7), and ecclesiastical (*1 Clem.* 1:3; 2:1; 37:1–5; 38:1; 57:1–2; Herm. *Sim.* 9.22.1–4; Ign. *Eph.* 2:2; *Magn.* 2:1; 13:2; *Trall.* 2:1–2; 13:2; *Pol.* 2:1; 6:1; Pol. *Phil.* 5:3) subordination (*hypotassō, hypotagē*). *1 Clement*, a writing preoccupied with the issue of order (chs. 1, 20, 37–40, 57) sees subordination in the civil realm, household (*oikos*), and religious community as in accord with the "rule of subordination" (*tōi kanoni tēs hypotagēs*, 1:3) and as a replication of the organization and order of the cosmos (20:1–12) in typical Hellenistic fashion.

to every human creature (*pasēi anthrōpinēi ktisei*). The expression is without parallel in secular as well as Biblical Greek and poses questions regarding both translation and meaning. The rendition of *ktisis* as "institution" (RSV, NRSV, NEB, Selwyn) is inappropriate, for the abstraction "institution" is a modern rather than an ancient concept. In secular Greek as a *nomen actionis*, it can denote the "founding" of a city (Strabo, *Geogr.* 12.4.8); in the biblical literature it is used of the act of divine creation (Rom 1:20; *Pss. Sol.* 8:7; cf. Josephus, *J.W.* 4.533) or the result of the creative act: individual persons or things created, "creature" (Tob 5:8, 15; Rom 8:29; 2 Cor 5:17; Heb 4:14), or the sum of everything created, "creation" (Mark 10:6, 13:19; 2 Pet 3:4; *Barn.* 15:3). Here in 1 Peter, its reference to persons rather than "institution" is clear from the qualifying words that follow, "whether to the emperor . . . or to governors"; see also 2:18; 3:1, 5; and 5:5a, where subordination is to human persons and not "institutions" (so Teichert 1949; Goppelt 1993, 182; and against Gielen 1990, 396–400, who favors institutionalized "order"). The rendition "creature," moreover, is consistent with the identification of God as "creator" (*ktistēs*) in 4:19. In connection with emperor and governors, *human creature* has a particular salience. With this expression, imperial power is subtly but decisively demystified, desacralized, and relativized (Goldstein 1973, 92). In contrast to devotees of the imperial cult who render obeisance to the emperor as "Lord and God" (*dominus et deus*, a title claimed by Domitian [Suet., *Dom.* 13.2]), Christians respect the emperor and his representatives only as human creatures, due only the deference owed to all human beings (stressed again in v 17). Ultimate supremacy is reserved for God the creator, and it is "because of him, the Lord," that Christians are subordinate (Schelkle 1976, 73; Gielen 1990, 401–2).

every (*pasēi*). The adjective *pas* applies the injunction to all types of human authority and bears this same implication in v 17 ("honor everyone"). This would include the relations of slave-to-master (2:18–20) and wife-to-husband (3:1–7) as well. But the following conditional phrases ("whether to the emperor or to governors," vv 13b–14) are the immediate qualifiers of this statement and argue against the likelihood that 2:13 is intended as a general heading for 2:13–3:7.

because of the Lord (*dia ton kyrion*). The phrase provides the motivation for the imperative, but its referent and meaning are uncertain. "Lord" (*kyrios*) could refer here to either Jesus Christ or to God. The former is suggested by the fact that *kyrios* elsewhere refers to Jesus Christ (1:3; 2:3; 3:15) except in the OT citation in 3:12. *Kyrios* is even substituted for *theos* in 1:25 to clarify the citation of Isa 40:8 as a reference to Jesus Christ. Moreover, in the following unit (2:18–25) Jesus is presented as a model for Christian behavior and subordination to God's will (2:21–25). On the other hand, Jesus is not called Lord in this later unit, and the further references to God in 2:13–17 (vv 15a, 16b, 17) together with the fact that "creature" (2:13a) implies God as creator (*ktistēs*, 4:19) make it more likely that God is meant here. Relating subordination in the civil realm to the ordering action (Rom 13:1–7) and will of God (1 Tim 2:3;

Titus 3:4) is typical of early Christian moral instruction. Further injunctions to subordination in 1 Peter also are supported by references to God's will and action (2:15, 18, 19, 20; 3:1, 4; 5:5ab). In the light of both 2:13–17 and 2:21–25, the difference in terms of motivation is negligible: subordination to authority is willed by God, with Jesus himself in his own act of subordination (2:22–23) providing the chief example of this obedient conduct.

The phrase could imply either "because this is God's will; he has ordered it so," as in the tradition (cf. also *dia syneidēsin theou* in 2:19 and other instances in 1 Peter where God's will is the motivation of Christian conduct [2:15; 3:17; 4:2, 19]); or, in conjunction with v 12, the implication could be that Christian subordination is a means of glorifying God. Ultimately, the honor of the God of the Christians is at stake in the behavior of his children (van Unnik 1964, 231). The ambiguity of the lapidary phrase could well be intentional.

13b. *whether* (*eite*). The conditional conjunction construction "whether"–"or" (*eite-eite*, v 13b, v 14a; cf. 1 Cor 3:21–22; Rom 12:6–8) qualifies the verb and introduces two specific civil authorities to whom subordination is due.

to the emperor as supreme (*basilei hōs hyperechonti*). In the Roman world of the first century, the Roman emperor was the highest instance of human authority. In the eastern regions of this world, the Greek term *basileus* (lit., "king") served as the equivalent for "emperor" (Lat. *imperator*; cf. John 19:15; Rev 17:9, 12; Dio Chrys. *Orat.* 7.12; 21.6, 8, 10). Three emperors are mentioned by name in the NT: Caesar Augustus (Luke 2:1); Tiberius (Luke 3:1); Claudius (Acts 11:28; 18:2); note also Caesar, used absolutely without a name (Matt 22:21 par.; Luke 23:2 [Tiberius]; Acts 17:7; cf. 18:2 [Claudius]; and with reference to Nero, Acts 25:8–12; 26:32; 27:34; 28:19; and Phil 4:22). *Hōs* ("as") here and v 14a (also v 16a and elsewhere) indicates an actual condition. The Greek participle *hyperechonti* (lit., "being superior") is translated "supreme" because it modifies "emperor" (the figure with highest political authority) and therefore contains the prefix *hyper-* (*super-*), which contrasts to the prefix *hypo* (*sub-*) of *hypotassō*; compare with Rom 13:1 *hyperechousiais* ("superior") and 1 Tim 2:2 ("kings and all in high positions" [*en hyperochēi*]).

14a. *or to governors as sent by him* (*eite hēgemosin hōs di' autou pempomenois*). The term "governors" (*hēgemosin*) can refer either to legates of the emperor (*legati Caesari*) in charge of imperial provinces or to proconsuls who adminstered senatorial or "public" provinces such as those in which the addressees resided, with the exception of Galatia. Four such governors are specifically named in the NT: Pontius Pilate (Matt 27:2, 11; 28:14; Luke 20:20); Antonius Felix (Acts 23:24. 26, 33); and Porcius Festus (Acts 26:30)—all Roman governors of the province of Judaea; for Syria, see Quirinius (Luke 2:2); for Bithynia, see Dio Chrys. *Orat.* 38.33; 40.22; 43.11. On the Roman provincial governors and their subordinates in the provinces of Asia Minor, see Magie 1950, 2:1579–1600.

sent by him (*di' autou pempomenois*). This phrase implies "dispatched and appointed to act through the emperor's mandate." Josephus, in recording the offenses of King Archelaus in Judea, uses similar language to describe the request of the Judeans to be freed of his rule and to "be made subject (*hypotassesthai*) to the governors sent (*pemponemois*) there" (*Ant.* 17.314). In a different, eschatological context, the combination "kings and governors" appears in a saying of Jesus concerning "kings and governors" before whom his followers will be brought to offer testimony of their faith (Luke 21:12–15).

14b. *to punish those who do what is wrong* (*eis ekdikēsin kakopoiōn*). This is the first of two basic sanctions, one negative, the other positive, the "stick" and the "carrot," employed by civil authority for the purpose of (*eis*) enforcing desired social behavior. The negative sanction entails the "punishment" (*ekdikēsin*) of those who do what is wrong (*kakopoiōn*)"—the only NT instance in which the role of civil authority is described in these terms; for a similar thought but with different language, see Rom 13:3–4. Elsewhere in the NT, *ekdikēsis* is used more generally of God's eschatological judgment of the immoral (Luke 21:22; Rom 12:19; 2 Thess 1:8; Heb 10:30; contrast Acts 7:24, of Moses' vengeance) or God's vindication of the elect (Luke 18:7, 8).

In contrast to its other appearances in 1 Peter, where *kakopoios* has the sense of "social deviant" (2:12; 4:15; cf. *kakopoieō*, 3:17), here the context (a statement of general fact concerning punishment meted out by civil officials) indicates that the wrongdoing is of a criminal nature; compare the trial of Jesus before Pilate, where Jesus is accused of "doing what is wrong" (*kakon poiein*, Mark 15:14/Matt 27:23/Luke 23:22; John 18:30).

Later manuscripts (C P etc.) secondarily add the particle *men* to explicitly balance this phrase with that of v 14c, which includes *de*.

14c. *or to praise those who do what is right* (*epainon de agathopoiōn*). This phrase presents the positive pendant to v 14b. The substantive *agathopoios*, like the related noun *agathopoiia* (4:19), is unique to 1 Peter in the NT (cf. Sir 42:14, its only LXX occurrence). This family of terms (including the verb *agathopoieō* [2:15, 20; 3:6, 17] occurs more frequently in 1 Peter than in any other NT writing)[96] and plays a major role in its ethical exhortation.

The substantive *agathopoios* can denote "one who does what is right" (rather than what is wrong), "one who does good" (rather than evil, wickedness), or, on rarer occasions, "one who does good for others" (as a benefactor). The association of "praise" (*epainos*) with the doing of good (also Rom 13:3) has been offered as a reason for regarding *agathopoiōn* as a reference to "generous benefactions" that are then publicly praised by the authorities (Selwyn 1947, 173; van Unnik 1954–55, 99; Winter 1988). These benefactions would then refute "unfounded rumours against Christians as being men of ill-will, subversive to the peace and well-being of a city" (Winter 1988a, 94). This interpretation, however, requires the assumption that "there must have been Christians of very considerable means to warrant Paul's imperative [in Rom 13:3] and also that of 1 Pet 2:15" (Winter 1988a, 94). But this assumption lacks specific support in the case of both Romans and 1 Peter.

---

[96] See Mark 3:4/Luke 6:9; Luke 6:33, 35; 3 John 11; also *poiēsatō agathon*, 3:11 and Gal 6:9.

On the other hand, the concept of the punishment of wrongdoers and the praise of the virtuous as the role of civil authorities, according to van Unnik (1955–1956, 1956–1957), was a commonplace of Greek popular philosophy (Lysias, *Or.* 31.30; Xen., *Mem.* 3.4.8, *Cyr.* 1.6.20, *Oec.* 9.14; Diod. Sic., *Hist.* 1.70.6; 5.71.1; 11.46.1; 15.1.1; Dio Chrys., *Orat.* 39.2) and could well have influenced the language of both 2:14 and 2:20. Thus, Socrates, according to Xenophon (*Oec.* 9.14), notes on the subject of social orders: "in cities subject to good laws the citizens do not think it enough merely to have fine laws, but in addition choose guardians of the laws to examine them, to praise the one who acts lawfully, and to punish the one who acts contrary to the laws." Similarly, Philo (*Legat.* 7) observes that "no law can be complete unless it includes two provisions: honors for things good and punishment for things evil" (*timēs agathōn kai ponērōn kolaseōs*; see also *Spec.* 4.77; *Mos.* 1.154; *Virt.* 227; and Josephus, *J.W.* 6.134; *Ant.* 6.267; see further Prov 14:35 and, in later Christian tradition, Arist., *Apol.* 13.7; Tat. *Orat.* 7.1–2). Christians, according to our author, concur on this function of civil government and thus share with their neighbors a common interest in respect for the law and the security of the social order.

Since in this context *agathopoieō* (v 14) is the positive antonym of *kakopoieō* (cf. also Mark 3:4/Luke 6:9; 3 John 11), it is best taken not as the conferring of benefactions but as "doing what is right" in contrast to "doing what is wrong," as in the similar contrasts of right and wrong behavior found elsewhere in the letter (2:20; 3:11–12, 17; cf. also 2:11–12; 3:6; 4:2–3, 19); so also Goppelt 1993, 187. In 2:20 the verb is used in conjunction with slaves—hardly persons capable of public benefactions. Moreover, as the following verse makes clear, the "right" behavior of which the author speaks is action that is not simply socially approved but that also is in accord with the will of God. The aim of doing what is right, as v 15b indicates, is not the garnering of public praise but the squelching of unfounded accusations of wrongdoing (cf. also 2:12; 3:16). For the contrast between the verbs *kakopoieō-agathopoieō* (here and 3:17), see also Mark 3:4/Luke 6:9; 3 John 11; and for the conceptual contrast, 1 Pet 2:20; 3:11 (cf. also *T. Benj.* 4:3; 5:2; *T. Ash.* 2:8; 3:1–2; *T. Jos.* 18:2). In commenting on the laws of the Pentateuch, Philo devoted an entire tractate to the subject of "rewards and punishments" (*De Praemiis et Poenis*). This Petrine description of the role of civil authorities is echoed in a modern prayer for civil authorities: "Grant also health and prosperity to all that are in authority, especially to the President and Congress of the United States, the Governor and Legislature of this commonwealth and to all our Judges and Magistrates, and endue them with grace to rule after Thy good pleasure, to the maintenance of righteousness and to the hindrance and punishment of wickedness, that we may lead a quiet and peaceable life in all godliness and honesty" (*Lutheran Book of Worship*).

In regard to the civil realm, urging subordination is hardly a call to "loyalty" to the state as Reicke (1964, 95) and others (Brox 1986, 115–16; Gielen 1990, 395; Prostmeier 1990, 396) would have it. The verb *hypotassō* involves only a recognition of and respect for order and assuming one's subordinate position vis-à-vis figures in authority. This is by no means equivalent to the emotional attachment that "loyalty" involves. In this context being subordinate to the emperor and his governors is to respect his authority and show him the honor due all persons (v 17)—nothing more and nothing less. Loyalty (*pistis, pisteuō*), on the other hand, is reserved for Christ and God alone (1:5, 7, 8, 9, 21; 2:6, 7; 5:9). Accordingly, it is references to the latter ("because of the Lord," v 13; "God's will," v 15; "as slaves of God," v 16) that serve here to motivate subordination and doing what is right.

This distinguishes the thought here from that of Rom 13:1–7, its closest NT parallel. On the one hand, both passages display certain linguistic and conceptual *similarities*. These include terms of the *hypotass-* root (1 Pet 2:13; Rom 13:1, 5);[97] *pas* ("every," 1 Pet 2:13; Rom 13:1); *hyperechonti*/*hyperechousais* ("supreme/superior," 1 Pet 2:13; Rom 13:1); *agathopoiōn, agathopoiountas* ("doing what is right," 1 Pet 2:14, 15)/*to agathon poiei* ("do what is right," Rom 13:3); *kakopoiōn* ("do what is wrong," 1 Pet 2:14), *kakias* ("evil," 1 Pet 2:16)/*tōi kakōi* (Rom 13:3), *to kakon poiēis* (Rom 13:4), *to kakon prassontai* (Rom 13:4); *epainos* ("praise," 1 Pet 2:14; Rom 13:3); *ekdikēsis* ("punish," 1 Pet 2:14)/*ekdikos* ("punisher," Rom 13:4); *timēsate, timate* ("honor," 1 Pet 2:17a, 17d)/*timēn* ("honor," Rom 13:7); and *phobeisthe* ("revere," 1 Pet 2:17)/*phobos, phobeisthai* ("fear," Rom 13:3); cf. also *kalōn ergōn*/*agathōi ergōi* ("good deed[s], 1 Pet 2:12; Rom 13:3). In addition they display "comparable ideas in a comparable sequence" (Schutter 1989, 62): (1) encouragement of subordination (*hypotassō*) to civil authorities (1 Pet 2:13; Rom 13:1, 5); (2) divine sanction (*dia ton kyrion* [1 Pet 2:13]; *dia tēn syneidēsin* [Rom 13:5]); reference to God's will (1 Pet 2:15) or God's action (Rom 13:5); (3) dual function of civil authorities (punishment of wrongdoing and reward of good behavior, 1 Pet 2:14; Rom 13:3–4); (4) incentives for doing what is right (1 Pet 2:15; Rom 13:3–5); (5) conclusion with injunctions that include showing honor and reverence (1 Pet 2:17; Rom 13:7). Finally, (6) the encouragement of mutual love in Rom 13:8–10 corresponds to 1 Pet 2:17 ("love the brotherhood").

On the other hand, these two texts also display notable *differences*.[98] 1 Peter makes no mention of paying taxes and revenues (compare Rom 13:7), makes no reference to divine wrath (compare Rom 13:4), uses *phobos* for "reverence" *for God* (compare Rom 12:3, 4, 7: "fear" *of humans*), includes concepts (2:15, 16) and terms (2:13b–14, 17) without parallel in Rom 13:1–7, and most importantly, makes no assertion that civil authorities are "servants" of God (contrast Rom 13:4) representing God's authority (contrast Rom 13:2, 4). The Petrine conception of the function of civil authority is a simple utilitarian one, devoid of divine warrant. The point of our Petrine text is not to discourage resistance

---

[97] In Romans, see also further terms for "set in order" (*tetagmenai*, 13:1; *diatagēi*, 13:2) and resisting order (*antitassomenos*, 13:2; cf. *anthestēken*, 3:2; *anthestēkotes*, 3:2).

[98] See Goldstein 1973; Lamau 1988, 234–42; Legasse 1988, 390–93; Gielen 1990, 435–74; Shimada 1993, 119–21. On Rom 13:1–7 see, most recently, Botha 1994.

to authorities established by God, as appears to be the case in Rom 13:2, but to encourage doing what is right as a sign of subordination to God's will and a means to silence detractors (2:15). The correspondences between these two texts, therefore, clearly are due not to literary dependence but rather to independent use of traditional parenetic material transmitted in oral form (Lohse 1954/1986, 43). 1 Peter, with its combination of civil (2:13–17) and domestic (2:13–3:7) instruction, appears closer to the *oikonomia* tradition in which civic and domestic responsibilities are united than does Rom 13:1–7, which addresses only the former issue.

On the whole, the Petrine author's view of civil government stands midpoint between the thoroughly positive position of Paul and the entirely negative view of the author of Revelation, who depicts civil authorities (Roman and local) as agents of Satan/the devil (2:10; chs. 13–18). Our author's more sober conception of Roman government may well reflect the change in political conditions after the composition of Romans (mid-50s) and Nero's actions against the Christians in connection with the fire of Rome (64 CE). However, its neutral stance concerning the emperor and his representatives would be inconceivable if, in fact, the Christian community throughout the world (5:9) were the target of official Roman prosecution. This passage thus provides one of several reasons for dating 1 Peter somewhere during the early Flavian period (73–92 CE), for which there is no evidence of Roman opposition to the messianic movement.

In v 15, a parenthetical comment, our author focuses specifically on "doing what is right" (*agathopoiōn*, v 14c; *agathopoiountas*, v 15c), applies this proper conduct to his readers, links it with the will of God, and notes its effect.

15a. *for thus it is God's will* (*hoti houtōs estin to thelēma tou theou*). "Thus" (*houtōs*) refers retrospectively (as in 3:5) to "doing what is right" (v 14c), and "for" (*hoti*) introduces a causal explanation (Hort 1898, 143) that, as elsewhere (1:16b; 2:21b; 3:9c, 12a, 18a; 4:1c, 8, 14b; 17a; 5:5c, 7b), presents "the theological ground of an ethical injunction" (Selwyn 1947, 217). "Doing what is right" is not simply a societal requirement; it is also, and most importantly, God's will (*to thelēma tou theou*) for his people, as is stressed also in 3:17 and 4:19 (cf. also 2:20; 4:2; 5:2; 2 *Clem.* 10:1; Herm. *Sim.* 9.18.1–2).

15b. *that by doing what is right you silence the ignorant talk of the foolish* (*agathopoiountas phimoun tēn tōn aphronōn anthrōpōn agnōsian*). The verb of the general statement in 14c, "doing what is right," is now applied specifically to the believers, and the effect of their honorable conduct on those who slander them (cf. 2:12) is indicated: you silence . . . the foolish. Righteous action speaks louder than words, a point repeated in 3:1–6. The accusative pl. part. *agathopoiountes* stands in apposition to "the will of God" and forms with *phimoun* ("silence") an accusative + infinitive construction with "you" as implied subject (made explicit in C and later MSS). "Doing what is right" (*agathopoieō*, *agathopoios*, *agathopoiia*) constitutes a key theme of the Petrine ethic (see also the conceptually related terms *dikaios* [3:12, 18; 4:18] and *dikaiosynē* [2:24; 3:14]). The verb is used again in conjunction with *hypotassomai* ("subordinate") in 2:18–20; 3:1, 5–6; and independently in 3:17; compare *poiēsatō agathon* (3:11; cf. also 2 *Clem.* 10:2; Herm. *Vis.* 3.5.4; 9.5; *Sim.* 9.18.1, 2). This family of terms forms part of a larger semantic field in 1 Peter involving such synonymous expressions as "holy conduct" or "honorable conduct" (1:14–16, 17, 18; 2:12; 3:1, 2, 16); "honorable deeds" (2:12); "zealots for what is right" (3:13); "doing what is right" (2:24c; 3:14a); "righteous" (3:12a, 18b; 4:18a); cf. also 2:22–23; 3:8–9; 4:8–11; 5:2–4, 5a). "Doing what is right," like avoidance of evil and wrongdoing (2:1, 12; 4:3, 15), describes the proper deportment of Christians in their social interactions with outsiders. By doing what is right Christians will not only silence their detractors, as indicated here, they will also be assuring outsiders that Christians share with their neighbors an earnest concern for proper and honorable conduct.

The verb *phimoō* literally means "muzzle" or "gag" (with demons as object in Mark 1:25; 4:39; Luke 4:35) and is used figuratively here, as in Matt 22:34, for "silencing" or "squelching" one's opponents. "The foolish" (lit., "foolish persons," *aphronōn anthrōpōn*), as implied by the context, are those outsiders who groundlessly accuse innocent Christians of wrongdoing (2:12). The generic term *anthrōpoi*, which is left untranslated here, elsewhere identifies those in opposition to Jesus Christ (2:4c) or "human" in constrast to divine standards (4:2, 6). Calling the detractors "foolish," as Michaels (1978, 128) notes, "is about as close as Peter comes to trading insults with his readers' enemies (something he expressly forbids in 3:9)." The outsiders' "ignorance" (*agnōsia*) of Christian virtue and of the God of the Christians (cf. 1 Cor 15:34) is akin to the ignorance (*agnoia*) of the believers themselves prior to their conversion (1:15). Israelites too, Josephus complained, had been the victims of slander born of ignorance and ill will (*Ag. Ap.* 2.145, 236, 258). In later time Tertullian continues to decry the ignorance of those responsible for injustices against the Christians (*Apol.* 1 and passim; *Nat.* 1.7: "It is more in keeping with the character of strangers both to be ignorant [of the true state of a case] and to invent [a false account]"). The verb "silence" implies that it is "ignorant talk" (*agnōsia*) that is to be squelched (cf. Titus 2:8). This is consonant with other terms such as "slander" (2:12; 3:16), "reviling" (3:9, 16; 4:4), and "reproach" (4:14), all of which indicate that it is primarily verbal abuse to which the believers have been subjected and which has occasioned their suffering.

The series of terms *agathopoiountes . . . aphronōn anthropōn agnōsian* is another alliterative chain manifesting the author's literary and rhetorical competence (cf. 1:4, 6; 2:12, 16, 18–20, 21; 3:17; 4:4).

16. The syntactical relation of v 16 to its context is not immediately clear. Lacking a main verb, it qualifies either what precedes it (Nestle-Aland) or what follows. Selwyn (1947, 173) and Brox (1986, 122) relate it to the initial verb of v 13: "be subordinate . . . as free persons." However, it could also qualify "doing what is right" in v 15b and form a unit consisting of vv 15 and 16 (so Beare 1970, 139, 143; Goppelt 1978, 180). Or it could qualify what follows in v 17: "as free persons . . . honor all" (so Reicke 1964, 95; Michaels 1988, 121; R. P. Martin 1992, 200–207). On the whole, the literary inclusion created by

references to God (v 15a and v 16c), the contrast of doing what is right (v 15b) with doing wrong (*kakia*, v 16), and the resulting coherence of vv 15–16 all favor the second option. In any case, the point is that respect for order, doing what is right, and showing honor are voluntary actions of free persons (*eleutheroi*) acting in accord with God's will.

16a. [*Do this*] *as free persons* (*hōs eleutheroi*). The ellipsis, with "do this" implied, extends the thought of v 15. The phrase *hōs eleutheroi* identifies the social and legal status of the specific persons here addressed (R. P. Martin 1992, 192); their freedom provides the premise for the preceding exhortation (vv 13–15). Occasionally it has been taken as a theological metaphor implying the addressees' freedom/ransoming from a meaningless or sinful past (cf. 1:18–19; so Goppelt 1993, 188; Michaels 1988, 128). But in this context, which concerns civil responsibility and which lacks any reference to the work of Christ, it is more likely that civil freedom is meant. Paul prominently contrasts free and slave in the theological sense (Rom 6:18–22; 5:1; Gal 4:7–10, 21–5:1); for the political sense, see Gal 3:28. However, it is not the Pauline concern with freedom from the Mosaic Law (Gal 5:1–13) that is under discussion here but, rather, the civil status of freedom that is the prerequisite of civil responsibility.

16b. *yet not using your freedom as a cover for wrongdoing* (*kai mē hōs epikalymma echontes tēs kakias tēn eleutherian*). This is the first of a pair of qualifications of the imperative in v 16a. Having the status of free persons should not be exploited as a "cover" (*epikalymma*), or more colloquially a "smokescreen," for wrongdoing (*kakias*; cf. *kakopoiōn*, v 14). For *kai* with the sense of "yet," see Matt 3:14; 6:26; Mark 12:12; 1 Cor 5:2; and esp. 2 Cor 6:9 (three *hōs* . . . *kai* formulations). The rare term *epikalymma* (Menander, frg. 90; 4 LXX instances) occurs only here in the NT; compare *kalymma akatharsias* in *T. Jud.* 14:5. The cluster of terms *eleutheroi* . . . *epikalymma echontes* . . . *eleutherian* constitutes another example of refined alliteration. Gielen (1990, 417–18), assuming Pauline influence, considers this phrase a "correction" of the addressees' position, which she presumes to be one of indifference to or withdrawal from society. But this confuses the phenomenon of societal "withdrawal" with that of social distinctiveness. The larger epistolary context suggests that the author is alluding to a claim of the outsiders that some Christians were using their freedom as a cover-up for illict or shameful behavior (see 2:12; 3:16; 4:4, 14–16). Reicke (1964, 96) imagined that our author was warning against "subversive activity" and revolts (like those of the Asia Minor "industrialized workers"). This is reading too much political subversion into the word *kakia*, a generic term for "wrongdoing" or "evil," which in 2:1 is associated not with rebellion but personal vices. In the present context, *kakia* could at most imply a lack of respect for established authority; hence the stress on subordination and honoring all persons. Sleeper (1968) offers a convincing critique of Reicke's revolution hypothesis.

16c. *but as slaves of God* (*alla hōs theou douloi*). This phrase constitutes the third of a triad of parallel *hōs* ("as") qualifications employed in this verse (see a similar triad in 4:15–16; cf. *T. Jos.* 2:5). Even Christians who enjoy civil freedom (v 16a) are ultimately bound by the will of God (v 15a) to avoid the misuse of this freedom (v 16b). The metaphor "slaves of God" has familiar OT roots. There it serves as a designation for all Israel (Deut 32:36) as well as its leading figures: Moses (1 Kgdms 8:53, 56; Mal 3:24); David (3 Kgdms 8:66); and the prophets (Jer 7:25; Amos 3:7). Followers of Jesus likewise adopted it as a self-designation (Acts 16:17; Titus 1:1; Jas 1:1); compare Paul's preference for "slave of (Jesus) Christ" (Rom 1:1; 1 Cor 7:22; Gal 1:10; Phil 1:10; see K. C. Hanson and Bartchy 1988). In this Petrine context concerning the obedience owed to civil authorities, on the one hand, and to God on the other, this expression takes on special force when compared to an observation of Philo. In referring to the treatment of Alexandrian Israelites under Emperor Gaius, he notes that civil "subjects are slaves of an absolute emperor" (*douloi de autokratoros hoi hypēkooi*) and are as cursed as is a slave when subject to a hostile master (*Legat.* 119). Our author, by contrast, reminds his audience that Christians are not slaves of the emperor or of the state but are the possession (2:9e) of the One who created them (2:13; 4:19), ransomed them (1:18), and gave them new life (1:3, 22; 2:5b). The notion of being both free and slaves of God expresses one of the great paradoxes of human life, as Philo also has noted: "For in truth he who has God alone for his leader, he alone is free" (*Prob.* 20). The concept is also consonant with Stoic thought; note Seneca, *Deo parere libertas est*, "To obey God is freedom" (*Vit. beat.*15.7). This paradox, echoed here in 1 Peter as well, is later captured in the phrase of a prayer traced to Augustine: "Whom (God) to serve is perfect freedom." On the subject of slavery as a metaphor of salvation in Paul see the study by D. Martin (1990). On the theological symbolic dimensions of freedom, see Malina 1978.

Verse 17 concludes this unit on civil duty and contains elements of the inclusion that frames vv 13–17. In addition to the recurrences of "emperor" (vv 13b, 17d) and an inclusive "everyone" (*pas*, vv 13a, 17a), the general principle that opens the unit is matched by a similar generalizing statement at the end in which the act of subordination (v 13a) is clarified as the conferral of honor (v 17a, d). Between these two parallel imperatives urging respect for all persons and then the emperor specifically, our author has interposed two further parallel injunctions concerning appropriate behavior within the community: love of the brotherhood (v 17b) and reverence for God (v 17c). With this carefully crafted chiasm (Bammel 1994–1965) involving four imperatives stated asyndetically, a distinction is drawn between the respect due to outsiders and the loyalty due within the community to fellow-members and God (Schröger 1981, 131–37; Légasse 1988, 385).

A. Honor everyone (external relations)
    B. love the brotherhood (internal relations)
    B′. revere God (internal relations)
A′. honor the emperor (external relations)

17a. *Honor everyone* (*pantas timēsate*). The verb *timēsate*, "honor," is a gnomic aorist stating a universally expected mode of behavior. To honor someone involves the showing of respect, acknowledgment of another's status, and deference to authority. The object of this action can be God (e.g., Matt 15:8/ Mark 7:6, citing Isa 29:13; John 5:23; 8:49) as well as humans (Matt 15:4/ Mark 7:10, citing Exod 20:12, as do Mark 10:19; Luke 18:20; Eph 6:2; cf. John 12:26; Acts 28:10; 1 Tim 5:3). As an Israelite sage observed, "Who is honored? He that honors mankind" (*m. ʾAbot* 4:1), and as Paul urged, "outdo one another in showing honor" (Rom 12:10), so the Petrine author notes that persons who have been honored by God (2:4–10) are to behave in honorable fashion (2:12) and render honor to *everyone* (*pantas*, lit., "all persons"). Honoring everyone is thus a way of being "subordinate to every human creature" (v 13a). For the equivalency of being subordinate and showing honor, compare Titus 2:9 ("Bid slaves to subordinate themselves to their masters") and 1 Tim 6:1 ("Let all who are under the yoke of slavery regard their masters as worthy of honor"); cf. also *1 Clem.* 1:3. The aorist of the latter verb (*timēsate*) also matches that of the former (*hypotagēte*) in contrast to the present tenses of the three following verbs. Plutarch, commenting on duties public and domestic (*Lib. ed.* 10; *Mor.* 7DE), makes a similar connection:

> For through philosophy and in company with philosophy it is possible to attain knowledge of what is honorable (*to kalon*) and what is shameful (*to aischron*), what is just (*to dikaion*) and what is unjust (*to adikon*), what, in brief, is to be chosen and what is to be avoided, how a man must bear himself in his relations with the gods, with his parents, with his elders (*presbyterois*), with the laws, with strangers (*allotriois*), with those in authority (*archousi*), with friends, with women (*gynaixi*), with children, with servants (*oiketais*); that one ought to reverence (*sebesthai*) the gods, to honour (*timan*) one's parents, to respect (*aidesthai*) one's elders, to be obedient to (*peitharchein*) the laws, to yield to (*hypeikein*) those in authority, to love one's friends, to be chaste (*sōphronein*) with women, to be affectionate with children, and not to be overbearing with slaves (*doulous*); and, most important of all, not to be overjoyful at success or overmuch distressed at misfortune, nor to be dissolute in pleasures, nor impulsive and brutish in temper.

The behavior required of Christian wives and husbands in 3:1–7 offers a further variation on this theme: the reciprocal relationship between being subordinate (3:1) and receiving honor (3:7).

It is not likely that this first clause is a general statement explicated by the following three clauses,[99] since 17b and 17c involve other, different actions concerning the brotherhood and God that are not illustrations of showing honor to all. The conjecture of J. P. Wilson (1942–1943) that "honor everyone" was an erroneous substitution for an original "do all things" (as slaves of God)

---

[99] Against the NAB; Légasse 1988, 384; S. Snyder 1991; and T. W. Martin 1992, 203–5 (following Theophylact [*Expos.* on 1 Pet 2:17]).

likewise misconstrues the syntax and structure of vv 16–17. Verse 17a instead forms with v 17d the framing clauses of a chiastically constructed unit in which honor to outsiders is contrasted with love of the brotherhood and reverence for God within the community.

17b. *love the brotherhood* (*tēn adelphotēta agapate*). The second (v 17b) and third (v 17c) imperatives concern two related actions within the Christian community: maintenance of emotional attachment to the group (love of the brotherhood) and of commitment to God. The action of love of which our author speaks (*agapate*) has as its object fellow-believers, not outsiders (cf. also 4:8). In the NT, as Lohfink (1984, 110–15) points out, "love," with only two exceptions (Matt 5:44/Luke 6:27; 1 Thess 3:12), "means *love for one's brother in the faith, love for one another*" (italics his), whereas "terms completely different from *agapē/agapan* (love/to love) [are used] to designate concern for people outside the church" (for the texts, see Lohfink 1984, 110, 193–94). In keeping with this fact, the object of the verb "love" here is "the brotherhood" (*tēn adelphotēta*). This collective noun depicts the believers as a surrogate kinship group whose members are committed to one another as are blood brothers and sisters. Love is the action by which they demonstrate this commitment. The term *adelphotēs* recurs in 5:9 and is implied in 5:13 ("the co-elect brotherhood that is at Babylon") but appears nowhere else in the NT, although the designation of fellow-believers as "brothers" and "sisters" is common; Silvanus is so identified as "faithful brother" in 5:12. In the LXX, *adelphotēs* can denote a political alliance (1 Macc 12:10, 17) or biological brotherhood (4 Macc 9:23; 10:3, 15; 13:19, 27). A contemporary, Dio Chrysostom of Prusa (*Orat.* 38.15), in describing the harmony that characterizes the household (*oikos*), speaks of "the concord of brothers" (*adelphōn homonoia*); see also the treatise of Plutarch, *De fraterno amore* (*Mor.* 478A–492D). The Petrine author, however, speaks not of loving "brothers" or "sisters" individually, but of loving the *brotherhood* (fraternal and sororal), using a unique *collective* term for the entire *community of brothers and sisters*, consonant with his employment of collective terms elsewhere in the letter ("household," 2:5; 4:17; "stock," "royal residence," "priestly community," "people," 2:9–10; "flock of God," 5:2a; cf. Spörri 1925). In addition, *adelphotēs* belongs to a broad semantic field of *familial* terms by which the believing community is identified as the "household" or "family" of God (throughout 1:3–2:10), a fictive kin group of brothers and sisters or "family of believers" (NRSV) united by divine rebirth (1:3, 23), faith (1:6, 8, 21; 2:7a), and election (1:1; 2:4–10; 5:13). "It was in the realm of the 'house churches' that brotherhood and sisterhood were lived concretely" (Lohfink 1984, 108). On the concept of fictive or surrogate kinship, see Pitt-Rivers 1968.

The familial love (i.e., emotional attachment and enacted commitment to surrogate kin) enjoined here (cf. Rom 12:9–10; 13:8–10; 1 Cor 13) is but one of several emphases on mutual brotherly (and sisterly) loyalty urged throughout the letter (1:22; 3:8; 4:8; 5:14; see respective NOTES). It is by means of this love and reciprocal sharing of resources (4:8–11), according to the author, that the internal cohesion of the Christian community is to be maintained and the brotherhood is to be distinguished from its surrounding society. On the concept of the church as fraternity, see Legido Lopez 1982 and K. Schäfer 1989. The identification of the believing community as a *brotherhood* at the end of the body of the letter (5:9) forms with its occurrence here one of the inclusive elements framing the hortatory portion of the letter (2:11–5:11).

The suggestion has been made (Puig Tarrech 1980, 384–87) that, from the vantage point of the outsiders, this brotherhood of Christians (4:16) may have been regarded as one of the many illicit associations (*collegia*; *hetairiai* [Pliny, *Ep.* 10.96.7]) that populated the social map of the early imperial period. While conceivable, there is no extant evidence that any such collegium designated itself as a "brotherhood"; nor can the suggestion be supported by any of the content of 1 Peter. Use of this unusual term in *1 Clem.* 2:4, along with numerous other terms common to 1 Peter and *1 Clement* (see GENERAL INTRODUCTION, 10), suggests the familiarity of Clemens Romanus with 1 Peter and the possible currency of this term as a self-designation of the Roman Christian community (cf. its use also in Herm. *Mand.* 8.10, another writing of Roman provenance).

17c. *revere God* (*ton theon phobeisthe*). Maintenance of familial solidarity within the community is matched by its members' exclusive devotion to God. The verb *phobeō* can mean "fear," but when used in conjunction with God it generally denotes the feeling of awe (in the presence of the Holy) and the demonstration of reverence and commitment.[100] A similar link between reverence for God and commitment to the brothers occurs in *T. Jos.* 11:1: "My children, have the fear/reverence of God in all your works before your eyes and honor your brothers." This Petrine clause and the one that follows (v 17d) may have been inspired by Prov 24:21: "My son, fear (*phobou*) the Lord and the king, and do not disobey either of them." The Petrine author, however, pointedly distinguishes the reverence appropriate for God from the honor due the emperor, as to all persons. Romans 13:7 likewise speaks of both revering and honoring but leaves the object unspecified. For our author, fear/reverence is reserved for God alone and is more prominent as a motivation for exhortation (1:17; 3:2, 6, 14, 16) than in any other NT writing (Goppelt 1993, 190).

17d. *honor the emperor* (*ton basilea timate*). The obligation to honor the emperor and respect his authority reflects general Christian as well as Israelite sentiment (see Matt 22:21 par.; Rom 13:1–7; Titus 3:1; *1 Clem.* 60:4–61:1; *Mart. Pol.* 10:2). One way Israel honored the emperor was to offer daily sacrifice for him in the Jerusalem Temple (Philo, *Legat.* 279–80; Josephus, *Ag. Ap.* 2.76–78). Another was to include him in the regular prayers for kings and rulers (cf. Ezra 6:10; 1 Macc 7:33; *m. ʾAbot* 3:2), a practice continued by the Christians as well (1 Tim 2:2; *1 Clem.* 61:1–2). This Petrine chiastic construc-

---

[100] See 3:2; Luke 18: 2, 4; Acts 10:2, 22, 35; 13:16, 26; Rom 3:18; 2 Cor 7:1; Rev 11:18; 14:7; 19:5; and the NOTE on 1:17d.

tion, however, indicates that the honor due the emperor is the same owed to all persons (v 17a) and is distinguished from the reverence that is due to God alone. This coincides with a similar distinction made in the Jesus tradition (Matt 22:21/Mark 12:17/Luke 20:25; *Gos. Thom.* 100; cf. Justin, *1. Apol.* 17.2) between what is due to Caesar and what is owed to God and likewise recalls the position attributed to Peter in Acts 5:29: "we must obey God rather than men." Earlier, Sirach had also noted the precedence given to fear of God: "The nobleman, the judge, and the ruler will be honored, but none of them is greater than the one who fears the Lord" (Sir 10:24). In the following century this Petrine contrast between honor for the emperor and reverence/fear for God is held up by the Christian martyrs of Scillium, near Carthage, as a principle of Christian conduct: "Pay honor to Caesar as Caesar; but it is God we fear" (*Acts of the Scillitan Martyrs* 9). The contemporary Christian apologist Tatian similarly observed, with reference to civil authority: "Man is to be honored as a fellowman; God alone is to be feared/revered" (*Orat.* 4).

The suggestion that this Petrine formulation might entail a subtle critique of the cult of the emperor (so Schneider 1961, 69; Goldstein 1973, 104; Gielen 1990, 420–35) remains only an interesting conjecture, given the complete absence in 1 Peter of any explicit reference to emperor worship. What is clear, however, is that the authority of the emperor is at least relativized, desacralized, and limited (Lamau 1988, 240–42; Gielen 1990, 420–21; Cervantes Gabarrón 1991a, 143). In contrast to the Pauline position reflected in Rom 13:1–7, our author asserts no divine warrant for imperial authority. Subordination is obligatory not because the emperor is divine or a minister of God but because he, like all creatures, deserves respect from subordinates. This is a respect that Christians can freely show when it does not impinge on the reverence that is due to God alone.

This clause completes the chiasm of v 17 and the literary inclusion formed by vv 13 and 17. Being subordinate is thus explained as a means of showing honor and thereby demonstrating a respect for social order and conventional roles so as to allay any suspicion of Christian disruptive social behavior. At the same time, the distinction between obligations toward outsiders, on the one hand, and toward the brotherhood and God, on the other, secures the firm boundary line between the messianic sect and the society at large (see also 1:14, 18; 2:6–10, 25; 4:3–4; and Légasse 1988, 385–86).

GENERAL COMMMENT

In this first exemplification of the honorable conduct called for in 2:12, the believers are enjoined to demonstrate respect for the social order and to honor civil authorities whose function is to preserve that order. This instruction is consonant in sentiment with a venerable Hellenistic moral tradition concerning appropriate conduct in both the civil and domestic spheres (see DETAILED COMMENT). The specific theological motivations that are provided ("because of the Lord" [v 13] or obedience to "God's will" [v 15a] as "God's slaves" [v 16c]; to "silence" ignorant detractors [v 15b]), along with elements of v 17 (v 17b, c), adapt this tradition to the values and strategy of the Christian movement. Respect for and subordination to civil authority in its function of rewarding good and punishing evil and doing what is right is fidelity to the will of God and a means for silencing ignorant detractors. These verses, however, explicate no theory of the state, nor do they present any critique of Roman or local political power. In contrast to the closest NT parallel, Rom 13:1–7, no divine warrant is assigned to political power, and authorities are not envisioned as the "servants of God." Only the *function* of political authorities is described: the punishment of wrongdoers and the praise of those who do what is right. A subtle but clear distinction is drawn between the honor that is due to the emperor as to all persons, and the reverence that is due to God alone. Believers are to exercise their freedom by choosing to do what is right rather than using their liberty as a pretext for evil, because they are slaves of God and subject ultimately to God's will. The effect of such conduct, which is a key concern of this exhortation, is that the uninformed slander of the outsiders will be muzzled. The final verse succinctly indicates how Christian subordination is a matter of demonstrating appropriate respect for all persons including the emperor, on the one hand, and of practicing reverence for God and love within the brotherhood, on the other.

The issue here is not the validity of social structures and authority as such, but how Christian believers as the children of God conduct themselves in relation to these unquestioned structures of social life. Our author, like all NT writers, accepts as a given the authority of emperor and governors and, later, the institution of slavery, the subordinate relation of wives to their husbands, and of younger persons to their elders, just as Jesus and his earliest followers did. Social order was a chief concern of ancient society because it secured the well-being and prosperity of the community. Given the suspicion and calumny Christians faced as strangers and resident aliens, it was essential that they assure their neighbors that they were in fact not malefactors and posed no challenge or threat to the social order. Their doing what was right would then effectively silence the charge that they were up to no good. The point the author impresses on his readers is that such authority and social orderings of relationships can be respected *insofar as* subordination to the will of God, the creator and ruler of all, is not compromised.

Finally, this passage offers strong incidental support for the conclusion that Rome played no discernible role in the hostility and sufferings encountered by the addressees. Encouragement of respect for the emperor and no mention of Roman persecution of Christians would be inexplicable if Roman "witch-hunts" were really the occasion of this Christian suffering. On the other hand, the tone of this exhortation is fully consonant with the previously expressed thought that honorable behavior can have a positive and winsome effect upon denigrating outsiders.

DETAILED COMMENT: THEORIES REGARDING THE TRADITIONS EMPLOYED IN 1 PETER 2:13–17 AND RELATED UNITS

The schematized form and subject matter of the ethical contexts in which the verb *hypotassō* and the theme of subordination appear in the NT have suggested to scholars their association with one of three possible forms of moral instruction: (a) a "code of subordination" associated with baptismal instruction;[101] (b) a formal "household code" treating domestic roles, relations, and responsibilities; or (c) a more general Greco-Roman ethical tradition concerning "household management" (*oikonomia*)[102] and often involving related conduct in the civil sphere (*politeia*) as well.

1. The "Subordination Code" Theory

The theory of the existence of a primitive "subordination code" involving the repeated use of the verb *hypotassō* and the use of this code by various NT authors was first advanced by Carrington (1940) and was subsequently expanded by Selwyn (1947, 419–49). Selwyn suggested that instruction on subordination formed part of a sixfold pattern of traditional baptismal catechesis that was variously adopted and adapted by NT authors. Traces of this code in 1 Peter, according to this theory, are found in 2:13–17; 2:18–20 (25); 3:1–6; and 5:1–5a. In two parallel instances in 1 Peter, the address to *specific* groups is followed by a *general* exhortation to humility on the part of all members (3:8–9; 5:5b), concluded in both instances with a citation of Scripture (3:10–12; 5:5c):

3:8–9	Finally, all of you (*To de telos pantes*)	5:5b	Finally, all of you (*pantes de*)
	be . . . humble-minded		clothe yourselves with humility
	(*tapeinophrones*)		(*tēn tapeinophrosynēn egkombōsasthe*)
10–12	for (*gar*)	5c	because (*hoti*)
	+ citation of Ps 33[34]:13–17		+ citation of LXX Prov 3:34

There are also significant *inconsistencies*, however, in this supposedly fixed "pattern." The content and sequence of the household instruction of 1 Peter

[101] See Carrington 1940; Selwyn 1947, 384–439, esp. 419–39 on *subiecti*; cf. also GENERAL INTRODUCTION, 2.4.2.

[102] See also GENERAL INTRODUCTION 2.4.2.

diverge from that found in its closest NT parallels. Our author reverses the more conventional sequence followed in Ephesians (wives-husbands, 5:22–33; children-fathers, 6:1–4; slaves-owners, 6:5–9), where slave exhortation occurs last; compare Colossians (wives, 3:18; husbands, 3:19; children, 3:20; fathers, 3:21; slaves, 22–25; owners, 4:1). By contrast, our author begins his domestic instruction by exhorting domestic slaves (*oiketai*, not *douloi* as in Ephesians and Colossians), with no reciprocal instruction of masters. To this initial exhortation is joined a lengthy and unique Christological substantiation (2:21–25) with no parallel in Ephesians and Colossians. The content of the exhortation to wives and husbands also varies appreciably from both the shorter text of Colossians and the longer text of Ephesians. Moreover, the exhortation to elders and younger members (1 Pet 5:1–5a), related to 2:18–25 and 3:1–6 by the theme of subordination (5:5), has no parallel at all in Ephesians and Colossians. Furthermore, in 1 Peter this instruction of household groups is explicitly integrated into a dominant conception of the believing community as the household of God (Elliott 1981/1990, 200–237), while this is not the case in Ephesians and Colossians.

These variations in the content and sequence of material in the NT writings supposedly following a fixed schema of instruction, coupled with the absence of evidence of any such code focused on "subordination" outside the NT, argue rather decisively against the existence and use of a fixed subordination code. These features point rather to the independent adaptation and expansion of a fluid form of instruction focused not primarily on the concept of subordination as such but on roles and relationships associated with the household and its management.

2. *The "Household Code" Theory*

Another explanation for the similarities in NT exhortation to husbands and wives, parents and children, and slaves and owners involves the assumption of the existence and common use of a "household code" or *Haustafel*. This hypothesis was developed by German scholars (beginning with A. Seeberg [1903] and particularly M. Dibelius [1913] and his pupil K. Weidinger [1928]) early in the 20th century.[103] On the basis of similarities in form and content between certain NT texts and Hellenistic, particularly Stoic, patterns of instruction, scholars imagined early Christian indebtedness to a parenetic form of instruction that they labeled the *Haustafel*. This term is found nowhere in the ancient literature but was adopted from Martin Luther's label for a list of

[103] Surveys of research on the NT "household codes" and theories of origin include: Weidinger 1928; Selwyn 1947, 363–466; Schroeder 1959; Crouch 1972; Lührmann 1975, 1980; Thraede 1977a, 1977b, 1980; Balch 1981, 1–10; 1988, 25–50; Elliott 1981/1990, 208–20; K. Müller 1983; Schüssler Fiorenza 1983a, 251–79; P. Fiedler 1986; Laub 1986; Hartman 1988; Lamau 1988, 153–80; Bosetti 1990, 47–72; Gielen 1990, 24–54; Prostmeier 1990, 181–326; Seim 1990; Goppelt 1993, 162–79 ("station codes" rather than "household codes").

duties, set out in his *Small Catechism*, that Christians should consider in their self-examination prior to attendence at the Eucharist. Although this theory has enjoyed wide popularity, more recent research has exposed its fatal weaknesses and inadequacies. While enumerations of duties are found in Stoic moral exhortation (e.g., Epict., *Diatr.* 2.14.8; 17.31; Sen., *Ep.* 94.1; Hierocles, in Stobaeus, *Ecl.* 1.3.53), little consistency is evident in the content and pattern of exhortation of the supposed parallels. The theory also fails to explain the close relation of instruction concerning both civil and domestic duties. Moreover, insufficient attention is paid to the relation of this instructional form to the larger contexts and themes of the documents in which it is found, particularly the theme of the household and household management. The accumulating evidence now points to an older and more encompassing type of moral instruction concerned with roles and relationships in the related areas of civil and domestic life.

3. The Theory of Indebtedness to a Flexible "Household Management" (Oikonomia) *Tradition*

Decades of research on this question have now decisively shown that early Christian instruction on domestic relations and roles has been influenced by a long-standing Greco-Roman tradition of instruction concerning appropriate behavior relevant to the two major domains of ancient society: the civil sphere (*polis*) and the related domestic sphere (*oikos*). This moral tradition concerning the guidelines of civil (*politeia*) and domestic (*oikonomia*) conduct treated the roles and responsibilities associated with political (*politikos*) and domestic (*oikonomikos*) persons and activities. After the Greek classical period, the household (*oikos*) and the city-state (*polis*) formed the fundamental and related building blocks of society and the models for all other kinds of human associations. Accordingly, in philosophical thought and moral exhortation, civil responsibilities (*politeia*) and domestic duties (*oikonomia*) were often discussed in tandem. Elements of this *oikonomia* or *oikonomos* tradition as it was expressed and developed over the centuries are found in a wide variety of authors from Plato to the first century of the Common Era (Plato, *Leg.* 3.690 A–D [and in Stobaeus 3–4]; Aristotle, *Pol.*, Book 1, 1253a [regarding the city-state], 1253b [regarding household management]; cf. also 3.10.2 [1285b]; *Eth. nic.* 8 [1160a 23–1161a 10]; 5 [1134b 1–14]; also Xenophon, *Oeconomicus*; Pseudo-Aristotle, *Oeconomica* [based on Xenophon's *Oeconomicus*] and Ps.-Arist., *Mag. Mor.* 1.1194b 5–28; Middle Platonists [Albinus, Apuleius, Diogenes Laertius]; fragments of the Neopythagoreans Bryson, Callicratidas, Perictione, and Phintys [cf. Wilhelm 1915]; Columella, *On Agriculture*; Antipater of Taurus, *On Marriage* [in von Arnim, *SVF*]; Seneca, *Ben.* 2.18.1–2; 3.18.1–4; Plutarch, *Conj. praec.* [*Mor.* 138B–146A]; Arius Didymus [2.148.16–19]; Dionys. Hal., *Ant. rom.* 2.25.4–5; 26.1.3–4; 27.1; and Hierocles [in Stobaeus]).

In the Roman period, the Roman statesman Cicero assumed a similar relation and sequence of topics in commenting on human responsibilities and obligations, treating responsibilities toward the immortal gods, then duties toward country, then toward parents, and so on (*Off.* 1.160). Again, when discussing the various bonds uniting human beings, he lists their common humanity; being of the same people, tribe, or tongue; being citizens of the same city; and being kindred united in the relations of husband and wife, parents and children, and forming one home (*domus*), which is "the foundation of civil government, the nursery, as it were of the state" (*Off.* 1.53–58). Philo of Alexandria also observed: "Organized communities are of two sorts, the greater, which we call cities, and the smaller, which we call households," *politeia* being the management of the former and *oikonomia*, that of the latter (*Spec.* 3.170).[104] Underlying this tradition of moral instruction is a fundamental concern for order (*taxis, kosmos*) in both the public and domestic realms that will ensure both the harmony and effective functioning of society and the favor of the gods.

The texts illustrative of this *oikonomia* tradition are listed and briefly discussed by Balch (1981, 29–62; 1988, 25–50).[105] He notes how elements of the triple reciprocal pattern (husband-wife, parents-children, owners-slaves) can be traced from Aristotle through the Peripatetics, eclectic Stoics, Epicureans, and Neopythagoreans. This undermines the theory advanced by K. H. Rengstorf (1953) that the NT "household codes" are a "genuine Christian creation" in structure as well as content. By the Roman period this combined instruction on civil (*politeia*) and domestic (*oikonomia*) conduct had become a commonplace of traditional ethical reflection. Israelite authors (Tob 4:3–21; Sir 7:18–35; Ps.-Phoc. 175–227; Philo, *Ios.* 38–39; *Decal.* 165–67; *Spec.* 2.225–27; 3.169–80; *Hypoth.* 7.3–8; Josephus, *Ag. Ap.* 2.199–210) also echoed aspects of this Hellenistic tradition and mediated it to early Christianity (Crouch 1972; Balch 1981, 51–59). It is the varied use of this flexible "household management tradition" that best accounts for the similarities and differences among the Greco-Roman, Israelite, and Christian materials.

In the Christian texts, elements of this tradition are reflected in moral exhortation on proper conduct and domestic roles, possibly as part of instruction for persons being baptized and initiated into the Christian community (so Selwyn 1947, 384–439). Christian recourse to this ethical tradition, with added stress on the concept of subordination, explains the similarities among the related NT texts, while the varying use of this flexible tradition explains the formal and material differences among the cultural spheres of instruction (Greek, Roman, Israelite, Christian) as well as among the NT texts themselves (varying subjects and sequences of roles and relations).

The verb *hypotassō* is prominent in the NT and later Christian echoes of this tradition but not in the earlier Hellenistic sources. However, the *idea* of subor-

---

[104] Cf. also Philo, *Opif.* 142; *Post.* 49–52, 181; *Mut.* 40; *Ios.* 38–39, 54; *Spec.* 3.31; Elliott 1981/1990, 222 n. 36.

[105] See also Lührmann 1975; Thraede 1977a, 1977b, 1980; Elliott 1981/1990, 208–20, 1986a; Laub 1982, 1986; Gielen 1990, 55–62, 122–28, 146–58; and Prostmeier 1990, 181–326.

dination is everywhere present, as would be expected in a tradition emphasizing order. The comment of Plutarch on public and domestic duties (*Lib. ed.* 10; *Mor.* 7DE) cited above in the NOTE on v 17a is representative. Subordination and respect for authority, he notes, are expected facets of honorable behavior. Cicero's consideration of the various motives by which people are led to submit to another's authority and power, in his treatise *On Duties* (*Off.* 2.22–23), makes a similar point. This tradition concerns not simply the issue of status, as Goppelt's categorization "station codes" (1993, 162–79; *Ständeparänese*) implies, but also the explication of roles and responsibilities in civil and domestic life.

The material of 1 Peter (2:13–3:7; 5:1–5a) reflects familiarity with this traditional and fluid pattern of Greco-Roman instruction and exhortation.[106] At the same time, 1 Peter is the only NT example of the explicit direct association of civil and domestic exhortation.

The affinities between 1 Peter and other NT writings in the appropriation of the Hellenistic *Oikonomia* Tradition may be set out in tabular form (see TABLE 1). In a seminal text of this tradition, Aristotle, following a discussion of the close relation between *politeia* and *oikonomia* (*Pol.* 1–2), notes concerning the household management (*oikonomia*): "The parts of household management correspond to the persons who compose the household, and a complete household consists of slaves and freemen. Now we should begin by examining everything in its fewest possible elements; and the first and fewest possible parts of a family are owner and slave, husband and wife, father and children" (*Pol.* 1.3.1253a–1253b; cf. also 1.3.1259a). For the same reciprocal pairs in Roman time, see also Seneca, *Ep.* 94.1–2.

The Petrine author also addresses similar pairs in reciprocal relationship (except in 2:18–20, where only slaves, not owners, are addressed) and in the same sequence (1 Pet 2:18–20, slaves; 3:1–7, wives and husbands; and 5:1–5a, elders/younger persons, reflecting the Petrine author's variation on "father and children"). There are, however, also notable differences: (1) Whereas Aristotle organizes his discussion around the roles of the male head of the family (*paterfamilias*) as owner, husband, and father, the Petrine author gives precedence to the inferior and subordinate agent: first, slaves with no instruction to masters; then wives followed by husbands. In 5:1–5 he reverts to the Aristotelian sequence of superordinate followed by subordinate. (2) Whereas Aristotle speaks of "rule" and "obedience" (1.6.1255b; 1.7.1255b), our author, like other NT writers, speaks of "subordination" and of "doing what is right" (slaves, wives), of husbands as "bestowing honor" on their wives, and of elders not "domineering" the flock. (3) As already observed, the verb *hypotassō* which is prominent here and in parallel NT texts is not found in the Hellenistic instances of the *oikonomia* tradition and constitutes a specific feature of the

---

[106] So also Balch 1981; Lührmann 1975; Thraede 1977a; Elliott 1981/1990, 208–20; Gielen 1990; Prostmeier 1990.

Table 1

1 Peter	*Other New Testament Passages*
2:13–17 Civil duty:	
All persons	Rom 13:1–7 1 Tim 2:1–3 Titus 3: 1–2
2:18–20 (25) Domestic duty:	
Slaves only, *oiketai*	Col 3:22–25; 4:1 (Slaves [*douloi*] and Masters) Eph 6:6–8, 9 (Slaves [*douloi*] and Masters) 1 Tim 6:1–2 (Slaves, *douloi*) Titus 2:9–10 (Slaves, *douloi*)
3:1–6 Domestic duty:	
Wives	Col 3:18 Eph 5:22–24 1 Tim 2:9–15 Titus 2:3–5 Cf. 1 Cor 14:34
3:7 Domestic duty:	
Husbands	Col 3:19 Eph 5:25–33
5:1–4 Domestic/Communal duty:	
Elders	Col 3:21 (Fathers) Eph 6:4 (Fathers) 1 Tim 5:17–19 (Elders) Cf. 1 Cor 16:15–16; 1 Tim 5:1a, 2a, 3–16; Titus 2:2–3
5:5a Domestic/Communal duty:	
Younger Persons	Col 3:20 (Children) Eph 6:1–3 (Children) Cf. 1 Tim 5:1b, 2b; Titus 2:4–6

Christian adaptation of this moral tradition, as do the various theological rationales supporting this instruction. Thus in 1 Peter the issue of order is brought explicitly into view, and the emphasis shifts notably from the householder's exercise of authority (as in Aristotle and other *oikonomia* texts) to the subordination of the social inferiors as illustrative of the mutual humility required of all the members of the household of God (3:8; 5:5b–6). (4) Of greatest significance, the Petrine author bases his instruction, not simply or mainly on the the respective roles as dictated by nature and custom, but on reverence for God (2:18; 3:2; cf. 2:13), submission to God's will (2:15, 19–20; cf. 3:4; 5:2–3), solidarity with Jesus Christ (2:21–25; 5:4) and the ancient matriarchs (3:5–6), copartnership in grace (3:7), and the concern for gaining converts (3:1)—all features that are typical of the entire believing community as the communal household of God.

Opinions vary as to the motive for the Petrine recourse to this *Oikonomia* tradition. Balch, claiming similarity between Josephus (*Ag. Ap.* 2.198–210) and 1 Peter in particular, maintained that both authors adopted this tradition to defend their respective communities against Roman suspicion that Israelites and Christians, like other eastern cults such as those of Dionysus or Isis, were reversing and undermining traditional views of order in the civil and domestic realms. To counteract these charges, these authors employed the *Oikonomia* tradition to demonstrate or urge Israelite or Christian conformity with Roman customs and values (Balch 1981, 63–116). In a somewhat related vein, Gielen (1990, 146–58) has proposed that, when at the turn of the eras, a Hellenistic "wave of female emancipation" was countered by Roman efforts at "restoration of male patriarchal authority," a body of teaching on household management emerged as a compromise position outlining the appropriate duties of husbands and wives, parents and children, owners and slaves. This mediating household management tradition was subsequently appropriated, modified, and equipped with theological rationale first by Christians of the Pauline mission field as a basis for regulating matters of internal domestic and ecclesial organization and order as well as matters of behavior in the related civil realm.

These theories suffer, however, from two serious weaknesses. First, they involve conjectures concerning the social situation (Roman fear of subversion; wave of female emancipation) that cannot be corroborated by the NT writings that employ elements of the household tradition. Second, and more seriously, both Balch and Gielen treat the function of the household codes in isolation from the material and strategy of the writings in which they are contained. They argue that the household codes were adopted in Israel and early Christianity for *apologetic* purpose—that is, to support a self-defense against those who accused Israelites and Christians of improper conduct. The codes and the NT writings in which they were included supposedly affirmed and encouraged *Christian accommodation* to Greco-Roman moral norms and styles of conduct. However the function of the code material in Josephus, Philo, and some NT writings may be judged, this is clearly not the case in 1 Peter. For here such an "accommodating" and conformity-urging aim of the code material is thoroughly incompatible with the exhortation of 1 Peter as a whole, which urges "holy nonconformity" (1:14–17) to former, preconversional modes of behavior, from which the readers/hearers have been redeemed (1:14–16, 17–18); abstinence from outsiders' vices (2:11); detachment from the conduct of Gentiles

(4:1–4); "resistance" to the Devil and the Gentiles under his thrall (5:8–9); and "standing fast in the grace of God" (5:12). Moreover, these scholars ignore the relation of the household instruction to the dominant metaphor of the community as household of God (Elliott 1981/1990, 200–266).

By contrast, when the role of this instruction is considered in conjunction with the strategy of the entire letter, a clear and coherent picture emerges. Following the depiction of the community as the family and household of God (1:3–2:10), the author utilizes elements of traditional household instruction in order to clarify how various members of the household of God are to conduct themselves honorably in both the civil and domestic realms. Where respect for authority and order is possible without compromise of one's loyalty to God, this respect ("honor" and "subordination") is appropriate. Where, however, adaptation to societal values and norms endangers exclusive commitment to God, Christ, and the brotherhood and obliterates the distinctive identity and boundaries of the Christian community, Christians are to stand fast and resist the encroachments of society, behind which stands the Devil (5:8–9). Keeping open the channels of communication between believers and nonbelievers is not to be confused with an advocacy of social assimilation (against Balch). Contacts between believers and nonbelievers are to be utilized as an opportunity for demonstrating the honorable character of the Christians and their God and are essential for recruitment to the Christian faith (2:11–12; 3:1–2). The household instruction of 1 Peter is of a piece with its portrayal of the community as the household of God. It serves to clarify areas and modes of recognizably honorable behavior that will foster the internal cohesion and stability of this household, demonstrate its respect for order, and attract erstwhile detractors to its number (cf. Elliott 1981/1990, 208–20; 1986a, 61–78).

1 Peter constitutes the sole NT example of the immediate association of civil (2:13–17) and domestic conduct (2:18–3:7; 5:1–5a) as it is found in the *Oikonomia* tradition and the only instance in which slaves are addressed first. Other NT instances of this moral tradition focus more discretely on the roles, relations, and responsibilities in the civil realm (Rom 13:1–7; 1 Tim 2:1–3; Titus 3:1–2), the domestic realm (1 Cor 16:16; Col. 3:18–4:1; Eph 5:22–6:9; Titus 2:1–10), or the ecclesial realm (1 Tim 3:1–13; 5:1–19; Titus 1:5–9; Heb 13:7, 17). In the Christian texts, the verb *hypotassō* also assumes greater prominence in this instruction.

Further features of this household management tradition as it is reflected in 2:18–25; 3:1–7; and 5:1–5a will be discussed in conjunction with these units. Familiarity with this household tradition may perhaps account for some of the material and structural similarities common to 1 Peter, Mark, *1 Clement* and Polycarp's *Letter to the Philippians* (cf. Elliott 1985, 197–98 and appended table, p. 209).[107]

[107] For research on the "household code" (*Haustafel*) and "Household Management" (*Oikonomia*) theories, see: Wilhelm 1915; Weidinger 1928; Selwyn 1947, 406–39; Spicq 1947; Dibelius 1953, 48–50, 93–96; 1955, 28–33; Rengstorf 1953, 1954; Schlier 1958, 250–88; Wendland 1958; Kähler 1959, 1960; Schroeder 1959; Strobel 1963; Daube 1966; J. W. Thompson 1966; Gülzow

For studies on 1 Pet 2:13–17, see Balch 1981, 1984, 1986; Bammel 1964–1965; A. Barr 1961; Dale 1896a; Elliott 1981/1990, 208–20; Gielen 1990; Goldstein 1973; Goppelt 1982, 161–76; Heiene 1992; Jossa 1996; Lamau 1988; Légasse 1988; Lugo Rodríguez 1991; Postmeier 1990; Puig Tarrech 1980; Richardson 1987; Schutter 1989; Sleeper 1968; S. Snyder 1991; Souček 1960; Teichert 1949; van Unnik 1955/56; J. P. Wilson 1942–1943; Winter 1988; Załęski 1984, 1985.

III. B. Honorable Subordinate Conduct in the Domestic Realm: Household Slaves and the Servant of God (2:18–25)

2:18a You household slaves:
be subordinate to [your] masters with all reverence,
18b not only to the kind and reasonable
18c but also to the cruel;
19a for this [is] creditable,
19b if one, mindful of God's will,
19c bears up under pain while suffering unjustly;
20a for what credit [is it],
20b if, when you do what is wrong and are beaten,
20c you patiently endure?
20d if, however, when you do what is right and suffer,
20e you patiently endure,
20f this [is] creditable in God's sight.
21a For to this you have been called,
21b because Christ also suffered for you,
21c leaving you an example,
21d that you should follow in his steps;
22a he "did no wrong,"
22b "nor was guile found in his mouth";

1969, 67–76; Kamlah 1970; Dupar 1971; Sampley 1971, 17–37; Crouch 1972; Goldstein 1973; Goppelt 1973, 93–106; 1993, 162–79; Schrage 1974–1975; Lillie 1974–1975; Lührmann 1975, 1980; Wicker 1975; J. T. Sanders 1975, 83–88; Balch 1977, 1981, 1982, 1984, 1986, 1988, 1992; Schweizer 1977, 1979; Thraede 1977a, 1977b, 1980; Herr 1978; Herzog 1981; Laub 1982, 1986; Legido Lopez 1982; Vogler 1982; K. Müller 1983; Schüssler Fiorenza 1983a, 243–342; Verner 1983; K. Berger 1984a, 135–41; 1984b, 1078–86; Bosetti 1986; 1987; 1990, 47–72; Elliott 1986a, 61–78; 1990, 208–20; P. Fiedler 1986; Hartman 1988; Lamau 1988, 153–230; Motyer 1989; Strecker 1989; Gielen 1990; A. McGuire 1990; Prostmeier 1990; Seim 1990; Adinolfi 1991c; C. L. Martin 1991; Malherbe 1992; von Lips 1994; Yoder 1994.

23a he, when insulted, did not insult in return;
23b when suffering, he did not threaten,
23c but rather committed his cause to the one who judges justly;
24a he "himself bore our wrongdoings" in his body on the tree,
24b so that we, having abandoned wrongdoing,
24c might live for doing what is right.
24d "By his bruise" you "have been healed."
25a For you "were straying as sheep"
25b but now "have been returned" to the Shepherd and Overseer of your lives.

INTRODUCTION

At this point in the line of thought, honorable conduct, subordination, and doing what is right remain leading themes, but attention shifts from the civic realm (2:13–17) to that of the household and the responsibilities of domestic slaves (2:18–20 [21–25]), wives (3:1–6), and husbands (3:7). This association of instruction on civic duties (2:13–17) and domestic responsibilities (2:18–3:7) is characteristic of the moral tradition on *politeia* and *oikonomia* that informs the structure and content of 2:13–3:7, as shown in the NOTES on 2:13–21 and the DETAILED COMMENT.

The unit is linked to the preceding one by several repeated or similar terms: slaves (*oiketai*, 2:18a; cf. *douloi*, 2:16); be subordinate (2:18a; cf. 2:13a); reverence, revere (2:18a; cf. 2:17); knowledge of God or God's will (2:19b; cf. 2:15a); do what is right (2:20d; cf. 2:14c, 15b); God (2:19b, 20f; cf. 2:15a, 16c, 17c). At the same time, the passage contains a number of terms that appear only here in the NT: *skolios* ("cruel," v 18), *adikōs* ("unjustly," v 19); *kleos* ("credit," v 20); *hypolimpanō* ("leaving," v 21, also absent in the LXX); *hypogrammos* ("example," v 21); *antiloidoreō* ("insult in return," v 23), and *mōlōps* ("bruise," v 24).

In terms of its structure, vv 18–25 comprise two distinct units embodying independent traditions that have been thematically united into one coherent statement:

A. Verses 18–20 constitute an exhortation to domestic servants/slaves that presents a general principle of conduct (v 18) supported by an initial rationale (vv 19–20) comprising mention of approval from God and an adaptation of a saying attributed to Jesus in Luke 6:27–36.
B. Verses 21–25 present further motivation for the exhortation of v 18, in which early Christian tradition concerning the vicarious suffering of Christ is expanded through language drawn from the fourth servant song of Isaiah (Isa 52:13–53:12).

Through this construction, the exhortation of v 18 is supported by a combined reference to God's approval and to Christ's action and example, whereby innocent suffering servants/slaves who are mindful of God's will are assured of being in solidarity with the innocent suffering servant of God.

NOTES

18a. *You household slaves* (*Hoi oiketai*). The construction of the article (*hoi*) with the nominative *oiketai* has vocative force (cf. also 3:1, 7). The persons addressed are slaves (*oiketai*) belonging to the household (*oikos*) and working as household servants (cf. Luke 16:13; Acts 10:7; Rom 14:4; Dio Chrysostom, *Orat.* 10, *Peri oiketōn*). In the LXX, *oiketēs* (56×) consistently renders the Hebrew *ʿebed* ("servant, slave"). Another term employed more frequently for "slave," *doulos*, occurs in similar early Christian master-slave instruction[108] and is used metaphorically in 1 Peter in the preceding pericope (*douloi tou theou*, 2:16).[109] The term *pais* ("youth," "servant") is another synonym (Gen 9:17; 24:5; Luke 7:7; 15:25; Ps.-Arist., *Mag. Mor.* 2.6.24; Dio Chrys. *Orat.* 10.1), a fact that assumes importance in view of the concept of the "servant of God" underlying the Christology of 2:21–25. *Oiketai*, the term used here, makes explicit the connection of these slaves to the "household" (*oikos*) and thus signals the shift of focus from the civic (2:13–17) to the related domestic realm (Elliott 1981/1990, 201–2; cf. also Selwyn 1947, 175). A linguistically related word, *oikonomoi* ("household stewards"), appears later as a metaphorical designation of *all* the believers of the household of God (4:10).

The issue of master-slave relations was an integral part of the household management (*oikonomia*) tradition[110] and is also addressed in NT writings that, like 1 Peter, reflect familiarity with this tradition.[111] Unlike its closest NT parallels (Eph 6:5–9 and Col 3:22–4:1), however, 1 Peter not only employs the term *oiketai* rather than *douloi* but also makes no mention of the reciprocal responsibilities of masters (i.e., owners) and concentrates attention on the servants/slaves alone. Whereas it was asserted that "the slave has no deliberative faculty" (Aristotle, *Pol.* 1.5.6; but cf. 1.5.11) and thus was not a free moral agent, the Petrine author, like other Christian writers (Eph 6:5–9; Col 3:22–25; cf. Titus 2:9–10), directly addresses slaves with a line of reasoning that presumes both their deliberative faculty and their moral responsibility. A further remarkable difference in this Petrine address to slaves is that it *commences* rather than concludes the instruction concerning household groups. This contrasts with the instructions in Ephesians, Colossians, 1 Timothy, and Titus,

---

[108] See Eph 6:5–9; Col 3:22–4:1; 1 Tim 6:1–2; Titus 2:9–10; *Did.* 4:10–11; Ign. *Pol.* 4:3; cf. 1 Cor 7:21–22.

[109] For the verb *douleuō* used with *oiketēs*, see Luke 16:13.

[110] E.g., Arist., *Pol.* 1.2.2–23; 5.1–12; Ps.-Arist., *Oec.* 5.1–6; Xen., *Oec.* 3.4; 12.1–14.10; Ps.-Phoc. 223–27.

[111] See Eph 5:21–6:9; Col 3:18–4:6; 1 Tim 5:1–6:2; Titus 2:1–10; cf. also *Did.* 4:9–11; Ign. *Pol.* 4:1–5:2.

which follow the more traditional sequence of the *oikonomia* tradition (husband-wife/parents-children/masters-slaves). This alteration, as will become clear, signals the unusual pride of place that our author attributes to the household slaves as paradigms for the entire household of faith.

Slaves in the period of Roman imperial rule formed the major part of the empire's labor force and the basis of its "slave economy." Roman Italy alone was home to 5–6,000,000 free citizens and 1–2,000,000 slaves (Veyne 1987, 33). The city of Rome itself at the end of the first century, it is estimated, included 400,000 slaves among its general population of 1,200,000 persons (Carcopino 1971, 74). Various factors account for the abundant supply of slaves at this time, including centuries of warfare and enslavement of the conquered; enslavement as a result of oppressive taxation and inability to pay off debts; abduction and sale into slavery; birth into slavery; sale into slavery of freeborn children or exposed infants; and voluntary enslavement as a means of procuring citizenship subsequent to manumission.

Because they lacked freedom, slaves were ipso facto disqualified from citizenship. They had no civil rights and could neither marry nor bear legitimate children, nor were there any legal limits on the punishment that could be inflicted upon them by their owners. Regarded and treated as chattel, they were branded, mutilated, castrated, raped, and subjected to the will and whim of their masters, including their physical and sexual abuse. Forcibly severed from their families and home and regarded as overgrown children, they were deprived of all honor and all means of support, except from their owners. They constituted the lowest rank of the household and of the general population, apart from foreigners and impoverished day laborers.

Israelite legislation, however, appears to have been designed to accord slaves some minimal forms of protection. Israelites who had sold themselves into slavery, for instance, nevertheless were to be treated as wage-earning guests (Lev 25:40) and were to be released after six years (Exod 21:2–6; Deut 15:1–6) and during the Jubilee, the fiftieth year (Lev 25:10–17). Moreover, slaves who were injured by their masters were to be set free (Exod 21:26–27); killing of slaves was punishable (Exod 21:20–21); and the life of a slave was to be considered on a par with the life of a free Israelite. In general, the treatment of slaves was to be motivated by the fact that, as God liberated Israelites, who were *oiketai*, from their "house of slavery" (*oikos douleias*) in Egypt, so Israelites should also show compassion to the slaves in their midst (Lev 25:35–55; cf. Exod 22:21; 23:9).

Slaves were used for the most physically demanding types of labor in agriculture, shipping (galley-slaves doing the rowing), mining, and construction work. In the domestic realm, where they formed part of the extended household (Gk.: *oikos*; Lat.: *familia*) under the complete control of the male head (*paterfamilias*), domestic slaves (*oiketai*) assisted the paterfamilias in his household management (*oikonomia*), occasionally also serving as nurses, tutors, and teachers of the young (Philo, *Spec.* 2.232). In Asia Minor the majority of slaves were used for such household purposes (Broughton 1938, 691, 840).

The number of domestic slaves (*oiketai, familiae serviles*) varied from 1 or 2 in families of simple means to 400 in wealthier households (Tacitus, *Ann.* 14.43) to over 4,000 in the home of one freed slave (Pliny, *Nat.* 33.135). The imperial household (*domus Caesari*) may have had as many as 20,000 slaves (cf. Carcopino 1971, 77–79).

Emancipation was a possibility through manumission granted by slave owners or through the slaves' purchasing their own freedom. In the Roman period, most urban and domestic slaves could anticipate being emanicipated by the age of 30. Such freedmen and freedwomen (*liberti, libertae*; *apeleutheroi*) assumed the name of their former owners and along with their progeny remained indebted to their former owners as clients who owed their patrons continued support and allegiance. The Emperor Claudius began the imperial strategy of using such freedmen in imperial administrative positions and thereby securing the personal loyalty of such administrators.

In addition to numerous freedmen (listed by Kyrtatas 1987, 73), there were many slaves among the ranks of the early Christians, perhaps the most well known being Onesimus in the household of Philemon. Jesus alluded frequently to slaves in his teaching (Matt 18:23–34; 24:45–51; Luke 14:15–24; 15:11–32; 17:7–10; 20:9–19; etc.), and Paul addressed the situation of slaves in his letter to the Corinthians (1 Cor 7:21–24; cf. Bartchy 1973) as well as in his missive to Philemon. The ransoming of slaves was counted among the Christian works of mercy (*1 Clem.* 55:2; Herm. *Mand.* 8.10), although the bishop Ignatius advises that slaves should be prepared to "endure slavery to the glory of God, that they may obtain a better freedom from God. Let them not desire to be set free at the Church's expense, that they be not found the slaves of lust" (Ign. *Pol.* 4.3). However, among the early Christians, as for the general population, "slavery as an institution was taken for granted and not questioned" (Osiek 1992), with the singular exceptions of the Essenes (Josephus, *Ant.* 18.18–22; Philo, *Prob.* 79) and the Egyptian Therapeutae (Philo, *Contempl.* 70). Paul speaks of the slave and the free person being one in Christ Jesus but never of the elimination of slavery itself. From a practical and political point of view, the messianic movement as a tiny minority was hardly in a position to alter this general situation. Christian teaching, at best, attempted to humanize slave-master relationships. Perhaps many shared the eschatological perspective of Paul on the matter that everyone should "remain in the state in which he was called . . . for the form of this world is passing away" (1 Cor 7:20, 31). It may also be that Christian slaves were encouraged to seek the "inner freedom" and spiritual indifference to external constraints of which the Greek moralists spoke (Socrates, Menander, Bion, Epictetus; cf. Philo, *Prob.*; 1 Cor 7:22–23; and Ign. *Pol.* 4:3). But the constraints themselves remained firmly intact, as odious as this might strike the modern reader. Only in the fourth century, under Constantine, were edicts first passed (316, 321 CE) declaring that Christians could emancipate the slaves of their own churches (Kyrtatas 1987, 70). Yet Augustine was still of the conviction that domestic tranquility in the "earthly city" required the obedience of wives to husbands, children to parents, and slaves to masters (*City of God* 19.14).

be subordinate to your masters (*hypotassomenoi . . . tois despotais*). The verb *hypotassomenoi* continues the stress on subordination begun in 2:13 and here refers to a specific instance of this conduct in the domestic sphere. This participle is unaccompanied by a main verb and functions as an imperative, as is the case with other such imperatival participles elsewhere in the letter (1:14b; 2:1; 3:1, 7, 9; 4:8, 10; on this usage, see the NOTE on 1:14b). As in 2:13–14, 3:1–6, and 5:1–5a, the advocacy of subordination is based on a conventional notion of social order that requires the subordination of the socially inferior to those in authority, here of domestic slaves to their masters/owners (cf. Titus 2:9; *Did.* 4:11). According to Aristotle in his comments on household management, the relation of master and slave is one of "authority and subordination, conditions [that] are not only inevitable but expedient" (Arist., *Pol.* 1.2.8; cf. 1.2.15); this relationship, moreover, is one that has been established by nature (*Pol.* 1.2.7, 8, 13, 15). This sentiment appears to have been the prevailing one in the social world of the NT as well, where the subordination of slaves to their masters was presumed to be a given feature of the social order. The kind of subordination (cf. Titus 2:9) that Christian slaves, as owned non-kin, render to their owners is obedience (cf. Eph 6:5; Col 3:22; 1 Tim 6:1) and submission to their authority rather than any kind of loyalty (which would presume some form of kin commitment).

The term *despotai* ("masters," actually "owners") designated persons who had complete power or authority over others, including householders who possessed slaves as chattel, a "live article of property" (Arist., *Pol.* 1.2.4; cf. Ps.-Arist., *Oec.* 5.1). For its occurrence in master-slave exhortation, see also 1 Tim 6:1–2; Titus 2:9; compare the subscript of Philemon in a few manuscripts (L 326 1241): "To Philemon and Aphia, masters of Onesimus. . . ."[112] The possessive pronoun "your" (masters), absent in most manuscripts, is implied by the use of the nominative *hoi oiketai* as a vocative. Its presence in a few manuscripts (א z vg^{mss} syr^{p} cop) is most likely a secondary clarifying addition.

There is no indication whether these masters/owners were Christian or not. As a general rule, slaves were obligated to the religion of their owners. The fact that 1 Peter contains no instruction for slave owners[113] and provides no indication of their religious allegiance would suggest that pagan masters are assumed. In any case, the effect of no further comment on the masters (except their qualities, v 18bc) is to focus attention exclusively on the behavior of the servants/slaves.

with all reverence (*en panti phobōi*). The term *phobos* could imply a fear of masters similar to that mentioned by Pseudo-Aristotle (*Oec.* 3.3), who con-

---

[112] For the juxtaposition of *oiketai-despotai*, see also Prov 22:7; Ps.-Arist., *Mag. Mor.* 1.33.15–56; 3.17.2.

[113] The same is the case in 1 Cor 7:21–23 and Titus 2:9, in contrast to Ephesians, Colossians, and *Didache*.

trasted the fear of the virtuous toward their superiors with the fear "felt by slaves for masters and by subjects for despots who treat them with injustice and wrong," a fear associated not with reverence and modesty but with "hostility and hatred." However, *phobos* was already used by our author in conjunction with God (1:17), who is also the object of the verb *phobeō* in 2:17. Consequently, it is best taken here (and 3:2) to denote not "fear of" or "deference to" (NRSV) owners but *reverence* for God, in line with the focus on seeking "credit" from God (vv 19a, 20f) and being mindful of God's will (v 19b; cf. also 2:15).[114] The domestic slaves are to be subordinate, then, not because of fear or force and not in pretense (*ophthalmodouleia*, Col 3:21), but because of their reverence for God and anticipation of divine approval (cf. *m. ʾAbot* 1:3).

18b. *not only to the kind and reasonable* (*ou monon tois agathois kai epieikesin*). Respect for the masters' authority is required by their status, not their demeanor. Obedience to the "kind" (*agathois*) and "reasonable" (*epieikesin*)—that is, to those who treat their slaves justly and humanely[115]—is less problematic than obedience to the cruel and unscrupulous.

18c. *but also to the cruel* (*alla kai tois skoliois*). "Also" (*kai*), absent in a few manuscripts including 𝔓[72], is nevertheless implied by the foregoing "not only" (*ou monon*) and here can have the sense of "even."

The word *skolios* ("cruel," lit., "crooked") is rarely used of persons in Classical Greek but in the LXX qualifies a generation as "crooked" (Deut 32:5; cf. the allusions in Acts 2:40 and Phil 2:15), in that it deviates from God's justice. The sense of "unjust" would fit here in the light of "suffering unjustly" (v 19c) and "suffer though doing what is right" (v 20d). But as a contrast to the qualities mentioned in v 18b, it probably describes masters who are unfair, cruel, or harsh, and inflict "pain" (v 19c).

The treatment of slaves is an issue conventionally discussed in instruction on household management (*oikonomia*). Thus Pseudo-Aristotle (*Oec.* 1.5–6) notes:

> Of property (*tōn de ktēmatōn*), the first and most indispensable kind is that which is also best and most amenable to household management (*oikonomatikōtaton*) and this is human chattel (*anthrōpos*). Our first step is to procure good slaves. Of slaves (*doulōn*) there are two kinds: those in positions of trust (*epitropos*) and the laborers (*ergatēs*). . . . In our interaction with slaves we must neither suffer them to be insolent nor treat them with cruelty. A share of honor should be given to those who are doing more of a freeman's work, and abundance of food to those who are laboring with their hands. . . . We may apportion to our slaves work, chastisement, and food. If men are given food but no chastisement nor any work, they become insolent. If they are made to work, and are chastised, but stinted of food, such

[114] See, similarly, Eph 6:5–8; Col 3:22–25 [Christ]; and *Did.* 4:11.

[115] On the just and compassionate treatment of slaves, see Seneca, *Clem.* 1.18; Philo, *Decal.* 167; *Spec.* 1.126–28; 3.136–43; Eph 6:9; Col 4:1.

> treatment is oppressive and saps their strength. The remaining alternative, therefore, is to give them work, and a sufficiency of food. Unless we pay men, we cannot control them; and food is a slave's pay.[116]

Verses 19–20, introduced by the conjunction *gar* ("for"), expand on the foregoing thought and provide the first of two motivations for the subordination urged in v 18 (the second of which is supplied in vv 21–25). The structure of these verses involves a carefully crafted inclusion embracing forms of both synonymous and antithetical parallelism contrasting unjust and just suffering. Verse 19 states a general principle ("one"), which is then applied specifically to the servants/slaves ("you") in v 20.

19a. *for this* [*is*] (*touto gar*). The conjunction "for" (*gar*) introduces a statement (vv 19–20) that provides motivation and support for the preceding imperative (v 18). The repetition of "this [is] creditable" (*touto charis*) in v 20f forms an inclusion with v 19a that frames the entire statement. Thus the demonstrative neuter pronoun *touto* ("this"), which can refer to either the foregoing imperative (v 18a) or the conditional statement that follows (v 19bc), in effect refers here to both related actions. An "is" is implied in the ellipses of vv 19a, 20a, and 20f.

creditable (*charis*). Elsewhere in 1 Peter and other NT writings, *charis* denotes the "grace" or unmotivated "graciousness" of God. In this particular context, however, *charis* (vv 19a, 20f) describes a human action of one who is *mindful of God's will* (v 19c) or a human action that is *creditable* "in God's sight" (v 20f). The parallelism of vv 19–20 indicates that *charis* functions as a synonym of *kleos* ("credit," v 20a; cf. "one is approved" [RSV]); "it is a credit" [NRSV]). This usage is classical (Sophocles, *Ajax* 522) but occurs also in a Lukan version of a saying of Jesus (Luke 6:32–34), where the expression *poia hymin charis esti* asks "what credit do you have (for doing good)?" (6:33; see the parallel *misthos*, "reward" (from God), in Luke 6:35; cf. Matt 5:46). Variations on this saying (*Did.* 1:3–5; Ign. *Pol.* 2:1; 2 *Clem.* 13:4) employ *charis* with this same sense (cf. also Herm. *Mand.* 5.1.5). Bigg (1902, 143–44) appropriately warns against attempting to harmonize the meaning of *charis* here with its sense in Paul and underscores its "secular" sense here as identifying something that is "thankworthy" or praiseworthy.[117] Goppelt's argumentation (1993, 199–201) for "grace," on the other hand, is typical of theologizing interpretations. The additional words "in God's sight" (*para tōi theōi*; cf. *para theōi*, v 20f) or "with respect to God" (*theōi*) found in some manuscripts are likely scribal additions meant to further explicate the parallelism of v 19a and v 20f.

[116] Regarding the treatment of slaves/servants in Israelite tradition, see Exod 21:2–11, 26–27; Prov 30:10; Sir 7:20–21; 33:30–31; *Ps.-Phoc.* 223–26; Philo, *Spec.* 1.126–28; 3.136–43; on the physical discipline of slaves, see the NOTE on v 20b.

[117] For similar usage, see also Luke 17:9 (a slave's credit) and Acts 2:27; 7:46 (credit/favor in the eyes of men or God). On the social implications of *charis* as a basic concept of the patron-client relationship underlying the God-human relationship, see Pilch and Malina 1993, 83–86.

19b. *if one* (*ei . . . tis*). This is the first of three conditional ("if," *ei*) clauses (cf. v 20b, d) in which creditable behavior (v 19b, v 20d) is clarified in contrast to conduct incurring no divine approval. This first clause states a general principle with an indefinite "one" (*tis*) as its subject.

mindful of God's will (*dia syneidēsin theou*). The phrase, literally, "out of (or because of) mindfulness of God," is without parallel in the NT and has prompted diverse scribal variants. Some witnesses (C 323 614 etc. syr) lack *theou* and read *syneidēsin agathēn*, "good/sound mindfulness." Other manuscripts contain the fuller reading, *syneidēsin theou agathēn* (A* Ψ 33) or *syneidēsin agathēn theou* ($\mathfrak{P}^{72, 81}$), "sound mindfulness of God." While the earliest witness ($\mathfrak{P}^{72}$) might represent the original text, with *agathen* subsequently inadvertently omitted through *homoeoteleuton* in later manuscripts (*syneidēsin agathēn*), it is also possible that *agathēn* was added secondarily under the influence of the formulation *syneidēsis agathē* (cf. 1 Pet 3:16, 21; Acts 23:1; and 1 Tim 1:5, 19). The fact that the briefer reading, *syneidēsin theou*, also has the strongest manuscript support (א A^2 B K L P most minuscules vg cop eth John Dam.) tips the balance in favor of its acceptance here. In the NT, *syneidēsis* has a range of meanings (Stelzenberger 1961, 94–95) including both "consciousness," "awareness of,"[118] and "conscience" in the sense of sensitivity to external norms or opinion (Acts 24:16; Rom 2:15; 2 Cor 4:2). This conception of "conscience," it should be noted, differs markedly from the modern psychological notion of conscience as an interior moral faculty. In the group-oriented culture of antiquity and its dyadic personality structure, assessment of self and of behavior was made in reference to the opinion of others, either one's primary group or God.[119] In 1 Peter (also 3:16, 21), as elsewhere in the NT (e.g., Acts 23:1; 24:15; Rom 9:1; 1 Tim 1:18–19; 2 Tim 3:1; Heb 13:18), *syneidēsis* implies not merely knowledge of God but also sensitivity to the divine will concerning conduct, or "compliance with God's will" (van Unnik 1983, 344–46; Brox 1986, 133).[120] For this reason the translation "mindful of God's will" is preferred (see also the explicit and related appeal to God's will in 2:15; 3:17; 4:2, 19). The phrase, introduced by *dia* ("because of," "out of"), modifies the verb that immediately follows it, "bears up under," and "provides a fortifying motive for the patient endurance of injustice" (Selwyn 1947, 177 and on *syneidēsis*, pp. 176–78). It likewise anticipates the following expressions, "credit" (*kleos*) and "creditable (*charis*) in God's sight."

19c. *bears up under* (*hypopherei*). The composite verb *hypopherō* ("bear" [*phero*] + "up under" [*hypo-*] a weight) can mean, metaphorically, "to submit to or endure danger, affliction, or injustice." It occurs in the LXX and literary Greek but only here in the NT (cf. 2 Macc 7:36; *1 Clem.* 5:4; 14:1; Herm. *Vis.* 3.1.9; 3.2.1; *Mand.* 10.8; 12.4.1; *Sim.* 7.4, 6). It is virtually identical in meaning

[118] See 1 Cor 8:7, 10,12; 10:25–29; Rom 2:15; 2 Cor 5:11; 1 Tim 1:5; Titus 1:15; Heb 9:9, 14; 10:2.

[119] See Malina 1993d, 63–89; Neyrey, ed. 1991, 67–96; Malina and Neyrey 1996, 153–201, esp. 183–87.

[120] See, in general, Zucker 1928; Pierce 1955; Stelzenberger 1961, 45–49.

with the similar composite and parallel verb *hypomenō* (v 20a, e), and both verbs involve the same preposition (*hypo-*) as in the composite *hypotassō*.

pain (*lypas*). The Greek *lypas* (also "grief," "affliction") recalls the related verb, *lypēthentes* (1:6, "you are afflicted"), describing the condition of all the believers. For the same phrase, see Herm. *Mand.* 10.2.6 (*lypēn hypopherei*, "endures grief").

while suffering unjustly (*paschōn adikōs*). Aristotle denied that a master's relation to chattel (slaves, property, children) was a matter of justice (*Eth. nic.* 5.10.8), but not so Israel (see Philo, *Spec.* 3.136–43) or the early Christians, who regarded slaves as human and therefore deserving of humane and just treatment. The experience of suffering unjustly (*paschōn adikōs*), here on the part of servants/slaves (also v 20d), will be stressed again in regard to Christ (2:21, 23; 3:18; 4:1; cf. also 1:11; 4:13; 5:1) and all the believers (3:14, 17; 4:19; 5:9, 10). In introducing this major theme of undeserved suffering in connection with the servants/slaves, the author presents slaves as paradigmatic of the entire community; their solidarity with the suffering of the innocent Christ (vv 21–24) is that of all innocent believers who share in this suffering (4:1, 13).

20a. *for* (*gar*). A repeated *gar* (cf. v 19a) introduces a statement that elaborates on the foregoing verse and applies its principle to the servants/slaves; for such explanatory twofold *gar* statements, see Matt 10:19–20; Luke 8:29; John 5:21–22, 46; Acts 2:15.

what credit [*is it*] (*poion . . . kleos*). The noun *kleos* occurs only here in the NT (and only in Job 28:22; 30:8 in the LXX) but in extrabiblical Greek belongs to the semantic field of terms for "honor" (*timē*) and its equivalents, such as "good report," "fame," "praise" (Plato, *Leg.* 633 A; Vermeulen 1981, 198). Like *charis*, which it parallels in this context, it denotes "credit," here in the sight of God. With the substitution of *kleos* for *charis*, the question *poion gar kleos* echoes the Lukan version of the Jesus saying concerning the doing of good to others and its question: *poia hymin charis*, "what credit is it to you?" (Luke 6:32, 33, 34; cf. also *Did.* 1:3, *poia gar charis*). The form of Jesus' sayings concerning love of enemies (Matt 5:43–48/Luke 6:27–30), nonretribution (Matt 5:43–48 and Luke 6:27–28, 32–36), and the golden rule (Matt 7:12/Luke 6:31) was fluid, not fixed. The structure and language of 1 Pet 2:19–20 are closest to, though not identical with, elements of the Lukan version of the saying regarding love of enemies (Luke 6:32–36). Each text states a principle for conduct (Luke 6:31 [declarative] / 1 Pet 2:19 [question]), followed by or including (1 Pet 2:19c) contrastive conditional clauses (Luke 6:32, 33, 34; 1 Pet 2:20bc, 20de) and a concluding statement (Luke 6:35–36/1 Pet 2:20f). The common vocabulary concerns the term *charis* ("credit," Luke 6:32, 33, 34/1 Pet 2:19a, 20f; cf. *misthos* [Luke 6:34] and *kleos* [1 Pet 2:20a, 20f]), the similar expressions *poia charis estin* (Luke 6:32, 33, 34) and *poion kleos* (1 Pet 2:20a), and the verb "doing what is right" (*agathopoieō*, Luke 6:33 [2×], 35; 1 Pet 2:20d). Terms from the same root occur in both (*hamartōloi*, Luke 6:32, 33, 34; *hamartanō*, 1 Pet 2:20b) but possibly with different senses (Luke: "sinners"; 1 Peter: "doing wrong"). Ultimately, the texts of Luke and 1 Peter have different thrusts, despite their similarities. 1 Peter 2:19–20 represents a substantial modification of a Hellenized version of the Jesus saying as found in Luke. Its aim is to motivate subordination and doing what is right, despite suffering for it, by appealing to what is creditable in God's sight.

20b. *if, when you do what is wrong* (*ei hamartanontes*). The first of two parallel conditional statements (v 20bc/20de) is a rhetorical question that presumes a negative answer; that is, no credit is due you for enduring a beating administered for wrongdoing. The pres. part. *hamartanontes*, in this context, refers primarily to "wrongdoing" in the eyes of masters, to which they respond with punishment, rather than referring to "sin" (as violation of God's will; cf. similarly van Unnik 1956, 100). However, since its parallel antonym, "do what is right" (*agathopoiountes*, v 20d; cf. 2:14; 3:6, 11, 17; 4:19), can also involve what is "right" in the sight of God (cf. also 2:14; 3:6, 11, 17; 4:19) as well as society, and, since its related noun *hamartia* in vv 21a and 24a also involves violation of divine ordinances ("sin"), the verb allows both implications.

and are beaten (*kai kolaphizomenoi*). The participle *kolaphizomenoi*, because of its superior manuscript support (א B C vg), is preferred over the similar-sounding variant *kolazomenoi* ("you are punished," in 𝔓^{72} א^{2} P Ψ), although the sense remains the same: the beating is punishment for wrongful conduct (cf. *Diogn.* 5:16, *hōs kakoi kolazomenoi*). Old Testament comments on the discipline of slaves reflect prevailing views; on the corporal punishment and torture of slaves, see Exod 21:26–27; Prov 29:19–21; Sir 23:10 ("a servant who is continually examined under torture will not lack bruises"); Sir 33:24–25, 26 ("Yoke and thong bow the neck and for a wicked servant there are racks and tortures . . . if he does not obey, make his fetters heavy"); see also Luke 12:45–47 (slaves severely beaten). The severity and anger that Greco-Roman masters often unleashed on their slaves were well known. In his discourse *On Anger*, Seneca criticized such cruel treatment: "You may take (a slave) in chains and at your pleasure expose him to every test of endurance; but too great violence in the striker has often dislocated a joint, or left a sinew fastened in the very teeth it has broken. Anger has left many a man crippled, many disabled, even when it found its victim submissive" (*Ira* 3.27.3).[121] In view of the fact that vv 22–24 recall the conduct of Jesus in his passion, it is noteworthy that the verb *kolaphizō* used here is also used in the description of the beating of Jesus prior to his execution (Matt 26:67/Mark 14:65); compare with the beating of Paul (1 Cor 4:11–12; 2 Cor 12:7).

20c. *you patiently endure?* (*hypomeneite*). The verb *hypomeneite* ("hold out," "patiently endure") is parallel to and synonymous with the foregoing verb, *hypopherei* (v 19c). Its future tense here and in v 20e has better manuscript attestation (א* A B C 049 𝔐 lat) than the present tense verb in some manuscripts, used in either or both places. Implied is the temporal sequence of present

[121] On the unjust suffering of slaves, see Sen., *Ep.* 47, and on the torture of slaves giving evidence, Brunt 1980 and Sir 23:10.

suffering that endures into the future. Like its accompanying *hypo-* composites (*hypotassomenoi, hypopherei*), all of which constitute another example of alliteration, *hypomeneite* also underscores the inferior position of the slaves.

20d. *if, however, when you do what is right and suffer* (*all' ei agathopoiountes kai paschontes*). Verse 20de forms the positive antithesis (*alla*, "however") to v 20bc; v 20def rephrases v 19. Thus, "when you do what is right and suffer" contrasts to "when you do what is wrong and are beaten." Both participles (*agathopoiountes, paschontes*), literally, "doing what is right and suffering," are subordinate to and prior in time to the main verb, "patiently endure," as is the case in the parallel construction of v 20bc. "Do what is right" (*agathopoinountes*) sounds a recurrent theme of the letter (2:14, 15; 3:6, 11, 17; 4:19; cf. 2:12; 3:2), as does the contrast of doing what is wrong and doing what is right (2:14; 3:11–12, 17; 4:14–16; cf. 2:11–12 and 4:2–3; cf. *Diog.* 5:16). "Suffering" (*paschontes*) when doing what is right, in turn, parallels "suffering unjustly" (*paschōn adikōs*, v 19bc) and typifies the fundamental dilemma faced not only by servants/slaves but by the addressees in general (3:14, 17; 4:1, 19; 5:10) as well as by their suffering Lord (2:21b, 23b; 3:18; 4:1; cf. 1:11; 4:13; 5:1). The contrast between deserved and undeserved suffering is also repeated in 3:13–17 and 4:14–16 in regard to the entire community.

20e. *you patiently endure* (*hypomeneite*). The future verb of v 20c is repeated and in the light of v 20d has the sense of "patiently endure" in the face of unjust treatment (as in Mark 13:13/Matt 24:9b–13; Rom 12:12; 2 Tim 2:10, 12; Heb 10:32; 12:2, 3, 7; Jas 1:12). It is not so much the idea of patient endurance that is central here, however, but the object that is endured; namely, suffering while doing what is right (cf. 3:14 and 4:16). In later writings, endurance itself in the face of affliction is given noticeably greater stress.[122]

20f. *this* [*is*] *creditable in God's sight* (*touto charis para theōi*). This final clause again underlines God's approval as the chief criterion for conduct. The term *charis* completes the thought of action creditable before God (vv 19a [*charis*], 20a [*kleos*]) and, in forming an inclusion (vv 19a/20f), concludes the first motivation for the imperative in v 18. Similar references to God's perspective on conduct are made in 3:4 ("very precious in God's sight") and 4:6 ("according to God's standard"), and similar positive assessments of innocent suffering are given again in 3:14, 17; and 4:12–16. Servants/slaves, in sum, are to be subordinate to their masters, not because this is simply their obligation as slaves or because of terror, but because of reverence for God and mindfulness of God's will and approval.

Verses 21–25 are joined syntactically and thematically with vv 18–20. The opening phrase, *for to this you have been called* (v 21a), refers retrospectively to the action enjoined in vv 18–20 and introduces a second, Christological motivation for the recommended behavior. Further syntactic, semantic, and

---

[122] See *1 Clem.* 34:8; 35:3, 4; 45:8; *2 Clem.* 1:2; 11:5; 17:7; *Did.* 16:5; *Barn.* 5:1, 2, 6, 12; 14:4; Ign. *Smyrn.* 4:2; 9:2; *Magn.* 1:3; 9:2; *Pol.* 3:1, 12; Herm. *Vis.* 2.2.7; Pol. *Phil.* 1:2; 8:1; 9:1; *Diogn.* 2:9; 5:5; 10:8; *Mart. Pol.* 2.2.4; 2.3; 13.3.

thematic links with the foregoing include: *also* (2:21b); innocent *suffering* (2:21, 22–23/2:19c, 20d); *example* (2:21c); *doing what is wrong* (2:22a, 24a,b/2:20b; *justly-unjustly* (2:23c/2:19c) and *just conduct* (2: 24c); commitment to God (2:23c), *reverence* for God (2:18), God's approval (2:19–20); and the relation of Christ as obedient servant of God with domestic servants/slaves. Elements of early Christian tradition (kerygmatic formulas concerning the vicarious suffering and death of Christ and tradition concerning discipleship) have been expanded through language derived from the book of Isaiah, one of the author's favorite OT writings. This material, drawn from Isaiah's portrait of God's suffering servant (Isa 52:13–53:12), is used to portray Christ as God's innocent suffering servant, who is then presented as both an example and an enabler for the conduct of the servants/slaves. This Christological unit, with its four relative clauses (vv 22, 23, 24abc, 24d) modifying Christ (v 21b), is framed by the inclusion formed by its opening and closing verses (vv 21 and 25). Though this Christological portrait is associated here specifically with household servants, affinities between this passage and other parts of the letter indicate that what is said here to household servants is true for the suffering community as a whole.

21a. *For* (*gar*). The conjunction "for" (*gar*) again (cf. vv 19a, 20a) introduces a statement (vv 21–25) that also supports the initial imperative of v 18 but that now cites the innocent suffering of Jesus Christ and his doing what was right as an illustration of the behavior and innocent suffering urged in vv 18–20. A final statement beginning with *gar* (v 25) completes vv 21–25 so that these two *gar* statements form an inclusion embracing vv 21–25 (Bosetti 1990, 87).

to this (*eis touto*). The reference is to some action of the foregoing (vv 18–20), either doing what is right and enduring undeserved suffering (Bigg 1902, 145) or, more generally, behavior mindful of God's will (Selwyn 1947, 178–79), both of which are illustrated in the description of Christ's behavior that follows. See the similar construction of 3:9d referring to 3:8–9c.

you have been called (*eklēthēte*). The verb is passive and implies God as subject; see elsewhere where God is the one who calls believers (1:15; 2:9; 5:10). This divine calling may well allude to the servants' hearing of the good news (1:12, 25) and their subsequent conversion and baptism. A repetition of the entire phrase *for to this you have been called* occurs in 3:9d with reference to all of the believers. Here, however, this calling is linked to and mediated through the vicarious suffering of Christ (v 21b).

21b. *because Christ also* (*hoti kai Christos*). This phrase, along with what follows, describes the Christological nature and basis of the divine calling and provides a further Christological ground for the ethical injunction of 2:18; see the similar function of its recurrence in 3:18a.

also (*kai*, with stronger MSS support for its inclusion than its exclusion;[123] cf. 3:18). The word serves here, as in 2:5a; 3:18a; and 4:1b, to express explicitly the relation between Christ and believers, here the commonality between Christ

[123] Probably through haplography: *hoti kai Christos.*

who suffered innocently and innocently suffering servants/slaves. A similar association of *diakonoi* and Christ the *diakonos* occurs in Pol. *Phil.* 5:2–3 (cf. also Mark 10:43–45/Matt 20:26–28/Luke 22:26–27, a tradition also reflected in 1 Pet 5:1–5a).

suffered for you (*epathen hyper hymōn*). Suffering slaves can bear their unjust suffering (2:19–20), the author assures them, first, because Christ, their Lord, also "suffered" (*epathen*) innocently and second, because he suffered vicariously on their behalf ("for you," *hyper hymōn*), an interpretation of suffering repeated later in the letter in regard to all of the believers (3:13–4:1; 4:12–16). The expression "Christ suffered for you" is unique in the NT. The manuscript evidence varies in regard to the verb (*epathen* ["suffered"] or *apethanen* ["died"]), the preposition (*hyper* or *peri*), and the plural forms ("your" [*hymōn*] and "you" [*hymin*] or "our" [*hēmon*] and "us" [*hēmin*]). In each case, the former of the two readings is supported by both superior external evidence and internal consistency.

The reading *epathen* (𝔓[72] A B C 33 81 etc. vg syr[h] cop) was replaced by *apethanen* in other witnesses (𝔓[81] ℵ Ψ 209* 2127 syr[p] arm), probably under the influence of the more common formulation "(Christ) died for our sins"; note the similar variation in 3:18. The earliest attestation of this formula is 1 Cor 15:3: *Christos apethanen hyper tōn harmartiōn hēmōn* (identified by Paul as already pre-Pauline in origin); for the construction "Christ (he) died for us," [*Christos*] *apethanen hyper hēmōn*, see also Rom 5:8; compare Rom 5:6 ("for the godless"); Rom 14:15 ("for whom"); 2 Cor 5:14, 15 ("for all"); and other related instances of "die" + *hyper* (as "for, on behalf of"): John 11:50, 51; 18:14; Rom 5:7 (2×). The similar formulation of "died" with the related preposition *peri* ("on behalf of") occurs in 1 Thess 5:10 (["our Lord Jesus Christ] died on our behalf"). In 1 Pet 3:18 the prepositions *peri* and *hyper* are used synonymously: "Christ suffered once for/on behalf of (*peri*) sins, a just one for (*hyper*) unjust ones. . . ." The construction of *pathein* with *hyper* (see also Ign. *Smyrn.* 7:1; *Mart. Pol.* 17:2) occurs elsewhere in the NT only in Acts 9:16; Phil 1:29; and 2 Thess 1:5, but in these instances *hyper* has the sense of "because of" rather than "on behalf of"; see also, however, Col 1:24, where *pathemata hyper hymōn* refers to Paul's sufferings "on behalf of" the Colossians. For equivalent expressions, see also *peri hamartiōn epathen* ("suffered for sins," 1 Pet 3:18a), *pathein heneka hēmōn* ("suffer for our sake," 2 *Clem.* 1:2), or *pathein tēs psychēs hēmōn* ("suffer for our life," *Barn.* 5:5).[124]

From this evidence, three things are clear. (1) The earliest and more frequently occurring formulation involves the verb "die" with *hyper* and thereby designates Christ's death as vicarious. Versnel (1989, 182) contends that *hyper* does not denote "in the place of" but has a military meaning: "in defense of," "in protection of." But this sense fails to fit v 24. (2) In formulations involving

[124] For further related instances of *hyper* in the sense of "for, on behalf of," see Mark 14:24; Rom 8:32; 1 Cor 5:7; Gal 2:20; 3:13; Eph 5:25; 1 Tim 2:6; Titus 2:14; Heb 2:9; 6:20; 1 John 3:16.

Christ's vicarious death, *hyper* and *peri* are virtually synonymous. (3) In the tradition, the object of the prepositions varies ("for us," "for [our] sins," "for many," "for you").

The Petrine author's preference for "suffered" rather than "died" is explained (1) by the connection he wishes to establish between the suffering of the servants/slaves (2:19–20) and the suffering of Christ and (2) by the central focus on suffering throughout the letter. The verb *paschō* (employed 12× in the letter—more than any other NT writing) appears three further times with Christ as subject (2:23; 3:18; 4:1); see also the sufferings (*pathēmata*) of Christ (1:11; 4:13; 5:1). Here, as elsewhere (Acts 17:3; Heb 2:9), Christ's suffering embraces his death as well (cf. 2:21–24; 3:18). The secondary scribal substitution of "died" for "suffered" could have been prompted by a desire to avoid any reduction of Christ's salvific act to only an example (thereby losing the unique soteriological signficance of Christ's act in contrast to the suffering of slaves and others) or by a wish to avoid the inference that suffering must be seen as necessary for salvation (Prostmeier 1990, 427–28). The reading *peri* (𝔓[72] A) may represent a scribal attempt to harmonize the formulation of 2:21a with that of 3:18a. The 1st- and 2d-person variants are perhaps the result of like-sounding vowels or of an attempt to reconcile v 21a with the "our" and "we" of v 24. The 2d-person plurals, however, are consistent with the focus on "you, your" throughout this unit (vv 18–20, 21a, 21d, 24d, 25). The hypothesis that these variants stem in part from the incorporation of hymnic or creedal material is unnecessary; see the DETAILED COMMENT.

Suffering, contrary to conventional opinion, was no proof or punishment of wrongdoing, for, as the following verses (vv 22–23) make clear, Christ was innocent of wrongdoing, as the servants/slaves were encouraged to be. However, his innocent suffering differed in one fundamental respect: it was a vicarious action on behalf of others ("for you," "our wrongdoing," v 24a), the mode and purpose of which are spelled out in v 24.

The concept of dying on behalf of others, especially one's comrades, was not unknown to Greeks and Romans.[125] However, the emphasis here on the *vicarious* character of Christ's suffering and death reflects a broad current of early Christological and soteriological Christian tradition that has its nearest roots in antecedent Israelite thought concerning the atoning power of virtuous conduct, suffering, and death.[126] While Israel had no concept of a suffering Messiah, the Israelite tradition concerning the atoning power of vicarious suffering was employed in early Christianity to assign a positive, soteriological significance to the scandal of Christ's ignominious death on the cross. The further elaboration of this tradition here, particularly through the use of Isa 53,

[125] See, e.g., Statius, *Thebais* 10.768–69; Livy 8.10.7; Hengel 1986, 192–220; on the notion of the "noble death," see Seeley 1990; and Droge and Tabor 1992.

[126] See, besides Isa 53; 4 Macc 1:11; 6:27–30; 17:22; *T. Benj.* 8:3; 1QS V 6; VIII 3–4, 10; IX 4; John 11:49–50; 18:14; and later, *b. Sanh.* 44b; *b. Sukkah* 20a; *b. Yebam.* 70a; see Lohse 1963; Hengel 1981; Breytenbach 1993; Seeley 1990; Droge and Tabor 1992, 69–165.

also reveals the creative hand of the Petrine author. This suffering and death, he affirms, is simultaneously vicarious (vv 21a, 24) and exemplary (vv 21c–23); the Lord to whom the servants/slaves and all of the believers are committed is both their example and their enabler. The phrase *hyper hymōn* ("for you," "on your behalf") once again illustrates the author's stress on the "for-you-ness" of the gospel (cf. 1:10–12, 18–21, 25b; 4:17–19).

21c. *leaving you an example* (*hymin hypolimpanōn hypogrammon*). At this point several rare or unique terms are employed to portray the behavior of Christ as a model to be followed (v 21c–d). The pres. act. part. *hypolimpanōn* has the sense of "leaving behind" (cf. Themistius, *Orat.* 10.139d). This verb, like the noun *hypogrammos* ("example"), appears only here in the NT, perhaps occasioning the variants *apolimpanōn* ("leaving behind," 𝔓[72]) and *hypolambanōn* ("taking up," a reading contained in P that is clearly a scribal mishearing of *hypolimpanōn*). The subsequent verb, *epakoloutheō* ("follow"), occurs elsewhere only in the longer, secondary conclusion to Mark (16:20) and 1 Tim 5:10, 24; and *ichnos* ("footsteps"), only in Rom 4:12 and 2 Cor 12:18. This unique constellation of terminology constitutes a formulation that is specifically Petrine. The Greek formulation *hyper hymōn hymin hypolimpanōn hypogrammon* ("for you . . . example") entails another elegant alliteration illustrative of the author's rhetorical competence (cf. 1:4, 6, 19; 2:12, 15, 16, 18–20; 3:17; 4:4.)

an example. The rare term *hypogrammos* appears only here in the NT and only once in the LXX, where it denotes the "outline" of the main lines of a story (2 Macc 2:28). In later time, Clement of Alexandria (*Strom.* 5. 675) uses it to denote a sample of handwriting to be traced by school boys learning to write the letters of the alphabet (*hypogrammos paidikos*, "writing-copy for a school child"; cf. Plato, *Prot.* 362D). With the figurative sense of moral example, it is also employed three times in *1 Clement*, twice of Christ as an example of humility (16:7) or of doing good deeds (33:8), and once of Paul as an example of endurance (5:7). Polycarp *Phil* 8:2 likewise depicts Christ as "example," with 8:1–2 clearly echoing 1 Pet 2:21–24. For Christ as example (*hypodeigma*), see also John 13:15; the same term is used earlier in Israelite martyr tradition of the noble example set by the aged martyr Eleazar (2 Macc 6:28, 31). On such NT terms for "pattern," see Lee 1962. In this Petrine context, the *example* provided by Christ involves an outline of behavior or moral "guidelines" (cf. Plato, *Leg.* 711B; Osborne 1983, 392). In the light of vv 22–23, this example includes innocent behavior, suffering without retaliation, and commitment of self to God, the just judge. In view of the association of vv 21–24 with vv 18–20, it is also possible that this example included Christ's subordination to God's will (cf. v 18) in his passion (Mark 14:36/Matt 26:29/Luke 22:12) and his obedience (1:2); compare Heb 2:8 ("he learned obedience through what he suffered") and texts affirming Christ's subordination to God (1 Cor 3:23; 11:3; 15:23–28). Later, Ignatius yearns to be an imitator of "the sufferings of my God" (*Rom.* 6:3).

21d. *that you should follow in his steps* (*hina epakolouthēsēte tois ichnesin autou*). The entire expression is unique in the Bible (but cf. Philo, *Virt.* 64: *tois autois ichnesin epakolouthēsai*, "follow in the same steps"). The verb *epakoloutheō* appears occasionally in the OT (of "following" God or idols; e.g., Josh 14:9; Lev 19:4; or following a way, Isa 55:3) and in the NT elsewhere only in the longer, secondary ending of Mark (16:20) and 1 Tim (5:10, 24; cf. Dio Chrys. *Orat.* 35:10, of a disciple). However, this verb is of the same family as *akoloutheō*, which is used in the Jesus tradition of those who respond to the call of Jesus to "follow" him, either in the physical sense of accompanying him as disciples (Mark 1:16–20 par.; 2:14 par.; Luke 9:57–62) or, figuratively, as going the way of the suffering Jesus or living in his spirit (Mark 8:34–9:1 par.; 10:38–39; cf. Luke 14:27). In view of the stress on suffering, which is also common to both this synoptic discipleship tradition and 1 Peter, this Petrine formulation appears to be a creative blending of the motifs of both imitation and discipleship together with the suffering it entails.

The term *ichnos* (lit., "sole" of the foot, 3 Kgdms 5:3; fig., "steps" [Prov 5:5], "tracks" [of an eagle, Prov, 30:19], "steps of truth" [Philo, *Gig.* 58]; "footstep[s]" as mode of behavior [Sir 21:6; Philo, *Opif.* 144]) occurs elsewhere only in Rom 4:12 (of following in the "footsteps" of believing Abraham) and 2 Cor 12:18 ("same steps" as "acting in the same spirit"; cf. Ign. *Eph.* 12:2 of Ignatius the martyr following in the "footsteps" of Paul; and *Mart. Pol.* 22:1 for following in the "footsteps" of the martyr Polycarp). In the Mishnah, figurative reference is made to "the footsteps of the Messiah" (*m. Soṭah* 9:15), which were understood to signal the end of the age.

The Petrine expression *follow in his steps* is also used metaphorically. But the context indicates that it is Christ's example of innocent behavior, his nonretaliatory suffering, and his commitment to God (vv 22–23) that is meant here. The expression is thus epexegetical and explains "pattern" or "example"; that is, retracing the pattern of his actions and following the guidelines he has established. Pliny (*Ep.* 8.13) gives somewhat similar advice to his young friend Genialis concerning the emulation of his father: "You have your model before you in whose footsteps you should tread, and are fortunate indeed to be blessed with a living example."[127]

The entire Petrine formulation, as noted, is similar in part to the concept of discipleship developed in the Gospels (similar verbs for "following," similar association between following Jesus and a "call" [either from Jesus, as in the Gospels, or from God, as here], a similar association between following and suffering, and a common emphasis upon Jesus as servant as an example for his followers [Mark 10:42–45 par.]). The accompanying terms here, however, are exclusive to 1 Peter and elements of a statement unique to 1 Peter. This statement differs notably from the language of Paul who, in addition to never speaking of the "suffering" of Christ, also never speaks of "following" (*akolouthein*) the historical Jesus. Instead, he employs the concept of imitation (*mimēsis*) of the Christ myth (1 Thess 1:6; 2:14; Phil 3:17; 1 Cor 4:16; 11:1; cf. Betz 1967, 137–89).

[127] Cf. also an inscription (SIG^3 708) that refers to following in the footsteps of the ancestors.

In 1 Pet 2:21c, Christ is portrayed not only as example but also, as vv 21a and 24 indicate, as the one who made emulation possible. To illustrate this correlation of Christ's roles as both example and enabler, E. Schweizer (1960, 11), in his classic study on lordship and discipleship, sketches the scenario of a child accompanying his father through a valley freshly blanketed with deep snow. The snow is too deep for the child to negotiate by himself, but by following step by step in the footsteps of his father he can make his way. In like manner, the Petrine author speaks here not only of Christ as vicarious sufferer but also as one who in his innocence and patient response to suffering provided the footprints in which those who have been called are to follow. His steps, in other words, have both kerygmatic and paradigmatic signficance.[128]

In later time, increased emphasis was placed on the exemplary "endurance" (*hypomenein*) of Christ (cf. *Barn.* 5:1, 5, 6, 12; Ign. *Pol.* 3:2; Pol. *Phil* 1:2; 8:1; Just. Mart., *1 Apol.* 50.1; 63.10, 16; *Dial.* 68.1; 121.2), and the thought of the martyr's imitation of the passion of the Lord eventually emerges (*Mart. Pol.* 1:1–2). In the spirituality of subsequent Christian generations, the thought, if not the precise words, of this Petrine text inspired centuries of popular piety such as the enormously popular *Imitation of Christ* by Thomas à Kempis (1379–1471) as well as Christian hymnody concerning the following of Jesus. This Petrine text also inspired the title of one of America's top religious best-sellers of modern time, Charles Monroe Sheldon's *In His Steps* (1896, reprinted 1967; see Elliott 1985). In the twentieth century, it was Dietrich Bonhoeffer (1948) who pointed out most forcefully the ethical as well as Christological dimension of the Christian's following of Christ, which entails not merely emulation but also the personal "cost of discipleship"—innocent suffering despite the doing of what is right in obedience to God (cf. also Yoder 1972, 115–34).

22a. *he "did no wrong"* (*hos hamartian ouk epoiēsen*). This is the first of four parallel statements commencing with the relative pronoun "who" (*hos*, rendered "he," vv 22a, 23a, 24a) or "whose" (*hou*, rendered "his," v 24d). This series of statements, inspired by Isa 53, is a creation of the Petrine author rather than a reproduction of an underlying source; see the discussion in the DETAILED COMMENT. The wording of v 22 echoes Isa 53:9 (*anomian ouk epoiēsen oude heurethē dolos en tōi stomati autou*) with the exception of the added initial relative pronoun "who" (*hos*), translated "he," and the substitution of *hamartian* for *anomian*. The latter terms are used synonymously in Isaiah (*hamartia*: 53:4, 5, 6, 10, 11, 12; *anomia*: 53:8, 9, 12). While *hamartia* could be translated "sin," it is likely that the Petrine substitution was intended to link this thought with v 20b and the verb "do what is wrong" (*hamartanontes*). This would then imply innocence of wrongdoing in respect to both God and humans (cf. also *hamartia* in 2:24a,b). For the equation of *hamartanō* and

[128] On the imitation motif in the NT, see also Larsson 1964; Schulz 1962; and Betz 1967; on the theme of discipleship in 1 Peter, see Elliott 1985.

kakopoieō, see 1 Chr 21:17. Earlier, Christ was compared to a flawless and faultless lamb (1:19; cf. John 1:19) and later, is described as "just" (3:18b); for the notion of the sinlessness of Jesus Christ, see Matt 4:14–15; John 8:46; 2 Cor 5:21; Heb 4:15; 7:26; and 1 John 3:5.

The clear use of material from Isa 52:13–53:12 here in v 22 as well as in vv 24a, 24d, and v 25a makes it likely that this Isaian passage has influenced much of the content of this section.[129] The Isaian portrait of the innocent suffering servant (*pais*, 52:13; *paidion*, 53:2) of God provides our author with a model for describing Jesus Christ as a similar innocent suffering servant of God who, in turn, serves as an apposite model for innocently suffering servants/slaves.[130]

22b. *"nor was guile found in his mouth"* (*oude heurethē dolos en tōi stomati autou*). These words, also from Isa 53:9, together with v 22a establish the innocence of Jesus and thus indicate how he serves as a model for innocently suffering servants/slaves (vv 19, 20; cf. 2 Cor 5:21; 1 John 3:5). All of the addressees were encouraged to renounce "guile" (*dolos*) in 2:1, and the thought is repeated in 3:10, citing Ps 33:14. On the verb "found" (*heurethē*) and its passive form, see the NOTE on its other occurrence in 1:7c.

in his mouth (*in tōi stomati autou*). This phrase refers to the anatomical place from which speech, either guileful or honest, emanates. Thus, Christ is said to have been innocent in his speech as well as in his behavior.

23a. *he, when insulted* (*hos loidoroumenos*). Literally, this clause is "being insulted" (*loidoroumenos*), with the present participle indicating repeated verbal abuse and reviling amounting to public shaming. As the servant of Isaiah was dishonored and degraded (Isa 52:14; 53:3, 8, 12), so Jesus in his passion is depicted as insulted, mocked, and humiliated (Mark 15:16–20 par.; 15:29–32 par.; Luke 22:65; Matt 27:39). This represents as well the experience of all of the Petrine addressees; see 3:9 and the related terms of public abuse in 2:12; 3:16; 4:4, 14.

did not insult in return (*ouk anteloidorei*). The preposition *anti-* when compounded with the verb *loidoreō* denotes reciprocal action, "to verbally abuse in return," with the imperfect indicating duration and endurance. The composite verb appears only here in the NT. Acts 23:4, describing Paul's encounter with the Jerusalem council, gives an example of the type of counterinsulting and threatening that is customary in an antagonistic culture, where slights to personal honor are dealt with and parried with counterthreats. Jesus in his silence proved an exception to this rule and by implication the servants/slaves were to follow suit. He himself, in the spirit of Deut 32:35–36, advocated the principle of nonretaliation (Matt 5:38–42; Luke 6:27–29) and, according to the tradition of his passion, exemplified it by meeting the abuse of his accusers

---

[129] Compare 2:21/Isa 53:3, 4, 5, 6, 8, 11, 12; 2:22/Isa 53:9; 2:23a/Isa 53:7; 2:23b/53:3–5, 7, 8, 11, 12; 2:23c/Isa 53:6, 12; 2:24a/Isa 53:4, 12; cf. 53:5; 2:24b,c/Isa 53:5; 2:24d/Isa 53:5; 2:25a/Isa 53:6.

[130] For the early Christian designation of Jesus Christ as "servant/child" of God (*pais theou*), see Matt 12:15–21; Acts 3:13, 26; 4:25, 27, 30 (speeches attributed to Peter); *1 Clem.* 59:2, 3, 4; *Did.* 9:2, 3; 10:2, 3. On Isa 52–53 and the other sources underlying 2:21–25, see the DETAILED COMMENT.

and tormentors with silence (Mark 14:61/Matt 26:63; Mark 15:5/Matt 27:12–14; Luke 23:9; John 19:9).[131] In this regard, as in other respects, Jesus serves as the model of the nonretaliation urged on all believers in 3:9 (see the NOTE on 3:9 and Zerbe 1993, 176–290 for further discussion).

23b. *when suffering, he did not threaten* (*paschōn, ouk ēpeilei*). In both its grammatical form (pres. part. + imperf. indic. act. verb) and its content this statement parallels v 23a, with the imperfects denoting repeated action. The statement "he did not threaten" (*ouk ēpeilei*, the verb occurs only here and Acts 4:17) may imply, parallel to v 23a, that Jesus did not threaten those causing his suffering with suffering in return. The verb *paschōn* ("suffering"; cf. also vv 19c, 21a) is the chief thematic link-word uniting vv 18–20 and 21–25. Though it is not used of the Isaian servant, other expressions do stress his suffering (53:3, 4, 5, 7, 8, 10, 12d), and suffering also is the leading theme of the narrative of Jesus' passion.[132] Christ's innocent suffering in subordination and obedience to the Father's will (cf. 1:2) links his experience with that of the suffering servant of Isaiah, the suffering servants/slaves of 1 Peter (2:18–20), and the suffering addressees of 1 Peter as a whole. Again, Christ serves as both example and enabler for all of those who share his experience and commitment to God.

In the view of the author's Mediterranean contemporaries, enduring reviling and suffering in silence could be variously interpreted. On the one hand, passivity and silence could be taken as an inability to respond and thus as something shameful. On the other hand, it could also be regarded as a mark of courage and honor. Thus Plutarch observes: "Silence cannot under any circumstances be called to an accounting . . . and in the midst of reviling it is dignified and Socratic, or rather Heraclean, if it be true that Heracles 'not so much as a fly gave heed to words of hatred.' Indeed there is nothing more dignified and noble than to maintain a calm demeanor when an enemy reviles one" (*How to Profit by One's Enemies, Mor.* 90D). The courageous bearing up under pain and punishment was esteemed as a sign of honor in the biblical communities as well (see Pilch 1991b, 71–94; 1995). The honorable Isaian servant of God endured suffering in silence (53:7), and the same thing is stressed about Jesus in his passion (Mark 14:61/Matt 26:53; Mark 15:5/Matt 27:14; Luke 23:9). Discipline and suffering were considered necessary for the training of children: "He who loves his son will whip him often, in order that he may rejoice at the way he turns out. . . . Bow down his neck in his youth

---

[131] Similar sentiments are expressed in Israelite tradition; see *T. Benj.* 5:4: "The holy man is merciful to his reviler, and holds his peace"; *Jos. Asen.* 28:7: "do not repay anyone evil for evil"; *b. Šabb.* 88b: "Those who are insulted but do not insult, hear themselves reviled without answering, act through love and rejoice in suffering, of them Scripture says, But they who love Him are as the sun when he goes forth in his might" (Judg 5:31). Cf. 1QS X 17; *2 En.* 50:2–4; *b. Giṭ.* 36b; *b. Yoma* 23a and Zerbe 1993, 34–173.

[132] See Matt 16:21/Mark 8:31/Luke 9:22; Luke 17:25; Matt 17:12/Mark 9:12; Luke 17:25; 22:15; 24:26, 46; cf. Acts 1:3; 3:18; 17:3; Heb 2:18; 5:8; 9:26; 13:12.

and beat his ribs while he is young, lest he become stubborn and disobey you" (Sir 30:1, 12).[133] According to a Hellenistic maxim, it was through suffering (*patheia, pathēmata*) that one achieved knowledge (*matheia, mathēma*); cf. Hdt. *Hist.* 1.207. Through discipline (i.e., "child-rearing," *paideia*) one learned how to be a proper (i.e., obedient) child (*pais*); note also the relation of *pais* and *paiein* ("beat").

This notion underlies the comment of the author of Hebrews, who sought to cast both the suffering of Christ and the suffering of his followers in a positive light: "as a son he (Christ) learned obedience through the things he suffered" (5:8). Christ's endurance of suffering is then presented as a model for his followers (12:3–11). Proverbs 3:11–12 ("The Lord disciplines him whom he loves and chastises every son whom he receives") is then cited in Hebrews to underline the point that

> it is for discipline that you have to endure. God is treating you as sons; for what son is there whom his father does not discipline. . . . Shall we not much more be subject to the Father of spirits and live? . . . he disciplines us for our good, that we may share his holiness. For the moment, all discipline seems painful rather than pleasant; later it yields the peaceful fruit of righteousness to those who have been trained by it. (Heb 12:5–11)

Here in 1 Peter as well, the suffering Christ is presented as a model for suffering believers, as one who through suffering demonstrates obedience and subordination to God's will.

23c. *but rather* (*de*). The particle *de* contrasts Jesus' actual response to abuse to what might have been expected, namely an effort at his self-defense. Instead Jesus relied on Another for the vindication of his innocence and honor.

committed his cause (*paredidou*). The verb *paradidomai* figures prominently in the passion tradition (of Jesus' being "committed" or "handed over" to the authorities, Mark 14:10; Luke 22:4–6; John 19:12; cf. also Luke 9:44; 18:32–33; Rom 4:25). Here, however, the verb is active and therefore is closer to the sense of Luke 23:46 (cf. Ps 30[31]:6): "Father, into your hands I commit my spirit" (cf. John 19:30). The verb appears also in Isa 53:6 and 12, but here in 1 Peter it is employed without a specified object. "Cause" renders the sense of the verb used absolutely and implies Christ's life's work and its vindication. The pronoun "himself" (*heauton*, $\mathfrak{P}^{81}$ r t vg Cyp. Aug.) was probably added secondarily as a clarification of the ambiguous sense of the verb used absolutely: "he committed himself" (cf. Gal 2:20; Eph 5:25).

to the one who judges justly (*tōi krinonti dikaiōs*). The phrase implies God as judge (see 1:17; 4:5, 6, 17–19) and expresses the conviction that God judges justly (cf. Jer 11:20 LXX; Zeph 3:5). The variant abverb "unjustly" (*adikōs*, in a few MSS, vg, Clem. Alex., Cypr., and several lectionaries)—perhaps in

[133] See also Prov 13:24; 23:13–14; 29:15, 17; and on the disciplining of servants, Prov 29:19–21.

parallelism with v 19b *paschōn adikōs*—indicates that a few scribes took this instead as an allusion to Jesus' unjust human judge, Pontius Pilate. Jesus' commitment of his cause to God, however, illustrates his obedient (1:2) subordination to his Father's will in his temptation (Matt 4:1–11/Luke 4:1–13) as well as his passion (Mark 14:36/Matt 26:39/Luke 22:42) and exemplifies the "reverence" (2:18) and "mindfulness of God" (2:19) that should characterize the behavior of the servants/slaves. As Jesus, so they too and all the believers (4:19) are to entrust themselves to a just God and faithful creator. Confidence in the just judgment of God thus provides a further compelling reason for the patient endurance of suffering (2:19–20).

Verse 24 states the effect of Christ's vicarious suffering and crucifixion: the transfer of human sins upon him and the consequence thereof; namely, liberation from the compulsion to do what is wrong and empowerment to live justly.

24a. *he "himself bore our wrongdoings"* (*hos tas hamartias hēmōn autos anēnegken*). The statement expands on v 21a and draws on the language of Isa 53: "he bears our wrongdoings/sins" (*houtos tas hamartias hēmōn pherei*, 53:4), "he shall bear their wrongdoings/sins" (*tas hamartias autōn autos anoisei*, 53:11), and "he himself bore the wrongdoings/sins of many" (*autos hamartias pollōn anēnegke*, 53:12). The verb *anapherō* ("bear," "bring," "take") can have, as in 2:5, the meaning of "offer" (sacrifice; cf. Lev 17:5; Isa 57:6; Jas 2:21; Heb 7:27; 9:28–29). However, Schelkle's proposal (1976, 85) that it here denotes Christ's offering of himself as a sacrifice on the "altar" of the cross is unconvincing. Nowhere in 1 Peter is the death of Christ interpreted as a sacrifice, and nowhere in the NT is the cross depicted as an altar. More generally, the thought resembles certain aspects of the scapegoat ritual of the Day of Atonement (Lev 16:1–34; so Goldstein 1974, 43–44). However, this ritual involves two goats with different functions, one that is slain as a sin offering for the people, making atonement (16:15–19), and a second that remains alive and bears (*lēmpsetai*) the inquities (*adikias*) of the people into the desert (16:20–22). *Barnabas* 7:6–10 offers an example of a clear reference to this ritual. The two goats are explicitly mentioned; but the "type" of Christ is not the one offered for sin but the scapegoat led into the wilderness. Isaiah 53, however, involves no evident allusions to this ritual, and it is Isa 53 that serves as the source of these words in 1 Peter (cf. Patsch 1969 and contrast Deissmann 1901, 88–91). The chief point here (as in v 21a and 1:18–19) is that Christ's action, like the action of the Isaian servant, was vicarious in nature.

our wrongdoings (*tas hamartias hēmōn*). The shift from the 2d-person pl. used throughout this passage (vv 18–20, 21, 24d, 25) to a 1st-person pl. "our" (*hēmōn*; compare the less well-attested "your" [*hymōn*]) and "we" (v 24c, *zēsōmen*) is striking. Some scholars trace these 1st-person plurals to an early hymn or creed (where "we" language is customary), which they theorize the author cited at this point. This theory, however, is neither necessary nor probable; see the DETAILED COMMENT. "Our wrongdoings" is derived from Isa 53:4 and 5 and therefore requires a 1st-person verbal form in the following purpose clause of v 24c ("we might live"), as Michaels (1988, 137) correctly notes. Moreover, the underlying Isaian text also varies between "you" (52:14; 53:10b) and "we," "our" (53:1–2a,c, 4–6; cf. also "my people" [53:8]; "I" [53:9]; "their" [53:11, 12]). The shift to the first person makes this statement inclusive of all believers. It expresses a conviction shared by both the senders and the addressees of the letter and emphasizes a cardinal feature of the faith that binds them together. It likewise demonstrates that this entire passage was formulated with both servants/slaves and all of the believers in mind. "Wrongdoings" (*tas hamartias*) repeats the same term as in v 22a (cf. also 3:18; 4:1, 8) and echoes the related verb, *hamartanontes*, in 2:20b. It includes wrong done against either humans or God ("sin").

In 1 Peter and its source, Isa 53, Christ or the servant of God, respectively, is said to bear the wrongdoings of the people as their representative and therefore as their substitute. Both texts assume the solidarity of the people with their servant-representative. This notion of solidarity in suffering receives particular stress in 4:1 and 4:12–16 (cf. also 2:4–10).

in his body on the tree (*en tōi sōmati autou epi to xylon*). This phrase conforms the foregoing terms, derived from Isa 53, to the crucifixion of Christ specifically. The words are reminiscent of Deut 21:22–23: "And if there be sin (*hamartia*) in anyone (deserving) the judgment of death, and he be put to death, you shall hang him on a tree (*epi xylon*). His body shall not remain all night on the tree (*ou koimēthēsetai to sōma autou epi tou xylou*), but you shall by all means bury it in that day, for everyone who hangs on a tree is cursed of God." The "tree" to which the Petrine author refers was the cross on which Jesus was hanged. The noun *xylon* can mean "tree," "wood," and objects of wood (pole, club, stake, gallows; cf. Gen 40:19; Deut 21:23; Josh 10:26; Esth 5:14; 6:4; Philo, *Somn.* 2.213; Josephus, *Ant.* 11.246). It is also used, however, as a synonym of *stauros*, a cross employed for crucifixion and specifically of Christ's cross (Acts 5:30; 10:39 [in speeches of Peter]; 13:29; Gal 3:13; *Barn.* 5:13; 8:5; 12:11; and Pol. *Phil* 8:1).[134] Use of "tree" or "wood" for "cross" is also now attested in the Qumran literature where, in allusion to Deut 21:22–23, crucifixion is prescribed for Israelites who betray or curse their own people (11QT^{a} LXIV 7–12).

In the light of this Deuteronomic passage ("cursed of God is everyone who hangs on a tree [*epi xylon*]," Deut 21:23), the equivalency of "tree" and "cross" presented a serious problem for the Jesus movement; namely, that Christ's crucifixion could be taken as a "scandal" (1 Cor 1:23) and an indication of his accursedness by God (Wilcox 1977; Sänger 1994). Paul is the first to address this problem. In his letter to the Galatians he asserts that Christ was indeed cursed in accord with Deut 21:23 because he was hanged on a tree. But, by "having become a curse for us," he "redeemed us from the curse of the law." The Petrine author also addresses this problem, but in a different fashion. He also acknowledges Christ's hanging on a cross and likewise affirms

[134] For sources on and discussion of crucifixion, see Reijners 1965; Hengel 1977; Adinolfi 1988, 88–90.

the vicarious nature of this action (2:24a). But he explains its salutary effect in different terms: by this act we can abandon wrongdoing and live for doing what is right (v 24b–d). The use of "tree" also distinguishes 1 Peter from Paul who, apart from Gal 3:13, employs *stauros*, never *xylon*, for the cross of Christ (cf. 1 Cor 1:17, 18; Gal 5:11; 6:12, 14; Phil 2:8; 3:18). By contrast, the Petrine author employs *xylon*, a term also occurring in the early tradition associated with Peter in Acts (Acts 5:30; 10:39).

The phrase *in his body* (*en tōi sōmati autou*) reflects *to sōma autou* in Deut 21:23. However, stress on the bodily aspect of Christ's suffering and death was also traditional (Col 1:22; Heb 2:14; 10:10). The formulation recalls the earlier references to his shed blood (1:2, 19).

The phrase *on the tree* (*epi to xylon*), as noted, likewise reflects the same phrase in Deuteronomy, with its implication of divine curse. The Romans, particularly their occupying armies, employed crucifixion as a means of state terrorism in order to deter resistance or revolt. It was employed particularly for the punishment of subversives, violent criminals, and rebellious slaves (*servile supplicium*, Val. Max. 2.7.12; Plaut. *Mil. Glor.* 372–73; *Most.* 358–60; Hengel 1977, 46–63). In Judea, thousands of Judeans were crucified as part of Rome's pacification program (Josephus, *J.W.* 2.75, 241, 253, 306–8; 5.449–51).[135] Accompanied by scourging and torture, crucifixion accomplished the complete public degradation and humiliation of its victims. Cicero (*Rab.* 4) specifically speaks of the cross as "the tree of shame" (*arbor infelix*; cf. Livy 1.26.7). Over against the abasement and shame that this mode of execution brought to the crucified Christ, a fact accentuated in all the passion narratives of the Gospels (Malina and Neyrey 1988, 88–91; Malina and Rohrbaugh 1992, 158–65), the Petrine author poses its life-giving effects. It is possible that Barnabas, who refers to the cross as "tree/wood" (8:5) and to the Son of God's "suffering on a tree" (5:13), was familiar with this text, and this is even more likely in the case of Polycarp in his letter to the Philippians (see below). Later Christian comments on the tree of the cross also reflect concern for casting it in a positive light. For example, Justin Martyr (*Dial.* 86.1–6) relates the tree on which Christ was crucified to OT passages regarding "tree" or "wood" (the tree of life in the Garden of Eden, the staff of Moses, Jacob's ladder, Aaron's blossoming rod, the stem of Jesse, etc.). He also observes that "Christians have been begotten anew [of Christ] by water and faith and wood, which contained the mystery of the cross, even as Noah also was saved by the wood of the ark when he was borne upon the waters" (*Dial.* 138.2). Further echoes of either the text of 1 Peter or its language and themes are evident in Melito's *Paschal Homily* (suffering [passim]; tree as cross [70, 71, 95–97, 104]; citation of Isa 53:7–8 [64; cf. 71]).

24b. *so that we, having abandoned wrongdoing* (*hina tais hamartiais apogenomenoi*). The bicolon of v 24bc states the double intention (*hina*, "so that")

---

[135] Hengel (1977) surveys the evidence for crucifixion in the Greco-Roman world, and Reijners (1965) traces the occurrences of *stauros* and *xylon* in the secular literature, LXX (where only *xylon* occurs), NT, and later Christian writings through Tertullian.

or moral result of Christ's vicarious suffering and bearing of wrongdoing. The subject "we" is contained in the main verb *zēsōmen*. The verb of the first colon, *apogenomenoi* (aor. middle part. and only biblical occurrence) can mean "get away from," "part from," "depart," or "part from life, die." While some sense of "dying" is implied by the parallel main verb "we might live" (*zēsōmen*, v 24c), the accompanying noun "wrongdoing" (*tais hamartiais*) indicates that some form of radical separation from unacceptable conduct is intended; hence, the translation "having abandoned wrongdoing" (cf. Selwyn 1947, 181). The parallel datives *tais hamartiais* and *tēi dikaiosynēi* accompanying the contrasting verbs *apogenomenoi* and *zēsōmen*, respectively, are best taken as datives of respect or relation: literally, "died *with respect* (or *in regard*) *to* wrongdoing," "might live *with respect* (or *in regard*) *to* doing what is right" (see Moule 1982, where this and related NT instances are discussed). The effect of Christ's bearing "our wrongdoings" (v 24a) is that believers ("we") are liberated from the control of and compulsion to wrongdoing/sin, which leads to deadly alienation from God. Consequently, Christ's bearing wrongdoing/sins enables believers to renounce wrongdoing and evil intentionally (2:1, 12, 16, 19–20; 3:9, 10–12, 17; 4:3, 15; 5:2–3, 8–9). A similar moral consequence of Christ's suffering is presented earlier in 1:17–19 and later in 4:1–3.

24c. *might live* (*zēsōmen*). This main verb with "we" as subject corresponds to the prior statement of v 24a that Christ bore "our" sins and indicates the second result of Christ's action. It recalls the motif of new life (and rebirth) stressed also in 1:3, 23; 2:2, 4, 5; 3:7. This experience is grounded in that of Christ who was himself "put to death" but also "made alive" (3:18de).

for doing what is right (*tēi dikaiosynēi*). The term *diakaiosynē*, used here as a dative of respect, is often rendered "righteousness" (KJV, RSV, NRSV, NAB, NEB). But in this context, as in 3:14, it has the sense of "just, upright behavior," "righteous living" (NJB: "uprightness"), "doing what is right." It is related semantically to the foregoing terms, "unjustly" (*adikōs*, 2:19c), "justly" (*dikaiōs*, 2:23c), as well as "just" (person) (*dikaios*, 3:12, 18; 4:18). In Israel and Christian circles still closely linked to Israel, *dikaiosynē* denoted the human fulfilling of divine ordinances (Job 27:6; 29:14; Ps 44[45]:7; Matt 3:15; 5:6, 10, 20; 6:1, 33; 21:32; Ign. *Smyrn.* 1:1; Pol. *Phil* 2:3; 3:1) and "doing what is right" (primarily in God's sight) (Acts 10:35; 1 John 2:29; 3:7, 10; Rev 22:11) in contrast to committing "lawlessness" (*anomia*, 2 Cor 6:14; Heb 1:9 [citing Ps 44:8]) or "injustice" (*adikia*, *2 Clem.* 19:2).[136] The Petrine author, like Isaiah (the servant establishes justice, 42:1–4) and Matthew (cf. Przybylski 1980; Giesen 1982), uses *diakaiosynē* in this latter sense of "upright conduct" and as a synonym for "doing what is right" (*agathopoieō*, 2:20; cf. also 2:15; 3:6, 11, 17; 4:19). See also the synonymity of "righteous" (*dikaious*) and "do what is right" (*poiēsatō agathon*) in 3:11–12 and the synonymity of *dikaiosynē* and "zealots for what is

---

[136] On Greek usage, see Bolkestein 1939, 102–5, 139–40; Danker 1982, 345–48, 354–55; Adinolfi 1988, 158–61.

right" (*zēlōtai agathōn*) in 3:13–14. He thus diverges substantially from Paul, who employs the term to denote the "righteousness of God" or the righteousness bestowed by God.[137] This variant use of common terminology, along with the differing treatment of "tree" and the use of the suffering servant theme not found in Paul, adds to the evidence throughout the letter illustrating the Petrine author's independence from the formulations of Paul and his sphere of influence.

Through his own upright behavior (vv 22–23) and vicarious suffering (v 24), Christ has made possible the believers' renunciation of wrongdoing and their living for doing what is right. The idea of abandoning wrongdoing/sinning and living uprightly summarizes succinctly the conversion and moral transformation entailed in baptism and reformulates common baptismal catechesis.[138] In the next century, these words of 1 Peter are echoed in Polycarp's *Letter to the Philippians* (8:1–2):

> Let us then persevere unceasingly in our hope, and in the pledge of our righteousness that is in Christ Jesus, who bore our sins in his own body on the tree, who did no sin, neither was guile found in his mouth, but for our sakes, that we might live in him, he endured all things. Let us then be imitators of his endurance, and if we suffer for his name's sake let us glorify him. For this is the example which he gave us in himself, and this is what we have believed.

24d. *"By his bruise" you "have been healed"* (*hou tōi mōlōpi iathēte*). A further effect of Christ's saving work is expressed again with language derived from Isa 53. The clause derives from Isa 53:5, with *hou* (lit., "whose," paralleling the relative pronouns of vv 22a, 24a) substituted for *autou, hēmeis* ("we") omitted, and a 2d-person pl. verb form ("you") substituted for the Isaian 1st-person pl. verb ("we have been healed"). The Greek term *mōlōps* (sole NT occurrence) denotes a "bruise" or "welt" caused by blows or a whip (Sir 28:17). According to Sir 23:10, "a servant (*oiketēs*) continually examined under torture will not lack a bruise (*mōlōps*)." Given the familiarity of the slaves of 1 Peter with the harsh reality of frequent beatings, this Isaian formulation could well have been included and modified with them specifically in mind. At the same time, this bruising recalls the scourging (Matt 20:19 par.; Matt 27:26/Mark 15:5; John 19:1) of Jesus in conjunction with his crucifixion. The relation of this crucifixion to Isa 53:5 is explictly stressed in *Barn.* 5:2 (cf. also *1 Clem.* 16:3–14, citing Isa 53:1–12). The chief point here, however, is that this bruise or bruising is a metonymy for Christ's entire ordeal of suffering and effects the

[137] See Rom 1:17; 3:21–22, 26; 4:25; 5:21; 9:30; 10:3; 1 Cor 1:30; 2 Cor 3:9; 5:21; Phil 3:9.

[138] See, e.g., Rom 6:1–12 (esp. 6:2, 4, 11, 12: "died to sin" . . . walk in newness of life . . . dead in sin and alive to God in Christ Jesus . . . let not sin reign in your mortal bodies, to make you obey their cravings").

healing of the servants/slaves that their own suffering could not. Along with 2:21a and 24 it further underlines the substitutionary nature and power of Christ's suffering and death (cf. also 3:18 and 4:1). Christ is not simply an example but an enabler, one whose own bruising brings about the healing of others, a healing that, as v 25 indicates, involves restoration of communion with God. In regard to the significance of this verse in modern time, it is worth noting that this was the text on which Dietrich Bonhoeffer's last sermon in Flossenbürg prison was based (April 8, 1945), one day before he was hanged by the Nazis (Doberstein 1954, 13).[139]

25a. *For you "were straying as sheep"* (*ēte gar hōs probata planōmenoi*). The conjunction "for" (*gar*) links this verse with the foregoing idea of healing, and the verse in its entirety appears to be formed on the basis of a conflation of images derived from Isa 53:6 and Ezek 34.

The straying sheep simile is adopted from Isa 53:6 (cf. Ps 118[119]:176; Isa 13:14; Jer 27[50]:17). An original 1st-person pl. verb (*eplanēthēmen*) is replaced with a 2d-person pl. construction (*ēte . . . planōmenoi*) that continues the 2d-person pl. subject in v 24d and preceding verses (vv 18–20, 21). This verbal construction (as found in ℵ A B etc.) is balanced by the following verb, "you were returned" (v 25b), and therefore is preferable to the alternative reading, "you were as straying sheep" (*ēte . . . hōs probata planōmena*, as found in 𝔓[72] C P Ψ and the majority of MSS). The images of Israel as lost, scattered, straying, or perishing sheep (Jer 27:6a LXX; Isa 13:14; Ezek 34) or sheep without a shepherd (Num 27:17; 1 Sam 22:17/2 Chr 18:16; Jdt 11:19) are traditional, as is the related symbolization of rulers and leaders as "shepherds" (2 Sam 5:2; Jer 3:15; 23:1–8; Ezek 34:1–31; Zech 10:3; 13:7). The image is also found in the Jesus tradition (Mark 6:34/Matt 9:36; Matt 10:6; 15:24). In conjunction with his passion, Jesus is portrayed as citing Zech 13:7 ("I will strike the shepherd and the sheep will be scattered") in anticipating the scattering of his disciples prior to his death (Mark 14:27/Matt 26:31; cf. John 16:32; *Barn.* 5:12). The image of the Christian community as God's flock recurs in 1 Pet 5:2–4, along with the image of Christ as the "chief shepherd" (5:4).

25b. *but now "have been returned" to the Shepherd and Overseer of your lives* (*alla epestraphēte nyn epi ton poimena kai episkopon tōn psychōn hymōn*). The verb *epestraphēte* ("you have been returned [by God]") and the image of the return of straying sheep do not occur in Isa 53. It appears to be derived from Ezekiel (34:4–11, 16), where mention is made of sheep (*probata*, 34:5, 6, 8, 10, 11), straying (*planōmenon*, 34:4), return (*apostrephō*, 34:4, 6, 10; *epistrephō*, 34:16 [God's returning the strayed sheep]; and *episkeptō*, 34:11, the verb related to the noun *episkopos* [overseer] in 1 Peter). The image of the future return and

---

[139] On NT teaching on the atonement and the vicarious quality of Jesus' death, see V. Taylor 1958; Olson 1979; Hengel 1981; 1986, 187–284; de Jonge 1988; Breytenbach 1993. On the atoning death of Jesus in 1 Peter and its ethical and ecclesiological implications, see Selwyn 1947, 90–101; Lohse 1963, 182–87; 1986; Goldstein 1974; and Cervantes Gabarrón 1991a, 363–92 and passim.

regathering of God's flock once scattered in exile appears also in Jer 23:1–8, and the verb *epistrephō* in this connection also appears in Jdt 5:19. The straying, scattering, and return of God's sheep eventually became one of several metaphors for the final gathering and salvation of God's scattered people.[140] In this Petrine construction, "straying" does not imply Christian defection *after* conversion but, rather, estrangement from God *prior to* baptism and rebirth. The return of those who have strayed is a composite metaphor for salvation as such.[141] This thought parallels the double contrast in 2:10, and the "now" (*nyn*) in both instances refers to the situation of those now under the care and mercy of God and God's Messiah. This "return" of the believers depicts a further aspect of their "healing" (v 24d) as not only personal health but collective unification with Christ.

The verb *epestraphēte* can be taken as either a passive or a middle. As a middle it is used figuratively of pagans who turn to God (Acts 14:15; 15:19; 26:18, 20; 1 Thess 1:9; cf. Gal 4:9) or of Israelites who turn to Jesus (Acts 9:35). Here, however, a passive use is more likely. Like *eklēthēte* (v 21a), which it balances, it serves as a divine passive implying God as agent (as in Ezek 34:16: "you have been returned by God"). The contrast in v 25a/b of former alienation and present reconciliation with God recalls the similar double contrast in 2:10.

to the Shepherd and Overseer of your lives. The expression *poimēn kai episkopos* is unique in the Bible and, hence, is likely a Petrine formulation. The related terms *poimainein* ("to shepherd") and *episkopein* ("to exercise oversight") also recur in 1 Pet 5:2 as functions of the elders, a text close in pastoral terminology to Paul's address to the elders of Miletus in Acts 20:17–35 (see the NOTE on 5:2). Both *poimēn* and *episkopos* are appropriate to the sheep metaphor employed here, and both can have been suggested by the language of Ezek 34 (*poimenes*, of human leaders, 34:2, 5, 7, 8, 9, 10; *episkeptō*, of God, 34:11).

It is not immediately clear whether these epithets refer to God or to Christ. The latter possibility, however, appears to have superior support and is favored by most scholars. In the OT, God is portrayed as shepherd of his people Israel[142] but not explicitly in the NT. Israelite tradition also depicts the messianic ruler as shepherd (Jer 23:1–4; Ezek 34:23–24; *Pss. Sol.* 17:40), and this appears to have influenced Christian conceptuality as well. It is Jesus Christ rather than God who is more frequently identified as shepherd in early Christian writings.[143] This pastoral image is also used to describe Jesus' teaching, activity, passion, and heavenly rule.[144] The expression "God's flock" occurs in 1 Pet 5:2

---

[140] See Ezek 11:14–21; 20:34; 28:25; 34:11–16, 28–31; Zech 10:1–12; Mic 2:12; 5:3–4; Sir 36:11; *Pss. Sol.* 8:28; 17:28; cf. 2 Macc 1:24–29; 2:18; Mark 13:27.

[141] See the use of this term for the conversion of the Gentiles (Acts 14:15; 15:19; 26:18, 29; 1 Thess 1:9) and of Israelites (Acts 9:35).

[142] See Gen 49:24 MT; Pss 23:1–4; 28:9; 76:21[77:20]; 78:52; 79:2[80:1]; Isa 40:11; Jer 27[31]:10; 31:10; Ezek 34; cf. Philo, *Agr.* 50–52.

[143] See John 10:1–16; 21:15–17; Heb 13:20; *1 Clem.* 16:1; 44:3; 54:2; 57:2; *Mart. Pol.* 19:2.

[144] See Mark 6:34/Matt 9:36; Matt 10:6; 15:24; 25:32; Mark 14:27/Matt 26:31; Luke 12:32; John 16:32; Rev 7:17; 12:5; 19:15; cf. also Matt 2:6; and *Barn.* 5:12.

(cf. Acts 20:28–29), but the context of this verse (1 Pet 5:2–4) also includes reference to the "manifesting" (by God) of Christ as "chief shepherd" (*archipoimēn*; see the NOTE on 5:4). The application of this unique pastoral term to Christ in 5:4 makes it likely that Christ also is implied as shepherd in 2:25.[145]

The term *episkopos* ("overseer") occasionally is used of God (Job 20:29; Wis 1:6; Philo, *Mut.* 39.216; *Somn.* 1.91; *1 Clem.* 59:3; cf. Ign. *Magn.* 3:1; 6:1), as is the verb *episkeptomai* (Ezek 34:11; cf. T. *Benj.* 6:6). But here in 2:25 it appears to be linked with *poimēn* as an epithet for Jesus Christ. Reference was made to God's *episkopē* (2:12), but the term concerned God's "visitation" in judgment not God's pastoral care. "Overseer" implies the protective function of a shepherd (as guardian). Its related verb *episkopountes* ("exercising oversight") appears in conjunction with the verb "shepherd" (*poimanate*) in 5:2 to depict the responsibility of the elders as "under-shepherds" of Jesus Christ, the chief shepherd; on this combination see the NOTE on 5:2. Thus *Shepherd and Overseer* in 2:25b are best taken as an hendiadys (two terms expressing one thought) symbolizing Christ's leading and protection of the servants/slaves as members of God's flock.

Structural features of this Petrine passage also support the identification of these terms with Christ. The verb *epestraphēte* is another divine passive implying God as subject. Thus, the sense here is that it is God who has returned the servants/slaves to Christ, who is their shepherd and overseer/guardian. This passive verb, "you were returned," parallels the similar divine passive verb, "you were called" (*eklēthēte*), in v 21a. The construction of both verses is identical ("for" + 2d-person pl. aor. pass. indic. verbs), and they are thematically related as well: both focus on the relation of the servants/slaves with Jesus Christ. Their being returned to the Christ, like their divine call, enables them to follow his lead. Thus, vv 21 and 25 form a literary inclusion that frames vv 21–25 and marks them as a coherent Christological unit joined to and substantiating vv 18–20.[146]

of your lives (*tōn psychōn hymōn* [having stronger MS support than *hēmōn*, "our"]). This phrase refers to the servants/slaves as whole persons, similar to the sense of *psychai* in 1:9 and 1:22 (see respective NOTES). The entire unit 2:18–25 ends on a pastoral note of encouragement: the Christ whose example the servants/slaves have been called to follow and whose suffering has freed them from wrongdoing and enabled them to live uprightly is the one to whom God has entrusted the shepherding and protection of the faithful.

---

[145] On extrabiblical and biblical use of the pastoral image in general, see Jost 1939; Jeremias 1968; Bosetti 1990, 227–58, Hamp 1990; and Engemann 1991. Jeremias (1968, 492–93) traces its Christian association with Jesus to Jesus' own teaching, whereas Tooley (1964–1965) considers this identification only a later development. In any case it is this Christian tradition that 1 Peter also appears to reflect. On the Petrine use of the pastoral motif, see Bosetti 1990, 117–223, 259–91.

[146] So also Bosetti 1990, 112–15; Ellul 1990, 28–30; Cervantes Gabarrón 1991, 177–78.

GENERAL COMMENT

This address to household servants/slaves is a skillfully composed passage, whose exhortation and encouragement apply first to servants/slaves but ultimately to the entire suffering community. In its fusion of biblical themes and motifs, kerygmatic formulas, and extensive use of Isa 52–53, this passage illustrates both an independence from Pauline thought and a theological formulation that is as creative as it is singular in the NT. The passage is noteworthy in several respects.

(1) The Petrine author, like other Christian writers, in no way shares the conventional notion that slaves are irrational brutes. He addresses them directly and not merely with a curt command but an extended line of argument assuming their rational competence, moral responsibility, and Christian commitment.

(2) He addresses them as *oiketai* rather than *douloi*, thereby stressing the household (*oikos*) sphere of their activity and significance.

(3) The affiliation of slaves with the Jesus movement apart from their masters inevitably would raise questions concerning their commitment to the subordination they owed to their owners. In regard to the vulnerable situation of slaves in general, the social historian Moses Finley (1968, 165–66) has observed:

> In principle the slave is an outsider, a "barbarian," and that set him apart from all the other forms of involuntary labour known to history—from the Egyptian peasants who were conscripted to build the pyramids, from the *clientes* of early Rome, from debt-bondsmen, serfs or peons. The slave is brought into a new society violently and traumatically, uprooted not only from his homeland but from everything which under normal circumstances provides human beings with social and psychological support. He is torn from his kin, from his fellows, from his religious institutions, and in their place he is given no new focus of relations other than his master, and, in a very unreliable way, his fellow slaves. Nor can he expect support from other depressed groups within the new society to which he has been transported. He has lost control not only over his labour but also over his person (and his personality).

The slaves of 1 Peter share this condition and illustrate, as no other group among the addressees does, the social and psychological predicament of the Christian community as a whole. Their uprootedness from home, lack of kin-group support, and exposure to the whims and abuse of their superiors, together with their suffering even when doing what is right typified the entire community's vulnerability in a hostile society.

(4) The *placement* of this exhortation diverges from the sequence of household instruction found in Ephesians and Colossians, where slaves (*douloi*) are addressed after wives-husbands and children-parents (Eph 5:21–6:9; Col 3:21–4:1). Thus our author gives exhortation to servants/slaves pride of place and uses it to initiate instruction on domestic relations.

(5) The point of this exhortation is not simply the subordination of household slaves, but also their doing what is right (v 20) and their endurance of unjust

suffering (vv 19–20). A double motivation supports this exhortation; namely: (a) appeal to "reverence" for God, "mindfulness" of God's will, God's "approval," and God's "calling" (vv 19–20, 21a); and (b) appeal to the solidarity between the innocent suffering servants/slaves and the innocent Christ as servant of God who suffered on their behalf and provided them an example to follow (vv 21–25).

(6) This double motivation involves the merging of diverse traditions: vv 19–20 allude to a saying of Jesus as preserved in Luke 6:32–34; v 21 echoes a tradition on discipleship; vv 21–24 entail formulations concerning the vicarious suffering of Christ, rooted and preserved in the eucharist tradition, that were expanded by material from Isa 52–53; and v 25 combines material derived from Isa 53:6 and Ezek 34:4–5, 16.

(7) This is the only domestic instruction of slaves in the NT to which such a lengthy Christological justification (vv 21–25) is added. In terms of its construction (2:18–20 + 21–25), 2:18–25 anticipates the similar construction in 3:13–22 (3:13–17 + 18–22). In terms of its length and specific Christological content, however, 2:21–25 constitutes the fullest Christological statement of the letter.

(8) Verses 21–25 incorporate an extensive amount of material drawn from the fourth servant song in Isaiah. This use of Isa 52:13–53:12 is noteworthy in at least two respects: (a) apart from Acts 8:32, these verses constitute the most extensive sustained allusion to Isa 52–53 in the entire NT; (b) the Christological portrait developed through use of this Isaian material is employed to substantiate instruction of household servants/slaves in particular, who also suffer despite their innocence and doing what is right. This association indicates that our author viewed Isa 52–53 as presenting a picture of an innocent yet humiliated servant of God who suffered vicariously on behalf of the people. In this picture he found a biblical model for portraying the innocent vicarious suffering of Jesus Christ and the solidarity that innocent suffering servants/slaves have with this figure of degradation and exaltation. Here it becomes clear that, from the author's point of view, Isaiah more than any other prophet represents the prophets who were concerned with the suffering and glorification of Christ mentioned earlier in 1:11–12 (so Hooker 1959, 198; Schutter 1989, 138–44).

(9) This passage, finally, has numerous terminological and thematic affinities with other parts of the letter. These include the ideas of subordination (v 18; cf. 2:13a; 3:1, 5; 5:5a) out of reverence for God (v 18; cf. 1:17; 3:2, 16); avoidance of wrongdoing/sin (vv 20a, 24a; cf. 4:1, 8 and 2:1, 12, 14, 16; 3:9, 10–12, 17; 4:15) and instead doing what is right (v 20b; cf. 2:14, 15; 3:6, 17; 4:19) in mindfulness of God's will (v 19b; cf. 3:16, 21); God as judge (2:23c; cf. 1:17; 4:5–6, 17); enduring unjust suffering (v 19c, 20d, 21b, 23b; cf. 1:6; 3:14, 17, 18; 4:1, 15, 19; 5:10), which has God's approval (vv 19–20; cf. 3:4); being called by God to such behavior (v 21a; cf. 1:15; 2:9; 5:10); Christ's suffering on the believers' behalf (v 21a, 23; cf. 1:11; 3:18; 4:1, 13; 5:1) and healing them (vv 21b, 24a,d) as the enablement for the renunciation of wrongdoing and for just conduct (v 24bc; cf. 1:14; 2:1, 11, 16; 3:11–12, 14, 17; 4:1–3, 16, 19); Christ's leaving servants (v 21cd) and all believers (3:18; 4:1) an example to

follow; Christ's stance of nonretaliation (v 23) as a model for slaves (v 20) and all believers (3:9); and his entrusting his cause to God (v 23c), as an example for all believers (4:19).

These affinities indicate that this passage has in view not simply servants/slaves but the entire community. The former are held up here as paradigmatic of the condition and vocation of the brotherhood as a whole.

The portrait of the atoning work of Jesus Christ (his innocence, his suffering on behalf of others, his submission to and trust in God, his wounding through which others are healed) and its saving effect provides a positive interpretation of the shame of his death on the cross, vindicates his uprightness, describes Christ as one who liberates from wrongdoing and enables living justly, recalls the kerygma that unites senders and recipients, and establishes the personal pattern of life that believers are to follow. In this unique exposition of Christ's atoning action, Christ, the antitype of the suffering servant of Isaiah, becomes the prototype for the servants/slaves, who in turn are presented as a model for the entire believing community.

What is said of and to slaves here at the outset of the domestic exhortation pertains ultimately to all within the household of God. The condition and experience, the attitude and the steadfastness, the vocation and the reward of the household slaves are all typical of and paradigmatic for the household of God as a whole. This may well provide the reason that the author departs from the conventional custom of reserving instruction of lowly slaves for the conclusion of domestic exhortation and instead gives these persons pride of place in his domestic instruction. As no other group addressed, these servants/slaves, in their uprootedness from home, lack of social support, and exposure to the whims of their superiors, together with their innocent suffering, typify the Christian comunity's vulnerability in a hostile society. In addressing these domestic slaves *first* in his household exhortation and in stressing their solidarity with the suffering Christ, our author lifts up the *oiketai* as paradigmatic of the entire *oikos* of God (Elliott 1981/1990, 205–8). The social condition and divine vocation of domestic slaves typify the condition and vocation of the community as a whole. Accordingly, these persons are addressed not as "slaves" (*douloi*), but as "household servants/slaves" (*oiketai*) who are linked with Jesus Christ as the suffering servant of God and they are presented as exemplary of the entire household of God (*oikos tou theou*) in regard to their vulnerable condition, their obligation of subordination, their doing what is right in mindfulness of God and his approval, their possible abuse and undeserved suffering, their vocation to follow in the footsteps of the suffering Christ, by whom they have been freed from sin and healed, and their divine return to the care of Christ. For servants/slaves, as for the entire community, Christ is the suffering servant of God who serves as both example and enabler. As in the case of the correlation between the social situation of the community addressed in Isa 53 and the Isaian portrait of the suffering but vindicated servant, so here as well, the thought of solidarity with Christ, the suffering yet vindicated servant, provides strength, hope, and motivation to a suffering community.

This exalting of lowly slaves as an example for the whole community is a powerful illustration of the author's conviction that "God opposes the proud and gives grace to the humble" (5:5c), a conviction fully consonant with the Lord's teaching concerning the reversal of status of the first and last (Matt 19:30/Mark 10:31; Matt 20:16), the servants and the served (Mark 9:35/Luke 9:48; Matt 20:26–28/Mark 10:43–45/Luke 22:26–27; cf. Matt 23:12; Luke 14:11; 18:14; John 13:1–15).

In view of the stance on slavery evident here—no censure of the institution but assumption of its continuation and legitimacy—this passage requires an awareness on the part of the present reader of the Bible of the historical, social, and cultural differences demarcating the perceptions and social structures of the world of the Bible from those of modern society and its principles and espoused rights of liberty and equality. Here, as throughout the Bible and the ancient world, slavery was perceived as a "given" and "natural" condition within a social order established by nature. Because this perception is no longer shared today and no longer informs contemporary political and legal arrangments, slavery and enslavement are no longer tolerated but instead are outlawed. This is true of ecclesial as well as political communities, however much in the not-too-distant past the Bible was indeed employed to provide divine warrant for slavery and policies of apartheid. The case of slavery, like that of the subordination of women (3:1–6), provides a graphic illustration of the constraints that the historical, social, and cultural contexts of both the Bible and its subsequent readers impose on its meaning and ethical implications for all generations.[147]

DETAILED COMMENT: TRADITION AND REDACTION IN 1 PETER 2:21–25

1 Peter 2:21–25 reflects a creative and original fusion of a variety of Israelite, Hellenistic, and primitive Christian traditions. The result of this merging of traditions is a portrayal of Jesus Christ as a personal model to be followed; as a servant of God, through whose vicarious suffering and death believers are freed from wrongdoing/sin, healed, and enabled to live justly; and as a shepherd and overseer of his followers. The image of Christ as an example whose pattern of innocent behavior is to be followed (2:21c, 22–23) represents a blending of a Hellenistic concept of a moral model with the primitive Christian

[147] On slavery in the Greco-Roman world, the Bible, and early Christianity, see Westermann 1935, 1955; Kehnscherper 1957; Bömer 1957–1963; Gülzow 1969; Bartchy 1973, 1988a, 1988b, 1992; Hopkins 1978; Finley 1980, 1987; Wiedemann 1981; Patterson 1982; Bradley 1987; Kyrtatas 1987, 25–74; Veyne, ed. 1987, 51–93; Hanson and Bartchy 1988a, 1988b; D. B. Martin 1990; Osiek 1992; Llewelyn and Kearsley, eds. 1992–1994, 163–96. On slavery in Asia Minor, see Broughton 1938, 636, 691, 839–49; D. B. Martin 1990, 1–49 and 151–73 (concerning occupations of slaves and duties of household slaves). On slavery and 1 Peter, see Carrez 1980; Laub 1982; Lamau 1986, 1988; Prostmeier 1990, 149–59, 405–32.

tradition of the disciple as one who follows the master, even to the point of solidarity in suffering (2:21d), as discussed in the NOTES above. The image of Christ as shepherd and overseer (2:25), in turn, is developed through a conflation of motifs derived from Isa 53:6 and Ezek 34 (see NOTES). The portrait, finally, of Christ as a "suffering just one" and suffering Servant of God, results from a unique expansion on various strands of antecedent biblical, later Israelite, and primitive Christian kerygmatic tradition in which Isa 52–53 in particular plays an influential role.

One major current of this tradition is the Israelite concept of the "suffering just one" or the theme of the suffering of the just (*passio iusti*). Developed in various stages over time, this concept related originally to Israel's king as the righteous one (Ps 18:21, 25; cf. 2 Sam 22) and subsequently included the suffering righteous who pray for God's justification (Pss 5, 7, 17, 25, 31, 71, 119, 143). The theme finds particular articulation in the fourth servant song of Isaiah (52:13–53:12) concerning the innocent servant of God, the "righteous one" (53:11; cf. 50:4–9), who is degraded, suffers though innocent, and is rejected by humans because of the message he brings. Applied to others who suffer but who are ultimately exalted, this theme is also given expression in Pss 33[34] and 36[37] and is echoed later in accounts of the suffering righteous one of Daniel (chs. 1–3, 6, 7–12) and the martyr theology of Susanna. However, only in late apocalyptic tradition does glorification clearly occur as a correlative to innocent suffering, when the concept of resurrection was already strong. In this tradition, the book of Wisdom, as L. Ruppert has shown (1972a, 1972b, 1973), played a significant role, with its focus on righteousness, the suffering of the righteous, and the contrast between the righteous and unrighteous. The date of this text suggests that the combination of the themes of suffering and glorification emerged in the first quarter of the first century BCE. The diptychs of Wis 2:12–20 and 5:1–7, on Ruppert's reckoning, appear to be an updating of Isa 52:13–53:12, applied to a lay, observant *ḥăsîd* or Pharisee persecuted by the Sadducees. Eventually the ideas of the "suffering righteous one" and martyrdom were combined in 4 Maccabees (18:6–19), which portrays the martyrdom of seven brothers under Antiochus Epiphanes as an experience of the "afflictions of the just" (18:16, citing Ps 33:20a). In Israelite responses to the suffering ensuing not only from the Maccabean revolt (e.g., *1 En.* 92–105) but also later from the Judean-Roman conflict of 66–73 CE (e.g., *2 Baruch*, *4 Ezra*), this theme of the suffering of the righteous, the *passio iusti/iustorum*, and its ultimate divine vindication likewise played a prominent role.[148]

Among the followers of Jesus, elements of this tradition were employed to provide scriptural and divine warrant for Jesus' suffering and death. Kerygmatic and creedal formulations were created through the use of both the *passio iusti* tradition and the fourth servant song of Isaiah.

---

[148] On this tradition in general, see Ruppert 1972a, 1972b, 1973. On the theme of the vicarious atoning effect of the death of the martyr in Israelite Hellenistic texts and later rabbinic sources, see Lohse 1963, 66–110; and Hengel 1986, 248–53.

In progressive stages of this development, the suffering and glorification of the Messiah/Christ were depicted as the fulfillment of Scripture[149] and of Isa 53 in particular.[150] At the presynoptic stage of development,[151] the "must" (*dei*) of the suffering, resurrection, and glorification of the Human One (Son of Man) or Christ implied the fulfillment of God's will.[152] This "must" also pertained to his being delivered (*paradidonai*) into human hands (Mark 9:31a; 14:41c; Luke 24:7; cf. Isa 53:12). At this stage of the formation of the passion tradition, there was reference to God's will but no trace yet of any soteriological significance of suffering and death. All allusions to Scripture at this point were to psalms concerning the suffering righteous one.[153] The term "the righteous one" (as vindicated by God) in six of seven occurrences is connected with Jesus' suffering (Luke 23:47; Acts 3:14; 7:52; Matt 27:19; 1 Pet 3:18; 1 John 2:1). Further OT echoes include Isa 50:4–9 (Mark 14:65; 15:19) and Wis 2 (itself a reflection on Isa 52–53), evident in Mark 14:55–65 par.

With the inclusion of the concept "he died for us, on account of our sins" (involving the *hyper* formulas), the atoning, soteriological aspect of Jesus' death was developed. The earliest pre-Pauline and pre-Synoptic traces of this tradition are the ancient kerygma of 1 Cor 15:3b–5, the words spoken over the cup in the Markan tradition of the Last Supper (Mark 14:24), and the "ransom for many" (Mark 10:45; cf. also Gal 1:4; Rom 4:25; 5:8; 8:32; Eph 5:2). The chief, and most likely oldest, Christian locus of the theme of the vicarious suffering of Jesus was the Lord's Supper tradition, which then formed the starting point for the Christian interpretation of Jesus' suffering and death as a self-giving act on Jesus' part that procures salvation for others. This vicarious character and power are expressed primarily through the *hyper* formula (Matt 26:26–29/Mark 14:22–25/Luke 22:15–20; 1 Cor 11:22–25): "this is my body for you" (*hyper hymōn*, 1 Cor 11:24); "my blood of the covenant which is poured out for many" (*hyper pollōn*, Mark 14:22; cf. Matt 26:28, *peri pollōn*); "this cup is the new covenant in my blood which is poured out for you" (*hyper hymōn*, Luke 22:20); cf. also Mark 10:45/Matt 20:28 ("ransom for many," *lytron anti pollōn*) and Titus 2:14 ("Jesus Christ who gave himself for us [*hyper hēmōn*] to redeem us").

Within this tradition, Jesus (the Human One/Son of Man) is also denoted as a "servant" (*diakonos*, *diakoneō*, Luke 22:24–27; cf. Mark 10:41–45/Matt 20:24–28; see John 13:1–20 [within the context of Jesus' death] and Luke 12:37b). Jesus is similarly declared to be "your (God's) servant (*pais*)" in the eucharistic

[149] See Matt 26:24; Luke 24:26–27, 46; Acts 10:39–44; 1 Cor 15:3–4; 1 Pet 1:11; cf. 5:1.

[150] See Acts 8:32–35; Luke 22:37; on Isa 52–53, see Dodd 1952, 90–96.

[151] On allusions to the *passio iusti* tradition in the pre-Markan passion history, see W. Pesch 1977, 13–15; for a comparison of scholarship on the pre-Markan Passion narrative, see Soards 1994.

[152] See Mark 8:31/Matt 16:21/Luke 9:42a; 9:12b; Luke 17:25; cf. esp. Luke 24:26: "Was it not necessary (*edei*) that the Christ should suffer these things and enter into his glory?"

[153] See Ps 22:2: Mark 15:34/Matt 27:46; Ps 22:8: Mark 15:29/Matt 27:39; Ps 22:9: Matt 27:43; Ps 22:19: Mark 14:24; Matt 27:35; Luke 23:34; John 19:24; Ps 41: Mark 14:18; Ps 42: Mark 14:34; Ps 69: Mark 15:23, 26; John 19:28.

instruction recorded in *Did.* 9–10 (9:2, 3; 10:2, 4). The appearance of this term in the fourth servant song of Isaiah (*pais*, 52:13; *paidion*, 53:2; cf. *paideia*, 53:5) together with the several affinities between this text and the eucharistic and passion tradition make it likely that Isa 52–53 served as a key OT source for providing scriptural warrant for Jesus' suffering, death, and divine vindication and the vicarious character of that suffering.[154]

In the NT, Luke 22:37 is the only instance in which Jesus himself is said to quote Isa 53: "He was reckoned among the transgressors" (Isa 53:12). Matthew (8:16–17, citing Isa 53:4) describes Jesus' healing as fulfillment of Isaiah's prophecy: "He took our infirmities and bore our illnesses." The account of Philip and the Ethiopian eunuch in Acts contains the fullest explicit citation of Isa 53 (53:7b–8b in Acts 8:32–33). This text pondered by the eunuch is interpreted by Philip as relating to the good news concerning Jesus (8:35), and a variant reading (8:37) contains the eunuch's confession, "I believe Jesus Christ to be the son of God" (where "son" [*huios*] is perhaps equivalent to *pais*). Besides these explicit citations, however, it appears that this passage provided Christian authors with a rich source of terminology, motifs, and themes for describing various features of Jesus' life, suffering, death, and exaltation as the fulfillment of Scripture and to substantiate aspects of the Christian mission.

Citations of and allusions to Isa 52–53 are found in early Christian comments on Jesus' ministry of healing (Matt 8:17, citing Isa 53:4), the disbelief of his audience (John 12:38, citing Isa 53:1), his identity as God's servant (*pais*, *paidion*) subordinate to God's will (Matt 12:18; Acts 3:13, 26; 4:27, 30; *Did.* 9:2, 3; 10:2, 3; *Diogn.* 8:9, 11; cf. Isa 52:13; 53:2, 11 [MT]); his submission to unjust treatment (Acts 8:32–33; 1 Pet 2:23; cf. Isa 53:7–8); his depiction as lamb (*amnos*, John 1:29, 36; 1 Pet 1:19; cf. Rev 7:17); his identity as "child" of God (Acts 3:13, 26; 4:25, 27, 30; *Did.* 9–10. and *1 Clem.* 16, which cites Isa 53 as an illustration of Jesus' humility) and as "righteous one" (*dikaios*, Acts 3:14; 1 Pet 3:18; cf. Isa 53:11 LXX); his innocence (1 Pet 2:22–23; 1 John 3:5; cf. Isa 53:9b); his being "handed over" (*paradidonai*, Mark 9:31/Matt 17:22/Luke 9:44; Mark 10:33/Matt 20:18–19/Luke 18:32; Mark 14:21/Matt 26:24/Luke 22:22; Matt 26:2/Mark 14:41/Matt 26:45; Luke 24:7, etc.; Rom 4:25; 8:32; 10:33 cf. Isa 53:6, 12); his degradation and humiliation (Mark 9:12; 10:34; Mark 15:16–20/Matt 27:27–31/John 19:2–3; Mark 15:29–32 par.; cf. Isa 52:14; 53:2–3, 8); his silence (Matt 26:62–63/Mark 14:60–61; Matt 27:12, 14/Mark 15:4–5; 1 Pet 2:23; *Barn.* 5:2; Just. Mart. *Dial.* 72.3; 90.1; 111.3; 114.3; cf. Isa 53:7); his being numbered with transgressors (Luke 22:37, citing Isa 53:12; cf. Matt 27:38/Mark 15:27/Luke 23:33; cf. Isa 53:12); his suffering and death and its vicarious quality (Mark 14:24/Matt 26:28/Luke 22:20/1 Cor 11:23–24; Matt 26:67–68/Mark 14:65/Luke 22:63–65; Matt 27:26–44/Mark 15:15–32; Luke 23:24–39; Acts

[154] Justin Martyr (*Dial.* 111.3, which explicitly cites Isa 53:7) illustrates the continued association of Isa 53 with this eucharistic tradition in later time as well.

10:43; Rom 4:25; 8:32; 1 Cor 15:3; Gal 2:20; Eph 5:2; Heb 9:28; 1 Pet 2:21, 24; *Barn.* 5:1–2; cf. Isa 53:4–8, 10–12) and his vindication, exaltation, and glorification (Luke 24:26; John 12:23, etc.; 1 Pet 1:11; cf. Isa 52:13; 53:12); the "going astray" of God's people/sheep (1 Pet 2:25; cf. Isa 53:6); and the proclamation of Christ to the Gentiles (Rom 15:21, citing Isa 52:15).

Within the NT, 1 Peter manifests the most extensive use of Isa 52:13–53:12 in elaborating the details, significance, and soteriological effect of Jesus' suffering and death and in presenting him as a model to be emulated. The correspondences in terminology and theme are abundant:

1 Peter	*Isaiah 53*
2:21	cf. 5:3, 4, 5, 6, 8, 10, 11, 12
2:22	53:9 (citation); cf. also 1 Pet 1:19 on Christ's sinlessness
2:23a	cf. 53:7 (silence)
2:23b	53:3–5, 7, 8, 11, 12 (suffering and death)
2:23c	53:6, 12 (2×) (*paradidou*)
2:24a	53:4, 11, 12 (citation); cf. 53:5
2:24b,c	53:5, 11 (*dikaiosai dikaion*; 1 Peter: *dikaiosynē*; cf. also 1 Pet 3:18: *dikaios*)
2:24d	53:5 (citation)
2:25a	53:6a

The Isaian text offers a scriptural portrait of, not only a suffering servant who nevertheless remains obedient to God, but one who in general was dishonored, despised, and shamed among humankind (52:14–15; 53:2–4, 7–9) but was nevertheless vindicated by God (52:13; 53:10–12). Thus, it provides an especially apposite biblical text for not only elaborating on the suffering and death of Jesus but also linking this innocent suffering with the suffering of servants/slaves and then with the suffering of the entire community.

The association of the Christological tradition in 1 Pet 2:21–25 with the servant/slave exhortation in 2:18–20 indicates that the Petrine author presumed an affinity between these household servants, the Isaian servant of God (*pais*, Isa 52:13; *paidion*, 53:2; cf. *douleuonta*, 53:11) and Jesus as servant. The term *pais*, denoting someone of inferior rank (including "child" and "servant") elsewhere in early Christian tradition, is used to identify Jesus as (1) "servant" of God (Matt 12:18; cf. Isa 42:1; *Barn.* 6:1 and 92; cf. Isa 50:10; *1 Clem.* 59:2, 3, 4; *Did.* 9:2, 3; 10:2–3); (2) "child" of God (*Mart. Poly.* 14:1, 3; 20:2; *Diogn.* 8:9, 11; 9:1); or (3) either "servant" or "son" (Acts 3:13, 26; 4:27, 30); cf. Israel as *pais* (servant or child) in Luke 1:54.

The *hyper* formula indicating vicarious suffering (2:21b) does not occur in Isa 52–53 but nevertheless reproduces the sense of several equivalent Isaian expressions: "he bears our sin and is pained for (*peri*) for us" (53:4); "But he was wounded on account of (*dia*) our sins and was bruised on account of (*dia*) our iniquities; the chastisement of our peace was upon him and by his bruise we have been healed" (53:5); "the Lord handed him over for our sins" (53:6); "and he shall bear their sins"(53:11); "he bore the sins of many and was handed over on account of (*dia*) their iniquities" (53:12; cf. *hyper*, however, in the text of *1 Clem.* 16:7, citing Isa 53:6).

In 1 Pet 2:21–25 we have "the earliest definite proof for the full identification of Jesus with the servant in all its Christological signficance" (Hooker 1959, 127). Given the association of this early Christian servant soteriology with Simon Peter (cf. the Petrine speeches in Acts 3:12–26; 10:34–43; cf. 4:24–30; Stanley 1965), the appearance of this theme in a letter attributed to Peter should come as no surprise. The notion of vicarious suffering found in 1 Peter does not appear in other NT texts that appeal to Isa 53 (Mark 14:61a; Matt 8:17; Acts 8:32–33) but seems to be a unique contribution of 1 Peter. Subsequent to and most likely reflective of 1 Peter, *1 Clem.* 16:3–14 cites the entirety of Isa 53 as a scriptural substantiation of Christ's humility. The author of *1 Clement*, as it were, follows in 1 Peter's footsteps. In the second century, Isa. 53:7–8 is cited by Melito of Sardis in his *Paschal Homily* (64; cf. 71).[155]

The patent extensive use of Isa 52–53 in 1 Pet 2:21–25 makes unnecessary the search for other sources underlying this passage, such as a pre-Petrine hymn or creed. Certain features of 1 Pet 2:21–24, nevertheless, have led some scholars to conjecture the use and modification of an earlier source construed as either a hymn or creed or catechetical instruction.[156]

This hypothesis is based on structural and syntactical features of this text:

1. the shift between "you" (2d-person pl., vv 21, 24d–25) and "we" (1st-person pl., v 24abc) and thus a seeming transition from hortatory ("you") to hymnic ("we") to hortatory ("you") style;
2. the repeated and paralleled occurrence of the relative pronoun *hos* ("who/he") in vv 22a, 23a, 24a, and 24d (*hou*, "whose/his"), which is typical in clauses in suspected hymns or creeds (see Col 1:15, 18; 1 Tim 3:16; cf. Phil 2:6);
3. a suspected thematic shift from Christ's example of innocent suffering and endurance (vv 22–23, as exemplary for slaves) to his vicarious suffering for sins (vv 21a, 24d, as relevant for all believers).

However, as other commentators have cogently noted (Best 1971, 120; Osborne 1983; Michaels 1988, 136–37), these features neither prove nor require the theory of use of an extant hymnic or creedal source. Consequently, I re-

---

[155] On the influence of Isa 52–53 on NT writings, see Dodd 1953, 92–94; Wolff 1950; Stanley 1965; Jeremias 1966d, 1967; Haag 1985; Hengel 1986, 245–48; Hofius 1993; Janowski and Stuhlmacher, eds. 1996. On the use of Isa 53 in 1 Peter, see Wolff 1950, 88–92; Schlosser 1980; Langkammer 1987; Hofius 1993. On the *pais theou* Christology of the early Church, see Hooker 1959; Lohse 1963; Jeremias 1966d; 1967, 79–104; D. L. Jones 1982.

[156] See, e.g., Windisch and Preisker 1951, 65; R. Bultmann 1947; Boismard 1961, 111–32; Schille 1962, 45–46; Deichgräber 1967, 140–43; Wengst 1974, 83–86, followed by others: Goldstein 1974; Millauer 1976, 15–84, 90–103; Schlosser 1980, 83–93; Brox 1986, 134; Goppelt 1993, 207–10.

tract my earlier acceptance of this hymnic theory (Elliott 1985) for the following reasons:

(1) No precise hymnic or creedal parallel to the entire text of 1 Pet 2:21–24 (25) is extant. The parallels that have been cited involve only isolated formulas or debatable thematic affinities (as in Boismard 1961) rather than complete correspondences and similarly structured texts. The similarity between 1 Pet 2:21–25 and the later text of Pol. *Phil* 8:1–2 is quite close, but the different structure and content of these similar texts argues against any common use of a fixed hymnic source and for the direct influence of 1 Peter upon Polycarp.

(2) There is no NT hymn or creed that incorporates the amount of material from Isa 53 found in 1 Peter. Moreover, reliance of the Petrine author upon Isa 52–53 extends beyond the limits of the suspected hymn (vv 21–24) and includes v 25a; see also further possible allusions to Isa 52–53 in 1 Pet 1:18, 19, 21; 3:18b.

(3) There is no agreement among proponents of this view regarding the content, form, and extent of the alleged source. Whereas Windisch and Preisker (1951, 65), for instance, see in vv 21–25 a "Christ hymn" of five strophes, R. Bultmann (1947, 12–14) differentiates more specifically between elements of hymnic tradition and prosaic redaction in vv 21–24; while Wengst (1974, 84–85) regards vv 21a, 22, 24ab as constituting a "catechetical formulation"; for differing views, see also Zerbe 1993, 279–84.

(4) The fluctuation between 2d-person and 1st-person subjects is due to the material employed from Isa 53 and the author's stress on the inclusiveness of Christ's saving work. The phrase *our wrongdoings/sins* (v 24a) is derived from Isa 53:4 and 5, and this then requires a 1st-person verbal form in the following purpose clause of v 24c ("we might live"), as Michaels (1988, 137) correctly notes. This "we" statement affirms the faith in Christ's vicarious suffering that unites senders and addressees. Furthermore, the underlying Isaian text also varies between "you" (52:14; 53:10b) and "we," "our" (53:1–2a,c; 4–6); compare also "my people" (53:8); "I" (53:9); "their" (53:11, 12).

(5) Relative pronouns indeed appear in suspected hymns (see 1 Tim 3:16; Col 1:15, 18; cf. Phil 2:6). However, they are also used frequently in 1 Peter in statements not reflective of hymnic sources (e.g., 1:8, 12; 2:8; 3:3, 4, 6, 20–21; 4:5; 5:9, 12) . Where the use of extant hymnic material is suspected elsewhere (1:20; 3:18, 22), the distinctive stylistic feature is the use of contrasting passive participles, not relative pronouns with finite verbs (Michaels 1988, 137).

(6) In regard to the four relative clauses (vv 22, 23, 24abc, 24d) and the statements of Christ's example of enduring innocent suffering (vv 21c–23) and his vicarious suffering (v 21b, 24), the terminology employed is derived primarily from Isa 53 (as is the terminology in v 25a). There is thus no pronounced "shift" in theme and hence no reason to suspect the use of a hymn or creed to account for this difference. Moreover, as is indicated elsewhere (in the NOTES and COMMENTARY), this entire unit (2:18–25) has both the servants/slaves and the entire community simultaneously in view.

(7) In contrast to such hymns as Phil 2:6–11 and 1 Tim 3:16, these Petrine verses lack such typical hymnic features as consistently parallel colons, a constant metrical or rhythmic pattern, and clear strophic arrangement of content.

(8) The *certain direct* source of much of this material, as indicated in the NOTES above, is Isa 52–53. The manner in which Isa 52–53 is used here, with Isaian terms and phrases interwoven with the author's own formulations, is consistent with the employment of the OT elsewhere in the letter (cf. 1:23–25; 2:4–10; 3:14; 4:8, 14; 5:8).

In sum, hymnic or creedal theories lack definitive proof and are unnecessary for accounting for the content of 1 Pet 2:21–25. These verses, rather, manifest an original and creative blending of tradition, concepts, and motifs that is marked by an extensive use of material from Isa 52–53 to present Christ as an innocent suffering servant of God and model for suffering believers. This unique NT construction is then used to provide apposite motivation for the exhortation of innocently suffering slaves in vv 18–20. The entirety of 2:18–25 forms a statement of exhortation and encouragement designed most immediately for servants/slaves and then, given the exemplary function of this group in the letter, for the community as a whole.

For studies on 1 Pet 2:18–25, see Achtemeier 1993; Bartina 1964; Betz 1967; Boismard 1961, 111–32; Bosetti 1990, 75–115; Braun 1940; R. Bultmann 1947; Burtness 1969; Carrez 1980; Cervantes Gabarrón 1991, 115–80; 1991a; Deichgräber 1967, 140–43; Elliott 1981/1990, 1985; Ellul 1990; Gielen 1990, 474–512; Goldstein 1974; Hall 1976; Hiebert 1982a; Hofius 1993; Hooker 1959; Jones-Haldeman 1988; Kirk 1981; Lamau 1986, 1988; Langkammer 1987; Lash 1982; Lohse 1986; Miguéns 1969; Millauer 1976; Ogara 1936c; Olson 1979; Osborne 1983; Patsch 1969; Prostmeier 1990, 149–59, 405–32; Schelkle 1961; Schlosser 1980; Schutter 1989, 138–44; Selwyn 1947, 90–101; Sisti 1968; Sywulka 1991; J. W. Thompson 1966; van Unnik 1956–1957; Wendland 1970, 101–4; Wengst 1974; Zerbe 1993, 270–91.

III. C. Honorable conduct in the domestic realm: subordinate wives (3:1–6) and respectful husbands (3:7)

3:1a Likewise you wives:
1b   be subordinate to your husbands,
1c   so that, even if some disobey the word,
1d   they may be won without a word
1e   by the conduct of their wives,
2   when they observe your reverent and chaste conduct.
3a   Do not adorn yourselves outwardly

3b by braiding [your] hair,
3c putting on gold ornaments,
3d and wearing fine clothing;
4a but rather let your adornment be the hidden person of the heart
4b with the imperishable [adornment] of a gentle and tranquil spirit,
4c which in God's sight is very precious.
5a For thus also the holy wives of old
5b who hoped in God
5c used to adorn themselves,
5d being subordinate to their husbands,
6a as Sarah obeyed Abraham,
6b calling him lord.
6c You became her children,
6d now doing what is right
and "not fearing any terror."
7a You husbands in turn:
7b live considerately with [your wives],
7c as with a weaker feminine vessel,
7d bestowing honor [on them]
7e as also co-heirs of the grace of life,
7f so that your prayers may not be hindered.

INTRODUCTION

Instruction regarding order and proper conduct in the civic (2:13–17) and domestic (2:18–25) realms continues now with an address to wives and husbands concerning their appropriate spousal roles. Connection to and continuity with the language and themes of the foregoing exhortation are maintained through a variety of means: the adverb "likewise" or "in turn" (*homoiōs*, 3:1a, 7a, respectively); the verb "be subordinate" (*hypotassō*, 3:1a, 5d; cf. 2:13, 18a); the concept of "disobeying the word" (3:1c; cf. 2:8); the accent on "conduct" (*anastrophē*, 3:1e, 2; cf. 1:15, 18; 2:12) and doing what is right (3:6; cf. 2:14, 15, 20); and the repeated mention of "reverence" (*phobos*) for God (3:2; cf. 1:17; 2:17, 18); gaining nonbelievers who "observe" (*epopteuō*, 3:1d, 2; cf. 2:12); holiness (3:2, 5a; cf. 1:14–16, 22; 2:5, 9); imperishability (3:4b; cf. 1:4, 23); divine approval (3:4c; cf. 2:19–20); hope (3:5b; cf. 1:3, 13, 21); obedience (3:6a; cf. 1:14a); and bestowing honor (3:7d; cf. 2:17).

The combined instruction to Christian wives (vv 1–6) and husbands (v 7) involves four main subunits: vv 1–2, wifely subordination and holy conduct and its winsome effect on nonbelieving husbands; vv 3–4, wifely subordination and conduct illustrated by adornment, with stress on internal character and divine approval; vv 5–6, present moral adornment and subordination illustrated by the conduct of the holy wives of old and especially Sarah; v 7, husbands' honoring their wives as co-heirs of divine grace.

The exhortation of wives in particular (vv 1–6) has a chiastic structure (Spicq 1966, 121):[157]

A. wives, be subordinate (v 1); holy conduct (v 2)
  B. your adornment (vv 3–4)
  B.′ the holy wives and their adornment (v 5a–c)
A.′ they were subordinate to their husbands (v 5d) as Sarah, your spiritual mother, obeyed Abraham (v 6abc); your good conduct (v 6d)

On the whole, the structure and vocabulary are quite similar to the structure and vocabulary of 2:18–25. In both cases an initial principle of behavior involving subordination (3:1ab; cf. 2:18a) is followed by two motivations (3:1c–4 [winning husbands, approval of God]; cf. 2:19–21a [approval of God, divine calling]) and an example (2:21b–25; 3:5–6); compare also reverence for God (3:2; 2:18), doing what is right (3:6d; 2:20d), and the antitheses of 3:3–4 and 2:20 (cf. Ellul 1990, 25).

The topic of marriage, marital relations, and the appropriate roles of wives and husbands was a prominent feature of early Christian instruction and exhortation, from the teaching of Jesus onward.[158] In general, this teaching is characterized by a conformity to prevailing cultural notions concerning males and females, their differing roles and status as determined by nature, and the features of proper marital relations and conduct. Certain NT texts, such as 1 Pet 3:1–7; Eph 5:22–33; and Col 3:18–20, appear to have been adaptations of a particular Hellenistic tradition concerning household management (see the DETAILED COMMENT on 1 Pet 2:13–17). The relation of husband and wife figured prominently in this *oikonomia* tradition.[159] Christian authors in adopting this tradition, however, also modified and "Christianized" it. Whereas this tradition mentioned wives only indirectly in advice addressed specifically to husbands/householders, early Christian authors address wives directly as responsible moral agents in their own right, as they do Christian slaves. Moreover, Christian writers, while sharing conventional notions of expected spousal behavior, also appeal to distinctly Christian rationales for this behavior. 1 Peter 3:1–7 represents this combination of conventional views and Christian motivation specifically designed for the situation in which the community found itself as a beleaguered messianic sect in Asia Minor.

[157] For a different, less probable view, see Schlosser (1983), who proposes v 5d as a second imperative paralleling v 1b and the two participles of v 6c as related to this second imperative, with a resulting parallelism of vv 3–5a/5b–6.

[158] See Matt 5:27–32; 19:3–12/Mark 10:1–12; 22:23–28; 1 Cor 5:1–11; 7:1–40; 14:34–37; Eph 5:22–33; Col 2:18–19; 1 Thess 4:3–8; 1 Tim 2:8–15; 3:11–12; 5:9–16; Titus 2:4–5; Heb 13:4; *1 Clem.* 1:3; 21:6–7; Herm. *Mand.* 4.1; Ign. *Pol.* 5:1–2; Pol. *Phil* 4:2.

[159] See Iamblichus, *Life of Pythagoras* 35–57; Arist., *Pol.* 1–2; Ps.-Arist., *Oec.*; Xen., *Oec.*; Philo, *Decal.* 165–67; *Spec.* 3. 169–71; *Hypoth.* 7. 14; Josephus, *Ag. Ap.* 2.189–209; Hier. (in Stobaeus, books 1–5; esp. 4.22.21–24; 4.502.1–507.5; cf. also 4.24.14; 4.603.8–24; 5.5–22; 5.696.23–697.3); and Balch 1981, 21–62.

NOTES

3:1a. *Likewise* (*homoiōs*). This adverb together with the verb "be subordinate" links this exhortation to Christian wives with the foregoing exhortation to civil subjects (2:13–17) and, more proximately, to household slaves (2:18–25). *Homoiōs* can serve as a simple connective with the sense of "in turn" (as in 3:7a and 5:5a). However, here it functions in its more usual manner (e.g., Mark 4:16; Luke 3:11; 10:32, 37; Jas 2:25) to introduce something similar to the foregoing, with the sense of "likewise," "so," or "similarly" (cf. *T. Naph.* 3:5; *T. Benj.* 6:7). The verb "be subordinate" and the parallel formulations of 3:1 and 2:18 (*hai gynaikes hypotassomenai/hoi oiketai hypotassomenoi*, "you wives be subordinate" / "you household slaves be subordinate") indicate that the similarity concerns the subordination and respect for order that wives, like domestic slaves and all the believers (2:13), are to demonstrate.

you wives (*hai gynaikes*). The definite article *hai*, found in the majority of ancient manuscripts ($\mathfrak{P}^{72}$ $\aleph^{2}$ C P Ψ etc.) but absent in others ($\mathfrak{P}^{81}$ $\aleph^{*}$ A B), is consistent with similar articular constructions in 2:18 and 3:7 and gives the expression *hai gynaikes* the force of a vocative: "you wives." The Greek noun *gynaikes* (vv 1, 5; cf. the related adjective *gynaikeios*, v 7b) can denote either "women" or "wives" depending on context, just as *andres* (v 1c, 5d, 7a) can denote either "men" or "husbands" (as is also the case in German and other modern languages). The adjective *idiois* ("your [own]") accompanying *andrasin* ("husbands," vv 1b, 5d) as well as the reference to the married couple Sarah and Abraham (v 5) indicate that "wives" and "husbands" are meant here (as in v 7) and that the instruction concerns marital relations and not male-female relations in general.

The instruction of wives and husbands that follows echoes sentiments and values concerning spousal roles and relations that prevailed in the Greco-Roman world of the day. These perspectives were enshrined in particular in moral instruction on "household management" (*oikonomia*), a tradition with which our author was clearly familiar. Xenophon's treatise *On Household Management* (*Oeconomicus*) has been described as "the most fully developed treatise on married life that classical Greece has left us" (Foucault 1985, 152). With its attention to marriage (ch. 7), domestic order (chs. 8–9), cosmetics (ch. 10), and the husband as gentleman (ch. 11), it illustrates the traditional place of these subjects in the household management (*oikonomia*) tradition of moral instruction. This is in accord with Aristotle's seminal observation (*Pol.* 1.5.1) that "the science of household management has three divisions, one the relation of master to slave . . . , one the paternal relation, and the third the conjugal, for it is part of the household science to rule over wife and children"; see also Ps.-Arist., *Oec.*, book 1 (1.2.1; 3.1–4.3) and book 3 (regarding the virtuous wife and honorable marital relations).

Our Petrine author, like Xenophon and others, treats the marital relationship within the context of instruction on household management. Again, however, as in the case of the household slaves, he diverges from the Hellenistic household management tradition in *addressing wives directly* (rather than charging husbands with their instruction), thereby acknowledging these wives as intelligent and responsible moral agents in their own right.

1b. *be subordinate to your husbands* (*hypotassomenai tois idiois andrasin*). The foregoing theme of order and subordination (2:13–17, 18–25) is continued and now concerns the respect of wives for the authority of their husbands and for order within the household. On the theme of subordination and social order, see 2:13 and the related DETAILED COMMENT. The verb *hypotassō* ("be subordinate"), here and in v 5, is also used elsewhere in the NT with reference to the subordination of wives to their husbands (1 Cor 14:34; Eph 5:21, 24; Col 3:18; Titus 2:5; cf. 1 Tim 2:11 [*hypotagē*]), though less frequently elsewhere.[160] Its participial form (*hypotassomenai*) here has imperatival force like other imperatival participles in 1 Peter (1:14b; 2:1, 18; 3:7, 9; 4:8, 10; see the NOTE on 1:14b).

This injunction concerning the subordination of wives "to their own husbands" (*tois idiois andrasin*; cf. the same phrase in Eph 5:22; Titus 2:4) and the portrayal of the manner in which this subordination is demonstrated (vv 3–4) reflect conventional norms and expectations regulating marital relations and uxorial conduct in the Greco-Roman and Israelite world. In their views of the different "natures" of males and females and the subordinate position of the latter, Christians shared the patriarchal constructs of gender, gender-determined status, and the gender-determined relations of the patriarchal society that they inhabited. This cultural context, so different from that of modern Western societies, is essential for contemporary readers to keep in mind, who may be inclined to read and evaluate biblical statements on wife-husband and female-male relations from the vantagepoint of their own historical and cultural settings. (For further discussion of this point see the DETAILED COMMENT.)

Subordination of wives to their husbands was universally regarded in ancient patriarchal society as being dictated by the differing physical and mental characteristics allotted by nature to males and females. These characteristics determined both their respective statuses and their roles in an ordered social hierarchy. Females (and thus wives), it was generally held, were *by nature* inferior to males (and husbands) physically, intellectually and morally, and were therefore consigned by nature to the authority, tutelage, and protection of the latter (Hesiod, *Op.* 695–705; Plato, *Tim.* 42AB, 91a; Xen., *Oec.* 3.11–14; 7.4–8; Plut., *Conj. praec.* 48; *Mor.* 145C–D). Aristotle, expressing "conventional (male) wisdom" on this subject, asserted: "As between the sexes, the male (*to arren*) is by nature the superior (*to kreitton*) and the female the inferior (*to cheiron*); he is the ruler (*to archon*) and she, the one ruled (*to archomenon*) (*Pol.* 1.2.12;

---

[160] See Josephus, *Ag. Ap.* 2.199–201; Plut., *Conj. praec.* 33 (*Mor.* 142E); and an Egyptian love-charm of the 3d–4th century CE (SEG 1717, l. 25).

1254b; cf. also 1.5.1–2; 1259a; 1.5.6; 1260a).[161] Plutarch, a contemporary of the NT period, similarly observes in his *Advice to Bride and Groom* (*Conj. praec.* 33, *Mor.* 142D):

> If they (wives) subordinate themselves (*hypotattousai*) to their husbands, they are commended, but if they want to have control, they cut a sorrier figure than the subjects of their control. And control (*kratein*) ought to be exercised by the man over the woman, not as the owner has control over a piece of property, but, as the soul controls the body, by entering into her feelings and being knit to her through good will. As, therefore, it is possible to exercise care over the body without being a slave to its pleasures and desires, so it is possible to govern (*archein*) a wife, and at the same time to delight and gratify her. (cf. also Ps.-Call. 1.22.4)

Such uxorial subordination was held to be a requisite for internal order and harmony in the household and was considered a badge of a family's honor and public reputation. Through their subordination, it was held, wives acknowledged and preserved the necessary order of the household, demonstrated loyalty to their husbands, assured a harmonious domestic life, and maintained the honor and good reputation of both their marital and natal families. Such domestic order, in turn, it was held, was a prerequisite for order and harmony in the political realm as well. As Aristotle noted in his discussion of the freedom of subordinates (slaves and women): "The freedom in regard to women is detrimental both in regard to the purpose of the *politeia* and in regard to the happiness of the state. For just as man and wife are part of a household, it is clear that the state also is divided nearly in half into its male and female population, so that in all *politeia* in which the position of women is badly regulated one half of the state must be deemed neglected in framing the law" (Arist., *Pol.* 2.6; 1269B). Although at the time of 1 Peter elite Roman matrons may have enjoyed a greater degree of freedom after their prepuberty confinement, "women in the provinces of Asia Minor would feel the tighter strictures imposed by Middle Eastern traditions" (Danker 1980, 147). Chastity, silence (in the public realm), modesty, obedient subordination, and familial loyalty were, in general, the prime virtues of an honorable woman or wife. (See the DETAILED COMMENT for further discussion.)

In Israelite and Christian circles, wifely subordination also was assumed to be a given fact of life and was more rigidly enforced. Israelite authors pointed to Gen 2–3 and creation of the woman from the man as the indication of her secondary and subordinate status. Philo (*QG* 1.27) observes that the serpent addressed the woman rather than the man because "woman is more accustomed

[161] See also Ps.-Arist., *Mag. Mor.* 1.33.18; 2.11.45, 52; 2.17.2; Euripides, *Trodes* 665–66; *Medea* 569–75; Ps.-Arist., *Oec.* 3.1; Xen., *Oec.* 9.18–19; 10.1; and generally the household management tradition from Aristotle onward.

to being deceived than man . . . because of softness she easily gives way and is taken in by plausible falsehood that resembles the truth" (cf. also *QG* 1.43). The Israelite sage Sirach advises the male: "Do not give yourself to a woman/wife so that she gains mastery over your strength" (Sir 9:2); "To son or wife or friend, do not give power over yourself as long as you live . . . while you are still alive and have breath in you, do not let anyone take your place" (Sir 33:19–20). Philo (*Hypoth.* 7.3) likewise asserts that "wives must serve (*douleuein*) their husbands, a servitude not imposed by violent ill-treatment but promoting obedience (*eupeitheian*) in all things" (cf. similarly *QG* 1.27, 29; see also *Let. Aris.* 250–51; and *Ps.-Phoc.* 175–206).

While sharing the biological views and social norms of their pagan contemporaries in this matter, Israelites and Christians pointed to the Torah as the legitimation for such subordination. Thus Josephus (*Ag. Ap.* 2.201) comments: "The wife, says the Law, is in all things inferior (*cheirōn*) to the husband. Accordingly, let her obey (*hypakouetō*), not for her humiliation, but that she may be ruled (*archētai*); for God has given the power (*to kratos*) to the husband." One important consequence of Eve's disobedience (Gen 3) according to Israelite and early Christian thought was her reduction to the authority and control of her husband: "yet your desire shall be for your husband, and he shall rule over you" (Gen 3:16), a status to which all future females and wives were assumed to be reduced.[162] Beyond appeal to the Mosaic Law, other rationales for the subordination of women and wives were also given: compare "the head of every man is Christ, the head of a woman is her husband, and the head of Christ is God" (1 Cor 11:3, 8: cf. Eph 5:23) . . . "man was not made from woman, but woman from man" (1 Cor 11:8); "wives, be subordinate to your husbands, as is fitting in the Lord" (Col 3:1); "wives, be subordinate to your own husbands as to the Lord" (Eph 5:21); or uxorial subordination is necessary, "so that the word of God may not be discredited" (Titus 2:5). Clement of Rome, writing to the Christians of Corinth observes: "To the women (or wives) you have instruction that they should do all things with a blameless and seemly and chaste mindfulness of God, yielding a dutiful affection to their husbands. And you taught them to remain in the rule of subordination (*en te tōi kanōni tēs hypotagēs*) and to manage their households with seemliness, in all circumspection" (*1 Clem.* 1:3). This expectation of wifely subordination remains constant in the Church throughout the following centuries. Generations later, Augustine voices the still current notion that wives must obey their husbands in the earthly city (*City of God* 19.14).

While the Petrine author likewise shares this universal view of the subordinate status of wives, the full rationale he gives for their subordinate behavior is decidedly Christian in content and without parallel in the NT: (1) subordination and holy conduct could win unbelieving husbands to the faith (v 1cde);

[162] See Philo, *QG* 1.37, commenting on Gen 3:16; 1 Tim 2:12–15; and 1 Cor 14:34: "wives should be subordinate, *as even the Law says.*"

(2) it has God's approval (v 4c); (3) it is consistent with the conduct of Sarah and the holy matriarchs of Israel (vv 5–6); finally, (4) Christian wives, whether or not married to believing husbands, are heirs of the grace of life (v 7e). In addition to this set of motivations, the following verses also clarify what this subordination entails: reverent and chaste conduct (v 2), a gentle and tranquil spirit (v 4b), emulation of the subordinate attitude of the holy matriarchs (vv 5–6a), and doing what is right without feeling intimidated (v 6c).

1c. *so that* (*hina*) introduces a statement (v 1c–2) indicating the strategic goal of wifely subordination; namely, the conversion of those husbands who are not believers.

even if some disobey the word (*kai ei tines apeithousin tōi logōi*). The conditional formulation "even if" (*kai ei*) indicates that the author allows for the fact that "some" (*tines*) of the husbands mentioned in v 1b may be nonbelievers, and it is on their reaction that he focuses attention. From the larger context of the letter it is clear that "disobey the word" (*apeithousin tōi logōi*) refers to disobedence to, or disbelief in, the word concerning Jesus Christ (2:7, 8) or the word of good news (1:23, 25; cf. 4:17).[163] This absolute use of *logos* to denote the Christian gospel in general is traditional (see Acts 6:4; 16:6; 18:15; Gal 6:6; Col 4:3; 1 Thess 1:6; Jas 1:21). The situation of mixed marriages is thus reckoned with here, similar to those encountered by Paul in Corinth (1 Cor 7:12–16), whereas in v 7 exclusively Christian spouses are presupposed. In the case of the mixed marriages, either believing women had married pagan males, or these wives had converted after having married. It is likely that at this time such mixed marriages were the exception to the rule of endogamous marriage (i.e., within the ethnic or religious community), as practiced generally in Israel[164] and the messianic sect.[165] As a defensive strategy, such endogamous marriages served to maintain the integrity of the group and to avoid "contamination" by outsiders.[166] Thus, it is more likely that the wives addressed in this chapter had become believers after having married.

Such conversions would have raised questions about domestic harmony, since wives were expected to venerate the gods of their husbands (Xen., *Oec.* 7.8; Dionys. Hal., *Ant. rom.* 2.25.1; Cicero, *Leg.* 2.8.19–22). This general expectation is illustrated in the observation by Plutarch in his *Advice to Bride and Groom* (*Conj. praec.* 19, *Mor.* 140D): "A wife should not acquire her own friends, but should make her husband's friends her own. The gods are the first and most significant friends. For this reason, it is proper for a wife to recognize

---

[163] Elsewhere in 1 Peter the verbal participle "disobedient" describes the imprisoned angelic spirits (3:20a) of primordial time.

[164] See Gen 24:3, 27; 27:46–28:1; Num 36:8; Deut 7:1–5; Ezra 9:10–12; 10:10; Tob 4:12–13; 6:10–12; *Jos. Asen.* 7:6; 8:5; *Jub.* 22:16–20; 25:1–10; 30:11–12; *T. Levi* 9:9–10; *T. Job* 45:3; Philo, *Spec.* 3.29.

[165] See Paul: "marry . . . only in the Lord" (1 Cor 7:39); "be not mismated with unbelievers" (2 Cor 6:14).

[166] See Malina (1993d, 117–48) on marriage strategies in general; on mixed marriages, see MacDonald (1990).

only those gods whom her husband worships and to shut the door to superstitious cults and strange superstitions. The performance of clandestine and secret rites by a woman do not ingratiate her to any of the gods." The second-century report (Just. Mart., 2 *Apol.* 2) of a Christian wife married to a pagan husband and the martyrdom of her instructor, Ptolemaeus, provides a later example of the kind of hatred that Christian wives and their fellow-believers could encounter from reprobate pagan husbands.[167] Thus, the regard that Christian wives demonstrate for domestic order and the authority of their husbands will be an important means for allaying any fears of disruption and insuring domestic tranquillity. In actuality, however, the stated goal of subordination is not simply marital harmony but the very conversion of nonbelieving husbands through their wives' chaste and reverent conduct (vv 1e–2) and gentle and tranquil spirit (v 4).

1d. *they may be won* (*kerdēthēsontai*). The verb *kerdainō* ("win," "gain") is used here in the sense of "winning over" or "convincing" persons, in this case the husbands, to become believers, as in 1 Cor 9:19–22.[168] This "winning" is not a process of compulsion but of attraction. Given their subordinate status, wives were hardly in a position to coerce their husbands. This reflects the situation of the messianic sect as a whole; hence its strategy of gaining converts through a winsome way of life (cf 2:12).

Rather than condemning these mixed marriages, the author views this situation as an opportunity for recruitment. Paul saw a similar potential in mixed marriages: "For the unbelieving husband is consecrated through his (believing) wife, and the unbelieving wife is consecrated through her (believing) husband. . . . Wife, perhaps you can save (*sōseis*) your husband? Husband, perhaps you can save (*sōseis*) your wife?" (1 Cor 7:14, 16, following Jeremias's [1966] proposed rendition of *ti gar oidas* as "perhaps"; cf. also Tert. *Ux.* 2.7). In such mixed marriages, the deportment of the wives was crucial because they may well have represented the first and perhaps only contact of the pagan husbands with the messianic sect. From the behavior of their Christian wives, these husbands would form their most powerful impressions of the Christian community. The honorable behavior of Christian spouses demonstrated respect for conventional marital norms. At the same time, it also gave compelling witness to commitment to God (3:4c) and to the holiness (3:2; cf. 1 Thess 4:3–8; 1 Cor 7:12–16; Heb 13:4; and *Diogn.* 5) and modest spirit (3:3–4) of the Christian community as a whole. Thus, wives in mixed marriages played an important role in the mission strategy of the sect in general. In their own domestic sphere they carry out the missionary charge committed to all believers in 2:12.[169] This encouragement of wifely conduct leading to spousal con-

[167] On domestic conflict, see also the *Acts of Paul and Thecla*; *Clem. Recog.* 2.29; and Tert. *Apol.* 3; and *Ux.* 2.2–8.

[168] See Daube 1947; cf. also Matt 18:15 on "winning" or convincing an errant brother.

[169] On the mission-orientation of 1 Peter, see Schröger 1981b, 137–42; Elliott 1981/1990, 73–84, 107–18.

version thus contrasts sharply with Greco-Roman household instruction which expected wifely devotion to the gods of the husband.

without a word (*aneu logou*) (being spoken by the wives). The phrase *aneu logou* qualifies the main verb *they may be won* and in conjunction with the stress on conduct illustrates the conviction that "actions speak louder than words" (cf. Philo, *Ios.* 86; John Chrys., *Hom. Heb.* 19.1). Silence was considered appropriate behavior for wives and for females in general. "Silence is a woman's glory" was a familiar adage (Soph., *Aj.* 293, cited also by Aristotle [*Pol.* 1.5.8. 1260a] in his discussion of household management; cf. Plut., *Conj. praec.* 32; *Mor.* 142D): "Pheidias made the Aphrodite of the Eleans with one foot on a tortoise to typify for womankind staying at home and keeping silent" (see also Val. Max., *Fac. dict.* 3.8.6; and Plutarch, *Lyc. Num.* 3.5). Israelite wisdom likewise affirmed that "a silent wife is a gift of the Lord" (Sir 26:14; cf. Philo, *Spec.* 3.174). Christians also saw silence in women as an appropriate sign of uxorial modesty and marital subordination (1 Cor 14:34; 1 Tim 2:11–12; *1 Clem.* 21:7).

1e. *by the conduct of their wives* (*dia tēs tōn gynaikōn anastrophēs*). From the author's vantage point, words were less important than the persuasive power of wifely conduct.[170] The double reference to "conduct" (*anastrophē*) in v 1e and v 2a (see also 1:15, 18 and 3:16) closely echoes the point made previously in 2:12 regarding the winsome influence of the *conduct* of all believers on nonbelievers. The behavior of wives is thus paradigmatic of the conduct required of the entire community. The accent on the convincing power of conduct is similar to Philo's comment on the winsome conduct of Joseph on his fellow Egyptian prisoners: "For by setting before them his life of temperance and every virtue . . . he converted even those who seemed to be quite incurable" (Philo, *Ios.* 87). Augustine's account of the influence of the conduct of his mother, Monica, on his pagan father, Patricius (*Conf.* 9.19–22) is frequently cited as a glowing illustration of the positive effect of the behavior encouraged here.

2. *when they observe your reverent and chaste conduct* (*epopteusantes tēn en phobōi hagnēn anastrophēn hymōn*). The specific quality of wifely conduct (v 1e) is now further clarified, and its observable quality is stressed. The manuscript evidence for the participle translated "when they observe" is divided. The aorist participle *epopteusantes*, preferred by *NTG*[27] (א[c] A B C P Ψ and the majority), is punctiliar, whereas the present participle *epopteuontes* (𝔓[72] א* and others) implies repeated observance. This variant perhaps has been conformed to the same present tense of the verb in 2:12, also with conduct ("good deeds") as its object. Here, as in 2:12, stress is placed on the direct, face-to-face observance by nonbelievers of the proper conduct of believers, by which the latter can positively impress and attract the former.

your reverent and chaste conduct. The stress on "conduct" (*tēn anastrophēn*; cf. v 1e) is reiterated, and the added "your" (*hymōn*) "resum[es] the directness

---

[170] On action and not simply words, see also Matt 7:21–27; 25:31–46; Jas 2:14–26; Ign. *Eph.* 10:1.

of the vocative" with which the verse began (Michaels 1988:158). The adjective "reverent" translates *en phobōi*, which functions adjectivally, and, as elsewhere (1:17; 2:18; 3:16; cf. 2:17), implies reverence for God, especially in conjunction with 3:4c ("in God's sight"). Contrast Eph 5:33, where it is husbands who are the object of fear. The adjective "chaste" (*hagnēn*) can denote a quality typically desired of all women, namely sexual purity, but in 1 Peter it is virtually synonymous with "holy" (3:5; cf. 1:22, "having purified yourselves by your obedience to the truth") and thus also invokes the broader and frequently stressed theme of holiness as a markedly Christian characteristic.[171] For Israelites and Christians, as for Greeks and Romans, the chasteness of wives involved their virginity prior to marriage and sexual fidelity to their husbands within marriage. In these essential regards, wives played their role in upholding the honor of the family. However, for members of the messianic sect, women as well as men shared in the holiness of the God who called and elected them (1:14–16; 2:4–10). It was this kind of holiness, manifested not only in their marital relations but in their behavior in general (1:22; 3:15) that, Christians insisted, set them apart from the lusts of the Gentiles (1 Thess 4:4–5; cf. 2 Cor 6:14–7:1; Eph 2:3; 4:22; Yarbrough 1985; MacDonald 1990). Stress on holiness in marital relations is found also in 1 Thess 4:3–8, Paul's earliest comment on marriage, and in 1 Cor 7:14, where he notes that the Christian wife could even sanctify her nonbelieving husband. Hebrews 13:4 likewise urges: "Let marriage be held in honor among all, and let the marriage bed be undefiled." *1 Clement* 21:7 appears to be a particularly close echo of the language here: "Let them (wives) exhibit the lovely habit of purity (*tēs hagneias*), let them show forth the innocent will of meekness (*tēs prautētos*), let them make the gentleness of their tongue manifest by their silence, let them not give their affection by factious preference, but in holiness (*hosiōs*) to all equally who fear (*phoboumenois*) God." In our author's stress on this theme, holy conduct is viewed as a powerful means of recruitment (cf. P. J. Robinson 1989).

1 Peter 3:1c–2, on the whole, is strikingly similar to the general exhortation of 2:12 in its structure, terminology, and expressed goal:

2:12b	so that when they slander you . . .	3:1c	so that, even if some disobey the word, . . .
2:12c	from observing your honorable deeds	3:2	when they observe your reverent and chaste conduct
2:12d	they may glorify God on the day of visitation	3:1d	they may be won

This correspondence makes three things clear: (1) the conduct of Christian wives is a particular instance of the honorable conduct required of *all* of the addressees; (2) nonbelieving husbands are a particular instance of nonbeliev-

[171] See 1:2, 14–16, 19, 22; 2:5, 9; 3:5; cf. also 1 Tim 5:22; 1 John 3:3; *1 Clem.* 1:3; 21:7; Pol. *Phil* 4:2.

ing Gentiles in general; (3) the goal of honorable conduct is the same in both passages; namely, the conversion of outsiders.[172]

While Reicke (1964, 94, 101) is correct in observing that proper conduct is viewed here, as in 2:12, as a means for evangelization, his claim (1964, 73) that "conversion of the non-Christians is one of the main interests of the author" exaggerates the role of this idea in relation to other, actually major, themes of the letter. What is clear from the correspondence between 3:1–2 and 2:12 is that, as in the case of the domestic slaves, subordination is a mode of "honorable conduct among the Gentiles." This conduct, moreover, is more effective than words alone for turning the hearts of nonbelievers, and the conduct of wives, like the conduct of domestic slaves, is exemplary of the behavior and spirit of the entire community.

Verses 3–4 illustrate what is meant by "reverent and chaste behavior" (v 2) by contrasting a preoccupation with *external* adornment to the *internal* disposition of the heart and spirit. While the comments on adornment echo traditional Greco-Roman moral teaching, v 4 provides a typical Christian motivation: what is precious in God's sight is not external cosmetics but internal character.

3a. *Do not adorn yourselves outwardly* (*hōn estō ouch ho exōthen . . . kosmos*). The Greek formulation of vv 3–4 is complex and reads, literally, "Let not yours be the outward adorning of braided hair and of wearing gold ornamentation and of donning clothing (*hōn estō ouch ho exōthen . . . kosmos*) . . . but rather the hidden person of the heart" (*all' ho kryptos tēs kardias anthrōpos . . .*). Modern versions, attempting to capture its sense, present a variety of translations. Syntactically, *ho . . . kosmos* embrace the words (v 3bcd) placed between the definite article *ho* and its following noun, *kosmos* (*adornment*). These are three phrases exemplifying external adornment. Then *ho kosmos* is contrasted with *ho kryptos tēs kardias anthrōpos*, "the hidden person of the heart" (v 4a) and its qualification (v 4bc). Since the focus here is on *adornment*, as indicated in the related verb "adorn" in v 5, the present translation attempts to make this clear in English with repetition of *let your adornment be* (v 4a) and *adornment* again in v 4b. The antithesis on the whole involves a contrast between external and internal adornment. The contrast of negative-positive statements is consistent with the contrasts evident elsewhere in the letter (see the NOTE on 2:2a).

In the imperatival formulation *hōn estō ouch ho exōthen . . . kosmos*, the relative *hōn* (lit., "yours") has "you wives" (v 1) as its antecedent, and *estō ouch* (lit., "let not") expresses a negative imperative. The noun *kosmos* means not "world" (as in 1:20; 5:9; and elsewhere in the NT) but "adornment" (as in Exod 33:5, 6; Isa 3:18, 19, 20, 24, 26; Jer 2:32; 4:30; Ezek 7:20; Sir 6:30; 21:21; Philo, *Migr.* 97; *T. Jud.* 12:1). This unusually formed imperative discourages a concern with outward, external adornment that involves ostentatious coiffure,

[172] See the comparative table and discussion in Gielen 1990, 356–607.

jewelry, and clothing, as expressed in three phrases (vv 3bcd) involving genitive nouns of action that depict "the expenditure of work and time that this way of making oneself attractive requires" (Goppelt 1993, 221).

3b. *by braiding [your] hair* (*emplokēs trichōn*). The braiding of hair (cf. 1 Tim 2:9), with the plaited hair upraised and interwoven with chains of gold or strings of pearls was "an art highly cultivated by Greek and Roman ladies" (Bigg 1902, 152; cf. Ovid, *Amat.*3. 136–38). Lollia Paulina, the future wife of Emperor Caligula, is said to have appeared at an ordinary banquet bedecked with emeralds and pearls on her head, hair, ears, neck, arms, and fingers. Terra cotta figures, cameos, statues, paintings, and even coins of the period display the various hair styles of style-setting, aristocratic women. In Israelite and Christian circles, the regulation of hairdos, like the insistence on veils and head coverings, was a means of ensuring the required modesty of wives (cf. 1 Cor 11:2–16; Billerbeck 1926–1961, 3:427–35). According to Paul (1 Cor 11:2–16), a woman's long hair was her "pride" and was "given to her for a covering of her head" (11:15). Women who pray, moveover, should do so with heads veiled (11:5–6), for a variety of reasons (11:7–15), the most compelling of which, it appears, was convention: "we recognize no other practice, nor do the churches of God" (11:16). The Petrine author likewise advises conformity to conventional norms of female modesty, presumably because this involved no sacrifice of Christian identity or principle, while it also secured public approval.

3c, d. *putting on gold ornaments, and wearing fine clothing.* The bedecking of oneself with gold ornamentation (*peritheseōs chrysiōn*), golden hairnets, rings, and gems, and the donning of fine clothing (*enduseōs himatiōn*) was an external and visible display of the possession of wealth and social status, as was the Roman toga with its broad purple stripe. In hair styling, jewelry, and clothing, lower-class women took their cues from the styles of the elites. Clothing, however, was also designed as a means of seduction; see Isaiah's excoriation of the "ruling daughters of Zion" and their seductive apparel (Isa 3:16–4:1). (On dress and ornamentation in general, see Edwards 1992.)

Censure of the love of finery (*philokosmia*), immoderate display, and extravagance was a commonplace of moral exhortation among Israelites, Greeks, and Romans alike.[173] In a comment on feminine attire and condemnation of lascivious conduct, Dio Chrysostom (*Orat.* 33.48–51) observes:

> Many of the customs still in force reveal, in one way or another, the sobriety and severity of deportment of those earlier days. Among these is the convention regarding feminine attire, a convention which prescribes that women should be so arrayed and should so deport themselves when in the street that nobody could see any part of them, neither of the face nor of the rest

[173] See Isa 3:16–4:1; *T. Reu.* 5:5; Philo, *Sacr.* 21; *Virt.* 39–40; *Mos.* 2.243; Plut. *Conj. praec.* 48 (*Mor.* 145A); cf. Juv., *Sat.* 2.6.50.2–3; Martial, *Epig.* 9.37; Strabo, *Geogr.* 17.7; Epict., *Ench.* 40; Sen., *Ben.* 7.9.

> of the body, and that they themselves might not see anything off the road. And yet what could they see as shocking as what they hear? Consequently, beginning the process of corruption with the ears, most of them have come to utter ruin. For wantonness slips in from every quarter, through ears and eyes alike. Therefore, while they have their faces covered as they walk, they have their souls uncovered and its doors thrown wide open. For that reason they, like surveyors, can see more keenly with but one of their eyes. And while this nasal affliction (ed. "snorting") is wholly manifest, it is inevitable that everything else also must be a fit accompaniment for a condition such as that. For you must not suppose that, just as other disorders often attack certain particular parts of other people, such as hands or feet or face, so also here among you a local disorder has assailed your noses; nor that, just as Aphrodite, angered at the women of Lemnos, is said to have polluted their armpits, so also here in Tarsus the noses of the majority have been polluted because of divine anger, in consequence of which they emit that dreadful noise. Rubbish! No, that noise is a symptom of their utter wantonness and madness, and of their scorn for all that is honourable, and their belief that nothing is dishonourable. So I assert that the talk of these women is quite in keeping with their gait and the glance of their eye. And if they cannot make anything so manifest by means of their eyes as to cause everyone to turn and gaze at them, or if they have not yet carried their art so far, still they are by no means the more respectable in other ways.

Regarding proper adornment, Plutarch, in his *Advice to Bride and Groom* (*Conj. praec.* 26; *Mor.* 141E) also recalls: "For, as Crates used to say, 'adornment (*kosmos*) is that which adorns,' and that adorns (*kosmei*) a woman which makes her more decorous. It is not gold or precious stones or scarlet that makes her such, but whatever invests her with that something which betokens dignity, good behavior and modesty (*hosa semnotētos eutaxias aidous emphasin peritithēsin*)" (cf. also *Conj. praec.* 48; *Mor.* 144A–146A).

Similar sentiments are expressed in a treatise attributed to a Pythagorean community in Italy (3d–2d century BCE, in Lefkowitz and Fant 1982, 104–5). The text illustrates prevailing conceptions of women and the kind of ideals to which an honorable woman was expected to conform, including honoring her husband and appropriate adornment.

> In general a woman must be good and orderly—and this one can become without virtue. . . . A woman's greatest virtue is chastity. Because of this quality she is able to honour and to cherish her own particular husband . . . women should keep house and stay inside and receive and take care of their husbands. But I believe that courage, justice and intelligence are qualities that men and women have in common. . . . The greatest glory a free-born woman can have—her foremost honour—is the witness her own children give to her chastity towards her husband, the stamp of likeness they bear to the father whose seed produced them. . . . As far as adornment of her

> body is concerned . . . she should be dressed in white, natural, plain. Her clothes should not be transparent or ornate. She should not put on silken material, but moderate, white-coloured clothes. In this way she will avoid being over-dressed or luxurious or made-up, and not give other women cause to be uncomfortably envious. She should not wear gold or emeralds at all; these are expensive and arrogant towards other women in the village. . . . She should not apply imported or artificial colouring to her face—with her own natural colouring, by washing only with water, she can ornament herself with modesty. Women of importance leave the house to sacrifice to the leading divinity of the community on behalf of themselves and their husbands and their households. . . . They keep away from secret cults and Cybeline orgies in their homes. For public law prevents women from participating in these rites, particularly because these forms of worship encourage drunkenness and ecstasy. The mistress of the house and the head of the household should be chaste and untouched in all respects.[174]

The echo here in 1 Peter of conventional sentiments concerning appropriate attire (cf. Prostmeier 1990, 439–40) reveals little if anything about the actual social status of the wives addressed (against Beare 1970, 155). Concern with external adornment serves primarily as a negative foil to the author's major point that it is the internal condition of one's heart that matters with God. Modesty in dress, however, like gentleness and quietness, is a socially approved mark of honorable female behavior that maintains the honor of the husband and the family. Cultivation of such attributes is a further way of demonstrating subordination and respect for one's spouse and thereby dispelling any notions that Christian wives, whose allegiance is to a God other than that of their husbands, represent a threat to familial cohesion and its honor rating.

Paul's strained remarks in 1 Cor 11:2–16 on the issue of female attire in general illustrate both the problems that this question presented and the general Christian concurrence in this matter with prevailing practice (11:16).

In some points the sentiment and content of vv 1–3 is similar to those of 1 Tim 2:9–10: "[I desire that] women should adorn themselves modestly and sensibly in seemly apparel, not with braided hair or gold or pearls or costly attire, but by good deeds, as befits women who profess piety. Let a woman learn in silence with all subordination. I permit no woman/wife to teach or to have authority over a man/husband; she is to keep silent." The remainder of this text (1 Tim 2:11–13), however, with its appeal to the sequence of the creation of Adam and Eve, Eve's deception and transgression, and a woman's salvation through bearing children, diverges sharply from the focus of 1 Peter on internal character, the solidarity of Christian wives with the matriarchs of old, and their status as joint heirs of the grace of life (cf. Scholer 1980).

[174] For similar sentiments, see also the comments of the Neo-Pythagorean Phintys (*Concerning the Temperance of a Woman* 153.19–22) and Perictione (*On the Harmony of a Woman* 143.26–28).

It is interesting to observe that the Church Fathers show more interest in this text in 1 Peter than in other passages that might be expected to draw attention, such as the letter's Christological statements or other soteriological formulations. Several Fathers regard this text as establishing an authoritative prohibition of external adornment for Christian women.[175] In general, later Christian attitudes toward female attire and modesty remained conservative and conventional in nature.[176]

4a. *but rather let your adornment be the hidden person of the heart* (*all' ho kryptos tēs kardias anthropos*). To the external physical adornment of the body is now contrasted (*alla*, "but rather") the internal (*kryptos*, "hidden") moral adornment of a person's heart. From adornment (*kosmos*) in the literal sense (v 3), the author now shifts to adornment in the figurative and moral sense (continued also in vv 5–6).

The expression "the hidden person of the heart" (*ho kryptos tēs kardias anthrōpos*) is unique in the NT but, like similar phrases such as "the inner person" (*ho esō anthropos*, Rom 7:22; Eph 3:16; cf. 2 Cor 4:16),[177] denotes the inner self and the sentiments and dispositions of the human heart, which was considered to be the organ of thought, disposition, and intention.[178] Similar appeals to the *heart* occur also in 1:22 ("with a pure heart love one another") and 3:14 ("in your hearts sanctify the Christ as Lord"). The external-internal contrast is reminiscent of Jesus' distinction between publicly demonstrative and privately concealed expressions of piety, only the latter of which are perceptible to God and have God's approval (Matt 6:1–18; 23:25–28; cf. also Mark 7:14–23; Luke 11:37–44; 12:1–3). See also the contrast of external-internal with respect to baptism in 3:21. Thus, while clothing and adornment are always a demonstration of social status, in the Christian scheme of things virtue outranks visible appearance as an adornment, and it is the approval of God (v 4c) that is ultimately decisive.

4b. *with the imperishable* [*adornment*] *of a gentle and tranquil spirit* (*en tōi aphthartōi tou praeōs kai hēsychiou pneumatos*). The phrase clarifies the desirable qualities of the inner person and the heart. The adjective "imperishable" (*aphthartou*) could be taken as a substantive ("imperishable quality"), but the contrast in vv 3 and 4 favors an implied "adornment" (*kosmos*) in this verse as well. The expression "imperishable seed" in 1:23 suggests that the imperishable adornment mentioned here likewise is the result of a regeneration from

---

[175] See, e.g., Clem. Alex., *Paed.* 3.11.66; Tert., *Or.* 20 (referring to 1 Pet 3:1–6); *Cor.* 14 (referring to 1 Pet 3:3); *Cult. fem.* 1.6; 2.2.7–14; Cyprian, *Hab. Virg.* 8.

[176] See, e.g., Tert., *To His Wife; On the Apparel of Women; On the Veiling of Virgins; On Modesty; On Monogamy; On Exhortation to Chastity*; Clem. Alex., *Paed.* 1.121.2–129.4; 2.8, 11–13; 3.56.1, 57.1–63.4, 64.1; and *Apos. Con.* (books 1, 3, and 8). Jerome (*Epist.* 127.3) contrasts Christian and pagan habits but also echoes traditional sentiments on attire and the message that attire sends.

[177] Cf. also *ho en kryptō Ioudaios* (Rom 2:29) and 1 Cor 14:25 (*ta krypta tēs kardias autou*).

[178] See Deut 15:9; Sir 13:24–26; Matt 6:21; 12:34; 15:8; Mark 7:21–23/Matt 15:10–20; Luke 12:33–34; John 12:40; Acts 11:23; 2 Cor 9:7 6:21.

hearing the word of the good news; see the other accents on imperishability in 1:4 (inheritance); 5:4 (crown); and the contrasts "corruptible"–"flawless" (1:18–19) and "perishable"–"imperishable" (1:23–25).

The noun "spirit" (*pneuma*) refers not to the divine Spirit (which would make no sense in connection with v 4c), but to a person's frame of mind, disposition, temperament, and "inward nature and essential character" (Beare 1970, 155).[179] For the virtual equivalence of "heart" and "spirit," see Ezek 36:26.

The adjective "gentle" (*praus*) has a range of meanings ("gentle," "humble," "modest," "unassuming, "meek") and refers to a highly prized virtue among the Greeks (Bolkestein 1939, 108–11, 140), as among Israelites. Of Leah, Jacob's wife, for example, it was said: "For he loved her very much after Rachel, her sister, died, since she was perfect and upright in all her ways, and she honored Jacob. And in all the days which she lived with him, he never heard a harsh word from her mouth because she possessed gentleness, peace, uprightness, and honor" (*Jub.* 36:23–24). According to the common expectations of the honor and shame code, the wife, in addition to her submission and deference to the authority of her husband and father and her protection of her chastity, was to display modesty and restraint in all things (Malina 1993d, 48–54). Compare again *1 Clem.* 21:7, "let them (wives) show forth the innocent will of gentleness (*tēs prautētos*)."

While the term *gentle* is used here in regard to females, as in *1 Clem.* 21:7, gentleness was valued as a *male* virtue as well (Ps 36[37]:11; Matt 5:5; Gal 5:23; Eph 4:2; Col 3:12; Titus 3:2). Jesus in fact describes himself as "gentle and humble" (Matt 11:29; cf. 21:5; 2 Cor 10:1). Paul likewise speaks of a "gentle spirit" in connection with himself (1 Cor 4:21) and other male believers (Gal 6:1; see Goppelt 1993, 222–23). This quality is urged on all believers in 3:16 so that here again the character and behavior of the wives are paradigmatic of the community as a whole.

The accompanying adjective "tranquil" (*hēsychios*, only here and in 1 Tim 2:2) denotes a state of inner peacefulness and calm, quiet serenity, and tranquility, unruffled by the vicissitudes and disturbances of the daily round. In 1 Tim (2:11, 13) a wife's quiet tranquility (*hēsychia*), as opposed to her teaching, is regarded as a feature of her subordination to her husband. This quality, however, is also urged elsewhere as an appropriate quality of all believers, male as well as female (2 Thess 3:12; 1 Tim 2:2; cf. 1 Thess 4:11). The terms *gentle* and *tranquil* are closely related and often combined (cf. *1 Clem.* 13:4 [cf. Isa 66:2]; *Barn.* 19:4; Herm. *Mand.* 5.2.3; 6.2.3; 11.8).

The valuation of wifely virtue is also a pendant to the critique of external adornment in Greco-Roman circles. Plutarch (*Conj. praec.* 46; *Mor.* 144E) advises that when a wife's body and physical beauty are invisible, "her virtue, her exclusive devotion to her husband, her constancy, and her affection ought to

[179] As in Matt 5:3; 1 Cor 4:21; 7:34; 16:18; 2 Cor 7:1; Gal 6:1, 18; Phil 1:27; 4:23.

be most in evidence" (cf. also his treatise *Brave Deeds by Women* [*Mulier. virt.*, *Mor.* 242E–263C]; and Sen., *Ep.* 106.7).

The qualities of a deceased wife inscribed on a second-century CE funerary epitaph by a mourning husband are a moving tribute to her virtuous qualities and her husband's profound sense of loss. Though the words are those of a non-Christian, the virtues extolled are strikingly similar:

> Farewell, lady Panthia, from your husband. After your departure, I keep up my lasting grief for your cruel death. Hera, goddess of marriage, never saw such a wife: your beauty, your wisdom, your chastity. You bore me children completely like myself; you cared for your bridegroom and your children; you guided straight the rudder of life in our home and raised high our common fame in healing—though you were a woman, you were not behind me in skill. In recognition of this your bridegroom Glycon built this tomb for you. I also buried here the body of [my father] immortal Philadelphus, and I myself will lie here when I die, since with you alone I shared my bed when I was alive, so may I cover myself in ground that we share. (cited in Lefkowitz and Fant 1982, 104–5)

Another funeral eulogy by a husband for his wife (Rome, 9 or 10 BCE [CIL 6.1527 = ILS 8393), the so-called *Laudatio Turiae*, includes a similar recounting of the departed's luminous virtues:

> Why recall your inestimable qualities, your modesty, deference, affability, your amiable dispostion, your faithful attendance to the household duties, your enlightened religion, your unassuming elegance, the modest simplicity and refinement of your manners? Need I speak of your attachment to your kindred, your affection for your family . . . you who share countless other virtues with Roman ladies most jealous of their fair name? These qualities which I claim for you are your own, equalled or excelled by few; for the experience of men teaches us how rare they are." (cited in Lefkowitz and Fant 1982, 209)

In commenting on this text, Horsley (1983, 33–36) calls it "the single most impressive personal statement of the depth of the marriage-bond known to me in the later Greco-Roman world" (Horsley 1983, 35; cf. also the *Laudatio Murdiae* [CIL 6.10230 = ILS 8394]). For similar, though less effusive, Israelite praise of a good and honorable wife, see Prov 31:10–31; Sir 26:1–4, 13–18 (in contrast to a shameless wife, Sir 25:15–26; 26:5–9).

which in God's sight is very precious (*ho estin enōpion tou theou polyteles*). The relative neuter "which" (*ho*) could have either *pneuma* ("spirit") or *to aphtharton* ("imperishable [adornment]") as its antecedent but probably refers to the entire preceding clause (v 4ab). "In God's sight" (*enōpion tou theou*) translated the similar expression *para de theou* in 2:5. Among several similar instances of this phrase in the NT, see especially Luke 12:6; Acts 4:19; 2 Cor 8:21; 1 Tim 2:3; 5:4; Rev 3:2. The ancients generally believed that "you could tell a book by its cover": "A man is known by his appearance, and a sensible man is known by his face when you meet him. A man's attire and open-mouthed laughter and a man's manner of walking show what he is" (Sir 19:29–30). But Israelites and Christians also knew that "the Lord sees not as man sees; man looks on the outward appearance, but the Lord looks on the heart" (1 Sam 16:7); see also Wis 1:6, "God is witness of his inmost feelings and a true observer of his heart," and Rev 2:23, "I am he who searches mind and heart."[180] Here, as in 2:19–20 (cf. also 5:2), it is God's approval that ultimately matters, a conviction that "reverence" for God (3:2; cf. 2:18) also entails.

The adjective *polyteles* ("very precious," "of great worth"), is also used of "expensive" perfume (Mark 14:3), clothing (1 Tim 2:9), and signs of status; note also *polytimoteros* (1:7), *timios* (1:19), *timē* (2:7), *entimos* (2:4, 6), all terms related to the semantic field of honor and worth. In contrast to what humans treasure, namely external adornment that perishes, God values the gentle and tranquil spirit of the inner person which alone has lasting worth. For similar contrasts between divine and human appraisal, see 2:4 and 4:2, 6.

The external-internal contrast also replicates the conventional identification of the female with the internal sphere of the home in contrast to the male's responsibility for the external affairs of public life. As roles and status were gender-specific and clearly demarcated, so was the social space that was proper to males (public) and females (domestic, private). It was woman's weaker physical constitution, it was maintained, that consigned females to the home and life indoors. Thus Aristotle (*Oec.* 1.3; 1343b–44a) explains, "For the divine made one stronger and the other weaker so that the latter would be more protected as a result of her timidity and the former more ready to defend as a result of his manliness . . . the one provides things from the outside, the other preserves the things inside." Moreover, in all ancient Mediterranean cultures, the wife and females of the family were regarded as symbols of the family's honor and its sensitivity toward shame. Males were conventionally seen to embody honor, authority, aggression, and courage and were expected to represent and defend the familial honor beyond the borders of the home. Females and wives were seen to embody the family's sensitivity to shame, deference to authority, modesty, and passivity and were expected to maintain their sexual integrity and the social integrity of the family within the domestic sphere. Therefore all honorable females were carefully sequestered in women's quarters separated from men's quarters, protectively clothed and kept from male sight, and rigorously restricted in their interactions with males outside the home. Males and females who violated these boundaries of role, status, and space were branded as "shameless" deviants acting contrary to "nature" (equated with conventional social ideals). This perception informs, for instance, Paul's argument against

[180] Cf. Ps 44:21; Matt 6:1–18; John 7:24; Rom 8:27; and 1 Cor 14:25.

males' and females' "unnaturally" exchanging or violating assigned roles (Rom 1:18–32; cf. also 1 Cor 11:2–16; 14:34–37; Philo, *Spec.* 3.37–42).

This prevalent conception of gender specificities and social space is illustrated by Philo of Alexandria, who comments:

> Market-places and council-halls and law courts and gatherings and meetings where a large number of people are assembled and open-air life with full scope for discussion and action—all these are suitable to men both in war and peace. The women are best suited to the indoor life which never strays from the house, within which the middle door is taken by the maidens as their boundary, and the outer door by those who have reached full womanhood. . . . A woman, then, should not be a busybody, meddling with matters outside her household concerns, but should seek a life of seclusion. (*Spec.* 3.169, 171; cf. also *Virt.* 19)

Similarly, Xenophon comments (*Oec.* 7.22–23, 30–31):

> God from the first adapted the woman's nature, I think, to the indoor and man's to the outdoor tasks and cares. For he made the man's body and mind more capable of enduring cold and heat, and journeys and campaigns; and therefore imposed on him the outdoor tasks. To the woman, since he has made her body less capable of such endurance, I take it that God assigned the indoor tasks. . . . It is a finer thing for the woman to stay indoors than to spend time in the open, while it is more disgraceful for the man to stay indoors than to concern himself with outdoor things. But when someone acts in a way contrary to what God has brought forth, perhaps in causing some disorder, he is noticed by the gods and pays the penalty for neglecting his own tasks or for doing the woman's tasks.

Within the home, the wife bore responsibility for tending the hearth, obtaining the water, preparing the meals, spinning wool, weaving cloth, sewing the clothing, and other tasks needed for the operation of the household as both a social and economic unit. In particular, the rearing of children was her responsibility. Consistent with this identification of the female and the wife with the internal sphere of the home, stress also was laid on the primary importance of the inward character and disposition of the wife herself. In Rome, the sequestered Vestal Virgins, who represented the purity of the Roman people, tended the hearth in the Temple of Vesta in the Roman Forum. Like the Vestal Virgins, the ordinary wife also maintained the heart of the home, the hearth; correlatively, her own heart and internal disposition could be said to be of far greater importance than her external appearance. See the explanation of baptism in 3:20 for a further contrast of external-internal spheres in 1 Peter.

Marriages, generally arranged by the male heads of the families of bride and groom, created new and mutually advantageous familial alliances. The chief aim of marriage in classical antiquity was to produce a male child who could inherit the family property. It is thus worth noting that the Petrine author says nothing about the wife's obligation of providing a male heir but focuses exclusively on her personal virtue.

As an illustration and model of appropriate uxorial subordination, holy conduct, and adornment, the author points to the example of the holy matriarchs of Israel, and of Sarah in particular. Once again the continuity of the messianic sect with the history of ancient Israel is presumed and affirmed (cf. 1:10–12; 2:4–10; 3:20–21). Contrast the comments of Brox (1981), who sees here only a "simple example," with no interest in the affirmation of continuity.

5a. *For thus also the holy wives of old* (*houtōs gar pote kai hai hagiai gynaikes*). The adverb *houtōs* ("thus"; cf. 2:15) and the conjunctions *gar* ("for") and *kai* ("also") introduce vv 5–6 as a support for the thought of vv 1–4. The adverb *pote* (lit., "once"), as in 2:10 and 3:20, refers to something of the ancient and hence authoritative past, in this instance to the holy wives *of old*, with whom the Christian wives are to see themselves in continuity and from whom they are to learn.

The phrase "the holy wives" (*hai hagiai gynaikes*) is unique in the NT, but the following reference to one of these wives, Sarah (v 6a), indicates that it is the honored matriarchs of the family of Abraham that are implied. Their holiness is a model of the holy Christian wives (v 2).[181]

5b. *who hoped in God* (*hai elpizomenai eis theon*). Minor textual variants amounting to no change in sense involve the addition of the definite article (*ton*) before "God" or the reading of *epi* for *eis*. While hope is not a quality of the matriarchs underscored in the OT, this characterization (*hai elpizousai eis theon*) is similar to the thought of Hebrews 11 regarding the great heroes of the past, including Sarah: "all died in faith, not having received what was promised but having seen it and greeted it from afar" (11:13; cf. also Philo, *Abr.* 8; *Praem.* 13–14). These matriarchs thus typify, in the view of the Petrine author, not only the holiness, but also the hope of the Christian wives and all of God's people (1:3, 13, 21; 3:15).

5c. *used to adorn themselves* (*ekosmoun heautas*). The moral adornment of Christian wives (v 4) has as its model the constant moral adornment (expressed by the imperfect tense, *ekosmoun*) of the Israelite ancestresses. The moral nature of this adornment, as the following indicates, consists in uxorial subordination (v 5d), explained as obedience (v 6a).

5d. *being subordinate to their husbands* (*hypotassomenai tois idiois andrasin*). The verb *hypotassomai* does not occur in the LXX descriptions of the matriarchs. It is employed here explicitly for the purpose of linking the subordinate conduct of the Christian wives (v 1) with that of their Israelite ances-

[181] On Sarah, Rebecca, Leah, and Rachel as exemplary figures, see also Philo, *Cher.* 41; cf. *1 Clem.* 55:3–6, which cites Judith and Esther as models of "manly valor" and humility. In Greek and Roman circles, notable women of the past (e.g., Theano, Timocleaia, Claudia, Cornelia, Laelia, Hortensia) likewise were held up as examples of female virtue and decorum; cf. Plut., *Conj. praec.* 48; *Mor.* 145 E–F; and Lefkowitz and Fant 1982, 206–8, 235.

tresses. The entire phrase mirrors that of v 1b, but here the participle functions, not as an imperative, as in v 1 (contra Schlosser 1983, 410), but as a normal participial phrase modifying the preceding verb, "adorn" (v 5c). "Being subordinate" thus explicates the sense of "adorn" in v 5a as *moral* adornment and is further clarified as marital "obedience" in v 6a. In their subordination to their husbands, Christian wives are to take their cue preeminently from the honorable matriarchs of old.

6ab. *as Sarah obeyed Abraham, calling him lord* (*hōs Sarra hypēkousen tōi Abraam kyrion auton kalousa*). The proto-matriarch Sarah is now cited as a specific instance of the subordinate and honorable behavior of the matriarchs. This is one of only four explicit references to Sarah by name in the NT (Rom 4:19; 9:9; Heb 11:14; cf. Gal 4:22–31). Sarah's obeying (*hypēkousen*) her husband Abraham and calling him lord (*kyrion auton kalousa*), according to our author, illustrate the subordination typical of all of the holy matriarchs. The instance alluded to is the event recorded in Gen 18, when Abraham and Sarah entertained three visitors, one of whom announced that Sarah, despite her old age, would nevertheless bear a son (Gen 18:1–15 LXX). Given the fact that Sarah was beyond childbearing age (Gen 18:11), "she laughed to herself, saying 'this has not yet happened to me even until now and my lord [*ho kyrios mou*, referring to Abraham] is old'" (Gen 18:12). The word "lord" (*kyrios*) also occurs earlier in this story (Gen 18:3) as a term of respect in Abraham's address to his visitor: "My lord (i.e., "worthy sir"), if indeed I have found favor in your sight, do not pass by your servant" (Gen 18:3; cf. also 19:2 and *T. Ab.* 5:12; 6:2, 5, 8). According to 1 Sam (1 Kgdms) 1:8, Hannah, the mother of Samuel, also addresses her husband Elkanah as "lord," or "sir" (*kyrie*; cf. also Ps 44[45]:11 and 1Qap Gen^{ar} II 8–9, 13, 24; XX 12, 14, 15, 25, where a wife also employs "my lord" as a respectful form of address for her husband). The Petrine author, interested not in the Genesis episode in general but only in Sarah's remark, takes it as an indication of her subordination and obedience to (*hypēkousen*) Abraham as her husband. In common Greek usage, a *kyrios* is a man of importance and high position, such as an owner of property (Matt 20:8; 21:40; Mark 12:9; Luke 20:13) or a master or householder with full control of something (Matt 9:38; Luke 10:2), including slaves (Matt 6:24; 13:27; Luke 12:46; John 13:16), children (Matt 21:29), and wife (Plutarch, *Mulier. virt.* 15; *Mor.* 252B; SIG^3 1189.7; 1190.5).

In the Hellenistic world, as in ancient Israel, the female was always under the tutelage and authority of some male known as *kyrios* ("owner, lord"), be it her father (or closest male relative) or her husband. In Roman society, the female was under the so-called *potestas patria* within different types of marriage (*ius matrimonium*, a legally valid marriage; *iniustum matrimonium*, cohabitation without a legal marriage). The traditional form of Roman marriage *in manum* involved either *usus*, life together for one year; *confarreatio*, a religious ceremony restricted to patricians and priests; or *coemptio*, a fictitious purchase of a wife by her husband (cf. Gaius, *Inst.* 1.108–13). A marriage with *manus* involved the legal transfer of a woman from the authority of her father to that of her husband, with each inheriting from the other at the other's death. In a marriage without *manus*, the woman's family retained control over her property during her lifetime and after her death. Because families with property (mostly elites) wanted to retain control of property within the family, marriages without *manus* became common as wealth increased from Republican times onward. The Emperor Augustus, concerned about the laxity of marriage customs in his day, passed specific legislation regulating adultery, divorce, and favoring the bearing of children (*Lex Julia de adulteriis* [18 BCE]; *Lex Julia de maritandis ordinibus* [18 BCE]; and *Lex Papia Poppaea* [9 BCE]).

Thus, the LXX text and its Petrine reformulation reflect the conventional view of wives as under the authority of their husbands/lords. In 1 Peter, Sarah is presented as a model for the same subordination appropriate for her spiritual offspring. This portrait of Sarah contrasts with that of Philo, for whom Sarah was not only a model of chastity (*Abr.* 98) and "wifely love" (*Abr.* 245–54), but also, in allegorical form, a symbol of virtue (*Abr.* 99, 206; *Leg.* 3.218, 244–45; *Congr.* 1–2; *Mut.* 77–80), wisdom (*Leg.* 2.82; *Cher.* 10), cleverness (*Migr.* 126), and authority (*Congr.* 2). According to D. I. Sly (1991), this was part of Philo's attempt to circumvent the fact that in Genesis Abraham is also said to have obeyed Sarah (16:2; cf. 16:6; 21:12), a fact problematic to patriarchal Israelites (cf. also Josephus' wrestling with this issue, *Ant.* 1.10.4). The Genesis text is later cited in *Apos. Con.* 6.29.1, with yet a different interpretation: "She honored him inasmuch as she would not call him by name, but called him lord, when saying 'My lord is old.'"

6c. *You became her children* (*hēs egenēthēte tekna*). This identification of Christian wives as the figurative "children" (*tekna*) of Sarah is unique in the Bible but is consistent with the depiction of all the believers as "children of obedience" (*tekna hypakoēs*) in 1:14 (cf. Mark as the figurative "son" of Peter, 5:13). Israelites knew the proverb "As is the mother, so is your mother's daughter" (Ezek 16:44) and traced their lineage, and hence their antiquity and honor, to their ancestors Abraham and Sarah: "Look to Abraham your father and to Sarah who bore you" (Isa 51:2); "Abraham is our father" (John 8:39; cf. 8:53; Matt 3:9). An Israelite woman could be described as a "daughter of Abraham" (4 Macc 15:28; Luke 13:16), just as a male Israelite was a "son of Abraham" (Luke 19:9; cf. Abraham as "father" [Luke 16:24, 27]). Philo, moreover, notes that "in the court where truth presides, kinship is measured not only by blood, but by similarity of conduct and pursuit of the same objects" (*Virt.* 195). In later rabbinic tradition, proselytes to Israel were known as the children of Abraham and Sarah.[182] Paul takes this notion further and declares all believers in Jesus Christ, Gentile as well as of the House of Israel, to be the "seed" of Abraham—that is, spiritual children and imitators of Abraham, the prototypical hero of faith and trust.[183] For Paul, believers are not only "Abra-

---

[182] See Montefiore and Loewe 1963, 573–74; cf. Philo, *Virt.* 219; Gen 17:16, where Sarah is to be "the mother of nations."

ham's offspring" (Gal 3:29) but also "children of the free woman," meaning Sarah (Gal 4:31; cf. 4:21–31). Hebrews 11:8–10 portrays Abraham as the prototypical resident alien (*paroikos*), who acted in obedience and faith in God's promise. While Sarah and her extraordinary bearing of Isaac are mentioned in this same context (Heb 11:11–12), it is only in 1 Pet 3:6 and Gal 4:31 that Christian believers are said to be the *children* of Sarah and thus sharers in the dignity and status of Israel's greatest ancestress. Even on this point, however, the Petrine author and Paul differ. For Paul, to be the children of Sarah, the free woman, is to be free of the Law (symbolized by Sarah's counterpart, Hagar, the slave woman). Our author, on the other hand, is concerned not with the issue of freedom from the Law but rather with the proper relation of wives to their husbands, for which Sarah and the other matriarchs serve as models.

Presumably the aorist verb *became* (*egenēthēte*) alludes to the moment of conversion, when the wives first became believers, and thereby heirs of the promise to Abraham and Sarah that through their progeny all the peoples of the earth would be blessed (Gen 12:1–3; 15:5–6; 17:4–7, 19; Isa 51:2). This, however, can only be inferred from the wider context (1 Pet 1:3–4; 2:4–10, 11; 3:9). The more immediate context (3:5–6) makes clear that it is in subordination, obedience, and the fearless doing of what is right that Christian wives emulate the exemplary model of the noble ancestress Sarah. Implicit as well, however, is the fact that Sarah and Abraham represent the quintessential resident aliens of Israelite-Christian history. Christian wives as the children of Sarah thus illustrate the solidarity that all Christian resident aliens have with their forebears as faithful resident aliens (cf. the NOTE on 2:11). Association of the believing wives with Sarah illustrates once again the continuity affirmed throughout this letter between the community and Israel, a continuity that provides a means for refuting any charge concerning the novelty of the Christian movement as a *nova superstitio*. Just as Sarah and the matriarchs are cited as examples for the believing wives specifically, so the description of all of the believers generally as "resident aliens and visiting strangers" (2:11) adopts language that describes Abraham in Gen 23:4. Thus, Sarah and Abraham are models not merely for one group but for the community in general. They represent the prototypical "aliens and strangers" of Israel's history, from whom the present aliens and strangers, as implied also in 2:11, are to draw inspiration and comfort (as recognized also by Puig Tarrech 1980, 378; and Kiley 1987).

6d. *now doing what is right and "not fearing any terror"* (*agathopoiousai kai mē phoboumenai mēdemian ptoēsin*). The present participles "now doing what is right" (*agathopoiousai*) and "not fearing" (*mē phoboumenai*) describe the present conduct and confidence consequent upon becoming Sarah's spiritual children through conversion. "Doing what is right" repeats a major theme of the letter (2:14, 15, 20; 3:10–12, 17; 4:17) and here represents the author's

---

[183] See Rom 4:1–25 (cf. Gen 15s:6); Gal 3:6–29; 4:21–31; Jas 2:21; see also Heb 2:16; 6:13–15; Jas 2:21; *1 Clem.* 31:2; Barn. 13:7.

summary of the appropriate behavior required of the wives, a form of conduct required as well of the entire community.

The accompanying phrase "not fearing any terror" (*mē phoboumenai mēdemian ptoēsin*) or, more colloquially, "not falling prey to terror," also has no relation to the story of Sarah and Abraham, despite the reference to Sarah's fearing in Gen 18:13.[184] The phrase is, rather, an adaptation of language from Prov 3:25, where the verb "fear" (*phobeō*) and the noun "terror" (*ptoēsis*, unique to 1 Peter in the NT; elsewhere in the LXX only Sir 50:4; 1 Macc 3:25) also occur: "And you (son) shall not fear (*ou phobēthēsēi*) the terror (*ptoēsin*) coming upon you." A further citation from this same chapter of Proverbs occurs in 1 Pet 5:5 (Prov 3:34), and a similar point about all the believers' "not fearing" is made in 1 Pet 3:14 (citing Isa 8:12). In both 1 Pet 3:6c and 3:14, where all of the believers are addressed, *phobeō* denotes not reverence for God (2:17, 18; 3:2) but fear of other *humans*. The thought is particularly apposite in regard to these wives of pagan husbands, who, like the Christian slaves, were especially vulnerable to the possible intimidation of their nonbelieving spouses (or masters). Their doing what is right, however, should allay any cause for intimidation. Again, wives, like the domestic slaves, illustrate the precarious situation faced by the community as a whole. Moreover, in doing what is right without fear, wives also serve as paradigms for the entire household of God.

In v 7 the author turns to the other partners of the marital union, the husbands. However, in contrast to the mixed marriages envisioned in vv 1–6, it is now believing husbands with believing wives that are in view, as the designation "co-heirs of the grace of life" (v 7e) makes clear (against Gross 1989).

7a. *You husbands in turn* (*Hoi andres homoiōs*). This exhortation to husbands fits together logically with the foregoing address to wives (vv 1–6) and illustrates the view that marriage entails *reciprocal* obligations. The sequence is also similar to that of household-management instruction, where discussion of the husband's responsibility follows that of the wife's (cf. Xen., *Oec.* [chs. 7–10 on *gynaikologia* and ch. 11 on *andrologia*]; Ps.-Arist., *Oec.* 3 [the role of the virtuous wife (3.1) followed by the honor to be shown by the husband (3:2–4)]).

The articular construction (*hoi andres*), as in 2:18 and 3:1, has vocative force: "you husbands." The adverb *homoiōs*, rather than introducing some aspect of similarity in the sense of "likewise" (as in 3:1a), serves here (as in 5:5a and occasionally elsewhere in Greek literature) as a simple connective with the sense of "in turn" or "also."[185] Subordination is no longer a point of comparison, for the conventional role of the husband is not to be subordinate but to manage the household, which includes showing respect and honor to one's spouse and co-worker. Noteworthy here, however, is the absence of any men-

[184] This was fear of divine punishment because of her denial that she had laughed at the thought of becoming pregnant, a motif to which our author gives no attention.

[185] See Radermacher 1926, 290–91 regarding this use of *homoiōs* in itemizations of related subjects; also BAGD 568.

tion of the "control" or "rule" of wives that is so often stressed in Hellenistic and Israelite marital exhortation.[186]

7b. *live considerately with* [*your wives*] (*synoikountes kata gnōsin*). The verb *synoikountes* ("live with," "dwell with") occurs only here in the NT but elsewhere of the cohabitation of husband and wife.[187] Its participial form has imperatival force similar to the participial imperatives in 2:18 and 3:1 and has stronger support than the variant *synomilountes* (א*), "converse with." As a term of the *oik-* family, *synoikeō* (lit., "make a home [*oikos*] with [*syn-*]"), like *oiketai* (2:18), is perhaps intentionally employed to underline the *household* realm of this body of instruction (2:18–3:7). The cooperation of husband and wife in household management (*oikonomia*) is noted by Philo (*QG* 1.26, commenting on Gen 2:22):

> Why does Scripture call the likeness of the woman "a building"? The harmonious coming together of man and woman and their consummation is figuratively a house. And everything that is without a woman is imperfect and homeless. For to a man are entrusted the public affairs of state; while to a woman the affairs of the home are proper. The lack of her is ruin, but her being near at hand constitutes household management (*oikonomia*).

The translation of v 7b presumes that "your wives" is the implied object of the verb, although the ellipsis in the Greek leaves this open. Danker (1980, 147) suggests that females in general (including female slaves) are under discussion. However, the immediate association between this verse and vv 1–6 (concerning wives and not females in general) and the verb *synoikeō* (referring to marital cohabitation) make it more likely that "wives" are meant. 1 Peter 3:1–7 as a whole concerns not male-female relations in general but wife-husband relations in particular.

considerately. The adverb translates *kata gnōsin* (lit., "in accord with knowledge, insight"; cf. *ennoia*, 4:1, and contrast *agnōsia*, 2:15). This considerateness or knowledge pertains not only to the assumed condition of wives as "weaker feminine vessels" but also and especially to their special status as "co-heirs of the grace of life." Therefore, it is unnecessary to suspect here a repudiation of the depreciation of women in various Gnostic circles (against Reicke 1954). The thought reflects conventional wisdom: "My soul takes pleasure in three things and they are beautiful in the sight of the Lord and humans: agreement between brothers, friendship between neighbors, and a wife and husband who live in harmony" (Sir 25:1); "happy is the one (male) who lives with (*synoikōn*)

---

[186] See Arist., *Pol.* 1.5.1.1259a; Gen 3:16; Sir 33:19; Philo, *QG* 1.29; Tac., *Ann.* 3.34; 4.20; 8.12; *Agr.* 16; *Germ.* 45; Juv., *Sat.* 6.242–43, 475–80; Martial, *Epig.* 8.12; see also the DETAILED COMMENT.

[187] See Gen 20:3 (Abraham and Sarah); Deut 22:13; 24:1; 25:5; Isa 62:5; Sir 25:8, 16; Hdt., *Hist.* 1.93; 4.168; Philo, *Sacr.* 20; Josephus, *Ant.* 17.14; 4.247; 8.191; Plut., *Conj. praec.* 34; *Mor.* 142F.

an intelligent wife" (Sir 25:8). See also Ps.-Arist., *Oec.* 3.4, where the unity of husband and wife is "allied with wisdom and understanding." On the mutuality of the marital relationship, see also 1 Cor 7:1–5, 10–16, 36; Eph 5:25–33; 1 Thess 4:4–6.

7c. *as with a weaker feminine vessel* (*hōs asthenesterōi skeuei tōi gynaikeiōi*). The phrase is unique in the Bible but nevertheless reflects conventional thinking regarding the female as the weaker gender. Literally, the phrase reads "as (living) with a weaker vessel, the feminine one," with the singular used collectively for all wives (v 7b). Here and again in v 7e the comparative particle "as" (*hōs*) introduces a phrase stating the reason for the action that is urged.

The adjective "weak" (*asthenēs*) and the noun "weakness" (*astheneia*) are used to describe humans as weak beings (Philo, *Deus* 80; *Spec.* 1.293–94; Clem. Alex., *Strom.* 2.15.62; 2.16.72; 7.3.16; *Paed.* 3.12.86), the female gender as weak (4 Macc 15:5; PLond. 971.4; Clem. Alex., *Paed.* 2.10.107), physical infirmity (Matt 25:43; Mark 6:56; Acts 5:15–16; 2 Cor 12:7–10), the weakness of human nature (Heb 5:2 ["ignorant and wayward"]; 7:28), weaker parts of the body (1 Cor 12:22), spiritual weakness or helplessness (Rom 5:6; 6:19; Heb 4:15), moral sensitivity (1 Cor 8:7–13), the weakness of the flesh in contrast to the power of the spirit (Matt 24:41; Rom 8:26), economic weakness or poverty (Acts 20:35; 1 Cor 1:27), and Christ as "crucified in weakness" (2 Cor 13:4).

Here the comparative adjective "weaker" (*asthenesterōi*) is linked conceptually with *gynaikeiōi* ("feminine," only NT appearance), with both adjectives modifying *skeuei* ("vessel"). Females were generally regarded (by males!) to be weaker than males physically, intellectually, and morally. Thus, it was held that "the male (seed) is stronger than the female (seed)" (Hippocratic Corpus, *Gen.* 6.1). "The female nature, in humankind," according to Plato (*Leg.* 6.781B), "is inferior in virtue to that of males." In fact, he claims, "the female is in all respects weaker (*asthenesteron*) than the male" (*Resp.* 5; 455D; also 451C–56A; *Meno* 71C–73C). Accordingly, female infants, because they are weaker (and less desirable) than males, comments Ovid (*Met.* 10.23), should be exposed. The weakness of females is also cited as a reason for their restriction to the home and indoor matters: "For Providence," it was noted (Ps.-Arist., *Oec.* 1.4, 1344a), "made man stronger and woman weaker (*asthenesteron*), so that he, in virtue of his manly prowess, may be more ready to defend the home, and she, by reason of her timid nature, more ready to keep watch over it; and while he brings in fresh supplies from without, she may keep safe what lies within." According to the Israelite *Letter of Aristeas* (250–51), "the female sex is bold, positively active for something it desires, easily liable to change its mind because of poor reasoning powers, and of naturally weak constitution," and thus the female requires a husband as a "pilot." Musonius Rufus, the Roman moralist, likewise comments (*Educ.*) that "in the human race, man's constitution is stronger and woman's weaker" so that "heavier tasks [gymnastics and outdoor work] should be given to the stronger and lighter ones [spinning and indoor work] to the weaker." According to the Roman jurist Gaius (*Inst.* 1.144), earlier generations wished women, even those of a mature age, to be under a guardian, because of the "innate weakness of their sex" (cf. S. Dixon 1984).[188]

Generally married soon after menarche, brides were also inferior in age to their older husbands and thus, it was held, inferior in experience and knowledge (e.g., Xen., *Oec.* 7.5). For this reason as well, it was thought, wives required the tutelage of their husbands in the practical affairs of household management. These notions, typical of male authors, it should be noted, supposedly were based on empirical evidence and, coupled with the force of custom, were generally employed by said males to legitimate and reinforce the social subordination of women. There is little evidence to indicate any sustained efforts to alter these views and social arrangements in the ancient world, or for that matter in many traditional societies of the modern age. This did not mean that the wife possessed no power in domestic and other relationships but only that this power, exercised through withholding her services or wielding influence through her husband, sons, family of origin, and friends, was real but covert and unassigned.

One last social aspect of the vulnerability of the wife in particular deserves mention. She never became a member of her husband's kin group. She remained an outsider to his family and could always be separated from her husband through divorce (a right reserved to the husband in Israel [Deut 24:1–4] but allowed to the wife as well in the Hellenistic Diaspora [Mark 10:12]). Plutarch (*Conj. praec.* 35–36; *Mor.* 143A–B) thus warns the bride concerning the jealous attitude of her husband's mother and not to feel indignant or resentful. In Israel, a husband could also annul his wife's vows (Num 30:3–15), and generally the wife enjoyed far less independence than her Roman counterpart. As a rule, her ultimate security and her closest emotional ties were not with her husband but with her male offspring (cf. Plut., *Conj. praec.* 36; *Mor.* 143B). As a result, wives were constantly in need of the respect and consideration of their husbands, as is urged in 1 Peter.

Fridrichsen (1947) sees a close affinity between 1 Pet 3:7 and 1 Tim 2:11–15 and explains the idea of weakness through reference to the biblical argumentation of 1 Timothy and its appeal to Gen 3:16 and Eve's deception. Thus, he takes "weaker" as referring to the woman/wife as an easier prey to the temptations and seductions of Satan. The affinity, however, is more apparent than real. In contrast to 1 Timothy, the Petrine author refers not to Gen 3 but to the example of Sarah and the matriarchs (vv 5–6) and stresses the possibility of wives' winning their husbands to the faith by their conduct (vv 1–2), the idea of divine approval of modesty (vv 3–4), and the fact that both wives and husbands are joint heirs of divine grace—all of which are thoughts absent in 1 Timothy. "Weaker" represents nothing more than the universally held notion

---

[188] On the weakness of the female, see also Cicero, *Mur.* 27; Tac., *Ann.* 3.34; Petron., *Sat.* 11; Juv., *Sat.* 6.475–80; Sen., *Hipp.* 559, 563–64; *Oct.* 868–69; Dio Chrys., *Orat.* 74.9; *b. Qidd.* 8b; *b. Šabb.* 33b; and Dean-Jones 1991.

that females, and thus also wives, are biologically weaker and more vulnerable than their male counterparts and thus require the particular consideration of the latter. The qualification of the Christian wives as "co-heirs of the grace of life" may also indicate that it is only *physical* weakness that the author has in mind. In the meantime, of course, modern science has proved that exactly the opposite is the case: males are in fact weaker than females biologically, sexually, and socially (Montagu 1953/1973).

The term *gynaikeios* ("feminine"), appearing only here in the NT, is used as a substantive plural in Gen 18:11 (*ta gynaikeia*), where it denotes "the custom of women" (menstruation and fertile period). In the *Testament of Reuben* it is used as both a substantive ("feminine looks," 3:10) and an adjective modifying nakedness (3:12). In the Greek medical tradition, *ta gynaikeia*, literally, "womens' things," was the term for gynecological recipes (Hippocratics) and in post-Hippocratic times for gynecological treatises on female diseases (see A. E. Hanson 1991). In the present passage, the singular is linked conceptually with *asthenesterōi* to identify the human "vessel" of which the author speaks: the wife, the feminine vessel.

The noun *skeuos* ("vessel") can denote a piece of property or furniture (Matt 12:29; Mark 3:27; Luke 8:16), a vessel for containing something (John 19:29) and, figuratively, a human instrument designed for a particular purpose (Acts 9:15), a vessel of the Spirit (*Barn.* 7:3; 11:9) or a human body (*T. Naph.* 8:6; Rom 9:22; 2 Cor 4:7; *Barn.* 21:8). In the closely related text of 1 Thess 4:4 ("that each male among you know how to take a vessel for himself in holiness and honor"), it denotes either "one's own body" or, more likely, "one's own wife" (as in rabbinical texts, e.g., *b. Meg.* 12b; *Midr. Esth.* 1:11), the "vessel" for the male's seed.[189] This usage implies nothing derogatory about the wives, since it is also used of males (Paul as God's vessel or instrument, Acts 9:15; cf. 2 Tim 2:21; and Jesus Christ, whose body is said to be a vessel of the Spirit, *Barn.* 7:3; 11:9). Elsewhere, the term is also associated with "honor" (Rom 9:21; 2 Tim 2:20–21).

7d. *bestowing honor* [*on them*] (*aponemontes timēn*). The participial form and structure of v 7de is fully parallel to that of v 7bc:

> live considerately with [your wives]
> as with a weaker feminine vessel
> bestowing honor [on them]
> as also co-heirs of the grace of life.

Thus, the participial formulation *aponemontes timēn* is either a second imperative paralleling *synoikountes kata gnōsin* or, as taken here because of the ab-

---

[189] For the former view, see Wanamaker (1990, 152–53), who follows those who regard "vessel" in 1 Thess 4:4 as a "euphemism for the (male) genitalia"; for the latter view, see Maurer 1971.

sence of a copulative, a subordinate adverbial phrase explaining *how* husbands are to live considerately with their wives.

The verb *aponemō* ("bestow") appears only here in the NT, but the phrase *aponemō timēn* appears later in *1 Clem.* 1:3 and Mart. *Pol.* 10:2 with the similar sense of bestowing or rendering honor (cf. also Soph., *Aj.* 1351 [*timas nemein*]; and Philo, *Spec.* 1.65).

A wife, who was not part of the husband's kin-group, remained an "outsider" on the periphery of his family until she bore him a son and thereby brought the family honor. Her honor generally was her chasteness, but it was also enhanced by the fidelity and respect of her husband (cf. Xen., *Oec.* 7.42; 9.11). Thus it was noted (Ps.-Arist., *Oec.* 3.2, 3), "Now a virtuous wife is best honored when she sees that her husband is faithful to her, and has no preferences for another woman; but loves and trusts her and holds her as his own . . . he should approach his wife in honorable wise, full of self-restraint and awe . . . advising her in a courteous and modest manner" (cf. similarly, Plut., *Conj. praec.* 47; *Mor.* 144F: The husband should show "no greater respect for anybody than for his wife"; and Ps.-Arist., *Oec.* 3.2: "Now to a wife nothing is of more value, nothing more rightfully her own, than honored and faithful partnership with her husband. Wherefore it befits not a man of sound mind to bestow his person promiscuously, or have random intercourse with women; for otherwise, the baseborn will share in the rights of his lawful children, and his wife will be robbed of her due honor, and shame will be attached to his sons").

In contrast to Col 3:19 and Eph 5:25, which urge husbands to "love" (*agapan*) their wives, here husbands are encouraged to render their wives "honor" (*timēn*), that fundamental act of respect in an honor-and-shame society. For our author, this honoring is a particular instance of the honor that all believers are to show to all persons (2:17a). The following thought (v 7e), however, indicates the chief reason that husbands are to honor their wives in particular: their common inheritance of the grace of life.

7e. *as also co-heirs of the grace of life* (*hōs kai sygklēronomois charitos zōes*). As in v 7c, a phrase commencing with "as" (*hōs*) provides a ground for the foregoing verb: believing wives deserve honor from their husbands because through God's mercy and through faith and baptism they are, with their husbands, co-heirs of the grace of life. The expression "co-heirs of the grace of life" is unique in the NT and here states the basis on which a Christian marital ethic is primarily founded. To honor one's wife is not only to be considerate towards one's "weaker" partner but "also" and especially (*kai*, which might be rendered "even") to respect her as a "joint heir" or "co-heir of the grace of life." The composite term "co-heir" (*syn-klēronomos*) is used both literally (Philo, *Legat.* 67, 75) and figuratively (Rom 8:17; Eph 3:6; Heb 11:9; Herm., *Sim.* 5.2.7–8, 11) and here matches the preceding composite, *synoikeō*. Christian cohabiters (*synoikountes*) are also co-heirs (*sygklēronomoi*). Our author displays a predilection for such *syn-* composites (cf. *synoikeō*, 3:7; *sympathēs*, 3:8; *sympresbyteros*, 5:1; *syneklektos*, 5:13), all of which are unique to this writing and all of which variously convey the commonalities that unite members of the Christian brotherhood. Several manuscripts (A C P Ψ and the majority witnesses) have a masculine nominative plural (*sygklēronomoi*) that would apply to the husbands alone, but superior witnesses (𝔓[72] 𝔓[81] ℵ[2] B vg and others) read a dative plural (*sygklēronomois*) that corresponds to the dative of v 7c and thus pertains to wives and husbands. The parallelism of the two phrases introduced by *hōs* likewise favors this latter reading. With this term, the author thus accentuates the *common* share that believing husbands and wives have in the inheritance (cf. *klēronomia*, 1:4) of divine grace. See also Titus 3:7 where "heirs in hope of eternal life" describes all believers, and compare Paul, who speaks of believers in general as "co-heirs with Christ" (Rom 8:17).

of the grace of life (*charitos zōēs*). In this expression, unique in the NT, "of life" (*zōēs*) serves as an epexegetical modifier of "grace" (*charitos*). Both are gifts of God to be enjoyed by all believers as a consequence of their divine regeneration in conversion and baptism ("grace": 1:2, 10, 13; 4:10; 5:5, 10, 12; "life": 1:3, 23; 2:5, 24). The addition of "eternal" to "life" in 𝔓[72] and the Syriac Peshitta perhaps was influenced by the stock expression "eternal life."[190] "Varied" (*poikilēs*) appears to have been added to "grace" by other scribes (ℵ A and others) on the analogy of 4:10.

The expression on the whole recalls 1:4, where the "inheritance" (*klēronomia*) of all of the believers is mentioned and anticipates 3:9, which also speaks of the blessing to be "inherited" by all of the faithful. Thus, the motif of inheritance involved in the word "co-heirs" links this passage with its broader context and the eschatological hope that pervades the letter.

Joint inheritance of divine grace is not the same thing as social equality, however. The principle espoused by Paul that baptism eliminates the distinction between Judean and Greek, male and female, slave and free (Gal 3:28) refers to the abolishment of previous social boundaries demarcating these pairs and to the unity they as believers enjoy "in Christ." But this affirmation of unity in Christ is not to be confused with an establishing of *social equality* (against Schüssler-Fiorenza 1983a, 205–18 and others who confuse unity with equality). Unity in Christ no more implies an equality of all members of the Christian community than family unity implies that parents and children are equal as social partners. 1 Peter 3:7, like Gal 3:28, and Paul's surprising assertion in 1 Corinthians that wives as well as husbands have authority over their spouses' bodies (1 Cor 7:4) represent "evangelical breakthroughs" beyond conventional perceptions which, however, fail to have led to actual social or legal alterations of power (see also Balch 1981, 143–49 on the lack of equality among enlightened Stoics as well). There is little if any evidence to indicate that within the Christian community any attempt was made to establish "equal

[190] See Matt 19:29; Mark 10:17; Luke 18:18 ("inherit eternal life"); cf. also Matt 25:46; Luke 10:25; John 3:16; Acts 13:46; Rom 2:7; etc.

legal or social or political rights" of males and females or their equal social status, as Paul's reflections on female attire (1 Cor 11:2–16) indicate, where custom and tradition remained the rule. The same holds true of the remaining social inequality between masters and slaves, elders and younger persons, leaders and followers. Conventional notions of the physical and social inferiority of females persisted among Christians, as the continuous history of early Christianity indicates. Here it was not equality but rather *equity* that remained the norm; that is, not the equal status of all but rather the just treatment of each according to his or her status. The common access of females and males to the grace of God found no practical or material expression in new, revolutionary social or legal arrangments, as lamentable as this might strike the modern reader. Therefore, it is historically unjustifiable to attribute to Jesus an "egalitarian" agenda from which his followers, including Paul and the Petrine author, supposedly diverged in their alleged "reinstitutionalization" of patriarchal order and control.

1 Peter 3:7 is indeed the first unequivocal expression of the commonality of husbands and wives as "co-heirs of the grace of life." But even this concept does not appear to have altered the presumed "weakness" and *social subordination* of Christian wives to their husbands in the early Church. The various NT texts relevant to this subject reflect a community still struggling to reconcile theological ideals and social practicalities, status, and roles within the community, especially at worship (1 Cor 11–14), and status and roles in the society at large. In the case of 1 Peter, as in the case of Paul (1 Cor 7:29–31), an awareness of living at the conclusion of the age (4:7, 17) may perhaps account for a disinterest in any fundamental alteration of structures in a world assumed to be in the process of passing away.

In 1 Peter, the unusual description of husbands and wives as co-heirs expresses the *commonality* rather than the equality of the marital partners. The harmonious domestic union of husband and wife and their joint inheritance of the grace of life serve as a mini-model for the solidarity and blessings of the entire household of God, whatever the members' respective social rankings.

7f. *so that your prayers may not be hindered* (*eis to mē egkoptesthai tas proseuchas hymōn*). This final phrase provides a third motivation for the conduct urged on husbands and links the harmony of husbands and wives with the effectiveness of their prayers and hence their relation to God. The plural pronoun "your" (*hymōn*), in the light of the concept "co-heirs," probably applies to the prayers of both husbands and wives. Prayer is mentioned also in 3:12 (God attends to the prayer [*deēsis*] of the righteous) as well as 4:7 (*proseuchai*), where praying is one of several communally fortifying acts of the household of God. Some manuscripts ($\mathfrak{P}^{81}$ B) read "so that you will not be hindered with respect to your prayers" (*tais proseuchais* instead of *tas proseuchas*), perhaps because the scribes assumed that the verb "is normally used in relation to persons rather than their activities" (Michaels 1988, 155). In 1 Cor 7:5, Paul also speaks of the prayer of spouses but as a reason for the temporary termination of sexual intercourse (cf. similarly *T. Naph.* 8:8: "There is a time for intercourse with one's wife and a time to abstain for the purpose of prayer").

The verb *egkoptō* is used of blocking with barricades and making something impassable; for the sense "hinder," see also Acts 24:4; Rom 15:22; 1 Tim 2:8; and Jas 5:4. This association between prayer and respectful (rather than sexual) conduct here in 1 Peter reflects the common Christian conviction that prayer, as an expression of one's relation to God and an act of praise, thanksgiving, confession, and petition, is directly affected by one's behavior toward other persons.[191]

Thus, in regard to 3:1–7, on the whole, the behavior of both wives and husbands is to aim for mutual respect of conventional marital roles in order to maintain the solidarity of the family and present an honorable face to outsiders, in order to win some to the faith, but also to gain the approval of God, to emulate the worthy matriarchs of old, to gain the inheritance of life, and to promote an effective life of prayer in relation to God.

GENERAL COMMENT

This exhortation to wives and husbands continues the focus on honorable conduct introduced in 2:12 and, more specifically, honorable conduct illustrated by the respect for order and authority in the public domain (2:13–17) as well as in the domestic sphere (2:18–3:7). With his exhortation to domestic slaves, the author introduced the domain of the household; his exhortation to wives and husbands now moves to its very center. The attention to marital order and harmony is typical of the Hellenistic household-management tradition, which this segment of the letter continues to reflect in its content and sequence of subjects. Notions here of the "weakness" of the female sex, the social subordination of wives to husbands, along with their expected chaste conduct, obedience, silence, modesty, and avoidance of ostentatious appearance mirror the prevailing perspectives, preferences, and conceptual constructs of the patriarchal cultures of the Greeks, Romans, Israelites, and early Christians. They are reflective of historical and social custom rather than of an absolute and abiding "order of creation" established by God, as Gielen (1990, 513–14) and Goppelt (1993, 218) also note. The same holds true for the respect that husbands are expected to show their wives. However, this address to Christian wives and husbands is animated by decidedly Christian values and goals as well. In particular, it is noted that (1) wives can "win" their pagan husbands to the faith through their holy behavior (3:1–2); (2) it is God who sees and approves their gentle spirit (3:4c); (3) they are to take the holy matriarchs and especially Sarah as their model, for through baptism and conversion they have become Sarah's children (3:5–6); (4) believing husbands are to honor their believing wives, not only because of the weakness of the latter, but because both partners, as a

[191] See Mark 11:25; Matt 5:23; 6:12, 14–15; 18:23–35; 1 John 4:18–20. On prayer, see von Severus et al. 1972, 1976.

consequence of their conversion, are "co-heirs of the grace of life" (3:7); and (5) because their marital relations have a bearing on prayer and their relation to God (3:7). Thus the behavior of wives as well as the harmony of Christian households serve as a model for the conduct and cohesion of the entire household of God.

This instruction to wives and husbands is in part similar to that found elsewhere in the NT (Col 3:18–19; Eph 5:22–33; 1 Tim 2:9–15; Titus 2:4–5; cf. Selwyn 1947, 432–35 and the comparative table on his pp. 432–33) and is consistent with concepts of domestic wifely subordination expressed in such texts as 1 Cor 11:2–16 and 14:33–37. However, the several differences among these texts, particularly the statements justifying these notions, rule out any possibility of direct literary dependence and point rather to varied use of common tradition. Thus, for example, both 1 Peter and Ephesians expand upon a briefer injunction to wifely subordination as contained in Col 3:18. But Ephesians, in contrast to 1 Peter, speaks of the "love" husbands owe their wives (cf. also Col 3:19) and grounds this love and wifely subordination in the relation between Christ and Church (wives representing the subordination of Church to Christ and husbands representing the love of Christ for the Church, 5:22–33). 1 Timothy 2 and Titus 2, on the other hand, contain no *direct* address to wives or husbands. And 1 Timothy, which, like 1 Peter, refers to wifely adornment, diverges significantly from 1 Peter in not mentioning the matriarchs and Sarah as models. Instead it justifies female subordination with the story of Eve's secondary creation and her transgression and concludes with the singular notion that the woman will be saved through bearing children (2:9–15). 1 Peter is the only text that speaks of husbands and wives as "co-heirs of the grace of life" and likewise is the only text that situates this wife-husband instruction within the larger concept of the Christian community as the "household of God." It thus is evident that these texts manifest varying adaptations of the Hellenistic household-management tradition.

Wives receive the lion's share of attention in 1 Peter for at least four discernible reasons. First, they represent the more vulnerable partner in the marital relationship, and this vulnerability is particularly acute for those who are married to nonbelieving husbands. Their *precarious situation*, like that of the domestic slaves, typifies that of the community as a whole. Second, the *conduct* and *character* encouraged of wives (respect for order, chasteness, virtuous comportment, gentleness, doing what is right without fear), like that of the domestic slaves, also is of a piece with the conduct and character required of all believers. Third, the Christian *goal* of wifely behavior likewise illustrates the behavior of all believers: leading a holy way of life that will win even nonbelievers to the faith. Finally, their *relation* to God (their holiness and reverence for God, their tranquil inner spirit precious in God's sight, their status as joint heirs of the grace of life) and their solidarity with Israel of old similarly illustrate the relationship to God and ancient Israel typical of the entire household of God. Thus, Christian wives, like the domestic slaves, are presented in the letter as poignant paradigms and moral examples for *all* of the believers addressed. The

Petrine author devotes noteworthy attention to these wives because they exemplify in their own particular way the vulnerable condition of all the faithful, because their role in the attraction of outsiders is a crucial one, and because in their conduct, character, and blessings they are representative of the entire household of God.

Accordingly, in this attention to wives it is unnecessary to suspect a concern for allaying social suspicion of domestic subversion customarily directed against Eastern religions (against Balch 1981, 65–116) or an intentional "reversion" from an alleged earlier stage of Christian "egalitarianism" to a patriarchal dominance motivated by a concern for promoting social conformity (against Schüssler Fiorenza 1983a, 260–66, whose position is also rejected by Prostmeier 1990, 454–55) or an attempt to counter a putative Hellenistic "wave of female emancipation" by urging "loyalty" in the domestic as well as the public realm (against Gielen 1990, 146–58, 512–28). It is true, as Balch (1981, 65–80) notes, that Roman elites, from their ethnocentric perspective, were generally critical of exotic religions and "superstitions" infiltrating from the East, one of which, the cult of Isis, because of its emphasis on the equality of females and males, held a particular attraction to women. But there is no evidence that the Christians of Asia Minor were associated with the Isis cult. Nor does 1 Pet 3:1–6, despite references to charges of wrongdoing elsewhere in the letter (2:12; cf. 2:15; 4:4), indicate any outsider criticism of Christian wives in particular. The behavior urged of wives is typical of the conduct generally expected of wives in Greek, Roman, Israelite, and Christian circles. Honorable wifely conduct in line with time-honored norms would assure the harmony and well-being of individual marriages and thereby allay possible suspicions of Christian disrepect for domestic order and conventional lines of familial authority. But the *explicit* concern of the author here is with the *conversion* of nonbelieving partners and not conformity for safety's sake (against Balch and Schüssler Fiorenza). In contrast to Titus 2:5, which expresses concern that "the word of God may not be discredited" (among accusatory outsiders), the Petrine author asserts the optimistic hope that Christian wives may even convert their unbelieving husbands through their conduct. In the case of Schüssler Fiorenza's theory that the use of the household tradition represented a "reversion" to patriarchal structures once abolished by Jesus, an original abolishment of patriarchal mentality and structures has yet to be demonstrated and thus talk of its resumption is premature. And in the case of all three authors (Balch, Schüssler Fiorenza, and Gielen), what they have failed to note is that any supposed interest on the author's part in promoting Christian accommodation to outsiders' standards of morality would be at variance with the argument of the letter as a whole. It is precisely holy nonconformity (1:14–16) and a distinctive communal identity and deportment (1:3–2:10, 17) that are urged to *demarcate* Christians from outsiders (2:11; 4:2–4, 12–19), along with exhortations to "resist" the enemy (5:8–9) and to "stand fast" in grace (5:12).

The perceptions of women that are evident in 1 Pet 3:1–7 are views that were shared universally in the ancient Mediterranean world. The author *pre-*

sumes these views, however; he does not argue them. What he does advance, on the other hand, are specifically Christian beliefs that *distinguish* this instruction from pagan views: reverence for God and concern for God's approval (3:2, 4), the conversion of nonbelievers (3:1), the solidarity of Christian wives with the holy matriarchs of old (3:5–6), and the status of Christian wives as coheirs with their Christian husbands of the grace of life (3:7). In acting on these beliefs, Christian wives are models for all believers. On the whole, this address to wives is a call not to wifely servility but to a courageous and winsome witness to their faith through a holy and decorous way of life, a call consonant with the call issued previously to all believers (2:12).

Husbands, in honoring their wives, likewise exemplify the honor that all believers are to render (2:17). They share with their wives, as with all believers (1:4; 3:9), in the inheritance of grace and life. The plural rather than singular vocatives ("wives," "husbands") indicate that this instruction has households in general in mind and is thus exemplary for all Christian marital situations. In addition, the links between this unit and its context indicate that the internal harmony and union with God that characterizes individual Christian households serves as a poignant example for the solidarity and prayer life of all the brotherhood. The union of husband and wife constitutes the core of the family and household. It is thus not surprising that much of what is said in 3:1–7 resonates with encouragement directed to the entire household of God. This marital exhortation thus undergirds two major social concerns in the letter: (1) the necessity for proper conduct that will overcome the suspicion and slander of outsiders and win some to the faith and (2) the need for order and harmony within the households, which in turn are models for the entire household of God. In the exhortation of the whole community that follows (3:8–12), this twofold focus on both the internal and external relations of the community receives still further accentuation.

DETAILED COMMENT: READING 1 PETER 3:1–7 TODAY—THE HERMENEUTICAL PROBLEM AND CONTEXTUALIZING GENDER CONSTRUCTS

1 Peter 3:1–7, like other biblical texts that presume the inferiority of women and urge their subordination, present the modern-day reader with an acute challenge involving both biblical interpretation and the use of these texts as moral guidelines today. These texts illustrate in an especially painful way a perennial hermeneutical problem facing modern readers of Sacred Scripture. On the one hand, the witness of these passages to the assumed inferiority of women and their secondary social status in ancient society is clear and indisputable. On the other hand, it is equally clear that this perception of the nature, status, and roles of women is no longer shared by many cultures of the modern world. The social world in which the biblical documents were composed was far different from the postindustrial society of most modern Bible readers. The

Renaissance and Reformation, the age of exploration, the rise of science, the Enlightenment, the Industrial Revolution, the collapse of monarchies, the onset of liberation movements, and the scientific advances of the last half millennium have all contributed to the radical restructuring of the political, economic, social, and cultural landscape of the planet. These fundamental restructurings of human life have been accompanied by shifting understandings of and attitudes toward the natural world, human biology and psychology, social relationships, time, space, and even the human-God relationship (as elaborated, for instance, by Roheim [1958] and the sociologists G. Lenski, Nolan, and J. Lenski [1995]).

As these massive changes remove the modern reader of the Bible ever farther from the world of antiquity, the biblical communities, and their world views, it becomes ever more problematic to determine in what way these ancient biblical documents may continue to serve as sources of spiritual inspiration and moral guidance at the outset of a new millennium. The hermeneutical problem is a perennial one: how do readers, who are removed from the texts they read in terms of time, place, and social-cultural circumstances, continue to derive meaning and motivation from this literature. It is this problem that biblical exegesis and theology have sought to address down through the ages. Making this complex issue even more complex is the fact that the texts of which we are speaking are parts of writings constituting Sacred Scripture, writings regarded as the inspired word of God, and therefore bearing fundamental ecclesiastical and spiritual authority.

Prior to the advent of modern biblical criticism, the images, valuation, and thought about women found in the Bible had been considered by those who regard the Bible as the inspired and authoritative Word of God as the final and decisive word about the female in God's economy and a reliable guideline for determining the status and role of women in both Church and society. Indeed, many Christians today still share this point of view. Given their inferior and subordinate status in the Bible, it is argued, wives today are to be subordinate to their husbands, are not to exercise authority in the Church or workplace, and are not to be ordained to ministry and priesthood. They are rather to regard the home, marriage, and bearing of children as the area of their divinely established calling. Or as a recent generation of Germans put it: women are good for Kinder, Küche, und Kirche ("children, kitchen, and church"). 1 Peter 3:1–7, along with other biblical texts speaking of the assumed inferiority of females and their subordinate role, is still read by many as supportive of this view.

On the other hand, increasing numbers of Bible readers have begun to regard 1 Pet 3:1–7 and related biblical texts as representing a demeaning, if not depraved, view of women that is contrary to the teaching and practice of Jesus and thoroughly inconsistent with the spirit of the gospel, to say nothing of the egalitarian spirit of our contemporary age. According to this view, this Petrine text and the related biblical passages impugn the status of women, contribute not to a joyful sense of the gospel's liberating and exalting power, but in all too many cases even become a tool for the justification of male abuse of females (Corley 1994). Such passages, it is argued, reveal a loss of evangelical vision, a reversion in the early Church to social structures that Jesus supposedly left behind, and represent a series of fateful steps leading to the devaluation, suppression, and silencing of women in the Church of the second and following centuries. When such texts are read in the Church today, it is said, they constitute not good news but decidedly bad news, not just for today's female population but for men as well who take these texts as biblical permission or mandate for "keeping women in their place," where "place" means a position of purportedly divinely ordained inferiority and subordination.

Given the yawning gap separating the modern age from that of the ancient biblical writings, some even go so far as to maintain that no hermeneutical bridge-building is possible: the Bible can provide no guidance whatsoever on modern social issues, be it atomic warfare, in vitro fertilization, slavery, or the roles and relationships of twentieth- and twenty-first-century men and women. Still others resist going so far and instead seek various ways of continuing to find inspiration and moral guidance in these sacred texts.

Thus, at present, we meet three distinct approaches to this issue. (1) One view insists on ignoring any chasms separating contemporary Christians from the biblical past and regarding the Bible as an absolute, timeless expression of the Word of God and as prescriptive for Christians of every time and place. As such, its statements on women are seen as unconditioned descriptions of the female nature and as infallible directives concerning the place, role, and behavior of women today.

(2) At the opposite extreme, a second view would see the Bible as reflecting a social and cultural world totally alien to our own and an understanding of gender, sexual nature, processes of reproduction, and all of their accompanying values and attitudes as incompatible with modern, scientifically-established knowledge. The negative views of women found in the Bible, like the assumption and toleration of slavery, are defective, obsolete, and in fact detrimental to an accurate, healthy, and just understanding of females today. Consequently, the Bible is a sleeping dog that should be allowed to lie, lest it be used to give theological sanction to the abuse and repression of women, just as it was used a century and a half ago to legitimate the abominable institution of slavery. A variation on this position would salvage some elements of the Bible by seeking a "canon within the canon" that embodies the "real" and unequivocal gospel, which in turn would serve as a critique and rejection of all patriarchal thinking, structures, and programs.

Each of these first two approaches finds numerous supporters today; but both are inadequate. The first position denies the actual conditioned character of the biblical writings as expressions of human authors inevitably constrained by their own time, place, social location, and culture. This includes all of the various views on females and males over the course of time and the varying explanations of male-female relations. Such an approach, however, not only flies in the face of sound historical consciousness, it also denies the theological and historical implications of the doctrine of the incarnation and God's self-revelation in, and not beyond, history. This is the double problem faced by any who would employ the Bible today as a source of "timeless truth" and a "timeless moral code" (L. T. Johnson 1987, 63–64).

The second position, on the other hand, while justified in its criticism of the misuse of the Bible in legitimating the abuse of and discrimination against women today, would reject any contribution of the Bible whatsoever to modern thought and conduct on the grounds that the Bible is hopelessly out of date, irrelevant to, and at odds with the sensitivities and changed social and legal structures of modern society. This, however, would be nothing short of relegating the Bible to the dustbin of history and denying any continuity whatsoever between the past and the present, to say nothing of dismissing any form of its authority as the word of God. The fatal weakness of the search for a canon within the canon is the subjectivity involved in deciding which and whose canon is to be preferred.

(3) In contrast to these radical and extremist positions, a third intermediate approach is the one taken by the majority of exegetes and ethicians today. This approach entails a contextualizing mode of exegesis and ethics in which biblical texts are read and understood in the light of their historical, social, and cultural contexts. Reading the Bible in its historical context has long been a staple of the historical-critical method. More recently, increased attention has been given to the social and cultural contexts as well (Elliott 1993 and its bibliography [pp. 138–74]). This approach in fact has been described and recommended in a study produced by the Pontifical Biblical Commission of the Roman Catholic church on *The Interpretation of the Bible in the Church* (1993).[192] "Religious texts," it notes, "are bound in reciprocal relationship to the societies in which they originate. This is clearly the case as regards biblical texts. Consequently, the scientific study of the Bible requires as exact a knowledge as is possible of the social conditions distinctive of the various milieus in which the traditions recorded in the Bible took shape" (1994, 506). Awareness of the social and cultural contexts proper to the biblical writings "allows one to distinguish more clearly those elements of the biblical message that are permanent, as having their foundation in human nature, and those that are more contingent, being due to the particular features of certain cultures" (1994, 507).

Taking this hermeneutical approach to the Bible first involves being clear about one's own personal perspectives and "horizon": how they have been shaped by one's own gender, age, race, social class, education, religion, and culture, and how different they may be from the perspectives, knowledge, experience, and world views of the biblical authors. A second step requires gaining clarity regarding the social and cultural world and "horizon" of the biblical authors. A third step involves a contextual reading of the biblical writ-

[192] Cited according to the English translation in *Origins* 23, no. 29 (Jan. 6, 1994) 498–524.

ings and a determination of the extent to which they reflected, modified, or rejected the conventional views of their contemporaries. Finally, the hermeneutical goal is an effective fusion of these disparate sets of horizons so that some degree of understanding is still possible. This involves a "dialogue" between reader and text—not a simplistic repetition of the words of the text but a genuine attempt to discover shared meanings and possible disagreements. In many instances the biblical texts continue to speak powerfully to the human condition. In other cases, where scientific knowledge has made decisive advances and where social, political, and legal conditions have undergone radical change, biblical conceptions and the presuppositions on which they were based will have to be critically assessed. This is the case, for instance, not only with the geocentric cosmology of the biblical authors and the erroneous conclusions drawn concerning the structure of the universe and the location of God, demons, and the deceased, but also with respect to their acceptance of the unalterable "given-ness" of slavery, the "natural" inferiority of females, and the social and moral consequences they drew from these erroneous assumptions, factors directly relevant to the reading of 1 Peter.

At the same time, the modern reader attempts to discern, even in these instances, the moral and spiritual principles at stake and the manner in which these principles produced a characteristically Israelite or Christian position on slaves and women in the economy of God. The diversity and discrepancies of positions expressed in the Bible even on these two issues require that modern readers must apply the so-called "axiological principle" and distinguish major from minor biblical themes—that is, predominating, consistent emphases running throughout the biblical writings from single or peripheral positions. This is an admittedly difficult and potentially subjective task but nonetheless essential. For those regarding the Bible as the inspired Word of God and inspiring guide for human behavior, this approach also requires an awareness that this holy Word of God is presented in the historically-, socially-, and culturally-contingent words of human beings and that meanings perceived in these texts are likewise historically, socially, and culturally contingent. Consequently, a contextual reading sensitive to the contexts of both the biblical writings and the current readers is an essential ingredient of the hermeneutical enterprise. Finally, reading the Bible as the Word of God requires a constant openness to the challenging and transforming, as well as comforting, power of these writings in relation to the reader today and to the particular issues of the present. Applying all of these steps to a reading of 1 Pet 3:1–7 is impossible here, but comment on a few of them may illustrate the direction and constructive results of such an approach.

In the world of biblical antiquity, patriarchal structures and patriarchal mindsets were the order of the day. This included the notion that females (and hence wives) were by nature and/or divine fiat inferior to males (and hence husbands) physically, intellectually, and morally. This assumed inferiority of the female, in turn, was used by Greek, Roman, Israelite, and Christian males alike to explain and justify women's subordination to father, husband, and brothers; the preference for male babies and the exposure of females; the female's "need" for male control and protection (given her "irrationality" and "enslavement to the senses," particularly the sexual drive); and hence her exclusion from governance, indeed from public life in general. She was restricted to the domestic realm, where her chief responsiblity was the bearing and nurturing of male children as legitimate heirs, with obedience and silent deference to the male head of the household in all things, so as to preserve and advance the honor of the household. This subordinate condition was to be manifested in all aspects of her behavior, including her chasteness, modesty, and decorous dress. Whereas males embodied the honor of the family in the public realm, females, it was held, embodied the family's potential shame. Thus this patriarchal view, articulated and promoted by males, found expression in a wide range of social institutions and cultural norms concerning female and male roles and relationships. Numerous illustrations of these notions held commonly by Greek, Roman, Israelite, and Christian authors have been cited above in the NOTES on 3:1–7.

This state of affairs is hardly unique to the ancient Mediterranean world, we might note. Indeed, anthropologists, including numerous female anthropologists, point out that asymmetrical gender-relations, the superordination of males and the subordination of females, are consistent features of *every* known society from ancient to modern time. "Female subordination" is a "cultural universal," states female anthropologist S. B. Ortner unequivocally (1974, 69, 71; cf. also M. Z. Rosaldo 1974, 19). What varies from one time and place to another is only how these asymmetical structures and the assumptions of female inferiority are construed and justified.

In the Bible, moreover, and in ancient sources generally, we have far more information on *ideas* about females and *rationalizations* of female status and roles than we do actual empirical descriptions of female conduct. These ideas, as historians, anthropologists, and theologians now realize, formed part of a "cultural construct," a way of construing the female that is not to be confused with reality (Dean-Jones 1991; see also Lerner 1986; Foucault 1985). As we now know with hindsight, this was a construct generally uninformed by accurate knowledge of female and male anatomy, biology, and physiology. Furthermore, the vast majority of the sources available to us was *produced by males* and conceived according to *male* perspectives, attitudes, values, and interests. This included their limited direct knowledge not only of female biology but of the inner social world of women. Finally, these ideas and idealizations are both reflections and justifications of the asymmetrical, stratified, male-controlled patriarchal society in which the ancients were at home. Consequently, given the perspectival, limited, selective, and ideological nature of the sources, we cannot be sure of the extent to which what they state concerning women accords with actual social reality. Nor is it the case that the specific norms and patterns governing female-male relations were everywhere the same throughout the ancient world. Nevertheless, it is clear that, in general, gender differentiation and gender inequality remained constant and were fostered by a broad array of male conceptions, gender constructs, and idealizations of how things supposedly are or ought to be. In traditional societies, this situation in fact has perdured down through modern times. Only recently have these constructs and institutional patterns been analyzed and challenged in postindustrial societies, as being ideologically driven.

This must be kept in mind when examining the information from antiquity and the Bible on the nature, roles, and status of women. In this regard, as in numerous other domains of social life, the biblical communities shared the prevailing views of their historical contemporaries, however they adapted and rationalized them. This leaves no room for singling out and criticizing the biblical authors as uniquely backward or depraved in their perspectives on women. They were, rather, children of their own times. They represent, unfortunately, a pervasive understanding of and attitude toward women that alarmingly perdures even into cultures of our own time, all our current scientific knowledge notwithstanding. Indeed, as Gerda Lerner underscores in her critical study *The Creation of Patriarchy* (1986, 220), it is only in modern and relatively recent time that a dramatic and comprehensive change in political, social, economic, and cultural conditions has made possible a critique and overturning of male domination and female subordination.

The actual position, activities, and influence of women in Greek, Roman, Israelite, and Christian societies were not static, of course, but varied to some degree according to historical periods, geocultural areas, ethnic groups, class, age, and even urban or rural location. There is some evidence, for instance, that, from Classical Greek time onward, in the aristocratic echelons of Greek and Roman society, upper-class women enjoyed relatively more freedom of movement and participation in public affairs than did their lower-class counterparts. They eventually began to assume a greater presence in civic magistracies, public benevolence as patronesses (sponsoring of salons and female priesthoods), greater proximity to their husbands in inheritance and property rights, relaxation of the rule of tutelage, and participation in symposia, women's clubs, and associations (Thraede 1972a, 197–224). To what extent this female involvement in public life penetrated the lower classes or the regions east of Italy is uncertain. The first-century CE Stoic Musonius Rufus asserted the equality of females and males in regard to sense-perception, intelligence, and virtue and encouraged the education of daughters as well as sons (*That Women Too Should Study Philosophy, Or.* 3). But this Roman champion of equality in marriage appears to represent the great exception that proved the rule as represented by the Aristotelian household-management tradition. And even for Musonius, the conventional distinctions between man and woman as stronger-weaker, ruler-ruled, better-worse still obtained (Mus. Ruf., *Sex. Ind., Or.* 12.86.38–88.4).

In the eastern realm of the Empire at any rate, older traditional modes of male control of females seem to have prevailed. Israelite society was resolutely patriarchal in structure and mentality. Torah was seen to warrant kinship structures of patrilineal descent, patrilocal residence, and patriarchal order and to legitimate the virtually total male control of females. Considered to be subject to the rule of the male, the source of sin and death, dangerous and "impure" because of their menstruation, females were marginal and not numbered among actual Israelites (male, Ezra 2:2–63), whose covenant with Yahweh was symbolized by circumcision, a male initiation rite. Like children, wives were considered as the property of their husbands (Exod 20:17; Lev 18:8, 16; Deut 5:21; 22:16, 30), a status reflected in the adultery laws that concerned violation of another man's property (Exod 20:14–15; cf. 20:17). During menstruation and childbirth they were regarded impure or unclean (Lev 15:19–31; 12:1–8), twice as long after the birth of a daughter as after the birth of a son. Such impurity disqualified them from the priesthood and from full participation in the Temple worship. In the Jerusalem Temple they were restricted to the Women's Court. They were not taught Torah, were disallowed from offering testimony in criminal cases, limited in initiating divorce proceedings, punished more severely for sexual offenses, secluded in the home, required to have their bodies totally covered, and considered in all respects to be inferior to males (Sir 22:3; 33:19–23) and to be the property of their husbands (Exod 20:17; Lev 18:16; Deut 5:21). "Sin," laments the Sage, "began with a woman, and thanks to her we all must die" (Sir 25:24; cf. Gen 3:1–7). "Many women, much witchcraft," declared Hillel (*m. ʾAbot* 1:5). Small wonder, then, that the Israelite male prayed thrice daily: "God I thank you that you have not made me a Gentile, one ignorant in Torah (*ʿam ha-aretz*), or a woman" (*t. Ber.* 7.18).

In their concurrence on the inferiority of the female, Israelites based their position on Sacred Scripture by pointing to the Creation story (Gen 2–3), according to which the woman was created from one of the man's ribs (Gen 2:21–22) and, because of her disobedience, was informed: "I will greatly multiply your pain in childbearing; in pain you shall bring forth children; yet your desire shall be for your husband and he shall rule over you" (Gen 3:16). Philo, commenting on the first text (*QG* 1.27), interprets these words in the light of conventional Hellenistic notions:

> Why was not woman, like the other animals and man, also formed from earth, instead of the side of man? First, because woman is not equal in honour with man. Second, because she is not equal in age, but younger. Wherefore those who take wives who have passed their prime are to be criticized for destroying the laws of nature. Third, he wished that man should take care of woman as of a very necessary part of him; but woman, in return, should serve him as a whole. Fourth, he counsels man figuratively to take care of woman as of a daughter, and woman to honour man as a father.

In explaining why the serpent spoke to the woman and not the man, Philo comments (*QG* 1.33 on Gen 3:1): "Woman is more accustomed to be deceived than man. For his judgment, like his body, is masculine and is capable of dissolving or destroying the designs of deception; but the judgment of a woman is more feminine, and because of softness she easily gives way and is taken in by plausible falsehoods which resemble the truth." In regard to Gen 3:8 he also observes (*QG* 1.43): "Why, when they hid themselves from the face of God, was not the woman, who first ate of the forbidden fruit, first mentioned, but the man. . . . It was the more imperfect and ignoble element, the female, that made a beginning of transgression and lawlessness, while the male made the beginning of reverence and modesty and all good, since he was better and more perfect" (cf. also *QG* 37 on Gen 3:6). Because of this disparity in nature and intelligence, Philo notes, in marriage the husband is "fitted to his spouse alone as if to a bridle. And especially because he, having the authority of a master (*kyrian echōn exousian*), is to be suspected of arrogance. But woman, taking the rank of a servant, is shown to be obedient to his life" (*QG* 1.29 on Gen 2:24). The woman, moreover, as other texts also stress, was the first sinner and cause of the death of the human race (Sir 25:24–26; cf. also *Apoc. Mos.* 7, 9; *Life of Adam and Eve* 3:258; 10:260; 18:264).

Consequently, it was assumed, males were assigned dominance and control of all females (Sir 33:19–23 [LXX 33:20–24]). Male vigilance was required concerning headstrong and wayward wives and daughters, who could bring shame upon the family (Sir 22:5; 26:12; 36:25; 42:6, 11, 12–14). For, stated Philo (*QG* 4.15 on Gen 18:11), "the female sex is irrational and akin to bestial passions, fear, sorrow, pleasure and desire, from which ensue incurable weaknesses and indescribable diseases." Thus Israel insisted that "wives must be in servitude to their husbands, a servitude not imposed by violent ill-treatment but promoting obedience in all things" (*Hypoth.* 7.3). Explaining why the Essenes did not marry, both Philo (*Hypoth.* 11:14–17, cited also in Eusebius of Caesarea, *Praep. ev.* 8.11.14–17) and Josephus (*J.W.* 2.121) rail on women's wantonness, jealousy, and seductiveness. "Women," declares the author of the *Testament of Reuben* (5:1–6:3), "are evil . . . and by reason of their lacking authority or power over men, scheme treacherously how they might entice with their looks . . . women are an incurable disease, but for us they are the plague of Beliar and an eternal disgrace."

To be sure, the qualities of a good wife did not go uncelebrated. Thus the Sages observed: "A wife's grace (*charis*) delights her husband . . . a silent wife is a gift of the Lord and there is nothing so precious as a disciplined soul. A modest wife adds grace (*charis*) to grace and no balance can weigh the value of a chaste soul . . . the beauty of a good wife is in the order of her home (*kosmōi oikias autēs*)" (Sir 26:13–16; cf. also 26:1–4). "A woman's beauty gladdens the countenance and surpasses every human desire. If kindness and humility mark her speech, her husband is not like other men. He who acquires a wife gets his best possession, a helper fit for him and a pillar of support" (Sir 36:22–24). The book of Proverbs concludes with an encomium of the ideal wife (31:10–31) summing up various praises of the virtuous female or honorable wife expressed elsewhere in the wisdom tradition.[193] On the whole, however, anxiety

[193] See Prov 5:15–19; 11:16, 22; 12:4; 18:22; 19:14; Sir 7:19, 26; 25:1, 8; 26:1–4, 13–18; 36:21–25; 40:19.

concerning shameful women and wives seems to have outweighed appreciation of the virtuous.

Israelite tradition likewise celebrated the virtues of Sarah and the matriarchs and recorded the heroic exploits of such women as Miriam, Deborah and Jael, Huldah, Esther, Ruth, Judith, and Susanna. Wisdom (*ḥokmâ*, *sophia*) and spirit (*rûaḥ*), moreover, were feminine rather than masculine idealizations (Prov 7:4–5; 8:1–36; 9:1–6; 14:1; Sir 4:11–19; 6:18–37; 9:3–9; 24:1–34; Wis 6:12–11:1). Nevertheless, it is not apparent that this extolling of heroines or the feminine personification of wisdom and spirit had any concrete impact on the social status of lower-class women, who were subject to their male superiors in all respects.

In the Jesus movement, women (Galilean, Judean, Samaritan, and Gentile) began to figure more prominently in Jesus' teaching and activity and in the organization of the movement. Jesus sought to strengthen the social position of women by reinforcing the command against adultery and prohibiting divorce (Matt 5:27–32/Mark 9:43–48/Luke 16:18; Matt 19:1–12/Mark 10:1–12). He welcomed women into his company (Mark 7:24–30; Luke 8:38–42; John 4:7–42), touched and healed impure females (Mark 1:29–31; 5:21–43)—all contrary to conventional norms dictating the avoidance of females by males. Nor did he ever speak a derogatory word about his female contemporaries. It was, in fact, certain women from Galilee who, according to Luke, provided the material support for his mission (Luke 8:1–3). Mark, moreover, recalls (14:9) that Jesus paid singular honor to the woman who anointed his body in anticipation of his death and burial by announcing that "wherever the gospel is preached in the whole world, what she has done will be told in memory of her" (see Schüssler Fiorenza 1983a).

The social and religious significance of these extraordinary interactions with women was not lost on the Evangelists. They did not suppress the memory of this unconventional and at points illicit behavior but, rather, emphasized it prominently as illustrative of the inclusiveness of Jesus' gospel and social agenda. Luke, in fact, went so far as to illustrate the reversal of values that Jesus' advent signaled by putting a key declaration of the gospel on the lips of a woman (Luke 1:46–55). All four Evangelists record that it was women who first witnessed the empty tomb and that it was they to whom the annnouncement of Jesus' resurrection was first made (Mark 16:1–8/ Matt 28:1–10/Luke 24:1–11). John, moreover, presents Mary Magdalene alone as the first witness of the resurrected Christ (John 20:11–18) and hence an honored witness to the central event of the Christian faith.

Such extraordinary honoring of the female, however, occurred within the ongoing social, political, and legal structures of a patriarchal society. Greater participation of women in the community and its cult was at best a challenge to, but not an eradication of, patriarchal arrangements. The notion advanced by Schüssler Fiorenza (1983a) and others that Jesus established a "community of equals" that escaped or overthrew prevailing patriarchal structures has no concrete social or material evidence to support it, as regrettable as this might be, viewed from our contemporary perspective. Such an overthrow of the prevailing social order, even within the messianic community, could hardly have been expected in the ancient world. While local rebellions occasionally occurred, wholesale revolutions of the political and social order did not. The material conditions necessary for such revolutions simply were not present.

As the messianic movement spread throughout Syria–Palestine and then the Diaspora, women continued to figure prominently in the growth, leadership, and organization of the messianic sect, as narrated in Acts and the letters of Paul. Their new status in the movement as full-fledged members of the household of faith without discrimination and as having direct access to the grace of God unmediated by males is affirmed in an early tradition cited by Paul: "For as many of you as were baptized into Christ have put on Christ. There is neither [the distinction any longer between] Judean and Greek, slave and free, male and female; for you are all one in Christ Jesus" (Gal 3:27–28; cf. 1 Cor 12:13; Col 3:11). His other writings make clear, however, that this principle of social inclusion was not regarded as an affirmation of the *social equality* of males and females. This is evident in his wrestling with the problem of the appropriate attire and behavior of females in the public, worshiping assembly (1 Cor 11:2–16). Here, instead of rejecting the traditional requirement of the veiling of women, the apostle resorts to an assortment of arguments from Scripture, tradition, and custom to insure the continued traditional attire of women and their silence in public (14:33–37) in accord with "nature" (1 Cor 11:14–15), "custom" (1 Cor 11:16), or Torah (1 Cor 11:7–10; 2 Cor 11:3). "The head of a wife," he claims, "is her husband. . . . Neither was man created for woman, but woman for man" (1 Cor 11:3, 9). A further Deutero-Pauline insistence on the necessary silence of women in the public worship assembly is the astounding notion articulated in 1 Tim 2:11: "Let a woman learn in silence with all submissiveness. I permit no woman to teach or to have authority over men; she is to keep silent. For Adam was formed first, then Eve; and Adam was not deceived, but the woman was deceived and became a transgressor. Yet a woman will be saved through bearing children, if she continues in faith and love and holiness with modesty."

Pauline and other Christian writings urging the subordination of wives to their husbands[194] indicate that, in regard to the regulation of both domestic order and order in worship, conventional notions concerning the physical and social inferiority of women, their subordination to the authority and tutelage of males, as well as conservative attitudes toward female attire and comportment prevailed in formative Christianity. Although attempts were made to extricate Christian marriage from traditional concepts of "ruler and ruled" through emphasis upon mutuality, love, the analogous relation of husband and wife to Christ and Church, and joint spousal inheritance of God's grace, principle was often at odds with actual practice. This socially conservative and ambiguous

[194] See 1 Cor 11:2–16; 14:33–36; Eph 5:22–24; Col 3:18; 1 Tim 2:11–15; Titus 2:5; 1 Pet 3:1; *1 Clem.* 1:3.

position, as the writings of the Church Fathers attest,[195] continued in orthodox Christian circles through late antiquity (Delling 1978, 794–82; cf. Thraede 1972a, 236–66).

This, to be sure, is primarily evidence from the *written* record, a record, as indicated above, produced by males, focused on males, and encoding male gender constructs. How women and wives actually negotiated with these male scripts, how they actually saw themselves, how they secured and advanced their personal interests and goals, how they formed networks of influence and support—these are urgent questions still calling for further research.

It is within this historical, social, and cultural context and its centuries-long and universally-prevalent view of women that we must understand 1 Peter and its specific exhortation to wives and husbands. In relation to this context, the Petrine author also is a child of his times, reflecting, like his Christian contemporaries, the views and expectations of a patriarchal society. He too assumes females to be inferior and requires that they be subordinate to their husbands for the sake of domestic harmony.

On the other hand, he too, like Paul and other Christian authors, appeals to *distinctly Christian reasons* in support of his conventional exhortation: Christian wives are to lead holy lives and are to be subordinate out of reverence for God (3:1–2, 4). As persons made holy through baptism, they are to live holy lives so that their unbelieving husbands may be won for the faith (3:2). As children of Sarah, they take their cues from the holy matriarchs. From their believing husbands Christian wives deserve respect and honor, because spouses together are "co-heirs of the grace of life." Their marital harmony is paradigmatic for that of the household of God as a whole. Thus, within the structures of social stratification and domestic hierarchy, Christian women are assigned a role exemplary of Christian reverence for God and moral holiness, the missionary focus of Christian faith, and the respect for order typical of the entire community.

Such Christian qualifications are overlooked by those who would decry 1 Peter as a piece of deplorable patriarchal propaganda unworthy of the gospel. One influential author representing this view is Elisabeth Schüssler Fiorenza (1983a and other writings). On the basis of a fanciful reconstruction of the Jesus movement from its inception, she has proposed a markedly different reading of 1 Peter from the one offered in this commentary. Imagining that Jesus overthrew the patriarchal structures of his society and ushered in a golden, though limited, egalitarian age, she assesses all later positions on women in the NT by the criterion of this fantastic premise which, it must be said, lacks any support whatsoever in the social data (as even acknowledged by other feminists [e.g., Heine 1987]). Beginning with Paul and extending through the post-Pauline letters and 1 Peter, she maintains, there was a slow

[195] See the texts cited in the above NOTES on 3:1–7.

but steady relapse back into patriarchal patterns and patriarchal thinking. In the case of 1 Peter she claims that this relapse was prompted by a concern to avoid persecution and suffering and to "lessen tensions" between the Christian community and its neighbors. The argument of the letter, she avers, is that "the distinctiveness of Christian faith and religion is maintained only insofar as slaves and wives must be prepared to suffer for being Christians. However, for the sake of the Christian mission, they should seek to reduce suffering and tensions as much as possible by a lifestyle that is totally conformed to the customs and ethos of their pagan household and state" (1983a, 261; similarly, pp. 317, 334).

This reading not only neglects to note that 3:1–6 never once mentions any suffering of women and that suffering is not the lot of any single group but of the community as a whole. More seriously, it completely misconstrues the aim of the letter, which is not to encourage conformity to secular society but precisely the opposite: to affirm the holiness and distinctiveness of the reborn family of God and to urge holy nonconformity with Gentile modes of thought and life. This sadly erroneous and arbitrary interpretation of 1 Peter must be mentioned not simply because it is an egregious example of ideologically driven exegesis but because this study, which on the whole has much positive to commend it, has had a pronounced influence on subsequent feminist commentary on 1 Peter, leading to a misreading and undeserved depreciation of this pastoral letter in general (e.g., the recent commentaries on 1 Peter by Sharon Dowd [1992] and Kathleen E. Corley [1994]).

Following the lead of Schüssler Fiorenza, Corley claims that the letter's encouragement of wives to be subordinate to their husbands "hints that they too [like slaves] should submit to sexual abuse" (Corley 1994, 353) and that suffering women along with slaves are told to "take the place of the sacrificial lamb" (1994, 355) in order to "protect the larger Christian community" (1994, 355). Criticizing the early Christian tradition of the vicarious suffering of Christ found in 1 Peter as portraying "God as an abusive patriarch who demands the punishment of his Son in order to satisfy his wrath and honor" (1994, 354), Corley claims that this "glorification of suffering . . . holds up the victim as a model for women" (1994, 354). Consequently, she concludes that "of all Christian texts, the message of 1 Peter is the most harmful in the context of women's lives. Its particular message of the suffering Christ as a model for Christian living leads to precisely the kinds of abuses that feminists fear" (Corley 1994, 355). This negative assessment of the theology of 1 Peter, its Suffering Servant Christology, and its exhortation to slaves and women is misplaced. On the whole, this view completely ignores the vicarious and substitutionary character of Jesus' suffering, erroneously claims that the Petrine author condones the suffering of women when in fact he never even speaks about women suffering let alone condones it, and overlooks the several ways in which wives in this letter are held up as exemplars of the winsome holy conduct, reverence for God, honor, courage and divine blessing characteristic of the entire community of faith. Such an interpretation appears to be driven more by an interest in present female liberation than by a desire to discover what the text really does say in its own time and place.

The weaknesses of this interpretation of 1 Peter stem not from an arbitrary reconstruction of nascent Christian history but from an antihistorical reading of this text altogether, coupled with subjective interests quite alien to those of this ancient text. With this we have now arrived at the knotty issue of the hermeneutical problem and the question of bridging the gap from past to present.

Of the three approaches to the Bible mentioned earlier, only the third, contextualizing approach is consistent with sound exegetical procedure. This is a procedure that acknowledges the historical, social, and cultural conditioning of all biblical writings, seeks to minimize an imposition of subjective interests on the reading and evaluating of the text, and takes seriously the incarnation of God and God's Word, in and not beyond history.[196]

Understanding that we are dealing with time-bound and place-bound human constructs of reality allows us to reckon with the actuality and even inevitability of change. Concepts and conceptual constructs change over time as knowledge and society change. And this is especially evident in the case of constructs of gender and human sexuality. To claim today that women are inferior to men and to insist for this reason on the subordination of women to men would fly in the face of everything we now know of human biology and of all of the structural social changes that have insured at least the legal equality of all genders and races (on the scientifically demonstrated "natural superiority of women" see, inter alia, Montagu 1973). 1 Peter cannot be enlisted to criticize or reject such developments as contrary to the will of God. Rather, what one seeks to discover with relation to 1 Peter is how the good news that once transformed and enlivened a people of old continues to exert transformative and redemptive power in the present. This letter is a message of evangelical encouragement and exhortation rooted in the death and resurrection of Jesus Christ and expressive of the solidarity that all believers, women and men alike, have with their suffering and exalted Lord. The Petrine instruction to wives and husbands must be seen as part and parcel of this broader evangelical message.

To be sure, there is an ancient construct of female inferiority or "weakness" and female subordination evident in 1 Peter and the Bible that is no longer plausible today or compatible with what we now know of human biology and the variability of societal systems. Gender asymmetry and social patterns of subordination and superordination are no longer viewed as established by nature or divine fiat. They are understood to be man-made, and more specifically,

---

[196] So also, e.g., Countryman 1988; Heine 1988; Brown and Schneiders 1990; Elliott 1993c and the numerous studies listed therein. On the hermeneutical issue involved in the ethical use of the Bible, see, inter alia, Ogletree 1983, 1985; Countryman 1988, 237–67; Donahue 1993; McDonald 1993; Curren and McCormick 1984; Spohn 1995.

male-made and therefore not inevitable but changeable. Moreover, we must also acknowledge the centuries-long misuse of 1 Peter and related biblical texts to justify the suppression and abuse of women and to keep them in their so-called "place." Such misuse of the Bible must be denounced and rejected as theologically deplorable and morally bankrupt. This misuse of biblical texts, however, in no way requires throwing out the evangelical baby with the cultural bathwater. We cannot restore the biblical past, so it is pointless to adore the biblical past. It is likewise pointless to deplore the past as incongruent with the values and visions of the present. Rather, we must explore the Bible in its cultural context with an openness to the way that the good news of the past may continue to animate the good news in the present.[197]

For studies on 1 Pet 3:1–7, see Balch 1981, 1984; Baltensweiler 1967, 243–49; Brox 1981; Fridrichsen 1947; Ghiberti 1988; Gielen 1990, 512–42; Gross 1989; Hutton 1922; Kiley 1987; Küchler 1986; Lamau 1988, 272–81; Lippert 1965; Manns 1984b; L. D. O'Connor 1991; Patterson 1982; Prostmeier 1990, 160–68, 433–48; Reicke 1954; Schlosser 1983; Scholer 1980; Seim 1990; Slaughter 1996a, 1996b; Sly 1991; Sylva 1983; Vander Broek 1985.

[197] For collections of primary sources on women in antiquity, see Clark and Richardson 1977; Lefkowitz and Fant 1982; Kraemer, ed. 1988; Sterling 1993; Dillon and Garland 1994, 373–412. On women in general in the ancient world, see Burck 1969; Thraede 1972; Pomeroy 1975, 1984a; Cameron and Kuhrt, eds. 1983; Peradotto and Sullivan, eds. 1984; van Sertima, ed. 1985; Fanthan et al. 1994. On the cultural construct of the female body in classical Greek science, see Dean-Jones 1991; Winckler 1990; A. E. Hanson 1991. On gender differentiation and honor and shame, see Delling 1978; and Malina 1993a, 28–62. On the status and roles of Greek and Roman women and marriage, see Balsdon 1962; Arthur 1977; Wicker 1975; MacMullen 1980; R. S. Kraemer 1983; Dixon 1984; Hallett 1984; Cantarella 1987; Veyne, ed. 1987, 32–50; Winckler 1990; Gardner 1991; Treggiari 1991. On women in the OT and Israel, see Oepke 1964; Loewe 1966; Jeremias 1969, 359–76; Swidler 1976; Meiselman 1978; Meyers 1988, 1992; J. B. Segal 1979; Brooten 1982, 1986; Brenner 1985; Kraemer 1986, 1988; Mayer 1986; Countryman 1988, 11–65, 147–67; Archer 1990; Engelken 1990; Sly 1990; Camp 1991; Levine, ed. 1991; Bird 1992; Hamilton 1992a; Mayer-Schärtel 1995. On women and marriage in the NT and early Christianity, see the bibliography of Lindboe 1990; see subsequently, Thurston 1989; Clark 1990, 1994; Wire 1990; Levine 1991; Malina and Neyrey 1991c; Wordelman 1992; R. F. Collins 1992; Witherington 1992; Corley 1993; Jacobs-Malina 1993; Malina 1993a, 1993b; Osburn, ed. 1993; Sterling 1993; Torjesen 1993; Castelli 1994; U. Wagner 1994. On women in rabbinic literature, see Billerbeck 1926–1961, 3:610–13, 435–43; Neusner 1979b, 1980; Brayer 1986; Wegner 1988; P. J. Haas, ed. 1992. On the household, public and private space, and respective male and female gender roles, see Verner 1983, 83–125; Foucault 1985, 141–84; Veyne, ed. 1987, 71–93. On patriarchy and male dominance, see Reeves-Sanday 1981; Lerner 1986. For relevant anthropological and ethnological studies of traditional societies inhabiting the circum-Mediterranean region and Middle East on gender distinctions, male and female roles, and social relations and embodiment of the values of honor and shame, see, e.g., Peristiany 1966; Pitt-Rivers 1977; Schneider 1971; Rosaldo (and Lamphere) 1974; Rogers 1975; Davis 1977, 1984; Bourguignon, ed. 1980; Gilmore 1982, 1987; Wikan 1982, 1984; Abu-Lughod 1985, 1986; Augsburger 1986, 175–213; Jowkar 1986.

III. D. HONORABLE CONDUCT IN CIVIL AND DOMESTIC REALMS: CONCLUDING EXHORTATION TO ALL (3:8–12)

3:8 Finally, all of you:
[be] like-minded,
compassionate,
loving of brothers [and sisters],
tenderhearted,
humble-minded.
9a Do not return evil for evil
9b or insult for insult;
9c but, on the contrary, bless,
9d because to this you have been called,
9e so that you may inherit a blessing.
10a For,
"Whoever wishes to love life
10b and see good days,
10c let that one keep the tongue from [uttering] what is wrong
10d and the lips from speaking guile;
11a let that one turn away from wrongdoing and do what is right;
11b let that one seek peace and pursue it."
12a For "the eyes of the Lord [are] upon the righteous,
12b and his ears [are open] to their prayer;
12c but the face of the Lord [is] against those
who do what is wrong."

INTRODUCTION

With the words of 3:8–12 our author brings to a close the exhortation concerning public and domestic conduct begun in 2:13. Following the instruction to specific groups (free persons [2:13–17]; slaves [2:18–25]; wives and husbands [3:1–7]), the community as a whole is now addressed regarding both relations with one another within the community (v 8) and relations with outsiders who abuse and insult (v 9). Verses 8–9 entail a series of five imperatival adjectives and a pair of parallel participial imperatives (v 9ab, c), followed by a substantiation (v 9de). The content of this exhortation is similar to the exhortation found elsewhere in the NT and reflects early Christian parenetic tradition (Selwyn 1947, 407–15; Piper 1979; Goppelt 1993, 229–32) unrelated to the household-management (*oikonomia*) tradition influencing the foregoing instruction. However, the hand of the author is evident in the precise formulation of this tradition: four of the five adjectives of v 8 occur nowhere else in the NT, and the content of vv 8–9 is closely related to that of other units of the letter. Together, these verses form an important part of the letter's stress on qualities fostering the mutual humility and internal cohesion of the community (see 1:22–23; 2:17b; 3:1–7; 4:7–11; 5:1–6) and on honorable interaction with outsiders (2:12, 13–17, 18, 23; 3:1–2). An extensive citation of Ps 33:13–17a[34:12–16a] in vv 10–12 ends this section, as biblical citations similarly function elsewhere in 1 Peter. The chief theme of this quotation is "doing what is right" in contrast to "doing what is wrong," an emphasis that pervades 2:13–3:9 (cf. 2:14–15, 20, 22–23, 24bc; 3:2, 6). Thus it is this concern, rather than subordination, that is the dominant and unifying theme of 2:13–3:12, and it continues to receive emphasis in what follows as well (3:13–4:19). On the whole, the coherence of this unit with its context is clear and in its address to the entire community touches on several key themes of the preceding and succeeding contexts.

NOTES

3:8 *Finally, all of you* (*To de telos pantes*). The phrase marks a transition (*de*) from instruction of specific groups to a general instruction of "all" (*pantes*) believers (3:8–12) that concludes (*to telos* employed adverbially: "finally") the foregoing units of exhortation (2:13–17; 2:18–20 [25]; 3:1–7). The proposal of Cervantes Gabarrón (1991a, 75–76, 97) that this phrase introduces a new section of the letter (3:8–22) focused on the theme of "the good" (*agathon*) is unconvincing for several reasons.[198] He is correct, however, in noting that these verses make no explicit mention of the foregoing theme of subordination. This fact has a bearing on the general thematic of 2:13–3:12, as will be discussed below.

The note of inclusiveness here (*pantes*, "all of you") parallels that in 2:13 ("every [*pasēi*] human creature") and perhaps is intended as a literary inclusion framing 2:13–3:12.

The first part (v 8) of a double injunction (vv 8, 9) is positive and concerns attitudes and actions vital for the internal cohesion of the community. These are expressed by five plural adjectives having imperatival force and implying a 2d-person plural verb "be" (*esesthe* or *ginesthe*; cf. Eph 4:32). Four of these adjectives are unique in the NT but are sufficiently similar in sense to other NT moral exhortations (esp. Rom 12:1–16) to suggest that they represent Petrine variations on a parenetic tradition, with Rom 12:9–18 constituting the closest parallel.

[198] This theme is also a focus of the foregoing material (2:14, 15, 20; 3:6); the exhortation of 2:13–3:7 is hardly less "specific" than that of 3:8–22; common terms such as "inheritance" (1:4; 3:9) are not sufficient to demonstrate the "parallelism" of 1:3–2:10 and 3:8–22; the verb "call" (3:9) is not used only to begin new sections (cf. 1:15; 2:9; 3:6; 5:10); scriptural citations (3:10–12) are used in this letter to conclude a line of thought rather than open new sections (1:16, 24–25; 2:3; cf. 2:6–8, 9–10, 17; 5:5c); finally, the concluding function of these verses is supported by the similar function of the same address to "all" (*pantes*) believers in 5:5–6, which concludes the exhortation of 5:1–5.

1 Peter		Romans 12	
v. 8	*homophrones* ("like-minded")	v. 16	*to auto . . . phronountes* ("of the same mind")
	sympatheis, eusplagchnoi ("compassionate," "tenderhearted")	v. 15	*chairein meta charontōn klaiein meta klaiontōn* ("rejoice with those who rejoice, weep with those who weep")
	philadelphoi ("loving of brothers and sisters")	v. 10	*tēi philadelphiai* ("brotherly and sisterly love")
	tapeinōphrones ("humble-minded")	v. 16	*mē ta hypsēla phronountes alla tois tapeinois* ("do not be haughty but associate with the humble")
v. 9	*mē apodidontes kakon anti kakou* ("do not return evil for evil")	v. 17a	*mēdeni kakon anti kakou apodidontes* ("Let no one return evil for evil"; cf. 1 Thess 5:15)
	tounantion . . . eulogountes ("but, on the contrary, bless")	v. 14	*eulogeite tous diōkontas* ("bless those who persecute you"; cf. 1 Cor 4:12)

Further similarities include 1 Pet 3:11a and Rom 12:9bc (also possibily based on Ps 33[34]:15a); 1 Pet 3:11b and Rom 12:18 (cf. Ps 33[34]:15b; cf. Heb 12:14); and the combination in both texts of prescribed conduct toward fellow-believers (1 Pet 3:8; Rom 12:3–13) with conduct toward hostile outsiders (1 Pet 3:9; Rom 12:14–21). On the other hand, Shimada (1993, 121–23) has pointed out several differences between these passages and the unlikelihood that there was any direct literary dependence by 1 Peter on Romans. Our author has the abuse from outsiders in mind and urges not "love" of persecutors but nonretaliation. Both 1 Pet 3:8–9 and Rom 12 have conceptual correspondences with the Jesus tradition.[199] Piper (1979) and Goppelt (1993, 229–32) discuss the history of this tradition and root its origin in the teaching of Jesus, which subsequently underwent expansion of various kinds as it was adapted to the varying situations and needs of the community. The substance of this Petrine material thus represents not precise quotations of words of either Jesus or Paul but sentiments that had become a common tradition inspired by the teaching of Jesus. The roots of nonretaliation in the Jesus tradition, at least in the mind of the Petrine author, is made likely by the similarity between 3:9 and 2:23; the

[199] Compare 1 Pet 3:8 and Rom 12:15 with Matt 5:4, 12; Luke 6:21, 23; 1 Pet 3:9 and Rom 12:14 with Luke 6:28; compare Matt 5:44; 1 Pet 3:9; and Rom 12:17, 19–21 with Matt 5:38–42; Luke 6:27–30.

former draws the ethical consequences from the latter and represents a further implied instance of Jesus serving as a model for all the believers.

[*be*] *like-minded* (*homophrones*). The Greek term *homophrones* (supported by weightier witnesses than its variant, *philophrones* ["friendly, kind"]), denotes, like the final adjective, *tapeinophrones*, a particular mentality or mindset (*phronēsis*, *phroneō*; cf. *sōphroneō* [4:7]) characterized by consensus and being of one mind; compare "arm yourselves with the same thought" (4:1; on the related concept of *homonoia*, see Thraede 1992). The term occurs nowhere else in the Bible but is found outside the Bible ; see Homer, *Il.* 22, 263; Strabo, *Geogr.* 6.3.3; Ps.-Phoc. 30; Plutarch, *Mor.* 432C. Since the second and fourth adjectives are also similar in sense, it is possible that the arrangement of these five adjectives is chiastic, with *philadelphoi* occupying the central emphasized position (so Cervantes Gabarrón 1991, 195).

homophrones: like-minded
sympatheis: compassionate, sharing feelings
philadelphoi: loving of brothers and sisters
eusplagchnoi: compassionate, good feelings
tapeinophrones: humble-minded

Paul prefers the equivalent expression to *auto phronein*, literally, "think the same" (Rom 12:16; 15:5; Phil 2:2; 4:2) but, like our author, repeatedly stresses the importance of unanimity among the believers. In view of the embattled situation of the addressees of 1 Peter and the likely diversity of opinion among the converts of different ethnic backgrounds, unanimity of thought and vision was essential for both the internal harmony and stability of the household of God and for the united front it should present to outsiders.

compassionate (*sympatheis*). The adjective *sympatheis*, literally, "suffer, feel with," is the term from which "sympathetic" derives and to which the Latin *compassio* is cognate. Like "like-minded," it occurs only here in the NT and similarly denotes the solidarity of affection valued by Greek and Roman authors for fostering group unity (Polyb. 2.56.7; Dionys. Hal., *Ant. rom.* 2.45.6; cf. Josephus, *Ant.* 19.330). Its family of terms also appears frequently in the martyriological text of 4 Maccabees. There it denotes, along with *philadelphoi* (13:21), the "compassion of brotherly love" (*sympathous philadelphias*) by which the seven martyred brothers were more compassionate (*sympathesteron*) toward one another.[200] In Hebrews, the related verb describes Christ's sympathizing with and sharing in human weakness (4:15) and the compassion believers had for imprisoned fellow-believers (10:34); cf. Plut. *Mor.* 140E, speaking of spousal sympathy. In 1 Peter, *sympathēs* is one of several rare or unique composites involving the preposition *syn* ("with," "together," "joint" or "co-"),[201]

---

[200] See also *sympatheia* (4 Macc 14:13, 14, 18, 20; 15:7, 11) and *sympathesteras* (15:4), regarding the compassion of a mother for her children.

[201] See *synoikeō* and *synklēronomos*, 3:7; *sympresbyteros*, 5:1; *syneklektos*, 5:13.

employed to stress aspects of the commonality and cohesion of the Christian brotherhood. Here it is akin in sense to its parallel *eusplagchnoi* ("tender-hearted") but, in the light of the suffering of the addressees, may further imply sharing the feelings, including the sufferings (*pathēmata*), of fellow-believers.[202]

loving of brothers [*and sisters*] (*philadelphoi*). If the adjectives are arranged chiastically, this constitutes the central term. The adjective *philadelphos* denotes here love of (i.e., emotional attachment and commitment to) fellow-believers who are regarded, figuratively, as "brothers" and "sisters" in the faith. This term is also unique in the NT but occurs in 2 Macc 15:14 (loving one's fellow-countrymen) and 4 Macc 13:21 (with *sympatheis*) and 15:10 (of the commitment of the seven martyred brothers to one another); cf. also Philo, *Ios.* 218. Plutarch devoted an entire treatise (*Frat. amor.*, *Mor.* 478–92) to the subject of "brotherly love" (*philadelphia*), in which he describes the familial relationship of blood brothers and the close link of family and friendship. To behave as a brother, he noted, involves the offer of mutual defense, assistance, and cooperation (*Frat. amor.* 1–2, *Mor.* 478DE). *Philadelphia*, the ideal relationship of brothers, involved *homonoia*, *symphonia*, and *harmonia* (*Frat. amor.* 2, *Mor.* 479A). According to a widely-cited proverb, "brothers have all things in common" (Arist., *Eth. nic.* 8.9.1–2) just as do friends (Arist., *Pol.* 2.2.4; *Eth. nic.* 9.8.2; Cicero, *Off.* 1.51; Dio Chrys., *Orat.* 3.110). In a home, notes Cicero, everything is common (*Off.* 1.54; cf. Hier., in Stobaeus 4.22.24).

In 1 Peter, *philadelphoi* belongs to the broad semantic field of terms that symbolize the believers as "brothers" and "sisters" in the faith (cf. *adelphos*, 5:12) and as constituting a spiritual brotherhood (*adelphotēs*, 2:17; 5:9; cf. 5:13) or a family or household of God (2:5; 4:17) whose unity is maintained through brotherly and sisterly love (1:8, 22; 2:17; 4:8; 5:14). The addition of *and sisters* in brackets explicates in English the ancient cultural assumption that references to males generally implied reference also to all of the females embedded in male kin or fictive-kin groups, unless only distinctively male traits were the issue under discussion. Like its paronym, *philadelphia* (1:22; cf. also *philēma*, "kiss," gesture of brotherly affection, 5:14), *philadelphoi* involves the *philia* ("affection," emotional attachment) of brothers and sisters of the brotherhood/family of God. This commitment also includes the material support typical of biological families, such as food, shelter, protection, and hospitality (see 4:8–9).[203] Such commitment and affective solidarity were essential within the fledgling messianic movement if it was to remain stable and grow. Thus the need for *philadelphia* receives repeated stress in early Christianity (Rom 12:10; 1 Thess 4:9; Heb 13:1; 2 Pet 1:7; *1 Clem.* 47:5; 48:1; cf. 2 Thess 3:14). This Christian regard of one another as brothers and sisters did not escape the

[202] Compare the Pauline expression "rejoice with those who rejoice and weep with those who weep" (Rom 12:15) and the use of the verb in Heb 4:15 and 10:34.

[203] See also Josephus' description of the Essenes, who shared their possessions "as brothers" (*J.W.* 2.122, 127).

notice of outsiders. Some years after 1 Peter, Lucian of Samosata (*Per.* 13), in commenting on the Christians, noted that "their first lawgiver persuaded them that they are all brothers of one another."

tenderhearted (*eusplagchnoi*). This adjective (elsewhere only in Eph 4:32), which is close in sense to the foregoing *sympatheis*, is a composite of the terms "good" (*eu-*) and "entrails" (*splagchna*). The ancients regarded the entrails, bowels, or inward parts as the seat of emotions and tender feelings, as people today speak of the feelings of the heart (cf. the KJV version of 1 John 3:17: "bowels of compassion"). The adjective (cf. also *T. Zeb.* 9:7; *T. Sim.* 4:4; *1 Clem.* 54:1; Pol. *Phil* 5:2; 6:1), the noun (*ta splagchna* [2 Cor 7:15; Phil 1:8; 2:1; Col 3:12; *1 Clem.* 23:1]), and the verb (*splagchnizomai*) all denote having good or tender feelings and caring concern for others, especially for kin, natural or fictive. Thus, like *sympatheis*, the adjective encourages the feeling and demonstration of affection and compassion toward fellow-believers.[204]

humble-minded (*tapeinophrones*). The adjective, like its less-well-attested variant *philophrones* ("friendly, kind, well-disposed"), is also unique in the NT.[205] The theme of humility will be stressed again in the general exhortation in 5:5b–6 (*tapeinophrosynē*, "humility"; *tapeinoi*, "the humble"; and *tapeinoō*, "be humble"). In *1 Clement*, being humble is associated with not being arrogant, subordinating oneself rather than subordinating others (*hypotassomenoi mallon ē hypotassontes*), and giving more gladly than receiving (2:1; cf. also 13:1–4). For our author as well, being humble is equivalent to being subordinate. Humility involves remaining within one's inherited social status and not seeking to transcend it (= "pride"), hence to respect the given social order. "Humble persons do not threaten or challenge another's rights, nor do they claim more for themselves than has been duly allotted them in life. They even stay a step below or behind their rightful status. Thus, humility is a socially acknowledged claim to neutrality in the competition of life" (Pilch-Malina 1993, 107). In the highly competitive and stratified world of Greco-Roman antiquity, only those of degraded social status were "humble," and humility was regarded as a sign of weakness and shame, an inability to defend one's honor. Thus the high value placed on humility by Israelites and Christians[206] is remarkable. It reflects confidence in God's favor for the lowly and in the radical divine transformation of status as expressed in 5:5b (citing Prov 3:34; cf. also Jas 4:6; Luke 2:52). For Christians, a humble posture was consistent with Jesus' favoring of the humble and Jesus' own humility (Matt 11:29; Phil 2:6–11). This stress on humility likewise recalls God's approval of lowly slaves in 2:18–20 and the privileged place our author ascribes to them as models for

---

[204] For the corresponding verb, see Luke 10:30 (of the good Samaritan), Luke 15:20 (of the father of the prodigal son), and Mark 1:41 (of Jesus).

[205] Occurrences elsewhere include Prov 29:23; *1 Clem.* 19:1; 38:2; Ign. *Eph.* 10.2; *Barn.* 19:3; Herm. *Mand.* 11.8.

[206] See also Prov 3:34; 11:2; 15:33; 16:19; 18:12; 22:4; 29:23; Sir 3:17–20; Gal 5:23; Eph 4:2; Phil 2:3; cf. Wengst 1988.

the entire community. Emphasis on the importance of the humble-mindedness of *all* thus constitutes an appropriate conclusion to a call for subordination here (2:13–3:7), as it does in 5:5–6.

Altogether the imperatival adjectives of v 8 urge dispositions that foster the mutual affection and commitment of the believers to one another and thus promote the social solidarity and cohesion of the community as a whole.

In v 9 the author turns to the relations of believers with *outsiders* and the appropriate response to hostility (cf. 2:12, 15, 18–20): not retaliation but, rather, blessing. The thought is akin to sayings of Jesus (Luke 6:27–28; cf. Matt 5:43–44), but the language is closer to expressions in the hortatory sections of Paul's epistles (Rom 12:14; 1 Cor 4:12; 1 Thess 5:15) and represents adaptation of traditional Christian parenesis.

9a. *Do not return evil for evil* (*mē apodidontes kakon anti kakou*). In the antithetical parallelism of the two participial clauses, v 9ab and v 9c, both participles (*mē apodidontes* ["do not return"] and *eulogountes* ["bless"]), like the foregoing adjectives, have imperatival force. The correspondence of this imperative with the content and form of Rom 12:17 and 1 Thess 5:15 points to its place in early Christian parenetic tradition:

Rom 12:17a		*mēdeni kakon anti kakou apodidontes*
1 Thess 5:15a	*horate*	*mē tis kakon anti kakou tini apodōi*
1 Pet 3:9a		*mē apodidontes kakon anti kakou*

In each case, the negative command is also balanced by a positive one (Rom 12:17b; 1 Thess 5:15b; 1 Pet 3:9c).

The OT *lex talionis* or law of retaliation (Exod 21:12, 23–25; Lev 24:17–21; Deut 19:21; cf. Gen 9:6; Judg 1:6–7) was itself a constraint on a previous principle of "might makes right." However, it was already blunted by the proscription of the retaliation of evil in other OT texts (Deut 32:35; Prov 20:22; 24:29; cf. 25:21–22) and was eventually rejected in postexilic Israel.[207] Jesus likewise opposed this code of retaliation (Matt 5:38–42/Luke 6:29–30; cf. *Gos. Thom.* 95), as did his followers,[208] although the formulations and examples of the principle tend to vary.[209]

The term *kakon* ("evil," "wrong") in this context refers to some kind of wrong done to a person, whether verbal or physical abuse or both. It recurs three times in the following scriptural citation of 3:10–12; see also the discouragement of *kakia* in 2:1 and 2:16. The *evil* or wrong that the believers experience

---

[207] See *Jos. Asen.* 23:9; 28:5, 10, 14; 29:3; *Apoc. Sedr.* 7:7; *T. Gad* 6:7; *T. Jos.* 18:1–2; 1QS IX 22, 23; X 17–18; *Let. Aris.* 225, 227; Ps.-Phoc. 75; *2 En.* 50:2–5; cf. 4 Macc 2:9–14, 16; Josephus, *Ant.* 4.8.33–35; *m.* *ʾAbot* 1:7).

[208] See Rom 12:14, 17–21; 1 Cor 4:12; 1 Thess 5:15; 1 Pet 3:9; *Did.* 1:4–5; Ign. *Eph.* 10:2; Just. Mart., *1 Apol.* 15.10–12; 16.1–2; cf. *1 Clem.* 2:1; *Let. Apos.* 58.

[209] See Piper 1979; Theissen 1992, 115–56; and Goppelt 1993, 229–32 for a comparison of the gospel and epistolary traditions; see also Luz 1989, 323–31 concerning Matthew's formulation, and Luz 1989, 331–37 on the nonretaliation principle in the postbiblical period.

but are not to repay is, like the following term *insult*, another allusion to the mistreatment they have encountered. Thus this element of general Christian parenesis has a direct bearing on the predicament in which the addressees of 1 Peter find themselves.

9b. *or insult for insult* (*ē loidorian anti loidorias*). The noun *loidoria* (elsewhere only in 1 Tim 5:14) denotes verbal abuse, insult, or reviling. The entire phrase echoes the formulation of 2:23a (*hos loidoroumenos ouk anteloidorei*) emphasizing Jesus' nonretaliatory stance ("when insulted, he did not insult in return"), but occurs nowhere else in the Bible and thus appears to be a specific Petrine expansion on the nonretaliation tradition. Consequently it provides an important indication of the kind of hostility that the author considers the believers to be experiencing: insult, defamation of character, and verbal abuse. These are the weapons typically employed in an agonistic honor-and-shame society for challenging the honor of others and publicly shaming and discrediting those who are different or regarded as one's competitors (Malina 1993, 28–62). Similar references to such verbal abuse mentioned elsewhere in the letter (2:12; 3:16; 4:4, 14) further indicate the level and informal nature of the hostility experienced by the Christians of Asia Minor. They argue decisively against the theory that the Christians were victims of any formal legal "persecution" initiated by the Roman government. It was rather insult, disrespect, contempt, reproach, and slander to which the Christians were subjected by their suspicious neighbors. See also the NOTES on 3:13–16 and 4:12–16.

The departure from the customary script of social interaction that this rejection of nonretaliation represents is also noteworthy. In a competitive society, where personal honor and the reputation of one's group was under constant scrutiny and challenge, a successful defense of honor normally required an immediate and crafty verbal riposte (Malina 1993d, 28–62; Malina and Neyrey 1988, 1991c). Our author, like Jesus (Matt 5:38–48; Luke 6:27–36) and Paul, rejected this prevailing practice and instead urged the unexpected; namely, speaking well of, or blessing, one's adversary. Thus Paul, whose formulations are closest to those of 1 Peter advises: "Bless those who persecute you, bless and do not curse. . . . Repay no one evil for evil [*mēdeni kakon anti kakou apodidontes*], but take thought of what is noble in the sight of all . . . never avenge yourselves, but leave it to the wrath of God. . . . No, 'if your enemy is hungry, feed him; if he is thirsty, give him to drink; for by so doing you will heap burning coals upon his head' [Prov 25:21–22]. Do not be overcome by evil, but overcome evil with good" (Rom 12:14, 17–21).[210]

According to our author, the insults encountered by the believers are akin to the insults experienced by the one in whose footsteps the believers follow (2:21–23). By not countering insult with insult (2:23), Jesus broke the vicious,

---

[210] See also 1 Thess 5:15 ("See that none of you repays evil for evil [*horate mē tis kakon anti kakou tini apodōi*], but always seek to do good to one another and to all") and 1 Cor 4:12–13 ("When insulted, we bless [*loidoroumenoi eulogoumen*]; when persecuted, we endure; when slandered, we try to conciliate"); cf. also *Diogn*. 5:15.

self-perpetuating cycle of vengeance and thereby enabled a similar course of action among his followers. The entire statement of 1 Pet 3:9ab and its sentiment of nonretaliation was later reiterated by Polycarp in his letter to the Philippians (2:2). In modern times, this spirit of nonretaliation captured the imagination of the Russian Leo Tolstoy, who in turn inspired the Indian Mohandas K. Gandhi, who in turn provided the moral prototype for Martin Luther King, Jr. and the United States civil rights movement. The spirit, if not the precise words, of 1 Peter and the tradition of Jesus that it echoes, were the power animating these advocates of pragmatic nonretaliation and nonviolence. Their commitment to this ancient vision of nonretaliation translated a biblical principle into a powerful force of political and social transformation.[211]

9c. *but, on the contrary, bless* (*tounantion de eulogountes*). The term *tounantion* (an elision of *to enantion*, "the opposite," used adverbially) underlines the contrast between the tit-for-tat behavior of v 9ab and the response of v 9c. This positive response to insult is rooted in Christ's teaching (Luke 6:28a; cf. *Did.* 1:3) more so than in his action (see his silence in 2:23). The imperatival participle *eulogountes* balancing *apodidontes* could have the conventional sense of "speaking well of" another. By such a tactic one ignores the insult as a challenge, thereby extricating oneself from the socially destructive cycle of challenge-retaliation, and shifts the subject from shame to honor, from defamation to praise. As a minority community with no apparent powerful patrons to lend them support, Christians stood little chance of succeeding in the public contest of negative challenge and riposte. Nor could it be imagined that matching insult with insult would be a promising means for winning hostile nonbelievers to the faith (2:12; 3:1–2). So, ignoring the insult and transforming the nature of the exchange was the wiser course. "Speaking well of" another is a gesture of conciliation and one of several ways of showing honor to others, the conduct encouraged in 2:17. However, in the context of biblical language, *eulogeō* can also denote the yet more conciliating action of "invoking the blessing of God on another"[212] as the opposite of cursing (invoking God's wrath on) someone (Gen 12:3; 27:29c; Deut 28; Matt 25:31–46). This response to insult, as previously noted, was also practiced and urged by Paul (Rom 12:14; 1 Cor 4:12) and was extolled as typical of Christians in *Diogn.* 5:15: "they are insulted and they bless; they are reviled and they render honor (*loidorountai kai eulogousin, hybrizontai kai timōsin*)"; see also Ign. *Eph.* 10:2.[213] Such a positive response to hostility was consonant with the principle of not being overcome by evil, but overcoming evil with good (Rom 12:21). The principle had Israelite

[211] On the texts and principle of nonretaliation in the NT and early Church, see the several relevant essays in Swartley 1992; cf. also Schottroff 1978; Wengst 1987, 68–72, 87–89; and Theissen 1992.

[212] Cf. the paternal blessings in Gen 27:18–29 and 49:1–28; see also Luke 1:42; 24:50–51.

[213] For also loving or praying for one's enemies, see Matt 5:43–48; Luke 6:27–28, 32–36; POxy. 1224; Ign. *Eph.* 10:2; Pol. *Phil* 12:3; *Did.* 1:3–5; 2 *Clem.* 13:4; Just. Mart. *1 Apol.* 1.15.

precedent as well: "If any man seeks to do evil to you, do well to him and pray for him, and you will be redeemed by the Lord from all evil" (*T. Jos.* 18:2); "the holy man is merciful to his reviler and holds his peace" (*T. Benj.* 5:4); see Zerbe 1993, 34–173 and the NOTE on 2:23. For the early Christians, the example and teaching of Jesus provided the chief precedent and inspiration for this way of confronting hostility, but among the letters of the NT it is only 1 Peter that makes this association explicit (note the relation of 3:9 and 2:23).[214]

However, in contrast to Christian texts that encourage "love" toward enemies (Matt 5:43–44/Luke 6:27, 32–35), love (i.e., emotional attachment and commitment) is reserved by the Petrine author exclusively for Christ (1:8) and the brotherhood (2:17b; 1:22; 3:8; 4:8), a feature also typical of the Johannine tradition.[215] In general, the tactic of countering evil with good is reminiscent of the conduct called for elsewhere (2:12, 15, 19–20; 3:13–17; cf. 4:14–16) and further exemplifies what it means to follow in the footsteps of the Christ (2:23). From a pragmatic point of view, such behavior was also much more likely to have a winsome effect on detractors (2:12).

9d. *Because to this you have been called* (*hoti eis touto eklēthēte*). A reason (introduced by *hoti*, "because") for the foregoing is now given.[216] The majority of later witnesses (P 𝔐 etc.) add a participle, "knowing" (*eidotes*), which, with *hoti*, would require the translation "knowing that" (cf. 1:18a). However, there is superior support (𝔓[72] 𝔓[81] א A B C etc.) for the simple *hoti*, with the sense of "because" or "since."

to this you have been called (*eis touto eklēthēte*). The demonstrative pronoun *touto* could refer either to the foregoing (vv 8–9c, or more specifically v 9c) or to the *hina* clause that immediately follows (v 9e). Instances elsewhere in the NT where *eis touto* is followed, as here, by a *hina* clause support this latter possibility,[217] as does the construction and sense of *eis touto* + *hina* in 1 Pet 4:6. In this case the sense would be: "you are to bless your insulters (v 9c) because it is this to which you yourselves have been called by God, namely to receive a blessing." This alternative makes the certainty of inheritance through God's calling the motive for blessing others and is favored by J. N. D. Kelly (1969, 137), Goppelt (1993, 234), and a majority of commentators.

There are weightier reasons, however, for preferring the first possibility (connection to the foregoing).[218] NT usage also demonstrates a retrospective

---

[214] On nonretaliation in 1 Peter, see Schertz 1992; and Zerbe 1993, 270–90, who discusses the primary Christological and eschatological warrants of this exhortation.

[215] Cf. John 13:34; 15:12, 17; 17:23; 1 John 2:15; 3:14, 23; 4:7, 12, 21.

[216] For similar enthymemes (a statement followed by a support [introduced with *gar, hoti, hina*]), see 2:12a/b; 2:13–14/15; 2:18a/19–20, 21–25; 3:1ab/c; 3:8–9c/9d; 3:15–1ba/16c, 17, 18–22; 4:1–2/3, 6; 4:8a/b; 4:11ab/c; 4:14a/b; 4:16/17–19; 5:2–3/4; 5:5b/c; 5:6a/b; 5:7a/b; cf. also 1:14–15/16; 17/18–21; 1:21, 22/23; 2:2a/b, 3.

[217] See John 18:37; Acts 9:21; Rom 14:9; 2 Cor 2:9; Eph 6:2; Col 4:8; 1 John 3:8.

[218] So Best 1971, 130; Michaels 1988, 178; Zerbe 1993, 286–87; and Piper 1980, 224–31, who convincingly refutes arguments for the second alternative.

function of *eis touto* (Mark 1:38; 2 Cor 5:5). More important, however, is the retrospective function of *eis touto* in the identical formulation of 2:21a, "For to this you have been called":

3:9d	*hoti eis touto*	*eklēthēte*	*hina . . .*
2:21a	*eis touto gar*	*eklēthēte*	*hoti . . .*

In 2:21a, *eis touto* can refer only to the conduct enjoined in 2:18–20, and this argues for its similar retrospective function here in 3:9d as well. This yields the sense: "you have been called to bless (or, less likely, to practice all of the conduct urged in vv 8–9c) in order that you yourselves may inherit a blessing." Inheriting a future blessing is thus contingent on blessing insulters, renouncing retribution, and fostering compassion and unity within the community here and now. The future blessing of present conduct is precisely the point of the psalm passage cited in the following verses (vv 10–12) and constitutes "the decisive factor" from the immediate context favoring this view (Piper 1980, 226–28). The thought is likewise consistent with future, teleological motivations of conduct occurring elsewhere in the letter (1:6–9; 2:12, 13–15; 3:1–2, 7, 10–12; 4:7b, 11c, 13b, 17–18; 5:4, 6b, 10). In contrast to Paul, who generally grounds imperatives on a prior experience of grace, our author varies references to a *present* experience of grace as a basis for conduct[219] with references to a *future* outcome. The latter is close to Israelite thought, including the perspective of Jesus (Matt 5:12; 6:1–18; 18:23–35; 25:14–30, 31–46; cf. also Heb 6:7).

In v 9d it is *all* believers who are reminded of their divine vocation to appropriate behavior; compare 2:21a (slaves alone).[220] The verb *eklēthēte* ("you have been called") here, as in 2:21a, is a divine passive, with God implied as agent.

9e. *so that you may inherit a blessing* (*hina eulogian klēronomēsēte*). This final clause states the purpose or envisioned outcome (*hina*, "so that") of the believers' doing what they were called to do. The phrase "inherit a blessing" appears also in Heb 12:7 in conjunction with Esau; see also the combination of blessing and inheriting in Ps 36[37]:22. The verb "inherit" (*klēronomēsēte*, a 2d-person aor. act. subj.) recalls the motif of "inheritance" in 1:4 and the more immediate "co-heirs" (*sygklēronomois*) of 3:7. "Inheriting a blessing (*eulogian*)" balances the action of "giving a blessing" (*eulogountes*, v 9c), reflecting a principle of the teaching of Jesus (e.g., Matt 6:14–15; 7:11; 25:31–46) concerning the relation of conduct and eschatological reward.[221] To inherit a blessing is tantamount to receiving a conferral of honor. The prospect of inheriting divine

---

[219] See also 1:14–16, 17–21, 22–23; 2:2–10, 24; 4:1–3; and 1:3–2:10 as the basis for 2:11–5:11.

[220] For similar NT examples of being called to a certain course of action, see 1 Cor 7:15; Gal 5:15; Eph 4:1; Col 3:15; 1 Thess 4:7.

[221] Cf. also Gal 5:19–21; 1 Cor 6:9–10; *1 Clem.* 35:4; and the texts in the above NOTE on *eis touto* (v 9d).

blessing and honor combines with God's calling and the model of Christ as a third and final motivation for the conduct encouraged in vv 8–9c.

10–12. At this point our author again uses a quotation of Scripture to substantiate ("for," *gar*, v 10a) and conclude preceding instruction. The text cited (Ps 33:13–17a) involves a segment of a psalm (Ps 33 LXX; Ps 34 MT) that sings of the suffering (33:7, 18, 20) of "resident aliens" (*paroikoi*, 33:5), "reverence" (*phobos*) for the Lord (33:8, 9, 10, 12), "hope" (*elpizō*, 33:9, 23), and blessing for the "just" (*dikaioi*, 33:16, 18, 20, 22)—all of which are terms and concepts that occur repeatedly in this letter. Another verse of the psalm (33:9) was cited in 2:3. Now vv 13–17a are quoted to provide biblical warrant for the thought of 1 Pet 3:8–9 as well as for the foregoing instruction to avoid "evil"[222] and to "do what is right."[223] The exaggerated claim (Bornemann 1919–1920) that 1 Peter contains no less than 51 references to Ps 33 has been convincingly rejected by Schutter (1989, 44–49), and the conjecture that the use of the psalm here was inspired by the early Christian baptismal catechesis in which it purportedly had a place (Selwyn 1947, 190, 408–14) still remains an open question. Nevertheless, the appropriateness of Ps 33[34] for the message of 1 Peter is beyond dispute.

The original acrostic form of the Hebrew of this psalm is not retained in the Greek version quoted in 1 Peter. The terms in brackets indicate, as usual, words implied but not expressed in the Greek. The Petrine modifications of the LXX psalm text involve the addition of "for" (*gar*, v 10a), introducing the quotation as a support for the foregoing, the replacement of an interrogative with a declarative statement (3:10a), the substitition of 3d-person imperatives for 2d-person imperatives (vv 10–11), and the addition of "for" (*hoti*) at the outset of v 12a.[224]

On the whole, vv 10–12 have the following structure:

v 10ab:	the desire for a good life
v 10cd/lla/11b:	three imperatives in which the antithesis between "doing what is wrong—doing what is right" (v 11a) is central
v 12a:	a substantiation ("for") involving the eyes, ears, and face of the Lord toward the righteous and against those who do what is wrong

Verses 10–12 also display a chiastic arrangment in which "righteous" is equivalent to "doing what is right":

[222] Compare *kakon* (Ps 33:11a) and *kakia* (2:1, 16).

[223] Compare *poiēsatō agathon* (Ps 33:11) and *agathopoieō* (2:14, 20; 3:6); see also the related expressions in 2:11–12, 14–15, 17, 18–20, 24bc; 3:2, 3–4, 6, 7.

[224] The remainder of Ps 33:17 ("to cut off the remembrance of them from the earth") is not included, perhaps because from our author's perspective the final outcome for the unrighteous nonbelievers remains an open question (compare 2:12; 3:1–2 and 2:8; 3:16; 4:5, 17–18).

A. keep from wrongful speech and action (vv 10–11a)
  B. "do what is right" and seek peace (v 11)
  B.′ God's favor toward the "righteous" (v 12ab)
A.′ God's opposition to "those who do what is wrong" (v 12c)

10ab. *For, "Whoever wishes to love life and see good days"* (*ho gar thelōn zōēn agapân kai idein hēmeras agathas*). The quotation begins without an explicit introduction (as in 1:16, 24; 5:5c; contrast 2:6). The particle "for" (*gar*), absent in the original psalm text, is added to link the citation to the foregoing verses as their biblical substantiation.

The original (Ps 33:13[43:12]) reads: "who is the person desiring life, loving to see good days?" This interrogative is changed into a declarative statement through the substitution of "whoever" (*ho*) for "who is the person who" (*tis estin anthrōpos ho*), the transformation of the participle "loving" (*agapōn*) into an infinitive (*agapan*), and the addition of a copulative (*kai*). The result is the creation of two balanced infinitive phrases ("to love life" [*zōēn agapan*] and "to see good days" [*idein hēmeras agathas*]), each governed by the participle *thelōn* ("[whoever] wishes," or "desires"). The masculine form of *ho* in Greek here, as often, has the generic sense of "the one (male or female) who." The stylistic improvement of "the crude barbarity" of the original is mentioned by Beare (1970, 161) as an indication of the literary competence of the Petrine author, whose mother tongue was clearly Greek rather than Aramaic.[225]

For the psalmist, the parallel expressions "life" (*zōēn*) and "good days" (*hēmeras agathas*) describe the full and prosperous daily life resulting from upright behavior (cf. also Tob 4:5–6 and *T. Ash.* 4:4). Bigg (1902, 157) considers this to be the sense of the words in 1 Peter as well. But in view of the future orientation of v 9d ("inherit a blessing") and the eschatological or regenerative sense of "life" (*zōē*) and "live" (*zaō*) elsewhere in 1 Peter (3:7; 1:3; 2:4, 5, 24; 4:6; cf. 3:18), it is more likely, as most commentators hold, that in the context of this letter these words are associated with the *future* life and blessing to be inherited *as a result of righteous behavior.*

In v 10cd the wording of the psalm (33:14[34:13]) also undergoes some stylistic improvement. To avoid the original inconsistency between the 3d-person subject of Ps 33[34]:13 and the 2d-person verbs of 33[34]:14 and 15, our author replaces the latter with 3d-person verbs (vv 10c–11) and omits the original 2d-person sing. pronouns ("your"). In their place, 3d-person sing. pronouns ("his/her") are implied (or secondarily supplied in some MSS).

10c. *"let that one keep the tongue from [uttering] what is wrong"* (*pausatō tēn glōssan apo kakou*). Wrongful speech is mentioned as the first hindrance to a blessed life. Therefore one must "keep from" (*pausatō apo*, lit., "cause to stop

[225] While the Petrine use of this psalm perhaps inspired its citation in *1 Clem.* 22:1b–7, with 22:7 adding the final words of Ps 33:17, *1 Clement* quotes Ps 33[34]:12–18 without alteration except for the substitution of 3d-person plurals for 3d-person singulars in the additionally cited v 18 of this psalm in *1 Clem.* 22:7.

from"; cf. Ps 36[37]:8; *1 Clem.* 8:4 [Isa 1:16]; Herm. *Sim.* 3.9.1) uttering *what is wrong* (*kakon*)—in other words, false or harmful words. "Tongue" (*glōssa*) and "lips" (*cheilē*) are organs of speech, and their use as instruments of evil was proverbial (see Ps 12:2–4; Prov 18:6–8, 21; Sir 28:13–26; Jas 1:26; 3:5–12). For a related use of the verb *pauein*, see 4:1: "ceased from sin." The threefold censure of wrongful speech and wrongdoing in this citation (v 10c, 11a, 12c) supports the warning against engaging in retaliatory wrongdoing and insult in v 9ab as well as in the admonitions of 2:1 and 2:16.

10d. *"and the lips from speaking guile"* (*kai cheilē tou mē lalēsai dolon*). The phrase, parallel to v 10c, is also governed by the verb "keep from" (*pausatō*). For the construction of *pauein* with the genitive of the infinitive (*tou lalēsai*, "speaking," lit., "to not speak"), see also Josephus, *Ant.* 3.218, and for *mē* with the infinitive in the sense of "from," see Gen 16:2; 20:6; Ps 38:2; 68:24; Rom 11:10.

guile (*dolos*). Deceitful speech was proscribed earlier in 2:1, where it joins "evil" (*kakia*) among a list of vices from which the believers are to distance themselves because they are nourished on the "guileless" (*adolon*) "milk of the word" (2:2). A similar combination occurs in 2:22 in a statement regarding the "wrongdoing" or "sin" (*harmartia*) and "guile" (*dolos*) from which Christ was free. In their avoiding guileful speech, the believers take Jesus as their model and follow in his footsteps (2:21). This thought of the psalm is also consonant with the attention given throughout the letter to the positive and negative aspects of words and speech (1:10, 12, 25; 2:1, 9, 12, 15, 17, 22–23; 3:6, 9, 10, 12, 15, 16, 19; 4:4, 5, 6, 7, 9, 11, 14, 16; 5:1, 12).

Verse 11ab, citing Ps 33:15[34:14], similarly replaces 2d-person with 3d-person sing. aor. imperatives and adds an adversative *de* (left untranslated but indicating the contrast to v 10cd), again according to the weightier manuscript witnesses (𝔓[72] A B C etc.).

11a. *let that one turn away from wrongdoing and do what is right* (*ekklinatō de apo kakou kai poiēsatō agathon*). Wrongful action is the second hindrance to a blessed life, and doing what is right, the gateway. The action "do what is right," which parallels "turn away from *kakon*" (cf. also Ps 36[37]:27; Prov 3:7), suggests that *kakon* involves wrongful conduct (cf. *poiountas kaka* in v 12c); hence the translation "wrongdoing."[226] This first clause supports the preceding prohibition of "returning wrong (*kakon*) for wrong (*kakon*)" in v 9a, but also is in line with similar directives to avoid wrongdoing given elsewhere (2:11, 16, 19–20; 3:3, 17; 4:2–3, 15; 5:2–3). The expression "do what is right" (*poiēsatō agathon*) is a linguistic variant of the relatively rare terms *agathopoieō* (2:15, 20; 3:6, 17),[227] *agathopoios* (2:12), and *agathopoiia* (4:19). The repeated use of this family of terms in 1 Peter is without parallel in the rest of the NT. In its totality,

---

[226] For the expression "turn away from wrongdoing" in conjunction with "loving life," see also Prov 16:17; for the contrast "doing what is wrong"—"doing what is right," see also Ps 36[37]:27; Amos 5:14, 15; 3 John 11; cf. also Rom 12:9bc, 17, 21; 1 Thess 5:21b–22.

[227] Cf. the MSS variants in Tob 12:13 (A: *agathon poiōn*; B: *agathopoiōn*) and 1 Macc 11:33 (S: *agathon poiēsai*; B, A: *agathopoiēsai*).

this central thought of the citation provides biblical support for an ethical theme that pervades 2:13–3:9[228] and that is in fact central to the letter as a whole.[229]

11b. *"let that one seek peace and pursue it"* (*zētēsatō eirēnēn kai diōxatō autēn*). This clause parallels and expands upon the foregoing clause. Doing what is right involves the quest for peace in all of its social, personal, and religious dimensions; compare 2 *Clem.* 10:2, where peace is seen as a consequence of doing what is right: "If we are zealous to do what is right, peace will pursue us" (cf. also the NOTE on 1 Pet 3:13). To the expression "seek peace" (*zētēsatō eirēnēn*) is added the intensification aggressively "pursue it" (*diōxatō autēn*), "strive for it." In the psalm, *peace* could involve harmonious relations with others (within or beyond one's group) and perhaps peace with God as well. In this sense it would describe the concord encouraged in v 8 and would be a consequence of the conciliatory conduct urged in v 9. For the early Christians, as for Israel, God is a God of peace (Rom 15:33; 16:20; 1 Cor 14:22; 2 Cor 13:11; Phil 4:7), who seeks peace among his people.

Beyond the notion of peace implied in Ps 33[34], the messianic movement considered the good news of Christ to involve the proclamation of a final eschatological peace (Acts 10:36; Eph 2:17; 6:15) and hailed Jesus as the messianic bringer of this peace (John 14:27; 16:33; Acts 10:36; Col 3:15; Eph 2:14) and God as "the God of peace [who] will soon crush Satan under your feet" (Rom 16:20). The pursuit of peace is a familiar NT theme (Rom 12:18; 14:19; Eph 5:15; 2 Tim 2:22; Heb 12:14; Jas 3:18) and echoes the teaching of Jesus (Matt 5:9; see Klassen 1992a). To pursue peace, from a Christian perspective, was to renounce unrighteousness (Rom 3:9–17), vengeance and retaliation (Rom 12:18–21), disorder and confusion (1 Cor 14:33), enmity, selfishness, and dissension (Gal 5:19–23; Jas 3:18–18), to terminate hostilities and to effect reconciliation and unity (Eph 2:11–22; 4:3–6)—all in the spirit of Christ.

The concept of peace receives no specific elaboration in 1 Peter. However, beyond the author's practical concern with social order and the internal concord of the community, it is possible, if not likely, that he shared these theological notions of peace, especially in the light of the spirit of the exhortation in 3:8–9 and the wording of his final greeting: "Peace to all of you who are in Christ" (5:14). Peace, like election, is a quality that unites senders and recipients and all the faithful (cf. also 1:2).

In the final verse of the citation, v 12, the favor of God toward the righteous (v 12ab) is contrasted to God's opposition to those who do what is wrong (v 12c). Except for the added conjunction "for," the words of the psalm (33:16–17a) are repeated exactly. In certain manuscripts (614 1505 2495 lat sy^h) the citation is extended secondarily to include the further phrase of 33:17b[34:16b], "to destroy their memory from the earth."

---

[228] See *kakopoios* vs. *agathopoios*, 2:14–15; *hamartanein* vs. *agathopoiein*, 2:20; *agathopoiein*, 3:6; *kakon*, 3:9a; cf. also 2:24bc (*hamartia vs. dikaiosynē*).

[229] See 2:1, 11–12, 13–17, 18–20, 24; 3:1–6, 7, 8–9, 13, 15–17; 4:1–3, 8–11, 15–16, 18–19; 5:2–3, 5–9, 12.

12a. *For* (*hoti*). The addition of this conjunction has the effect of identifying v 12 as a motivation for the foregoing imperatives.

"the eyes of the Lord [*are*] *upon the righteous"* (*ophthalmoi kyriou epi dikaious*). Anthropomorphic references to the "eyes," "ears," and "face" of the Lord concern imagined aspects of God's disposition. The face is the part of the anatomy through which one's attitudes are most clearly expressed. Eyes, like ears, were regarded as the organs of perception and "emotion-fused thought," as part of a traditional three-zone concept of human (and divine) personality (Malina 1993d, 73–81). Each of these three related zones is present in vv 10–11: thought (eyes-heart: desiring life); self-expressive speech (tongues, lips: not speaking evil, guile); outward purposeful action (hands-feet: turning from evil, doing what is right, seeking and pursuing peace). The mention of all three zones implies a reference to the *total* personality. The fact that God can look upon (*epi*) all creatures with either favor (cf.2:20; 3:4, 10) and care (cf. 5:7) or judgment (cf. 1:17; 4:6, 17–18) provides a motive for the conduct urged in vv 10c–11; cf. Sir 17:2, 19, "He set his eye upon their heart . . . his eyes are continually on their ways."

righteous (*dikaious*). In the OT, the *righteous* are those who observe God's will and lead upright lives. In the chiasm of vv 10–12, where v 12ab corresponds to v 11, the "righteous" (*dikaious*) of the psalm are those who *do what is right*. That our author shares this notion is evident from the sense of *dikaiosynē* in 2:24 and 3:14 and from the same association of terms in 3:13–17 (*dikaiosynē* [v 14] and *agathopoiountas* [v 17]) and 4:18–19 (cf. *dikaios* and *agathopoiia*). "Lord" (*kyrios*) in both the LXX version of the psalm and its citation in 1 Peter refers to Yhwh, whereas in formulations of the Petrine author, except for 2:13, it designates Jesus Christ (1:3, 25; 2:3, 13; 3:15).

12b. *"and his ears* [*are open*] *to their prayer"* (*kai ōta autou eis deēsin autōn*). The thought parallels v 12a and expresses the openness (verb supplied according to sense) and attentiveness of God to the prayer (*deēsin*) of the righteous. This establishes the confidence for the offering of prayer (cf. 3:7 and 4:7) and is consistent with the emphasis on divine care in 5:6–7 and 5:10 (cf. also 1:5).

12c. *"but the face of the Lord* [*is*] *against those who do what is wrong"* (*prosōpon de kyriou epi poiountas kaka*). This final clause contrasts (*de*, "but") to vv 12ab, and the antithesis of v 12 as a whole parallels in sense the central imperative of v 11a. Here *those who do what is wrong* are contrasted with *the righteous* (v 12a) and the one who *does what is right* (v 11a), with *poiountas kaka* providing the negative counterpart to *poiēsatō agathon*. For the combination of hearing prayer and not turning the face, see Ps 101[102]: "Hear my prayer, O Lord, and let my cry come to you. Turn not away your face from me." The combination of *eyes, ears and face* describes the full awareness and attentiveness of God to those who do right and those who do wrong, the divine blessing of the former and the divine opposition to the latter. This focal thought of the psalm lends support not only to the injunctions concerning wrongdoing and doing what is right that precede vv 10–12 but also those that follow, including repeated mention of God's judgment (4:5–6, 17–18). Its words in general describe not only the eschatological blessing to be inherited (v 9) but also the divine basis for the confident perseverance in uprightness and doing what is right (3:13–17).

GENERAL COMMENT

With this appeal to *all* the members of the community, a first section of instruction treating the honorable conduct of specific groups of the household of God in society (2:13–3:7) is brought to a moving conclusion. Exhortation of a final set of persons of the brotherhood, elder and younger members (5:1–5a), is reserved until later (5:1–5a) and likewise is concluded with a similar call for the mutual humility of all that reproduces the content and structure of 3:8–12 (appeal to *all* members [*pantes de*], call for humility, and substantiating biblical citation).

Here in 3:8–12, the addressees are urged to cultivate the characteristics that foster the internal cohesion and solidarity of the community: oneness of mind, tenderhearted compassion, emotional commitment to brothers and sisters of the faith, and humility (v 8). Toward hostile outsiders, on the other hand, mistreatment and insult are not to be paid back in kind, but instead believers are to bless their detractors.

This marks a radical departure from the prevailing social script that prescribed retaliation, vengeance, vendettas, and blood feuds for violations of personal or group honor. Following the lead of postexilic Israel, Jesus had also urged and practiced the renunciation of retaliation, and his followers, as early Christian tradition indicates, did likewise. Such unusual conduct short-circuited the vicious cycle of retribution and escalating violence. Blessing one's detractors, from the vantage point of the Petrine author, also would contribute to the possibility of Christians' having a positive and winsome effect upon those who maligned them, as envisioned in 2:12 (cf. 3:13–17). In adopting this course of action, they will not only be following in the footsteps of their Lord, who refused to repay insult with insult (2:21–23), but they also will be acting in accord with their divine calling (v 9d) and ensuring for themselves God's blessing (v 9e, supported by the biblical citation of vv 10–12). The virtues encouraged in v 8, like the renunciation of retribution urged in v 9, echo emphases of early Christian exhortation also rooted in the teaching of Jesus. However, the specific vocabulary employed, the interweaving of themes, and their combination with an explicit citation of Ps 33[34] reveal the creative hand of the Petrine author. The author's hand is also evident in the manner in which this unit repeats and underlines ideas and themes already presented. Thus, nonretaliation roots the conduct of believers in the nonretaliatory behavior of Christ (2:23); the fact of their divine calling to such action (v 9d) repeats the thought of 2:21a (cf. also 1:14–16 and 2:9); and the notion of inheriting a blessing recalls the concept of "co-heirs of the grace of life" in 3:7 (cf. also 1:4).

The quotation of Ps 33[34] in vv 10–12 provides biblical warrant for the exhortation that precedes it. The relevance of this psalm concerning the deliverance of suffering resident aliens (33:5) to the suffering resident aliens in 1 Peter may well account for its repeated use in this letter. Beside its citation in 3:10–12 and 2:3, echoes of its language and thought occur elsewhere, including stress on reverence for God, avoiding wrongdoing and doing what is right, and hope of divine blessing. Psalm 33[34], as noted earlier (DETAILED COMMENT on the traditions underlying 2:21–24), had a place in the tradition concerning the "suffering of the just." Another text of this tradition, Isa 52:13–53:12, was used in 2:21–25 to describe the innocent suffering of Jesus, the innocent and just one who made possible the new life and upright behavior of the believing community. Now in 1 Pet 3:10–12, Ps 33, another text of this tradition, is cited to provide biblical assurance to suffering just ones of the divine blessing that follows upon righteous behavior and blessing of detractors. In terms of its immediate context, the citation provides scriptural support for the conduct urged in vv 8–9 and shows how divine blessing follows upon upright conduct. At the same time, its central command to "turn away from wrongdoing and do what is right" also provides biblical warrant for the general injunction to avoid what is wrong and do what is right, the theme that pervades much of the letter (2:13–17, 18–20, 22–23; 3:1–6, 7, 8–9). Accordingly, this concluding emphasis on "doing what is right" rather than "doing what is wrong" indicates that it is *this* theme, rather than the theme of subordination (not mentioned in vv 7, 8–12), that is the basic theme pervading and uniting 2:13–3:9. Subordination is only *one* important form of doing what is right and behaving honorably. The importance of doing what is right and behaving honorably is underlined further in 3:13–4:19 with a continued focus on Christian behavior toward hostile nonbelievers. Thus the unit 3:8–12 represents not so much a climax as a minor conclusion within a longer and more embracing line of thought.

For studies on 1 Pet 3:8–12, see Bornemann 1919–1920; Cervantes Gabarrón 1991a; Dale 1896; Lecomte 1981; Piper 1979, 1980; Schertz 1992; Schwank 1966; Schutter 1989, 44–49, 144–53; Sisti 1966b; Zerbe 1993, 270–90.

IV. DOING WHAT IS RIGHT IN THE FACE OF HOSTILITY (3:13–4:6)

◆

IV. A. DOING WHAT IS RIGHT DESPITE SUFFERING (3:13–17)

3:13a Who then shall harm you
13b if you are zealots for what is right?
14a If, however, you should suffer for doing what is right,
14b how honored [you are]!
14c "Have no fear of them, nor be frightened";
15a "sanctify the Lord," that is, the Christ, in your hearts.
15b Always [be] ready for a reply to everyone who requests of you
an account of the hope that fills you;
16a but [offer it] with gentleness and reverence.
16b Maintain a sound mindfulness of God's will,
16c so that, when you are slandered,
16d those who persist in disparaging your good conduct in Christ
may be put to shame.
17a For it is better to suffer for doing what is right,
17b if this should be God's will,
17c than for doing what is wrong.

INTRODUCTION

The previous section called for honorable behavior (2:13–3:12) and concluded with a quotation from Ps 33[34], stressing the importance of "doing what is right" (cf. also 3:6). Expanding on this point, our author now relates upright behavior to the issue of handling abuse from outsiders and the suffering that it brings. This problem of suffering despite doing what is right was already touched on earlier (1:6; 2:12b, 15b, 19–20, 21–24; 3:9ab) but now becomes the subject of sustained attention.

Our unit is joined to, and continues the thought of, the foregoing through other means as well: the linking copulative "and" (*kai*, v 14a) and the link-words "wrong(doing)," "harm" (*kakoō* [3:13a], *kakapoieō* [3:17c]; cf. *kakon*, *kaka* [3:9, 10c, 11a, 12c]), and their opposite, "(doing) good" (*agathos*, *agathopoieō* [3:13b, 17a]; cf. 2:12, 14, 15, 20, 24d; 3:6, 8–9, 10–12). The affinities with the exhortation of wives (3:1–6) in particular are also striking.[230] The behavior earlier urged of wives is now required of the entire community. Here, however, it is suffering despite doing what is right that becomes the focus of attention and that constitutes the issue that frames and demarcates this unit as a whole (vv 13–14/17).

The 2d-person plural imperative verbs and the pronounced focus on "you" in this section indicate the hortatory mood that distinguishes this unit from the indicative unit that follows (vv 18–22). A threefold inclusion, moreover, marks its boundaries (*kakōsōn/kakopoiountes*, vv 13/17; *agathou/agathopoiountas*, vv 13/17; and *paschoite/paschein*, vv 14/17; cf. also *ei* + optative, vv 14/17) and signals its central theme of doing what is right, now in the face of suffering. There is, however, a clear connnection and no major break between 3:13–17 and 3:18–22, for the theme of innocent suffering continues in 3:18 in regard to that of Jesus Christ, who after his innocent suffering and death was raised and exalted to honor and power. The relation of vv 13–17 and vv 18–22 thus repeats the similar relationship of 2:18–20 and its following supportive Christological statement (2:21–25). 1 Peter 4:1–6, in turn, draws out further moral and social implications of sharing in the suffering of Christ and his vindication. Thus, 3:13–17; 3:18–22; and 4:1–6 comprise distinct but related pericopes, which unfold one coherent line of thought, with the idea of doing what is right in accord with God's will, despite abuse and suffering, as the chief theme pervading and framing 3:13–4:6.

NOTES

3:13a. *Who then shall harm you* (*kai tis ho kakōsōn hymas*). A rhetorical question now draws out a positive implication of the foregoing biblical citation (3:10–12), especially God's favor toward those who do what is right (v 12). The copulative *kai* joins this verse with the foregoing and has the inferential sense of "then" (cf. BAGD 392), that is, "in the light of what has been said" (cf. Mark 10:26; John 9:36; 2 Cor 2:2). The Greek future active participle *kakōsōn* ("shall harm," "do wrong to") is a verb form of the preceding term *kakon* (3:10c, 11a, 12c; see also v 9) and serves as a further term linking this unit with 3:10–12. Here, however, it is the wrong done by *others* to the believers and their ensuing suffering (vv 14, 17) that is brought into view. The verb is used in connection with the Isaian suffering servant (Isa 53:7), but the rhetorical question in which it occurs here is closer to that of Isa 50:9: "Behold the Lord will help me; who shall harm me (*tis kakōsei me*)?" The verb *kakoō* occurs elsewhere only in Acts (of harmful actions against Jesus' followers: 12:1 [Herod Agrippa against

[230] Compare "not fearing" (3:14c; cf. 3:6d); "hearts" (3:15a/3:4a); "hope" (3:15b; 3:5b); "gentleness" (3:16a; 3:4b); "reverence" (3:15b; 3:2a); "conduct" (3:16d; 3:1, 2); and "doing what is right" (3:17a; 3:6c).

James and Peter]; 14:2; 18:10). Its further use in Acts 7:6 is particularly interesting since it refers to the mistreatment of Israel as a resident alien people (*paroikos*), citing the divine prediction to Abraham (Gen 15:13). The addressees of 1 Peter, as resident aliens (*paroikoi*, 2:11; cf. 1:17) and the spiritual progeny of Abraham and Sarah (3:6), now find themselves in a similar situation.

Since our author had previously indicated that believers are already experiencing abuse and insult (2:12, 19–20; 3:9; cf. 1:6), and since v 14 allows for the possibility of suffering, it is likely that he is speaking of "harm" to one's ultimate status and favor with God; that is, of being deprived of the grace of life, hope, inheritance, and salvation at the final appearance of Jesus Christ. Jesus, according to Matthew (10:28–31), also distinguished an ultimate hostile action from a proximate one: "Do not fear those who kill the body but cannot kill the soul . . . are not two sparrows sold for a pittance? And not one of them will fall to the ground without your Father's will . . . fear not, therefore; you are of more value than many sparrows." More generally, see Rom 8:31: "If God is for us, who is against us?" The point of the rhetorical question, directly following the comforting words of 3:10–12, is that, since God cares for those who do what is right, when you are zealots for what is right no one can thwart this divine protection (cf. also the similar comforting words in 2:25 and 5:7). Socrates's remark to his judges offers a classical parallel: "no harm can befall a good man, either when he is alive or when he is dead, and the gods do not neglect his cause" (Plato, *Apol.* 41d). More apposite to 1 Peter and Christian teaching, however, is the Israelite tradition concerning God's protection and vindication of the suffering righteous ones (Isa 52:13–53:12; Wis. 1–5; 2 Macc. 7; cf. the NOTE on 2:21 and the related DETAILED COMMENT).

13b. *if you are zealots for what is right?* (*ean tou agathou zēlōtai genēsthe*). The phrase "zealots for what is right" (*tou agathou zēlōtai*) is unique in the NT but has a near counterpart in Titus 2:14 ("a special people zealous for good deeds" [*zēlōtēn kalōn ergōn*]; see also Pol. *Phil* 6:3, "Let us be zealots for what is right" [*zēlōtai peri to kalon*]). In these instances, the noun can also be rendered as an adjective: "zealous for, devoted to, eager to do" what is right (cf. also Sir 51:18; Philo, *Virt.* 175). It commonly is used in the encouragement of moral excellence: be ardent pursuers of truth (Epict., *Diatr.* 3.24.40), virtue (Isoc. *Ep.* 4b; Philo, *Praem. 11*), piety (Philo, *Spec.* 1.30), the law (Acts 21:20), or ancestral traditions (Gal 1:14). The noun can also designate an enthusiastic adherent of a person or cause (Josephus, *Life* 12; Dio Chrys., *Orat.* 55.4). In Israelite history, Phineas, the grandson of Aaron (Num 25:6–18; Ps 105 [106]:30–31; Sir 45:23–24; 4 Macc 18:4; Philo, *Mut.* 108), and the later high priest Onias III (2 Macc 4:2) were revered as prototypical zealots for the law, and Phineas as a forefather of the Maccabees (1 Macc 2:26, 54), who were also zealous for the law (1 Macc 2:24, 26, 27, 50). One follower of Jesus, Simon "the zealot" (Luke 6:15; Acts 1:13), is identified as also being associated with this tradition of zeal for the law, and Paul the Pharisee describes himself as a "zealot for the traditions of his fathers" (Gal 1:14; cf. also Acts 22:3; 21:20). Josephus used the term to designate Judean nationalists active in the first revolt against Rome (66–70 CE; cf. *J.W.* 2.651; 4.160–61, 302–10; etc.). Reicke's claim (1964, 107), however, that the Petrine author has in mind "these Jewish fanatics and warns against [the Christian adoption of] their terroristic methods" is pure speculation that finds no support in this text or its wider context. In 1 Peter the phrase represents the author's restatement of words in the foregoing citation ("doing what is right" [3:11] and "righteous" [3:12a]), a further reason to prefer "zealots" over the variant reading "imitators" (*mimētai*), with its weaker manuscript attestation.

The verb *genēsthe* (aor. middle subj.) likewise has stronger support than its variants *este*, *genesthe* (pres. middle indic.) and *genoisthe*, an optative probably prompted by the accompanying optative *paschoite* (v 14), and has the force of "show oneself to be." Being zealous for what is right in this context (see also vv 16, 17) and elsewhere in the letter is being eagerly engaged in doing what is right in accord with God's will (2:15), conduct that has God's approval (2:20) and blessing (3:9, 10–12). The antithesis of such behavior is not political terrorism but, as v 17 indicates, wrongdoing—that is, any act contrary to the will of God (2:15–16, 19–20; 3:11).[231]

14. Following a general statement of assurance (v 13), the author now considers the possibility of suffering, which believers face for doing what is right. Verse 14ab together with v 13 forms a minor chiasm involving a parallelism of the *internal* conditional clauses and "doing what is right" (v 13b, v 14a), and the framing *external* clauses contrasting harm from humans with honor from God (v 13a, v 14b):

A. Who then shall harm you
    B. if you are zealots for what is right?
    B.′ If, however, you should suffer for doing what is right,
A.′ how honored [you are]!

14a. *If, however, you should suffer for doing what is right* (*all' ei kai paschoite dia dikaiosynēn*). With these words, the author returns to, and addresses more systematically, the predicament that was the primary motivation for the letter; namely, the suffering of Christians despite their innocence (1:6; 2:12, 15–16, 18–20; 3:9; 4:12–16; 5:9). The *possibility* of this suffering is expressed by the conditional particle "if" (*ei*) and the rare optative mood of the verb *paschoite*: "if perchance you should suffer." The optative mood is employed in Classical Greek to express a conceivable possibility but appears far less frequently in the NT (see BDF §385.2 on the potential optative). This conditional statement mirrors the conditional formulations of 1:6 ("while now for a brief time, *if* it must be [*ei deon*], you are afflicted by various trials") and 2:19–20 ("*if* one bears

---

[231] The expression also occurs in 2 *Clem.* 10:2, which appears to entail a combination of elements in 1 Pet 3:11 (citing Ps 33:15) and 1 Pet 3:13 to produce a somewhat different thought: "If we are zealous to do what is right, peace will pursue us" (contrast 1 Pet 3:11b: "seek peace and pursue it").

up under pain while suffering unjustly . . . *if* when you do good and suffer") as well as the conditional form and optative of 3:17. These two optatives, however, point less to what is possible than to what is desirable; namely, upright behavior even if it leads to suffering (so Danker 1967b, 100). This is made likely by the full statements of vv 14 and 17 and by the fact that abuse and suffering are already a present reality (2:12, 15, 19–20; 3:9, 16; 4:12–19; 5:9, 10).

The thought of suffering "for doing what is right" (*dia dikaiosynēn*; lit., "on account of" or "because of [*dia*] upright behavior") echoes the earlier concern with *innocent* suffering (2:19–20; cf. 2:12, 16, 22–23)—not simply suffering in general but suffering unjustly for doing what is right (2:19). The noun *dikaiosynē* (see also 2:24c) is related to the foregoing substantive *dikaioi* ("righteous," 3:12) and functions as a synonym of *agathopoiein* (v 17a), just as these terms are related in 3:10–12 (*dikaious* [v 12] synonymous with *poiēsatō agathon* [v 11]). The chiastic construction of vv 13–14b also makes it clear that *dikaiosynē* is synonymous with the formulation "zealots for what is right" and that both expressions are further Petrine expressions for "doing what is right" (*poiēsatō agathon*, 3:11; *agathopoieō*, 2:15, 20; 3:6; cf. *agathopoiia*, 4:19); hence, the translation "doing what is right." *Dikaiosynē* has the same sense here as in the word of Jesus recorded in Matthew, a saying that the first half of v 14 appears to echo: "Blessed/honored are those who are persecuted for doing what is right" (Matt 5:10).[232] This upright conduct is made possible by Christ's vicarious death, which enabled the abandonment of wrongdoing and living "for doing what is right" (2:24). Now in 3:14 the author stresses that suffering for doing what is right is actually honorable in God's sight. The fact that he has already noted that the role of provincial governors is the approval of doing what is right (2:14) makes it unlikely that the suffering mentioned here is thought to be the result of state persecution. Further evidence in the following verses concerning the mode of harassment adds to the conclusion that the suffering is the result of sporadic, local, unorganized assaults of a verbal nature.

14b. *how honored* [*you are*]! (*makarioi*). Suffering for doing what is right is not a stigma of social disgrace but a badge of divine honor. This statement, in terms of its form, is a "makarism" (Greek: *makarismos*), an ascription of honor or a declaration of the honored status of a person or group. In such declarations of honor, *makarios* (sing. or pl.) functions either as an adjective or a substantive, and often, as here and in the parallel makarism of 4:14, the verb ("is" or "are") is absent but implied (see also Matt 5:3–10; Rom 4:8; Jas 1:12). Here the verb "are" (*este*) has been supplied secondarily in a few textual witnessses. Makarisms, similar but not identical to blessings, are a prominent biblical as well as extrabibical figure of speech (Hauck and Bertram 1967; Käser 1970). In the LXX, makarisms declare the honor of the elect people (Ps 32:12; 143:15; 145:5), of the pious who fear the Lord and observe his ways (Ps 1:1–2; 2:12; 39:5; Prov 14:21; Sir 25:7–11; 4 Macc 7:22) or of those who trust in God (Ps 40:5;

[232] On its dissimilarity from Pauline usage, see the NOTE on 2:24.

Prov 3:13; 8:34; Isa 30:18; Sir 14:20; 31:8). Makarisms in eschatological texts place special emphasis on the final salvation of the upright.[233] In the honor-shame society of the biblical communities, makarisms express the value judgments of a group as they relate to specific conceptions of honor and shame; for *makarios* as a contrast to being shamed, see LXX Ps 126:5.

The NT contains over 40 instances of such exclamations of honor, all of which involve the social imputation of esteem to an individual or group for manifesting desirable behavior and commitments. What is remarkable about the makarisms of Jesus and early Christianity is that they so often challenge conventional expectations and values. Instead of acknowledging the honor of the wealthy and the powerful, Jesus and his followers regularly attribute honor to the despised, the destitute, and the oppressed. This is a particular feature of the familiar makarisms introducing Jesus' Sermon on the Mount (Matt 5:3–12/Luke 6:20–23). In regard to the NT makarisms, 1 Pet 3:14 is closest in sense to that of Matt 5:10a ("How honored are those who are persecuted for doing what is right," *makarioi hoi dediōgmenoi heneken dikaiosynēs*), which is also echoed in Pol. *Phil* 2:3; cf. also *Gos. Thom.* 68, 69a; Clem. Alex., *Strom.* 4.6.41.2; see the NOTE on 4:14. Both formulations assert the paradoxical honor of "you" (1 Peter) or "they" (Matthew) who suffer (1 Peter) or who are persecuted (Matthew) for doing what is right. Thus, they represent divergent reformulations of a makarism of Jesus that was variously preserved and employed in early Christian tradition, perhaps in association with baptismal catechesis.[234] The makarism of Jesus, moreover, echoes a theme of earlier Israelite tradition concerning the "suffering of the righteous," a tradition echoed from Ps 33 cited in 1 Pet 3:10–12 and, earlier, from Isa 52–53 employed in 2:22–24.[235] Since Ps 33:13–17 was just cited in 1 Pet 3:10–12, it is conceivable that the makarism of the psalm ("How honorable is the one who hopes in him [the Lord]," 33:9b) also inspired the Petrine author here. The thought, however, is different. The psalmist continues, "revere (*phobēthēte*) the Lord, you his holy ones" (33:10), whereas our author discourages fear of human agents who could cause the suffering of the believers.

This is the first of two such "makarisms" employed in the letter, the other occurring in 4:14, which is similar in form and content:

> 3:14 if you should suffer for doing what is right, how honored you are!
> 4:14 if you are reproached because of Christ, how honored you are!

---

[233] See, e.g., *Pss. Sol.* 4:23 ("Honored are they that fear the Lord in their avoiding wrongdoing; the Lord shall deliver them from guileful persons and sinners, and shall deliver us from every stumbling-block of the lawless") and *2 En.* 81:4 ("How honored is the man who dies righteous and upright, against whom no record of oppression has been written, and who received no judgment on that day"); cf. also *2 En.* 82:4; *4 Ezra* 7:45.

[234] See also Selwyn (1947, 439–58), Nauck (1955), and the NOTES on 4:13–14 concerning the early Christian appropriation of the "joy-in-suffering" tradition.

[235] On the marginalized of Palestine as the object of Jesus' makarisms, see Kloppenborg 1986.

In each case, conditional statements ("if . . .") are followed by assertions of honor or blessing, with the potential suffering in 3:14 (expressed by the optative *paschoite*) balanced by the actual experience of reproach in 4:14 (expressed by the indicative *oneidizesthe*). On the history of biblical makarisms, including the two in 1 Peter, see Millauer 1976, 145–65. Translations often render *makarios* as "blessed" or "happy," but since makarisms are actually acknowledgments or conferrals of honor, *makarios* is best rendered "how honorable" or "how esteemed" (you are). The present contrast between honor and suffering at the hands of human adversaries suggests that it is honor from God that is meant, as is generally the case in biblical makarisms. See similar contrasts in 2:4c/d and 4:2b/c and the contrast of the Christ and believers (honored by God) with nonbelievers (shamed by God) in 2:4–10. The parallel expression in 4:14 makes this divine honoring explicit: "how honored you are, because the divine Spirit of glory rests upon you." God, our author has already affirmed, has honored the believers by rebirthing, electing, sanctifying, and knitting them together as his honored family (1:3–2:10). This honor is certain, even when they suffer for their upright behavior.

The parallel statements in vv 13–14b are followed in vv 14c–15a by a second pair of parallel formulations concerning an appropriate response to innocent suffering. The words entail a modified citation of the final line of Isa 8:12 and the opening line of 8:13. The author has made earlier use of this text in 2:8 (citing Isa 8:14). This passage in Isaiah warns of the threatening advance of the Assyrian army (8:7–8) but assures Israel that "God is with us" (8:10). Therefore Israel is told: "have no fear of what this people fear [lit., 'do not fear its fear'], nor be terrified; sanctify the Lord himself" (*ton de phobon autou ou mē phobēte oude mē tarachthēte; kyrion autōn hagiasate*, 8:12d–13a). This first portion of the Petrine citation (v 14a) replaces a singular pronoun "its" (*autou*, referring to the people [*laos*]) with a plural "their" (*autōn*, serving as an objective genitive, *fear of them*) and reads *mē* and *mēde* in place of *ou mē* and *mēde*, respectively. The second portion of the citation (v 15a) interpolates the words *de ton Christon* between *kyrion* (*Lord*) and *hagiasate* (and adds the phrase "in your hearts").

14c. *"Have no fear of them, nor be frightened"* (*ton de phobon autōn mē phobēte mēde tarachthēte*). Since righteous believers are honored by God, they need not fear those who cause their suffering. The words derive from Isa 8:12c, with a plural *autōn* ("their") replacing an original singular *autou* (referring to *laos*, "this people"). Here, as in the following verse, the author draws again on Isa 8 (8:14 cited earlier, in 1 Pet 2:8). The inclusion of "nor be frightened" rather than its exclusion (𝔓[72] B L Jerome) has superior manuscript support; the latter may have been a result of haplography occasioned by similar verb endings (*phobēte, tarachthēte*). The subjunctive mood of "fear" (*phobēte*) and "be frightened" (*tarachthēte*) with the negative (*mē, mēde*) is used to form a prohibition. The clause *ton de phobon autōn mē phobēte* involves a cognate accusative (*phobon . . . phobēte*) that reads, literally, "do not fear their fear," with *autōn* in this context having the force of an objective genitive; hence the translation "have no fear of them," with "them" now referring to the readers' abusive neighbors. The verb *fear,* as in 3:6c, denotes not "reverence" for God, as elsewhere in 1 Peter, but fear of hostile humans, as in 3:6. The idea of fearlessness before maligners recalls Matt 10:26–33 and Luke 12:4–7. But here in 1 Peter, all fearless believers take their cue from the fearlessness of Christian wives (3:6).

15a. *"sanctify the Lord," that is, the Christ, in your hearts* (*kyrion de ton Christon hagiasate en tais kardiais hymōn*). This positive counterpart to v 14c likewise embodies language from the same Isaian context (8:13a), but with greater modification. The expression "the Christ" (*ton Christon*) replaces an original "himself" (*autōn*); "in your hearts" is added as a modification of "sanctify"; and an added particle *de* serves either to explicate the contrast between vv 14c and 15a or, more likely, to mark "the Christ" (*ton Christon*) as appositive to and explanatory of *kyrion.*[236] As a result, "Lord" (identifying God in Isa 8:13a) is specifically identified here as "the Christ," and an Isaian statement concerning the sanctifying of God is transformed into a statement concerning the interior sanctifying of Christ the Lord. The fact that this expression is unique in the Bible may have prompted certain scribes ($\mathfrak{M}$, including the later uncials K L P and most minuscules) to substitute "God" (*theon*) for "Christ" (cf. Howard 1977, 76–82). But "Christ" has earlier and diversified external attestation ($\mathfrak{P}^{72}$ ℵ A B C Ψ 33 614 1739 it 65 vg syr^{p,h} cop^{sa} bo arm Clement) as well as transcriptional probability (the more familiar expression [*kyrion ton theon*] replacing the less usual formulation [*kyrion ton Christon*]). The articular form "the Christ" appears also in 4:13 and 5:1, and two earlier instances where Jesus is identified as *Lord* display a similar modification of their sources. In 1:25 the citation of Isa 40:8 is altered (substitution of "Lord" for "God") to transform a reference to "the word of God" into a reference to "the word of the *Lord,*" that is, the gospel concerning Jesus Christ (see the NOTE on 1:25). A similar shift in the referent of "Lord" occurs in 2:3 (referring to God in the source [Ps 33:9] but to Christ in 1 Peter 2:3 and its context [2:4]).

The verb *hagiazō* ("sanctify," "regard as charged with sacred power," "acknowledge the holiness of," "venerate," "keep holy") occurs predominantly in Biblical Greek and related texts (Philo, *Leg.* 1.18; *Spec.* 1.167). It can denote the actions of "consecrating," "setting apart," or "sanctifying" special times (e.g., Sabbath, Gen 2:3; Exod 20:8–11; Num 20:12; 27:14; Isa 8:13; 29:23; *Barn.* 15:1, 3, 5–6), places (e.g., Mt. Sinai, Exod 19:23), persons (e.g., priests and others, Exod 13:2, 12; 29:1; 30:3; Josh 7:13), or objects (e.g., sacrifice, Matt 23:17, 19; 1 Tim 4:5). God, the Holy One, sanctifies his people (Exod 31:13; Lev 20:8; 21:8, 15, 23; 22:9; Ezek 20:12; John 17:17; 1 Thess 5:23) and is sanctified among his people (Sir 36:3). God also enables his name to be kept holy; see "may your name be sanctified" (Isa 29:23; Ezek 36:23) and the first petition

---

[236] For this function of *de* ("that is"), see Rom 3:22; 9:30; 1 Cor 10:11; 15:26; and Phil 2:8. For the use of the article with proper names employed as appositives when referents are to be distinguished, see Matt 3:1; 11:1; Acts 21:8, 16 and BDF §268.

of the Lord's Prayer (Matt 6:9; Luke 11:2; *Did.* 8:2), reminiscent of the first-century prayer of Israel's liturgy, the Kaddish: "Exalted and hallowed be his great name."[237] Jesus is sanctified by God the Father (John 10:36) and sanctifies himself (John 17:19) as well as the church (Eph 5:26) through his atoning death (Heb 2:11; 13:12). Believers have also been sanctified or purified by the Holy Spirit (Rom 15:16; 1 Cor 6:11) or the word of God (1 Tim 4:5; cf. also Acts 20:32; 26:18).

To sanctify Christ the Lord is to "honor as holy" the one whose holiness has already been established (1:19). The term and concept belong to the large semantic field of 1 Peter concerning the holiness of God and Christ, the divine sanctification of the readers, and their obligation to a holy way of life. Inasmuch as the readers have been sanctified by the Spirit of holiness (1:2) and through faith in Christ have become God's elect and holy people (2:4–10), they now are called to a holy way of life (1:14–16; cf. 1:22; 3:2) that includes venerating Christ the Lord as the faultless agent of redemption (1:18–19; 1:2; 3:18). The reference to Christ here and in v 16 anticipates the Christological unit that follows (3:18–22).

in your hearts (*en tais kardiais hymōn*). This phrase, which does not derive from the cited Isaian text, makes it clear that the sanctification of Christ as the Lord commences in the believers' hearts, the organ of thought, disposition, and intention (see also 1:22 and 3:4 and their respectives NOTES). What was said earlier to wives (3:4) is now implied of all believers: it is the internal disposition of the heart (which God alone can see) that matters most and that has God's approval; cf. Matt 6:3, 6, 18.

The syntactical relation of v 15b–16a to its context is uncertain. A finite verb is lacking, and thus these words could be seen as modifying the nearest finite verb, "sanctify the Lord . . . always being ready for a reply . . . but with gentleness and reverence." This, however, would constitute an awkwardly long and complex construction as well as a formulation in which v 15b–16a would provide a rather inappropriate qualification of v 15a, since v 15a focuses on *internal disposition*, whereas v 15b–16a speaks of *external communication*, interaction with outsiders. Preference therefore is given to a second possibility, whereby v 15b (and v 16b) are taken as related but independent clauses with imperatival force, similar to the imperatives of vv 14c and 15a (so also Beare 1970, 164).

15b. *Always [be] ready for a reply to everyone who requests of you an account of the hope that fills you* (*Hetoimoi aei pros apologian panti tōi aitounti hymas logon peri tēs en hymin elpidos*). This formulation, while an independent imperatival clause, extends the foregoing line of thought. Fearlessness toward outside detractors is to be manifested in a readiness to provide a public account of oneself, especially regarding the hope that arouses their curiosity. The pl. adj. "ready" (*hetoimoi*) pertains to the readers referred to as "you" in the verbs of

[237] See Billerbeck and Strack (1926–1961, 1:411–18) on the Israelite concept of "sanctifying God's name" as an equivalent for glorifying God.

vv 14–15 and the pronoun *hymas* ("you," v 15a). When combined with the preposition *pros* ("for"), it denotes readiness for something (Xen., *Mem.* 4.5.12; Aelianus, *Var. Hist.* 14.49; Tob 5:17 BA; Titus 3:1). In the present imperatival context, the adjective *ready* has imperatival force similar to the adjectives in 3:8, with the verb "be" implied.

a reply to everyone who requests of you an account of the hope that fills you (*apologian panti tōi aitounti hymas logon peri tēs en hymin elpidos*). Occasionally in the NT the noun *apologia* ("reply") is used in reference to a personal "defense" before juridical officials (Acts 22:1; 25:16; 2 Tim 4:16).[238] Elsewhere, however, it denotes a reply to accusations of a general rather than a legal nature (1 Cor 9:3; 2 Cor 7:11; Phil 1:7, 16).[239] The term *apologia* is used here in this latter sense, as the context demonstrates. First, the generalizing expressions "always" (*aei*) and "to everyone who requests" (*panti tōi aitounti*) point to an ongoing state of preparedness for a response to inquiry from any quarter. The situation envisioned is "a running debate in everyday life with people who have a different way of thinking" (Goppelt 1993, 244; so also Selwyn 1947, 193–94; and Michaels 1988, 188). In contrast to Luke 12:11 and 21:12–15, which refer to "rulers and authorities," "kings and governors," before whom a defense is to be made, our author speaks of "any and all" (*panti*) who are curious. Second, the verb *aiteō* ("request," "ask," "seek"), occurring with a double accusative of the person asked and of the thing requested,[240] involves the action of *requesting* (contrary to Beare 1970, 164) rather than of demanding or commanding, as would be the case in official hearings. Third, in this context the question and the reply concern "an account (*logon*) of the *hope* that fills you." Curiosity about *hope*, a personal attitude rather than a legal crime, indicates that the author is referring here not to formal defenses before legal authorities (who would be concerned not with expectation concerning the future but culpable behavior in the present) but rather to replies to informal inquiries concerning the nature and basis of Christian hope, whenever and from whomever they should come. This focus on hope is acknowledged by Balch (1981, 90), but his speculation that "the 'defense' anticipated in 1 Pet 3:15 would include the ethics of the household code" is supported neither by this text nor its immediate context, where no allusion to household ethics as such is to be found. Fourth, the *manner* in which believers should offer this response, namely with "gentleness and reverence for God," presupposes not official inquests, where courage and fortitude would be required, but occasional queries, where modesty and commitment to God would be designed to underline the nature of Christian hope and to attract a positive response on the part of the curious.

---

[238] For a similar use of the verb *apologeomai* (exclusively in Luke–Acts), see Luke 12:11; 21:14; Acts 19:33; 24:10; 25:8; 26:1, 2, 24; cf. Lamau 1988, 64–66.

[239] For the verb with this sense, see Acts 19:33; Rom 2:12; 2 Cor 12:19; cf. also PWisc. 55.1 (Horsley 1981–1982, 2:92).

[240] As in Josh 4:12; 1 Esd 6:11; Josephus, *Ant.* 12.24; Mark 6:22–23; cf. Matt 5:42; 6:6; Luke 11:13; John 4:10.

Accordingly, the term *apologia* is best rendered "reply," "answer," or "response." The presupposed situation is an ongoing one always facing the believers. It involves not formal trials and the demands of official magistrates requiring evidence of nonculpability but occasions when outsiders, out of curiosity, ask for explanations of the hope that animates these believers (against Reicke 1964, 107–8; Beare 1970, 164–65).[241]

an account (*logon*). The common term *logos* has a broad range of meanings depending on context ("word," "statement," "speech," "reckoning," etc.); for an "account" given in private, see Plato, *Pol.* 285e. With the accompanying words "of the hope that fills you," it denotes that which the believers are requested to provide curious inquirers: an *account* of the hope that fills them. It is employed again with the same sense in 4:5 in reference to the "account" that those who malign the believers will themselves have to give to the One ready (*hetoimōs*, an adverb related to the adjective *hetoimoi* of the present verse) to judge the living and the dead. Together, these two texts point to an eventual "turning of the tables," when those who once requested an account from the believers will themselves be called to account by God.

of the hope that fills you (*peri tēs en hymin elpidos*; lit., "concerning the hope that is in you [*en hymin*]"). It is their hope, the author indicates, that distinguishes these believers in the eyes of outsiders and arouses their curiosity, a hope within each believer or among the believers as a community. In the light of a prevailing uncertainty or pessimism concerning the future ushered in with the advent of Roman rule, this interest in hope, particularly among the subjugated peoples of the provinces, would come as no surprise. This period of Greco-Roman history following the collapse of the native city-states and kingdoms had seen the erosion of traditional values and norms and the rise and perpetuation of military conflict. This was accompanied by a loss of confidence in previous institutions, skepticism regarding their supporting myths, a sense of failure, resignation to the capricious powers of fate or chance, and "a progressive loss of hope in the world" (G. Murray 1955, 4). A perception of the Gentiles as "those without hope" also appears to have been widespread among the early believers (1 Thess 4:13; Eph 2:12). If, as may be assumed, this spiritual malaise characterized the populations of Asia Minor as well, their particular curiosity about a religious movement focused on hope and a positive sense of the future might be expected.

Hope, as a distinguishing feature of Christian life, is stressed repeatedly in the NT[242] and is associated specifically with "Christ our hope" (Col 1:27; 1 Tim 1:1; Titus 2:13; 3:7) and the good news (Col 1:23). Hope figures prominently in 1 Peter as well. Already at the outset of the letter, our author listed a "living

---

[241] "Apology" as a genre of Christian composition similar to the Apology of Socrates by Plato does not emerge until the second century; see the Apologies of Justin, Aristides, Tatian, Athenagoras, Theophilus, Minucius Felix, and Tertullian, the *Epistle to Diognetus*.

[242] See Rom 5:2–5; 8:24; 12:12; 15:4; 2 Cor 3:12; Gal 5:5; Eph 4:4; Col 1:5; 1 Thess 1:3; 5:8; 2 Thess 2:16; Titus 1:2; Heb 3:6; 6:11, 18; 10:23; 1 John 3:3.

hope" as the first of the benefits accruing to the believers as a result of their rebirth (1:3) and described it as an anticipation of the divine grace to appear at the final revelation of Jesus Christ (1:13). Hope as well as trust in God is made possible by Christ's suffering, death, and resurrection (1:21). Hope in God is also mentioned as a characteristic of the exemplary matriarchs (3:5). The author envisions outsiders fastening onto this particular quality of Christian belief and evident confidence, and presumably it is these features of hope that the author expects the addressees will emphasize in their reply to the curious. The hope awakened by Christ's resurrection and the believers' rebirth is not merely a positive anticipation of the future but the very "life principle" of present Christian existence according to 1 Peter (Schröger 1981b, 198–207).[243]

16a. *but [offer it] with gentleness and reverence* (*alla meta prautētos kai phobou*). The words involve not a contrast (note the omission of *alla* in 𝔓[72]) but a qualification of the *manner* in which the believers are to reply. Accordingly, the force of the particle *alla* (included in most witnesses) is not adversative as in v 14a but qualitative or asseverative ("but surely"). The qualification implies some verbal expression such as "offer it" or "do so." This reply to any and all is to be marked by the same qualities urged earlier of Christian wives: *gentleness* (cf. 3:4) and *reverence for God* (cf. 3:2). Such gentleness (*prautēs*) was a prized Christian virtue,[244] while the stress on *reverence for God* repeats that of 1:17; 2:17, 18; and 3:2.

It may be, as Knox suggested, that these words imply that believers are to "avoid both contemptuous silence and insolent speech" (Knox 1953, 189). But his assumption that the situation is that of an official Roman inquiry similar to the one Pliny held in Pontus at a later time (*Ep.* 10.96, ca. 111 CE) overlooks the manifest dissimilarities between 1 Peter and Pliny's account of his formal inquiry concerning the Christians of Bithynia-Pontus (see the NOTES on 4:12–19). The situation presumed here and throughout 1 Peter, as Goppelt notes (1993, 238, 243–44), is one of "social discrimination," not official incriminations (see also the NOTE on v 16d below). In giving an account with restraint and reverence for God of the hope that animates them, believers would be taking their cue from the everyday behavior of gentle and reverent wives in particular. Like these wives, they might thereby hope to win over the nonbelievers (cf. 3:1–2 and 2:12).

16b. *Maintain a sound mindfulness of God's will* (*syneidēsin echontes agathēn*). The formulation could be taken as a further qualification of how the believers are to respond. It is more likely, however, that the present participle *echontes* here, as in 2:12a and 4:8, has imperatival force (so also Brox 1986, 161; Reichert 1989, 186–89) and introduces a related but further thought. This injunction is then followed by a purpose clause (v 16cd), whose words "your

---

[243] See also Piper 1980; Land 1981; Kendall 1987. On the concept of hope in general, see Woschitz 1979.

[244] See also 1 Cor 4:21; 2 Cor 10:1; Gal 5:23; 6:1; Eph 4:2; Col 3:12; 2 Tim 2:25; Titus 3:2; Jas 1:21; 3:13; and specifically in response to outsiders, Ign. *Eph.* 10:2.

good (*agathēn*) conduct in Christ" describe action in accord with a "sound (*agathēn*) mindfulness of God's will."

The noun *syneidēsis* (also 2:19 and 3:21) often is rendered "conscience" in the translations. Such a rendering, however, is misleading to modern, individualistically oriented readers, who associate "conscience" with an internal state and an interiorized moral sensitivity, such as the "superego." For group-oriented cultures like those of the ancient world, it was sensitivity to and mindfulness of the evaluation of significant *others* that guided moral behavior (Malina 1993d, 63–73; Malina and Rohrbaugh 1992, 113). For the early Christians, it was God who represented the most "significant other." Thus here, as in 2:18–20, *syneidēsis* is associated with "reverence" for God (*phobos*) and, as in 2:19, denotes *mindfulness of God* and compliance with God's will (rather than "good will toward society," as Reicke [1964, 138] suggests). The same expression is employed in 3:21 to describe the nature of baptism: "a pledge to God to maintain a sound mindfulness of God's will." This imperative of v 16b is thus rooted in the pledge believers once made in their baptism. For our author, this divine will concerns "doing what is right" (2:15, 19–20; 3:11, 13, 17; 4:19) and "good conduct" (1:15, 17; 2:12; 3:1–2). On *syneidēsis*, see also the NOTES on 2:19 and 3:21.

16c. *so that, when you are slandered* (*hina en hōi katalaleisthe*). This final clause expresses the purpose or intended result of the preceding injunction. Whereas vv 15b–16a allow for a possible positive outcome to the clarification of the hope that fills the believers, a negative response with negative consequences is also considered. The phrase *en hōi katalaleisthe* echoes that of 2:12b ("when they slander you," *en hōi katalalousin hymōn*) and here, as there, *en hōi* functions adverbially ("in a case or circumstance when") in connection with the verb that follows. Elsewhere it is also used cirumstantially, but in reference to the foregoing (1:6; 3:19; 4:4; see P. R. Fink 1967, 34 and Michaels 1988, 190). The single verb *katalaleisthe* ("you are slandered"), a rare passive form of the verb, is preferred over the longer variant reading, "when they slander you as those who do what is wrong," chiefly on transcriptional grounds: it is likely that the earlier statement *en hōi katalalousin hymōn hōs kakopoiōn* (2:12) prompted copyists to expand the shorter reading by adding *hōs kakopoiōn* (syr^{h} cop) or by altering the person of the verb and adding *hymōn* (vg arm) or *hymōn hōs kakopoiōn* (א A C K P 049 etc.).

Given the similarity between 2:12a and 3:16c, it is likely that the "slander" of which 3:16 speaks involves the same denigration of the believers as mentioned in 2:12b ("they slander you as those who do what is wrong"). But at this point an alternative consequence is presented. In 2:12 and following verses, the author allows for the prospect that detractors, upon viewing the good behavior of the believers, may be led to join them in glorifying God (see also 3:2) or that such proper behavior at least will reduce them to silence (2:15). Here, on the other hand, the possibility is expressed that the slanderers could also *persist* in disparaging the good conduct of Christians. In this case, the result would not be their conversion but their condemnation, as the remainder of this verse indicates.

16d. *those who persist in disparaging your good conduct in Christ may be put to shame* (*kataischynthōsin hōi epēreazontes hymōn tēn agathēn en Christōi anastrophēn*).

those who persist in disparaging (*hōi epēreazontes*). The verb *epēreazō* ("speak disparagingly of," "act despitefully toward," "insult") appears in the NT only here and in Luke 6:28b ("Pray for those who disparage you," which parallels "Bless those who curse you," Luke 6:28a, a thought echoed earlier in 1 Pet 3:9).[245] In both instances the verb concerns a verbal mode of abuse and, in the case of 1 Peter, disparagement of the *good conduct* of the believers. The translation, "persist in disparaging," conveys the continuous action implied by the present tense of the verb. The term is also later used by Justin Martyr (*1. Apol.* 1) of the abusive treatment of Christians. This form of behavior, verbal disparagement, along with "slander," provides further evidence of the situation confronted by the addressees. The believers are the victims not of formal juridical inquiries but of slander, denigration, insult, and public shaming. This is consistent with 2:12 and the references to the verbal abuse of the believers that occurs elsewhere in the letter (*loidoria*, "insult," 3:9; *blasphēmeō*, "malign," 4:4; oneidizō, "reproach," 4:14; cf. *loidoreō*, "insult," and *antiloidoreō*, "insult in return," 2:23). Such abusive speech is not characteristic of "Roman authorities" holding official examinations (as Reicke 1964, 108 imagines) but of the informal means employed by one group to shame and discredit others in the court of public opinion. Neither here nor in the parallel statements of 2:12 and 4:14 (reproach, malignment of character and name) does 1 Peter indicate anything other than the insults and shaming strategies of the crowd. The implication of shame is further explicated by the accompanying reference to the denigrators themselves being *put to shame* (v 16d). Along with the absence in 1 Peter of any explicit mention of formal legal proceedings against the Christians, these numerous references to verbal abuse paint a consistent picture of the type of opposition and oppression encountered by the Asia Minor believers: suspicion, slander, and insult designed to demean and discredit persons perceived as different, deviant, and potentially dangerous to the common good. This evidence again argues decisively against any theory of formal trials or official Roman "persecution" as the situation envisioned in 1 Peter.

your good conduct in Christ (*hymōn tēn agathēn en Christōi anastrophēn*). The phrase echoes the previous formulations of 2:12 ("your honorable conduct" [*tēn anastrophēn hymōn . . . kalēn*]) and 3:2 ("your reverent and chaste conduct [*tēn en phobōi hagnēn anastrophēn*]), referring, respectively, to the conduct of all believers and that of the wives in particular. In its more proximate context, *good conduct* captures the sense of being "zealots for what is

---

[245] Cf. also variant MS readings of Matt 5:44a and 44b.

right" (v 13a) and "doing what is right (3:11a, 14a, 17a). Here, as in v 14 and v 17 (as also in 4:2–4), the believers' "good conduct" and "doing what is right" are the object of disparagement leading to suffering. On *anastrophē*, see also the NOTES on 1:15b and 2:12a.

in Christ (*en Christōi*). This added qualification now makes it clear that the "good behavior" of the believers is a result not only of their devotion to God but also of their allegiance to Jesus Christ, a point that prepares for the Christological statement that follows (vv 18–22). It is possible that Paul, who frequently employs this expression[246] to circumscribe the entire Christian life in unity with Christ, introduced it into Christian parlance (cf. also "those of Christ," 1 Cor 15:23; Gal 5:24). It is likely, however, as K. Berger (1971, 403–8) has shown, that Paul was Christianizing antecedent Israelite formulas, such as "in the law"[247] or "in God,"[248] which describe the community identified and bound by the upright obedience to God's will. Whereas Paul, however, often expands on the ecclesial implications of being "in Christ," the Petrine author does not. He instead employs it in unelaborated fashion as a stock phrase (here and in 5:10 and 5:14) signaling the communal Christian identity of the believers: the righteous who are "in Christ," those embedded in the story and destiny of Jesus Christ. Thus the phrase functions like the name "Christian" (*christianos*, 4:16), though "in Christ" represents a *self-designation* of the believing community, whereas "Christian" is a label originating with *outsiders* (see the NOTE on 4:16a).

Evidence from the following centuries indicates that good Christian conduct was often slandered and maligned: the nocturnal Christian worship assemblings were decried as occasions for orgies; the love of Christian brothers and sisters for one another was maligned as incest; baptism as a ritual of death and rebirth was decried as murder; the Eucharist was criticized as cannibalism; and Christians continued to be slandered as "wrongdoers" and enemies of the common good, (see, e.g., Tert., *Apol.*, *Nat.*; Min. Fel., *Oct.*; Origen, *Cels*).

may be put to shame (*kataischynthōsin*). Those who persist in shaming the Christians and disparaging their honorable behavior will themselves be put to shame. The verb *kataischynō* (here an aor. pass. subj. within a purpose clause, "be put to shame, be shamed") could refer to an immediate social shaming of those whose unjustifed denigrations of the believers are exposed as false and groundless and thereby silenced (see 2:15; cf. also Titus 2:8). It is more likely, however, that the verb serves as a divine passive similar to its use in 2:6 and therefore, like 2:6, as a reference to the *divine shaming* of the nonbelievers at the final judgment; for a similar point, see also 2:7–8; 4:5; and 4:18. This eschatological sense is also favored by 3:12. In the honor-and-shame culture of the

---

[246] E.g., Rom 9:1; 12:5; 1 Cor 3:1; 4:10, 15; 15:18, 19; 2 Cor 5:17, 19; Phil 2:1; etc.

[247] See Ezra 10:3; Sir 9:15; Ps.-Philo, *L.A.B.* 9:13, 19; 30:4; *T. Jud.* 23:5; 24:3; *T. Naph.* 2:6.

[248] See 2 Kdgms 22:30; Ps 17[18]:30; Ps.-Philo, *L.A.B.* 6:9; *T. Naph.* 8:10; cf. 1 Thess 1:1; Jude 1:1.

biblical world, shaming as well as honoring actions are ascribed also to God (Elliott 1995a). To be "shamed" or "put to shame" by God (as also in 2:6d) is to experience the ultimate in censure and degradation for acting contrary to God's will and oppressing God's people, with its consequence of condemnation and lasting death at the final judgment.[249] For this sense of divine shaming in the NT, see Mark 8:38/Luke 9:26; Rom 9:33 and 1 Pet 2:6 (citing Isa 28:16); Phil 1:20; 1 John 2:28.

This divine shaming of nonbelievers was already stressed in 2:6–8, and in the light of references to divine judgment in 1:17; 4:5; and 4:17–18 probably also implies here the final condemnation of those who persist in rejecting the Christ and oppressing his followers. Just as faith in Jesus Christ as God's elect results in honor and glory (2:4–7a), so disobedience and reproach of those in Christ results in shame and punishment at the final reckoning. The thought thus further underlines the concept of an eventual "turning of the tables" (Danker 1980, 149), when those who presently shame the Christians will themselves be put to shame. The relation between 3:15 and 4:5, as has been noted, expresses the same idea: those who once required an account of believers will themselves be called to account by God. The eventual fate of the nonbelievers is thus left an open question in the letter and made dependent on their response to Christ and his followers. Joining Christians in their honoring of God will result in life; persistence in rejecting Christ and disparaging his followers will result in divine shaming and eternal condemnation.

17. This unit on suffering for doing what is right is now brought to a close with a maxim affirming the superiority of suffering for doing what is right over suffering for doing what is wrong. It thus applies a similar principle underlying the exhortation of slaves (2:18–20) to the entire community. Some scholars[250] take v 17 with vv 18–22 as the first of three coordinated arguments for the instruction of vv 13–16, but this is highly unlikely. The conjunction *gar* ("for") here, as elsewhere (2:20, 25; 4:6), introduces a statement that *concludes* the unit. The verb *agathopoieō* relates to kindred terms in vv 13, 14, and 16 but does not reappear in vv 18–22. Rather, with the other terms of v 17 and v 13–14 it forms an inclusion framing vv 13–17. Thus, the exhortatory unit 3:13–17, supported by the following Christological substantiation (vv 18–22), replicates the pattern evident in 2:18–20 supported by 2:21–25.

---

[249] See Ps 6:11 ("Let all my enemies be put to shame [*aischyntheiēsan*] and troubled; let them be turned back and severely be put to shame [*kataischyntheiēsan*]"); Ps 70[71]:13 ("May my accusers be put to shame and consumed; with scorn and disgrace may they be covered"); Jer 17:18 ("Let those who persecute me be put to shame . . . bring upon them the day of evil; destroy them with double destruction!"); and further, Ps 21:6[22:5]; 24[25]:2, 3, 20; 30:2, 18[31:1, 17]; 33[34]:6; 36[37]:19; 39:15[40:14]; 43:8[44:7]; 52:6[53:5]; 69:3, 4[70:2, 3]; 70[71]:1, 24; 82:18[83:17]; 126[127]:5; Isa 28:16.

[250] E.g., Reicke 1964, 128–30, 211–19; Cervantes Gabarrón 1991, 181.

17a. *For it is better to suffer for doing what is right* (*kreitton gar agathopiountes . . . paschein*). "For" (*gar*) links this concluding statement with the foregoing. The adverb *kreitton* ("better," the comparative of *agathos*, with "it is" implied; cf. 1 Cor 7:9; 2 Pet 2:21), together with *ē* ("than") in v 17c, forms a proverb-like statement comparing two different reasons for suffering. In its formal characteristics, the formulation is similar to other "better-than" axiomatic statements appearing in the NT (see Snyder 1977; K. Berger 1984b, 1064).[251] Here in 1 Peter it is the superiority of suffering for doing what is right over suffering for doing what is wrong that this comparison stresses, a point made earlier in 2:19–20 and later in 4:14–16.

to suffer for doing what is right (*agathopoiountas . . . paschein*). The infinitive *paschein* ("to suffer") is a substantival infinitive functioning as the subject of an implied "is" and governs the participles "doing what is right" (*agathopoiountas*) and "doing what is wrong" (*kakopoiountas*). In the Greek text, however, the first participle is separated from its controlling verb by the intervening clause "if this should be God's will." The participle *agathopoiountas*, like its parallel *kakopoiountas*, is an accusative plural agreeing with the implied plural subject "you" associated with the infinitive: "it is better for *you* to suffer for doing what is right. . . ." The Greek text does not make it explicit that suffering is specifically *for* doing what is right, but this causal sense is implied by the context; see v 14: "suffering for (*dia*, "on account of") doing what is right." *Doing what is right* and *if it should be God's will* also correspond in sense to "mindfulness of God's will" (v 16b) and "your good conduct in Christ" (v 16d), as well as to the points of 3:9 and 3:10–12. The accent on *doing what is right*, here as elsewhere (2:18–20; 3:6, 11; 4:19), brings the unit to a close. Balancing "zealots for what is right" (v 13) and "doing what is right" (v 14), it forms part of the inclusion framing vv 13–17 as a whole, (cf. also "suffer" [vv 14, 17] and *kakopoiountas* [v 17] / *kakōsan* [v 13]).

17b. *if this should be God's will* (*ei theloi to thelēma tou theou*). This conditional clause, interjected between the two parts of the comparison proper (vv 17a, 17c), involves a second optative verb (*theloi*; cf. *paschoite*, v 14a) and a pleonastic formulation—literally, "if the will of God should will it," namely, suffering for doing what is right. As observed in the NOTE on v 14, the classical optative rarely occurs in the common dialect Greek of the NT. Like the alliteration formed by the juxtaposition of the Greek terms *theloi, thelēma, theou,* it is a mark of the author's literary refinement and his sensitivity for mood. Here, as in the qualifying formulation of 1:6 ("if it must be," *ei deon*), Christian suffering is viewed in relation to the will of God. In 1:6, as in 4:12, moreover, suffering is interpreted as a means of the divine testing (*peirasmos*) of faith and

---

[251] The features of such comparisons, Snyder notes, include their introduction by *kreitton* ("better"), with "it is" implied, as in 1 Peter (cf. 1 Cor 7:9; 2 Pet 2:21), or an equivalent (e.g., *sympherei* ["it is profitable," Matt 5:29, 30] or *kalon* ["it is good," Mark 9:42, 43, 45, 47]); present tenses; an exaggeration of some kind in their protasis; *ē* or *kaimē* as the connective particle; and often in their *apodosis* a moral or religious admonition that can have an eschatological overtone.

fidelity. In the present context the author twice makes it clear (vv 14, 17) that God's will involves not suffering for suffering's sake but suffering for doing what is right. It is *innocent* suffering for doing what is right, as modeled by Christ himself (2:21–24; 3:18; 4:1) in obedience to the Father's will,[252] that has God's approval (2:20) and that ultimately will be vindicated by God (5:10), as Christ himself was vindicated (3:18–22).

17c. *than for doing what is wrong* (*ē kakopoiountas*). *Doing what is right* is contrasted with *doing what is wrong*; for related antitheses, see 2:14–16, 19–20, 3:11. The contrast appears in the LXX [253] as well as in the NT.[254] The related noun *kakopoios* ("wrongdoer") has already been employed in 2:12 and 2:14 and appears again in the contrasts in 4:14–16 (see the respective NOTES).

The principle expressed in the "better-than" parts of this verse is reminiscent of earlier moral sentiment; see, for example, Cicero's dictum (*Tusc.* 5.56), "It is better to accept injustice than to do injustice," or that of Socrates, "To act unjustly is worse, insofar as it is more disgraceful, than to be treated unjustly" (Plato, *Gorg.* 508b). Our author, however, speaks specifically of "suffering" and puts this principle into both a theological (God's will) and a Christological (vv 15, 16 and 3:18–22) perspective.

This theologically modified principle underlies the instruction of this unit as a whole. It is Reicke's misconstruing of the situation that leads him to see in this verse a warning that believers are not to seek "the glory of martyrdom through stubborn opposition to the power of the state" (Reicke 1964, 108). The issue is rather the problem of suffering for doing what is right in everyday interaction with nonbelievers, with no mention of "martyrdom" or "opposition to the power of the state." The qualification, *if this should be God's will*, refers to suffering *for doing what is right* and not simply suffering per se. The point is not that God wills suffering but that *God wills doing what is right* rather than doing what is wrong (see 2:15–16, 19–20; 3:11–12; 4:2, 19), even if and when this results in suffering. This sense of v 17 is made clear by the parallel expression of v 14 and by the accented location and contrast of the chief terms *doing what is right—doing what is wrong*, echoing the similar contrast of 3:11a. Viewed in the light of the missionary goal emphasized in 2:12 and 3:1–2, it is only innocent suffering for doing what is right that constitutes exceptional moral behavior that could conceivably attract detractors to the Christian faith, should they not persist in their slander. "Such patient endurance is *better* because, being so unexpected to unbelievers and so unnatural in their view, it constitutes a convincing witness to the power of the gospel to transform and empower human lives" (Hillyer 1992, 110).

---

[252] See also Mark 14:36, 39/Matt 26:38, 42/Luke 22:42–44.

[253] See Lev 5:4; Judg 19:23–24; Jer 4:22; 10:5.

[254] See Mark 3:4/Luke 6:93; note esp. 3 John 11: "Beloved, do not imitate what is wrong (*to kakon*) but rather what is right (*to agathon*). He who does what is right (*ho agathopoiōn*) is of God; he who does what is wrong (*ho kakopoiōn*) has not seen God."

This verse is similar to the statement of 2:20 in structure, content, and sense. Both contrast *doing what is wrong* with *doing what is right*; both speak of suffering for doing what is right; both refer to God's approval (2:20) or will (3:17); both statements are followed and supported by appeals to the action of Christ introduced by the words *hoti kai Christos*; and both underline the preference for suffering for doing what is right over suffering for doing what is wrong, a point made again in 4:14–16. Michaels (1966–1967; 1988, 191–92, following Gschwind 1911, 104–10) argues for an eschatological sense here: it is better to suffer now for doing what is right than to suffer at the final judgment for doing wrong (i.e., betraying the Christian cause; so also Best 1971, 135). In the light of v 16 (God's shaming of disparagers) and the wider context (3:9e, 10–12; 4:5–6, 17–19), this eschatological overtone is possible but not certain. *Doing what is right* summarizes the behavior urged in vv 13–16. Within this context, the statement of v 17 is focused more on present action than on its future consequences. It represents a continued accentuation on the larger theme of doing what is right, now in the face of suffering. With vv 13–14 it forms an inclusion framing and expressing the key thought of this entire unit (3:13–17).

Attributing a positive value to suffering for doing what is right, however, calls for some justification, as Reichert (1989, 198) notes, and this is provided by the Christological statement that follows (3:18–22).

GENERAL COMMENT

Doing what is right in contrast to doing what is wrong remains the focus of attention in this pericope, which also reprises other leading themes in the foregoing exhortation. Now the possibility of *suffering* for such upright behavior (cf. 2:19–20; 3:9) is more fully addressed. Undeserved suffering could lead to discouragement, despair, and even defection from the Christian community. Therefore, in continuity with Israel's teaching concerning the divine protection of the suffering righteous, the author assures his readers that even in the face of unjust suffering no harm can ultimately befall those who remain faithful to God's will. Indeed, innocent suffering for upright conduct is honorable in the sight of God, as Jesus had already assured his followers. Consequently, the beleaguered believers have no cause to fear (cf. 3:6), but should rather sanctify and honor the Lord Christ in their hearts. This internal attitude (cf. 3:4), moreover, is to be reflected in a readiness to respond to any who seek an explanation of their remarkable hope, with gentleness, reverence for God, and mindfulness of God's will. On the whole, the conduct that is to characterize the entire community in general is identical to that required earlier of wives (3:1–6) and domestic slaves (2:18–20) in particular. Here again it becomes clear that wives and domestic slaves are paradigmatic for the community as a whole.

Despite their upright and honorable conduct, the Christians may nevertheless be exposed to attempts to slander, malign, and publicly shame them, as the author had noted earlier (2:12). But God who honors them will ultimately turn the tables and put persistent detractors themselves to shame. The envisioned situation involves not formal accusations or legal proceedings before Roman officials or local magistrates, but the general climate of popular hostility to the Christians as strangers, curiosity about their hope, and the malicious intent of outsiders to demean, discredit, and disparage them. The addressees nevertheless are urged to persist now in doing what is right, even in the face of slander and suffering, for in actuality they are under God's protection and subject to his will, with the implication that their innocent suffering will indeed be vindicated. The primary model for this behavior and the surety of the vindication of those "in Christ" are the conduct and experience of their suffering and resurrected Lord, the point of the following pericope, vv 18–22.

For studies of 1 Pet 3:13–17, see Caviglia 1981; Dalton 1970; K. C. Hanson 1996; Hofius 1975; Johnston 1961; Kloppenborg 1986; Knox 1953; Lumby 1890; Michaels 1966–1967; Mildenberger 1979; Millauer 1976; Ogara 1937; Omanson 1982; Peeters 1986; Reichert 1989, 179–99; Reicke 1946; Schweizer 1868; Steuer 1938; Talbert 1991.

IV. B. Christ, the Suffering Righteous One: His Suffering, Death, and Resurrection as the Basis of Believers' Salvation and Vindication (3:18–22)

18a Because Christ also suffered for sins once for all,
18b a righteous one for unrighteous ones,
18c so that he might bring you to God.
18d Having been put to death in the flesh,
18e having been made alive, however, in the spirit,
19a having gone in this connection also to the spirits in prison,
19b, 20a he announced to these [spirits] who once disobeyed
20b when God's patience waited in the days of Noah,
20c during the building of the ark,
20d in which a few
20e —that is, eight persons—
20f were saved through water.
21a Corresponding to this, baptism now saves you too
21b —not [as] a removal of filth from the body
21c but [as] a pledge to God of a sound mindfulness of God's will—
21d through the resurrection of Jesus Christ,
22a who is at the right [hand] of God,
22b having gone into heaven,
22c with angels and authorities and powers subordinated to him.

INTRODUCTION

To strengthen the resolve of addressees who suffer for doing what is right (3:13–17), the author again recalls the suffering of their innocent Lord (cf. 2:21–25) and shifts from imperative to indicative mood. The pattern of exhortation followed by Christological substantiation repeats that of 2:18–20/21–25, except that 3:13–17 concerns not one particular group (slaves) but the entire community. Furthermore, the experience of Christ recounted here involves not only his innocent and vicarious suffering and death (v 18ab, d) but also the divine vindication of his suffering and death; namely, his resurrection, ascension, and exaltation at God's right hand (vv 18e, 21d, 22), which demonstrates his ability to bring believers to God (v 18c). His ultimate exaltation and glorification at God's right hand is the surety of their vindication as well.

These verses are joined with 3:13–17 syntactically (causal conjunction *hoti* ["because"] and the connective *kai* ["also"]), terminologically, and thematically: the *innocent suffering* of Christ (v 18a) is a model for that of the believers (vv 14a, 17a); his righteousness (*dikaios*, v 18) is a paradigm for theirs (*dikaiosynē*, v 14a; cf. 3:12a). Further links include "mindfulness of God" (*syneidēsis*, vv 21c and v 16c) and the subjects *Christ* (vv 18a, 21d; cf. vv 15a, 16d), *God* (vv 18c, 20b, 21c, 22a; cf. v 17b), and *you* (vv 18c, 21a; cf. vv 13–16). At the same time, the indicative mood of these verses, the double mention of *Christ* (v 18a, 21d–22) and *God* (vv 18c, 22a) forming an inclusion that frames this unit, and its predominantly Christological focus and function distinguish this pericope from the exhortation that precedes (3:13–17) and follows (4:1–6) it.

A further distinguishing feature of this unit is its merger of early Israelite and Christian traditions to form a statement without parallel in the NT. Between the related traditional formulas of v 18e and v 22, which affirm Christ's resurrection (v 18e), journey to heaven (v 22b), and exalted position at God's right hand (v 22a) over the cosmic powers (v 22c), is a series of interrelated thoughts comparing Christian baptism (as the saving event through which believers share in the resurrection of Christ) with the event of the primordial Flood, the disobedient spirits whose evil brought it on, and Noah and his family whose salvation through water prefigured that of the Christian believers.

This complex passage has long challenged scholars and poses a host of questions concerning the syntax and structure of these verses, their sources and conceptual background, their coherence and meaning, their relation to 4:1–6, their rhetorical function, and their relation to the concept of Christ's "descent into hell," despite the fact that neither "descent" nor "hell" is mentioned here.[255]

As most translations and commentators indicate, our passage begins with v 18, not v 17 (against Cervantes Gabbarón 1991a, 181–252 and a few others). 1 Peter 3:17 forms part of an inclusion framing 3:13–17. 1 Peter 3:18–22, like 2:21–25 in relation to 2:18–20, opens with a reference to Christ and provides

---

[255] On the history of the diverse interpretations of these verses, see Holzmeister 1937, 306–51; Selwyn 1947, 314–62; Reicke 1946, 7–51; Brox 1986, 182–89; Dalton 1989, 25–66.

a Christological basis for the foregoing call for doing what is right despite suffering. 1 Peter 3:18, moreover, has the same structure as 2:21; compare 3:18a and 2:21b; 3:18b and 2:21c; 3:18c and 2:21d; as well as the modifying phrases or clauses of 3:18d, e, f, 22 and 2:22, 23, 24. The structure of 3:19–22 involves a series of subordinate clauses or qualifying phrases similar to those in 1:3–12 and 1:17–21.

Differing explanations have been offered for the connection of 3:18–22 to what goes before. Reicke's claim (1946, 118–25, 211–19; 1964, 11) that 3:18–22 was intended to support 3:14–15 (which call for a "fearless" witness to nonbelievers) by indicating that Christ too "announced good news" (3:19) is unconvincing, for it ignores the fact that it is "suffering" that explicitly links these units and arbitrarily regards "announce" (*ekēryxen*) as proclamation of "good news." Spitta (1890, 8–10) and Gschwind (1911) see 3:18–22 as providing Christological support *only* for the truth of 3:17, adding that the "disobedient spirits" (vv 19–20) are possibly an example of those who "do what is wrong." In fact, however, as the numerous affinities between 3:18–22 and 3:13–17 indicated above make clear, 3:18–22 rather provides a Christological support for the *entirety* of 3:13–17, similar to the function of 2:21–25 in relation to 2:18–20 (so also Dalton 1989, 101).[256]

NOTES

18a. *Because Christ also suffered for sins once for all* (*hoti kai Christos hapax peri hamartiōn epathen*). A Christological motivation (vv 18–22), once again introduced with the causal conjunction *hoti* ("because," "for"; cf. 2:21b), provides support for the foregoing exhortation concerning doing what is right despite suffering. The conjunction "also" (*kai*, omitted in $\mathfrak{P}^{72}$), as in 2:21a, links this statement with the foregoing. The variant of an articular noun ("the Christ," $\mathfrak{P}^{72}$ and a few other witnesses) was perhaps influenced by the articular formulation of 3:15a.

Verses 18–22 support not simply the "better" course of action mentioned in 3:17 alone, since in these verses Christ himself is not said or implied to have faced such an alternative; they rather provide a Christological basis for the entire exhortation of 3:13–17. The initial four words, "because Christ also suffered" (*hoti kai Christos . . . epathen*), are identical to those of 2:21b, and their contexts also have further points in common. Both involve Christological statements linking the suffering of believers with the suffering of Christ (2:21–25 in support of 2:18–20 and 3:18–22 in support of 3:13–17). Both refer to Christ as the supreme example of innocent suffering for doing what is right (v 18ab and 4:1; cf. 2:21–23). Both also stress the vicarious ("for unrighteous ones," v 18ab; cf. 2:21, "for you") and atoning ("for sins," v 18a; cf. "he himself bore our sins,"

[256] On 3:13–17, 18–22, see also Reichert 1989, 96–143, 179–354; the convoluted interpretation of Vogels (1976, 34–44), on the other hand, has been effectively critiqued by Dalton 1977.

2:24a) nature of Christ's suffering. And both include a statement of the intended result of this vicarious suffering (*hina . . . theōi*, v 18c; cf. *hina . . . zēsōmen*, 2:24b) and of its saving consequences (*nyn sōizei*, v 21a; cf. *hou . . . iathēte*, 2:24d) as a basis for Christian conduct. At the same time, 3:18–22 goes further in its emphasis on (1) the once-for-all nature of Christ's suffering (v 18a); (2) the cosmic scope of Christ's action (vv 19–22); and (3) the divine vindication of Christ's suffering—his resurrection, ascension to heaven, and presence at God's right hand with power over the cosmic forces and the link of these events with baptism (vv 21–22). Thus, Christ is presented here not simply as an example but as one who through his exaltation and superiority over the cosmic powers assures Christians of their union with God (v 18c), their salvation (v 21), and thereby their ability to bear the suffering that might confront them.

Here, as in 2:21, there are also a number of further textual variants to the preferred reading "suffered for sins" (*peri hamartiōn epathen*, 𝔓[72] B P 𝔐). These include: "died for sins on our (your) behalf" (*peri hamartiōn hyper hēmōn* [*hymōn*, 𝔓[72] A 1241, 2495] *apethanen*, 𝔓[72] ℵ A C[2] L 33614, 630, 945, 1241, 1739 syr[h] bo [81 and a few others: "suffered"]); "died for you for sin" (*peri hymōn hyper hamartias apethanen*, Ψ); "died for sins" (*peri hamartiōn apethanen*, vg[st] Cyp?); "died for our sin" (*peri hamartias hēmōn apethanen*, C* a few others vg[cl] syr[p] Aug). These variants, some of them conflated, reflect a substitution of the more traditional formulation ("he died") for the less customary ("he suffered"; see also the NOTE on 2:21b).

Although the use of *paschō* with the sense of "die" is known since Plato (*Ax*. 369; cf. also Luke 24:46; Ign. *Smyrn*. 2:1b; *Barn*. 7:11), *epathen* here has the sense of "suffered" and, as in 2:21b, is preferred to the variant *apethanen* ("died," which occurs nowhere else in 1 Peter). The point of comparison ("Christ *also* suffered") here in the context of 3:13–17 and throughout the letter is not a common experience of dying–no mention is made of Christians' "dying"—but of *unjust suffering*.[257] This theme of suffering, moreover, is resumed in 4:1. The thought thus reflects early Christian affirmation of the vicarious death of Christ,[258] which the Petrine author has modified here and in 2:21 by replacing "died" with "suffered" in accord with his thematic emphasis upon the innocent *suffering* that unites Christ and his followers.

The expression "suffered for sins" (*peri hamartiōn epathen*) is unique in the NT but is close to the formulation of 2:21b, "Christ suffered for you" (*Christos epathen hyper hymōn*).[259] In both instances it is in his innocent suffering for doing what is is right that Christ serves as a model ("Christ also suffered . . .") for the innocent suffering believers (3:14, 16, 17; cf. 2:19–20).

---

[257] See 2:19, 20, 21, 23; 3:14, 17; 4:1, 13, 15, 16, 19; 5:1, 9, 10; cf. also 1:6; 2:24.

[258] See Rom 4:25; 5:6–8; 1 Cor 15:3; 2 Cor 5:14–15; Gal 1:4; 2:21; 1 Thess 5:10; Heb 10:12; 1 John 2:2.

[259] For the interchange of *peri* and *hyper* with *hamartia*, see Ezek 43:21 and 22, 25. See also the NOTES on 2:21a and 2:24a and the accompanying DETAILED COMMENT.

The phrase *peri hamartiōn* is used for a sacrifice for sins (Heb 5:1, 3; 7:27; 10:18, 26; 1 John 2:2; 4:10), as is the related phrase *peri hamartias* regarding a propitiatory sin-offering (Lev 5:6, 7; 6:30; Ezek 43:21). In Isa 53, which provided much of the language for 2:21–25, it is the suffering servant who is described as bearing the sins of the people (53:11), and this thought may well have inspired the formulation here. The phrase serves to stress again both the redemptive nature of Christ's suffering (cf. 1:2, 18–19; 2:24a, d) and its vicarious character. Here *peri* occurs in conjunction with the sins atoned for (cf. 1 Cor 15:3), while *hyper* is used of the persons benefited (v 18b; cf. 2:21b; Mark 14:24; Luke 22:19, 20; John 15:13; and the texts listed below regarding v 18b).

once for all (*hapax*). This further qualification of *suffered*—namely, "once for all time" (Heb 9:26, 28; cf. 9:12; 10:10) or "once only" (cf. *ephapax*, Rom 6:9–10, with reference to Christ's death)—expresses the singular, comprehensive, and conclusive aspect of Christ's suffering. Along with the formulations "for sins" and "for unrighteous ones," it also underlines the uniqueness of Christ's atoning suffering in contrast to the suffering of others.

18b. *a righteous one for unrighteous ones* (*dikaios hyper adikōn*). This pregnant phrase parallels and expands upon v 18a. Again our author emphasizes that the suffering of the innocent Christ is not only paradigmatic but vicarious and atoning in nature (v 18a; 2:21b, 24). Omitted in one manuscript (044), perhaps due to haplography but otherwise attested unanimously, it contains two anarthrous adjectives functioning as substantives.

The substantive *dikaios* ("righteous one" or "just one"), one who is obedient to God's will, recalls the earlier Christological statement of 2:21–25, which was seen to be reliant on the portrait of the Suffering Servant of Isaiah (Isa 53), identified as the "righteous one" (*dikaios*, Isa 53:11). This concept of the suffering righteous one, as noted there, belonged to a broader Israelite tradition, eventually assumed messianic import (Wis 2:18; *1 En*. 38:2, 3; 53:6 ["the Righteous and Elect One"]), and was subsequently applied as a messianic designation to Jesus by his followers.[260] The term also expresses the innocence of Christ as recognized by outsiders (Luke 23:47; cf. Matt 27:19; Mark 15:14; Luke 23:4, 14, 22; John 19:4, 6) and is related to the notion of his sinlessness as well (cf. 2 Cor 5:21; Heb 4:15; 1 John 3:5).[261]

In line with this traditional concept of the just or righteous one, "righteous one" identifies Christ as the innocent (1:19; 2:22) and obedient (1:2c) one, who does what is right in accord with God's will. In his steadfast uprightness as well as his suffering, Christ serves as the model for those also called to be

---

[260] See Acts 3:14 (by Peter); Acts 7:52 (by Stephen); Acts 22:14 (by Paul); cf. also Jas 5:6; 1 John 2:1, 29; 3:7; *Diogn*. 9:2; Just. Mart., *Dial*. 17; and Melito, *Peri Pasch*. 94: "the unjust murder of the just."

[261] On the theme and tradition of the "suffering righteous or just one" with respect to Jesus and his passion, see Ruppert 1972a, 1972b, 1973; Lohse 1963, 64–110; Kleinknecht 1984, 177–92; de Jonge 1988; and the NOTES on 2:22–24.

righteous (2:24; 3:12, 14; 4:18) and to do what is right (*agathopoiein*, 2:15, 20; 3:6, 17; *agathopoiia*, 4:19). With this term is forged yet another conceptual link between Christ and the believers and a further literary link between vv 18–22 and 3:13–17.

for unrighteous ones (*hyper adikōn*). The phrase reiterates the vicarious and atoning effect of Christ's suffering while also contrasting the innocence of Christ with the unrighteousness of those for whom he has suffered and died (*dikaios-adikōn*). The term *unrighteous* covers all humans acting contrary to what is right or consonant with the will of God.[262] A related contrast occurs in 4:18, where the citation of LXX Prov 11:31 sets the "impious" and the "sinner" over against the "just/righteous person"; for the juxtaposition of *dikaios-adikoi*, see Matt 5:45; Acts 24:15. The preposition *hyper* ("for," "on behalf of," "for the sake of") occurs here, in 2:21b, and regularly in Christian kerygmatic formulas to express Christ's substitutionary atonement *for* or "on behalf of" others.[263]

In its entirety, the phrase is unique in the Bible but constitutes a succinct description of Christ who, like the righteous suffering servant of Isaiah (53:11; cf. 2:21–25), lived in fidelity to God's will but also suffered on behalf of the unrighteous.[264] It likewise reflects in its conceptuality the notion of Israelite martyr theology that "the martyrs represent Israel with their lives and through their death divert the wrath of God from the people" (Lohse 1963, 67–68).[265] While this Christological formulation of v 18a and 18b serves to support the exhortation of 3:13–17, it also, as in 2: 21–24, distinguishes Christ as the one who removes sin and thereby enables upright behavior (2:21–25; 3:8–12, 13–17; 4:1).

18c. *so that he might bring you to God* (*hina hymas prosagagēi tōi theōi*). A *hina* clause, similar to that of 2:21d (following 2:21bc) and 2:24bc (following 2:24a), brings this first line of thought to a conclusion by succinctly expressing the intended result or consequence of Christ's innocent vicarious suffering: to bring believers into God's presence. The reading "you" (*hymas*, $\mathfrak{P}^{72}$ B P Ψ 𝔐 z vg^{mss} syr) is preferred to the variant "us" (*hēmas*, $\aleph^{2}$ A C K L etc. vg syr^{hmg} Cyprian Cyril), since the former is consistent with the focus on "you" in v 21 and the surrounding context (3:13–17; 4:1–6). Once again the author stresses here the "for-you-ness" of the gospel (cf. 1:12, 20–21).

---

[262] See Philo, *Abr.* 33; Josephus, *J.W.* 2.139; 5.407; Matt 5:45; Acts 24:15; 1 Cor 6:9; Herm. *Mand.* 6.1.1–2; *Diogn.* 9:2.

[263] See Rom 5:6 (*hyper asebōn apethanen*) and 5:7 ("for one will hardly die for a righteous person" [*hyper dikaiou*]), 5:8 (*hyper hēmōn apethanen*); cf. also Rom 14:15; 1 Cor 11:24; 15:3; 2 Cor 5:15, 21; Gal 2:20; 3:13; Eph 5:25; 1 Thess 5:10; Titus 2:14; John 11:50, 52; and the NOTE on 2:21b.

[264] Note its incorporation in the later *Letter to Diognetus* (9:2): "He [God] gave his own son as a ransom for us (*hyper hēmōn*), the holy for the lawless (*ton hagion hyper anomōn*), the innocent for the guilty (*ton akakon hyper tōn kakōn*), the righteous for the unrighteous (*ton dikaion hyper tōn adikōn*), the incorruptible for the corruptible (*ton aphtharton hyper tōn phthartōn*), the immortal for the mortal (*ton athanaton hyper tōn thnētōn*). For what else could cover our sin but his uprightness (*dikaiosynē*)?"

[265] On the atoning power of suffering and death in postexilic Israel, see also the NOTE on 4:1.

The verb *prosagō* (here a subjunctive with *hina*) occurs only occasionally in the NT (Matt 18:24; Luke 9:41; Acts 12:6; 16:20; 27:27) and has a variety of meanings: "lead" or "bring to"; "provide persons access to another person"; "bring before a tribunal or present before a royal court" (Classical Greek and LXX); "bring" sacrifice before God (Exod 29:10; Lev 1:2); "bring" persons before God to be consecrated for cultic service (Exod 29:4, 8; 40:12; Lev 8:24; Num 8:9–10). Dalton (1989, 135), recalling the earlier designation of the believers as a "holy priestly community" (2:5, 9), sees in *prosagagēi* a possible "implict reference to the consecration of the Christian priesthood." The thrust of this verse and its context, however, is soteriological rather than ecclesiological, and the idea of priesthood is nowhere evident. There is, moreover, a different correspondence between this verb and 2:4–10, which Dalton fails to mention. The verb *prosagō* appears in the covenantal formula of Exod 19:3–6, from which the terms of 2:9 (and 2:5) derive. God declares: "You have seen what I did to the Egyptians, and how I bore you on eagles' wings and brought you to myself" (*prosēgagomēn hymas pros emautōn*, Exod 19:4). The expression describes God's saving act, and it is likely that *prosagagēi* in 3:18 and its context has this same soteriological implication (Cervantes Gabarrón 1991a, 232).[266] The kindred noun *prosagōgē* is used similarly to denote "access to" and union with God.[267] The Petrine expression thus indicates that the goal of Christ's vicarious suffering as the righteous one is to bring or lead believers to God; for similar expressions, see Heb 10:19–20 and 6:19–20; 7:25. As vv 19–22 will make clear, because the resurrected Christ himself has entered heaven and is at God's right hand, he is able to lead others into God's presence. Baptism, through Christ's resurrection, now saves (3:21) believers by uniting them with God and setting them on the course of salvation.

to God (*tōi theōi*). This fuller reading has weightier manuscript support (𝔓[72] A P 𝔐 lat syr) than the omission of the phrase in Codex Vaticanus or the variant "to the father" (a few MSS). For the dative with *prosagō*, see also Gen 27:25; 1 Kgdms 15:32; 2 Chr 35:12; Prov 24:15; Sir 14:11; 45:16; 2 Macc 14:4.

While the thought as a whole is close to other NT formulations, it does not derive from any fixed formula. It is, rather, one of three Petrine statements declaring an intended result of Christ's vicarious suffering, in this case the union of believers with God, the ultimate goal of salvation according to 1 Peter. The same is true of all of the content of v 18 examined to this point. The thoughts echo Christian tradition, but the formulations are specifically those of the Petrine author.

---

[266] Against the cultic sense of this verb here, see also Selwyn 1947, 196; Michaels 1988, 203; and Goppelt 1993, 252.

[267] See Rom 5:2 ("through him [Christ] we have obtained access to this grace in which we stand"); Eph 2:18 (persons once alienated from God and persons once near both "have access in one Spirit to the Father"); and Eph 3:12 ("in whom [Christ Jesus our Lord] we have boldness and confidence of access through our faith in him").

The function of the verses that follow (vv 18d–22) is to show that Christ's bringing the believers to God is a consequence of his own death, resurrection, and ascension to God's right hand, an event in which believers participate through baptism.

Verse 18de, the first element of this explanation, consists of a pair of parallel phrases asserting Christ's death and resurrection:

thanatōtheis men sarki	Having been put to death in the flesh,
zōiopoiētheis de pneumati	having been made alive, however, in the spirit

The couplet contains two parallel aorist participles but no finite verb. Although *Christ* (v 18a) is the implied subject of both participles, the phrases are juxtaposed asyndetically and also lack any particle specifically linking this couplet with v 18c. In form and content the couplet is actually more closely related with what follows. The two aorist participial phrases are followed by and linked with a third aorist participle, "having gone . . ." (v 19a). The actions of death, resurrection, and ascension are logically related, and "having been made alive" is echoed in "resurrection of Jesus Christ" in v 21d. Accordingly, it appears that vv 18de–22, and in particular the fact of Christ's resurrection, ascension, and presence with God (vv 18d, 19a, 21d, 22), are designed to provide a unified and fitting explanation of v 18c. Christ can lead believers to God because after his death he himself was made alive by God and ascended to God's right hand. More on the relation of this couplet to vv 19 and 22 will follow below.

The couplet itself is unique in the NT. Nowhere else do these phrases occur either independently or in combination, nor are the verbs alone joined elsewhere. Nevertheless, its articulation of the very center of the early Christian kerygma—Jesus' death and resurrection—indicates that this couplet is a unique Petrine formulation of a common Christian tradition. 1 Corinthians 15:3 is the earliest attested stage (pre-Pauline) of this tradition: "For I [Paul] delivered to you what I also received, that Christ died for our sins . . . that he was raised." In various formulations it appears in a diversity of other texts as well; see Rom 8:34 ("died . . . was raised"); 2 Cor 5:15 ("died and was raised"); 1 Thess 4:14 ("died and rose"); Rom 6:9 ("Christ raised from the dead no longer dies"); Rom 6:10 ("died . . . lives"); Rom 14:9 ("died and lived"); Mark 8:31; 9:31; 10:34 ("be killed and rise"); Luke 24:7 ("be crucified and on the third day rise"); Luke 24:46 ("suffer and on the third day rise"); Acts 2:23–24 ("killed by the hands of lawless men but God raised him up"); Acts 4:10 ("whom you crucified, whom God raised from the dead"); Acts 5:30–31 ("The God of our fathers raised Jesus whom you killed by hanging him on a tree. God exalted him at his right hand"); Acts 10:39–40 ("They put him to death by hanging him on a tree, but God raised him on the third day"); compare *Ascen. Isa.* 3:13; 9:14; 11:20.

18d. *Having been put to death in the flesh* (*thanatōtheis men sarki*). The verbal form *thanatōtheis* is an aor. pass. part. of *thanatoō* ("intentionally kill," "put to death"), with Christ's executioners the implied agents of the passive.[268] The aorist of both verbs of the couplet matches the aorist of the preceding verb, "might bring" (*prosagagēi*) but refers to events that logically precede and form the basis of this action. The absence of both *thanatoō* and its parallel *zōiopoieō* elsewhere in 1 Peter, and their use in the kerygma recounting Jesus' death and resurrection point to Christian tradition as the source of both terms.

The particle *men* is omitted in some manuscripts (𝔓[72] A* and Ψ), but its inclusion has superior manuscript support and is likely because of the correlative *de* in the second half of the couplet (v 18e). Such *men-de* combinations occur elsewhere in the letter (1:20; 2:4; 4:6) and are typical of the author's predilection for explicit antitheses. Here the contrastive particles underline the antithesis of both the verbs and their qualifying states. In particular, they underscore the contrast between the differing types of treatment Christ received from humans (v 18d) and God (v 18e), as does the similar contrast made in 2:4 (rejection by humans but election and honoring by God).

in the flesh (*sarki*, lit., "with respect to [his] flesh"). The term *sarx* designates the tissue, muscle, or fleshly part of one's anatomy, in contrast to bones, blood, and internal organs. When contrasted, as here, to *spirit*, it refers more generally to the physical (and mortal) dimension of one's life. The balance of the term *flesh* by the term *spirit* in the second half of the couplet requires an identical grammatical function of both terms. This rules out regarding *flesh* as an instrumental dative ("he was put to death *through* his flesh") and *spirit* as a reference to the Holy Spirit as subject ("he was made alive by the Spirit"). Nor can *sarx* and *pneuma*, as pointed out by Michaels (1988, 204), denote differing material and immaterial parts of Christ's person (his "body" and "soul"), since each is associated with a different verb. Both terms instead function as datives of respect qualifying "put to death" and "made alive," respectively, and denote the differing but complementary physical and spiritual states of Christ's existence (similar to the contrasts between *sarx* and *pneuma* in Rom 8:10; 1 Cor 5:5; Gal 5:16–25; 1 Tim 3:16; cf. also the similar comparisons of states in 1 Cor 15:42–44). Thus, *sarki* indicates that it was in respect to his physical mortal existence that Christ was put to death (as in 2 Cor 4:11; Heb 5:7). The expressions *kata sarka*[269] and *en sarki*[270] function similarly. In 1 Pet 1:24, *sarx* designates all human mortals, and later in 4:1, 2 and 6 the dative of respect, *sarki*, again denotes the physical, mortal dimension in which Christ and the believers experienced suffering.

In accord with a common contemporary view of death as entailing a descent into the underworld realm of the dead (Sheol or Hades), Jesus' death could be

---

[268] Cf. Matt 26:59; 27:1; Mark 14:55; and the synonymous passive formulation *apoktantheis* in Mark 9:31.

[269] Indicating Christ's nature as a human being (2 Cor 5:16); cf. also Rom 4:1 (of Abraham) or Christ's *physical* descent from the line of David (Rom 1:3; cf. 9:5).

[270] Referring to one's physical and mortal body (1 Cor 7:28; 2 Cor 4:11; 10:3; Gal 2:20; 4:13, 14; Phil 1:22, 24).

thought to have included a "descent into hell" (as in Acts 2:24–28, 31, alluding to Ps 16:10; cf. Matt 12:39–40) during the period (the *triduum mortis*) prior to his resurrection. This notion lies behind the later words of the Apostolic Creed, "he was crucified, died and was buried; *he descended into hell*; on the third day he rose again from the dead." This view of Christ's death associated with a "going" to the realm of the dead (allegedly referred to in 1 Pet 3:19) emerged only in the late second century and will be discussed in connection with v 19. Here reference to the death of Christ is followed immediately by reference to his resurrection (v 18e). The death of Christ is mentioned not as a model for believers to emulate as willing martyrs (against Reicke 1946, 218); their connection with Christ is in *innocent suffering* (3:14, 16, 17; 4:1), not death. His death is rather the presupposition of and necessary prelude to his resurrection (v 18e), which is the chief focus of the remaining verses (vv 18d–22).

18e. *having been made alive, however, in the spirit* (*zōiopoiētheis de pneumati*, lit., "with respect to [his] spirit"). The ignominy of Christ's having been put to death by human opponents was removed by his having been made alive and honored by God (cf. 2:4). The verb *zōiopoieō* occurs 11× in the NT, with God, Christ, or the divine Spirit as subject. Its use in parallelism with *egeirō* ("raise"),[271] the verb more frequently used of God's raising Jesus from death to life, suggests that it serves here as as a synomyn for *egeirō*, so that "having been made alive" is equivalent to "having been raised from the dead." Its passive form (cf. also 1 Cor 15:22, 36), like that of *egeirō*,[272] implies God as the raising agent (see John 5:21 and Rom 4:17 for the verb in the active voice and God as subject). The fact that the verb *zōiopoieō* ("make alive") appears only once in 1 Peter but repeatedly in other NT kerygmatic formulas suggests its derivation from early Christian tradition.

This mention of Christ's resurrection reformulates the thought in 1:21 ("God who raised him from the dead and gave him glory"), recalls the stress on Christ's resurrection at the outset of the letter (*anastasis*, 1:13), and prepares for its repeated mention in 3:21d and its elaboration in 3:22. Taken together, these formulations provide the logic for regarding Christ as the "*living* stone" (*lithon zōnta*, 2:4).

in the spirit (*pneumati*, lit., "with respect to [his] spirit"). The form *pneumati*, like its parallel, *sarki*, is a dative of respect qualifying its foregoing verb. This parallelism of *sarki-pneumati*, as already noted, rules out the possibility of regarding *spirit* as a reference to the Spirit of God. The second of two senses of the variant reading *en pneumati* ("in his spirit" or "by the Spirit [of God]") could suggest this, but this variant is poorly attested ($\mathfrak{P}^{72}$ Or^{lat}) and undoubtedly secondary and would disrupt the balance with the first clause of the couplet which cannot mean "having been put to death by the flesh." Nor is there any

[271] See John 5:21; Rom 8:11; 1 Cor 15:20–22; 35–36, 42–45.

[272] See Matt 27:64; 28:6, 7; Mark 16:6; Luke 24:6, 34; John 21:14; Rom 4:25; 6:4, 9; 1 Cor 15:4, 12, 13.

basis in 1 Peter for regarding *pneuma* as a reference to Christ's divine nature in contradistinction to his human nature, or his "soul" in contradistinction to his body, views justly rejected by Dalton (1989, 136–37, 140–41) and Michaels (1989, 204). The term *pneumati* rather refers to that state of Christ's existence most demonstrably controlled and animated by God's life-giving Spirit, (cf. Ezek 37:14, "And I shall give you my spirit and you shall live"). This interrelation of human spirit as animated by the divine Spirit is articulated most extensively by Paul in Rom 8:1–27 (for the contrast of one's body [that dies] and one's spirit [that lives], see esp. 8:10 and also 1 Cor 5:5). In his comment on Christ's resurrection in 1 Cor 15, Paul further describes this contrast of death with respect to one's flesh and life with respect to one's spirit in terms of "perishability-imperishability," "dishonor-glory," "weakness-power," "sown a physical body–raised a spiritual body" (15:42–46). A similar contrast appears in 1 Tim 3:16bc ("he [Christ], was manifested in the flesh [*en sarki*], vindicated in the spirit [*en pneumati*]"). In 1 Peter, *sarki* and *pneumati* recur in 4:6, again as contrasted datives of respect. The experience of Christ (3:18c) is thus established here as the basis for that of the believers as well (4:6b). The second-century *Letter to Diognetus* appears to make this same point when it repeats the two verbs of this Christological couplet to describe the experience of Christ's followers: "they are put to death and they are made alive" (*thanatountai kai zōiopoiountai*, 5:12).

In the context of vv 18–22, Christ's resurrection and the accompanying motif of his ascension into heaven (*zōiopoiētheis . . . poreutheis*, "having been put to death . . . having gone" [vv 18e–19a] / *anastaseōs Iēsou Christou . . . poreutheis eis ouranon*, "resurrection of Jesus Christ . . . having gone into heaven" [vv 21d, 22b]) thus constitute the determinative event in connection with which vv 19–21 are to be understood. Verses 18de and 22, reformulations of primitive Christian kerygmatic tradition, constitute the framework and set the immediate context for the thought of vv 19–21.

Verses 19–21, in turn, are distinguished from vv 18 and 22 by the abrupt stylistic shift from balanced phrases to a series of subordinated or parenthetical phrases and clauses and by certain ideas associated not with the kerygmatic tradition echoed in vv 18 and 22 but rather with an independent Israelite body of tradition amplifying on Gen 6–8. Although suspected of being an interpolation (Cramer 1891) or a "digression" (Beare 1970, 170), these verses in fact do "cohere closely with the writer's main objectives" (J. N. D. Kelly 1969, 152). Because of the numerous and seemingly intractable problems these verses pose, they have long been regarded as a notorious *crux interpretum*. Martin Luther, that master biblical expositor, when struggling with v 19 exclaimed: "This is a strange text and certainly a more obscure passage than any other passage in the New Testament. I still do not know for sure what the apostle meant" (Luther 1967 [1523], 30:113 = *Weimarer Ausgabe* 12:367). Subsequent scholars likewise viewed this passage as one of the most perplexing and vexatious texts in all of Holy Scripture.

The passage indeed poses a staggering number of difficult questions:

(1) the Greek text of *en hōi kai*; (2) the antecedent or sense of *en hōi*; (3) the place of the pause between v 19 and v 20; (4) the event to which Christ's "having gone" refers, including its occasion, time, and direction; (5) the identity of the disobedient spirits in prison and the occasion and nature of their disobedience; (6) the location and nature of this prison; (7) the content of Christ's announcement to them, the time of this annnouncement, and the relation between 3:19 and 4:6; (8) the nature of the relation between the Flood and baptism, and between Noah's family and present believers; (9) the sense of the explanation of baptism; (10) the syntactic and semantic coherence of vv 19–21 and their relation to vv 18 and 22; (11) the possible sources underlying this material; (12) the relation of vv 18–22 as a whole to both the foregoing (3:13–17) and following (4:1–6) units; and (13) the theological and rhetorical function of this passage in the broader context of the letter.

These difficult questions have generated an enormous body of literature and a wide diversity of proposed solutions. On the whole, four main views have been advanced, with some of these views also having finer nuances of interpretation. Dalton (1989, 17–66) offers the fullest survey and critique to date (but see also Grudem 1988, 203–39; and, for earlier overviews, Holzmeister 1937, 306–51; and Reicke 1946, 7–51).

View 1. When Christ descended (*poreutheis*) to the realm of the dead in conjunction with his death and prior to his resurrection (i.e., during the so-called *triduum mortis*), he, "in the spirit" (*en pneumati*), made an announcement (*ekēryxen*) to the deceased humans ("spirits") whose souls were imprisoned in the lower world (*infera*), the realm of the dead (Hades, hell). Frequently this view also assumes a direct relation between 3:19 and 4:6.

Among the many scholars espousing this view, however, opinions diverge regarding the more precise identity of the spirits and the content of Christ's announcement. Some (1A) hold that Christ's spirit preached to the spirits of the deceased of Noah's generation to convert them and bring them to salvation. Others (1B) view Christ as offering good news only to those of Noah's generation who were converted before death (or to all of the OT righteous and patriarchs who died prior to Christ). Still others (1C) claim that Christ announced condemnation to the unbelieving contemporaries of Noah, who presumably died without conversion.

View 1A first emerged with Clement of Alexandria at the end of the second century. Prior to this, 1 Pet 3:19 was never understood as a reference to Christ's descent to the underworld, and when the descent of Christ was mentioned, for instance by Irenaeus (*Haer.* 4.22.1; 4.27.2; 5.33.1), 1 Pet 3:19 was never cited. However, from the time of Clement of Alexandria onward, View 1A became the prevailing view until Augustine.[273]

---

[273] For representatives of this view in the early Church, including Origen and Athanasius, see Dalton 1989, 29–32; for modern supporters, including Bigg, Windisch, Cranfield, Beare, Schneider, Schelkle, Galot, Spicq, Beare, Hanson 1981–1982, and Goppelt 1993, 258–60, see

View 1B is less clearly attested in the early Church (the Jeremiah logion in Justin [*Dial.* 72, Ps.-Jeremiah agraphon] and Irenaeus [*Haer.* 3.20.4; 4.22.1; 4.33.1; 4.33.12; 5.31.1; *Epid.* 78?]; *Gos. Pet.* 10:4?; *Easter Homily* of Hippolytus?; see Reicke 1946, 14–27; Dalton 1989, 34–37). In later centuries this view was supported by, among others, Calvin, Blenkin (1914, 17), Wohlenberg (1915, 105–15), and Johnson (1960, 49).

View 1C was preferred by certain representatives of 17th-century Lutheran Orthodoxy (listed by Reicke 1946, 44–45), by Lenski (1966, 160–69), and by a few Roman Catholic scholars (see Dalton 1989, 41).

View 2. Christ, in his *preexistent* nature, went to Noah's contemporaries during their lifetime, particularly through the person of Noah, and preached repentance to these human spirits who were imprisoned in sin. Augustine (*Ep. Eud.* 64, chs. 14–17) proposed this allegorical interpretation only hestitatingly. Nevertheless, eventually it became the dominant view in the Western Church.[274] Although abandoned by the majority of modern commentators, this view, in various nuanced forms, still finds occasional supporters.[275]

View 3. In order to resolve some of the obvious difficulties involved in the Augustinian view, the Roman Catholic scholar Robert Bellarmine (1586) advanced the view that after Christ died his soul descended to the realm of the dead and announced salvation to those humans of Noah's generation who, he conjectured, had repented of their sins just prior to their death (*Disp. R. Bellarmini de Controversiis, Tom.* 1, *Cont.* 2, *Lib.* 4, ch. 13). This theory was adopted subsequently by various Roman Catholic commentators (listed by Holzmeister 1937, 315; Reicke 1946, 42–44; and Dalton 1965, 30–31). The notion that these humans had undergone a purging of sin has been argued in recent time by Vogels (1976).

View 4. Pioneered by the study of F. Spitta (1890), this view is based on the recognized proximity of the thought in 1 Pet 3:19–20 to early Israelite tradition concerning the Flood and in particular the widely influential book of *1 Enoch*. Here the "spirits in prison" are regarded as the sinful angelic spirits whose transgression, according to Genesis 6 and subsequent tradition, preceded and instigated the evil that was destroyed in the Flood. To them Christ announced some form of his triumph over death and their condemnation.

Spitta himself followed Augustine in seeing in 1 Pet 3:19 a reference to the activity of the preexistent Christ (1890, 21–22, 32–33) prior to his incarnation. Among the numerous scholars, however, who followed his lead in identifying the "disobedient spirits" with the sinful angels associated with the Flood story, some

---

Dalton 1989, 33–34. On the topic and scholarly discussions of Christ's descent, see the overviews of Holzmeister 1937, 317–43; Bieder 1949; Selwyn 1947, 339–53; Brox 1986, 182–89; Goppelt 1993, 26–63; and DETAILED COMMENT 2.

[274] See Bede; Thomas Aquinas, *Summa Theologica*, part 3, question 52, art. 2, reply to objection 3; W. Kelly 1872, 3–89.

[275] See Wohlenberg 1923, 106–15; Patterson 1982, 134–46, 195–99; Feinberg 1986; Grudem 1988, 203–39; Erickson 1995; Skilton 1996.

(4A) located the announcement of Christ within the period after his death and *before* his resurrection (e.g., Knopf, Gunkel, Windisch, Reicke, Selwyn, Best, Schrage), with "spirits" sometimes taken to include both sinful angels and humans (Reicke, Selwyn, Windisch). Many others (4B), however, considered this announcement as having occurred *after* his resurrection in the course of his ascension to heaven ("having gone," 3:19a, 22b).[276] Calvin, like Luther, had also located the preaching of Christ after his resurrection but regarded it as addressed to the souls of the OT faithful in the realm of the dead (1963, 292–95). Michaels, who likewise favors the ascension hypothesis, identifies the "spirits" of 1 Pet 3:19 with the *demonic progeny* of the angels of Gen 6:4.

The variety and nuances of these views reveal the numerous exegetical problems posed by these verses, raise the question of the original conceptual background of these thoughts, and illustrate the specific dogmatic positions seen to be at stake by the interpreters. Any adequate interpretation therefore must take into consideration all of these issues. The significant advance instigated by Spitta was to identify the body of literature—the apocryphal and pseudepigraphical Israelite writings of the intertestamental period and their amplification of the Flood narrative of Genesis—that provided the closest and clearest conceptual background for understanding the references to the Flood and its surrounding events present in 1 Pet 3:19–20. As proponents of the fourth view have long recognized, a reading of these Petrine verses in the light of this extensive Flood tradition provides the most productive basis for deciphering these enigmatic verses. Consideration of the manner in which the Petrine author integrated concepts related to this tradition with the kerygmatic formulas in vv 18 and 22 will clarify the structure, import, and function of vv 18–22 as a whole. Dalton (1964a, 1965/1989, 1968, 1979, 1984) has presented the most convincing interpretation of this material. The NOTES that follow expand on his research and conclusions, with only minor points of disagreement.[277]

In anticipation of what follows, a brief summary of the general thrust of these verses may be helpful. In vv 19–21 the author expands on the implications of Christ's having been put to death, having been made alive (v 18de), and having gone into heaven (v 22). In the course of going into heaven (*poreutheis*, v 19a, 22), Christ confirmed the condemnation of the disobedient spirits imprisoned in one of the heavenly realms (v 19b). These spirits were the sinful angels who had disobeyed (v 20a) prior to the primordial Flood, when Noah and his family were saved (v 20b–f). Baptism, which corresponds to this primoridal saving event, now saves the believers through the resurrection of Jesus Christ (v 21a–d). Framed by the double occurrence of the verb "having

[276] So Luther (*LW* 30:113); Jensen 1903, 181; Gschwind 1911, 88–89, 97–114; Dalton 1964a, 1965, 1968, 1979, 1984; 1989, 47–48, 161–63, 182–84 (viewing the announcement of Christ as confirmation of the disobedient angels' condemnation); J. N. D. Kelly 1969, 175–76; Elliott 1982, 98–99; Michaels 1988, 205–11; Davids 1990, 140–41; and as a possibility, Brox 1986, 175.

[277] Several of the issues are discussed more fully in DETAILED COMMENT 1. The NOTES presume the conclusions reached in these detailed discussions.

gone" (*poreutheis*, vv 19a, 22b), referring to Christ's ascension into heaven following his death and resurrection, vv 19–22 spell out the implications of Christ's resurrection for the cosmic powers as well as for baptized believers. In particular, a correspondence is affirmed between the salvation of the family of Noah in primordial time (v 20) and the salvation of the believing community of the end time, a salvation effected through the resurrection of Jesus Christ in which the believers participate through baptism (v 21). With this comment completed, the author concludes by reverting to the remaining elements of the kerygmatic tradition introduced in v 18de. Having been put to death, having been made alive, and having gone into heaven, the resurrected Christ is now at the right hand of God, with the cosmic powers subordinated to him (v 22a, c).

19a. *having gone in this connection also to the spirits in prison* (*en hōi kai tois en phylakēi pneumasin poreutheis*). As the structure of the translation indicates, this participial phrase, together with the two preceding participles (vv 18de), states the prelude for the main clause, "he announced to these (spirits) who once disobeyed" (v 19b–20a), with a pause or comma between *poreutheis* ("having gone") and *ekēryxen* ("announced").

The aor. participle "having gone" (*poreutheis*) could be taken as an auxiliary to the verb "announced" (*ekēryxen*): "having gone, he announced to the spirits in prison" (as assumed in *NTG*[27] and most translations; for the construction, see also Matt 10:17). However, it is more likely that *having gone* is linked directly with *spirits in prison* and completes the initial phrase (*having gone . . . to the spirits in prison*), which is then followed by the main clause initiated by the finite verb "announced" (*ekēryxen*): "he announced to these (spirits) who once disobeyed." This alternative is favored by the fact that the construction of an initial participial phrase or phrases followed by a main verb and clause is typical of the author's style (see 1:8, 13, 22; 2:20 [2×], 23 [2×]; 3:10; 4:1; 5:4; 10cd). Moreoever, the verb *kēryssō* more commonly appears with a following dative of person (Mark 16:15; Luke 4:18; Acts 8:5; 10:42). The spirits in prison (see below) are those to whom Christ went; for this construction of going to another person or persons, see also Luke 14:31 and Acts 28:16. Thus the opening participial phrase (together with v 18de) sets the stage for the action of the main clause: "having gone . . . to the spirits in prison, he announced to these (spirits) who had once disobeyed."

in this connection also (*en hōi kai*). These initial words join this verse and what follows to v 18de. The conjunction *kai* ("also") clearly links the participle "having gone" with the preceding participles "having been put to death" and "having been made alive." The syntactic function of *en hōi* is less obvious. The relative dative *hōi* could have as its antecedent the preceding term "spirit" in v 18e ("in which sphere of the spirit" [of Christ in his risen state]).[278] This

[278] So Dalton 1989, 145 and J. N. D. Kelly 1969:152, appealing to the opinion of ancient commentators.

possibility, however, is weakened by the rarity of such a dative of reference serving as antecedent of a relative pronoun (cf. Acts 2:8; Eph 2:2, 3; 2 Pet 1:4; 3:1). Moreover, the focus of vv 19–22 is not on the *mode* of Christ's going ("in his spirit") but on events involved with the *occasion* of his going, namely his resurrection (vv 18e, 21d) and ascension into heaven (v 22). This likewise eliminates the possibility of a reference to a preexistent spirit of Christ (against Spitta 1890, 21–22 and others who follow Augustine). It is more likely that *en hōi* functions here, as elsewhere in the letter (1:6; 2:12; 3:16; 4:4), as a temporal or circumstantial conjunction ("in this connection," "in the course of which," "in the case or circumstance when," "on which occasion."[279] Thus *en hōi*, rendered "in this connection," links Christ's "going" and what follows with the foregoing event of his "having been made alive" (v 18e), a linkage strengthened by the accompanying conjunction "also" (*kai*). The construction of *kai* with a following verb occurs in 3:14; in 4:14, *kai* and its verb are likewise separated by intervening words.

This analysis of the syntax makes conjectures of textual emendation unnecessary. In 1763 J. Bowyer published a Greek New Testament[280] in which he conjectured that the present phrase *ENŌKAI* (*En hō kai*) was a substitute for an original *ENŌCHKAI* (*Enōch kai*, "Enoch also"). At the outset of the twentieth century, J. Rendel Harris (1901, 1902a, 1902b) hypothesized a text with the letters *ENŌKAIENŌCH* (*En hō kai Enōch*, "in which also Enoch"), with "Enoch" subsequently omitted by later scribes due to haplography. This proposal was accepted in the biblical translations of Moffatt (1928) and Goodspeed (1923). In defense of this conjecture Goodspeed (1954) appealed to the similarity of 1 Pet 3:19 and the Enoch legend in *1 En.* 12–16. Neither conjecture, however, has found favor with scholars. Neither is supported by any manuscript evidence; neither accounts convincingly for a sudden and unexplained reference to Enoch in a text that has Christ as subject (vv 18, 21d); and neither is necessary to account for the text as it stands (see Metzger 1968, 185). These objections apply also to W. D. Morris (1926–1927), who, in responding to Harris, favored the reading *ENŌNŌE* ("in which Noah . . ."). The proximity of this verse to the tradition concerning Enoch, however, requires closer attention.

The sense, then, of vv 18de–20a is: "(Christ), having been put to death, having been made alive, and in this connection also having gone to the spirits in prison, announced to these (spirits) who once disobeyed. . . ." The syntactical ambiguity evident here may well be the result of the merger of thoughts deriving from different traditions, with vv 18 and 22 reflecting Christian kerygmatic tradition and vv 19–21 expanding on elements of an Israelite Flood tradition to

---

[279] So Gschwind 1911, 118; Reicke 1946, 108, 113–15; Selwyn 1947, 197, 315; Michaels 1988, 206; Goppelt 1993, 255–56. For this usage, see also Mark 2:19/Luke 5:34; Luke 19:13; John 5:7; Rom 2:1.

[280] See also the second edition of his *Critical Conjectures* (1772).

be discussed below. An earlier passage, 2:5, illustrates a similar syntactical uncertainty resulting from a combination of tradition and authorial comment.

In itself, the verb *poreuomai* does not indicate the direction of movement (such as "descend" or "ascend"); this must be determined by context. In the present immediate context, the aor. part. *poreutheis* occurs again in v 22b, clearly referring to Christ's ascension or "having gone into heaven." Thus the context offers compelling reason for regarding the *poreutheis* of v 19 as also referring to Christ's ascension. This is further supported by the use of *poreuomai* elsewhere in the NT of Christ's ascension into heaven (Acts 1:10, 11) or his "going" to God [who is in heaven] (John 14:2, 3, 12, 28; 16:7, 28). On the other hand, in the NT *poreuomai* never has the sense of "descend," and there is no reason to imagine with Bultmann (1947, 5) a confused author speaking of two different journeys of Christ, one to the underworld (v 19) and one to heaven (v 22). Finally, this conclusion is also supported by the logical relation of this verb to v 18de: reference to the ascension of Christ here in v 19 logically follows reference to his death (*thanatōtheis*, v 18d) and resurrection (*zōiopoiētheis*, v 18e), a point made centuries ago by Luther: "Now He did not descend again into hell after he had assumed a new existence. Therefore one must understand these words to mean that He did this after his resurrection" (*LW* 30:113).

The double use of *poreutheis*, referring to Christ's having gone into heaven and completing the threefold action of death-resurrection-ascension, thus frames the thought of vv 19–21:

v 19a *poreutheis* to the spirits in prison
  v 20 Noah and family saved through water
  v 21 baptism now saves you through the resurrection of Jesus Christ
v 22 *poreutheis* into heaven with cosmic powers subjected to him

Consequently, the material concerning Christ's announcement to the imprisoned disobedient spirits, the days of Noah, the preparation of the ark, the salvation of Noah's family, and the corresponding salvation of the baptized believers is directly linked to the event of Christ's resurrection (vv 18e, 21d, 22) and his having gone or ascended into heaven (vv 19a, 22b) and clarifies the implications and effects of this resurrection-ascension event. Elements of vv 19–20, moreover, have their closest analogy in a broad current of Israelite and Christian tradition concerning the Noachic Flood and its surrounding events, as narrated initially in Gen 6–8 (see *1 En.* 6–22; 64–69; 85–89; 106; Wis 10:4; Sir 16:7; *Jub.* 4:24; 5:1–6:3; 7:20–33; 10:1–6; *2 En.* 7:1–5; 18:1–9, 34–35; 73; *T. Reu.* 5:6; *T. Naph.* 3:5; 1QapGen; 1Q19; 1Q19bis; 1Q23–24; 4Q201–207, 212; 4Q530, 531; 6QapGen II 18–21; CD II 17–21; Philo's two treatises on the subject [*On the Giants* and *The Unchangeableness of God*; cf. also QG 1.92–2.55]; Josephus, *Ant.* 1.72–95; *Ag. Ap.* 130; *2 Bar.* 56:8–16; *3 Bar.* 4:10–15; *Apoc. Ab.* 13–14; *Sib. Or.* 1:97–104, 125–282; 7:7–15; 1 Pet 3:19–20; 2 Pet 2:4–5; 3:6; Jude 6, 13–15; Just. Mart., *1 Apol.* 5; *2 Apol.* 5. Regarding Noah alone, see also Matt 24:37–39/Luke 17:26–27; Heb 11:7; *1 Clem.* 7:6; 9:4).

Salient features of this tradition included the rebellion of angelic spirits against God, their departure to earth and illicit mating with human women, their introducing evil into the world and the announcement of their condemnation and imprisonment, the destructive punishment of the Flood, and the salvation of Noah and his family; see DETAILED COMMENT 1 for further discussion of the texts.

One important representative of this tradition, *1 Enoch*, describes its protagonist, Enoch (cf. Gen 5:21–24), as ascending into heaven and "going" (*poreuein*, 12:4; 13:3; 15:2) to the disobedient angelic spirits of the Flood period with the announcement of their divine condemnation (*1 En.* 12:4–6; 13:1–10; 14:1–7; 15:1–16:3; cf. *2 En.* 7). This heavenly journey of Enoch and his announcement to the sinful angelic spirits constitutes the closest analogy for the action of Christ as described here in 1 Peter and in all likelihood provided the conceptual model for the Petrine author. The verb *poreutheis* forms the first link in the merger of (1) the Christian kerygmatic tradition echoed in vv 18de and 22 and (2) tradition, represented by *1 En.* and related writings, concerning events surrounding the Noachic Flood. The Petrine author, intent on assuring the readers of their salvation (3:18abc), compares their salvation to the prototypical salvation of Noah and his household at the time of the great Flood. Preceding and prompting this destructive Flood was the rebellion of the angelic spirits, those to whom Enoch, upon his "going" (*poreuein*) to heaven, announced their condemnation and imprisonment. Our author, with this tradition in mind, depicts Christ in similar terms. Upon his resurrection and ascension to heaven, Christ "went" (*poreutheis*) to the disobedient angelic spirits of the Flood period and announced to them his victory over death and their condemnation (3:19–20).

This noteworthy affinity between 1 Pet 3:19–20 and the Flood tradition argues decisively against regarding *poreutheis* as a reference to a "descent" of Christ into the underworld in conjunction with his death and prior to his resurrection (Views 1–3, 4A) or to some "going" of Christ in a preexistent state before his incarnation (the Augustinian view). The term *poreutheis* of v 19 is, rather, the first of two references here to Christ's ascension (View 4B), and it is the event of Christ's resurrection (vv 18d, 21d, 22a, c) and ascension to heaven (v 19a, 22b) that frames vv 19–20c and controls their meaning.

In depicting Christ ascending through the heavens to the right hand of God in the highest heaven (v 22), the Petrine author appears to share with his Israelite and Christian contemporaries the notion of a plurality of heavens.[281] This cosmology, under increasing Hellenistic influence, also could locate even

---

[281] See *1 En.* 18:4, 10; 71:1; *2 En.*; *3 En.* (seven heavens, 12:4; 17:2; 18:1; etc); *T. Levi* 2:7–8; 3:1–9; 13:5; 14:3; etc.; *T. Dan* 5:13; *T. Ash.* 2:10; 7:5; *T. Benj.* 10:7; *Ascen Isa.*; *Apoc. Mos.*; *3 Bar.*; *Apoc. Zeph.*; *4 Ezra*; 2 Macc 15:23; 3 Macc 2:2; Wis 9:10; Tob 8:5; 2 Cor 12:2; and 43 other occurrences of "heavens" (pl.) in the NT, including 1 Peter (1:4); on this notion, see Gundel 1950, 834; Lumpe and Bietenhard 1991.

Hades, the realm of the dead, no longer *under* the earth but *above* the earth (Plut., *Fac.* 28, 943CE) or in the heavens.[282] The idea of an ascent of Christ through the heavens is likewise consistent with the theme of heavenly journeys or ascents as found in numerous writings contemporary with 1 Peter.[283] The comparable heavenly ascent of Levi as described in the *T. Levi* (2:6–5:2) is particularly noteworthy. Levi is described as passing through three lower heavens on his way to God in the "uppermost heaven" (3:4). In similar fashion, Christ is portrayed in vv 19 and 22 as "having gone" to and through a plurality of heavens before reaching the final heaven, where God resides. This cosmology is also reflected in Heb 4:14 ([Jesus, the Son of God] "who has passed through the heavens"] and Eph 4:10: ("He [Christ] who descended is he who also ascended far above all the heavens"). See also the Christian components of the *Ascension of Isaiah* (3:13–4:2; 9:6–18; 10:7–11:33), which describe the resurrected Christ passing through six heavens and being enthroned at God's right hand in the seventh heaven; on the location of God in the seventh heaven, see 7:17; 10:14; 11:33.

to the spirits in prison (*tois en phylakēi pneumasin*). The plural *spirits* is preferable to the less-well-attested "spirit" ($\mathfrak{P}^{72}$ 614 1881 vg^{mss}), which apparently was seen as linked with *en hō* ("in which spirit"). Manuscript support for *phylakēi* is superior to that for *tōi hadēi* ("Hades," 614 a few other MSS and Ambrosiaster). The reading "locked" (in prison) (C other MSS vg^{mss} Augustine) appears to be a secondary addition. In regard to the *identity* of these spirits (*pneumasin*) and their *location*, the immediate literary context supplies information that is further clarified by details of the Flood tradition. The spirits are located "in prison" (*en phylakēi*, v 19a) and are identified as "those who once disobeyed" (*apeithēsasin pote*, v 20a) in conjunction with *the days of Noah* and the Flood (v 20b–d). The adverb "once" (*pote*), as in 3:5a, refers to a time of the distant past—in this case the Noachic Flood and what preceded it: the rebellion/disobedience of angelic spirits, their imprisonment, and the announcement of their condemnation.

The biblical account of angelic rebellion, their instigation of evil on earth, the punishment of the Flood, and the salvation of Noah and his family were the focus of intense interest in the Second Temple Period as a prototypical example of God's condemnation of evil and salvation of the righteous, as the numerous texts indicate. The terminological and thematic affinities of 1 Pet 3:19–20 with this tradition are clear and make it virtually certain that the content of vv 19–20 represents early Christian allusion to and variation on this tradition.

---

[282] See Heraclides Ponticus, *Frgs.* 96; Plut., *Sera* 30–31, 566E; *2 En.* 10:1–5; *3 Bar.* 3–9. On this new Hellenistic cosmology with its increased focus on the heavens as the locality of the spirits, see Oden 1992; Colpe et al. 1995a, 1995b, 1995c; and Lumpe and Bietenhard 1991.

[283] See 2 Cor 12:2–4; Rev 4:1; 1 *Enoch*; 2 *Enoch*; *Apocalypse of Abraham*; *Testament of Abraham*; *Apocalypsis of Moses*; 3 *Baruch*; *Ascension of Isaiah*; *Life of Adam and Eve/Apocalypse of Moses*; cf. Himmelfarb 1983, 1993; and Tabor 1992.

At the same time it is evident that this Petrine text as a whole (vv 19–22) has no complete parallel in either Israelite or contemporary Christian sources and represents an *original contribution* of the Petrine author. Petrine nuances on this tradition become apparent as the author's thought continues to unfold.

Taking these affinities into account, the "disobedient spirits" are best taken as a reference to the angelic spirits of the pre-Flood period in whose rebellion and punishment Israel and early Christianity displayed so much interest. Several factors make this virtually certain. For one thing, "spirits" (*pneumata*) is a highly unusual term for speaking of human beings but a thoroughly conventional one for referring to *supernatural beings*, both angels and demons. The plural "spirits" (*pneumata*) is used only once in the NT of deceased human beings (Heb 12:23). But there the term is qualified by an accompanying phrase ("of just ones made perfect") in contrast to the absolute term in 1 Peter and refers not to disobedient but "just" persons (cf. also the qualification "[spirits] and of all flesh," Num 16:22; 27:16). On the other hand, "spirit" is used of a heavenly being in 3 Kgdms 22:19–23, and in the NT "spirits" frequently designates supernatural beings, both benevolent angels (Heb 1:14; Rev 1:4; 3:1; 4:5; 5:6) and malevolent "unclean spirits" or demons.[284]

In the Flood tradition to which the Petrine author alludes, the term "spirits," when occasionally referring to humans, is never used absolutely but is always qualified; for example, "spirits of humans" (*1 En.* 20:6; 22:13); "spirits of the souls of the dead" (*1 En.* 22:3; cf. 22:9). On the other hand, when used *absolutely* as in 1 Peter, "spirits" denotes the defiant angel-spirits (called "sons of God" in Gen 6:1–4), who abandoned their heavenly dwelling-place, engaged in illicit intercourse with human women, and together with their offspring initiated the evil destroyed in the Flood.[285] Where in Israelite tradition the fall of these Watchers or angelic spirits is featured, the Noachic Flood is regularly represented as the remedy for the evil introduced. The extensive interest in these disobedient angel-spirits and their imprisonment in this Flood tradition coupled with the explicit reference to the Flood and Noah in 1 Pet 3:20 argue decisively for regarding the *pneumata* of v 19 as a reference to these defiant angel-spirits.[286] In v 19, as in the Israelite Flood tradition and Jude 6 and 2 Pet 2:4–5,[287] these spirits represent the angelic forces of primordial time whose

---

[284] See Matt 8:16; 10:1; Matt 12:45/Luke 11:26; Mark 1:27; 3:11; 5:13; 6:7; Luke 4:36; 6:18; 7:21; 8:2; 10:20; Acts 5:16; 19:12–13; Rev 16:13–14; and in the singular, Matt 12:43/Luke 11:24; Mark 1:23, 26; 3:30; 5:2, 8; 7:25; Luke 8:29; 9:39, 42; 13:11; Acts 16:16, 18; 19:15–16.

[285] See*1 En.* 15:4, 6, 7, 8, 10a; 16:1; *Jub.* 10:7; 10:3 ("evil spirits"); Philo, *QG* 1.92 ("angels," "sons of God," "spirits," *pneumata*); *1 En.* 19:1 ("spirits of the angels"); cf. also God as "Lord of the spirits," *1 En.* 54:5, 6; 55:3; etc.; for other designations of these angelic spirits ("[evil] angels," "Watchers," "demons"), see the numerous texts listed in DETAILED COMMENT 1.

[286] So Spitta, Gschwind, Gunkel, Holtzmann, Hart, Knopf, Hauck, Windisch, Bieder, Stibbs, Margot, Reicke, Selwyn, Dalton, J. N. D. Kelly 1969; Best, Schrage, Elliott, Brox, Michaels (their demonic progeny), Davids; Bauckham 1992b.

[287] See DETAILED COMMENT 1 on these two related NT texts.

transgression and union with human women led to the spread of evil and the punishment of the Flood.

On the other hand, there are no compelling reasons for taking *pneumata* as a reference to deceased humans alone or to deceased humans along with sinful angels (against Views 1–3). As indicated above, use of "spirits" for human beings is very rare, and even then it is always qualified. In the Bible and related literature, when reference is made to deceased humans in Hades or the underworld, the term used is not *pneuma* but *psychē*.[288] Furthermore, in the Flood tradition, it is only the angelic spirits and not deceased humans who are said to be "in prison," bound, or in chains.

This sense of "spirits" is consistent with the Petrine context as well. The correspondence between vv 19 and 22 indicated by the double use of the verb "having gone" also involves a correspondence between the angel-spirits of v 19 and the "angels, authorities, and powers" of v 22, the totality of cosmic powers subordinated to the risen and ascended Christ. It is not human beings but cosmic spirits over whom Christ is said to have control. Reference to this control thus appears to be included in Christ's announcement (v 19). Finally, an identification of "spirits" with human dead because of a presumed association of the *pneumata* of v 19 with the human dead (*nekrois*) of 4:6 involves an arbitrary and indemonstrable assumption concerning a relation between these two verses.Thus ordinary word usage, detail from the Flood tradition, and Petrine context speak against Views 1–3 and favor taking *pneumata* (v 19a) as referring to the rebellious angels of primordial time.

in prison (*en phylakēi*). In the NT, *phylakē* denotes "guarding" as an action (Luke 2:8), "guard" or "sentinel" (Acts 12:10), "watch" of the night (Matt 14:25; Mark 6:48), "haunt" (Rev 18:2), and mostly frequently "prison" (e.g., Matt 14:3, 10; 25:36, 39, 43–44; Mark 6:27; Luke 3:20; 21:12; 22:33; Acts 5:19, 21; Rev 2:10; 20:7). It never designates the abode of the dead in general, hell, or Hades (as rightly stressed by Gschwind 1911, 85, 88). In fact, MS 614 (and a few other witnesses, including Ambrosiaster), assuming a reference to Hades here, intentionally replaced *phylakēi* with *tōi hadēi*. In Rev 20 a future "binding" of Satan for a millennium is envisioned (20:2), along with his release from his "prison" (*phylakēs*) thereafter (20:7). But this text makes no mention of "spirits," concerns the future not the past, and in general is unrelated to the thought of 1 Peter.[289]

---

[288] See Acts 2:27; cf. also Ps 48:16[49:15]; Josephus, *Ant.* 6.332; *4 Ezra* 4:35, 42; 7:32; *2 Bar.* 30:2–5.

[289] Michaels (1988, 208–9) appeals to a further text of Revelation (18:2) as a reason for rendering *phylakē* in 1 Pet 3:19 as place of "refuge." But there the term is used to denounce Babylon as a "haunt (*phylakē*) of every unclean spirit (*pneumatos*), a haunt of every foul and hateful bird." These presently active spirits, however, are different from the primordial spirits of which the Petrine author speaks, and the thought as a whole is quite unrelated to that of 1 Pet 3:19–20.

The concept of disobedient spirits confined to prison is clarified best by the Flood tradition. There it is repeatedly stressed that the primordial sinful angelic spirits, as a consequence of their transgression, were "bound" (*deō, desmoi*) or put into "chains" (*1 En.* 69:28; *2 Bar.* 56:13) or cast into "prison" (*desmōtērion*) or "confinement" (*sygkleisis*), where they will be locked up forever.[290] In other NT texts, this imprisonment of the angels is similarly described as their being kept by God "in eternal chains (cf. *1 En.* 69:28; *2 Bar.* 56:13) in the nether gloom until the judgment of the great day" (Jude 6; cf. 2 Pet 2:4: "God cast them into Tartarus [the realm of the dead] and committed them to chains of nether gloom to be kept until the judgment"). In 1 Pet 3:19a this thought is given expression in the phrase *in prison*.

This prison or confinement of the rebellious spirits is assigned varying locations in the Flood tradition; see DETAILED COMMENT 1. 2 *Enoch* 7:1–3 and *T. Levi* 3:3 locate these confined and condemned angels in the second heaven, and this would fit the scenario of Jude, 2 Peter, and 1 Peter as well (so also Dalton 1968, 34–35). In the course of his "having gone" (*poreutheis*) to God in the highest heaven (v 22b), Christ had passed through the lower heavens and "had gone" (*poreutheis*) to the disobedient spirits in the second or nether heaven with an announcement of their final condemnation. On the prevalence of the notion of the plurality of the heavens (reflected also in 1 Pet 1:4 ["heavens," *ouranoi*]), see the foregoing NOTE on *poreutheis*.

19b, 20a. *he announced to these [spirits] who once disobeyed* (*ekēryxen apeithēsasin pote*). The phrase *who once disobeyed* is a further qualification of "spirits in prison," with the dative aor. act. part. *apeithēsasin* modifying the preceding "spirits" (dative). The accompanying adverb "once" (*pote*), as already noted, points to an event in the distant past (as in 3:5 and 2:10). In this case the reference is to "the days of Noah" and the Flood (v 20b–d), thereby relating these spirits and their disobedience to the event of the Flood. The verb "disobey" is the author's summary term for the rebellion of the angelic spirits portrayed in Gen 6:1–4 and variously described in the Flood tradition as transgression, illicit intercourse, boundary violation, impurity, or sin.[291] According to this tradition, human sin followed that of the angel-spirits, but primary attention is directed to the transgression of the angel-spirits as the instigation of all subsequent evil eradicated by the Flood. Thus an appeal to human transgression is an unconvincing basis for contending that *pneumata* refers to Noah's contemporaries and that *apeithēsasin* can "only" describe their sin (against Grudem 1988, 215–17). Again the Israelite Flood tradition argues decisively for regarding the "spirits who once disobeyed" as a reference not to disobedient humans who perished in the flood or to spirits or souls of the dead generally

[290] See *1 En.* 10:4, 12, 13, 14; 13:2; 14:5; 18:13–16; 14; 21:1–10; 54:4–6; 67:4; 69:28; 88:1, 3; *2 En.* 7:1–3; 18:3; *Jub.* 5:6–11; 10:4–11; 4QEnoch I 6, 22; VII 1; *Sib. Or.* 1:100–104.

[291] See *1 En.* 6:3; 9:7–9; 10:11; 12:4; 15:3–4, 8–9, 11, 12; 16:1; 18:15; 21:4, 6; 106:14; *Jub.* 5:1–11; 7:21; 10:1–6; *T. Reu.* 5; *T. Naph.* 3:5; *2 Bar.* 56:12; CD II 18, 21; Philo, *Gig.* 6; *QG* 1.92; 2 Pet 2:4; Jude 6; cf. also *Haer.* 1.10.1.

and certainly not to the "righteous dead" (since they are described as *disobedient* spirits) but to the sinful angel-spirits whose disobedience inaugurated the evil resulting in the Flood.

The Petrine author does not elaborate further on this disobedience of the angelic spirits, but there are some indications of what he may have had in mind. First, in the Israelite Flood tradition the disobedience of these angelic spirits included their violation of the boundaries separating angels and humans through their intercourse with human women (*1 En.* 6:1–8; 9:7–8; 10:11; 12:4; 15:3; *Jub.* 7:21; *T. Reu.* 5:6; *T. Naph.* 3:5; Jude 6). The *Testament of Naphtali* (3:3, 5) specifically states: "The Gentiles wandered astray and forsook the Lord, having changed the order. . . . In like manner the Watchers departed from nature's order; the Lord produced a curse on them at the Flood. On their account he ordered that the earth be without dweller or produce." This text refers explicitly to the "writing of holy Enoch" (4:1) and warns that God's people will likewise experience punishment for "living in accord with every wickedness of the Gentiles and committing every lawlessness of Sodom" (4:1). The same association is found in Jude 6–7 and 2 Pet 2:4–6, where both the disobedient angels and Sodom are cited as negative warnings for the present community. The author of 1 Peter also may have envisioned these angelic spirits as primordial "boundary violators." Their imprisonment and condemnation would serve as a warning for his audience to keep separate from the sins of disobedient Gentiles, as 1:14–17 and 4:2–3 also urge.

The concept of angelic disobedience also should be seen in connection with reference to disobedience elsewhere in 1 Peter. Those who reject Christ as the elect cornerstone are said to have "disobeyed" the word concerning him (2:7–8). The verb is used again in 3:1 of "disobedient" (i.e., nonbelieving) husbands and appears once more in 4:17 in regard to those who "disobey the good news of God." It is thus disobedience that characterizes all agents, both human and divine, who oppose God or God's agent of salvation, with the implication that the fate of those who continue to disobey will be that of the disobedient spirits of primordial time, a note of judgment sounded more immediately in 3:16 (cf. also 4:17). The disobedient spirits and their condemnation thus underline the importance of two key points of the letter: the necessity of maintaining clear social boundaries between believers and nonbelievers (1:14–16; 4:2–3) and the certainty of divine judgment on disobedience.

he announced (*ekēryxen*). This is the only finite verb in vv 19–20a and therefore expresses the main thought of these verses. As the sequence of the foregoing participles "having been put to death"–"having been made alive"–"having gone (into heaven)" indicates, this announcing took place in connection with Christ's resurrection and ascension to heaven. This alone rules out the the possibility that the announcing occurred during some putative "descent" of Christ into the realm of the dead in connection with his death but *before* his resurrection—that is, between Christ's death and resurrection (against Views 1 and 3). The one who announces, as the context indicates, is the resurrected Christ (3:18a, 18c, 19a; cf. also v 21d), not a preexistent Christ (against View 2), let alone Noah or Enoch. The recipients of this announcement were the angelic spirits, further described (as discussed above) as "those who once disobeyed" in the days of Noah.[292]

The absolute use of *ekēryxen*, however, with no additional indication of content, has led to much speculation concerning the *substance* of this announcement. The verb *kēryssō* frequently appears in the NT in connection with the verb *euaggelizō* and the noun *euaggelion* to denote the "heralding" of the good news of salvation (Matt 24:14; Mark 1:14; 13:10; 14:9; Luke 8:1; Col 1:23; 1 Thess 2:9). Since *euaggelizō* appears in 4:6 (*euēggelisthē*), it has been proposed that *ekēryxen* is to be interpreted in the light of *euēggelisthē* in 4:6 and implies Christ's preaching of repentance or forgiveness or salvation to deceased humans (View 1). But several facts argue against this conclusion. (1) When the content of *kēryssō* is the good news, this customarily is made explicit (see Matt 4:23; 9:35; 24:14; 26:13; Mark 1:14; 13:10; 14:9; 16:15; 1 Thess 2:9; cf. Luke 8:1, *kērussōn kai euaggelizomenoi* . . .). (2) There is no demonstrable correspondence between the thought in vv 19–20 and 4:6 and thus no reason for assuming an association between *ekēryxen* and *euēggelisthē*. Christ is the subject of *ekēryxen* but not of *euēggelisthē*, which has Christian preachers as its implied subject, as in 1:12 and 25. The human "dead" (*nekrois*) of 4:6 are not equivalents of the "spirits in prison" (v 19) who, as we have seen, are the rebellious angelic spirits rather than the human sinners of the Flood period or deceased humans generally. Nor can "judged in the flesh according to human standards" (4:6b) describe the fate of the disobedient angels in vv 19–20 who, according to the Flood tradition, were condemned by God rather than according to human standards. With no demonstrable association between vv 19–20 and 4:6,[293] there is no demonstrable equation of *ekēryxen* and *euēggelisthē*. Thus *ekēryxen* is best taken in the more neutral sense of *announce* ("proclaim," "act as a herald" [*kēryx*], as in Luke 12:3, Rom 2:21, and Rev 5:2), with no reference to the proclaiming of good news.

This neutral sense of *ekēryxen*, however, still leaves open the question of the *content* of this announcement, and again a text of the Flood tradition, *1 Enoch* (cf. also *2 Enoch*), provides the most satisfactory answer. According to this writing, as already noted, Enoch undertook a journey to heaven, during which he went to the angelic spirits whose defiance of God led to the evil resulting in the Flood, and announced to them their *doom and condemnation* (*1 En.* 12:4–6; 13:1–10; 14:1–7; 15:1–16:3; cf. *2 En.* 7). This declaration of condemnation by Enoch[294] is a consistent theme of the Flood tradition in both its Israelite and Christian (Jude 6; 2 Pet 2:3–4) elaborations, where it served as a warning for present human behavior. The judgment of these angels and their illicit offspring, who were considered the patrons of the mighty rulers of the world, was

---

[292] For a similar use of *kēryssō* with the dative of the indirect object, see Mark 16:15; Luke 4:18; Acts 8:5; 10:42; 1 Cor 9:27.

[293] So also Spitta 1890, 63–66; Selwyn 1947, 337–39; Best 1971, 144; Dalton 1989, 154–59.

[294] Or by one or more of the righteous angels; see *1 En.* 10:4 (Sync.), 11; 12:4; 13:1, 3; 15:2.

presented as a prototype of the coming judgment of the heathen rulers and oppressors of God's people, as *1 En.* 67:4–69:1 and especially 67:12 make clear: "This judgment with which the angels are judged is a testimony for the kings and the mighty who possess the earth." The affinity of 1 Pet 3:19–20 with this Flood tradition and with *1 Enoch* in particular, makes it most likely that the content of Christ's announcement, like that of Enoch, involved the *condemnation* of the disobedient spirits. This position, advanced variously by Spitta (1890, 26–27) and Gschwind (1911, 71–85, 111, 116, 130), has found favor with more recent scholars as well, including Selwyn (1947, 200), Dalton (1965, 1968, 1979, 1989), France (1977, 271–72), Davids (1990, 140–41), and others.

The notion that *erkēryxen* involved a proclaiming of repentance or the offer of salvation has far less to commend it (against the various versions of View 1, as articulated most recently by Goppelt 1993, 257–60). This only would make sense if "spirits" referred to deceased humans, which it does not. But even in this unlikely case, the thought of a second opportunity for repentance and salvation—offered to the deceased, no less—would be unique in the NT. It would also contradict later rabbinic teaching concerning the condemnation of the Flood generation (*m. Sanh.* 10:3), and it would be completely inconsistent with the outlook of 1 Peter, which envisions divine judgment according to one's deeds (1:17; 4:17–18) and condemnation of the disobedient (2:7–8; 4:17–18). Moreover, the alleged equation of *ekēryxen* and *euaggelisthē* (4:6) used to buttress this notion has already been noted as indemonstrable.

Reicke (1946, 120) speculated that *ekēryxen* (taken to mean "preached or proclaimed the Gospel") had as its content "the secret about Himself as the humbly suffering, and thereby victorious, Messiah." Others saw the announcement chiefly as a declaration of Christ's victory or glory (e.g., Jensen 1903, 185; Gschwind 1911, 125–25; Selwyn 1947, 200). Dalton takes the entire statement, "he announced to the spirits in prison," to refer to "Christ's self-presentation as risen Lord to the hostile angelic powers in the heavens on the occasion of his ascension, an idea, echoed in different terms, in the subjugation of the 'angels, authorities and powers' in 3:22" (1989, 26; cf. also 154–59; and J. N. D. Kelly 1969, 156). Indeed, the correspondence of the verbs *poreutheis* in v 19 and v 22 does suggest a further correspondence between the *disobedient spirits* in v 19 and the cosmic spirits in v 22. Their subordination to Christ in v 22 would then be a demonstration of their condemnation announced in v 19b.

Ultimately there is little difference between an announcement of subjugation or of victory or of condemnation, for the point is the same: Christ's complete containment of and control over these angelic spirits. However, the weight of the Flood tradition to which 1 Peter alludes favors *condemnation* as the content of Christ's announcement.[295] This would be consistent with the

---

[295] In *1 Clem.* 9:4 this same verb *kēryssō* is used absolutely of Noah, but the point made there differs significantly from that of 1 Peter: "Noah was found faithful in his service, in announcing (*ekēryxen*) a new beginning to the world, and through him the Master saved the living creatures which in concord entered the ark." The description of Christ's resurrection in the second-century

fate of the persistently disobedient, as described throughout 1 Peter. The idea that the announcing constituted a proclamation of *good news* arose only at the end of the second century, in connection with a new question concerning the fate of the righteous who lived before Christ; see DETAILED COMMENT 2. 1 Peter, along with Jude 6 and 2 Pet 2:3–4, reflects an earlier stage of the Christian appropriation of the Flood tradition, in which the accent falls exclusively on the condemnation of the disobedient angelic spirits and the rescue of Noah and his family alone. Any notion of a possibility of conversion or salvation after death would seriously undermine the letter's consistent stress on the necessity of righteous behavior here and now. On the other hand, assurance of the condemnation of all those who disobey, both angels and humans, along with the certainty of Christ's control of the cosmic powers would provide significant comfort to Christian believers who were under attack by disobedient Gentiles and who were wondering about the certainty of God's justice.

20b. *when God's patience waited in the days of Noah* (*hote apexedecheto hē tou theou makrothymia en hēmerais Nōe*). This clause qualifies the foregoing text in regard to time and circumstances: the "spirits" are those angelic spirits who once disobeyed in the primordial time of the Flood. Here, as in 2 Pet 2:4–5 and the Flood tradition in general, mention of the disobedient angelic spirits is immediately followed by and linked with the event of the Flood. This is the first in a remarkable series of subordinate phrases or clauses, each qualifying and expanding upon its predecessor, extending through the final words in v 22.[296]

The reference to *the days of Noah* locates the disobedient spirits in terms of time[297] and prepares for the correspondence drawn between the salvation of Noah and his family and the salvation of the baptized. The story of Noah and the Deluge (Gen 6:5–8:22) served both Israelites and Christians as the primordial and prototypical event of the destruction of the unrighteous (Gen 6:11–13, 17; 7:21–23a; 8:21) and the salvation of the righteous (Gen 7:23b; 8:1–22). According to the Genesis narrative, Noah stood at the end of the primordial 1,500-year era extending from the creation of the world to its conclusion in his own day. In Genesis, Noah figures as "an epoch divider figure as well as a bridge between the quasi-mythological history and a more humanly accountable history" (Kikawada 1992, 1123), just as parallel figures serve in other eth-

---

Gospel of Peter (10:1–4), with three men leaving Christ's tomb followed by a cross and a voice from heaven asking, "Have you preached to those who sleep?" also is irrelevant. This later narrative is unique in the early Christian tradition and, aside from the verb "preached/announced," has nothing in common with 1 Pet 3:19. Consequently, it offers no aid for clarifying the substance of Christ's announcement to the angelic spirits here in 1 Peter.

[296] For other, more inclusive, theories of this "step construction" (embracing 3:17–21 or 3:17–22), see Perrot 1980, 244–45 and Cervantes Gabarrón 1991, 190, respectively.

[297] For the expression "the days of Noah" as a reference to the event of the Flood, see also Isa 54:9; Matt 24:37/Luke 17:26.

nic Flood traditions.[298] Elsewhere in the Bible and related tradition, Noah is held up as an exemplar of uprightness,[299] a model of God's compassion and covenant,[300] a preacher of repentance,[301] or a preacher of the beginning of a new generation.[302] His rescue also served as a model for the story of Moses' rescue in his "ark" or basket (Exod 2:1–10), the rescue of the Israelites at the Reed Sea (Exod 15), and the rescue of Jonah.[303] In Israel's apocalyptic writings, the salvation of Noah, Enoch's grandson (*1 En.* 65:1–5, 9; 68:1), and the condemnation of the rebellious angels serve as the combined example of divine deliverance and destruction (*1 En.* 106; *Jub.* 5:12–19; *3 Bar.* 4:10–11; *Sib. Or.* 1:125–282). The reference to Noah in the *Genesis Apocryphon*, one of the seven major scrolls found in Qumran Cave 1, is an important illustration of the merger of the accounts of the disobedient angels and the story of Noah that had taken place by this time.[304] It relates the anxiety of Lamech, Noah's father, that Noah might have been the product of his mother's intercourse with one of the Watchers/Holy Ones/Nephilim/sons of heaven (1QapGen[ar] II 1–26; III 3; IV 4; V 3–27; cf. *1 En.* 106). In the NT, the "days of Noah" and the Flood serve as an example of the coming of the Son of Man and as an instance of eschatological warning (Matt 24:37–39/Luke 17:26–27; 2 Pet 2:4–5; 3:5–6). Beside 1 Pet 3:20 and 2 Pet 2:5, the theme of Noah's deliverence figured prominently in early Christian art.[305]

The Petrine author makes no mention of Noah as "herald." Thus there is no exegetical reason for imagining any association of the verb *ekēryxen* in v 19b with the "heralding" of Noah or, for that matter, any association of Christ with Noah, contrary to the once dominant theory of Augustine (Christ "in the spirit" preaching through Noah, View 2) revived recently by Feinberg (1986), Grudem (1988, 160, 204, 218–20), and Erickson (1995). Here the emphasis falls not on Noah alone but on the salvation of his *entire family* (see the NOTE on v 20d). The Pauline writings, by contrast, contain no references to Noah or to the Flood in the days of Noah.

when God's patience waited (*hote apexedecheto hē tou theou makrothymia*). The expression is without exact parallel in the biblical literature. The verb

[298] Traditions from Mesopotamia, Sumeria, Iran, India, and Greece (righteous Deucalion and his wife Pyrrha; cf. the explicit equation of Noah and Deucalion made by Justin Martyr, 2 *Apol.* 7).

[299] See Ezek 14:14, 20; Wis 10:4; Sir 44:17; Tob 4:12; Philo, *Abr.* 27–46; *Migr.* 125; Josephus, *Ant.* 1.75–79, 99; Heb 11:7 (exemplar of faith); *1 En.* 106:18; 107:3; *2 En.* 35:1–3; *Jub.* 7:20–39; 10:17; *4 Ezra* 3:9–11; *Sib. Or.* 1:125–282; cf. 7.7–15; *2 Clem.* 6:8.

[300] See Isa 54:9–10; Jer 31: 35, 36; Sir 44:18; *Jub.* 6:4–16.

[301] See Josephus, *Ant.* 1.74; Heb 11:7; 2 Pet 2:5; *1 Clem.* 7:6; *Sib. Or.* 1.128–29, 147–98.

[302] See Philo, *Abr.* 46; *Mos.* 2.60, 65; cf. also Ps.-Philo, *L.A.B.* 1:3–10.

[303] On Noah and the Flood, see J. P. Lewis 1968, 1984, 1992; and Bailey 1989, 1992.

[304] For further examples of this merging of accounts, see *1 En.* 54:1–6/7–10; 64:1–2/65:1–69:29; 85:1–88:3/89:1–9; 106:13–14/15–107:3; *Jub.* 7:20–25.

[305] See Fink 1955; Hooyman 1958; Kötzsche-Breitenbach 1976, 51–54 and plate 4a (Via Latina catacomb).

apexedecheto ("wait out," "await") occurs elsewhere in the NT (1 Cor 1:7; Gal 5:5; Phil 3:20) but never with God as subject. Elsewhere reference is also made to the patience or magnanimity (*makrothymia*) of God.[306] The expression as a whole, however, is a unique Petrine formulation. Genesis 6 makes no explicit reference to God's "patience" or "forbearance." Israelite interpreters regarded Gen 6:3 ("The Lord said, 'My spirit shall not abide in humanity forever, but its days shall be one hundred and twenty years' "), an indication of the length of human life, in a different sense—as an instance of God's allowance of time for repentance (*Tg. Neof.*, *Tg. Onq.*, and *Tg. Ps.-J.* on Gen 6:3.; *m. ʾAbot* 5:2). Philo seems to express a similar thought (*QG* 2.12) and goes on to describe the "seven days" of Gen 7:4 ("in seven days I will send rain upon the earth") as a period of grace in which God "kept back the flood after their entering the ark" and as a "reminder of the genesis of the world" brought about by "God's goodness and kindness" (*ho agathotēs kai hē chrystotēs*); for a similar combination of the motifs of Flood, God's patience, and repentance, see also 2 Pet 3:6 and 9. The idea of repentance, however, is absent in 1 Peter, so that Noah and his family, rather than human sinners, appear to be the implied beneficiaries of this divine forbearance (against Grudem 1988, 218). Here in 1 Peter this divine patience then would refer to God's restraint of his destruction of a corrupted earth until the ark had been completed, a reference to which occurs in the following phrase.

20c. *during the building of the ark* (*kataskeuazomenēs kibōtou*) or "while the ark was being constructed." This second in a series of subordinate qualifying statements is a genitive absolute construction modifying *in the days of Noah*; for the construction, see also 4:1a; 4:4b; 5:4a.

ark (*kibōtos*). The term denotes the protective vessel occupied, according to the Genesis account, by Noah, his family, and the pairs of creatures taken aboard (Gen 6:14–9:18, with "ark" mentioned 28×). Its size, according to Gen 6:15, was 300 cubits long, 50 cubits wide, 30 cubits high (i.e., 450 feet by 75 feet by 45 feet). Its enormous size is illustrated by its comparison with the Mayflower, which, as Bailey (1992, 1131) observes, was only 90 feet long. Josephus (*Ant.* 1.93), noting that "this flood and the ark are mentioned by all who have written histories of the barbarians," quotes the Hellenized Babylonian priest Berosos (ca. 330–250 BCE), who refers to a legend stating that "a portion of the vessel still survives in Armenia on the mountain of the Gordyaeans and that some people carry off pieces of the bitumen which they use as amulets" (cf. also *Ant.* 1.90, 92). The ancient association of the ark with Mt. Ararat in northeastern Turkey (Gen 8:4; *Jub.* 5:8; 1QapGen[ar] X 2) still holds a fascination for those today on a quest for the lost ark (see Bailey 1978 and 1992, 1131–32). Another legendary tradition, on the other hand, traced the ark's resting

[306] See Rom 2:4; 9:22; cf. Ign. *Eph.* 11:1; see also the related adjective used of God in Exod 34:6; Num 14:18; Ps 102[103]:8; *1 Clem.* 19:3; Herm., *Sim.* 8.11.1; *Barn.* 3:6; *Diogn.* 8:70.

place and Ararat to the "dark mainland of Phrygia" (*Sib. Or.* 1:262–82; 7:12).[307]

Josephus (*Ant.* 1.77–78) described Noah's ark as "the means of salvation (*pros sōtērian*)," and in Israel's martyrological tradition the renowned mother of the seven martyred sons who bore up amidst the storms against piety is compared with the ark of Noah, which bore up against the waves (4 Macc 15:31; cf. *Sib. Or.* 1:225–41). In the period following 1 Peter, some Christian texts present the ark as a *type*, either of the cross[308] or of the Church.[309] J. N. D. Kelly's suggestion (1969, 158), however, that this latter association appears here in 1 Peter "in embryo" claims more than is apparent in the text.

The verb *kataskeuazō* ("make ready," "construct," "build") does not occur in the Genesis account of the Flood. It is, however, employed by Josephus (*Ant.* 1.77), who speaks of Noah as "having built" (*kataskeuasas*) the ark (cf. also Philo, *QG* 2.1 for *kataskeuē*).[310]

20d, e, f. *in which a few—that is, eight persons—were saved through water* (*eis hēn oligoi—tout' estin oktō psychai—diesōthēsan di' hydatos*). This is the third in a series of qualifications modifying what goes before. In this case, "ark" is the antecedent of the relative "which" (*hēn*). The use of *eis* ("in, into") in place of an expected *en* ("in") may have been occasioned by the recurring expression *eis tēn kibōtēn* ("into the ark") in the Genesis narrative (7:1, 7, 9, 13, 15). In any case, the locative use of *eis* as a replacement for *en* was already common in the NT period (Mark 1:9; Luke 11:7; John 1:18; Acts 8:40, etc.; see BDF §205) and appears again in 1 Pet 5:12. Cook (1980) favors the normal sense of *eis* as "into" and translates "into which a few . . . came safely through water," taking the expression to state that Noah and his family passed through water to step into the ark. But this proposal unconvincingly takes "water" to indicate only the water already on the ground rather than the entirety of the Flood in the midst of which Noah and his family were saved. The Petrine expression, with *eis* replacing *en*, parallels the formulation of Josephus (*Ag. Ap.* 1.130): "the ark in which (*larnakos en hēi*) Noah, the founder of our race, was saved (*diesōthē*)."

20d. *a few* (*oligoi*, masc. pl.). This Greek word is the subject of the following verb, "were saved." The masculine substantive *oligoi* (generic for "a few persons") has better manuscript support (𝔓[72] א A B and others) than the variant feminine *oligai* (C P Ψ 𝔐 and others), which probably was regarded as an adjective modifying the following feminine term "persons" (*pyschai*). Bishop

[307] On local Phrygian traditions concerning the Flood and on locally minted coins of Apamea in Phrygia (already known as *Apamea kibōtos*, Strabo, *Geogr.* 12.569, 576; Pliny, *Nat.* 5.106) depicting Noah and the ark, see Trebilco (1991, 86–90).

[308] The "wood" on which Noah was borne to safety, Justin, *Dial.* 38.2; cf. Wis 14:5–7 for the equivalency of "ark" and "wood."

[309] See Tert., *Bapt.* 8.4; Cyprian, *Unit. eccl.* 6.

[310] For Noah as the builder, see also *1 En.* 89:1 and Heb 11:7; contrast *1 En.* 67:2 (constructed by angels "working with wood").

(1951) takes *few* as indicating here and in Mark 8:7 a number between three and ten. Although his point is based on later Arabic usage, it is consistent with the following Petrine qualification, "eight persons."

20e. *that is, eight persons* (*tout' estin oktō psychai*). This is a fourth in the series of qualifying formulations, in this case modifying the preceding expression, *a few*. It is interjected parenthetically between the subject *few* and its predicate *were saved through water*; a similar parenthetical clarification is made of "baptism" in v 21bc.

The term *psychai* ("persons") denotes living beings (as in Gen 46:15; Exod 1:5; Lev 7:27; 23:29; Acts 2:41; 7:14; 27:37; and elsewhere in 1 Peter: 1:9, 22; 2:11, 25; 4:19; see the NOTE on 1:9). The Genesis account expressly named these persons as Noah, his wife, his three sons, and their wives. 1 Peter, having just mentioned Noah (v 20b) and stressing the group's number as "eight," implies that it is Noah and his family that is meant.

eight (*oktō*, apparently inadvertently omitted in $\mathfrak{P}^{72}$) is the number of the group saved, embracing Noah, his wife, their sons and their wives.[311] The number "eight" (*oktō*) gradually came to symbolize completeness and perfection and was associated with other significant times or events[312] and especially with Sunday, the "Lord's Day," as the day of Jesus' resurrection, marking a new beginning in time (Just. Mart., *Dial.* 138.1; see Reicke 1964, 112–13; Hillyer 1992, 119). According to Irenaeus (*Haer.* 1.18.3), speculation concerning numbers, including the eight persons saved in the Flood (with the ogdoad regarded in itself as a symbol of salvation), was a typical heretical trait. The Petrine author, however, uses the number *eight* not figuratively but literally to clarify the preceding term, *few*. He thus underscores the exceedingly low number of those saved in the Flood.

20f. *were saved through water* (*diesōthēsan di' hydatos*). With these words, our author reaches the chief point he wishes to make concerning Noah and his family: this small household *was saved by God*. In the Genesis account of the preservation of Noah and his family, the verb "save" does not occur. It is present, however, in numerous other texts recounting the Flood.[313] The composite verb *diasōzō* functions as a synonym for the simple verb *sōzō*, with the same meaning of "save," "rescue" from a perilous situation (2 Macc 1:25 and 2:17; Matt 14:36; Luke 7:3; Acts 23:24; 27:43, 44; 28:1, 4). Josephus uses both verbs

---

[311] See Gen 6:18; 7:7, 13; 8:16, 18; and *1 En.* 106:18; cf. also *1 En.* 10:2; 65:2; 67:2; 89:1; *Jub.* 5:19; *Sib. Or.* 1.280–81 (Noah came out eighth); 2 Pet 2:5 ("Noah and seven other persons"); Just. Mart., *Dial.* 138; Theoph., *Autol.* 3.19; and Iren., *Haer.* 1.18.3.

[312] Circumcision on the eighth day (Gen 17:12; Luke 2:21); a healed leper declared clean on the eighth day (Lev 23:36; John 7:37).

[313] See *1 En.* 106:16 (*sōthēsetai*); *Jub.* 7:34 ("my God who has saved me from the water of the Flood") and 10:3 ("[God] has acted mercifully with me and saved me and my sons from the water of the Flood"); Josephus, *Ant.* 1.76, 78, 89; *Ag. Ap.* 1.130; *Sib. Or.* 1.136; Heb 11:7 (*eis sōtērian*); *1 Clem.* 9:4 ("through him [Noah] the Master saved [*diesōsen*] the living creatures which in concord entered the ark"). For the idea, see also *1 En.* 10:1–3; 67:1–4; 89:1–9; 106:18; 107:1–3; *Sib. Or.* 1.199–282; 2 Pet 2:5.

synonymously in describing Noah's being saved (*Ant.* 1.76 [*sōzetai*], 78 [*dia-sōzetai*]; cf. 1.89 [*diasōthēnai*]; *Ag. Ap.* 1.130 [*diesōthē*]). In the present Petrine context, the composite verb is balanced by the simple *sōizei* in 3:21. Its passive form here implies God as the saving agent, as does the passive *sōizetai* in 4:18.

through water (*di' hydatos*). The formulation *were saved through water* contains a double use of the preposition *dia* (*di' hydatos* and the composite verb *dia-sōizō*) and poses a question as to whether "through water" (*di' hydatos*) has instrumental or local force.[314] With instrumental force, *dia* would indicate that the household of Noah was saved *by means of* water (favored by Michaels 1988, 213). In this case, *dia* would have the same instrumental force as it does in the succeeding parallel phrase, "baptism saves . . . through the resurrection of Jesus Christ" (v 21):

diesōthēsan di' hydatos	were saved through water (20f)
sōizei . . . di' anastaseōs Iēsou Christou	saves . . . through the resurrection of Jesus Christ (21a, d)

The similarity is more formal than substantive, however, since "through the resurrection of Jesus Christ" indicates the saving power behind baptism, whereas "through water" can hardly connote the power by which the family of Noah was saved. The passive of the verb *diesōthēsan* clearly implies God as the saving Agent, a use of the passive typical of Petrine style. Moreover, the idea that Noah's family could have been saved "by" water runs contrary to the entire Flood tradition, which stresses a rescue *from* the destructive effect of the Flood. Thus *Jubilees*, for example, states that Noah and his sons were "saved *from* the water of the Flood" (7:34; 10:3), and this is the sense implied by Josephus as well: "The ark had stout sides and roof so as not to be overwhelmed from any quarter and to defy the violence of the waters. Thus was Noah saved (*dia-sōzetai*) with his family" (Josephus, *Ant.* 1.78; cf. also 4 Macc 15:31).

Therefore, it is more likely that *dia* functions in combination with its verb *diesōthēsan* as a *locative* indicating that the household of Noah was saved while "passing through" water.[315] This sense of being saved "in the midst of" the waters is supported by the reference to Noah's ark and the salvation of its occupants in Wis 14:1–7. Wisdom 14:5 reads: "therefore do persons entrust their lives to a small piece of wood and *passing through the rough sea* in a weak vessel were saved" (*dielthontes klydōna schediai diesōthēsan*). As Selwyn (1947, 202–3) and J. N. D. Kelly (1969, 159) aptly note, however, the problem of this grammatical issue should not be exaggerated and it is even conceivable that the author intentionally employed an ambiguous formulation so that it could be taken in either sense. The ambiguity of the phrase would assist the transition

---

[314] Gen 7:7 provides no answer because there *dia* is used with a different, causal sense: "Then Noah, with his sons and his wife and his sons' wives, entered into the ark *because of* (*dia*) the water of the flood (*dia to hydōr tou kataklysmou*)."

[315] So also Reicke 1946, 141–42; Beasley-Murray 1963, 259; Goppelt 1993, 265–66.

from a condensed version of the OT story to its Christian counterpart. Whereas the original Flood story entailed the rescue of those in the ark and the destruction of others by water, the Petrine author focuses exclusively on the aspect of salvation. It is this divine act of salvation that constitutes the chief analogy between the experience of the family of Noah and that of Christian believers.

21. The parallel to v 20 in v 21 represents the first time in Christian thought that a correspondence (signaled by *kai* and *antitypon*) is drawn between the Flood and Christian baptism and, specifically, their correspondence as events of divine salvation. Several features of v 21, however, are not immediately clear. These include (1) the textual presence and/or case of the Greek pronoun *ho* or *hōi*, the question of its antecedent and of its relation to either *antitypon* or *baptisma*; (2) the meaning and grammatical function of *antitypon* and its relation to *baptisma*; and (3) the semantic as well as syntactic relation of v 21a to what precedes it.[316] The conclusions reflected in the following NOTES can be summarized as follows:

(1) The terms *kai* and *antitypon* signal some kind of correspondence between the thought of v 21a and the foregoing. The double appearance of verbs meaning "save" (*diesōthēsan*, v 20d; *sōizei*, v 21a) is the most explicit indication of the correspondence intended: namely, the salvation of the believers ("you") as analogous to the salvation of Noah and his household ("a few, that is, eight persons"). In vv 20–21 a correspondence is established between the protological salvation of Noah and his family and the eschatological salvation of the present believers through the resurrection of Jesus Christ and baptism.

(2) Verse 21a involves two text-critical problems. The first concerns the presence or absence of an initial pronoun and, if present, the question of its case. There are three chief possibilities: (a) *ho*, a neuter nominative ("which," with the weightier MS support of א^{c} A B C K P and the majority of MSS); (b) *hōi*, a neuter dative ("to which," with the inferior MS support of 69 206 216 241 630 1518); or (c) the absence of the pronoun altogether (𝔓^{72} א* 255 436 eth). Of these variants, the dative *hōi*, despite its weaker external attestation, is conceivable as the original reading with which a later nominative was inadvertently confused because of the similarity in sight and sound between *hōi* and *ho*; its grammatical function as the object of the adjective *antitypon* ("corresponding to this") accords best with the remainder of this verse.

The second textual problem involves the variants "you" (*hymas*) and "us" (*hēmas*). The pronoun *hymas* (𝔓^{72} A B P Ψ and others) has earlier and stronger manuscript support than does *hēmas* (C L 514 630 𝔐) and better accords with the context (the stress on "you" in v 18c and vv 13–17).

(3) The term *antitypon*, which could function as either an adjective or an independent substantive, is best taken as an adjective modifying "baptism" and as linked with the dative pronoun *hōi* with this sense: "corresponding to this

[316] On the scholarly discussion, see Selwyn 1947, 203–24, 298–99; Reicke 1946, 144–45.

[namely the salvation of Noah and his family through the water], baptism now saves you too."

(4) The phrase *kai hymas* ("you too") is accented in Greek through its location at the earliest possible place in the Greek sentence (between *hōi* and *antitypon*). This is reflected in its accented position in English at the end of the sentence.

21a. *Corresponding to this* (*hōi. . . antitypon*). The correspondence that these terms entail is indicated by the structural correspondence between elements in v 20 and v 21 and primarily by the parallel use of verbs meaning "save" (*diesōthēsan*, v 20d; *sōizei*, v 21a):

v 20	v 21
oligioi	*hymas*
diesōthēsan	*nyn sōizei baptisma*
di' hydatos	*di' anastaseōs Iēsou Christou*
a few	you
were saved	baptism now saves
through water	through the resurrection of Jesus Christ

The parallel terms for "save" provide explicit evidence that the correspondence concerns two analogous saving events: the earlier saving of Noah and his family ("a few—that is, eight persons—were saved through water") and the present saving of the believers effected by baptism ("baptism now saves you too . . . through the resurrection of Jesus Christ").

This, in turn, helps to decide the questions involving the relative pronoun (*ho* or *hōi*) and its antecedent. The reading *ho* (neuter nominative), as indicated, has superior manuscript support and as the most difficult reading could account for the origin of *hoi* as a simplifying replacement. This nominative in turn either could have "water" (a neuter noun, "which water . . .") as its antecedent or could be linked with baptism (also a neuter noun, "which baptism . . ."). In both cases, however, the absence of a verb leaves unclear the syntactical relation between "which (water)" or "which (baptism)" and the remainder of the sentence. Connecting *ho* with "water" ("which water") generally results in a translation that must supply additional words not present in the text in order to produce a clear statement (e.g., Windisch 1951, 72). In addition, this option regards the "water" of the Flood as the instrument of Christian salvation, as though it were equivalent with, rather than comparable to, baptism. But the moral qualification of baptism in 3:21b rules out this equation.

The alternative "which baptism" (taking *ho* with *baptisma*), though a bit more felicitous syntactically, likewise leaves in question the relation of baptism to the term *antitypon*, so that those preferring this option also are required to add words not contained in the text. Reicke (1946, 145), who links *ho* with *baptisma*, views *antitypon* as an adjectival attribute to *baptisma* but regards the entire formulation (*ho . . . baptisma*) as "an apposition to the previous sentence drawn into the relative clause" (a construction illustrated by Greek and NT texts that he subsequently lists [1946, 146–72]). This results in the translation: "which antitypical baptism now saves you." But this is not the sense of *antitypos* in Heb 9:24, which Reicke cites as support. Perhaps to obviate this difficulty concerning the pronoun, other manuscripts (𝔓[72] ℵ and a few other MSS) deliberately omitted it.

On the other hand, it is also possible to regard the third textual reading, *hōi* (neuter dative), as the original reading, which eventually underwent inadvertent corruption or substitution by the nominative pronoun *ho*.[317] In this case, *hōi* ("to which," "to this"), referring not to the preceding word "water" but to the entire foregoing statement concerning the salvation of the family of Noah, would have a function similar to that of the relative phrase *en hōi* elsewhere in the letter (1:6; 2:12; 3:16; and 4:4). This would create no further syntactical problems and would be consistent with the parallelism of the two verbs for "save." For these reasons, this third option is preferred; "to this" (*hoi*) refers to the immediately foregoing statement concerning the salvation of Noah and his family (v 20d).

This leads to the related question concerning the meaning and syntactical function of the term *antitypon*. The rare term *antitypon* was used as both an adjective (Soph., *Phil.* 693, 1460; Lucian, *De domo* 3; Polyb., *Hist.* 6.31.8) and a predicate noun. In its only other NT occurrence, Heb 9:24, it is used to describe the Israelite "sanctuary (*hagia*) made with hands" as an inferior and secondary "copy" (*antitypa*) of the true one in the heavens (with *antitypa* [plural] synonymous with the plural *ta hypodeigmata* ["copies," Heb 9:23]).[318] Its kindred term *typos* is used later in 1 Pet 5:3 of elders who are to be positive "types" or models for the community. An antitype in general is that which corresponds to or is the counterpart of a (proto)type (*typos*). Each term when used independently of the other can denote either something original or its copy, with its actual meaning determined by its context (Selwyn 1947, 298–99). In Acts 7:44 and Heb 8:5 (citing Exod 25:40), *typos* identifies the complete (original and superior) type that serves as the "pattern" for the earthly tent of witness in the wilderness. Alternatively, *typos* can denote Adam as the foregoing imperfect "type" of Christ (Rom 4:14), or the ancient Israelites in the wilderness as "types" (*typoi*, 1 Cor 10:6; cf. *typikōs*, 10:11) for the experience and warning of present believers (1 Cor 10:1–13). For *typos* as "copy," see *Barn.* 19:7; *Did.* 4:11; Ign. *Trall.* 3:1.

In general, *typos* and *antitypon* were employed by the early Christians to signal some perceived correspondence between events of the sacred past and the present and some assured continuity between God's action in past, present, and future; for example, Adam-Christ (Rom 5:12; 1 Cor 15); Elijah–John the

[317] So Gschwind 1911, 139; Beare 1970, 174; Beasley-Murray 1963, 260; and earlier, Erasmus and Hort.

[318] Cf. also 2 *Clem.* 14:3 and Esth 3:13 (a secondary erroneous variant).

Baptist (Matt 11:14; 17:12); Jonah-Christ (Luke 11:29–32)); Israel "baptized in Moses in the cloud and in the sea" and Christian baptism (1 Cor 10:1–3); Israel in the wilderness as a warning for present believers (1 Cor 10:5–13); the Israelite high priest and Christ as high priest (Heb 5:1–10); or Melchizedek-Christ (Heb 7:1–17; cf. Goppelt 1982).

In this Petrine context, *antitypon* also could function as either a predicate noun or as an adjective. The former is preferred by Goppelt (1993, 266), who takes *antitypon* as a substantive in apposition to *baptisma*, with a nominative *ho* referring to the entire preceding statement ("as an antitype to this, baptism now also delivers you" [Goppelt 1993, 247]). But in this case the sentence would then contain two nouns (*antitypon, baptisma*) whose relation, even if appositional, is unclear given the absence of any linking term, so that Goppelt is forced to add the comparative "as," which is not in the text. The problem is that this construction of a relative pronoun with an epexegetic substantive introducing a new idea has no Greek precedent. In addition, although Goppelt takes the relative pronoun *ho* as a nominative ("which"), his translation implies the assumption of a dative *hōi*: "as an antitype *to this*, baptism now also delivers you" (Goppelt 1993, 247).

J. N. D. Kelly (1969, 160) and Michaels (1988, 214), on the other hand, are representative of those who take *antitypon* as an adjective and the phrase *ho antitypon* as referring to "water" of the preceding verse, with *baptisma* as appositional to *antitypon* (cf. also BAGD 76 sub *antitypon*). However, Kelly's translation ("which thus prefigured now saves you too [I mean] baptism") is at best an awkward rendition of what he claims is "a clumsy construction" in the original. Moreover, his statement that "the *water* [emphasis mine] of the Flood prefigures that of baptism" (J. N. D. Kelly 1969, 161) claims a correspondence that is not explicitly indicated in the text. Michaels aptly comments, "that which now saves Christians is not of course the same water that once saved Noah, but something 'corresponding' to it." But even Michaels' translation ("this water—or baptism, which corresponds to it—now saves you as well" [Michaels 1988, 214]) obscures this distinction while also implying a syntactical construction not present in the text. The adjustment of punctuation to include *ho kai hymas antitypon* with v 21 (so Brooks 1974, 291) separates this clause from *baptisma* and, hence, also must be rejected.

The preferable solution, therefore, is to take *antitypon* as an adjective ("corresponding") modifying *baptisma* (so also Reicke 1946, 145) but joined with *hoi* ("to which"[319]) "corresponding to this" (i.e., "a few—that is, eight persons—were saved through water"), "baptism now saves you too." For a similar use of *en hōi* to refer to the foregoing statements, see 3:19 as well as 1:6; 2:12; and 3:16. For other examples of *antitypon* with the dative, see Polybius 6.31.8; Nonnus, *Dion*. 26.327. The dative pronoun need not be seen as an intentional substitution for a more difficult original nominative but can be regarded as the

[319] In contrast to Reicke, Selwyn, J. N. D. Kelly, and others, who prefer *ho* to *hoi*.

original reading with which a later term (*ho*), similar in both sight and sound, was *inadvertently* confused. As Hort observed (cited by Selwyn 1947, 203), the connection of *hōi* and *antitypon* may well have been overlooked because of the intervening words "also you" placed at the the beginning of the verse for the sake of emphasis. This alternative was favored by Beare (1970, 174) and earlier by Hort (following Erasmus and Beza), Bernard (in Selwyn 1947, 203), and Gschwind (1911, 139). Conceivable on text-critical grounds, it avoids the problems posed by alternative interpretations. Without violence to the word order and syntax of the text, it yields a clear sense consistent with the remainder of this verse.

The chief weakness of other proposals is their failure to convey the explicit correspondence of *saving actions* evident in vv 20–21. This applies also to Selwyn's preference (1947, 203) for *antitypon* as a substantive "in apposition with *hymas*," thereby claiming a correspondence between the "company of Noah" (the type) and the Christian community (the antitype; cf. also Gschwind 1911, 131). Thus he translates: "And water now saves you too, who are the antitype of Noah and his company, namely the water of baptism." Besides the awkwardness of this translation and its abitrary addition of "water" (not in the original Greek), this proposal accentuates a correspondence between *persons* over a correspondence between *saving events*. But it is baptism as a saving act, rather than a saved group, that is further clarified in v 21bc. The chief *explicit* correspondence is between the verbs of the same root (*diasōzō, sōzō*).

Thus, the primary focus is on corresponding *saving events* rather than a correspondence of groups, or persons (Christ and Noah), or the Flood water and baptism, or the one ark of Noah as a type of the one true Church (Cyprian, *Ep.* 73.11; 74.15; 75.2), or the wood of the ark and that of the cross (Just. Mart., *Dial.* 138.2). This Petrine passage is the earliest association between the Flood and baptism in Christian literature (see Danielou 1950, 74–85; 1956, 70–85 for later developments). While this association and the presence of the term *antitypon* in v 21a may have invited such typological interpretations, it must also be recognized that they represent imaginative elaborations that go beyond the actual words and explicit correspondence present in the Petrine text.

The correspondence announced by *antitypon* is expressed as follows: "baptism now saves you too . . . through the resurrection of Jesus Christ" (*kai hymas . . . nyn sōizei baptisma di' anastaseōs Iēsou Christou*). Inserted into this statement is the couplet of v 21bc, which is added immediately after *baptism* in order to clarify the nature of baptism.

The noun *baptisma*, literally, "dipping," "immersion," and akin to *baptismos* ("dipping," "washing"), appears nowhere outside the NT (Oepke 1964, 545; on baptismal terminology in general, see Ysebaert 1962). In the Gospels and Acts it is used predominantly of the baptism of John the Baptist (13×). In the Pauline and Deutero-Pauline letters it is used exclusively of the messianic community's rite of initiation and incorporation. In the early Church in general, the rite of baptism was seen as putting believers into contact with the power of God, who raises the dead and gives life, the cardinal demonstration of which is the resurrection of Jesus Christ (1:3; 3:21; Rom 6:1–11).

Previously in the letter, our author already alluded to various aspects of the addressees' conversion and baptism (sanctification, rebirth, purification, etc.) and its moral implications (leading holy lives, desisting from evil, practicing what is right, etc.) through the employment of early Christian catechetical and parenetic tradition associated with baptism. It is, however, only at this point that he *explicitly* mentions baptism, clarifies its specific nature, and notes its correspondence to a saving event of primordial time.

The relationship drawn between the saving of the household of Noah and the saving of the believers establishes a correspondence and continuity between protological and eschatological events of salvation. The former serves typologically as a paradigm for the latter, so that *Endzeit gleicht Urzeit* ("end time resembles primordial time"). Paul also linked Christian baptism with an earlier event of deliverence in Israel's history. However, it was not the rescue of Noah's family to which he referred but rather Israel's passing through the Reed Sea (1 Cor 10:1–2). Moreover, with a greater sense of eschatological reservation he spoke of the resurrection of believers as only *anticipated* in baptism as an event yet to be experienced in the future (Rom 6:3–5; 1 Cor 15:22). This Petrine formulation, on the other hand, is the first Christian association of baptism with the salvation of Noah's household, an association that was to inspire Christian theology and art for generations to come.[320] The impact of this Petrine association on Christian liturgy was evident as late as the era of the Reformation, when Martin Luther in his German translation of the traditional liturgy of baptism, "The Order of Baptism," added the "Flood prayer" (*Sintflutgebet*) celebrating the preserving of Noah and his family as "prefiguring this bath of thy baptism" (*LW* 53:95–103, esp. p. 97 [= *WA* 12:42–48]).

As a ritual of conversion, baptism was the public celebration of both a personal transformation and a social transition. It signaled, according to 1 Peter, a personal spiritual and moral transformation from a life of conformity with the futile customs of the ancestors, hopelessness, and alienation from God to a life in union with God the gracious and Holy One, Jesus Christ the Resurrected one, and incorporation into a new fictive kin group, a brotherhood of faith (1:2; 1:3–2:10; 2:17; 5:9). It simultaneously inaugurated a transition from one set of social allegiances and alliances to another that included termination of conformity to modes of behavior characteristic of those alienated from God (1:14–21; 2:11–12; 4:1–4). The sanctification that baptism effected (1:2, 22; 2:4–10) was to be manifested in lives of holy conduct, obedience to God's will, upright behavior, and renunciation of wrongdoing (2:11–5:11). As a rite of initiation and incorporation into the people of God, baptism replaced a ritual

---

[320] See Just. Mart., *Dial.* 138.2–3; Tert., *Bapt.*; Cyprian, *Ep.* 68.2; Ambrose, *Myst.* 10; *Sacr.* 2.1; John Chrys., *Hom. Laz.* 6; and Danielou 1956, 70–85.

available only to males (circumcision) with a rite available to both genders, thus signaling the inclusive character of the new community (3:1–7). Symbolized as a "regeneration" or "rebirth," it marked a passage from death to life (1:3; 2:5; 2:24) and incorporation into and growth within a new family of God (1:3–2:10). Because in baptism believers are unified with Jesus Christ, they share in both his innocent suffering and his glorious exaltation, in both his human shaming and his divine honoring (2:4–10; 2:18–25; 3:13–22; 4:1, 12–16). Many of these aspects of baptism are typical of early Christian baptismal teaching in general and are reflected in virtually every section of this Petrine letter. Although it is first here that baptism is mentioned explicitly, the fact of the readers' baptism has been, from the letter's outset, a basic premise of its consolation and encouragement. At this point in the letter, baptism is declared to be a present saving action corresponding to the primordial saving of Noah and his family and rooted in the resurrection of Jesus Christ.[321]

now saves (*nyn sōizei*). The statement that *baptism saves* is unique in the NT, but Mark 16:16 ("he who believes and is baptized will be saved") and Titus 3:5 ("He [God our Savior] saved us . . . by the washing of regeneration and renewal in the Holy Spirit") at least attest a similar association of ideas (cf. also Acts 16:30–33). The verb *sōizei*, like the preceding *diesōthēsan*, also means "save," or "preserve," "rescue," or "deliver" from a perilous situation. The use of synonymous verbs for "save" and the paralleling of their clauses (v 20def/v 21a, 21d) indicate that the "correspondence" of which our author speaks (v 21a) is that between the salvation of Noah's family and the salvation of the addressees. This correspondence is without precise precedent, though an appeal to Noah as a warning for the present generation is found in a saying of Jesus (Matt 24:37–39/Luke 17:26–27).

The earlier antithesis of "once-now" (*pote-nyn*) in 2:10 could suggest that "now" (*nyn*) stands in contrast to the "once" (*pote*) of v 20a. But in actuality, the point here is not a contrast between the spirits (who once disobeyed) and baptism (which now saves) but a comparison between a protological event of salvation in the past (*diesōthēsan*, aorist) and its present, eschatological counterpart (*sōizei*, present tense).[322] This "now" is the present now, when Jesus Christ has been revealed (1:12), the now of the experience of God's mercy (2:10) and the now of Christ's gathering of the flock (2:25); that is, the time of the present saving of the believers, a saving (*sotēria*) inaugurated but yet to be

---

[321] For the less likely possibility that "baptism" here is a metaphor for suffering, see Nixon 1968; and Cyril of Jerusalem (*Myst. Cat.* 22.6), who describes baptism as the "antitype of the sufferings of Christ" (*tōn tou Christou pathēmatōn antitypon*).

[322] Preisker (Windisch and Preisker 1951, 73), postulating that 1 Peter represents a baptismal liturgy, proposed that the adverb *now* refers to a performance of baptism that "now" takes place at this point in the liturgy; cf. similarly Brooks (1974, 294–305) who, however, regards 1 Peter to be not a liturgy but a "baptismal instructional sermon." This interpretation, however, founders not only on the implausibility of the liturgy and homily theories but also on the fact that the addressees are assumed from the outset of the letter to have *already* undergone conversion and baptism (cf. 1:1–2, 3, 14–16, 22–23; 2:2–3).

completely realized (1:5, 9, 10; 2:2). It is "through the resurrection of Jesus Christ" (v 21d) that baptism now saves, and the implications of this complete thought will be considered below in the NOTE on 3:21d.

you too (*kai hymas*). The term *kai* could be taken with the distant term *baptism* ("baptism *also* saves you") but is more likely linked with its proximate term, *you* (cf. 1:15; 2:5, 21; 3:5, 7, 18; 4:1). The stress that this phrase, *you too*, receives through its initial position in the Greek sentence is conveyed in English through its emphatic location at the end of the sentence. The variant "us" (*hēmas*) (supported by C L 514 etc. 𝔐) might have been original if the words of this sentence derived from a hymnic source; see the same reasoning regarding the "you" or "us" in v 18c. But there is no NT "hymnic" equivalent to the statement "baptism now saves us" and no certainty that an extant hymn is a source here. Since the reading "you" (*hymas*) has stronger manuscript support ($\mathfrak{P}^{72}$ ℵ A B P Ψ etc. vg syr^{h}) and accords with the contextual stress on "you" (3:13–17; 4:1–4), it may be regarded as original.

Although the explicit correspondence established here concerns two acts of salvation, it is conceivable that some similarity between the groups that are saved is also implied, as Selwyn has suggested (1947, 203), though for different reasons. In v 20 the author refers, not just to a single person, Noah, but to his entire household of eight persons and stresses the small number of those saved ("a few"). Altogether, this group of eight comprised the household (*oikos*) of Noah.[323] The addressees likewise comprise only a small minority of believers within a nonbelieving society at large. The positive implication of this similarity would be that the believing community, though a household of God small in number in a hostile environment, can take comfort in the fact that, once before, another household, also small in number in a hostile environment, was the object of God's saving action. Such a similarity, while consistent with the author's imagery and the thrust of the letter as a whole, nevertheless is at best implicit.[324]

The statement "baptism now saves you too" is brought to completion with the phrase "through the resurrection of Jesus Christ" (*di' anastaseōs Iēsou Christou*, v 21d). The same formulation was used in 1:3, where Christ's resurrection was portrayed as mediating "salvation" and "rebirth," a metaphor for baptism.[325] Included parenthetically within this larger statement is a couplet (v 21bc) that immediately follows and describes *baptisma*. This couplet will be examined separately.

The association between baptism and resurrection, like the earlier link between baptismal rebirth and resurrection (1:3), reflects traditional Christian teaching, according to which undergoing baptism was the ritual means for

[323] See Gen 7:1: Noah "and all your household" (*kai pas ho oikos sou*); Philo, *QG* 1.96 (*oikou*), 2.11 (*oikia, oikōi*), 2.26 (*en tēi oikiai*); and Heb 11:7 (*eis sōtērian tou oikou autou*).

[324] Other "parallels" between the situation of Noah and that of the Petrine addressees that Grudem (1988, 160–61) mentions are rather forced and unconvincing.

[325] For the construction "save through" (Christ, him), see also John 3:17; Acts 15:11; Rom 5:9; 1 Cor 1:21, 15:2; cf. Eph 2:8 (saved through faith).

identifying personally with the crucified and resurrected Christ (Rom 6:4–5, 8–11; Col 2:12; cf. 1 Cor 15:20–28, 29–34). This association between baptism and Christ's resurrection makes it clear that it is the resurrection of Jesus Christ that gives baptism its saving efficacy and makes human rebirth possible. Baptism is thus the *instrument* rather than the agent of salvation, for it is ultimately God who raises Jesus Christ from the dead (1:21; 2:4d) and through his resurrection (1:3) confers new life and living hope on those who bear Christ's name (2:5a, 24; 4:6c), as consistently attested throughout the NT.

Baptism "saves" by bringing believers into contact with the saving power of God manifested in the resurrection of Jesus Christ and unifying believers with the resurrected Christ (Rom 6:3–5, 8–11; Col 2:12–14). The House of Israel also associated God's resurrecting and saving activity, as is clear in Benediction Two of the Eighteen Benedictions, one of the oldest parts of the synagogue service: "You, O Lord, are mighty forever; you quicken the dead, you are mighty to save." For the messianic community and the Petrine author, this act of divine salvation is effected through the power manifested in Christ's resurrection (1:3). Thus baptism can be seen as a "rebirth" (1:3; cf. 1:23; 2:2; John 3:1–16; Titus 3:5), a transforming action by which persons are regenerated as the "children" of God (1:14), sanctified with his holiness (1:2, 14–16, 22; 2:5, 9), honored by his grace (1:3–12; 5:5b), incorporated into his household (2:4–10), and protected by his power (1:5; 5:6–7, 10b). Within the context and thrust of the letter as a whole, the saving power of baptism entails aspects of transformation, identification with the suffering and resurrected Christ, incorporation into a holy community, protection by a heavenly Father, and commitment to a new way of life subordinated to the will of God—powerful comfort indeed to strangers and aliens in a hostile society.

That baptism "now saves" in no way implies, however, that the Petrine author views the salvation of the believers as an accomplished fact, for he has already indicated that it is actually a goal yet to be realized (1:5, 9, 10–11; 2:2). Moreover, as he clarifies in what follows, baptism involves a commitment on the part of the faithful to a constant mindfulness of God's will. Thus baptism represents the *commencement* of a process of rebirth and growth toward salvation. For the early Christians, it was particularly worship and the acts of baptism and eucharist that served as the vehicle for rooting life in the present and hope concerning the future in the saving events of the past. This formulation of 1 Peter thus illustrates the point that "in Christian worship the anticipated goal of final, eschatological deliverance was drawn into the sphere of the present experience and celebrated as if it had been fully and finally achieved" (Aune 1992, 596).

The resurrection of Jesus, according to early Christian teaching, is the decisive divine acceptance and vindication of Jesus' life, his teaching and ministry, and his innocent suffering and death (Moule 1968; Hoffmann 1979; P. Perkins 1984; Nickelsburg 1992c). From the outset of 1 Peter (1:3–5, 11), it is God's raising of Christ to life, honor, and glory (1:3–5, 11, 21; 3:18e; 5:1, 10) that is declared to be the power that transforms Christian believers from death to life

(1:3; 2:5), that gives them reason to hope (1:3, 21), that makes them beneficiaries of God's mercy (1:3; 2:10) and incorruptible inheritance (1:4; 3:7), and that sets them on the course of salvation (1:5, 9; 2:2; 3:21). The following verse (3:22) elaborates on the further cosmic implications of Christ's resurrection, and this concluding stress on resurrection unites with v 18e ("having been made alive") to set the thought of vv 19–21 within the context of Christ's resurrection and ascension to heaven.

21bc. Within the formulation, "baptism now saves you too through the resurrection of Jesus Christ" (v 21a, 21d) a parenthetical explanation of baptism is provided (v 20bc), similar in function to the parenthetical comment of v 20d ("that is, eight persons") explaining the term "few." The Greek text reads literally: "baptism—not a removal of dirt from the body but a pledge to God of a sound mindfulness of his will—now saves you through the resurrection of Jesus Christ." This clarification of baptism, unique in the NT, consists of a couplet of balanced phrases, one negative and one positive, focusing on the moral signficance of baptism, stating what it is not and what it is:

ou *sarkos apothesis rhypou*
alla *syneidēseōs agathēs eperōtēma eis theon*

not [as] a removal of filth from the body
but [as] a pledge to God of a sound mindfulness of his will

This parenthetical couplet is also set off by dashes in the translations of Beare (1970, 170) and Goppelt (1993, 247). The fact that this carefully balanced couplet has no precise NT parallel and that two of its terms (*rhypos*, *eperōtēma*) appear only here in the NT (and *apothesis* only in 2 Pet 1:14) identifies this as a unique statement of the Petrine author, for whom such negative-positive contrasts are also typical (see the NOTE on 2:2a).

21b. *not [as] a removal of filth from the body* (*ou sarkos apothesis rhypou*). An added "as" in the translation conveys the fact that both phrases are qualifications of the term *baptism*. The noun *apothesis* ("removal," "putting aside," "getting rid of") occurs only here and in 2 Pet 1:14 (but as part of a metaphor for death). It is related, however, to the verb *apotithemi* ("rid yourselves of") employed in 2:1. The use of this verb in early Christian baptismal catechesis[326] might account for the use of the related noun to explain the nature of baptism. The language is similar to that of Jas 1:21, but the point is different. James encourages "getting rid of (*apothemenoi*) all filth" (*pasan rhyparian*), whereas here baptism is expressly described as *not* a removal of filth from the body. A closer affinity to James and the baptismal tradition would be present if the terms "only" and "also" were included here, with the sense that baptism is "not *only* a removal of filth from the body but *also* the pledge . . . ," but in fact these terms are not present.

[326] So Selwyn 1947, 204, 393–400; cf. Eph 4:22, 25; Col 3:8; Jas 1:21; cf. Rom 13:12; Heb 12:1.

The noun *sarx* denotes the physical body (as in 3:18d, 4:1, 2, 6) and *rhypos*, the only NT occurrence of this term (cf. *rhyparos*, Jas 2:2; Rev 22:11; *rhyparia*, Jas 1:21), means "filth," "dirt" (Aristopho 10.4) or, metaphorically, moral "uncleanness" (Job 14:4; Isa 4:4; *1 Clem.* 17:4; *Barn.* 11:11). Since our author gives no indication elsewhere of regarding the physical body as filthy in itself, the expression is best rendered "not a removal of filth *from* the body" (so also Goppelt 1993, 267), reflecting the force of *apo* (*apo-thesis*), rather than "filth *of* the flesh" (e.g., Michaels 1988, 215). Selwyn's translation (1947, 204), "not a fleshly putting away of dirt," has even less to commend it.

If *removal* implied "washing," this statement could entail an intentional contrast to the "washing of the corruption of the world by the Flood," an image found in *1 En.* 106:17.[327] Our author would then be contrasting the interior character of the washing of baptism to the external washing of the world's filth effected by the Flood. But since *apothesis* in itself does not mean "washing" and since reference here is to the personal "body" rather than the "earth" and to *rhypos* rather than *phthora*, this idea is unlikely.

The thought of a removal of filth from the personal body could be closer to the ceremonial cleansings practiced by Israel or to the consecrations of the pagans, especially in the Mystery rites. The *Rule of the Community* of Qumran speaks of a person who has humbled himself to God as having his "flesh" or body purified: "He will be sprinkled with the waters of purification and sanctified by the waters of washing" and thereby purified of all his iniquities (1QS III 7–9). Purification in this case involved both an external cleansing of the body and an internal purification from sin (cf. Thiering 1980).[328] But in contrast to this Qumranic concept, the Petrine author specifically *rejects* the equation of baptism with a removal of bodily filth.

Dalton (1965, 215–24; 1989, 199–206), followed by J. N. D. Kelly (1969, 161–62), sees here an allusion to circumcision. He takes *sarkos apothesis* as referring to the "putting off" of the "foreskin," that "unclean" part of the body and symbol of impurity (cf. Jer 4:4; Philo, *Spec.* 1.2–7; Billerbeck 1928, 4:31–37). This idea, he suggests, also lies behind Jas 1:21 and especially Col 2:11–12, where a direct connection is drawn between circumcision and Christian baptism: "In him you too were circumcised with a circumcision made without hands, by putting off the body of flesh in the circumcision of Christ; and you were buried with him in baptism, in which you were also raised with him." The proposal, however, has been rejected for good reason.[329] The terms *apothesis* and *rhypos* are never used of circumcision. The explicit comparison of baptism and circumcision in Colossians is unique in the NT and appears spe-

[327] "There shall be a great plague (= Flood, 106:15, with a reference to the salvation of Noah and his three sons [106:16]) upon the earth, and the earth shall be washed clean from all the corruption" (*kai praunei tēn gēn apo tēs ousēs en autēi phthoras*); cf. also 10:20–22 and Philo, *Det.* 170.

[328] For purification through water, see also CD X 10–13.

[329] See Michaels 1988, 215–16; Davids 1990, 144; and Goppelt 1993, 268.

cifically designed to contest the position of the Judean-Christian heresy rampant in the Colossian church. Since the Petrine author makes no mention of this heresy, it is difficult to imagine what readers would make of such a cryptic allusion to circumcision. Moreover, Colossians *compares* baptism and circumcision, whereas these words of 1 Peter state what baptism is *not*, with no indicated interest or motive for contrasting baptism to circumcision.

This first half of the antithetical couplet instead explains that baptism is not an action affecting the external condition of one's body. The point of the contrast lies in the antithesis between an *external cleansing* of one's body and an *internal pledge* of one's commitment to God. This has a certain similarity to the point made by Jesus in his conflict with the Pharisees over the required washing of hands before dining (Mark 7:1–23/Matt 15:1–20/Luke 11:37–41) and the internal rather than external location of evil. The Lukan version employs the verb *baptizō* to describe the position of a Pharisee who "was astounded to see that he (Jesus) did not wash (*ebaptisthē*) before dining" (11:38; see the same thought in different terms in Mark, Matthew, and POxy. 840). The lexical similarity between *baptizō* and the *baptisma* of 1 Peter is insufficient to suggest any literary relation between these texts, not to mention the absence of any parallel to the specific words of 1 Pet 3:21bc. But the common point of these texts—the contrast of external-internal and a stress on internal disposition—provides a possible cultural frame of reference for the thought of 1 Peter: Christian baptism differs markedly from ritual ablutions as practiced by outsiders. It likewise recalls the contrast made in 3:3–4 between external adornment and the internal disposition of the heart.

21c. *but* [*as*] *a pledge to God of a sound mindfulness of God's will* (*syneidēseōs agathēs eperōtēma eis theon*). In contrast to the phrase in v 21b, this positive qualification of baptism accentuates its internal, cognitive and moral nature.

pledge to God (*eperōtēma eis theon*). Determining the meaning of *eperōtēma* is difficult because it occurs only here in the NT and only once in the LXX.[330] The plural *ta eperōtēmata* appears in Herm. *Mand.* 11.2 with the sense of "requests."[331] Its related verb, *eperōtaō*, appears frequently in the NT (56×), mainly as "ask" (a question, e.g., Mark 9:32; 12:34), "request" someone for something (Matt 16:1), or "inquire" (concerning God's will or purpose, Rom 10:20; cf. Isa 65:1).[332] Since there is no instance in which the verb means "pray," the rendition of *eperōtēma* as "prayer" or "petition" to God is unconvincing (against Greeven

---

[330] See Dan 4:14 Theod. ("demand"); cf. Sir 36:3 as a variant for *erōtēma* ("oracle," explaining "law").

[331] Cf. the similar meaning of the simple *erōtēsis* in *1 Enoch* (10:10; 13:2; 14:4, 7).

[332] The verb also occurs in 2 Kgdms 11:7 with *eis*: "David inquired (*eperōtēsen*) concerning (*eis*) the well-being of Joab and concerning (*eis*) the people and concerning (*eis*) the progress of the war." But this provides no analogy, since *eis* here is followed by *theon* (as in 1:21), and it is not likely that the author is describing baptism as an "inquiry" concerning God to those already united with God.

1964, 688). Moreover, this would introduce a view of baptism (as supplication to God) without parallel in the NT or early church.

Evidence from contracts preserved on papyrus, on the other hand, indicates the use of both the verb and the noun as part of a stipulatory legal formula involving a formal question followed by an acknowledgment of consent (*eperōtētheis homolēsa*, POxy. 6.905; 10.1273; *eperōtēma ēi engegra*[*mmenon*], PCairo [Preisigke 1.16]).[333] Although *eperōtēma* (or its verb) specifically describes the first part of this contract, it can also identify the transaction as a whole. In this latter case it denotes a contract involving a pledge or assent given to specific questions, similar to the Latin *stipulatio* or *adstipulatio* (Hill 1976, 187). On this analogy, *eperōtēma eis theon* denotes a *pledge to God* in which, at the occasion of baptism, assent is given to certain behavioral requirements such as moral commitment, obedience to God's will, and doing what is right. This pledge would resemble the oath taken by initiants entering the Qumran community to commit themselves to the law of Moses and God's will (1QS V 8–10; CD XV 6–11; XVI 1–2, 4–5). The combination of *eperōtēma* and *syneidēseōs agathēs* ("sound mindfulness of God's will"), further strengthens this interpretation. Thus, "pledge" appears to be the most satisfactory rendition of *eperōtēma*.[334]

This notion of baptism as entailing a pledge perhaps was also a first step toward the application of the term *sacramentum*, "military oath" in secular parlance,[335] to both baptism and eucharist (Selwyn 1947, 205; Beasley-Murray 1963, 261). Epictetus had made reference to the soldier's oath of allegiance to the emperor (*sacramentum*) as a model for the philosophical life dedicated to God.[336] It is also perhaps such a "pledge" or "oath" to which Pliny later (ca. 111–112 CE) makes reference in his letter to Emperor Trajan, as he describes the testimony of Christians regarding their practices: "They bound themselves by a solemn *oath* (*sacramento*) not for any criminal purpose, but that they would commit no fraud, theft, or adultery, that they would not violate their

---

[333] See LSJ *sub* words and MM 231–32 for further examples.

[334] So also MM; Richards 1931; Reicke 1946, 182–85; Selwyn 1947, 203; Spicq 1966, 141–42; J. N. D. Kelly 1969, 162–63; Best 1971; Hill 1976, 187–88; Dalton 1989, 206–10; Davids 1990, 144–45; Hillyer 1992, 119 .

[335] See Servius, *Aen.* 8.614; Pliny, *Ep.* 10.29 (*sacramento militari*); Tac., *Hist.* 1.76.2 (oath of allegiance to Emperor Otho); 2.79 (oath of allegiance to Emperor Vespasian); cf. Helgeland 1978, 1478–80.

[336] "To this God (who is within) you ought to swear allegiance, as the soldiers do to Caesar. They are but hirelings, yet they swear that they will put the safety of Caesar above everything; and shall you, indeed, who have been counted worthy of blessings so numerous and so great be unwilling to swear, or, when you have sworn, to abide by your oath? And what shall you swear? Never to disobey under any circumstances, never to prefer charges, never to find fault with anything that God has given, never to let your will rebel when you have either to do or to suffer something that is inevitable. Can the oath of the soldiers in any way be compared with this of ours? Out there men swear never to prefer another in honour above Caesar; but here we swear to prefer ourselves in honour above everything else" (Epict. *Diatr.* 1.14.13–17).

word, that they would not refuse to return a deposit when called upon to do so" (Pliny, *Ep*. 10.96).

of a sound mindfulness of God's will (*syneidēseōs agathēs*). The noun *syneidēsis*, literally, "consciousness," "awareness," here, as in 2:19 and 3:16, denotes *mindfulness* of God and compliance with God's will; see the NOTES on 2:19 and 3:16. Reicke (1946, 187) renders the phrase "pledge before God of a loyal attitude of mind" (cf. Brooks 1974, 292: "an appropriate awareness toward God"). While the contrast between external removal and internal disposition seems reminiscent of the external-internal contrast of 3:3–4, "internal purity" alone[337] fails to convey the sense of moral commitment implied in the combination of *syneidēsis* and "pledge." Other instances of this stock phrase occur in Acts 23:1; 1 Tim 1:5, 19; and *1 Clem*. 41:1.[338] The modifying adj. *agathēs* (lit., "good") defines *mindfulness* here as *sound* (as in 3:16) in the sense that it is focused on God and God's will.

The phrase *syneidēseōs agathēs* can be taken either as a subjective genitive ("a pledge to God proceeding from a sound mindfulness of God's will") or as an objective genitive ("a pledge to God to maintain a sound mindfulness of his will"). The latter, preferred here and by Best (1971, 148), is favored by the similar thought in 3:16 ("maintain a sound mindfulness of God's will," *syneidēsin echontes agathēn*; cf. also 2:19) and is consistent with the understanding of baptism as involving, first, instruction concerning God's will and, then, a pledge to maintain a constant mindfulness of this will. The mindfulness of God's will does not precede baptism, but follows from baptism. Those who so pledge themselves to being ever mindful of God's will stand in stark contrast to the "disobedient spirits" of 3:19.

The association of *syneidēsis* with baptism perhaps was traditional. This is suggested by its use in Heb 10:22, which speaks of drawing near to God with "bodies washed with pure water" and "hearts sprinkled clean of an unsound consciousness (*syneidēseōs ponēras*). This formulation of Hebrews, however, actually is closer to Qumranic thought[339] than to 1 Peter. 1 Peter makes no mention of "washing," and over against the equation of washed bodies and purified hearts the Petrine author expressly *contrasts* an internal pledge to an external cleansing.

The point of this unique couplet, then, is that baptism concerns not the external *sarx* but the internal *syneidēsis*; not cleansing of the *corpus* but consciousness of God and commitment. Baptism, our author insists, is a *moral* action entailing a pledge of constant mindfulness of and compliance with God's will. Within the context of the letter as a whole, such compliance is manifested in obedience (*hypakoē*, 1:14, 22), upright conduct (*dikaiosynē*,

---

[337] So Stelzenberger 1961, 56–68, appealing to Heb 9:9, 14; 10:2, 22; and 2 Tim 1:3.

[338] Cf. also *kathara syneidēsis* (1 Tim 3:9; 2 Tim 1:3; *1 Clem*. 45:7) and *kalē syneidēsis* (Heb 13:18).

[339] See 1QS V 8–10; CD XV 8; XVI 7; 1QH[a] XIV 17.

2:24c; 3:14; *kalē anastrophē*, 2:12; 3:2, 17; *kala erga*, 2:12), and doing what is right (*agathopoiia*, 4:19; cf. 2:15, 20; 3:6, 11, 17). Baptism as a pledge implies the necessity of continued fidelity; the new life it confers in rebirth (1:3, 23) and the transformation it entails (1:14–16) are to be manifested in ongoing obedience to God's will (1:2, 14, 22; 2:15; 3:17; 4:2, 19). Likewise, the salvation mediated through baptism is not an accomplished fact but an ongoing process (2:2) to be fully realized only in the future (1:9). On the whole, this Petrine formulation, "baptism now saves you too through the resurrection of Jesus Christ," and its accompanying clarification ("not as removal . . . God's will") has no precise NT parallel and thus reflects a specific contribution of 1 Peter to the baptismal theology of the early church. In fact, as Dunn (1970, 219) notes, this verse "is the nearest approach to a definition [of baptism] that the NT affords." At the same time, the claim that this verse concerning baptism contains the interpretive "key" to 1 Peter (Brooks 1974) exaggerates its importance and undervalues other dominant emphases of the letter, such as suffering and doing what is right; see also the critique of Hill 1976.[340]

22. The concluding verse of 3:18–22 is joined syntactically and thematically to the preceding phrase, "through the resurrection of Jesus Christ." The relative pronoun "who" (v 22a) has "Jesus Christ" (v 21d) as its antecedent, and three formulations, all, like v 18de, reflective of Christian kerygmatic tradition (Shimada 1966, 375–95; 1979), express interrelated implications of Christ's resurrection: Christ, as the resurrected one, has ascended to God in heaven; he has been exalted to a privileged position at God's right hand; and this exaltation involves his superiority over the cosmic powers. This concluding stress on Christ's resurrection (v 21d, 22), together with v 18e ("made alive"), frames the content of vv 19–21c and puts the entire set of verses within the context of Christ's resurrection and ascension to heaven. This makes clear that the function of vv 19–21 is to explain the implications of Christ's resurrection for both the disobedient spirits and the baptized believers.

With respect to temporal sequence, the second phrase of this verse, "having gone into heaven," (v 22b), already anticipated in v 19a, logically precedes the actions indicated in v 22a and v 22c. Rather than deriving from a preexisting hymn or creed, this verse, like v 18, is composed of formulations reflective of early Christian kerygmatic tradition concerning Christ's resurrection, ascension and presence at God's right hand, and the subordination to him of the cosmic powers. On this verse, see also Dalton 1989, 215–18.

22a. *who is at the right* [*hand*] *of God* (*hos estin en dexiai* [*tou*] *theou*). The antecedent of "who is" (*hos estin*) is "Jesus Christ" (v 21d). The entire clause, including the definite article *tou*[341] (accompanying God), occurs also in Rom

---

[340] On the significance of 3:20–21 for 1 Peter's theology of baptism, see also Beasley-Murray 1963, 258–62 and Dunn 1970, 215–19. On later baptismal texts of the early Church reflecting affinity with 3:21, see Reicke 1946, 191–98. For a recent survey of baptism in the nascent church, see Benoit and Munier 1994.

[341] Omitted in ℵ* B 044 33, possibly due to haplography.

8:34 and reflects early Christian tradition depicting Christ's resurrection as an exaltation to privileged status at the right hand of God.[342] This tradition involves an appropriation of the language of Ps 109[110]:1, which describes the elevation of David as king to God's right hand with the bestowal of royal honor and power as God's human vice-regent and the subordination of David's enemies ("Sit at my right hand until I make all your enemies a stool for your feet"). This psalm is one of the most frequently cited OT texts in the NT. Hay (1973) in his instructive overview of the use of this psalm in early Christianity lists no less than 22 NT citations or allusions to the first verse of this psalm alone,[343] together with 10 instances of the use of Ps 110:4 (exclusively in Heb.). This OT psalm, in turn, along with Ps 2 and 2 Sam 7:14,[344] reflects Israelite adoption of an oriental enthronement tradition in which kings were often depicted as being seated at the right hand of the god, signifying that they were bearers and exercisers of divine power. Israel appropriated this tradition to express symbolically the divine adoption of David as king, his elevation to God's right hand, and the full extent of his royal authority (Rengstorf 1962, also referring to earlier studies).

As part of this Davidic tradition, Ps 109[110]:1 featured prominently in the Christological kerygmatic, creedal, and hymnic tradition of the early Church to interpret one or more of three implications of Jesus' resurrection-ascension: (1) his divine vindication and glory at God's right hand and/or the accompanying glory or empowerment of the believers; (2) his identity as Messiah/Christ; and (3) the subjection of the cosmic powers to the resurrected Christ (Hay 1973, 44–47). The first and third of these uses are evident here in 1 Peter.

The *right hand* conventionally was regarded as the favored and honorable hand (in contrast to the left or "sinister" or shameful hand) and was the proper hand used for eating and showing or receiving honor, blessing, and salvation (Ps 16:11; Prov 3:16; Plut., *Lib. ed.* 7, *Mor.* 5A; *Alex. fort.* 5, *Mor.* 99D). Metaphorically, God is depicted as using his "right hand" to save (Ps 107:7[108:6]; 59[60]:7; 97[98]:10; 107[108]:7).[345] The *right hand* thus signified the hand of power (Rev 1:16, 17, 20; 2:1; 5:1, 7), honor (Acts 3:7; Gal 2:9; Rev 10:5), and the place of privilege (Sir 12:12; Mark 10:40/Matt 20:23). For Jesus Christ to be at God's right hand, as in the case of King David, meant his enjoying of

---

[342] See Mark 14:62/Matt 26:64; Mark 16:19; Acts 2:31–36; 5:30–31; 7:55; Eph 1:20–22; Heb 1:3; 8:1; 10:12; 12:2. The clause is close to the formulation of Col 3:1 ("Christ . . . seated at the right hand of God"), which subsequently was incorporated into the Church's creed ("seated at the right hand of God").

[343] See Matt 22:41–46; 26:64; Mark 12:35–37; 14:62; 16:19; Luke 20:41–44; 22:69; Acts 2:33–36; 5:31; 7:55–56; Rom 8:34; 1 Cor 15:25; Eph 1:20; 2:6; Col 3:1; Heb 1:3, 13; 8:1; 10:12–13; 12:2; 1 Pet 3:22; Rev 3:21; cf. also Mark 16:19 (longer conclusion); Pol. *Phil* 2:1; *Apoc. Pet.* 6; *Sib. Or.* 2.243; *Apocr. Jas.* 14:30–31; Hegesippus, in Eusebius, *Hist. eccl.* 2.23.13. See also Dodd 1953, 34–35, 120–21.

[344] See the collocation of all three texts in Heb 1:1–14, describing the privileged position of the resurrected Christ at the right hand of God.

[345] Cf. also Ps 117[118]:15–18, a psalm cited earlier in 1 Pet 2:7 (Ps 117[118]:22).

God's favor[346] or being elevated and enthroned by God as God's vice-regent to whom supreme authority is committed.[347] This enthronement at God's right hand likewise entailed a conferral of "glory."[348] Psalm 110:1 served the early Christians in making this point about the resurrected Christ as well;[349] hence, the appropriate title of Hay's study of Ps 109[110], *Glory at the Right Hand*. The association of resurrection and glory, however, was also made apart from reference to this psalm text,[350] and "glorify" can serve as a synonym for "raise, exalt."[351] In 1 Peter, this traditional understanding of resurrection as glorification appeared in 1:21 ("God who raised him from the dead and gave him glory"), and is implied in the several other references to Christ's "glory" (1:11; 4:13; 5:1). When, as in 1:11 and 5:1, "glory" is combined with "sufferings," it also implies the idea of Christ's divine vindication, a thought present here in 3:18–22 as well. Through resurrection (cf. also v 18e and 2:4) God vindicates Jesus Christ, his suffering righteous one (v 18ab; cf. also 2:4, 21–24).[352] This, in turn, provides the suffering baptized who share in his resurrection (v 21) with a firm basis for confidence in their own vindication and glory; for the suffering and glory of the believers, see 1:6–8; 4:13; 5:10.

Following "at the right hand of God," the Vulgate adds "swallowing up death, that we might be made heirs of eternal life." In all likelihood the addition is a Latin translation of a Greek gloss (so Metzger 1975, 693–94) similar in content to 1 Cor 15:54: "death is swallowed up in victory" (cf. also 2 Cor 5:4; for discussion, see Beare 1970, 177).

22b. *having gone into heaven* (*poreutheis eis ouranon*). The expression echoes early Christian kerygmatic or creedal tradition linking Christ's resurrection and ascension into heaven and constitutes a fuller formulation of the action referred to by the *poreutheis* of v 19. Together these verbs and the action of Christ's *having gone into heaven* form an inclusion framing the thought of vv 19–22 and relating it to v 18de.

The verb *poreuomai* (simply "go" or "depart") is combined with a prepositional *eis* ("to," "toward") phrase over 36 times in the NT to indicate the direction of the going.[353] Here, as in Acts 1:10 (*eis ton ouranon poreuomenou*) and

---

[346] See Ps 15[16]:11; 17[18]:36; *T. Benj.* 10:6 (of Enoch, Seth, Abraham, Isaac, and Jacob "being raised up at the right hand"); Matt 20:21, 23; 25:33, 34.

[347] See the texts listed in n. 342.

[348] See the descriptions of the heavenly Messiah in the book of the *Similitudes of 1 En.* (chs. 37–71) as "the Elect One" or "Son of Man" sitting on the "throne of (his) glory" (61:8; 62:5).

[349] See Acts 7:55–56; Eph 1:20; Heb 1:3, 13; *1 Clem.* 36:5–6; Pol. *Phil* 2:1; *Apocr. Jas.* 14:30–31; Hegesippus (in Eusebius, *Hist. eccl.* 2.23.13).

[350] See Matt 19:28; Mark 10:37; Mark 13:26/Matt 24:30/Luke 21:27; Luke 24:26; Rom 6:4; 1 Tim 3:16.

[351] See John 7:39; 12:16, 23; 13:31, 32; 17:1, 5; Acts 3:13–14 (God "glorified his servant Jesus . . . the holy and righteous one . . . whom God raised from the dead").

[352] A theme prominent in earlier Israelite apocalyptic tradition (P. Perkins 1984, 39–47) and basic to the concept of resurrection generally (Nickelsburg 1992c); cf. esp. 2 Macc 7:9, 12.

[353] See, for example, going to a region (Matt 28:16; Acts 20:1), a city (Acts 20:22; 22:5); or, figuratively, going to death (Luke 22:33) or to eternal fire (Matt 25:41).

Acts 1:11 (*analēmphtheis . . . eis ouranon* and *poreuomenon eis ton ouranon*), the phrase denotes Christ's "having gone into heaven."[354] The aorist form of the verb *poreutheis* indicates that Christ's having gone into heaven temporally *preceded* his being (*estin*, present tense) at the right hand of God (cf. Mark 16:19). Although the final phrase, v 22c, also involves an aorist verb, its place after v 22b reflects the traditional sequence of these two motifs as influenced by Ps 109[110]:1 (cf. Mark 16:19; Acts 2:32–35; Eph 1:20–22; Heb 1:3–4, 13; 10:12–13).

The image of Christ's ascending into heaven was inseparably related to the concept of his resurrection, exaltation to the right hand of God, glorification, and supremacy over the cosmic powers (Danielou 1964, 248–63). NT and early Christian references to the ascension of Christ employ a variety of further related terms and expressions: "leaving" (*metabainō, aperchomai, exerchomai*) the world and "going (up)" (*anabainō, hypagō*) to God;[355] "going up, ascending" (*anabainō*), being "taken up" (*anapherō*) into heaven;[356] being "lifted up" (*hypsoō*) from the earth (John 12:32, 34; cf. 3:14); "ascending (*anabainō*) above all the heavens" (Eph 4:10); and "passing through the heavens" (Heb 4:14). Luke is the sole NT author to depict Christ's ascension as a physical event available to the senses (Luke 24:50–51; Acts 1:9, 10, 11; cf. Luke 9:51 and Acts 1:2, 22). In all other cases, including 1 Pet 3:19 and 3:22b, Christ's going into heaven is a further metaphorical elaboration on the nature and significance of his resurrection; namely, his elevation to the presence of God in the highest heaven.

The notion that certain privileged figures journeyed or ascended to and through the heavens had wide currency in Second Temple Israel and early Christianity. Prominent figures of the OT said to have ascended into heaven during their lifetime or following their death include Enoch (*1, 2 Enoch*; Heb 11:5; cf. Gen 5:24), Elijah (2 Kgdms 2:1–12), Isaiah (*Ascension of Isaiah*; cf. Isa 6:1–13), and Ezekiel (Ezek 11:1).[357] Among the early followers of Jesus, Paul during his lifetime ascended to the third heaven (paradise, 2 Cor 12:2; cf. *2 En.* 8–9), and the author of Revelation likewise ascended to the heavenly regions (4:1).[358] Early Christianity merged the notion of ascension with the concept of

---

[354] For *poreuomai* used alone for Christ's ascension, see John 14:2, 3, 12, 28; 16:7, 28; for equivalent NT expressions, see below.

[355] See John 6:62; 7:33; 8:14; 13:1, 3, 33, 36; 14:1–4; 16:7, 28; 20:17.

[356] See Mark 16:19; Luke 24:51; John 3:13; Acts 1:11 (cf. Acts 1:2, 22; Luke 9:51); 1 Tim 3:16; *Ascen. Isa.* 9:16–18; 3:18 (ascension to the seventh heaven); the Christian interpolation of *T. Benj.* 9:4; and *Sib. Or.* 1.381; cf. also Rev 12:5.

[357] For the concept, see also Exod 24:9–11; Tob 12:20; *2 Bar.* 46:7; 48:30; *T. Levi* 2:1; *L.A.E.* 25:3; *Apoc. Mos.* 37:5; *Apoc. Ab.* 15:4.

[358] On the motif of the heavenly journey and associated features, see Segal 1980; Himmelfarb 1983, 1991; Tabor 1992; Colpe et al. 1995, 407–543. On the ascension of Christ and its conceptual background, see Larrañaga 1938; S. L. Davies 1958; Lohfink 1971; Parsons 1987; Colpe 1991; Colpe et al. 1995, 445–66.

Christ's resurrection as a way of conceptualizing his exaltation and elevation to a privileged position with God.

For the Petrine author, Christ's resurrection involved not only his having been made alive by God (3:18e; cf. also 1:21) but also his celestial journey to God in the highest heaven (possibly the seventh heaven; cf. *Ascen. Isa.* 3:16–20; 9:16–19; 11:32) and his exalted presence at God's right hand. In the context of 1 Peter, it is Christ' presence with God that assures the believers that he can and will bring them to God as well (3:18c).[359]

The concepts of being "raised," "ascending" to God, and exaltation to God's right hand are images for symbolically describing something that transcends mundane human experience and history. They thus belong to the realm of myth, that is, symbolic language used to convey the ultimate meaning of human life. In this case they are employed to declare the ultimate meaning of Jesus' life, his divine approval and final vindication in particular. To celebrate Jesus as raised to life by God, ascended to God's right hand, and superior to the powers of the universe is, in accord with the mythopoetic conceptuality of the time, to proclaim Jesus and his life as vindicated by God the author of life and as the ultimate ground for the life, blessing, and hope of Jesus' fellow mortals.

22c. *with angels, and authorities, and powers subordinated to him* (*hypotagentōn autōi aggelōn kai exousiōn kai dynameōn*). This third and final phrase, another genitive absolute construction (cf. 3:20c; 4:1a), likewise echoes early Christian tradition in its affirmation of the *cosmic* implications of Christ's resurrection-ascension: the powers of the universe are subordinated to the authority of him who is now at the right hand of God.[360]

angels, and authorities, and powers (*aggelōn kai exousiōn kai dynameōn*). The first two terms of this triad, taken separately, could refer to either human or spiritual agents, messengers of humans or of God (*aggeloi*), or bearers of authority (*exousiai*). Together with "powers" (*dynameis*), however, they form a triad of terms denoting, like the triad of 1 Cor 15:24 ("every rule and every authority and power"), the *inimical spiritual powers* (1 Cor 15:25) that have been subordinated to the rule of the resurrected Christ.[361] A later replication of this triad appears in *Ascen. Isa.* 1:3 ("the prince of this world and his angels and his authorities and his powers") as part of a Christian interpolation comprising *Ascen. Isa.* 1:2b–6a.

A prominent feature of Israelite and early Christian conceptions of the universe and the agency of evil, as already noted, was belief in the existence of superhuman spirits, ranks of angels, and demonic forces inhabiting the sky

[359] For a similar thought, see also Heb 4:14–16; 9:11–14; 12:2; Col 3:1–3; and Eph 4:8–13.

[360] For the traditional combination and sequence of the motifs of resurrection and subjection of the cosmic powers, see also Phil 2:9–11; Heb 1:3–13; 2:5–9; 10:12–13.

[361] Further traces of the resurrection tradition underlying both 1 Cor 15:2–28 and 1 Pet 3:18, 22 include "Christ," "resurrection" (1 Cor 15:20, 21/1 Pet 3:21d); "died"/"was put to death" (1 Cor 15:22/1 Pet 3:18d); "was made alive" (1 Cor 15:22/1 Pet 3:18e); "subordinated to him" (1 Cor 15:24–28/1 Pet 3:22c). On the relation between the two texts, see Zeilinger 1987.

and the heavenly regions,[362] their alliance with the Devil/Satan,[363] and their presumed influence over human lives and fortunes.[364] In the Bible and related literature, these cosmic forces are designated with a variety of terms,[365] including both *exousiai* (spiritual "authorities")[366] and *dynameis* ("powers").[367]

A fundamental affirmation of the Christian kerygma, reflected here in v 22, is that Christ's resurrection entails the final subordination or vanquishing of these cosmic powers.[368] Prior to this conclusive subordination of the hostile spirits, Jesus had demonstrated his power over them during his ministry, a motif frequently stressed in the Gospel tradition.[369] According to Luke 10:17–20, the demons (*ta daimonia*, 10:17), alias the spirits (*ta pneumata*, 17:20), were subject (*hypotassetai*, 10:17, 20) to the followers of Jesus as well.

This motif of Christ's subordination of the cosmic spirits was a thought developed with the help of Ps 8:6–7 LXX[370] and Ps 109[110]:1.[371] Psalm 8:5–7 LXX is cited explicitly in Heb 2:6–8 and applied to the resurrected Christ in Heb 2:9.[372] The subordination of *enemies* in particular is a thought derived from the latter half of Ps 109[110]:1, which is cited in Heb 1:13 and likewise is applied to the resurrected Christ.[373] Thus, motifs from the David tradition (Pss 2, 109[110]) concerning David's elevation and enthronement as king and subjection of his enemies provided the model for conceptualizations not only

---

[362] See *1 En.* 6–16 and passim; *2 En.* 7:1–5; 18:3–6; *Jub.* 5:1–11; and the NOTE on "spirits" in 3:19; cf. also *T. Levi* 3:1–10; Philo, *Gig.* 16; *Conf.* 171–82; Eph 2:2; 6:12.

[363] See *1 En.* 54:6; Matt 25:41; Eph 6:11–12; Rev 12:7–9; *Ascen. Isa.* 1:3.

[364] See Manson 1952; MacGregor 1954–1955; Caird 1956; Ziegler 1957; Morrison 1960; Schlier 1961; and Wink 1984 (who rightly contests the contrary view of Carr 1981).

[365] E.g., "the rulers of this age" (1 Cor 2:6, 8); "demons" (1 Cor 10:20–22); "angels, principalities . . . powers" (Rom 8:38); "elemental spirits of the universe" (Gal 4:3, 9; Col 2:8, 20; 2 Pet 3:10, 12); "rule, authority, and power" (1 Cor 15:24); "thrones, dominions, principalities, authorities" (Col 1:16); "rule, authority, power, and dominion" (Eph 1:21); "the prince of the power of the air" (Eph 2:2); "principalities and powers in the heavenly places" (Eph 3:10); "principalities, powers, world rulers of this present darkness . . . spiritual hosts of wickedness in the heavenly places" (Eph 6:12).

[366] See *T. Levi* 3:8; *T. Sol.* 20:15; Rom 13:1; 1 Cor 15:24; Eph 1:21; 3:10; 6:12; Col 1:16; 2:10, 15; Titus 3:1.

[367] See 4 Macc 5:13; Philo, *Conf.* 171; *Mut.* 59; Rom 8:38 (combined with "angels"); 1 Cor 15:24; Eph 1:21 (combined with *exousia*); Ign. *Eph.* 13:1 ("the powers of Satan"); *Mart. Pol.* 14:1 ("God of angels and powers"); cf. Rev 13:2; 17:12–13; and Wink 1984, 159–63.

[368] See 1 Cor 15:24–28; Eph 1:19–22; Col 1:15–20; 2:10–15; Heb 1:3–4, 13–14; 2:5–9; 10:12–13; cf. Matt 28:18; Luke 10:22; Phil 2:9–10; 3:21; Rev 17:11–21; 20:1–3; Pol. *Phil* 2:1.

[369] See Mark 1:23–28/Luke 4:33–37; Mark 1:32–34/Matt 8:16–17/Luke 4:40–41; Mark 3:7–12/Luke 6:17–19; Mark 3:22–27/Matt 12:22–30/Luke 11:14–23; Mark 5:1–20/Matt 8:28–34/Luke 8:26–39; Mark 7:24–30/Matt 15:21–28; Mark 9:14–29/Matt 17:14–21/Luke 9:37–43; Luke 13:32.

[370] "You [God] have crowned him with glory and honor . . . you have put all things under his feet" (*panta hypetaxas hypokatō tōn podōn autou*).

[371] "The Lord says to my lord: 'Sit at my right hand, till I make your enemies your footstool.'"

[372] Other implicit appropriations of Ps 8:7 include 1 Cor 15:27; Eph 1:22; and Phil 3:21.

[373] See also 1 Cor 15:25; Eph 1:20; Heb 10:12–13; Rev 3:21; *1 Clem.* 36:5–6; Pol. *Phil* 2:1; *Apoc. Pet.* 6; and *Sib. Or.* 2.243 as listed and discussed by Hay 1973, 122–29; for the rabbinic messianic interpretation of this OT text, see Billerbeck 1928, 4/1:452–65.

of the elevation and enthronement of Jesus Christ and his privileged position at God's right hand of power, but also of his superiority over his enemies—in Jesus' case, the cosmic forces of the universe. The subordinating agent, as the contexts of these passages make clear, is God so that the passive here in 1 Peter (*hypotagentōn*) is a further divine passive with God as implied subject.

In its totality, this Petrine verse echoes a broad current of early Christian tradition concerning the implications of Christ's resurrection, including his ascension to heaven, his elevation to God's right hand, and his divinely established supremacy over the cosmic powers. Within the context of 3:13–22, this verse expresses the basis for persistence in doing what is right despite suffering: Christ who himself suffered can lead the believers to God because he already is in the presence of God.

Two further features of v 22c are also noteworthy. First, the inclusion of *angels* within the triad of cosmic powers occurs only here in the NT and thus appears deliberate. This intentional mention of *angels* in all likelihood is to be understood in relation to the reference to the "disobedient angel spirits" in v 19; for the synonymity of "angels" and "spirits," see the NOTE on v 19. In the context of vv 19–22, the term *angels* appears to embrace the angel "spirits" of v 19. This equation of "spirits" and "angels" is further supported by the correspondence of vv 19 and 22 signaled by the double occurrence of the verb *poreutheis* and the resulting chiasm (similarly, Schertz 1992, 277–78):

A. condemnation of angel spirits by Christ
  B. salvation then of Noah and family
  B.′ salvation now of believers
A.′ subordination to Christ of angels, principalities, and powers

Through the combination of *angels* with *authorities* and *powers*, the author thus appears to have included the disobedient angelic spirits in v 19 among the powers subordinated to the rule of the resurrected Christ (so also Dalton 1989, 215–18). Christ's resurrection to power is the final confirmation of their condemnation; compare the earlier but similar thought in *1 En.* 55:4 concerning "The Elect One" who "sits on the throne of glory and judges Azazʾel and all his company and his army (i.e., the rebellious angels of Gen 6:1–4) in the name of the Lord of the Spirits."

Second, the idea of subordination occurs elsewhere in the letter in connection with civic (2:13) and domestic (2:18; 3:1, 5; 5:5a) order. Here, however, in line with Christological kerygmatic tradition, the stress is on the new order established in the cosmos as a result of Christ's resurrection. This concluding phrase thus represents a further note of assurance for the beleaguered believers. Not only are the baptized enlivened and set on the course of salvation through the resurrection of Jesus Christ; not only is their ultimate vindication prefigured in the exaltation and vindication of Christ. The subordination of the cosmic powers to the resurrected Christ also assures the believers of their freedom from the power of all those spiritual forces that once controlled human lives. If, as was conventionally thought, these cosmic forces were viewed as the powers working through human agents (1 Cor 2:6–9; 2 Cor 6:15; Eph 2:2), this would further imply that, with the subordination of these cosmic powers to Christ, the power of their human agents ultimately to harm God's righteous people had also been broken (Reicke 1946, 200–201). Hence, the readers have no cause to fear any who would do them harm (cf. 3:13–14).

This affirmation of the solidarity of innocent suffering Christians with the innocent suffering Christ (3:13–17, 18–22) thus concludes with the resounding assurance that the resurrection, exaltation, vindication, and cosmic rule of the suffering Christ constitute both the basis for confidence in their own vindication by God and the motivation for their continued perseverance in doing what is right, whatever suffering this might involve.

GENERAL COMMENT

In this complex and moving passage, the fact of Christ's innocent suffering, expounded upon previously (2:21–25) as a model for household slaves (2:18–20), is now reemphasized as a model for the entire suffering community (3:13–17). Thus this passage resembles 2:21–25 in its content and function. As 2:21–25 provides Christological support for the exhortation of 2:18–20, so 3:18–22 offers Christological support for the exhortation of 3:13–17. At the same time, the thought of this passage moves beyond a notion of the suffering Christ as model to an emphasis on his death, resurrection, journey to heaven, exaltation, and the soteriological implications for the baptized believers. Christ, our author affirms, is the suffering righteous one (v 18ab) whose innocent and vicarious suffering has been vindicated through his having been made alive and raised by God to heavenly glory, honor, and power (vv 18e, 21, 22). Those who share in innocent suffering shall also share in the glory of his resurrection. Because of the divine vindication of the suffering Christ, suffering believers can anticipate their own vindication if they persevere in doing what is right. His own resurrection and ascension to heaven assures the believers that he can lead them to God as well (v 18c). As Christ's innocent suffering is the model for Christian suffering, so his resurrection and presence with God are the basis of Christian hope.

It is through baptism that believers participate in this power of Christ's resurrection and are set on the course of salvation (v 21a, d). This baptism is an eschatological act of salvation corresponding to the protological salvation of Noah and his family in the event of the Flood (v 20b–21a). To those disobedient and imprisoned angelic spirits, on the other hand, who first instigated the evil eliminated in the Flood, the resurrected Christ, in the course of his ascension to God, announced their condemnation (v 19–20a). His superiority over them and all cosmic spirits is confirmed by his exaltation to God's right hand of glory, honor, and power.

This statement entails a unique combination of motifs and themes deriving from independent Israelite (Flood tradition) and Christian (kerygmatic tradition) sources. Within an affirmation of Christ's resurrection and ascension to heaven (3:18e, 19ab, 21d, 22), the author has included motifs of the Flood tradition (3:19–20) that enable a correspondence to be drawn between the saving of the family of Noah and the salvation of the present believers who in baptism are saved through the resurrection of Jesus Christ. This correspondence and continuity between the protological and eschatological events of salvation wrought by God also include a correspondence between the condemnation of the primordial angelic spirits annnounced by Christ (3:19–20a) and the final subordination of all cosmic spirits to the power of this exalted Christ (3:22c). This emphasis on the resurrection and heavenly ascension of Christ, in turn, serves to support and encourage confidence in the assertion of v 18c: it is as the raised and exalted one that Christ can lead others to God. Although vv 18 and 22 in particular echo early Christian kerygmatic tradition, attempts to demonstrate that vv 18–22 incorporate or reflect a fixed literary source such as a creed or hymn have proved inconclusive; see DETAILED COMMENT 1. Here, as elsewhere (1:18–21; 2:4–10, 21–25), is a unique creative merger of Christian and Israelite tradition. We are dealing here with a theological statement not only distinct from Paul but without complete parallel in the entire early Church.

Conclusions regarding the several controverted issues posed by these verses can be summarized as follows:

(1) In 3:19, the antecedent of *en hōi* is not the foregoing term "spirit" (*pneumati*) but the foregoing statement of v 18 as a whole and especially its last words referring to Christ's resurrection, "he was made alive in the spirit." Verses 19–22, framed by the verbs "having gone," therefore describe events (Christ's annnouncment to the disobedient spirits, the saving of Noah and family, and the saving of the believers) associated with Christ's resurrection and ascension to heaven.

(2) Verses 19–22 thus refer not to a "descent" of Christ to the underworld between his death and resurrection but to the *ascent* of Christ to the right hand of God as one major aspect of his resurrection. The verb "having gone" in vv 19 and 22 denotes Christ's going into the uppermost heaven, in the course of which he passes through inferior heavenly regions where the disobedient spirits were imprisoned, in accord with the cosmology of *1 Enoch*, Israelite, and Christian tradition and cosmology.

(3) The disobedient spirits, also in accord with Israelite and early Christian tradition, are the fallen angels or spirit-powers of Noah's time who were disobedient to God's will before the Flood and therefore imprisoned until the final judgment. Here in 1 Peter they are associated with the cosmic spirits who have been subordinated by God to the exalted Christ.

(4) The "announcement" to these disobedient spirits (*ekēryxen*, 3:19a) concerns not the proclamation of the good news of their salvation but word of their condemnation and subordination to the power of the exalted Christ.

(5) In 3:21, *antitypon* announces a correspondence between the saving of Noah and his family and the baptismal saving of the believing addressees through the resurrection of Jesus Christ.

(6) In the explanation given of baptism, *eperōtēma* denotes the pledge to God of a sound and constant mindfulness of God's will (*syneidēseōs agathēs*).

(7) Verse 22, like v 18, echoes the early Christian Christological tradition that provided the theological frame for vv 18–22. This tradition adapted Ps 109 [110]:1 (pertaining to David's exaltation as king) to symbolize the resurrection of Christ as an exaltation to God's right hand. The subordination of the cosmic powers is also a Christian theme associated with Christ's resurrection adapted from Ps 109[110]:1 and Ps 8:6.

(8) The passage is linked to 3:13–17 and supports its exhortation in several compelling ways.[374] At the same time it reiterates and expands on themes found elsewhere in the letter. In actuality, vv 18–22 support the foregoing exhortation in a variety of interrelated ways:

(a) Here (esp. 3:18ab), as in 2:21–24, the suffering of the innocent Christ provides a model and motive for the patient suffering of his innocent followers (3:13–17; cf. 2:18–20 and 4:1–2, 12–13). 1 Peter 4:1 makes the same point but is not a "hinge" joining 4:1–6 to 3:13–17, since 4:1–6 is not structurally parallel to 3:13–17. Verse 4:1 rather introduces a unit describing the moral and social implications of innocent suffering. Christ as the righteous one (3:18b) likewise serves as a paradigm for all those enjoined to be righteous (3:13–14; cf. 3:12; 2:24c).

(b) Here (3:18ab), as in 2:21b, 24, it is the *vicarious* nature of Christ's suffering that is said to effect the salvation of the unrighteous and make possible their upright behavior and endurance in suffering. Once unrighteous and alienated from God, those joined by faith with the suffering and exalted Christ are now reconciled through Christ's death with their Creator and enabled to lead lives of righteous and innocent obedience to their Father's will (cf. also 1:14–21; 4:1–4, 19, and their respective NOTES).

(c) This salvation, moreover, is described as Christ's "bringing you to God" (3:18c), an action that is supported by reference to Christ's resurrection and ascension to God. Christ provides access to God because he himself has been exalted to God's right hand in heaven (3:18e, 19–20a, 21d, 22). Through their baptism, believers share in the salvific power of Christ's resurrection (3:21), and this eschatological salvation is analogous to the salvation of Noah and his

[374] Some scholars find here primarily a support for the moral injunction of 3:17 (so Spitta 1890, 8–10; Gschwind 1911, 117, 126; Vogels 1976, 34–44, 137–38). Reicke, on the other hand, suggests that Christ's preaching of the gospel (*sic*) to the spirits is presented as a motive for "a bold [contemporary] communication of the Gospel to the pagans" (1946, 118–25, 130–31, claiming a relation of v 19 to 3:15; see also pp. 211–19). Reicke, however, focuses too narrowly on the issue of preaching, and both theories ignore the content of vv 18–22 *in their entirety*, especially the implications of the climactic focus on Christ's resurrection, ascension, and exaltation to power and its significance in particular for the exhortation of 3:13–17.

family in primordial time (3:20b–21). Baptism thus entails not only "rebirth" (cf. 1:3, 23; 2:2) and adoption as children of God (cf. 1:14–16), but salvation and commencement of a new life characterized by commitment to God and compliance with God's will (3:21bc; cf. 2:15, 19; 3:16, 17; 4:2, 19).

(d) This salvation contrasts with the condemnation of the primordial angelic spirits (v 19–20a), the prototypically disobedient ones, that Christ announced in the course of his ascension to heaven and that exemplifies the condemnation of all the disobedient (cf. 2:7–8; 3:1; 4:17) who oppose God (4:2–3) and God's people. God's subjection of these spirits, along with all of the cosmic powers and their human agents, to the authority of the resurrected Christ (3:22) thus assures believers that they are safe from the power of any forces (cosmic or terrestrial) who might harm them (3:13). They thus have no reason to fear (3:13–14) the hostility of outsiders (Reicke 1964, 115, 219). Those who disparage the Christians now (3:16) and cause their suffering (3:14) will in the final judgment be called to account (4:5) and put to shame (3:16) by the God who vindicated the suffering Christ and subordinated all powers to his authority. Consequently, the believers are free to serve God alone in doing what is right (3:21c; cf. 2:15, 20; 3:13, 17; 4:19) .

(e) The vindication and glorification of the innocent suffering Christ and his exalted presence with God (3:22; cf. 1:11; 4:13; 5:1) assure the suffering believers (3:13–17; cf. 1:6; 2:18–20; 3:9; 4:12–14, 16, 19; 5:10) of their eventual vindication, glorification, and presence with God (3:18c; cf. 1:7; 4:13; 5:10). The vindication of the innocent suffering Christ lays the basis for the vindication of the innocent suffering believers (Michaels 1988, 220–21). His being made alive (3:18e; cf. 2:4) is the surety of their life as well (4:6b; cf. 1:3; 2:5; 3:7).

The thematic and terminological links uniting 3:18–22 with its foregoing exhortation are numerous, and it is this rich integration of exhortation and Christological confirmation that makes the passage one of the most rhetorically powerful statements of the entire letter. As a foundation for the foregoing exhortation of 3:13–17, vv 18–22 present the beleaguered believers both a comprehensive basis for their hope and a powerful motivation for their continued perseverance in doing what is right. Christ's full experience, from suffering and death to glorification, is the illustration and the prototype of that which awaits the Christian believer according to 3:13–22 (cf. Michaels 1966–1967, 400).

This grandiose Christological and soteriological statement affirms the *universal* scope and result of Christ's death, resurrection, and ascension. Together with 4:1–6, Dalton (1989, 105) notes, it is "the only text in the whole letter which formally gives the theological basis for the victory of Christians in the stress of persecution," and its "underlying presupposition is *Christianus alter Christus* ['the Christian is a second Christ']."

The resurrection of Jesus Christ in which the beleaguered believers share through baptism, is a source of their salvation, a promise of their vindication and exaltation to glory, and a confirmation of the continuity and universal scope of God's power in world history. Sustained by this assurance, the suffering addressees can persevere in doing what is right and remaining mindful of God's will, for such innocent suffering and obedience will indeed be vindicated.

DETAILED COMMENT 1: TRADITIONS AND REDACTION IN 1 PETER 3:18–22

Various features of the terminology, style, focus, and content of 3:18–22 distinguish this unit from its surrounding contexts (3:13–17; 4:1–6) and point to a creative combination of two independent currents of tradition. In contrast to the hortatory tone of 3:13–17 and 4:1–6, this unit is indicative in mood and focuses primarily on the experience of Jesus Christ as a substantiation for the foregoing exhortation. Furthermore, it contains a strikingly large number of terms and phrases not occurring elsewhere in the letter (*hapax* ["once for all"], *peri hamartiōn* ["for sins"], *prosagō* ["bring to"], *apothnēskō* ["put to death"], *zōiopoieō* ["make alive"], *phylakē* ["prison"], *pneumata* [pl., "spirits"], *kēryssō* ["announce"], *apodechomai* ["wait"], *makrothymia* ["patience"], *en hēmerais Nōe* ["in the days of Noah"], *kataskeuazō* ["build"], *kibōtos* ["ark"], *oktō* ["eight"], *diasōzō* ["save"], *hydōr* ["water"], *antitypon* ["corresponding to this"], *baptisma* ["baptism"], *apothesis* ["removal"], *rhypos* ["filth"], *eperōtēma* ["pledge"], *hos estin en dexiai theou* ["who is at the right hand of God"], *poreutheis eis ouranon* ["having gone into heaven"], *exousiai* ["authorities"], *dynameis* ["powers"], and the notion of the subordination of the cosmic powers to Christ). Third, as indicated in the NOTES above, virtually every phrase or clause in these verses has conceptual or terminological parallels elsewhere in the NT or Israelite tradition.

Within 3:18–22, vv 18 and 22 and vv 19–21 differ in terms of both form and content. Verses 18 and 22 embody loosely connected kerygmatic formulas focused on the action of Christ, whereas the latter verses, with v 19 serving as a transition, form a series of subordinate phrases or clauses focused on a comparison of two events of salvation, the salvation of Noah and his family (v 20b–e) and that of the present addressees (v 21). The formulas of vv 18 and 22, moreover, are reminiscent of early Christian kerygmatic tradition. Verses 19–20, on the other hand, display affinity with a different stream of tradition; namely, Israelite amplifications on the narrative of Gen 6.

1. Christian Tradition in 1 Peter 3:18, 22

In modern times, two main theories have been advanced regarding the possible Christian sources underlying vv 18 and 22. One view is that the Petrine author made use of independent Christian kerygmatic formulas affirming Christ's passion, death, resurrection, ascension into heaven, session at God's right hand, and subordination to him of the cosmic spiritual powers. An alternate view is that underlying vv 18–22 was a single, unified creed or hymn similar to those in Phil 2:6–11; Col 1:15–20; and 1 Tim 3:16. Both theories reckon with varying degrees of authorial redaction.

1a. Christian Kerygmatic Formulas

Verses 18 and 22 are related in regard to their *form* (loosely connected [in instances asyntactic, parallel] brief kerygmatic formulas), *focus* (Jesus Christ), and *content* (Christ's vicarious suffering, death, resurrection, ascension into heaven, and presence at God's right hand with cosmic powers subordinated to him). In these three features they are closely similar to numerous Christian kerygmatic formulas employed elsewhere in the NT:

3:18ab	vicarious suffering/death of Jesus Christ:[375]
	"a righteous one"[376]
	"for unrighteous ones"[377]
3:18c	"bring you to God"[378]
3:18de, 22a	
3:18de	"having been put to death . . . having been made alive"[379]
3:22a	"at the right [hand] of God"[380]
3:22b	"having gone into heaven"[381]
3:22c	"with angels and authorities and powers subordinated to him"[382]

These common characteristics of vv 18 and 22 suggest that this formulaic material derived from a reservoir of early Christian Christological and kerygmatic oral tradition upon which most of the NT authors drew.

1b. A Hymnic or Creedal Source?

Some scholars suspect, however, that this material derived from a more unified extant source such as a creed or hymn. Hymns and creeds played a significant

---

[375] See Rom 8:3; 1 Thess 5:10; 1 John 2:2; 4:10; cf. Mark 14:24 and numerous other passages explicating the vicarious power of Christ's passion (Shimada 1979, 172 nn. 26 and 28).

[376] See Acts 3:14; 7:52; Jas 5:6; 1 John 2:1,29; 3:7; cf. also Luke 23:47; 2 Cor 5:21; Heb 4:15; 1 John 3:5.

[377] For the *hyper* formula see: "for you": Luke 22:19; 1 Cor 11:24; "for us": 2 Cor 5:21; Gal 3:13; Eph 5:2; "for me": Gal 2:20; "for many": (Mark 14:24; Heb 2:9; "for the ungodly": Rom 5:6; "for the people": John 11:50; 18:14; "for the nation": John 11:51; "for our sins": 1 Cor 15:3; Gal 1:4; 1 John 2:2; "for the church": Eph 5:25; "died for us": Rom 5:8; "died for our sins": 1 Cor 15:3; "for whom Christ died": Rom 14:15b; 1 Cor 8:11; "died for the ungodly": Rom 5:6.

[378] See Rom 5:2; Eph 2:18; 3:12; Heb 10:19.

[379] See Mark 8:31; 9:31; 10:34; Luke 24:7, 46; Acts 2:23–24; 4:10; 5:30–31; 10:39–40; Rom 6:9; 8:11; 14:9; 1 Cor 15:3–4; 2 Cor 5:15; Phil 2:8–11; Thess 4:14; Rev 1:18. See esp. Acts 2:32 ("killed . . . raised up . . . exalted at the right hand of God"); Rom 8:34 ("died, was raised, is at the right hand of God").

[380] See Mark 14:62/Matt 26:64; Mark 16:19; Acts 2:33–35; 5:30–31; 7:55, 56; Rom 8:34; Eph 1:20; 2:6; Col 3:1; Heb 1:3; 8:1; 10:12; 12:2.

[381] See Acts 1:9–11; Eph 1:20; Phil 2:9–11; Col 1:18b–20; 2:15; 1 Tim 3:16; Mark 16:19 and *poreuomai* of Christ's ascension (John 14:2, 3, 12, 28; 16:7, 28; Acts 1:10, 11).

[382] See 1 Cor 15:24–28; Eph 1:21; Col 1:16–18; 2:10; Heb 1:3–4, 13–14; 2:5–9; 10:12–13; cf. Phil 2:9–11; 1 Tim 3:16.

role in the worship, instruction, and self-definition of the early Church (Cullmann 1943; Delling 1962, 77–91; Lietzmann 1966, 41–60). Among the NT writings are numerous instances of hymnic or confessional formulas[383] or more complete hymns or creeds.[384] Hymns[385] were confessional as well as celebratory in nature and, like creeds, are marked by such features as parallel colons with parallelism of the members; metrical or rhythmic consistency; pronominal or adjectival phrases referring to the subject of the hymn; asyndeton; strophic arrangement; and concerted focus on the nature or action of God or Christ, or salvation.[386]

A Petrine use here of a preexistent unified creedal or hymnic source has been suspected for a variety of reasons: (1) the presence of terms occurring only here in 1 Peter (as noted above), suggesting derivation from a source; (2) the focus on Christ, as typical of NT hymns and creeds; (3) the presence of a relative pronoun (v 22a), adjective (v 18b), and participles (vv 18de, 22bc) referring to Christ; (4) the presence of parallel colons with some parallelism of the members (v 18a/b; 18d/e/19a/22a/b/c) found in other NT formulations; (5) the affinity of these colons with other Christian texts regarded as hymns or creeds (e.g., Phil 2:6–11; Col 1:15–20; 1 Tim 3:16).

The triad of aorist participial phrases *thanatōtheis men sarki/zōiopoiētheis de pneumati/poreutheis eis ouranon* is particularly noteworthy. These three phrases succinctly express the three related actions of Christ's death, resurrection, and ascension. In their form as well as general content they are similar to three of the aorist participial phrases of the hymn of 1 Tim 3:16 ("manifested in the flesh/pronounced righteous in the spirit/taken up into glory"). In a comparison of 1 Pet 3:18–22 and 1 Tim 3:16, Selwyn (1947, 325) considered further possible parallels but ultimately rejected the theory that 1 Pet 3:18–22 was based on any hymnic source.[387]

The absence of any precise and extensive parallels between 1 Pet 3:18–22 and any earlier hymn or creed nevertheless has not deterred a number of scholars from suspecting Petrine dependence on some form of hymn or creed in 3:18–22. H. Windisch (1930, 70–72), for example, saw underlying these verses a four-strophe "Christ hymn" (or "baptismal hymn") interpolated between

[383] See Acts 8:37D; 10:36; Rom 1:3–4; 10:9; 1 Cor 1:9; 8:6; 12:3; 15:3–8; 2 Cor 4:5; Eph 4:4–6; 1 Tim 1:12; 6:11–12; 2 Tim 2:8; Heb 3:1; 4:14; 10:23; 1 John 4:2.

[384] See Phil 2:6–11; Col 1:15–20; 1 Tim 3:16; Heb 1:3; Rev 4:11; 5:9–10; 11:17–18; 14:3; 15:3–4; cf. also Luke 1:46–55; 1:68–79; 2:29–32; Cullmann 1943; Deichgräber 1967; Wood 1979.

[385] On hymns in Christian worship, see 1 Cor 14:15, 26; Col 3:16; and Pliny, *Ep*. 10.96.

[386] See the 21 criteria of hymnic, creedal, or formulary material listed by Shimada (1979, 155–56) and, earlier, Stauffer (1943, 338–39) and Schille (1962, 18–20).

[387] Michaels (1988, 198) suspected a later parallel to the Petrine triad in the second-century Valentinian *Epistle to Rheginos or Treatise on the Resurrection* (45:25–28), probably composed in Rome ("So then, as the Apostle said, we suffered with him, and we arose with him, and we went to heaven with him"). However, the idea of solidarity in this formulation is closer to the thought of Paul (Rom 6:8; 8:17; cf. 2 Tim 2:11) and thus implies Paul, not Peter, as the "apostle" in mind, so that this text also sheds no light on the hymnic or creedal nature of the text of 1 Peter.

3:13–17 and 4:1 and incorporating a myth of a descent into hell (v 19) with gnostic, anti-Jewish, and anti–Jewish-Christian overtones.

O. Cullmann (1943, 14–15), on the other hand, modifying Windisch's theory, considered these verses to reflect not a hymn but a creed treating Christ's death (v 18), descent to hell (v 19), resurrection (v 21d), ascension, and session at God's right hand (v 22). Verses 20–21 he regarded as an interpolation of a brief baptismal instruction suggesting that this confession was employed in the baptismal ritual.

R. Bultmann (1947), expanding further on Windisch, presented the first detailed analysis of vv 18–22 and concluded that the underlying source of these verses and 1:20 was a confession of gnostic coloration. Distinguishing units of the original source from elements of Petrine redaction, he theorized that the source began with the words "I believe in the Lord Jesus Christ who" and thereafter ran as follows:

ton proegnōsmenon men pro katabolēs kosmou (1:20a)
  phanerōthenta de ep' eschatou tōn chronōn (1:20b)
hos epathen hapax peri hamartiōn (3:18a)
  hina hēmas prosagagēi tōi theōi (3:18c)
thanatōtheis men sarki (3:18d)
  zōiopoiētheis de pneumati (3:18e)
en hōi kai tois en phylakēi pneumasin ekēryxen (3:19)
poreutheis (*de*) *eis ouranon ekathisen en dexiai theou* (3:22b,a)
  hypotagentōn autōi aggelōn kai exousiōn kai dynameōn (3:22c)

was foreknown before the foundation of the world (1:20a)
  was manifested at the end of the ages (1:20b)
who suffered for sins once for all (3:18a)
  so that he might lead us to God (3:18c)
was put to death in the flesh (3:18d)
  was made alive in the spirit (3:18e)
in which he also announced to the spirits in prison (3:19)
having gone into heaven he sat at the right hand of God (3:22b, a)
  with angels and authorities and powers subordinated to him (3:22c)

The Petrine author, according to Bultmann, cited the first two lines of the source in 1:20 and its remainder in 3:18, 19, 22, with redactional modifications ("you" for "us," 3:18c; inversion of word order in 3:18a, 22) and additions (*hoti kai Christos, dikaios hyper adikōn*, vv 20–21). Bultmann's theory was accepted by some other scholars but with various types of modifications.[388]

[388] See Boismard 1961, 61–67; Schille 1962, 38–39 (a "Savior hymn"); Hunzinger 1970, 142–45; Reichert 1989, 355–74. Wengst (1974, 161–65), while following Bultmann's lead, found more traces of Petrine redaction in the hymn than Bultmann allowed (v 18abc; vv 19–20; v 22b) and classified the hymn as a "Weglied" (a hymn on Christ's departure).

A substantial number of scholars, however, has found these studies inconclusive and unconvincing. In contrast to 1 Tim 3:16, as a clear example of a hymn/creed, the present verses of 1 Pet 3:18–22 display no metrical consistency, no consistent parallelism of the members, and no clear strophic divisions so that a hymn or creed must be reconstructed hypothetically and then distinguished from subsequent redactional elements. But on these vital points there is no agreement whatsoever. Nor has a satisfactory explanation been offered on why the first couplet of the source should have been used separately in 1:20. Thus, in addition to the absence of any extant written source representing a precise and complete parallel to 1 Pet 3:18–22, the chief problem with these theories is the patent lack of consensus regarding the genre of the suspected source, its original content and strophic arrangement, the nature and extent of Petrine redaction, and the manner and motive of its use in 1 Peter.

This lack of agreement is the result not only of the conjectural nature of the method of these analyses but also of the complex nature of the text under examination, the presence of both poetic and prosaic material, and the combination of ideas deriving from different streams of Israelite and Christian tradition. With no convincing case at hand for the existence and use of a fixed creed or hymn in vv 18–22, the most that can be said with certainty is that vv 18 and 22 echo independent and fluid formulas of primitive Christian kerygmatic or creedal-hymnic tradition.[389]

The author's procedure here is similar to his practice evident elsewhere in the letter, where various kergymgatic formulas (1:2–21; 2:21–25) and traditions (2:4–10) are merged to form unique coherent units of thought. Verse 18ab, echoing traditional formulations of Christ's passion, links vv 18–22 with 3:13–17 as its Christological substantiation; v 22, embodying kerygmatic formulas declaring Christ's resurrection, ascension, and presence with God, provides the basis for the statement in v 18c that he leads believers as well to God, and together vv 18 and 22 provide the context (resurrection and ascension) within which the protological event of the Flood and the eschatological event of baptism (vv 19–20) are assigned corresponding soteriological significance.

Verses 19–20 are related to a different body of tradition, and it is to this unit that we now turn.

2. *Traces of Noachic Flood (and Enochic) Tradition in 1 Peter 3:19–20*

Verses 19–20 (21) differ from vv 18 and 22 in terms of their form (a series of prosaic subordinate clauses including parenthetical comments), as well as their focus and content (the Noachic Flood and related elements, correspondence of

389 So also Reicke 1946, 126; Selwyn 1947, 195; Jeremias 1949, 196; Shimada 1966, 303–95; 1979; Deichgräber 1967, 169–73; J. N. D. Kelly 1969, 147; Best 1971, 135–36; Goldstein 1974, 40; Schelkle 1976, 110–12; Brox 1986, 165–66; Dalton 1989, 109–19; Cervantes Gabarrón 1991a, 208–18; and Goppelt 1993, 248–50. For a word of caution on "hymn-hunting" in 1 Peter, see Lash 1982.

the saving of Noah's family and the saving of the addressees with parenthetical qualifications of each). The details concerning the Noachic Flood indicate our author's familiarity with and allusion to elements of a broad Israelite tradition in which this Flood story of Genesis 6–8 underwent extensive amplification.

The Genesis Flood account, the evil leading to the Flood, and the salvation of Noah and his family were the focus of intense interest in the Second Temple period as a protoypical example of God's condemnation of evil and salvation of the righteous. The widely influential book of *1 Enoch* (second century BCE–first century CE) and related Enoch legendary material had a particular significance in this regard (cf. VanderKam 1984). The text of *1 Enoch* is known through extant Ethiopic and Greek translations of a Hebrew-Aramaic original.[390] This writing, as well as *2 Enoch* (preserved in Slavonic), recounts journeys that Enoch undertook to and through multiple heavenly regions and describes his visions of the fate of the inhabitants (supernatural angel-spirits, "watchers," and their hybrid progeny in addition to deceased just and unjust humans) with particular stress on the contrasting fates of the sinful angels of Gen 6:1–4 and of righteous Noah and his family (*1 En.* 6–22; 64–69; 70; 85–89; 106; *2 En.* 1–68).

1 Enoch 1–36 takes as its biblical point of departure Gen 6 and its description of the fall of the angels, the introduction and increase of evil leading up to the Flood, and the story of the rescue of Noah and his family. The evil leading to the Flood is said to have commenced with 200 angels, the *Bene Elohim* ("sons of God," Gen 6:4), who initially formed part of the heavenly divine court. Under the prompting of their chief, Semyaz, they descended to earth, lusted after, and mated with human women in violation of the divine order. The product of this "polluted" union was a race of bastard hybrids and "giants" (*Nephilîm*, Gen 6:4), who revealed eternal secrets and filled the earth with blood, oppression, and sin. As a result, these disobedient angels, also known as "Watchers,"[391] were confined to prison, "where they will be locked up forever" (*1 En.* 10:13; cf. 13:2; 14:5). The Flood of Noah's time was the divine punishment and eradication of this initial evil.[392]

Traces of this writing have also been found at Qumran (4QEnoch [Aramaic] and other fragments), and it was likewise known and read in the early Church. The letter of Jude (vv 14–15) explicitly cites *1 Enoch* (1:9) as an ancient and reliable witness to the certainty of divine judgment of the godless.

---

[390] English translations are contained in the volumes of Charles, ed. (1913, 2:163–281) and Charlesworth, ed. (1993, 1:5–89, where the components of this composite writing [1–5, 6–36, 37–71, 72–82, 83–90, 91–104, 105–8], its structure, themes, and its extensive influence are also discussed); see also Nickelsburg 1992a.

[391] See *1 En.* 10:9, 15; 12:4; 13:10; 14:1; 15:2, 9; 16:1.

[392] On *1 Enoch* and Enoch tradition in general, see Nickelsburg 1981b, 46–55, 90–95, 145–51, 214–23; 1992a; and VanderKam 1984; on the figure of Enoch and his legend, see Grelot 1958; on the relation between the figures of Enoch and Peter, see Nickelsburg 1981a; on *1 En.* 6–11, see Nickelsburg 1977; P. D. Hanson 1977; Dimant 1978. On writings recounting "tours of Hell" and heavenly ascents, see Segal 1980; Himmelfarb 1983, 1993; Tabor 1992.

Thus it is likely that its earlier description of the sinful and bound angels of the primordial period (Jude 6, 13, 15; cf. 2 Pet 2:4–5) reflects familarity with *1 Enoch* material.[393] Knowledge and adaptation of the Enochic Watcher tradition (chs. 1–36) is evident as well in 2 Peter (2:4–5) and several later Christian writings.[394] Codex Panopolitanus (4th–5th century, Egypt), which contains combined sections of *1 Enoch* 1–36, the *Gospel of Peter*, and the *Apocalypse of Peter*, attests to the continued association of Enochian and Petrine tradition down through later time (Nickelsburg 1990).

References to the Flood story, often with amplifications similar to those in the Enoch tradition concerning the sin and fate of the disobedient angelic spirits in Gen 6:1–4, appear in numerous other Israelite writings of this period.[395]

Several features of this tradition expanding on Gen 6–8 are relevant to vv 19–20 of 1 Pet 3 and their interpretation:

(1) In this tradition, the "sons of God" in Gen 6:1–4 are identified not only as "angels" (*1 En.* 6:2; 67:4 and passim)[396] or "evil angels" or "demons"[397] or "Watchers"[398] or "stars" (*1 En.* 21:3, 6) but also as "spirits" (*pneumata, 1 En.* 15:4, 6, 7, 8, 10a; 16:1)[399] or "spirits of the angels" (*1 En.* 19:1).[400]

(2) The defiance of these angelic spirits entailed their transgression of God's command through abandonment of their heavenly abode, their violating the boundaries between angelic and human species and engaging in illicit intercourse with human women, and their spawning of giant sons (Heb., *Nephilîm*, "fallen ones"; LXX, "giants").[401] These hybrid fallen ones/giants are also identified as "(evil) spirits" (*1 En.* 15:8, 9, 11, 12; 16:1; *Jub.* 10:3–5) or "demons" (*Jub.* 7:22; 10:1, 2) who, together with the angelic spirits who spawned them, were responsible for the evil purged by the Flood.[402] This act of boundary violation (cf. also *T. Reu.* 5:6; *T. Naph.* 3:5; Jude 6), self-defilement, impurity, lust, and instigation of corruption on the earth is condemned as "great sin"

---

[393] For references to *1 Enoch* see also *Barn.* 16:5; Tert., *Idol.* 15.6; Clem. Alex., *Ecl.* 3.

[394] See, e.g., *Gos. Pet.* 39–42; *Apoc. Pet.*; *Ps.-Clementine Homilies* 8.10–20 (in a sermon attributed to Peter); cf. also Zuurmond 1991.

[395] See Wis 10:4; 14:1–7; Sir 16:7; *Jub.* 4:24; 5:1–6:3; 7:20–33; 10:1–6; *T. Reu.* 5:6; *T. Naph.* 3:5; 1QapGen; 1Q19; 1Q23; 1Q24; 4Q201–207; 4Q212; 4Q530; 4Q531; 6Q8; CD II 17–21; *2 En.* 7:1–5; 18:1–9, 34–35; 73; *2 Bar.* 56:8–16; *3 Bar.* 4:10–15; *Apoc. Ab.* 13–14; *Sib. Or.* 1:97–104, 125–282; 7:7–15; Philo, *On the Giants* and *The Unchangeableness of God*; *QG* 1.92–2.55; Josephus, *Ant.* 1.72–95; *Ag. Ap.* 130; 1 Pet 3:19–20; 2 Pet 2:5; Jude 6; Just. Mart., *1 Apol.* 5; *2 Apol.* 5. For mention of Noah and the Flood generation, see Matt 24:37–39/Luke 17:26–27; Heb 11:7; *1 Clem.* 7:6; 9:4.

[396] See also *Jub.* 5:1, 6; 1QapGen III 3; IV 4; *2 Bar.* 56:10; Josephus, *Ant.* 1.73; Jude 6; 2 Pet 2:4.

[397] See also *Jub.* 10:2; Philo, *Gig.* 6, 16.

[398] See *1 En.* 10:9, 14; 12:4; 13:10; 14:1, 3; 15:2, 9; 16:1; *Jub.* 7:21; 10:5; *T. Naph.* 3:5; CD II 18.

[399] See also *Jub.* 10:7; 10:3 ("evil spirits"); Philo, *QG* 1.92 ("angels," "sons of God," "spirits" [*pneumata*]).

[400] Cf. also God as "Lord of the spirits," *1 En.* 54:5, 6; 55:3; etc.

[401] See *1 En.* 6–7; 9:7–9; 10:11; 12:4; 15:3; Sir 16:7; *2 En.* 18:1–9; *Jub.* 5:1–11; Philo, *Gig.*

[402] See *1 En.* 6–16; 15–16; 18:14–15; 19:1–3; 21:4–6; 39:1; 54:4–6; 64–69; 84:4; 85–88; 90:21, 24; 106:13–15; *Jub.* 5:1–11; 7:21–22; 10:1–6; *T. Reu.* 5; *T. Naph.* 3:5; *2 Bar.* 56:12.

(*1 En.* 6:3; 21:4; cf. 2 Pet 2:4) or "transgression of the commandments of the Lord" (*1 En.* 18:15; 21:6; 106:14; *2 En.* 7:3; CD II 18, 21; Philo, *Gig.* 6; *QG* 1.92), words equivalent to "disobedient" (*apeithēsasin*), the term employed in 1 Pet 3:20a.

Although the rebellion of the angel-spirits or "Watchers" preceded the days of Noah by several generations, the Flood was seen as a consequence of the defiance they initiated (Huggins 1995, 104), and the two events were viewed as correlative and telescoped in the tradition (Gen 6:1–4, 5–8:22; *1 En.* 10:2–3 [announcement of Flood] and 10:3 [binding of Azazʾel, one of the leaders of the rebellious angelic host]).[403] 1 Peter 3:19–20 (as well as 2 Pet 2:4–5) likewise reflects the direct association of these events.

(3) As punishment for their rebellion, these angelic spirits and a portion of their demonic descendants (*Jub.* 10:1–6) were "bound" (*deō, desmoi*), put into "chains" (*1 En.* 69:28; *2 Bar.* 56:13) or cast into prison (*desmōtērion*) or "confinement" (*sygkleisis*), where they were to be locked up forever.[404]

Josephus (*Ant.* 1.73) notes the similarity between this story of the sin of the angels in Gen 6 and the Greek myth of the Titans, a race of giants produced from the blood of Uranus falling on Earth (*gē*; Hesiod, *Theog.* 185, 617–735; cf. Homer, *Od.* 7.59). In punishment for their rebellion against Chronus, they too were bound in chains (in dark Tartarus). This binding of the angelic spirits is also mentioned in Jude 6 and 2 Pet 2:4 (where "Tartarus" may reflect a merger of Israelite and Greek myths). In 1 Peter, this motif of the binding and imprisonment of the angels from Gen 6 is expressed in the phrase "in prison" (*en phylakēi*, v 19a). This early Christian appropriation of the Flood tradition likewise stresses the final condemnation of these angelic spirits (Jude 6, 13, 15; 2 Pet 2:5) as a warning for present believers, a motif crucial to the sense of *ekēryxen* in 1 Pet 3:19a. Earlier, their punishment was cited as "a testimony to the kings and rulers who control the world" (*1 En.* 67:12) or to those who were under the influence of their offspring, the demonic evil spirits (*Jub.* 10:1–6).

(4) The *location* of these bound or imprisoned angel-spirits and their demonic offspring is situated variously in the tradition.[405] *1 Enoch* on one occasion, however, has Enoch describing his being "lifted up" (17:1) to a place "where the heavens come together," where he saw "the prison house" (*desmōtērion*) of the transgressing angelic stars and powers of heavens (18:14–16; cf. 21:1–10). *2 Enoch*, more specifically, describes how Enoch, in the course of

---

[403] See also *1 En.* 54; 64:1–69:29; 85:1–89:9; 106:13–107:3; *Jub.* 5:1–5; 10:1–6; *2 Bar.* 56:12–15; *T. Naph.* 3:5; Josephus, *Ant.* 1.72–74.

[404] See *1 En.* 10:4, 12, 13, 14; 13:2; 14:5; 18:13–16; 21:1–10; 54:4–6; 67:4; 69:28; 88:1–3; 90:23–24; *2 En.* 7:1–3; 18:3; *Jub.* 5:6–11; 10:4–11; 4QEnoch I 6, 22; VII 1; *Sib. Or.* 1.100–104.

[405] E.g., "underneath the rocks of the ground" (*1 En.* 10:12; cf. 1QH[a] III 17–18; Rev 20:1–3); "inside the earth" (*1 En.* 14:5; *Jub.* 5:6), "on the earth" rather than below it (*1 En.* 13:9), "in the west" (*1 En.* 67:4), or some terrible "place" along Enoch's journey (*1 En.* 21:1–10); cf. "nether gloom," Jude 6; "held captive in Tartarus," 2 Pet 2:5.

his journey through the seven heavens saw in the second heaven, a realm of darkness greater than earthly darkness, those apostate angels "who did not obey the Lord's commandments" and who "had turned away with their prince" (*2 En.* 7:1–3, longer recension; cf. *T. Levi* 3:3, which also locates "the spirits [*tois pneumasin*] of error and of Beliar" in the second heaven). The "gloom" (*zophos*) of which both Jude (vv 6, 13) and 2 Pet 2:4 speak may also refer to this lower heaven of darkness.

(5) To these imprisoned angelic spirits or "Watchers," Enoch announced divine condemnation and judgment (*1 En.* 12:4–6; 13:1–10; 14:1–7; 15:1–16:3; cf. Josephus, *Ant.* 1.75). This stress on the condemnation of the angelic spirits, whether by Enoch or one or more of the righteous angels,[406] is a consistent theme of this tradition in both its Israelite and Christian elaborations.

The similarities between 1 Peter, Jude, and 2 Peter in this regard are particularly noteworthy and indicative of how the words of 1 Peter are best understood. Jude, in recounting three examples of ungodliness in ancient time as a warning for his own generation (vv 5–7), refers to the disobedient angelic spirits of primordial time and underscores their imprisonment.[407] Then, referring explicitly to *1 Enoch* (1:9), he observes, "It was of these also that Enoch . . . prophesied, saying, 'Behold, the Lord came with his holy myriads, to execute judgment on all, and to convict all the ungodly of all their deeds of ungodliness which they have committed in such an ungodly way'" (vv 14–15). These are the fallen angels of Gen 6, who did not keep their own position but left their proper dwelling in heaven and cohabited with the daughters of men (cf. Gen 6:1–4; *1 En.* 6–16). 2 Peter 2:4–5 represents an expansion of Jude and a further elaboration on this tradition. Again examples from the past are cited, now in chronological order (2 Pet 2: 4–8)—the sinful angels held captive in Tartarus for judgment (v 4), the Flood, and the preservation of Noah and his household (vv 4–5)—as illustrations of the fact that "the Lord knows how to rescue the godly from trial and to keep the unrighteous under punishment for the day of judgment" (v 9). As in Jude, the examples are applied to the ungodly of the author's day and especially to "those who indulge in the lust of defiling passion and despise authority" (2 Pet 2:10a and 10b–22). Thereafter, reference also is made to "an earth formed out of water and by means of water . . . through which the world that then existed was deluged with water and perished" (2 Pet 3:5, 6; cf. 1 Pet 3:19) and to the "patience" of the Lord (3:9; cf. 1 Pet 3:19). Common to 1 Peter, 2 Peter, and Jude are references to the errant angels who sinned and mention of their condemnation and enduring bondage or imprisonment. 1 Peter and 2 Peter also make a common reference to Noah, the family of eight, its salvation, and the patience of God. In 1 Peter, these

---

[406] See *1 En.* 10:4 [Sync.], 11; 12:4; 13:1, 3; 15:2; and the texts listed in no. (4) above.

[407] "And the angels that did not keep their own position but left their proper dwelling have been kept by him in eternal chains in the (nether) gloom for the judgment of the great day" (v 6). They were "errant stars for whom the (nether) gloom of darkness has been reserved forever" (v 13).

sinning angels are described as "disobedient spirits." In the light of Jude and 2 Peter, it is also possible that these disobedient spirits were mentioned, not only because they had a decisive role in the Flood story on which 1 Peter focuses, but also to illustrate the condemnation of the "disobedient" nonbelievers of the author's own time (cf. 2:7b, 8b; 3:1c; 4:17c). In terminology, theme (judgment), and function (example for disobedient of the present), 1 Peter, Jude, and 2 Peter represent similar early Christian appropriations of this Flood tradition and identify the angel-spirits as examples for the disobedient and ungodly of the end time. This similarity strengthens the likelihood that for 1 Peter (1) the disobedient spirits are the angels who sinned at the time of Noah and the flood; (2) the "prison" of 1 Peter corresponds to the commitment or keeping of these sinning angels in eternal chains of (nether) gloom; and (3) Christ's announcment to these angel-spirits (*ekēryxen*, 1 Pet 3:19b) was not one of salvation but of divine judgment, as in Jude and 2 Peter. If, as is likely, 3:22c refers to these spirits as well, their subordination to Christ is one decisive aspect of this judgment.

When 1 Pet 3:19–20 is examined in conjunction with this Israelite tradition and its Christian appropriation, greater clarity is gained on a number of questions:

(1) In the light of this entire tradition, the reference in 1 Pet 3:19–20 to the "spirits in prison . . . who once disobeyed . . . in the days of Noah" is best taken as a reference to the disobedient angelic spirits and their hybrid progeny whose transgression led to the rampant evil destroyed in the Noachic Flood. The preoccupation with these disobedient angelic spirits in the author's time, his explicit association of these spirits with the Flood, and further aspects of their description make this identification virtually certain. A reference here to deceased humans (or an ensemble of angelic and human sinners) on the other hand is far less likely. In *1 Enoch*, as noted above, these angelic spirits are consistently identified as *pneumata* (Greek text of *1 Enoch*), used absolutely, as in 1 Peter. When, on the other hand, *pneumata* is used in *1 Enoch* to designate deceased humans, the term is qualified by various clarifying expressions.[408] Moreover, when the fate of the human deceased is mentioned in *1 Enoch* (22:1–14; 27:1–5; 65:6–11; 102–4; 108:6), human and angelic sinners are distinguished, and the sin and punishment of the primordial *angel-spirits* and their hybrid progeny receives the lion's share of attention.[409]

(2) The Petrine location of these spirits "in prison" (*en phylakēi*), not equivalent to "in hell," as Gschwind rightly stressed (1911, 85, 88), corresponds to the intermediate fate of the disobedient angelic spirits described in the Flood tradition as their being "bound" or "imprisoned" until their final condemna-

[408] Such as "spirits of humans" (20:3; 22:13); "spirits of the souls of the dead" (22:3; cf. 9:3); "spirits of the dead, spirits of the just" (22:9); cf. also 20:6; 22:12, 13 ("souls of the people"); for two possible exceptions, see 98:3; 103:4.

[409] See *1 Enoch* (chs. 6–16, 17–21; 54:1–4; 69:1–21; 85:1–89:9; 106:1–19); see also Jude and 2 Peter.

tion, a punishment not associated with deceased humans.[410] Just as these angelic spirits are described in the tradition as having "sinned" and "transgressed" against the commandment of God, so the Petrine author expresses this with the formulation "those who once disobeyed" (*apeithēsasin pote*). This constellation of details argues decisively for seeing in *pneumata* a reference not to the human deceased of Noah's generation or to the deceased in general or to an ensemble of sinful angels and humans but solely to the angelic spirits of Gen 6:1–4 as portrayed at greater length in *1 Enoch* and the Flood tradition.

(3) According to the sequence of the verbs *thanatōtheis*, *zōiopoiētheis*, and *poreutheis* in 1 Pet 3:18–19, Christ's "having gone" to these disobedient spirits *followed* not only his "having been put to death" but also his "having been made alive." The occasion of this "going" therefore cannot refer to any time *prior* to his resurrection. This argues decisively against the Augustinian theory, revived in recent time, that Christ in some putative preexistent state ("in the spirit" or "through Noah") or in connection with his death and prior to his resurrection "descended" into the underworld and announced salvation to deceased humans there. This is all the more unlikely because the "having gone" of v 19 is repeated and further clarified in v 22d as "having gone into heaven." With this repetition of verbs the author frames the thought in vv 19–22 and expressly links its content to Christ's resurrection (v 18e, 21d). The theory of a descent of a preexistent Christ claims a connection between Christ and Noah not stated in the Petrine text and imputes to this text a concept of Christ's preexistence nowhere in evidence in the letter. Analogous rather to the description of Enoch in *1 Enoch* and *2 Enoch*, the Petrine author portrays Christ as having announced to the disobedient angelic spirits in the course of his ascension into heaven (as shown definitively by Dalton 1965/1989).[411] The sequence of verbs, in brief, requires that Christ's announcement occurred in conjunction not with his death but with his resurrection and ascension to heaven.

(4) In accord with the Israelite and Christian conception of multiple heavens[412] and the earlier reference to "heavens" in 1 Pet 1:4, the Petrine author appears to have envisioned Christ's passing through several heavens on his

[410] For the equivalency of *phylakē* and *en desmois*, see *T. Levi* 8:4–5 (of Joseph in Egypt), and for the *phylakē* of Satan involving his being bound (*edēsen*), see Rev 20:2, 7. The term *phylakē* occurs in *1 En.* 100:5, but the passage is not relevant, since there it is used not of *disobedient* spirits but of the "righteous and holy ones" whom God "shall set under the guard" (*taxei phylakēn*) of the holy angels until the tribulations are over.

[411] The 2d-century *Peri Pascha* by Melito of Sardis, referring to Christ's death, resurrection, and ascension, contains a similar juxtaposition and sequence of aorist verbs, including reference to his burial but not to his "descent into hell": "It was he . . . that was hanged on a tree (cf. 1 Pet 2:24), that was buried in the earth, that was raised from the dead, that was taken up (*analēmphtheis*) to the heights of the heavens" (*Peri Pascha* 70; cf. also 104).

[412] See 2 Cor 12:2 ("third heaven"); cf. also Eph 1:10; 3:15; 4:10; 6:9; Phil 3:20; Col 1:5, 16, 20; 1 Thess 1:10; Heb 4:14; 1 Pet 1:4; 2 Pet 3:3–13; and 55 references to plural "heavens" in Matthew and 7 in Hebrews.

journey to God in the highest of the heavens (as also in Heb 4:14). The ascending Christ then would have encountered the disobedient spirits in a lower heaven where they were confined and bound. 2 *Enoch* 7:1–3 and *T. Levi* 3:2–3 locate these condemned and imprisoned angel-spirits in the second heaven, and this location appears to be presumed here in 1 Peter as well.

(5) The fact that Israelite and earliest Christian tradition unanimously stressed the final condemnation and judgment of these rebellious angel-spirits is the strongest reason for concluding that the unqualified verb *ekēryxen* (v 19b) entailed Christ's announcement of condemnation as well. Within the closer context of this verse, only an equation of this verb with the distant verb *euaggelisthē* in 4:6 would suggest that Christ's announcement in v 19b entailed a message of "good news." It is on this proposed but unlikely equation of terms that the theory of Christ's preaching repentance and salvation to the "spirits" of deceased humans has been based. But such an equivalency of these verbs in this context, though often assumed and asserted, has never been satisfactorily demonstrated.[413] The same is true of the proposed correspondence between the human dead of 4:6 and the imprisoned spirits of vv 19–20 and the assumption of "in prison" as a moral metaphor ("imprisoned in sin"). Moreover, the notion of Christ's preaching good news to disobedient angelic spirits (or for that matter deceased humans) of the Flood generation for the purpose of their repentance and salvation would be an idea thoroughly alien to the Flood tradition, the thought of 1 Peter, and that of the NT as a whole.

Accordingly, the substance of Christ's announcement to these disobedient angel-spirits is best construed not as an offer of repentance and salvation but as a confirmation of their divine condemnation and judgment. Just as Enoch and the good angels "had gone" (*poreuein*) to the evil angelic spirits with the announcement of their punishment and imprisonment (*1 En.* 10:1–4 [Sync.]; 12:4; 13:1–3; 15:1–16:3), so Christ is depicted as "having gone" (*poreuein*) to these now imprisoned spirits with a confirming announcement of their condemnation.[414] Such a message of judgment would not only be consistent with the Israelite and early Christian tradition but also with the following stress on the subordination of the cosmic spirits to the resurrected Christ at God's right hand (v 22). All cosmic spirits, including those imprisoned, it is affirmed, are now subject to the power of the exalted Christ. The condemnation and subordination of the disobedient spirits as prototypical rebels of primordial time prefigure the final condemnation of all those who disobey God's word and will (2:7b–8; 3:1, 16; 4:17–18). Their condemnation also serves as a contrast to the salvation in store for the obedient children of God.[415]

[413] As also stressed by Dalton 1989, 51–60, 184–88; and Hillyer 1992, 122.

[414] So Gschwind 1911, 130–32; Selwyn 1947, 200, 322–33; Dalton 1965, 135–201 (slightly modified in the 2d ed., pp. 47, 158–59); and against Bigg 1902, 162–63; Reicke 1946, 90–91, 118, 120–22, 130–31; Beare 1970, 172; Best 1971, 144; Grudem 1988, 223–25.

[415] See 1:2c, 3–12, 14–16; 2:2, 15–17, 20, 24; 3:5–6, 7, 10–12, 14; 4:2–3, 6; 12–19; 5:4, 5, 10.

While the foregoing conclusions regarding the terms of 1 Peter are inferences based on their close similarity to concepts and themes of Israelite and Christian tradition, their likelihood is strengthened by their consistency with both the content and the structure of the Petrine text as a whole. At the same time it is clear from this comparison that the Petrine text as a whole (vv 19–22) has no exact parallel in either Israelite or contemporary Christian sources and represents an original contribution of the Petrine author.

3. The Petrine Combination and Redaction of This Traditional Material

In 1 Pet 3:18–22 the author has merged concepts, motifs, and formulas reflecting two distinct traditions: early Christian kerygmatic formulations (vv 18, 22), on the one hand, and motifs of the Flood tradition (vv 19b–20) combined with Christian baptismal tradition (v 21), on the other. Dalton (1989, 109–19) speaks less felicitously of the combination of two "sources" (vv 18 and 22, which he sees deriving from a hymn or creed and vv 19–21 reflecting "baptismal catechesis"). But he is correct in noting (1989, 119) that this combination "accounts for the elements of repetition in 3:19a–20 and 3:22." These repetitions were the syntactical means by which our author merged this material into a unified whole. Further redactional elements by which our author combined traditions and linked them to their immediate and more remote contexts include the following: (1) *kai*, v 18a ("Christ *also*"); (2) "suffered," v 18a (a leitmotif of 1 Peter as well as an element of Christological tradition); (3) *en hōi kai*, v 19a (a circumstantial link joining v 18 to vv 19–21); (4) "also having gone," v 19a (derived from and anticipating the same term of the tradition, "having gone [into heaven]," used in v 22b); (5) "disobedient," a modifier of "spirits" in v 19a (in accord with the Flood tradition) and the same term for nonbelievers who reject Christ and "disobey" the word (2:7–8; cf. 3:2; 4:17); (6) the typological relation established in vv 20– 21 between the salvation of Noah and his family through water and the salvation of the baptized through the resurrection of Jesus Christ, both representing small groups that are saved, in contrast to disobedient evil angels who are condemned; and (7) the phrase "through the resurrection of Jesus Christ," which echoes the same phrase in 1:3, thereby thematically linking the topics of baptism and rebirth.

Kerygmatic material concerning Christ's death, resurrection, and ascension to heaven provided the traditional basis and literary framework for the entire statement in 3:18d–22. Into this framework the author incorporated the material of vv 19–21, which presents a different set of ideas with affinity to a different body of thought, namely Israelite tradition amplifying on Gen 6–8.

Thus 3:18–22 in its entirety, like 2:21–25, represents another creative merger of traditions designed to substantiate a preceding exhortation. The identification of the substance of these traditions and then of the manner of their combination has helped to clarify not only the thrust of the passage as a whole but also several of its syntactical and semantic problems.

DETAILED COMMENT 2: 1 PETER 3:19 AND THE DOCTRINE OF CHRIST'S DESCENT INTO HELL (*DESCENSUS CHRISTI AD INFERA/INFEROS*)

1 Peter 3:19, within the context of 3:18–22, refers to the *ascension of Christ* following his resurrection, rather than to a descent of Christ to the realm of the dead following his death and prior to his resurrection. The idea of Christ's *descensus ad infera* (descent to the underworld) or *inferos* (to the dead) developed independently of 1 Peter in the NT. Its elaboration in post-NT time involved a variety of concepts and theological concerns quite alien to 1 Peter.

According to one of the oldest cosmological views of the ancient world, the abode of the humans who died was the "underworld," known as *Hadēs* in Greek, *infera* in Latin (with *inferi* designating the inhabitants of the infernal regions), and *Sheol* in Hebrew.[416] Thus, to die and join the dead was thought to involve a "descent" (*katabasis, descensus*) into the infernal regions. According to this view, Jesus' death would entail his "descent" to the underworld, a mythological thought expressing no more than the reality of his death and his place among the dead (e.g., Matt 12:40; Acts 2:23–31; Rom 10:7; Eph 4:9[?]). Where death was seen as also involving punishment for an unjust life, the realm of the dead accordingly could be viewed as a place of punishment and retribution (Hebrew: *gehinnom*; Greek: *gehenna*; cf. also *Tartaros* [a sublevel of Hades]), as with the later Anglo-Saxon term, *hell*. Various myths throughout the ancient Near East recount the descent of gods, heroes, and seers to the underworld to communicate with the dead or to retrieve loved ones or to battle the infernal forces (cf. Kroll 1931; Bauckham 1992c, 145–54).

A mingling and modification of cosmological views beginning with the Hellenistic period resulted in occasional relocations of the realm of the dead. While many still reckoned with an underworld realm of the dead below the earth's surface, others located this realm in one of the lower of the seven heavens. For the latter, including Second Temple Israelite authors (e.g., *1 Enoch*, *2 Enoch*, *3 Baruch*), a journey to the realm of the dead and imprisoned angel-spirits would entail not a descent but an *ascent* to one of these nether regions of the sky (cf. Himmelfarb 1983; Bauckham 1990; 1992, 154–55). The Petrine author is among the Israelite and Christian authors sharing this modified view.

This diversity of views prevailed in the post-NT period as well. At this time, moreover, soteriological significance began to be associated with Christ's presence in the realm of the dead prior to his resurrection and ascension. For numerous Christian authors, Christ's descent to the realm of the dead still signified his sharing fully in the lot of all mortal beings, namely death (e.g., *Sib. Or.* 8:312; Iren., *Haer.* 5.31.2; Tert., *An.* 55.2). Others, however, addressing the theological question of the final fate of the OT righteous, speculated that

[416] See Billerbeck 1928, 4/2:1016–1165; Bauckham 1992c; T. J. Lewis 1992; Watson 1992.

Christ, on the occasion of his death and descent to the realm of the dead, proclaimed deliverance to the righteous of Israel who had died prior to Christ.[417] This thought, however, "is unknown to the NT" (Danielou 1964, 233, concurring with Bieder 1949, 128; and Reicke 1946, 115–18), and 1 Pet 3:19, as Selwyn (1947, 340) notes, was never among the NT texts eventually used to support it. When Irenaeus, for instance, does refer explicitly to 1 Pet 3, it is 3:20 that he cites in reference to the Flood, "through which eight persons are saved" (*Haer.* 1.18.3), with no identification of the "spirits" in 1 Pet 3:19 as dead humans to whom Christ preached. On the other hand, to support the notion of Christ's proclamation to the OT righteous, Irenaeus cites not 1 Peter but Matt 12:40 and Eph 4:9 (*Haer.* 5.31.1).

It appears that it was Clement of Alexandria at the end of the second century who first introduced 1 Pet 3:19–20 into this developing speculation about Christ's activity in the realm of the dead prior to his resurrection. In the economy of a just God, Clement asserted, all persons have the possibility of hearing the gospel, of repenting, and of being saved (*Strom.* 6.6). This included not only Israelites but also Gentiles "that were righteous according to philosophy," and not only the living but also the dead. To the dead this opportunity was offered when "the Lord preached the Gospel (*euēggelisato*) to those in Hades" (*Strom.* 6.6 [44,1]). Without citing 1 Peter explicitly, he appears to be alluding to 1 Pet 3:19 here and when he further states that "the Lord descended to Hades for no other purpose than to preach the Gospel" (*ho kyrios di' ouden heteron eis aidou katēlthen, ē dia to euaggelisthai, Strom.* 6.6 [46,1–2]). If an allusion to 1 Pet 3, then Clement has viewed the "having gone" (*poreutheis*) of 1 Pet 3:19 as equivalent to "descended" (*katēlthen*) and the Petrine verb *ekēryxen* as equivalent to "preach the Gospel" (*euēggelisato, to euaggelisthai*). That Clement had 1 Pet 3:19–20 in mind is made further likely by his preceding remark, "do not they (the Scriptures) show that the Lord preached the Gospel to those that perished in the flood, or rather had been chained, and to those kept in prison and guard" (*tois en phylakēi te kai phrourai synechoumenois, Strom.* 6.6 [45,4–5]). The language clearly echoes the Petrine references to the Noachic Flood and the term "prison." If, as seems likely, Clement is alluding to 1 Pet 3:19–20 in *Strom.* 6.6, this is an illustration of how the Petrine passage was appropriated, indeed misappropriated, early in the Church's history to make a case for the universality of salvation, a thought quite contrary to the original thrust of this passage and of the letter as a whole. 1 Peter's reference to Christ's "going" was presented as a "descent," "spirits in prison" were considered to be deceased humans imprisoned in Hades, and Christ's announcement was seen not as the condemnation of disobedient angelic spirits but as the

---

[417] See *Gos. Pet.* 10.41–42; Melito, *Peri Pascha* 17.13–19; a fragment of the *Apocrypon of Ps.-Jeremiah* cited by Justin Martyr (*Dial.* 72.4) and Irenaeus (*Haer.* 4.22.1; contrast 3.20.4, attributed to Isaiah); Christian additions to *T. Dan* 5:10–11; *Odes Sol.* 42:11–20; and *Sib. Or.* 1.377–78; 8.310–12; Iren., *Haer.* 1.27.3; 4.27.2; 4.33.1, 12; 5.31.1; *Epid.* 78; Tert., *Ani.* 55; Origen, *Cels.* 2.43; *Ep. Apos.* 27–28; *Acts Pil.* 17–27; possibly also Ign. *Magn.* 9:2.

preaching of good news leading to the repentance and salvation of all. If this initial linking of 1 Pet 3:19–20 with the doctrine of Christ's *descensus* in the service of a universalist theory of salvation represents an ingenious contribution of Clement, it also represents a fateful departure from the original thrust of this Petrine passage and its mooring in Israelite and nascent Christian thought.

Origen took the thought of Clement one step further by appealing to 1 Pet 3:18–20 as support for the idea that as a result of Christ's descent and preaching in the underworld even the wicked are ultimately saved (Origen, *Princ.* 2.5.3).

Another theme eventually associated with the *descensus Christi* was Christ's storming of the stronghold of Hades; his overthrow of Satan, his minions, and death; and his release of the captives.[418] This idea received later elaboration in the theme of the "harrowing of hell" so popular in the Middle Ages (see MacCulloch 1930). Still other related themes included the proclamation of the apostles to those in Hades (Herm. *Sim.* 9.16.5–7; Clem. Alex., *Strom.* 6.6) and the association of Christ's *descensus* and proclamation of salvation to the dead with their baptism (Herm. *Sim.* 9.16.1–4; Clem. Alex. *Strom.* 2.43.5; 6.6; *Ep. Apos.* 26–27).

Not until the 4th century do the first creedal references to Christ's descent to hell make their appearance (the Fourth Creed of Sirmium in 359; the Creeds of Nike and Constantinople in 360). The Old Roman Creed (in the *Apostolic Tradition* of Hippolytus, died 235) still makes no mention of it, but eventually it was included in the Aquileian Creed commented upon by Rufinus (ca. 345–410; *Comm. Sym.*) and thereafter in the Apostles Creed and Athanasian Creed of the same period. On the other hand, it is absent from the Niceno-Constantinopolitan Creed.[419]

In sum, the idea of Christ's *descensus ad infera* underwent various stages of development and diverse modes of theological elaboration in the first four centuries. 1 Peter speaks of Jesus' death, but nowhere of his *descensus ad infera.* It was only at the end of the second century and first in the school of Alexandria that 1 Pet 3:19 was enlisted as biblical support for a doctrine of universal salvation proclaimed by Christ in conjunction with his death and *descensus ad infera.* Later Fathers who commented on this doctrine referred to 1 Pet 3:19 only in passing.

The absence of any reference to 1 Pet 3:19 in connection with this doctrine until 190 CE and its minimal role in subsequent patristic discussion of the *descensus*, therefore, are serious reasons for doubting any original association of

---

[418] See the Christian additions to *T. Levi* 4.1 and *T. Dan* 5.10; see also *Ascen. Isa.* 9.16–18; *Odes Sol.* 42:11–20 (contrast, however, *Odes Sol.* 17:8–12 and 22:4, where Christ's overthrow of the Devil is associated with his *ascension*, rather than his descent); Melito, *Peri Pascha* 17:13–17; 102; cf. 11:9–10; Origen, *Comm. Rom.* 5.10; *Acts Thom.* 10; *Teach. Silv.* 110:19–24; Cyril Jerus., *Myst. Cat.* 4.11; 14.17–19; *Gos. Nic.* 1 [17].1–11 [27] 1 (a fourth-century work containing some second-century material and the *Acts Pil.* [5–10]); the Creed of Sirmium; and Cyril Alex., *Pasch. Hom.* 6.7.

[419] On the creedal history of the descensus doctrine, see J. N. D. Kelly's basic study, *Early Christian Creeds* (1960, 378–83).

this verse with a descent of Christ into the underworld. In contrast to views from Clement of Alexandria onward, which were informed more by dogmatic than exegetical concerns, it is now generally agreed that the content and immediate context of vv 19–20 itself, with its reference to "the days of Noah" and its affinity with early Israelite elaborations on Gen 6–8, provide the most certain basis for the interpretation of these enigmatic verses. Further, stronger reason for doubting any relation between 1 Pet 3:19–20 and universalist views associated with the *descensus* concept is the particularist perspective of 1 Peter in general. The Petrine author consistently emphasizes an immiment and conclusive judgment according to one's deeds (1:17; 4:6, 17–19) and one's obedience to the will of God in the present (1:2, 22; 2:15; 3:17; 4:2, 19). It is this obedience and union with the resurrected Christ in baptism (3:21) that alone form the basis of salvation according to 1 Peter, a notion hardly compatible with the idea of a universal salvation or a postmortem opportunity for repentance. In this Petrine literary and theological context and in the light of the traditions merged (Israelite and Christian Flood tradition, vv 19–20 and Christian kerygmatic traditions concerning Christ's suffering, death, resurrection and heavenly ascension, vv 18, 19, 22), Christ's "having gone" in v 19, as in v 22, is a reference to the *ascension* of the resurrected Christ into heaven rather than to his descent into the underworld prior to his resurrection. The "disobedient spirits in prison" are not deceased humans but the angelic spirits whose disobedience led to the destruction through the Flood, and Christ's announcement entails a confirmation of their eternal condemnation and confinement. The subsequent development of the *descensus* theory and its theological interests should not be allowed to determine or obscure the meaning of 1 Pet 3:19 in its original historical, literary, and theological context.[420]

For studies on 1 Pet 3:18–22, see Aalen 1972; Arvedson 1950; Banks 1966; Barth 1951, 111–16; Barton 1950; Bauckham 1992b; Beasley-Murray 1963, 258–62; Bernard 1916; Bieder 1950, 1963; Bindley 1929; Bishop 1951; Boismard 1961, 57–109; Bornhauser 1921; Braun 1940, 18–35; Brinley 1987; Brooks 1974; Brox 1986, 182–89; Brusten 1905; Bullinger 1960, 141–63; Bultmann 1947; Cervantes Gabarrón 1991a, 181–252; Chaine 1934, 418–28; Clemen 1902; Cook 1980; Cramer 1891; Cranfield 1958; Cullmann 1943; Dalton 1964a, 1964b, 1965/1989, 1965b, 1968, 1979; Danielou 1947; 1956, 70–85; Davidson 1981, 313–36; Deichgräber 1967, 170–73; de la Bonnardière 1980; Delling 1963,

[420] On the *descensus Christi ad infera* concept, its history, and diverse interpretations, see Dietelmair 1762; Güder 1853; Schweizer 1868; Brusten 1897; Huidekopper 1890; W. Kelly 1970; Lauterburg 1900; Jensen 1903; Monnier 1904; B. Schmidt 1906; Turmel 1908; Gschwind 1911; Quilliet 1911; Nordblad 1912; Bousset 1919–1920; C. Schmidt 1919; MacCullough 1930; W. Kroll 1931, 1–132; Chaine 1934; Holzmeister 1937, 306–51 (earlier literature, pp. 307–9); König 1942; Odeberg 1944; Reicke 1946, 7–51, 231–48; Selwyn 1947, 339–59; Bieder 1949; Rousseau 1951–1952; Biser 1959; Reicke 1959; Galot 1961; Kürzinger 1962; J. M. E. Robinson 1962; Danielou 1964, 233–63; Vorgrimmler 1966; Perrot 1969; Rödding 1970; Strynkowski 1972; Grillmeier 1975; Maas 1979; Vogels 1976, 183–235; A. T. Hanson 1980; Perrot 1980; Miller 1981; Brox 1986, 182–89; Dalton 1989, 27–50; Colpe 1991; Bauckham 1992, 156–58.

82–96; de Ru 1966; Diderichsen 1975; Erickson 1995; Feinberg 1986; France 1977; Frings 1925; Galot 1961; Giesen 1989; Goldstein 1974; Goodspeed 1954; Gourges 1978, 75–87; Griffith-Thomas 1916; Grudem 1986; 1988, 203–29; Gschwind 1911; Hanson 1981–1982; Harris 1901, 1902a, 1902b, 1911; Hiebert 1982b; Hill 1976; Hunzinger 1970; Ittig 1730; Jensen 1891; Jeremias 1949; S. E. Johnson 1960; W. Kelly 1872; Kira 1960; Knapp 1887; Kowlaski 1938, 1949; Kvanvig 1985; Landeira 1966; Lundberg 1942, 98–116; W. D. Morris 1926–1927; Nixon 1968; Odeland 1901; Otto 1883; Papa 1980; Patton 1882; Perrot 1980; Pinto da Silva 1984; Plooij 1913; Plumptre 1885; Reichert 1989, 144–568; Reicke 1946; Richards 1931; Rigaux 1973; Rubinkiewicz 1982; Rudrauf 1685; Salvoni 1971; Scharlemann 1989; Schertz 1992; Schwank 1973b; Schweizer 1868; Selwyn 1947, 298–99, 313–62; Shimada 1966, 303–95; 1979; Skilton 1996; Skrade 1966; M. L. Smith 1912; Spitta 1890; Spoto 1971; Stemmler 1894; Steuer 1938; Synge 1971; Tripp 1981; van Unnik 1979; Usteri 1886; Vitti 1927; Vogels 1976; Volpi 1988; Zeilinger 1987; Zezschwitz 1857.

IV. C. Obedience to God's Will Distinguishing Suffering Believers from Sinful Outsiders; God's Condemnation of Sinners and Vindication of the Faithful (4:1–6)

4:1a Therefore, since Christ suffered in the flesh,
1b you too arm yourselves with the same understanding,
1c because whoever suffered with respect to the flesh
1d has ceased from sinning,
2 so as to live out the remaining time in the flesh
no longer in accord with human cravings
but in accord with the will of God.
3a For the time that has passed [is] sufficient for
carrying out the will of the Gentiles,
3b having pursued immoderate conduct,
selfish cravings,
drunkenness,
reveling,
carousing, and
lawless idolatries.
4 In this situation they are surprised at your no longer joining them
in the same torrent of dissipation, [and] they malign;
5 they shall have to give account to him
who is ready to judge the living and the dead.
6a For to this end the good news was proclaimed also to the dead,

6b so that though they were judged in the flesh
according to human standards
6c they might live in the spirit
according to God's standard.

INTRODUCTION

Having established the divine vindication of the suffering Christ, our author returns once more to Christ's having suffered (3:18a) and died in the flesh (v 18d) as a model for Christian suffering in the flesh and now spells out the moral and soteriological implications of this thought. The focus on the behavior of both believers (upright conduct in accord with the will of God) and nonbelievers (Gentile vices) as well as the theme of innocent suffering (v 1; cf. 3:14a, 17b, 18a) unites this unit with both 3:13–17 and 3:18–22.[421] Further links with the foregoing include: *Christos* (v 1a; cf. 3:15, 16, 18a, 21d); "flesh" (*sarx*, vv 1a, 1c, 2, 6b; cf. 18d); "sin" (*hamartia*, v 1d; cf. 3:18a); God (vv 2, 6; cf. 3:17b, 18c, 20b, 22a); "will of God" (v 2; cf. 3:17b); *poreuō* (v 3b; cf. 3:19a, 22b, but different senses); "malign" (*blasphēmountes*, v 4; cf. the synonyms *katalaleō* ["slander"], *epēreazō* ["disparage"], 3:16); "account" (*logos*, v 5a; cf. 3:15b); and the contrast *sarx-pneuma* (v 6b; cf. v 18de). At the same time, 4:1–6 is distinguished from the Christological exposition of 3:18–22 by its hortatory tone (similar to that of 3:13–17) and by both the double mention of the term *sarx* (vv 1, 6) and the double contrast "humans-God" (vv 2, 6) that frame the unit.[422]

NOTES

4:1a. The theme of innocent suffering is resumed (3:13–17, 18a), and the inferential conjunction *oun* ("Therefore") introduces a hortatory line of thought, as in 2:1; 4:7b; 5:1, 6, developing the moral implications of 3:18–22.

since Christ suffered in the flesh (*Christou . . . pathontos sarki*). Christ, who suffered innocently (cf. 3:18ab), is now presented as the model according to whom the believers are to view their own suffering, repeating the pattern of 2:18–20, 21–25. The phrase is unique in the NT, though close in language to such texts as Acts 1:3; 3:18; 17:3; Heb 13:12, as well as to previous formulations in our letter (cf. 2:21, 23; 3:18a). As in the case of 2:21 and 3:18, the several textual variants, including the substitution of "died" for "suffered," reflect the

[421] Against Cervantes Gabarrón (1991a, 79–81), who sees here the beginning of a new unit (4:1–11) that concludes 1:13–3:22.

[422] S. E. Johnson (1960, 48–51; followed by Hillyer 1992, 118), claims that 4:1–6 is structurally related to 3:18–22 through an elaborate chiastic arrangement. The parallelisms he alleges, however, are superficial and involve only a few terms rather than clearly correlated clauses and ideas. Furthermore, 3:18–22 and 4:1–6 differ in both mood (indicative vs. hortatory) and chief focus (Christ vs. believers), and each unit is bounded by a different set of inclusions (3:18/22; 4:1–2/6).

influence of familiar traditional formulation on the scribal tradition.[423] The simple *pathontos sarki* (supported by 𝔓^{72} B C Ψ 323 1739 a few other MSS, cop^{sa}?; Nic.) best explains the origin of the variants and is preferred as the likely original reading. The participle *pathontos*, morever, echoes the *epathen* of 3:18a, although now, as v 1b indicates, it is not the expiatory nature of Christ's suffering but its paradigmatic character that once again is stressed (cf. 2:21–23).

The phrase, a further genitive absolute construction (cf. 3:20, 22c), combines in one formulation the terms "suffer" and "flesh" appearing in v 18a and v 18d, respectively. As in 3:18d, the dative of *sarx* modifies its foregoing participle as a dative of respect (lit., "with respect to the flesh") and denotes the human, mortal frame in which Christ underwent suffering, the same sense *sarx* has in 4:1c, 2, and 6. This qualification thus prepares for what follows.[424] Altogether, "flesh" is used four times in vv 1–6, with its appearances in vv 1 and 6 forming part of the inclusion framing the unit.

Once again an inseparable connection is affirmed between the suffering of Christ and the suffering of his followers. In 3:18a the suffering of Christ is stressed to *support* the foregoing exhortation of the suffering believers (3:13–17). Here it serves as the *premise* for the exhortation that follows (4:1b–3).

1b. *you too arm yourselves with the same understanding* (*kai hymeis tēn autēn ennoian hoplisasthe*).

you too (*kai hymeis*). Consistent with the previous pattern of exhortation, the experience of Christ once again serves as a motivation for the behavior of the addressees (2:4/5; 2:18–20/21–25; 3:13–17/18–22; cf. 4:12–16). Here, as in 2:4–5, the sequence is Christ-believers. Both "too" (*kai*) and "same" (*autēn*) make this correlation explicit.

The verb *hoplisasthe* ("arm yourselves with") occurs only here in the NT; it is the verbal counterpart of "hoplite," an arms-bearing foot soldier in the Greek army. The expression is used here metaphorically to describe the struggle of the moral life, as is the verb *strateuō* ("war against") employed in 2:11b (see the NOTE on 2:11). Such figurative use of military language in moral contexts was common among the Greek and Roman philosophers[425] and occurs frequently in the NT as well.[426] Paul's thought in 2 Cor 10:3–5 is typical:

> For though we are subject to all human limitations (*en sarki*), we do not wage war (*strateuometha*) according to these limitations (*kata sarka*); for the

[423] See "suffered on our behalf with respect to the flesh" (ℵ^{2} A P 𝔐 syr^{h} cop^{bo}; Cyril Didymus Augustine^{pt}); "suffered on your behalf with respect to the flesh" (69 1505 2495 a few others vg^{ms} syr^{p}); "suffered in the flesh" (049$^{(c)}$ [it], vg cop^{sa}?); "died on your behalf with respect to the flesh" (ℵ*).

[424] For this Hebraic sense of *sarx*, see also 1:24; 3:21; 4:6; and in Israelite writings besides the OT, *T. Sim.* 6:2; *T. Jud.* 18:4; 19:2 ("as human, as flesh"); *T. Naph.* 1:4 ("my flesh shall die"), and *T. Gad* 7:2 ("all flesh dies"; cf. 1 Pet 1:21). On the varied senses of *sarx* in the NT, see Schweizer et al. 1971.

[425] See Plato, *Apol.* 28d.5–29a.1; Sen., *Ep.* 59.7–8; 96.5; cf. also Wis 5:17–20.

[426] See Kamlah 1964, 189–96; Pfitzner 1967, 157–86; and Krentz 1993.

> weapons of our warfare (*ta hopla tēs strateias hēmōn*) are not human and weak (*sarkika*), but have power through God to destroy strongholds, demolishing arguments and every proud obstacle to the knowledge of God, and taking captive (*aichmalōtizontes*) every thought (*pan noēma*) to obey Christ.[427]

Puig Tarrech (1980, 360–68) notes that military metaphors in 1 Peter are consonant with the military presence in Asia Minor.

the same understanding (*tēn autēn ennoian*). The noun *ennoia* appears only here and in Heb 4:12 (plural) in the NT but frequently in Proverbs and the *Testaments of the Twelve Patriarchs* with the sense of "understanding," "thinking," "reason," or "mind-set" leading to resolve.[428] Both the noun and its verb *ennoeō* ("have in mind," "think of," "conceive a plan"; cf. *T. Reu.* 4:1; *T. Iss.* 3:5, 4:5; *Diogn.* 8:9) are related to *nous* ("mind," "understanding," "way of thinking") and kindred terms in 1 Peter (*dianoia*, "mind" [1:13]; *agnoia*, "ignorance" [1:14]), terms expressing the cognitive dimension of behavior.

The adjective "same" (*autēn*), like the preceding conjunction "also," establishes some connection between this understanding with which believers are to fortify themselves and the suffering of Christ. Since v 1a, however, speaks not of an "understanding" of Christ but of his "act" of having suffered, "same understanding" must refer to the attitude of mind and commitment that the author believed prompted Christ to endure suffering. From what the author has already stated, this mind-set could have involved Christ's subordination to the divine will during his innocent suffering (1:2c; 2:21–23 [as God's servant]; 3:17–18), his resistance to wrongdoing and retaliation (2:22–23b), and his trusting commitment of his cause to God (2:23c). These features of Christ's attitude and behavior have already been held up as paradigmatic for the believers and therefore may be implied here as well. The invoking of Christ as model is typical of NT instruction, particularly on the subject of discipleship.[429]

1c. *because whoever suffered in the flesh has ceased from sinning* (*hoti ho pathōn sarki pepauetai hamartias*). Having urged the believers to espouse the same mind-set that motivated the action of the suffering Christ, the author now focuses on the action of physical suffering itself, its implication and consequence. Both the syntactical relation of this clause to its immediate context

---

[427] See also 2 Cor 6:7 (*hopla tēs diskaiosynēs*, "weapons of righteousness"); Rom 6:13 (*hopla adikias*, "weapons of wickedness"); 13:12 (*ta hopla tou phōtos*, "the weapons of light"); and further, 1 Thess 5:8; Eph 6:11–17 [Isa 59:17–18]; Phil 2:25; Col 4:10; Phlm 1, 23; 2 Tim 2:3.

[428] See Prov 2:11 ("good counsel shall guard you and holy understanding [*ennoia*] shall keep you to deliver you from wrongdoing"); also 3:21; 4:1; 5:2; 8:12; 16:22 (understanding is a fountain of life to its possessors"); 18:15; 19:7; 23:4, 19; 24:7; Wis 2:14; *T. Reu.* 4:8, 11; *T. Zeb.* 1:4; *T. Naph.* 2:5; *T. Gad* 5:5; *T. Jos.* 9:2; *T. Benj.* 2:8 [A]).

[429] See Matt 10:24–25, 38–39; 20:25–28/Mark 10:42–45/Luke 22:24–27; Mark 8:34–38; 10:38–39; Luke 9:23–27; 14:27; John 13:12–15; Rom 15:1–3, 7; 1 Cor 11:1; Phil 2:1–11.

and its meaning can be variously construed. Syntactically, its function depends upon whether its initial preposition *hoti* has the epexegetical sense of "that" or the causal sense of "because." In the former case, the clause would explain the *content* of "understanding"; in the latter case, it would provide a *reason* for the imperative "arm yourselves with the same understanding." The first alternative, favored by several scholars,[430] is suggested by the fact that *hoti* can function epexegetically in connection with terms of thought and mental perception (BAGD 588 1b) such as *ennoia* (Philo, *Praem.* 42), *ennoeō*,[431] and *noeō*.[432] On this reading, *hoti*, linked with *ennoian*, would introduce a clause indicating the substance of *tēn autēn ennoian*: "be armed with the same understanding, namely, that the one who has suffered physically has put an end to sinning." The problem with this alternative, however, is that the clause speaks not of an understanding or mental attitude but of an *action* of physical suffering and its implication—ceasing from sinning. This focus on action rather than mindset continues through vv 2–4. Content and context therefore favor the second alternative (so the majority of commentators). The second question concerning its meaning will be treated below.

whoever has suffered with respect to the flesh (*ho pathōn sarki*). The phrase is similar to the foregoing phrase in v 1a (*pathontos sarki*) but, as we shall see, is not a second reference to Christ but part of a statement of proverbial wisdom applicable to anyone who suffers innocently. Since this 3d-person sing. formulation differs from the 2d-person pl. verb "arm yourselves" (v 1b), it is often set off in translations by a set of dashes, with v 2 generally taken as indicating the purpose of "arm yourselves." In view of the fact that the author speaks consistently of *innocent* suffering throughout the letter, this must be the implication of the participle *pathōn*, which likewise means "suffered (innocently)" and not "died" (against Goppelt 1993, 282; and Martin 1992, 230). *Sarki* ("with respect to the flesh"), as in vv 1a, 6, and 3:18d, is a dative of respect,[433] and *sarx* again, as in all these instances as well as 3:21 and 4:2, denotes the physical, mortal frame in which one experiences suffering (cf. also *sarkikos* in 2:11).

has ceased from sinning (*pepauetai hamartias*). The aorist (*pathōn*) expresses a punctiliar action, and the perfect (*pepauetai*) expresses its continuing effect, the same function of the perfect verbs in v 3. The verb *pepauetai* is a middle rather than passive perfect, meaning not "has been delivered from sin" but "has ceased from sinning." It is used with the genitive of the thing ceased or separated from (cf. Exod 32:12; Philo, *Decal.* 97; Josephus, *Ant.* 7.144), here

---

[430] See Windisch and Preisker 1951, 73; Best 1971, 151; J. N. D. Kelly 1969, 166; Davids 1990, 148; T. W. Martin 1992a, 228–29.

[431] See Plato, *Theaet.* 161b; Xen., *Anab.* 6.1.29; Herodotus 1.86; Philo, *Praem.* 42.

[432] See Matt 15:17; 16:11; Mark 7:18; Acts 16:10 D; *1 Clem.* 27:3); cf. 1 Pet 1:18: "knowing that . . ." and *hoti* as "that" in 1:12, 1:16 and 2:3.

[433] Some MSS (K P 69 𝔐 zvg[mss]) read "suffered in the flesh," adding the preposition *en*; but the shorter version, has stronger manuscript support and is to be preferred.

hamartias,[434] and approximates the sense of its earlier occurrence in 3:10 ("let that one keep the tongue from [uttering] what is wrong," with the preposition "from"). In contrast to Paul (e.g., Rom 5:12–13, 20–21; 6:1, 10, 12–14; 13:14), the Petrine author views *hamartia* not as a condition or external power, but as active wrongdoing contrary to the will of God (see 2:22, 24; 3:18; 4:8; cf. 2:20). Thus, it is best rendered here with the active term "sinning."[435]

What, however, is the meaning of this enigmatic statement, especially in conjunction with the suffering of Christ as the actual means of release from sinful behavior (v 1a; cf. also 1:17–21; 2:21–25; 3:18)? Various explanations have been proposed (in addition to the commentaries, see Millauer 1976, 112–34; and Dalton 1989, 220–25). Once again the Petrine context must be considered the chief arbiter of meaning; therefore, the statement must be understood in the light of innocent suffering for doing what is right in accord with God's will (2:20, 21–24; 3:14, 16, 17; cf. 4:15–16).

At the outset it is clear that this statement cannot refer to Christ and v 1a (despite the similarity of the phrases *pathontos sarki* and *pathōn sarki*), since Christ has already been declared "righteous" (3:18) and free from sin (2:22–23) and therefore cannot be said to have "ceased from sin."[436] Moreover, if Christ had terminated the sins of others there would be no point in urging the abandonment of sinning, as is done in vv 2–4. The statement instead refers to something considered true of the human condition in general and is to be taken as connected with, and preparatory for, vv 2–3 and their stress on a proper Christian conduct differing from the sinful behavior of the Gentiles.

Although the statement does not refer to Christ, it also cannot be understood as referring to the substitutionary and atoning power of suffering and death as this was stressed in Israel's martyrological tradition. According to this tradition, the suffering and especially the death of the righteous were thought to make atonement for Israel.[437] Such atonement, however, generally involved not simply the suffering but specifically the *death* of the righteous, whereas our author speaks here and elsewhere only of suffering and never of the death of the believers. More importantly, according to 1 Peter and the Christian kerygma

---

[434] The genitive sing. *hamartias* ("sin," or better "sinning") has stronger support ($\mathfrak{P}^{72}$ א* A C P 𝔐 cop[sa] and others) than the dative pl. *hamartiais* (א[2] B Ψ a few other uncials), which is a probable assimilation to the following *epithymiais* (a concretization of "sinning"). The other variant, *apo hamartias* (049 056 0142 1881 a few others; Jerome), is a secondary strengthening of the partitive sense of the simple genitive, perhaps on the analogue of 3:10c.

[435] Cf. the contrast of *hamartiai* and *dikaiosynē* ("doing what is right") in 2:24b and *hamartanontes* as the antonym of *agathopoiountos* ("doing what is right") in 2:20.

[436] Against Sieffert 1875; Strobel 1963; Schrage and Balz 1973, 107; Davids 1990, 149; and Michaels 1988, 226–27, who regards these words "almost as an afterthought."

[437] See 2 Macc 7:37–38; 4 Macc 1:11; 6:28–29; 9:23–24; 17:21–22; 1QS V 6–7; VIII 1–6; IX 4; 1QSa I 3); cf. also the statement of Caiaphas with reference to the pending death of Jesus (John 11:50, 51; 18:14). For later rabbinic teaching, see Montefiore and Loewe 1963, 223–29; and Büchler 1967, 119–211, 337–74; and for further discussion, Lohse 1963, 66–110.

in general, it is the substitutionary suffering and death of Christ that alone has atoning power (1:18–19; 2:21–24; 3:18). Having just referred to Christ's suffering (v 1a), the author could hardly be implying in the same breath that human suffering also has atoning power.

It is also unlikely that this thought has any relation to Rom 6:7, which on the surface appears similar ("one who has died is freed from sin"). This formulation, occurring within the context of Rom 6:1–11, speaks not of suffering but of "dying" (*apothanōn*) as the action that liberates (*dedikaiōtai*, lit., "acquits") from sin, and it is dying, not suffering, on which Paul focuses throughout this passage (6:2, 3, 4, 5, 6, 7, 8, 9, 10, 11). Moreover, this dying that Paul emphasizes is a *metaphorical dying with Christ* in baptism (6:3–5). Our Petrine verse, on the other hand, speaks of *actual physical suffering* and makes no reference to baptism. In addition, *hamartia* ("sin," "sinning"), as elsewhere in 1 Peter (2:22, 24; 3:18; 4:8), denotes a concrete act of disobedience rather than, as in Paul, an independent power over humans, from which baptismal incorporation into Christ's death sets the believer free (Rom 6:1–14; cf. also 5:12–13, 20–21; 6:15–23; 7:13). The Petrine clause speaks not of being liberated from sin's control but of ceasing sinful behavior.[438]

Some scholars[439] see here a reference to the purifying effect of suffering: innocent suffering in the flesh purifies the flesh from sin. But the texts cited to illustrate this thought (*1 En.* 67:9; *2 Bar.* 13:10; 78:6) are irrelevant, since they speak of suffering that is *deserved* rather than undeserved.[440] The Hebrew text of Prov 20:30 (not included in the LXX) could also be mentioned ("Blows that wound clean away evil; strokes make clean the innermost parts"). It is more likely, however, that this thought is related to a broader concept reflected here: the idea that suffering has a disciplining function and assists in the control of the flesh, which is prone to sinning.

The disciplining function of suffering is a prominent idea in Israelite conventional wisdom, particularly in the area of parental child-rearing.[441] The book of Proverbs is replete with such injunctions as "Do not withhold discipline from a child; if you beat him with a rod, he will not die. If you beat him with the rod, you will save his life from Sheol" (Prov 23:13–14; cf. also 13:24; 19:18; 29:15, 17). Similarly Sirach advises: "He who loves his son will whip him often, in order that he may rejoice at the way he turns out" (Sir 30:1; cf. also 22:33–4;

[438] See also Best (1971, 151–52) and Millauer (1976, 122–30) for further discussion of the differences. For other unconvincing attempts to interpret this Petrine verse in the light of Pauline theology (e.g., Reicke 1964, 117 [suffering as "mortification of sinful flesh"]; J. N. D. Kelly 1969, 168–69; Beare 1970, 179; also Bigg; Knopf; Windisch), see the comments of Goppelt (1993, 280–81).

[439] E.g., Selwyn 1947, 209; Best 1971, 151; Millauer 1976, 114–30; Vogels 1976, 142–59.

[440] Millauer (1976, 114–19, 122, 129–30) points to two Qumran texts (1QS IV 20–21; X 9–11, 22), only the first of which explicitly refers to a divine purification of the flesh; cf. also, however, 1QS VIII 3–4. But these passages refer to purification "through the holy spirit" (1QS IV 20–21) or to substitutionary suffering (1QS VIII 3–4), neither of which is implied here.

[441] See Pilch 1993; and for the Greco-Roman world as well, Plutarch, *Lib. ed.* 12.16 (*Mor.* 12 A–D).

30:13) and notes that "chastising and discipline (*paideia*) are wisdom at all times" (Sir 22:6). Behind what appears to us modern readers as nothing short of unpardonable parental abuse lies the ancient notion that "a son unrestrained turns out to be willful" (Sir 30:8) and will bring shame to his parents and family (Sir 22:3; 30:13; 42:11; cf. 1 Tim 3:4). For this reason children (*paides*) require discipline (*paideia*), since learning (*mathēma*) comes from suffering (*pathēma*).[442] Or as the modern maxim has it, "no pain, no gain." Israel applied this notion to the divine parent's disciplining of his children as well: "My son, do not despise the Lord's discipline (*paideias*) or be weary of his reproof, for whom the Lord loves he reproves and scourges every son whom he receives" (Prov 3:11–12).[443] This proverb is explicitly quoted by the author of Hebrews (12:5–6) in order to give a positive interpretation to the suffering the Christian readers are enduring: "It is for discipline (*paideian*) that you have to endure. God is treating you as sons; for what son is there whom his father does not discipline (*paideuei*)? . . . They [our earthly fathers] disciplined (*epaideuon*) us for a short time at their pleasure, but he [God] disciplines us for our good, that we may share his holiness. For the moment, all discipline (*paideia*) seems painful rather than pleasant; later it yields the peaceful fruit of uprightness to those who have been trained by it" (12:7–11). According to Hebrews, even the innocent Christ, as God's son, "learned obedience through what he suffered" (5:8). That Christ did not sin, as both Hebrews (9:14) and 1 Peter (2:22–23; 3:18b) affirm, in no way vitiates the significance of this concept as a general pedagogical principle relevant for the believers. Paul, too, may reflect this notion of the disciplining effect of suffering when he states: "we rejoice in our sufferings, knowing that suffering produces endurance, and endurance produces character, and character produces hope" (Rom 5:3–4).

Our verse makes eminent sense in the light of this concept of the disciplining effect of suffering (so also Frankemölle 1987, 61). The statement is neither a piece of baptismal theology nor an echo of Israel's martyr theology. The author is not claiming that the suffering of a righteous person atones for sin (either one's own or others') or that it purifies from sin, but rather that suffering, especially innocent suffering, disciplines the physical body (*sarx*) by which sinning is carried out and and thereby trains one to cease from sinning. As Christ's vicarious suffering has liberated believers from the proclivity to sin (1:18–19; 2:21b, 24; 3:18; 4:1a) so that they might live uprightly (1:17; 2:18–20, 24c; 3:13–17), so now they are reminded that their own innocent suffering sustains this break with sinning and wrongdoing. On the whole, this statement, in conjunction with v 2, recalls and builds on the thought of 2:24: "He himself bore our

---

[442] See Herodotus 1.207 (Croesus to Cyrus: "my sufferings [*pathēmata*] are disagreeable, [but] they have been instruction [*mathēmata*] for me").

[443] See also *Pss. Sol.* 10:1–2, which specifically mentions the constraint of suffering on sinning ("How honorable is the one whom the Lord remembers with reproving and protects from the way of evil with a whip"); cf. further, Prov 20:30; Wis 11:9–10.

wrongdoings in his body on the tree, so that we, having abandoned wrongdoing, might live for doing what is right." This adapted piece of conventional wisdom in v 1c thus explains the reason that the believers should "arm themselves with the same understanding" that guided Christ in his suffering and prepares as well for the moral instruction that follows in vv 2–4.

2. This verse now states the intended consequence ("so as to live") of the foregoing imperative in v 1b. The entire statement is a complex formulation in the original Greek. Verse 2a of the English translation renders those words that in the Greek begin (*eis to mēketi*) and end (*ton epiloipon . . . chronon*) this verse and that express its main thought. These words embrace the intervening and qualifying contrast, "no longer in accord with human cravings but in accord with the will of God."

2a. *so as to live out the remaining time in the flesh* (*eis to . . . ton epiloipon en sarki biōsai chronon*). The implied subject of the verb "live out" is either the "whoever" in v 1c (so Bigg 1902, 167), with v 2 extending the thought of v 1c or, more likely, the "you" in v 1b (so J. N. D. Kelly 1969, 169; Goppelt 1993, 275). The latter is more likely because the content of this verse echoes earlier exhortation to the addressees and is joined by an explanation (vv 3–4) concerning their relation to the Gentile nonbelievers (vv 3–4). For this reason some commentators[444] regard the 3d-person sing. statement in v 1c, which intervenes between the 2d-person pl. statements in v 1b and 2, as a parenthetical comment (similar to 3:20d and 3:21bc) and set it off with dashes. Verse 2 then states the purpose for which the readers are to arm themselves (v 1b), while also making specific for the readers what was implied by the gnomic statement in v 1c, especially by "ceased from sinning."

so as to live out (*eis . . . to biōsai*). The preposition *eis* with the articular infinitive (*to . . . biōsai*) expresses a purpose or intended result (BDF §402; cf. 1 Pet 3:7 and elsewhere in the NT).[445] The verb *bioō* (only here in the NT), in combination with "remaining time" has the sense of not simply "live" but *live out*; for the combination of *bioō* and *chronon*, see also Job 29:18. The verb (cf. Wis 12:23), like its noun *bios*,[446] denotes the pursuit of the daily round.

the remaining time in the flesh (*ton epiloipon en sarki . . . chronon*). This phrase refers to the period of time (*ton . . . chronon*) "remaining" (*epiloipon*, only here in the NT) for the believers' mortal existence (*en sarki*) until the imminent end (4:7,17; cf. 1:20b). It recalls the similar formulation in 1:17: "conduct yourselves with reverence throughout the time (*ton chronon*) of your residence as aliens." The distinction made in that context between the believers' life before (1:14b, 18a) and after (1:14a, 15–17a, 18–21) their conversion is

[444] E.g., Windisch and Preisker 1951, 72; Michaels 1988, 223; Goppelt 1993, 275.

[445] See Matt 20:19; 26:2; 27:31; Mark 14:55; Luke 5:17; Acts 7:19; Rom 1:11, 20; 4:18; Jas 1:18; 3:3.

[446] See Mark 12:44; Luke 8:14, 43; 15:12, 30; 1 Tim 3:2; 1 John 2:16; etc.

implied here as well. "Remaining time" is contrasted with the "time that has passed" (v 3).

2b. *no longer in accord with human cravings but in accord with the will of God* (*mēketi anthrōpōn epithymiais alla thelēmati theou*). Since suffering with respect to the flesh gives one control over one's flesh and hence over the urge to sin, the suffering believers can now choose "to live out their remaining time in the flesh" no longer (*mēketi*) in accord with human cravings (a graphic depiction of what "sinning" involves) but in accord with the will of God (the opposite of "sinning"). The contrasting phrases "human cravings" (*anthrōpōn epithymiais*) and "will of God" (*thelēmati theou*) describe the opposing standards that govern the believers' lives before and after conversion, as well as the norms between which they must continue to choose.

Thus, "no longer in accord with human cravings" (*mēketi anthrōpōn epithymiais*) recalls the earlier expressions "the cravings of your former ignorance" (1:14b) and "the futile conduct inherited from your ancestors" (1:18a), descriptions of the believers' preconversion life-style (cf. also 2:11). Similarly, "but in accord with the will of God" (*alla thelēmati theou*) recalls the expression "but in conformity with the Holy One who called you" (1:15a), which describes the new standard of Christian behavior following conversion. In addition to these correspondences between 4:1–6 and 1:13–25, others are also evident.[447] The thought here thus echoes the thought in 1:14–19 and reemphasizes the theme of transformation. Earlier the believers' renunciation of the cravings that dominated their former life (1:14a, 18b) was motivated by the fact of their calling by God (1:15–16) and their redemption by the blood of Christ (1:18–19). Here our author adds that their suffering in the flesh strengthens their resolve to cease from sinning and consequently to have done once and for all with the cravings of the past. They are to live exclusively in accord with the will of God who called them to holiness (1:14–16; 2:4–10). This succinct formulation thus reprises key points made earlier in the letter, while also clarifying the effect of having "ceased from sin" as a result of "suffering in the flesh" (v 1c).

The noun *epithymiai* occurs twice in this context, here in v 2 as the author's generalizing description of human life alienated from God, and in the traditional catalogue of vices that follows (v 3), as one of several sins typical of a dissolute way of life (on *epithymia* see also the NOTES on 1:14 and 2:11). Implied in the generic term *anthrōpōn* (lit., "of humans") are the "Gentiles" in v 3 (cf. 2:12). As the antithesis to "human cravings," "the will of God" once again is underscored as the central criterion of Christian conduct (cf. 2:15; 3:17; 4:19). A similar contrast between humans and God is made in 2:4, where the word "humans" comprises all nonbelievers (cf. 2:7b–8).

---

[447] See *dianoia* (1:13) and *ennoia* (4:1); *mē-alla* and *epithymiai-theos* (1:14; 4:2); present time (*chronos*, 1:17; 4:2); past time (1:18; 4:3); God judges (1:17; 4:5); and good news (1:25; 4:6).

3a. *For the time that has passed* [*is*] *sufficient* (*arketos gar ho parelēlythōs chronos*). An explanation ("for," *gar*) supports the foregoing injunction (v 1b–2) and *chronos* (vv 2, 3), *ethnōn* (v 3 = *anthrōpōn*, v 2), and *epithymiais* (vv 2, 3) serve as link-words.[448]

the time that has passed (*ho parelēlythōs chronos*). The "time" (*chronos*) remaining to the believers (v 2) is now contrasted with an earlier period of time (*chronos*) prior to their conversion, when they lived in accord with "human cravings" (v 2b; cf. also 1:14), now elaborated on and described as conduct typical of Gentiles.

The perfect tense of the participle *parelēlythōs*, modifying "time," like the accompanying perfect verbs *kateirgasthai* and *peporeumenous*, underlines the sense that this earlier phase of their life is over. As persons called and sanctified by God (1:2, 14–16; 2:4–10) and redeemed by the blood of Christ from a futile and hopeless existence (1:2, 18–19), their past is now a closed chapter of their life.

[*is*] *sufficient* (*arketos*). In this context, *arketos* ("sufficient") is used ironically with the implication of "more than enough";[449] for *arketos* with this sense, see also Matt 6:34. The elliptical formulation implies the verb "is." On the construction of the sentence, see also BDF §405.2.

for carrying out the will of the Gentiles (*to boulēma tōn ethnōn kateirgasthai*). The verb *kateirgasthai* is a perf. middle infin. of *katergazomai* ("carry out," "produce, accomplish, achieve").[450] The perfect tense of *kateirgasthai* matches the perfects of *peporeumenous*[451] and *parelēlythōs* ("has passed"). This initial thought, like the following expression "no longer joining them" (v 4), has in view the present nonconformity of Christians with Gentile modes of behavior (cf. 1:14 and 2:11).

The phrase *boulēma tōn ethnōn* (unique in the NT) contrasts with the foregoing *thelēmati theou* ("will of God"), so that *boulēma* (lit., "intention," "purpose"; cf. Acts 27:43; Rom 9:19) in this context is tantamount to "will," as in Rom 9:19.[452] Some manuscripts (P 𝔐) in fact read *thelēma* ("will") in place of *boulēma*, though the latter has far superior manuscript support. As the present time for the believers is marked by conduct in accord with the will of God, the preconversion phase of their life was spent carrying out the will and expectations of Gentiles. "The will of the Gentiles," as Goppelt (1993, 284) aptly

[448] The secondary addition, "of life" (*tou biou*), following "time" (P 049 𝔐), most likely was prompted by the foregoing verb *biōsai* and was intended to explicate further the relation of vv 2 and 3.

[449] Some MSS add "to you" (*hymin*) or "to us" (*hēmin*) following "sufficient," but the shorter reading has stronger MS support (𝔓[72] ℵ[c] A B Ψ latt syr cop[sa]) and is preferred.

[450] Cf. Rom 1:27 ("committing shameless acts"); Rom 2:9 ("producing what is wrong").

[451] Preferred to the variant present tense verb *poreumenous*.

[452] For *boulēma* meaning "will" (of God), see *1 Clement* (8:5; 19:3; 23:5; etc.); for the similar meaning of the kindred *boulē*, see Luke 23:51; Acts 5:38–39 (contrast between *boule* of humans and of God); Acts 13:36; 20:27.

notes, "manifests itself especially in those forms of social and religious custom that become requirements through the power of habit and the pressure for conformity."[453]

It is clear from the equation of *ethnōn* and *anthrōpōn* (vv 2–3) and the contrast of *anthrōpōn* ("humans") and *theou* ("God") in v 2 that "Gentiles" denotes all who are opposed to the will of God as taught and carried out by Jesus Christ—that is, all non-Christians, including not only pagans but Israelites as well. This is its sense also in 2:12, where it was noted that the function that the word "Gentiles" had for Greek-speaking Israelites (namely, to designate all non-Israelites) was appropriated by followers of Jesus to designate all those outside the Christian brotherhood and thus served as a synonym for the "disobedient" (2:7; 3:2).[454]

The types of conduct enumerated in what follows are vices commonly associated by Israelites and Christians with the dissolute behavior of all outsider "Gentiles," especially "lawless idolatries." These vices are often regarded by commentators as evidence of the former non-Israelite background of most of the addressees, especially in connection with the earlier reference to their "former ignorance" (1:14) and the "futile conduct inherited from your ancestors" (1:18a). But this conclusion is made uncertain by the fact that Israelites themselves in contravention of the Torah engaged in idolatry on more than one occasion, as well as in the other vices mentioned. Moreover, as Kamlah (1964, 180) notes, v 3 does not say "you were Gentiles" but "you carried out the will of the Gentiles." Given this ambiguous state of the evidence, it is best to take "Gentiles," which corresponds with "humans" in v 2, as a reference not simply to Greeks and Romans but to all non-Christians, as in 2:12. The remainder of this verse describes at length the characteristics of this Gentile—that is, non-Christian and God-opposed—style of life. This second use of *ethnē*, along with the reference to *epithymiai* and the military metaphor in v 1, links this verse closely with 2:11–12, where all three words appear.

3b. *having pursued* (*peporeumenous en*), literally, "having walked in (the way of)." The perf. middle pl. part. of the verb *poreuō* has "you" (v 1b and implied in v 2) as its antecedent subject and commences an enumeration of various vices in which the believers were engaged in their preconversion stage of life. In 3:19a and 3:22b, *poreuō* was used to denote Christ's going into heaven, in the course of which he went to the angelic spirits in prison. Here, on the other hand, it is used in the Hebraic sense of a moral "going," proceeding along a certain behavioral path, conducting one's life in a moral or immoral manner.

---

[453] For similar exhortation, see Eph 4:17–5:14 ("you must no longer live as the Gentiles do" [4:17], followed by a description of their ignorance and licentiousness, 4:18–19; cf. 5:3–14) and 1 Thess 4:4–7 (living in accord with God's will versus being motivated by "the passion of lust like Gentiles who do not know God").

[454] For the Gentiles as a negative reference group, see also Matt 6:32; Matt 20:25–28/Mark 10:42–45/Luke 22:24–27; Mark 12:29–31; Rom 9:30; 1 Cor 10:20; 1 Thess 4:11.

In conjunction with the preceding terms *boulēma* and *thelēma*, it recalls the formulation of Ps 1:1: "Blessed is the man who has not walked (*poreuthē*) in the counsel (*boulēi*) of the ungodly . . . but his will (*thelēma*) is in the law of the Lord."[455] It is likewise linked with *epithymiai* in Jude 16, 18; and 2 Pet 2:10; 3:3. Its perfect tense (preferred over the weakly attested present participle), matches the perfect tenses of the foregoing verbs *parelēlythōs* and *kateirgasthai* in describing conduct that is, or should be, past history.

The six modes of immorality enumerated here (cf. also the earlier list of vices proscribed in 2:1) are vices typically associated in the thinking of Israel and members of the messianic movement with the conduct of outsider "Gentiles." Lists of these vices[456] were adopted and adapted by the NT writers for hortatory and instructional purposes.[457] In the NT, as elsewhere, vice lists such as these were often balanced with lists of virtues in order to illustrate acceptable and unacceptable modes of Christian conduct.[458] Most of the six vices here, all plurals in Greek, involve acts of excess that in actuality were abhorred by Greek and Roman moralists as well. The Epistle of Titus similarly cites a standard list of vices to describe the former, pre-Christian conduct of its readers ("We ourselves were once . . . ," Titus 3:3).

immoderate conduct (*aselgeiais*). The noun *aselgeia* denotes libertine behavior lacking moral restraint such as wanton violence or insolence, dissoluteness, debauchery, licentiousness,[459] including transgression of sexual norms (Philo, *Mos.* 1.305; Rom 13:13). It appears in several NT lists condemning a variety of related vices, including idolatry, immorality, impurity, fornication, and the like[460] and was combined with *epithymiai* already in Polybius (36.15.4 [*aselgeia peri tas sōmatikas epithymias*]; cf. also Herm. *Vis.* 3.7.2). *Testament of Judah* 23:1–2 warns that even Israelites will engage in this vice, along with witchcraft, idolatry, making their daughters into musicians and common women, and becoming "involved in revolting Gentile affairs."

selfish cravings (*epithymiais*). The noun *epithymia* (see also 1:14; 2:11; 4:2; and their respective NOTES) denotes physical appetites and cravings (Plato, *Crat.* 419D) focused on self-indulgence, including but not restricted to sexual

[455] For this Hebraic sense of *poreuō*, see also Lev 18:3; Ps 25[26]:1, 11; 80[81]:13; Prov 10:9; Luke 1:6; 10:37; Acts 9:31; and of immoral conduct, Acts 14:16 (of Gentiles); 2 Pet 2:10; 3:3; and Jude 11, 16, 18.

[456] See Wis 14:25–27; Sir 7:1–21; *1 En.* 8:1–4; *2 En.* 10:4–6; 34:1–2; *2 Bar.* 73:4; 1QS IV 9–11; X 21–23; *T. Reu.* 3:3–6; *T. Dan* 1:6; *T. Sim.* 3:1; *T. Dan* 2:4; *T. Jud.* 16:1; Philo, *Sacr.* 32; Josephus, *Ag. Ap.* 2.19–28; *T. Mos.* 7:3–10.

[457] See Matt 15:19/Mark 7:21–22; Rom 1:29–31; 13:13; 1 Cor 5:10–11; 6:9–10; 2 Cor 12:20–21; Gal 5:19–21; Eph 4:25–31; 5:3–13; Col 3:5–9; 1 Tim 1:9–10; 6:4–5; 2 Tim 3:2–5; Titus 3:3, 9; Rev 21:8; 22:15; cf. also *Did.* 2–5; 5:1–2; Herm. *Mand.* 8.3; *Sim.* 6.5.5; 9.15.3; Pol. *Phil* 4:3; 5:2, 3; 6:1.

[458] On catalogues or stock lists of vices and virtues and their employment by Greek and Roman moralists as well as Israelite and early Christian authors, see Vögtle 1936; Wibbing 1959; and Kamlah 1964.

[459] See Polybius 1.6.5; 5.28.9; Wis 14:26; 3 Macc 2:26; Josephus, *Ant.* 4.151; 8.252; 20.112.

[460] See Mark 7:22; Rom 13:13; 2 Cor 12:20–21; Gal 5:19; Eph 4:19; cf. also 2 Pet 2:2, 7, 18; and Jude 4.

desire.[461] In v 2 the expression "human selfish cravings" denoted the generic type of self-indulgence in which the believers should no longer be engaged. Its place in coventional lists of vices such as v 3 may account for its repetition here, where it also serves as a link-word joining v 3 to v 2. It also represents an orientation diametrically opposed to the well-being and cohesion of the community as a whole, a point of vital concern throughout this letter.

drunkenness (*oinophlygiais*). This and the following two terms concern vices of immoderation connected with dining and drinking. The rare term *oinophlygia* occurs only here in the NT[462] and its verb *oinophlygeō*, only in Deut 21:20 (of a son who disobeys and shames his parents by reveling and getting drunk). It is a composite of *oinos* ("wine") and *phlygia* (from *phylyō*, "boil over," "overflow") and, akin to the adjective *oinophlyx* ("given to drinking," "drunken"), denotes excessive indulgence in wine: "winebibbing," "boozing."[463] Concern about the dangers of wine and intemperate imbibing was typical of Israelites [464] as well as early Christians.[465] Clement of Alexandria, commenting on drinking (*Paed*. 2.2), paints a lurid picture of pagan winebibbing and revelry:

> But the miserable wretches who expel temperance from conviviality, think excess in drinking to be the happiest life; and their life is nothing but revel, debauchery, baths, excess, urinals, idleness, drink. You may see some of them, half-drunk, staggering, with crowns around their necks like wine jars, vomiting drink on one another in the name of good fellowship; and others, full of the effects of their debauch, dirty, pale in the face, livid, and still above yesterday's bout pouring yet another bout to last till next morning. It is well, my friends, it is well to make our acquaintance with this picture at the greatest possible distance from it, and to frame ourselves to what is better, dreading lest we also become a like spectacle and laughing stock to others.

Excessive drinking, furthermore, leads to stupefaction, the opposite of the alertness or sobriety for which the Petrine author calls in 1:13; 4:7; and 5:8.

reveling (*kōmois*). The noun *kōmos* originally denoted a festal procession in honor of Dionysus, the god of wine, and then a meal or banquet. In the LXX it is used of the "revelings of strange rites" (*thesmōn kōmous*) by the godless

---

[461] The term occurs frequently in the moral instruction of the *Testaments of the Twelve Patriarchs* (*T. Reu*. 1:10; 2:4; 4:9; 5:6; 6:4; *T. Jud*. 13:2; 14:1, 3; 16:1; *T. Ash*. 3:2; 6:5; *T. Jos*. 3:10; 4:7; 7:6, 8; 9:1), in the catalogue of 4 Macc 1:22–23, and that of Epict., *Diatr*. 2.16.45; 2.18.8.

[462] Cf. Xen., *Oec*. 1.22; Polybius 2.19.4; Philo, *Mos*. 2.185; *Spec*. 4.91.

[463] For the related *oinoposia*, see *T. Jud*. 14:7.

[464] See Prov 23:29–35; Sir 31:25–31; Tob 4:15; *T. Reu*. 1:10; *T. Levi* 8:5; 9:14; *T. Jud*. 9:8; 11:2; 12:3; 13:6; 14:1, 2, 3, 6, 7; 15:4; 16:1, 2, 3, 4; *T. Iss*. 7:3; *T. Jos*. 3:5; cf. also Philo's treatise *On Drunkenness*.

[465] For other NT warnings against drunkenness, designated by the more common synonym *methē* and related terms, see Luke 21:34; Rom 13:13; 1 Cor 5:11; 6:10; Gal 5:21; Eph 5:18; cf. 1 Thess 5:7. See also 1 Tim 3:2, 8, 11; Titus 2:3. On intoxication in the view of Greeks and Romans, see the texts cited by Adinolfi (1988, 138–40).

(Wis 14:23) or of the Seleucid "revelings" that were included among the desecrations of the Jerusalem Temple in the time of the Maccabees (2 Macc 6:4; see the reference to the "feast of Dionysus" in 6:7). The *reveling* of which the Petrine author speaks thus may well imply "drunken orgies" and carousing associated with the notorious Dionysian feasts.[466] The term also appears in the NT vice lists in Rom 13:13 and Gal 5:21, in each case combined with *methai* ("drunkenness"); see also its use in Eph 5:18 in connection with drunkenness and *asōtia* ("dissipation," used later in this Petrine verse as well).

carousing (*potois*). The noun *potos* (lit., "drinking," "drinking parties") occurs only here in the NT[467] but belongs to the same semantic field as the two preceding vices and elsewhere is also linked with *kōmos*.[468] All three Petrine terms pertain to the dissolute carousing typical of the Gentile occasions of feasting and drinking, from which Christians are to distance themselves.

and lawless idolatries (*kai athemitois eidōlolatriais*). This concluding phrase, an apparently Christian formulation found only here and in subsequent Christian writings, reveals the Christian perspective according to which this enumeration of vices is presented. By the word "idolatries" (*eidōlolatriais*), the author could have in mind the libations made to Dionysus/Bacchus, the god of wine, in the context of meals and drinking bouts (cf. 1 Cor 8:4–13 and 10:14–22 for idolatry in conjunction with meals). For Christians, as for the House of Israel, idolatry was the chief mark of the outsider alienated from God (1 Cor 5:11–12; 1 Thess 1:9–10) and for Paul (Rom 1:18–32), as for the author of the Wisdom of Solomon (14:27), the source of all other vices.[469] In its present final and emphatic position here in v 3, "idolatries" serves to summarize in one condemning expression the futility and fatuity of life lived in opposition to God. The modifier *athemitois* ("lawless," "abominable," "grossly wicked"),[470] Beare (1970, 180) notes, "means not so much 'illegal' as 'unholy'—violating the divine ordering of life (contrary not to *nomos* [law], but to the more fundamental *themis*)." In Peter's remark to the Gentile Cornelius in Acts, it seems to imply both: "You yourselves know how unlawful/unholy it is for a Judean to associate with or to visit anyone of another people" (Acts 10:28; cf. also 2 Macc 6:5–6; 7:1; 10:34).

---

[466] The fondness for reveling at *symposia* ("banquets") was recorded on the famous red-figured Greek vases as well as on drinking cups for wine and water. Philo offers a particularly vivid and critical portrayal of conventional Greek and Roman banquets, with their drinking orgies, gluttonous excesses, and sexual frenzies, to which he contrasts the circumspect festal meetings of the contemplative Israelite Therapeutae of Egypt (*Cont.* 40–89); cf. also *T. Jud.* 8:2.

[467] Cf. Gen 19:3; *Let. Aris.* 262; Philo, *Contempl.* 46; Josephus, *Ant.* 5. 289; *T. Jud.* 8:2.

[468] See Diog. Laert. 10.132; Plut., *Lib. ed.* 16; *Mor.* 12B. Kindred terms include *symposia* ("drinking party"), *symposiastai* ("fellow-drinkers"), *oinoposion* ("drinking of wine").

[469] On *eidōlolatria*, see also *T. Jud.* 19:1; 23:1; *T. Benj.* 10:10; and on *eidōlon* ("idol"), see *T. Reu.* 4:6; *T. Jud.* 19:1; *T. Zeb.* 9:6; *T. Jos.* 4:5; 6:5.

[470] See also Acts 10:28; *1 Clem.* 63:2; *Did.* 16:4; and Josephus, *J.W.* 4.562 (with *aselgeia*).

Some of these idolatrous drinking parties could have taken place during meetings of the well-known associations, clubs, and guilds (*eranoi, koina, collegia*) that were a common feature of Greco-Roman society from the fourth century BCE onward. These clubs, both public (sanctioned by the state) and private, were voluntary associations that provided occasions for socializing, occupational and business linkages, conviviality, religious devotion, and group pursuit of common interests and mutual aid, including the burial of the dead. They thus provided an important means of social networking. It is conceivable that the Petrine author presumed that some of the addressees had been members of associations such as these, where banquets, wine bouts, and the like were a matter of course (so Reicke 1964, 117–19).[471] As part of his evidence, Reicke cites the report of Philo (*Flacc.* 136), who reflects Israelite sensibilities and views: "In the city there are clubs with a large membership. Their fellowship is founded on no sound principles, but on strong liquor, drunkenness, sotted carousing and on their progeny, wantonness—'synods' and 'divans' they call them" (cf. also *Ebr.* 20–26, 29, 95; *Spec.* 2.44). However, clubs and corporations generally were concerned with the "due observance of the established customs"[472] and were vigilantly regulated by the state (see Pliny, *Ep.* 10.33–34, 92–93). Thus, while it is possible that the addressees may have been involved in such associations, this cannot be stated with certainty, as Danker (1992, 502) stresses. In any case, the Petrine list of vices specifies from an Israelite and Christian point of view modes of behavior considered typical of persons alienated from God and therefore thoroughly inappropriate for the reborn people of God.

4a. *In this situation* (*en hōi*). The phrase *en hōi* again functions adverbially and, as in 1:6 and 3:19, refers to a circumstance described by the foregoing, in this case to the fact that the believers are no longer behaving like the Gentiles (vv 2–3).

they are surprised at your no longer joining them in the same torrent of dissipation (*xenizontai mē syntrechontōn hymōn eis tēn autēn tēs asōtias anachysin*). Ceasing conformity to Gentile behavior (vv 2–3) also involves dissociating from them, for bad company breeds bad morals. This termination of both Gentile-like conduct and Gentile contacts, in turn, evokes the surprise of the believers' erstwhile cronies.

they are surprised (*xenizontai*). The "Gentiles" in v 3 are the implied subject of this 3d-person pl. verb. In the active voice, *xenizō* means to "entertain a stranger [*xenos*]" as a guest. But in the passive voice, as here, it means "to be surprised," "astonished," or shocked at something because of its unusual or unexpected nature, with the possible overtone of anger and resentment. The verb is used again in 4:12 in connection with the believers, who are told not to be

---

[471] Elsewhere, Reicke (1951, 320–38, 347–52) tends to exaggerate their violent and "anarchic" nature.

[472] As attested by an association of Ephesian devotees of Demeter; cf. Danker 1982, 288.

surprised or upset at the fiery ordeal coming upon them. The verb's present tense, like that of the accompanying participle, "malign," and the expression "you no longer join them," conveys the sense of an ongoing situation.

at your no longer joining them (*mē syntrechontōn hymōn*). This genitive absolute construction (cf. also 4:1a; 3:20c, and 21c) describes what prompts the resentful astonishment and indicates an important stimulus for the invective directed against the addressees. The verb *syntrechō*, literally, "run with," involves the verb *trechō*, which is used elsewhere in the NT of the moral effort of believers (Heb 12:1; 1 Cor 9:24; cf. also Gal 2:2; 5:7; Phil 2:16). The composite verb used here (*syn-trechō*) can denote people converging from all sides (Mark 6:33 and Acts 3:11). Here, however, the participle conveys the idea of joining and associating with others in their immoral activity (cf. Ps 49[50]:18; *Barn.* 4:2). The translation "no longer joining" expresses the continuing dissociation implied in the present tense of the Greek participle *syntrechhontōn* and its negative adverb, *mē* ("not"). Conversion has required a break from Gentiles and the unholy behavior entailed in such associations. This is a point already made earlier in this letter (1:14–16; cf. also 2:11–12) and frequently within the NT.[473]

in the same torrent of dissipation (*eis tēn autēn tēs asōtias anachysin*). This is the author's summarizing description of the vices listed in v 3. The vices were those conventionally condemned by Israel and the messianic movement. Their description here, on the other hand, involves an expression unique to 1 Peter. The negative image is a graphic one that underscores the wild excesses involved in these practices. Again *eis* ("in") substitutes for the more classical *en* (cf. 3:21d; 5:12f).

The noun *anachysis*, another unique NT term, denotes a "pouring forth" or "outpouring." It is used of rock pools filled up by the sea at high tide (Strabo, *Geogr.* 3.1.9; cf. 2.5.24) or of a swamp formed by the pouring forth of waters (Beare 1970, 181). Here, as a figurative description of immoral behavior, it has a more active sense: "torrent," "flood," or "wild outpouring (of dissipation)" (cf. Philo, *Aet.* 102; *Somn.* 2.278).

The noun *asōtia* ("dissipation," "profligacy," "debauchery")[474] can denote that which is ruinous to health (*sōtēria*; cf. the related adverb *asōtōs*, used in Luke 15:14 of the prodigal son's "riotous living"). In Eph 5:18 it refers to drunkenness in particular, but here it covers all of the foregoing vices as manifestations of frenzied and reckless living. These final words also involve

---

[473] See 2 Cor 6:14–18 ("Do not be mismated with nonbelievers . . . come out from them and be separate from them," 6:14, 17); Eph 5:7 ("do not associate with them," in connection with a warning against vices typical of the "sons of disobedience," 5:3–13); 2 Tim 3:5b ("Avoid such people," in connection with a list of sinners, 3:2–5a); cf. also Titus 3:10 and a similar disengagement urged by Philo, *Ebr.* 29. See also the social dissociation implied in 1 Cor 6:11–12; and Rev 22:14–15; cf. Rev 21:8; and 22:10–11.

[474] See Arist. *Eth. Nic.* 4.1.3; Prov 28:7; 2 Macc 6:4; *T. Jud.* 16:1; Eph 5:18; Titus 1:6.

another of the letter's several refined rhetorical alliterations (*autēn, asōtias anachysin*; cf. 1:4, 6, 19; 2:12, 15, 16, 18–20, 21; 3:17).

[*and*] *they malign* (*blasphēmountes*). As a result of the believers' no longer joining them in their wild and reckless living, their erstwhile cronies are surprised and estranged and respond with maligning. Cessation of engagement with nonbelievers provokes censure and hostile response on the part of the abandoned.

The connection of this plural participle to its context is not immediately clear. In place of a participle, some manuscripts (א* C* 81 323 and others) have a finite verb and a copulative ("and they malign" [*kai blasphēmousin*]). This reading links the verb more clearly with what precedes it and thus appears to be a secondary attempt at improvement. However, it does accurately represent the implication of the participle, which should be retained as the more difficult and therefore preferred reading (𝔓[72] א corrected A B C K L P 044 𝔐 latt syr cop). Beare (1970, 178, 181) treats the participle as a substantive used as an interjection and sets it off with dashes ("—blasphemers that they are—"). Michaels (1988, 224) also regards it as a substantive but takes it with what follows: "Blasphemers, they will have to answer. . . ." Such a substantival function of a participle however, would be singular in 1 Peter; its customary verbal sense as a modifier of something preceding it, in this case "they are surprised," is more likely here. This is in keeping with the use of participles elsewhere in the letter.[475]

The verb *blasphēmeō*, the opposite of "to honor" or "to praise" (Philo, *Migr.* 115), means "malign," "defame," "insult," "revile," "vilify," "heap abuse" (Hillyer 1992, 124), with either God or humans or both (Josephus, *Ant.* 8.358–59) as the object. When God or the gods or angels are the stated object, the verb is generally rendered "blaspheme" (i.e., to speak profanely and disparagingly of something sacred).[476] When humans are the object, it has the sense of "malign" or "insult," as in the case of the maligning of Jesus (Mark 15:29/Matt 27:39; Luke 22:65) or Paul (Acts 13:45; 18:6; Rom 3:8; 1 Cor 10:30).[477] Since the Petrine author speaks so consistently of the verbal abuse directed against the believers, it is likely that they are the implied object here as well, with *blasphēmountes* best rendered "malign (you)." The verb is similarly employed by Josephus to refer to the unjust maligning of Israel by outsiders (*Ag. Ap.* 1.223; 2.32).

This maligning of the believers because of their dissociation from former practices and alliances is of a piece with other forms of verbal abuse (slander, disparagement, reproach, insult) which, according to the author, the Gentiles

---

[475] See also 1:18a, 20a, 21b, 23a; 2:4a; 3:2a, 6b, 7d, 18de; 4:3b; 5:2b, 12c. For a similar construction, including the terminal position of *blasphēmountes*, see Acts 13:45 and 2 Pet 2:10.

[476] See Isa 52:5; Acts 19:37; 26:11; Rom 2:24; 1 Tim 6:1; Titus 2:5; 2 Pet 2:10; Jude 8, 10; Rev 13:6; 16:9, 11, 21; 2 *Clem.* 13:2–4.

[477] For the verb elsewhere, see Jas 2:7; 2 Pet 2:2, 12; Ign. *Trall.* 8:2.

heap on the believers (2:12; 3:9, 14a, 16; 4:14, 16; cf. 2:23) and reflects the persistent effort of the outsiders to defame and dishonor the Christians (see also the NOTES on 2:12; 3:9, 17; 4:14–16).

Behind this maligning lay the suspicion that the Christians were no longer maintaining expected modes of conduct and social alliances. The situation recalls a similar predicament faced by Diaspora Israel, whose neighbors were thought to plot:

> Let us lie in wait for the righteous man, because he is inconvenient to us and opposes our actions. . . . He professess to have knowledge of God and calls himself a child of the Lord. He became to us a reproof of our thoughts; the very sight of him is a burden to us, because his manner of life is unlike that of others and his ways are strange. We are considered by him as something base, and he avoids our ways as unclean. The final end of the righteous he calls happy and boasts that God is his father. (Wis 2:12–16)

According to Josephus (Ag. *Ap.* 2.255), Israel was condemned by the Greek Apollonius Molon for "refusing admission to persons with other preconceived ideas about God, and for declining to associate (*mēde koinōnein ethelomen*) with those who have chosen to adopt a different mode of life (*tois ath' heteran synētheian biou zēn proairoumenois*)". Other Greeks and Romans also censured the "apartness" of Israelites (*amixia*, 2 Macc 14:38) and decried it as a manifestation of their "misanthropy" (*misanthrōpia*).[478]

The Christian sect, like its parent, the House of Israel, had to demonstrate to its suspicious neighbors that its termination of former practices and alliances was by no means a case of misanthropy and in no way prompted by a disdain for

[478] Thus Diodorus Siculus (*Hist.* 34–35.1.1, 2) states: "They [Israel] alone of all nations avoided dealings with any other people and looked upon all men as their enemies . . . the nation of the Judeans had made their hatred of mankind (*to misos to pros tous anthrōpous*) into a tradition"; cf. also 34–35.1.3, 4 for their alleged "misanthropy" and "laws hateful of strangers" (*ta misoxenia nomina*). The slanderous criticism of Tacitus (*Hist.* 5.5.1–2) is particularly harsh but also typical of how Israel could be viewed by outsiders: "The Judeans are extremely loyal toward one another, and always ready to show compassion, but toward every other people they feel only hate and enmity. They sit apart at meals and they sleep apart, and although as a race they are prone to lust, they abstain from intercourse with foreign women. . . . They adopted circumcision to distinguish themselves from other peoples by this difference. Those who are converted to their ways follow the same practice, and the earliest lesson they receive is to despise the gods, to disown their country, and to regard their parents, children, and brothers as of little account." Cf. also Philostratus (*Vit. Apoll.* 5.33), commenting on the first Judean revolt: "For the Judeans have long been in revolt not only against the Romans but against humanity; and a race that has made its own a life apart (*bion amikton*) and irreconcilable, that cannot share with the rest of mankind in the pleasures of the table (*trapeza*) nor join in their libations (*spondai*) or prayer (*euchai*) or sacrifices (*thysiai*), are separated (*aphestasin*) from ourselves by a greater gulf than divides us from Susa or Bactra or the more distant Indies." See also Diod. Sic. 40.3.4; Strabo, *Geogr.* 16.2.37; Dio Cass., *Hist. Rom.* 37.17.1–2. For Israel's promotion of social distinction and separation, see Dan 1:8–21; 6:1–28; Jdt 12:1–2; Tob 1:10–11; 3 Macc 3:4; *Jub.* 2:19–20; 22:16–18; 1QS V 1–2, 10–13, 15–20; VIII 11; IX 8–9; CD VI 4–6, 14–15; Josephus, *Life* 74–76; *J.W.* 2.591–92; Acts 10:28.

honorable behavior and the obligations of civic and domestic responsibility. The respect for authority, order, and doing what is right that the Petrine author so persistently urges is surely intended as a practical means for allaying such suspicions and fears in the face of Christian modes of nonconformity and dissociation.

5. *they shall have to give account* (*hōi apodōsousin logon*).[479] Those who presently malign will be held accountable at the end. The verb *apodōsousin*, a 3d-person pl. future act. indic. of *apodidōmi* ("give," "pay out [wages]," "render"), like "they are surprised," also has the Gentile nonbelievers in v 3 as its subject. The expression *apodidōmi* logon ("give, render account") is also used of an employee's rendering account to an employer (Luke 16:2) or of a mob answering to civil authorities (Acts 19:40), but here it has an eschatological sense similar to its use in Matt 12:36 ("on the day of judgment people will give account for every careless word they utter") and Heb 13:17 (leaders watching over you "will have to give account"; cf. also Rom 14:12). The statement forms a foil to 3:15, which speaks of the outsiders' requesting of the Christians an "account" (*logon*) of their hope and, like 3:15–16, again envisions an eschatological turning of tables: those who once sought an account from others and maligned them will themselves be called to account by God at the final judgment. Again the thought of 1 Peter runs parallel to that of the Wisdom of Solomon: "But the ungodly will be punished . . . who disregarded the righteous man and rebelled against the Lord. . . . They will come with dread when their sins are reckoned up, and their lawless deeds will convict them to their face" (3:10, 4:20).

to him who is ready to judge the living and the dead (*tōi hetoimōs echonti krinai*). The universal judge is the one to whom this account will have to be rendered. Some manuscripts (B [C] Ψ [81] 614 630 1852 others syr[h]) read *hetoimōs krinonti* ("readily judging"). In place of the adverb *hetoimōs* found in the superior textual witnesses (א A C^2 P 𝔐), other manuscripts read *hetoimōi krinai* ("to him who is ready to judge") ($\mathfrak{P}^{72}$ 945 1241 1739 1881 a few others cop?). Because it creates a smoother text, this reading is probably secondary but nevertheless captures the original sense intended. The combination of the adverb *hetoimōs* with the verb *echō* (lit., "have") and an accompanying infinitive (here *krinai*, "to judge") is an idiom meaning "ready to do X."[480] The dative *echonti* indicates the one to whom account is given and *krinai* ("to judge"), the action for which he is ready; "ready," in turn, implies the imminence of the day of judgment, as stressed in 4:7 and 4:17.

The identity of the judge is not stated and could be either God or Jesus Christ. Christ is the subject of 3:18–22 (cf. also 4:1a) and elsewhere in the NT is described as "judge of the living and the dead" (Acts 10:42 [speech of Peter];

---

[479] The first hand of Codex Sinaiticus omits all three Greek words, and $\mathfrak{P}^{72}$ omits *logon*, but the full reading has superior attestation (א[c] A B C P Ψ 𝔐 latt syr cop).

[480] For this construction, see Acts 21:13; 2 Cor 12:14; and Josephus, *Ant.* 12.163; cf. also Dan 3:15 LXX.

Pol. *Phil* 2:1; 2 *Clem.* 1:1) or as the one "about to judge the living and the dead" (2 Tim 4:1; cf. *Barn.* 7:2).[481] However, the more traditional Israelite view of God as judge also occurs in the NT[482] and is reflected elsewhere in 1 Peter (1:17 and implied in 2:23 and 4:17–19), while Jesus nowhere is depicted as judge but rather as the one who submits to God's will as his servant (2:21–24; cf. 1:2c). Thus God appears to be the implied subject here as well.

the living and the dead (*zōntas kai nekrous*). This stock expression refers to all humanity, the totality of those physically alive or physically dead (Acts 10:42; 2 Tim 4:1; *Barn.* 7:2; Pol. *Phil* 2:1; 2 *Clem.* 1:1; cf. Rom 14:9). Here it expresses the universality of God's judgment, from which none are exempt, including the nonbelievers of vv 3–4.

Verse 6, which concludes this unit, presents the interpreter with several notoriously difficult problems: (1) the subject and content of the verb "proclaim"; (2) the identity of the "dead"; (3) the relation of 4:6 to 3:19; and (4) the sense of the antithesis of v 6b. Scholarly opinion on these issues is divided, with one school of thought seeking to interpret 4:6 in the light of 3:19 (and 3:19 in the light of 4:6)[483] and another rejecting any relationship between the two verses.[484] The deficiencies of the first view have already been discussed in the NOTES and COMMENT on 3:19–20 and can be summarized as follows:

(1) The verbs *ekēryxen* (3:19) and *euaggelisthē* (4:6), though often used in conjunction in the NT, are not intrinsically synonymous but have different meanings ("announce" and "proclaim good news," respectively); in 3:19 and 4:6 they also have different voices (active and passive, respectively) and different subjects (Christ and an unnamed subject, respectively). Therefore, they are not necessarily related to each other.

(2) The indirect objects of these two verbs ("spirits" and "dead," respectively) are also different and not equivalent. The "spirits" referred to in 3:19 are not deceased humans but the angelic spirits of primordial time whose disobedience and rebellion against God led to the evil destroyed in the Noachic Flood (as stated in Gen 6–8 and the extensive Flood tradition that 1 Pet 3:19–20 reflects). The term "dead" (*nekrois*) in 4:6, a link-word joining v 6 to v 5, has the same meaning as in v 5, where "dead" (*nekrous*) denotes all of the *human* deceased. Furthermore, in the biblical and related literature, the term "dead" (*nekroi*) regularly refers to human dead but never to "spirits."

---

[481] For Christ as judge, see also Mark 8:38; Matt 25:31–46; Luke 21:34–36; John 5:27; Acts 17:31; 1 Cor 4:4–5; and the Apostles' Creed.

[482] See Rom 2:6; 3:6; 14:10; 1 Cor 5:13; Heb 10:30; 13:4; Rev 18:8; cf. Jas 4:12; 2 *Clem.* 2:1.

[483] So Bigg 1902, 171; Gunkel 1917, 284; Reicke 1946, 204–10; and 1964, 119; Jeremias 1949, 196–97; Windisch 1951, 75; Hauck 1957, 73; E. Schweizer 1952, 152–54; Cranfield 1960, 110; S. E. Johnson 1960; Spicq 1966a, 138, 146; Michl 1968, 144; Beare 1970, 173, 182; Schrage 1973, 108; Schelkle 1976, 116; Vogels 1976, 81, 142–59; Frankemölle 1987, 62–63; Goppelt 1993, 289.

[484] So Spitta 1890, 63–66; Gschwind 1911, 23–144; Selwyn 1947, 214, 337; J. N. D. Kelly 1969, 173; France 1977, 269; Elliott and Martin 1982, 95–101; Michaels 1988, 235–38; Dalton 1989, 57–60, 149–50, 225–26; Davids 1990, 153; Hillyer 1992, 122. For a survey of interpretation, see Dalton 1989, 51–66; see also pp. 225–41.

(3) There is also no *structural* correspondence between 3:19 and 4:6. In actuality, 3:19 and 4:6 belong to different and independently circumscribed units of thought.

(4) Finally, whereas 3:19–20 speaks of an announcement of condemnation to the disobedient angelic spirits (and their subordination to the resurrected Christ, 3:22), 4:6 sounds a note of hope by contrasting a judgment of the dead according to human standards to their living according to God's standard. Thus the implication of 4:6 and the term "dead" are best determined in relation to the immediate context of 4:1–6.

The interest in a possible correspondence between 3:19 and 4:6 appears motivated more by dogmatic than by exegetical concerns; namely, a desire to find here a biblical expression of the universality of salvation, including especially the salvation of the righteous in the OT (see DETAILED COMMENT 2 on the Doctrine of Christ's Descent into Hell in connection with 3:18–22). The representative statement by Beasley-Murray (1963, 258) succinctly expresses the theological implication of this view:

> [T]he primary reference of both statements [3:19 and 4:6] is the same and the primary lesson in the writer's mind is to exemplify the universal reach of Christ's redeeming work and the divine willingness that all should know it. The preaching of Christ between his cross and his Easter is intended to prove that the wickedest generation of history is not beyond the bounds of his pity and the scope of his redemption, hence there is hope for *this* generation, that has sinned even more greatly than the Flood generation in refusing the proclamation of a greater Messenger of God and that faces the *last* judgment (4.7).

Such a thought, however, along with the notion of a second opportunity for repentance and life offered to those who died before Christ (e.g., Beare 1970, 182; Best 1971, 156–57), is thoroughly inconsistent with the theology, ethics, and aim of 1 Peter as a whole. In this letter the stress consistently falls on the performance of the will of God here and now, and judgment according to one's behavior in the present. Moreover, any "second chance" for the salvation of humans after death, as Best himself admits (1971, 156), "would hardly encourage those who are being persecuted to resist unto death." "The question at issue," Selwyn (1947, 337) aptly observes, "was not one of eschatological theory, but of personal and practical importance, namely the vindication of God's justice through the punishment of the wicked and the oppressors and the deliverance of the faithful and persecuted, whether or not they had died before Christ's coming." For these several reasons the questions presented by 4:6, like those posed by 3:19, are best treated separately, without recourse to any putative correspondence between these verses.

6a. *For to this end* (*eis touto gar*). The same phrase was employed earlier in 2:21a and here, as there, introduces a thought supporting a preceding point. This second use of *gar* in this context (cf. v 3), rendered "for," signals an inferential connection between the present thought and what precedes it (either v 5 or vv 1–5; cf. BAGD 152 §3.). Whereas in 2:21a and 3:9d *eis touto* refers to what precedes it, here, in conjunction with the following *hina* clause,[485] it refers to the content of this purpose clause (v 6bc), with the sense of "to this end" or "for this reason." This verse is further linked with v 5 by the conjunction "also" (*kai*) and the link-words "dead" (*nekrois*; cf. *nekrous*) and "judge" (*krithōsi*; cf. *krinai*). Now, however, the focus shifts from the dead in general (v 5) to those dead to whom the good news was proclaimed. Moreover, the agent of judgment is not God (as in v 5) but humans, and this judgment according to human standards is contrasted with living in the spirit according to God's standard.

the good news was proclaimed also to the dead (*kai nekrois euēggelisthē*). A form of *euaggelizomai* ("proclaim good news," "evangelize," "preach the gospel") that was also used earlier in 1:12 and 1:25, *euēggelisthē* is a rare impersonal passive with the proclaimer(s) left unstated. If the one "who is ready to judge the living and the dead" (v 5) was Christ, he could be the implied subject here also. Selwyn (1947, 214–15) favors this option but curiously translates "he [Christ] was preached" rather than "the good news was preached by Christ," referring to the fact that in the NT Christ is predominantly the object (Acts 5:42; 8:35; 11:20; 17:18; Gal 1:16) rather than the subject (Luke 4:18 [citing Isa 61:1]; 4:43; 8:1; 20:1) of this verb. Neither alternative is likely, however, since God appears to be the judge implied *in v* 5. "Almost invariably," J. N. D. Kelly (1969, 174) notes, "'preaching the gospel' is an activity carried out by Christian evangelists, always in this world," and earlier uses of this verb in 1 Peter favor this alternative here as well. Verse 1:25b involves a related passive form of this verb: "This 'word' is the good news that was proclaimed (*to euaggelisthen*) to you," and this statement, in turn, harks back to the statement in 1:12b "things (concerning Christ's sufferings and glories [1:11b]) that now have been announced to you by those who proclaimed good news (*euaggelisamenōn*) to you." The fact that these earlier instances clearly refer to evangelizing by Christian missionaries suggests that their agency is implied here as well. Both the meaning and point of this verb have no relation to the meaning, content, and context of *ekēryxen* in 3:19. Here, in contrast to Christ's announcement of condemnation in 3:19, the proclaiming of good news by Christian preachers has as its goal life in the spirit.

also to the dead (*kai nekrois*). The identity of the "dead" to whom the good news was proclaimed has been vigorously debated among scholars (cf. Dalton 1989, 51–66). In this debate the question of the relation of 4:6 to 3:19 has also played a substantial role. Scholars who assume a relation between 4:6 and 3:19 (listed above) claim that the "dead" (*nekrois*) in 4:6 are identical to or include the "spirits" (*pneumasin*) in 3:19. Also taking *euēggelisthē* (4:6a) as equivalent

---

[485] As in John 18:37; Acts 9:21; Rom 14:9; 2 Cor 2:9; Eph 6:2; Col 4:8; 1 John 3:8.

to *ekēryxen* (3:19b) and Christ as the subject of both verbs, they see 4:6 as a second reference to a putative proclamation by Christ to the "dead" when he was in the realm of the dead prior to his resurrection. These dead are variously identified as the deceased human "spirits" of Noah's generation, the OT righteous, or all of the human deceased prior to Christ's coming.

The several exegetical and theological problems associated with this view have already been discussed above as well as in the NOTES and COMMENT on 3:19–20 and the related DETAILED COMMENTS. Its most serious weakness is the initial premise on which it is based: an assumed correspondence of 4:6 and 3:19. This premise, however, is mere conjecture.

With no certain relation between 3:19–20 and 4:6, the "dead" in 4:6 have no connection with the "spirits" of 3:19, and their identity must be ascertained on other grounds. In respect to the immediate context, the "dead" (*nekrois*) in v 6 are related in some way to the "dead" (*nekrous*) in v 5, and the verb *euēggelisthē* is to be understood in relation to the purpose clause that follows (4:6b).

This relation of "dead" in v 5 to "dead" in v 6 militates against the proposal that "dead" in v 6 be taken metaphorically as a reference to the *spiritually* or *morally* dead (cf. Eph 2:1; Col 2:13; Rev 3:1) to whom the gospel had first been preached by ministers of the Church. This view was first proposed by Clement of Alexandria (*Adum.* 4:6, "to us, namely, who were at one time unbelievers"). It was adopted also by Cyril of Alexandria (cited with approval by Theophylact (PG 125.1237, 1240), Augustine (*Ep. Eud.* 164.21; PL 33, 717–18), Bede (PL 93.6A), Erasmus, Luther, and others and has been defended in more recent time by Gschwind (1911, 24–40).[486] Its fatal weakness, however, is attributing different meanings to two adjoining uses of "dead." As one of the terms linking v 6 to v 5, "dead" (*nekrois*) in v 6 must have the same meaning as its precedessor in v 5; namely, *humans* who are presently *physically dead.* (For further problems with the metaphorical interpretation, including its irrelevance to the point of vv 1–6, see J. N. D. Kelly 1969, 173; and Dalton 1989, 56–57.)

Best (1971, 156–57) takes the term inclusively of "all who are physically dead and who are in this state when they hear the Gospel" and claims that "the Gospel is now offered to those who never had the opportunity of hearing it when alive." He admits the weakness of this interpretation, however, by granting that this would imply a "second chance" for persons after they had died. This notion, he correctly observes, would contradict clearer statements in the letter (1:3–4; 3:10; 4:5, 18; and 5:8) and would hardly be an encouragement for suffering addressees to remain faithful in the present.

Taking the "dead" of v 6a in connection with both v 5 and the remainder of v 6, however, provides a satisfactory solution. In this case, the "dead" of v 6 refers to a *portion* of those now deceased (cf. v 5), namely the deceased among

[486] See also Holzmeister 1937, 364–65; Bieder 1949, 120–28.

the letter's addressees. The fact that the author stressed earlier that the addressees themselves were the privileged recipients of the good news (*euaggelisamenōn hymas*, 1:12, and *euaggelisthen eis hymas*, 1:25) makes it likely that the entire statement in 4:6 also pertains to the addressees, but here to those among the addressees who, once having heard and accepted the good news, are at present among the dead. This view was first advanced by Spitta (1890, 63–66) and subsequently was adopted by several other scholars.[487]

The remainder of the verse then states the consequence of this proclamation for these deceased believers: though they too were judged by hostile outsiders and died without apparent vindication, they nevertheless, because of their reception of the good news prior to their death, will, with all believers, enjoy vindication and life from God. This contrast is consistent with the foregoing contrasts Gentiles-believers and humans-God (vv 2–4), and only this interpretation accords with both the earlier references to the "proclaiming of good news" and the letter's stress on faith as requisite for salvation. The situation envisioned is thus similiar to the situation presupposed in Paul's first letter to the Thessalonians (1 Thess 4:13–18). In both instances, *some* believers who had heard and accepted the gospel had died. The Petrine author, like Paul, addresses this issue with words of assurance concerning their resurrection to life (1 Pet 4:6c; cf. 1 Thess 4:14b, 16), based on the resurrection of Jesus Christ (1 Pet 3:21d, 22; cf. 1 Thess 4:14a).

While many have been tempted to see here a reference to the universality of salvation, balancing a universality of judgment, there is no basis for this in the text of 1 Peter. The remainder of this verse underscores the fact that it is the justice of God and the vindication of oppressed believers that the author has in mind (so also Dalton 1990, 908). The thought here is thus consonant with the eschatological outlook of the letter and the author's aim of consolation. Even those who once heard and were reborn by the good news but who have since died, even these believers shall live. Adversaries, like all creatures, will be held accountable to the One who judges all, the living and the dead. It is believers, however, whether alive or dead, who will enjoy eternal life. Thus, the point of the verse is to assure the divine vindication of Christians who suffer from the abuse of their adversaries so that they can stand firm in the midst of their innocent suffering.

6b. *so that though they were judged in the flesh according to human standards they might live in the spirit according to God's standard* (*hina kritōsi men kata anthrōpous sarki zōsi de kata theon pneumati*). This formulation, which brings vv 1–6 to a close, states the purpose or intended result (*hina*, "so that") of the proclamation of the good news (v 6a). Both parallel verbs, *krithōsi* and *zōsi*, are

---

[487] See Selwyn 1947, 214, 338–39; Dalton 1989, 57–60, 236; J. N. D. Kelly 1969, 174–75; Danker 1980, 153; Hillyer 1992, 122; cf. Bengel (1773, 1194–95), who saw here a reference to deceased Christians even beyond the addressees of 1 Peter. Michaels (1988, 237) also favors this view but unconvincingly includes among these Christian dead the prophets (1:10–12) and the holy matriarchs (3:5) as "Christians before Christ."

subjunctives, as is appropriate for *hina* purpose clauses (BDF §369.1). The former verb, an aor., is prior in time and subordinate in sense to the latter verb, a pres. act. indic. with a future sense. The subject of both verbs is the "dead" Christians in v 6a, their fate at human hands and their future before God. On the whole, the formulation is an antithetical parallelism involving two balanced clauses with three sets of contrasts:

4:6b	*krithōsi*	*men*	*kata anthrōpous*	*sarki*
4:6c	*zōsi*	*de*	*kata theon*	*pneumati*
	though they were judged		according to human standards	in the flesh
	they might live		according to God's standard	in the spirit

This compact statement also has been variously interpreted, but not always with sufficient attention to the manner in which its structure controls the meaning of its parts. The meaning of each of the terms in the three sets of contrasts in this balanced couplet (*krithōsi-zōsi, kata anthropous-kata theon, sarki-pneumati*) is conditioned by its contrasting term. This provides an important guideline for translating and assessing the meaning of each term and for determining the gist of the statement as a whole. The similarity of this formulation to the form and content of the earlier balanced couplet in v 3:18de (referring to Christ's death and resurrection), as we shall see, provides yet a further clue to its meaning:

4:6b	*krithōsi*	*men*	*kata anthrōpous*	*sarki*
3:18d	*thanatōtheis*	*men*		*sarki*
	put to death			in the flesh
4:6c	*zōsi*	*de*	*kata theon*	*pneumati*
3:18e	*zōiopoiētheis*	*de*		*pneumati*
	made alive	however		in the spirit

The death and resurrection of Christ, as affirmed in the early Christian tradition and mentioned in 3:18, thus seems to have inspired a similar formulation concerning the deceased Christian believers in 4:6.

though (*men*). The adversative particles *men* and *de* underline the contrast of the two parallel clauses (as also in 3:18de), with the first clause having a concessive sense: "though. . . ." The *men* clause is parenthetical, however, with the *de* clause stating the intended result to which *eis touto* points.

they were judged (*krithōsi*). The idea of judgment introduced in v 5 is continued and now applied to the deceased believers in particular. The verb *krithōsi*, a form of *krinō* ("pass unfavorable judgment on, be critical of, find fault with, condemn"),[488] is a 3d-person pl. pass. (cf. Rom 3:7; 1 Cor 10:29), with the dead

---

[488] See Matt 7:1–5/Luke 6:37; Rom 2:1, 3; 14:3–4, 10, 13; 1 Cor 4:5; Col 2:16; Jas 4:11–12.

Christians of v 6a as its subject. As an aor. pass., it describes their having been judged or faulted as an event of the past, prior to their death, and contrasts with its parallel, "might live" (v 6c), a present-tense verb with future import.[489] Although *krinō* is used elsewhere of God's judging activity (1:17; 2:23; cf. 4:17) and although v 5 speaks of God as the eschatological judge, the accompanying mention of "human standards" indicates that here *human judging* is in view, since God can hardly be said to judge according to human standards. The verb has the sense of "pass an unfavorable judgment on, criticize, find fault with" (BAGD 452; see also below).

in the flesh (*sarki*). Both *sarki* (cf. 4:1a, c) and its counterpart, *pneumati* ("spirit," v 6c), are datives of respect (cf. 3:18de); literally, "with respect to their flesh, their spirit." Both datives modify their preceding verbs, but both also occur last in their respective Greek clauses. This may be for emphasis' sake, but in the case of *sarki* it may also be due to the fact that the construction of *krinō* + *kata* ("judge according to") was felt to require the proximity of *kata anthrōpous* to *krithōsi*. To maintain the balance of the couplet, its second half was similarly constructed. In any case, to avoid the impression that "flesh" and "spirit" modify their immediately preceding phrases ("according to human standards," "according to God's standard"), it is more stylistically appropriate in English to reverse the sequence and translate "were judged in the flesh" and "might live in the spirit," respectively.

As elsewhere in this letter, *sarx* denotes not the "sinful flesh" of which Paul speaks, but the physical existence in which mortals are subject to abuse and suffering. As in 3:18de, it denotes a mortal mode of life in contrast to life in the spirit after death. This repeated stress on the present mortal life of the believers (cf. also v 1c, 2 and Christ's mortal suffering, v 1a) forms part of the inclusion framing vv 1–6, which concerns how Christians in the light of Christ's suffering should behave in the remaining time of their mortal existence.

according to human standards (*kata anthrōpous*). The preposition *kata* in this formulation and its parallel, *kata theon*, "expresses conformity with some standard, model, rule or will" (Selwyn 1947, 215), as also in 1:2, 3, 15, 17; 3:7; 4:19; and 5:2. The phrase qualifies "judged" (*krithōsi*).[490] The noun *anthrōpous* (lit., "humans") names the norm and identifies the subjects of the judging. In the present context (vv 1–6), *anthrōpous* refers not simply to humans in general but to the Gentiles who malign the believers, as the equation of "Gentiles" and "humans" in vv 2–4 makes clear. Both of these terms identify the hostile "outsiders," nonbelievers who have rejected Christ (*anthrōpoi*, 2:4) and slandered the believers (*ethnē*, 2:12). The equation of "humans" with "Gentiles" indicates that the "human" standards are those of the Gentiles who have maligned

---

[489] On the omission of the movable *nu* in *krithōsi*(*n*) and its parallel *zōsi*(*n*), see Gignac 1976, 114–15.

[490] For the construction of *krinō* + *kata* + standard of judgment, see John 8:15; 18:31; Acts 23:3; 24:6.

and faulted the Christians in the past and present. Echoing the contrast between humans/Gentiles and God in vv 2–4, *human standards* are now contrasted with *God's standard.*

The phrases *kata anthrōpous . . . kata theon* describe contrary standards of reckoning, that of the Gentiles versus that of God. The contrast does not mean "like men . . . like God" (as though the author were saying "they were judged like men but might live like God")[491] or "according to the nature or manner of men . . . according to the nature or manner of God."[492] Moreover, with the aorist of the verb *krithōsi,* the author is referring not to a future eschatological judgment of God when all mortals will be judged as humans (against Reicke 1946, 206) but to a judgment of the *past* rendered according to human standards. Goppelt's translation (1993, 276) "might be judged" is also inaccurate and misleading. Best's paraphrase (1971, 158) is not much better: "though judged at death in the sphere of the flesh according to human standards, they might live in the sphere of the Spirit as God lives." Instead, the phrase *kata anthrōpous* emphasizes that the deceased Christians were faulted by the Gentiles according to Gentile standards (and, by implication of what follows, not according to God's standard). Selwyn (1947, 215) contradicts his own comment on the meaning of *kata* (see above) by rendering *kata anthrōpous* "humanly speaking"; and his translating the parallel expression *kata theon* "in God's likeness" fails to capture the parallelism of these two phrases in the Greek. Goppelt's (1993, 276) translation ("judged humanly . . . with regard to God might live") is deficient on the same score. Dalton's (1989, 50) alternative, "in the eyes of people . . . in the eyes of God," preserves the parallelism but obscures the active role of the humans/Gentiles.

Our author is referring in this first half of the couplet not to the end time judgment by God when all of the dead are raised in the flesh and judged as humans are judged (against Reicke 1946, 204–10; Goppelt 1993, 289; and others). There is little to commend taking "were judged" as reference to "a purifying punishment" experienced by all the deceased in the "prison" of purgatory (against Vogels 1976, 44; see the convincing critique by Dalton 1977). Dalton (1989, 238) and a few others (Beare 1970, 182; Best 1971, 158) regard "were judged" as implying the "judgment" that the dead suffered *in death* as a divine judgment on the sinful flesh. In support of this view, Dalton notes that the idea of death as a form of condemnation is biblical (citing Gen 2:7; 3:19; Wis 2:23–24; Rom 5:12; 6:23). He takes the statement to represent the position of the Gentiles that the physical death of the believers was actually a proof of their condemnation: "for the pagans the order of the flesh is the final order; death is the final verdict on human destiny" (Dalton 1989, 238). But this view assumes that the Gentiles were more *observers* of the judgment of the believers than its *perpetrators.* It is also inconsistent with Dalton's own recognition of

---

[491] Against Arichea and Nida 1980, 135–36 and others.

[492] Against Reicke 1964, 118; Goppelt 1993, 290.

"the close link between 4:6 and the preceding context, where the main idea is the hostile attitude of the pagans to the newly converted Christians" (Dalton 1989, 239). This latter observation, however, grasps the nub of the issue. The Gentiles, according to the Petrine author, were not simply observing the condemnation of the believers as bystanders; they were the ones who with their maligning, slander, and reproach (4:4; cf. 2:12; 3:9, 16; 4:14) actively faulted the Christians according to their own God-opposed norms (so also Davids 1990, 155). This, by the way, is a further point against the view (equating 4:6 with 3:19) that this verse is a reference to God's judgment of the dead (of Noah's time or all the dead), to whom then Christ supposedly preached salvation upon his "descent into Hades." Moreover, as Dalton stresses (1989, 240), "were judged" does not precede "good news was preached" (v 6a), as this flawed theory would require, but follows it.

6c. *they might live in the spirit according to God's standard* (*zōsi de kata theon pneumati*). This second half of the couplet and final clause of the unit states the goal of the proclamation of good news and shifts the focus from suffering, being maligned, and being judged, to the prospect of life with God. Deceased Christians who had heard and embraced the good news, though wrongfully faulted by Gentile outsiders, will nevertheless enjoy eternal life. Their life and vindication follow Christ's and presage the life and vindication of all who remain faithful.

they might live (*zōsi*). The verb *zōsi*, an act. pres. subjunctive (with *hina*), has the deceased Christians as its subject, and in conjunction with *hina* ("so that") describes the intended result of the proclaiming of the good news (v 6a). Whereas the verb *bioō* in v 2 referred to the present mortal existence of the believers, the verb *zaō*, as elsewhere in 1 Peter, denotes the life of resurrection conferred by God. Christ "was made alive" (*zōiopoiētheis*, 3:18e) and became a "living stone" (*lithon zōnta*, 2:4). The believers have shared proleptically in this resurrection of Christ since their rebirth to a "living hope" (1:3; cf. 3:21), as "living stones" (2:5a), and as those "living for doing what is right" (2:24c). Here, as in 3:7, the final and full realization of resurrection life is in view. Within the overall context of 1 Peter, this life is synonymous with the final salvation (1:5, 9, 10; 2:2; 4:18), exaltation (5:6b), and glorification (1:7c; cf. 5:10) in store for all believers, the deceased as well as those presently living. The thought recalls the resurrection hope expressed by the oppressed righteous of an earlier time: "It is good, being put to death by humans, to look for hope from God of being raised up again by Him" (2 Macc 7:14; cf. also 4 Macc 7:19); for this Christian hope regarding both the deceased and the living, see Rom 14:8; 1 Cor 15:20–23, 51–57; 1 Thess 4:16–18; 5:9–11.

in the spirit (*pneumati*). The formulation "might live in the spirit" parallels the kerygmatic formulation in 3:18e concerning Christ ("he was made alive in the spirit"), and thus the experience of Christ once again serves as the basis for that of the Christians. As in 3:18e, "spirit," as the antithesis of "flesh," refers to a *human* dimension of existence and not to the Spirit of God. It denotes a sphere of existence contrasted with physical mortal existence (3:18e; 4:1a, 1c, 2), a human state after death animated by the life-giving Spirit of God (see Ezek 37:14; Rom 8:10; 1 Cor 5:5; 15:42–46; and the NOTE on 3:18e).

according to God's standard (*kata theon*). This expression forms a contrast with "according to human standards" (*kata anthrōpous*), and *kata* again implies accordance with a standard, in this case, God's standard or will. It recurs with the same sense in 5:2c; see also 4 Macc 15:3; Rom 8:27; and 2 Cor 7:9, 10, 11. The expression "live to God" (*zōsi tōi theōi*, 4 Macc 7:19; 16:25) appears similar but lacks *kata* and, thus, the sense of standard implied by this term. The contrast between human and divine standards echoes the contrasts "humans" and "God" in v 2 and "will of Gentiles–will of God" in v 3. Thus, this final antithesis represents an appropriate conclusion to the distinction between God and humans pervading these verses. In v 2 and elsewhere, the will of God is held up as the norm by which Christians are to live in the present (2:15; 3:18; 4:2, 19; cf. 5:4). Here, however, *resurrected* believers are in view, and the point of *zōsi de kata theon* is not that they will live in obedience to God's will but that it is God's will that they will live. This differs from the sense of *kata theon* in Eph 4:24 ("in God's likeness;" cf. Col 3:10) and implies not *similarity* ("as God lives," so Selwyn 1947, 216; cf. also Vogels 1976, 167–68]) but *conformity* to God's intention.

At the outset of the letter, the rebirth of the addressees to a living hope through the resurrection of Jesus Christ is said to have occurred "in accord with God's lavish mercy" (*kata to poly autou eleos*, 1:3), and this mercy may be the divine standard implied here as well, where life and resurrection are also in view. Similar expressions in 1 Peter denoting the divine perspective or standard include *enōpion tou theou* (3:4) and *para de theōi* (2:4, 20), each rendered "in God's sight." The expression in 2:4 is particularly noteworthy, since there too God and humans are contrasted in regard to their differing views and treatment of Christ. This similarity would lend weight to Dalton's translation (1989, 236, 238–39) "in the eyes of God." In any case the point is that God's impartial judgment (1:17; 4:17), will (2:15; 3:17; 4:2, 19), intention (1:2b), and disposition of mercy (1:3; 2:10) supersede and reverse all erroneous and malicious human criticism.

The statement as a whole is hardly based on alleged *verba Christi* incorporated in John 5:19–29 as Selwyn (1947, 215, 346–53) claims. The "judgment" from which "life" is distinguished in John 5 is the final judgment by God (and Christ), which believers will not experience according to John 5:24, whereas our author speaks of a *past* judgment-as-criticism that deceased believers have already undergone. The structure and content of 4:6 instead echo the structure and content of the kerygmatic formula in 3:18de and the Christological formulation in 2:4, with the result that the experience of the believers, the deceased as well as the living, is linked inseparably with that of Jesus Christ (cf. also 1 Cor 15:12–18; 1 Thess 4:13–18). As God raised, honored, and vindicated the "living stone" rejected by humans, so it is God's will that believers who have been maligned and judged by humans nevertheless shall live in the spirit. Verse 6 thus expresses the second of two aspects of divine reversal in this passage. On the one hand, those who malign the believers and have called them to account (3:15) will themselves be called to account by God (v 5). On the other hand, suffering believers who, like Christ, have been rejected and judged by these detractors will, also like Christ, be raised to life.

While the thought in v 6 is grounded Christologically in God's raising of Jesus Christ (3:18, 22), its perspective is reminiscent of an earlier confidence in the vindication of the oppressed righteous expressed in the Wisdom of Solomon:

> But the souls of the righteous are in the hand of God, and there shall no torment touch them. In the eyes of the ignorant (*en ophthalmois aphronōn*) they seemed to die and their departure is taken for misery and their going from us to be utter destruction. But they are in peace. For though they be punished in the sight of humans (*en opsei anthrōpōn*), yet is their hope full of immortality. And having been a little chastised, they shall be greatly rewarded, for God has proved them and found them worthy for himself. As gold in the furnace he has tested them [cf. 1 Pet 1:6; 4:12] and received them as a burnt offering. (Wis 3:1–6)[493]

As already noted in connection with 2:21–25, the tradition of the suffering of the righteous and their divine vindication is reflected at several points in this letter in both the portrait of Christ and the consolation of the suffering faithful.

This concluding verse provides a final theological warrant for the foregoing exhortation. Confident in the life that awaits all believers, both the dead and the living, the addressees, strengthened by their union with Christ and by the disciplining effect of suffering, can make a complete break with the conduct and contacts of the past and devote themselves single-mindedly to carrying out God's will in the time remaining.

The terms "human" (*anthrōpous*), "flesh "(*sarki*), and "God" (*theon*) in this verse together with their counterparts in vv 1–2 form an inclusion that frames the unit as a whole and demarcates it from 4:7–11, which turns from the relation of believers and their adversaries to the internal life of the community.

GENERAL COMMENT

Although 3:13–17; 3:18–22; and 4:1–6 are discernible units of thought, each framed by literary inclusions, they all form related parts of a larger pattern of thought moving from exhortation to substantiation back to exhortation. Hav-

[493] See also Wis 5:1, 15–16: "Then the righteous man will stand with great confidence in the presence of those who have afflicted him. . . . The hope of the ungodly is like dust that is blown away with the wind. . . . But the righteous live (*zōsi*) forever and their reward is with the Lord; the Most High takes care of them. Therefore they will receive a glorious kingdom [or crown, *to basileion*; cf. 1 Pet 2:9] and a beautiful diadem (cf. 1 Pet 5:4) from the Lord's hand because with his right hand he will cover them and with his arm he will shield them."

ing shown how God's exaltation and vindication of the suffering Christ (3:18–22) serve as basis and motivation for the suffering readers to persevere in doing what is right despite innocent suffering (3:13–17), our author resumes the imperative mood of 3:13–17 and returns to the theme of suffering and its moral and social implications. Once again (4:1a) the suffering Christ is held up as a model for the suffering believers (cf. 3:13–17/18–22 and 2:18–20/21–25), and now the emphasis falls on the break from sinning that suffering enables. The addressees are urged to finalize in their present conduct the break with the sinful ways of the past that their baptismal conversion and divine rebirth has initiated (1:14–19; cf. 2:11–12). This is possible because innocent suffering, like the suffering of Christ (v 1ab), disciplines the physical body and facilitates ceasing from sinning (v 1c). This forms one of several positive interpretations that the author gives to Christian suffering throughout the letter; see also innocent suffering as a divine test of fidelity (1:6, 4:12); innocent suffering while doing what is right as approved by God (2:18–25; 3:13–17; 4:16, 19), as solidarity with the suffering Christ (2:18–25; 3:13–17, 18–22), and as an occasion for glorifying God (4:16). On this point, see also the NOTES and GENERAL COMMENT on 4:12–19.

The sinning to be abandoned (vv 2–3) balances the behavior to be embraced in 3:13–17. The demarcation of the preconversion and postconversion phases of the readers' existence (vv 2–3; cf. 1:14–19) is to be marked by distinctively different modes of conduct: living no longer in accord with the human cravings of the Gentiles but in accord with the will of God. Christian conversion means nonconformity with society's immoral life-style, a point made earlier, in 1:14–16. The several antitheses employed here reinforce this call for demarcation and separation (human cravings–will of God, v 2; the remaining time–the time that has passed, vv 2, 3; Gentiles–you, vv 3, 4; judged in the flesh–live in the spirit, v 6; according to human standards–according to God's standard, v 6). To cease from sinning like the Gentiles entails dissociating from them as well. Dissociation, however, arouses the astonishment and resentment of the Gentiles, resulting in their malicious maligning of the believers (v 4). This maligning, like the other expressions of verbal abuse, does not yet include any physical harm to the believers; nevertheless, it represents no small threat to their physical well-being and their ability to survive in a hostile environment. Any temptation to avoid disparagement and discrimination by maintaining ties with the outsiders and their godless ways or by reversing previous severance of alliances must be assiduously resisted, even if this results in further suffering, for accommodation would undermine the very existence and viability of the community.

So the author concludes with an assuring word of comfort and consolation: this state of affairs eventually will be reversed by God. Those who malign and shame the Christians and call them to account will themselves be called to account by the universal Judge of all. Believers, on the other hand, can anticipate the same future as their rejected yet resurrected Lord. Those who have already died, though judged by their human adversaries according to human standards, will live in the spirit according to God's standard, a great reversal to which all believers, whether dead or alive, can look forward.

The view that claims a relation between 4:6 and 3:19 and finds here in 4:6 an accent not only on universal judgment but also *universal salvation*, however, runs contrary to the thought of 1 Peter in general and to the point of vv 1–6 in particular. Throughout the letter, salvation is made contingent upon faith in Jesus Christ and fidelity to the will of God here and now, with no hint of a second opportunity of repentance after death. The author's intention here, as throughout the letter, is the exhortation and consolation of the faithful, those who in their lifetime have heard the gospel and are "in Christ." Here attention is given to the deceased among the believers as examples of the prospect facing all the community. The point of 4:6 is not the universal judgment and salvation of all but the vindication of oppressed believers, the deceased as well as the living, as Christ himself was vindicated (2:4; 3:18, 22). The concept of a universal salvation is a noble idea but is not advocated in this letter and ought not to be read into this passage.

Having concluded this first piece of exhortation concerning the problematic relation of the believers to their detractors (3:13–4:6), the author turns next to the relation of the believers to one another (4:7–11).

For studies on 1 Pet 4:1–6, see Blazen 1983; Bullinger 1895; Cervantes Gabarrón 1991a, 253–88; Cramer 1891; Cranfield 1958; Dalton 1965/1989, 1977, 1979; Frings 1925; Kira 1960; Millauer 1976; Pinto da Silva 1984; Plooij 1913; Reicke 1946; Salvoni 1971; E. Schweizer 1952; Selwyn 1947, 313–62; 1956; E. A. Sieffert 1875; Stemmler 1894; Strobel 1963; Usteri 1886; Vitti 1927; Vogels 1976; see also the studies listed on 1 Pet 3:18–22.

V. MAINTAINING THE SOLIDARITY OF THE HOUSEHOLD OF GOD TO THE GLORY OF GOD (4:7–11)

◆

4:7 The end of all, moreover, is at hand.
7b Therefore exercise sound judgment and be alert as an aid to praying.
8a Above all, maintain constant love toward one another
8b because "love covers a multitude of sins."
9 [Be] hospitable to one another without complaint.
10a Inasmuch as each has received a gift of grace,
10b serve one another with it
10c as honorable household stewards of God's varied grace:
11a whoever speaks, [let that one do so]
as [uttering] oracles of God;
11b whoever renders service, [let that one do so]
as from the strength that God supplies;
11c so that in all things God may be glorified through Jesus Christ.
11d His is the glory and the power forever, amen.

INTRODUCTION

Moving from the subject of the readers' suffering due to the hostility of *outsiders*, the author now turns to the *internal* life of the community as seen in the light of the nearness of the end. These verses have only a loose connection with the foregoing, though the idea of the nearness of the end (v 7a) is related thematically to the foregoing mention of judgment (4:5) and the time remaining (4:2). The hortatory mood (marked by a string of imperative finite verbs [v 7b], imperatival participles [v 8a, 10a], and one imperatival adjective [v 9]) continues the hortatory mood in 4:1–6 with the difference that, whereas 4:1–6 focuses on the relation of believers to outsiders, 4:7–11 concentrates on the internal life of the community (cf. 1:22; 2:17b; 3:8; 5:1–7).[494]

The form (a series of staccato-like injunctions) and content of these verses suggest reliance on a broad stream of early Christian hortatory tradition

[494] For a list of the terms that 4:1–11 has in common with 1:13–3:22, see Cervantes Gabarrón 1991a, 79–80, who unconvincingly regards 4:1–6 and 4:7–11 as a "double conclusion" to a major section, 1:13–4:11.

(Goppelt 1993, 293–94), which, however, is structured and theologically grounded in a fashion unique to 1 Peter. The connection and unity of these injunctions are created by means of an internal series of link-words (*pantōn/pantōn* [vv 7a/b]; *agapē/philoxenoi* [vv 8/9]; *eis autous/eis allēlous/eis autous* [vv 8/9/10]; *diakonountes/diakonei* [vv 10/11]; *theou/theou/theos/theos* [vv 10c/11a/11b/11c]; *doxazetai/doxa* [vv 11b/c]) as well as by the symmetry of vv 11a and 11b. A comprehensive stress on "all" (vv 7, 8, 11) frames the unit as a whole, and a final doxology marks a minor conclusion to this part of the letter.

NOTES

4:7. *The end of all, moreover, is at hand (Pantōn de to telos ēggiken).* The particle *de* ("moreover"), serving as a transitional particle as in 3:8 and 5:5b, forges a loose connection with the foregoing, with "end" (*telos*) related to the motif of judgment in 4:5 and the "remaining time in the flesh" in 4:2. The theory that this verse forms the conclusion of 4:1–6 (Holzmeister 1937, 362–70; R. P. Martin 1992, 235–36) is rightly rejected by the vast majority of commentators and translators. While the idea of the imminence of the end is compatible with the foregoing theme of judgment (4:5), in the expresssion "end of all," "all" (as in vv 8a and 11c) refers not to persons but things, and the expression as a whole, as indicated below, refers not to the personal "end" of individuals but the eschatological end of the ages. As elsewhere in the NT, appeal to the imminence of the end provides an eschatological motivation for Christian conduct.

In the NT, *to telos*, meaning "the end," can have various senses depending on the context: "termination" or "cessation"; "consummation" or "fulfillment"; "close" or "conclusion"; "maturity," "goal," or "intended outcome" (BAGD 811). The semantic range in other Greek literature includes such meanings as "achievement," "power," "perfection," "obligation," "offering" (for the gods), "tax," "tribute," "toll," and "detachment" or "group" (Delling 1972b). Elsewhere in 1 Peter, *telos* denotes "goal" (of faith, 1:9) or "end result" of disobedience (4:17) or "finally," in an adverbial sense (3:8). Here, however, in conjunction with the verb *eggizō*, it is used in an eschatological sense and refers to the end of the ages that is now viewed as being at hand.

In Israel's history, anticipation of an eventual moment in time when justice and God's rule would once again be established accompanied the gradual corruption and decay of the monarchy. Following the collapses of both the Northern and Southern monarchies in 722 and 587 BCE, respectively, attention began to focus increasingly on a future, final epoch of history as the time of the divine punishment of evil, reestablishment of justice, and the salvation of the just.[495] This expectation was nurtured defiantly in the face of Judah's ongoing control by foreign powers and comprised a cluster of events associated with this

[495] See Jenni 1962; Petersen 1992; Nickelsburg 1992b.

final age referred to variously as the "latter days,"[496] or the "day" of the Lord,[497] or the "end" (*synteleia*).[498]

Early Christianity, in its perception of God, of time, of Jesus as the messianic agent of the end time, and of its own role in history's final phase, was fundamentally inspired and shaped by this eschatological perspective (Bowman 1962; Schüssler Fiorenza 1976b; Nickelsburg 1992). And as the content of 1 Peter illustrates, this is true of our author as well. Thus *to telos* has the same eschatological sense that it bears elsewhere in the early Church.[499] The verb accompanying *to telos*, namely *eggiken*, is likewise a stock term in early Christian eschatological thought,[500] expressing the imminence or nearness of the end.

of all (pantōn). Reicke (1964, 120) takes "all" to refer to persons—namely, all the members of the community—and translates: "For all, however, the end is near."[501] This translation, however, presumes a dative rather than the actual genitive, which is more appropriately taken with "end": "the end of all" (as in most translations and commentaries). Moreover, the other two references to "all" in this passage (vv 8a, 11c) also refer not to persons but things.[502] The formulation is close in syntax and sense to the expression "the end of the ages" (*ta telē tōn aiōnōn*) in 1 Cor 10:11 (cf. *T. Levi* 14:1).[503] These ages (*aiones, chronoi*[504]) were generally conceived as periods or epochs of world history (e.g., *1 En.* 91:12–17; 93:1–10; *2 En.* 33 *inscr.*; *Acts Pil.* 28) or identified as weeks of years (Dan 9:24–27) and associated with the rise and fall of specific empires (Dan 7:1–28; 10:13–14, 20–11:1; 11:2–12:13). The earlier statement in 1:20b that Christ "was made manifest at the last of the ages" (*phanerōthentos de ep' eschatou tōn chronōn*) makes it likely that here in 4:7 "the end of all" refers not to the "end of the *world*" but to the end and conclusion of all of the foregoing "periods of time" or "ages" (*chronōn* or *aiōnōn*). The explicit mention of *aiōnes*, "ages" (synony-

---

[496] See Ezek 38:16; cf. Isa 2:2; Jer 23:20; 30:24; Hos 3:5; Mic 4:1.

[497] See Isa 61:2; Joel 1:15; 2:1–11; 3:14; Zeph 1:7–18; 2:2–3; 3:8; Zech 12–14; Sir 36:7; cf. Amos 5:18–20; Mic 4:1–6.

[498] See Dan 11:35, 40; 12:4, 13; *T. Zeb.* 9:9; *T. Benj.* 11:3; *T. Levi* 10:2; Heb 9:26; cf. also *4 Ezra* 3:14; 14:5; *2 Bar.* 29:8.

[499] See Matt 10:22; Matt 24:6/Mark 13:7/Luke 21:9; Matt 24:13/Mark 13:13; Matt 24:14; 1 Cor 15:24; Jas 5:11; Rev 21:6, 22:13; Herm. *Vis.* 3.8.9; Ign. *Eph.* 14:2; *Rom.* 10:3. Other related expressions for the final epoch of time include "last days" (Acts 2:17; Heb 1:2), "last time" (*eschatou tou chronou*, Jude 18) and "last hour" (1 John 2:18).

[500] See Matt 3:2; Matt 4:17/Mark 1:15; 10:7; Luke 21:31; Rom 13:12; Phil 4:5; Jas 5:8; Rev 1:3; 22:10.

[501] See also R. P. Martin 1992, 235–36, following Theophylact and regarding 4:7 as the conclusion of 4:1–6.

[502] The formulations "whose end" (*hōn to telos*, 2 Cor 11:15; Phil 3:19) or "its end" (*hēs to telos*, Heb 6:8) are not analogous, since in these instances "all" refers to nominal antecedents, which is not the case here.

[503] See also the related and virtually identical expressions *synteleia aiōnos* (Matt 13:39, 40, 49; 24:3; 28:20; *T. Benj.* 11:3; *T. Levi* 10:2) or *synteleia tōn aiōnōn* (Heb 9:26).

[504] For *chronoi* (pl.), like *aiōnes*, denoting "periods of time" or "aeons" or "ages," see *T. Iss.* 4:3; Wis 7:18; Acts 1:7; 3:21; 17:30; Rom 16:25; 1 Thess 5:1; 2 Tim 1:9; Titus 1:2.

mous with *chronoi*) in v 11d may strengthen this likelihood. The phrase *eis tous aiōnas tōn aiōnōn* (lit., "to the ages of ages") is a formula with which doxologies, like those in 4:11d and 5:11, often end. However, since these words of 4:11d conclude the unit begun in v 7, an implied "ages" in v 7 would have matched an explicit "ages" in v 11 and would have formed part of the the literary inclusion framing this unit.

is at hand (ēggiken). The verb *eggizō* means to "be near," "draw near," or "approach," either temporally or spatially. In the perfect tense, as here, it has the sense of "is at hand," "is imminent," "has drawn near." In the NT it appears regularly in statements concerning the nearness or imminence of God's rule or reign (Mark 1:15/Matt 3:2; Matt 4:17; 10:7; Luke 10:9, 11; 21:31) or the nearness of redemption (Luke 21:28).[505] This combination of *eggizō* and *to telos* occurs nowhere else in the NT, but the association is fitting, given the eschatological use of both terms in the NT.

The statement as a whole, in its terms and conceptuality, echoes the eschatological conviction of the early Christians that the advent of the Christ has ushered in an end time conceived either as the conclusion of all history or as the end of preceding eras and the prelude to a new era to follow. This critical moment in human history involves, from an Israelite and Christian perspective, events traditionally associated with the initial and final appearances of the Messiah/Christ, the commencement of the reign of God, salvation, and judgment—events expressly mentioned elsewhere in this letter as well (salvation: 1:3–5, 9, 10; 2:2; 3:22; judgment: 1:17; 2:23; 4:5, 17–18; first [1:11–12, 20] and final "revelation" of Christ: 1:7, 13; 4:13; 5:1, 4). The present time of the Christian community, from the letter's perspective, is thus located at the intersection of a period of human history now concluded and a new period of salvation soon to commence.

For the Romans, a sense of the end of the ages was stimulated by catastrophes such as the great fire in Rome in 64 CE or the cataclysmic struggle for imperial power in 68 CE or the devastating eruption of Mt. Vesuvius in 79 CE, when the towns of Pompeii and Herculaneum were annihilated. For Israel as well as members of the messianic community, the destruction of Jerusalem and the Temple, the "desolating sacrilege," was seen as a signal of the end (Mark 13:14–27/Matt 24:15–31/Luke 21:20–28). The Petrine author reflects this event in referring to Rome as "Babylon" in 5:13, a connection made in Israelite and Christian writings only after the destruction of Jerusalem and the Temple in 70 CE (see the NOTE on 5:13).

On the whole, however, our author refers to no portents or cosmic signals of the end time and indulges in no apocalyptic calculation concerning its occur-

---

[505] Cf. also "the day has drawn near/is at hand" (Rom 13:12); "for salvation is nearer [*eggyteron*] to us now than when we first believed" (Rom 13:11); "the coming [*parousia*] of the Lord has drawn near / is at hand" (Jas 5:8); "as you see the Day drawing near" (Heb 10:25); "the Lord is near / at hand" (Phil 4:5) and "the time is near / at hand" (Rev 1:3; 22:10).

rence.[506] His sense of the imminence of the end of the ages is rooted Christologically in the conviction of the Messiah's first appearance (1:12, 20), inaugurating the end time, and of the imminence of his final manifestion (5:4; cf. also 1:7, 13; 4:13; 5:1), bringing this age to a close. The interval between these first and final appearances is accompanied by the tribulations and sufferings of the just (1:6; 2:19–20; 3:14, 17; 4:1, 6, 12–19; 5:10), otherwise known as the "messianic woes," and the divine judgment of humankind now in process (4:17–18; cf. 1:17; 4:5) as a prelude to the final manifestation of Christ (1:7; 5:1), salvation (1:5b, 9; cf. 2:2), and the glorious vindication of the faithful (1:8; 5:1, 4, 10). His view of the end appears to involve not an eradication of the world but a termination of the current order of life and a transition to a new and glorious future. This intense eschatological consciousness, which our author shares with primitive Christianity in general,[507] serves here as elsewhere as a compelling motivation for behavior that is consonant with the conduct of Christ, the inaugurator of salvation, and the will of God, the judge.

W. Meeks (1993, 174–210) offers a brief but elegant survey of "senses of an ending" in the early Church. He aptly notes that this eschatological sense joins other religious features distinguishing the social boundaries of the Christian community from a pagan world "worried more about the beginning of the world than about its possible end" (Meeks 1993, 175, citing R. Lane Fox). Even more, this sense of an ending "disestablishes the world," with eschatological scenarios that "undermine the cultural system that masquerades as common sense," and helps to justify innovative Christian practices, as well as relativizing claims to power in the present and orienting all Christian moral behavior to "the divinely appointed future moment" (Meeks 1993, 180, 186–88). While 1 Peter is not treated explicitly in Meeks's discussion, the demarcating and dissestablishing roles of eschatology of which he speaks are evident in this letter as well, where the distinction between believers and nonbelievers is so clearly stressed.

This eschatological conviction was relaxed in later time. Therefore, this view, which is so determinative in 1 Peter, locates the letter within the early stage of the Christian movement and thus supports its dating in the last third of the first century.[508]

7b. *Therefore exercise sound judgment (sōphronēsate oun).* Awareness of the nearness of the end lends special eschatological urgency to the exhortations that follow. Similar use of the *oun pareneticum* to introduce exhortation is made in 2:1; 4:1; 5:1, 6 (cf. Nauck 1958).

---

[506] This is in contrast to such texts as Mark 13 par.; 1 Cor 15:20–28; 1 Thess 4:15–17; 2 Thess 2:1–12; 2 Pet 3:3–13; Rev 4:1–22:5.

[507] See Matt 24:45–25:13; Mark 13:33–37; Rom 13:11–14; Phil 4:5; Heb 10:25; Jas 5:8; 2 Pet 3:1–18; 1 John 2:28–29; see also Meeks 1983, 171–80; 1993, 174–88.

[508] On eschatology in Israel and Christian circles, see Davies and Daube 1954; Bowman 1962; Schüssler Fiorenza 1976b; Aune 1992; Petersen 1992; Nickelsburg 1992b; Allison 1994; and on the eschatological perspective of 1 Peter, Selwyn 1954.

exercise sound judgment (sōphronēsate). The imminence of the end is no cause for eschatological fever but requires clear-mindedness, sound judgment, and vigilance. Here the verb *sōphroneō* means not so much "keep sane" (as an alternative to being deranged [Mark 5:15/Luke 8:35; 2 Cor 5:13]) as "exercise sound, balanced judgment and self-discipline" (see Plato, *Gorg.* 491d). The related noun *sōphrosynē* likewise denoted self-control governed by moderation and a sense of balance and proportion. This self-control was made possible by self-knowledge and was reckoned by the Greeks as one of the four cardinal virtues (along with prudence, justice, and courage) characterizing the honorable person (cf. Danker 1982, 361–62). Self-control and avoidance of excess were regarded as essential for social harmony and group concord (Dio Chrys., *Orat.* 77–78; Thraede 1994). While in the Classical period *sōphrosynē* denoted the middle way in politics as a means for balancing conflicts, especially between commoners and elites, in the Hellenistic period it came to mean an individual's self-mastery, especially in regard to desire (for food, drink, sex), and was stressed by moralists as the antithesis to love of luxury, greed, and sexual immorality. In Israelite literature, the *Testament of Joseph,* as its assigned title (*peri sōphrosynēs*) indicates, was considered a treatment of this theme and Joseph its exemplar (*sōphrosynē, T. Jos.* 4:1, 2; 6:7 9:2, 3; 10:2, 3; *sōphrōn, T. Jos.* 4:2; cf. also *T. Benj.* 4:4; and for *sōphronōs, T. Jud.* 16:3).

Early Christianity likewise stressed the necessity of sound judgment and mastery of appetites and desires (1 Tim 2:9; 3:2; 2 Tim 1:7, 15; Titus 1:8; 2:2, 4, 5, 6) as an expression of personal holiness. But *sōphrosynē* was also used in the older Classical sense as an antithesis to hybris, the breach of social limits and of one's assigned status that was so deterimental to the unity of the community (Rom 12:3; cf. Dio Chrys., *Orat.* 3.80). Since the addressees have already abandoned the excesses of the Gentiles (4:3–4), it is more likely that here the author is urging sound judgment rather than moderation. As in the occurrence of the verb in Rom 12:3, the focus is on the Christian community rather than the individual, its harmony and well-being, and *sōphronein* in both instances involves a behavior contributing to communal solidarity.

and be alert (kai nēpsate). This is the second of three calls for alertness or vigilance (see also 1:13 and 5:8 and respective NOTES), all three of which are eschatologically conditioned. The same is true of the use of the verb *nēphō* in 1 Thess 5:6, 8, where "being alert" is contrasted with spiritual stupor.[509] Selwyn (1947, 380–82, 396, 453) hypothesizes that this motif of vigilance had a place in early Christian baptismal catechesis and instruction on persecution. In 1 Peter, being alert is complementary in sense to exercising sound judgment (cf. 1 Tim 3:2), and both verbs emphasize, in the light of the imminent end, the need for a disciplined life focused on the urgencies of the moment.

---

[509] On the necessity of eschatological watchfulness, see also Matt 24:42; 25:13; Mark 13:33, 35, 37; Acts 20:31; 1 Cor 16:13; and 1 Thess 5:1–10.

as an aid to praying (eis proseuchas). One urgency of the moment is a sound life of prayer. Earlier the author referred to the prayers of husbands and wives (3:7). Here the prayers of the entire community are in view and are said to require sound-mindedness and alertness (cf. Col 4:2–3; Eph 6:18). In 5:8 being alert (*nēpsate*) is combined with and close in sense to being vigilant (*grēgorēsate*), another action that is necessary for prayer (see Mark 14:39 par.). In the phrase *eis proseuchas* (lit., "for prayers") the preposition *eis* indicates purpose, as elsewhere in the letter (1:3, 4a, 5, 7, 22; 2:5, 7, 8, 9, 14, 21; 3:7f, 9; 4:2, 6, 7). Reicke (1964, 121) regards *eis proseuchas* as consecutive: "so as to bring about prayers," "so that it leads to prayers" (Reicke 1964, 139).[510] But sound judgment and alertness do not bring *about* prayer as much as they *determine and aid* its effectiveness, just as domestic harmony affects prayer in 3:7. The plural *proseuchas*[511] implies the plurality of acts of praying; for the singular *eis proseuchēn*, see *T. Naph.* 8:8. The association of prayer with sound judgment and alertness in the light of the eschatological hour is recurrent in the NT.[512] For a more conventional link between sound-mindedness and prayer, see *T. Jos.* 10:2.[513]

The concern for prayer is one of several topics that this unit of exhortation has in common with the exhortation in Rom 12. This exhortation enjoins not only sound-mindedness (Rom 12:3) and constant prayer (Rom 12:12c) but also love (Rom 12:9a, 10a; cf. 1 Pet 4:8); hospitality (Rom 12:13; cf. 1 Pet 4:9) and service (Rom 12:7; 1 Pet 4:9, 10–11) in connection with a discussion of the gifts (*charismata*) from God (Rom 12:3–8; cf. 1 Pet 4:10–11); compare also Rom 12:1–2 and 1 Pet 1:14–16. The similarities are not the result of literary dependency, however, but rather of the varying use of common tradition. Selwyn (1947, 375–419), noting further NT texts similar to 1 Pet 4:8–11, suspected reliance here, as elsewhere in the letter, on a "common catechetical tradition." But the texts vary too much in both form and terminology to demonstrate with certainty the existence, content and structure of a fixed catechetical tradition (see Goppelt 1993, 291–94). In the case of vv 7–11, "the most that can be cautiously claimed is the varied employment and adaptation of a common oral pattern of parenetic exhortation" concerned with the "reinforcement of internal group solidarity" (Elliott 1981/1990, 162).

8–11b. In conjunction with prayer as an expression of the relation of believers to God, attention is next directed to actions that maintain a sound relation

---

[510] So also Davids (1990, 156) and Beare (1970, 183): "so that you may give yourself to prayers."

[511] The presence of a definite article (*tas*) accompanying *proseuchas* is uncertain. It is contained in some MSS (P 049 𝔐) but is absent in several weighty other MSS (𝔓[72] א A B 044 etc.), though it may have been lost through haplography resulting from homoeoteleuton (*eis tas proseuchas*). No difference in meaning, however, is involved.

[512] See Matt 26:41/Mark 14:38; Luke 21:36; Col 4:2; 1 Thess 5:8, 17.

[513] On prayer in the Bible and its role in the life and worship of the biblical communities, see Delling 1962, 104–27; von Severus et al. 1972, 1976; Koenig 1992b. For a Christian treatise on prayer, see Tertullian, *On Prayer* (*De Oratione*).

of believers to one another, a combination recalling 2:17bc (reverence toward God and love of the brotherhood). Here, as in 3:8 and 5:5b, dispositions and behavior necessary for fortifying group cohesion are encouraged—specific actions of social and material support of fellow members that serve to express and sustain the internal solidarity of the household of God. Maintenance of internal cohesion and support was absolutely essential if Christians were to resist the reproach and encroachments of their environment (2:12, 15; 3:9, 13–17; 4:2–4, 12–16; 5:8–9) and to give a concerted witness to the glory of God (v 11; cf. 2:12; 4:16).[514]

8a. *Above all, maintain constant love toward one another (Pro pantōn tēn eis heautous agapēn ektenē echontes).* In the following call for community-maintaining actions, the community-reinforcing act of love is given priority ("above all," *pro pantōn*; cf. 1 Cor 12:12b–13:13).[515] The participle *echontes* ("maintain") is another participle used imperativally (see the NOTE on 1:14b) and, as elsewhere (2:12, 16; 3:16), conveys the sense of ongoing practice. This is reinforced by the adjective "constant" (*ektenē*), modifying "love," just as the adverb *ektenōs* functions in the virtually identical injunction of 1:22: "love one another constantly."

Love (agapē) is the emotional commitment and loyalty of believers to one another as fictive kin, brothers and sisters of the household of God. "Love," Clement of Alexandria observed (*Strom.* 2.9), is "consent to what pertains to reason, life, and manners, or in brief, fellowship in life, for it is the intensity of friendship and affection, with right reason, in the enjoyment of associates." Love lay at the heart of Jesus' teaching;[516] Paul reckoned love as "the more excellent way" (1 Cor 12:29; 13:1–13); and its indispensability is stressed continually in the NT.[517] Here in 1 Peter, the readers are reminded once again of the essential role love plays in uniting the communities of Asia Minor (see 1:22; 2:17; 3:8; and respective NOTES) as well as in linking these "beloved" recipients with the senders of the letter (2:11; 4:12; 5:14; and NOTES; cf. Spicq 1965, 359–63).

toward one another (eis heautous). This is the first of three such phrases (see also *eis allēlous*, v 9, and *eis heautous*, v 10) stressing the reciprocity and mutuality of love and of the other acts enjoined.

8b. *because "love covers a multitude of sins" (hoti agapē kalyptei plēthos hamartiōn).* The call for love is supported by an allusion[518] to Prov 10:12 (closer to the Hebrew text ["hatred stirs up strife, but love covers all offenses"] than to

[514] See Elliott 1981/1990, 145–48, 161–64; and Lamau 1988, 283–307.

[515] The same phrase occurs in Jas 5:12 where, however, it is the renunciation of oaths that is given priority.

[516] See Matt 5:43–48/Luke 6:32–36; Matt 19:19; Mark 12:28–33 par.; John 13:34–35; 15:12, 17; *Gos. Thom.* 25.

[517] E.g., Rom 12:9, 10; 13:8, 10; 1 Cor 16:14; Gal 5:14; Col 3:14; 1 Thess 4:9–10; 5:13; Heb 13:1; Jas 2:8; 1 John passim; cf. *1 Clem.* 49:1–50:7.

[518] Our author uses *hoti* (*because*, "for") to introduce biblical citations or allusions (cf. 1:16b and 5:5c); compare the similar function of *dioti* in 1:16a, 24a; and 2:6a.

the LXX). Since the LXX normally is cited in this letter, including quotations of or allusions to Proverbs (1 Pet 2:17; 3:6; 4:18; 5:5c), it is likely that the Hebrew form of this proverb had passed into Christian usage as a detached maxim (Best 1971, 159). The maxim is cited here as well as in Jas 5:20 (whose future verb "will cover" perhaps influenced the same variant here [𝔓[72] ℵ P 049 𝔐]).[519] The phrase "multitude of sins" (*plēthos hamartiōn*) occurs in neither the Hebrew nor the Greek version of the proverb but could have been derived from Ezek 28:17–18 or Sir 5:6.

The sense of the proverb is best understood in the light of Ps 32:1[31:1, LXX]: "Blessed is he (those, LXX) whose transgression(s) is (are) forgiven, whose sin(s) is (are) covered (*epekalyphthēsan*)" (cited also in Rom 4:7) and Ps 84:3 LXX: "You (God) have forgiven the people their transgressions; you have covered (*ekalypsas*) all their sins." Thus, "covers" (*kalyptei*) here and in all references to Prov 10:12 has the sense of "forgive" or "cancel."[520] The majority of manuscripts (including 𝔓[72] ℵ L P) read "will cover" (*kalypsei*), perhaps in assimilation to Jas 5:20, but the present tense is also well attested (A B C K and others) and fits the context which focuses on present conduct. Whether the "covering" or forgiveness involves the sins of the one who loves (Luke 7:47; *1 Clem.* 50:5; *2 Clem.* 16:4) or of those loved (*T. Jos.* 17:2) is not a relevant issue here, since the mutuality of Christian relations is in view and the forgiving of *all* sins is implied (so Reicke 1964, 122). As a loving God has covered (forgiven) believers' sins, so they are to cover (forgive) the sins of their brothers and sisters (cf. 1 Cor 13:7).[521] Mutual forgiving of sins, like constancy in love and loyalty, was essential to the ongoing cohesion of the community if it was to present a united front against attack from without.[522]

9. *[Be] hospitable to one another without complaint (philoxenoi eis allēlous aneu goggysmou).* "Akin to love," Clement of Alexandria noted (*Strom.* 2.9), "is hospitality, being a congenial art devoted to the treatment of strangers." Hospitality in fact is one practical expression of constant love (von Harnack 1908, 1:177–81), is associated with love also in Rom 12:9–13 and Heb 13:1–2, and constitutes another essential means for maintaining the cohesion of the community. Between "be hospitable" (*philoxenoi*) and "brotherly love" (*philadelphia*, 1:22), both terms from the root *phil-*, there is a social as well as linguistic relationship (see also *philēma*, "kiss of familial affection," 5:14).

The plural adjective *philoxenoi* in this imperatival context has imperatival force like the adjectives in 3:8, with a 2d-person pl. "be" (*este*) implied. *Philoxenos* (also 1 Tim 3:2; Titus 1:8) and its kindred noun *philoxenia* (Rom 12:13;

[519] Cf. also *1 Clem.* 49:5, and *2 Clem.* 16:4; and further, Tert., *Scorp.* 6.11; Clem. Alex., *Quis div.* 38; *Paed.* 3.12.91; Origen, *Hom. Lev.* 2.4; *Didask. Apost.* 2.3.3.

[520] Cf. *1 Clem.* 50:5; *Did.* 4:6; Pol. *Phil* 10:2; and for a related thought involving Peter, Matt 18:21–22.

[521] The association of both acts of forgiveness is traditional; see also Matt 6:12/Luke 11:4; Matt 6:14–15; 18:21–35; Luke 6:37; 7:47.

[522] On practical manifestions of love in the ancient Church, see von Harnack 1908, 1:147–98.

Heb 13:2) denote the generous receiving, sheltering, feeding, and support extended to a guest or stranger (*xenos*).

Hospitality, opening one's home to others, was a highly regarded virtue in the ancient world and the sign of generous and honorable families and groups. For the Greeks it was a sacred duty. "Zeus himself under the title *Zeus Xenios* guarded the sanctity of the relation between host and guest, and pursued any breach of hospitality with the vengeance of heaven" (Beare 1970, 185; cf. Homer, *Il.* 13.624; *Od.* 14.389). *Philoxenia,* in fact, often was associated with *philanthropia.*[523] Ancient Israel had been urged to be hospitable to the resident aliens among them on the grounds that they themselves had been vulnerable resident aliens in the land of Egypt (Exod 22:21; 23:9; Lev 19:33–34; Deut 10:18–19). Violations of the sacred hospitality code by the people of Sodom (Gen 19) and the Benjaminites (Judg 19) reckon among the most shocking of biblical stories, with the Sodomites often cited as a lurid example of gross immorality punished by God.[524] On the other hand, Abraham (Gen 18:1–18), Lot (Gen 19:1–8), Rahab (Josh 2:1–21), the widow of Zarephath (1 Kgs 17:8–16), and the Shunammite woman (2 Kgs 4:8–10), among others, served as glowing examples of generous hosts (see Heb 12:31; *1 Clem.* 10:7; 11:1–2; 12:1–8). The hospitality prized in Israel (see also CD VI 20; *T. Zeb.* 6:4–5; Josephus, *Ant.* 1.250–51) also was vigorously promoted in early Christianity.[525] Jesus singled out for praise women who showed him hospitality (Mark 14:3–9; Luke 7:36–50), chided one niggardly male host (Luke 7:44–46), and expected his disciples to be properly received and hosted (Matt 10:1–16/Mark 6:8–11/Luke 9:2–5; Luke 10:1–12), as he had been hosted (e.g., Mark 1:29–31 par.; 9:33; Luke 10:38–42; John 11:6; 12:1–8).

Christianity as a mobile missionary movement was especially dependent on the hospitality of its own members. Private households were the focus, locus, and basis of this mission.[526] The willingness of its members to offer hospitality to fellow-members was absolutely essential to its consolidation and growth and the condition sine qua non of the mission and expansion of the early Church. Both Peter[527] and Paul and his companions[528] were reliant on generous hosts. Other itinerant missionaries and bearers of the Christian message, such as traders, traveling artisans, and couriers of Christian correspondence, likewise were dependent on hospitable homes for their lodging, meals, and material support (*Did.* 11:3–6, 9, 12; 12:1–5; 13:1–7) and for further "networking." Hospitality, in fact, has been called "the chief bond which brought the churches a sense

---

[523] See Heraclides Ponticus, *Frg.* 3.6; Bolkestein 1979, 111–12, 121–22, 214–31.

[524] See Jer 23:14; Ezek 16:48–50; Matt 10:15; Luke 10:12, 17:29; Rom 9:29; 2 Pet 2:6; Jude 7.

[525] See Matt 25:31–46; Rom 12:13; 16:1–2; 1 Tim 3:2; 5:10; Titus 1:8; Heb 13:2; 3 John 5–8; *1 Clem.* 1:2; chs. 10–12; *Did.* 11:1, 4; 12:1; 13:1–3.

[526] See Acts 16:15, 31–34; 18:8; Rom 16:2, 3–5, 10, 11, 14–15, 23; 1 Cor 1:14, 16; 16:15–16, 19; Col 4:15; 2 Tim 4:19; Phlm 1–2; 2 Tim 4:19; 2 John 1, 13; 3 John 5–8.

[527] See Acts 9:32, 43; 10:32, 48; 12:12–17.

[528] See Acts 16:15, 32–34; 17:5; 18:1–3, 7; 20:7–12; 21:5, 8–14; Rom 15:24; 16:2, 3–5, 13, 23; 1 Cor 16:5–9; 2 Cor 1:16; Phil 1:5; 4:15–18; 2 Tim 3:13; Titus 3:12.

of unity" (Kooy 1962, 654). The shameful failure to offer hospitality, as in the case of Diotrephes (3 John 9–10) in contrast to the graciousness of Gaius (vv 3–8), came under severe censure (cf. Malherbe 1977 and Malina 1985, 1993a). Down through Late Antiquity and beyond, hospitality remained a cardinal feature of Christian service as, for instance, the Rule of St. Benedict illustrates.

In the present context, hospitality is a concrete expression of the love enjoined in the foregoing verse and a further means of maintaining the cohesion of the community. Like the content of the household tradition (2:18–3:7), this injunction calls for a practical demonstration of the familial integrity of the household of God. As strangers and resident aliens, the addressees of 1 Peter would be especially sensitive to the need for (or absence of) hospitality. Moreover, a reminder about its importance is especially appropriate in a circular letter such as 1 Peter, where the housing and hosting of its courier (5:12) and the sharing of the letter from one community to the next would be involved.

This stress on hospitality in a letter coming from Christians in Rome is consonant with the reputation that the Roman Church eventually gained as "preeminent in love" (Ign. *Rom. inscr.*) and a model of hospitality (letter of Dionysus, bishop of Corinth, to the Roman Church [in Eusebius, *Hist. eccl.* 4.23.10]). Von Harnack (1908, 1:178–90) in fact attributes the rapid rise of the Roman Church to supremacy in Western Christendom, not simply to its geographical position at the capital of the Empire or to its location as a seat of apostolic activity, but also to its generous hospitality and support of communities abroad.[529]

without complaint (aneu goggysmou). Goggysmos,[530] literally, "grumbling," "murmuring," "muttering" (see Exod 16:7–9; Acts 6:1; Phil 2:14; cf. Matt 20:11; John 6:41, 43; 1 Cor 10:10), would represent a veiled rather than direct expression of complaint; it would signal a hospitality offered only grudgingly rather than gladly. Hospitality, though a duty, could also be a burden, especially when accommodations and supplies were limited. The author of the *Didache* also encouraged hospitality (chs. 11–13) and giving without grumbling (4:7). He nevertheless was aware of itinerant freeloaders masquerading as apostles and prophets and provided his readers with a practical guideline for distinguishing the true from the phony: the latter ask for money (11:2) and seek more than two days of hospitality (11:5; 12:2).

10a. *Inasmuch as each has received a gift of grace (hekastos kathōs elaben charisma).* The adverb *kathōs* could mean "to the extent to which," "to the degree that" (BAGD 391, 392). But it is more likely that it has the same sense as the kindred adverb *katho* ("inasmuch as," 4:13), which introduces something

---

[529] On hospitality and its protocols in the ancient world, Israel, and Christianity, see also Hiltbrunner et al. 1972; Bolchazy 1977; Malherbe 1977; Koenig 1985, 1992a; Malina 1985, 1986b, 1993a; Matthews and Benjamin 1993, 82–95. On the hospitality of the Roman Church and its bearing on the place of origin of 1 Peter, see Elliott 1981/1900, 162–63, 281.

[530] The singular rather than the plural *goggysmōn* has superior manuscript attestation; for the phrase *aneu goggysmou* in connection with human kindness, see also *Pss. Sol.* 5:13.

already known and established. Here *kathōs* introduces the known fact that each has received a gift of grace, and this fact forms the basis of the imperatives that follow (vv 10b–11b).

Linguistically, *charisma* is a concrete manifestation (*-ma*) of *charis* ("grace") and the present statement makes this relation explicit. The "gift of grace" (*charisma*) that "each" (*hekastos*) member of the community has "received" (*elaben*) is a concrete manifestation of the *charis*, the grace and favor of God (v 10c) lavished on each and every believer (1:10, 13; 3:7; 5:5, 10, 12). A similar connection between *charismata* and *charis* is made by Paul in Rom 12:6 (Brandt 1931, 126). The expressions *received, of God's varied grace* (v 10c), *oracles of God* (v 11a), and *which God supplies* (v 11b) make it clear that a *charism* is indeed a *gift* of grace from God rather than an innate talent or inherited quality. As the following also makes clear, these gifts have the service of fellow-members as their purpose.

Elsewhere in the NT it is only Paul and Deutero-Pauline authors who employ the term *charisma*.[531] Paul, who may have introduced the term into Christian parlance, also considered a "charism" (*charisma*) to be a manifestion of divine "grace" (*charis*, Rom 12:6; cf. 12:3), bestowed by God (1 Cor 12:4–6, 28) on individuals (Rom 12:3; 1 Cor 7:7; 12:7–11). However, Paul's elaborations of several diverse forms of these gifts of grace and his connecting them with the Holy Spirit and the image of the body of Christ (Rom 12:6–8; 1 Cor 12:4–11, 28, 30) have no parallel here, so that any direct dependence of our author on these texts must be ruled out. In contrast to Paul, our author mentions only two charismatic actions, speaking and serving (v 11ab), makes no mention of the Spirit or the Lord, and relates these gifts not to the image of the body of Christ but to the root communal metaphor of this letter; namely, the community as the household of God. Believers are to exercise their charisms as "honorable household stewards of God's varied grace." The present context also makes clear that *charisma* is understood not as a gift conferring an authority that distinguishes some believers from others (contrast 2 Tim 1:6). It is, rather, a concrete manifestation of the divine grace given to *each* and every believer (v 10a) that makes them *all* stewards of divine grace. The use of this term thus reveals nothing concerning the structural organization of the Petrine communities or a possible notion of "charismatic authority," as Schröger (1981b, 110–14) has correctly observed.[532]

10b. *serve one another with it (eis heautous auto diakonountes)*. The plural participle *diakonountes*, like the foregoing adjective *philoxenoi*, does not mod-

---

[531] See Rom 1:11; 5:15, 16; 6:23; 11:29; 12:6; 1 Cor 1:7; 7:7; 12:4, 9, 28, 30, 31; 2 Cor 1:11; cf. 1 Tim 4:14; 2 Tim 1:6.

[532] On *charisma* in the NT, see Piepkorn 1971; Conzelmann 1974a; Wambacq 1975; Koenig 1978; Laurentin 1978; du Toit 1979; R. P. Martin 1992; K. Berger 1993. On the sociological concept of "charismatic authority" (which is not in view here), see the classic thesis of Weber (1978, 212–301; Eisenstadt 1968) and the study of Holmberg (1980) for its application to the issue of structure and authority in the early church.

ify a proximate finite verb (against S. Snyder 1995, 195–96) but has imperatival force, with "each" (*hekastos*) as its subject.[533] The imperative insists that the gift that each has received is to be exercised not for self-aggrandizement but for the service of others. The later exhortation to community elders (5:2–3) involves the same altruistic principle.

The verb *diakoneō*, along with its kindred terms *diakonos* and *diakonia*, is used with a range of meanings in the NT ("serve," "wait on someone at table," "care for," "help, support," "minister to," "aid," "act as spokesperson or emissary," "deliver something to a delegating authority"). Earlier in this letter it was used of the OT prophets, who were said to "serve" the believers in their prewitnessing to the sufferings and glories of the Christ (1:12). Here it has *gift of grace* as its object, "it" (*auto*) referring back to *charisma*. A literal rendering would be "serve it (i.e., the received gift of grace) for the good of one another (*eis heautous*)." In his first letter to the Corinthians, Paul spoke of "varieties of service" (*diakonōn*, 12:5) parallel with "varieties of charisms" (*charismatōn*, 12:4), and in Romans he mentioned "service" (*diakonia*, 12:7) as one of the various charisms evident in the community. In contrast to Paul, however, our author links "gift of grace" and "serving" not with the communal image of the body of Christ but with the communal image of the household ("as honorable household stewards," v 10c). This association is more natural than Paul's, since in the NT *diakoneō*, *diakonia*, and *diakonos* frequently are used of the task of domestic duties and of serving persons at table.[534]

J. N. Collins (1990), analyzing the use of this family of terms in non-Christian as well as early Christian sources, has challenged the conventional view that in the NT the words refer primarily to humble service. He contends that "the root idea expressed by these words is that of go-between, mediation, and authorized representation (Collins 1990, 193–94), a sense found in the NT as well as extrabiblical sources" (1990, 193–252). This conclusion, however, tends to minimize the importance of the non-Christian (1990, 150–68) and Christian texts where this family of terms also refers to menial domestic duties. Moreover, in the Lukan and Johannine tradition, according to which Jesus at the Last Supper (Luke 22:14–38; John 13–17; cf. Matt 20:26–28/Mark 10:43–45) compares himself to a servant (*diakonos*) serving (*diakoneō*) at table as a model for his followers to emulate (Luke 22:24–27; John 13:1–17), these terms have the clear sense of humble service, and allowance must be made for the influence of this critical Christological tradition on other NT use of these terms. In regard to our Petrine verse, Collins proposes the translation "communicating each gift among themselves" (1990, 232). But it is more likely that here and in v 11 *diakoneō* has the sense of the humble and mutual serving of gifts on each other's

---

[533] For the construction of the sing. *hekastos* with pl. verbs or pronouns, see also Matt 18:35; John 16:32; Acts 11:29; Eph 4:25; Heb 8:11; Rev 2:23; 5:8; 20:13; and BAGD 236.

[534] See Matt 8:15/Mark 1:31/Luke 4:39; Luke 10:40; 12:37; 17:8; John 2:5, 9; 12:2; Acts 6:2; Ign. *Trall.* 2:3; cf. Herm. *Sim.* 8.4.1; 8.4.2; see also Philo (*Contempl.* 71, 75) regarding the table service of the Israelite Therapeutae and *T. Job* 12:2, "to attend on the poor at table."

behalf. This would be consistent with the repeated emphasis on mutual humility (3:8; 5:5b, 6), the depiction of the believers as "household stewards" (see below), the image of the community as the household of God (2:5; 4:17 and passim), and the elevation of lowly household slaves as paradigms for the entire community (2:18–25).

10c. *as honorable household stewards of God's varied grace (hōs kaloi oikonomoi poikilēs charitos theou).* The comparative particle *hōs* ("as") occurs three times in this context (also 4:11a and 4:11b) and in all three cases indicates an actual quality or condition. For similar multiple uses of *hōs,* see also 1:24; 2:11–12, 13–14, 16; 3:7; 4:15–16.

honorable household stewards. An *oikonomos* was a domestic steward (usually a reliable slave [*oiketēs, doulos, diakonos*], Plut., *Lib. ed.* 7; *Mor.* 4B; Xen., *Oec.* 1.2; cf. Matt 24:45–51) who managed a household (*oikos*) with authority delegated by the householder (*oikodespotēs*; cf. Luke 12:42; 16:1, 3, 8; Gal 4:2). In a transferred sense the term could also designate a public official, such as a city treasurer (e.g., Erastus as *oikonomos* in Corinth, Rom 16:23), steward of the grain supply or, within the Mystery cults, a person in charge of household management and food distribution (Reumann 1958, 342–49).[535] Jesus used the example of a household steward to encourage in his listeners the virtues of both reliability (Luke 12:42–43, in conversation with Peter, 12:41) and shrewdness (Luke 16:1–8) at the present eschatological hour (cf. also Matt 24:45–51). Paul described himself, Apollos, and Cephas figuratively as "servants (*hyperētas*) of Christ and household stewards (*oikonomous*) of the mysteries of God" (1 Cor 4:1–2), who as such were obliged to be trustworthy. In Titus 1:5–10, community leaders (elders, overseers, vv 5, 6) were urged to serve as "stewards in God's household," possessing the qualities that would ensure sound household management: blameless character, respect for order, integrity, humility, patience, hospitality, not given to greed, and so on.[536] The term was not reserved for leaders alone, as Ignatius illustrates. In his letter to Polycarp of Smyrna, he applies the term to *all* of the Symrneans: "Labor with one another, struggle together, run together, suffer together, rest together, rise up together as God's household stewards and assessors and servants" (Ign. *Pol.* 6:1).

In similar fashion, the kindred term *oikonomia tou theou* ("management of the household of God") was employed metaphorically to depict Paul's responsibilty and service to the community conceived as "household" (Col 1:25; cf. 1 Cor 9:17; Eph 3:2; 1 Tim 1:4) or God's arrangements for human redemption—the plan and process of divine salvation (Eph 1:9–10; 3:9–10; cf. Reumann 1957, 1959, 1985; Michel 1967, 151–53). In these several cases the community is envisioned as a household and its members and leaders as

---

[535] For Hellenistic usage, see Landvogt 1908; Magie 1950, 2:850–52, 1026–27, 1513–14; and Reumann 1957, 1958, 1966–1967; for the LXX, NT, and early Church, see Michel 1967, 149–51; Reumann 1959, 1985; and Tooley 1966.

[536] For its application to bishops, see Ign. *Eph.* 6:1.

responsible household stewards/slaves. These stewards are subordinate to the Lord of the household and manage what God has provided.

In the network of house churches that comprised early Christianity, including the believers of Asia Minor, this kind of household agent would have been quite familiar. Used here metaphorically of all the believers (so also Reumann 1958, 339), *oikonomoi* is a particularly appropriate characterization of those who serve one another in a community symbolized as the "household [*oikos*] of God" (2:5; 4:17). It is also consistent with the familial terminology describing the community throughout the letter, the use of household management tradition (2:18–3:7), the idea of the community as being "built up" (*oikodomein*) by God (2:5; 5:10), and the encouragement of familial-like love (4:8) and hospitality (4:9). Just as *oiketai*, household servants/slaves, were addressed earlier as exemplary of the entire household of God (2:18–25), so here all believers are reminded of their common, mutual responsibilities in and to this household. Reciprocal love, hospitality, and mutual service are typical examples of the "generalized reciprocity" prevailing in a natural family, where members react generously to need without reckoning in terms of quid pro quo. This same kind of reciprocity should prevail as well in the household of God.[537]

The adjective *kaloi* modifying *oikonomoi* means "honorable," "manifestly excellent," as in 2:12 (see NOTE), where all the believers are also addressed. Here "honorable" would entail the responsible and trustworthy sharing of their respective gifts of grace on behalf of the entire household of God, as then illustrated in v 11.

of God's varied grace (poikilēs charitos theou). The expression, unique in the NT, makes clear the divine origin of the gifts of grace, playing on the relation of *charis* and *charisma*, as noted above. "Grace" (*charis*) is one of the chief terms employed in this letter to depict the favor, generosity, and beneficence that the believing community has experienced from God their Father and patron (1:2, 10, 13; 3:7; 5:5, 10, 12). It is this grace that has brought the household of God into existence and that is shared through household service. The divine source and empowerment of this service is emphasized again in v 11b.

The word *varied* (*poikilēs*) describes God's grace as having diversified facets or aspects or modes of concretization (cf. "the God of all grace," 5:10a). The adjective *poikilos* occurs only here in the NT in connection with *charis* and *charisma*; see also 1:6 ("various [kinds of] trials"); and Matt 4:24 ("various [kinds of] diseases"); Heb 2:4 ("various manifestations of power"). Beare (1970, 186) correctly observes that no use is made here of "the Pauline doctrine of the Spirit as the giver of the charismata." But having insisted incorrectly throughout his commentary that the author of 1 Peter is generally dependent on Pauline thought, he can only conclude that "it is remarkable how little he [the

[537] On the social implications of the relation among fraternity, hospitality, and household management, see also Elliott 1981/1990, 146–48; on Christian stewardship in general, see also Brattgard 1963.

Petrine author] understands, or at least how little he applies, the doctrine of the Spirit as it had been expounded by St. Paul." Rather than a cause to impugn the Petrine author's opaqueness, this text, like so many other theological formulations of this letter, constitutes clear evidence of the author's independence from Paul and his own form of appropriation of the common tradition.

11. God's varied grace is concretized in a plurality of gifts of grace (*charismata*). Paul lists many of these gifts (seven in Rom 12:6–8 and nine in 1 Cor 12:7–11; cf. Eph 4:11) and integrates them through use of the ecclesial metaphor of the "body of Christ." Our author, by contrast, makes no use of this metaphor and mentions only two kinds of gifts: speaking (v 11a) and serving (v 11b). This represents an early and still rudimentary division of labor, similar to that found in Acts 6:1–6 (cf. also Jas 2:12, "so speak and so act . . .") and the word-deed juxtapositions in Rom 15:18; Col 3:17; 1 Thess 1:5; 2 Thess 2:17. Thus in this regard also, 1 Peter belongs to a relatively early stage of ecclesiastical development, an issue that will be discussed further in connection with 5:1–5a.

Verse 11ab forms a balanced couplet of actions illustrating the general injunction in v. 10. The parallelism of this couplet is marked by balanced conditional statements, followed by elliptical clauses referring to God ("whoever . . . God") and a balanced use of *hōs* ("as"), introducing the similar actual quality of both actions, namely their divine source:

whoever speaks,
  [let that one do so]
    as [uttering] oracles of God;
whoever renders service,
  [let that one do so]
    as from the strength that God provides.

11a. *whoever speaks (ei tis lalei)*. The Greek in both v 11a and v 11b involves a conditional *ei* ("if"); in both cases, *ei tis* (lit., "if anyone") is rendered by "whoever."

speaks. The common verb *lalein* occurs some 298 times in the NT with reference to a wide diversity of speech and in this context could cover a variety of acts: proclaiming the good news and articulating convictions of faith; evangelizing as missionaries; speaking critically as prophets; speaking in tongues; instructing as teachers; sharing words of admonition, correction, encouragement, or comfort; defending the community verbally; or praying and praising God. Here the focus is on speaking and serving within the community, with *all* community members in view rather than just leaders in particular. This is made clear by the term "each" (v 10a) and the stress on mutuality ("one another," vv 8a, 9a, 10b).

[let that one do so] as [uttering] oracles of God (hōs logia theou). This formulation, like its parallel (v 11b), is an ellipsis in which the words in brackets appear implied. *Hōs* ("as") in both v 11a and v 11b identifies an actual quality, as it does elsewhere in this letter (see the NOTE on 1:14a; and BAGD 898 III.1).

Logia, the Greek plural of *logion*, are brief "sayings" or "utterances." When qualified by "of God" (*theou*), the term *logia* assumes the sense of "oracles" of God, that is, weighty words or promises originating with God.[538] Like its counterpart, "that God supplies" (v 11b), the phrase *logia theou* emphasizes God as the One who makes possible both speaking and serving. God supplies, as "householder," the grace that his "household stewards" put into action.[539]

11b. *whoever renders service (ei tis diakonei)*. The second half of the couplet similarly concerns a broad category of activity, namely, acts of practical service (cf. Brandt 1931, 125–32). J. N. Collins (1990, 215–16, 232) regards also this second occurrence of *diakoneō* as devoid of humble implications and renders the verb "ministering." But the same qualifications of his argument registered in the NOTE on v 10b apply here as well. The frequent use of *diakoneō* in the NT for menial serving and 1 Peter's stress on humility favor regarding the verb as designating a humble service to fellow household members. Its parallelism with the preceding verb "speak," moreover, is similar to the complementarity of "preaching the word of God" and "serving tables" mentioned in Acts 6:2; for the complementarity of serving and teaching, see Rom 12:7.

The charism of such service (see Rom 12:7; 1 Cor 12:5), like that of speaking, could embrace a variety (1 Cor 12:5) of related activities,[540] all related to meeting the material needs of fellow-believers.[541] Persons providing services as well as persons who preached or taught could assume positions of leadership. Paul denoted his apostolic work and that of his colleagues a "ministry" (*diakonia*) of "servants" (*diakonoi*).[542] Luke also spoke of the "ministry" (*diakonia*) of Paul and others (Acts 1:17, 25; 12:25; 20:24; 21:19). Eventually *diakoneō* and *diakonos* came to designate specific functions and functionaries within the community.[543] The Latin terms *minister* (translating *diakonos*) and *ministrare*

[538] See Ps 106[107]:11; Isa 5:24; Rom 3:2; Heb 5:12; *1 Clem.* 13:4; 19:1; *2 Clem.* 13:3.

[539] Bigg (1902, 174) regarded *logia* here as a reference to Scripture (cf. *1 Clem.* 53:1, where "oracles of God" [*logia tou theou*] could be taken as parallel to "the Sacred Scriptures" [*tas hieras graphas*]; cf. also 62:3). The readers he claimed, were being encouraged to speak as Scripture speaks, "with sincerity and gravity." But the parallel of this statement in v 11b does not allow this sense. The point of both qualifications is that the gifts of both speech and service are supplied by God.

[540] E.g., providing food, shelter, and hospitality (Acts 6:1–2; cf. Matt 25:43–44; Jas 2:15); aiding the poor and needy (Matt 25:43–44; Acts 6:1; 11:29; 2 Cor 8:4; 9:12–13; Jas 1:27); healing of and caring for the ill (Matt 25:44–45; Jas 5:14–15); visiting the imprisoned (Matt 25:43–44; Heb 13:3); providing a house for assembly (1 Cor 16:15, 19); serving as supportive patrons (Mark 15:41; Luke 8:3; Rom 16:1–2—all are women). On occasion Paul identified the collection that he gathered for the poor in Jerusalem as a *diakonia* (1 Cor 16:15; 2 Cor 8:4; 9:1, 12, 13; 11:8; cf. also Rom 15:25, 31; 2 Cor 8:20; and Acts 11:29; 12:25).

[541] See also Acts 19:22; 2 Tim 1:18; 4:11; Phlm 13; Heb 6:10; Rev 2:19; cf. also Reicke 1951, 19–164.

[542] See Rom 11:13; 1 Cor 3:5; 2 Cor 4:1; 5:18; 6:3; 2 Cor 6:4; 11:23; 1 Thess 3:2; cf. Eph 3:7; 4:12; 6:21; Col 1:7, 23, 25; 4:17; 1 Tim 1:12; 4:6; 2 Tim 4:5.

[543] See Phil 1:1; 1 Tim 3:8, 10, 12, 13; *1 Clem.* 42:4, 5; *Did.* 15:1; Ign. *Eph.* 2:1; *Magn.* 2:1; 6:1; 13:1; *Trall.* 2.3; 3:1; 7.2; *Phld.* 1:1; 4:1; 7:1; 10:1, 2; 11.1; *Smyrn.* 8:1; 10:1; 12:1, 2; *Pol.* 6:1; Pol. *Phil* 5.2; Herm. *Vis.* 3.5.1; *Mand.* 2.6; 12.3.3; *Sim.* 9.26.2.

(translating *diakonein*) form the basis of the English "minister" and "to minister," respectively. These terms today are applied ecclesiastically to an ordained minister or politically to a functionary of the state. Neither of these modern usages, however, should be confused with the sense of the family of *diakon*-terms employed in the NT to refer to various forms of service and mutual aid practiced by all believers.

In our Petrine text it is clear that the author is referring not to leadership roles of specific members but to the mutual responsibilities *of all of the believers to and for one another* (*eis heautous, eis allēlous*; cf. Cothenet 1974, 144–47). The charismatic quality of this serving lies in the fact that, like speaking, it illustrates the general statement of v 10 and, like speaking, is made possible by God.

[let that one do so] as from the strength that God supplies (hōs ex ischyos hēs chorēgei ho theos).[544] Like its foregoing parallel, this is another elliptical statement in which some words, such as "let that one do so," are implied. Again, as in v 10, God is explicitly identified as the one who enables Christian serving, a fact that determines the sense of v 11a as well. For God as the source of *ischys* ("strength," "power," "might"), see also Ps 117[118]:14 and for the idea in general, Phil 2:13. Stress on God's power also occurs at both the beginning (1:5) and end (5:6, 10, 11) of the letter.

supplies. The verb *chorēgeō* (only here and in 2 Cor 9:10 in the NT) originally meant "to be in a chorus" (performing on the Greek stage), then "to supply a chorus," and eventually "to furnish or supply" anything. A wealthy citizen, as *chorēgos*, provided for the equipment and training of a chorus making a dramatic or religious presentation (Arist., *Pol.* 8.4.6) such as the Great Dionysia at Athens. The verb belongs to a broader semantic field of terms indicating the generosity of a benevolent patron (Danker 1982, 323–36). Thus the concept of God as a benevolent patron aiding human undertakings could be behind this expression (cf. 2 Macc 1:24–25, where a prayer refers to God as both *ischyros*, "powerful," and "the only provider," *ho monos chorēgos*).[545]

Speaking and serving with the awareness that God makes this possible are further examples of being "mindful" of God (see 2:19; 3:21; cf. also 3:4c and 5:2c). Together these actions constitute basic forms of mutual service within the Christian community. The rudimentary and generalized forms of this activity—speaking and serving—as well as the fact that these charisms are exercised by each member (v 10) rule out any possibility that specialized ministries or "offices" of leadership are in view here (against Windisch and Preisker 1951, 76–77; and Reicke 1964, 121). Here it is all of the members of the community that are addressed, and only later in his exhortation to elders (5:1–4) does the author turn to the issue of leaders and their responsibilities. Nor is there any indication that at this time the terms *diakoneō* (*diakonia, diakonos*), *lalein*, or

---

[544] The reading of some later MSS (P 𝔐), "as from the strength *as* God provides," most likely has resulted from a mistaking of *hēs* ("which," referring to *strength*) for the similar-appearing term *hōs* ("as"), a misreading occasioned by the initial *hōs* in this phrase.

[545] For a similar sense of *epichorēgeō*, see 2 Cor 9:10; Gal 3:5; Col 2:19; 2 Pet 1:11.

oikonomos had become technical terms reserved for church leaders. As Schröger (1981b, 110–14) has aptly noted in criticism of contrary views, vv 7–11 have no bearing on the vexed issue of charismatic versus hierarchical authority or "a Spirit-controlled freedom of the Church's life" in contrast to a "one-sided, authoritarian conception of church government" as von Campenhausen (1969, 82) and others (Goldstein 1975, 12–17) would have it. The issue here is not ecclesiastical structure and authority but mutual acts of service necessary for ensuring a united front against external hostility.

1 Peter reflects a period of the Church's development when, apart from elders, there was no development of specialized ministries, offices, and hierarchical organization (so Selwyn 1947, 219; contrast Holmberg 1980, 109–11). This points to a date of composition preceding this development and thus prior to *1 Clement* (cf. chs. 40–41, 42), approximately 96 CE, and the letters of Ignatius (ca. 110 CE) that presume a hierarchical distinction of single bishop, presbyters, and deacons.[546]

11c. *so that in all things God may be glorified through Jesus Christ (hina en pasin doxazētai ho theos dia Iēsou Christou).* A final purpose clause (*hina* "so that") with the pres. pass. subjunctive (*doxazētai*) sums up the goal of all of the previously encouraged conduct. All charisms originate with God and have the glorification of God as their ultimate goal.

The phrase *in all things (en pasin)* embraces all of the actions and aspects of congregational life described in the foregoing verses. With the *all* (*pantōn*) of vv 7 and 8, *pasin* forms part of the literary inclusion framing this unit and underlines the inclusivity of its thought.

God may be glorified. The idea of the glorification of God through behavior is traditional in Christian as well as in Israelite circles[547] and is prominent in 1 Peter as well. The sentiment of the present verse echoes the idea of 2:12 that the glorification of God is the goal of Christian life. Glorifying God with action is stressed also in 4:16; and the glory that is God's is acknowledged in 4:11d. The enumeration of reciprocal duties in *1 Clem.* 38:1–4 concludes on a similar note: "Since, therefore, we have everything from him [God], we ought in everything to give him thanks; his is the glory forever and ever. Amen." In later time this vision of Christian life as focused on the glorification of God is admirably reflected in the mottoes of the Order of St. Benedict, *in omnibus*

---

[546] On the relation between the serving mentioned in 4:10–11 and the leadership of the elders treated in 5:1–5, see Elliott 1966b, 192–96. For a refutation of the proposal (Schröger 1976) that 4:10–11 and 5:1–5 derive from different letters of different authors and that the presbyterial form of leadership discussed in ch. 5 was intended to supplant the charismatic form of service presumed in 4:10–11, see Elliott 1981/1990, 163–64. On the "distribution of power" within the local Pauline churches, charismatic authority, and its institutionalization, see Holmberg 1980, 95–121, 137–204. On ministry and ministries in the NT, see Schweizer 1961; Delling 1962, 151–62; Delorme, ed. 1974; Schröger 1976; 1981b, 110–24.

[547] See Matt 5:16; John 15:8; Rom 15:6; 1 Cor 6:20; 10:31; 2 Cor 9:12–13; Gal 1:24; 2 Thess 3:1; 1 Cor 10:31. Philo (*Spec.* 1:317) similarly held up the "honoring of God" as the goal of life and "the indissoluble bond of all the affection which makes us one."

glorificetur Deus, and of John Calvin and the Society of Jesus, *ad maiorem Dei gloriam*.

The formula *through Jesus Christ*, as in 2:5, expresses the mediatorial role of Jesus Christ, as also in the doxologies of Rom 16:27 and Jude 25 (cf. also *1 Clem.* 58:2; 61:3). Just as believers offer spiritual sacrifices acceptable to God "through Jesus Christ" (2:5), so they who are one "in Christ" (3:16; 5:14; cf. 5:10) glorify God through Jesus Christ.

Together vv 10–11 thus stress the divine origin of the gifts of grace, their distribution among all believers, their contribution to the support of the household of God, and their ultimate goal, the glorification of God. The purpose clause summing up this goal of glorification logically is followed by a glorifying doxology.

11d. *His is the glory and the power forever, amen (hōi estin hē doxa kai to kratos eis tous ainōnous tōn aiōnōn, amēn)*. A doxology acclaiming the glory and power of God ends this unit of exhortation, similar to the doxology in 5:11 with which the letter as a whole concludes. The expression is not a wish (as the RSV and NIV suggest) but a statement of fact. NT doxologies never employ optatives; when verbs are included in doxologies (e.g., Rom 1:25; 2 Cor 11:31), they are indicative. The indicative is consistent "with the NT conviction that God's glory and honour are His by right" (J. N. D. Kelly 1969, 182).

Some scholars regard Jesus Christ as the antecedent of "his" (*hōi*, lit., "to him") and thus the object of the doxology (e.g., Selwyn 1947, 220; Michaels 1988, 252–54). In the NT, however, only rarely are doxologies addressed to or statements about Christ (2 Tim 4:18; 2 Pet 3:18; Rev 1:6), and giving honor both *to Christ* (v 11d) and *through Christ* (v 11c) would be contradictory. On the other hand, God as the focus of the doxology (so J. N. D. Kelly 1969, 181–82; Davids 1990, 162; Goppelt 1993, 306) is in keeping with the predominant number of NT doxologies and eulogies, which are offered to God, not Christ.[548] Moreover, it is God, not Christ, to whom the doxology of 5:11 refers (*autōi* looking back to *autos* [referring to God] in v 10). Finally, God as the antecedent of *his* is supported by the threefold mention of "God" in vv 10–11 and the fact that it is God who is glorified in v 11c (as in 2:12 and 4:16; cf. also 4:14, referring to God's glory). The theology of 1 Peter is fundamentally theocentric (Frankemölle 1987, 64), with God viewed as the source of life (1:2, 3; 2:13; 4:19; 5:5c–7, 10) and central object of Christian worship and praise (1:3, 21; 2:9, 12; 4:16; 5:11). Jesus Christ, on the other hand, is the one raised, glorified, and honored by God (1:3, 21; 2:4; 3:18, 22; cf. 1:11; 4:13; 5:1) and mediator of the believers' relation to God (1:3; 3:18d, 21; 4:11c).

the power (to kratos). *Kratos*, here and in the doxology of 5:11, denotes "power," "might," "authority," "rule," and "dominion." Absent in Pauline dox-

---

[548] See Luke 2:14; Rom 1:25; 9:5; 11:36; 2 Cor 1:3; 11:31; Eph 1:3; 3:20–21; Phil 4:20; 1 Tim 1:17; 6:16; 2 Tim 4:18; Heb 13:20–21; Jude 24–25; 1 Pet 1:3; 5:11; Rev 5:13; 7:12—all still under the influence of synagogue prayer.

ologies, "power" does appear in other doxologies, along with "glory."[549] Our author uses the kindred term *krataian* in speaking of the "powerful hand of God" (5:6). Earlier he referred to God's power (*dynamis*), by which the believers are guarded (1:5), as well as more immediately to the "strength" that God provides (v 11b).[550]

forever (eis tous aiōnas tōn aiōnōn), literally, "to the ages of ages." *Tōn aiōnōn* is absent in several manuscripts, including 𝔓[72], which also omits the definite articles with "power" and "glory" and *tōn aiōnōn* again in the doxology of 5:11. The fuller phrase, however, is frequent in the Psalms (*eis ton aiōna tou aiōnos*: 9:6, 37; 44[45]:7, 18; 47[48]:15; 51[52]:10; 111[112]:3, 9; 144[145]:1) and functions here, as elsewhere (Gal 5:4; Eph 3:21; Phil 4:20; 1 Tim 1:17; 2 Tim 4:18; Heb 13:21; Rev 1:6), as a solemn formulaic ending to the doxology by affirming the everlasting nature of God's glory and power.

amen (amēn). This Hebrew term, which was taken over in transliterated form in Greek, Latin, and modern languages, means "firm," "reliable," "valid." As a confirmatory response ("So be it!" "It is indeed true!"), it expressed acceptance of a commission (1 Kgs 1:36; Jer 11:5), subjection to a curse or threat (Num 5:22; Deut 27:15, 26), or confirmation of a eulogy, promise, prayer, doxology, or benediction.[551] It was employed frequently by Jesus as an affirmation of the certainty of a statement (Matt 5:18, 26; Mark 10:15, 29; John 1:52; etc.). In Greek it is translated *genoito* (Deut 27:15–26; 3 Kgdms 1:36; Jer 11:5; Ps 106:48) or *alēthōs* (Jer 35:6). Its use in Israelite synagogue worship influenced Christian liturgical usage (1 Cor 14:26), especially as a response to or conclusion of doxologies.[552] Here, as in other letters of the NT, *amēn*, though reflecting the language of worship, appears to have lost its original character of a congregational response and serves as the precatory affirmation by the writer himself of the foregoing doxology (Shimada 1966, 420–21).

The doxology logically follows the idea of glorifying God and punctuates one major section of the letter. It echoes the doxological note on which 2:11–4:11 began (2:12) and precedes a similar doxology with similar function in 5:11. Both doxologies conform to the general pattern involving four elements (Deichgräber 1967, 25–32): (1) an addressee (most frequently God) in the dative case (*tōi, hōi, autōi, soi*); (2) ascription of honor ("glory," alone or with other synonyms); (3) duration of praise, usually "forever"; and (4) a confirmatory

---

[549] See 1 Tim 6:16; Jude 24–25; Rev 1:6; 5:13; *1 Clem.* 64; 65:2; *Mart. Pol.* 20:2; cf. also Eph 1:19; 6:10; Col 1:11; *2 Clem.* 17:5; and the alternative *hē dynamis kai hē doxa* in variants of the secondary conclusion of the Lord's Prayer (Matt 6:13).

[550] For a similar association between *ischys* and *kratos*, see Job 12:16, and the expression "the power of his strength" in Eph 1:19 and 6:10.

[551] See 1 Chr 16:36; Neh 8:6; 2 Esd 18:6; Tob 8:8; 3 Macc 7:23; 4 Macc 18:24; 1QS I 18b–20; Matt 6:13; and Stuiber 1992.

[552] See 1 Pet 5:11; Rom 1:25; 9:5; 11:36; 16:27; Gal 1:5; Eph 3:21; Phil 4:20; 1 Tim 1:17; 6:16; 2 Tim 4:18; Heb 13:21; Jude 25; Rev 1:6; 5:14; 7:12; 19:4; Shimada 1966, 415–21.

"Amen."[553] In 1 Peter, both doxologies illustrate the doxological tone of the letter as a whole and its repeated celebration of the honor and glory of God.

GENERAL COMMENT

This unit of thought shifts the focus of attention from the relation of believers toward society (2:11–4:6) to their relations with one another within the Christian community. Certain terms and concepts in this unit are reminiscent of Pauline thought, but the passage as a whole displays affinity with a broader body of oral Christian catechetical and hortatory tradition (Selwyn 1947, 363–466) known to the Christians of Rome (Elliott 1981/1990, 162–63, commenting on Selwyn's thesis). However similar to scattered Pauline motifs this material might be (an adaptation of the "Pauline heritage," according to Goldstein [1975, 11–24], but rejected by Schröger 1981b, 112–14), the exhortation in its structure, combination of motifs, and rationale is uniquely Petrine. The positive injunctions here present an alternative to the negative imperatives in 4:1–6 (so Schutter 1989, 71–74). But whereas 4:1–6 concerns the believers' relation to *outsiders*, 4:7–11 focuses on behavior *within the community*.

A reminder at the outset that "the end of all things is at hand" lends special eschatological urgency to the exhortations that follow. Along with exclusive worship of God, allegiance to Jesus as the Messiah, and dedication to mutual support, it was this sense of finality and imminence of divine judgment that set the messianic community so much apart from its contemporaries. At the same time, the encouragement to sound-mindedness, vigilance, love, forgiveness, hospitality, communication, and service has as its aim the securing of the unity of the community so necessary for its confronting hostility with a unified front. This focus on the internal cohesion of the community reinforces similar exhortation occurring earlier (1:21–22; 2:1, 17bc; 3:7, 8) and later (5:1–5a, 5b–7) in the letter.

The forms of reciprocal conduct encouraged here—love, hospitality, mutual service, and communication—are those characteristic of a biological family and are now required of the family of faith. The communal solidarity maintained by this conduct will not only ensure internal unity but will also put the lie to any accusations of disregard for social harmony. Indeed the actions of mutual support encouraged here could even make the community attractive to outsiders (2:12). These actions are conceived not as expressions of innate personal qualities but as behavior made possible by God. They are "charisms," concrete actualizations of divine grace (*charis*) intended for the nurturing of the entire community. In contrast to Paul, however, these charisms are not linked to the Pauline ecclesial image of the "body of Christ" but to the chief communal metaphor of this letter, the household of God. The believers are

[553] On the formulary character of the doxologies in 4:11d and 5:11, see also Shimada 1966, 396–421.

exhorted to exercise their charisms as "honorable household stewards of God's varied grace."

The several references to "each" (v 10) and "anyone" (translated "whoever," v 11) are inclusive and make no distinction between sex or class or status; all members of the community are inclusively in view. The "charisms" of which 1 Peter speaks are not phenomena that distinguish some members from others in status but are gifts of divine grace enjoyed by each member equally. Inasmuch as each member of the community is said to have received a charism, the concern here is not with any form of "charismatic authority" (distinguishing "charismatics" from other members) but with the mutuality and reciprocity of the believers' aid to one another ("toward one another," "serve one another").

At the same time, as manifestations of "God's varied grace," these gifts are not uniform but pluriform in nature. Their rudimentary differentiation here—speaking words that God supplies and serving with the strength provided by God—points to a rudimentary division of labor within the community and to activities involving all Christians rather than simply the leaders. The responsibilities of the latter, identified as elders in 5:1, will be treated later in 5:1–4. None of the terms employed in the present context (such as *charisma, oikonomoi, diakoneō,* or *laleō*) exclusively designates functions of leadership, authority, or "office." What is in view here is not the social structure of the community but its unity. Like the maintaining of love and the offering of hospitality, these terms instead describe activities of *every* believer for the *mutual* edification and cohesion of the community. *Diakoneō, diakonia,* and *diakonos* (rendered in Latin *ministro, ministerium, minister,* respectively) constitute the most predominant family of terms in the NT for designating Christian service to one another on behalf of the gospel. While used also of leaders, they are not reserved for denoting leadership functions in particular. Their usage and contexts, however, form the proper biblical starting point for any subsequent conception of Christian ministry, whether general or clerical. They express the unequivocal conviction of the nascent church that the ministration of the gospel is shaped by the paradox of a *crucified* Messiah and a *servant* Lord. "Service" is the operative word for followers of the servant Lord, not "rule" and certainly not "domination" (cf. 5:3). Service is discipleship always exercised in the shadow of the cross.

The idea of humility stressed so frequently in 1 Peter in all likelihood determined the sense of the service spoken of in 4:7–11: mutual acts of humble service of all believers to one another made possible by the benevolent grace of God. Support for one's fellow household members is a manifestation of having been graced by God. Whatever form this support might take, be it acts of speech or actions of mutual service, it is essential to remember that it is God who has made it possible. For this reason and in this way God is to be glorified. All the actions enjoined here contribute to the cohesion of the community but have as their ultimate goal the glorification of God (v 11c). Just as all charisms derive from God, so all are to be exercised for the greater glory of

God. Glorification of God is the chief aim of Christian conduct according to this letter (see also 2:12; 4:16) and forms a key theme by which 2:11–4:11 is framed and in turn united with the exhortation that follows. A solemn glorification of God (v 11d, "his is the glory . . .") evoked by this reference to glorification (v 11c) brings the unit to a fitting doxological close.

The material that follows (4:12–5:11), as will be seen, does not introduce new subjects but reprises, recaptitulates, and expands upon ideas and themes central to 1:3–4:11, often with the very same terminology. The doxology in 4:11 and its accompanying "amen" by no means serve as end-markers for 1:3–4:11.[554] In the NT writings, doxologies occur at various places within a document and only rarely in a final position. In the great majority of cases they provide, as here, a solemn conclusion *only to a foregoing unit of thought.*[555] Of the more than twenty-five doxologies in the NT, only three conclude a document.[556] Likewise, of the ten doxologies in *1 Clement,* nine are internal (20:12; 32:4; 38:4; 43:6; 45:7–8; 50:7; 61:3; 64:1), and only the last (65:2) concludes the letter (see also *Mart. Pol.* 22:3; and *Diogn.* 12:9). There is thus no compelling reason for viewing 4:11 as anything more than a formal glorification of God prompted by the immediately preceding verse, which affirms that "in all things God is glorified." This in turn eliminates a key building block of the theories postulating the composite rather than integral nature of 1 Peter. The doxology of 1 Pet 4:11 constitutes not a punctuation but a pause, a glorification of God that also prepares for what immediately follows (4:12–19). The glory that is God's is also the glory that rests upon suffering believers (4:14) and is the glory that they will acknowledge in their suffering as Christians (4:16).

For studies on 1 Pet 4:7–11, see Cothenet 1974; Elliott 1966b, 192–96; 1981/1990, 145–48, 162–64; Hiebert 1982c; Kline 1963; Lamau 1988, 283–307; Ogara 1936b; Schmauch 1967; Schröger 1976, 1981b; Selwyn 1954; Shimada 1966; Sisti 1965; Spicq 1965, 1966.

---

[554] As noted by Shimada (1966, 407–15), Dalton (1969, 1251), Lohse (1954/1986, 50), and Goppelt (1993, 307).

[555] See Rom 11:36; Gal 1:5; Phil 4:20; Eph 3:20–21; 1 Tim 1:17; 6:16; 2 Tim 4:18; Heb 13:20–21.

[556] See Rom 16:25–27 (v 27 constituting a secondary, non-Pauline addition); Jude 24–25; and 2 Pet 3:18.

VI. Honor and Joy in Suffering, Communal Unity, and Trust in God (4:12–5:11)

◆

VI. A. Suffering and Doing What Is Right as Joyous Solidarity with Christ and Honor with God (4:12–19)

4:12a Beloved,
do not be surprised at the fiery ordeal coming upon you to test you,
12b as though something surprisingly strange were happening to you;
13a but, inasmuch as you share in the sufferings of the Christ,
13b rejoice now
13c so that you may also rejoice with exultation when his glory is revealed.
14a If you are reproached because of Christ,
14b how honored [you are]
14c because the divine Spirit of glory rests upon you.
15 To be sure, let none of you suffer as a murderer,
or a thief,
or a wrongdoer,
or as a meddler in the affairs of others.
16a If, however, [any of you suffers] as a Christian,
16b you should not feel shamed,
16c but should rather glorify God with this name.
17a For [now is] the propitious time for judgment to begin
with the house(hold) of God.
17b And since [it begins] first
with us,
17c what [will be] the end
of those who do not obey the good news of God?
18a And "since
the righteous person is saved only with difficulty,
18b what will become of
the impious and sinner?"
19a So then, let those suffering in accordance with God's will
19b also entrust their lives to a faithful Creator in [their] doing what is right.

INTRODUCTION

In the foregoing unit (4:7–11), our author instructed the addressees on their responsibilities toward *one another* in the interest of the *internal unity* of the community. Now he returns to the knotty issue of their relation to hostile *outsiders* and the suffering they are undergoing. The positive value of this suffering is stressed, along with the joyful prospect of the ultimate salvation and vindication of those who persevere in doing good and entrust themselves to God's care.

1 Peter 4:12–19; 5:1–5a; and 5:5b–11 form the concluding section of the letter. The topic of suffering forms an inclusion (4:12–13/5:11) framing 4:12–5:11 and is taken up in each of the three subunits (4:12, 13, 14, 15, 16, 17; 5:1b; 5:9, 10). Each of these subunits likewise stresses the relation of believers to God (4:14, 16, 17–18, 19; 5:2; 5:5b–7, 10–11), and each makes reference to the future glory, salvation, or blessing awaiting the faithful (4:13, 18; 5:1c, 4; 5:6, 10). The letter thus concludes with an intensified eschatological assurance that the innocent suffering of the faithful will ultimately be vindicated by a faithful Creator.

The structure of 4:12–5:11 mirrors that of 2:11–4:11. Both sections open with a direct address, "beloved" (4:12; cf. 2:11), which is followed by a general exhortation to all concerning their conduct in the public sphere (4:12–19; cf. 2:11–12, 13–17). This is followed by instruction to specific domestic or internal groups (5:1–4, 5a; cf. 2:18–25; 3:1–6, 7), which in turn is followed by a resumed appeal to all believers (5:5b; 6–9; cf. 3:8–9), supported by a biblical citation (5:5c; cf. 3:10–12) or allusion (5:7, 8). Both sections end with a concluding doxology (5:10–11; cf. 4:11d). The consistency of the compositional pattern further illustrates the literary integrity of the letter in its entirety.

Thematic connections between 4:12–19 and 1:3–4:11 include the focus on unjust suffering (4:12–19; cf. 2:19–20; 3:13–17) resulting from reproach (4:14, 16; cf. 2:12; 3:9, 16; 4:4), the testing of faith through suffering and joy in suffering (4:12; 1:6–7), and honor for the righteous sufferer (4:14; cf. 3:14); the community as the house(hold) of God (4:17; cf. 2:5); salvation of believers (4:17; cf. 1:5, 9; 2:2; 3:21) and judgment of the disobedient (4:17b; cf. 1:17; 2:7b–8; 3:16, 20a; 4:5); and perseverance in doing what is right (4:19; cf. 2:20; 3:6, 11, 13, 17). On the whole, 4:12–5:11, in its language, themes, eschatological orientation, and function, reiterates, recapitulates, and amplifies central issues of the foregoing sections of the letter. Balancing the introduction of 1:3–12, it forms with this opening section a literary inclusion framing the body of the letter as a whole (1:3–5:11).

Indications of the literary, thematic, and rhetorical continuity between 4:12–5:11 and 1:3–4:11 were insufficiently appreciated by earlier scholars, who postulated a definitive break between 4:11 and 4:12 and regarded 1:3–4:11 and 4:12–5:11 as originally independent units of material, only secondarily combined. Evidence alleged to indicate a definitive break between 4:11 and 4:12 included the following: (1) The doxology of 4:11 and its "amen" mark the literary conclusion of the material in 1:3–4:11. (2) The suffering mentioned in

1:3–4:11 appears only potential, while from 4:12 onward actual suffering is presupposed. (3) In 1:6 and 8, joy is presented as a present reality, but in 4:13 as lying in the future. Thus 4:12–5:11 presumes a historical situation different from 1:3–4:11. (4) The notation in 5:12, "I have written briefly," seems an apt description of 4:12–5:11 but not of an entire letter of some 1675 words. The supposedly different bodies of material, in turn, were variously described as a baptismal homily[557] (1:3–4:11) addressed to newly baptized believers, to which a letter (4:12–5:11) was later attached, when their suffering had become an actual reality;[558] differing parts of a eucharistic liturgy (Windisch and Preisker 1951; Cross 1954); or parts of two independent letters composed at different times and subsequently combined (Moule 1956–1957).

The fatal weaknesses of these partition and compilation theories, however, are their exaggeration of alleged "discontinuities" in the present writing and its presumed situation and their lack of consensus on the genre of the original components of 1 Peter. The combination of a baptismal homily and a letter, moreover, lacks any analogy in the literature of the early Church. Finally, "there is not the least textual support in extant manuscripts for hypotheses of this nature" (Hillyer 1992, 6). For these compelling reasons, these theories have been justly rejected by the majority of recent scholars.

The doxology in 4:11d does not mark the finale of a document but only the conclusion of a major unit of this letter, as is the case with most NT doxologies that occur at various places in a writing (see the NOTE on 4:11). The doxology is motivated by the doxological point of 4:11c, that in all things God is to be glorified.

Second, the nature and cause of the suffering envisioned from 4:12 onward is no different from that assumed in 1:3–4:11; thus, a similar situation is assumed throughout the letter. Earlier the *possibility* of suffering is allowed for in some cases (1:6 [*ei deon*, but note the aorist *lypēthentes*]; 3:14, and 17). But in other, more frequent instances (2:12, 15, 18–20; 3:9, 16; 4:1, 4, 6), actual reproach and suffering, as in 4:12–5:11, are envisioned in 1:3–4:11 as well. 1 Peter 4:12 does not introduce a new situation but deals extensively with the positive value of suffering when it occurs. The fact that this letter is addressed to numerous communities dispersed across four provinces of Asia Minor may explain why the author reckons with the actuality as well as potentiality of Christian suffering, since conditions could vary from one locality to the other.

Third, the focus, themes, and terminology in 4:12–5:11 are throughly consistent with those in 1:3–4:11. This concluding section also has in view the end (4:17; cf. 1:20; 4:7), judgment (4:17–18; cf. 1:17; 2:23; 4:5–6), and the imminent

[557] This was because of the explicit mention of baptism in 3:21 and the appearance of baptismal allusions elsewhere in 1:3–4:11.

[558] For this theory with varying modifications, see Perdelwitz 1911; Bornemann 1919/1920; Streeter 1929, 129–34; Jülicher-Fascher 1931, 199–200; Windisch 1930, 82; Fransen 1960, 28–38; Reicke 1964, 74–75; Beare 1970, 25–28, 188; Marxsen 1968; Duling-Perrin 1994, 475, 477.

revelation of Jesus Christ (5:1, 4; cf. 1:7, 13). Several other foregoing themes are also resumed and expanded upon.[559] Specific textual correspondences are also evident; compare the content of 4:12–13; 5:10; and 1:6–7, as well as that of 5:1 and 1:11–12. These correspondences suggest that the units of which they are a part, 1:3–12 and 4:12–5:11, form a literary inclusion involving the opening and concluding sections of the body of the letter. On the comment in 5:12 ("I have written briefly"), see the NOTE on this verse.

Finally, the thematic, terminological, and compositional consistency between 4:12–5:11 and foregoing sections of the letter indicates that this unit constitutes, not a shift in content or situation or a secondary imitation of the content of 1:3–4:11 (against Carrington 1940), but a climactic resuming and amplification of the foregoing.[560] As Goppelt (1993, 311–12) aptly notes, 4:12 introduces "not a new situation but new aspects of the interpretation of suffering." Here in 4:12–19, as in 5:1–5, and 6–11, principles outlined earlier "are connected to circumstances in a more concrete and direct way." 1 Peter 4:12–19 recapitulates and expands on what has already been stated on the issue of suffering. This unit does not mark a caesura or break in the line of thought but a crescendo.

This consistency of situation, language, and theme, in addition to the fact that the doxology in 4:11d forms only a minor pause rather than a major conclusion, argues decisively against all theories questioning the original connection and continuity between 1:3–4:11 and 4:12–5:11. Given the original integrity of the letter, there is no motivation or basis for regarding 4:12–5:11 as a later, secondary addition to 1:3–4:11, let alone for assigning these sections to originally different genres.

The subunits of 4:12–19, a series of six imperatival statements, consist of vv 12–13 (injunction and substantiation); vv 14–16 (positive/negative/positive types of suffering); vv 17–18 (motivation); and v 19 (concluding moral principle and final injunction). The inclusion formed by *pathēmasin* (v 13) and *paschontes* (v 19) frames the unit as a whole.

---

[559] See the contrast between believers and disobedient (4:17bc; cf. 2:4–10, 12, 15; 3:1–2, 13–16; 4:2–4); reproach and abuse from outsiders (4:14a; 5:9; cf. 2:12; 3:9, 16; 4:4) and the related contrast between shame and honor (4:16; 5:5c; cf. 2:4–10); the contrast between just and unjust suffering (4:15–16; cf. 2:20; 3:17); suffering for obedience to God's will (4:19a; cf. 3:14, 17; 4:2); innocent suffering as a test (4:12a; cf. 1:6–7), as a sharing in the sufferings and glory of Christ (4:12b–13; 5:1, 10; cf. 2:18–25; 3:13–22; 4:1; see also 1:11 and 2:4–10), and as an experience or occasion of honor (4:14, 16; 5:4, 6, 10; cf. 1:7c; 2:12; 3:9, 14) and joy (4:13a; cf. 1:6–8); the experience of the Spirit of God (4:14c; cf. 1:2, 12; 2:5); the community as God's house(hold) (4:17; cf. 2:5) and household instruction (5:1–5a; cf. 2:18–3:7); accent on the good news (4:17c; cf. 1:12, 25) and the grace of God (5:5b, 10, 12; cf. 1:2, 10, 13; 3:7; 4:10); the glorification of God through conduct (4:16c; cf. 4:11c and 2:12); and self-entrustment to a faithful and caring Creator (4:19; 5:7, 10; cf. 2:13, 23).

[560] So Nauck 1955, 79–80; van Unnik 1956–1957, 80; Stibbs and Walls 1959, 51; Shimada 1966, 414; J. N. D. Kelly 1969, 183–84; Elliott and Martin 1982, 56–58, 104; Brox 1986, 210–212; Lohse 1954/1986, 50; Michaels 1988, 257–58.

NOTES

4:12a. *Beloved* (*Agapētoi*). As earlier (*Agapētoi*, 2:11), our author again opens a unit of exhortation with a direct and intimate address of his readers. The vocative plural "beloved" (cf. TEV, "my dear friends") underscores the bond of affection uniting author and audience as the problem of innocent suffering is again taken up. This term of affection is consistent with the stress on love (*agapē*) and familial loyalty throughout the letter (1:8, 22; 2:17; 3:8; 4:8; 5:14; see also the NOTE on 2:11).

do not be surprised (*mē xenizesthe*). Earlier the author employed the same verb in his reference to the Gentiles' "surprise" (*xenizontai*, 4:4) that the believers were dissociating from them. Now he turns to the surprise that the believers could feel at the persistence and intensity of their suffering. The verb *xenizō*, related to the noun *xenos* ("stranger," "alien"), sometimes means "receive (a stranger) as a guest," but here, as in 4:4, it involves a reaction to something regarded as "strange" (*xenos*) or foreign. The point is that intense suffering should not (*mē*) be considered something "alien" or surprising to followers of the suffering Christ (2:21–24; cf. 1:11; 3:18a; 4:1a; 5:1).[561] Beare's references (1970, 189) to "paralyzing shock" and "numb inability to understand" claim more than the verb implies, do not fit its sense in 4:4, and are prompted by the invalid assumption that a new and different crisis is in view here. In what follows, several reasons are given or reprised for regarding suffering as no surprise but an experience with positive value. The first involves the concept of the testing function of the fiery ordeal of suffering.

at the fiery ordeal coming upon you to test you (*tēi en hymin pyrōsei pros peirasmon hymin ginomenēi*), literally, "at the fiery ordeal among you coming upon you for a test."[562] The term *pyrōsis* ("fiery ordeal") is related linguistically to *pyr*, "fire," and has a range of meanings in the Bible and extrabiblical literature,[563] the most relevant of which is the "fiery process" by which metal ore is separated from dross, freed of its impurities and refined; see Prov 27:21, "the fiery ordeal is the test of silver and gold" (*dokimion argyrōi kai chrysōi pyrōsis*); *Did.* 16:5, "the fiery ordeal of testing" (*hē pyrōsis tēs dokimasias*). Its related verb, *pyroō*, is often used in this same sense of "testing, refining by fire."[564]

---

[561] Such imperatives in the present tense are common in negative commands (Moulton 1908–1976, 1:122–23); see also *mē paschetō*, v 15a; *mē aischynesthō*, v 16b.

[562] 𝔓[72] includes an *epi* before *tēi* . . . *pyrōsei*, but *xenizō* normally appears with the dative of the thing causing the surprise (see Polyb. 1.23.5; 3.68.9; and BAGD 547–48).

[563] Exposure to fire (e.g., cooking; cf. Prov 21:12) or burning (Amos 4:9; Josephus, *Ant.* 1.203); destruction by fire (cf. Rev 18:9, 18); "heated passion" (*T. Jud.* 16:1).

[564] See Ps 65[66]:10–12; "For you, O God, have tested (*edokimasas*; cf. 1 Pet 1:6); you have refined (lit., "fired," *epyrōsas*) us, as silver is refined by fire (*hōs pyroutai to argyrion*) . . . you laid afflictions (*thlipseis*) on our back. You let people ride over our heads; we went through fire (*pyros*) and water"; Ps 16[17]:3, "You tested my heart . . . you refined me" (*edokimasas tēn kardian mou* . . . *epyrōsas me*); Zech 13:9, "I will try (*pyrōsō*) them as silver is tried (*pyroutai*); I will prove (*dokimō*) them as gold is proved (*dokimazetai*)"; cf. Rev 3:18 ("gold refined by fire"); Herm. *Vis.* 4.2.4; and *Mart. Pol.* 15:2.

Since our author has already used this metaphor in 1:6–7 in speaking of faith as more precious than "perishable gold tested by fire," this sense of *pyrōsis* is clearly implied here as well. In both passages the analogy of a metallurgical process is used to provide a positive interpretation of innocent suffering (*pathēmasin*, v 13; cf. *lypēthentes*, 1:6) as a divine testing of faith's constancy. In the context of this letter, *fiery ordeal* thus serves as a graphic comprehensive image for all of the hostility, slander, and abuse directed against the faithful and the suffering it has caused.

coming upon you (*hymin ginomenēi*), literally, "happening to you." The dative participle *ginomenēi* (of the verb *ginomai*, "happen," "take place") modifies the dative noun *pyrōsei* and occurs with the dative *hymin* ("to you"), indicating the persons affected (BAGD 159). In the Greek text, this phrase is separated from its antecedent by the phrase *pros peirasmon*, which indicates the purpose of the fiery ordeal.

to test you (*pros peirasmon*), literally, "for the purpose of testing," with "you" implied and *pros* indicating purpose.[565] Just as intense fire refines precious metal, so the fiery ordeal tests and proves the genuineness and constancy of faith-as-commitment. That this is the object and purpose of this testing was indicated in 1:6–7, where it was stated that the aim of "various testings" (*poikilois peirasmois*) was the ascertainment of "the tested genuineness of your faith" (*to dokimion hymōn tēs pisteōs*). The terms *peirasmos* and *peirazō* are virtually synonymous with *dokimasia* and *dokimazō*, and both latter terms also appear in combination with *pyrōsis* or *pyroō*, as *peirasmos* occurs with *pyr* in 1:6–7 (cf. Ps 25[26]:2, "Prove [*dokimason*] me, O Lord, and test [*peirason*] me; purify [*pyrōson*] my mind and heart").[566] An echo of these Petrine verses appears later in *Ep. Apost.* 36 ("if they suffer torment, such suffering will be a test for them, whether they have faith").

The term *peirasmos* has a different sense in the final petition of the Lord's Prayer: "lead us not into temptation/testing (*peirasmon*)" (Matt 6:13/Luke 11:4), a situation to be avoided (cf. also Mark 14:38/Matt 26:41/Luke 22:40, 46; Luke 8:13). In Matthew's version, the term also is linked with evil or the "Evil One," meaning the Devil as tempter/tester (cf. Matt 4:1–11). James (1:13–14; cf. also 1:2–3), on the other hand, understands *peirasmos* as coming not from God or the Devil but from within the self. Since in 1 Peter *peirasmos* is interpreted positively here and is described in 1:6–7 as a "testing" or "proving" (parallel in sense to *dokimion* and *dokimazō*, 1:7) of the genuineness of faith, it is clearly God who is envisioned as the one who tests.[567]

---

[565] See also 3:15b; Josephus, *J.W.* 4.573; 2 Cor 1:20; 10:4; Eph 4:29; 2 Tim 3:16.

[566] Cf. also Pss 11[12]:6; 16[17]:3; 65[66]:10; Prov 27:21; Jer 9:7; Zech 13:9; *Did.* 16:5. See also the combined use of *peirazō* and *pyroō* for God's testing and refining in Jdt 8:25–27.

[567] See similarly *T. Jos.* 2:7 and Wis 3:5–6 ("God tested [*epeirasen*] them and found them worthy for himself. As gold in the furnace he has tried [*edokimasen*] them"). For God as the source of testing and its positive effect, see also Sir 2:1–6; 4:17; 33:1; Wis 3:5–6; 11:10a; Jdt 8:25–27; 1 Macc 2:52; 2 Macc 6:12, 16; 4 Macc 9:29–32; 1QS I 17–18; VIII 3–4; 1QM XVII 8–9; 1QH[a] V 16;

E. T. Sander (1966, 43–50, 67, 85–96, 103–4) proposed a shift in the sense of *pyrōsis* from "refinement-test" to a designation for the eschatological ordeal of the end time, as indicated at Qumran (*mazrep* = *pyrōsis*) in its view of end-time affliction.[568] Paul stated that the day of judgment "will be revealed with fire, and the fire will test (*dokimasei*) what sort of work each one has done" (1 Cor 3:13; cf. also Rev 3:10 and *4 Ezra* 16:73–74). It is possible that *pyrōsis* and *peirasmos* have an eschatological overtone, especially in the light of vv 17–18 and the eschatological perspective of the letter in general, but this is not certain. Kuhn (1952, 202–3) shows that *peirasmos* is also used to characterize the daily ongoing situation of believers (Luke 8:13; 1 Cor 7:5, 10:13; Gal 4:14; 6:1; 1 Thess 3:5).[569]

The repetition of the same word in 1:6 (*peirasmois*) is a further indication of the close relation of these two passages. The terminological and thematic similarities between 4:12–13 and 1:6–7 indicate the presupposition of a similar situation, so that 4:12 cannot be said to introduce a new, actual crisis, even though 1:6–7 refers to the potentiality of suffering and 4:12–13 to its actuality. Beare's contention to the contrary (1970, 26–27, 188–93) is now rejected by virtually all subsequent commentators. Both passages and their similar terms (*pyrōsis/pyr, peirasmos/dokimazō*) qualify the nature of innocent suffering and indicate its constructive functions. 1 Peter 4:12–19 differs from 1:6–7 only in describing more fully the circumstances of this suffering and the Christian behavior required. Given the traditional nature of this language and the absence of any accompanying mention of organized persecution, there is no reason for seeing in *peirasmos* any reference to a "persecution" initiated by Rome or *pyrōsis* as an allusion to Nero's execution of the Christians of Rome by fire (*pyr*) as arsonists (against Beare 1970, 190; Leaney 1967, 65; and others). The terminology and images employed here and in 1:6–7 are instead traditional means[570] for depicting the tribulations and testing of God's people. The divine test of faith (trust in God and commitment to Jesus Christ) through suffering proves faith's genuineness and durability.

12b. *as though something surprisingly strange were happening to you* (*hōs xenou hymin symbainontos*). This is another genitive absolute construction (cf. 3:20c; 4:1a, 4b; 5:4a, 10c) with the substantive *xenou* functioning as the subject of the participle *symbainontos*. In this formulation, *hōs* ("as"), as in 2:16b,

1 Cor 10:13; Heb 3:8. In *1 En.* 108:8–14, the abuse, insult and suffering experienced by the faithful of God (cf. the similar terms of 1 Pet 4:12–14) are likewise depicted as a testing from God, which will then be followed by blessing, recompense, and honor.

[568] See 1QS I 17; VIII 4; 1QM XVI 15; XVII 1, 8–9; 1QH[a] IV 16; 1QpPs XXXVII 2, 19; 4QFlor II 1; CD XX 27. However, the affinities that Sander claims between 1 Peter and Qumran are exaggerated and not as precise as she suggests.

[569] His associating *peirasmos* with the attack of the Devil in 5:8 is unconvincing, however, since the constructive testing of 1:6 and 4:12 is of divine origin.

[570] Selwyn (1947, 221, 439–58), following Carrington (1940, 51–54) sees in 1 Pet 1:6–7 and 4:12 traces of a "persecution form" underlying numerous NT texts (1947, table 14, pp. 442–49) but his data point more to fluid tradition than to a fixed, structured schema.

introduces something that is not true; this is expressed in the translation by *as though . . . were happening*. The translation also seeks to express the linguistic kinship of *xenou* ("something surprisingly strange") and the foregoing verb *xenizesthe* ("do not be surprised"). The participle *symbainontos*, like *xenizesthe* and *xenou*, echoes the language of 4:4 (*syntrechontōn, xenizontai*). But here *hymin symbainontos* ("happening to you")[571] forms a contrasting parallel to the preceding participial phrase *hymin ginomenēi*, so that both participles have virtually the same meaning, and *hymin* in both instances emphasizes the addressees ("you") who are affected. The present tense of both *symbainontos* and *ginōmenēi* presumes a continuing situation rather than a new and sudden crisis. The threefold stress on "you" (*hymin*, 2d-person pl. dative) in this verse shows that the author is not simply passing on general teaching about suffering but is concerned with the suffering of the addressees in particular.

Converts of Gentile origin might find suffering for the faith something strange and unexpected, since this was not part of their previous experience (Windisch and Preisker 1951, 77). This would not have been the case for converts of Israelite origin, on the other hand, since suffering was an integral dimension of Israel's experience, as indicated especially in the Israelite tradition of the suffering righteous (see the NOTES on 2:21–24 and 3:18b). The author extends this tradition to include the sufferings of Christ the righteous one and his righteous followers as well. The verse contains the first of several positive interpretations of suffering offered in vv 12–19. The ordeal of suffering, our author states at the outset, is a familiar means for the divine testing of faith and constancy and hence should come as no surprise. A second immediately follows: through their suffering, believers are united with the suffering Christ (v 13).

Verse 13 and its main verb *chairete* presents a positive contrast to v 12 and its main verb *mē xenizesthe*: joy rather than surprise should be the believers' response to the fiery ordeal.

13a. *but, inasmuch as you share in the sufferings of the Christ* (*alla katho koinōneite tois tou Christou pathēmasin*). As the author has already indicated (2:18–25; 3:13–22; 4:1), believers suffer as did their suffering Lord; suffering is nothing alien to those who "follow in the footsteps" of the suffering Christ (2:21bcd). Thus the sense of *katho* is not "in the measure which" (Selwyn 1947, 221) or "in so far as" (Grudem 1988, 178) but "inasmuch as" or "since." Rejoicing, similarly, is not contingent on the degree of suffering but is based on the actuality of this commonality of suffering.

you share in the sufferings of the Christ. Moving beyond the comparison of the sufferings of the believers to those of Christ (2:21–23; 3:18a; 4:1), the author now speaks of their "sharing in" (*koinōneite*) these sufferings (*pathēmata*). The verb *koinōneō* means "have, take a share in" something, "partake, participate in" something (with that which is shared in the dative case, as here).[572]

---

[571] For this sense of the phrase, see also Mark 10:32; Acts 3:10; 1 Cor 10:11; for its occurrence with *peirasmoi*, see Acts 20:19.

[572] See Rom 15:27, Heb 2:4; for the verb see also Rom 12:13; 15:27.

The verb, the related adjective/substantive *koinōnos*, and noun *koinōnia* are used in the NT to express various aspects of fellowship and solidarity that believers have with God, Christ, and one another. Our author employs the related noun *koinōnos* in describing himself as a "sharer in the glory about to be revealed" (5:1).[573]

the sufferings of the Christ (*tois tou Christou pathēmasin*). The same phrase recurs in 5:1 and a similar expression, "the sufferings [destined] for Christ," was employed in 1:11. In this letter *Christos* (without a definite article) normally is employed as a proper name (1:11, 19; 2:21; 3:16, 18; 4:1, 14; 5:10, 14). Here, however, as in 3:15 and 5:1, the articular form, "the Christ" (*tou Christou*) is used. This formulation reflects an older stratum of tradition in which *the Christ* still functioned as a title for Jesus as *the Messiah*. In Israel and early Christianity, suffering by the righteous and great tribulations ("woes") were expected to accompany the advent of the Messiah and the end time.[574] However, Israel never expected the Messiah himself to suffer but, rather, to be the victorious deliverer of his people from the control of Israel's enemies. Followers of Jesus who saw in him the Messiah transformed this notion to include not only themselves but the Messiah himself among the sufferers of the endtime.[575] The references to "the sufferings (*pathēmata*) of (the) Christ," meaning, Jesus the Messiah, in this letter (also 1:11; 5:1) reflect this thought as well. At the same time, the further use of "Christ" without the article in the similar phrase in 1:11b (*ta eis Christon pathēmata*), like its other instances of unarticular *Christos* (1:11a, 19; 2:21; 3:16, 18; 4:1, 14; 5:10 [Christ Jesus?], 14), reflect the gradual development within early Christianity of the term *Christos* from title to personal name. Thus, for the Petrine author, both "Christ" and "the Christ" are equivalent designations for the same person, Jesus the Messiah. Christians sharing in the sufferings of the Christ participate in the sufferings of their Lord Jesus Christ.

Paul uses the verb *koinōneō* in connection with sharing things with one another (Rom 12:13; 15:27; Gal 6:6; Phil 4:15; cf. 1 Tim 5:22) but not for sharing in the sufferings of Christ.[576] The Gospels express this idea of solidarity in suffering with the language of discipleship, taking up one's cross, and experiencing

---

[573] On the *koinō-* word field in the NT, see J. Y. Campbell 1932; Seesemann 1933; Hauck 1965; McDermott 1975; Popkes 1976; Panikulam 1979; Hainz 1991; Wall 1992.

[574] See Ezek 38, 39; Dan 7:21–27; 12:1; Joel 2; Hab 3:3–16; Zeph 1–3; Zech 11–14; *T. Levi* 10; *T. Dan* 5; 2 Esd 5:1–13; 6:18–24; 13:16–52; *2 Bar.* 29:2; Mark 13 par.; 2 Thess 2:3–12; Rev 6–18; cf. also Billerbeck 1926–1961, 2:284–91.

[575] See Mark 8:31; 9:31, 32–34; and their synoptic parallels; Mark 13:7–27 par.; Luke 24:45–46; John 16:20–24, 32–33; Rom 8:18–25; 1 Thess 1:10; 5:1–3; 2 Thess 2:3–12.

[576] For this he uses the expression *perisseuei ta pathēmata tou Christou eis hēmas* (lit., "the sufferings of the Christ abound for us," 2 Cor 1:5) or *gnōnai . . . koinōnian pathēmatōn autou* ("to know . . . share in his sufferings," Phil 3:10). For the idea of suffering with Christ, see also Rom 8:17 and 2 Cor 4:8–12; Wolter 1990; for sharing the sufferings of other believers, see 2 Cor 1:7; cf. 1 Pet 5:9.

the fate of Jesus (Mark 8:34 par.; cf. also Matt 10:24; John 15:18–20), an echo of which occurs in 1 Pet 2:21–23.

In 1 Peter this notion of sharing the sufferings of Christ is added here to the ways in which the author stresses the solidarity of suffering believers with their suffering Lord (cf. also 2:18–25; 3:13–22). In the present context it states yet another way in which innocent suffering is given positive value and explains (1) why suffering is nothing strange to followers of Jesus Christ, their suffering Lord (v 12), and (2) why believers, even in the face of suffering, have reason to be joyful (v 13b).

13b. *rejoice now* (*chairete*). Since their innocent suffering unites them with their suffering Lord, believers have cause for exuberant joy both now and at the future revelation of Christ's glory. The vocabulary and theme of this verse echo those in 1:6–8 (cf. *chairō, chara*, 1:6; *agalliaō*, 1:6, 8; *apokalypsis*, 1:5, 7; *doxa*, 1:8).

In view of the earlier passage (1:6–8), where mention was made of present rejoicing despite suffering, there is possibly an iterative sense to the present tense of *chairete* here: "continue to rejoice now." Joy, like honor, is not only a future hope but an already present reality. Of the 74 times that the verb *chairō* is used in the NT, it appears in connection with suffering only in 4:13b (cf. also *chara* and *lypēthentes* in 1:6, 8), Col 1:24, and a dominical saying (Matt 5:11–12/Luke 6:22–23) apparently known to our author and echoed in vv 13–14.

1 Peter 1:6–8 and 4:12–14, as well as this related Jesus saying and other NT passages, represent Christian adaptations of an Israelite tradition that emerged sometime in the second-century BCE confrontation of Israel with Greek domination. This tradition interpreted suffering positively as a divine testing of constancy and often as reason for rejoicing.[577] The origin of this fluid oral tradition antedates the teaching of Jesus (so Nauck 1955, 73; against Selwyn 1947, 450). Its distinctive Christian adaptation is characterized by affirmation of the present (rather than only the future) experience of divine blessing and its Christological basis and focus (Nauck 1955, 76–77; Brox 1986, 214).[578]

1 Peter represents a fuller adaptation of this tradition than does its closest NT parallel, the Jesus saying of Matt 5:11–12/Luke 6:22–23. It has been suggested, moreover, that 4:14ab could be an earlier form of the Q saying ("How honorable are you when you are reproached because of me") that was then expanded in a different manner by the evangelists (so Millauer 1976, 157; and Schröger

[577] Texts reflecting elements of this tradition include 2 Macc 6:28, 30; 4 Macc 7:22; 9:29; 11:12; Tob 13:13–14; Jdt 8:25–27; Wis 3:4–6; 1QH[a] IX 24; 2 *Bar.* 48:48–50; 52:5–7; 54:16–18; Matt 5:11–12/Luke 6:22–23; Acts 5:41; 14:22; Rom 5:3–5; 8:18; 2 Cor 4:17–18; 6:10; 8:2; 1 Thess 1:6; 2 Thess 1:4–6; Jas 1:2, 12; Heb 10:32–36. Echoes of this tradition may also be found in the later rabbinic comments on suffering cited in Montefiore and Loewe 1963, 541–55.

[578] For discussion of this tradition, see Selwyn 1947, 439–58, later qualified and expanded upon by Nauck 1955; Millauer 1976, 165–87; and Goppelt 1993, 316–21. On suffering more generally, see Wichmann 1930; Sutcliffe 1953; Braun 1940, 36–56; J. A. Sanders 1955; Filson 1955; Braun 1962; Lohse 1963, 29–58; Villiers 1975; Millauer 1976; Horbury and McNeil, eds. 1981; Talbert 1991.

1981b, 186; see also the NOTE on 4:14a). According to the Petrine author's formulation, rejoicing is not a condition for being honored (as in Matthew and Luke) but a result of sharing in the sufferings of Christ (v 13a). Being honored (by God), on the other hand (v 14b), is a direct contrast with being reproached and shamed by others. This honor is manifested in the fact that the divine Spirit of glory rests upon those reproached (v 14c). In these two respects this Petrine adaptation of the tradition is unique in the NT.

13c. *so that you may also rejoice with exultation when his glory is revealed* (*hina kai en tēi apokalypsei tēs doxēs autou charēte agalliōmenoi*). The verb "rejoice" is repeated but now as an aorist subjunctive (as is fitting for verbs in *hina* purpose clauses) with a future reference. The conjunction *hina* ("so that") has the same value as *hōste* in 4:19 and 1:21. Rejoicing in the midst of present suffering is a prelude to joy at the final revelation of Christ's glory. The tense of *charēte* ("you may rejoice") can be either present or future, but this issue is immaterial to its sense. As J. N. D. Kelly (1969, 57) notes, "By any ordinary assessment their exultation should belong to the future, when the Lord will appear to reward the saints; but for the writer the joy of the end overflows into the present, irradiating the wretched plight of those to whom he writes."

with exultation (*agalliōmenoi*). This present participle modifying *charēte* (lit., "you may also rejoice, *exulting*") emphasizes through repetition the overflowing exuberance of this joy. The verb *agalliaomai*, appearing also in the parallel unit of 1:6–9, is used in the OT of the eschatological jubilation of the redeemed (Ps 95:12; 96:1, 8; Isa 25:9; 66:10). The same combination of joy and exultation, occurring both here and in 1:6–9 (*agalliasthe*, vv 6, 8; *chara*, v 8), is found in Ps 95[96]:11–12; 125[126]:2; *T. Levi* 18:5, 14; and *1 En.* 104:14, but more importantly in Matt 5:12 (*chairete kai agalliasthe*, "rejoice and exult"), the text of the "joy in suffering tradition" to which 1 Peter is closest in form and content. Thus, *agalliōmenoi* also appears to reflect knowledge and adaptation of the dominical logion recorded in Matt 5:11–12 and Luke 6:22–23.

when his glory is revealed (*en tēi apokalypsei tēs doxēs autou*). The substance of this temporal clause has no affinity with the dominical saying preserved in Matthew/Luke but reflects other early Christian tradition.[579] It echoes the thought of 1:8 (*en apokalypsei Iēsou Christou*), where the same connection between present and future rejoicing is made (1:6–9). In the case of Christ as well, suffering was followed by glory (1:11, 19–21; 2:4; 3:18–22; 5:1bc). Therefore, believers who share in his innocent sufferings likewise can look forward to sharing in his glory at his final revelation (cf. 1:7–8, 13; 5:1, 4, 10).

The glory of Jesus Christ involves his divine election (2:4), resurrection (1:3, 21; 2:4; 3:18e, 21), and ascension to God's right hand of honor (3:22)—all constituting his divine vindication by God. Such is also the glory in store for his followers. According to Cervantes Gabarrón (1991, 301), this is the clearest

---

[579] The combination of present suffering with Christ and future glorification with Christ is found also in Rom 8:17–17; for varied expressions of this thought, see also 2 Cor 1:5–7; 4:17; Phil 3:8–11; 2 Tim 2:11–12; Heb 2:9–10; 10:32–39; 12:1–11.

and most succinct statement in the NT of the relation of the passion and glory of Christ to the life of his followers.

In this verse, moreover, two further positive features of suffering are presented: believers who suffer innocently (a) share in the sufferings of the innocent Christ and consequently (b) have cause for exuberant joy both now and in the future. Joy now and at the final revelation of Christ's glory are the believers' paradoxical response to present *pathēmata*, *pyrōsis*, and *peirasmon*, a paradox that complements that of their being at home with God despite existing as aliens in society.

In vv 14–16, specific cases of sharing or not sharing in the sufferings of Christ are now given, along with experiences of receiving or giving glory here and now. The parallel conditional statements in vv 14 and 16 form an inclusion and mark vv 14–16 as a minor subunit. Parallel types of appropriate conduct (vv 14, 16) are contrasted to four types of unacceptable behavior (v 15). In addition, reproach because of association with Christ (v 14a) and suffering as a "Christian" (v 16a) are contrasted with being honored by God (v 14b) and rendering God honor with this name (v 16b). The subunit is structured as follows:

A. If (*ei*) you are reproached because of Christ (v 14a)
  B. how honored [you are] (positive) (v 14b)
    C. But let none of you suffer as . . . (negative) (v 15)
A.′ If (*ei*), however, [any of you suffers] as a Christian (v 16a)
  B.′ you should not feel shamed, but should rather glorify
    God with this name (positive). (v 16bc)

14a. *If you are reproached because of Christ* (*ei oneidizesthe en onomati Christou*). These words and the following makarism ("how honored you are") parallel the statement in 3:14, with the indicative mood of the verb *oneidizesthe* balancing the optative in 3:14 (*paschoite*). Since this verse, along with terms in v 13 (*chairete, agalliōmenoi*), is close to the dominical saying reworked in Matt 5:11–12/Luke 6:22–23, the force of *ei* may be less conditional ("if") than temporal ("when," as *hotan* in Matthew and Luke).[580]

you are reproached (*oneidizesthe*). The verb *oneidizō* ("reproach," "revile," "heap insults on") is a standard term for verbal abuse and public shaming.[581] Josephus (*Ag. Ap.* 2.148) uses a combination of the verbs *oneidizō* and *loidoreō* in his portrayal of the scorn heaped upon Israelites because of their "superstition," separateness, and alleged misanthropy (see also *Ag. Ap.* 2.236, "the Lysimachuses and Molons and other writers of that class . . . insult [*loidorousin*] us [Israelites] as the very vilest of mankind"). Jesus himself was reproached in his

[580] Cf. the possible temporal force of *ei* also in 2:19, 20; 3:2; 4:11, 16.

[581] See Pss 68[69]:10; 78[79]:12; 88[89]:51–52; 118[119]:42; Isa 37:3; Matt 5:11/Luke 6:22; Matt 11:20; 27:44; Rom 15:3; Heb 11:26; 13:13; Jas 1:5. For the equivalency of "reproach" (*oneidos, oneidismos*) and "shame" (*aischynē*), see Ps 68[69]:7–8, 10, 20; Prov 19:26; Isa 30:5, 6; 54:4; Dan 3:33, 12:2; Luke 1:25; Lattke 1991.

passion (Mark 15:32/Matt 27:44; Rom 15:3), and his followers could encounter the same treatment (Matt 5:11/Luke 6:22; 1 Tim 3:7; Heb 10:33; 13:13).

The verb is virtually synonymous with other terms used earlier to describe the treatment experienced by the addressees ("slander" [*katalaleō*, 2:12; 3:16]; "insult" [*loidoreō*, *loidoria*, 2:23; 3:9], "disparage" [*epēreazō*, 3:16]; "malign" [*blasphēmeō*, 4:4]). This indicates once more that the suffering presumed in this letter was a result of verbal abuse and public humiliation rather than of offical incrimination. "The most serious and pressing form of suffering as yet is reproach, not imprisonment or death" (Bigg 1902, 177; similarly, Best 1971, 163). The situation envisioned here, as elsewhere in the letter (see also the NOTES on 3:16 and 4:4), is not one of formally organized, legal persecution or prosecution but the informal and sporadic public shaming of those who follow the Christ and bear his name. This shaming and its converse, honor, receive further explicit stress in the following term, *makarioi* (v 14b), and the language of v 16.

because of Christ (*en onomati Christou*). These words indicate the basis of the reproach directed against the believers. This Greek phrase is unique in the NT and has been rendered in various ways: "for the name of Christ" (KJV, NAB, RSV, NRSV); "because of the name of Christ" (NIV; Reicke 1964, 124); "for bearing the name of Christ" (JB, NJB); "for the sake of Christ" (Goodspeed, NAB). Such translations, however, presume the presence of a definite article with *onoma*, when in actuality it is lacking. This poses a problem, then, concerning the sense and function of the phrase *en onomati*.

It is clear that *en onomati Christou* cannot be taken instrumentally ("if you are reproached with the name of Christ"), since no article is present, and it is not the name "Christ" by which they are labeled but the term *Christianos*, as v 16 makes clear. This applies also to Goppelt's (1993, 309) rendition "for the sake of Christ's name." Normally and predominantly in the NT, *onomati* occurring with *en* is articular, *en tōi onomati* (28×).[582] In these cases, *onoma* is appropriately translated "name," and the expression implies some action done "in the name" and on behalf of the authority of another. This is not the case here, however, since those doing the reproaching are hardly acting "in the name" of Christ and his authority. Consequently, *en onomati* has a different sense and function and in all likelihood operates as an idiom.[583]

Of the four other NT occurrences of *en onomati* (Mark 9:41; Acts 16:18; Eph 5:20; 2 Thess 3:6), Mark 9:41 offers the closest parallel to its use here. The Markan verse reads, literally, "Whoevever gives you a cup of water because,

---

[582] In some other instances the article is lacking but appears to be implied (Matt 21:9/Mark 11:9/Luke 19:38/John 12:13; Matt 23:39; Luke 13:35 [all citing Ps 117:26]; cf. also Acts 16:18; Eph 5:20; Col 3:17; 2 Thess 3:6; 2 Tim 3:6).

[583] Selwyn (1947, 226) cites Thucydides 4.60 (*onomati ennomōi xymmachias*, "under the fair name of alliance") as a classical instance of an idiomatic use of *onoma*. This instance, however, is not germane, since the believers were not being reproached "under the name 'Christ'" but, as v 16 indicates, under the name "Christian."

since you are Christ's, will by no means lose his reward." In this redundant expression, the phrase *en onomati* ("because") is followed and explained by the phrase *hoti Christou este* ("since you are Christ's"). The Matthean parallel (Matt 10:41–42) expands on Mark by creating a threefold statement, eliminates the Markan redundancy, and replaces *en onomati* with *eis onoma* (which, however, has the same sense): "He who receives a prophet *because he is a prophet* (*eis onoma prophētou*) will receive a prophet's reward. He who receives a righteous man *because he is a righteous man* (*eis onoma dikaiou*) will receive a righteous man's reward. And whoever gives one of these little ones a cup of cold water *because he is a disciple* (*eis onoma mathētou*), truly I say to you, he will not lose his reward." In both cases the unarticular phrase *en onomati* or *eis onoma* has the idiomatic meaning "because" (J. N. D. Kelly 1969, 186, 190–91; cf. also Moule 1960, 78–79). The Markan version, in which *mou* originally may have accompanied *onoma* ("because of me") makes this causal sense evident by its following phrase, "because you are Christ's." Since Jesus nowhere refers to himself as the Christ, this phrase must represent a later Christian formulation and is thus synonymous in sense with our Petrine formulation "because of Christ"—that is, because you belong to, are affiliated with, Christ. The Petrine formulation *en onomati* thus is best taken as an idiom meaning "because" (cf. J. N. D. Kelly 1969, 186; Davids 1990, 167; Goppelt 1993, 323).

This rendition of *en onomati Christou* is further supported by the fact that vv 13–14 constitute an independent redaction of the dominical saying reworked also in Matt 5:11–12/Luke 6:22–23, where the term "reproach" also occurs and is linked with similar causal phrases ("because of me" [*heneken emou*, Matt 5:11b] or "because of the Son of Man" [Luke 6:22b]) and where the expression "how honorable" (*makarios*, cf. 1 Pet 4:14a:) also appears.[584] In addition to Matt 5:11/Luke 6:22 and our verse, numerous other NT passages show that the

[584] The main similarities that 1 Pet 4:13–14 share with Matt/Luke include *chairein* followed by *agalliasthai* (contrast *skirtēsate*, Luke 6:23), *makarioi*, *oneidizein* followed by a reason for reproach ("because of me" [Matt], "because of the Son of Man" [Luke], "in the name of Christ"/ "because of [your association with] Christ [1 Peter]), and a use of *chairein* in relation to a compensatory reward. Differences, however, are also evident. 1 Peter 4:13–14 involves some but not all of the substance of Matthew/Luke and this material is presented in a different sequence. In 1 Peter the call for rejoicing *precedes* rather than follows the makarism. Rejoicing *in both the present and the future* is stressed and is associated with the *revelation of Christ's glory* rather than with the prospect of a heavenly reward. The explanatory clauses of Matthew (*hoti* . . .) and Luke (*idou gar* . . .) following *chairete* (Matthew) or *charēte* (Luke) do not accord with the *hina* purpose clause following *chairete* in 1 Peter, but parallel in function the *hoti* explanatory clause following *makarioi* in 1 Pet 4:14bc. The *basis* for the makarism in 1 Peter, the presence of the divine Spirit of glory, has no parallel in the Gospel logion. According to 1 Peter, rejoicing is not a consequence of being honored (as in Matthew and Luke) but a result of sharing in the sufferings of Christ. Being honored (by God), on the other hand, is in direct contrast to being reproached and shamed by others, and this honor is manifested in the fact that the divine Spirit of glory rests upon those reproached. Matthew and Luke, moreover, make no mention of *peirasmoi* (1 Pet 4:12, 1:6), a feature of the tradition, nor of sharing in the sufferings of Christ (1 Pet 4:13a). On the other hand, they link the

idea of suffering or being maligned because of one's association with Christ was expressed in a variety of similar or equivalent Greek formulations with causal force and translated "because of," "on account of," "on behalf of," "in the name of" followed by "me," "Christ," and so on.[585] The Petrine statement reflects this traditional idea, traced back to Jesus, that association with him will result in the same treatment that he himself encountered (cf. 2:23) and has the sense: "if you are reproached *because of* (*being associated with*) *Christ*."

Whereas the term *onoma* in v 14a is part of an idiom (*en onomati*) and hence should not be translated "name," the expression in v 16c, *en tōi onomati toutōi* ("with this name"), refers back to the name *Christianos* (v 16a). Both *en onomati Christou* and *Christianos*, however, are expressions concerning the same phenomenon—association with Jesus Christ. Whereas *Christianos* is a label fabricated by outsiders (see below), *en onomati Christou* is the author's insider expression, like the expression *en Christōi* (3:16; 5:10, 14). Thus, in this verse our author contrasts reproach from outsiders because of believers' affiliation with Christ and honor conferred upon these believers by God.

14b. *how honored* [*you are*] (*makarioi*). This "makarism," or declaration of honor, as Hanson (1996) has shown, is similar in form and thrust to the earlier makarism of 3:14ab, which also contrasts honor and suffering. Here too the construction is elliptical, with "you are" implied:

3:14 if, however, you should suffer for doing what is right,
how honored [you are]!
4:14 if you are reproached because of Christ,
how honored [you are]!

---

reproach of the followers of Jesus with the persecution of the ancient prophets, a motif absent in 1 Peter. These several differences rule out the likelihood of the Petrine author's dependence on Matthew/Luke (against Metzner 1995, 35–48). The correspondences and differences, taken together, suggest instead our author's independent redaction of a Q logion (so Millauer 1976, 145–55) in which the motif of "joy in suffering" was prominent (Nauck 1955). He apparently was familiar with the makarism and the associated motif of rejoicing but not with the substantiations contained in Matthew and Luke, so that his formulation actually could antedate the final redactional formulations of the saying in Matthew and Luke (so Millauer 1976, 157; and Schröger 1981b, 186). From an historical and social perspective, all three versions of the saying fit less the lifetime of Jesus than the situation of the post-Easter community, so that it may have been a community construction rather than a word of Jesus. On the history of the tradition of the saying and its transformations for different social settings, see Millauer (1976, 154–64), Boring (1985, 20–32), and Kloppenborg (1986).

[585] See, e.g., (1) *dia to onoma mou*: Matt 10:22; Matt 24:9/Luke 21:17 (you will be hated "on account of my name" [*dia to onoma mou*], i.e., because of your association with me; note the equivalency of *heneken emou* and *dia to onoma mou* in Matt 10:18, 22, resp.); cf. also Mark 13:13; John 15:20–21; Rev 2:3; (2) *heneken*: Mark 10:29 (*heneken emou*) / Matt 19:29 (*heneken tou emou onomatos*); Mark 13:9 / Matt 10:18 (*heneken emou*) / Luke 21:12 (*heneken tou onomatos mou*); Matt 5:11/Luke 6:22 (*heneken emou/heneka tou hyiou tou anthrōpou*); (3) *hyper*: Acts 5:41 ("suffer dishonor on behalf of [*hyper*] the name"); 9:16 ("suffer on behalf of [*hyper*] my name"); 21:13 ("to die in Jerusalem on behalf of [*hyper*] the name of the Lord Jesus"); cf. also Acts 15:26; Phil 1:9.

Both statements also involve conditional formulations, but the likely temporal force of *ei* and the indicative mood of the verb make clear that at this point the actuality of suffering and reproach is foremost in view, in line with the overall perspective of 4:12–19.

Prototypes of such makarisms include Dan 12:12; Tob 13:14; Sir 25:7–10; and *1 En.* 58:2.[586] Makarisms are prominent as well in the joy-in-suffering tradition that vv 13–14 reflect (cf. Matt 5:11–12/Luke 6:22–23; Jas 1:12). Since vv 13–14 accord most closely with the dominical saying recorded by Matthew and Luke, it is probable that *makarioi*, like the verbs "rejoice" and "reproach," echoes this saying of Jesus in its earliest Q formulation. Recalling the words of his Lord, our author likewise paradoxically ascribes honor to believers despite their shameful public reproach. The basis for this ascription of honor is next explained in v 14c with words that no longer echo the dominical logion but that introduce a theme (glory) typical of this letter.

14c. *because the divine Spirit of glory rests upon you* (*hoti to tēs doxēs kai to tou theou pneuma eph' hymas anapauetai*). The Greek phrase, literally, "the Spirit of glory and that of God rests upon you," is unique in the Bible but appears to be an expansion of the statement in Isa 11:2. This passage speaks of the branch from Jesse—that is, someone of David's lineage (11:1)—who will bring justice and peace (11:1–9): "the Spirit of God shall rest upon him" (*kai anapausetai ep' auton pneuma tou theou*).[587] In applying this statement to his readers, our author modified it by revising the word order, adding two definite articles and the words "of glory" (*tēs doxēs*), and substituting "you" (*hymas*, pl.) for "him" (*auton*). The additions created a hendiadys (two formulations [*of glory, of God*] used [in modification of *Spirit*] to express one idea). Both formulations could be treated as appositives ("the Spirit of glory, the Spirit of God," so JB, Selwyn, Goppelt) but, since both *of glory* and *of God* qualify *Spirit*, this pleonastic construction can also be rendered more smoothly as *the divine Spirit of glory*. The added *of glory* is consistent with the stress on *glory* in this section (4:13, 14, 16; cf. 4:11d) and throughout the letter and may also have been prompted by the desire to ground the addressees' honor (*makarioi*) explicitly in the honor (*doxēs*, "glory") of God, thus once again linking glory to suffering (1:11; 5:1, 10; cf. similarly, 2 Cor 4:17). The glory that is God's (4:11) and Christ's (1:11, 21; 5:1) rests now on the suffering faithful and soon will be revealed in all its fullness (1:7; 5:1, 4). Thus "the Spirit turns reproach into glory" (Bigg 1902, 177).

---

[586] For further instances, and observations on their function, see Hanson 1996 and the NOTE on 3:14.

[587] The diverging variants following *of glory*—namely, "and of power" (א A P 33 81 etc.), "the name of the glory and power of God and (the Spirit)" (614 630 1505 etc.), as well as the addition at the end of this verse, "(the Spirit who was) blasphemed among them but honored among you" (P Ψ 𝔐 lat syr[p] cop[sa])—are all less well attested and appear to be homiletic supplements to or, in the case of the latter, an explanatory gloss on the original shorter text. Arguments for the originality of the final longer reading by Rodgers (1981) are effectively countered by Davids (1990, 168); cf. also García del Moral 1961a.

This is one of the few references to the divine Spirit in the letter (see 1:2b, 12). The thought reflects the OT notion of God's Spirit resting on God's people and its leaders (cf. Num 11:25–26 [*epanepausato to pneuma ep' autous*]; so also Goppelt 1993, 324) rather than a "trinitarian" sense of *Spirit of God* (against García del Moral [1961a, 1961b, 1961c]). The substitution of the present *rests upon*[588] for the original "shall rest upon" in Isa 11:2 relates the honor of the readers to a present reality: reproach because of Christ is a sure sign of the Spirit's immediate presence.[589]

Verses 15 and 16 continue the focus on suffering and draw a further contrast. Verse 15 indicates activities in which believers should *not* be involved and which do not fall under the category of the innocent suffering referred to in v 14. Verse 16, on the other hand, returns to the point of v 14 and indicates the honorable character of suffering as a "Christian."

15. *To be sure, let none of you suffer* (*Mē gar tis hymōn paschetō*). When suffering comes, it should not be for the wrong reasons. The focus on suffering (cf. v 13) continues, and the particle *gar* ("to be sure"; cf. Josephus, *Ant.* 11.8) functions as a connective (BAGD 152, §4) introducing a thought that is patently self-evident. The verb *paschetō* ("suffer"), like the following verbs *aischynesthō* (v 16b) and *doxazetō* (v 16c), is a cohortative (imperatival) 3d-person sing., with "none of you" (*Mē tis hymōn*, lit., "not any of you") as its subject.

as a murderer, or a thief (*hōs phoneus ē kleptēs*). These first two of the four nouns of this verse involve acts expressly proscribed by the Decalogue (Exod 20:13, 5; cf. also Philo, *Decal.* 168–73; *Spec.* 4.1–40) and Greco-Roman law and that are condemned in other NT vice lists as well.[590] The final two nouns, however, do not occur in those lists but are unique to 1 Peter. Thus, they in particular may involve types of misconduct of which the author suspects the believers had been or could have been directly accused. This is certainly the case with *kakopoios* ("wrongdoer"), as 2:12 makes clear. Taken together, all four miscreants are involved in actions contrary to the will of God, the author's ultimate moral criterion, and are listed in descending order of gravity and specificity. On the whole, v 15 serves as a negative foil for the injunctions of v 14 and v 16. It indicates types of conduct obviously not qualifying as causes of innocent suffering, the only type of suffering in mind throughout the letter (1:6; 2:19, 20, 21, 23; 3:14, 17, 18; 4:1, 16, 19; 5:10).

---

[588] The verb *anapauetai* has better support (א* B P 𝔐 lat Clem Tert) than its variants (*epanapauetai* [A Ψ 81 etc.]; *anapepauetai*, or *epanapepauetai* [𝔓[72] א[2] 33 623 etc.]; *anapempetai* [049]).

[589] On the presence of the Spirit with those who suffer, see also Matt 10:20; Acts 7:55; and in later time in connection with the martyrs, *Mart. Pol.* 2:2; *Pass. Perp. Fel.* 1.3; Eusebius, *Hist. eccl.* 5.1.34. cf. also Iren., *Haer.* 4.33.9. Later rabbinic teaching expresses the same thought. Rabbi Jose b. Judah (fifth generation of Tannaites) taught: "Beloved are sufferings before God, the glory of God rests upon sufferers" (*Sipre Deut.* 6:5 §32, f. 73b); see also *Midr. Pss.* 24.3 (102b, §3) "The Holy Spirit does not rest where there is idleness or sadness or ribaldry or frivolity or empty speech, but only where there is joy" (cited by Hillyer 1992, 135).

[590] Earlier our author twice listed vices to be avoided (2:1; 4:3), vices also conventionally proscribed in other NT and Israelite writings (see the NOTES on 2:1 and 4:3).

as a murderer (*hōs phoneus*). The particle *hōs* ("as") here, as elsewhere in 1 Peter (see the NOTE on 1:14a), serves to identify an actual condition, in the present case suffering punishment for being an actual murderer. It is hardly likely that the author thinks he must dissuade his readers from engaging in murder or theft. These crimes, along with wrongdoing, are mentioned as misdeeds self-evidently to be avoided.

or a thief (*ē kleptēs*).[591] Early Christianity, like the House of Israel, proscribed both murder[592] and theft.[593] Paul, prior to his call by God, however, was said to have had murderous intentions (Acts 9:1; cf. 1 Cor 15:9; Gal 1:13; Phil 3:9). Judas Iscariot proved to be a thief (John 12:6), and other believers had been thieves prior to their conversion (1 Cor 6:10–11; Eph 4:28). Jesus' followers had been suspected (Matt 27:64) or accused (Matt 28:13) of stealing Jesus' corpse. Other allegations of theft or murder (as in Acts 28:4) could have been made by ignorant, slandering outsiders similar to the accusations leveled against Israel. "The Jews," Tacitus (*Hist.* 5.3.2) sneered, "regard as profane all that we hold sacred; on the other hand, they permit all that we abhor." Pagan vitriol against Israel eventually was transferred to the Christians as their offspring.

or a wrongdoer (*ē kakopoios*). In contrast to the two previous terms, *kakopoios* and *allotriepiskopos* involve less clearly defined offenses, activities that, depending on their meaning and usage, were not condemned by law but were contrary to prevailing custom and standards.

As indicated in the NOTE on 2:12, *kakopoios* is a term unique to 1 Peter (2:12, 14) in the NT. Its sense is broad and varies according to context. Tertullian (*Scorp.* 12) and Cyprian (*Quir.* 3.37) translate it with *maleficus*, which could mean, besides "wrongdoer," "sorcerer."[594] Since sorcery had been criminalized by the Romans, being a "sorcerer" (favored by Selwyn 1947, 225; Bauer 1978a, 109–10; and the NEB) would then be a third illegal act against which our author warns. This would also hold true for the translations "malefactor" (Reicke 1964, 124) and "criminal" (Goodspeed, JB, NRSV, NIV). It is by no means certain, however, that the generic term *kakopoios* always implied criminality. Beare (1970, 193) opts for "thug," but "rogue" (Phillips) could fit as well if the author had no illegal act in view.

Earlier our author had spoken of the believers' being slandered as "wrongdoers" (*kakopoioi*, 2:12) and had stated that it was the responsibility of provincial governors to punish wrongdoers (2:14), thus allowing for the possibility that such wrongdoing could involve legally proscribed offenses. The wrongdoing, however, is not further specified, and no mention is made in 2:14 of Roman

---

591 The particle *hōs* ("as"), added by some MSS before "thief" (𝔓[72] 𝔐 cop[bo]) and before "wrongdoer" (𝔓[72]), seems to be supplied for consistency's sake and is therefore most likely secondary.

592 See Mark 10:19 par.; Rom 13:9; Jas 2:11; cf. Matt 15:19/Mark 7:21; Rom 1:29; Rev 21:8, 22:15.

593 See Mark 10:19 par.; Rom 2:21; 13:9; 1 Cor 6:10; Eph 4:28; cf. John 10:1, 8, 10.

594 Cf. Tac., *Ann.* 2.69.3 (*malefica*, "sorceries"); Lact., *Inst.* 2.16.4.

authorities' charging believers with such offenses. In the NT, the kindred verb *kakopoieō* has the more general sense of "doing what is wrong" in contrast to "doing what is right" (*agathopoieō*, Mark 3:4/Luke 6:9; cf. 3 John 11), and this is its sense in the contrast in these two verbs in 1 Pet 3:17 as well. Thus, it is likely that *kakopoios* here refers in general to "one who does what is wrong," acting contrary to prevailing custom and norms of conduct. To counter any suspicion of wrongdoing, the believers are repeatedly urged to avoid wrongful behavior (2:1, 12, 20; 3:9, 11) and to "do what is right" (2:20; 3:17; 4:19). Both "doing what is wrong" and "doing what is right" in 1 Peter are broad in their connotations and are measured ultimately by the will of God (2:20; 3:6, 13–14, 17; 4:19; van Unnik 1954).

or as meddler in the affairs of others (*ē hōs allotriepiskopos*). Whereas the preceding three nouns identify stock types of unacceptable conduct, the noun *allotriepiskopos* occurs nowhere else in all of Greek literature and raises questions about what the term means and why it was included in this list. As variants of this term, which is unique but nevertheless contained in the best manuscripts, a few manuscripts have the slightly different spelling *allotrioepiskopos* (K P and many cursives); others substitute a less unusual expression such as "alien overseer" (*allotrios episkopos*, A Ψ 69 and a few others) or "overseer with respect to others" (*allotriois episkopos*, $\mathfrak{P}^{72}$).[595] The term does not appear again until it is used by Epiphanius in the fourth century (*Anc.* 12.5; cf. *Pan.* 67.85.6) and Dionysius the Areopagite in the fifth (*Ep.* 8), neither of whom is referring to this text (cf. Holzmeister 1937, 386). The term thus appears to be a Petrine coinage, though its precise meaning is not immediately clear.

Although our term follows "murderer" and "thief," this is no proof that it too designates some criminal act (against Bauer 1978a, 111; and Brox 1986, 219; similarly, Goppelt 1993, 326). A repeated *hōs* ("as") accompanying *allotriepiskopos* links it to, but also distinguishes it from, the foregoing three terms; see the similar function of *hōs* in 2:16. Selwyn (1947, 225) and Michaels (1988, 268) take this as indicating that the noun refers to something less legally culpable. The distinction, however, may lie elsewhere. Murder, theft and wrongdoing are patently actions that all believers would regard as unacceptable conduct. On the other hand, *allotriepiskopos* is a unique coinage whose moral implications would be less clear but nevertheless relevant to the situation envisioned by our author. He may well be referring here to actions in which the addressees could have been engaged or behavior of which they could more easily have been accused.

The varying renditions of *allotriepiskopos* in the commentaries and biblical translations reflect a range of assumed spheres of meddling and attribute to it varying degrees of gravity (cf. Bauer 1978a, 110–15). Some envision some form

---

[595] The Syriac Peshitta omits it altogether.

of illicit political activity;[596] others, illegal activity of an economic nature.[597] K. Erbes (1919, 1921) saw a reference to a bishop (*episkopos*) who misappropriated funds for the poor; Sander (1966), on the other hand, a bishop misleading the flock. Michaels (1988, 268) appropriately objects, however, that nothing here indicates that church leaders in particular are in view. The uncertainty of the term's connotation of illegal activity, on the other hand, may have led to a preference for the more general translation "mischief maker" (RSV, NRSV).

What appears most likely is that *allotriepiskopos* denotes a "meddler" (NIV) or "busybody in other men's affairs" (KJV, Michaels). Linguistically, *allotriepiskopos* involves a combination of *episkopos* ("overseer") and some form of *allotrios* ("belonging to another," "strange"), a combination, however, unattested prior to 1 Peter. Analogous combinations, such as *allotriophagos* ("eating another's bread"), *allotriophthoneō* ("envy another's possessions"), *allotrionomeō* ("live according to foreign customs"), *allotriopragia* ("meddling in another's affairs")," and *allotriopragmosynē* ("meddlesomeness"), indicate that in such constructions *allotrios* always qualifies the activity as *involvement in something alien to the doer*, or engagement in matters not of one's proper concern (Beyer 1964, 621).

The term has been construed as akin to *allotrios episkopos* (lit., "another kind of overseer"), one who assumes oversight in a strange, improper fashion (K. Erbes 1919, 39–40; 1921, 249). But in analogous composite constructions the prefixed *allotrio-* refers to the *object* of the term that follows, not the subject. Thus *allotriepiskopos* would rather have a sense similar to *episkopos allotriōn* (lit., "an overseer of others or the affairs of others"). More specifically, it appears to be modeled on composite terms having the sense of "meddling in another's affairs."[598] According to Epictetus, Cynic philosophers were accused of being self-appointed censors of the morality of others. His words in the Cynic's defense (*Diatr.* 3.22.97), may contain the original charge and are strikingly close to the components of our term *allotriepiskopos*:

> for this reason he that is so disposed is neither a busybody (*periergos*) nor a meddler (*polypragmōn*), for he is not meddling in alien matters (*ou gar ta*

[596] E.g., "revolutionary" (Moffatt; Goodspeed; Bischoff 1906); "agitator" (Beare); "intriguer" (NAB 1990); "spy" (Phillips; cf. Tert., *Scorp.* 12, *alieni speculator*); "informer" (JB, NJB); "destroyer of another's rights" (NAB 1970); "infringing on the rights of others" (NEB).

[597] See Cyprian, *Quir.* 3.37 (*curas alienas agens*, one who defrauds when "taking care of others' affairs"); Vulgate (*alienorum appetitor*, "one eager for the money of others"); cf. "embezzler" (Erbes 1919, 1921; Bauer 1978a, 112; Brox 1986, 220); and "depository of foreign assets" (suggested tentatively by Reicke 1964, 124–26).

[598] These composite terms include *allotrioprageō*, *allotriopragia* ("meddling in other people's business," Plut., *Adul. amic.* 14; *Mor.* 57D); and *allotriopragmosynē* ("meddlesomeness"), which Plato combines with a more conventional term having a similar meaning, *polypragmosynē* (*Resp.* 444b). For *polypragmōn* meaning "meddlesome," "busybody," see Eupolis 222; Aristoph., *Aves* 471; Lysis, *Ep.* 24.24; Isoc., *Ep.* 15.98, 230, 237; Epict., *Diatr.* 3.22.97; see also *polypragmoneō*, "to be meddlesome, a busybody" (Aristoph., *Plut.* 913; Plato, *Resp.* 433a), "to interfere" (IG 5.1208.24), or "to meddle in state affairs" (Hdt. 3.15; Xen., *Anab.* 5.1.15).

allotria polypragmonei) when he oversees human affairs (*hotan ta anthrōpina episkopēi*), but is attending to matters that concern him as well (*alla ta idia*).

To illustrate, Epictetus points to a general who oversees (*episkopēi*), reviews, watches over his troops, and punishes the guilty (cf. also *Diatr.* 3.22.72, 77).[599]

On the basis of this evidence, *allotriepiskopos* is best taken as designating "one who meddles in the affairs of others" (people outside the immediate range of family, friends, and associates). Plutarch's treatise *On Being a Busybody* (*Peri Polygramosynēs*, *Mor.* 515B–523B) is representative of the condemnation of busybodies by Greek and Roman moralists. The busybody or meddlesome person, he observes, pries into the private and domestic affairs of others. He desires to learn the troubles of others (*Polyg.* 1; *Mor.* 515E); he shows no respect for domestic privacy but pries into secrets and blabs them to outsiders (*Polyg.* 2–4; *Mor.* 515D–517C).[600] Cicero, commenting on the duty of the private citizen, (*Off.* 1.124), notes that "the private individual ought first, in private relations, to live on fair and equal terms with his fellow-citizens, with a spirit neither servile and groveling (*neque summissum et abiectum*) nor yet domineering; and second, in matters pertaining to the state, to labor for her peace and honor; for such a man we are accustomed to esteem and call a good citizen." Then with a statement that would be particularly germane to resident aliens such as those addressed in 1 Peter he continues (1.125): "As for the foreigner or the resident alien (*peregrini, incolae*), it is his duty to attend strictly to his own concerns, not to pry into other people's business, and under no condition to meddle in the politics of a country not his own."[601]

Being a "snoopy busybody" and a "meddler in the affairs of others" was condemned not only by Hellenistic moralists but by Israelite and Christian authors as well, with similar terms, such as *periergos* and *periergazomai*,[602] and Paul urged, "mind your own affairs . . . so that you may command the respect of outsiders" (1 Thess 4:10).

In the context of 1 Peter, the "others" in whose affairs believers should not meddle would be the nonbelieving outsiders.[603] These outsider "Gentiles" (2:12; 4:3) would have seen such behavior as particularly offensive when

[599] See also Xen., *Mem.* 3.7.9, concerning many who rush to oversee the affairs of others (*to skopein ta tōn allōn pragmata*) without scrutizing their own affairs.

[600] See also Plut., *Polyg.* 6; *Mor.* 518B; *Polyg.* 7; *Mor.* 518E; and *Polyg.* 15; *Mor.* 523A (busybodies "investigate and make public even the involuntary mischances of their neighbors").

[601] See also Philo's warning (*Spec.* 3.170–71) that a woman in charge of household management (*oikonomia*) should not be a busybody (*mēden . . . polypragmoneitō*) in affairs outside the household.

[602] See Sir 3:23 ("do not meddle [*mē periergazou*] in what is beyond your task"); *T. Iss.* 5:1 ("do not meddle [*mē periergazomenoi*] in the affairs of your neighbors"); cf. *T. Reu.* 3:10; 2 Thess 3:11 (against "mere busybodies," *periergazomenos*); 1 Tim 5:13 (against "busybodies," *periergoi*).

[603] *Allotrios* is the antonym of *oikeios*, and in this letter terms from the *oik-* root regularly designate the believing community and its members.

practiced by persons such as the addressees, who in fact were considered strangers and aliens. A missionary movement seeking recruits inevitably ran the risk of appearing to prescribe for others how they should manage and conduct their own affairs. Censuring the behavior of outsiders on the basis of claims to a higher morality, interfering with family relationships, fomenting domestic discontent and discord, or "tactless attempts at conversion" (Selwyn 1947, 225; and Windisch and Preisker 1951, 77; cf. also Spörri 1925, 71) could all have fallen under the label of "meddling." Seen in this light, this proscription of meddling may well have been intended to warn the addressees to respect the social boundaries distinguishing them from outsiders, to keep their own house in order and beyond reproach, and to focus on attracting others rather than on criticizing them or meddling in their affairs. Meddling would only exacerbate an already tense relationship with outsiders. The thought would be similar to that expressed by Paul: "What have I to do with judging outsiders? Is it not those inside the church whom you are to judge? God judges those outside" (1 Cor 5:12).

Only the first two of the four misdeeds listed in v 15 unquestionably refer to criminal acts, with the latter two likely involving offenses against expected decorum. Consequently, there are no valid grounds for assuming that any suffering resulting from all of these activities would have been the result of an official prosecution of Christians as criminals undertaken by Rome. Nor does the author indicate that any of the addressees had in fact been so charged. The statement is not a description of what has taken place but a warning against what must not occur. Reicke's claim (1964, 127) that in vv 12–19 and v 15 in particular the author is warning that "Christian martyrs should not be anarchists" introduces a notion of political subversion hardly in keeping with the tenor and focus of the remainder of his exhortation.

The point here is that the addressees should lead irreproachable lives (so also 2:1, 11; 4:2–3) and offer no occasion for justifiable accusation on the part of outsiders.[604] All of the terms in v 15 concern modes of misconduct that, within the context of this letter, are incompatible with being "in Christ" (3:16; 5:14), being associated with Christ (4:14), being mindful of God's will (2:15, 19; 3:16–17, 21; 4:2, 19), and doing what is right" (4:19; cf. 2:15, 20; 3:6, 11, 17). These actions are to be avoided not primarily because they violate Roman law or custom but because they transgress the will of God, the fundamental moral criterion of this letter (so also van Unnik 1954–1955, 100–102). To engage in any of these actions would be disgraceful, and suffering would be a just penalty. Not so, however, suffering as a "Christian." With the foil of proscribed shameful behavior established, the author arrives at his main point (v 16): suffering as a Christian is no cause for feeling shamed but actually an opportunity for honoring and glorifying God. Once again, as in v 14; 2:4–10; and 3:16, the

[604] On this theme, see van Unnik 1964 and the NOTE on 2:11.

relation of believers to outsiders and to God is described in the contrasting terms of shame and honor, respectively.

16a. *if, however, [any of you suffers] as a Christian* (*ei de hōs Christianos*). As a contrast to v 15 (with *de* ["however"] having adversative force), this elliptical formulation implies a repetition of the words "any of you suffers" (*tis hymōn paschei*) in v 15, and "suffers as a Christian" contrasts with "suffer as a murderer, or a thief, or a wrongdoer, or as a meddler in the affairs of others." A final *hōs* ("as") links *Christianos* to but also distinguishes it from the preceding terms; see its similar function in 2:16. The 3d-person sing. imperatives *mē aischynesthō* and *doxazetō* in v 16 match the 3d-person sing. imperative *paschetō* in v 15. At the same time, this verse also parallels the conditional statement in v 14 so that "if any of you suffers as a Christian" reformulates "if you are reproached because of Christ," with suffering being a consequence of being reproached and the injunction to "glorify/honor God" (v 16c) corresponding to the declaration "how honored you are" (v 14b). Verses 14 and 16 thus form an inclusion embracing this subunit (A/B/A′).

as a Christian (*hōs Christianos*). The parallel structure of vv 14 and 16 indicates that "as a Christian" parallels "because of (your association with) Christ," but the expressions reflect different perspectives. "Because of Christ" is our author's formulation, whereas "Christian," as will be shown, is a label applied to members of the messianic sect by outsiders. *Christianos*, an adjective used here as a substantive,[605] appears only twice elsewhere in the NT (Acts 11:26 and 26:28). These three instances are the first attested appearances of the term in all of Greek literature. The term was never used by and was apparently unknown to Jesus, Paul, and virtually all other NT writers (except the authors of 1 Peter and Acts), yet in time it became the most common name for members of the messianic movement.

Christianos involves a borrowed Latin ending (*-ianos* [Gk.] from *-ianus* [Lat.]) or an underlying Latin formation in its entirety (Karpp 1954, 1132). This indicates its origin within Latin-speaking circles (Peterson 1982, 69–77 and most scholars), where "Christ" was regarded as a proper name (not a title, against Peterson 1982, 76), and the suffix *-ianus* designated a partisan, adherent, or client of the one named. Such Latin formations (proper name + *-ianus*) were numerous.[606] Hellenistic practice was to copy this by attaching *-ianos* (pl. *-ianoi*) to the name of a leader, as in the case of *Hērōdianoi* (Mark 3:6; 12:13; Matt 22:16) and *Kaisarianoi* (App., *Bell. Civ.* 3.91]) for partisans of Herod or

[605] The alternate readings *Chrēstianos* (Codex Sinaiticus, here as well as in Acts 11:26 and 26:28) and *Chreistianos* (Codex Vaticanus) are itacisms reflecting the identical pronunciation of the Greek letters *ē*, *i*, and *ei* in the Hellenistic period (BDF §21; Horsley 1981–1989, 3:129). Compare also *Chrestus* for *Christus* (Suet., *Claud.* 25) and see also the NOTE on the readings *christos* and *chrēstos* in 2:3.

[606] E.g., Augustianus, Brutianus, Caesarianus, Catonianus, Ciceronianus, Crassianus, Drusianus, Galbianus, Lepidianus, Marianus, Milonianus, Neronianus, Pisonianus, Pompeianus, Varonianus (Zahn 1909, 193–94).

clients of the emperor, respectively (cf. also the gnostic groups named after their leaders as mentioned by Justin [*Dial.* 35]: *Markianoi, Oualentinianoi, Basilidianoi, Satournilianoi*). The term *Christianos* (pl. *Christianoi*) thus appears to have been a similar appellation originating in Latin-speaking or Latin-influenced circles, and was applied to members of the messianic sect as "followers, partisans, or clients of Christ."

The first use of "Christian," according to Acts, was in Antioch of Syria. Following his account of the dispersion of the messianic movement from Jerusalem northward to Antioch (Acts 8:1–11:25), the author of Acts states, "and in Antioch the disciples were for the first time called Christians" (Acts 11:25). In the chronology of Acts this is linked with the reign of King Agrippa I (41–44 CE), to whom reference is made in the immediately following verse, Acts 12:1. A few scholars have contended that *Christianos* originated with the followers of Jesus as a self-designation.[607] Bickermann (1949, 110–16) argued that the verb *chrēmatisai* in Acts 11:26 is active and has the sense of "called themselves." This view was effectively countered by Haenchen (1971, 367–68 n. 3) and Taylor (1974, 83), who have shown that *chrēmatizō* in the active voice also was used of persons being called certain names by others.[608] Such use of *chrēmatizō*, together with the Latin rather than Greek or Aramaic origin of *Christianos*, make it more likely that the sense in Acts 11:26 is that it was first at Antioch that the disciples "were called Christians" *by others*, as most scholars now agree.[609] This likelihood is strengthened by the second occurrence of *Christianos* in Acts 26:28. In the account of Paul's hearing at Caesarea in Palestine, King Herod Agrippa II responds to Paul's self-defense with the sneering words, "In a short time you think to make me a Christian!" (26:28). In this passage of Acts it is clearly an outsider to the movement who employs the term, a person aligned with Roman authorities (the governor Festus) and Latin-speaking circles.

Among those outside the movement, the appellation cannot have been coined by members of the House of Israel, since they would hardly have acknowledged that Jesus was the Christ/Messiah and therefore would never have named Jesus' followers "Christians." Indeed, its Latin origin points instead to its invention by Gentile residents of Antioch, the third largest city of the Roman Empire with a rich admixture of cults and groups from east and west. With this label, members of the messianic sect were singled out from other Israelite factions and Gentile groups by pagan outsiders, perhaps including Roman authorities, and designated "partisans of Christ." The mocking tone of Herod Agrippa's remark suggests that the label had a derogatory overtone from

[607] See Bickermann 1949; Moreau 1949–1950; Spicq 1961; Lifschitz 1962.

[608] See Plut., *Mulier. virt.*; *Mor.* 248d; Philo, *Deus* 121; Josephus, *Ant.* 8.157; POxy. 3.505; Origen, *Cels.* 8.25; Eusebius, *Hist. eccl.* 1.2.14; Athan., *Serm.* 32; John Chrys., *Hom. Act.* 25.1.

[609] See von Harnack 1908, 11; Gercke 1911; Karpp 1954, 1132; Mattingly 1958; Downey 1961, 275–76; Spicq 1961; Penna 1967; Haenchen 1971; Searle 1975–1976; Cadbury 1979; Dickie 1979; Elliott and Martin 1982, 107; Peterson 1982; Wilkins 1992; J. Taylor 1994.

the outset, so that it meant, not simply "partisans of Christ," but something like "Christ-lackeys," shameful sycophants of Christ, a criminal put to ignominious death by the Romans years earlier, in 30 CE. Mattingly (1958, 32) proposed that, with this name, persons professing allegiance to Christ were ridiculed in a fashion similar to the Roman knights called *Augustiani*, who devoted themselves to the praise of Nero, the self-proclaimed spiritual heir of Augustus. The wanton reputation of these *Augustiani* was well known (Tac., *Ann.* 14.15), and Roman sources indicate a similar negative odor of the label *Christiani* (see Pliny, *Ep.* 10.96–97; Tac., *Ann.* 15.44; and Suet., *Nero* 16.2).

Negative odor, however, should not be confused with criminality. Peterson's claim (1982, 76–87) that at Antioch the label "Christian" was coined by Roman authorities as a designation of the Christians as political subversives and criminals goes beyond the available evidence. The same objection applies to J. Taylor's related claim (1994, 94) that after Antioch "the name was thenceforth synonymous with sedition and crime." If the label had had this sort of connotation for Herod Agrippa and Festus, Paul, as a Christian, would have stood condemned. In actuality, however, he was not condemned but instead was allowed to plead his case before Nero in Rome. Against Peterson's view, Haenchen (1971, 367–68 n. 3) makes the further telling point that a Roman view of Christians as political subversives is impossible to reconcile with Acts' portrayal of the favorable treatment of Christians at the hands of Roman authorities. In the course of the first century, the label followed the messianic sect from Syrian Antioch (Acts 11:26)[610] to Caesarea in Samaria (Acts 26:28) to Rome (Tac., *Ann.* 15.44; Suet., *Nero* 16.2) and Asia Minor (1 Pet 4:16). The coinage of "Christian" by outsiders as a term of opprobrium explains its absence in most of the NT and its markedly slow acceptance as a self-designation in the course of the second century.[611]

The significance of the term *Christianos* in v 16 is conditioned by the fact that here too it likely has a denigrating overtone. At the same time, its use here, as Dalton (1990, 908) indicates, "does not mean that being a Christian was a public crime." There is no evidence proving that, at this early point in Christian history, merely being a Christian violated some putative Roman law or edict. For in fact no such edict or law universally proscribing Christianity existed. The use of *Christianos* by outsiders as a derogatory label was, rather, a tool in the arsenal of nonbelievers for demeaning the honor and impugning

[610] Gercke (1911) argued unconvincingly for its origin in Rome, not Antioch.

[611] For its earliest use as a self-designation, see *Did.* 12:4 and the letters of Ignatius of Antioch (*Eph.* 11:2; 14:2; *Magn.* 4:1; *Rom.* 3:2; *Pol.* 7:3; *Trall.* 6:1); see also *Mart. Pol.* 3:2; 10:1; 12:1, 2; *Diogn.* 6:1–10; cf. also *ho Christianismos* ("Christianity") in Ign. *Magn.* 10:1, 3; *Rom.* 3:3; *Phld.* 6:1; *Mart. Pol.* 12:1. On the origin, meaning, and early use of the term *Christianos*, see Lipsius 1873; Le Coultre 1907; von Harnack 1908, 410–14; Zahn 1909, 191–94; Gercke 1911; Labriolle 1929–1930; Bickermann 1949; Moreau 1950; Karpp 1954; Mattingly 1958; Peterson 1982; Downey 1961, 275 n. 19; Spicq 1961; Haenchen 1971, 367–68; Grundmann et al. 1974, 536–37, 576–80; Cadbury 1979; R. E. Brown and Meier 1983, 35; Benko 1985b, 1–29; J. Taylor 1994. On its use as a sectarian designation, see Elliott 1981/1990, 79, 95–96; and 1995b.

the moral character and reputation of these strangers and aliens. It was not a term by which they were legally accused. In the case of Nero's attack on the Christians in Rome (64–65 CE), the adherents of Jesus Christ, despite being despised by the mob, were not incriminated for simply being "Christians" (as they were called) but as purported arsonists (Tac., *Ann.* 15.44).

Some scholars, nevertheless, have claimed a similarity between 1 Pet 4:12–16 and the circumstances described in an exchange of letters between Pliny the Younger and Emperor Trajan (*Ep.* 10.96–97) concerning Pliny's encounter with Christians in Pontus (ca. 111–112 CE). Both Pliny and our author write about a situation in Pontus (although for 1 Peter this is only one region of the letter's much more inclusive address). Both refer to persons labeled "Christians," and both mention shameful deeds with which the Christians may have been associated (Pliny) or in which they should not be involved (1 Pet 4:15). Could not Pliny and the Petrine author be contemporaries referring to the same situation, and might not Pliny show that merely being a "Christian" was a crime under Roman law? (so Knox 1953; Beare 1970, 32–34, 175, 193; Downing 1988). Close comparison of the writings, however, reveals that the situation described by Pliny bears no substantive resemblance to the situation portrayed in 1 Peter and that the Pliny-Trajan exchange has no bearing on the import of the label "Christian" in 1 Peter.

Pliny the Younger was a legate commissioned by Emperor Trajan to assist in the ordering of affairs in the province of Bithynia-Pontus. On arriving in Pontus (ca. 112 CE), Pliny learned that local residents were denouncing others among them as Christians (*Christiani*). Unsure of how to handle the situation, he wrote to Trajan describing his actions to that point and requested information on how to proceed. Because of an acknowledged uncertainty concerning any criminal implications of the name "Christian," he submitted those denounced as "Christians" to an examination (a *cognitio extra ordinem*) to ascertain possible culpability of shameful acts (*flagitia*) and crimes. Giving them the opportunity to renounce being Christian, he was struck by their "stubborness and unshakable obstinacy," which he thought should not go unpunished. But he found no evidence of punishable "shameful acts" (*flagitia*) and "nothing but a degenerate sort of cult carried to extravagant lengths" (*superstitionem pravam et immodicam*). In his response (Pliny, *Ep.* 10.97), Trajan made no mention of any official Roman policy proscribing Christianity and commended Pliny's procedure, indicating the impossibility of laying down "a general rule to a fixed formula." He furthur insisted that Christians were not to be hunted down but, if any charges of shameful acts against them were proved, they must be punished. Moreover, anonymous charges were not to be admitted, since this would be incompatible with the tolerant "spirit of our age."

This correspondence makes clear that for Roman authorities in the early second century Christianity was still an unknown quantity. Considered members of a degenerate sort of cult or sordid alien superstition, Christians may have been suspected of engaging in disgraceful acts or crimes, but this remained to be proved. In the meantime, "they were to be treated fairly and not made to suffer from calumny or slander" (Wilken 1984, 28). This exchange of letters likewise demonstrates the absence of any imperial edict proscribing Christianity worldwide.

On the other hand, the content of this correspondence bears little similiarity to the situation described in 1 Peter. (1) The situation that 1 Peter envisions is not simply that of Pontic Christians (as in Pliny) but of Christians in Galatia, Cappadocia, Asia, and Bithynia (1 Pet 1:1), as well as throughout the world (5:9). (2) The Petrine author, like Pliny, knows of the label "Christian" attached to persons in Pontus but speaks only of the "reproach" and "suffering" of these persons and says nothing of their delation by others, their arrest or examination by Roman governors/legates, their trials, or their execution. In contrast to Pliny, he also makes no mention of tortured deaconesses or of any Christians who have renounced their faith at an earlier time. He likewise says nothing about desertion of temples or refusal to sacrifice, matters of special concern to those delating the Christians according to Pliny. Nor does he present any critique of Rome anywhere in the letter, an omission difficult to imagine if Roman authorities were indeed executing innocent Christians as criminals.

What the Petrine author *does* state also bears little resemblance to the situation described by Pliny. Rather than citing formal denunciations of Christians, our author speaks only of verbal "reproach" (4:14) aimed at publicly shaming the believers in the court of public opinion, the consistently portrayed situation in this letter. The conduct warned against in 4:15 included two crimes (murder and theft) but also two vaguer behaviors, "wrongdoing" and the still vaguer "meddling in the affairs of others," neither of which was per se a legally defined crime or an equivalent of Pliny's *flagitia*. Suffering public ridicule by being stigmatized as a "Christ-lackey" (4:16) is several steps removed from being legally denounced, arrested, and punished as a criminal. Our author speaks only of the former, and Pliny, only of the latter. In the single instance in which reference is made to the Roman emperor and his governors (2:13–14, 17), no mention is made of trials before Roman governors, nor is Roman rule subjected to any criticism. Believers instead are urged to be subordinate to imperial authority and to give the emperor honor.

In sum, the details in 1 Pet 4:12–16 diverge significantly from those in the Pliny-Trajan correspondence. This correspondence is of little use in clarifying the situation in 1 Peter or the implication of the label "Christian" in 1 Pet 4:16 and provides no basis for the notion that the Petrine author and Pliny were contemporaries. Pliny, writing about 111–12 CE, reflects a later situation when, for the first (attested) time, Christians were being denounced to and tried by a Roman provincial authority in Bithynia-Pontus. 1 Peter reflects a different, earlier situation than that of Pliny (so also Lepelley 1980, 56–59). Since Pliny states, without providing further detail, that some Christians in this province had apostatized "twenty years ago" (*Ep.* 10.96.6), the letter of 1 Peter, whose address includes Pontus but that makes no mention of such apostasy, must have been written prior to 92 CE. This provides a useful *terminus ad quem* for the composition of 1 Peter.

The circumstances presumed in 4:12–19, moreover, are not different from but the same as those described earlier in this letter (against Beare and all partition theorists). The situation entails intense verbal abuse and incessant maligning and reproach, including the smearing of followers of Jesus Christ with the opprobrious label "Christian" or "Christ-lackey." With no evidence of any official Empire-wide Roman proscription of Christianity prior to Decius (249–251 CE), and with no mention in 1 Peter of local arrests, trials, or executions, there is no basis for claiming that at the time of 1 Peter Christianity had been officially proscribed by Rome and that being labeled a Christian implied being charged as a criminal. If being a Christian were itself a crime, then its consequence would be legal punishment, not shame (v 16a).

The point of our author is that suffering "as a Christian"—that is, being demeaned and shamed as a "Christ-lackey"—is a different cause for suffering from those mentioned in v 15. Instead, it is related to the reproach mentioned in v 14 but described with different language and reflecting a different perspective. The Petrine author himself designates the believers as persons who are "in Christ" (3:16; 5:10, 14) or who are suffering "because of (their association with) Christ" (4:14). With *Christianos*, on the other hand, he is referring to a shaming label applied by reproaching outsiders. Thus, v 14 describes the predicament from the perspective of the author, whereas v 16a records the language of the outsiders. In both verses the issue is one of shame and honor, with a shift from the former to the latter (v 14a/14bc, v 16a/16b).

16b. *you should not feel shamed* (*mē aischynesthō*). Together with the preceding adversative particle *de* ("but"), the negative *mē aischynesthō* forms an antithetical parallel to the negative imperative in v 15, "let none of you suffer . . ." (*mē gar tis hymōn paschetō* . . .). The imperative, as that in v 16c, is a 3d-person present pass. imperative with *tis* ("any [of you]," v 15) still presupposed as grammatical subject, so that a literal translation would be, "let this person not feel shamed . . . but let this person glorify . . ." (as in many translations). However, the expression "any of *you*" (*tis hymōn*, v 15) also allows treating *aischynesthō* and *doxazetō* according to sense as 2d-person sing. imperatives: "you should not feel shamed, . . . but (you) should rather glorify . . ." (as preferred here and by Michaels 1988, 268–69; cf. also Luther, NRSV, NIV, LB). This is also consistent with the 2d-person verbs in vv 12, 13, and 14.

Believers should not suffer for violations of the law and ignoble behavior, and if they do so suffer it would be shameful both in God's sight and the eyes of society. But there is no cause for feeling shamed if suffering results solely from being labeled a "Christian." The verb *aischynō*, often used interchangeably with the virtually synonymous verbs *kataischynō* (which appears in 2:6 and 3:16) and *epaischynomai*, can be taken as either a passive or, as here, a middle-voiced verb. In the passive voice it means "be put to shame," "be shamed, disgraced" by another.[612] In the middle voice it means "to feel shamed, disgraced," "to be ashamed (of something)" (Gen 2:25; Prov 1:22; 13:5; Luke 16:3; 1 John 2:28).[613] The passive has the external act more in view; the middle, the internal subjective reaction. Philo (*Migr.* 225) offers an example of the sense of the passive *aischynthēnai* in speaking of the soul "that had seemed to have been shamed." Neither the voices nor the senses, however, are always clearly distinguishable.[614] The present context suggests aspects of both external act and internal reaction. The passive verbs *kataischynthēi* and *kataischynthōsin* in 2:6 and 3:16, respectively, imply God as the shaming agent. Here, however, in the light of v 14, it is those who reproach the Christians who are the implied shaming agents. With their reproaching (v 14a) and their application of the disparaging label "Christ-lackey" (v 16a), they attempted to discredit the addressees and put them to public shame.[615] This is a further indication that legal proceedings are not in view here. Such proceedings would have involved far more than the public shaming of victims, namely arrest and trial (so also Best 1971, 165).

Our author urges the believers not to feel shamed, not to consider themselves as actually disgraced (J. N. D. Kelly 1969, 188). A similar sentiment is expressed by a contemporary moralist, Musonius Rufus. A philosopher, he points out (*Pers. Inj.* 10.15–23), ought not to regard suffering personal injuries (being reproached or struck or spit upon) as actual injuries: "For what does the man who submits to insult do that is wrong? It is the doer of wrong who forthwith puts himself to shame, while the sufferer, who does nothing but submit, has no reason whatever to feel shame or disgrace." The reason that the addressees of 1 Peter should not feel shamed has been stated earlier: God, not society, is the ultimate arbiter and conferrer of shame and honor (1:21; 2:4–10; 3:14, 16; 5:10). In their reproach and suffering, believers share in the insult (2:23), rejection (2:4c; 3:18d), and suffering (4:14) of Christ. Appraisal by society is of less account, and it is the would-be shamers themselves whom God will actually put to shame (3:16; cf. 4:5–6).

The addressees' appropriate response to attempts at shaming them, as the remainder of this verse indicates, is to acknowledge God's honor and glory, even with the very name by which they are reproached and caused to suffer (v 16c).

16c. *but should rather glorify God with this name* (*doxazetō de ton theon en tōi onomati toutōi*). Suffering as a "Christ-lackey" is not a reason for feeling

---

[612] See 1 Kgdms 13:4; 27:12; 1 Chr 19:6; 2 Chr 12:6; Sir 51:18; 2 Cor 10:8; Phil 1:20.

[613] Cf. the similar sense of *epaischynomai*, linked explicitly with suffering and being ashamed of Jesus Christ in Mark 8:38/Luke 9:26; 2 Tim 1:8, 12; cf. R. Bultmann 1964, 189; Horstmann 1990, 42.

[614] For overlapping senses, see Vorster 1979, 68–69; and on *aischynomai* and kindred terms in the NT, Vorster 1979, 66–140.

[615] For shame associated with reproach, see also Ps 43:16–17[44:15–16]; 68:7–8[69:5–6]; and Prov 20:4.

shamed but an opportunity for honoring and glorifying God. This is a deft transvaluation of shame into honor, similar to the contrast "reproach-honor" in v 14, and constitutes yet another positive value assigned to innocent suffering: it is an opportunity to glorify God. The verb *doxazetō* is a 3d-person present act. imperative but because of *tis hymōn* ("any of you," v 15) is rendered, like *aischynesthō*, according to sense as a 2d-person verb: "(you) should rather glorify. . . ." It contrasts with *aischynesthō*, as *doxa* in v 14 contrasts with *oneidizesthe*; for the association between "suffering" and "glory," see also 1:11; 4:13–14; 5:1, 10. The concern for glorifying or honoring God, especially through an honorable way of life,[616] is a continuing theme of the letter (cf. 2:9, 12; 4:11) but now is related to the experience of reproach and stigmatization with the contemptuous label "Christian."

with this name (*en tōi onomati toutōi*). This is an adverbial phrase modifying "glorify God." "This name" refers not to *onomati Christou* in v 14, despite the recurrence of *onoma*, but to *Christianos*, the nearest antecedent for the demonstrative adj. "this" (*toutōi*), as J. N. D. Kelly (1969, 190–91) and Davids (1990, 170) have observed. The differing translations of the entire phrase reflect three different ways of considering the function of the preposition *en*: (1) *en* with *instrumental* force ("with," "by," or "through this name"; so Goodspeed); (2) *en* with locative force ("in the sphere of this name," "by virtue of bearing this name"; so Selwyn 1947, 225–26; or "under that name let him glorify God," RSV); (3) *en* with causative force ("because of the name," NAB 1990).[617]

J. N. D. Kelly (1969, 190–91) favors an idiomatic sense for the entire phrase, translating *en tōi onomati toutōi* "in this capacity," "on this account." The variant reading *en tōi merei toutōi* ("on this account," "in this case"; cf. 2 Cor 3:10; 9:3) in some later manuscripts (P 049 𝔐), he holds, indicates that later scribes also took the phrase in this sense. His chief support for this view, however, involves different Greek phrases, which actually better explain the expression *en onomati Christou* in v 14 (see NOTE on 4:14). Michaels (1988, 269–70) goes further and actually regards *merei* (rather than *onomati*) as original and translates "in this manner." This reading, however, has weak manuscript support and appears actually to be a secondary substitution for what scribes considered a more difficult reading.

Since *en* frequently is used instrumentally in this letter (1:2, 5a, 6b, 12, 17, 22; 2:2, 18; 3:2, 4; 4:19; 5:14) and since this usage fits this context as well, preference is given here to the first named option. "Glorify" is used with an instrumental *en* also in John 13:31, 32; 17:10; Rom 15:6; and 1 Cor 6:20. The issue addressed here is not the sphere in which the believers find themselves or the cause for which they glorify God but a specific name (*Christianos*) with which they are stigmatized. Any and all kinds of ignominy and wrongdoing of which

---

[616] Cf. also Matt 5:16; John 15:8; 17:4; 21:19; Rom 15:6; 1 Cor 6:20.

[617] Cf. "in virtue of that name," NAB 1970; "let him glorify God on this behalf," KJV; "he should thank God that he has been called one," JB; "for bearing this name," NJB.

believers and Christ their Lord were falsely accused would have been associated with this contemptuous label "Christian." Since the faithful know the baselessness of such slander, however, they can turn even this instrument of reproach into a means of glorification. Thus, a contemptuous label employed to shame paradoxically can become an honorable name used to honor God. Just as joy is contrasted with surprise (vv 12, 13), and divine honor is contrasted with human reproach (v 14), so honoring God is contrasted with being shamed by outsiders.

This, then, constitutes a fifth positive valuation of innocent suffering mentioned here. Not only is suffering innocently a divine test of faith (v 12), a sign of solidarity with the suffering Christ (v 13a), a cause for rejoicing (v 13bc), and a mark of the Spirit's presence (v 14); it is also an opportunity for actively glorifying God. Reproached believers who are honored by God (v 14bc), honor God in return.

17a. *For [now is] the propitious time for judgment to begin with the house(hold) of God (hoti ho kairos tou arxasthai to krima apo tou oikou tou theou)*. "For" (*hoti*) introduces a thought that provides an eschatological warrant for the foregoing exhortation (vv 12–16), just as earlier in the letter the impartial judgment of God (1:17a) provided an eschatological warrant for the imperative that followed (1:17b) (cf. also 4:7a, establishing the eschatological perspective for 4:7b–11, and 4:5, stressing the nearness of the moment of judgment). This initial clause is elliptical, with *nyn esti* ("now is") apparently implied.

the propitious time (*ho kairos*). The noun *kairos*[618] denotes a "propitious" or "critical" point in time. As in 1:5, 11; and 5:6 (see respective NOTES), it has eschatological coloration and refers here to the critical moment when the anticipated divine judgment of humanity begins.[619]

for judgment to begin (*tou arxasthai to krima*). The nature of this "propitious time" is explained by a construction[620] involving a genitive of the articular infinitive (*tou arxasthai*) and its subject (*to krima*): "a propitious time for judgment (*to krima*) to begin (*tou arxasthai*)." The noun *krima* ("judging action") occasionally is used, as here, with the sense of *krisis* ("judgment"; see also Acts 24:25; Heb 6:2; and Rev 20:4). As Bigg (1902, 181) comments, "verbals in *-ma* and *-sis* not infrequently interchange meanings." The judgment is the final divine assize (cf. Rom 2:2–3; 2 Pet 2:3; Jude 4; Rev 17:1; 18:20), an event already affirmed as being at hand (4:5–6; cf. 1:17) and linked traditionally, as in this letter, to the end time (4:7) and the suffering of the righteous (4:12–14, 16;

[618] The manuscripts vary in regard to the exclusion (א A and others) or inclusion (𝔓[72] B P Ψ 𝔐) of the definite article (*ho*) with *kairos*, perhaps reflecting a scribal confusion caused by the sequence of the Greek letters *O-T-I-O* (cf. also 5:5c). Elsewhere *kairos* is anarthrous, but here the manuscript evidence tips in favor of the article's inclusion. Whether it was omitted inadvertently or added for emphasis sake, no difference in meaning is evident.

[619] Cf. Matt 21:34, 41; Mark 13:33; Luke 21:8; Rom 13:11; 1 Cor 7:29; Rev 1:3; 22:10.

[620] On the construction, see BDF §400.1; and for further NT examples, see Luke 1:57; 2:6; 10:19; 22:6; Acts 27:20; 1 Cor 9:10; Rom 15:23.

cf. Hiers 1992). Suffering for the faith as a mark of the end time, "a distinctly Christian view" according to Selwyn (1947, 301), is a recurrent NT theme,[621] as is the conviction that the current moment is the commencement of divine judgment (John 16:11; 1 Thess 2:16). Our author shows no interest in premonitory signs or cosmic upheavals, traditonally viewed as announcements of the end time, but focuses on the suffering of the righteous (including both Jesus [3:18b] and his followers [4:12–16]) as the sure indication that the end is near and that the judgment of God is at hand.

with the house(hold) of God (*apo tou oikou tou theou*). The preposition *apo* ("with," lit., "from"), when accompanying the verb *archō* ("begin"), conventionally indicates the starting point of the action (Ezek 9:6; Matt 4:17; 16:21; 20:8; Luke 14:18; John 8:9; Acts 1:22; 8:35; 10:37). Here the starting point of divine judgment is said to be the very house(hold) of God, God's own people. Once again the Christian community is portrayed as the house(hold) or family of God, just as *oikos pneumatikos* (2:5) denoted the believing community as the "house(hold) of the Spirit."

The idea of judgment's commencing with God's own people is traditional, as Israelite writings illustrate.[622] These texts, however, envision the *punishment* of God's people for their disobedience, whereas 1 Peter looks to the *saving* of the righteous (v 18; cf. 1:5, 9; 2:2; 3:21). Thus judgment, as relating to the believers, is not condemnation but evaluation, testing, and vindication, as already indicated (4:12; 1:6–7; cf. Mal 3:1–5).

This contrast is also important for considering the relation of 1 Pet 4:17 to Ezek 9:6, which has been claimed to have inspired this verse (L. T. Johnson 1986; Schutter 1987; 1989, 156–63; Michaels 1988, 271), and for determining the sense of *oikos tou theou*. The words of our text, *tou arxasthai to krima apo tou oikou tou theou*, bear some resemblance to the language of Ezek 9:6 (*apo tōn hagiōn mou arxasthe*). But the correspondence is so limited and the points of each passage so different that any connection between 1 Pet 4:17 and Ezek 9:6 is highly unlikely.

Ezekiel 8:1–11:25 describes visions regarding the Jerusalem Temple, associated abominations, the slaying of the disobedient, the defiling of the Temple, and God's departure. In this section of Ezekiel, the term *oikos* appears frequently and designates either God's people or the Temple. Chapter 9 in particular describes the slaying and defiling action of the "executioners" of the city

---

[621] See Rom 8:18, 22; 1 Cor 7:26; Phil 1:29–30; 1 Thess 3:3–4; 5:3; 2 Thess 1:4–10; 2 Tim 3:1, 12; Heb 13:13; Rev 2:10; 3:10; 12:1–8.

[622] See Jer 25:29 (32:29 LXX: "For behold I begin to work evil at the city that is called by my name . . . you shall not go unpunished"); Ezek 9:5–6 and *T. Benj.* 10:8 ("for the Lord first judges Israel for the sins she has committed and then he shall do the same for all the nations"); and later rabbinic texts (*Midr. Qoh.* 45a; *b. B. Qam.* 60a; *b. Roš Haš.* 8b; *Midr. Pss.* 17a, 44b, 212a; *Exod. Rab.* 88d); more generally, see Amos 3:1–2, 14; Jer 1:13–16; 25:8–38; Ezek 21:7–22; Mal 3:1–18; *2 Bar.* 13:9–10; cf. Millauer 1976, 106–10.

of Jerusalem and God's destruction of the city's inhabitants. Those who groaned over the abominations committed in the Temple, the Lord said, were to be spared. All others (elders, youth, children and women) were to be slain (vv 1–6a). The text said to be relevant to 1 Pet 4:17, Ezek 9:6b–7, recounts further instructions from God, and then continues:

> "And [you executioners] begin with my holy ones [or sanctuary] (*apo tōn hagiōn mou arxasthe*)." So they began with the elder men who were within the house (*Kai ērxanto apo tōn andrōn tōn presbyterōn hoi ēsan esō en tōi oikōi*). Then he [God] said to them, "Defile the house (*ton oikon*) and go out and fill the ways with dead bodies and strike."

Two chief problems concerning this section of Ezekiel and its possible relevance for 1 Pet 4:17 are (1) the ambiguity of *tōn hagiōn* ("holy ones" [masc. pl. noun] or "sanctuary" of the Temple [neut. pl. noun]) and (2) the ambiguity of *oikos* ("house" of Israel [Judah] or "Temple"). Regarding the first issue, the parallelism and juxtaposition of *apo tōn hagiōn* and *apo tōn andrōn tōn presbyterōn* clearly favors taking *tōn hagiōn* as a masc. pl. substantive ("holy ones") of whom the "elder men" were an instance. The translation using this option would read: "And begin with my holy ones." Slaughter was to begin, and indeed did begin, with *persons* in front of the house/Temple.

The polyvalent term *oikos* is used in this section of Ezekiel for both the people as "house of Israel" or "house of Jacob"[623] and the Jerusalem Temple as "house of the Lord."[624] The expression in 9:7, "defile the house," in this context could refer to either the Temple or the people. Verse 9:6b would support the former ("in front of the house" = Temple), while the remainder of 9:7 would support the latter ("and so they went out and killed in the city"; with the persons killed being members of the house of Israel; cf. 9:8–9). This ambiguity is overlooked by those who claim a Petrine dependency on Ezek 9 and argue that *oikos* in 1 Pet 4:17 must mean "Temple" since that is its meaning in Ezek 9:6–7. Moreover, if the Petrine author had been thinking of this passage of Ezekiel, he was remarkably free in its adoption and made a point quite different from that of the prophet. Our author makes no reference to the slaying of the elder men within the house (contrast Ezek 9:6) or to the defiling of the house itself (contrast Ezek 9:7). He speaks rather of an evaluating *judgment* and, indeed, of the *salvation* of the righteous (v 18). Furthermore, he expressly states that it is the faithful people of God, "us" (v 17b), with whom this judgment begins, relating *oikos* to "persons," not a place ("temple" or "sanctuary"). Finally, although the Jerusalem Temple may be the focus of Ezekiel, *oikos* as "temple"

---

[623] "House of Israel" (*oikos Israel*, 8:10, 11, 12; 11:1, 5, 15), "house of Judah" (*oikos Iouda*, 8:17), or "house of Israel and Judah" (*oikos Israel kai Iouda*, 9:9).

[624] "House of the Lord" (*oikos Kyriou*, 8:14, 15, 16; 10:19; 11:1, 5) or simply "house" (9:3, 6, 7, 9; 10:3, 4, 18); cf. "Temple of the Lord" (*naos Kyriou*, 8:16, 17).

is clearly not the "operative metaphor" in 1 Peter (against Michaels 1988, 271). The Petrine author shows no interest in portraying the Christian brotherhood as a cultic or temple community in this context or elsewhere in the letter. The dominant root metaphor for community in this letter, as illustrated by the recurrent use of the *oik-* family of terms and related familial imagery, is not "temple" but "house(hold)" or "family," a sense of *oikos* that fits here as well. This domestic sense of *oikos* is also consistent with its sense in 2:5 (see NOTE), where it designates the believing community as the "house(hold) of the Spirit."

The factors distinguishing the texts and points in Ezekiel and 1 Peter therefore cast serious doubt on any direct relationship between 1 Pet 4:17 and Ezek 9:6. Two linguistic similarities, "begin from" and *oikos*, do not outweigh the differences between these two texts. The more general point that they have in common, that divine judgment begins with God's own people, is a traditional thought attested in other writings as well. The term *oikos* here in 1 Peter is best rendered "house" or "house(hold)" (with no allusion to temple), a sense that fits the immediate and broader context of the letter.[625]

It is more likely that 1 Pet 4:17, like vv 12–14, incorporates and adapts traditional motifs and themes, with *oikos tou theou* designating the believing community as the "house(hold) of God" (so also Bigg 1902, 181; RSV, NRSV, NEB), in accord with the domestic metaphors so typical of this letter. This ecclesiastical metaphor reflects an image found in numerous NT writings, from Paul onward (Gal 6:10; Heb 3:1–6; 10:21; 1 Tim 3:15) going back to Jesus' redefinition of his new family of faith (Mark 3:31–35 par.), and one given special profile in 1 Peter in particular. Here, as in 2:5, the believers are assured that, although they are vulnerable and harassed *paroikoi* in society, in the Christian community they constitute the honored *oikos tou theou*. God commences judgment with his own household, but those who in their suffering persist in doing what is right can look forward to salvation (v 18) and entrust themselves to a faithful Creator (v 19).

Verses 17b–18 constitute two parallel statements drawing a similar conclusion from the fact that judgment has now commenced with the house(hold) of God: the precariousness of the fate of the disobedient in comparison with the salvation of the righteous. Divine judgment, executed on the basis of a perfect justice, is all-encompassing in scope, including both the godly and the godless. It is likewise just in nature, involving both the vindication of the righteous and the condemnation of unrepentant sinners.

[625] L. T. Johnson (1986), followed by Grudem (1988, 181–84), though allowing that the *language* of 1 Peter was influenced by Ezek 9, finds the concepts in 1 Pet 4:12–19 closer to the scenario in Mal 3, which speaks of the Lord coming suddenly to his Temple (*ton naon heautou*), "refining" the sons of Levi "like gold and silver" and judging sinners (3:1–5). All of these motifs, however, are also traditional, occurring in numerous other biblical writings as well; see the NOTE on 4:12. The Greek version of Malachi, moreover, involves *naos* rather than *oikos* and makes no explicit mention of "judgment" or where it begins. Thus, there is no evidence of any direct literary connection between 1 Peter and this prophetic text.

17b. *and since [it begins] first with us* (*ei de prōton aph' hēmōn*). This statement, like v 17a and v 17c, involves another ellipsis. Since it parallels v 17a, the implied words are "it" (referring to the foregoing noun "judgment") and the verb "begins." The particle *ei* here and in v 18a is not truly conditional ("if") but positive ("since"), as elsewhere (1:17; 2:3; 4:14), because both vv 17b and 18a repeat in different words the point of v 17a. The phrase "with us" (*aph' hēmōn*) parallels "with the house(hold) of God" (*apo tou oikou tou theou*), thereby indicating that our author includes himself and his group in Rome (5:13) within the house(hold) of God, with whom God's judgment has begun (cf. also 5:9).

17c. *what [will be] the end of those who do not obey the good news of God?* (*ti to telos tōn apeithountōn tōi tou theou euaggeliōi*). The rhetorical question differentiates "those who disobey the gospel" from the foregoing "us," the "household of God," a differentiation echoed in the following verse as well. A third ellipsis implies some verb such as "will be" or "is." Here *to telos* ("the end") means not the temporal "end" of the ages (as in 4:7) but the "outcome" of one's personal life, as in 1:9 (for this sense, see also Josephus, *Ant.* 9.73; *T. Ash.* 1:3; Matt 26:58; 1 Tim 1:5).

of those who do not obey (*tōn apeithountōn*). Since obedience (*hypakoē*, 1:2, 14, 22) in 1 Peter is tantamount to "trust-belief" (*pistis*, 1:5, 7, 9, 21; 5:9; *pisteuō*, 1:8; 2:6, 7), disobedience is a refusal to believe or trust God, Jesus Christ, or the good news concerning both (*apisteuō*, 2:7; *apeitheō*, 2:8; 3:1). A similar expression for nonbelievers is used in 2 Thess 1:8, which speaks of the punishment of "those who do not know God and those who do not obey (*tois mē hypakousousin*) the good news of our Lord Jesus Christ." This contrast between believers and the disobedient will be paralleled by a similar contrast between "righteous" and "impious and sinner" in v 18.

the good news of God (*tōi tou theou euaggeliōi*). The term *euaggelion* ("good news," "gospel") is a traditional and technical term in the NT (76 occurrences) for the joyous message concerning God's gracious dealing with humanity, especially through Jesus Christ. The specific content of this good news is spelled out in a variety of ways in relation to a variety of specific circumstances (see Elliott 1969). This differs from its less frequent use in the LXX (in the plural, *euaggelia*) and extrabiblical Greek, where it has the meaning "tidings of victory" (2 Kgdms 18:22, 25 [both pl.]); or "recompense for a good report" (2 Kgdms 4:10; Homer, *Od.* 14.152). First employed among Diaspora communities of believers, it belonged to early Christian tradition predating Paul (see 1 Thess 1:9b–10; 1 Cor 15:1–5; Rom 1:1–3, 9). Then, along with the verb *euaggelizō*, it was employed frequently by Paul (48×; 8× in the Deutero-Paulines), the Evangelists (12×), our author (1 Pet 4:17), and the seer of Revelation (14:6).

The particular formulation "the good news of God" occurs also in Mark 1:14; Rom 15:16 (cf. 1:1); 2 Cor 11:7; 1 Thess 2:2, 9 (cf. 1 Tim 1:11). While *tou theou* ("of God") could be taken as a subjective genitive (the good news "from God"; so BAGD 318), an objective genitive here in 1 Peter and in the other uses of *to euaggelion tou theou* is equally possible, if not more likely (the good news "concerning God"). Analogous constructions of *euaggelion* accompanied by objective genitives are frequent in the NT.[626] All instances of *to euaggelion tou theou*, moreover, are employed in writings addressed to believers in predominantly Gentile-dominated areas, where reference to the good (and novel) news concerning the God known to Israel and the messianic community would be most fitting. The function of *tou theou* as an objective genitive also is consistent with the Petrine author's theocentric focus throughout the letter. The kindred verb "proclaim good news" (*euaggelizomai*) was employed earlier (1:12, 25; 4:6). It is clear from several statements (1:10–12, 21, 23–25; 2:2–3) that this good news also concerned the "sufferings" and "glories" of the Christ (1:10–12), whom God raised from the dead (1:21), and which constituted the "word" of good news (1:25b; 2:2a) through which the believers were reborn (1:23; 2:2). Thus for 1 Peter, and in line with most NT writings, the good news concerns the proclamation of the power, mercy, and grace of God manifested preeminently in the resurrection, exaltation, and honoring of the suffering Christ and now available to all who follow obediently in his footsteps.[627]

Verse 18ab provides scriptural support for the statement in v 17bc and mirrors its antithetic structure. The text cited is the Septuagint version of Prov 11:31. This Greek text varies somewhat from its Hebrew counterpart, which reads, "If the righteous is requited on earth, how much more the wicked and the sinner!" The LXX version substitutes the idea of the difficulty (*molis*) of salvation for the Hebrew accent on recompense, and in this processs the semantic relation of the verse halves is somewhat obscured (on the reasons for this LXX substitution, see J. Barr 1975). The sense of the LXX text and of its adoption in 1 Peter nevertheless is still intelligible: the salvation of the impious and the sinner is more precarious than that of the righteous. As employed here in 1 Peter, the contrast "righteous person" versus "impious and sinner" parallels the antithesis "house of God . . . us" versus "those who do not obey the good news of God" (v 17). The arguments in both v 17bc and v 18ab are a fortiori arguments, similar to the argument in Luke 23:31. This form of argument was known among the rabbis as a *qal waḥomer* ("light and heavy") argument: "if X is true, how much more is Y also true."

18a. *and "since the righteous person is saved only with difficulty"* (*kai ei ho dikaios molis sōizetai*). A second "since" statement parallels, reiterates, and re-

[626] E.g., the good news concerning God's rule (Matt 4:23; 9:35; 24:14), concerning God's grace (Acts 20:24), concerning (Jesus) Christ (Mark 1:1; Rom 15:19; cf. 1:9; 1 Cor 9:12; 2 Cor 2:12; 9:13; 10:14; Gal 1:7; Phil 1:27; 1 Thess 3:2; cf. 2 Cor 4:4; 2 Thess 2:14), concerning your salvation (Eph 1:13), concerning peace (Eph 6:15).

[627] On the content of the gospel as presumed and unfolded in this letter, see also the NOTES on 1:12 and 1:25. On *euaggelion* and paronyms and NT usage, see Schniewind 1927–1931; Friedrich 1964; Stuhlmacher 1968; Martin 1982; Strecker 1991 (with, however, an inadequate explanation of the meaning and function of *euaggelion* in 1 Pet 4:17).

inforces the point of v 17bc. Although the thought is taken from Prov 11:31 LXX, it has, because of its context (v 17), an eschatological sense lacking in the original. As in v 17b, *ei* again is positive ("since," "seeing that") rather than conditional ("if") because this clause as well presumes the positive statement of v 17a. In this Petrine context, "the righteous person" (*ho dikaios*) refers to everyone included within "the household of God" ("us"), just as "the righteous" in 3:12a (citing Ps 33:16 LXX) applies to the readers of whom "uprightness" is required (2:24; 3:14). Such righteous persons are related to Christ, the "righteous one" (3:18b; cf. 2:21–24). The verb "is saved" (*sōizetai*) is another passive verb implying God as agent. Although the verb of the proverb is a present tense, here in the context of 1 Peter it has eschatological future force (cf. 1:5, 9, 10; 2:2).

with difficulty (*molis*). The notion of the difficulty of salvation, in the context of this letter, pertains to the fact that salvation is gained only in the course of human opposition and unjust suffering and hence requires constant vigilance, trust in God's supportive power, steadfastness in suffering, and perseverence in doing what is right according to the will of God (v 19). This difficulty, however, does not vitiate the fact that the righteous will indeed be saved if they remain faithful. Thus here we have yet another positive valuation of innocent suffering: those who continue to live uprightly in the course of their suffering will in fact be saved and vindicated by God. On the limits of those saved see also Jesus' warning in Matt 22:14; Luke 13:23–24.

18b. *"what will become of the impious and sinner?"* (*ho asebēs kai hamartōlos pou phaneitai*), literally, "where will the impious and sinner appear?" These words from the remainder of Prov 11:31 LXX parallel the terms in v 17c. This word order is preferred to the textual variant ($\mathfrak{P}^{72}$ and other less weighty witnesses), which reads "sinner and impious." The contrast between the righteous and the impious is the dominant thought of this entire chapter of Proverbs. The terms *asebēs* ("impious") and *hamartōlos* ("sinner") are virtually synonymous, and in Prov 11 the "impious" is described as one who "does what is unrighteous/ unjust" (11:18; cf. 11:5) or what is "wrong" (11:15) and whose fate is death (11:19) (cf. Ps 9:6, the impious perish). For similar traditional contrasts between *dikaios-asebēs*, see Prov 24:16 and Wis 1–5 (cf. also Ps 10[11]:5).

Within the present immediate context, the contrast *righteous person–impious and sinner* mirrors the antithesis "household of God . . . us"—"those who do not obey the good news of God" (v 17). Together, both sets of antitheses belong to a broader pattern of "we-they" contrasts so prominent in this letter (2:7–10, 12; 3:1–2, 9, 12, 13–16; 4:2–4, 6, 14–16; cf. 5:5c). This differentiation of society into simple we-they categories—believers versus unbelievers, oppressed versus oppressors, righteous versus sinners, insiders versus outsiders—is typical of sectarian social perception and thus provides another illustration of the sectarian perspective of this letter. Awareness of an imminent divine judgment with its sifting of righteous and sinner serves here as elsewhere in the NT to validate and reinforce social distinction and demarcation from the godless.

The judgment of God, the author has already indicated, is both inclusive (4:5–6) and impartial (1:17), involving the living and the dead, nonbelievers and believers everywhere. The honor or shame it brings will be meted out according to each one's deeds (1:17) relative to God's will and each one's response to Jesus Christ (2:4–10; 3:16). All creatures (cf. 2:13) are accountable to God their Creator (4:19). This universality and impartiality of divine judgment is firmly accented in early Christian tradition and is stressed repeatedly in 1 Peter. While the implication of the present statement is that the salvation of sinners is more difficult than that of the righteous, the interrogative form of the statement nevertheless leaves open the final outcome of the former. Their final condemnation, while possible (2:8; 3:17), is not necessarily a foregone conclusion. In the author's mind it apparently hinges on their negative or positive response to the witness of the believers and their possibly being won to the Christian faith (2:12; 3:2).

19. All of the preceding thoughts on the positive value of innocent suffering, the advent of God's just judgment, and the certainty of the salvation of the righteous are now brought to an affirmative and comforting conclusion as the author assures his readers that they can confidently entrust their lives to God their faithful Creator. As a conclusion, this verse reiterates and combines several prominent foregoing topics: innocent suffering,[628] the will of God (2:15; 3:17; 4:2; cf. 3:21), doing what is right (2:14, 15, 20; 3:6, 11, 13, 16, 17; cf. 2:12), and self-commitment to a faithful God (1:21; 2:23c).

19a. *So then, let those suffering in accordance with God's will* (*hōste kai hoi paschontes kata to thelēma tou theou*). With the sense "so then" or "consequently," *hōste*, as in 1:21c, expresses the intended outcome of the foregoing (vv 12–18). As a logical consequence of the inaugurated judgment of God and the positive value of suffering, believers are to entrust themselves to God and persevere in doing what is right.

those suffering (*hoi paschontes*) is the subject of the main verb "let . . . entrust" (*paratithesthōsan*). This participle refers particularly to the addressees but can embrace all suffering believers everywhere (cf. 5:9).

in accordance with God's will (*kata to thelēma tou theou*). The suffering to which the author refers here, as throughout the letter, is *innocent suffering* for doing what is right in obedience to the *will of God* (cf. 2:15; 3:17; 4:2), hence the link between *suffering* and *doing what is right* (as in 2:20 and 3:17). Such innocent suffering (cf. also 1:6; 2:18–20; 3:9, 13–17; 4:12–16) mirrors that of the obedient and innocent Christ (1:2c; 2:18–25; 3:18; 4:1). The point is not that suffering *as such* is God's will, as might be inferred from 1:6 and 3:17, but rather that obedience to God can entail innocent suffering as a consequence and that such suffering is part of a larger divine purpose—the conquest of sin (4:1), the testing of faith's probity (1:6–7; 4:12), the sharing in Christ's experi-

[628] *Paschontes*; cf. 2:19, 20, 21, 23; 3:14, 17, 18; 4:1, 15; *pathēmata*, 1:11; 4:13; *lypeō, lypē*, 1:6; 2:19.

ence (2:21–25; 3:18–22; 4:1, 13), and the glorification of God as vindicator of all innocent suffering (2:12, 23c; 3:9, 10–12, 13, 18c, 22; 4:6b, 16; 5:10). Like the Lord's own passion, this innocent suffering is the cup that the Father has given (Mark 14:36/Matt 26:39/Luke 22:42) in order that children of God might learn and demonstrate obedience (cf. Heb 5:7–10 and 12:5–11; cf. 4:1–2). To be sure, their detractors could not effect this suffering unless this were allowed by God (John 19:10–11; cf. Matt 26:54–56; John 18:11). However, God's will involves not only the freedom of believers from ultimate harm (3:13) but also their final passage from suffering to glory (1:6–9; 4:13–14; 5:10). In the meantime, suffering will be of only short duration (1:6; 5:10) because the end is at hand (4:7) and the final judgment is already in process (4:17). Thus, those suffering innocently in accordance with God's will can entrust themselves confidently to a faithful Creator in doing what is right.

19b. *also entrust their lives to a faithful Creator in doing what is right* (*kai . . . pistōi ktistēi paratithesthōsan tas psychas autōn en agathopoiiai*). The conjunction *kai* ("also") could be taken with "those who suffer" (which it immediately precedes in Greek). But since this entire unit concerns suffering believers, it is not likely that they are singled out here for additional or special mention. Therefore Bigg's proposal (1902, 181–82) has merit. He takes *kai* with the main verb *paratithesthōsan,* regarded as a parallel to the similar cohortative 3d-person verb *doxazetō* in v 16c, thus yielding the thought: "Let them (him) not only glorify God, but also entrust themselves to God." At the same time, this clause also balances v 19a: the God whose will believers obey even when enduring suffering is the faithful Creator to whom they can entrust their very lives.

let . . . entrust (*paratithesthōsan*). The verb is a 3d-person pl. pres. middle imperative (cohortative),[629] with *hoi paschontes* ("those suffering") as its subject. In Classical literature, *paratithēmi* is used of giving one's possessions into the safe-keeping of a friend. A "deposit" (*parathēkē, parakatathēkē*) entailed a sacred obligation not to be violated. The verb occurs in the NT with the sense of "entrust" or "commit" something precious (Luke 12:48, 1 Tim 1:18; 2 Tim 2:2), including entrusting people to God (Acts 14:23; 20:32), with Acts 14:23 and 2 Tim 2:2 making the connection with trustworthiness.

their lives (*tas psychas autōn*). What believers are urged to entrust to God is the most precious item of all, their very lives, as Jesus entrusted himself to God (2:23c; Luke 23:46). Behind the present verse and Luke 23:46 (cf. also Acts 7:59) lies the thought expressed in Ps 31:5[30:6 LXX], "Into your hand I entrust my spirit." As elsewhere in this letter (1:9, 22; 2:11, 25; 3:20), *psychē* designates the total living person.

to a faithful Creator (*pistōi ktistēi*). The noun *ktistēs* appears only here in the NT. In Hellenistic Greek it designates a "founder" of a city (SIG[3] 751.2; 839.8;

---

[629] For similar instances of *hōste* followed by imperatives, see 1 Cor 10:12; 11:33; 14:39; 15:58; Phil 2:12; 4:1; and 1 Thess 4:18.

Dionys. Hal., *Ant. rom.* 1.1.126; Josephus, Ag. *Ap.* 2.39), a patron who brought a city imperial favor or other benefits (Merkelbach and Sahin 1988, no. 28a–b, pp. 119–20), and a Roman emperor as "founder of the world" (CIG 2.2572), or a deity (PGM 4.591; 5.248; 7.963). In the Bible and related writings it is used exclusively of God as "Creator" of the world or "founder" of all things.[630] In 1 Peter, the idea of God as Creator informs the injunction in 2:13 requiring the subordination of every human "creature" (*ktisei*) "because of the Lord" (see the NOTE). As Procreator, God has given the believers new life (1:3); as Creator of all things (cf. also 1:20a), God has the power (cf. 1:4–5; 5:6, 10–11) to preserve those who entrust themselves to his care (cf. 5:7).

faithful (*pistōi*) underscores the reliability and fidelity of God as Creator. The adjective is used of God elsewhere in the NT (1 Cor 1:9; 10:13; 2 Cor 1:18; 2 Tim 2:13; Heb 10:23) and in 1 Peter of Silvanus as well (5:12). "Faithful creator"—how fitting and comforting is this concept of God for this letter of encouragement and comfort! Because God is the Creator, he has the power to sustain; because God is faithful, believers have reason to trust (cf. also 1:21).

in [*their*] *doing what is right* (*en agathopoiiai*). As the final word of this sentence and this unit, the importance of *doing what is right* is strongly accentuated. "All of the Christians' convictions about God, about creation, about human destiny, about the meaning of suffering should lead them to persevere in their active witness of leading a good life" (Senior 1980, 85). The phrase modifies *let them entrust their lives* and has either temporal or instrumental force: "*while* doing what is right" or "*by* doing what is right." "Their" is not stated but is nevertheless implied.

The noun *agathopoiia* is used only here in the Bible but appears once in *T. Jos.* 18:2 ("And if anyone wishes to do you harm [*kakopoiēsai hymas*], you should pray for him, along with doing what is right [*tēi agathopoiia, v.l.*], and you will be rescued by the Lord from every evil"). In 1 Peter it belongs to one of the letter's most prominent and distinctive fields of terms for behavior consonant with the will of God.[631] With this final term of v 19 the author sums up the forms of conduct encouraged in 2:11–4:19: honorable behavior (*kalē anastrophē*, 2:12; 3:2, 16); good deeds (*kala erga*, 2:12; cf. 1:17); respect for order and persons in authority (*hypotassesthai*, subordination, 2:13–17, 18–20; 3:1–6; cf. 5:5a); obedience (*hypakouō*, 3:6; cf. *hypakoē*, 1:2, 14, 22); husbandly respect for wives (3:7); and the actions in vv 8–12; 3:13–17; 4:8–10, 12–16, including uprightness (2:24c; 3:12, 14).[632]

[630] See 2 Kgdms 22:32; Jdt 9:12; Sir 24:8; 2 Macc 1:24; 7:23; 13:14; 4 Macc 5:25; 11:5; *Let. Aris.* 16; Philo, *Spec.* 1.30; *Somn.* 1.93; *1 Clem.* 19:2; 59:3; 62:2); cf. Mal 2:10, "Have you not all one father? Did not one God create (*ektisen*) you?"

[631] In addition to its paronyms *agathopoieō* (2:15, 20; 3:6, 17) and *agathopoios* (2:14), see also its synonym, *dikaiosynē* (2:24; 3:14; cf. *dikaios*, 3:12, 18; 4:18).

[632] The use of this rare term *agathopoiia* in *1 Clement* as well (2:2, 7; 33:1; 34:2) is one of the several factors suggesting the influence of 1 Peter on Clemens Romanus.

With this final phrase, the author also indicates that suffering in accord with God's will is not a matter of passive resignation but active obedience. Persistence in doing what is right despite suffering, a thought reprising the point of 2:19–20 and 3:17, is the concrete means for demonstrating trust in God's fidelity and entrusting oneself to God's care. The eloquent combination of exhortation and consolation contained in this final verse expresses quintessentially the spirit and substance of the entire letter: innocent suffering and perseverance in doing good in fidelity to God's will are possible for those who trust in God's care and entrust themselves, as did Jesus (2:23), to God as a trustworthy Creator.

GENERAL COMMENT

This initial unit of the concluding section of the letter (4:12–5:11) reiterates, recapitulates, and amplifies major points made earlier. In bringing the letter to a close, the author returns once more in 4:12–19 to the issue of innocent suffering, its inevitability for followers of Jesus Christ, its positive value, and its glorious outcome. The situation presumed here is likewise consistent with the situation presumed in 1:3–4:11—namely, an early period of Christianity, when the unfounded reproaches of outsiders led to undeserved suffering, which in turn caused surprise and distress that the security and salvation so fervently desired was so little in evidence.

Tempering exhortation with consolation once again, our author offers one of the most sustained comments on Christian suffering to be found in the NT (see Elliott 1990, 142–45; Davids 1990, 30–44; Talbert 1991). The key points he stresses can be summarized as follows:

(1) The addressees should not be surprised at their suffering (v 12) because it is nothing alien to those in communion with the suffering Christ (v 13a).

(2) Reproach, being labeled "Christ-lackey," and innocent suffering are instead to be viewed as a divine test of the probity of faith and trust in God (v 12).

(3) Inasmuch as innocent suffering effects solidarity with the suffering Christ, it is a cause for rejoicing both now and in the future, when his glory will be revealed (v 13b; cf. 1:7). Suffering should lead, not to grief or despair, but to "rejoicing with exultation."

(4) Such suffering is an experience blessed by the presence of the divine Spirit of glory (v 14b) and, hence, a sign of being honored by God (v 14; cf. 3:14). Thus 1 Peter offers a biblical example of that lovely thought of Leon Bloy, that "joy is the infallible sign of the presence of God."

Believers, of course, should not be engaged in forms of misconduct for which they would justly suffer punishment (v 15), behavior that would be inconsistent with the will of God and incompatible with their union with Christ. Their life must be irreproachable and offer no occasion for justifiable accusation on the part of outsiders.

(5) If they nevertheless are maligned and suffer as "Christians," this is not a cause for feeling shamed but an occasion for glorifying God (v 16). From a

weapon of shame the label "Christian" can be transformed into a means for giving God honor.

(6) This suffering is a sign of the divine judgment that has begun with God's own people, "us," the household of God. It is thus a further indication of the presence of the end and the nearness of salvation (v 18), and with it a termination of suffering; note also 1:6 and 5:10 on the brief duration of this suffering.

(7) Finally, all who suffer innocently can confidently entrust their lives to their faithful Creator and thereby persevere in doing what is right.

Martyrdom, on the other hand, is not an issue here. Our author is neither encouraging a "preparation for martyrdom" (against Reichert 1989) nor forestalling a quest for "the glory of martyrdom" (against Reicke 1964, 126). Our author's statements involve no glorification of suffering as such. Innocent suffering is seen as a means to an end—union with Christ, demonstration of faith's probity, and glorification of God. In contrast to Ignatius of Antioch and the Christian martyrs of the second and following centuries, for our author joy *in* suffering had not yet transformed into a joy *for* suffering. At the same time, our author makes no attempt to divert attention from the pain of present suffering by focusing exclusively on future joy "in the sweet by and by." Nothing like a theology of "pie-in-the-sky" is presented here, where a blessed future compensates for a wretched present. Rather, suffering is addressed with utmost earnestness but also confident hope. So that it not be seen as utterly meaningless and a reason for despair and defection, the issue of innocent suffering is addressed within the framework of the encompassing story of salvation, the testing of faith, the suffering of the Christ, union with the Christ in suffering and in vindication, and the reliable sustenance of a faithful Creator. Offering positive meaning to innocent suffering was not to value suffering as such or to promote it as something "good for the soul" or for a "strengthening of character." The suffering of innocent believers, like that of their suffering Lord, was a result of human opposition to God's action and God's agent of salvation. But this suffering, the Petrine author insists, can be courageously endured, welcomed with joy, and even embraced as an occasion for glorifying God. Salvation is not liberation *from* suffering but the goal attained *through* suffering and in the midst of suffering. With eyes fixed on this goal, suffering Christians can persist in doing what is right, confident of God's sustenance.

For studies on 1 Pet 4:12–19, see J. Barr 1975; Bauer 1978a, 1978b; Best 1969–1970; Bischoff 1908; Borchert 1982; Braun 1940; Busto 1993; Cervantes Gabarrón 1991a, 299–310; Diderichsen 1975; Dierkens 1919; Downing 1988; Elliott 1969, 1995a, 1995b; K. Erbes 1919, 1921; Filson 1955; García del Moral 1961a, 1961b, 1961c; García del Moral and Garrido 1962; Hill 1976; Holzmeister 1929; J. T. Johnson 1986; R. B. Jones 1949; Knox 1953; May 1967; Michaels 1966–1967; Millauser 1976; L. Miller 1955; Molthagen 1995; Penna 1967; Rodgers 1981; Sander 1966; Schutter 1987; Schwank 1973a; Selwyn 1947, 299–303; van Unnik 1954–1955.

VI. B. Maintaining the Unity of the Community: Responsible Elders and Subordinate Younger Persons (5:1–5a)

5:1a Therefore, the elders among you I exhort,
as co-elder
1b and witness to the sufferings of the Christ,
1c and sharer in the glory about to be revealed:
2a shepherd the flock of God among you
2b by exercising oversight
2c not because compelled
but willingly in accord with God;
2d not for shameful gain,
but eagerly;
3 not as domineering those allotted [to you],
but being examples for the flock.
4a And when the chief shepherd is made manifest,
4b you will receive the unfading crown of glory.
5:5a You younger persons in turn: be subordinate to the elders.

INTRODUCTION

The conclusion of the body of the letter (4:12–5:11) ends with an address to two related groups within the community, elders (5:1–4) and younger persons (5:5a), followed by a final exhortation to all the addressees (5:5b–9) and a benediction (5:10–11). Following a section focused on the relation of believers to *outsiders* (4:12–19), the author now directs attention *primarily to the internal life of the community* (5:1–5a, 5b–7) and its support by God (vv 10–11). The arrangement thus follows the pattern established earlier in the letter: exhortation concerning interaction with outsiders is balanced by advice concerning life within the brotherhood.[633]

Verses 1–5a, introduced with a threefold identification of the author (v 1), focus on the appropriate conduct of elders (vv 1–4) and younger persons (v 5a). This subunit is thus demarcated from its immediately adjacent contexts (4:12–19 and 5:5b–11), both of which address the entire community. The commencement of a new line of exhortation is likewise signaled by the initial *oun* ("therefore," as in 2:1a; 4:1a, 7b; 5:6a) and the 1st-person sing. declaration "I exhort" (v 1a, identical to the one in 2:11a, which also begins a new unit).

---

[633] Besides the contrast in 2:17 (see NOTE), see the larger balanced units of external (1:14–17; 2:1, 12, 13–16; 2:17a, d; 2:18–20; 3:1–6; 3:9; 3:13–17; 4:1–6; 4:12–19; 5:8–9) and internal (1:18–25; 2:2–10, 11; 2:17b, c; 2:21–25; 3:7; 3:8, 10–12; 3:18–22; 4:7–11; 5:1–7, 10–11) exhortation.

At the same time, this subunit is linked logically and thematically to the foregoing through the particle *oun* ("therefore"), the repeated phrase "sufferings of Christ" (*tou Christou pathēmata*, v 1a; cf. 4:13 and also 1:11; 2:21, 23; 3:18; 4:1), and the idea of sharing in this suffering (v 1c *koinōnos*; cf. 4:13 *koinōneite*; see also 2:19–20; 3:14, 17; 4:1, 15, 19). It likewise reprises earlier language and thought: anticipation of an imminent final revelation (vv 1c, 4; cf. 1:5, 7, 13; 4:13) and glory (vv 1c, 4; cf. 1:7, 8, 11; 4:13, 14); subordination (v 5a; cf. 2:13, 18; 3:1, 5); the shepherd-flock motif (vv 2, 4; cf. 2:25); and the letter's general focus on suffering. The reciprocal pairing of elders-younger persons and the call for subordination and regard for order (v 5a; cf. 2:13, 18; 3:1, 5), moreover, recall the domestic instruction in 2:18–3:7 and the reciprocal pairing of wives-husbands (3:1–6/7). Finally, the broader literary pattern evident here (exhortation of specific groups [vv 1–5a] followed by an exhortation of all [5:5b] and a supporting OT citation [5:5c]) mirrors the literary pattern in 2:18–3:12 (2:18–25; 3:1–6; 3:7 [domestic slaves, wives, husbands] followed by 3:8–9 [exhortation of all members] and a supporting OT citation [3:10–12]). Verses 1–5a, 5b–7, 8–9, and 10–11 form discernible subunits combining elements of both exhortation and encouragement. They are loosely joined by a series of link-words, inferential particles, and related themes (suffering, care of God, and eventual reception of glory and honor). The terms "suffering" (vv 1, 10), "Christ" (vv 1, 10), "God" (vv 2, 10; cf. v 11), and "glory" (5:1, 10) form an inclusion embracing these final verses.

Traces of various types of tradition are evident in these verses. The exhortation of elders and younger persons as a reciprocal pair within the household suggests the influence of the household management (*oikonomia*) tradition also reflected in 2:13–3:7. Elsewhere in the early Christian teaching, domestic instruction concerning familial relations and conduct includes exhortation of parents and children (Eph 6:1–4; Col 3:18–21; *Pol. Phil* 4:1; cf. Mark 10:2–16 par.) and/or of older and younger persons (1 Tim 5:1–2, 17–18; Titus 2:1–6; *1 Clem.* 1:3; 21:6–8; Pol. *Phil* 5:3–6:1); see also Philo, *Decal.* 165–67; *Spec.* 2.225–27. In 1 Peter, which portrays the entire community as a household and adapts this household management tradition as well, an appeal to community elders and those younger in faith thus has a natural place.[634] Selwyn (1947, 435–47) proposed that 1 Pet 5:5a with its call for the subordination of younger persons to their seniors "belonged to teaching on Church order," which was part of early baptismal catechetical instruction, with a *verbum Christi* (Luke 22:26) as the primary inspiration for 5:5a. In regard to vv 2–3, Nauck (1957), on the other hand, noted terminological and thematic affinities with Israelite

[634] Boismard (1957, 179; 1966, 1423) sought to support his theory of an original connection of 1 Pet 5:1–9 with 2:13–3:6 by appeal to the similarity of this instruction with Titus's: cf. exhortation of presbyters (Titus 1:5–9/1 Pet 5:1–4); of wives (Titus 2:4/1 Pet 3:1–6); of slaves (Titus 2:9–10/1 Pet 2:18–20); and concerning civic duty (Titus 3:1–3/1 Pet 2:13–17). The alleged correspondence, however, is too vague to be compelling, and his attempt to identify a hymn behind these similarities and those of 1 Pet 5:5–9 and Jas 4:6–10 (Boismard 1961, 133–63) fails to convince.

(especially Qumran) and early Christian teaching concerning community leaders. This suggested the use of "a primitive Christian instruction on office" (*Amtsanweisung*; see below in 1 Peter 5). As evidence for such a tradition, he cited affinities with the communal arrangements at Qumran reflected in earlier and later Christian texts. The affinities with Qumranic material, however, are minimal, and correspondences with Christian texts involve similar terms for leaders and similar combinations of roles but no fixed and formal scheme of "instruction for office." Thus, the Petrine formulation represents at best a stage in the development of a ministry and order tradition, rather than dependency upon an already fixed tradition. Expanding on both Selwyn and Nauck, I proposed (1969) that vv 2–3 reflected part of an early, flexible ministry and Church order tradition that was shaped by teaching concerning leadership, status, and humility and Jesus as model, teaching associated by Luke and John with the Lord's supper (Luke 22:24–27; John 13:1–20) and with the Apostle Peter (John 13:1–20; 21:15–21).

The content and form of the traditions possibily adopted here are still open to debate. There is no single source that combines all of the elements found here. The most that can be stated with certainty is that 1 Peter represents a growing coalescence of thought on Christian leadership and mutual responsibility, elements of which were associated with the Apostle Peter in particular. Our author has drawn on a diversity of traditional terminology, images, and motifs and has united them in a statement on the responsibilties of elders, recent converts, and the entire community that in its totality is without parallel in the NT. The accompanying presence of an inordinately large number of unique terms as well (*sympresbyteros* [v 1a], *anagkastōs* [v 2c], *aischrokerdōs* [v 2d], *prothymōs* [v 2d], *archipoimēn* [v 4a], *amarantinos* [v 4b]; cf. also the rare terms *episkopeō* [only here and in Heb 12:15]; *hekousiōs* [only here and in Heb 10:26]), along with the unique triad of vv 2c–3, reveals again the creative hand of the Petrine author and his skillful blending of diverse material into a unified and rhetorically compelling line of thought.

NOTES

5:1 *Therefore, the elders among you* (*Presbyterous oun en hymin*). The particle *oun* ("Therefore") introduces an exhortation (as in 2:1a; 4:1a, 7b; 5:6a) linked in some fashion with the foregoing. Not all manuscripts contain this particle, but its original presence seems likely.[635] The nature of the connection, however, is not immediately clear.

---

[635] The majority of later MSS (P Ψ 𝔐) omit "therefore" and have a definite article (*tous*) following "elders" ("the elders who are among you"). However, the earliest and superior MSS (𝔓[72] A B and others) include "therefore," and its presence is attested as well in Codex Sinaiticus and other conflate readings ("The elders therefore who are among you"). The definite article may be a secondary addition or, as seems more likely, may have been inadvertently omitted as a result of haplography resulting from homoeoteleuton (*presbyterous tous*). In any case, the presence of "therefore" appears original.

Several possibilities have been proposed. Scholars who claim a dependence of 1 Pet 4:17 on Ezek 9:6 (Michaels 1988, 277–79; Grudem 1988, 185–86; Schutter 1989, 78–79) theorized that an address to "elders" here was prompted by the mention of "elder men" (*presbyteroi*) in Ezek 9:6. This proposal, however, fails to convince. The uncertain dependency of 4:17 on Ezek 9:6 (see the NOTE on 4:17) is an inadequate basis for viewing Ezekiel's mention of slain elder men of Jerusalem as a stimulus for our author's address to Christian elders regarding their appropriate mode of leadership.

On the other hand, Davids (1990, 174–75) holds it conceivable that elders/leaders would have been a target for the hostility mentioned in 4:12–19 and for this reason were immediately addressed. There is, however, no reference to elders' suffering in vv 1–5a. It is more likely that the foregoing discussion of suffering in 4:12–19 led naturally to an appeal to elders as leaders of the flock, for the suffering readers would need reliable leaders to guide them in their predicament.

Still other scholars[636] have called attention to the conceptual link of elders and younger persons and the call for subordination (v 5a) with 2:13–3:7, where specific groups also are addressed and subordination likewise is urged in an instruction echoing the tradition of "household (*oikos*) management" (see the NOTES on 2:13–17).[637] The relationship between elders and younger persons is also treated in Israel's appropriation of the *oikonomia* tradition in connection with responsibilities appropriate to the fourth commandment (honoring of parents and elders as parents; see Philo, *Spec.* 2.236–38, 240, 247; 3.155; *Flacc.* 80; Prostmeier 1990, 453–57). Combined exhortation of presbyters/elders, youth, and wives also occurs in other Christian exhortation; see *1 Clem.* 1:3; 21:6, 8; Pol. *Phil* 4:1–6:1 (wives, 4:2; *neōteroi*, 5:3; *presbyteroi*, 6:1; and the chart in Elliott 1985, 209). While an address to elders and younger persons would have been appropriate following 3:7, its placement here is consistent with the renewed stress on the community as the "household of God" in 4:17. It is also possible that this appeal to elders was reserved for the conclusion of the letter in harmony with similar final exhortations to or mention of church leaders in other NT writings.[638]

---

[636] See Boismard 1957, 179; Bosetti 1990, 45; and Prostmeier 1990, 453–57.

[637] While elder and younger persons were not often mentioned in the Greek and Roman versions of the *oikonomia* tradition, Plutarch (*Lib. ed.* 10; *Mor.* 7DE) illustrates how conventional moral instruction on appropriate behavior in the civic and domestic realms includes elder and younger persons as well: "For through philosophy and in company with philosophy it is possible to attain knowledge of what is honorable (*to kalon*) and what is shameful (*to aischron*), what is just (*to dikaion*) and what is unjust (*to adikon*) . . . how a man must bear himself in his relations with the gods, with his parents, with his elders (*presbyterois*), with the laws, with strangers, with those in authority, with friends, with women/wives (*gynaixi*), with children, with servants (*oiketais*); that one ought to reverence (*sebesthai*) the gods, to honour (*timan*) one's parents, to respect one's elders, to be obedient to the laws, to yield to those in authority, to love one's friends, to be chaste with women/wives, to be affectionate with children, and not to be overbearing with slaves."

[638] See 1 Cor 16:15–18; 1 Thess 5:12–15; 1 Tim 6:11–16, 20–21; Heb 13:7, 17; cf. also Rom 16:1–16; Col 4:7–14; Jas 5:14; John 21:15–23; and Acts 20:17–35 (located in the final part of Acts).

On the whole, several combined factors may have been at work here, including the foregoing reference to the "household of God," of which elders and younger persons were a logical component, the epistolary convention of a final address to leaders, and the need for responsible leadership in the face of suffering. Finally, the conduct required of these elders and younger persons is also illustrative of the *agathopoiia* ("doing what is right") urged on all believers in the preceding verse, 4:19 (cf. Beare 1970, 197).

the elders among you (*Presbyterous oun en hymin*). Elsewhere in the letter, when specific groups are addressed, the noun ("household slaves," 2:18; "wives," 3:1; "husbands," 3:7) is accompanied by a definite article. Here and in v 5a ("younger persons"), by contrast, the article is absent in some manuscripts (𝔓[72] A B etc.) but is present in others (5:1a: P Ψ 𝔐; 5:5a: 33 323 614 630 945 1241 etc.). Michaels (1988, 276, 279) therefore translates "any elders" (who might be leaders in the congregations addressed). But this indefinite "any" does not fit with the correlate group "younger persons," as Michaels's translation of v 5a recognizes ("You in turn who are younger"). In both cases haplography possibly accounts for the unintentional omission of the definite article.

elders (*presbyterous*). The adjective *presbyteros* ("older") is a comparative form of *presbys* ("old"). When used substantivally, as here, *presbyteros* could mean "older" in biological age (Luke 15:23; John 8:9; Acts 2:17; 1 Tim 5:1, 2) or a notable person of a past generation (Matt 15:2; Mark 7:3; Heb 11:2). Since in the ancient world age conferred status and hence qualification for leadership, it also was the term for one who functioned as a community leader ("elder"), as are the cognates *zaqēn* (Heb.), *gērōn* (Gk.), and *senior* (Lat.). It is thus a polyvalent term with implications of either age or function or both (on semantic developments in its usage, see Gomez 1962). The instruction that accompanies this address to *presbyteroi* (vv 2–4), however, makes it clear that the author, who goes on to identify himself as a "co-elder," presumes that these are persons functioning as leaders/shepherds/overseers among the Asia Minor addressees.

In the Hellenistic world *presbyteroi*/elders served as community functionaries (Deissmann 1901, 154–57, 233–35; R. A. Campbell 1994, 67–98). In Second Temple Israel, elders likewise served as village, city, or community leaders,[639] as members of the Great Sanhedrin,[640] and as leaders in the synagogue communities (Luke 7:3).[641] Paul makes no mention of Christian elders,

---

[639] See Ezra 5:5, 9; 6:7, 14; 10:7; 1 Esd 5:60; 6:5, 8, 10, 26; 7:2; 9:4, 13; Sir 7:14 (assembly of elders); Jdt 10:6; 1 Macc 1:26; 7:33; 11:23; 3 Macc. 1:8, 23, 25; 6:1; *Let. Aris.* 32, 310; Josephus, *Ant.* 11.105.

[640] See Matt 16:21; 21:23; 26:3, 47, 57, etc; Mark 8:31; 11:27; Luke 9:22; 20:1; Acts 4:5, 8, 23; 6:12; 23:1–10, 14; 24:1; 25:15.

[641] See G. H. Davies 1962; Bornkamm 1968; Coenen 1972; Jeremias 1969, 222–32; Schürer 1973–1987, 199–226, 423–39; Reviv 1989; Matthews and Benjamin 1993, 121–31; Rohde 1993; R. A. Campbell 1994, 20–66. On elders (*presbyteroi, gerontes, seniores*) in the Greco-Roman society, see Deissmann 1901, 154–57; R. A. Campbell 1994, 67–98.

though it is possible that with the term *hoi proistamenoi* (1 Thess 5:12; cf. Rom 12:8) he is referring to such leaders. However, according to the author of Acts, Paul and Barnabas appointed elders in each congregation on their missionary journey (Acts 14:23), and the church in Jerusalem was led by "apostles and elders" (15:2, 4, 6, 22, 23; 16:4; cf. 11:30; 21:18; cf. R. A. Campbell 1993, 1994). Further evidence indicates that within a generation or more of Paul's death elders functioned as traditional leaders within the messianic movement, as they did in the House of Israel.

Leadership by elders is well attested for the Christian communities of Asia Minor in particular and in several texts beyond 1 Peter. In Miletus and Ephesus, elders headed the church (Acts 20:17; 1 Tim 5:17–22). Their responsibilities there and elsewhere included preaching, teaching, support of the poor (Acts 20:28–30, 35; 1 Tim 5:17–19; cf. Titus 1:5–9), and perhaps also caring for the ill (cf. Jas 5:14). Both 2 John and 3 John were letters dispatched by leading Asian elders (2 John 1; 3 John 1). Asian elders are also attested later in the letters of Ignatius (*Magn.* 2:1; 3:1; 6:1; 7:1; *Trall.* 3:1; 7:1, 2; 12:2; *Phld. inscr.*; 7:2; 10:2; *Pol.* 6:1) and Polycarp (*Phil inscr.*; 5:3; 6:1). Elders were likewise in place in Corinth (*1 Clem.* 1:3; 3:3; 21:6; 44:5; 47:6; 54:2; 55:4; 57:1; cf. *2 Clem.* 17:3, 5) and Rome (Herm. *Vis.* 2.4.2, 3; 3.1.8). Collectively, Christian elders comprised a "council of elders" known as a *presbyterion*,[642] analogous to the Israelite council of elders in Judea (Acts 22:5; cf. Luke 22:66).[643]

As R. A. Campbell (1994) and others (A. E. Harvey 1974; Sobosan 1974; Powell 1975; M. Karrer 1990) aptly note, in Israel and the Greco-Roman world generally, elders (*zeqenîm*, *gerontes*, *presbyteroi*, *seniores*) were *heads of households* and senior persons of honor and significance. Elders were not "officeholders" but men who, by virtue of their age and the prestige of the families whose heads they were, exercised "an authority that is informal, representative and collective" (R. A. Campbell 1994, 65; cf. also pp. 111–14, 160–62, 514–16). This was authority conferred *by tradition* rather than charismatic quality or legal prescription, to follow the well-known distinction established by Max Weber (1978, 1:212–301).

Given the existence of elders throughout the Greco-Roman world, there is no necessity for assuming that it was the synagogue alone that provided the model for Christian elders or their alleged "office" (against Michaelis 1953; von Campenhausen 1969, 76–123; and others). That Christian elders were modeled after the seventy elders mentioned in Num 11:16–25 (so Karrer 1990) is even more farfetched (for a critique, see R. A. Cambell 1994, 161–62). The more immediate social context within which Christian elders emerged, as R. A. Campbell (1994, 117, 162) has pointed out, was the context of the household.

---

[642] See 1 Tim 4:14; cf. Ign. *Eph.* 2:2; 20:2; *Magn.* 2:1; 13:1; *Trall.* 2:2; 13:2; *Phld.* 4:1; 5:1; 7:1; *Smyrn.* 8:1; 12:2.

[643] On elders in the early Church, see Michaelis 1953; Bornkamm1968; Coenen 1972; Delorme, ed. 1974; A. E. Harvey 1974; Sobosan 1974; Powell 1975; Jay 1981; M. Karrer 1990; R. A. Campbell 1993, 1994; Rohde 1993.

In Palestine and the Diaspora, it was households that served as the matrix, locus of assembly, and focus of mission in the early messianic movement.[644] This connection of elders with house churches is reflected in such texts as 1 Tim 5:1–22 (cf. 3:1–7) and Titus 1:5–9; 2:1–10; as well as 2 John and 3 John, where elders address communities described along household and family lines ("elect lady and her children . . ."; "the children of your elect sister greet you"; "brothers . . . my children"), as in 1 Peter.

R. A. Campbell (1994, 126–31) offers a plausible scenario for the claim that "It is the household structure of the earliest churches which is both the factor that makes the calling of people 'elders' inappropriate in the first generation [Paul], and inevitable in the second." As the movement grew and the number of individual households increased, "the leaders of these house-churches would need to relate and act together in a *representative* capacity and at this point nothing could be more natural than to refer to their leaders collectively as 'the elders'" (R. A. Campbell 1994, 130, 153). Paul's activity at a stage prior to this development could explain, according to R. A. Campbell (1994, 110), the absence of mention of elders in his writings. The elders' role as "overseers" (*episkopoi*) "overseeing" (*episkopountes*) the flock, likewise suggests a household context, since community oversight was so regularly associated with household management (see below under *episkopountes* v 2b). (For a different view of "the system of elders and the beginnings of official authority," see von Campenhausen 1969, 76–123.)

Within the developing messianic movement, it was neither the elders' endowment with the Spirit nor their accomplishments that earned them status and roles of leadership but their age and the prestige of the households of which they were heads. But since being an elder was not solely a factor of age (so also R. A. Campbell 1994, 66), it is also probable that, when leaders of house churches were designated "elders," the term "elder" was extended beyond seniority in age to include those who were "seniors" in the faith (see Elliott 1970, 382–85; 1981/1990, 190–91; and the NOTE on v 5a below).

In any case, the elders addressed here in 1 Peter exercised a traditional form of authority, including that of "oversight" (*episkopountes*, v 2). The qualities enumerated in v 3 are not qualifications for persons applying for the role of elder/overseer but attitudes according to which the elders are to lead and shepherd the flock. The elders do not occupy positions in a hierarchalized organizational structure, of which there is no hint in 1 Peter. It is thus inappropriate and anachronistic to speak of them as "officials" or "office-holders." They are, rather, leaders whose authority is conferred by tradition and who exercise traditionally associated roles and functions. It is conceivable that, as

---

[644] See Acts 1:13; 2:1–42; Acts 2:46 and 5:42 (*kat' oikon*); 4:31; 8:3; 9:36–42, 43; 12:12–17; 16:15, 40; 17:5; 18:7; 20:7–12, 17–38, 20 (teaching from house to house); 21:8–14, 16; 28:17–31; see also house churches (*hē kat' oikon ekklēsia*, Rom 16:5; 1 Cor 16:19; Col 4:15; Phlm 2) and the conversion of entire households (John 4:53; Acts 10:24–48; 11:13–18; 16:31–34; 18:8 [cf. 1 Cor 1:14–16]); cf. Klauck 1981a, 1981b, 1982; Elliott 1981/1990, 187–200; 1984, 146–50; Verner 1983.

elders, the leaders of the communities could have been particular targets of hostility, but 1 Peter says nothing of this and focuses exclusive attention on their responsibilities *within* the communities. The absence of any Pauline mention of elders and shepherds is a further factor distinguishing 1 Peter from the Pauline writings and the Pauline mission field.

These community elders our author now exhorts and instructs in his threefold capacity as co-elder, witness to Christ's suffering, and sharer in the glory about to be revealed. These characteristics establish, in rhetorical terms, the *ethos* of the author, ostensibly the Apostle Peter, and his personal qualifications for addressing the elders as he does. This self-identification expresses both the bond uniting the author with the elders and the basis for his instruction and thus is designed to secure a favorable hearing from his fellow-leaders.

I exhort (*parakalō*). The verb *parakalō* is employed here, as in 2:11 (also 1st-person sing.), to open a new unit of exhortation. Ranging in tone between a request and a command, it serves to establish the proper diplomatic atmosphere for the author's exhortation of his fellow-elders with remarks that are both directive and reassuring (Bjerkelund 1967). It is used one final time in 5:12 to characterize the consolatory-hortatory aim of the letter as a whole. These three passages (including *logizomai*, "I regard," 5:12) are the sole instances in which the author speaks in the 1st-person singular.

The three phrases that follow establish the personal qualifications of the author for exhorting the elders, with each conveying some aspect of his solidarity with these leaders. These qualifications are the only attempt in the body of the letter to bring forward the personal status of the author and belong, as do 1:1 and 5:12–13, to the apparatus of pseudonymity (Beare 1970, 198)—that is, to details characterizing the presumed author, the Apostle Peter. While "co-elder" is a unique formulation with its own motivation, the accompanying two terms, along with the pastoral imagery employed in vv 2–4, reflect features associated with the Apostle Peter in early Christian tradition.

as co-elder (*hōs sympresbyteros*). With the particle *hōs*[645] the author indicates that he speaks "as" or "in the capacity of" a co-elder, a witness to the sufferings of Christ, and a sharer in the glory about to be revealed (see also Michaels 1988, 276, 279; and others). A reading lacking "as" and containing the definite article, however, has the same sense, with all three following nouns ("the co-elder and witness . . . and the sharer . . .") qualifying the "I" of "I exhort."

The unique noun *sympresbyteros* ("co-elder," "co-presbyter," "fellow-elder/fellow-presbyter") occurs nowhere else in Greek literature and represents an-

[645] Although *hōs* ("as") is contained only in several later manuscripts (P 1 630 1243 1505 2495 syr[h] cop[sa]), it probably was original but was lost at an early stage through haplography: [*parakal*]*ō ōs s*[*ympresbyteros*], with *ho* ("the") inserted afterwards. Such a probability is supported by the resulting symmetry of *presbyteros* with *martys* (v 1b), which also lacks a definite article. The secondary addition of *ho* following the inadvertant omission of *hōs*, in turn, could have been prompted by the definite article *ho* associated with *koinōnos* and introducing v 1c.

other coinage by the author.[646] The definite article accompanying both this term and "sharer" (v 1c) in Greek makes them specific and implies that their bearer is well known to the addressees, as Peter could be presumed to be. The term "co-elder" is particularly striking, however, given the fact that in the letter's salutation (1:1) Peter is identified by the more prestigious term, "apostle." If R. A. Campbell (1993, 516–28) is correct in claiming that the apostles were at an early stage also known as elders, this would be less surprising; note Papias (in Eusebius, *Hist. eccl.* 3.39.4), who in speaking of the apostles, including Peter, refers to them as "elders." But this theory has yet to be convincingly demonstrated. In any case, it is likely that *sympresbyteros* was coined by our author to accentuate the responsibility common to the author and the elders addressed. He has already displayed a predilection for such composite terms involving the preposition *syn.*[647] All of these terms express some form of commonality and underscore the unity and internal cohesion of the community that is such a prominent concern of the author. Like *synklēronomos* ("co-heir") and *syneklektos* ("co-elect") in particular, *sympresbyteros* also conveys a sense of solidarity, in this case the solidarity and collegiality between the author and the elders addressed. Paul used similar *syn-* composite terms in referring to his "co-workers" and associates in ministry (Rom 16:3, 9, 21; 2 Cor 8:23; Phil 2:25; 4:3; Phlm 24; Col 4:11), terms that likewise conveyed the sense of collaboration and collegiality (see also the series of six *syn-* composites in Ign. *Pol.* 6:1).

Proponents of either the genuine or the pseudonymous authorship of the letter have speculated about this unusual term and its bearing on the issue of authorship. The difficulty facing scholars who suppose Petrine authorship on the basis of 1:1 is that Simon Peter the Apostle is never identified as an "elder" in the NT, let alone "co-elder." Nor is there any basis in the letter for supposing that Peter identifies himself as "co-elder" out of modesty[648] or as an ingratiating ploy. Among those assuming the letter's pseudonymity, Brox (1986, 228–29) claims that with this term the *actual author* (who is writing in Peter's name) was referring to *himself*, an actual elder, and thereby partially lifting the mask of pseudonymity. His identity as co-elder supposedly gave him the competence to address fellow-elders. What accounts for this admitted "inconsistency" in the execution of the "literary fiction" of the letter, however, Brox leaves unexplained.

---

[646] For much later instances of the term used of others, see Eusebius, *Hist. eccl.* 5.16.5; 7.5.6; 7.11.3, 20.

[647] See *synkleronomos* ("co-heir," 3:7); *syneklektos* ("co-elect," 5:13); cf. also *syschēmetizō* ("molded," 1:14); *synoikeō* ("live with," 3:7); *sympathēs* ("compassionate," 3:8); *syntrechō* ("joining," 4:4); *symbainō* ("happening," 4:12). Four occur only here in the NT (*synoikeō, sympathēs, sympresbyteros, syneklektos*).

[648] Against Knopf 1912, 188; Windisch and Preisker 1951, 78; Beare 1970, 198; Grudem 1988, 186; and Davids 1990, 176, citing as analogues Rev 19:10; 22:9; and Ign. *Eph.* 2:1; *Magn.* 2:1; *Phld.* 4:1; *Smyrn.* 12:2.

Marxsen (1979) goes several steps further. He takes "co-elder" to be the self-designation of a later pastor in Asia Minor, who wrote a letter (4:12–5:11) that originally was distinct from 1:3–4:11 but that was eventually combined with this earlier material in later time, with 1:1–2 and 5:12–14 added as the epistolary framework. The right of this "fellow-elder" to address the other elders of Asia Minor was his experience of suffering in persecution. He stood in the same "tradition of suffering" as did the present audience and as did Peter, who was martyred in Rome. The composite writing, Marxsen theorized, was ascribed secondarily to Peter, in order to lend apostolic authority to the letter. The theory, however, entails the fatal flaw of all partition theories: their indemonstrability and lack of necessity, given the evident literary integrity of the document. Within this integral letter, the words *witness*, *co-elder*, *sharer*, and *apostle* all serve as self-designations of the same implied author of the letter.

A variety of factors indeed favor the likelihood of the letter's pseudonymity (see GENERAL INTRODUCTION, 7.1). But the fiction of Peter as "co-elder" need not be seen as inconsistent with his identification as "apostle" in 1:1, for what "co-elder" brings to expression is the *solidarity* that binds Peter, the presumed author, with the elders he addresses. By appealing to the "elders" (*presbyteroi*) as "co-elder" (*sympresbyteros*), he affirms a collegiality that puts him on an equal rather than superior footing with the elders in respect to leadership and responsibility. This in turn provides a common and courteous basis for the exhortation that follows. He is thus exhorting fellow-leaders as peers, with perhaps the further implication that they too are witnesses to the suffering of the Christ and sharers in the glory to be revealed. In actuality, the term "co-elder" by itself proves nothing regarding the authenticity or pseudonymity of the letter. This is an issue that must be settled on other grounds.

1b. *and witness to the sufferings of the Christ* (*kai martys tōn tou Christou pathēmatōn*). The second and third ways that the author identifies himself relate to two associated and fundamental emphases of this letter: Christ's suffering and his glory as the basis for the hope of glory on the part of the suffering believers addressed. The correspondence between the language of 5:1 and 4:12–13, in particular, is striking, with *en hymin*, *tōn tou Christou pathēmatōn*, and *apokalypsis/apokalyptesthai doxēs* occurring in both. Our author's identification of himself as "witness" (*martys*), furthermore, relates to his stated aim in writing (5:12). There he employs a kindred verb, *epimartyroō*, to indicate that, along with exhortation, his aim in this letter is to "bear full witness" to the grace of God experienced by the believers. Here (5:1) his witness pertains to Christ's suffering, a reason for the grace experienced.

A witness (*martys*) is one who observes and testifies to the actuality and veracity of something (cf. Strathmann 1967; Danker 1982, 442–47; Beutler 1991c). The term *martys* is used with the genitive of the thing observed or attested (Luke 24:48; Acts 1:22; 2:32; 3:15; 5:32; 10:39). In the passages in Acts (cf. also 10:41), it is Peter who is the one witnessing to Jesus' activity, crucifixion, and resurrection. The identification of Peter as the preeminent witness in nascent Christianity to Jesus' suffering, death, and resurrection was an element of the early Petrine tradition (see Cullmann 1958, 70–152; and the NOTE on 1:1) and hence is appropriately stressed in this "Petrine" letter. Paul, by contrast, never identifies himself as a *martys* to Christ or his sufferings; for his use of the verb with respect to Christ's resurrection, see 1 Cor 15:15.

In the NT, *martys* can mean either "eye-witness" *of* something (Matt 18:16; Luke 24:48; Acts 1:8; 7:58; 10:39, 41; 22:15, 20) or "one who bears witness" *to* something. In view of the Gospel traditions about Peter's denial and desertion of Jesus during his passion, it is unlikely that the author, speaking in the name of Peter, is claiming to be an eye-witness *of* the sufferings of Christ (against Bigg 1902, 186; Selwyn 1947, 228; Beare 1970, 198; Trites 1977, 213–16). It is rather the latter sense that is implied here, in keeping with the NT tradition concerning Peter as one who in his preaching witnessed to the reality of Christ's having suffered, died, and having been resurrected and glorified (see especially the speeches by Peter in Acts 2:14–36 [2:32]; 3:12–26 [3:15]; 4:8–12; 5:30–32; 10:34–43 [10:39–41]), a sense of *martys* found also in Luke 24:46, 48; Acts 1:8, 22; 22:15, and 20. This is also consonant with our author's repeated testimony to the sufferings of Christ in this letter (1:11; 2:21, 23, 24; 3:18a; 4:1, 13).

Eventually the term *martys* came to designate a "blood witness," one who *dies* for bearing witness to her/his convictions, but it is unclear when it took on this sense, though in any case it was later than 1 Peter.[649] Nothing in 1 Peter, moreover, suggests this sense (so also Brox 1986, 229; against Marxsen 1979, 381–93). The letter contains no mention of any believers, let alone Peter, having died for the faith. If this were an allusion to Peter's dying a martyr's death in Rome (as mentioned in *1 Clem.* 5:2–7 and later Christian tradition),[650] its use in this sense would be singular in the NT. Elsewhere in 1 Peter, the related verbs *promartyreomai* (1:11) and *epimartyreomai* (5:12) still have the more

[649] Suffering and dying in witness to one's convictions was a staple of Israel's experience from its confrontation with Hellenization onward (Frend 1967, 22–57; see 1–4 Maccabees; Heb 11:32–38). However, with the possible exception of the Alexandrian manuscript of 4 Macc 12:16 and Rev 11:3 (if an Israelite source), *martys* "was apparently not used by Jewish writers to describe the act of those who die for Torah" (Frend 1967, 66). The remark by Paul in Acts 22:20, "when the blood of Stephen your witness was shed," and the references in Revelation to "Christ the faithful witness" (1:5; cf. 3:14), "Antipas my witness . . . who was killed" (2:13) and "the blood of the witnesses of Jesus"(17:6), show that being a witness *could* lead to death, but in none of these cases does the term *martys* itself mean "blood witness." Acts states (5:18, 40–41; 12:1–11) that Peter *suffered* for his witness, but the tradition of Peter as a "blood witness" arose outside the NT. It is first attested in *1 Clement* (5:2–7), which in a listing of Christian martyrs (5:2–6:2) refers to Peter and Paul as "the greatest and most righteous pillars [who] were persecuted and contended unto death." Peter in particular is described as he "who because of unrighteous envy suffered not one or two but many trials and, having given his witness (*martyrēsas*), proceeded to his due place of glory" (5:4), with the latter two expressions implying his death and resurrection. The terms *martys, martyreō, martyria*, and *martyrion* are clearly used of witnessing with one's *death* in the mid-second-century *Martyrdom of Polycarp* (1:1; 2:1, 2; 13:2; 14:2; 15:2; 16:2; 17:1, 3; 18:3; 19:1; 21:1; 22:1).

[650] See Lietzmann 1936; Cullmann 1958, 70–152; and the NOTE on 5:13.

traditional sense (unconnected with suffering and death) of "bearing prior witness" or "bearing full witness," respectively. Moreover, Peter, the implied author, is stressing here in v 1 what he has in common with his fellow-elders. This could involve suffering resulting from bearing witness to the sufferings of Christ but not death, since the letter contains no reference to the latter. Hence *martys* here has the sense of one who witnesses in word and possibly deed but not in giving up one's life in the martyrological sense. As the author shares with the addressees in Christ's glory (v 5c), so in his own experience of suffering he shares with them and the entire brotherhood in the sufferings of Christ (cf. 4:13; 5:9).[651]

The phrase "the sufferings of the Christ" (*tōn tou Christou pathēmatōn*) is identical to the phrase in 4:13a, just as v 1c echoes the language of 4:13c. Here, however, "witness" is linked with the first phrase, and "sharer" (cf. 4:13a, "share") is connected with "glory," rather than with "the sufferings of the Christ." Our author views the resurrection of Christ as the fundamental manifestation of God's power and the basis of the believers' new life (1:3, 21; 2:4; 3:18, 21–22). Here, however, he again refers to the *sufferings* of Christ (cf. 1:11; 4:13; see also 1:2c, 19; 2:4c, 21–24; 3:18a; 4:1) as the object of his witnessing, since innocent suffering is the chief problem addressed in this letter. The articular expression, *the Christ* (as in 4:13), is noteworthy. As mentioned in the NOTE on 4:13, the virtually identical formulations of 5:1b and 4:13a represent an older tradition in which "Christ" is not yet a personal name but still a label applied to Jesus by his followers.

1c. *and sharer in the glory about to be revealed* (*ho kai tēs mellousēs apokalyphthēnai doxēs koinōnos*). The third self-identification, like the second, expresses the solidarity that the author has with Christ and all believers (including the elders), who also will share in Christ's glory. Thus the definite article (*ho*) acompanying *koinōnos* does not set off the author from other "sharers" and is omitted in the translation. Both qualifications (v 1b, 1c) mirror the earlier association of the "sufferings" with the "glories" of Christ (1:11; cf. 2:4) and thus also appear linked in the author's mind. The same combination also appears in 4:13, where believers who "share in the *sufferings* of the Christ" can also look forward to the revelation of his "glory." There the believers are said to "share" (*koinōneite*) presently in Christ's sufferings. Here the author describes himself as one who shares (*koinōnos*) *in the glory about to be revealed.*[652] Selwyn takes this as an allusion to Peter's participation in Jesus' transfiguration (Mark 9:2–8 par.). But this would require some past-tense for-

[651] So also Luther; Calvin; von Harnack 1897, 452; Brox 1961, 38; 1986, 229; Strathmann 1967, 494–95; Michaelis 1967c, 934. On witness and martyrdom in the NT and early Church, see von Campenhausen 1964; Frend 1967, 58–76; Horbury and McNeil, eds. 1981. On *martys* and its family of terms, see Brox 1961; Strathmann 1967; Trites 1977; Beutler 1991a, 1991b, 1991c.

[652] For the construction of *koinōnos* with the genitive of the thing shared (*tēs . . . doxēs*), see also Sir 6:10; Esth 8:12; 1 Cor 10:18; and 2 Cor 1:7.

mulation, such as "one who was a sharer of. . . ." Moreover, the *glory* spoken of here (see also 1:7–8; 5:4, 10) is a glory to be revealed in the *future* to *all* believers rather than one revealed in the *past* only to Peter (and the other two apostles), as Best (1971, 168–69) aptly notes. Emphasis on this common experience and expectation serves to unite the author with his addressees (elders, but also all believers), while also providing a basis for the exhortation to follow (v 4).

The substantive *koinōnos* means "sharer," "partaker," "participant," "partner," or "associate"[653] and recalls the kindred verb *koinōneō* ("share"), used of the addressees in 4:13. There too "sharing" occurs in a context concerned with suffering and subsequent glory. Paul once spoke of other believers as "sharers in our suffering" (2 Cor 1:7) but never employed the expression "sharer in glory." In later time, *koinōnos*, like *martys*, was used specifically of blood martyrs in Asia Minor.[654]

in the glory about to be revealed (*tēs mellousēs apokalyphthēnai doxēs*). The "glory" (*doxa*)—that is, the honor—shared is that of Jesus Christ (cf. 1:11, 21; 4:13, 14; 5:4) but in the light of 1:7 and 5:10 also involves the final glory and honor awaiting all who are in Christ. The combination *sufferings of the Christ* and *glory* expresses once again (cf. 1:11 and 4:13) the essential features of Christ's life according to this letter: his passion and his divine vindication, which set the pattern for the experience and hope of his followers.

The idea that this glory is "about to be revealed" (*tēs mellousēs apokalyphthēnai doxēs*) is related to the expectation of the imminent revelation of Christ (1:7, 13; 4:13; 5:4; cf. Rom 8:18; Titus 2:13) and further illustrates the *future* as well as present orientation of the letter's consolation and exhortation. The formulation is especially close to that of Rom 8:18 (*tēn mellousan doxan apokalyphthēnai*, "the glory about to be revealed").[655] The implied agent who reveals is God, with the verb representing yet another divine passive.

With these three designations our author affirms his solidarity with the elders (and their communities) in three respects: collegiality with the elders, in particular, and then solidarity with all of the addressees in bearing witness to the suffering of Christ through one's own suffering and in sharing in the glory of Christ soon to be revealed. 1 Peter 5:1 reprises themes and formulas in 1:3–4:19 and thus further illustrates the thematic and literary integrity of 1:3–4:11 and 4:12–5:11.

In vv 2–3 our author instructs the elders on the manner in which they are to exercise their leadership. It is likely that the terminology and concepts of these verses have been influenced by Israelite and early Christian tradition

---

[653] See Matt 23:30; Luke 5:10; 1 Cor 10:18, 20; 2 Cor 8:23; Phlm 17; Heb 10:33; 2 Pet 1:4.

[654] See *Mart. Pol.* 6:2 and Montanist circles (Buschmann 1995, 251–64). On the *koino-* word field in the NT, see J. Y. Campbell 1932; and the literature cited in the NOTE on 4:13a.

[655] On the grammatical construction in which the participle (*mellousēs*) is separated from its adjunct (*doxēs*), see BDF §474 (5a) and Rom 3:25; 8:18; and Jas 1:5 for similar examples.

concerning community leaders and their responsibilities, though theories vary concerning the precise form and content of such tradition. The triad of antitheses in vv 2–3, however, constitutes a unique Petrine formulation.

2a. *shepherd the flock of God among you* (*poimanate to en hymin poimnion tou theou*). The terms employed here involve a single pastoral image of the community as the "flock (*poimnion*) of God," with Christ as "chief shepherd" (*archipoimēn*, v 4a) and the elders as "shepherding" (*poimainein*) the flock and exercising oversight (*episkopountes*). See Riggenbach 1889; Bosetti 1990, 159–223. A similar though not identical cluster of terms is found in the account of Paul's farewell address to the elders/shepherds of Miletus (Acts 20:17–38).

This pastoral imagery, rooted in Israel's long history as a people of shepherds as well as farmers, figures prominently in both the OT and the NT in portrayals of the people of Israel, their leaders, and their relation to God as shepherd.[656] Thus, in the OT and related writings Israel frequently is portrayed as a "flock" (*poimnē*, *poimnion*) or as "sheep" (*probata*) under the guidance and care of God and/or human leaders depicted as "shepherds" (*poimanes*, *poimainein*)[657] or as sheep scattered and without a shepherd.[658] Jesus applied the metaphor to himself and his disciples,[659] and his followers followed suit (see also 2:25 and 5:4 and their respective NOTES).

In our verse, *poimanate* is a 2d-person pl. aor. act. imperative of the verb *poimainō* ("shepherd," "act as shepherd," "tend"), with "flock of God" as its object. Employed 54× in the LXX, it appears in the NT only here and in Heb 12:15 but belongs to a widely-employed pastoral metaphor in both Old and New Testaments. Shepherding included such activities as leading, guiding, gathering, feeding, and defending a flock, whether used literally (Luke 17:7) or figuratively (Ezek 24:10; Acts 20:28; John 21:15–17; Rev 2:27; 7:17). In a secondary sense, the verb also had the sense of "rule" or "govern" when applied figuratively to God, the gods, or humans in authority (2 Sam 7:7; Ps 2:9; Philo, *Det.* 8.25; Matt 2:6). In the OT, both God[660] and human rulers (2 Sam 7:7; Isa 44:28; 63:11; Jer 22:22; Ezek 34) are depicted as shepherds. The latter often are denounced by the prophets as unfaithful shepherds leading the people astray (Isa 56:11–12; Jer 23:1–4; 50:6–7; Ezek 34:2–10; Zech 11:4–17). In the anticipated messianic restoration, on the other hand, God would give his people "shepherds after my own heart" (Jer 3:15; cf. 23:1–4) or one shepherd

[656] See Jost 1939; Botterweck 1960; Bosetti 1990, 227–58; Engemann 1991, 577–607.

[657] See 2 Kgdms 5:2; 24:17; 3 Kgdms 5:2; 22:17; 1 Chr 11:2; Pss 2:9; 23; 27[28]:9; 47[48]:14; 76[77]:20; 77[78]:52, 70–72, etc.; Isa 27:10; 40:11; 63:11; Jer 3:15; 13:17, 20; 23:1–4; 27[28]:6, 17; 28[51]:23; 38[31]:10; Ezek 34:2–31; 36:37–38; Hos 13:5; Mic 2:12; 4:8; 5:4, 7; 7:14; Zech 9:16; 10:3; 11:3–17.

[658] See Num 27:17; 3 Kgdms 22:17; Ezek 34:5, 6, 12; Zech 10:2; 13:7; cf. also *1 En.* 89–90; CD XIII 10; XIX 8–9.

[659] See Matt 9:36/Mark 6:34; cf. also Matt 26:31/Mark 14:27, referrring to Zech 13:7; John 10:1–18; 21:15–19; and Tooley 1964–1965.

[660] See Gen 49:24 MT; Pss 23; 28:9; 77:20; 78:52; 80:1; Isa 40:11; Jer 31:10; Ezek 34.

over all the people (Ezek 34:23–24; 37:34), a concept linked to the symbolization of the Messiah as shepherd (see the NOTE on v 4 below).

Jesus, besides applying the image to himself (Tooley 1964–1965), also commissioned Peter to "feed my lambs . . . , shepherd [*poimaine*] my sheep . . . , feed my sheep" (John 21:15–17). In addition to this Johannine passage and the present Petrine verse, "shepherd" as either a noun (*poimēn*) or a verb (*poimainō*) is also used elsewhere of Christian leaders.[661] One such instance, Paul's farewell address to the elders of Miletus (Acts 20:17–35), is especially noteworthy because of the cluster of terms it shares with our Petrine text: "elders" (Acts 20:17), "the flock (*tōi poimniōi*) in which the Holy Spirit has made you overseers (*episkopous*) to shepherd (*poimainein*) the church of God" (20:28). Paul's further mention of "fierce wolves . . . not sparing the flock" (Acts 20:29) can also be compared to the devouring, roaring lion in 1 Peter (5:8). The affinities are likely due to use of early Christian tradition, in which the community and its elders/leaders are depicted as flock of God and shepherds, in continuity with OT symbolism.

The correspondence between 1 Peter and John 21 illustrates how this tradition was associated with the Apostle Peter in particular. According to John 21:15–17, the resurrected Christ enjoins Peter three times to feed his lambs or sheep. This threefold commission contrasts to Peter's threefold denial (John 18:17–18, 25–27) and restores the apostle to a position of authority and leadership. The pastoral metaphor and focus on Peter, along with other common terms and motifs,[662] point to a coalescence of tradition concerning ministry and leadership associated with the Apostle Peter and the beginning of a "Petrine motif" that continues in later time.[663]

The Greek noun for "shepherd," *poimēn*, was rendered in Latin as *pastor*, a term that was taken over in ecclesiastical parlance for a clerical leader—hence, the association today of the Christian "pastor" with the role of shepherd. Beginning with the 2d century, the term "shepherd" gradually came to be associated with the role of bishop (*episkopos*) exclusively, a terminological development made possible because of the earlier association of "shepherd" with "overseer" (*episkopos*) and of "shepherd" with *episkopountes* here in 1 Peter. Thus Ambrose, in his letter to the presbyter Evangelus (*Ep*. 146), cites 1 Pet 5:1–2 in noting that *episkopeuontes* (*sic*!) means "oversee" but is also the term from which "bishop" derives. A century earlier, Cyprian, bishop of Carthage,

---

[661] See Eph 4:11; Ign. *Phld.* 2:1; *Rom.* 9:1; *Ascen. Isa.* 3:23–27; Herm. *Sim.* 9.31.5–6; see also the "shepherd" who authored the *Shepherd of Hermas*, Herm. *Vis.* 5.5 and *Sim.* 9.31.6.

[662] See *neōteros* ("younger," John 21:18; 1 Pet 5:5a); girding metaphor (John 21:18; 1 Pet 5:5b); reference to the Lord's coming (John 21:20; 1 Pet 5:4); see also "follow me" (*akolouthei mou*, John 21:19, 20, 22; 1 Pet 2:21, "follow in his footsteps," *epakolouthēsēte tois ichnesin autou*) and reference to the glorification of God (John 21:19); cf. glory, 1 Pet 5:1; glorification of God, 1 Pet 2:12; 4:11, 16.

[663] On the early Christian tradition of Peter as shepherd, see R. E. Brown, Donfried, and Reumann, eds. 1973, 139–47, 163–64.

in a letter to Stephan, bishop of Rome, observes: "Although we shepherds are many, we feed one flock" (Cyprian, *Ep.* 68.3).

the flock of God among you (*to en hymin pomnion tou theou*). As a component of this pastoral metaphor, the people under the leadership of shepherds are identified as "sheep" (*probata*), "lambs" (*arnia*) or, as here, "flock" (*poimnion*). The term *poimnion* (lit., "little flock," a diminutive of *poimnē*) appears 75× in the LXX but in the NT only here (vv 2, 3) and in Luke–Acts (Luke 12:32; Acts 20:28, 29)—in all cases figuratively of the believing community.[664] The paronym *poimnē* (3× in the LXX), on the other hand, appears in Matt 26:31 (citing Zech 13:7); Luke 2:8; John 10:16; and 1 Cor 9:7, with Matthew and John applying "flock" or "little flock" to Jesus' followers. The added qualification "of God" (*tou theou*) makes clear to the elders/shepherds that the flock is not theirs to supervise as they choose, but God's. They are in reality only "under-shepherds" (of the chief shepherd, v 4) to whom the flock has been "allotted" (v 3).

It is unlikely that *en hymin*, the same phrase as in v 1, refers to some capacity "within" the shepherds personally ("as far as in you lies," so Calvin, Erasmus) or that it means "in your charge" (e.g., RSV, NRSV). As in 4:12 and 5:1, the phrase instead has distributive force: the flock of God that is *among you*; that is, in your towns or villages or household communities (so also Bigg 1902, 188; Knopf 1912, 189; Selwyn 1947, 230).

2b. *by exercising oversight* (*episkopountes*). This verb, a pres. pl. part. of *episkopeō*, is subordinate to and modifies the "you" of the main verb, "shepherd." Since flocks of sheep and goats are by nature vulnerable to attack or going astray (cf. 2:25), effective shepherding includes vigilant watching and oversight. In the NT, *episkopeō* ("watch" [*skopeō*] "over" [*epi-*], "exercise, engage in, provide oversight"; cf. "super-vise") occurs only here and in Heb 12:15 (but in a different sense); the related verb *episkeptomai* ("look at," "visit") appears more frequently (11×; cf. Beyer 1964). Earlier our author used the kindred noun *episkopos* of Jesus Christ as "overseer" of believers' lives and the related noun *episkopē* of (the day of) God's "visitation" (2:12).[665] A similar combination of terms in Acts 20:17–38 (*presbyteroi*, v 17; *poimnion, episkopous, poimainein*, v 28) reflects a traditional association of terms in the *episkept-* family with

---

[664] Cf. also *1 Clement*, figuratively of Christ's flock (16:1; 44:3; 54:2 ["only let the flock of Christ have peace with the presbyters set over it"]; 57:2); Hermas, *Sim.* 6.1.6; 9.31.6; *Mart. Pol.* 14:1.

[665] In some important MSS (א* B 33 323 cop[sa]) *episkopountes* is absent, but the witness of normally reliable Codex Vaticanus (B) in particular is suspect, since it also omits *kata theon* and the entirety of v 3. Manuscript support for its inclusion, on the other hand, is early and extensive (𝔓[72] א [second hand] A P Ψ 33 69 81 945 1241 1739 and others, as well as the Old Latin, Vulgate, Syriac [syr[p]], and Coptic [cop[bo]] versions). The variant *episkopeuontes* (614 630 1505 2495 and a few others; Ambrose) is a virtually synonymous though secondary reading, also pointing to the initial presence of *episkopountes*. An addition of *episkopountes* at a later time when presbyters/elders had been distinguished from *episkopoi* ("bishops") is unlikely, whereas its exclusion at that later time for this same reason is more plausible; so also J. N. D. Kelly 1969, 200; and Beare 1970, 202. Its original presence is also consistent with the author's fondness for qualifying main verbs with modifying participles and with his pairing of "shepherd" (*poimēn*) and "overseer" (*episkopos*) in 2:25.

shepherding a flock.[666] In the LXX, the verb (2 Chr 34:12) and its paronym, *episkopos* ("overseer," Num 31:14; Neh 11:9, 14, 22; and 1 Macc 1:51), connote administrative responsibility. Plutarch also used the verb *episkopein* in speaking of the task of *presbyteroi*: "elders [*presbyteroi*] oversee [*episkopousin*] public affairs [*ta koina*], for what they bring to the task is reason, judgment, frankness, and 'sapience profound,' as poets say" (*An Seni* 28; *Mor.* 797E). Polycarp, describing the duties of *presbyteroi*, included their "caring for" (*episkeptomenoi*) the weak (Pol., *Phil* 6:1). In the Greek world, *episkopeō* and *episkopos* were used of urban and state functionaries and their administrative and cultic responsibilities (Deissmann 1901, 230–31; MM 244–45; Beyer 1964, 611–14), a usage that could account for the Christian adoption of these terms in areas of the Diaspora.[667]

A functionary at Qumran known as the *mĕbaqqēr* offers an instance of leadership from Palestinian provenance that also may have influenced the combining of the elder and oversight roles in nascent Christianity. This person, a man of between thirty and fifty years of age, thus "elder" in age, and a trained interpreter of the Law, had the responsibility of examining and admitting applicants to the community.[668] He was to care for the members like a shepherd; he also received and distributed money given for charity:

> He shall instruct the congregation in the works of God. . . . He shall love them as a father loves his children, and shall carry them in all their distress like a shepherd his sheep. He shall loosen all the fetters which bind them so that in his congregation there may be none that are oppressed or broken. He shall examine every man entering his community with regard to his deeds, understanding, strength, ability and possession, and shall inscribe him in his place according to his rank in the lot of the L[igh]t. (CD XIII 9–10)

This leader "presided" (a verbal form related to *pāqîd*) over the community assembly and was called "overseer" or "supervisor [*mĕbaqqēr*] of the Many" (1QS VI 12, 14).[669] The affinity between *mĕbaqqēr* and oversight is clear in the Greek OT, where words related to *episkopein* translate terms from the Hebrew roots *bqr* and *pqd*.[670]

---

666 See Ezek 11:16; 34:1–31 (*episkepsomai* [v 12] and *poimenes, poimnion, probata* passim); Num 27:16; Jer 13:2–21; 23:2; Ezek 34:11–12; Zech 10:3; CD XIII 7–9; *1 Clem.* 44:3; Ign. *Rom.* 9:1; *Phld.* 1:1–2:1.

667 On the history of usage from Homer onward, see Gomez 1962; on NT usage, see Zisioulas 1983.

668 See 1QS VI 13–23; XV 11; 5Q13, frg. 4; CD IX 18, 19, 22; XIII 6, 7, 13, 16; XIV 8, 11, 13; XV 8, 11, 14; cf. von der Osten-Sacken 1964.

669 CD XIV 6–9, on the other hand, distinguishes between the "supervisor (*mĕbaqqēr*) over all the camps" and "the priest who is made to preside (verbal form related to *pāqîd*) at the head of the Many."

670 Thus Ezek 34:11 LXX *episkeptesthai* translates *baqar* in a passage about Israel's shepherds that "probably lies behind the picture of the *mĕbaqqēr* in the first place" (R. A. Campbell 1994, 156); cf. also Lev 13:36; 2 Esd 4:15, 19; 5:17; 6:1; 7:14; Ps 26[27]:4.

This combination of the roles of older male, overseer, and shepherd by both the *mĕbaqqēr* of Qumran and the *presbyteros* of nascent Christianity is striking enough to have suggested to several scholars[671] that the former figure was the most immediate model for the Christian elder. Both were older male leaders; both exercised oversight. Just as the Qumran *mĕbaqqēr* was responsible for community property, so the Christian overseer (*episkopos*) was to be a "steward over household affairs" (*oikonomos*, Titus 1:7) and an efficient manager of his own household (1 Tim 3:4–5). Both also supervised proper behavior (1QS VI 13–23; CD XIII 9–10; Acts 20:29–31; Titus 1:9–10). Finally, both were compared to shepherds guiding the flock (CD XIII 9–10; Acts 20:28; 1 Pet 5:2). In extrabiblical Greek, by contrast, the association between "shepherd" and words from the *episkept-* group is not found (R. A. Campbell 1994, 158–59). On the other hand, Lohse (1980, 70–71), typical of scholars who see in the Qumran *mĕbaqqēr* only an analogy but not the basic model for the Christian overseer, stresses the overwhelmingly Hellenistic provenance of the *episkopos* as functionary and the Christian adoption of this terminology only in writings of the Hellenistic Diaspora.

However one judges the significance of the Qumran overseer as a model for nascent Christianity, it is explicitly "elders" (*presbyteroi*) to whom 1 Peter and other Christian writings attribute "oversight" and the role of "shepherding" the flock. Paul's genuine letters contain only one reference to Christian leaders as overseers (Phil 1:1, *episkopoi*). Acts 20:17–38, however, describing Paul's farewell address to the elders of Miletus (Ephesus), contains, as noted above, a constellation of terms similar to the terms in 1 Peter and represents its closest NT parallel. The similarity of terminology and themes illustrates a developing tradition concerning community leadership in early Christianity and suggests for both Acts and 1 Peter a similar stage of ecclesial development.[672] Like our Petrine author (5:5a, 10a, 12), the Paul of Acts also testifies here to the good news of the grace of God (Acts 20:24, 32), while concurrently stressing his humility (Acts 20:19; cf. 1 Pet 5:3, 5b, 6) and the fact that he desired no one's silver or gold (Acts 20:33; cf. 1 Pet 5:2c). Here too "elders" (v 17) are addressed as "overseers" (*episkopoi*), who as shepherds are to "feed the church of the Lord" and protect the "flock" (v 28). This role of elder as overseer is likewise found in the Pastorals, where the overseer (1 Tim 3:1–7; Titus 1:7–11) appears to be one of the "elders" (1 Tim 5:17–19; Titus 1:5); note also the juxtaposition of "elders" and "overseer" in Titus 1:5, 7.[673] The evidence thus indicates that the status of Christian elders was a high and honorable one and that their role as overseers/shepherds included instruction in the faith, moral guidance, protection of the flock, organizational leadership, and management of community resources.

[671] E.g., Nauck 1957, 203–7; R. E. Brown 1970, 67–69; R. A. Campbell 1994, 155–59.

[672] So also Goppelt 1993, 338; against Bornkamm 1968, 666.

[673] At the same time, the possibility that in some places only *some* elders functioned as overseers is raised by 1 Tim 5:17: "Let the elders who lead be considered worthy of double honor"; cf. R. E. Brown 1970, 66.

The Greek verb *episkopeō* and its noun *episkopos* form the basis of the Latin *episcopus* and the English term "bishop" (bi- = *epi*-; -shop = *skopos*). In the earliest stages of ecclesial organizational development reflected in the NT, oversight (*episkopē*) was exercised by *all* elders. Eventually, however, this responsibility was associated with and restricted to one elder among the elders as *the* "overseer" or "bishop" of an area. This post-NT development was a gradual one and varied from place to place. In the NT at any rate, *episkopeō* and *episkopos* were terms designating not "bishop" or the "functioning of a bishop" but the oversight responsibilities of elders. *1 Clement* still describes "presbyters" functioning as *episkopoi* (44:1–6), as does the *Letter of Polycarp to the Philippians* (6:1). Ignatius, on the other hand, distinguished the plurality of elders and the "council of elders" from the singular *episkopos* (Ign. *Eph.* 4:1 and passim). He envisioned elders and deacons as subordinate to the overseer/bishop (*Magn.* 6:1; *Trall.* 2) and established the pattern that was gradually adopted thereafter. This hierarchical pattern included the restriction of the shepherd role to the bishops alone.[674]

In contrast to this later development, 1 Peter and Acts 20, and perhaps also the Pastorals, represent a stage of organizational development in which elders still functioned as overseers, a situation "typical for the area from Rome to Asia Minor during the period A.D. 65–80" (Goppelt 1993, 338). The association of elders and oversight with management of the affairs of the household (*oikos*) (as in 1 Tim 3:4; 3:15; 2 Tim 2:20; Titus 1:7) is also significant in 1 Peter. It illustrates the logic of the elders' serving as leaders of the household of God and the relation of this exhortation with the household exhortation in 2:18–3:7.

The precarious situation faced by the Asia Minor communities required pastoral leadership of a high quality. Accordingly, the author qualified the act of shepherding and exercising oversight with a triad of negative-positive antitheses ("not . . . but"), clarifying the ideal spirit, proper motive, and appropriate manner of Christian leadership (vv 2c–3):

mē anagkastōs	*alla hekousiōs kata theon*
mēde aischrokerdōs	*alla prothymōs*
mēd' hōs katakyrieuontes tōn klērōn	*alla typoi ginomenoi tou poimniou*
not because compelled	but willingly in accord with God
not for shameful gain	but eagerly
not as domineering those allotted [to you]	but being examples for the flock

[674] See, e.g., Hipp., *Trad. ap.* 3 and esp. the *Didaskalia Apostolorum* and the *Constitutiones Apostolorum* (*Apostolic Constitutions*) of the 4th century (*Didask. Apost.* 4 = *Apos. Con.* 2.1.1; 2.6.5; *Didask. Apost.* 7 = *Apos. Con.* 2.20.8; *Didask. Apost.* 9 = *Apos. Con.* 2.28.2; *Didask. Apost.* 10 = *Apos. Con.* 2.42.1; 2.43.3); cf. Nauck 1957, 201–2. For discussion of the qualifications and role of the bishop, see *Didaskalia Apostolorum* (chs. 4–12, 17–18). On the history and features of this development, see Schnackenburg 1949; R. E. Brown 1970, 47–86; Stalder 1971; Lohse 1980; Vogt 1982; Dassmann 1984; Lane Fox 1987, 493–545.

Though partially reflecting early Christian tradition (v 3), the triad as a whole is unique in the NT and corresponds in its triadic form to the author's threefold identification of himself in v 1. The repeated term "flock" (*poimnion*, v 3b; cf. v 2a) forms an inclusion framing vv 2–3. The point of vv 2–3 in general is that pastoral leadership must be freely undertaken and devoid of self-serving and domination.

2c. *not because compelled* (*mē anagkastōs*). The first of the three antithetic formulations calls for willingness to lead in contrast to being compelled to do so. The adverb *anagkastōs* is another of the unique NT terms employed in this unit. Its kindred noun *anagkē* means "compulsion," "necessity"; its verb *anagkazō*, "compel" or "force"; and its adjective *anagkaios*, "necessary." Its contrasting term, *hekousiōs* ("willingly"), indicates that the point here is that elders should not feel compelled or constrained to take up the task of shepherding but do it willingly. Persons might avoid leadership not simply out of modesty but because of the burden that leadership, like acts of benevolence to the community, entailed. They might also fear being singled out for special abuse as leaders in a movement already under attack. In later time this was precisely the fate of the overseers/bishops Ignatius and Polycarp.

but willingly in accord with God (*alla hekousiōs kata theon*). Responsibility is to be taken on willingly (*hekousiōs*) rather than because of compulsion to do so. Similar contrasts between compulsion and willingness are made by Philo and Paul. Philo (*Contempl.* 68) describes aged virgins of the contemplative Israelite Therapeutae, who kept their chastity "not because of compulsion . . . but of their own free will" (*ouk anagkēi . . . mallon ē kath' hekousion*). Paul in his letter to Philemon (v 14) hopes that Philemon's compliance with his request "might be not by compulsion . . . but of your own free will" (*mē hōs kata anagkēn . . . alla kata hekousion*).[675] The Petrine mention of willingness may indicate that the function of leadership "was conferred by designation or election" (Senior 1980, 87; cf. Acts 14:23; Titus 1:5; *1 Clem.* 42:1, 44). In this case, even if selected by others as leaders, the elders were not to feel that this responsibility was foisted upon them but were to accept it willingly.

The phrase *kata theon*,[676] as in 4:6c (see NOTE), means literally, "in accord with God" or "with respect to God"; for *kata* with God with the sense of "according to" or "in accord with," see also 1:1, 3, 15; 4:19. The phrase disturbs the structural balance of the first two qualifications and appears to have been added intentionally by the author to underline the divine orientation of this willingness. The looser translation "as God would have you do it" (NRSV) aptly captures its sense. In the context of this letter, it indicates that to which Christian volition is fundamentally oriented; namely, the will of God (cf. 2:15; 3:17; 4:2, 19; cf. also Ign. *Eph.* 2:1; *Phld.* 4:1).

---

[675] For similar contrasts, see also Xen., *Cyr.* 4.3.7; Artem. 5.23; *Let. Aris.* 104; 2 Macc 15:2; Philo, *Prob.* 60–61; Josephus, *Ant.* 3.223; *T. Dan* 4:6 (*hekousiōs ē akousiōs*). Cf. also Heb 13:17.

[676] It is omitted in some MSS (B K L most minuscules syr^{p}), but its inclusion is favored by the variety of other MSS representing different text types ($\mathfrak{P}^{72}$ ℵ A P Ψ 33 81 1739 it^{h,r} vg syr^{h} cop arm eth).

2d. *not for shameful gain* (*mēde aischrokerdōs*).[677] This second antithetical qualification touches on motive and contrasts calculation with spontaneity. The elders are not to be leaders for lucre or ministers for mammon. The adverb *aischrokerdōs* appears only here in the Bible, but the adjective *aischrokerdēs* appears in 1 Tim 3:8 and Titus 1:7, also in connection with "servants" and "overseers," respectively (cf. also Titus 1:11 concerning the "shameful gain" [*aischrou kerdous*] of greedy teachers).[678] This family of terms expresses the conventional opinion that the gaining (*kerdainō*) of wealth for oneself alone is highly shameful (*aischros*).[679] Thus, Luke's description of the Pharisees as "lovers of money" (*philargyroi*, 16:14) constitutes a shaming condemnation. Such love of money (*philargyria*), "money-grubbing," would be shameful for Christians as well and thus is regularly proscribed, especially where leaders are involved (*philargyria*, 1 Tim 6:10; 2 Tim 3:2; 2 *Clem.* 6:4; Pol. *Phil* 2:2; 4:1, 3; 6:1; *philargyros*, *Did.* 3:5; *aphilargyros* ["not avaricious"], 1 Tim 3:3; Heb 13:5; *Did.* 15:1; Pol. *Phil* 5:2).[680]

The warning is appropriate, given the fact that Christian leaders generally received some form of compensation for their labors on behalf of the community, be it meals and shelter (Matt 10:10; 1 Cor 9:7b, 9–10, 13; *Did.* 11:4–6; 13:1–3, 5–6), clothes (Acts 20:33; *Did.* 13:7), or some other material form of "wages" or honor (Luke 10:7; 1 Cor 9:7a; 2 Cor 11:9; Gal 6:6; 1 Tim 5:17–18; *Did.* 12:2–3). It is in this light that Paul asks, "Who shepherds a flock without drinking some of its milk?" (1 Cor 9:7), and advises the Galatians, "Let him who is taught the word share all good things with him who teaches" (Gal 6:6). Presbyterial oversight could also entail some responsibility for community finances and common property (Acts 4:32; 5:1–5 [Peter]; see also 2 Cor 8:20; and Acts 6:1–3). Such compensation and involvement with funds could invite a quest for leadership out of greed; hence, the warning against "love of money" and "shameful gain"—that is, personal gain from apparent godliness (1 Tim 6:5) or, as *Didache* put it, "making business on Christ" (*christemporos*, 12:5) and being prophets for profit (cf. chs. 11–13).

but eagerly (*alla prothymōs*). Elders are to be motivated not by an "itch to get" but by a spontaneous eagerness to give. The adverb *prothymōs* means "eagerly," "readily," "enthusiastically willing."[681] In Tob 7:8 it describes hospitality offered "cheerfully." Its kindred noun *prothymia* (Acts 17:11; 2 Cor 8:11, 12, 19; 9:2) and adjective *prothymos* (Matt 26:41/Mark 14:38; Rom 1:15) likewise convey the sense of eagerness, readiness, and willingness. Philo's description of the

---

[677] In place of *mēde* some MSS read a simple *mē* (A L 1243 etc.), but no difference in meaning is involved.

[678] For the related noun *aischrokerdia*, see *T. Jud.* 16:1 and Dio Chrys., *Orat.* 7.110–11; 31.37.

[679] Cf. Soph., *Ant.* 1055–56; Arist., *Pol.* 3.10.8, 1286a; *Eth. nic.* 4.1, 43; Theophr., *Char.* 30.1–2.

[680] See also Acts 20:33–35, referring to Paul's not coveting anyone's silver or gold or apparel, and *T. Jud.* 17:1, "do not love money" (*mē agapan argyrion*). In his letter to the Philippians, Polycarp regrets the avarice of the presbyter Valens as a negative example for others and sees it as a prelude to defiling idolatry (Pol. *Phil* 11:1–2).

[681] See Josephus, *Ant.* 12.133; 18.374; Herm. *Sim.* 9.28.2, 4; and *Mart. Pol.* 13.1.

Therapeutae employs a contrast similar to that of our verse. At their banquets, he notes, their members serve at table "not under compulsion nor yet waiting for orders, but with deliberate goodwill, anticipating with attentiveness and eagerness (*meta spoudēs kai prothymias*) the demands that may be made" (*Contempl.* 71). In this thought, the spontaneity implied in eagerness comes to expression. In a similar vein, Danker (1982, 321) observes the synonymity of the nouns *prothymia* and *spoudē* as noted qualities of benefactors and patrons and notes that *prothymōs* here in v 2c implies "spontaneous interest and enthusiasm." In this light, the point of the Petrine contrast appears to be that what should motivate the elders/shepherds is not a calculating quest for personal gain but a spontaneous eagerness to serve the needs of God's flock.

3. *not as domineering those allotted* [*to you*] (*mēd' hōs katakyrieuontes tōn klērōn*). This third and final qualification[682] mirrors the negative-positive sequence of the two preceding qualifications and proceeds from a warning against love of money to a warning against love of power. Elders are not to exercise oversight as domineering lords (*kyrioi*) of the flock but as its influencing exemplars (*typoi*). The antithesis as a whole contrasts a hierarchical exercise of authority to a horizontal demonstration by example.

The particle *hōs* ("as") is part of a negative injunction (*med'*), as in 4:15 and 2:16, indicating here in 5:3 how shepherding and oversight (v 2ab) are *not* to be discharged; namely, as an act of domination. The composite verb *katakyrieuō* (lit., "lord it over," "have dominion over") has the sense of "dominate"[683] or "domineer" (ruling with insolence or arbitrary sway, especially over the poor, Pss 9:26[10:5]; 9:31[10:10]). Paul used the simple *kyrieuō* to express a similar thought: "Not that we domineer (*kyrieuomen*) your faith; we work with you for your joy" (2 Cor 1:24). Given their recognized position of authority, elders, like other leaders, could be tempted to exploit it.

Aside from Acts 19:16, where *katakyrieuō* is used of an "overpowering" evil spirit, the only other NT appearances of this composite verb are in a saying by Jesus recorded in Mark 10:42–45/Matt 20:25–28/Luke 22:25–27. Hence, the first half of the bicolon is likely a Petrine reminiscence of Jesus' critique of a preoccupation with precedence on the part of his disciples and his holding up the ideal of service as exemplified by himself as servant. The Petrine verse and the Jesus saying are close in language (*katakyrieuousin*, Mark 10:42/Matt 20:25; compare Luke 22:25, *kyrieuousin*; *hōs*, Luke 22:26; *neōteros*, Luke 22:26; cf. 1 Pet 5:5a), form (contrast between negative and positive), and point (model of conduct: Jesus, Mark 10:45/Matt 20:28/Luke 22:27; elders, 1 Pet 5:3; see Elliott 1970). These similarities, which cannot be traced to literary dependence, indicate the influence of an early Christian tradition on ministry (concerning rank, humility, example, eschatological reward) going back to the teaching of Jesus, a tradition perhaps also echoed in John 13:1–20 and 21:15–23.

---

[682] Codex Vaticanus is alone among the textual witnesses in omitting this entire verse.

[683] See Pss 18:14[19:13]; 109[110]:2; *T. Dan* 3:2; *T. Naph.* 8:6; *T. Benj.* 3:3, 5.

Use of elements of this tradition in a letter ascribed to Peter indicates a tendency, already apparent in the NT, to associate issues of ministry, leadership, and shepherding with the Apostle Peter.[684]

those allotted [*to you*] (*tōn klērōn*). In the Bible, *klēros* means "lot" (as in lots that are cast)[685] and then, by extension, "that which is assigned by lot," an allotted "portion" or "share"[686] or "place" (Wis 3:14; 5:5). In Classical Greek, *klēros* could designate an allotment of land assigned to a citizen by the civic authorities (Arist., *Pol.* 2.3.7, 1265b 15), usually determined by the casting of lots. In the present verse, however, the parallelism of the phrases involves the correspondence of *tōn klērōn* and *tou poimniou*. Accordingly, *klēroi*, like "flock," refers to *people*, as in Deut 9:29, where the singular *klēros* together with *laos* designate Israel as God's "people and portion," whom God brought forth from Egypt.[687] As the majority of commentators have rightly concluded, with this term our author is portraying the members or communities of the flock of God as having been "allotted" by God to the care of the elders/shepherds, a unique use of this term in the NT. It is ironic that in later time, when leaders of worship had begun to be differentiated from the "layperson" (*ho laikos anthrōpos*, *1 Clem.* 40:1–5; Hipp., *Trad. ap.* 19), the term *klēros* became a designation for ecclesiastical "office" (e.g., Hipp., *Trad. ap.* 3.5; 9.8; 19.1). Thus, the term "clergy" (deriving from *klēros*, *klēroō*) eventually came to designate leaders of the church in contradistinction to the "laity," the remainder of the people (*laos*) of God.[688]

In 1 Peter, on the other hand, the Greek term *klēroi* designates, not ordained or appointed leaders, but community members allotted or assigned to the care of the elders/leaders. In the history of ecclesiastical development, this eventual shift in the use of *klēroi* or *clerus* is matched in a yet later time by the use of the term "priest" (a cognate derived from the term *presbyteros*) as a designation not for an unordained "elder" but for one who (as *hiereus* or *sacerdos*) presides at the Eucharist, understood metaphorically as sacrifice.[689]

---

[684] See, e.g., the prominence assigned to Peter in the the Gospel of John, the latest of the Gospels, in its narratives recounting Jesus' exemplary humility at the footwashing (13:1–11), Jesus' postresurrection commission to Peter to "feed my lambs, sheep" (21:15–19), and the abundant haul of fish (21:1–14; cf. Luke 5:1–11). On the "Petrine trajectory" in the NT, see R. E. Brown, Donfried, and Reumann, eds. 1973.

[685] See 1 Chr 25:8; 26:14; Ps 21[22]:18; Matt 27:35/Mark 15:24/Luke 23:34/John 19:24; Acts 1:26. The casting of lots was one means employed for ascertaining the will of God.

[686] See Deut 10:9; 12:12; 1 Chr 25:9; Isa 57:6; Acts 1:17; 8:21; 26:18; Col 1:12.

[687] This is preferable to the theory of Nauck (1957, 210–13) that *klēroi* refers to "ranks" or "positions" in the community similar to those over which the priests of Qumran disposed (1QS IX 7; cf. V 20–24; VI 22; CD XIII 12–13). The meticulously stratified hierarchy at Qumran and demarcation of ranks find no counterpart in 1 Peter. For other unconvincing theories regarding *klēroi*, see those listed by Nauck 1957, 210; and Schröger 1981b, 118.

[688] See Lampe (*PGL* 757) for texts; on the history of this development in general, see Osborne 1993, 7–47.

[689] On this development, see Blum 1963; von Campenhausen 1968; R. E. Brown 1970, 18–20; Jay 1981; Noll 1993.

but being examples for the flock (*alla typoi ginomenoi tou poimniou*). The elders are to lead not by domination but by inspiration. The pres. pl. part. *ginomenoi* ("being"), like its counterpart *katakyrieuontes*, modifies "exercising oversight," which in turn qualifies the verb "shepherd."

The noun *typoi* ("examples") is the plural of *typos* ("type," "model," "exemplar," "example"; cf. *antitypos*, 3:21a). The term is rare in the OT, but in the NT belongs to the semantic field of discipleship and moral imitation (see Lee 1962; Schulz 1962; H. D. Betz 1967). It can mean "prototype" (Rom 5:14, of Adam) or "model" or "pattern" to be imitated or copied (Acts 7:44; Heb 8:5), especially a model of behavior to be emulated (Phil 3:17) or avoided (1 Cor 10:6;[690] see Lee 1962). Paul used the term, often in conjunction with *mimetēs* ("imitator"), in urging believers to follow his example (Phil 3:17; 2 Thess 3:7–9; cf. Acts 20:33–35) or to be examples for others (1 Thess 1:7; cf. 1 Tim 4:12; Titus 2:7).[691] This is the counterpart to the language of discipleship and modeling of which Jesus spoke, according to the Gospel tradition (cf. Schulz 1962; H. D. Betz 1967).

These words also appear to reflect the sense of the dominical saying preserved in Matt 20:25–28/Mark 10:42–45/Luke 22:25–27. The disciples, warned against imitating Gentiles who "domineer" others (*katakyrieuousin*, Mark 10:42/Matt 20:25; *kyrieuousin*, Luke 22:25), are positively urged to take Jesus and his servant role as their example. He did not come to be served but to serve, and they were to follow suit. Earlier our author spoke of having Jesus as an example (*hypogrammos*) and "following in his footsteps" (2:21; cf. also 3:21 and 4:1). Now it is the leaders who, following Christ's example, are to be models for those allotted to their care. The element of humility implied in Jesus' instruction and example (cf. also John 13:13–17) is also echoed here and in vv 5–6, where the mutual humility of all believers is enjoined.

Those who domineer (*katakyrieuein*) do so as *kyrioi*; that is, as persons having power or legal authority. By contrast, those who lead by example do so with a moral authority deriving only from their own integral life-style. This authority is not intrinsic but conditional upon one's ability to inspire in others the desire to follow and obey. In the Greek and Roman philosophical tradition, teachers were to be living examples of their teaching. Followers of Jesus thought of him in this same sense and required it of their leaders as well. One followed Jesus, not simply because he had the power or authority to demand this allegiance, but primarily because his disposition, teaching, vision, and way of life evoked the desire to follow and emulate him. In 1 Peter, the notion of leadership by example is extended from Jesus the chief shepherd (v 4) to

[690] Cf. 4 Macc 7:19, where Eleazar, the 85-year-old martyr-to-be, warned his fellow-Israelites against becoming "an example of impiety to the young" (*genoimetha tēs tois neois asebeias typos*).

[691] For *mimetēs*, cf. also 1 Cor 4:16; 11:1; Eph 5:1; 1 Thess 1:6; 2:14; Heb 6:12; for *mimeomai*, Heb 13:7 ("remember your leaders . . . and imitate their faith") and 3 John 11.

under-shepherds. As he served with humility (2:21–24), so humility is required of *all* the faithful (vv 5b–6), and this includes elders as well.[692]

This Petrine instruction thus relativizes and limits the authority of elders/leaders. A domineering mode of leadership can be avoided only when leaders practice what they preach, or as is said today, when they not only "talk the talk" but "walk the walk." The Pharisees' failure to do this, in Jesus' estimation, led to their condemnation as hypocrites who urged a reverence for the law that, in his opinion, they themselves failed to demonstrate in their own behavior.

4a. *and when the chief shepherd is made manifest* (*kai phanerōthentos tou archipoimenos*). The future result of obedience to the foregoing injunctions (vv 2–3) is now indicated. The shepherd metaphor now is also applied to Christ, with the implication that elders/shepherds are subordinates to Christ, the chief shepherd. The formulation is another genitive absolute construction (cf. 3:20c; 4:1a, 4b), here with temporal force ("when").

In Israel's anticipation of the messianic restoration, the notion of the establishment of one shepherd over the flock of Israel was prominent (Ezek 34:23–24; 37:24) and contributed to the identification of the Messiah as "shepherd" (*Pss. Sol.* 17:40); see also 2 Esd 2:34: "Await your shepherd; he will give you everlasting rest, because he who will come at the end of the age is close at hand." In early Christianity, this pastoral, messianic image was applied to Jesus as the Christ.[693]

The term *archipoimēn*, in which *archi-* ("chief") is combined with "shepherd" (*poimēn*), however, occurs only here in the Bible. Elsewhere it is used by Symmachus in his translation of 2 Kgs 3:4, and in *T. Jud.* 8:1 it identifies a certain Hiram the Adullamite as "chief shepherd." It also has been found in misspelled form on the mummy label (Roman period) that identifies a simple Egyptian peasant youth: "Plenis, the younger, chief shepherd (*archipoimenos*). Lived . . . years" (Deissmann 1923, 77–79 and plate 9).[694] The closest NT parallel to our term is Heb 13:20, which refers to the resurrected Lord Jesus as "the great shepherd of the sheep" (*ton poimena tēn probatōn ton megan*;

[692] An echo of this Petrine passage may be contained in Polycarp's letter to the Philippians (*Phil* 5:1–6:3). In an even more extensive list of presbyteral virtues and duties (6:1), Polycarp urges that elders (cf. 1 Pet 5:1, 5a) be "compassionate, merciful to all, bringing back those that have wandered, caring (*episkeptomenoi*; cf. 1 Pet 5:2a) for all the weak, neglecting neither wisdom, nor orphan nor poor, but 'ever providing for that which is good before God and humans' (citing Prov 3:4), refraining (cf. 1 Pet 5:2c–3) from all wrath, respect of persons, unjust judgment, being far from all love of money (*philargyrias*; cf. 1 Pet 5:2d), not quickly believing evil of any, not hasty in judgment, knowing that 'we all owe the debt of sin' " (6:1), with a view to the final judgment calling all to account (Pol., *Phil* 6:2; cf. 1 Pet 5:4).

[693] See, besides 1 Pet 2:25, Mark 6:34/Matt 9:36; Mark 14:27/Matt 26:31; Matt 2:6; 10:6; 15:24; 25:32; Luke 12:32; John 10:1–18; 16:32; 21:15–19; Heb 13:20; Rev 7:17; 12:5; 19:15; *Barn.* 5:12; *Mart. Pol.* 19:2.

[694] A similar construction is represented by *archiboukolos*, "chief herdsman" (scholion on *Iliad* 1.39) or president of a college of *boukoloi* (tenders of kine; SIG[3] 1115.3, Pergamum, 1st century CE).

cf. Herm. *Sim.* 9.31.6, "master of the flock"). Here in 1 Peter, the metaphor is adopted to fit the present pastoral context and implies that the elders as "under-shepherds" of the flock of God are responsible to, and take their cues from, Christ the chief shepherd, the *princeps pastorum* or *pastor pastorum.*

is made manifest (*phanerōthentos*). The previous association of the verb *phaneroō* with Christ in 1:20b and his identification as shepherd in 2:25 make it clear that it is Christ who is implied as the chief shepherd. "Made manifest" already in human history (1:20b; cf. also 1 Tim 3:16), Christ now as the resurrected one is soon to be manifested or revealed (1:7, 13; 4:13; cf. 5:1) at the age's close. In both instances the pass. part. of *phaneroō* implies God as the one who makes manifest. In Col 3:14 and 1 John 2:28 the verb is also used of Christ's final manifestation in glory.

4b. *you will receive the unfading crown of glory* (*komieisthe ton amarantinon tēs doxēs stephanon*). With the arrival of the chief shepherd, under-shepherds will receive their glorious recompense. The middle form of *komizō* ("get," "receive") conveys the sense of receiving something *for oneself.* A similar middle of this verb was used at the outset of the letter (1:9) in respect to the salvation that all believers will receive for themselves as the goal of their faith. Here, as in 1:9 and most NT instances (e.g., Eph 6:8; Col 3:25; Heb 10:36; 11:13, 39), it is used of eschatological recompense (see the NOTE on 1:9). God, the one who makes the chief shepherd manifest, is likewise the one from whom the under-shepherds will receive this reward.

The "crown of glory" that faithful elders are to receive signifies great honor and blessing (see Grundmann 1971b; Pfitzner 1967, 51–52). Proverbial wisdom held that "a grey head is a crown of glory" (Prov 16:31; 17:6). In regard to elder men (*presbyteroi*), Plutarch (*An Seni* 10; *Mor.* 789EF) makes the same point: "Just as the law places diadem and crown [*ton stephanon*] upon the head, so nature puts grey hair upon it as an honorable symbol of the high dignity of leadership." Our author, however, speaks not of a natural crown but of one received for honorable services rendered.

The term *stephanos* can designate various types of head adornment, depending on context: regal crown or diadem (2 Kgdms 12:20; 1 Chr 20:2; Isa 22:17), the corona worn by a priest (Zech 6:11, 14) or a bridegroom (Song 3:11), a garland worn at special festivals (Isa 28:1, 3; Ezek 23:42), or a crown or wreath borne by gods and outstanding mortals as an emblem of dignity, power, and glory. Crowns or honorific wreaths or garlands, along with statues, portraits, and seats of honor, were regularly conferred by urban assemblies upon victorious military leaders, athletes, and benefactors in pubic recognition of their outstanding courage, prowess, achievements, or generous contribution to the common good.[695] With such honor came distinction, privilege, and high sta-

[695] See Dio Chrys., *Orat.* 66.2; Josephus, *Ant.* 14.152; Tert., *Cor.*; Deubner 1933; cf. Baus 1940; Blech 1982; Danker 1982, 468–71 and passim.

tus. The prizes conferred at the Olympic, Pythian, Isthmian, and Nemean games (cf. 1 Cor 9:25; 2 Tim 2:5) were crowns or wreaths of wild olive, laurel, pine, celery, or parsley, and in some cases elaborate headbands of gold, often emulating laurel leaves. Reference to a crown in the figurative sense is common in the OT,[696] often signifying the conferring of blessing and honor (Isa 28:5; 62:3; Wis 4:9) and the reward for a righteous life.[697]

In 1 Peter, the image of the crown belongs to the theme of honor that plays such a prominent role in this letter (see Elliott 1995). The crown to which our author refers is not a perishable wreath but a metaphorical *unfading crown of glory* to be conferred at the conclusion of the ages. The adjective *amarantinos* (a denominative adj. formed from *amarantos*) appears only here in the NT and technically means "made of amaranath," "amaranthine," the unfading flower symbolizing permanence. The related adjective *amarantos* was employed in 1:4 to identify the inheritance in heaven as something "unfading," and that sense fits *amarantinos* here as well; see also the "imperishable crown" (*aphtharton stephanon*) of which Paul speaks (1 Cor 9:25). An *unfading* crown, one that never loses its luster, is also consonant with the contrast between the imperishable and perishable means by which believers have been given new birth (1:23). Imperishability in this letter is a feature of the new life in Christ from its inception to its close.

of glory (*tēs doxēs*). The genitive phrase is epexegetical, explaining the *crown* to be the *glory* and honor awaiting faithful elders at Christ's final coming. The expression *crown of glory* is unique in the NT, but in Israelite tradition its metaphorical use as an image of honor was common (Isa 28:5; Jer 13:18; Sir 47:6; 1QH^a IX 25) and also, as here, in an eschatological sense.[698] "Crown of life" (Rev 2:10; Jas 1:12) and "crown of righteousness" (2 Tim 4:8) represent equivalent expressions and illustrate the commonness of the concept of a crown conferred on faithful believers at Christ's coming. In the 2d and 3d centuries, it was the Christian martyrs in particular who were celebrated as having gained, by their constancy, a "crown" of immortality or incorruptibility.[699] In 1 Peter, just as glory is a primary attribute of God (4:11, 14, 16; cf. 2:12), so the glory that Christ himself received from God in his exaltation to life (1:11, 21; 4:13; 5:1) is the glory also to be bestowed upon both leaders and the believing community as a whole (1:7; 4:14; 5:10). "Glory," in fact, used

---

[696] See Prov 4:9; 12:4; 14:24; 16:31; 17:6; Sir 1:11, 18; 6:31; 15:6; 25:6.

[697] See Wis 5:16; 4 Macc 17:15; cf. *Let. Aris.* 280; *T. Levi* 8:2, 9; Philo, *Migr.* 113–34; *4 Ezra* 2:43–45.

[698] Cf. *T. Benj.* 4:1 ("Be imitators of him [the good man] in his goodness because of his compassion, so that you may wear crowns of glory"); 1QS IV 6–8; *2 Bar.* 15:8. For further Christian usage of the phrase, see Ign. *Magn.* 13:1; *Ascen. Isa.* 9:10–12; 11:40; and for the eschatological conferral of crowns generally, Herm. *Sim.* 8.2.1; 8.3.6; *Ascen. Isa.* 7:22; 9:24–25. For similar rabbinic usage, see *b. Ber.* 17a, 34.

[699] See *Mart. Pol.* 17:1; 19:2; Tert., *Cor.* 1; *Mart.* 3; Eusebius, *Hist. eccl.* 5, Preface, 5.1.36.

here and in v 1, forms an inclusion framing the entire instruction to elders in vv 1–4.

From the elders, our author now turns to a reciprocal group within the community, recent converts, identified as "younger persons."

5a. *You younger persons in turn* (*Homoiōs neōteroi*). The adverb *homoiōs* ("in turn"), is used not with the meaning "likewise" (as in 3:1)[700] but as a connective term joining related but distinct items in a series, as in 3:7 (see the NOTE). Here it connects the exhortation to younger persons with the foregoing instruction to elders. The subject "you" (pl.) is contained in the verb *hypotagēte*.

The term *neōteroi* is a substantival use of the adjective *neōteros* ("younger," 10× in the NT), a comparative form of the adjective *neos, nea* ("young"). The comparative sense of the adjective,[701] however, often is muted so that *neōteros* or *neōtera* (fem.) as a substantive also can mean either "younger (male or female) person" or simply "young person," "youth" (Acts 5:6; 1 Tim 5:14; Pol. *Phil* 5:3). This is also the case when it is juxtaposed with the term *presbyteros* as "younger person" distinguished from "older person/elder" or "youth" versus "the aged" (1 Tim 5:1, 2; Titus 2:6).[702] Younger persons formed a natural counterpart to older persons or elders.[703] This reciprocal pair was considered when familial or communal roles and obligations were under discussion.[704]

The identity of these *neōteroi* of 1 Peter is not immediately clear, and the term has been interpreted in a variety of ways.[705]

(1) Some take the terms *presbyteroi* and *neōteroi* in v 5a to refer to persons older and younger in *age*, respectively.[706] This requires that *presbyteroi* here has a different sense from v 1, where it clearly designates elders as *leaders* of the community and not simply those older in age. The author, however, gives no indication of such a sudden shift in the sense of *presbyteroi*. Nor does the variation in the sense of *presbyteros* in 1 Tim 5:1, 17 offer an apposite analogue. J. N. D. Kelly (1969, 204) attributes a difference in the senses of *presbyteroi* in vv 1, 5 to the likelihood that v 5a is "a detached fragment of the community code paraphrased in ii.13–iii.9 which the writer has transferred here for reasons of his own" but fails to clarify what these reasons might have been. It is

---

[700] Cf. also Titus 2:6 (*tous neōterous hōsautōs*) and Pol. *Phil* 5:2, 3 (*homoiōs kai neōteroi*).

[701] See Luke 15:12, 13; 22:26; John 21:18; 1 Tim 5:11; *Barn*. 13:5.

[702] The term *neaniskos* (Matt 19:20; Mark 14:51; 16:5; Luke 7:14; Acts 5:10; 23:18, 22; 1 John 2:13, 14), is linguistically related and likewise means "young man." Both terms designate youths, generally between 18 and 20 years of age; cf. Spicq 1969, 508–10.

[703] For the combination, see Gen 19:31, 34; 29:26; 44:12; Josh 6:21; 2 Chr 10:13–14; 15:13; Job 32:6; Ps 148:12; Isa 20:43:5; Ezek 16:61; 1 Esd 1:53; 2 Macc 5:13; Philo, *Prob*. 81.

[704] See Sir 32:1–9; Philo, *Decal*. 166–67; *Spec*. 3.134; 1 Tim 5:1–22; Titus 2:2–6; 1 John 2:12–14; *1 Clem*. 1:3; 3:3; 21:6; Pol. *Phil* 5:3–6:3.

[705] For further discussion of positions and advocates, see Holzmeister 1937, 397–98; and Elliott 1970, 378–79.

[706] So Bigg 1902, 190; Selwyn 1947, 227, 233; J. N. D. Kelly 1969, 204–5; and others listed in Elliott 1970, 378.

indeed conceivable that the instruction of elder and younger persons once belonged to a traditional instruction for households, akin to the exhortation for parents and children (cf. Eph 6:1–2 within the household instruction of 5:21–6:9, and Col 3:20 within 3:18–4:1) and that 1 Pet 5:1–5a represents an adaptation of this part of the household tradition for instructing community elders/leaders and younger persons.[707] It is also possible that 1 Peter represents an early stage of development, when civic and domestic instructions was expanding into community instruction, a development evident also in the Pastorals (1 Tim 3:1–15; 5:1–6:2; Titus 1:7–9; 2:1–10; 3:1–2), *1 Clement* (1:3; 21:6–8; 37:1–4; 57:1–2), and Polycarp (*Phil* 4:1–6:3). Kelly might have suggested that it was the address of *presbyteroi* as elders in vv 1–4 that attracted the reference to *presbyteroi* in the "fragment," but this would undermine the likelihood that the same term had different meanings in these connected verses and thus would defeat his point. Consequently, whatever the connection between 5:1–5a and 2:13–3:9 might have been, it sheds no light on the meaning of *presbyteroi* and *neōteroi* in 5:5a. With no indication given that the *presbyteroi* in v 5a are different from those in v 1, the proximity of both terms requires the sense of "elders" (as leaders) for both verses.

(2) Others regard *presbyteroi* in both vv 1 and 5a as identifying community leaders and the *neōteroi* simply as those who are "young in age" (e.g., Leconte 1961, 115; Bornkamm 1968, 66). In this case, however, it is not clear why it is younger persons *alone* who are urged to be subordinate to the elders. It is true that the impetuosity and rebelliousness of youth were proverbial in antiquity (see Philo, *Sobr.* 16, 23; Plut., *Virt. mor.*; *Mor.* 450F).[708] In a forecast of anarchic times, Isaiah warned that "the youth will be insolent to the elder and the base fellow to the honorable" (3:5). *1 Clement* 3:4 appears to allude to this Isaian verse in a description of the rebelliousness against elders that arose in the church of Corinth (cf. also 44:3–6; 47:6). However, no such problem of youthful insubordination is evident elsewhere in 1 Peter, and it is more likely that the call for subordination of the *neōteroi* belongs to the more conventional pattern of household instruction followed earlier in the letter.

(3) Still others regard the *neōteroi* as comprising *all community members* other than the elders (e.g., Windisch and Preisker 1951, 79; Reicke 1964, 130;

---

[707] See Philo's discussion of the subordinate relation of youth to elders in connection with his instruction on the command of the Decalogue calling for the honoring of parents and social relations in general: "old to young, rulers to subjects, benefactors to benefited, slaves to masters" (*Decal.* 165–67); cf. also *Spec.* 2.224–27, "elders (*presbyteroi*) are set above younger persons (*neōteroi*); and Ps. Phoc. 207–21. Aristotle's comment (*Pol.* 1.5.1–2) on the three basic units of household management (*oikonomia*) as concerning the relations of owners-slaves, parents-children, and husbands-wives is seminal; see also his observation that by nature "the older (*presbyteros*) is more fully developed (and fit to rule) than is the younger (*neōteros*) and immature" (*Pol.* 1.5.2; cf. also 7.133).

[708] A term from the same root, *neōterismos*, in fact meant "uprising, "rebellion," "rebelliousness"; see *Let. Aris.* 101; Philo, *Flacc.* 93; Josephus, *Ant.* 5.101; *T. Reu.* 2:2; *1 Clem.* 30:1.

Goppelt 1993, 351). While the pairing of *presbyteroi* and *neōteroi* allows this possibility, such a collective use of *neōteroi* would be without parallel in the NT; see also *1 Clement* and the letter of Polycarp (*Philippians*), where in all cases *neōteroi* or *neoi* designates youth *within* the larger community. Furthermore, this theory would not fit the present context, since it is v 5b that first introduces an appeal to "all" (*pantes*) members of the community. Thus, the *neōteroi* must constitute a specific group within the larger community.

(4) Yet other scholars, pointing to Acts 5:6, take the *neōteroi* as "minor officials," corresponding to the elders regarded as "major officials."[709] But the fact that elders themselves were not yet "officials" occupying some defined "office" applies all the more to the *neōteroi*, who are not even assigned a discernible function here or elsewhere in the NT. The young men who carried out the corpses of Ananias and Sapphira (Acts 5:6, 10) were performing a menial ad hoc task and hardly formed an institutionalized group. The differentiation in 1 John among "children" (2:12, 13), "fathers" (2:14a), and "young persons" (2:14b) concerns distinctions according to age, not function. Nothing, moreover, in 1 Peter suggests an equation of *neōteroi* with *diakonoi*; in fact, the two groups are explicitly distinguished by Polycarp (*Phil* 5:2–3); against this view, see also Beare 1970, 201; and Davids 1990, 183.

(5) It is also highly unlikely that these younger persons formed a particular group analogous to associations of *neoi* ("young men") in Hellenistic society (against Spicq 1969, 518–27) or that these persons had "belonged lately to a Gymnasium and were regarded as now in training for the responsibilities attaching to citizenship of the Church" (against Selwyn 1947, 436). Clubs of younger males (*neoi* between 20 and 30 years of age) who trained in the *gymnasia* did exist among groups of urban citizens,[710] and an inscription from Hypaepa in Lydia (CII 755, 2d–3d century CE) mentions also young Judean males (*Ioudaiōn neōterōn*) who were active in the local gymnasium. But nothing in the literature of early Christianity indicates recruitment of these young club members or the existence of analogous formations within the messianic movement.

(6) There is, however, evidence to suggest that *neōteros* here is similar in sense to "neophyte" (*neophytos*), with both terms designating someone "young or younger in the faith" and hence a *recent convert* (see Elliott 1970). The terms *neos and neōteros* can mean "new," "fresh," "not long there," "recent," as well as "young" (Behm 1967, 896). A 3d-century BCE inscription from Ptolemais draws a distinction between *hoi neōteroi* and *hoi alloi p*[*olit*]*ai*; the former appear to be "citizens recently introduced into the city, but not yet officially

---

[709] E.g., Kühl; Weiss; Holtzmann; Moffatt; and later, Holzmeister 1937, 392; E. Schweizer 1961, 199.

[710] See, e.g., SIG^3 959.10–30; Forbes 1933, 4; Behm 1967, 897; Spicq 1969, 519–20; Schürer 1973–1987, 3:103.

enrolled in the demes" (MM 425–26). At Qumran, persons seeking membership formed a specific group under the tutelage of the "overseer" (*měbaqqēr*), a man senior in years and eminent in status. These novices underwent a two-year period of instruction in the Mosaic Law and testing prior to their admission to the community (1QS VI 13–23; CD XIII 7–13). Appropriate behavior during this period included a display of humility and respect for order and for men older in age and rank (CD XIV 3–12), the person of lesser rank obeying his superior (1QS V 23–25), as was required of the membership in general (1QS II 20–24; VI 8–13). The process of admission began with the person's twentieth year (1QSa I 1–19), thereby indicating that these novices were relatively young in age. In terms of their association with the Qumran community, however, they were also *recent initiants*. Determination of status according to one's seniority of membership in the community was, according to Philo, also typical of the Therapeutae, a contemplative Israelite group in Egypt. At their banquets, he reports, "the seniors/elders (*presbyteroi*) recline according to the order of their admission (to the community)" (Philo, *Contempl.* 67), indicating that status here too was determined by longevity of membership.

Two NT texts, 1 Cor 16:15–16 and 1 Tim 3:6, indicate that also within the Christian community distinctions were made between those who where seniors in the faith or in length of membership in the community and those who were recent converts (see Elliott 1981/1990, 190–91). In 1 Cor 16:15–16, Paul exhorts the Corinthians to "be subordinate" (*hypotassēsthe*) to the household of Stephanas, for Stephanas and his household were the first converts ("firstfruits," *aparchē*) in Achaia (16:15). The implication is that Stephanas was "older in the faith" and that his seniority and experience as a believer qualified him for leadership. In this sense he was an "elder" by implication, if not in title, keeping in mind that the title (*presbyteros*) was not used by Paul. In Corinth, Stephanas would correspond in rank and function to the *presbyteroi* of 1 Peter. A similar implication concerning this same term is found in *1 Clement*, where the author states that "overseers" (equivalent to elders) and deacons were selected from the *first converts* ("firstfruits" [*aparchas*], 42:4).

1 Timothy, like 1 Corinthians 16, implies something similar about Christian leaders as "elders in faith" and specifically insists that the overseer (*episkopos*) must not be a "recent convert" (*mē neophyton*, 3:6), a "neophyte in the faith." "Otherwise he would be puffed up with conceit and fall into the condemnation of the devil" (1 Tim 3:6). Thus, he must be "older in the faith." Moreover, Timothy himself, though a leader, was clearly not older in years, since Paul advises him, "let no one despise your youth" (4:12). But Timothy was, like Stephanas, an early convert to the messianic movement (Acts 16:1–5). This indicates that a qualification for leadership was not simply seniority in biological age but also maturity in the faith, a condition not met by the neophyte, who only recently had joined the community.

In the light of this evidence it is most likely that the *presbyteroi* (vv 1, 5a) were, as leaders, not simply older in years but also seniors in the faith and that the *neōteroi* were recent converts, "young in the faith."[711] This would be akin to the distinction made by Hermas who, in speaking of groups within the Christian community, differentiates between "apostles, overseers, teachers, and deacons" (*Vis.* 3.5.1) and "those who are young in faith" (*neoi eisin en pistei*, *Vis.* 3.5.4).[712] While *all* of the addressees in 1 Peter were characterized as "newborn babies" in 2:2a, the *neōteroi* addressed here would constitute the *most recent* converts of the community.

be subordinate to the elders (*hypotagēte presbyterois*). The verb *hypotagēte* is a 2d-person aor. imperative like the verb in 2:13. The same verb in the middle voice was used also in 2:18 and 3:1, where subordination and respect for order is urged of household slaves and wives, respectively. Respect for and subordination to the aged, parents, and leaders were basic and universal expectations in antiquity.[713] "Youth," Plutarch observed, "is meant to obey, and old age to rule" (*peitharchikon gar hē neotēs hēgeminikon de to gēras*"; *An Seni* 10; *Mor.* 789E).[714] Philo, commenting on Lev 19:32 ("You shall rise up before the grey-headed and honor the aged"), notes that "By 'elder' is meant he that is worthy of honor and privilege and high place" (*Sacr.* 77). Respect and subordination of younger persons to elders and superordinates, he noted, were especially evident among the Essenes (*Prob.* 81, 87; *Hypoth.* 11.13; cf. 1QS V 23; VI 2, 8–9). The author of Ephesians likewise urges: "Children, obey your parents in the Lord; for this is right. Honor your father and mother, which is the first commandment with a promise, that it may be well with you, and that you may live long on the earth" (Eph 6:1–3).

Applying this universal notion to leaders of the Christian community, Paul had urged his readers to "subordinate yourselves" (*hypotassēsthe*) to such persons as Stephanas (a first convert of Achaia and hence elder in the faith), for they had "devoted themselves to the service of the holy ones" (1 Cor 16:15–16); for submission to leaders, see also Heb 13:7, 17. The author of 1 Tim 3:4–5 insists that an overseer (*episkopos*) must "keep his own children subordinate (*en hypotagēi*) and respectful in every way; for if a man does not know how to manage his own household, how can he care for God's church?" (3:4–5), thereby using the household and its ordering as an analogy for order in the church. Subordination to elders similarly is praised and urged in *1 Clement* (1:3; 57:1, 2; 61:1; cf. also 2:1; 21:6; 37:2; 38:1). Polycarp likewise instructs *neōteroi* to "be subordinate (*hypotassomenous*) to the elders (*tois presbyterois*)

---

[711] For the additional possibility that *neōteros* in John 21:18a refers to the *initial stage* of Peter's life *as a disciple*, in contrast to the end of his life and his death (21:18b–19) and for further associations of John 21:15–23 with 1 Pet 5:1–5a, see Elliott 1970, 382–84.

[712] See also the expressions *neōsti katēchoumenos* and *neokatēchētos* used by Clement of Alexandria (*Paed.* 1.36.3; *Strom.* 6.130.1) for new catechumens under prebaptismal instruction.

[713] See, e.g., Prov 23:22; Sir 6:32–34; 8:6, 9; Philo, *Decal.* 165–67; *Spec.* 2.225–27, 237–39; Josephus, *Ag. Ap.* 2.206–7.

[714] Cf. also Plato, *Resp.* 412C; 425A; 465A; Cicero, *Off.* 1.122–23.

and deacons as to God and Christ" (Pol. *Phil* 5:3).[715] In both *1 Clement* and Polycarp's letter, the call for subordination of specific groups is followed by an urging of the humility of all (*1 Clem.* 1:3–2:7; 21:6–8; 38:1–4; Pol. *Phil* 4:1–6:3), as in 1 Pet 5. In both writings, the household domain at the root of this ecclesial instruction, as in 1 Timothy, is clear and likely reflects what underlies the exhortation of 1 Peter as well.[716] In all of these texts, moreover, it is elders as community leaders rather than simply as older males to whom the young or recent converts are urged to be subordinate. Subordination in these instances involved a respect not only for age but also for the leadership capacity of the elders and hence a regard for social order and harmony within the community, as in the Petrine case of slaves (2:18), wives (3:1), and the believers in general (2:13–17). This respect for order would have been especially important to impress upon the newly converted, who would have been least familiar with the values and norms of the believing community. Within a century, Clement of Alexandria in an address to the newly baptized (*Protr. hyp.*) similarly instructed such persons to "submit to elders just as to fathers" (*hypeike presbyterois isa patrasin*).

In 1 Peter this urging of deference to authority is immediately relativized by the following injunction (v 5b), calling for the mutual humility of *all* members of the community. Thus, leaders as well as recent converts are constrained by a humility required of all the faithful.

GENERAL COMMENT

In view of the social hostility encountered by the addressees, pastoral leadership of high quality was required. To remain consistent in their commitment, persistent in doing what is right, and unified as a single cohesive movement, they needed leaders devoted not to their own self-interests but to the cause of the community as a whole. This required collegiality and cooperation among the leaders, a collegiality underlined by the author, who addresses the elders as "co-elder." Use of this unique term may well have a further implication. Having associated himself with the elders as "co-elder," our author could also be implying that in his additional roles as witness to Christ's suffering (in his own life as well as his teaching) and as "sharer in the glory about to be revealed" he is one whom his fellow-elders are to emulate in their own behavior.

---

[715] Ignatius too calls for subordination to the elders (*Trall.* 2:2; *Pol.* 6:1) as well as to the overseer/bishop in particular (*Eph.* 2:2; *Magn.* 2:1; 13:2; *Trall.* 2:1).

[716] The similarities among the exhortations in 1 Peter, *1 Clement*, and Polycarp's *Letter to the Philippians* are numerous and striking enough in content, terminology, and sequence to suggest, if not a reminiscence of 1 Peter in the two later writings, then common reflection of a tradition in which instruction on domestic duties was developed into teaching on relations and responsibilities within the ecclesial community as a whole, a development attested by the Pastorals as well.

The focus on the elders' conduct in vv 2–3 and on the glory that will be theirs in v 4 supports this likelihood.

The unit as a whole (vv 1–5a) constitutes a creative blending of a variety of motifs and traditions (people of God as flock, leaders as shepherds and overseers, Jesus' teaching on status and humble leadership, tradition concerning Peter as shepherd, and instruction on domestic duties extended to elder-younger roles within the community).

The elders addressed were not holders of an "office" but, as elsewhere in the Greco-Roman world, including Israel, household heads whose seniority and family status earned them positions of prestige and leadership within their local communities. This involved not only seniority in biological age but also length of years as believers. Employing the pastoral imagery of flock, shepherding, and exercising oversight, our author instructs these elders concerning appropriate and inappropriate attitudes of leadership. The threefold form by which he describes himself (co-elder, witness to the sufferings of the Christ, sharer in the glory about to be revealed, v 1) is matched by a triad of qualifications for leadership that is unique in the NT (vv 2c–3).

The flock that these elders oversee as shepherds is not theirs to exploit or dominate as a means for self-aggrandizement. This flock belongs to God, who has allotted its members to the elders, who are under-shepherds of Christ, the chief shepherd. They are to lead, not because compelled to do so, not for personal gain, and not as domineering lords, but willingly as God would have it, eagerly, and as inspiring examples for those in their charge. The reward for such leadership is not the transient honors that society confers, but an unfading crown of glory bestowed at the chief shepherd's final appearance.

Recent converts, in turn, are to be subordinate to the elders, a theme relating this unit to the instruction on domestic roles in 2:18–3:7 and underscoring once again the importance of order and respect for authority within the believing community.

Respect for the authority of superordinates, however, in no way exempts elders and superordinates from the humility required of all members toward one another. Thus, this exhortation to elders and novices is immediately balanced and conditioned by the following call for mutual humility, with which all members are to be clothed (5:5b–7; cf. 3:8–12).

1 Peter 5:1–5a (along with 4:7–11) has relevance for the issue of the letter's date of composition and its integrity. Both passages reflect a still early, rudimentary stage of ecclesiastical organization and leadership (so Selwyn 1947, 56; J. N. D. Kelly 1969, 197). Leadership by persons older in age and in the faith (*presbyteroi*, "elders") was typical of the early period of the Church's development[717] and antedated the institution of the differentiated ecclesias-

[717] See also Acts 20, the Pastorals, 2 John, 3 John, *1 Clement*, and Polycarp's *Letter to the Philippians*. As far as Rome, the likely place of origin for 1 Peter, is concerned, the 2d-century writing of Hermas still speaks only of *episkopoi* in the plural (*Sim*. 9.27.2) and indicates that still at this

tical offices of bishop, presbyter, and deacon, a development anticipated by the writings of Ignatius of Antioch (early 2d century). At this early stage, elders exercised *roles* and *functions* of *traditional* authority rather than "offices" (*legally defined positions* within a specified institutional and bureaucratic order).[718] At this point in time, the conditions necessary for bureaucracy and offices[719] were not yet in place. Thus, it is premature and misleading to speak of "offices" during the earliest period encompassed by the NT writings,[720] since none of these writings presumes these conditions. Nor do the writings employ a uniform nomenclature for leaders or speak uniformly of their qualifications or their responsibilities.[721] Only in the course of the following centuries, as the church grew in size and complexity, was leadership eventually institutionalized, and traditional or charismatic modes of authority developed into well-defined "offices."

1 Peter presupposes only one form of *community leaders*, besides apostle; namely, elders (5:1–5a). Those addressed in 4:7–11 are *all* members of the community. From the beginning of the messianic movement and onward, forms of both charismatic activity (cf. Rom 12:6–9, 9–20; 1 Cor 12:4–11, 28–31; 14:1–39) and traditional leadership by elders operated in tandem, as in the situation presumed in 1 Peter. The *charismata* mentioned in 4:10–11 are not charisms restricted to "charismatically endowed" leaders but manifestations of divine grace (*charis*) conferred upon all members and gifts that are to be mutually shared (see the NOTES on 4:10–11). Nor does our author associate these gifts of speaking and serving with any form of "organizational structure" or "charismatic church order," in dependency on Paul (against Goldstein 1975, 11–24).

Since 4:10–11 speaks not of leadership roles but of endowments of grace and modes of action pertinent to *all* believers, these verses represent no alternative to the leadership tasks outlined for elders in 5:1–4. This argues decisively against the notion (Schröger 1976) that 4:10–11 and 5:1–5a represent contrary forms of ecclesial organization (charismatic versus presbyteral, respectively) in different writings (1:3–4:11; 4:12–5:11) reflecting different historical situations,[722] a position Schröger later retracted (1981, 112–14). The

---

time it was presbyters-as-overseers (*Vis.* 3.1.8) who constituted the collegial leadership of the Roman church.

[718] On the distinction between traditional authority and the legal-rational authority of offices, see the seminal study of Max Weber (1978, 1:212–301).

[719] Such conditions included the consolidation of regional communities, standardization of qualifications and nomenclature for specific roles, stratification of functions in a hierarchical order, and legitimation of this order through legal means.

[720] Against Holmberg (1980, 109–11 and passim) and many others who speak indiscriminately of "offices" in the NT period.

[721] On the inappropriateness of the word "office" for elders in particular, see also R. A. Campbell 1994, 65, 111–14, 160–62, 514–16.

[722] See the critique of Elliott 1981/1990, 163–64.

responsibilities described in 4:7–11 and 5:1–5a are thus complementary rather than contradictory (cf. Elliott 1966b, 192–96). Since these two units do not represent "alternative modes of organization," they also cannot be used to support theories postulating the original literary independence of 1:3–4:11 and 4:12–5:11. That 5:1–5 contains an "interpolation" of material from a later "pastoral (trito-Pauline) stratum of tradition" added to 1 Peter and the Pauline letters sometime between 90 and 140 CE, as argued by W. Munro (1983), is a conjecture with little to commend it. The theory is unsupported by the manuscript witnesses, and there is no clear evidence for the independent existence of such a stratum of tradition. The theory is highly speculative, complexifies rather than simplfies matters, and is unnecesary for explaining affinities among the texts concerned (see the cogent critique of Dijkman 1987). It offers no convincing evidence of a 2d-century final redaction of 1 Peter.

The stage of development of ecclesiastical organization reflected in 1 Peter is later than the time of Paul, who makes no reference to elders/shepherds/overseers (except for Phil 1:1, "overseers and servants," *episkopoi kai diakonoi*), on the one hand, and is less defined and standardized than the arrangements evident in Christian writings of the 2d century. Thus the content of 1 Pet 4:7–11 and 5:1–5 suggests that 1 Peter was written at an early stage of the subapostolic period (70–100 CE), when acknowledgment of the charismatic endowment of all believers had not yet disappeared, as it did in later time, and when the role of overseer as "bishop" had not yet been distinguished from the role of elder. 1 Peter reflects an early stage of organizational development, akin to that of Acts 20. At this time the terms and images for leaders were gradually coalescing, but the nomenclature was still fluid and leadership tasks were still minimally defined and not hierarchically differentiated.[723]

For studies on 1 Pet 5:1–5a, see Boismard 1957, 1966, 1961; Bosetti 1990, 159–223; R. E. Brown, Donfried, and Reumann, eds. 1973; Cervantes Gabarrón 1991a, 310–18; Cothenet 1974, 147–52; Elliott 1970; Goldstein 1975, 17–24; Gryglewicz 1957; Harris 1919; Hiebert 1982d; Lamau 1988, 201–3; Marxsen 1979; Michl 1973; Nauck 1957; P. Perkins 1994, 131–50; Prostmeier 1990, 169–77, 449–71; Riggenbach 1889; Schröger 1976, 1981b, 114–20; Silvola 1978; Spicq 1969; Spörri 1925, 104–29.

---

[723] On leadership and ministry in the NT and Apostolic Fathers in general see, int. al., Schnackenburg 1949; Nauck 1957; Schweizer 1961; Shepherd 1962; von Campenhausen 1969; R. E. Brown 1970; Quinn 1970; Bourke 1970; Lemaire 1971; Delorme, ed. 1974; Roloff 1978; Holmberg 1980; Noll 1993; Osborne 1993; Ysebaert 1994.

VI. C. The Mutual Humility of All, Resisting the Devil, and Trusting in God (5:5b–11)

5:5b Finally, all of you:
clothe yourselves with humility in your relations with one another,
5c because
"God opposes the arrogant
but gives grace to the humble."
6a Allow yourselves, therefore, to be humbled under the powerful hand of God,
6b so that at the propitious time he may exalt you.
7a "Cast all your anxiety upon him"
7b because he cares about you.
8a Stay alert, remain watchful!
8b Your adversary, the Devil, prowls about "as a roaring lion"
8c seeking someone to devour.
9a Resist him, firm in [your] faith,
9b knowing that these same sufferings are being accomplished in the case of your brotherhood throughout the world.
10a The God of all grace, however,
10b who has called you to his eternal glory in Christ,
10c after you have suffered for a brief time,
10d will himself complete,
reinforce,
strengthen, [and]
establish [you].
11 His is the power forever, amen.

INTRODUCTION

From his exhortation to elders and recent converts, our author now turns to address *all* the believers (*pantes de*, 5:5b). The pattern is similar to the earlier appeal to the whole community in 3:8–12, following the exhortation to specific groups (2:13–3:7). Thus, the break between vv 1–5a and 5b–11, like the break between 3:7 and 3:8, is a minor one. 1 Peter 5:5bc also resembles 3:8–12 in content and structure, containing a call for the humility of all (vv 5b, 6; cf. 3:8), followed by a causal *hoti* clause (v 5c; cf. 3:9d) and a supporting scriptural citation (v 5c [Prov 3:34 LXX]; cf. 3:10–12 [Ps 33:13–17 LXX]; see also v 7 [Ps 54:23]). Terms and themes joining this subunit to 5:1–5a include "finally" (v 5b), "God" (vv 5c, 6–7, 10–11), "suffering" (vv 9, 10; cf. 5:1b), "Christ" (v 10; cf. 5:1b), and "glory" (v 10b; cf. 5:1c, 4b). Although a "therefore" (*oun*) opened new units elsewhere in the letter (2:1; 4:1, 7; 5:1), this is not the case in v 6, since this verse clearly extends the stress on humility found in v 5b. Throughout this subunit the focus is on the entire community: its relation to God, on the one hand (vv 5b–7, 10–11), and to the Devil on the other (vv 8–9). The terms "God" (v 5c, 10 [–11]), "grace" (vv 5c, 10a), and "powerful"/"power" (vv 6a, 11) form an inclusion framing these final verses.

NOTES

5:5b. *Finally, all of you* (*pantes de*). An address to two specific groups, elders (5:1–4) and younger persons (5:5a), is now followed by a concluding ("finally," *de*) exhortation directed to the entire community (*pantes*, "all of you"). The fact that this compositional pattern[724] mirrors that of 2:8–3:7 (specific groups) followed by 3:8–9 (all) argues against regarding the words *pantes de* plus *allēlois* as part of the imperative in v 5a ("Younger persons, be subordinate to the elders, and all of you to one another"); "all of you" rather is connected with the following verb "clothe yourselves."

clothe yourselves with humility in your relations with one another (*allēlois tēn tapeinophrosynēn egkombōsasthe*). This call for mutual humility involves a 2d-person pl. imperative verb (*egkombōsasthe*) that occurs only here in the NT. The verb means to "put or tie something on oneself," such as a tunic or apron (BAGD s.v.). Linguistically, *egkombōsasthe* is related to the nouns *komba* ("knot") and *egkombōma*, denoting an "apron" tied on over other garments, as by a slave (Pollux, *Onom.* 4.119), and so an article of clothing equivalent to a *lention* ("linen cloth," "towel"; cf. John 13:4; Suet., *Cal.* 26.2). The verb thus denotes the binding of an apron, as done by slaves in performance of their domestic duties, including washing the feet of guests. The clothing metaphor recalls 1:13, where the verb *anazōnnymi* also was used figuratively in the expression "having girded your minds for action."

The image of clothing oneself with humility (*tēn tapeinophrosynēn*) appears also in Col 3:12 but seems especially close to John's description of Jesus' action at the Last Supper (13:1–20). Jesus bound himself with an apron or towel (*lention*) in preparing to humbly wash the feet of his disciples (vv 4–5). This act of demonstrating not simply hospitality but humility, Jesus noted, was to serve as an example "that you should do as I have done to you" (13:14–15). The prominent role of Peter in this scene (vv 6–11) along with the accent on humility in this Petrine letter (see also 3:8) and its call for emulating the example of Jesus the servant Lord (2:21–23; 3:18; 4:1) suggest that a stress on mutual humility grounded in Jesus' humility (see also Mark 10:35–45 par.; and 1 Pet 5:3) was one of the several features of the tradition associated with Peter in the early Church. Humility is not to be confused with self-degrading humiliation.

---

[724] See also the same pattern in *1 Clem.* 1:3–2:1, where subordination to elders and of wives to husbands (1:3) is immediately followed by a reference to the humility of *all* persons (2:1); cf. also 21:6–8.

It is, rather, an acceptance of one's social position, with no attempt to lord it over others or to better oneself at the expense of others (Pilch and Malina, eds. 1993, 107–8). For Israel and the messianic community, "humility goes before honor" (Prov 15:33; 18:12), and humility gains God's approval and favor, as the following contrast between the "arrogant" and the "humble" (v 5c) makes clear. This positive valuation of humility,[725] so typical of Jesus' teaching, stands in absolute contrast to its negative valuation in the Greco-Roman world.[726] For the latter, humility was typical of slaves and an unworthy, servile attitude for those who were free (see Grundmann 1972, 1–3). For the former, humility was an acknowledgment of one's assigned place in the divine scheme of things, renunciation of ambition and domination over others, submission to God's will, and trust in God's generous favor and support, all of which contribute to the social harmony and cohesion of the community (see Grundmann 1972, 6–26; Wengst 1988; Pilch and Malina, eds. 1993, 107–8).

In 1 Peter, humility is repeatedly urged (3:8; 5:5–6) and circumscribes submission to both God (5:6–7) and human superiors (2:13, 17, 18; 3:1, 6, 8; 5:5a) in obedience to God's will (1:2, 14, 22; 2:13, 15, 16; 3:17; 4:2, 19). The model for this humility is Jesus Christ, who in 2:18–25 is presented as the humble servant of God, the exemplar for lowly domestic slaves, who in turn are paradigmatic for the entire household of God.

in your relations with one another. These words translate the sense of the single reciprocal pronoun *allēlois*, a dative pl. of respect, literally, "in respect to others" or "in respect to your relations with one another." The term is used similarly in 1:22; 4:9; and 5:14 to express the idea of mutuality (see the NOTES on 1:22 and 4:9). In the Christian household of God, as distinct from the society at large, our author notes, order and harmony are maintained not simply by respect for superiors. Rather, even social superiors are to demonstrate humility toward their social inferiors, for before God all mortals, regardless of their social station in life, are humble subjects. Thus, a call for subordination to those in authority (5:5a; cf. 2:13–17, 18–20; 3:1–6) is followed and balanced by an insistence on the humility of *all toward one another* (cf. 3:8; 5:5b–6). Mutual humility of all members would defuse any attempts at domination on the part of husbands and leaders and ensure the harmony, unity, and cohesion of the community (cf. Phil 2:3–11; and Best 1971, 172).

5c. *because "God opposes the arrogant but gives grace to the humble"* (*hoti ho theos hyperēphanois antitassetai, tapeinois de didōsin charin*). Humility (*tapeinophrosynē*, v 5b) is essential because it is the humble (*tapeinois*) whom God especially favors. In accord with his procedure throughout the letter, our author again supports and wraps up a preceding exhortation with a concluding citation of Scripture (cf. 1:16, 24; 2:3; 3:10–12; 4:8, 18). Again *hoti* ("because,"

[725] See also Isa 57:15; 66:2; Acts 20:19; 2 Cor 11:7; 12:21; Eph 4:2; Phil 2:3, 8; 4:12; Col 3:12; Jas 4:10.

[726] E.g., Epict., *Diatr.* 3.24.56; Plut., *Arist.* 27; *Sull.* 1; *Alex. fort.* 4; Josephus, *J.W.* 4.9.2 (concerning Galba).

"for") introduces a theological motivation for a moral injunction (cf. 2:15a, 21b; 3:9d, 12a, 18a; 4:8b, 14c, 17; 5:7b). And again, as in 3:8–12, behavior required of the believers (v 5b; cf. 3:8–9) is followed and motivated by behavior typical of God (v 5c; cf. 3:10–12).

The citation is from the Septuagint version of Prov 3:34, with *ho theos* ("God") substituted for *kyrios* (LXX), since *kyrios* ("Lord") in this letter generally designates Jesus Christ (1:3, 25; 2:3; 3:15), except for 2:13 (God) and 3:6 (Abraham). The alteration is consistent with that of 1:25, where the author replaces *theos* with *kyrios* (referring to Christ) in his citation of Isa 40:8. This same proverb is cited also in Jas 4:6 with the same substitution. Prov 3:34 LXX is quoted again more fully in *1 Clem.* 30:2 and partially (Prov 3:34a) in Ignatius, *Eph.* 5:3, so that it appears to have had a firm place in early Christian parenesis. Here in 1 Peter the proverb supplies a weighty reason for humility toward fellow-believers (v 5b) as well as toward God (v 6a).

The verb *antitassetai* ("oppose," "resist") expresses God's opposition to the "arrogant" (a better translation of *hyperēphanois* than "proud") and divine resistance to their succeeding. Terms of the *hyperēph*-root occur frequently in the Bible, always with a negative sense ("arrogant," "haughty," "presumptuous," "blasphemous," etc.), and generally of persons opposed to God (cf. Schoonheim 1966). Elsewhere in the NT, arrogance is also contrasted with humility (Luke 1:51; Jas 4:6) and proscribed in vice catalogues (Mark 7:21; Rom 1:30; 2 Tim 3:2). As noted by Goppelt (1993, 354), arrogance and pride are virtually synonymous with the Greek concept of *hybris* and people characterized by it (cf. Isa 13:11, *hybris hyperphanōn*; Prov 8:13; etc.). The "humble" (*tapeinois*), by contrast, are the recipients of God's "grace" or "favor" (*charin*).[727] Thus, humility is the only proper stance before God and the necessary prelude and precondition to exaltation.

The concept of God's counterconventional opposition to the arrogant and favoring of the humble is a commonplace in Israel's story of God's favor toward the poor and humble[728] and God's reversal of their plight.[729] The reversal theme was prominent in Jesus' teaching,[730] and, as Jas 1:9–11 and the present text (cf. also Jas 4:6) indicate, shaped Christian moral teaching as well. Stress on the exaltation or salvation of the humble also occurs in Ps 33:19, a psalm cited earlier in 1 Pet 3:10–12 and 2:2. The idea had special resonance for a harassed and disparaged community of strangers and aliens, such as those of 1 Peter.

[727] Note the repeated accent on believers as the objects of divine *grace/favor* in this letter: 1:2, 10, 13; 3:7; 4:10; 5:10, 12; cf. also 2:19, 20 (divine "credit" or "approval").

[728] See Num 12:3; Judg 6:15; Prov 22:4; Sir 3:17–20; 10:7–18.

[729] See, e.g., 1 Sam 2:7–8 echoed in Luke 1:46–55; Job 5:11; Pss 17[18]:27; 30[31]:23; Ezek 17:24; 21:31 LXX; Sir 3:18; 10:14–15.

[730] See Matt 5:3–12/Luke 6:20–23; Matt 19:30/Mark 10:31; Matt 20:16; Matt 23:12/Luke 18:14; Matt 25:31–46; Mark 9:35/Luke 9:48; Luke 14:11; 18:14.

Beginning with this citation of Prov 3:34, 1 Pet 5b–9 displays a number of similarities with Jas 4:6–10.[731] The differences accompanying the similarities argue against direct literary dependence and for the varied and independent adaptations of primitive Christian hortatory tradition (so also Goppelt 1993, 356). The present tenses of v 5c as well as the gnomic character of Prov 3:34 make this statement a reference to the present. But in the light of its context, which looks to the future (vv 4, 6, 10), it appears to have implications for the future as well.

The following pair of imperatives, vv 6–7, introduces new thoughts but at the same time continues the call for humility in v 5b and expands on its term "grace." Consequently, the literary break between vv 5 and 6 is a minor one. The structure of vv 6 and 7 is identical (you be humble—God will exalt; you cast anxiety on him—he cares for you), and "exalt" and "care" elaborate on "he gives grace" (v 5c). Verse 5bc urged humility toward others; now humility toward God is in view.

6a. *Allow yourselves, therefore, to be humbled under the powerful hand of God (Tapeinōthēte oun hypo tēn krataian cheira tou theou).* The fact that God

[731] Both texts cite Prov 3:34 LXX, with identical substitution of *ho theos* for LXX *kyrios* (Jas 4:6b; 1 Pet 5:5c). Both contain a similar following imperative clause: *hypotagēte oun* (Jas 4:7a); cf. *tapeinōthēte oun* (1 Pet 5:6a, acutally closer in content and form to Jas 4:10). Both associate a call for humility and subordination to God with an imperative to resist the Devil (Jas 4:7b; 1 Pet 5:8–9a). While the terminology, verse structure, and general hortatory tone are strikingly close, the differences in formulation and sequence rule out literary dependency and argue for varied adoption of common tradition (so also Goppelt 1993, 356). (1) In 1 Peter, the citation supports the encouragement of communal *humility*, whereas in James the proverb substantiates the *grace* that God gives (*didōsin charin* in 4:6a and 4:6b). (2) Echoes of Prov 3:34 are contained in the wider context of Jas 3:13–4:10 (Johnson 1995, 283) but not in 1 Peter. (3) In James, reference to the Devil (*diabolos*) is prepared by the characterization of earthly wisdom as "demonic" (*daimoniōdēs*, 3:15), a notion without parallel in 1 Peter. (4) Whereas for James the Devil represents dangerous dissension *within* the community, for 1 Peter the Devil represents the threat of *external* hostility. (5) The vigilance and watchfulness called for in 1 Peter (5:8), on the other hand, have no parallel in James; nor does the depiction of the Devil as a "roaring lion" or the community as a "brotherhood" suffering throughout the world (1 Pet 5:9). (6) Finally, James balances resisting the Devil with drawing near to God in purity (5:8), whereas 1 Peter surrounds the thought of resisting the Devil with appeals to trusting in God's power, care, and support (5:6–7, 10). James, moreover, repeats and rounds off the call to humility in 4:10 (cf. 4:6), an inclusion without parallel in 1 Peter. Bigg (1902, 191–92), assuming literary dependency, assigned priority to 1 Peter (so also Beare 1970, 202), but it is far likelier that both passages reflect independent use of common parenetic tradition. Boismard (1957, 177–79; 1961, 133–63) supposed that 1 Pet 5:5b–9 contained a baptismal hymn that concluded an alleged baptismal liturgy incorporated in 1 Peter. The chief support for this theory, however, the similarity of vv 5b–9 with Jas 4:6–10 and the common citation of Prov 3:34, involves only a similarity of hortatory content but no traces of hymnic or liturgical structure (such as parallelism, rhythm, or relative clauses) so that this proposal was rejected by most commentators. The language of 1 Peter and James is too prosaic, hortatory, and varied to indicate reliance on an underlying rhythmically structured hymn, let alone its association with baptism. The tradition variously adapted in 1 Peter and James is, rather, hortatory in nature, inspired by Prov 3:34 and perhaps a saying of Jesus (so Goppelt 1993, 357, pointing to Luke 14:11), and unfixed in oral or written form.

is gracious toward the humble (v 5c) leads naturally to a call for humility before God. Thus, *tapeinōthēte* and *theos* link this verse with v 5bc, and "therefore" (*oun*) annnounces this logical connection. The sense of the pass. imperative aor. *tapeinōthēte* is not "humble yourselves" (which would require a reflexive middle form) but "allow yourselves to be humbled," literally, "be humbled" (so also Selwyn 1947, 235), with God ("under . . . God") implied as the one who humbles.

The expression "the powerful hand of God" (*tēn krataian cheira tou theou*) is used in the OT of God's disciplining his people (Ezek 20:34–35; cf. Ps 31[32]:4), and the thought of Job 30:21 ("they [Job's critics] attacked me without mercy; you have scourged me with a powerful hand") could suggest that being humbled by God is an allusion to the fiery ordeal that the believers are undergoing (4:12). But the point of vv 6–7 is more consolatory than admonitory, so this expression more likely is meant to recall the exodus and the analogous great acts of deliverance by God's "powerful hand" (Exod 3:19; 6:1; 13:9, 14, 16; Deut 3:24; 4:34; 9:26, 29; 26:8; Dan 9:15) as well as his power to protect and sustain his people (cf. Acts 4:28, 30; 11:21). God's power (*kratos*) is also stressed in v 11, and thus these kindred terms frame this concluding unit of the body of the letter with an emphasis on the divine power by which the believers are upheld and protected (cf. also 1:5).

6b. *so that at the propitious time he may exalt you* (*hina hymas hypsōsēi en kairōi*). Since God "gives grace to the humble" (v 5c), humble believers can anticipate their future exaltation. Appeal to a blessed future serves here, as in 3:9, 10–12; and 4:13, as motivation for action in the present. As in 4:18, the author gives an eschatological orientation to conventional wisdom expressed in a proverb. This is the last of the several *hina* constructions of the letter, taking the subjunctive (*hypsōsēi*) or future (BDF §369.1, 2) and expressing purpose or intended result.[732]

at the propitious time (*en kairōi*).[733] In Classical Greek, *kairos* means "opportune time" (Thucydides, *Hist.* 1.21; 4.59; 6.9). In 1 Peter (cf. also 1:5; 4:17), as elsewhere in the NT (Matt 8:29; Mark 13:33; Luke 21:8; 1 Cor 4:15; Rev 1:3), this noun has eschatological import. Here, as in 1:5, it refers to that final event of the endtime, the resurrection of the faithful to life eternal.

he may exalt you (*hymas hypsōsēi*). The verb *hypsoō* is used of God's exalting or "lifting up" of the humble (Ps 149:4; Luke 1:52) and often occurs, as here, in the contrast between humility and exaltation (Matt 23:12/Luke 14:11; Luke 18:14; 2 Cor 11:7; Jas 4:10). It is also used of God's exalting/raising Jesus from the dead (John 3:14; 12:32, 34; Acts 2:33; 5:31; cf. Phil 2:9) and here in 1 Peter refers similarly to God's exalting/raising of the believers. As God raised Jesus Christ (1:3, 21; 3:18, 21–22) and honored him (2:4), so God will exalt

---

[732] See also 1:7; 2:2, 21, 24; 3:9; 4:11, 13 for *hina* + subjunctive; and 3:1 for *hina* + future.

[733] Following *kairōi*, several witnesses (A P [Ψ] 33 104 etc. vg syr^{h} cop^{bo} eth Ephraem Bede) add *episkopēs* ("of visitation"), but this reading is absent in other important MSS ($\mathfrak{P}^{72}$ ℵ B K L 0205 most minuscules $syr^{p\ h}$ cop^{sa} Origen) and was probably derived from 2:12 ("day of visitation").

and honor those who share in Christ's life (1:3; 2:5, 24; 3:18c, 21; 4:13–14; 5:1, 10). The pattern humility-exaltation replicates the patterns of suffering-glory (1:11; 3:18, 22; 4:13, 14; 5:1, 10) and shame-honor (2:4–10; 4:14, 16). Thus, in the context of this letter, to be exalted is equivalent to being raised, honored, glorified, saved, and receiving a crown of glory. This anticipation of future exaltation expresses the optimism that is voiced explicitly in v 10 and that characterizes this letter as a whole.[734]

7a. *"Cast all your anxiety upon him"* (*pasan tēn merimnan hymōn epiripsantes ep' auton*). The thought expresses a further mode of humility and of being under God's mighty hand. Verse 7a parallels the gist of v 6a, and v 7b, that of v 6b. The formulation appears to be a modified adaptation of LXX Ps 54:23 [MT 55:22] (*epiripson epi kyrion tēn merimnan sou, kai autos se diathrepsei*, "cast your anxiety upon the Lord and he will sustain [or nourish] you").[735] The verb "cast" (*epiripsantes*) is yet another participle with imperatival force (so also RSV, NRSV, NEB, NIV; see the NOTE on 1:14b). Some see it as modifying the main verb, "humble yourselves" ("humble yourselves *by casting* all your anxiety upon him"; so Michaels 1988, 296 and Davids 1990, 187). But its imperatival force is made more likely by the 2d-person sing. imperative of Ps 54:23, which it replaces. The verb *epiriptō*[736] means "throw something upon something else," such as clothes upon an animal for riding (Luke 19:35); here, its only other NT occurrence, it is used figuratively.

all your anxiety upon him. "Anxiety" (*tēn merimnan*) repeats the language of the source, Ps 54:23 LXX, but our author has added "all" (*pasan*) and has substituted a plural "your" (*hymōn*) for a singular (*sou*) and "him" for *kyrion* ("Lord"). The words are thus modified to apply to plural readers (as in Herm. *Vis.* 3.11.3) and adjusted to context ("him" referring to "God" in the previous verse), and the thought is extended in comprehensiveness (*all* your anxiety). The kindred verb *merimnaō* appears repeatedly in Matt 6:25–34, where Jesus urges his followers not to be anxious about the basic requirements of daily life, since "the Father knows that you need them all" (Matt 6:32), a sentiment similar to the one expressed here. But this is inadequate grounds for suspecting a derivation of this Petrine verse from Matthew (against Metzner 1995, 103–6). The Petrine formulation instead adapts Ps 54[55]:23, which underlies Jesus' words as well. The psalm verse is also cited in Herm. *Vis.* 3.11.3 and 4.2.4, 5. Philippians 4:6 presents a similar sentiment: "Have no anxiety (*mēden merimnate*) about anything, but in everything by prayer and supplication with

---

[734] This verse may underlie the later thought in the *Acts of the Martyrs of Vienne and Lyon* (177 CE): "They [the martyrs] humbled themselves under the mighty hand, by which they are now greatly exalted" (Eusebius, *Hist. eccl.* 5.2.5).

[735] Modifications include a revision of word sequence, an addition of "all" (*pasan*); the replacement of a 2d-person sing. with a 2d-person pl. to fit the full audience of 1 Peter; a substitution of "him" (*auton*) for *kyrion*; and replacements of "and" (*kai*) with "because" (*hoti*) and an original "will sustain you" (*se diathrepsei*) with "he cares for you" (*melei peri hymōn*).

[736] The variants *aporipsantes* (𝔓[72], "cast away") and *epiripsate* (2d-person pl. imperative) are less well attested.

thanksgiving let your requests be made known to God." (On *merimnan* and *merimna*, see also Goppelt 1993, 358.)

In the case of 1 Peter, entrusting all anxiety to God is another mode of humble submission to God and God's paternal care. With the term "anxiety," our author could be presupposing worry on the part of his beleaguered addressees concerning their present well-being and their future fate, though this is not explicitly stated (cf. Luke 12:11). His point in any case is that they can divest and free themselves of anxiety because they are under God's care and protection.[737]

7b. *because he cares about you* (*hoti autōi melei peri hymōn*). This statement does not derive from Ps 54 ("and he shall sustain you," *kai autos se diathrepsei*, v 23b) but offers a similar thought, closer to the expression in Wis 12:13 (*hōi melei peri pantōn*, "he [God] cares for all"). The readers, who are urged to be humble vis-à-vis one another and before God, can comply with this command not only because they will be exalted in the future but also because God takes care of them in the present. The verb *melei*, a 3d-person sing. pres. act. indic. of the verb *melō*, is used here impersonally with the dative (*autōi*) and the prep. *peri*; literally, "there is care to him about you" (for the construction, see also Matt 22:16/Mark 12:14; John 10:13).

The idea of God's providential care for all was common in Israel (Wis 12:13; Philo, *Flacc.* 102; Josephus, *Ant.* 7.45). Philo (*Spec.* 1.318) employed the kindred terms *epimeleia* and *epimeleō* in making a similar point: "(God) protects and provides for you as would a father. And how much this watchful care (*epimeleia*) will exceed that of humans is measured, believe me, by the surpassing excellence of the one who cares (*epimeloumenos*)." Jesus likewise stressed God's fatherly care for his creatures as the reason for not being anxious (Matt 6:25–34/Luke 12:22–34). A hireling, in contrast to a good shepherd, he also observed, "cares nothing for the sheep" (John 10:13). "The conception of God as concerned with the afflictions of man," Beare (1970, 204) aptly notes, "is the peculiar treasure of Judaic and Christian faith; Greek philosophy at its highest could formulate a doctrine of His perfect goodness, but could not even imagine in Him an active concern for mankind."

The two halves of v 7 form a minor "you"/"him" chiasm: (A) "*You* cast your anxiety upon (B) *him*, because (B′) *he* cares about (A′) *you*." The thought as a whole recalls the idea of God's guarding the believers, mentioned at the letter's outset (1:5) and the injunction to entrust their lives to a faithful Creator (4:19). With 5:10 it establishes the basis for the exhortation to resist the Devil (vv 8–9). Threatened by the Devil and a hostile society, believers can unload their anxiety upon God because the One who has called them (v 10a) is also the powerful One (vv 6a, 11) who constantly cares for and sustains them (v 10d).

---

[737] This Petrine thought is perhaps echoed in Herm. *Vis.* 4.2.4–5, which follows 1 Peter in combining the thought of casting anxiety upon God with a warning concerning a "beast" (*thērion*; cf. Devil as lion, 1 Pet 5:8–9), representing "the great persecution to come"; cf. also Herm. *Vis.* 3.11.3.

The assurance that our author offers here and throughout this concluding unit is characteristic of the consolatory thrust of the letter as a whole.

From God's care for the community, our author now turns to the persistent threat posed by the Devil and the society under his thrall, with an urgent call for alertness and vigilance (vv 8–9).

8a. *Stay alert, remain watchful!* (*Nēpsate, grēgorēsate*). Divine protection does not eliminate the need for constant vigilance. The two 2d-person pl. aor. imperatives are joined asyndetically and are virtually synonymous in meaning. The verb *nēphō* ("be alert," "be sober," "stay awake," "be self-controlled") occurs more often in 1 Peter (see also 1:13; 4:7; and NOTES) than in any other NT writing (cf. 1 Thess 5:6, 8; 2 Tim 4:5). It involves being self-possessed, clear-headed, and attentive to what is going on. The verb *gregoreō* ("remain watchful," "be vigilant") and the call for vigilance appear repeatedly in Jesus' eschatological discourse (Mark 13:34–37; Matt 24:42; 25:13), the Gethsemane episode (Matt 26:36–41/Mark 14:34–38), and other NT eschatological contexts.[738] It is likely that both verbs, combined also in 1 Thess 5:6, belong to early Christian hortatory tradition linked with the teaching of Jesus concerning the dangers of the end time and the vigilance required (Lövestam 1963, 60–64 and passim). Selwyn (1947, 375–82, 452–56) saw this theme of vigilance as a hortatory element of early baptismal catechesis.

The need for this vigilance is indicated in v 8b. In some manuscripts ($\mathfrak{P}^{72}$ Sin^2 L Ψ 049^c etc.) the two imperative verbs are directly joined to what follows by a conjunction (*hoti*, "because") that is absent in other, weightier manuscripts (ℵ* A B P 049* 𝔐). The conjunction may have been added secondarily to make the logical connection explicit. On the other hand, it is also possible that *hoti* was original and inadvertently omitted through haplography (homoeoarcton): *hoti ho antidikos*. In either case, v 8b has a causal sense: vigilance is necessary especially because "there is a demonic dimension to the hostility experienced by Christ's followers" (Danker 1980, 158).

8b. *Your adversary, the Devil* (*ho antidikos hymōn diabolos*). Though sustained by God, the believers still face a formidable enemy, the prince of all evil forces terrestrial and celestial. The noun *antidikos* designates an "opponent" or "plaintiff" in a lawsuit (Prov 18:17 LXX; Matt 5:25/Luke 12:58; Luke 18:3) or, secondarily, an "adversary" generally.[739] While *diabolos* could be taken as an adjective ("slanderous") modifying "adversary" ("your slanderous adversary"), it more likely functions here, as generally elsewhere in the Bible, as a substantive ("Devil") standing in apposition to "adversary." The definite article added by $\mathfrak{P}^{72}$ was no doubt intended to make this clear. This is the only NT instance in which the Devil is called "your adversary," although this role is implied in the tradition cited below as well as Rev 12:9–10, where the Devil/

[738] See Luke 12:37, 39; 21:34–36; Acts 20:31; 1 Cor 16:13; Col 4:2; 1 Thess 5:6, 10; Rev 3:2, 3; 16:15.

[739] See 1 Kgdms 2:10; Isa 41:1; Esth 8:11 LXX; Sir 36:16; Josephus, *Ant.* 13.413; for the enemy as "our adversary," see *Acts of John* 108.

Satan is designated *katēgōr* ("accuser"). This is also the only NT instance where the Devil is compared to a lion. Paul, by contrast, never speaks of the "Devil" but only of "Satan"; "Devil" occurs only in the Deutero-Paulines (Eph 4:27; 6:11; 1 Tim 3:6, 7, 11; 2 Tim 2:26; 3:3; Titus 2:3).

Used without an article and therefore virtually as a proper name, *diabolos* (from which the English cognate "Devil" derives) literally means "slanderer." In the LXX, *diabolos* renders the Hebrew words *ṣār, ṣōrēr* (Esth 7:4; 8:1, a human slanderer, Haman), but more often the Hebrew noun *śāṭān* (18×), referring to a celestial agent who tests loyalties for the king, with the sense of "tester," "adversary," "opponent," or "accuser" of humans.[740] The Hebrew *śāṭān*, transliterated in Greek as *satanas*, was used both of humans (2 Sam 19:22; Ps 108[109]:6) and of celestial figures (Job 1:6–12; 2:1–7; Zech 3:1–2; cf. Num 22:22, 32). Originally, the celestial or angelic figure referred to as *śāṭān*/*diabolos* was seen as a heavenly prosecutor under God's control (Job 1:6–12; 2:1–7; cf. Num 22:22, 32). His function was to question and test the genuineness of human virtue and loyalty. In later postexilic time, however, this figure was envisioned as an evil force independent of and opposed to God and God's people (1 Chr 21:1; Zech 3:1–2) and as an afflicter of humankind.

This postexilic period was marked by the development of an elaborated angelology and demonology, conceptions of the existence and agency of not only good but evil spirits that inhabited the sky and heavenly regions and affected human affairs. At this time, the conceptualization and depiction of evil as a personalized force developed under the influence of Persian dualism and became increasingly prominent in the two centuries before the turn of the era. By the 1st century CE, Israel reckoned with a myriad of pernicious superhuman spirits led by one personalized as a masculine spirit and known variously as Satan, Devil, Belial/Beliar, Beelzebul, Sataniel, Sammael, Semyaz, Azazel, Mastema, Abaddon, Apollyon, and Lucifer. Traditions expanding on Gen 6:1–4 imagined a host of evil angelic spirits, with Satan at their head, who had rebelled against God, abandoned heaven, and wreaked constant havoc among humans, causing illness, envy, hatred, dissension, war, and death (see especially *1 En.* 6–16 and other texts discussed in the NOTE on 3:19).

In this demonology, "Satan" and "Devil" were prominent among the terms applied to that demonic power considered to be the "prince of demons" or chief of the evil spirits (*1 En.* 6:3; *Jub.* 10:8; *T. Dan* 5:6; *T. Naph.* 8:4, 6; *T. Ash.* 3:2). This personification of evil was identified as the tempter and envier of Adam and Eve (Wis 2:24; *The Life of Adam and Eve*; *2 En.* 31:4–7; *Apoc. Mos.* 15:1–19:3). Originally an angel of the heavenly court of God, he had rebelled against God, was cast down from heaven (*2 En.* 29:4–5; *L.A.E.* 12:1), inhabited the "lower places" of the sky (*2 En.* 31:3–4), and influenced humans to

[740] See 1 Chr 21:1; Job 1:6, 7 (2×), 9, 12 (2×) 2:1, 2 (2×), 3, 4, 6, 7; Ps 108[109]:6; Zech 3:1, 2, 3; Wis 2:24; 1 Macc 1:36; cf. also *T. Naph.* 8:4, 6.

similar rebellion against their Creator prior to the Flood and thereafter (*1 En.* 6–16; 69:1–19; *Jub.* 10:7–11).[741] Through the Devil and his envy, it was believed, "death entered the world" (Wis 2:24). In league with other spirits known as "principalities," "rulers," or "powers" (see the NOTE on 3:22c for related texts), he held the world under his sway (*Mart. Isa.* 2:1–5). He could disguise himself as a human (*T. Job* 6:4; 17:2; 23:1), and unrighteous humans were under his rule (1QS I 18, 23–24; 1QH[a] II 16, 22; IV 10, 13; V 26; VI 21; 1QM I 1, 5, 13; IV 2; etc.). Ultimately, however, this evil force and his minions, it was believed, would be vanquished (Isa 14:12–15; *T. Levi* 3:3; 18:12; *T. Dan* 5:10–11; *T. Zeb.* 9:8; *T. Benj.* 3:8).

Early Christianity adopted and adapted this body of thought. In the NT, *diabolos* (37×) and *satanas* (36×) are used interchangeably for the chief supernatural adversary of God and God's people (Matt 4:1, 10/Luke 4:2; cf. Mark 1:13; Mark 4:15; cf. Luke 8:12; John 13:2, 27; Rev 2:9–10; 12:9; 20:2, 7, 10).[742] This figure who "has the power of death" (Heb 2:13) claims that all the kingdoms of the world are in his power (Luke 4:6). His power, however, is the power of darkness (Luke 22:53), opposed to the power of light (Acts 26:18). He is the originator of sin and wickedness (Mark 4:15; Luke 22:3; John 8:44; 13:27; Acts 5:3; 1 Tim 5:15) and the great deceiver of nations (Rev 20:3, 8), who effects massive delusion (2 Thess 2:9–12).

Besides causing all manner of illness (e.g., Luke 13:16; Acts 10:38; 2 Cor 12:7), the Devil/Satan removes the good news from those who receive it (Matt 13:19; Mark 4:15; Luke 8:12). He put the betrayal of Jesus into the heart of Judas (John 13:2); he misled Peter, whom Jesus called "Satan" (Matt 16:23; Mark 8:33), and sifted Peter and the disciples like wheat (Luke 22:31); he filled the heart of Ananias with deceit (Acts 5:3); tempted and seduced the believers (1 Tim 5:15) with desire, wiles (1 Cor 7:5; 2 Cor 2:11; Eph 6:11), and snares (1 Tim 3:7; 2 Tim 2:26); deceived humans by disguising himself as an angel of light (2 Cor 11:14); sowed cockle in the field of the Lord's wheat (Matt 13:39;

---

[741] This figure, identified primarily as "Beliar" in the *Testaments of the Twelve Patriarchs* but known also as the "Devil" (*T. Naph.* 3:1; 8:4,6; *T. Ash.* 3:2) and "Satan" (*T. Dan* 5:1–6:1), was the spirit of impurity (*T. Reu.* 4:11; 6:3; *T. Sim.* 5:30), falsehood (*T. Dan* 3:6), deceit (*T. Jud.* 19:4; *T. Benj.* 6:1), duplicity (*T. Benj.* 6:7), hatred (*T. Gad* 4:7), and all evils (*T. Ash.* 1:8; 3:2; *T. Benj.* 7:1–2), the enemy of God (*T. Levi* 19:1; *T. Dan* 5:1; *T. Naph.* 2:6; *T. Ash.* 3:2), and diverter from the observance of God's will (*T. Sim.* 4:8; *T. Dan* 6:1; *T. Naph.* 3:1; 8:4, 6).

[742] This personification of evil was known also as *Beliar* (2 Cor 6:15), *Beelzeboul* (Matt 10:25; 12:24, 27; Mark 3:22; Luke 11:15, 18, 19), *Abaddōn* and *Apollyōn* (Rev 9:11), "prince of demons" (Matt 12:24–27/Luke 11:15–19; Matt 10:25), "the ancient serpent, who is called the Devil and Satan, the deceiver of the whole world" (Rev 12:9; cf. 20:2); "the accuser" (Rev 12:10); "the ruler of this world/age" (John 12:31; 14:30; 16:11; Acts 26:18; 1 John 5:19; Ign. *Eph.* 17:1; 19:1; *Magn.* 1:2; *Rom.* 7:1; cf. his minions as "the rulers of this age," 1 Cor 2:6); "the god of this age" (2 Cor 4:4); "the ruler of the dominion of the air" (Eph 2:2); "the strong one" (Matt 12:29; Mark 3:27; Luke 11:21); "the evil one" (Matt 13:19; 1 John 5:18; *Barn.* 2:10; 20:3); the "enemy" (Matt 13:39; Luke 10:19; cf. Acts 13:10); and "a liar and the father of lies" (John 8:44).

Luke 8:12); hindered Paul's mission (2 Cor 2:11; 1 Thess 2:18); blinded the minds of nonbelievers (2 Cor 4:4); and laid snares to entrap the faithful (1 Tim 3:7; 2 Tim 2:26; Ign. *Trall.* 8:1). Those under his sway are denounced as children of the Devil (John 8:44; Acts 13:10; 1 John 3:8) or "the synagogue of Satan" (Rev 2:9; 3:9). This malevolent power was identified with the great dragon of ancient mythology and the serpent cast down from heaven by Michael (Rev 12:9). As the "ruler of this age," the Devil is behind the nonbelievers who abuse and harass the Christian brotherhood (Eph 2:2; 6:11–12; 2 Thess 2:9–10; Rev 12–18; Ign. *Magn.* 1:2; cf. Ign. *Eph.* 10:3). The one who tempted Jesus, God's son (Matt 4:1–11/Mark 1:12–13/Luke 4:1–11), tempts Jesus' followers as well (1 Cor 7:5; 1 Thess 3:5; Rev 2:10; *2 Clem.* 18:2; Herm. *Mand.* 4.3.6). Jesus, however, appeared in order to destroy the work of the Devil (1 John 3:8c). He contended with Satan and his demonic allies, demonstrating his superior power over them (Matt 4:1–11/Mark1:12–13/Luke 4:1–13; Luke 11:14–22 and passim in the healing stories of the Gospels). The Devil/Satan, whom Jesus saw "fall like lightning from heaven" (Luke 10:18) has already been judged (John 16:11), and at the final judgment he and all those belonging to him will depart into eternal fire (Matt 25:41; Rev 20:10).

Followers of Jesus, therefore, can resist the seduction and temptations of the Devil because Christ has vanquished this foe and limited his power to injure and kill. Believers should allow him no room to work (Eph 4:27). If they resist the Devil, he will flee from them (Jas 4:7; 1 Pet 5:8); God will crush Satan under their feet (Rom 16:20). Sinners and human adversaries of the believers, on the other hand, are delivered to the authority of Satan (1 Cor 5:5; 1 Tim 1:20) and are labeled the "synagogue of Satan" (Rev 2:9; 3:9) and "of the Devil" (John 8:44; Acts 13:10; 1 John 3:8, 10).[743]

It is likely that the Petrine author regarded the Devil, as did his Israelite and Christian contemporaries, as the chief of all the cosmic powers, including those powers and disobedient spirits subordinated to the rule of the resurrected Christ (3:19, 22). Since this is not explicitly stated in the letter, however, it can only be surmised. What is stressed here is the deadly threat that this evil adversary poses to the flock of God through the comparison to a ravenous lion.

prowls about "as a roaring lion" seeking someone to devour (*hōs leōn ōruomenos peripatei*). The comparison of the Devil to a lion is unique in the Bible[744] and communicates the adversary's deadly ferocity and devouring capacity. Elsewhere in the NT, it is wolves who are said to threaten the flock of God (Acts 20:29; see also Matt 7:15; 10:16/Luke 10:3; John 10:12; *4 Ezra* 5:18).

[743] On the Devil/Satan in biblical, Israelite, and early Christian tradition, see Langton 1949; Ling 1961; Gaster 1962; Foerster and von Rad 1964, 72–81; H. A. Kelly 1968; Foerster and Schäferdieck 1971, 151–65; Böcher 1972, 1990, 1993; Russell 1977, 1981; 1988, 28–55; Haag 1980; Ferguson 1984; Wink 1986; Fuller 1988; Pagels 1991, 1992; Baumbach 1992; Hamilton 1992b; McGinn 1994, 9–56; Page 1995.

[744] *Testament of Job* 27:1, where Satan is compared to a lion, represents only a partial analogy; cf. Michaelis 1967a.

The lion is a symbol of even greater power and rapacity. As the mightiest of all beasts (Prov 30:30), it too was the bane of the flock (Amos 3:12; *T. Gad* 1:3; *T. Jud.* 2:4) and an instrument of death (Daniel in the lions' den, Dan 6:16–28). Its roaring inspired fear and terror. Occasionally God (Job 10:6; Lam 3:10; Hos 13:7; Amos 1:2; 11; 3:7–8), Judah and its kings (Gen 49:9; Ezek 19:2–9), or the Messiah, the "Lion of the tribe of Judah" (Rev 5:5), were compared to the powerful lion. But more frequently it was wicked persons (Ps 10:9; 17:12) and Israel's enemies who were depicted as lions attacking the righteous or God's flock.[745] The frequency of this biblical image outweighs the use of a lion to symbolize the Phrygian goddess Cybele as the most likely stimulus for its application here to the Devil (against Perdelwitz 1911, 101–2). The association of shepherd, sheep, and threatening lion in Amos 3:12, moreover, indicates the logical connection between the lion metaphor in 1 Pet 5:8–9 and the shepherd-sheep image in vv 2–4: "Thus says the Lord: 'As the shepherd rescues from the mouth of the lion two legs, or a piece of an ear, so shall the people of Israel who dwell in Samaria be rescued, with the corner of a couch and part of a bed'" (Amos 3:12).

It is particularly Ps 21[22]:14, however, that has influenced the terms employed here. This psalm figured prominently in the theological formulations of Christ's passion.[746] Here it supplies the image of the ravenous lion that the Petrine author applies to the Devil, an image that, as the psalm suggests, encompasses human adversaries as well. The psalmist describes the *human* enemies who surround him as "bulls" (21:13[22:12]), "dogs" (21:17, 21[22:16, 20]), and "wild oxen" (21:22[22:21]). About these bulls he states, "They open wide their mouths at me, *like a ravenous and roaring lion*" (*hōs leōn ho harpazōn kai ōruomenos*, 21:14[22:13])[747] and prays for deliverance from the mouth of the lion and the horns of the wild oxen" (21:21–22[22:20–21]). This comparison of human enemies and roaring lion makes it likely that the Petrine author in similar fashion associated the threatening lion with human agents under the Devil's power (so also Goppelt 1993, 362). This likelihood is further supported by other associations of *antidikos* and *Devil* with the enemies of God's people (cf. 1 Kgdms 2:10; Isa 41:11; Sir 36:6; Ign. *Rom.* 5:3; *Mart. Pol.* 2:4) and by other NT instances of lion imagery as well. Paul, according to 2 Tim 4:7, speaks of being "rescued from the lion's mouth," which Eusebius (*Hist. eccl.* 2.22.4) took as an allusion "to Nero, on account of his cruel nature." The author of Revelation (13:1–2) similarly equates the beast from the

---

[745] Pss 7:2; 17:8–12; 22:13, 21; 35:17; 57:4; Isa 5:29; Jer 2:15; 4:7; 5:6; 49:19[30:13]; 50[27]:17, 44; 51[28]:38; Joel 1:6; Ezek 32:2; Nah 2:11–12; Dan 7:4, 17; Mic 5:8; *1 En.* 89:55–66; 1QH[a] V 5–19; 4Q169 on Nah 2:11–12; Targums on Isa 35:9, Jer 4:7, 5:6, Ezek 19:6; *Jos. Asen.* 12:9–11; *1 En.* 89:65–66; 2 Tim 4:17; Heb 11:33.

[746] See Matt 27:35/Mark 15:24/Luke 23:23/John 19:24; Matt 27:39 par.; Matt 27:43; Matt 27:46/Mark 15:34.

[747] For enemies or wayward leaders as "roaring lions," see also Jer 2:15 and Ezek 22:25; cf. Janowski 1995.

sea having a "mouth like a lion's mouth" with the Empire of Rome.[748] The Seer's earlier statement that "the Devil is about to throw some of you in prison" (2:10) also clearly presupposes human agents under the sway of the Devil. 1 Peter, in contrast to Revelation, expresses no anxiety over or hatred for the power of Rome and in fact encourages a respect for the authority of Roman rulers (2:13–14). The author instead appears to have in mind the nonbelieving Gentiles responsible for the harassment and suffering of the Christian brotherhood.[749] Behind the slander and abuse perpetrated by these Gentiles lies the aggression of the cosmic "slanderer" and adversary of God's people. The social implication of this simile of aggression is ignored when it is seen only as an image for a personal near-death experience or "spiritual death or apostasy" (against Horsley 1983, 50–51). This image is, rather, an example of early Christianity's defensive demonizing of its enemies.

This tactic of demonizing hostile outsiders as agents of the Devil is typical of minority sects, such as the Jesus movement, that are pressured to conform and assimilate to the surrounding society, and is evident throughout the NT.[750] Such vilification of critics and hostile outsiders was part of a process whereby the identity and distinctiveness of the in-group were affirmed, the social boundaries demarcating "us" (the Christian in-group) from "them" (the hostile society, as out-group) were clearly affirmed, and slandering outsiders were implied to be pawns of the slandering and abusive Devil, seeking to disparage, devour, or decimate the believers.

seeking someone to devour (*zētōn tina katapiein*). The manuscripts vary regarding the function of the pronoun *tis* and the form of its accompanying verb. The form *tina* is an accusative of the pronoun *tis* and could function here either as an interrogative (*tína*, "whom to devour") or an indefinite pronoun serving as a substantive (*tinà*, "someone to devour"). Uncertainty on this issue has led, in turn, to variants concerning the verb "devour." There are three main variant readings: (1) "someone to devour" (*tinà katapiein*, supported by ℵ[c] [K P 049] 81 181 326 1739 cop[bo] Origen), with *tinà* as an accusative of the pronoun *tis*; (2) "whom he may devour" (*tína katapiēi* [𝔓[72] A Byz and most early versions]), with *tína* as an interrogative; an alternate finite verb, *katapíei*, is a transcriptional error either for the infinitive or, by itacism, for the subjunctive; and (3) simply "to devour" (*katapiein*, with *tina* omitted [B Ψ Origen[lat]]). The second reading could be seen as an attempt to alleviate the difficulty of

---

748 See also *Ascen. Isa.* 4:1–6 (of Beliar, "the king of this world," appearing in the likeness of Nero) and Justin (*Dial.* 103), who identifies the "ravening and roaring lion" of Ps 21[22] with Herod Antipas or the Devil.

749 A later apparent echo of this verse took it in a similar sense. In a letter from the churches of Vienne and Lyons, reference is made to human adversaries of the Christians, intent on "devouring" them (Eusebius, *Hist. eccl.* 5.1.52; 5.2.6); cf. also the previous echo of 1 Pet 5:6 in *Hist. eccl.* 5.2.5.

750 See Matt 16:33/Mark 8:33; John 6:70; 8:44; Acts 13:10. 1 John 3:8–10; Rev 2:9, 13, 24; 3:9; 12–18; 20:2–3, 7–10; cf. Freyne 1985; Malina and Neyrey 1988; and Elliott 1995b, 84–89.

the absolute use of *katapiein* or could have arisen at a later time, when the indefinite *tina* ("someone") was taken as the interrogative *tína* ("whom"). The constancy of *tina* in the overwhelming majority of the manuscripts, however, makes probable its original presence and its omission in other manuscripts a case of accidental oversight (against Beare 1970, 205; and Michaels 1988, 292–93, who regard the briefer reading [3] as original). Selwyn (1947, 237–38) considered variant (2) more "colorful," but an interrogative at this point yields an awkward expression in Greek. This points to (1) as the most likely original reading, with *tinà* resembling its use in Mark 15:35; Luke 8:46; Heb 3:4 (so also Robertson 1919, 742; Metzger 1971, 696–97; Goppelt 1993, 361).

The verb *katapiein* is an infinitive of purpose, a use of the infinitive also occurring in 2:5 (*anenegkai*). The verb *katapinō* ("devour," "swallow down, eat up") is used of a beast swallowing its prey (Jonah 2:1; cf. Tob 6:2) and appropriately fits the image of the Devil as lion. It is also used figuratively, however, of human enemies hostile to Israel who "devour" God's people.[751] This lends further support to the likelihood that our author envisioned an alliance between the Devil and the believers' human enemies.

9a. *resist him, firm in [your] faith* (*hōi antistēte stereoi tēi pistei*). As God opposes (*antitassetai*) the arrogant (v 5c), so believers are to oppose and resist (*antistēte*) the demonic promoter of arrogance and hostility against God's people. The pronoun *hōi* ("him," "whom"), omitted only in 𝔓[72], has as its antecedent "your adversary the Devil," thereby linking v 9a to v 8. The dative case is required by the verb *antistēte* ("resist"). The verb *antistēte*, an act. 2d-person pl. imperative of *antistēmi* ("stand up against, withstand," "resist"), is an aor., probably with ingressive force: "take your stand against." This and similar commands to resist the Devil (Jas 4:7; Eph 6:11, 12, 16; cf. also Eph 4:27; *Barn.* 4:9; Herm. *Mand.* 12.5.2) reflect early Christian hortatory tradition, which Selwyn (1947, 238), following Carrington, associated with the baptismal catechesis of the early Church (so also J. N. D. Kelly 1969, 210–11). This association continued in baptismal rituals of later time that required the one baptized to "renounce the Devil and all his pomps and all his ways."

firm in [your] faith (*stereoi tēi pistei*). The adjective *stereoi* modifies the "you" contained in the foregoing imperative verb. Used of physical objects, *stereos* means "hard" or "solid"; compare "solid food" (Heb 5:12, 14) and "solid foundation" (2 Tim 2:19). Used figuratively of humans and their character, as here, it has the sense of "firm," "steadfast" (BAGD 766), or even "stubborn." Perhaps to avoid this latter sense, 𝔓[72] reads *hedraioi*, a term that means "firm," "steadfast" (cf. Quinn 1965). The kindred verb *sterizō* is used of God in v 10; God himself will *reinforce* their firmness in faith.

---

[751] See Pss 9:30[10:5]; 34:25; 123:3; Hos 8:8; Hab 1:13; Isa 16:8 LXX; 49:19; Jer 28[51]:34, 44; Lam 2:16. Cf. Rev 12, where the Devil/Satan is depicted as a great dragon seeking to devour (*kataphagēi*) the child (12:4) of the woman clothed with the sun (12:1–6), symbolizing either Israel or the Christian community.

The term *tēi pistei* is best taken as a dative of respect: "firm *with respect to* your faith," with "your" unstated but implied.[752] *Pistis,* as throughout the letter (1:5, 7, 9, 21), means, along with its verb *pisteuō* (1:8; 2:6, 7) and its adjective *pistos* (1:21), trust in and unwavering commitment to God and Christ.

The Devil here is not yet a cipher for the "intimate enemy" lurking *within* the Christian community (on this concept, see Pagels 1991, 1992), for the letter contains no polemic against any kind of deviant teaching and practice within the messianic movement. Nor is this reference to the Devil to be taken as an allusion to Rome. In contrast to the seer in Revelation, who associates Rome with the Devil/Satan (Rev 12–13, 17–18), our author makes no such equation and in fact urges respect for Roman authority (2:13–17). The image of the Devil as a powerful lion seeking someone to devour instead serves as a potent means for depicting a hostile society as under the sway of the Devil, the arch-enemy of God and God's people, and intent on absorbing or annihilating the brotherhood. The image thus labels and demonizes hostile outsiders who attack the Christians for separating from them (4:2–4) and not conforming to their modes of behavior (1:14–17; 4:2–4) as agents of the Devil. The conflict between the Devil and the brotherhood replicates the repeated contrasts between hostile nonbelievers and the suffering faithful (2:4–10, 12; 3:1–2, 13–16; 4:2–4, 6, 14–16). Resistance to the Devil and firmness in faith include resistance to pressures urging conformity to a style of life that believers have renounced and resistance to the temptation to "go along in order to get along." Should Christians succumb to this pressure, they would indeed be "devoured" and absorbed by the society at large, and this would have meant the end of the Christian movement in Asia Minor (cf. Elliott 1981/1990, 81, 108, 114–15, 144–45); hence the urgent need for vigilance, resistance, and firmness in faith.

According to U. Holzmeister, 1 Pet 5:8 was the most frequently cited of all of the passages in 1 Peter (for the citations, see Holzmeister 1937, 404–5). Eventually, this verse was given an honored place as the scriptural reading for the order of Compline, the prayer of the Church at the close of the day. Here at the close of this letter, these words encourage the believers to resist the devilish adversary and his human agents with the aid of God's power (vv 6–7, 10–11) and with the knowledge that their experience is that of the worldwide brotherhood.

9b. *knowing that these same sufferings are being accomplished in the case of your brotherhood throughout the world* (*eidotes ta auta tōn pathēmatōn tēi en tōi kosmōi hymōn adelphotēti epiteleisthai*). As a motivation for the foregoing call to resistance, the addressees of Asia Minor are reminded that their experience of suffering is that of the brotherhood throughout the world. They are not alone, and solidarity in suffering should help strengthen their resolve.

The entire formulation bristles with grammatical problems that have prompted textual variants and differing attempts to resolve the issues. The verb

---

[752] For analogous expressions see Rom 11:20, 2 Cor 1:24; Col 1:23; Acts 15:5; cf. also Col 2:5; Ign. *Eph.* 10:2.

oida (of which *eidotes* is the perf. act. part.) followed by an infinitive, as here, can mean either "know that" or "know how to"; the infinitive *epiteleisthai* can be either middle or passive, with a range of possible senses; *ta auta tōn pathēmatōn* is a technically incorrect construction, and *ta auta* can be taken either as a subject or object of the infinitive; and the function of the dative *adelphotēti* is not immediately clear.

The participle *eidotes* introduces a thought supporting the foregoing (v 9a) and bringing it to a conclusion, as in 1:18. As in this earlier instance, the author reminds his audience of a fact already known to them. The participle stands alone but is equivalent to "knowing that," as it is in Luke 4:41; *1 Clem.* 43:6; and 62:3 (cf. BDF §397.3). The addition of *hoti* ("that") in 𝔓72 was probably prompted by the fuller formulation in 1:18. The Greek involves a conventional accusative (*ta auta tōn pathēmatōn*)-with-infinitive (*epiteleisthai*) construction as the object of what is known; literally, "knowing these same sufferings to be accomplished. . . ."[753]

The formulation *ta auta tōn pathēmatōn* itself is unusual, involving a neut. pl. pron. substantive (*ta auta*) with a neut. pl. partitive genitive (*tōn pathēmatōn*), which reads literally, "these same of sufferings." The formulation is "strictly speaking incorrect" (BDF §164.1), but the sense intended is either that expressed by the proper formulation *ta auta pathēmata* ("these same sufferings") or "the same sort of sufferings" (so Robertson 1919, 687). These are the sufferings mentioned most immediately in 4:13, 19; namely, the sufferings that all believers experience as a consequence of their allegiance to the suffering Christ (5:1).[754]

are being accomplished (*epiteleisthai*). Some manuscripts (א A B* K etc.) read *epiteleisthe* ("you are completing") or *epiteleitai* (𝔓72 and a few others), both finite verbs rather than infinitives. Other later minuscules (322 323 1241) read *epimeleisthe* ("you are being cared for"). But the majority tradition (B2 P Ψ 𝔐 latt syr), reading *epiteleisthai*, is weightier and represents the more difficult reading, which then prompted the secondary variants.[755]

The present infinitive *epiteleisthai* could be either a middle or passive. The verb *epiteleō* (cf. also Rom 15:28; 2 Cor 7:1; 8:6, 11; Gal 3:3; Phil 1:6; Heb 8:5; 9:6) is a denominative of *telos*, which can mean either "end," "goal," or "tax." Thus the verb can mean "bring to an end," "complete," "accomplish," or secondarily, "perform" (rituals), "lay something upon someone" (in the dative case), with these senses also expressible in the passive.[756]

---

753 For this construction with this verb, see also Luke 4:41; *1 Clem.* 43:6; 62:3; and, with related verbs of perceiving or knowing, John 12:18; 1 Cor 11:18; and Heb 10:34. On the construction, see BAGD 556 and BDF §397.1.

754 For *ta auta* used absolutely, see also Luke 6:23; for the singular *to auto*, see Matt 5:47.

755 Quinn (1965, 247–49) reads the 𝔓72 variant *epeiteleitai* as *epei teleitai* ("because [it, the brotherhood] is being perfected"). However, *epei* is not used elsewhere in 1 Peter, and the spelling could just as well involve an itacism in which *ei* stands for *i*; cf. BDF §§22–23 and Davids' (1990, 194) justifiable reservations.

756 See, e.g., Lev 6:15; 1 Esd 4:55; 6:14, 28; 8:21; Tob 12:1 [S]; *1 Clem.* 40:2, 3.

As a middle, the verb was also used of "paying a tax in full" (cf. Xen., *Mem.* 4.8.8, *ta tou gērōs epiteleisthai*, "to pay the tax of old age") or of "fulfilling one's religious duty." Beare (1970, 206), who takes it in this latter sense, regards *ta auta* as a cognate accusative with *epiteleisthai, tōn pathēmatōn* as a "genitive of definition," *adelphotēti* as dependent on *ta auta*, and translates: "showing yourselves able [for *eidotes*] to fulfill the same meed of sufferings as your brotherhood in the world" (Beare 1970, 203; cf. also Bigg 1902, 194; and Best 1971, 175, "knowing how to pay the same tax of suffering").[757] The economic metaphor of "paying a *tax* (or *meed*) of suffering," however, is alien to this letter, which makes no mention of taxes, either figuratively or literally.

On the other hand, taking the infinitive as passive and as comprising with *ta auta pathēmatōn* an accusative-with-infinitive construction (with *tēi adelphotēs hymōn* as a dative of respect or agency) is equally possible and yields a sense that is not dependent on assuming that a term such as "meed" or "tax" is implied by the verb *epiteleisthai* (see also Goppelt 1993, 363). This is also preferred by BAGD, who allow the renderings "knowing that these same sufferings *are being laid upon* your brotherhood" or ". . . *are being accomplished* in the case of your brotherhood." The sufferings to be accomplished or completed are, most likely, the messianic woes inaugurating the end time (see the NOTE on 4:13), of which the sufferings of all the believers of the brotherhood are a part.

in the case of your brotherhood throughout the world (*tēi en tōi kosmōi hymōn adelphotēti*). The translation takes *tēi adelphotēti* in connection with the passive verb *epiteleisthai* as a dative of respect, rendered "in the case of." Alternatively, it could also function as a dative of agent ("by your brotherhood");[758] for the construction of a passive verb with a dative of respect, see Phil 2:7 (*schēmati heuretheis hōs anthrōpos*, "found as a human with respect to form") and Rom 7:10 (*heurethē moi*, lit., "[it] was found in respect to me").

Once again "brotherhood" (*adelphotēs*) rather than "church" (*ekklēsia*) is used to depict the entire Christian community (cf. Giaquinta 1980). Occurring only in 1 Peter, it was employed in 2:17 and was probably also implied in 5:13 ("co-elect [brotherhood]"; cf. also *1 Clem.* 2:4). Together with the collective formulations "household of the Spirit" (*oikos pneumatikos*, 2:5) and "household of God" (*oikos tou theou*, 4:17), "brotherhood" expresses the familial nature and solidarity of the believing community, whose members are "children of God" (1:14) who are to be obedient to God their father (1:14–17; cf. 1:2, 3) and loving toward one another (1:22 [*philadelphia*]; 2:17; 3:8 [*philadelphoi*]; 4:8).[759] The Asia Minor believers are a vital part of this worldwide

[757] Reicke's translation (1964, 131) of *epiteleisthai*, "confront (your brothers)," is unprecedented and ignores the difficulties altogether.

[758] For the construction of a passive infinitive and dative of agent, see Matt 6:1 (*to teanthēnai autois*, "to be seen by them"); similarly Matt 23:5; Luke 23:15 (*estin pepragmenon autōi*, "nothing deserving of death was done by him"); and 2 Pet 3:5 (*autōi heurethēnai*, "to be found by him").

[759] On the concept of brotherhood (but not the term *adelphotēs*) in Paul, see K. Schäfer 1989.

brotherhood ("your brotherhood"); their share in Christ's suffering is that of all brothers and sisters worldwide. Thus, their predicament is not atypical or unique, as they might be tempted to think, but characteristic of all those in solidarity with the suffering Christ. In this unity there is strength. Paul consoles the Philippians with a similar thought (Phil 1:29–30).

throughout the world (*en tōi kosmōi*). The noun *kosmos* here, as in 1:20a (see NOTE; contrast 3:3, "adorning"), has the neutral global sense of "inhabited world" (as in Mark 4:8; 14:9; Rom 1:8; 1 Cor 14:10; 1 Tim 1:15; 3:16; 6:7; Heb 10:5). The preposition *en* (lit., "in") has a distributive sense here: "throughout" (as in Matt 26:13; Rom 1:8; 1 Cor 14:10; 2 Cor 1:12; Col 1:6). The connection of "Devil" (v 8 and "him," v 9a) and "world," together with the contrast between Devil and God in this context seem similar to the statement in 1 John 5:19, "We know that we are of God and the whole world is in the power of the evil one." But the adjacent thought in 1 John 5:18 ("We know that anyone born of God does not sin, but he who was born of God keeps him, and the evil one does not touch him") varies fundamentally from the Petrine author's understanding of sin as a reality to be resisted and his portrait of the Devil as indeed touching and threatening believers. The Johannine and Petrine senses of "world" also are disparate. For the Petrine author, *kosmos* designates, not a society alienated from God,[760] but the physical world as founded by God (1:20a) and the inhabited regions, where believers too are to be found.[761] For inhabitants of the Circum-Mediterranean region, this world, as most knew it, comprised the area that was ruled by Rome and extended from the Levant in the east to Spain in the west, and from Britain and Gaul in the north to the African Sahara in the south.

On the whole, v 9b thus affirms the communal and familial character of the messianic movement, the worldwide extent of its growth, and the universal experience of Christian suffering. These were crucial features of the movement of which the Asia Minor Christians were a part and important aspects for them to keep in mind as they engaged in the task of nonconforming resistance to evil, both demonic and human. The consolatory force of this statement is strengthened by the thought of its surrounding context. The addressees, though exposed to the threat of the enemy of God, are ultimately in the hands of a protective Creator (vv 6–7, 10). With their brothers and sisters in the faith everywhere they can resist the encroachments of the Devil and his agents because the powerful God (vv 6, 11) who called them into being as a brotherhood of believers will forever sustain them (vv 6–7, 10).

Cervantes Gabarrón (1991a, 434), viewing 4:12–5:9 as the final section of the body of the letter, characterized vv 10–11 as a "theological doxological epilogue." While vv 10–11 indeed reprise salient themes of the letter as a

---

[760] For this sense, see John 15:18–19; 16:33; 1 John 2:15–17; 3:1; 4:1–17; 5:4–5, 19; 2 John 7; and Beare 1970, 206.

[761] For this sense, see 2 Macc 3:12; Matt 24:14; Mark 14:9 par.; Rom 1:8; 1 Cor 14:10. In favor of this sense are also Johnston 1964 and Goppelt 1993, 363.

whole, they nevertheless are also directly linked to their immediate context. The author assures his readers in v 10 that, despite the threat posed by the Devil, God will strengthen and secure them. Thus v 10 presents a positive counterpart to vv 8–9 and repeats the theme of God's care sounded in vv 6–7. Verse 11, in turn, constitutes a concluding doxology of God similar to the doxology of 4:11. Here, however, the doxology focuses on God's "power" (*kratos*), a term related to the "powerful" (*krateian*) hand of God in v 6, terms that form an inclusion embracing vv 6–11. Verse 10 is further united with the preceding verses by the linking terms *pas* (cf. v 5b), *theos* (cf. vv 5b, 6), *charis* (cf. v 5c), *hymeis* (cf. v 6; *hymōn*, vv 7, 8), and *stērizō* (cf. *stereos*, v 9). All but these last two terms, furthermore, form components of the literary inclusion framing vv 5b–11.[762]

10a. *The God of all grace, however* (*Ho de theos pasēs charitos*). From the threat of the Devil, the author turns once more to the care, protection, and support provided by God, with vv 10–11 expanding further on the thought of vv 6–7. These final verses of the body of the letter also reprise some of its chief emphases and thus form a fitting assurance and doxological close to the letter as a whole. The particle *de* was used with the sense of "finally" in v 5b, which introduced this concluding exhortation to the entire community (cf. also 3:8a). An illogical redundancy would be created by rendering it "finally" once again in the present verse. Here in 10a, it has adversative force ("however") and introduces a statement that contrasts the strength and support provided by God to the danger posed by the believers' devilish adversary. Under attack by the Devil (vv 8–9), the believers are surrounded and sustained by the power and care of God (vv 6–7, 10–11).

The "grace" (*charis*) or generous "favor" of God of which the addressees are beneficiaries has been mentioned often in this letter (1:2, 20, 13; 3:7; 4:10; 5:5; cf. 2:19, 20, divine approval) and in 5:12 summarizes in one word the focus of the letter's witness as a whole. This grace is varied in its manifestations (4:10) so that "all" (*pasēs*) covers every aspect of grace experienced by the believers from the time of their baptism onward. The threefold use of *all* in vv 5b–11 also underlines the comprehensive scope of these concluding sentiments ("all persons," "all anxiety," "all grace") and forms a part of the inclusion framing this unit.

10b. *who has called you to his eternal glory in Christ* (*ho kalesas hymas eis tēn aiōnion autou doxan en Christōi*). The phrase modifies "the God of all grace," and "who has called you" stresses the divine calling of the believers one final time (1:15; 2:9, 21; 3:9) with emphasis here, as in 3:9, on the final goal of the believers' calling (see the NOTES on these verses in regard to *kaleō* and the traditional notion of Christians as "called" by God).

---

[762] Selwyn (1947, 239) claimed, unconvincingly, that terminological affinities here with 1 Thess (5:23–28) and 2 Thess (2:13–17) "point to the pen of Silvanus." Against Silvanus as author of 1 Peter, see the NOTE on 5:12.

to his eternal glory. The eschatological goal of the divinely-called reborn believers is once more expressed: sharing in the glory of God (1:7; 4:11, 13, 14, 16; 5:4), as does Jesus Christ (1:11; 5:1). 2 Thessalonians 2:13–14 expresses a similar sentiment: "God chose you . . . he called you through our gospel, so that you may obtain the glory of our Lord Jesus Christ" (cf. also Rom 8:30; 9:23; 1 Thess 2:12).

The phrase *in Christ*[763] has been taken instrumentally by some commentators ("who called you . . . through Christ"), but our author uses *dia* to express an instrumental function of Christ elsewhere (2:5f; 4:11c). *Dia* has also been taken with the word "glory," which immediately precedes it: "the glory manifest in Christ." Since, however, the expression is used also in 3:16 and 5:14 to designate those who are *in union with* Christ (5:14) or the conduct of those *united with* Christ (3:16), a trace of this sense may be present here as well. Christ has been glorified (1:11, 21; 4:13; 5:1) and shares in the glory of God (4:11d, 14, 16; 5:10b; cf. 2:12), so that all who are "in Christ"—that is, united with Christ—are called to share in both God's glory and Christ's (1:7; 4:13, 14; 5:1, 4). The glory of God manifest in Christ belongs to those in union with Christ. On the phrase "in Christ," see also the NOTES on 3:16 and 5:14.

The aorist formulation with a following *eis* phrase indicating purpose or goal ("to, for") is similar to 1:3 in structure and thrust:

5:10 The God of all grace . . .
  who has called (*kalesas*) you
    to (*eis*) his eternal glory
1:3 (Blessed is) the God and Father of our Lord Jesus Christ
  who . . . has caused us to be born again (*anagennēsas*)
    for (*eis*) a living hope,
    for (*eis*) an inheritance . . .
    for (*eis*) a salvation . . .

10c. *after you have suffered for a brief time* (*oligon pathontas*). The participle *pathontas* ("suffered") has *hymas* ("you") as its antecedent. It is the last of the numerous references to the suffering and malignment of the believers (1:6; 2:12, 19, 20; 3:9, 14, 16, 17; 4:1, 6, 12–16, 19; 5:9) and is accompanied by the assurance that their suffering will be brief and concluded with God's ultimate strengthening and fortifying of the faithful (cf. 2 Cor 4:17). The expression repeats the similar remark in 1:6 ("for a brief time . . . you are afflicted," *oligon . . . lypēthentes*), so that the author reiterates at the close what he has stated at

[763] There is weightier MS support for the longer reading "in Christ Jesus" ($\mathfrak{P}^{72}$ A P Ψ 𝔐 latt syr[h] cop) than for "in Christ" (א B ["in the Christ"] 614 630 1505 2495 and a few others). However, the formulation "Christ Jesus" occurs nowhere else in 1 Peter and, given the tendency of copyists to expand the sacred name, this fuller formulation could well be secondary. Moreover, the shorter reading is consistent with "in Christ" in 3:16 and the shorter reading of 5:14, where a similar set of variants occur. It also accords with the regular use of "Christ" absolutely throughout the rest of the letter (1:11, 19; 2:21; 3:15, 16, 18; 4:1, 13, 14; 5:1, 14 [?]).

the outset: suffering is a reality, as acknowledged and addressed throughout the letter, but is of brief and limited duration. This thought, along with the accompanying stress on the eternal glory in store (v 10a; cf. 1:7), forms part of the inclusion framing the entire body of the letter, 1:3–5:11; see also mention of the power and protection of God (1:5; 5:6–7, 10–11); Christ (1:3, 7, 10; 5:10); faith (1:7; 5:9); grace (1:10; 5:10); and the eulogy of God (1:3) matched by the doxology of God (5:11).

10d. *will himself complete, reinforce, strengthen,* [*and*] *establish* [*you*] (*autos katartisei, stērixei, sthenōsei, themeliōsei*). The focus now returns to God, the primary subject of this verse. With a concluding cluster of four future-tense verbs, the author assures the readers repeatedly that God "himself" (*autos*, an emphatic reference back to "God," v 10a; cf. 1 Thess 5:23; 2 Thess 2:16) will surely fortify and consolidate the community in the future, as in the present. The four actions mentioned are specific manifestations of God's grace (vv 5c, 10a) and care (v 7b); the implied object of these verbs is the plural "you" of v 10b.

will complete (*katartisei*).[764] The verb *katartizō* has a range of meanings, including "put in order," "mend" (nets, Mark 1:19/Matt 4:11; figuratively, 2 Cor 13:11), "fully train" (Luke 6:40), "restore" (Gal 6:1), "unite" (1 Cor 1:10), "make whole," "complete" (1 Thess 3:10; Heb 13:10). The sentiment it expresses here is especially close to the thought of Heb 13:20–21, "may the God of peace . . . complete you with everything good that you may do his will." If suffering has caused any faltering of faith or discord, God surely will make the believers whole.

reinforce (*stērixei*). This and the following two verbs have similar, overlapping senses. The verb *stērixei* is a future form of *stērizō* ("set up, fix firmly"; figuratively, "establish," Sir 3:9; "hold up," Sir 13:21; 2 *Clem.* 2:6), which is used most frequently with the meaning "reinforce," "support, confirm, strengthen," often in the face of adversity.[765] It is related linguistically to *stereos*, which appears in v 9a: those urged to be "firm in faith" are now assured that God himself will make this possible. The verb also appears in Luke's account of Jesus' words to Peter prior to his denial: "Simon, Simon, behold, Satan sought you all out to sift you (pl.) like wheat, but I have prayed for you (sing.) that your (sing.) faith may not fail; and when you yourself have returned, reinforce (*stērison*) your brothers" (Luke 22:31–32). While it is possible that this notion of

[764] A few MSS (P 𝔐) have an optative, *katartisai* ("might complete"), and add "you" (*hymas*), which is implicit in any case. Other, later MSS (614 630 1505 2495 and others) record scribal changes of one or more of the accompanying future indicative verbs to optatives. The third verb (*sthenōsei*) is omitted in some MSS (𝔓[72] 81 some Lat. versions) and the fourth (*themeliōsei*) in others (A B Ψ some cursive and the Vulg.), both probably inadvertent omissions due to the similar verb endings. The presence of all four verbs as future active indicatives has the best support (א 33 945 1241 1739 etc.) and is favored by *NTG*[27] and most commentators.

[765] See 1 Macc 14:14; Luke 22:32; Acts 18:23; Rom 16:25; 1 Thess 3:2; 2 Thess 3:3; Rev 3:2.

reinforcing, common to 1 Peter and the Peter episode in Luke, represents an element of the NT Petrine tradition, it must be acknowledged that here in v 10 it is God, rather than Peter, who reinforces.

strengthen (*sthenōsei*). The virtually synonymous verbs pile up as the author seeks to assure readers, who could be anxious about their ability to remain steadfast, of God's unswerving support. This third verb is a future form of *sthenoō* ("strengthen," "make strong," "fill with strength"). It is used only here in the NT and rarely elsewhere in Greek literature, where *sthenō* ("be strong") is more common (in the LXX only in 3 Macc 3:8). It overlaps in sense with the previous verb.

[*and*] *establish* [*you*] (*themeliōsei*). "You" as direct object is implied, as it is for all four verbs, and in fact is added secondarily by P and 𝔐. The verb *themelioō* ("make, provide a solid foundation," "ground firmly," "establish") belongs to the semantic field of building activity and often is used figuratively of being grounded in something and being stable (Eph 3:17; Col 1:23; Heb 1:10; Herm. *Vis.* 3.13.4; 4.1.4).[766] The verbs *themelioō* and *oikodomeō* appear together in Matt 7:24–27, and *oikodomeō* and *themelion* appear in the Lukan parallel, 6:48–49 (cf. also Rom 15:20; 1 Cor 3:10–15; Eph 2:20). In 1 Peter, *themelioō* is thus close to the sense and use of the verb *oikodomeisthe* in 2:5 ("you are being built up"); the related noun, *themelia* ("foundation"), appears in Isa 28:16, a portion of which is cited in 1 Pet 2:6. In 2:5, *oikodomeisthe* is a passive implying God as subject (as Isa 28:16 explicitly states); here in 5:10, God also is the explicit subject of the kindred verb *themelioō*. This final verb denoting building activity suggests that all four actions pertain to the securing, fortifying, and upbuilding of the community as the household of God, the metaphor employed in 2:5 and 4:17.

11. *His is the power forever, amen* (*autōi to kratos eis tous ainōnas amēn*). Having assured his beleaguered readers of God's certain care and support, the author concludes these consolatory words and the letter as a whole with a celebratory doxology. Similar in form to the doxology of 4:11, where *to kratos* ("the power") also appears, this praise of God affirms in particular the power that is God's to accomplish the actions enumerated in v 10. The pronoun *autōi* ["him"], like the foregoing *autos* in v 10, has God (v 10a) as its antecedent. The implied verb of the ellipsis is *estin* ("is"), as in 4:11, rather than *estō* ("to Him be"). Similar doxological formulations appear in *Pss. Sol.* 17:3 (*to kratos tou theou hēmōn eis ton aiōna met' eleous*, "the power of our God is forever with mercy") and 1 Tim 6:16 (*hōi timē kai kratos aiōnion, amēn*, "His is honor and eternal power, amen"; cf. Shimada 1966, 396–421). The noun "the power" (*to kratos*) recalls the "powerful (*krataian*) hand of God" in v 6; the

---

[766] See also its figurative use for God's "founding" of the earth (Heb 1:10) and the figurative use of its paronym *themelion* ("foundation," 1 Cor 3:10–15; Eph 2:20; 1 Tim 6:19; 2 Tim 2:19; Heb 6:1; 11:10).

two related terms belong to the inclusion framing vv 5b/6–11.[767] By contrast, *kratos* never appears in Pauline doxologies but is found in the doxologies of the Deutero-Pauline 1 Timothy (6:16) as well as Jude 25 and Rev 1:6 and 5:13.

forever (*eis tous aiōnas*). The fuller reading, "forever and ever" (*eis tous aiōnas tōn aiōnōn*), has extensive attestation (א A P Ψ 𝔐 latt syr cop^{sa} cop$^{bo^{ms}}$), but this probably is a harmonization with the longer reading of 4:11d. In light of the scribal tendency to enlarge doxologies, the shorter reading (𝔓^{72} B a few uncials and cop^{bo}) is preferred.

The doxology ends with an *amen*, as in 4:11d. *Amēn*, originally an affirmation of what had been spoken by another ("It is indeed so!"), eventually lost its function as a congregational response and was incorporated into doxological statements themselves (see Shimada 1966, 415–21 and Delling 1962, 71–76). This doxology concluding the body of the letter matches the eulogy (1:3–5) with which it began. These liturgical formulas reflect the language of the synagogue and its praise of God[768] and here provide the words that form a literary inclusion embracing the body of the letter and that give it its prevailing note of divine praise.

GENERAL COMMENT

Our author brings the body of his letter to a close with another masterful blend of exhortation (vv 5b, 6a, 7a, 8–9a) and encouragement (vv 5c, 6b, 7b, 9b, 10–11), a combination exemplifying the twofold aim of the letter as a whole (5:12d). The goal of this exhortation and encouragement is the galvanizing of the internal social cohesion of community, not only through a proper exercise of leadership (vv 1–4) and a respect for order (v 5a), but also through the mutual humility of all (vv 5b–6), the resistance of the encroachments of a Devil-driven society, and a collective confidence in the sustaining power of God. A call to resistance of the Devil (and his agents) is surrounded by assurances of God's favor toward the humble and of God's sustaining of the community. Though attacked by the Devil, believers are embraced by the power and care of God.

Turning once again from specific groups (5:1–5a; cf. 2:18–3:7) to the community as a whole, he repeats his call for humility toward one another (v 5b; cf. 3:8) and toward God (v 6a). Such humility before God is a condition of and prelude to being exalted (v 6). This reversal in circumstances echoes an underlying motif in the story of God's relation to his people and in this letter in particular. The anxiety, which might naturally fill the harassed believers and lead

[767] Some MSS have a fuller formulation, "the glory and the power" (א P 𝔐 vg^{cl} [syr^{p}] cop^{sa}), or "the glory, power" (K 049 and others), or "the power and the glory" (33 69 81 etc. syr^{h} cop^{bo}). The briefer reading (𝔓^{72} A B Ψ vg$^{st, ww}$), omitting "the glory," is more likely original, whereas the fuller expressions are the result of harmonization with 4:11 and traditional doxologies.

[768] On doxologies and eulogies as liturgical formulas and on their use in early Christianity, see Delling 1962, 61–70; Deichgräber 1967, 25–43.

to resignation and despair, is not something inescapable. It can be unburdened upon God because God indeed cares for them (v 7) and strengthens them (v 10).

Being under God's care, however, does not mean escape from a hostile society and its demonic dimension. The precarious predicament in which the addressees find themselves calls for vigilance and resistance to hostility in its demonic and human forms. For one last time, the problem of suffering is addressed and put into a cosmic as well as social context (vv 8–9). Behind the efforts of a hostile society intent on absorbing, neutralizing, and eliminating the Christian movement by forcing its conformity to standards and values alien to the Gospel and the will of God, lurks the Devil, who as a ravenous lion seeks to devour the brotherhood. The social stakes concerning the endurance of the Christian movement throughout the world were high. Accommodation to alien forms of conduct could lead to assimilation and assimilation to the demise of the Christian movement altogether. Resistance to pressures urging conformity, therefore, was essential to preserving the distinctive holy identity, solidarity, and exclusive commitment of the community and thereby securing not only its viabilility but also its growth. Resistance to the Devil involves not only withstanding evil in all its forms, natural and supernatural, but also resisting pressures to conform socially to outsiders' modes of behavior (4:2–4) and leading lives of holy nonconformity (1:14–16). Such resistance is necessary because Christian believers are God's holy children (1:14–16) and household (2:4–10), with no attachments or allegiances to their former associations. That such resistance is possible has been demonstrated by Jesus Christ (2:22–23), to whom God has subjected all powers, terrestrial and celestial (3:22), including the Devil and his minions.

The faithful in Asia Minor, moreover, are not to think that they alone are ones who suffer innocently for their faith and estrangement. Not only does such suffering unite them with the suffering Christ; it also unites them with their estranged brothers and sisters in the faith throughout the world. In this solidarity there is strength for the concerted opposition to evil, demonic and human. This suffering, furthermore, is only "for a brief time" and will end shortly (v 10), given the nearness of the end of the ages (4:7), the commencement of judgment (4:17; cf. 4:5), and the imminence of the Lord's appearance (5:1c, 4; cf. 1:5, 7, 13). In the meantime, the addressees can trust in the care and power of God (vv 6–7, 10–11) and in the certainty that the God who called them to his eternal glory will restore, establish, and strengthen them. In their engagement with evil (vv 8–9), they are surrounded by the care and support of God (vv 6–7, 10), as the structure of these verses so graphically indicates.

A final doxology extolling the power of God (v 11) appropriately brings to an end the body of this letter, so focused on the glorification of God (2:9, 12; 4:11, 16), and balances the note of praise (1:3–5) with which the letter began.

For studies on 1 Pet 5:5b–11, see Bergh 1784; Boismard 1961, 133–63; E. F. Brown 1907; Dumas 1970; Giaquinta 1980; Golebiewski 1965; Harris 1919; Ogara 1936a; Quinn 1965; Richardson 1987; Schwank 1962a.

EPISTOLARY POSTSCRIPT (5:12–14)

5:12a Through Silvanus, the faithful brother,
12b as I regard [him],
12c I have written briefly to you,
12d exhorting and witnessing fully
that this is the dependable grace of God.
12e Stand fast in it!
13a The co-elect [brotherhood] in Babylon sends you greetings;
13b and [so does] Mark, my son.
14a Greet one another with the kiss of love.
14b Peace to all of you who are in Christ.

INTRODUCTION

The letter, now completed, is brought to a close with the identification and commendation of its bearer, Silvanus (v 12ab), a succinct statement regarding its aim (v 12c), the sending of fraternal greetings from the brotherhood in Rome, including Mark (v 13), the urging of a gesture of familial affection (v 14a), and a wish for peace (v 14b). The pattern and features of this postscript are similar to those of the Pauline letters and, like those missives, vary from the briefer postscripts of conventional Greco-Roman letters, which simply contain a final wish ("live well," *errōsthe*; cf. 2 Macc 11:21, 33; Acts 15:29) and the letter's date.[769] The terminology and fraternal tone here match that of the letter as a whole. As the epistolary postscript, it balances the letter's prescript (1:1–2) and its terminology ("Peter"/"I," "elect"/"co-elect," "strangers in the Diaspora"/ "Babylon," "peace"). Prescript and postscript form an epistolary inclusion framing the letter as a whole and demonstrate the epistolary genre of this composition.

The reiteration of additional earlier terminology and concepts further indicates the conceptual and literary coherence of this postscript with the remainder of the letter ("faithful" [v 12a; cf. 4:19]; "brother" [v 12a; cf. "brotherhood," 2:17; 5:9; "brotherly love," 1:22; 3:8]; "exhorting" [v 12d; cf. 2:11; 5:1]; "witnessing fully" [v 12d; cf. "witness," 5:1b]; "true" [v 12d; cf. "truth," 1:22]; "grace of God" [v 12d; cf. 1:10, 13; 3:7; 4:10; 5:5, 10]; "son" [v 13b; cf. "children," 1:14; 3:16]; "one another" [v 14; cf. 1:22; 4:9; 5:5]). There are no compelling linguistic or literary grounds, therefore, for seeing in these verses a secondary addition of material by a later redactor (against von Harnack 1897, 451–65; Marxsen 1979; and others) or a literary fiction simply serving the purposes of pseudonymity (against Brox 1986, 240–41).

[769] On epistolary postscripts and conventions, see Roller 1933, 68–70, 114–16, 481–88; Koskenniemi 1956; J. L. White 1972, 1983, 1986; Doty 1973, 39–40; K. Berger 1974; Schnider and Stenger 1987, 108–67.

NOTES

5:12a–c. *Through Silvanus, the faithful brother, as I regard [him], I have written briefly to you (Dia Silouanou hymin tou pistou adelphou, hōs logizomai, di' oligōn egrapsa).* With these words, the courier of the letter is identified and commended to the addressees.

Silvanus. Except for the brief commendation that follows, nothing further is said of this person, thus suggesting that he was known to the addressees. Paul's letters also mention a person named Silvanus, who accompanied Paul on his mission to certain regions of Asia Minor and Greece, and who is identified, along with Paul and Timothy, as co-author of the letters of 1 and 2 Thessalonians (2 Cor 1:19; 1 Thess 1:1; 2 Thess 1:1). Since these are the only occurrences of the name *Silvanus* in the NT, it is likely that they refer to one and the same person. In Acts, as most scholars agree, this person is identified as "Silas," a Grecized form of the Aramaic *Šĕʾîlāʾ*, the name by which Silvanus was earlier known in the Jerusalem community (Acts 15:22, 25–27). In regions of the Diaspora to which the letters of Paul and 1 Peter were addressed, this companion of Paul referred to as Silas in Acts (16:19, 25, 29; 17:4–15; 18:5) was also known as *Silouanos*, a like-sounding Grecized form of the Latin name *Silvanus*.[770] Bigg (1902, 84) conjectures that "Silvanus or one of his ancestors [was once a slave who] had been manumitted by one or other of the Roman [family] Silvani," but he provides no support for this supposition.

In Acts, Silas/Silvanus and his colleague Judas Barsabbas are identified as "leading men among the brothers" of the Jerusalem church (15:22) and "prophets" (15:32). As men of high prestige in Jerusalem, they were commissioned to deliver to the church of Antioch the letter conveying the decision of the Jerusalem church validating Paul's mission to the Gentiles (15:22–34). Thereafter, Silas/Silvanus was chosen by Paul as his associate on his journey to Asia Minor and Greece (15:40–18:21; 18:23–23:35), and in 2 Cor 1:19 he is mentioned as a cofounder of the Corinthian church. Acts indicates that Silas/Silvanus also possessed Roman citizenship (16:37) but records nothing of his further activity following his work with Paul. His earlier association with Peter and Mark in Jerusalem (Acts 15; cf. also 12:12–17) could have provided the stimulus for a later resumption of this association in Rome, a situation against which nothing in the historical record would argue. What *is* explicit in the NT evidence is his high standing in the early Jerusalem community, his later service with Paul as a missionary to areas of the Diaspora, including Asia Minor, and finally, his collaboration with Peter and Mark in Rome.[771]

---

[770] On Silas/Silvanus, with differing views of his role in 1 Peter, see Seufert 1885b; Strahan 1918; Rademacher 1926; Barnikol 1931; Selwyn 1947, 9–17, 241–42; Best 1971, 55–59; Elliott 1980; 1981/1990, 270–80; Gillman 1992. See also below.

[771] A 2d- or 3d-century Gnostic writing bearing the name *Silvanus* is contained in the Nag Hammadi library, *The Teachings of Silvanus* (NHC VII:84,15–118,7), though the identity of this figure is unclear. Apart from NHC VII:89.16–17 (cf. 1 Pet 5:7) and 91.19 (cf. 1 Pet 5:8), this Gnostic text bears little resemblance to 1 Peter or the letters of Paul; cf. Peel and Zandee 1972.

The Petrine phrase *dia Silouanou*, "through Silvanus," belongs with the following words, "I have written briefly to you," with v 12b forming an intervening commendation. This phrase has figured prominently in the debate over the letter's authorship, with many scholars taking it to identify Silvanus as the secretary or *amanuensis* of a letter dictated by Peter or of a communication incorporating Peter's thought (see below). This hypothesis was advanced first in modern times in response to growing doubts about the direct Petrine authorship of this letter. A decisive body of evidence, however, indicates that in this phrase Silvanus is instead identified as the *courier* or *emissary* of the letter. This position is held both by scholars favoring Peter as author[772] and by those favoring the letter's pseudonymity.[773]

The construction "I/we have written through X" (*egrapsa/egrapsamen dia* + Name) was a conventional formula for identifying *not* the secretary of a letter but *its bearer* or *courier*. This epistolary convention is attested frequently in papyrus letters,[774] and a virtually identical expression occurs in yet other letters. The letter of a certain Serapion addressed to Herakleides states: "I sent (*epempsa*) two other letters to you, one through Nedymos (*dia Nēdymou mian*) and one through Kronios (*dia Kroniou*)" (CPJud 2.152 [= BGU 4.1079]; see also PAmh. 2.131, lines 21–23; PMich. 8.481, lines 8–10). The formula employed in 1 Peter also appears in later Christian letters to identify their couriers; see Ignatius' letters to the Romans ("Now I am writing these things to you from Smyrna through the blessed Ephesians," *dia Ephesiōn*, 10:1); to the Philadelphians ("I am writing [from Troas] to you through Burrhus [*dia Bourrou*], who was sent with me by the Ephesians and Smyrneans as a mark of honor," 11:2); and to the Smyrneans ("I am writing [from Troas] to you through Burrhus (*dia Bourrou*), whom you together with the Ephesians your brothers sent with me, and he has in every way refreshed me," 12:1). See also Polycarp's letter to the Philippians ("I have written this to you through Crescens [*per Crescentum*], whom I commended to you when I was present and now commend again. For he has behaved blamelessly among us and I believe that he will do the same with you," 14:1).[775] A similar formula employed in Acts 15:23 (*grapsantes dia cheiros autōn*) also refers to Silvanus as courier of a letter and is discussed below.

Some scholars (J. N. D. Kelly 1969, 215; Davids 1990, 198; Goppelt 1993, 369) cite one rare case in which the *dia* formula identifies an author of a letter; namely, a letter by Dionysus of Corinth (in Eusebius, *Hist. eccl.* 4.23.11), in

[772] E.g., Stegmann 1917, 21–32; Schlatter 1937, 174–75; Selwyn 1947, 241; Dalton 1990, 908.

[773] E.g., Smothers 1926–1927, 419; Schrage 1973, 62–64; Elliott 1981/1990, 267–95; 1982, 64–66, 113–14; Brox 1975, 84–90; 1986, 241–43.

[774] See, e.g., PWisc. 2.69, lines 4–5; CPR 6.80, lines 9–10; PMich. 8.466, lines 6–8; 14.751, lines 4–7; POxy. 42.3067, lines 4–5; 939; PAnt. 94, line 8.

[775] See also *Mart. Pol.* 20:1 and a Christian papyrus letter of the 1st century (Milligan 1910, 39). For further, numerous texts illustrating this convention, see also Llewelyn and Kearsley, eds. 1992–1994, 7:54.

which Clement is identified as the author of *1 Clement* (*tēn proteran hymin dia Klēmentos graphein*). Regarding Clement as having written "under the commission of and in keeping with the desires of the church in Rome," Goppelt suggests that "something corresponding to this is said here of Silvanus." But this exceptional case from the 2d century is outweighed by the vast preponderance of instances in which the *dia* formula indicates the bearer rather than the author of letters. Hence, *dia Silouanou* is best understood as indicating Silvanus as the courier rather than the author or "drafter" (J. N. D. Kelly) of 1 Peter.[776]

This letter-bearing role of Silvanus in 1 Peter is akin to the role he played in Jerusalem, where he and Judas Barsabbas were chosen to deliver the letter from the Jerusalem church to the church of Antioch (Acts 15). According to this account, "apostles and elders with the whole church" prepared a letter addressed to the Gentile believers in Antioch, Syria, and Cilicia (15:23) and, selecting Judas called Barsabbas and Silas, "wrote through their hand" (*grapsantes dia cheirou autōn*, 15:23; compare *dia Silouanou*). Thereafter, "when they were sent off, they went down to Antioch and, having gathered the congregation together, they delivered the letter (*epedōkan tēn epistolēn*)" (15:30). The context makes it clear that the phrase *grapsantes dia cheirou autōn* identifies Judas and Silas not as the authors but as the couriers of the Jerusalem letter, a sense accurately conveyed by the RSV: "they sent Judas . . . and Silas . . . with the following letter." The similar expression, *dia Silouanou . . . egrapsa*, in 1 Pet 5:12 has the same sense.[777] With the elimination of the chief textual basis for the hypothesis that *dia Silouanou* designates Silvanus as the secretary of the letter, there is little else to commend it. While Paul (Rom 16:22), Pliny (*Ep*. 9.36), and others used secretaries on occasion,[778] this was not the role of Silvanus in 1 Peter.

N. Brox (1975a, 87–88; 1978b, 111; 1986, 241–43), while correctly understanding *dia Silouanou* to indicate Silvanus as the bearer not secretary of the letter, views this phrase, nonetheless, as part of the "fictional apparatus" of 1 Peter, with the choice of Silvanus perhaps reflective of a tradition linking

[776] Other NT letters also contain references to their couriers: 1 Cor 4:17 appears to identify Timothy as the bearer of 1 Corinthians. 2 Corinthians was brought by Titus and an unnamed brother (2 Cor 8:16–19; 9:3–5), while Titus may have been the bearer of the earlier, painful letter (2 Cor 2:12–13; 7:6–13). Tychicus and Onesimus served as the bearers of Colossians (4:7–9) and Tychicus, the courier of Ephesians (6:21–22). Epaphroditus was the bearer of Philippians (2:25–30). Zenas the lawyer and Apollos were the bearers of the letter to Titus (3:13). Romans 16:1–2 commends Phoebe, possibly the bearer of the letter, with the request that she be received and helped. On letter-carriers in the early church, see M. R. P. McGuire 1960; Llewelyn and Kearsley, eds. 1992–1994, 7:50–57.

[777] Beare's opposition to Silvanus as courier (1970, 209) rests solely on the supposition that a single courier would require "months or even years to accomplish such a task," an exaggeration left unsupported.

[778] See Doty 1973, 41; cf. also Roller 1933; E. R. Richards 1991; on co-authorship, see Murphy O'Connor 1993.

Peter with Silvanus (cf. also Brox 1975, 89–90). However, he provides no evidence for this alleged tradition and offers no compelling argument against seeing in the name *Silvanus* a reference to the *actual* bearer of the letter. On the face of the available evidence, it is just as likely that these words identify the *actual* courier, as is discussed below. Other scholars suspected that reference to a fictive Silvanus was prompted by the author's desire to link the letter with Paul, Pauline tradition, or Pauline Asia Minor communities (e.g., Barnikol 1931, 18; Trilling 1971, 122–23; Schrage and Balz 1973, 60). This idea of Silvanus as "mediator," however, rested on the invalid assumption, going back to F. C. Baur, that the aim of 1 Peter was to unify Petrine and Pauline poles in the Church, an assumption convincingly refuted by Brox (1978b, 116–19). When the integrity of 1 Peter was doubted and its inclusion of a baptismal homily was assumed, the mention of Silvanus was taken as a reference to the original homilist (Bornemann 1919–1920). Since, however, the homily theory is untenable, and *dia Silouanou* indicates a different role for Silvanus, this theory too has no merit.

In sum, the textual evidence concerning the epistolary use of the *dia* formula makes it virtually certain that *dia Silouanou* identifies Silvanus as the *courier* of the letter. There is no cogent evidence, however, that the name was simply part of the "device of pseudonymity" (against Beare 1970, 48–50 as well as Brox). The NT evidence that is available suggests that the Silvanus in 5:12 was the historical Silvanus, a former leading member of the Jerusalem church, and erstwhile colleague of Paul. Having subsequently joined Peter and Mark in Rome (see below) and belonging to the Petrine circle responsible for the composition of 1 Peter, he was the one who brought the letter to the various Christian communities of Asia Minor.

the faithful brother (*tou pistou adelphou*). Affirming the reliability of Silvanus as a *faithful brother*, this comment serves to commend the courier to the communities he will be visiting. The genitive *tou pistou adelphou* accords with the genitive of the name *Silouanou*, which it modifies. "Brother" (*adelphos*) identifies Silvanus as a fellow-believer, a "soul brother," "one of our own." "Brother" and "sister" are used frequently in the NT as designations for the believers (e.g., 133× in the Pauline and Deutero-Pauline letters; 10× in Hebrews; 19× in James; 20× in 1–3 John).[779] They belong to the broad group of familial terms used regularly by the followers of Jesus to depict the movement as a family-like community, with family-like relations and obligations. This sense of believers' constituting a surrogate family of faith is traceable to the comment by Jesus that "whoever does the will of God is my brother, and sister, and mother" (Mark 3:35; cf. Matt 12:50; and Luke 8:21). Paul also employed "brother" and "sister," often as terms for his co-workers and colleagues

[779] On the meaning and use of the term "brother," see Schelkle 1954; von Soden 1964; Horsley 1981–1989, 4:250–55.

in leadership.[780] As applied to Silvanus, "brother" could convey either or both of these senses, thereby identifying Silvanus as both a fellow-believer and an associate in ministry. This use of "brother" is especially appropriate in this letter, where the root metaphor for the community as a whole is "brotherhood" (2:17; 5:9, 13) and "household" or family of God (2:5; 4:17), where Mark is characterized as "son" (5:13), and where so much stress is laid on "brotherly (and sisterly) love" (1:22; 3:8; cf. 2:11; 4:8, 12).

faithful (*pistos*). This word affirms Silvanus's reliability and trustworthiness. The adjective is used with this sense for God, in 4:19. For its use in commendations of other Christian co-workers, see also Eph 6:21 and Col 4:7, 9.

12b. *as I regard* [*him*] (*hōs logizomai*), literally, "as I think," "in my opinion," or "by my reckoning" (cf. 1 Cor 4:1; Rom 8:18). This further qualification of Silvanus, with "him" implied, is part of the personal endorsement on the author's part (supposedly Peter) of Silvanus's trustworthiness and reliability. The verb *logizomai* is used for acts of reckoning, calculating, evaluating, estimating, and opining (BAGD 476). Silvanus's commendation here, which parallels other commendations of emissaries of Christian letters,[781] assures the recipients that this trusted brother knew the mind of the apostle and would expound the letter faithfully (Bigg 1902, 195; Selwyn 1947, 242). It likely was also intended to secure for Silvanus the hospitality he would require, a hospitality such as is urged in 4:9. This commendation poses another fatal problem for those who regard Silvanus as the actual author of the letter, for this would then constitute a bizarre form of self-commendation without parallel in the literature.

In addition to delivering the letter, Silvanus would also serve as representative of the community sending the letter, clarifying and perhaps supplementing its content with encouragement of his own. This would be similar to his activity in delivering the letter of the Apostolic Council to the church in Antioch, as narrated in Acts 15:22–34: "We have therefore sent Judas and Silas (cf. 15:22), who themselves will tell you the same things by word of mouth (15:27) . . . they delivered the letter (15:31) . . . and Judas and Silas, who were themselves prophets, exhorted the brothers with many words and strengthened them" (15:32). This practice of letter-couriers' supplementing the content of the letters they delivered with words of their own apparently was conventional in the early Church.[782] As emissary, Silvanus would also gather information

---

[780] See, e.g., 1 Cor 16:19; 2 Cor 2:13; 2 Cor 8:23; 9:5; 12:18; Phil 2:25; 4:21; cf. also Acts 16:1; 17:14; Eph 6:21; Col 4:7; 2 Tim 4:21; and E. E. Ellis 1971.

[781] See Rom 16:1–2; 1 Cor 4:17; 2 Cor 8:16–19, 23; Eph 6:21–22; Col 1:7–8, 4:7–9; Ign. *Rom.* 10:1; *Smyrn.* 11:1.

[782] "Chloe's people," who probably delivered a letter from the Corinthians to Paul (1 Cor 1:11), also added further information orally (1 Cor 1:11). The same is true of the courier of Ephesians, Tychicus, whose function and commendation are similar to those of Silvanus: "Now, that you also may know how glad I am and what I am doing, Tychicus the beloved *brother* and *faithful* servant

from his journey that could then be shared with the community in Rome (cf. *1 Clem.* 65:1). On the whole, he would thus play a vital role in strengthening the personal ties uniting the brotherhood in Asia Minor and the brotherhood in Rome.

The "I" involved in the verb "I regard," along with "I have written" (v 12c) and "I exhort" (2:11; 5:1), are the four instances in which the inscribed author, Peter (1:1), speaks directly in the first-person singular to the audience; see also the reference to Mark as "*my* son" (5:13). As the foremost figure in whose name the letter was written, "Peter" speaks in his own voice, and with his personal authority confirms the reliability of its bearer, Silvanus.

12c. *I have written briefly to you* (*hymin . . . di' oligōn egrapsa*). The verb *egrapsa* is an epistolary aorist ("I have written," "I am writing").[783] Its aorist mood is consistent with the aorist of verbs referring to the "sending" or "going" of the letter-bearer.[784]

briefly (*di' oligōn*). Those who imagine 1 Peter to be a composite writing maintain that this reference to brevity does not fit a letter of 105 verses and thus can refer only to the "appended" section, 4:12–5:11. The claim, however, is unpersuasive. 1 Peter has fewer words (1,669) than Ephesians (2,425) and far fewer than Hebrews (4,942), where similar remarks about brevity occur (*en oligōi*, Eph 3:3; *dia braxeōn*, Heb 13:22). Brevity in letter-writing was a sign of authorial respect for the hearers'-readers' patience and hence was duly noted.[785] While comment on one's brevity was a rhetorical convention (cf. Acts 24:4), "the author might also have had in mind the vastness of the subjects he has tackled. How much more could have been said!" (Hillyer 1992, 151; cf. Beare 1970, 209). Silvanus, however, would supplement it with further words of his own; hence, his commendation. NT letters are replete with such authorial references to the act of writing itself.[786]

The "I/you" underscores the personal relation between sender and addressees. The establishment and maintenance of a personal relation between writer and reader (*philophronesis*), making a writer present to an audience (*parousia*), and inscribed communication (*homilia*) are three components of a genuine letter (Koskenniemi 1956, 35–47). The presence of all three features here is further confirmation that 1 Peter constitutes a genuine letter. This letter is

---

in the Lord will tell you everything. I have sent him for this very purpose, that you may know how we are, and that he may encourage your hearts" (Eph 6:21–22).

[783] For this epistolary aorist, see also Rom 15:15; Phlm 19, 21; 1 John 2:21, 26; 5:13; also 1 Macc 15:19; 2 Macc 2:16; *Mart. Pol.* 1:1 (*egrapsamen*); cf. Robertson 1919, 845–46.

[784] See 1 Cor 4:17; 2 Cor 8:17, 18; Eph 6:22; Phil 2:28; Col 4:8; Phlm 12; *1 Clem.* 63:3; cf. BDF 334.

[785] See also Ign. *Rom.* 8:2; *Pol.* 7:3; *Barn.* 1:5; Isoc., *Ep.* 2.13; 8:10; Pliny, *Ep.* 3.9.27 and K. Berger 1974, 227; Schnider and Stenger 1987, 110.

[786] See also Acts 13:23; Rom 15:15; 16:22; 1 Cor 5:9, 11; 14:37; 2 Cor 1:13; 2:3, 4, 9; 7:12; 9:1; 13:10; Gal 1:20; 6:11; Phil 3:1; 1 Thess 4:9; 5:1; 2 Thess 3:17; 1 Tim 3:14; Phlm 19, 21; 2 Pet 3:1; 1 John 1:4; 2:1, 7, 8, 12, 13 (2×), 14 (3×), 21, 26; 5:13; 2 John 5, 12; 3 John 9, 13 (2×); Jude 3 (2×); cf. Rev 2:1, 8, 12, 18; 3:1, 7, 14.

just one of numerous written communiqués by which separated groups of the early Christian movement established and maintained contact and thereby fortified the bond of communal solidarity.[787]

The stated purpose of 1 Peter expressed in the following words (v 12def) is fully consistent with the mood, style, and message of the letter in its totality. It is a message of exhortation and witness concerning the grace of God of which the letter speaks and its dependability.

12d. *exhorting and witnessing fully* (*parakalōn kai epimartyrōn*). This succinct concluding statement of the aim of the letter involves two pres. participles modifying "I have written," the first of which is used absolutely. Both participles recall the content of 5:1. The participle *parakalōn* ("exhorting") reprises the use of the verb in 2:11 and 5:1 and aptly characterizes the hortatory thrust of the letter as a whole. It has the sense of "encourage" more than "command," belongs to the hortatory tradition of the early Church, and is employed frequently in NT letters[788] as well as sermonic addresses (Acts 13:15; Heb 13:22). Bjerkelund (1967) notes that the verb is a diplomatic term used to exhort in a fraternal manner.

The second participle, *epimartyrōn* ("witnessing fully"), is an intensified form of *martyreō* ("to bear witness, "attest," "testify") and occurs only here in the NT (cf. *synepimartyreō*, Heb 2:4). It has the sense of "bear full (*epi-*) witness (*martyrōn*)," "fully attest" something to be factual and true.[789] The use of this verb accords with the author's identification of himself as a "witness" (*martys*) in 5:1. Danker (1982, 442–48) points out that *martyreō* and its paronyms frequently are used in connection with attesting to the benefactions of generous patrons. Its association here with the grace or patronal favor of God is thus fitting. With his authoritative witness, the author thus confirms the proclamation of those who first announced the good news to the addressees in an earlier time (1:12). The suffering that had followed their conversion, the author assures them, in no way puts into question the divine grace by which their lives are changed and blessed.

that this is the dependable grace of God (*tautēn einai alēthē charin tou theou*). This object of the preceding participle *epimartyrōn* is another accusative (*tautēn*)-with-infinitive (*einai*) construction (cf. also 5:9). Literally it reads, "(witnessing) this to be the dependable grace of God." This construction of the accusative + infinitive with verbs of speaking occurs frequently in the NT[790]

---

[787] On the extensive exchange of letters and literature in early Christianity beyond the NT, see von Harnack 1908/1962, 369–80. On letters, including those by Christians, in the Greco-Roman world, their structure, conventions, and conveyance, see J. L. White 1972, 1983; 1986, 187–220; Llewelyn and Kearsley, eds. 1992–1994, 7:48–57.

[788] See Rom 12:1; 15:30; 16:17; 1 Cor 1:10; 4:16; 2 Cor 10:1; Eph 4:1; Phil 4:2; Col 2:2; 1 Thess 4:1; 1 Tim 2:1; Phlm 9, 10.

[789] See Neh 9:29, 30; and *T. Reu.* 1:6, "I call the God of heaven to bear full witness to you this day."

[790] See Mark 8:27/Matt 16:13; Mark 8:29/Matt 16:15; Mark 12:18/Matt 22:23; Mark 14:64; John 12:29; Acts 12:14; Rom 3:9; cf. BDF §397,3.

(for its use with paronyms of *epimartyreō*, see Acts 10:43; 18:5; Eph 4:17; 1 Thess 2:12).

In this compact statement, it is not immediately clear to what the demonstrative pronoun "this" (*tautēn*) refers. Some take the demonstrative pronoun to refer to the letter itself ("this letter") or its chief point.[791] The term *epistolē* ("letter") is a feminine noun, to which the feminine pronoun *tautēn* could refer, but *epistolē* is not present here, and its implied presence is far from clear. Reicke (1964, 133) takes "this" to refer to the suffering experienced by the believers. Brox (1986, 244–45) attempts to support this by claiming a parallel here to the formulation in 2:19–20, where he sees *charis* explained (*touto charis* . . .) as bearing undeserved suffering. But the similarity is more apparent than real. The demonstrative pronouns are different (*touto* in 2:19, 20; *tautē* here in 5:12d), and 2:19–20 reflects a specific tradition (see NOTE) in which *charis* means God's "approval" of human action. In the present verse, on the other hand, and the immediate context (5:10), *charis* means the "grace" initially or finally conferred by God as benevolent gift, not approval. Moreover, there is no mention of suffering in 5:12 and, without any connection to 2:19–20, no reason to see it implied here, as Davids (1990, 200) aptly notes. It is more likely that *tautēn*, a fem. sing. demonstrative, has as its antecedent the proximate fem. sing. noun *charis* ("grace") in v 10, which has the same meaning as the following noun *charis* in v 12d and the other instances of *charis* throughout the letter other than 2:19–20. The point being made is that *this* ("grace," v 10) is the *dependable grace of God* (v 12d) that envelops the believers, sustains them, and constitutes the basis for their hope.

grace of God (*charin tou theou*).[792] The phrase refers to the lavish favor of "the God of all grace" (5:10), which believers experience in the present (1:2; 4:10, 14; cf. 1:10) and anticipate enjoying fully at Christ's return (1:6; 3:7; 5:5) as a consequence of their calling by God and union with Jesus Christ. This grace "of," or "from" (so Michaels 1988, 305), God is emphasized from the beginning of the letter to its close (1:2, 10, 13; 3:7; 4:10; 5:5, 10). As in Greek parlance generally, "grace" is virtually synonymous with "glory" (*doxa*, 1:7, 11, 21; 4:11, 13, 14; 5:1, 4, 10), "praiseworthiness" (*aretē*, 2:9), and "honor (*timē*, 1:7; 2:7; 3:7; 5:10; cf. *entimos*, 2:4, 6), all of which in this letter are attributes of God, Christ, and God's elect people. The Paul of Acts summarizes his ministry with a similar expression: "to witness to the good news of the grace of God" (Acts 20:24).

dependable (*alēthē*). The adjective *alēthēs*, when used of things, means "true," "genuine" (cf. the noun *alētheia*, "truth" in 1:22). Often, however, it describes something that, because truthful and genuine, is therefore "dependable" (Josephus, *Ant.* 4.219; John 5:31–32; 21:24; Titus 1:13; 3 John 12), and this sense is conceivable here as well. Ultimately these senses converge. The

---

[791] E.g., Bigg 1902, 196; Berger 1974, 192–93; Michaels 1988, 309–10; Davids 1990, 200.

[792] The definite article accompanying "God" is lacking in some MSS (𝔓[72] Ψ and some cursives), but its original presence is favored by the majority of MSS (including א A B).

author, as a "witness" (5:1b), whose function is to bear testimony to the truth, assures his audience of the truth of God's grace. At the same time, the grace of God to which he points throughout the letter is a reality upon which the beleaguered community can continually depend.

12e. *Stand fast in it!* (*eis hēn stēte*). The relation of this clause to the foregoing words is difficult to state with certainty. Several factors are involved in determining whether it is best translated "in which you stand" or "stand fast in it." As J. N. D. Kelly (1969, 217) has noted, the preceding expression, "this . . . grace," "almost asks to be defined by a relative [indicative] clause, and 'in which you stand' would fill this gap admirably," whereas an imperative at this point seems abrupt. Certain manuscripts (K L P 𝔐 majority of minuscules and versions), perhaps sensing this abruptness, replaced *stēte* with *hestēkate* ("you stand"); others substitute *este* ("you are," 1505 2495 and syr^{h}) or *aiteite* ("you seek," Ψ). However, *stēte*, an intransitive 2d-person pl. 2d aor. imperative or hortatory subjunctive of *histēmi* ("stand fast, firm," "hold one's ground"), has superior textual attestation (𝔓^{72} ℵ A B and others). The variants are clearly secondary efforts at providing a smoother reading or at accommodating this formulation to the similar expression in Rom 5:2. There, however, the verb is not *stēte* but the perfect *hestēkamen* ("through him we have obtained access to *this grace in which we stand*," *eis tēn charin tautēn en hēi hestēkamen*), a formulation similar to 2 Cor 1:24 ("you stand firm in your faith," *tēi gar pistei hestēkate*). A few scholars, nevertheless, take this Petrine clause as an indicative statement (e.g., Spicq 1966, 178; Frankemölle 1987, 70).

On the other hand, in the only other NT instance in which the form *stēte* appears, Eph 6:14, it has *imperatival* force, calling for resolutely holding one's ground: "stand fast, therefore, having girded your loins with truth." Thus, the imperatival force of the verb and its parallel use in Eph 6:14 in a similar hortatory context favor regarding v 12e as an independent imperative statement but joined to v 12d through "it" (*hēn*), which has "grace" (v 12d) as its antecedent. This is the position held by the majority of commentators.[793]

The phrase *eis hēn* ("in it") involves, as in 3:20d (see NOTE), a use of the preposition *eis* (usually indicating direction) where *en* (indicating locality) would have been expected.[794] This is a development typical of the vernacular Greek of this period (Robertson 1919, 591–93; BDF §205); for *eis hēn* used in this fashion, see also Acts 7:4. Reicke's translation (1964, 132), "*in view of it* remain steadfast," is not supported by the use of *eis hēn* elsewhere. In several NT instances, the verb *histēmi* occurs with a prepositional phrase involving *en* rather than *eis* to indicate in what one stands firm (Rom 5:2 [grace]; 1 Cor 15:1

---

[793] E.g., Bigg 1902, 196; Selwyn 1947, 243; Reicke 1964, 133; J. N. D. Kelly 1969, 213, 217; Best 1971, 177; Brox 1986, 240; Michaels 1988, 305, 308; Davids 1990, 201. Goppelt's rendition "so that you may stand in it" (1993, 367, 373) is somewhat misleading, since it conveys a tentativeness ("may stand") that is hardly intended in the original Greek.

[794] For this use of *eis*, see also Mark 13:3, 9, 16; 14:60; Luke 6:8; John 20:7, 19, 26; Acts 2:27, 31; 7:4, 9, 12; 8:40; 21:13, 17; 23:11; Rom 5:2; Heb 11:9.

[the gospel]; 16:1 [the faith]; Phil 4:1 [the Lord]; cf. Pol. *Phil* 10:1). Here it is the dependable grace of God in which believers are directed to stand fast. This imperative, typifying a feature of the author's "exhorting" (*parakalōn*), is akin to the imperative in 5:9 to resist the Devil and remain firm in faith.

In this verse the author succinctly condenses the heart of his message: those who have been reborn to new life through the resurrection of Jesus Christ and incorporated into the family of faith are what they are by the grace of God. Until their final salvation, they must now live in and through this grace as the graced people of God. Their challenge is to stand fast in the divine grace that shapes their past, their present, and their future.

This explicit indication of the letter's aim makes it clear that its purpose can hardly have been to establish a theological consensus between "Petrine and Pauline wings" of the church, as some scholars have argued (for discussion and critique, see Brox 1978b; 1986, 50–51). If this had been the goal of this letter, our author failed grievously in making this clear. Not only is there no mention whatsoever of Paul (compare 2 Pet 3:15), as would have been required in an *Unionsdokument* and effort at theological "reconciliation"; even more telling is the complete absence of the emphases typical of Pauline theology (justification by faith, freedom from the Mosaic Law, the relation of the Church and Israel, etc.) as well as any effort at "reconciling" them with features of Petrine tradition. The letter's aim, as indicated here and as is evident throughout the letter, is a pastoral not a dogmatic one. Its intention is to reassure suffering believers of God's sustaining grace and to motivate them to an honorable yet distinctive way of life worthy of their identity as the household of God.

Having summarized the purpose of his writing, our author now adds personal greetings from those with him, a conventional feature of letters as media of *personal* communication.

13a. *The co-elect [brotherhood] in Babylon sends you greetings* (*Aspazetai hymas hē en Babylōni syneklektē*). The inclusion of greetings (*Aspazetai hymas*) from associates at a letter's close is conventional and is found in the letters of Paul as well,[795] as is reference to sharing a kiss[796] and a peace wish[797] or a benediction.[798] "The co-elect" (*hē . . . syneklektē*) is the first mentioned among those sending greetings. The composite term *syneklektē* ("co-elect," "fellow-chosen") occurs only here in the Greek Bible. Its choice and formation appear motivated by the theme of election that is so prominent in this letter. Just as the addressees are identified as "elect" in 1:1, so the community sending the letter is characterized as the "co-elect"; both groups are members of the all-encompassing elect and holy household of God (2:4–10). The composite formation (*syn-eklektē*) conveys the solidarity stressed here and elsewhere in the

[795] See 1 Cor 19:19–20a; 2 Cor 13:13; Phil 4:21–22; Rom 16:3–15.

[796] See 1 Thess 5:26; 1 Cor 16:20b; 2 Cor 13:12; Rom 16:16.

[797] See 1 Thess 5:23–24; 2 Cor 13:11b; Gal 6:16; Phil 4:7–9; Rom 15:33.

[798] See 1 Thess 5:28; 1 Cor 16:23–24; 2 Cor 13:14; Gal 6:18; Phil 4:23; Rom 16:20.

letter through the numerous similar *syn-* composites (*synoikeō, synklēronomos,* 3:7; *sympathēs,* 3:8; *syntrechō,* 4:4; *symbainō,* 4:12; *sympresbyteros,* 5:1).

With its feminine gender, this substantive could refer either to an unnamed female person ("she," "sister," "wife") or a collectivity of the feminine gender in Greek. Some translations render the term with a simple "she who is likewise elect/chosen" (RSV); others suppose a reference to a co-elect "sister" (*adelphē;* JB) or "sister-in-the-faith," just as Silvanus is identified figuratively as "brother" and Mark as "son." However, the anonymity of this person would be inconsistent with the explicit naming of Silvanus and Mark. This objection also argues against seeing here a reference to Peter's wife (*gynē;* cf. Mark 1:29–31 par.; 1 Cor 9:5), who according to Clement of Alexandria (*Strom.* 7.11) later suffered a martyr's death. If "wife" were implied (so Bengel 1742; Bigg 1902, 197; and a few others), "with me" rather than "in Babylon" would have been appropriate; "co-elect," moreover, implies a co-election with the *addressees,* not with the author. Why, moreover, would the author mention the names of Silvanus and Mark but not that of his own wife?

Similarly unconvincing on these and further grounds is the suggestion (Applegate 1992) that this was a reference to a woman well known to the audience, who was "a missionary and church leader in Asia Minor" and who was mentioned "to authorize the [letter's] household code because this code was expected to find resistance from women who were Christian leaders in Asia Minor" (1992, 604). Not only does this speculative proposal involve an undue preoccupation with the "household code" of the letter, but Applegate herself admits that in any case this woman would have been seen by the recipients as a "traitor" or one whose "title and reputation" were betrayed by those who misused her authority to sanction use of the household code (Applegate 1992, 604)—a situation that hardly would have won a receptive hearing for the letter.

The context, however, allows an implied collective term embracing a plurality of believers, and this would better parallel the plural term "elect" (persons) in 1:1. Most commentators and translators opt for the feminine term *ekklesia,* "church."[799] "Church" already was added in the ancient textual tradition (א a few other uncials vg^{mss} syr^{p} arm), but its inclusion lacks widespread manuscript attestation and must be regarded secondary. Even an implied *ekklēsia* is unlikely, since this term, though current in early Christianity, is noticeably absent in this letter. The expressions "elect lady," "elect sister" in 2 John 1, 13 refer to a community and/or its leader as elect but involve the term "elect" (*eklektē*) not "co-elect," *kyria* ("lady") and "sister" (*adelphē*), not *ekklēsia;* consequently, they offer no significant parallel, especially since "sister" and "lady" do not occur in 1 Peter. It is methodologically unsound to assume that a term is implied when it appears nowhere else in a writing.

---

[799] E.g., Jerome; KJV; Goodspeed; TEV; and NRSV ("your sister church"); Bigg, Selwyn, Kelly, Beare, Best, Brox, Michaels, Goppelt; cf. Reicke 1964, 133: "the congregation."

There is, however, another feminine collective term that in fact appears *only* in this letter, that admirably fits the context, and that appears to be the term implied here; namely, the noun *hē adelphotēs*, "brotherhood." "Brotherhood" as a designation for the believing community appears twice in 1 Peter, nearest in the preceding unit (5:9) and earlier in 2:17. Moreover, it is a term consistent with the metaphorical familial language in vv 12–14 ("brother," "son") as well as with the familial metaphors so characteristic of the letter as a whole. The fact that mention was made already of the brotherhood as worldwide (5:9) would allow for one branch of this brotherhood in Rome as well. Though the term appears nowhere else in the NT, it does appear in two other writings associated with Rome, *1 Clement* (2:4) and the Shepherd of Hermas (*Mand*. 8.10), its only uses in the Apostolic Fathers. T. W. Martin's preference (1992a, 145–46) for "Diaspora" (cf. 1:1) is unpersuasive, since it rests on the unconvincing claim that "the controlling metaphor of 1 Peter is the Diaspora" (1992, 144; cf. pp. 144–61) rather than the household of God and its related term "brotherhood."

With "brotherhood" as the term most likely implied here, it is then members of the co-elect brotherhood located in Rome (see below) that send their collective greetings to the fellow-elect (1:1) members of the brotherhood dispersed throughout Asia Minor. This greeting constitutes yet another reinforcement of the unity of senders and recipients, their common divine election, and their common membership in the worldwide brotherhood. 1 Corinthians 16:20 offers an interesting parallel in which a greeting from the *brothers* (and sisters) is immediately followed, as here, with a near-identical statement: "greet one another with a holy kiss."

in Babylon (*en Babylōni*). A few minuscules dating from the 9th century and beyond (4^{mg} 1518 2138) replace "Babylon" with "Rome." The substitution is clearly secondary, though reflective of the likely function of "Babylon" here as a figurative expression for Rome. Other theories regarding the identity of "Babylon," whether the term is taken literally (for sites in Mesopotamia or Egypt) or as a general allusion to a "place of exile," are mere speculations, with little to commend them (see Cullmann 1958, 82–86; D. W. O'Connor 1969, 15–18; and GENERAL INTRODUCTION, 8. Place of Composition).

Babylon in Mesopotamia, once capital of the great Babylonian Empire, was at this time a mere shadow of its former self. Toward the middle of the 1st century CE, Judeans resident there (Philo, *Legat*. 282; Josephus, *Ant*. 15.14, 39) had departed for the larger city of Seleucia (Josephus, *Ant*. 18.371–72).[800] By the time of Trajan's visit (115 CE) it was virtually desolate.[801] This location was first proposed by Erasmus and Calvin and later was favored by B. Weiss, Kühl, and Schlatter, but by few others. There is no evidence of any connection of Peter, Silvanus, or Mark with this Mesopotamian region. Nor was this

[800] On Judeans in Babylonia, see also Josephus, *Ant*. 11.131–33; 18.310–73; Neusner 1964; and Schürer 1973–1987, 3.1:5–13.

[801] See Pliny, *Nat*. 6.121–22; Dio Cass., *Hist. Rom*. 68.30.1; cf. also Strabo, *Geogr*. 16.739.

possibility envisioned in the early post-NT tradition; contrast the later, singular, highly suspect *Acts of Philip* (ca. 400 CE). Syriac tradition, closest in geographical location to this Babylon, connects Peter not with Babylon but with Rome.

Another place named *Babylon* was a small military stronghold located at the head of the Nile Delta in Egypt, near Memphis, a location favored by Manley (1944). According to Josephus (*Ant.* 2.315), this Babylon was founded by Cambyses when he subjugated Egypt. Strabo (*Geogr.* 17.1.30) knew it as a fortress founded by refugees from Mesopotamian Babylon, and Diodorus of Sicily (1.46.3), as a colony founded by Babylonian captive laborers in Egypt. In Strabo's day (early 1st century CE), it was the garrison of one of the three Roman legions in Egypt. This Babylon is identified with the Roman ruins in Old Cairo. Later Church tradition linked Mark with the Egyptian city of Alexandria (Eusebius, *Hist. eccl.* 2.16.1) as well as Rome, but there is no evidence or tradition linking either Peter or Silvanus with this Babylon of Egypt.

By contrast, the figurative identification of Rome as *Babylon* is widely attested in Israelite and Christian literature composed after the Roman conquest of Judea and destruction of Jerusalem in 70 CE (Hunzinger 1965) and the association of Peter (and Mark) with Rome as Babylon finds consistent and unquestioned attestation in subsequent Christian tradition. The association of Rome with Babylon builds on the memory of Babylon the Great as portrayed in the OT. The city of Babylon was the capital of the Neo-Babylonian Empire that in the 6th century BCE had defeated Judah and laid waste to Jerusalem and the Temple (2 Kgs 24–25; 2 Chr 36:17–21; Jer 20–21). Culminating in the year 587 BCE, this was a watershed event in Israel's history and a catastrophe from which it was never to fully recover. In the postexilic period, Babylon then became a symbol for the dominant world power in whose thrall the scattered people of God found themselves.[802] Half a millennium later, doleful history repeated itself. This time it was the armies of Rome under Vespasian and Titus who, as Babylonian armies once before, conquered Judea in 70 CE, devastated the Holy City, and razed the Temple, the physical symbol of Israel's national and religious identity. Thus, for Israel and the messianic movement it was inevitable that Rome, capital of the new world power and destroyer of Jerusalem, should be seen after 70 CE as a latter-day Babylon, and this equation is in fact found in Israelite and Christian writings composed after 70 CE. *2 Baruch* relates the events of 70 CE to 587 BCE as well as Rome to Babylon. Rome, the ravager of Zion, is addressed as "Babylon" (*2 Bar.* 11:1) and is alluded to again in 67:7: "But the king of Babylon will arise, the one who now has destroyed Zion, and he will boast over the people and speak haughtily in his heart before the Most High" (cf. also *2 Bar.* 79:1 and references to the displaced "brothers in Babylon," 77:12, 17, 19; 80:4). *4 Ezra* also equated these

[802] See Dan 1–5; Bel and the Dragon; *Prayer of Azariah*; Song of the Three Young Men; Susanna; Baruch; Epistle of Jeremiah; cf. Kuhn 1964.

events and denounced Rome under the symbol "Babylon" as the destroyer of Jerusalem (3:1–5:20; 10:19–48; 15:43–63; 16:1–34). Its eagle vision (11:1–12:51) reapplied the vision of Dan 7 and the affliction of God's people to Rome and the events of 66–70 CE. Similar equations occur in the *Sibylline Oracles* (5:137–78 regarding Rome-Babylon; 3:63–74 and 5:137–54 regarding Nero; cf. 3:303–13; see Galling and Altaner 1950, 1129). Josephus, writing after 70 CE, also related Rome's destruction of Jerusalem to the devastation of the city by the Babylonians as an illustration of the nonintervention of God when Israel depended on its own military might (*J.W.* 5.376–400). He also paralleled the two catastrophes by locating their occurrences on the same day of the same month, the 10th of Ab (*J.W.* 6.250–51). In the rabbinic literature, the Midrash on Lamentations (*Lam. Rab. Proem* 23) identified the legions of Nebuchadnezzar as the *Joviani* and *Decimani* (i.e., Roman-named legions); see also *Esth. Rab.* 1:19 (*Decimani* and *Augustiani* or *Joviani* and *Herculani*) and *Lam. Rab. Proem* 30, where the siege of Jersusalem by Nebuchadnezzar is said to have lasted 3.5 years, the length of time of the siege of Jerusalem conducted by Vespasian. The Midrash on Isa 47:1–2 in *Lam. Rab.* 1:13 applies equally well to Babylon and Rome (cf. also *b. Taʿan.* 29a; *b. ʿArak.* 11b; *S. ʿOlam Rab.* 30).[803]

Particularly for former Israelites within the messianic movement, Babylon as a symbol of Rome, the destroyer of Jerusalem and the Temple, would have recalled that notorious city of ancient memory that most poignantly epitomized power and conquest and the heart of Israel's Diaspora existence far from the homeland.[804] Writing in this same post-70 period, the author of Revelation also refers to Rome as "Babylon" (14:8; 16:19; 18:2, 10, 21) but with an anti-Roman animus not present in 1 Peter and likely reflective of developments subsequent to 1 Peter.

Further support for the equation of "Babylon" with Rome in 1 Pet 5:13 is provided by the early and consistent tradition in both the east and the west, which associates Peter and Mark with Rome, and identifies this city as the site of the final phase of Peter's ministry and his eventual death. Ancient Asian tradition, transmitted by Papias of Hierapolis, attests a final collaboration between Peter and Mark in Rome (in Eusebius, *Hist. eccl.* 2.15.2; 3.39.15). Commenting on 1 Pet 5:13, Papias (in Eusebius, *Hist. eccl.* 2.15.2) recorded that "Peter mentions Mark in his former epistle, which also it is said he composed at Rome itself, and he indicates the fact when he calls the city, somewhat metaphorically, 'Babylon' in these words: 'The co-elect that is in Babylon greets you, and so does Mark my son.'"[805] Peter's presence in Rome also is

[803] On the typological meaning of Babylon, see also Uhlig 1974. On the equation of Rome with Babylon (as symbol of luxury and intemperance) also in Roman sources, see Thiede 1986, 533–35.

[804] See 1 Chr 9:1; 2 Chr 36:20; Ps 137; Isa 12–13; 43:14–21; Jer 20:4–6; 24:1–7; 27; 50–51; Lamentations; Ezek 4–5; 7; 12:8–16; Mic 4:10; cf. Matt 1:11–12.

[805] For similar comments on 1 Pet 5:13, see also Clem. Alex., *Hyp.* 6 (in Eusebius, *Hist. eccl.* 2.15.2); Origen, *Comm. Matt.* 1 (in Eusebius, *Hist. eccl.* 6.25.5), and Jer., *Vir. ill.* 8.

implied in the letter by Ignatius of Antioch to the community at Rome, dispatched on his way to Rome (ca. 106 CE). Peter and Paul, he noted, were apostles who had the authority to command the Romans (Ign. *Rom.* 4:3), presupposing the apostles' presence in Rome. Although the messianic sect had already established itself in Rome prior to Paul's letter to the Romans (ca. 56–58 CE), a letter from Dionysius, bishop of Corinth, to Christians in Rome records the belief that Peter and Paul indeed had *founded* ("planted") the church at Rome as well as the one at Corinth (in Eusebius, *Hist. eccl.* 2.25.8, cited below). Irenaeus likewise speaks of "Peter and Paul . . . preaching at Rome and laying the foundations of the Church" (*Haer.* 3.1.5); see also the comment of Gaius, presbyter of Rome (preserved in Eusebius, *Hist. eccl.* 2.25.6–7).[806] Eusebius (*Hist. eccl.* 2.14.6) attests a notion that Peter first arrived in Rome during the reign of Claudius (41–54 CE), a date perhaps harmonized with the account of Peter's contending with Simon Magus in Rome (cf. Acts 8:9–24). According to Justin Martyr (*1 Apol.* 26), Simon Magus also came to Rome during the reign of Claudius. In Jerome's version of Eusebius's *Chronicle*, Peter is said to have arrived in Rome in the 2d year of Claudius (42 CE) and to have died with Paul in the 14th year of Nero (67–68 CE).[807] This notion of a 25-year stay of Peter in Rome is a later element of the tradition that falls far short of historical demonstration. However uncertain the beginning and length of Peter's time in Rome, the tradition is nonetheless unanimous in regard to his death there.

If, as is probable, Peter's martyrdom took place in connection with the great fire of Rome in 64 CE and Nero's execution of Christians as the purported arsonists,[808] his death occurred at some point in the period from 64 to 67 CE. Clement of Rome (ca. 96 CE), speaking of Christian martyrs (*1 Clem.* 5:2–6:2), mentions in one breath the *recent deaths* of Peter and Paul, "the good apostles" (5:3–7). Eusebius explicitly mentions the tradition connecting the deaths of Peter and Paul in Rome with Nero's persecution (*Hist. eccl.* 2.25.1–8, citing the testimony of Gaius, a Roman presbyter, and of Dionysius, bishop of Corinth, in his letter to the Roman Christians). The likely place of his execution was northwest of the city, beyond the Tiber, in the circus and gardens of Nero (Vatican Hill), where, according to Tacitus (*Ann.* 15.44), Nero put to death Christians held responsible for the burning of Rome (cf. also Eusebius, *Hist. eccl.* 2.25.5–7). Traditions vary regarding the location of his burial,

---

[806] On Peter in Rome, see also Tertullian (*Marc.* 4.5; *Bapt.* 4) and Origen (in Eusebius, *Hist. eccl.* 3.1.2–3); D. W. O'Connor 1969, 18–22; and Bauckham 1992a.

[807] Compare the Armenian version of the *Chronicle*, which lists Peter's arrival in Rome in the 3d year of Gaius (39 CE) and his death, with Paul, in the 13th year of Nero (66–67 CE); see the tables and discussion in Finegan 1964, 307–11. For later testimony, including Jerome (*Vir. ill.* 1, 5) and the *Liber Pontificalis*, the "Book of Popes," see D. W. O'Connor 1969, 27–35; and Finegan 1964, 311–15.

[808] On this combination of events, see Tac., *Ann.* 15.41, 44. Suetonius also mentions Nero's execution of Christians in Rome (*Nero* 16.2) but independently of his account of the fire (*Nero* 38.1–3).

although literary and archaeological evidence make it most likely that Peter was buried in the necropolis on Vatican Hill, the site of his execution.[809]

Just as the association of Peter with Rome supports the equation of "Babylon" (1 Pet 5:13a) with Rome, so do the references to Mark's link with Peter and Rome (see the NOTE on 5:13b below). Other considerations that point to Rome as the place of origin of 1 Peter, of course, would also favor regarding "Babylon" as referring to Rome.[810] In the light of this weighty evidence, linking Peter, Mark, and 1 Peter with Rome and hence pointing to the equation of "Babylon" with Rome proves fatal to theories proposing "Babylon" as a metaphor for Jerusalem, one supposed location of Peter's death (so von Harnack 1897, 459; Erbes 1901; Schmalz 1952), or "Babylon" as a reference to the world in general as a place of exile (so Heussi 1955, 36–41; Boismard 1957, 181; Prete 1984; cf. Selwyn 1947, 304–5).[811] The use of "Babylon" for Rome, in turn, pro-

---

[809] Gaius, a presbyter of the Roman church under the bishop Zephyrinus (ca. 199–217 CE) stated: "I myself can point out the trophies (*tropaia*) of the apostles [Peter and Paul]. For if it is your will to proceed to the Vatican or to the Ostian Way, you will find the trophies of those who founded this church" (in Eusebius, *Hist. eccl.* 2.25.6–7). These "trophies" presumably were the burial places and memorials of victory of the martyred apostles. While Peter was venerated at a *triclinum* situated on the Via Appia just south of the city, the tradition of his burial at the site of his execution at the Vatican has far greater support. Gaius's mention of the "trophy" at the Vatican in all likelihood was a reference to the simple niche with columns in the so-called "Red Wall," a venerated shrine dating to about 160 CE that was discovered in the course of excavations under St. Peter's basilica in the 1960s (Kirschbaum 1959, 63–81). A graffito inscribed in the plaster of the Red Wall not long after 160 CE has been deciphered as reading: *PETR*[*OS*] *ENI* (with *ENI* possibly a contraction of *ENESTI*), thus stating, "Peter is within," that is, "Peter is buried inside here" (so Guarducci 1960, 131–36). While this reading of the graffito is justly contested, there is now general agreement among scholars that the shrine attests the *popular belief* that Peter was buried there and that, in the 4th century, the emperor Constantine expended enormous effort to erect a basilica over the shrine (over which the present basilica of St. Peter is located) because he took this belief to be accurate. Thus, support for Peter's burial in the necropolis on Vatican Hill, while not conclusive, is stronger than for any other scenario. On Peter's final ministry, martyrdom, and burial in Rome, including the literary, archaeological, and liturgical evidence, see von Harnack 1897, 240–43, 703–10; Lietzmann 1927, 1936; Heussi 1936, 1937, 1949; Holzmeister 1937, 37–71; Appolonj-Ghetti et al. 1951; Klauser 1956; Toynbee and Perkins 1956; Cullmann 1958, 70–152; Kirschbaum 1959; Aland 1960; Guarducci 1960, 1982; de Marco 1964; Finegan 1964, 302–15; Carcopino 1966; D. W. O'Connor 1969, 1975; G. F. Snyder 1969; 1985, 141–47; R. E. Brown, Donfried, and Reumann, eds. 1973, 20–21; Redigonda 1977; J. Fink 1978; Dockx 1984, 175–78; Walsh 1982; Sakkos 1989; Bauckham 1992a; Ghiberti 1992; Goppelt 1993, 9–14.

[810] See the GENERAL INTRODUCTION, 8. Place of Composition, where reasons also are given against taking "Babylon" as a supposed "code name" for Rome designed to conceal its place of origin.

[811] Some of the advocates of this theory assumed that 1 Peter was a message for believers who were homeless in the world and seeking a home in heaven, but this assumption is unfounded. Moreover, such a lack of specificity regarding the place of this letter's origin would ill accord with the specific locality of its address (provinces of Asia Minor, 1:1) and the specific persons mentioned (Peter, Silvanus, Mark). If "Babylon" meant the world in general, the addressees would also be "in Babylon," but in fact they are located in Asia Minor. Finally, the term "Babylon" here is never viewed in this way in later tradition, which consistently sees it as a reference to Rome and links Mark and Peter with this specific city.

vides a further reason for dating 1 Peter sometime after 70 CE and thus after the death of the apostle (ca. 65–67 CE), factors that argue for the pseudonymity of 1 Peter as well.

13b. *and* [*so does*] *Mark, my son* (*kai Markos ho hyios mou*). The foregoing verb *aspazetai* ("sends you greetings," "greets," v 13a) pertains to Mark as well. "My son" is hardly meant literally.[812] Just as Silvanus is characterized figuratively as "faithful brother," so Mark is described figuratively as Peter's *son*, both terms being consistent with the familial language of the letter as a whole. "Son" could imply that Mark was Peter's disciple.[813] This would be similar to Paul's use of familial language in speaking of those to whom he has introduced the gospel. Timothy, one of his early converts, he calls "my beloved and faithful child (*teknon*) in the Lord" (1 Cor 4:17; cf. also 1 Tim 1:2, 18; 2 Tim 1:2). His similar references to Onesimus (Phlm 10) and Titus (Titus 1:4), each as his "child," and to himself as "father" of his Thessalonian, Galatian, and Corinthian "children" (1 Thess 2:11; Gal 4:19; 1 Cor 4:14–15) could have the same implication. On the other hand, his observation that Timothy, "as a son with a father . . . has served me in the gospel" (Phil 2:22), stresses more the initimate relationship of both co-workers, and this may be the point implied by "son" here as well: it expresses the bond of intimacy and affection uniting the older apostle with his younger colleague.

The absence of any further identification indicates that Mark is presumed to be known to the addressees. The only Mark mentioned in the NT and concerning whom this might have been the case is the John Mark referred to in Acts 12 and 15 and elsewhere in the NT (see R. P. Martin 1986; Jefford 1992). According to Acts 12:1–17, it was in Jerusalem at the home of a certain Mary, "the mother of John surnamed Mark," where Peter sought refuge following his escape from Herod Agrippa I (41–44 CE). This John Mark, also nephew of Barnabas (Col 4:10), was enlisted to accompany Barnabas and Paul on a missionary journey to southern Asia Minor (12:25–14:25). He returned with them to Antioch and Jerusalem, where a council convened to assess the mission to the Gentiles (Acts 15), a council in which Peter (15:7–11) and Silas-Silvanus (15:22, 27, 30–34) had prominent roles. Following this council, as related in Acts, Paul declined to take Mark along on a return trip to regions visited earlier because Mark had "withdrawn from them in Pamphylia and had not gone with them to the work" (15:38; cf. 13:13). Separating from Barnabas, who took Mark with him to Cyprus (15:39), Paul chose Silas-Silvanus and returned to the churches founded in Syria and Cilicia (15:40). The account of Acts thus indicates the association of Peter, Mark, and Silvanus in Jerusalem, a

---

[812] Against Haselhurst (1926), who would also regard Mary, the mother of Mark (Acts 12:12), as Peter's wife.

[813] According to the rabbis, "he who teaches the son of his neighbor the Torah, Scripture ascribes it to him as if he had begotten him" (*b. Sanh.* 19b; cf. 99b); cf. also Clem. Alex. (*Strom.* 1.1.2): "we call our religious instructors fathers"; and "everyone who is educated in obedience to his instructor becomes a son" (*Strom.* 1.1.3).

brief association of Mark with Paul, and a subsequent longer collaboration of Paul and Silas-Silvanus as missionaries in Asia Minor, Macedonia, and Greece (Acts 15:36–18:22). Years later, Mark apparently had rejoined Paul, who was in prison, possibly in Rome (Col 4:10; Phlm 24; cf. 2 Tim 4:11). Although "Mark" was an extremely common name, these eight NT passages form a consistent picture, with no compelling cause for doubting that they refer to the same person (Martin 1986). The last stage of Mark's activity in Rome would have put him in contact again with Peter, during the final phase of the apostle's life.[814]

Post-NT tradition concerning Mark emphasizes his collaboration with Peter in Rome during this final period of Peter's ministry. Papias of Hierapolis (ca. 60–130), transmitting early tradition from Asia Minor, indicates in his *Exposition of the Oracles* of the Lord that Mark, to whom the second Gospel was attributed (in Eusebius, *Hist. eccl.* 3.39.14), was known by Papias's source, an Asian elder, to be the "interpreter (*hermeneutēs*) of Peter" (Eusebius, *Hist. eccl.* 3.39.15; so also the *Anti-Marcionite Prologue* on Mark). Papias, moreover, as noted above, referred directly to 1 Pet 5:13 and to Mark as Peter's "son" (in Eusebius, *Hist. eccl.* 2.15.2). Many others followed Papias in regarding Mark as the interpreter of Peter, transmitting in writing the preaching of Peter in Rome.[815] Origen (*Comm. Matt.* 1, cited in Eusebius, *Hist. eccl.* 6.25.5) reflects the same tradition ("Mark who wrote it [his Gospel] in accordance with Peter's instructions") and identifies this Mark as the one "whom Peter acknowledged as his son in the catholic epistle, speaking in these terms: 'The co-elect in Babylon greets you along with Mark my son.'"

1 Peter 5:13 is the earliest written reference to such an association of Mark and Peter in Rome and, it has been argued by some, could have been the starting point of the post-NT tradition maintaining their collaboration in Rome (Körtner 1980; 1983, 206–20). The apologetic intent behind Papias's associating the second Gospel with Mark as Peter's interpreter (in Eusebius, *Hist. eccl.* 3.39.14–15), thereby securing it apostolic authority, makes its historical value open to question. The same is not necessarily true, however, of Papias's statement concerning 1 Pet 5:13 (in Eusebius, *Hist. eccl.* 15.2). Körtner is correct in separating the Mark of 1 Pet 5:13 from the question of the authorship of the Markan Gospel. But his speculation that the Peter-Mark tradition recorded in Eusebius *Hist. eccl.* 3.39.15 is "perhaps older than 1 Pet 5:13" (Körtner 1983, 212) is unsubstantiated, as is the claim that "the figure of Mark" derives from Pauline tradition rather than representing an actual collaborator with Peter (Körtner 1983, 211). On the whole, the most that can be said with certainty on this controverted issue is that from Acts onward and throughout the patristic

---

[814] On the chronology of Mark's life, see Dockx 1984a, 179–98.

[815] E.g., Justin Martyr (*Dial.* 106.3); Irenaeus (*Haer.* 3.1.2, cited also in Eusebius, *Hist. eccl.* 5.8.3); Clement of Alexandria (*Adum. on 1 Pet* 5:13; *Hyp.* 6, in Eusebius, *Hist. eccl.* 6.14.5–7); Tertullian (*Marc.* 4.5.3); Epiphanius (*Pan.* 51.6.10); and Jerome (*Vir. ill.* 8, referring both to Mark and to Rome as Babylon; *Epist.* 120.11).

period the knowledge of a Peter-Mark connection was a constant one. What our Petrine text indicates is that Mark, like Silvanus, was an associate of Peter in Jerusalem, joined Peter and Silvanus in Rome at the close of Peter's ministry there, and eventually was included in 1 Peter among those sending greetings to fellow-believers in Asia Minor.[816] However the historical reliability of the Lukan and post-NT tradition is to be judged, the bulk of the evidence illustrates the presumed association of Mark and Peter from their early contacts in Jerusalem to their final collaboration in Rome before Peter's death. The Peter-Mark connection is also relevant to the association of "Babylon" and Rome. Even if the early post-NT witness to the association of Mark with Peter in Rome was based exclusively on their association in 1 Peter, it would still illustrate the early consensus that in 1 Peter "Babylon" was a reference to Rome.

Finally, the explicit reference in 1 Peter to Mark and Silvanus as intimate associates of Peter indicates that the letter originated not simply with one individual but with a group including Silvanus and Mark, with Peter as its leading figure. Since numerous literary and historical factors argue against authorship of the letter by Peter himself and indicate a date of composition after Peter's death, 1 Peter is best viewed as a letter emanating from this Petrine group and sent in the name and under the authority of the Apostle Peter, its most prominent leader.

Just as Paul in his missions did not work alone but operated with a team of "co-workers" (E. E. Ellis 1971), this Petrine group too functioned as a team. All three persons had early contacts in Jerusalem, if the evidence of Acts (12:1–17; 15:1–29) is given credence, and now all three were together once again in Rome. Along with Peter, Silvanus and Mark represented leading figures of the early Jerusalem community through whom the Palestinian Christian tradition of Jesus' teaching, suffering, death, and resurrection was transmitted from Jerusalem to Rome. All three thus represent in their personal careers the spread of the gospel from Jerusalem (Acts 12:1–17; 15:1–29) and Antioch (Acts 15:36–41; Gal 2:11–14) to Asia Minor (Acts 13–14; 16:1–18:22; cf. Acts 2:9–19) and eventually to Rome. Thus, they represented and authenticated for the Asia Minor addressees what they stood for earlier in Jerusalem and what is expressed in this letter: the universal dimension of God's grace, the furtherance of a community open to believers of all peoples and classes, and the unity of believers in one common brotherhood and family of God. Their association in Jerusalem as well as later in Rome attests to the cohesion and personal cooperation of which their letter speaks. Their activities from east to west and their present concern for the movement in Asia Minor confirm the ecumenical dimension of the universal grace of which they write. Their own experience of suffering gives personal witness and authority to the message of comfort and hope they send to their suffering fellow-believers.

---

[816] Any role of Mark in the actual writing down of 1 Peter, however, can only be conjectured; see Gamba 1982.

The proposal that 1 Peter was the letter of a Petrine group in Rome was advanced more than thirty years ago and, with several arguments to commend it, continues to gain supporters (see the GENERAL INTRODUCTION, 7.1. Authorship). In regard to the question of authorship, this proposal shifts the focus of attention from the specific writer of the letter to the group responsible for its composition and dispatch. It likewise takes into consideration the tradition employed in this letter, a tradition current in the Christian community of Rome.[817] This Petrine group at Rome, intimately associated with Peter and personally familiar with his teaching, writes a letter in the name of Peter that reflects both the diversity of tradition current in Rome and the legacy of the great apostle who was martyred there. While we can speak here only of possibility rather than certainty, this proposal is sociologically plausible and logically compelling. It avoids the problems militating against Peter as direct writer while simultaneously accounting for traces in the letter of tradition associated with the apostle; it is compatible with NT evidence regarding Silvanus and Mark and consistent with post-NT evidence concerning the association of Peter and Mark in Rome; it explains the reasons for, and functions of, the references to Silvanus and Mark; and it adequately accounts for the letter's ascription to Peter.

14a. *Greet one another with the kiss of love* (*aspasasthe allēlous en philēmati agapēs*). Besides receiving greetings from the brotherhood in Rome, the recipients are also encouraged to greet one another (*aspasasthe allēlous*) with a "kiss of love" (*philēmati agapēs*), a physical expression of brotherly love (cf. *philadelphia*, 1:22; *philadelphos*, 3:8) and family-like affection. Such a request was often included in the conclusion of Christian letters.

In Greco-Roman culture, the kiss (*philēma*) was an expression of affection (*philia*) among family members and close friends (*philoi*; see Adinolfi 1988, 183–86). The etiquette of the kiss varied in expression (lips to lips; lips to hand; lips to feet; cheek to cheek; kiss as embrace or hug) and according to social situation. It could serve as a gesture of greeting; of farewell; of respect, honor, and deference; of familial or fraternal affection; of sexual ardor; of reconciliation; or of friendship and solidarity.[818] As the letters of Paul also show, the Christian community adopted the kiss as a regular physical manifestion of their affection for one another, not as a perfunctory ritual but as a genuine expression of love within the brotherhood. Paul, however, preferred the expression "holy kiss" (*philēma hagion*, Rom 16:16; 1 Cor 16:20; 2 Cor 13:12; 1 Thess 5:26).[819] For both authors, however, this kiss was an expression of the familial affection typical of the Christian community, whose members regarded one another as sisters and brothers in the faith.

---

[817] See J. N. D. Kelly 1969, 33–34, 215–16; Best 1971, 34, 36; R. E. Brown and Meier 1983, 128–39; Lohse 1954/1986, 53–55; R. E. Brown 1990; Mullins 1991, 94–365; Goppelt 1993, 32, 48, 370.

[818] On the kiss, sacred and profane, see Neal 1885; Nyrop 1901; W. Kroll 1931; Löw 1967; Perella 1969.

[819] Some witnesses (a few minuscules vg syr^{p}) read "holy" here as well, but this appears to be a case of inadvertent or intentional harmonization with the formulation of Paul.

Probably exchanged within the context of assemblies gathered in the homes for worship, the gesture could involve either a kiss on the lips or, more likely, a *hugging embrace* as shared among kin and friends.[820] The author's encouragement of this greeting may suggest the presumption that the letter would be read during a worship assembly. Reference to the kiss in combination with the reading of letters, probably during the worship assembly, is found already in 1 Cor 16:19–20 and 1 Thess 5:26–27; cf. also Acts 20:37. Later evidence clearly attests the sharing of the kiss in the setting of the Eucharistic liturgy.[821] Modified in various ways, the kiss of peace or of love has remained a part of the eucharistic liturgy down to the present day.[822] This intimate expression of solidarity is especially appropriate in 1 Peter, where the chief ecclesial symbol of community is that of the household or family of God and where love and familial loyalty are so frequently stressed (1:8, 22; 2:11, 17; 3:8; 4:8, 12).

14b. *Peace to all of you who are in Christ* (*Eirēnē hymin pasin tois en Christōi*).[823] The letter ends in conventional epistolary fashion with a wish for peace (cf. Eph 6:23; Heb 13:20; 3 John 15; and Koskenniemi 1956, 148). Just as the author wished his readers "peace" at the beginning of his letter (1:2), so he concludes on the same note. "Peace" (*eirēnē*) thus forms, along with other terms (personal names [Peter, Silvanus, Mark, 5:12–13; 1:1]; grace [5:12; 1:2]; co-elect/elect [5:13; 1:1]; Babylon/Diaspora [5:14; 1:1]; Christ [5:14/1:1]) part of the grand literary inclusion framing the letter as a whole. The greeting contains no verb, but in such formulations its omission is conventional.

"Peace" (*eirēnē*; Heb. *šālôm*) is the concluding term of the ancient Aaronic benediction (". . . and give you peace," Num 6:24–26). The wishing of *peace*

---

[820] This sense of *philēma* (cf. Luke 7:45; 22:48) is conveyed by the related verbs *phileō* (Matt 26:48) and *kataphileō* (Matt 26:49; Mark 14:45; Luke 7:38, 45; 15:20) as well as by *enagkalizomai* ("embrace, hug, put one's arms around," Mark 10:16) and *symperilambanō* ("embrace, hug," Acts 20:10). According to Acts 20:37, Paul received such a kiss in the context of worship: they "hugged (lit., 'fell on his neck') and kissed (*katephiloun*) him."

[821] Justin (*1 Apol.* 65.1–4 [ca. 160 CE]) notes: "Having ended the prayers, we salute one another with a kiss" (prior to the consecration). Regarding the Eucharist at Rome (ca. 225), Hippolytus observes: "And when the catechumens finish their prayers, they must not give the kiss of peace, for their kiss is not yet pure. Only believers shall salute one another, but men with men and women with women; a man shall not salute a woman." Cf. also Tert., *Or.* 14, 18 (*osculum pacis*); Cyril Jerus., *Myst. Cat.* 5.3–5; *Apos. Con.* 2.57; 8.11; John Chrys. *Hom.* 30.2.

[822] On the kiss of peace or love, see Hofmann 1938; Spicq 1965, 363–65; Thraede 1968–1969; 1972b; Benko 1985a; Ellington 1990; Klassen 1993.

[823] The entire statement is absent in 𝔓^{72}, which, however, is not necessarily an indication of its later addition (against Quinn 1965, 246), since NT letters usually conclude with some kind of prayer or blessing. As in the case of 5:10a, some MSS read only "in Christ" (A B Ψ 33 a few others vgst syr^{p} cop$^{sa, bo^{ms}}$) while others read "in Christ Jesus" (ℵ K P 𝔐 it^{h} vg^{cl} syr^{h} cop^{bo} arm) or "in the Lord Jesus" (629). Given the tendency of copyists to expand rather than shorten the sacred name, the longer readings appear secondary; the shorter reading would also be consonant with 3:16 and the shorter reading of 5:10b. Many MSS (including ℵ K P 614 1739 *Byz* it$^{h, r}$ vg syr$^{p, h}$ cop$^{bo^{mss}}$ arm) also add a concluding "amen." This addition, perhaps prompted by liturgical practice, was resisted by other copyists (A B Ψ 81 323 629 945 1241 1881 cop$^{sa, bo}$ eth).

reflects a conventional Israelite and Christian greeting (cf. "go in peace," Mark 5:34; Luke 7:50; 8:48; Acts 16:36; Jas 2:16). "Peace" was also the salutation of the risen Lord (Luke 24:36; John 20:19, 21, 26). Paul, by contrast, normally used "grace" as the concluding term in his postscripts, with 2 Cor 13:11 forming a singular exception.[824] Peace, the sound state of a person and the prosperity of one's affairs as well as the state of mutual concord, naturally was precious to Israelites and Christians alike. The great sage Hillel taught: "Be of the disciples of Aaron, loving peace and pursuing peace, loving your fellow-creatures, and drawing them near to the Torah" (*m. ʾAbot* 1:12).[825]

However, the eschatological and Christological dimensions of peace typical of the Christian gospel (see the NOTE on 3:11) are also likely to be implied here. This peace, like grace, election, holiness, glory, and salvation, is a divine gift (cf. Phil 4:7) effecting the union of God with his children. These reborn believers, in turn, are to be instruments and purveyors of this peace in the world (3:11). The peace that our author wishes for his addressees is grounded in their relationship with Christ, as the final words of the letter indicate.

to all of you who are in Christ (*hymin pasin tois en Christōi*).[826] "In Christ" has the sense of "in union with Christ." The phrase was similarly used in 3:16 (cf. 5:10) in reference to the conduct of those who are united with Christ. The formulation is the author's succinct inclusive expression for the followers of Christ and his alternative to the term "Christian" employed by outsiders (4:16). Here, as the final phrase of the letter, it expresses collectively and profoundly the union of all those enjoying personal fellowship with Christ. Reicke's claim (1964, 135) that this peace wish was prompted by "dangerous tendencies toward disturbance [that] actually existed in the communities of the recipients" strains credibility. These alleged internal disturbances are more imagined than real, as Sleeper (1968) has convincingly shown. On the other hand, in a letter so focused on conflict and struggle with *outsiders*, it is a mark of the consolatory character of 1 Peter that it concludes, as it began (1:2), with a wish for peace. Those who are reborn through Christ's resurrection, who live according to his example, and who share in his glory are now wished the peace that is available for all who are "in Christ." Even in the face of fierce hostility, their hearts may be at peace, assured of God's unceasing protection and care.

GENERAL COMMENT

In his epistolary postscript, our author succinctly states the purpose of his writing, names the persons involved in its composition and dispatch, and extends greetings "from our part of the household to yours." These formal features

[824] Unless Phil 4:7 and 4:9 concluded letters now contained in canonical Philippians; cf. also Rom 15:33 and 2 Thess 3:16.

[825] See Montefiore and Loewe 1963, 530–37 for further rabbinic sentiments regarding peace.

[826] The majority of later MSS (including ℵ K P) read "Christ Jesus" (rather than "Christ" alone) and "amen," both of which are secondary additions.

of the postscript are conventional elements of genuine letters and together with its epistolary prescript (1:1–2) mark this writing as a genuine letter. Postscript and prescript are also similar in language and imagery; compare "co-elect"/"elect"; "Babylon"/"Diaspora"; the familial imagery of "brother," "brotherhood," "son," familial "kiss"/"Father"; and "grace" and "peace." Consistent with accents in the letter as a whole, the similar structure and content of 1:1–2 and 5:12–14 form a literary inclusion framing the entire letter and manifesting its thematic integrity. Summing up the letter as a message of exhortation and witness concerning the grace of God, our author urges his addressees to stand fast in this grace. The commendation of Silvanus, the courier of the letter, is designed to gain him a cordial welcome and a favorable hearing. Greetings sent from the co-elect brotherhood and from Mark, Peter's colleague, who along with Silvanus was part of the Petrine group responsible for the composition and dispatch of 1 Peter, express the warm affection uniting the senders of the letter with the brothers and sisters in Asia Minor. "Babylon," employed metaphorically, locates the senders at Rome, the present center of worldwide power similar to the Babylon of old. Although separated by geography, the believers in Rome and those in Asia Minor belong to a single, worldwide brotherhood (5:9) solidified by a common predicament as dispersed strangers and aliens and by a common experience of divine blessing: their divine election, their membership in a household of God in which persons are "brothers" and "sons" and embrace one another with familial affection, and their mutual experience of the grace and peace from God that bind and sustain all who are "in Christ."

This letter from Rome is the earliest-known document expressing the concern of Christians in the capital for their beleaguered brothers and sisters in Asia Minor. This effort toward solidifying the bond between the community in Rome and the brotherhood abroad was one small but significant step in the construction of a bridge joining the Roman church with congregations elsewhere in the Empire.[827] This bridge was to be traveled many times in both directions in the subsequent course of Christianity's history.

For studies on 1 Pet 5:12–14, see Applegate 1992; Bornemann 1919–1920; Brox 1975, 1978; Elliott 1979; 1981/1990, 267–95; 1983; 1992a; Fedalto 1983; Gamba 1982; Haselhurst 1926; Hunzinger 1965; Knoch 1990, 1991; Körtner 1980; Marxsen 1979; Manley 1944; Prete 1984; Quinn 1965; Radermacher 1926; Selwyn 1947, 303–5; Seufert 1885a, 1885b; Smothers 1926–1927; Soards 1988; Stegmann 1917; Thiede 1987a; Thurston 1974.

---

[827] On subsequent correspondence and traveling to and from Rome, see von Harnack 1908/1962, 1:369–76.

Index of Subjects

◆

INDEX OF SCRIPTURAL AND OTHER ANCIENT REFERENCES

◆

Bold italic page numbers denote pages on which a large number of individual verses from the source (sometimes all of the verses) may be found. Ranges of page numbers denote either a (real) continuation of the discussion of a reference or a conflation (artificial) of successive pages containing the same reference.

OLD TESTAMENT

Genesis

Exodus

Song of the Three Young Men (Sg Three) . . .

Susanna (Sus)

Tobit (Tob)

Wisdom of Solomon (Wis)

OLD TESTAMENT PSEUDEPIGRAPHA

Apocalypse of Abraham (Apoc. Ab.)

Apocalypse of Moses (Apoc. Mos.)

Apocalypse of Sedrach (Apoc. Sedr.)

Apocalypse of Zephaniah (Apoc. Zeph.) . . .

Ascension of Isaiah (Ascen. Isa.) . . . 685

OTHER ISRAELITE WRITERS, WRITINGS

Josephus

Philo

Mark

Romans

2 Corinthians

Philippians

Colossians

1 Thessalonians

2 Thessalonians

1 Timothy

2 Timothy

1 Peter [*Greek Vocabulary*] . . . *42–68*

2 Peter . . . *140–1*

1 John

2 John

OTHER CHRISTIAN WRITINGS

INSCRIPTIONS AND PAPYRI

GREEK AND LATIN WRITERS, WRITINGS